Praise for previous editions of

SAD mACs, BOMBS, AND OTHER DISASTERS

MacAddict magazine (September 1997; p. 89) called Sad Macs "the best book on and definitive guide to Mac troubleshooting." It also listed it as one of nine "great" Mac books in its holiday gift guide (December 1997; p.38).

Computer Shopper magazine (December 1997; p. 516) called Sad Macs "an indispensable reference for any Mac user."

Mac Home Journal magazine (September 1997; p. 51) wrote that Sad Macs "details just about every Mac problem you could possibly think of. Impressively, Ted Landau wrote the book so that anyone can understand it."

ComputerEdge Online (November 1997) wrote that Sad Macs "should be bundled with every Macintosh computer. If you own a Mac, you should own this book."

BMUG Newsletter (Fall 1997) wrote that Sad Macs "is the book to go to when things go bump in the night. Sad Macs is a definite must-have. Apple ought to bundle it with their entry level machines (although it would benefit veterans, too)."

Amazon.com lists Sad Macs as a "recommended book," writing that Sad Macs "is the definitive guide to have on hand when your Apple Macintosh rolls a bomb in your general direction. If you've got a Mac, this is an essential utility, and a must-have desktop reference guide." A reader adds: "Of the many Mac-related books I own, this is the one Mac book I would least want to do without."

In **Beyond the Little Mac Book** (Peachpit Press, 1997), authors Steve Broback and Robin Williams write: "For an exhaustive reference guide to almost any Mac problem and its solution, get Sad Macs. Author Ted Landau is the most knowledgeable I know of when it comes to troubleshooting Macs, and his book is terrif

Ted Landau

SAD mACs, B♦mBs, AND OTHER DiSASTERS

AND WHAT TO DO ABOUT THEM

4th Edition

Peachpit Press

Sad Macs, Bombs, and Other Disasters, 4th Edition
Ted Landau

Peachpit Press
1249 Eighth Street
Berkeley, CA 94710
(510) 524-2178
(510) 524-2221 (fax)

Find us on the World Wide Web at: http://www.peachpit.com

Peachpit Press is a division of Addison Wesley Longman

Copyright © 2000 by Ted Landau

Editor: Marty Cortinas
Production Coordinator: Amy Changar
Copy Editors: Tracy Brown, Wendy Sharp
Compositor: Owen Wolfson
Indexer: Emily Glossbrenner
Cover Design: Mimi Heft

ISBN: 0-201-69963-X

0 9 8 7 6 5 4 3 2 1

Printed and bound in the United States of America

To Naomi

Acknowledgments

This fourth edition of *Sad Macs* has been by far the most difficult one for me to write. The main reason for this is that my Web site, MacFixIt, has grown tremendously since the last edition of *Sad Macs* was published. And with this growth has come an ever increasing demand on my time. It got to the point where it was almost impossible for me to write the book and work on my Web site at the same time. Somehow, I still managed to finish the book, months later than I had originally hoped, but still finished.

For this reason, my first acknowledgment must go to Marty Cortinas and all the editors and staff at Peachpit Press that put up with a near constant series of delays and broken promises of meeting deadlines. Thanks for not giving up on me altogether!

And similarly, thanks to Nancy Peterson, my editor at *Macworld* magazine where I had been a columnist for the Secrets section, for allowing me to delay writing several months of columns so that I could have more time to work on the book.

A thank you also to Oakland University, where I work as a professor, for granting me the leave time I needed so that I could work on *Sad Macs*.

And my biggest thanks to my wife, Naomi, who somehow managed to put up with my nearly 24/7 work schedule and not only did not divorce me but actually gave me the support and encouragement I needed to finish the task.

A warm thanks to all of the public relations people and product managers for the various products that are mentioned in this book. They answered my technical questions and sent me the software and hardware when I needed it.

I also offer my gratitude to all of the readers of the previous editions of *Sad Macs* who have patiently waited for this delayed new edition to finally get published

And a special note of gratitude to all of the readers of the MacFixIt Web site who, through their emails to me, have contributed to the database of information on the site. This information provided much of the background for the new material in this edition of *Sad Macs*. Without this help, the book would have been almost impossible to complete.

Finally, I offer my personal thanks to Steve Jobs. When the third edition of *Sad Macs* was published, Apple had entered a dark period where its sales were sinking, red ink was mounting, and critical promised software (most notably the original "Copland" Mac OS) had been cancelled. The media were all but writing Apple's obituary. Then Steve Jobs returned to the company he had founded and worked to re-create it. He told us to "Think Different." The result was the iMac, the iBook, Mac OS X and all of the other fantastic products of the past few years. This triggered a resurgence in Apple sales and prestige that is still growing. Without this, there might not have been a reason to write a fourth edition of *Sad Macs*.

Ted Landau
May 2000

Contents

Chapter 13   Road Service for the Infobahn:
The World Wide Web, Email and Beyond 547

Chapter 14   Think Different: the iMac, iBook,
Power Mac G4 and Beyond 623

What's New in This Edition?

"Since the publication of the previous edition of this book, the Macintosh landscape has changed substantially." Those were the opening words of this section of the two previous editions of this book. If anything, these words vastly underestimate the extent of change that has occurred in the last few years. For starters, there have been *three* major upgrades to the Mac OS (OS 8, OS 9 and now OS X) and a complete overhaul of the Mac hardware (starting with the iMac). And of course, the importance of the Internet has grown exponentially.

With all of this change, it has become impossible to retain all of the relevant information in previous editions and still add the new information. The book would be too large to publish as a single volume. As such, in cases where information is different across different hardware and software, I have limited coverage to PowerPC Macs only and to Mac OS 8.0 or later. For troubleshooting help that predates this, you'll have to rely on older editions of *Sad Macs*.

Second, due to the accelerated rate of change, it has reached the point where material becomes obsolete almost as soon as I am done writing it. Still, I tried to make this book as current as possible, making changes up to the last hours before the book went to press. To find out about something that is newer than what made the deadline for this edition, my best advice is to check my MacFixIt <http://www.macfixit.com> Web site. For example, it will certainly have the latest information about the forthcoming Mac OS X.

Those caveats aside, the fourth edition of Sad Macs represents, once again, an almost complete rewrite of previous editions. However, the basic structure of previous editions remains the same. This means that a cursory glance at the table of contents hardly hints at all of the changes that lie just beneath the surface. To give you a better idea of what's new, here's a list of some of the more noteworthy additions:

- Every chapter has been updated to include information about Mac OS 8 and Mac OS 9

- Where relevant, all chapters have been updated to include new information about the iMac, the iBook, USB, FireWire and all of the other recent hardware innovations.

- Chapter 2 has new information on creating emergency startup disks.

- Chapter 5 has new information on DVD drives.

- Chapter 6 has new information on Navigation Services dialog boxes.

- Chapter 7 has new information on troubleshooting inkjet and USB printers.

- Chapters 9 and 10 have been substantially revised to eliminate out-of-date material and replace it with more recent information.

- Chapter 11 has been rewritten almost from scratch to include new information about Mac portables, including the iBook, and an expanded section on file sharing (with new material on Ethernet and on AirPort connections).

- Chapters 12 and 13 are expanded versions of what was previously one chapter on Internet-related troubleshooting. I am particularly pleased with how these chapters turned out. For those of you with Internet-related problems (which is just about everyone!), these two chapters alone are likely to be worth the price of this book.

- Chapter 14 covers issues specific to the iMac, iBook, new PowerBooks, and Power Mac G3/G4.

- Chapter 15 covers issues specific to Mac OS 8.x, Mac OS 9.x and Mac OS X.

- The 18 original Fix-Its have been reorganized into 16 Fix-Its.

- Fix-It #4 has been revised to cover recent changes in installing the Mac OS.

- Fix-It #6 has been revised to cover the new viruses (such as the AutoStart virus) that emerged in the last few years. It also describes the new versions of anti-virus software.

- Fix-It #10 is a completely revised Fix-It on dealing with Directory damage.

- Fix-It #13 has new information on HFS Plus formatting.

- Fix-It #14 is an almost entirely new Fix-It that covers troubleshooting SCSI, IDE, USB, FireWire, serial and ADB connections.

- Fix-It #15 has new information on G3 and G4 processor upgrades.

- Fix-It #16: has a completely revised section on getting troubleshooting help from the Web.

This list is far from complete. Every chapter and Fix-It has at least some changes. Summarizing all of this, I once again find that what I said here in previous editions still applies: "I believe you hold in your hands the most comprehensive book on Macintosh troubleshooting that is available anywhere."

Preface

In previous editions of this book, the Preface went to great lengths to explain what exactly this book is about and who the book's target audience is. Given that the book is now entering its fourth edition, I suspect that most prospective buyers already know this stuff. So I decided to save a few pages of text and cut most of it out.

For those who are completely new to *Sad Macs*, I will simply say that it is designed to help you solve problems with your Macintosh. It is not a general introduction to the Mac, nor is it a comprehensive encyclopedia of tips. It's a fix-it-yourself book for the Mac. Its emphasis is not on hardware repairs, but on the much more common and primarily software troubleshooting that any end user can do without any special tools and without voiding their warranty. Further, its focus is more on OS-level problems that affect virtually all Mac users than those specific to a single application, such as Word or Photoshop.

Along the way, you'll learn that many Mac "problems" are not really problems at all. The apparent problem is one of understanding. When you learn more about how your Mac works, the unexpected will transform into the expected, and the problem is "solved." It's like discovering that the reason you are getting no sound from your TV is because someone pressed the mute button. Nothing's really wrong. That's the way it is supposed to work!

While not exactly intended for a novice Mac user, neither is this book intended for the Mac expert. Instead, it is for that broad middle audience that knows the basics of how the Mac works, but wants to learn much more.

Though this book does not specifically mention every possible problem you might have (no book could do that!), it does teach you the general skills needed to diagnose and solve even those problems that are not mentioned.

How This Book Is Organized

This book has three main parts:

- **Part I: Background and Basics** deals with general background information and some problem-solving basics. This is designed to bring all users up to speed so that any relevant gaps in your knowledge get filled before you proceed.

- **Part II: Symptoms, Causes, and Cures** covers the whole range of Macintosh problems, what their symptoms are, what causes them, and what you can do to solve them.

- **Part III: Disaster Relief** focuses on specific problem-solving tools, called Fix-Its, rather than on symptoms. Each Fix-It contains all the necessary information about how and when to use it and why it works.

These three sections are followed by an appendix, called "Stocking Your Troubleshooter's Toolkit," that provides the information needed to obtain any of the troubleshooting software mentioned in this book.

On a Related Note

Throughout this book, you will find three types of text set off from the main text. Each of these has a different purpose:

TAKE NOTE ▶ An Example

These notes contain important information directly relevant to the topic under discussion. For example, they may include definitions or explanations of terms used in the main text.

BY THE WAY ▶ An Example

These notes contain more tangential information than you will find in the Take Note boxes. For example, they may list changes expected in a forthcoming version of the software under discussion.

TECHNICALLY SPEAKING ▶ An Example

These notes contain supplementary information that is at a more technical level than the rest of the book. Less technically inclined readers may choose to skip them.

See: What I Mean

This book contains numerous cross-references. Some of these references direct you to a continuation of the steps needed to solve a problem, such as, "If the system error continues to recur, see 'Solve It! Recurring System Errors,' later in this chapter." Others inform you where you can find more information about a subject, such as:

SEE: • Chapter 8 for more details on invisible files.

Still others point to the location of the initial description of a term or item.

On the one hand, the sheer number of these references may seem disconcerting at first, especially if you are in a hurry to solve a problem. However, not all of these references demand immediate attention. Many of them are only suggestions. Thus, if you can solve your current problem without needing to know more about invisible files, for example, you need not bother with that particular cross-reference.

See Also: The Fix-Its

If you have just started browsing through this book and have come across a reference such as

SEE: • Fix-It #8 for more on rebuilding the desktop.

you may be a bit mystified. What's a Fix-It? Where is it? The Fix-Its, as just mentioned, make up the Part III (Disaster Relief) section of this book. This book is deliberately designed so that the Chapters make frequent reference to them. Each Fix-It covers a different troubleshooting topic, such as rebuilding the desktop or solving extension conflicts. They are the central location for all information on their given topic.

If a particular chapter section includes a long list of Fix-It references, you probably won't wind up needing all of them. As soon as one of them fixes your problem, you can stop. If the length of a particular list seems daunting, remember that the longest lists cover the most general cases, when the information at hand provides little or no guidance on which direction to go. Usually, if you can describe your problem more specifically, you can find more specific advice, with a narrower range of Fix-It choices, elsewhere in the book.

On the Web: *MacFixIt*

This book makes frequent reference to my **MacFixIt** <http://www.macfixit.com> Web site.

MacFixIt began in 1996 as the **Sad Macs Update Site**. Its purpose was to provide readers of *Sad Macs* with access to the otherwise-hard-to-find shareware and freeware utilities mentioned in the book, as well as to offer updated troubleshooting information about topics too new to have been covered in the latest edition of *Sad Macs*.

As time went on, the site began to attract an audience that extended well beyond *Sad Macs* readers. In response, the site gradually evolved into a more general Mac troubleshooting site, featuring nearly daily updates of the latest tips and news. To reflect this change, the site was renamed MacFixIt.

Despite these changes, the site retains its original benefits for *Sad Macs* readers: it still has a Download Library where you can get troubleshooting utilities, and it still is a source of information newer than what is in *Sad Macs*. In fact, by combining the encyclopedic material in *Sad Macs* with the latest tips from MacFixIt, you have the best of both worlds.

A Final Note: Feedback

I encourage you to send me your comments about this book. Did you find the book helpful? Was the information easily accessible? Were you disappointed that certain topics were omitted? Were some topics covered in too little or too much detail? Or were you impressed with the breadth and depth of the coverage? Were you pleased to find just what you were seeking in just the right amount of detail? Any suggestions, criticisms, or compliments are welcome.

The best way to reach me is by email: *sadmacs@macfixit.com*.

PART I

Background and Basics

Chapter 1 is an overview of basic computer terms, concepts, and operations. It explains the essentials of the different types of memory that your Macintosh uses, and the different methods used to store data, as well as some specifics about other common hardware, especially monitors and printers. It also delves into the mysteries of the System Folder.

Chapter 2 covers preventative maintenance. It begins with an overview of the causes of Macintosh problems. The middle section describes the important software tools you need to make your repairs. The final section describes a general set of routine maintenance procedures designed to keep your Macintosh out of trouble.

Chapter 3 provides a set of general strategies for solving problems. With these skills, you will be ready to tackle almost any problem that comes your way, even if it is not specifically covered in this book.

1

Macintosh Basics: Hardware and Software

Exactly How Did I Get Here?

You turn on your Macintosh. The smiling Macintosh icon appears briefly and is soon replaced by the Welcome to Macintosh display. Eventually, this too disappears and is replaced by the desktop, a display where your disk icon appears in the upper right corner of the screen and the various files on your disk are listed in any number of windows. In one of these windows, you find the file icon for your word processor. You double-click on the file and it opens. You create a new document and save it. You quit the application and shut off the machine.

That's a typical brief session with your Macintosh.

If you are relatively new to using computers (and even if you are not), you have probably wondered exactly how all this happens. Where does the Welcome to Macintosh display come from? How does the Macintosh know what to do next? What happens when you open an application? Where was the information stored before you opened it, and where is it now? What exactly happens when you save something, and why isn't it saved automatically as you create it?

These are big questions, and they can be answered on many levels. It is a bit like the little child who asked his parent, "Where do I come from?" After the mother made several uncomfortable attempts at answering the question, the boy blurted out, "But Billy said he comes from Cleveland. I want to know where I come from."

Similarly, behind many Macintosh questions is a desire for a much simpler answer than the question may seem to imply. It is with this desire in mind that I attempt to answer these "big" questions. The focus of this book is always limited to what you need to know to understand the problem-solving material presented in the chapters to come. It does not pretend to be more comprehensive.

The Macintosh's ability to strut its stuff, whether to create sophisticated page layouts or display incredibly detailed color graphics, is the result of an intricate interplay between hardware and software. If you are going to solve the problems that will confront you in your day-to-day life with the Macintosh, you need some minimal understanding of how all this works. That's what this chapter is all about.

Macintosh Models and Computer Systems

Over the years, Apple has experimented with a wide variety of Macintosh models and styles. In the mid-'90s, Apple developed a dizzying array of models, with names such as Performas, Quadras, and Duos. However, since Steve Jobs' return to Apple in 1997, its product line has been trimmed into four main categories, each with few if any variations:

- **Consumer desktops** are represented by Apple's smash success, the iMac. It is an "all-in-one" unit, which means that the monitor is built into the basic "box" that holds the computer. It's designed to appeal to the typical home user. While it has limited expansion options, it has more than enough juice to get you on the Internet, play today's graphic intensive games, and do basic school, home, and office tasks. The main dilemma is choosing a color for your new iMac.

- **Consumer portables** are represented by the sleek new iBook. Its marketing slogan, "an iMac to go" pretty much sums it up: the dimensions are similar to a thin standard portable and it was the first Mac to support the AirPort wireless communication device.

- **Professional desktops** are represented by the striking Power Macintosh G3 and G4 units. Monitors are sold for these models separately. These Macs come with numerous expansion options, including bays for additional drives and PCI card slots (see Fix-It #15 for details about slots).

- **Professional portables** refer to Apple's esteemed PowerBook series. Variously called laptop or notebook Macs, today's PowerBooks compare favorably in features to Apple's desktop machines.

The term *computer system* typically refers to the essential combination of hardware components needed to use the computer: the computer "box" itself, a monitor, input devices such as a keyboard and mouse, and any disk drives. An almost essential additional component is a printer.

In recent years, Apple's line of Macintoshes has undergone a major overhaul. Such standard options as SCSI ports, ADB ports, serial ports, and even floppy disk drives have been abandoned. In their stead are newer and/or superior technologies, such as USB, FireWire, and Ethernet ports.

SEE: • **Fix-It #14 for more on ports.**

Finally, for a few years Macintosh clones were available from companies such as Power Computing. This era appears to be over. At present, only Apple is making Macintoshes.

Computing and Storage Hardware

The CPU and ROM

If you opened up any Macintosh model, the most distinctive object you would see is a board full of soldered circuits. It looks like the electronic equivalent of an aerial view of New York City. This is called the *main logic board* (or *motherboard*).

Many items are on this board. For now, you are concerned with just two of these items: the *central processing unit* (or *CPU* or *processor*) and the *read-only memory* module (or *ROM*). The expression *read-only* means that the information stored in the module cannot be altered in any way; it can only be read. A compact disc is another example of a read-only storage medium.

Simply put, the CPU makes a Macintosh a computer, and ROM makes a Macintosh a Macintosh.

The Processor Is the Computer

The processor is where most computations take place. Essentially, all programs are simply a set of instructions that get executed by the processor to produce the desired result.

All Macintoshes today are Power Macs. This means that they use a PowerPC processor. But this does not mean that they all have the exact same processor. The original Power Macintosh processor was called the PPC 601. This was followed by several 603 and 604 processors (there never was a 602 model released). These in turn were followed by the G3 processors.

Within each designation, there are different speeds of the processor (as measured by megahertz). Thus, there is a 300 MHz G3 and a 400 MHz G3.

All of these processors are compatible with whatever Mac software you choose to use. The major difference among them is speed. The newer versions (and within a type, those with higher MHz) are faster. However, these days, even the slower G3 processors are sufficiently fast enough that I would not recommend spending the extra money to get the fastest processors.

Before the arrival of the Power PC processor, the Mac used another processor series, now referred to as the 680x0 series (with specific names such as 68030 and 68040). These older processors cannot run software specifically written for the Power Mac. They are also significantly slower than Power Macs, especially G3 series Macs. If you are still using a 680x0 Mac, it's time to get a new Mac if you wish to use software designed for Power Macs.

SEE: • **Fix-It #15 for more on Power Macintoshes.**

The Nature of the Mac ROM Has Changed

The ROM contains the essential instructions needed to create the windows, menu bars, scroll boxes, dialog boxes, and graphics that make up what is commonly called the *Macintosh user interface*. All other programs can be designed to access this information. This is a great time-saver for programmers, since they don't have to keep reinventing the wheel. It also ensures that all programs have a similar look and feel.

Until the arrival of the iMac, the ROM was largely contained in the hardware of the Mac, on a "ROM chip" located on the logic board. However, the iMac signaled a major change - which has been followed by all subsequent Macs. Now, most of the ROM (that is, all of it except for the parts needed to start up the Mac) is contained in software, within a file called *Mac OS ROM*.

One implication of this change is that the Mac now easily starts up using an entirely different OS. For example, it can shift between Mac OS 9.x, Mac OS X, or Linux. It does this by taking advantage of another Macintosh technology buzzword: *Open Firmware*. More details about Open Firmware and Mac OS ROM, and the advantages of the changes introduced above, are described in Chapter 14).

For problem solving:

The most important thing to know is that the existence of different processors and different ROMs across different models of Macintoshes may lead to incompatibilities. For example, because of ROM and processor differences, certain programs may work fine with some Macintosh models, but not with others.

RAM: Electronic Storage

RAM stands for *random access memory.* When you hear people talking about how much memory their Macintosh has, they are talking about RAM. When a manual says that a program needs a certain amount of memory to run, it is referring to RAM.

When you turn on your computer for the first time, the RAM contains nothing at all. The startup process consists largely of loading the needed information into RAM. This is because almost all program instructions must be loaded into RAM before they can be carried out.

Similarly, when you open an application, you are transferring the instructions contained within that file from its storage location (usually a disk) to RAM.

The hardware that determines the amount of RAM in your machine is located on the main logic board inside your computer. These hardware components are often referred to as *memory chips* or *memory modules.*

By the way, some Macs have separate RAM just for creating the monitor's display, called video RAM or just VRAM (I'll have more to say about this in Chapter 10 and Fix-It #15).

Measuring RAM

RAM is usually measured in megabytes (MB). The more (or higher capacity of) RAM in your machine, the more megabytes of memory you have.

This RAM measurement has nothing directly to do with the physical size of the memory chip. Instead, it refers to the capacity of the chip to hold information.

All Macs currently being sold are not sold with the maximum amount of RAM that they can use. If you decide that your Mac needs more memory, you can easily add more.

TECHNICALLY SPEAKING ▶ Byting Off More Than You Can Chew

The *byte* is the basic unit of measurement for computer memory and storage. In particular, 1 megabyte equals 1,024 kilobytes (K) and 1 kilobyte, in turn, equals 1,024 bytes.

As a rough guideline, one page of text, single spaced, requires about 5K of memory.

Older Macintoshes have as little as 1MB of RAM. (The original Macintosh had only 128K!) A typical minimum amount of RAM on current Macintoshes is 64MB.

The first popularly priced hard drives for the Mac were 20MB in size. Today, the most popular hard disk capacity exceeds 4 Gigabytes(GB), or 1,000 megabytes, in size.

These "average" sizes grow larger every year. You can never have too much disk space or memory!

RAM Is Fast

The *random access* in RAM means that you can almost instantly get to any portion of what is stored in RAM. Most familiar storage mechanisms are *not* random access. For example, with a cassette tape, you must fast-forward or rewind to get where you want, which can take a considerable amount of time. Even a compact disc, which has a much faster access time, technically still works on the same principle as the cassette tape.

Thus, RAM access speed far exceeds any other alternative method the computer could use. This speed advantage is the main rationale for using RAM. Without it, all computer operations would slow down immensely, if they could be completed at all.

RAM Is Electrical

One reason RAM can achieve such a speed advantage is that information is stored in RAM in a purely electronic manner. Theoretically, information in RAM can be accessed at the speed at which electricity travels, which is quite fast!

Information in RAM Is Not Read-Only

Information in RAM can be easily modified or erased. To do so is just a matter of altering the path of electrical current flow in the memory chip.

With all of these advantages, you might wonder why anyone would use something other than RAM to store data. Actually, there are two very good reasons:

RAM Is Expensive

Memory chips are expensive. Even though RAM is far cheaper than it was a few years ago, it is still expensive compared to storing the same information on a hard drive.

RAM Is Temporary

Because RAM is electrical in nature, anything in RAM is lost forever when you turn the computer off, restart the computer, or interrupt the flow of electricity in any way (though if you use RAM disks, as described in Fix-It #5, you may know that they are a partial exception to this generalization). Thus, an unexpected power failure could result in the loss of several hours of work—if it is stored only in RAM and nowhere else! To permanently save your information, you need another form of storage, or disks, as described in the next section.

For problem solving:

The most important thing to know is whether you have enough memory for what you want to do and what to do if you do not.

RAM limitations are generally the bottleneck that limits how much you can do at one time. Whenever you open an application, the RAM that it occupies becomes temporarily unavailable for any other use. Since everything you want to use needs to load into RAM first, you can only work with as much as can fit into the available RAM.

Of course, information in RAM can be removed. The information you remove is then no longer available for immediate use, but the RAM is freed up. For example, quitting an application removes it from RAM and leaves that RAM available for another program.

Some programs may not run at all on your machine because you do not have sufficient RAM to open them, even if nothing else is running already. When that happens, it's time to buy more memory!

The minimum amount of RAM you need to effectively run the latest software keeps increasing as the software evolves. If you have an older Mac model and still run older software, you may be able to get by with as little as 8MB. For everyone else, double digit RAM is a necessity. As I write this, 64MB should be considered the absolute minimum; 128MB is already almost a necessity. Without enough RAM, you will keep getting "out of memory" messages throughout your workday. That's why adding more RAM is one of the best investments you can make.

See: • **Fix-It #15 for more on adding and replacing RAM, RAM Caches, and related issues.**

Disks: Physical Storage

Disks are used to store information permanently. That is, the information is retained even after the computer is turned off. This stored information on disks is commonly referred to as *software*.

Most Macintosh models have a type of disk, called a *hard disk*, built into the computer box itself. This disk is *not* in any way part of the main logic board (which holds the processor, ROM, and memory chips). A hard disk is a totally separate unit, though it connects to the main logic board. In fact, it is only a matter of convenience that it is inside the box at all. The Macintosh could work just fine without this internal hard disk, accessing instead a separate hard disk unit connected to the Macintosh on an outlet in the rear of the machine.

Still, though not technically correct, many users lump all of these components together as the internal hardware of the Macintosh. Whether in RAM, ROM, or on a hard disk, information is viewed as being stored somewhere inside the machine.

As mentioned in the section on RAM, when you *open* an application stored on a disk, you are copying its information from the disk to RAM. From here, its instructions can be sent to the processor as needed, which essentially means that the program will *run*.

Conversely, when you use an application's Save command to save a document, you are taking a copy of the document's information, which is currently at least partially in RAM, and transferring it to a disk.

Measuring Storage Capacity

If RAM is normally referred to as *memory,* disk space is normally referred to as *storage capacity.* Thus, you may be asked, "What is the storage capacity of your hard drive?" or simply, "How large is your hard drive?" Like RAM, storage capacity is measured in *kilobytes* (K) and *megabytes* (MB) and even *gigabytes* (GB). This can be a source of confusion. When talking about megabytes, it may not be immediately clear whether someone is referring to RAM (memory) capacity or disk (storage) capacity. Once you understand the context, however, it is usually clear how to distinguish between these two alternatives.

By the way, don't expect the amount of space a file occupies on a disk to be the same as the amount of space it needs when it loads into RAM. For various reasons, the numbers may be different. A program may load only part of its instructions into RAM at one time, thus requiring less RAM than you might expect. Alternatively, a program may need a lot more space than the storage size of the file to accommodate documents that you may open with the application.

Disk Storage Is Temporarily Permanent

A disk works in a way that is metaphorically similar to a cassette tape. You can write to a computer disk just as you can record to a cassette tape. When you turn off your cassette recorder, the information remains on tape. Later, you can play back the tape, or erase it and record something else. You can do the same thing with most types of computer disks.

Thus, disk storage is temporarily permanent: information written to it remains on the disk until you change it. That is, as with RAM, you can both read and write information to a disk. But, unlike RAM, information on disk is not stored electronically. Instead, as with cassette tape, an actual physical change to the disk occurs when you write new information to it. This is why, after you save a document to a disk, the information is retained even after you turn the computer off.

For problem solving:

The most important thing to remember is this: as you go through a typical computer session, a frequent two-way flow of information takes place from disk to RAM and back again. Understanding the distinctions between these two ways of holding information is often critical to isolating the causes of a problem and thus solving it.

For example, an application that cannot open because of insufficient memory is basically a RAM-related problem. An application that cannot open because the instructions stored on the disk have been damaged in some way is essentially a disk-related problem. The methods used to solve these different types of problems are, as you will see, quite different.

TECHNICALLY SPEAKING ▶ Putting It All Together

With this information now digested, you can now answer the initial questions asked in the "Exactly how did I get here?" section with more clarity.

When you turn on your machine, the processor and the ROM kick in immediately. They continue to play an essential role in all operations until the moment you shut down. Everything your computer does ultimately depends on instructions being sent to, and carried out by, the processor.

Almost immediately after this initial step, information (particularly from the System Folder files that I describe later in this chapter) stored on disk (most likely the hard disk inside your machine) begins to load into RAM. As this occurs, the smiling Macintosh icon appears briefly, indicating a problem-free start, followed by the Welcome to Mac OS display. Eventually, the desktop appears as the program called the Finder opens.

When you launch your word processor or any other software, this too is transferred from its disk storage location to RAM, so that you can now use it (assuming you have enough RAM for that program to run). The menu bars, windows, and dialog boxes that appear are produced by information taken from the program itself in combination with standard information accessed from the ROM (and, in some cases, from system software, as described later in this chapter).

When you work on your document and save it, the information is transferred out of RAM to disk storage, so it remains there even after you turn your Macintosh off. When you quit your application, you free up the RAM it occupied, which can then be used by another program.

Types of Disks and Disk Drives

The term *disk* refers to the actual medium that stores the information used by the computer. It is the metaphorical equivalent of the tape in a cassette tape player. The term *drive* refers to the mechanism used to read and write information to and from the disk. That is, the drive is like the cassette tape player itself. In component stereo systems, to hear the tape, you must connect the deck to a receiver and speakers. Similarly, to use information on a disk, the disk drive must be connected to the Macintosh.

Four basic categories of disks are considered here: hard disks, floppy disks, CD-ROM (and DVD) disks, and other removable cartridges/disks. (Note before proceeding: Check out Fix-It #14 if you need more background on terms such as SCSI, IDE, and USB).

Hard Disks

A hard disk, like its floppy disk counterpart, is simply a means of storing information—except that it can hold a lot more information than a floppy disk. These days, drives of 10 Gigabytes (that's more than 10,000 MB) or more are common. To put this in perspective, a 10 GB hard disk can hold the equivalent of more than 7,100 high-density floppy disks.

A hard disk drive (usually referred to as simply a *hard drive*) is a mechanism that contains the hard disk storage media inside its case. The typical hard disk drive mechanism has a hard disk permanently encased inside it. You cannot remove it or insert another one. Thus, for many people, the terms *hard disk* and *hard disk drive* seem synonymous, though technically they are as different as the terms *floppy disk* and *floppy disk drive*.

Every Mac comes with an *internal* hard drive, that is, one that is installed inside the case of the Mac itself. It is sold with the Mac OS and additional software preinstalled on it. This is the drive that you typically use as your startup drive (see Chapter 5,). Additional hard drives may be added internally or externally, depending upon which Mac model you have.

Amazingly, drive prices keep getting cheaper. You can buy a 20GB drive today for less money that you could buy a 20MB drive 12 years ago! Like memory, get the largest hard drive you can afford. You won't regret it.

Hard drives can be connected to your Mac via one of several types of connections: SCSI, IDE, FireWire, or even USB. Within a particular type of connection, there may be various subtypes. For example, you can increase the basic transfer speed of SCSI by using SCSI Fast (this doubles the maximum speed that data can travel over an SCSI connection from 5MB per second to 10MBper second). However, FireWire (which is much faster than even the fastest SCSI drive) is already replacing SCSI as the preferred connection for external drives. It can transfer data in speeds in excess of 100MB per second.

SEE: • **Fix-It #14 for more on the different ways to connect a hard drive to a Mac.**

Floppy Disks

Floppy disks are on the Mac's endangered species list. They are no longer included with the iMac or any Mac released since the iMac. Apple's position is that floppy disks are an ancient technology that should no longer be actively supported. However, for those of you who still desire a floppy disk drive, you can add one as an external device connected to the Mac's USB port.

SEE: • **Fix-It #14 for more on ports in general.**

For all of you faithful floppy disk users out there, here's what you need to know about these disks:

The standard size for floppy disks in use today are 1.44MB; they are also referred to as high-density (HD) disks. The other type you may see are 800K disks. These names refer to the approximate maximum storage capacity of the disks.

If you hold an 800K or HD disk with the front facing you, and with the metal slide on the bottom, you should see a small square hole visible in the upper right corner. On the rear side of this hole is a slide tab. When the tab is up, so that you can see through the hole, the disk is locked, which means that you cannot modify the contents of the disk in any way (see Chapter 6 for more on locked disks). HD disks include a second square hole on the upper left-hand side. There is no slide tab here; this hole is simply used by the floppy disk drive to identify the disk as an HD disk. HD disks also have the HD symbol to the side of the metal slide. Otherwise, the two types of disks look virtually identical.

HD and 800K disks are both *double-sided* disks. This means they store information on both sides of the disk.

A third type of floppy disk is a 400K (*single-sided* or *one-sided*) disk. Single-sided disks are identical to 800K disks except that they are designed to store information on only one side of the disk. Single-sided disks are almost never available anymore.

Current floppy disk drives and current versions of the Mac OS no longer recognize 400K disks. Some may not recognize 800K disks. Stick with HD disks exclusively, if you must use floppy disks at all.

Floppy disks that are formatted to run on PC computers (and typically running Windows) will not be recognized by your Mac unless you have certain software installed, most notably, Apple's File Exchange (as described more in Chapter 6).

Where Is the Flop? Looking at the hard-shell plastic case of a floppy disk, it may seem that the disk does not live up to its name. It's not floppy. This is because the term *floppy*

refers to the truly flexible, thin, plastic, circular disk encased inside the hard plastic shell. You can see this when you slide the metal shutter back. This floppy part actually stores the information.

The metal shutter is automatically pulled back when you insert the disk into a disk drive. This gives the disk drive access to the critical floppy media.

Figure 1-1 An 800K floppy disk (left) and an HD floppy disk (right). The HD symbol is upside down here. The lock tab on both disks is in the unlocked position (you cannot see through the hole)

CD-ROM and DVD-ROM Discs

CD-ROM Discs CD-ROM stands for Compact Disc-Read Only Memory. CD-ROM discs (the word *disk* often becomes *disc* when referring to CD-ROMs) are now the most common disk format for the Mac. All current models of Macintoshes come with a CD-ROM drive. If you purchase any software beyond that which came with your Mac, it almost always comes on a CD-ROM disc.

Basically, CD-ROM discs look identical to the compact discs that are now standard in the music industry (in fact, a CD-ROM drive can also play ordinary music CDs). A CD-ROM disc can hold over 600MB of data (or about as much as you could hold on more than 400 floppy disks). This is a major reason for the shift from floppy disks to CD-ROM discs. Much of today's software has grown so large that it requires at least one CD-ROM disc, sometimes more, to hold it all. To install software from a CD-ROM disc to your hard drive is a snap. Installing software from a set of 50 or more floppy disks is not something you would ever want to do.

A traditional disadvantage of CD-ROM discs is that they are slow—at least compared to hard drives. However, CD-ROM drives keep getting faster. You will see terms such as *24X drive* (which means that it is 24 times faster than the original CD-ROM drives). However, constraints imposed by the software on the disc and the connection of the drive to the Mac typically can mean that your drive is operating at a much slower speed than its theoretical maximum.

The second traditional disadvantage of CD-ROM discs is contained in the name "Read Only." This means that you can read from a CD-ROM disc, but not write to it. The data is written once to a disc, by the vendor who created the disc, and it can never be modified again. Fortunately, this limitation is changing. There are now CD-R (Recordable) and CD-RW (Read/Write) drives available for the end-user market. CD-R drives allow you to write to the drive only once. While this is obviously not ideal, these drives use the same inexpensive discs as are used with traditional CD-ROM drives, which means that the discs you create are cheap to make and can be used in virtually any CD-ROM drive. CD-RW drives can write to a disc multiple times. However, these drives require special (much more expensive) discs that typically cannot be used in ordinary CD-ROM drives.

CD drives typically connect to the Mac either via SCSI or, more often in newer Macs, IDE ports. FireWire CD drives are now also available.

DVD discs DVD stands for Digital Video Disc (or Digital Versatile Disc, depending upon who you ask). They look almost exactly like CDs, but they have a far greater capacity: up to 17GB! As a result, these discs can hold an entire movie, which is their major consumer use right now. However, the same basic DVD format can be used to store computer data. Because DVD drives can also play CDs, they are likely to ultimately replace CD drives over the next few years. As with CDs, there are multiple formats for DVD. These include DVD-Video (for movies), DVD-ROM (the DVD equivalent of CD-ROM), and DVD-RAM (an erasable read/write version of DVD format).

SEE: • **Chapter 5 and Chapter 10 for more on mounting and playing DVDs.**

Other Removable Storage

Floppy disks, CDs, and DVDs are all "removable." That is, you can eject one disk from its drive and insert a different one. However, the term "removable" drive has more commonly been used to apply to the remaining world of removable storage devices. Here is an overview of the more common examples:

Iomega drives Iomega makes the Zip and Jaz drives. These are currently the two most popular removable media formats.

Zip disks look somewhat similar to floppy disks. The original Zip disks hold 100MB of data; the newer ones can hold 250MB of data. In either case, they are significantly slower than hard drives. They are used mainly as a backup medium or to hold large files (such as graphics images or QuickTime movies) that would not fit on a floppy disk. You can make a Zip disk act as a startup disk, but you would only want to do this in an emergency (for example, if your normal startup disk stops working).

Jaz cartridges look almost like a casing for a hard drive mechanism. And that is fairly close to what they are. They come in either 1GB or 2GB capacities and they are almost as fast as the fastest of hard drives. As such, they can substitute for a hard drive in most situations. Plus, they have the advantage of being replaceable: you can simply eject one and replace it with another when it gets full. As with all removable media, they can also be used to transfer material from one computer to another (as long as both machines have access to the appropriate drive). However, Jaz cartridges are more easily damaged than most other removable media. You would not want to simply throw one in a briefcase or otherwise toss it around.

Zip drives come in SCSI, IDE, and USB versions. Jaz drives come in SCSI and USB versions for the Mac. Many Mac models offer an internal Zip drive as an option. For awhile, it appeared that Zip disks would replace floppy disks as the coin of the realm. Now, with other competing formats gaining popularity (such as SuperDisks and erasable DVD), a single standard seems less certain.

TAKE NOTE ▶ Using Zip 100MB disks in a Zip 250 drive

While the Zip 250 drive is basically compatible with 100MB Zip disks, there are some limitations:

- Write times to 100MB disks can be up to 10 times longer than to 250MB disks.

- There is no guarantee that a 100MB disk written to a Zip 250 drive will be able to be read by a Zip 100 drive. The Iomega manual reads: "If you write information to a 100MB Zip disk using a 250MB Zip drive, and later find that the disk cannot be read by a 100MB Zip drive, try reading the disk again using your 250MB Zip drive."

- The Iomega Tools software includes options for a short and a long format. The long format is preferred if you are having any problems using the disk. However, you cannot long format a 100MB Zip disk in a Zip 250 drive. Only short format is supported.

- Getting the drive to boot from a 100MB disk is a bit tricky. The Iomega manual actually recommends moving all your information from 100MB disks to 250MB disks and using only 250MB disks in your drive to "optimize performance."

SuperDisk drives A SuperDisk looks almost identical to a floppy disk. However, it holds 120MB of data, instead of a floppy disk's paltry 1.44MB. As a bonus, SuperDisk drives (such as the one by Imation) can also read and write to HD floppy disks. As such, these drives are especially popular as an add-on to an iMac (connected via the USB port), where they serve both as a means of using traditional floppy disks plus as an alternative to something such as a Zip drive for storing larger amounts of data. However, they are significantly slower than a Zip drive.

Other removable formats Other removable formats include *magneto-optical drives* and *digital tape drives* (used mainly for backing up data from your hard drive). Also gaining in popularity is the *ORB drive*. The cartridges for these drives hold 2GB of data and features speed comparable to the Jaz cartridge, but the disks are priced significantly less. Keep your eye on this one.

TAKE NOTE ▶ What About Monitors and Printers?

In addition to the basic components described here, virtually all computer systems include some type of a monitor and a printer. Check out Chapters 7, 9, and 10 for more information about these additional components.

System Software

The term *system software* most commonly refers to the basic set of files included with each Macintosh. These files come pre-installed on your hard drive. They are also included on the CD-ROM disc that comes with your Macintosh. Finally, you can purchase system software packages independent of any hardware purchase.

A few system software files are essential for the use of your Macintosh. Without access to them, your Macintosh typically will not even start up. Others are nearly essential, needed for routine operations such as printing. In most cases, these and related files are contained in a special folder called the *System Folder*. A disk that contains such a folder is called a *startup disk* (a topic discussed more in Chapter 5).

Many users are not familiar with what is contained inside a System Folder. Some users may not even be aware they have one. If this describes you, your awareness is about to change. **To effectively solve problems on the Macintosh, understanding the basics of the System Folder and its contents is essential!**

System Software Versions

Apple periodically releases new versions, or upgrades, to its system software, which is referred to as *Mac OS*. Often, rather than releasing a completely new version of the system software, Apple may release a special subset of files typically called *Mac OS Updates.* In either case, there are at least three reasons for releasing these upgrades:

1. To fix problems with the previous version of the software.

2. To provide support for new models of Macintosh that have been released.

3. To add new features that improve on the previous version.

The differences in the features of these versions is most relevant to the problem-solving issues in this book. These differences affect what problems you may have and what problem-solving tools are at your disposal.

Every time a significant revision occurs, Apple assigns it a new numerical name. Thus, users may refer to system software by its version number, such as version 8.6 or version 8.5.1. The version number indicates the extent of the difference of the new version from its predecessor. Thus, changes in the number after the second decimal indicate the most minor changes. Really major upgrades call for a change in the first digit.

As of this writing, Apple is preparing to offer a major fork in the road regarding your choice of Mac OS: *Mac OS 9.x* continues the tradition of the Mac OS that dates back to the original Mac of 1984. *Mac OS X*, on the other hand, is a radical departure, a fundamentally different OS (although still Mac-like in its appearance). We'll discuss Mac OS X more in Chapter 15.

SEE: • **Fix-It #4 for more on installing and upgrading your system software.**

The Essentials: The System File, The Finder, System Resources, Mac OS ROM, and Other Important Files

All of the files in this section are absolutely essential. Without them, your Mac would never complete a successful startup.

The System File

The System file is the single most critical file in your System Folder. The System file contains a wealth of information regarding icons, dialog box messages, fonts, keyboard layouts, sounds, and much more that affect your Mac every second that it is on.

System

Figure 1-2 The System "suitcase" file icon.

Unlike the other files in this section, you can actually "open" the System file from the desktop. Double-click the file and it will open a window that lists all the keyboard layouts and sounds installed. There's a lot more in the System file that is hidden from view. You would need a utility such as ResEdit to access it. But don't worry; you rarely, if ever, need to dig this deep into the System file.

SEE: • **Chapter 8 for more on ResEdit.**

The Finder (and the Desktop)

The Finder is the second most critical file in the System Folder. This is because the Finder creates the Macintosh *desktop*. The desktop is where you find the disk icons, the Trash, and the various windows that display the contents of all mounted disks. Actually, the words *Finder* and *desktop* are often used interchangeably. When you are in the Finder, the menu bar contains the familiar File, Edit, View, and Special menus.

The Finder is your main way of navigating around your disks. It is from here that you locate files, open files, copy files, and delete files. In general, you would not want to do without it, even if you could.

The Finder is also a great problem-solving tool. Beginning in the next chapter, and continuing throughout this book, I describe numerous Finder features, such as its Get Info command in the File menu, which can be used for fixing problems.

BY THE WAY ▶ Finder Preferences

Finder preferences have expanded greatly in Mac OS 8.5, as compared to previous versions. What follows is just a sampling of the customization you can accomplish:

View menu: Icons and button view You probably already know what an icon is; icons are small graphic images. Their most prevalent use is for files on the Finder's desktop.

You use the Finder's View menu to determine how icon files on the desktop are displayed. Select either "as Icons" or "as Buttons." The main difference between these two choice is that you double-click on an icon and single-click on a button to launch a file. You can also choose from different sizes of icons from the View Options command in the View menu.

To arrange the order of icons, select the Arrange command from the View menu and choose how you want the icons listed from the hierarchical menu (for example, by Name, by Size, and so on).

From View Options, you can select a choice that causes icons to automatically snap to an invisible grid whenever you move them, or you can choose to move icons to whatever location you wish.

View menu: List Views Alternatively, you can view a window's contents "as List." Even here, the icons of the files are displayed along the left border of the listing. Once again, you can choose different sizes of the icons from the View Options window.

To see the contents of a folder in List View, you can either double-click the folder (to open up a new window) or click the triangle to the left of the folder icon (to list the contents within the same window).

List View offers numerous options, both directly from the window itself and from the View Options window. For example, if you click on the title of any column, you sort the listings by the contents of that column. Clicking the pyramid triangle at the end of the row of titles will reverse the order of the sort (for example, A-Z changes to Z-A). You can also use the mouse to adjust the width and location of each column and (from the View Options menu) select which columns you wish to display at all.

The option to Calculate Folder Sizes, while occasionally useful, is best left disabled. Leaving it on can significantly slow down how long it takes for a folder to open.

Preferences View Options changes only affect the selected window. To make a change to the default selections for all windows, select Preferences from the Finder's Edit menu, and select the View tab. From the General tab, you can select whether the spacing between icons in the grid should be tight or wide.

Appearance From the Fonts tab of the Appearance control panel, you can select the large and small System Fonts (used for menus and headings, for example) and the View Font (used for icon names and list view text). From the Appearance tab, you can select the text highlight color. From the Desktop tab, you can select the desktop background.

  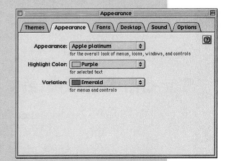

Figure 1-3 Some of the different Appearance and View Options for modifying the look of the desktop: View Options (left); Finder Preferences (middle); Appearance control panel (right).

System Resources

Starting with the Mac OS 8.5, Apple split some of the resources that you would expect to find in the System file into a new file called System Resources. It is just as essential as the System file itself. A special version of Disk First Aid that can run at startup is stored here. Data needed for the new Open and Save dialog boxes used in Mac OS 8.5 or later are also located here.

SEE: • **Fix-It #10 and Chapter 8.**

Mac OS ROM

If you are using an iMac, or any newer model of Mac, you will also have a file called Mac OS ROM. This file (as described earlier in this chapter in "The CPU and ROM") contains information that was formerly in the hardware ROM file on the logic board. If your Mac uses this file, you can be sure that it is essential (see also Chapter 14, for more on this file).

Other Important Files

Recent versions of the Mac OS will likely not start up unless you have the *Text Encoding Converter* extension installed. This file is mainly used to make sure that text characters are displayed correctly on your Mac, even if the text originates from another computer that uses a different set of "encodings" to describe the characters. As I understand it, the Text Encoding Converter is only essential for drives formatted using HFS Plus (see Fix-It #13) because this format uses a new system for naming files, called *Unicode*, which requires the Text Encoding Converter. Still, to keep things simple, the Mac OS now requires this extension, whether you use HFS Plus or not.

As described in Fix-It #4, if you have a Mac model that was released subsequent to the OS version you are using, you may also need an *Enabler* file. Occasionally, depending upon what version of the OS you are using, and what Mac you are running, other files may also be deemed "essential." For example, the Appearance extension was essential in Mac OS 8.0 and 8.1 (but is no longer used in Mac OS 8.5 or later).

If you are unable to start up your Mac because an essential file is missing, the Mac will usually give you a message at startup informing you of what is missing. At this point, the main solution is to start up with another disk (such as a bootable CD), reinstall the missing file, and then start up again from the original drive. For help in reinstalling files, check out Fix-It #4.

Special Subfolders

The System Folder depends heavily on the use of several special subfolders that now contain most of the Macintosh system software. These folders, together with the standard files that Apple places in them, are all installed automatically when you first create the System Folder with the Mac OS Installer.

Which Item Goes Where?

When you put a new item in your System Folder, you generally don't need to know which special subfolder it belongs to, if any. Simply place the file destined for the System Folder *on* the System Folder icon (*not* in the System Folder window). When you see the System Folder icon highlighted, release the mouse. The Macintosh then checks if it knows where the file should go. If it does, you get a dialog box informing you of the file's intended destination and asking you to confirm that this is correct. Click OK, and you are done.

Helpful Hint: Watch out for some newer files that are supposed to be in the Control Panels folder but are really ordinary applications in disguise. When you drag these to the System Folder icon, they may *not* be placed in the Control Panels folder. Instead, they will be left in the root level of the System Folder. If this happens, you will have to drag them to the Control Panels folder yourself (of course, they will work fine whether or not they are in the Control Panels folder; you just won't see them listed in the folder if they are not placed there).

SEE: • **Fix-It #3 for more on extensions and control panels.**

The main System Folder subfolders are named as follows: Apple Menu Items, Extensions, Control Panels, Startup Items, Shutdown Items, Preferences, Fonts, Control Strip Modules, Contextual Menu Items, and Internet Search Sites. Also noteworthy (and this does not exhaust the list) are Appearance, Favorites, Application Support, Launcher Items, Scripts, and Help.

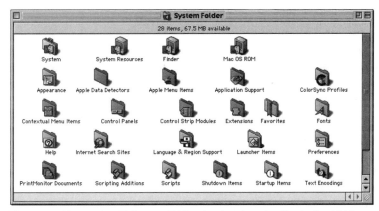

Figure 1-4 The inside of a System Folder showing the many files and subfolders mentioned in the text.

Apple Menu Items Folder

Any file placed in the Apple Menu Items folder appears in the Apple menu. This menu, located on the left side of the menu bar and denoted by an Apple logo, is available in almost every application. In the old days, this is where special files called "desk accessories" appeared. Now, this folder can hold just about anything you want. Especially important items found in the Apple menu (which are all discussed throughout this book) are the Chooser, Network Browser, Scrapbook, and Notepad.

Extensions Folder

The Extensions folder now contains several types of files. The most common are *system extensions* and *Chooser extensions*.

System Extensions System extensions accomplish a variety of specialized tasks, mostly by working in the background the entire time the Macintosh is on.

SEE: • "Take Note: What's an INIT?" later in this chapter.

For these types of extensions to work, they must load into memory at startup. Thus, when you first place a new system extension on your disk, it has no effect. You must restart your Macintosh before the extension can perform its function. Furthermore, during startup, the Macintosh looks for these extensions only in certain locations. The main location, of course, is the Extensions folder. However, it also checks the Control Panels folder (see below) as well as the top level of the System Folder (that is, not in any subfolder). System extensions in any other location will not load at startup and, therefore, will not work.

SEE: • Fix-It #4 for more on problems with startup extensions.

Chooser Extensions To understand the meaning of Chooser extensions, you first have to understand the Chooser itself. The Chooser is a desk accessory found in the Apple Menu Items folder. Its primary function, as the name implies, is to let you *choose* which printer (or networking server) you intend to use.

When you select the Chooser, a selection of icons (such as LaserWriter, ImageWriter, or AppleShare) is typically displayed on the left side of the Chooser window. Each icon represents a Chooser extension located in your Extensions folder.

The most common type of Chooser extension is called a printer driver. These files are necessary so that the Macintosh and the printer can talk to each other. Printer drivers for all of Apple's printers come with the Macintosh system software. Printers from other companies may require their own drivers.

AppleShare is a Chooser extension that has functions related to networking and file sharing. By the way, unlike most Chooser extensions, AppleShare loads into memory at startup together with system extensions.

By the way, the Chooser is likely to be on the way out and may not be included in upcoming versions of the Mac OS. Check Chapter 15, for possible late-breaking information on this development.

SEE: • Chapter 7 for more on the Chooser and printing in general.
• Chapters 9 and 10 for more details on the Page Setup and Print dialog boxes.
• Chapter 11 for more on AppleShare.

Other "Extensions" The modern Extensions folder also contains a variety of other files, especially Shared Libraries. These files function as extensions, except that they typically do not load into memory at startup. They are loaded only when needed by one of the applications that "share" the file.

SEE: • Fix-It #3 for more information on these other extensions.

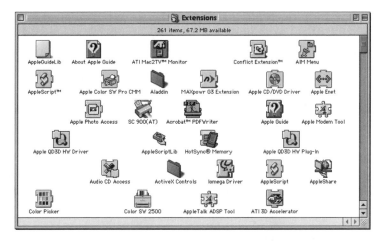

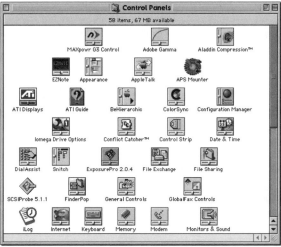

Figure 1-5 A peek inside an Extensions folder and a Control Panels folder.

Control Panels Folder

As its name implies, the Control Panels folder holds special files called *control panels.*
They are sometimes more technically referred to as *control panel devices,* or *cdevs.*
What do these control panels do? Many of those that come with the system software,
such as General Controls, Mouse, and Sound, set basic preferences for the operation of
the Macintosh. These include such settings as the cursor blinking rate, mouse tracking
speed, and sound volume. Most of the remaining control panels function similarly to
system extensions. That is, they perform some task(s) while working in the background,
and they must be loaded into memory at startup before they can perform their task.
In these cases, each control panel's window is primarily used to select among options
that modify how its background activity works.

SEE: • **"Take Note: What's an INIT?" below.**

Several control panels that are particularly relevant to problem solving are described in more detail in the next chapter. In recent versions of the OS, most control panels function similarly to ordinary applications. That is, you can launch them no matter where they are stored. Unless they contain an INIT portion that loads at startup, there is no need to keep them in the Control Panels folder. However, it is still convenient to do so. If nothing else, it makes it easy to access control panels from the Control Panels (alias) item in the Apple menu. Also, a few applications that work with a specific control panel may not find the control panel unless it is in its expected (Control Panels folder) location. Similarly, be careful about renaming extensions and control panels. In most cases, there is no harm in doing so. However, in some cases, an application that works with the control panel will not find it unless it has its "given" expected name.

TAKE NOTE ▶ What's an INIT?

The term INIT is generally used to describe programs that, when correctly located in a System Folder, load into memory during the Macintosh's INITial startup process. Usually, they remain there until you select Shut Down. In particular, virtually all system extensions and the majority of control panels fall into this category.

INITs typically perform functions that require a constant presence and availability throughout a session. For example, a given INIT may place a digital clock on the menu bar. The clock continues to work in the background, remaining on the screen no matter what application is active, as long as the menu bar is visible. Similarly, Apple's QuickTime extension is an INIT. Unless it is present in the background, no application can run QuickTime movies. Other INITs act to modify particular components of the Macintosh interface. For example, an INIT may add new features to the Macintosh's Open and Save As dialog boxes (ACTION Files, from Power On Software, is a popular example).

The term INIT has fallen out of favor. Apple currently prefers to refer to these programs simply as *extensions.* However, there is a good deal of potential confusion here. Not all extensions function by loading into memory at startup. System extensions do, but Chooser extensions generally do not. Conversely, not all programs that load into memory at startup are technically called extensions. Some control panels also work this way. The only real difference between these startup control panels and system extensions is that the control panels provide a dialog box (the control panel!) for selecting various options, while system extensions typically do not. It is as if there is a system extension component contained within the control panel, which is actually pretty much the case. Thus, I find it preferable to group all of the files that load into memory at startup (system extension or control panel) under the umbrella term of INITs. This is the convention I have used in previous editions of this book. However, the term INIT has now become so rarely used elsewhere, that I am abandoning it. Instead, bowing to convention, I will refer to these files as *(startup) extensions* (some more technical aspects of this terminology are described in Chapter 8).

By the way, there is no way to immediately identify which control panels function as extensions and which do not. You can usually tell what's going on because most system extensions and most control panels that function like system extensions place a small icon along the bottom of the Welcome to Macintosh screen as the file loads into memory. However, not all of these files do this and even those that do usually have an option to turn off this feature. A more reliable alternative is to check the listing of a startup management utility (as explained in Fix-It #4). These utilities either list only those extensions and control panels that are truly startup extensions or clearly identify which ones are and which ones are not. Another alternative is to check something called a file's Finder flags (a method that I describe in Chapter 8).

Startup Items Folder

Any application or document file that you place in the Startup Items folder automatically opens as part of the startup process. Thus, if you want your word processor to be opened automatically each time you turn on your Macintosh, place the word processor file (or its alias) in this folder. (For more about aliases, see Take Note ▸ Aliases on page 30.)

These files are distinctly different from the system extensions and control panels that load into memory at startup. Placing an item in the Startup Items folder is simply a shortcut method for getting the file to open. This folder confers no special properties on the file. Any file to be opened can be placed in the Startup items folder. On the other hand, system extensions, as described earlier, are special types of files that must be loaded into memory at startup in order to work at all.

Shut Down Items Folder

Complementary in function to the Startup Items folder, any applications in the Shut Down Items folder are launched just after you select Shut Down, but before the Mac actually shuts down. You might set up some AppleScript files to run just before you shut down, but there's not much practical use for this feature.

Preferences Folder

Many programs, including the Finder, allow you to change the default settings of the program. That is, these changes are remembered even after you quit the application, and they are still in effect the next time you use it. For example, a word processor may normally open with its text ruler visible. However, you can usually select a Hide Ruler command to get rid of it. In some cases, you may even be able to set a Preferences option so that the ruler is automatically hidden from view whenever the program opens, thus eliminating the need to select the Hide Ruler command each time. This is a change from the default setting.

Generally, the program remembers these settings by placing the information in a special preferences file, which the program accesses whenever it is opened.

These preferences files, together with miscellaneous other accessory files, are typically located in the Preferences folder. However, preferences files can also be found at the root level of the System Folder. Occasionally, a preferences file can be located not in the System Folder at all, but within the same folder as the application to which it is linked.

The Mac OS itself comes with a dizzying array of preferences files, including files for Apple Menu Options, Apple Video Player, AppleCD Player, AppleScript, and AppleVision (and those are just the files that begin with A!).

Fonts Folder

Fonts placed in this folder appear in the Font menu and thus are used by any application that has a Font menu. If you use a utility such as Adobe Type Manager Deluxe or Suitcase, you can access fonts stored in other locations. Otherwise, except for a few fonts stored in the System file or directly in applications, the Font folder is where all your fonts will be.

Control Strip Modules

The Control Strip is the bar of icons, each with its own pop-up menu, that provides access to settings for monitor resolution, color depth, sound level, AppleTalk (on or off), and more. The functions that appear in the Control Strip are determined by which Control Strip modules (CSMs) appear in the Control Strip Modules folder. The Mac OS ships with a set of these modules preinstalled. Various third-party programmers have created yet other modules.

In recent versions of the Mac OS, you can directly add or remove items from the Control Strip by Option-dragging the icon from the Strip or Option-dragging the file to the Strip, bypassing the need to deal with the folder directly.

A Control Strip control panel can turn the feature on and off.

Contextual Menu Items

This Mac OS feature is accessed by holding down the Control key and clicking the mouse. A pop-up menu then appears. The items included in this menu are a function of two factors.

First, it depends on where you are when you click (hence, the name "context"). For example, if you Control-click on the desktop background, one of your choices will be "Change Desktop Background." If instead, you click on a file icon, you will have choices such as Make Alias or Get Info. If the file is an alias, one of the choices will be Show Original. If you are in an application other than the Finder, you may find application-specific commands in the contextual menu (if the application was written to take advantage of this feature). In general, the items in these contextual menus duplicate what is available from the menu bar at the top of the window. It is provided as a more convenient way to access these commands.

The second factor that determines what menu items appear is what Contextual Menu Item Plug-ins are in the Contextual Menu Items folder. Once again, many of these come from developers other than Apple. For example, a Virex plug-in adds the ability to scan a selected file for viruses. A StuffIt Deluxe plug-in adds StuffIt's Magic menu choices to the contextual menu. **Note:** In a couple of cases, it is possible to add items to contextual menus via a control panel. FinderPop is the best known example of this.

SEE: • **Chapter 15 for more on troubleshooting contextual menus.**

Internet Search Sites

The most eye-popping new feature introduced with Mac OS 8.5 was Sherlock. At its core, Sherlock is a replacement for Apple's older Find File function. But what was most compelling about Sherlock was completely new: its ability to search the World Web Web right from the desktop. If you are already online, simply select Sherlock's Search Internet tab, enter a search term, and click the Search button. In a matter of seconds,

Sherlock posts results simultaneously gathered from Alta Vista, Excite, Apple's own Tech Info Library, and a collection of other Web sites. Click on any item and Sherlock displays a brief look at its contents. Double-click an item and Sherlock opens your Web browser to the selected page!

Essentially, any Web site that has its own search engine can be included in a Sherlock search. All that is needed is a Sherlock plug-in. The Mac OS comes with a collection of these plug-ins, located in the Internet Search Sites folder. Once again, many additional ones are available. In fact, chances are good that every Mac-oriented Web site worth its salt has its own Sherlock plug-in.

SEE: • **Chapter 15 for more on Sherlock's Internet features.**

Launcher Items

When you turn on Launcher, from the Launcher control panel, the items that appear in the Launcher window are determined by what items are in the Launcher Items folder. Similar to the Control Strip, you can drag items directly into and out of the Launcher window. Hint: to create multiple launcher "windows," place a folder in the Launcher Items window and precede the name of the folder with a bullet (•).

Appearance

The Appearance folder contains the Desktop Pictures, Sound Sets, and Themes that you can select from the Appearance control panel.

Favorites

When you highlight an item and select Add to Favorites from the Finder's File menu (or from a Contextual Menu), the name of the highlighted item is added to the Favorites item in the Apple menu. What actually happens is that an alias of the item is placed in the Favorites folder inside the Apple Menu Items folder of the System Folder. You can now access that item directly from the hierarchical menu that appears when you scroll down to Favorites in the Apple menu.

Application Support

Numerous programs create a folder in the System Folder to house accessory files for the application. Apple now encourages programmers to house all of these files in the Application Support folder. If you have AppleWorks or Adobe products, you will see such support files here. Other developers will likely follow this lead in the future.

Help

When you need an answer to a basic question about your Mac, your first thought may be to reach for the manuals that came with your computer. Unfortunately, Apple's printed documentation gets skimpier with each new version of the Mac OS. It is now almost non-existent. In contrast, Apple's digital help keeps expanding all the time .

Begin your search for help with the ReadMe files and other related online documents that come with each OS release. Beyond that, the primary way to get help is via the

Help menu. If you are in the Finder, the first choice in the menu will be Help Center. If you select this, you should see further choices: such as AppleScript Help and Mac Help. Select one to get a further list of help topics. You can also select Mac Help directly from the Help Menu. Depending on what software you have installed, other Help files may also be available. For example, on my Mac, I have an option for the HP LaserJet Printer Guide.

If you select the Help menu when something other than the Finder is active, you are likely to see a Help option for the active application.

The Apple Help documents, accessed via the Mac OS Help Center, are located in the Help folder of the System Folder. Other Help documents may be stored in other locations in the System Folder or even in the folder of the relevant application.

Currently, there are two basic types of Help files. Initially, in Mac OS 7.5 when this feature was first introduced, help files were based on a format called Apple Guide. Apple Guide is an interactive help system. From a list in the main Guide window, you select the topic for which you want help. The Guide then uses a series of windows to take you step-by-step through the process of answering your question. In many cases, if it tells you to do something (such as "Select the Apple menu"), it further assists you by indicating on screen exactly what to do (by "circling" the Apple menu icon). You carry out the suggested steps while Apple Guide remains active. This is what is meant by "interactive help."

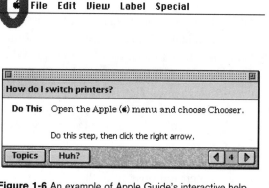

Figure 1-6 An example of Apple Guide's interactive help.

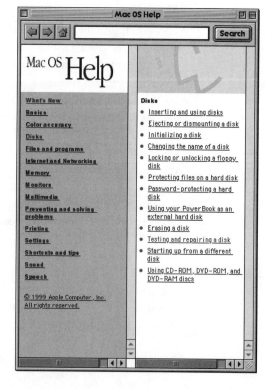

Figure 1-7 An example of a
Mac OS Help HTML window.

However, developers beyond Apple were reluctant to spend the time needed to write Apple Guide Help files. As a result, the feature was never widely adopted. This is probably why, in Mac OS 8.5, Apple shifted its Help to a Web page system (based on HTML documents). Now, you select Help items via hypertext links that work exactly the same way as links in a Web browser do.

Currently, both the Guide-type and HTML-type help can be accessed from the Help menu. What appears depends upon what the programmer of the Help decided to use.

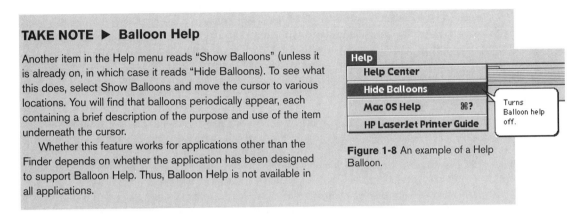

TAKE NOTE ▶ Balloon Help

Another item in the Help menu reads "Show Balloons" (unless it is already on, in which case it reads "Hide Balloons). To see what this does, select Show Balloons and move the cursor to various locations. You will find that balloons periodically appear, each containing a brief description of the purpose and use of the item underneath the cursor.

Whether this feature works for applications other than the Finder depends on whether the application has been designed to support Balloon Help. Thus, Balloon Help is not available in all applications.

Figure 1-8 An example of a Help Balloon.

Still More Folders

The list just keeps growing. It seems that with each new version of the Mac OS come new OS folders. Among the remaining examples are Color Sync Profiles, and Scripts. Almost all of the System Folder subfolders will be mentioned again in the relevant sections of later chapters of this book.

Remaining System Folder Files

The remainder of the System Folder contains items of varying degrees of significance. Some of these files are part of the Macintosh system software and are installed at the same time that the System and Finder files are installed. The Scrapbook File, which is used in conjunction with the Scrapbook desk accessory, is an example. The Scripts folder is another.

The remaining items in your System Folder come from other companies. I have already mentioned most of these possibilities: extensions, control panels, and third-party plug-ins for such features as Sherlock, Control Strip, and Contextual Menus.

Is It Apple or Not Apple? You can generally tell whether an application in the System Folder comes from Apple by selecting Get Info from the Finder's File menu for that file. If the file is part of the system software, the information usually indicates this at the top of the window (where it says something like *Mac OS 9.0*, for example) and/or at the bottom, next to the word *Version* (where it says that the file is copyrighted by Apple). If the item is a document created by a Mac OS application, such as the Note Pad file, the creating application should be indicated in the Kind line of the Get Info window listing (which should read, "Note Pad document," for example).

With so many possible files, if you open your System Folder now, you will almost certainly find some files that are unfamiliar to you. For now, leave them alone. Later on in this book, especially in Chapter 2, I discuss how to decide whether you need them or not.

TAKE NOTE ▶ Aliases

You can create an alias of any file on your drive. Here's the what, how, and why of aliases:

In the File menu of the Finder is a command called Make Alias. When you select a file (or folder) and then select this command, the Finder creates a new file that superficially looks identical to the original file. However, its name is in italics rather than plain text, and the word *alias* is attached to the end of the name. More important, the file is as little as 1K in size. It does not contain any of the information of the original file; it is simply used as a pointer to the original file. That is, you can move this alias around as you like. Whenever you double-click on an alias, the Macintosh locates the original file (even if it is now in a different folder) and launches it.

Among other uses, placing a collection of aliases together in a single folder is a convenient way of having access to a variety of applications that may be scattered in a variety of different locations on your hard drive.

Of course, if you delete the original file, the alias becomes useless and double-clicking the alias does not open anything. However, renaming the original file does not break the connection.

Do you want to find the location of the original file of an alias on your hard drive? Use contextual menus to do so. Select the file, access the contextual menu, and select Show Original. (Prior to Mac OS 8, there was a Show Original option in a file's Get Info window.)

Do you want to create an alias in a location other than the same location where the original file sits? You can simply create the alias and drag it to the new location. Or you can do it in one step: simply hold down the Command-Option keys while dragging the file. This instantly creates an alias, rather than a copy, at the new location.

If the Finder ever loses track of which original file is linked to an alias, a dialog box will appear when you double-click the alias file. From here, you will have the option to reselect the alias's "original" file. You can even choose a different file from the one that was initially selected.

Figure 1-9 QuickTime Player: the icons for the "real" file and its alias.

SEE: • **Chapter 6 for more tips on using aliases.**

TAKE NOTE ▶ Applications and Documents

In addition to the software categories already described in this chapter, there are two other major types of files: applications and documents. Typically, applications are the programs that are used to create documents. For example, AppleWorks is an application, while a letter that you create with AppleWorks is called an AppleWorks document.

This distinction can get blurry around the edges. For example, some applications never create documents (such as a utility application that is used just to check whether a disk is damaged or not). Further, many applications use accessory files (such as translator files and plug-in modules) which are a special type of document file, even though they were not created by the application.

2

Be Prepared:
Preventing Problems

Preventive Maintenance *(continued)*

Tooling Up

This chapter is about troubleshooting tools and preventative maintenance.

For hardware repairs, you can't do much without the proper tools. You need screwdrivers, pliers, and wrenches whether the hardware is a computer, a television, a refrigerator, or a car. The same idea is true for computer software repairs—except that your main tools are electronic, not metal. In either case, first you need to gather the relevant tools required for the repair, and then you must become familiar with how to use them.

Solving problems also means trying to avoid the problem in the first place. Do you regularly change the oil filter in your car to prevent problems caused by dirty oil? Well, the same logic applies to computer maintenance.

Damage Control

I describe many types of problems in this book, but certain themes keep recurring. These include *damaged disks, corrupted files, software bugs,* and *software conflicts.*

If these terms are not familiar to you, they can seem a bit confusing. What, exactly, gets damaged if the disk looks okay physically? How does this damage occur? Where do bugs come from? Why do conflicts occur? Here are the answers.

Damaged Files and Disks

A *damaged* (or *corrupted*) *file* means that the data contained in the file has, at least partially, been lost or incorrectly altered. The result is that the Macintosh can no longer "understand" the file correctly. This damage usually means that the file either will not open at all or will not function properly if it does open. In some cases, trying to use a damaged file may result in the Mac abruptly coming to a halt—an event typically referred to as a *system crash. There are some files on your Mac that are so critical that damage to them can prevent the entire disk from being "read" by your Mac.* If the disk is your startup disk, you may not be able to start up – this situation is often referred to as a *crashed disk.*

In most cases, damage to files is essentially *software damage.* No physical damage to the disk itself has occurred. Consider the following analogy: an entire scene of a movie you taped is somehow lost or erased. The videotape machine is still fine. The actual videotape is still fine. But the movie is not fine. This missing scene is similar to a damaged file on a computer. However, in some cases, special software can be used to "fix" damaged files. At this point, our videotape analogy starts to break down a bit.

Software damage can occur if a file is being saved, or even being accessed, at the time of some unexpected interruption, such as a power failure or a system crash. The result is that the file is saved incorrectly. The wrong data are written to the file. Software damage can also occur because of seemingly random and unpredictable changes that can happen to a disk over its lifetime. For example, stored electronic information is vulnerable to almost any sort of electromagnetic interference, and even a minor alteration can have serious consequences.

A related problem is referred to as *media damage* or *bad blocks.* Here, the cause of the problem is a defect in the physical disk media. If a part of the surface of a disk gets marred, for example, any file that occupies that area is damaged. Although it is true that the file itself is damaged, the actual cause of the problem is with the disk. It takes only the smallest amount of damage to cause total loss of access to a file. Like software damage, media damage can also result in system crashes and disk crashes.

Scratches or flaking of the magnetic surface of a disk are also common causes of media damage. Damage may be present from the first time you use a disk, or it may occur over time. A specific event, such as an accidental bumping of the drive while it is in use, may damage the drive media. More often, defects occur simply as a consequence of normal use or aging of the disk.

Returning to the videotape analogy, imagine a scene in a movie suddenly becoming blurred or distorted because the tape had been stretched or crumpled in that area. The movie scene is probably irrecoverably damaged, and you can no longer use that section of the tape for future recordings (you may, in fact, choose to splice it out). If the damage is severe enough, you may even have to discard the tape altogether. Still, you do not need to bring in the recorder itself for repairs. In this case, tape damage is clearly distinct from damage to the mechanical or electronic components of the recorder.

Similarly, media damage, while technically a hardware problem, is separate from damage to the mechanisms of the disk drive itself. As with videotape damage, media damage can often be resolved without requiring a trip to the repair shop; only software tools are needed. However, media damage to a hard drive, if the software techniques fail to work, will require repair or replacement of the entire drive.

Finally, a damaged disk may be "true" *hardware damage* to some component of the disk drive. This will almost certainly require replacement of the drive.

SEE: • **Fix-Its #10 and #11 for more information on file and disk damage.**

Software Bugs and Conflicts

A software bug is simply an error made by the programmer when the program was written. Thus, it is caused by the people who created the program, not by you. There is no way that you can repair a bug yourself. The only permanent solution is to get a new version of the software that has fixed the problem, when it becomes available. In the meantime, you may find some acceptable work-around solutions.

Software bugs vary in their level of seriousness. Less serious bugs may have only a cosmetic effect on the display and can often be ignored (though caution is advised even here, as these bugs may be harbingers of more serious problems). More serious bugs may prevent you from using the program entirely.

A software conflict is a special case of a software bug. Typically, what happens is that one program is written in a way that fails to take into account something that another program may do. If both of these programs are in use at the same time, they conflict with each other. A common result of such a conflict is a system crash. A conflict may also occur between a software program and a hardware component (such as a particular monitor). That is, some programs may not work when certain hardware is in use.

If all software programs were written perfectly, none of these bugs or conflicts would occur. But software programs are written by humans, so bugs and conflicts do occur—all too frequently.

A Troubleshooter's Toolkit

In the early days of personal computing, solving computer problems required that you be a programmer who had developed your own problem-solving tools. Thankfully, these days, the tools have already been designed for you. You simply need to acquire them. Many of them are free while a few require a relatively inexpensive purchase. These tools cannot solve every problem. On the other hand, there are many problems you can solve without them.

The problem-solving tools (or *utilities*) described here are designed for users who have little or no technical skills. Some of the utilities are so easy to use that they practically run themselves.

TAKE NOTE ▶ **What's a Utility?**

Most applications that you use probably fall in the productivity category. That is, their purpose is to allow you to do something on the computer faster, easier, and better than you could do it without the computer. Word processors and spreadsheets are typical examples.

However, some programs exist only to accomplish tasks that you would never do if you did not use a computer. These programs are called utilities. For example, you can get utilities to help you back up your software (that is, to make a second copy that you keep in the event something goes wrong with the first copy). Unless you use a computer, you obviously have no reason to make backup copies of computer disks.

Hundreds of utilities are available to assist you in almost every imaginable task, from backing up files, to undeleting files, to recovering damaged files. Some are designed to make your computer life easier. Others are designed to help solve problems. I describe many of them in this chapter.

Many beginning users balk at using these utilities. They feel that utilities are primarily for experienced or professional users who have the time and interest to learn how to master them. This is not true. Every user, regardless of skill level, can learn how to use—and benefit from—the utilities described in this chapter.

Table 2-1 gives a summary of useful troubleshooting tools. However, it is not the last word on the subject; other utilities are mentioned throughout the book.

Make sure that your Toolkit includes at least one example of each of the following categories:

- data repair and recovery package
- anti-virus utility

- back-up utility

- disk formatting utility

- extensions manager

- a SCSI mounting utility (if your Mac has a SCSI port)

The other categories of utilities in Table 2-1 are also valuable, but you may not need them right away. Some you may never need. But the time to start stocking your Toolkit is now. Details on how to get these products are described in the Appendix.

Table 2-1 ▶ A Catalog of Troubleshooting Utilities

NAMES/ TYPE OF UTILITY	USE IT TO:	FOR MORE INFORMATION, SEE:
Macintosh System Software		
Mac OS Help	Get interactive help for problem solving	Chapter 1
Functions built into the Mac OS	Rebuild desktop, zap parameter RAM, reset Power Manager (on PowerBooks), and more	This chapter, Fix-It #8 Fix-It #9
Finder	Determine pertinent information about files (such as version number), locate files, copy files, delete files, set memory allocations for files, erase floppy disks, restart, shut down, and more	This chapter, Chapter 4 Chapter 5 Chapter 6 Fix-It #5 Fix-It #15
Installer	Do a clean reinstall of system software	Fix-It #4
Memory control panel	Access disk cache, virtual memory, and RAM disk settings	Fix-It #5
Startup Disk control panel	Select which disk is to be the startup disk, if more than one potential startup disk is available	Chapter 5
Control panel for Monitor and Sound, and related Control Strip options	Adjust the depth of the display (how many colors or grays are displayed)	Chapter 10
General Controls control panel	Automatically lock Application and System Folder files, hide the Finder when in the background, and more	Chapter 6
Chooser	Turn on AppleTalk, select printer, access AppleShare, and related functions	Chapter 7 Chapter 11
Disk First Aid	Check for, and possibly repair, damaged disks	This chapter Fix-It #10
Drive Setup	Update disk driver, check for media damage, reformat disk	Fix-It #12 Fix-It #13
Extensions Manager	Manage extensions (which ones are on or off at startup)	Fix-It #4
Disk Copy	Copy disks and mount disk image files	This chapter Chapter 6 Fix-It #4
PowerBook control panel and Control Strip options	Access settings that affect battery conservation and related PowerBook-specific features	Chapter 11
Apple System Profiler	Profiles contents of your disk and characteristics of your hardware	Fix-It #15 Fix-It #16
File Exchange control panel	Helps in opening files that otherwise can not be opened, especially PC formatted files	Chapter 6

Table 2-1 ▶ A Catalog of Troubleshooting Utilities *continued*

NAMES/ TYPE OF UTILITY	USE IT TO:	FOR MORE INFORMATION, SEE:
Data Protection, Repair, Recovery and/or Diagnostic Utilities		
Norton Utilities for Macintosh, TechTool Pro, DiskWarrior and Data Rescue	Check for and repair damaged files and disks. Other functions include undeleting files, optimizing disks and backup up files, and exactly copying floppy disks	This chapter Chapter 6 Chapter 8 Fix-It #8 Fix-It #10 Fix-It #11
Data Protection, Repair, Recovery and/or Diagnostic Utilities		
Norton AntiVirus, Virex	Detect and eradicate viruses	This chapter, Fix-It #6
General System Enhancement Utilities		
ACTION Utilities, Default Folder	Enhance Open and Save dialog box features, add options to Apple menu, and more	This chapter Chapter 6
Extension Managers		
Conflict Catcher	Manage extensions (it has many more features than Apple's Extension Manager)	Fix-It #3
Backup Utilities		
Retrospect and Retrospect Express	Back up the data on a hard disk	This chapter
Disk Format Utilities		
Hard DiskToolKit, Silverlining (or whatever custom utility comes with your hard drive)	Update disk driver, check for media damage, reformat disk, partition disk (use instead of Apple HD Setup for non-Apple drives)	Fix-It #12 Fix-It #13 Fix-It #15
Selected List of Other Troubleshooting Utilities		
Spell Catcher's GhostWriter	Recover text unsaved at the time of a system crash	This chapter, Chapter 4
Spring Cleaning, Yank	Clean up superfluous files in System Folder, uninstalls files, and more	This chapter Fix-It #2
SCSIProbe, Mt. Everything	Conveniently list and mount SCSI devices	Chapter 5, Fix-It #14
HellFolderFix, Rename Rescue, Unlock Folder	Fix problems with renaming or deleting files	Chapter 6
DiskTop, Snitch, InvisiFile Save A BNDL, File Buddy	Do specialized work with invisible files and file attributes	Chapter 8
Font Box, Font Reserve, Adobe Type Manager, Suitcase	Fix damaged fonts and related font problems	Chapter 9
Reaper, MacOS Purge	Do specialized work for fixing certain system heap memory problems and/or giving more memory to the Finder	Fix-It #5
TechTool	Rebuild desktop and zap Parameter RAM (it's better than using Apple's methods)	Fix-It #8 Fix-It #9
Can Opener	Recover text and graphics from damaged and unopenable files	Fix-It #11
ResEdit (Apple)	Edit resources; can do all sorts of wonderful things	Chapter 8
Peek-a-Boo	Be a process manager; useful for closing "faceless" applications	Fix-It #3
TattleTech	Profiles contents of your disk and characteristics of your hardware, similar to Apple System Profiler	Fix-It #15

Troubleshooting with the Finder

We begin our survey of troubleshooting-related software with a closer look at the many helpful features of the Mac OS Finder.

Get Info

When in the Finder, select any file on your disk (click its icon once). Then select the Get Info command from the File menu (or type its keyboard shortcut: Command-I). This brings up a window for that file called, appropriately enough, the Get Info window. It is filled with important information.

You can also view some of the same Get Info information directly in a folder window, if you select a non-icon view (such as By Name) from the Finder's View menu.

Apple redesigned the Get Info window a bit starting with the Mac OS 8.5. There is now a pop-up Show menu. At the top of the window, regardless of which item is selected, you will see the name of the file and its icon. If the file selected is part of Macintosh system software, such as the Finder, the name should also include the version of the system software to which the file belongs (such as *Mac OS 8.6*). The file name can be edited directly unless the file name is locked. You can also change the icon of the file by selecting the icon box and pasting another graphic.

General Information The default selection for Show is General Information. The first line here will be *Kind*. Most commonly, the Kind is either *application program* or *document.* If it is a document, and the Finder recognizes it as belonging to a particular application, it probably says so (such as *AppleWorks document*). If you don't know what application created a particular document, this can be a quick way to find out. (Alternatively, if you enable Help's Show Balloons and move the cursor over the document file's icon on the desktop, this also tells you the name of the creating application.)

For system software, all sorts of additional Kind names are possible, such as *control panel* or *system extension.* The System file itself is listed as a *suitcase.*

The *Size* and *Where* lines refer to how much disk space the file occupies and where on the disk the file is located.

The *Created* and *Modified* lines tell you when the file was first created and the last

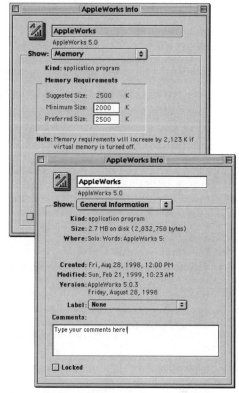

Figure 2-1 Two examples of Get Info windows.

time that it was modified (changed in any way). Every time you save a document, its modification date changes. Sometimes even applications get modified. Thus, the modification date for an application on your hard drive may be different from the date on your backup copy of that same application. This date difference may be just fine and normal. However, unexpected changes in the modification date may be a warning sign of trouble, such as damage done to the file.

The *Version* line identifies the particular version number of a program. This information can be essential when you are trying to determine incompatibilities. For example, suppose you are told that version 2.0 of BusyWorks (a fictitious application I use in some examples) is incompatible with System 8.6. The version line can tell you whether or not you are using the problematic version 2.0.

BY THE WAY ▶ Finding the Version Number

Sometimes programmers forget to include version information in the Get Info window. You should be able to find it, however, by launching the application and then selecting About (name of program) from the top of the Apple menu. The window that appears usually indicates the version number.

The *Label* pop-up menu lets you assign a label color for the file in the same way that you can from the Finder's File menu.

The *Comments* box may contain text placed there by the creator of the file, or you may add your own text. Most often, it is empty.

The *Locked* box, which can be checked, is used to lock the file. This simply prevents the file from being deleted when you place it in the Trash and select Empty Trash. You can still delete a locked file either by first unlocking it (by unchecking the box) or by holding down the Option key when you attempt to empty the Trash that contains the locked file. Documents provide you with a *Stationery Pad* box. If checked, this means that if you launch the file from the Finder, it will open an untitled copy of the file, rather than the original file itself. However, this feature does not work with all applications. If it isn't compatible, it will open the original file instead.

TAKE NOTE ▶ Locking Floppy Disks

You can lock an entire floppy disk, which prevents you from adding, deleting, or even modifying any and all files on the disk. Even holding down the Option key while you select Empty Trash does not allow you to delete a file from a locked disk. The only way to delete a file from a locked disk is to unlock it first.

To lock a floppy disk, first hold the disk with the front of it facing you. Then, slide up the square plastic tab, which is located in the upper right-hand corner of the disk, so that you can see through the hole. Sliding the tab back down unlocks the disk again.

SEE: • **Chapter 6 for more information on deleting locked files.**

For most documents, General Information is the only choice in the Show menu. For folders, a Sharing choice is added. For applications, the Show pop-up menu includes General Information, Sharing, and a third choice: Memory.

Memory If you select Memory, a box appears that is titled *Memory Requirements*. It includes three numbers: *Suggested size, Minimum size,* and *Preferred size*. These numbers refer to the amount of memory (RAM) that the program occupies when it is opened.

The default values of all three numbers are initially set by the application itself. The Suggested size can never be altered. This is the recommended amount of memory needed to run the program under normal conditions.

The user can alter the remaining two values simply by typing a new number in the appropriate box. You can increase or decrease these values as long as the application itself is not currently open. If it is open, quit the application and then make the change.

The Minimum size is the minimum amount of memory the program needs to open. This number can be set to less than the Suggested size (helpful for those times when memory is tight), but some of the program's features may not work, or serious problems (such as system crashes) may develop. If the program's default Minimum size is already set lower than the Suggested size, certainly don't set the Minimum size any lower.

You can set the Preferred size for considerably more than the Suggested size. When a program opens, it uses its Preferred memory size if that much memory is available. This helps applications, such as graphics and multimedia programs, which can run faster or work with larger documents with additional memory available.

If, when you open an application, the available free memory is less than the application's Preferred size (as might happen, for example, if other applications are already open), the application uses whatever free memory still remains. However, if the free memory is less than the Minimum size, the program does not open at all. Once an application launches, its memory allocation cannot change until the next time you use it, even if more memory frees up while you are running the application.

Thus, on a given launch, the amount of memory occupied by an application can vary anywhere between the Minimum and the Preferred size, depending on the available memory at the time you launch the application. If you don't like this degree of uncertainty, you can guarantee that the program always uses the same amount of memory by setting the Minimum size and Preferred size to the same number. Otherwise, to find out exactly how much memory an open application is using, you have to check the About This Macintosh window (as described in the next section).

In most cases, you will probably do just fine if you leave the memory values the way they were initially set by the program's publisher. However, some adjustments may occasionally be required. For example, an application's memory allocation includes the amount available to the application plus all of its open documents. For some programs, you may need to increase the Preferred size in order to be able to open several documents at once or to open a single large, complex document.

For Power Macintoshes, you will see a note at the bottom of the screen concerning virtual memory. The significance of this is explained in Fix-It #5.

SEE: • **Chapter 6 and Fix-It #5 for more information on memory management.**

Sharing This option is available for applications and folders/volumes.

If selected for a folder, it allows that folder to be shared over a network, if file sharing has been turned on via the File Sharing control panel. To allow a selected folder to be shared, check the *Share this item and its contents* option and select the desired privileges settings.

If selected for an application, it allows the application to be shared via the Program Linking option of the File Sharing control panel. In this case, your only choice is to check (or not) the *Allow remote program linking* option.

SEE: • **Chapter 11 for more on sharing.**

About This Computer

If the Finder is the active application, the first item in the Apple menu is *About This Computer*. Select this item, and a new window opens. From this window, you can sometimes learn the name of the Macintosh model you are using (in case you didn't already know it). It is still another location where you can get the exact version number of the system software you are using.

More importantly, About This Computer tells you the settings for Total Memory and Largest Unused Block. The Total Memory is equivalent to the amount of RAM you have installed in your computer.

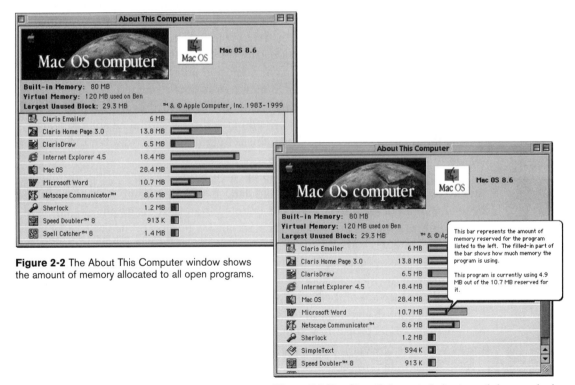

Figure 2-2 The About This Computer window shows the amount of memory allocated to all open programs.

Figure 2-3 Use Show Balloons to find out exactly how much of Microsoft Word's memory allocation is actually in use.

TECHNICALLY SPEAKING ▶ Built-in Memory And Virtual Memory

If you are using virtual memory (set in the Memory control panel, as described in Fix-It #5), another line above the Total Memory line reads Built-in Memory. In this case, the Built-in Memory refers to the amount of RAM installed in your computer. Total Memory then refers to the sum of the Built-in Memory plus virtual memory or RAM Doubler extended memory.

The Largest Unused Block is similar to the quantity of RAM that is currently not in use and therefore available for use by other applications.

The remainder of this window shows a series of bar graphs that indicate the memory usage of every currently open application plus the system software. The number after each file name is the memory allocation for that file. This value can range from the application's Minimum size to Preferred size, as listed in the Memory Requirements area of the application's Get Info window. For example, AppleWorks may open in a memory allocation of 1850K, larger than its Minimum size (1000K) and smaller than its Preferred size (2400K). This could be because AppleWorks was the last of all the programs listed to be opened and this was all the memory left at that time. If 2400K or more of memory were available, AppleWorks would have used the full 2400K. Actually (again, as explained more fully in Fix-It #5), the maximum length of the bar may exceed its Preferences size (due to such things as temporary memory).

One item you will always find in this bar graph is Mac OS. It lists the combined amount of memory currently used by the System file, the Finder, and various other system software (as well as third-party extensions and control panels). Its size varies depending on which system software version you are using, and how many extensions/control panels you have installed. Mac OS memory is in a state of constant flux.

By the way, you might think that the size of the Largest Unused Block plus the sum of the memory allocation of the items listed in the display should be approximately equal to the Total Memory value. Often, this is indeed the case. However, there are exceptions to this rule, as you will discover in Fix-it #5.

The bar graphs also indicate how memory is currently allocated within each application. The total length of a bar (light- and dark-shaded areas combined) represents the total amount of memory assigned to an application (it is the graphical equivalent of the number to the left of the bar). The dark-shaded portion of the bar represents how much memory is currently in use by the application.

Every time you open an additional document within an application, for example, you use more of the memory allocation for that application. Graphically, this means the light-shaded section of the bar graph gets smaller.

When the light-shaded section of the bar gets very small, you are approaching the memory limits of the program. You may be unable to open any more documents (unless you close one first). Taxing the application's use of memory further will result in *out of memory* alert messages.

Be aware that even if a program is not using most of its assigned memory at the moment, the assigned memory cannot be used by any other program. It simply sits there, waiting for the program to use it, until you quit the application.

If you want to know precisely how much memory the light- and dark-shaded sections of each bar represent, select Show Balloons from the Balloon Help menu and then move the cursor over a section of the bar. A balloon appears that gives you the amount of memory currently being used as well as the total allocation of memory for that particular application.

Window Headers

Underneath the title of each window in the Finder is a line that lists two items: the number of *items* in the window, and the amount of disk space currently *available*. The number of items listed varies depending on how many items are in the selected folder. The other number refers to the entire disk and is the same no matter what folder is selected. This number is useful, for example, when you are trying to determine whether you have sufficient space available for an operation that you are attempting, such as copying files to the disk.

By the way, hidden within the window title is a useful feature that can help you locate where you are on the disk and quickly navigate you to a related location. To access it, hold down the Command key when you click the name of the window in the header. This brings up a pop-up menu showing the hierarchy of folders starting from the current folder and working backward to the root level. Selecting any folder immediately takes you there. (Also, if you hold down the option key when opening a new folder, the window that contains the current folder will close as the new one opens, thus aiding navigation and preventing screen clutter.)

If you click and hold on the folder icon to the left of the folder's name, you will be able to drag the icon to any location, moving or copying the folder just as if you had selected the folder icon itself from the desktop. Conversely, if you drag an item to the icon, it moves or copies that item to the folder.

Finally, note the three small boxes in the header. The little square on the left is the *Close* box (click it and the Finder window closes). The first of the two boxes on the right is the *Grow* box (click it and the window will expand or contract in size). The third box is the *WindowShade* box (click it and the window "rolls up" so that only the title bar is visible. Note, too, that if you select "Double click title bar to collapse windows" in the Options panel of the Appearance control panel, double-clicking the title bar also rolls the window up (or down).

Figure 2-4 Top: the top of a window, showing the window header information just below the title. Bottom: the pop-up menu that appears when you click on a window title while holding down the Command key.

Sherlock

Beginning with Mac OS 8.5, the Mac OS's original Find File feature has been expanded into a sparkling new addition called Sherlock. When you open Sherlock (either from the Finder's Find menu or the Sherlock item in the Apple menu), you will find three main options (or tabs):

Find File This option is essentially the same as the previous Find File utility/feature. It is an essential tool for finding a file that you cannot otherwise locate or to check if a certain file even exists on your disk. Using the default selection, Name contains, you type text

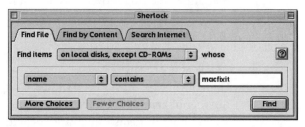

Figure 2-5 Sherlock's Find File tab.

into the text block, and click Find. Sherlock now locates any file on your "local disks" with a name that contains your text. The list of found files appears in a separate Items Found window. Clicking any file listed in the upper part of the window shows the hierarchical location of the file in the bottom half of the window. You can double-click any item in the pathway to go to that location, or you can double-click the file itself to open it. You can even directly drag a file name from the window to any location on your disk (such as the Desktop or the Trash) and the file immediately moves to the new location.

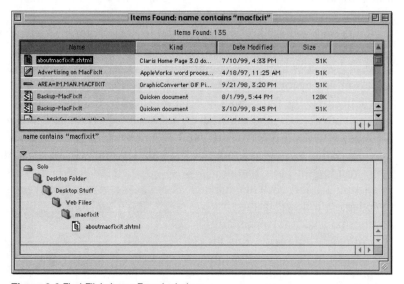

Figure 2-6 Find File's Items Found window.

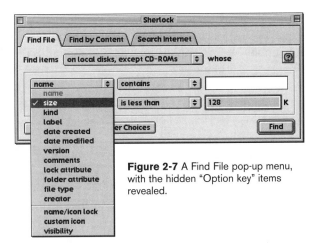

Figure 2-7 A Find File pop-up menu, with the hidden "Option key" items revealed.

Returning to the original Find File window, you can use the pop-up menus to select a variety of different search criteria, basing searches on such attributes as file size or date created. Using Sherlock's Save Search Criteria command (in Sherlock's File menu), you can even save your current search criteria for future use, so you don't have to set it up again next time. Just double-click the file that is created and it will automatically launch Sherlock and perform the search.

SEE: • Chapter 6, "When You Can't Locate a File," for a step-by-step example of using this
         feature.

BY THE WAY ▶ Hidden Search Options in Find File

Hold down the Option key while accessing the Name pop-up menu. If you do, you will get four additional attributes that you can select as search criteria: name/icon lock (locked files and icons); custom icon (files that have a custom icon); visibility (invisible files); and contents (text within a file, up to 30 characters).

Find By Content   Find by Content searches the actual text content of most types of text files on your drive (including word processing documents from popular applications such as AppleWorks and Microsoft Word). Because searching can be a very time-consuming task, you should index a volume before you begin a search on it. When you index, Sherlock creates an invisible file that stores all the needed data to perform a search. It can scan through this file much faster than actually searching your drive, so a search does not take very long. However, this means that if you have made changes to the contents of your drive since the last time it was indexed, the search will not reflect the changes.

To make indexing more convenient, you can schedule it at a time when you would not be using the computer, such as late at night. To schedule an index, select the Index Volumes button and then, from the window that appears, select the volumes you want to index and click the Schedule button. Set the schedule as desired.

Once a volume is indexed, you can perform a search by typing any text into the Words box (see Figure 2-8), select which volumes you want searched, and click Find. An Items Found window will eventually appear. It is similar to the Find File Items Found window, except that items are ranked according to relevance, or how closely the text of the document matches the words being searched.

To find files that contain similar words to the listed file, select the file and click the Find Similar Files button.

Search Internet Search Internet is the third of Sherlock's tabs. This feature lets you search specified Web sites for pages that contain your selected search terms—

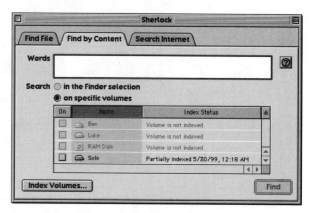

Figure 2-8 Sherlock's Find by Content tab.

assuming you are online of course. With Sherlock, you can check multiple search engines at once and see the results without even launching a Web browser. Spectacular!

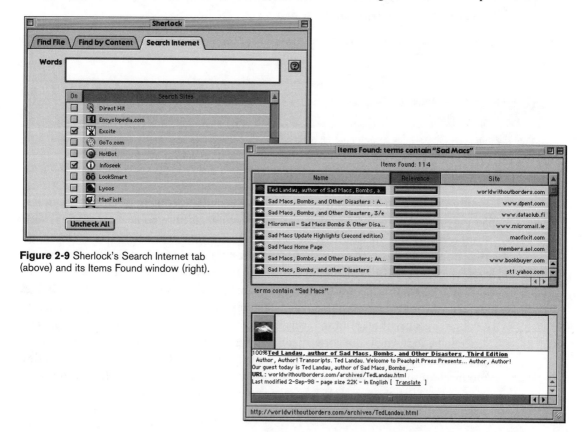

Figure 2-9 Sherlock's Search Internet tab (above) and its Items Found window (right).

Sherlock 2 With the release of Mac OS 9, Sherlock was upgraded to Sherlock 2. Most of the main features remain the same, although how you access them has changed. The three tabs (Find File, Find by Content, and Search Internet), for example, are now gone. The new Find File and Find By Content share the same display (see Figure 2-10); you shift between them by clicking radio buttons (now called File Names and Content). You shift to one of several Internet search sets by clicking the various icons along the top of the window.

Troubleshooting issues regarding Sherlock's Internet features will be covered in Chapter 15.

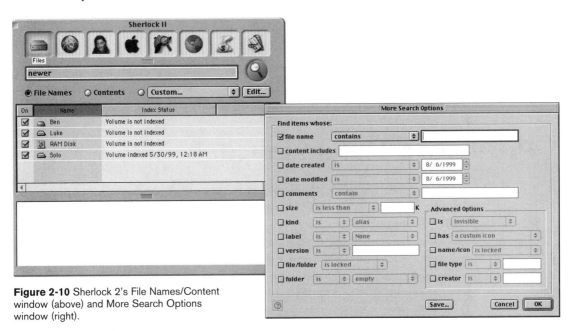

Figure 2-10 Sherlock 2's File Names/Content window (above) and More Search Options window (right).

Figure 2-11 An Internet search window from Sherlock 2.

The Erase Disk and Empty Trash Commands

The Erase Disk and Empty Trash commands are found in the Finder's Special menu. The Erase Disk command is primarily used to reformat floppy disks and USB-connected drives. That is, the entire disk is erased and recreated as if you had started with an unformatted disk.

The Empty Trash command deletes only the files currently in the Trash. To place a file in the Trash, you drag the file's icon to the Trash icon until the Trash icon is highlighted. Release the mouse button. The Trash icon bulges to show that it contains file(s).

The Trash is never actually emptied until you select Empty Trash. Until the Trash is emptied, you can remove files from the Trash. Just double-click the Trash icon to open up its window and drag the file out again.

By the way, if you want to bypass the message that appears each time you empty the Trash, select Get Info for the Trash and then uncheck "Warn before emptying."

SEE: • **"Protect Against Accidentally Deleted Files" later in this chapter.**
           • **Fix-It #13 for more information on erasing disks.**

Preventive Maintenance

As is often the case, you can avoid big headaches later on by enduring some small headaches now. This is what preventive maintenance is all about: solving problems before they happen.

I am certainly sympathetic to those who abhor routine maintenance. I am one of them. When I purchase a piece of equipment, such as an air conditioner or a microwave oven, one of the first things I want to know is how long I can happily ignore any maintenance whatsoever that might take up more than five seconds of my time.

Thankfully, your Macintosh doesn't require very much physical maintenance. Occasionally cleaning your monitor's display with a soft cloth may be the extent of such maintenance for most users.

Then there's electronic maintenance, which is the focus of the remainder of this chapter. True, electronic maintenance can be just as tedious as any other kind of maintenance. But ignoring the following procedures can seriously hamper the performance of your computer and (without wanting to sound too alarmist) possibly result in the irrecoverable loss of invaluable data.

Have an Emergency Startup Disk Ready

If your one-and-only hard drive is your startup disk and it develops a serious problem, you will not be able to use it to startup the Macintosh. Similarly, many troubleshooting utilities can only make alterations or repairs to a disk if it is not the current startup disk—which will be a problem if your current startup disk is the one that needs repairing. For these reasons, you need to have a special, emergency startup disk (or disks). Having one of these disks *before* trouble strikes is wise, preventive maintenance.

Apple's Disk Tools Startup Floppy Disk (and related startup floppy disks)

With Apple's abandonment of the floppy disk drive, floppy disk emergency startup disks may soon go the way of the dinosaur. Nevertheless, for those users who still have floppy disk drives, the Mac OS CD (prior to Mac OS 9) includes a DiskScript called "Make Disk Tools Floppies." It works with Apple's Disk Copy utility to make a floppy disk (based on the Disk Tools.img disk image file also on the CD) that contains Disk First Aid, Drive Setup Lite (a smaller version of Drive Setup), and a special modified System Folder that is reduced in size enough to fit on a floppy disk. As of Mac OS 9, "Disk Tools" has been dropped from Mac OS CDs.

Once you have created a Disk Tools startup floppy disk, you can create customized disks by copying the original disk and then changing its contents. For example, you can delete Disk First Aid and Drive Setup and replace it with another utility (or utilities) of your choice - as long as there is room on the disk. Unfortunately, given the small size of floppy disks and the large size of most current utilities, very little of value will fit on these disks.

One solution to this lack of space is to chuck the Finder in favor of a Finder substitute that is much smaller in size. With these substitutes, you will not be able to go to the desktop, but you will be able to launch the applications on the disk. The best of these programs is called MiniSubstitute. Even with this program, you will likely find that a floppy disk cannot hold everything you would like. But it's the best you can do with this arrangement.

Helpful hint Do not try to make a startup disk by dragging the System, Finder, and other needed System Folder files from your hard drive to a floppy disk. They won't fit. Similarly, don't ever drag the System Folder files from a startup floppy disk to use on a hard drive. The System Folder files on a floppy disk are usually special versions designed to work only on floppy disks and should not be used on a hard drive.

Another helpful hint If you use a Disk Tools disk that belongs with a Mac model other than your own, it may not work with your Mac. There are several possible reasons for this incompatibility. One is that your Mac needs a specific Enabler file (as described in Fix-It #4), and the Disk Tools disk you are trying to use does not have it. Also, it is possible that the System Software on another disk is too old a version to be used on your (newer) Mac.

TAKE NOTE ▶ Use Disk Copy to Make Disks

Disk Copy started as a simple utility to make *exact* copies of floppy disks (including the disk name, locations of icons and any invisible files). Over the years, it has developed into a much more sophisticated copy utility. Here's a brief primer on how to use it:

Making a copy of a disk Making a copy of a floppy disk is basically a two step process. First you convert the contents of the floppy disk to a disk image file. Then, you copy the disk image file to a new floppy disk.

To make a disk image from a floppy disk:

1. Insert the floppy disk you wish to copy.
2. Launch Disk Copy.
3. Select "Create Image from Disk" from Disk Copy's Image menu.
4. Locate the floppy disk, select the floppy disk and click Choose.
5. From the next window that appears, click Save. A new file is created and saved as a .img file. The file contains the contents of the floppy disk.

Note: The Size pop-up menu that appears in the Save box lists a variety of sizes up to 2 GB, plus special CD-ROM sizes. Conversely, Disk Copy's Create New Image command (in the Image menu) has a similar set of size options to use when creating a blank image file. There is also a Create Image from Folder command. Clearly, with Disk Copy, you can create images from, and make copies of, much more than just floppy disks.

To create a floppy disk from a disk image:

1. Select Make a Floppy from Disk Copy's Utilities menu.
2. Select the image (.img) file you just created.
3. Click Choose. Disk Copy will prompt you to insert a floppy disk to make a copy.

Note: To make a copy of floppy disks with USB drives, make sure the disk is in the drive before selecting the Make a Floppy command.

Mounting and using disk images Disk image files (.img files) have a use beyond being a way station on the road to creating a disk copy. You can *mount* a disk image file. Simply double-click the file and you will see a new icon appear. It will look similar to a disk icon. Double-click the new icon and a window will open that contains the contents of whatever you copied when making the image file. This mounted image can be used in just the same way as the original disk.

Apple, for example, uses image files for almost all of the files in its software updates ftp site. You download the image file, mount it, and run the installer directly from the mounted image (see Fix-It #4 for more information).

Here's a tip: have you ever tried to install software that uses two or more floppy disks and then got caught in a trap where your computer incessantly asks you to swap floppy disks in and out of the drive? For this and other similar situations, just make image files of the floppy disks (or at least of the disk that contains the Installer application). Then run the Installer from the image file. The constant swap requests should vanish.

CD-ROM Startup Discs

The Mac OS CD-ROM disc that comes with all Mac models can be used as a startup disc. This is because it has special "boot block" data written to the disk. To use it, simply insert the disc, select Restart, and then hold down the "C" key until the Mac starts to load from the CD. If this does not work, sometimes holding down Command-Option-Shift-Delete should work.

SEE: • **Chapter 5 for more details.**

If your Mac has not yet started up, and especially if you are getting a system crash at startup that prevents you from selecting the Finder's Restart command, eject the CD-ROM tray as soon as you hit the power button. How you do this varies with different Mac models. With the iMac, simply push the button on the CD tray. With other models, holding down the mouse button will do the trick. Once you have ejected the tray, insert the CD, close the tray, and restart (see Chapter 4 for more information on restarting after a system crash).

You will always start up from the CD. You can now run Disk First Aid or Drive Setup directly from the CD, eliminating the need for the floppy disk. This is the preferred method for use with iMacs and other Macs that do not have a floppy disk drive.

All other major disk repair utilities (such as Norton Utilities, TechTool Pro, and DiskWarrior) are also sold on a bootable CD-ROM disc. This allows you to use similar disks for repairs at those times when you need to start from an alternate disk (see Fix-It #10 for more details on this issue).

What happens if the repair utility is updated to a newer version than the one on the CD—and the update is more conveniently available if you download it from the Internet than if you order an updated CD? You download the utility but how do you use it when starting up from the CD, especially if (because of the problem you are trying to repair) you cannot access it from your hard drive? There are several possible alternatives here.

- If you have a floppy disk drive, and the utility fits on a floppy disk, you can copy the updated utility to the floppy disk. Insert the disk after starting up from the CD and run the utility from the disk. A similar arrangement can be made via a Zip disk or any other similar removable media that you may have.

- Alternatively, you may be able to create a removable media startup disk. However, this may be a problem with certain Mac models. For example, the original iMacs cannot startup from an external USB device. This would prevent creating a startup disk for a USB Zip drive (see Chapter 5 for more details).

- If you are lucky enough to have a CD-R or CD-RW drive, you can create your own CD-ROM discs. With the right software (such as Adaptec's Toast), you can even create your own bootable CD-ROM discs. For an emergency startup disc, simply create a bootable CD with the utilities you want. However, be sure to read the CD-R software's instructions carefully. Creating a bootable CD-ROM disc is not as simple as copying a valid System Folder to the disc. You also need to copy the special bootable code from the Apple CD-ROM driver. If you select Toast's "Bootable" option and the driver is available on your hard drive, Toast will copy the special code automatically.

- If you have no other media, and you can at least successfully access your hard drive after starting up from any bootable CD, create a RAM Disk large enough to hold the utility (see Chapter 11). Then copy the utility from the hard drive to the RAM Disk and run the updated utility from there.

- If all else fails, you can order an updated CD-ROM disc from the vendor. Hopefully, if the update itself is free, the vendor will supply this at a nominal charge (usually around $10 or $20). Another reason for getting an updated utility CD is if you get a new Mac that requires a newer version of the Mac OS than the one on the CD. In this case, the original CD will no longer be able to startup your Mac.

Secondary Hard Drives or Partitions as Startup Disks

If you have two hard drives, you can always set up System Folders on both of them using the System Software Installer disks. You can then use one as an Emergency Startup Disk when the other fails to work. A removable cartridge drive may also be used as a startup drive (as mentioned in the previous section). Using this method, you don't have to worry about how to squeeze everything you need onto one disk.

If you have only one hard drive, you can do almost as well by dividing your drive into two partitions and setting up a System Folder on each. This won't help you if your drive fails altogether, but if you just need to run from a different startup drive (to do repairs with DiskWarrior, for example) the partition method will work fine.

See: • **Chapter 5, "Understanding the Startup Sequence," for more details on starting up with alternate hard drives and partitions**

Universal Startup Disks

If you work with more than one Macintosh model, you may wish to have a single Emergency Startup Disk (on a Zip or Jaz drive cartridge for example) that is compatible with all (or at least most) Mac models. To do this, create a Universal System Folder by doing a Customized Installation of the Mac OS, and then selecting Universal Installation from the popup menu at the top of the window.

See: • **Fix-It #4 for more information on installing system software.**

Save and Back Up Your Work

Saving your work simply means using the Save command to save a file to disk. Backing up your work means making a copy of the file to a separate disk location.

Regularly saving and backing up your work is Preventive Maintenance Rule #1.
It supersedes every other rule by a wide margin. I cannot emphasize this rule enough. Save often. Back up everything. Regularly. The dire consequences of almost every type of disaster that could possibly befall you can be avoided if you frequently save your files while you work and back up everything when you are finished for the day.

Almost everyone has a horror story to tell about how their only copy of an important document, representing weeks of work, was lost or destroyed just before it was to be printed out. Don't add your name to the roster. Save the document. Back it up. Losing precious work can happen to you.

I wouldn't have to emphasize this advice so vigorously if it wasn't ignored so routinely—even by people who should know better. Why is this? The usual excuses are time and money: users often complain that it either takes too much time to back everything up or costs too much money to buy the equipment needed to do it at a reasonable speed.

But ask anyone who has lost critical data (maybe it's happened to you already) about the time and/or money spent to replace it. Then reconsider your attitude.

Save Your Work... Often

The simplest of all disaster prevention methods is to make generous use of the Save command (which is found in the File menu of almost every application). It is important to remember that unsaved data exists in RAM, or electronic memory, only. It will disappear into digital hyperspace if there is an unexpected (is there any other kind?) system crash or power failure. Yes, hours of unsaved work can vanish in an instant—unless you have already saved it.

So, when you are working on a file, save it frequently—at least every ten minutes. Alternatively, if your program has an *autosave* feature, you can use it. An autosave function automatically saves documents, without giving any prompting or requiring any input from the user, at any specified interval. Some people like this idea. Personally, I prefer to do my saving the old-fashioned way. If I am experimenting with strange formatting, for example, I would not want it to be saved automatically before I decided whether I preferred to revert to the previous format. Still, for some people, autosaving can be just the ticket.

If your program does not include a built-in autosave function, some shareware utilities allow you to include this function in virtually any program.

SEE: • **Chapter 6 for more information on the use of the Save and Save As commands.**
• **"Protect Against Loss of Data Due to System Crashes" later in this chapter.**

Selecting backup software and hardware

To do it right, backing up your work (especially full disk backups) requires specialized backup software and hardware.

Software Don't depend on the Finder alone. Use a software utility specifically designed for backing up your files. Backup software offers several advantages beyond the Finder's capabilities. It can keep track of the source and destination locations of files. It can split large files across disks if needed. When you wish to restore a file, backup software can quickly locate which disk (of multiple backup disks) contains the particular file you are seeking—and it can even automatically restore the file to its original location on your drive. It can also copy invisible files that the Finder does not copy. Finally, backup software can copy to some storage devices (such as tape) that the Finder cannot access. The best of the lot is Dantz' Retrospect or, for personal non-networked backups, the less expensive Retrospect Express.

For quick backups of important, frequently modified files, I have also used Speed Doubler's Copy Agent feature (which sadly may not be updated to work in Mac OS 9 or X). You can use this feature to create and save a set of all the files or folders you want to copy. You can also set it up to copy only those files that have changed since the last time you made a backup, thus speeding up the copying process. Other synchronization utilities, such as Apple's own File Synchronization do a similar job, but not as quickly or easily as Speed Doubler.

Hardware After you have installed the backup software of your choice, you will need a good backup media to use with the utility. In choosing hardware, there are four features to consider: speed, capacity, reliability, and cost.

- **Speed** The faster the medium, the less time you need for backing up or restoring.

- **Capacity** The larger the capacity of the medium, the less often you will need to use more than one disk, tape, or cartridge to complete a backup. Large capacity is particularly useful for unattended backups (such as late-night copying, while you sleep).

- **Reliability** Good-quality hardware is essential. There is no point in backing up your work if, when you finally need the backup, you find that the media is damaged and you can no longer retrieve data from it.

- **Cost** Addressing the first three concerns is easy if money is no object. For most of us, however, money is a big obstacle. As a result, you will have to weigh the costs of the above features against your peace of mind, and make some compromises.

Here are some popular backup hardware choices to consider:

- **Back up to another hard drive** A fast hardware alternative, this backup method is obviously limited in its capacity. Once the drive is full, you are finished. It is also not very useful for backing up more than one drive. However, it may be the most cost-effective way to back up a very large hard drive.

- **Back up to Zip disks or SuperDisks** This hardware can be useful for selective backups. However, the capacity of each type of disk is too small to make it effective for whole disk backups of multi-Gigabyte drives. At the very least, a large backup will require you to manually eject and reinsert many disks. There are also some reliability issues (see "Take Note: Reformatting Zip/Jaz Cartridges..." in Fix-It #13). This method is very slow.

- **Backup to Jaz cartridges or ORB disks** The capacity of this hardware is decent, but its reliability remains a concern. Jaz cartridges are notoriously delicate devices.

- **Back up to specialized tape devices (such as HyperDAT tape drives)** These devices feature great capacity (20GB or more) and speedy copying. They are also very reliable. The best models can cost thousands of dollars, but the moderately priced ones are still very good. A negative feature is that you cannot use this hardware for anything but backing up.

- **Back up to a writable CD or DVD** Very slow compared to other hardware options, this media, however, is very reliable. Its capacity is also on the small size only when compared to specialized tapes. This is an especially good choice for backing up something that you will not need to back up often, such as a completed manuscript. As they become more widely used, writeable DVDs may prove to be a very astute choice of backup hardware because of their much greater capacity than CDs.

- **Back up to floppy disks** Don't make me laugh. Except for small documents (such as some word processing files or spreadsheets), a floppy disk has too small a capacity and is too slow to be a useful backup device. That's assuming you even have an example of this endangered species.

Devise a Good Backup Strategy

How, how much, and how often should you back up your files? Everyone has their own recommendation for the best way to back up the most data with the least hassle. Here are the two most important pointers:

Back Up All Personal Document Files Your personal files, such as manuscripts and illustrations, are unique creations and thus, are irreplaceable. Back them up frequently (as in every time you modify them) and maintain multiple backups if feasible. This can be done by using the Finder and any storage medium separate from where the original data are stored. This backup method should be done in addition to any global backups.

Maintain a Global Backup of Your Hard Drive(s) Ideally you want to use special backup software that can create a *mirror image* global backup. This type of backup can be used to recreate your entire hard drive, down to every customized preference file and every invisible file, with all files and folders in their original hierarchical location. This is a tremendous time saver if you ever have to reformat your hard drive. If you work on your computer almost every day, update this backup at least once a week, more often if you make frequent, major changes to the contents of the drive.

After doing an initial global backup, your backup software/hardware may provide the option to do either an *incremental* or *archival* backup on subsequent updates. An incremental backup backs up only newly added and modified files (deleting the old version of any modified files). Archival backups work similarly except that they never delete anything, not even files that have been modified or deleted since the last backup. This allows you to revert to versions prior to the most recent version, if desired.

Helpful hint: try a restore before you have a problem Try restoring some files to your hard drive using your specialized backup software. If you can, get a spare hard drive or cartridge and try a global (or full) restore. If doing so reveals that the restore will fail because of procedural problems, you can easily address and fix these problems now. However, if you wait until a crisis occurs, it you may end up with a very difficult problem to solve, or it may be too late.

Prune Your Hard Drive

Delete Unnecessary Data and Application Files

As you back up your hard drive, you won't want to keep useless and outdated files. That's why you should periodically go through your hard drive and delete these unnecessary files.

If you never delete anything, you probably still have that 1994 letter to your Aunt Millie sitting in a folder somewhere. Get rid of it. In fact, delete any applications and documents that you rarely or never use. If you haven't used a file for the last six months or more, get rid of it. Maintain a copy on a floppy disk, if desired, but get it off your hard drive.

Why bother getting rid of these useless files? First, it will be easier to locate your useful files, since you won't have to wade through "garbage" files. Second, depending on your work habits, you may free up a surprising amount of space. If you already have a nearly full hard drive, the extra space can allow you to add other, more important, files. Even if you don't need more space, a nearly full hard drive is subject to all sorts of minor problems. Certain activities, such as printing for example, may create temporary files in order to work, and often require free disk space to hold these files. I'm getting ahead of myself a bit here, but less than a minimum of empty disk space can hasten fragmentation of the files on your disk, which can slow down your Mac. Conversely, discarding unnecessary files prior to rebuilding your desktop will create a more compact Desktop file, which will speed things up.

SEE: • **"Give Your Macintosh a Tune-up" later in this chapter for more information on fragmented files and rebuilding the desktop.**

With today's larger-capacity multi-Gigabyte hard drives, try to keep at least 100MB of space unused. If you find yourself regularly going below 50MB, it's time to get a larger hard drive. Need to know how much free space you have left? Remember, you can check the current amount, which is usually visible in the header of any open Finder window on your hard drive.

Delete Items from the System Folder

Storing extraneous files in the System Folder can be a huge waste of space. Here's what to look for:

Application-Related Files Suppose you decide to discard a word processor you have been using in favor of another one. You may forget that your old word processor included a special dictionary file to be used with the processor's built-in spelling checker, and which is buried somewhere in your System Folder. After awhile, you can build up quite a collection of these unnecessary files. Similarly, you probably still have preferences files for deleted applications. The Preferences Folder is often a rich source of files that can be deleted.

If the initial placement of an application on your disk required an Installer utility, your System Folder may be storing many application-related files that you did not even know existed. Once the application is deleted, these can all be removed as well.

Some application installers may have a Custom Remove option that will assist you in making sure that most associated software gets deleted when you remove the application. Otherwise, utilities such as Yank and Spring Cleaning can assist in these tasks.

SEE: • **Fix-It #2.**

System Software Files Similarly, when your system software was installed on your hard drive, it probably installed many files that you never use. For example, if you find a printer driver (such as StyleWriter or ImageWriter) for a printer that you do not have or use, delete it. The same space-saving principle applies to any extensions, control panels, fonts, and Apple menu items that you no longer use. Get rid of them. Doing so often has the side benefit of reducing the amount of memory occupied by the system software, freeing up more RAM for other uses.

However, the current Mac OS has become sufficiently complex that it is often hard to tell what is needed and what is not. For example, I have read of situations where Apple's File Sharing software needs to be installed (even if it is not turned on) to prevent a conflict with some other software. Also, if you delete system software files and then need them back at some point, finding and reinstalling what you previously discarded can be a pain. A simple solution here is to save these discarded files to a separate disk (such as a Zip disk). Still, especially given today's large hard drives, I would lean to leaving most system software files where they are.

Delete Mystery Files

What if you can't identify the purpose of a file? How do you know if it is safe to delete it? For applications and documents, this is usually easy to figure out. Just open the file and see what it contains.

If a data document cannot be opened, it probably belongs to an application that is no longer on your hard drive. However, many System Folder files cannot be opened from the Finder under any circumstances. You may have trouble identifying the purpose of these files. In these cases, select Get Info for the mysterious file. Check for any information that might give you a hint about the source and purpose of the file. This may tell you all you need to know to make a decision about deleting it. Even if Get Info only identifies the origin of the file, you can presumably go to the relevant documentation for more help.

Also try turning on Balloon Help and placing the cursor over the mystery item. This is particularly useful for system extensions. If you are unlucky, you will get the generic message that says only that the file in question is an extension. If you are lucky, you may learn exactly what the extension does.

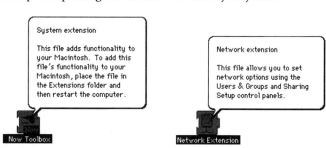

Figure 2-12 Balloon help messages may (right) or may not (left) help you identify a mystery file.

A related note: Software installers for applications may install more than the application and its associated files. They may also install third-party extensions (often without clearly telling you they have done so) that, while potentially needed by the application, may also affect other programs on your drive. Sometimes, they may install older versions of extensions that you already have (overwriting your newer version), or they may install extensions that cause conflicts with other software on your drive. These problem and/or outdated extensions will likely need to be disabled or deleted.

SEE: • Fix-Its #3 and #4 for more detailed advice on this topic.

BY THE WAY ▶ What's With Folders With Names Like Duplicate Items and Deinstalled?

Occasionally, in your System Folder, you may find folders with names like Duplicate Items or Deinstalled 4/10/99. These folders were created at the time you ran an Installer utility of some sort (such as when upgrading your system software). In many cases, an Installer replaces existing older versions of software with the newer versions. However, in some cases (as a protection to you in case you still want to preserve the older versions), it will move the older versions to a special folder it creates and give the folder a name like Duplicate Items. In general, if you discover this folder, you can probably delete it and its contents, because you already have other versions of its contents somewhere else (such as in the Control Panels folder). This is another way to free up some disk space.

Similarly, if you find a file called Installer Cleanup, you can delete it. It is a temporary file that should have been automatically deleted when you quit the Installer and restarted.

SEE: • Chapter 6 for more information on opening and identifying files.

Other Ways to Save or Get More Space

If you discard all unnecessary files and there is still not enough free space on your hard drive, you have two alternatives:

• Replace your hard drive with a larger one (or just add another one).

• Use an automatic compression utility.

The rationale behind increasing your hard drive space is obvious. And with drive prices falling faster than a two-ton rock in water (especially if you figure it on a cost/megabyte), getting a larger drive is definitely the way to go if you are running short on space.

I would only recommend automatic compression utilities as a last resort. These utilities reduce the size of files stored on your disk by eliminating the "redundancy" in the file's data. When you really need to use the file, the compression utility uncompresses it to its normal state, without any data loss.

The leading automatic compression utility has been SpaceSaver from Aladdin. But even Aladdin has recognized the diminishing returns of this methodology; they no longer market SpaceSaver. Taking a cue from their lead, I am omitting any further discussion of these utilities from this edition of *Sad Macs*—other than to say that I recommend against using them.

> **BY THE WAY ▶ Archival compression utilities**
>
> For just occasional compression of a few infrequently used files, for archival storage of files, or for transmitting files across networks (where reduced size means less transmission time), consider manual archival compression utilities (such as Aladdin's StuffIt Deluxe, or its freeware/shareware counterparts, Expander and DropStuff). Currently, these utilities are used mainly in conjunction with sending email or downloading files from the Internet. As such, I discuss them again in Chapter 13 (Road Service for the Infobahn: The World Wide Web and Email).

Install Protection Utilities

Typically, protection utilities are control panels and system extensions that can do their intended job only if they are installed on your startup disk before a problem occurs. Thus, getting them installed is part of preventive maintenance. None of these utilities are essential. Still, depending on your work situation, all are worth considering.

Protect Against Virus Infections

To protect yourself against computer viruses, you need to use an anti-virus utility. The most popular ones are Norton AntiVirus and Virex.

Of course, these utilities can be used at any time to check for and eradicate an existing virus infection. However, when properly set up, they can also monitor your disk and block a virus infection before it occurs. That's why I mention them here as part of preventive maintenance.

SEE: • Fix-It #6 for more details on checking for viruses.

Protect Against Accidentally Deleted Files

Have you ever unintentionally or deliberately deleted a file that you subsequently wished you could get back? Sure you have. Luckily, utility packages such as Norton Utilities provide a means of recovering files that have been deleted via the Finder's Empty Trash command.

These utilities can accomplish their magic because when you empty the Trash, you do not immediately remove the dumped file from the hard drive. Only its name is removed from a special area of the drive (where the computer looks to find out what is on your drive). The file data remain on the drive, intact, until the data is overwritten by a new file. Undelete utilities can find these deleted files, even though the Finder cannot, and restore them to their undeleted condition.

Keep in mind that eventually you will write new information over that particular area of the hard drive, and then the file *will* be irrecoverable. Thus, these utilities work best if you use them as soon as possible after deleting the file. You should not depend on this method as a guarantee for the recovery of deleted files!

Norton Utilities To make maximum use of the UnErase capability of Norton Utilities, you need to install the Norton FileSaver control panel (included with Norton Utilities; see Figure 2-13) using the following steps:

1. To set FileSaver in motion, place it in the Control Panels folder.

2. Open the control panel and click the On button (if it isn't already on).

3. Check the "Update Directory Disk Info" checkbox for each volume you wish to be protected by FileSaver.

4. Click the Preferences disclosing triangle to open the Preferences section of the window. Select the Update Schedule tab and select when you want FileSaver to perform the Update ("At Shutdown" is a suitable time). Or, if you leave your computer on all night, schedule the Update for some time while you are asleep.

5. Close the control panel and restart.

6. When you need to undelete files, launch Open UnErase from the Finder (or, alternatively, select UnErase either from the main menu window of Norton Utilities or from the Utilities menu). More details on using UnErase are outlined in Chapter 6. If FileSaver has been installed, Norton Utilities will use the saved FileSaver data to facilitate UnErase's search for files that can be recovered.

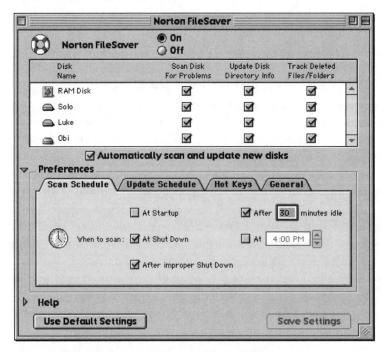

Figure 2-13 The FileSaver control panel of Norton Utilities.

Two final important points to remember: first, if you wait until you need to recover a file before you install FileSaver, it may be too late. The critical point here is prevention. The undelete feature of Norton Utilities work best if their associated control panel or extension is installed before you need to use it! While you still may be able to recover files even without this prior installation, your chances are slim. Second, only files that have been saved can be undeleted. These utilities are not useful for recovering work that was lost because of a system crash that occurred before you saved the file.

SEE: • **"Protect Against Loss of Data Due to System Crashes" later in this chapter.**
      • **Chapter 6 for more information on undeleting files.**

Protect Against Accidentally Erased Hard Drives

It's hard for me to imagine how you could erase a hard drive by accident. To do this, you would first have to inadvertently select Erase Disk from the Finder's Special menu. Then you would have to click OK on the prompt asking if you really want to do this. Even the Macintosh itself tries to prevent you from making such a mistake by prohibiting you from erasing the current startup disk (which is often your one and only hard drive). Still, I suppose it may happen to some poor soul somewhere.

Installing the FileSaver of Norton Utilities prior to the accidental disk erasure will facilitate any file recovery. It may also help with other problems such as crashed disks (described in the next section), where you cannot access a drive. (See the previous section, "Protect Against Accidentally Deleted Files," for details on how to set FileSaver up.)

Assuming FileSaver is installed, you recover a disk via the Volume Recover feature (rather than the UnErase feature described in the previous section). Volume Recover can quickly restore an entire disk in one step, rather than via a file-by-file selection. This feature is similar to restoring a disk from a global backup, except it's much faster and you don't need separately stored backup files. However, the effectiveness of this recovery feature depends on having the relevant invisible files (maintained by FileSaver) periodically updated. The more recently they have been updated, the better the recovery. You also need to be able to access the disk sufficiently to access the invisible Volume Recover data.

SEE: • **Chapter 5 for more information on disk crashes.**
      • **Fix-It #10 for more information on repairing and restoring disks.**
      • **Fix-It #11 for more information on file recovery.**
      • **Fix-It #13 for details on formatting disks.**

Protect Against Disk Damage

The most critical use for disk repair utilities (e.g., Disk First Aid, Norton Utilities, TechTool Pro, and DiskWarrior) is to repair a damaged or crashed disk. These terms primarily refers to disks that have damage to the disk's invisible Directory. Disk damage can cause any number of symptoms, including (in the worst cases) a failure of the disk to startup. In many cases, directory damage causes few, if any, initial symptoms. Eventually, symptoms worsen and become more obvious. To prevent these more serious symptoms from developing, you should use the above utilities to check your disks on a regular basis. I have often been surprised by how often it reports that a repair is needed—especially when I did not suspect a problem existed.

All of these utilities can be "manually" launched to check a disk at any time. Disk First Aid is the best place to start. It is free (it came with your Mac) and, because it comes from Apple, the latest version is occasionally able to fix newly discovered problems that others utilities can not. Conversely, if you have other disk repair utilities, such as Norton Utilities, run them as well. Additional utilities may spot and fix problems that Disk First Aid misses or cannot fix. DiskWarrior (and now TechTool Pro) has the bonus of actually "optimizing" the Directory files, which should lead to slightly faster performance (this type of optimization is separate from the more general disk optimization of a utility such as Norton Speed Disk, as described below and in Fix-it #7).

Norton Utilities and TechTool Pro include an option to automatically scan a disk at scheduled times (such as just prior to shutdown) or in the background (when the computer is otherwise idle). DiskWarrior now has a similar feature with its DiskSheild extension. If a problem is spotted, an alert message appears on the screen that informs you of the problem and typically suggests a course of action A sample message might read: "There is a problem on the disk... Run Norton Disk Doctor."

Personally, I prefer to "manually" schedule my own checking. But for those users who prefer an automatic setup, it's easy to set up. With Norton Utilities, for example, simply enable the "Scan Disk for Problems" checkboxes in the FileSaver control panel and set a schedule from Preferences. This is a separate function from the "UnErase" feature described previously in "Protect Against Accidentally Deleted Files."

SEE   • **Fix-It #10 for a description of how to using disk repair utilities.**
       • **Chapter 8 for more information on invisible files, including the Directory files.**

Protect Against Data Loss Due to System Crashes

Following seemingly sadistic logic, a system crash or bomb typically occurs when you are in the middle of some important task.

Yes, even if you take all the previous precautions, there will probably come a day when you are working on some important document, so engrossed in what you are doing that you forget to save your work. Suddenly, WHAM!—the infamous system bomb appears. Or maybe there is just a brief power failure. Whatever the case, all your work is lost.

Recovering from a system crash is usually as simple as restarting your computer. This gets you up and running again, but it does not resurrect any data that was unsaved at the time of the crash. The probability of recovering this unsaved work is almost zero—unless you have previously installed certain protection utilities (and even then, the probabilities may not be all that good!).

Save Text Data After a System Crash The GhostWriter option of Spell Catcher (as set from the Preferences command) saves all text input to a special, continually updated file. You can set it to do so for specific applications only, or for all applications. If a system crash or power failure occurs, this file has a copy of all of your work up to (or almost up to) the point of the interruption.

This feature has its limits. For example, text is saved in the order you typed it, which may not be the order it appears in the document. However, in times of crisis, whatever is saved may be worthwhile.

A new utility called Search & Rescue may be able to recover text directly from RAM, even if you have not saved the text in any form and even after a system crash. But don't expect miracles. It will certainly not resurrect an entire document, complete with text formatting.

Recover from a Crash Without Loss of Data: CrashGuard and MacsBug Over the years, various utilities have purported to help you recover from a system crash. Most of them are no longer actively updated and may no longer work effectively. The last major survivor was CrashGuard, included with Norton Utilities. However, Symantec dropped CrashGuard from Norton Utilities 5.x (although it says CrashGuard may return).

For those who may still be able to use it, here's a brief look at how CrashGuard works: with this control panel installed, when you get a system crash, CrashGuard intervenes and puts up its own alert box. One option offered is to "Fix" the cause of the crash. If this works, you may be able to save currently unsaved data. One other feature of CrashGuard worth mentioning: open the CrashGuard control panel and select "Show Details." You will get a log of all your recent system crashes, what application was active when the crash occurred, and the technical description of what caused the error. This log may assist you in diagnosing the cause of frequent seemingly random system crashes (see Chapter 4 for more details).

Another recovery possibility is to install Apple's MacsBug debugger (available from Apple's public online software libraries). While this is really designed for programmers (to help them debug errors in their programs), it can be helpful for anyone. It may allow you to recover from a system crash without having to restart.

To install it, just place the MacsBug file in your System Folder and restart. When you get a system crash, your screen fills with what appears to non-programmers as gibberish. However, at the bottom of the screen is a place where you can enter keyboard input. Type "ea" (for "exit application"). With some luck, you will be returned to the Finder, from where you should at least be able to save data in open applications other than the one that crashed. Otherwise, typing "rs" will force a restart.

Use an Autosave Feature An autosave function, such as the shareware Auto-Save, can be viewed as a means of protecting you against loss of data after a system crash. That's assuming it has automatically saved your otherwise unsaved data just prior to a crash.

SEE: • **Chapter 4 for more details on system errors in general.**

Give Your Macintosh a Tune-up

The following sextet of procedures should be done, ideally, on a regular basis, even if your machine seems to be running smoothly:

- Run a disk repair utility (such as Disk First Aid)
- Check for viruses
- Defragment/optimize your disk
- Rebuild your desktop
- Check and/or replace the System file
- Stay up-to-date

Think of them as the equivalent of giving your car a tune-up. Many users have merrily gone along without ever having done any of these things. I don't recommend this approach. How often should these procedures be run? Some (such as running Disk First Aid) should be done every month or so. Others (such as defragmenting a disk) need to be performed only a couple of times a year.

The first two items on this list, running a disk repair utility and checking for viruses, have already been covered (see "Install Protection Utilities"). What follows is an overview of the remaining four items.

All of these procedures are more than preventive measures. You can also use them to solve problems after the problems have occured. Thus, I discuss these procedures again, from a more specific problem-solving perspective, in Part III, especially in Fix-Its #4, #6, #7, #8, #10, and #16. To avoid repetition, I save most of the details for these later Fix-Its.

Defragment/Optimize Your Disk

It may surprise you to learn that when you write a file to your hard drive, the file may be split and saved in several sections, and scattered across your drive. This typically occurs when there is not enough disk space in a single unused chunk to hold the entire file. While not a problem by itself, if too much fragmentation exists, you may see a slowdown in performance or an inability to open a file. At the very least, less file fragmentation tends to improve chances of recovering files after a disk crash. Optimizing a disk is more complex than defragmenting: it means reordering the location of the files on the disk to "optimize" access to the files and minimize the rate of future defragmentation, thereby getting a further speed boost.

You usually defragment and/or optimize a disk by using a special disk-optimizing utility. In Norton Utilities, the optimizing application is called Speed Disk. TechTool Pro also has an optimizing feature. Disk Express is another alternative.

By the way, whenever you reformat your hard drive and restore files from your backup copies, you have also defragmented the files on your disk.

SEE: • **Fix-It #7 for details on how to defragment a disk.**

Rebuild Your Desktop File

Rebuild your desktop. Rebuild your desktop. Almost a mantra of Macintosh problem solving, rebuilding your desktop is usually one of the first recommendations you will hear, no matter what your problem is. It is as if to say, "Well, even if it doesn't do anything, it can't hurt to try."

So what does it really mean to rebuild your desktop? The Desktop file(s) are invisible files that the Finder uses to keep track of information required to create the Finder's desktop display. Basically, rebuilding your desktop means updating or replacing your existing Desktop file.

Rebuilding the desktop is a useful tool for solving a variety of problems, especially those related to the functioning of the Finder (such as an inability to launch files). However, it is also useful as a maintenance measure, even if you don't suspect anything is wrong at the moment.

To rebuild the desktop, hold down the command and option keys just prior to the mounting of a disk (hold them down at startup for the startup disk) until an alert box appears asking if you want to rebuild the desktop. Click OK.

SEE • **Fix-It #8 for more information on how to rebuild the desktop.**
 • **Chapter 8 for more information on invisible files, including the Desktop files.**

Check and/or Replace the System File

The System file is the most essential and probably most complicated file on your disk. Unfortunately, it is also one of the most frequently modified. The Macintosh modifies the System file quite often, as part of the Mac's normal operation. You get no special notification that this has happened, so you may not even be aware of it. With every modification, there is a chance that an error will occur and that the System file will be corrupted. This can lead to a variety of problems whose cause may not be easily diagnosed as due to a corrupted System file. Sometimes, these problems may not even appear until weeks after the damage first occurred. Thus, it is usually a good idea to replace the System file every three or four months, even if you are not yet experiencing any symptoms. The easiest way to do this is if you keep a special backup copy of your System file (that you are confident is not damaged) maintained for just this purpose. Otherwise, you will have to reinstall the System file from your system software disks, using the Installer utility — which can be less than ideal if you have customized the System file from its original state. If your System Folder also has a System Resources file, you should similarly maintain a backup copy of it.

If you are reluctant to replace a System file as a preventive measure, especially since the file may be perfectly fine, at least check it out. The freeware program, TechTool, can check the integrity of the System file. Just make sure you have a version of TechTool that is newer than the version of the system software you are using. Otherwise, it may be unable to check it.

SEE: • **Fix-It #4 for details on how to reinstall system software and more information about checking for damaged system software.**

Stay Up-to-Date

Regularly check sources (such as those described in Fix-It #16) to find out if the vendors of your software have recently released bug-fixed upgrades. These upgrades can solve problems that cannot be fixed in any other way.

Especially check for update fixes to Apple's system software, as these are likely to have the most wide-ranging effect on your Mac's behavior. For example, an iMac Update 1.1 (released in late 1998) fixed an assortment of problems users were having with connecting USB devices to the iMac. Similarly, Font Manager Update 1.0 (released in the summer of 1999) fixed a font problem with Mac OS 8.6 that was causing numerous system crashes.

The ReadMe file that accompanies an update should explain exactly what the update fixes and what, if any, new features it introduces.

Generally, when a new version of the Mac OS is available, installing it eliminates the need to worry about older updates. Thus, if your iMac is running Mac OS 9, you needn't worry about whether or not you have iMac Update 1.1. In fact, with Mac OS 9, you can regularly run the Software Update control panel to make sure you are always completely up-to-date.

SEE: • **Chapter 15 for more information on the latest system software.**
• **Fix-It #4 for more details on installing System Updates and Enablers.**
• **Fix-It #16 for more information on how to keep up-to-date with the latest software.**

3

Problem Solving:
General Strategies

Uh-Oh...

Something has gone wrong with your Macintosh. You are sitting and staring at your screen, trying to figure out exactly what has happened and (more important) what you can do to fix it. That's exactly what you are about to find out.

Five Steps to Solving Macintosh Problems

1. Read Alert Box Messages

Often, after something unexpected has occurred with your Macintosh, an alert box error message appears. These messages often contain valuable information.

TECHNICALLY SPEAKING ▶ What's an Alert Box?

An *alert box* pops up on your screen to warn you or inform you about the consequences of what you have just done (*Your file has been successfully transferred*) or what you are about to do (*Erasing the disk will permanently erase all data on it. Do you still want to erase it?*). It is usually accompanied by either the "! in a triangle" icon (which means "caution") or the "hand in a stop sign" icon (which is more serious and means "stop and read this before proceeding").

Usually, you cannot do much in response to an alert box message other than click an OK or Cancel button.

Alert boxes are a normal and expected part of the Macintosh's operation. Their appearance doesn't necessarily mean that you have a problem. When you do have a problem, however, they are particularly likely to appear. In such cases, they are often referred to as *error messages*.

A terminology note: a cousin to the alert box is the *dialog box*. A dialog box usually appears after you've chosen a command from a menu. The box that appears after you choose Print from the File menu, for example, is a dialog box. Dialog boxes are distinguished from alert boxes both by the different functions and by the fact that dialog boxes usually have many more options than the one or two choices typical of an alert box.

The alert box may inform you of an action you need to take (*Please select Page Setup before printing your document*). It may also inform you why you cannot perform a command you requested (*The disk cannot be erased because the disk is locked*). Or it may tell you what has just gone wrong (*The application unexpectedly quit*). In any case, it can also provide advice on how to successfully carry out the command or fix the problem.

Suppose you have an application that does not open when you try to launch it, and you get an alert box message that says there is not enough memory available.

The alert box may offer a suggested solution to the problem and may even provide a button for enacting that solution (Quit Application).

For another example, consider a message that tells you that the Trash cannot be emptied. It may not only tell you why you could not empty the Trash, but also may give you a *keyboard shortcut* that you can use to solve the problem quickly. This keyboard shortcut works faster than going to the Get Info window of each locked file and unlocking it.

What if you don't understand the meaning of the alert box message or if it doesn't offer any useful advice? This is where the rest of this book can help. This book describes dozens of alert box messages and explains how to deal with them. You can look up any error message in the Symptom Index at the back of this book. This book does not list every possible alert message you might get; no single book could do that. But it does describe and explain the most important and most common alert messages you are likely to encounter.

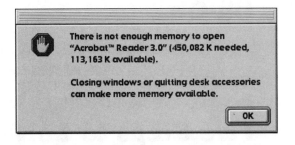

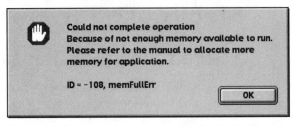

Figure 3-1 Two examples of alert boxes indicating that there is insufficient memory available to open an application. Workaround solutions are offered.

One final note: alert boxes that accompany some of the more serious problems you can get, such as a system crash or an unexpected quit, often include esoteric information about the cause of the problem (such as *An error of Type 11 occurred*). Although I generally recommend ignoring this information, because it is rarely helpful for most users, I do describe examples of what these messages mean in Chapter 4.

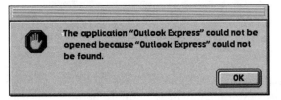

Figure 3-2 Sometimes the Mac gets confused. This alert box started to appear when I tried open an application for which not enough memory was available. Closing some open applications eliminated the error.

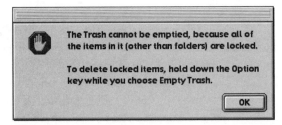

Figure 3-3 An alert box that may appear when you try to empty the Trash. It not only tells you the problem, but also provides a solution.

2. Check If the Problem Repeats

Clearly, not all problems can be solved by reading error messages (especially if your problem did not result in any error message!). Still, the solution to your problem may be close at hand, often just a few clicks away.

First off, many Macintosh problems are one-time-only occurrences. They happen for reasons that may never again be exactly duplicated and that no one will ever fully understand. So before you run off and spend hours trying to solve a problem, make sure you really have a problem to solve: see whether you can get the problem to recur.

If the problem involves an application, quit and then relaunch it. If the problem involves a floppy disk, eject and then reinsert it. And so on. Then see whether the problem recurs.

If your problem is a system crash or other equally debilitating event, you will have to restart the Macintosh before you can find out whether the problem recurs. Even for less serious errors, it is usually good advice to restart the Macintosh before checking for a recurring problem. A restart solves a surprising array of problems all by itself. But beware: a restart may sometimes only appear to solve a problem. The symptoms may return again the next day or the next week.

If the problem does not recur, be happy! You probably had one of those once-in-a-lifetime unknown causes that may never happen again. Chalk it up as one of life's cosmic mysteries. If it does continue to recur, you have more work to do.

3. Isolate the Cause

From a general perspective, there are relatively few types of Macintosh problems. System crashes and system freezes alone probably account for more than half of what people complain about. The problem is that figuring out the exact cause of a particular crash is not always easy. Many causes can produce the same symptom.

On the other hand, I continue to be surprised by how often a seemingly inexplicable problem turns out to be due to a simple-to-fix common cause. You may get a symptom that is so rare that no one has ever heard of it happening before. Yet the cause could be something quite basic—perhaps a lack of proper termination on your SCSI chain (as described in Fix-It #16). No one knows all the many symptoms that this SCSI cause could produce.

To take another example, someone may ask me for advice on why he suddenly started to get a system freeze when choosing Print in his favorite word processor. After checking my database of troubleshooting notes and failing to find any mention of this specific problem, I am unsure what to suggest. But a little basic experimenting soon uncovers the cause: a previously unknown (at least to me) conflict with an extension that the user had recently added to the System Folder. It had nothing to do with the printer, the printer driver, the application in use, damaged software or any other cause that I might have thought was more likely to provide the solution.

So before searching for odd explanations for odd symptoms, make sure you have covered the basics.

In any case, your job is to progressively narrow the range of possible causes of your problem until you succeed in isolating the precise cause. Although the general problem-solving strategies described here are useful no matter what the specific nature of your problem is, they are most critical when you are trying to diagnose and solve problems on your own, on those occasions when seeking help did not provide the answer.

SEE: • **Chapter 4, "Solve It! Recurring System Errors," for more detailed strategies on diagnosing recurring system errors.**

Look for Recent Changes or Unusual Circumstances

Suppose that while you are trying to save a BusyWorks word processing document, a system crash occurs. You have saved many documents with BusyWorks before and have never had a system crash. What's going on? Usually, some recent change in your software or hardware is precipitating the crash. The culprit may be a newly added system extension or a recently connected hardware peripheral. The problem may even be due to a change you recently made in existing software, such as changing an application's default preferences setting or turning on a new option in a control panel. Thus, if you are aware of any recent changes to your computer system, focus your search on them.

If you don't know of any recent changes to your computer system, consider whether any unusual circumstances, not previously duplicated, could have caused the problem. Perhaps you were trying to save a particularly long BusyWorks document, for example, when the crash occurred. If you have never before tried to save a document that long, the size of the document may be the problem.

Assess the Specificity of the Problem

Suppose that you cannot open a particular document file currently stored on a floppy disk. What's the cause? The problem could be with the particular file, the particular application used to open the file, some related file stored in the System Folder, the floppy disk that contains the file, or even the disk drive hardware.

Often, the exact symptom or error message (if one appears) helps you choose among these possibilities. Otherwise, you need to assess the specificity of the problem. Thus, to see whether the problem is specific to that file, try opening another file. To see whether it is specific to that application, try opening files in other applications. To see whether it is specific to that disk, try using other disks. I think you get the point by now. There are no exact rules. In the end, isolating the cause of a problem is often more of an art than it is a science.

TAKE NOTE ▶ Risk Management

Whenever you try to fix a problem, there is at least a small risk that what you do will somehow succeed only in making matters worse. Always look for ways to minimize this risk. As stressed in Chapter 2, for example, always back up your files before you attempt to fix a problem.

In general, try the simplest, easiest, and most-likely-to-be-successful techniques first. Then proceed to the more powerful, difficult-to-use, more time-consuming, lower-probability-of-success ones, if necessary. This not only saves you time and hassle, but also is generally safer. The more powerful techniques tend to be the riskier ones.

4. Go for Help

You need not wait to try this step until you have exhausted all your attempts to isolate the cause in the preceding step. Similarly, you don't always need to go for help before you can go on to the next step and solve the problem. You can think of these last two steps as being more parallel than sequential. You can skip from one to the other in whatever order gets you to the solution fastest.

Check the Manual!

I know—at best, people use the manual for a while when they start using a new program and then never glance at it again. Whole sections of the book remain untouched by human hands. Many Macintosh users are proud of how much they can accomplish without *ever* looking at the manual. The fact that they can accomplish anything at all is touted as evidence of how easy the Macintosh is to use.

And yes, most manuals are not fun to read. They are reference books, after all—not science-fiction adventures.

Despite all this, I am telling you to read the manual. Check whatever manuals, for hardware or software, seem to be potentially relevant to your problem. No, you don't have to read the whole thing cover to cover. Just check for the part relevant to the problem you are having. Check the opening pages of the manual—the ones that discuss how to install the program. In these pages, you can find vital details about where files should be located and possible incompatibilities. Check the troubleshooting section, if there is one. Use the index, if necessary. You will be amazed how many problems you can solve this way. Sometimes, you will even discover helpful tips that make it easier to complete your task, regardless of any problems you may be experiencing.

These days, checking the manual does not mean simply the printed documentation. The current trend is to minimize the use of printed manuals and shift instead to documentation available as a file (which you can print if need be) on the application CD or help accessible via the Mac's Help menu.

If a feature of a program doesn't work the first time you try it, don't immediately assume that there is a problem with the program. Often, the problem is that you did not understand how to use the program correctly. Reading the manual almost invariably solves this type of problem.

SEE: • **Chapter 1 for more on the Help menu.**

Get Outside Help

Often, this means calling a vendor's technical-support line. Almost all companies maintain a phone number to help answer your technical questions. The number should be included somewhere in the documentation that came with the program.

These days, if you have Internet access, checking a vendor's Web site is probably the best way to start. Commercial online services (such as America Online) also offer a wealth of help via bulletin boards and/or update libraries.

Technical support should not be used as a substitute for reading manuals or developing your own problem-solving skills. it can be helpful, however, in providing information about undocumented features or recently discovered bugs in the software—information that's not readily available anywhere else. The company may even be able to supply an updated version of the software that fixes the bug.

SEE: • **Fix-It #16 for more on technical support and seeking outside help.**

Consult This Book

This is an obvious bit of advice. After all, solving problems is the purpose of this book.

5. Fix the Problem

Identifying the cause of a recurring problem is often the most difficult and time-consuming step in this whole procedure. Obviously, it is not the last step. You next need to fix the problem so that it no longer recurs.

I can make broad generalizations here. A problem that is unique to a particular application is usually solved by replacing or upgrading the application and/or its preferences file(s). Otherwise, it is probably due to a conflict with an extension or some aspect of the system software. Symptoms that span most applications are usually caused by system software. This is especially likely if the problem involves activities (such as printing) that depend heavily on system software files. Solutions to these problems often involve replacing or updating system software files. Conflicts with extensions and control panels also cause these problems. Problems that affect the entire disk or affect basic system operations (such as an inability to empty the Trash) are usually due to damage to special invisible files on the disk. You should try to repair this damage, if possible (using special repair utilities). If they can't be repaired, you will probably have to reformat the entire disk.

The Troubleshooter's Cure-Alls

As an alternative to searching for a precise cause of and solution to a given problem, many experts suggest working your way through a familiar list of likely cures, a list supposedly guaranteed to fix almost any problem you might encounter: rebuild the desktop, do a clean reinstall of your system software, turn off all your extensions, run Disk First Aid, and so on. It certainly can't hurt to try at least some of these procedures. Indeed, I already advised (in Step 3) not ignoring these basics, even for apparently rare problems.

Still, just following these procedures blindly often results in wasting time trying things that have little or no hope of helping you. Sure, I describe these all-purpose panaceas, in extensive detail, in the Fix-Its section of this book. It also helps you figure out when certain "cures" would be a waste of time to try and when they might be useful.

BY THE WAY ▶ If You Can't Fix It, Maybe You Can Work Around It

If the exact circumstances that must be repeated to get the problem to recur are sufficiently unusual, you may be able to live without ever repeating those circumstances. Maybe the problem occurs only when you have Word, Excel, and Canvas all open at the same time, for example, and you try to open an Excel document immediately after trying to print a Word document.

If necessary, you probably can prevent this problem without having to find the cause. Just don't duplicate those events in the future. This type of solution is often called a *workaround* because you have worked around the problem rather than actually fixing it.

Preventing Problems

Get to Know Shortcuts

Almost anything you can do with the Macintosh, you can do in more than one way. Do you want to close a window on the desktop, for example? Simply choose the Close command from the Finder's File menu. Or click the close box in the top-left corner of the window. Or use a keyboard shortcut—in this case, Command-W (this shortcut is listed in the File menu next to the word Close). Other shortcuts are more obscure and can be found only by consulting an application's manual.

The Command (⌘), Option, Control, Shift, and Escape keys, in combination with other keys, often produce a variety of strange and wonderful results and shortcuts, depending on which application you are using.

Familiarity with at least the most common of these shortcuts is invaluable in negotiating many problem-solving tasks, not to mention making your daily work with the Macintosh considerably more

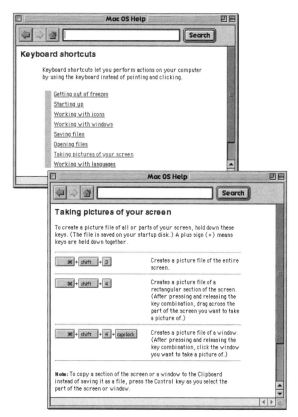

Figure 3-4 Did you forget the key combination to zap your PRAM? Don't despair. Check out the Mac OS Help Shortcuts list (Starting Up is one the one that tells you how to zap the PRAM). Or, if you want to take a snapshot of the screen, check out the instructions in the bottom window of this figure. There are more options than you probably realized.

pleasant. For starters, go to the Help menu when you are in the Finder, choose Mac Help and then select "Shortcuts and Tips." Especially check out the "Keyboard shortcuts" item in the list that appears. Also check out the "Common Troubleshooting Keyboard Shortcuts" table in the Appendix at the end of this book. Beyond this, check the manuals of your applications for details, or simply explore on your own and see what happens.

Go Exploring

The topic of exploring is worth discussing a bit more. The design of the Macintosh, with its pull-down menus and point-and-click approach, encourages exploring, because it minimizes the need to memorize anything or to type long, obscure commands. Take advantage of this situation. Even if you never look at an application's manual, spend some time exploring its menus and dialog boxes. Try out potential shortcut commands.

You may feel that you do not have the time to spend on this sort of frivolity. Time spent exploring, however, can be an investment repaid several times over in preventing future frustration. Often the biggest benefit of exploring is the pleasant surprise of discovering that there is a way (perhaps an easy way) to do something that you thought was impossible. The "I didn't know you could do that" reaction itself can be considered to be a form of problem-solving.

Still, if you are a relatively inexperienced user, this may sound like dangerous advice—like advising a novice tightrope walker to practice without a net. If you use a little common sense, however, the risks are minimal at best. Here's some common-sense advice to use while exploring.

Work Only with Duplicates

Work only with a duplicate copy of any important document (or use a document that you don't mind losing). That way, even if the document gets deleted or corrupted in some way, it does not matter. Even if your entire machine crashes and you have to start all over again, no harm is done.

Use Undo

Remember that most actions can be reversed by the Undo command and that (usually!) no changes are saved until you choose Save from the File menu. When in doubt, undo.

Use Cancel

Almost all potentially "dangerous" operations on the Macintosh, such as erasing a disk, are preceded by a warning and an opportunity to cancel. If you get too anxious about what you might be about to do, just choose Cancel.

PART 2

Symptoms, Causes, and Cures

When preventive measures are not enough and a problem occurs anyway, this is the section to turn to first. Here, you will find a listing of symptoms that cover a broad range of both the most common and the most serious problems you are likely to confront, together with step-by-step instructions for what to do to solve them. Again, the solutions require only a few simple software tools and no particular expertise on your part.

Chapters 4 and 5 cover the problems that are the most disruptive to your use of the Macintosh.

Chapter 4 covers system errors (also called system crashes), typified by the infamous bomb alert box. Chapter 4 walks you through exactly what to do after specific system errors. It may surprise you to learn that you can often do more than simply give up and restart your Macintosh.

Chapter 5 covers what is probably the most anxiety-provoking problem to confront any computer user: a total inability to start the machine. The Macintosh may successfully turn on, but the startup sequence may never begin or never reach a successful conclusion. Chapter 5 also describes what to do for any crashed disk, whether it is a startup disk or not. The chapter concludes with a look at a few other general disk-related problems, such as problems with ejecting floppy disks or shutting down the Macintosh.

From launching applications to printing documents, Chapters 6 through 8 explain what can go wrong and how you can make it right again.

Chapter 6 covers the most common and yet most frustrating file-related problems. Are you having trouble locating a particular file? Or if you do locate it, do you find that it refuses to open? Maybe there is insufficient memory to use the Clipboard. Perhaps you want to copy or delete a file, but the Macintosh refuses to let you do it. If you are having any of these problems, Chapter 6 guides you to a solution.

Chapter 7 Even after you complete and save your masterpiece, your problems may not be over. You probably want to print your work. This introduces a new host of potential problems. Chapter 7 is devoted to what to do when you cannot get a document to print.

Chapter 8 is a more technical look at some of the Macintosh's more esoteric (yet still comprehensible and certainly useful) topics: file types, creators, and attributes. As always, the focus remains on how you can apply this knowledge to solve problems.

Most Macintosh productivity applications can be boiled down to one or two basic components. Either you are using text and numbers, or you are using graphics. Whether the work is dashing off a memo or writing a novel, whether it's creating a chart in a spreadsheet or creating a full-page ad for a magazine, virtually all Macintosh users spend most of their time with these two prime functions. Chapters 9 and 10 explore these basics.

Chapter 9 covers text problems. Although they're most likely to crop up when you're using a word processor, text problems can appear when you are using any application that contains text, including spreadsheets and databases. The chapter begins with an overview of the different categories of fonts and how they determine the appearance of your text. It concludes with a description of common text-related problems and their solutions.

Chapter 10 deals with graphic-related problems that can confront even the most non-graphic Macintosh users. It begins with an explanation of the types of graphics files and the basics of how your computer displays grayscale and color documents. The chapter also discusses QuickTime and movie/video troubleshooting. It concludes with a collection of common graphics-related problems and how to solve them.

Chapters 11 through 13 cover problems that go beyond the individual Macintosh. It explores troubleshooting issues that can occur when you connect your Macintosh to other Macintoshes, to a larger network, or to the Internet.

Chapter 11 deals with problems related to transferring files from one Mac to another (file sharing) via a variety of different methods, including LocalTalk and Ethernet networks. There is also a special focus on PowerBooks, extending into PowerBook issues not directly related to file sharing.

Chapter 12 covers problems with Internet connections. It offers advice on setting up all of Apple's Internet-related software (such as the TCP/IP and Remote Access control panels) and how to successfully get and stay online.

Chapter 13 covers the 2,000-pound gorilla of the Internet: Web browsers and the World Wide Web. It also delves into problems with email and downloading files.

The final two chapters deal with Apple's latest hardware and software.

Chapter 14 covers troubleshooting the latest Apple hardware: the iMacs, iBooks, and Power Mac G3s and G4s.

Chapter 15 covers troubleshooting problems specific to the latest Apple software: Mac OS 8.x, 9.x, and Mac OS X.

As you go through these chapters, you will find frequent references to other parts of the book, particularly the Fix-Its in Part III. Part II emphasizes the diagnosis of a problem and, in general, how to go about solving it. The Fix-Its describe more specifically the tools used to solve these problems. By analogy, if this book were about home repair, Part II might tell you that the squeak in your flooring is caused by a loose floorboard and that you have to hammer in some nails to fix it. Part III, by contrast, would explain what hammers are and the general techniques for using them. So if any explanations in these chapters seem to be less than complete, check out the Fix-Its for the rest of the story.

4

System Errors: Living with the Bomb

The Mac's Worst-Kept Secret

If you are new to the world of computers, you may think that a *system crash* is the sound your computer makes after you throw it to the floor in frustration. No, that's not it exactly—though a series of system crashes can certainly get you thinking about sending your Macintosh into free fall. Actually, a system crash refers to any time your computer's processing gets so messed up that it stops whatever it was doing and no longer responds to further user input.

What to do when you have this type of system crash, or any other of several related *system errors,* is the subject of this chapter. System errors are the Macintosh's worst-kept secret. Many software manuals barely mention the possibility that system errors can occur. Yet they do occur, all too frequently.

If (or, more realistically, when) you get any sort of system error, it is the equivalent of seeing a "Road Closed" sign at the end of a long stretch of highway. There's no going forward, and you have to spend some time heading back before you can make progress again.

I am not going to delve much into what causes these system errors. My goal is simply to explain how to rid yourself of them. Still, it may make you feel better to know that system crashes are not the result of some mistake on your part. It is either the result of faulty hardware or (much more likely) damaged or less-than-perfectly designed software. Your freedom from guilt is at best only small consolation when a system error does occur. This knowledge doesn't save any of your data or eliminate any of the frustration.

Helpful hint: No software is perfectly designed. Therefore, all software is potentially a source of a system error. Trust no one. But wait! Don't get overly alarmed by this warning. Programming for the Macintosh is not the easiest thing in the world to do, and it is almost impossible to anticipate every potential circumstance that might lead to a system crash—especially when programmers have to contend with the ever-growing number of Macintosh models, a dizzying assortment of potential peripherals, and a seemingly endless variety of software, all of which may be combined in a nearly infinite number of permutations. The real surprise is that things work just as expected most of the time.

Your immediate concerns probably are the following:

- What permanent damage has been done to the machine, if any?
- What data have I lost, if any?
- How do I get the Macintosh working again?
- How do I prevent the system error from occurring again?

The answer to the first question is good news. System errors never cause any permanent damage to your hardware. A system crash can result from damaged hardware, but it never causes it. And although a system crash may damage (or, as it is sometimes called, *corrupt*) your software—particularly anything you were using at the time of the crash—it is much more likely that everything on your disks is still OK. In general, you should be able to get your Macintosh up and running again in a matter of minutes.

The answer to the second question is potentially bad news. Barring a few exceptions (to be discussed shortly), everything you were working on at the time of the crash that you did not save to disk is forever lost in space, never to be seen again. If you spent the past hour writing the opening chapter of your next novel and never saved it, it is probably gone forever. Actually, any file that's open at the time of the crash, saved or unsaved, is at some risk of damage.

Helpful hint: save frequently. Saving is your greatest protection against the worst-case scenario of a system crash. So if you plan to spend the day working on your Great American Novel, don't forget to use the Save command every few minutes.

The answers to the remaining two questions depend on the cause of the system error. The main thing you do after most system crashes is restart the Macintosh. Happily, in many cases after you restart, the system error does *not* recur, because the specific combination of events that led to the system error are not repeated. Even if you think you are repeating what you did before the system error, the Macintosh may see matters differently. Sometimes, however, a system error occurs repeatedly. In such cases, you must track down the cause of the error so that you can find a way to prevent its recurrence.

Solve It! A Catalog of System Errors

System Crashes

 Symptoms:

The Bomb Alert Box Appears

The bomb alert box is the best-known of all system errors. The alert box includes an icon of a bomb, as well as a text message apologizing for what has just occurred (*Sorry, a system error has occurred.*). Users typically refer to this unhappy event by saying, "My computer crashed" or "My Mac just bombed."

Sometimes, an bomb alert box may appear with no text at all in it. It's still a crash.

This is not a warning that your computer may explode. But it does mean that your Mac's activity has come to a grinding halt.

Breakup of Screen Display

The other type of system crash is so severe that the Macintosh cannot even muster the strength to display

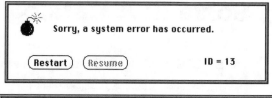

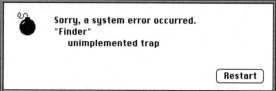

Figure 4-1 Two examples of system bomb alert boxes.

the bomb alert message. Instead, the screen display may break up into an unintelligible mess, complete with flashes of light and crackling noises. (This phenomenon is less common on the newer Macintosh models.) Despite the pyrotechnics, it is still a system crash. Again, no permanent harm has been done to your machine.

 ## Causes:

Most crashes are due to a software bug or a conflict between two active programs. Bad memory management is the likely immediate culprit in most of these cases.

System crashes can also have some hardware-related causes, including defective memory chips, a defective power supply, and SCSI device problems.

 ## What to Do:

Understanding System Error Alert Box Messages (Or What the Heck Is a "Bad F Line Instruction," Anyway?)

Besides offering its apologies, the bomb box error message typically describes the cause of your crash. You are not likely to be impressed by the description. Depending on the exact circumstances of the system error, descriptions either define the problem by name (such as *bad F line instruction* or *unimplemented trap*) or by number (such as *ID = 02* or *an error of Type 1*). Not very informative, are they? On a scale of understandability, this information ranks slightly lower than the instructions for calculating depreciation on your tax return.

The truth is, this information was not meant to be easily understood by the masses. It was meant for programmers to understand, so that they can figure out why their programs are crashing. Most of the time, the numbers simply mean that there is a mistake (or bug) in the program that needs to be fixed. (This is what typically causes a *bad F-line instruction* or *unimplemented trap* message, for example.) Correcting a program's instruction code is not something that you can do yourself, so the ID information is almost always of little value to you.

If, despite all this, you are still curious about what the error-code numbers mean, several places list their "meaning." Unfortunately, the translation usually is not much more illuminating than the error code itself. You will learn, for example, that an ID 1 error is a *bus error* and that an ID 2 error is an *address error.* Coming to the rescue, Table 4-1 lists several common error codes, together with a non-jargonese explanation of

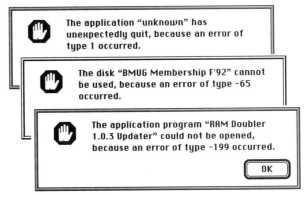

The application "unknown" has unexpectedly quit, because an error of type 1 occurred.

The disk "BMUG Membership F'92" cannot be used, because an error of type -65 occurred.

The application program "RAM Doubler 1.0.3 Updater" could not be opened, because an error of type -199 occurred.

OK

Figure 4-2 System error ID numbers as they appear in a variety of alert messages. In case you are curious, Type 1 means "bus error," -65 means "read/write requested for an offline drive," and -199 means "map inconsistent with operation." Aren't you glad you asked?

what they mean and what you might do about them. Otherwise, check out a shareware utility such as Black & Bleu or MacErrors for a more complete listing. Black & Bleu is especially noteworthy, as it attempts to explain many errors in less technical language.

Theoretically, understanding these error codes might help you track down the cause of a system error. But the error code itself may not be accurate. A system crash can mess things up so much that the Macintosh may put up a code that doesn't describe the true cause of the problem... in which case, the information is (once again) useless.

Helpful hint: don't waste much time trying to interpret the error message.
Understanding these messages *never* helps in the immediate crisis of recovering from the crash. It only rarely helps in diagnosing the ultimate cause of the crash. At best, jot down the number for later reference.

Positive vs. Negative Error Codes

Not all error codes are associated with system crashes (the focus of this section!). Actually, error codes come in two basic varieties: positive and negative. *Positive error codes* most often accompany system crashes or unexpected quits.

Negative error codes occur after a variety of less disruptive problems, such as a failure to copy or delete a file. Negative error codes are more likely to point you in a useful direction for solving the problem than positive error codes are. In the most benign cases, the message may inform you why you can't do what you are trying to do (such as copy a file or open an application), but it allows you to proceed with using your Mac.

Table 4-1 provides a few examples of common negative error codes. File system errors (-33 to -61) are probably the most common. Later sections of this chapter (as well as other chapters, especially 5 and 6) include more examples of negative error codes.

There are literally dozens more negative codes, some of which are undocumented, and even calling Apple tech support for help may not lead to an explanation of what they mean. Utilities such as MacErrors list most of them, however. If you want to know what a given negative error code means, keep this (or a similar) utility handy.

Table 4-1 ▶ Some Common System Error Codes*

ID/ERROR NAME	WHAT IT MEANS	WHAT TO DO**
Positive Error Codes		
01/ Bus error 02/ Address error	Most often due to a software bug, extension conflict, or insufficient memory assigned to an application. The exact cause varies with when the error occurs. Immediately at startup: probably a problem with an externally connected SCSI device (possibly an incompatible disk driver); while the extensions are loading: probably an extension conflict; while in the Finder: probably corrupted system software; any other application: a bug in the application. Most common on 680X0 Macs.	If problem is specific to one application, try increasing its memory size (Fix-It #5). Otherwise, call the manufacturer to find out about a possible bug. If the error happens across many applications, replace system software (Fix-It #4). See Fix-Its #3, #14, and #15 for more on extension conflicts, SCSI problems, and logic-board problems, respectively.
03/Illegal instruction	Most likely, a software bug. Technically, the Macintosh is trying to execute an instruction that is not in its processor's vocabulary.	Problem is usually specific to a single application. Contact the manufacturer for information about a bug-fixed upgrade.
04/Divide by zero error	A mistake in the program code caused the program to attempt to divide a number by zero. Because this is impossible, the system error results.	Problem is almost assuredly specific to the program in use. Contact the manufacturer for information about a bug-fixed upgrade. Also, see Fix-It #3 to check for possible extension conflicts.
08/Trace mode error	A debugger (such as MacsBug) isn't installed, and the processor is accidentally placed in Trace mode (a mode that should ordinarily be used only by programmers when debugging a program). Assuredly, a software bug.	Installing MacsBug (see: "Protect Against Data Loss Due to System Crashes," in Chapter 2) can work-around the error. Otherwise, upgrade the software.
09/Line trap (A-line) error 10/F-line instruction error 12/Unimplemented trap of core routine (operating system)	Typically, an extension conflict or a software bug. A program may assume, for example, that the Mac's ROM contains information that is only available in newer Macs; thus, it bombs when run on an older model. Technically, it typically means that a call was made to the Macintosh's ROM for an entry that doesn't exist. Type 10 errors are essentially the same as "No FPU Installed" errors.	Problem is usually specific to a single application. Contact the manufacturer for information about a bug-fixed upgrade.
11/Miscellaneous hardware exception error	An error generated by the processor and not covered by IDs 1 to 10. Exact cause unknown. This error is much more common on Power Macintoshes than on 680X0 Macs.	Problem is usually specific to a single application. Contact the manufacturer for information about a bug-fixed upgrade. Before Mac OS 8.0, this error was common and could be caused by any number of unrelated problems. It is now relatively rare.

Table 4-1 ▶ Some Common System Error Codes* *continued*

ID/ERROR NAME	WHAT IT MEANS	WHAT TO DO**
Positive Error Codes *(continued)*		
15/Segment Loader Error	Macintosh programs can be broken into segments that may be separately loaded, so as to minimize RAM use. The system software's Segment Loader, in conjunction with instructions from the program, determine how this is done. A bug in the system software and/or the program can cause this error.	Upgrade the program or system software. If an extension is the cause, disabling the extension is a workaround.
25/Out of memory 28/Stack ran into heap	Although this error should be caused by an application running out of memory, the Macintosh may be "fooled" by other causes into thinking that there is a memory problem	Increase the application's memory allocation (see Fix-It #5). Otherwise, try the more general solutions described in this chapter.
Negative Error Codes		
−34/Disk is full	Not enough room on the disk (typically occurs when you are trying to save a file to a disk). Otherwise, the disk may be damaged.	Delete or transfer files on the disk to free more room for what you are trying to do. Otherwise, try to repair the disk (see Fix-Its #10).
−39/End of file	Indicates a discrepancy between the actual and expected sizes of a file. Usually means that the file is hopelessly corrupted.	If it is an application, replace it and its preferences file (if any). See Chapter 6 (on deleting files) and Fix-It #2. For a data file, recover data, if possible; then delete it (see Fix-It #11). Otherwise, try replacing the System and Finder (see Fix-It #4) (either from backup copies or by reinstalling from the Mac OS CD) and/or check for disk damage (see Fix-Its #10).
−43/File not found	A file you are trying to use could not be located.	Unless the file is really missing, it probably means you have disk damage (see Fix-It #10).
−97/Port in use	Most likely, a problem with a serial port (printer or modem) connection; possibly a problem with an SCSI device.	Turn off the serial-port peripheral device and turn it back on again. Restart the Mac. Try again. If problem persists, zap Parameter RAM (see Fix-It #9). Otherwise, check for disk driver (Fix-It #12) or other SCSI problems (Fix-It #14)
−108/Out of memory	Although this error should be caused by an application running out of memory, the Macintosh may be fooled by other causes into thinking that there is a memory problem.	Increase the application's memory allocation (see Fix-It #5). Otherwise, try the more general solutions described in this chapter.

Table 4-1 ▶ Some Common System Error Codes* *continued*

ID/ERROR NAME	WHAT IT MEANS	WHAT TO DO**
Negative Error Codes *(continued)*		
−127/Internal file system error	Usually due to a corrupted directory.	Try repairing the disk with Disk First Aid or other repair utilities (Fix-It #10). Otherwise, reformatting the disk will probably be necessary (Fix-It #13).
−192/Resource not found	Usually due to a corrupted application.	If it happens with only one application, the application is probably corrupted. Replace it. A bug in an extension or control panel can also cause this error.

* *Most other positive number error codes imply either a bug in an application (especially likely with IDs 5–7, 16, or 26) or a damaged file, particularly the System file (especially likely with IDs 17-24 or 27). Negative number error codes have a variety of specific, usually technical, meanings. See a utility such as MacErrors for a more complete list, if needed. Also see Chaoter 15 for a discussion of the Type 119 error and Mac OS 9.*

** *Refer to main text for more complete explanations of suggested actions.*

TAKE NOTE ▶ System crashes at startup

If a system error occurs during startup, skip the rest of this chapter for now. Instead, go immediately to Chapter 5, which deals with startup problems.

TAKE NOTE ▶ Protected Memory

One of the most annoying problems with system crashes is that even though the problem may be restricted to only one of several applications that are currently open, the crash brings down the entire system, forcing a restart. If this happens several times in one day, you could be wasting an hour or more of your time just waiting to return to where you were before each crash. How much better it would be if a crash caused only the problem application to crash, leaving everything else fully functional, with no restart required or even recommended.

If this is your dream come true, it's about to become a reality. It's called *protected memory,* and it's one of the new features of Mac OS X (see Chapter 15).

For now, the rest of this chapter assumes that you are still working with Mac OS 8.x's or 9.x's "unprotected" memory.

TAKE NOTE ▶ Power On, Power Off

The Restart and Shut Down Commands Before getting into restarting your Mac after a system crash, let's go over how to restart and shut down your Mac when things are going well.

The most common method is simply to choose Restart or Shut Down from the Finder's Special menu.

Restart essentially turns off your machine momentarily and then immediately restarts it. This technique may be useful, for example, when you add system extensions to your System Folder. These extensions require the Macintosh to be restarted before they can work.

Shut Down turns your machine off–period. In most Macintoshes, the Shut Down command completely shuts off the machine. No further action is necessary. In certain (mostly older) Macintosh models, however, choosing Shut Down results in a message that says *It is now safe to turn off your Macintosh.* You then have to turn off your machine by using the machine's on/off switch (power button). The location of this button varies from model to model.

As discussed in later sections of this chapter, choosing Shut Down is a more complete shutdown than when you choose Restart. On some Macs, the contents of a RAM disk, for example, may be preserved after Restart, but not after Shut Down. For this reason, if you are having any problems with your Mac, and you want to Restart to see whether that fixes the problem, choose Shut Down and then turn your Mac back on, rather than choosing Restart. Shut Down is more likely to clear up whatever the problem may have been.

The other common way to shut down your Mac is to press the Power key (discussed next). This brings up the Shut Down alert box, which asks, *Are you sure you want to shut down your computer now?* This alert box has four options: Restart, Shut Down, Sleep, and Cancel. Choosing Restart, Shut Down, or Sleep does the same thing as choosing these commands from the Finder's Special menu.

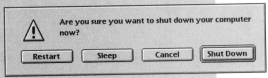

Figure 4-3 This alert box appears when you press the Power key on the keyboard.

Power buttons and Power keys There are two types of power buttons on Macintoshes. Some Macs have only one of these buttons; others have both. One is usually on the machine itself (it's on the front of iMacs and Power Mac G4s). I refer to this button simply as the *Power button.* The other button is on the keyboard. On ADB keyboards, the button is in either in the top-right corner or the top middle of the keyboard and usually has a triangle symbol on it (yes, it's similar to the symbol on the Reset button). On the USB keyboard (used with the iMac and all newer Macs), the button is on the top of the keyboard between the main keys and the numeric keypad; its symbol is an open circle with a vertical line through the opening. I refer to all these buttons as the *Power key.*

Pressing the power key when the Mac is off typically turns the Mac on. Pressing the Power key when the Mac is on does different things, depending upon the specific Mac model. On some older Mac models, it does nothing at all. Most typically, it brings up the Shut Down alert box (as described in the previous section).

Similarly, the exact function of the Power button varies from model to model. In some cases, it functions like the Power key–shutting down the Mac if it is on (either directly or via the Shut Down alert box) and turning it on if it is off. On the original iMac models, the Power key brings up the Shut Down alert box, whereas the Power button bypasses this alert box and shuts down the Mac directly. On the newer iMacs (those with the slot loading CD/DVD drives) and on all newer Macs, pressing the Power button normally puts the Mac to sleep if it is up and wakes it up if it is asleep.

Under most circumstances, do *not* use the Mac's Power button to directly shut down the machine. Choose one of the Restart or Shut Down commands instead. These commands do some final cleanup, updating, and proper closing of files before they turn off your machine. Using the Power button without first choosing Shut Down bypasses these actions and may result in the loss of data and possibly damaged files.

Restart the Macintosh

There is no way to completely undo the effects of a system crash or other serious system error! It would be wonderful if you could simply choose an Undo command and return your Macintosh to exactly where it was before the crash, with all your data still intact, but this is not possible. Even if it were, though, the crash might recur a few moments later.

Here's what you can do: Restart the Macintosh. To do this, try the following solutions. If one doesn't work, or if it is not applicable, try other options until you are successful.

- **Click the Restart button in the System error alert box** System bomb alert boxes usually include a Restart button. Clicking this button, as its name implies, should restart the Macintosh just as though you chose Restart from the Finder's Special menu. This button, however, works only about half the time at best.

    If the Restart button does work, you probably notice that it takes longer for the Welcome to Macintosh screen to appear after a system-crash restart than after you choose the Finder's Restart command. This is largely the result of the startup sequence's partially compensating for the lack of cleaning up (including saving and closing all files, updating directory files, and so on) that would normally have been done after you chose Restart or Shut Down from the Finder. In recent versions of the Mac software, however, I have noted a trend toward the Restart button's resulting in a proper shutdown that *does* prevent the long disk access time at the beginning of the next startup.

    Note: If you installed Norton Utilities CrashGuard or Apple's MacsBug, you may get something other than the system bomb alert box. Refer to Chapter 2, "Protect Against Loss of Data Due to System Crashes," for more details.

- **Click the Reset button (not the Interrupt button)**

    The (physical) Reset button Most, although not all, Macs have a physical Reset button located somewhere on the Mac's case. It is one of a matched pair of buttons—the one of the pair that is identified by a triangle symbol. The other button (the Interrupt button) is identified by a circle symbol.

    On some Mac models, you can actually press these buttons with your finger. In other cases, the button is a recessed button that you can access only by inserting the end of an unbent paper clip into the hole. On an iMac, for example, the Reset button is in the panel on the side where the USB and modem ports are located. For the first generation iMacs, you did need a paper clip to access it. With the newer iMacs (such as the iMac DV), it is accessible by your fingers.

    Pressing the Reset button restarts the Macintosh in almost the same way as clicking the bomb box's Restart button. Unlike the Restart button in the bomb box, however, the physical Reset button is almost a sure thing. One exception is the iMac; it is not uncommon for the Reset button to do nothing.

The (physical) Interrupt button The partner of the Reset button is called the Interrupt button (identified by a circle symbol). In most cases, you can just ignore the Interrupt button; it is rarely, if ever, useful to you. If you press it by accident, when you meant to press the Reset button after a system crash, don't fret. Just press the Reset button next. Alternatively, if you should press the Interrupt switch by accident, when nothing is actually wrong with the Macintosh, you should be able to return to where you were, with no data lost, by typing **G** and then immediately pressing Return. (**Note:** If you have MacsBug installed, pressing the Interrupt button invokes MacsBug.)

The keyboard Reset and Interrupt commands As already implied, one notable problem with using the Reset or Interrupt buttons is finding them. The hardware designers at Apple occasionally amuse themselves by devising ways to hide these buttons. Some models have no Reset and Interrupt buttons at all. On some of these Macs, however, you can use keyboard equivalents to mimic the effects of these buttons:

Command-Control-Power (all three keys held down at the same time) acts as a Reset button.

Command-Power acts as an Interrupt button. If this does not work on your Mac, you can still add this capability via a freeware extension called Programmer's Key.

Helpful hint: The Reset button/command is designed to be used after system crashes. It is not the ideal way to restart your Macintosh routinely. Use the Finder's Restart command for routine restarts. The Finder's Restart command has the advantage of prompting you to save all unsaved work before the restart. Also, there is a small chance that restarting with the Reset button may cause some software damage to files on your disk (especially if you press the button while something is being written to a disk). This has never actually happened to me, and I use the Reset button quite often, so the risk must be quite small. But why take it at all, unless you must?

• **Turn the Macintosh off and then back on with the Power button** If the Reset button ever fails to work, and if your Mac has a separate Power button (see: "Take Note: Power On, Power Off"), use it. It may turn the Mac off. Then wait about 10 seconds (to make sure that everything has really shut down). Next, depending on your model of Macintosh, either press the Power button again or press the Power key on your keyboard. Doing this initiates a restart that is similar to using the Reset button— that is, it does not do the cleanup (such as saving and closing all open files) that occurs after you choose the Finder's Restart command.

At this point, you may well wonder why you should bother with the Reset button at all. Why not always use the alternative of turning the Macintosh off and then back on again? Won't this do pretty much the same thing as the Reset button? The short answer is, "Yes, it will." So go ahead and turn the Macintosh off and on again to restart it after a system crash, if you want.

Still, the official view is that using the Reset button is preferred, because by not actually shutting down the system, it places less strain on the computer's electronic circuitry, thereby prolonging the life of the components. It may also extend the life of the on/off switch (although you would have to be having a lot of system crashes for this to be relevant). Personally, I believe that this threat is highly exaggerated and suggest that you not worry about it too much. Nevertheless, I use the Reset switch whenever possible. Why take chances, especially when (on most models) the Reset switch is more conveniently located than the on/off switch?

● **Pull the plug** If everything else has failed to shut down and/or restart your Mac, simply unplug the Macintosh from the wall outlet. Wait a few seconds (or minutes), and plug it back in. You should now start up successfully. If not, you probably have a hardware problem. Start by checking Chapter 5 for how to deal with startup problems. Otherwise, contact Apple or an authorized Apple dealer for help.

● **Special case: the iMac (and other Macs with USB keyboards) and restarting after a system error** On the iMac and all newer Macs that use a USB keyboard, Command-Control-Power no longer works to restart the Mac after a system crash. It works only as a normal Restart command (as if you chose Restart from the Finder's Special menu). Thus, after a system crash, this keyboard combination does nothing. (As Apple explains: "On ADB-equipped Macintosh computers, the ADB keyboard has a hardware line to the circuitry, which controls the reset of the computer. In all but the most extreme cases, it is possible to reset the Macintosh via the keyboard at any time. With the iMac (and other Macs with USB keyboards), this direct hardware line to the reset circuitry does not exist but is emulated in software. If the iMac has reached a state where the low-level software is not able to interpret the reset signal, the keyboard reset will not work.") The Interrupt keyboard combination should still work, however.

When you're trying to restart your iMac after a system crash, do the following until one method works:

1. Try the Power key. It will likely do nothing, but give it a try.

2. Try the Power button on the front of the Mac. It may restart your Mac even when the Power key fails—especially if you hold it in for about 5 seconds or so.

3. Try the Reset button (the one that's recessed in the side panel).

4. Pull the plug and then replug; then press the Power key.

Some people report that Command-Shift-Power restarts these Macs after a system crash. I have not found this to be the case.

Finally, pressing these keys (or even either of the Power keys) does not interrupt a normal startup sequence on these Macs. Instead, when the startup is over, the Shut Down message appears or a Shut Down initiates.

Command-Control-Power does work to restart an iBook after a system crash.

SEE: • **Chapter 11, "Saving the Contents of Your RAM Disk after a restart" and "Restarting a PowerBook After a System Error," for more on special restart situations**

BY THE WAY ▶ The Shut Down Warning Message

If you restart after a system crash (or, really, any time you shut down in a way other than choosing the Shut Down command), you will probably get a message during your next startup sequence, telling you what you already know: that you did not restart your Mac last time in the normal fashion. Typically, this also triggers an automatic check of your disk by Disk First Aid. (You do not see the Disk First Aid window at this point; the only way you know this is happening is that excessive disk activity takes place, prolonging the time it takes for you to start up.)

If you don't want to keep seeing this message every time you have a system crash, you can turn it off by unchecking the Shut Down Warning checkbox in the General Controls control panel.

By the way, here's how the Mac knows that you crashed: there is an invisible file of size 0 bytes called Shutdown Check at the root level of the startup volume. The presence or absence of this file determines whether the warning message appears on your next startup. The file normally gets deleted at shutdown. In such cases, the warning message does not appear. If you restart after a system crash, however, the file is *not*

Your computer did not shut down properly. Disk First Aid is checking your hard disk and will repair any problems.

If your computer is having problems, see Mac Help for troubleshooting information.

You can turn off this warning in the General Controls

Figure 4-4 This message may appear after restart following a system crash.

deleted, so the warning message *does* appear. This also means that the warning message appears the first time you start up with a disk after it has crashed, even if you started up successfully with other disks in the meantime.

The Shut Down warning dismisses itself automatically after two minutes, so the startup warning does not remain on the screen until you dismiss it.

Occasionally, the Shutdown Check file gets corrupted and does not get deleted as it should. In this case, you see this message at each restart, even if you did not have a system crash. Or you may see some error message that appears to be unrelated to Disk First Aid (including one that refers to International Utilities). In either case, the solution is to manually delete this invisible file. You can do this in numerous ways. The simplest is to use a utility (such as File Buddy) that lists and allows you to delete invisible files.

SEE: • Chapter 8 for more information on working with invisible files

BY THE WAY ▶ When not to turn on or off your Macintosh

- Don't turn the Mac on during a thunderstorm. If a power failure occurs during the storm, the Macintosh may restart itself when power returns. This is the equivalent of using the on/off switch under normal power conditions. During a storm, however, the return of power may be accompanied by a power surge that could damage your hardware even if you are using a surge-protected outlet. Because a power failure may be momentary—too short for you to react to it by turning the Macintosh off—your safest action is to turn off and unplug the Macintosh until the storm is over. Then you can turn the Mac back on.

  I have ignored this advice myself many times, and nothing has ever happened. You'll make your own decision on what risks you want to take.

- Never turn the machine off (or press the Reset or Interrupt button) while the Macintosh is reading from or writing to a disk. You may damage the data files that are currently in use.

BY THE WAY ▶ **Energy Saver and Shut Down/Restart**

Apple's Energy Saver control panel is used mainly to put the Mac in various stages of sleep. There is a separate Sleep setting for the display and for the hard drive. This difference explains why sometimes when waking up from sleep, the computer seems to "snap" awake (display sleep), while at other times, it seems to drag itself back to action (hard drive sleep).

Energy Saver can also be the source of some surprises. Does your Mac start up or shut down seemingly spontaneously? If so, check the Scheduled Startup and Shutdown panel of this control panel. You (or someone else) may have set this feature to turn your Mac on or off automatically. Similarly, check the Server Settings Preferences control panel, which includes an option labeled Restart Automatically After a Power Failure. If this option is enabled, it can also lead to some unexpected restarts of the Mac, even when you have not had an actual power failure.

Various problems have been attributed to Energy Saver. If someone ever recommends that you try disabling this control panel, take note: simply disabling it (via Extensions Manager) does not really disable it entirely. The preferred technique is to set its Sleep settings to Never. Then restart. Then disable the file. Sleeper, a shareware application, is an often-recommended alternative.

SEE: • **"Take Note: The iBook and Preserving Memory Contents on Sleep and Restart," in Chapter 11, for related information about Energy Saver options.**

Recover Unsaved Data After a Restart

OK, you're back in the saddle again. You've successfully restarted your Macintosh and returned to the Finder's desktop. What now? If you didn't lose any unsaved data or didn't care about what you did lose, just return to whatever you were doing before the crash and hope that it doesn't happen again. In the meantime, be careful to save your work frequently.

You can also try to recover any data that wasn't saved before the crash. I know—this sounds almost impossible. It also seems to contradict my own previous statements that unsaved work at the time of a system crash cannot be recovered, because unsaved work is present only in RAM, and information in RAM (other than, perhaps, RAM disk contents) evaporates when you restart the Macintosh. Nevertheless, you may yet be able to recover some unsaved data.

A word to the wise before you start trying the options that I am about to describe: they really are good only for rescuing text data, and even then, they are often unsuccessful. Even if they do work, they typically save only part of your data or save them in a form that requires deleting unwanted text, rearranging paragraphs, and reformatting (fonts, margins, and so on) before the file resembles the way it appeared originally. All this takes time. If you lost only a small amount of work, you may be better off simply starting from scratch and redoing the work. When you really are desperate, try the following techniques.

Check for temporary files Many (but far from all!) programs create temporary files (sometimes called *work files*) that hold part or all of a document's data while the document is open. Ordinarily, you are unaware of the existence of these files. The software manual may not even refer to them. This is usually OK, because these temporary files should be deleted automatically when you quit the program. You never see a trace of them. After an unexpected quit, a forced quit, or a reset after a system crash, however, these temporary files typically do not get deleted and remain somewhere on your hard drive.

These temporary files may contain data from the document you were working on before the crash, even if you had not yet saved the data! On the other hand, these temporary files are more often useless, containing virtually no data at all. Still, it can't hurt to try.

Often, temporary files are invisible—that is, you never see them on the Finder's desktop or in most Open or Save dialog boxes. This arrangement prevents you from using them inadvertently during normal operation of the Macintosh. Deleting a temporary file while the application that is using it is still open, for example (assuming that the Macintosh lets you do this), could cause a system crash! The downside, however, is that this invisibility makes these files more difficult to find when you do want to use them.

Some temporary files on your disk may be left over from system errors that are now ancient history. These files, obviously, are of no value to you in recovering data from your current system error. Ideally, you are looking for the one temporary file that contains data from the document you were working on at the time of the system error. Often, you can figure this out by checking file names, which tend to give away the files' origin and nature (such as Word Work File for Microsoft Word temporary files). To be certain that you have ferreted out all these files, look for both visible and invisible temporary files.

BY THE WAY ▶ **Word Work Files Hassles**

Word 98 has an annoying habit of creating multiple (visible) Word Work files in some seemingly random fashion, located in the same folder as the document you are working on. Certainly, the more often you click the Save button, the more of these files you start to collect.

Normally, this situation is not much of a problem. When you close the document, the Work files evaporate. If you get a system crash while the document is open, however, these files will still be there when you restart. Now you have to drag them to the Trash to get rid of them. Don't worry—you don't need them.

Finally, if too many of these Work files open, you may get an odd error that says that you cannot save your document because too many files are open or because of insufficient memory. This can be a real annoyance. Even choosing Save As will not work. There are two possible solutions. The first solution is to close other open applications. This technique may allow Save to work. If so, close the document as soon as you save it; then reopen it. This will get rid of the Work files associated with the document. The second solution is to choose Save As and use a different file format, such as Word 6 or Rich Text Format (assuming that you have no special Word 98-only formatting that would be lost when you do this). Again, if this technique works, close and reopen the document. Then you can save it again in Word 98 format.

By the way, one suggestion for preventing this buildup of Work files is to turn off Word's Fast Save option (in its Preferences window). When I tried this, however, it only made matters worse.

SEE: • **Chapter 6 for more information on problems with opening and saving files.**

- **Look for visible temporary files (check the Trash!)** After a system crash, the first place to look for visible temporary files is in the Trash! I'm not kidding. The Mac OS creates a special folder called Temporary Items. Any programs that are written to be aware of this folder place their temporary files in this folder. This folder, and the files within it, are normally invisible.

  After a system crash and a subsequent restart, however, the Macintosh automatically places all the items in the Temporary Items folder in a new folder called Rescued Items from <*name of your disk*>. This folder is visible and is placed in the Trash. It contains the files that were in the invisible Temporary Items folder at the time of the system error. In some cases, the folder may simply be named Temporary Items.

  The Macintosh places the Rescued Items folder in the Trash for a good reason: deleting these files is usually the best way to deal with them. Still, the point of this discussion is that these rescued files may contain some of your unsaved data. So if you find the Trash contains items in it immediately after a restart, double-click the Trash icon to open its window. If you find a Rescued Items folder in the Trash, remove it and place it in any other location. All the temporary files in the folder should be from applications that were open at the time of the system error, so it should be relatively easy to check for one that is useful to you.

  Occasionally, visible temporary files on your disk do not make it to the Trash. They are typically in your System Folder, in the same folder as the application that was active at the time of the crash, or at the root level of your disk. You can use the Finder's Find command to locate these temporary files, if necessary. If you are unsure what the name of the temporary file might be, try search words such as **Temp** or the name of the application itself. Even better, search by creator (as explained in Chapter 8).

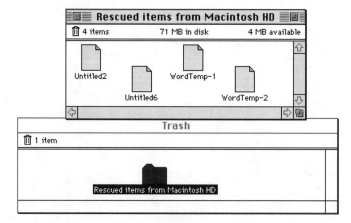

Figure 4-5 A Rescued Items folder, normally located in the Trash following a restart after a system crash.

- **Look for invisible temporary files** If you are having trouble locating the temporary file you want, it may be invisible. Invisible files can still appear in the Open dialog boxes of some applications. Microsoft Word can do this (as described in the following paragraphs). Otherwise, your main hope of finding invisible temporary files is a special utility (such as Norton Utilities and File Buddy) that lists them. For text data files, these utilities may be able to extract and save the text to a separate visible file, using the same technique you would use to recover text from a damaged file. Alternatively, these utilities can change the invisible file to a visible file. The probability of successfully recovering any data from these files is fairly low, however. Unless the lost data is important, don't feel compelled to learn how to do this.

  SEE: • **Fix-It #11 on extracting data from damaged files.**
  • **Chapter 8 for more information on invisible files and folders.**

- **Recover data from temporary files** After you locate the appropriate temporary file by any method, open it to view its contents. To do this, your best bet is to open the application that was in use at the time of the crash. See whether it lists the relevant temporary file in its Open dialog box. If so, open the file.

  Some applications do not list their temporary files as openable. Others do so, but only after a bit of fiddling. To see temporary files listed in Word, for example, choose the All Files option from the List Files of Type pop-up menu in the Open dialog box. Otherwise, for text files, try any other application you have that can read text files. In general, choose the option that shows the broadest range of file types.

  If you are successful in opening the temporary file, you may find some useful data in it (primarily only text data), even if it is only a partial recovery. If so, edit and save the data as you would in any other file. If you find any garbage data along with the real data, you can cut it.

  Temporary files that remain on your disk after a system error are not used again as temporary files. Rather, the program creates a new temporary file the next time one is needed. Thus, if there is nothing worth saving in these recovered temporary files (which, unfortunately, is all too often the case), delete them. Otherwise, they remain on your disk, taking up space. As long as you are doing this, you might as well delete any other old temporary files that you find.

  Delete these temporary files only when the program that created them is *not* open, however. This practice ensures that you do not accidentally delete a temporary file that is currently in use, which (as mentioned earlier) can lead to a system crash.

Use special recovery utilities You can recover text by using utilities such as Spell Catcher's GhostWriter feature (described in Chapter 2). To briefly review, this feature records each keystroke that you make as you type. The resulting text is automatically saved in a special file that is typically stored in your System Folder. This is done every minute or so, without your having to choose any command. This feature is separate from any auto-save function you might have. Auto-save saves the actual file you are using, whereas these utilities save data to a separate file, even if the file itself was not saved. After a system crash, locate these special files and open them in a word processor. With luck, you will find your unsaved text. The recovered data may not be in perfect shape (some data may be missing or garbled), but it should be far preferable to having nothing at all. On the other hand, if you remember to use the ordinary Save command often enough, these utilities will probably not be of much extra benefit.

What If the System Error Keeps Recurring?

After completing all the previous advice, you can typically return to what you were doing before the system crash and continue your work. Most often, another crash will not occur. But what if it does? What, most especially, if it keeps recurring every time you get back to the same point? Ah, yes. If this unfortunate event happens to you, you will have to spend some time trying to determine the source of the error. The only other alternative is to stop doing whatever caused the system error. Sorry.

To solve recurring system-error problems, skip to the last section of this chapter.

SEE: • **"Solve It! Recurring System Errors" later in this chapter.**

System Freezes

 Symptoms:

The Macintosh appears to lock up. Without warning, everything on the screen display comes to a complete halt. If the cursor is animated, like the watch cursor, all animation has stopped. At best, the cursor may continue to respond to the mouse, but you can't get it to do anything. Menus do not drop down; applications do not open. Typically, keyboard input has no effect, either. At worst, everything, including the cursor, refuses to move or respond to any input. For the moment, your computer screen has become little more than an expensive paperweight.

When any of these things happen, you have a *system freeze* (also called a *hang*).

 Causes:

A freeze is almost always caused by a software bug. But identifying the program that contains the bug can be tricky. The bug can be in the application, it can be in the system software, or it can be a conflict between two programs that are active at the same time. Most often, the bug is related to problems with the way a program is trying to access RAM memory.

Damaged files, particularly damaged System, Finder, or font files, may cause a freeze. A damaged directory may similarly lead to a system freeze. Trying to defragment a disk with a damaged directory can result in a system freeze. A loosened and disconnected cable can cause the same symptoms as a freeze, although no system error has occurred. A multitude of other causes remain, including low memory and SCSI problems.

What to Do:

Try to Save Your Work (Press Command-S)

Despite the system freeze, you may still be able to save your unsaved work. Presumably, you cannot actually choose the Save command from the File menu because of the freeze. Sometimes, however, the Macintosh responds to certain keyboard input even though it seems to be frozen. By pressing Command-S (the keyboard shortcut for Save), you may be able to save whatever document you were using at the time of the freeze. Otherwise, the data is almost certainly lost. In either case, you still have a frozen Macintosh that needs to be unthawed.

Try a Force Quit (Press Command-Option-Escape)

To do a force quit (or forced quit, as it is often called), press Command-Option-Escape. An alert box should appear. Its message asks whether you want to force the active application to quit and tells you that any unsaved changes in that application will be lost. Because you have few other alternatives at this point, go ahead and do it.

This technique should return you to the Finder's desktop. The Macintosh should be functioning fairly normally now, except that the application you were using has been closed, and any unsaved work is lost. Still,

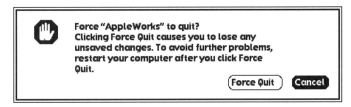

Figure 4-6 The "force quit" alert box

if you had other applications besides the active one open at the time, you should be able to return to them and save any previously unsaved documents in these other applications.

A force quit is designed to work primarily after either a system freeze or an endless loop (described in "Endless Loops" later in this chapter). I have never seen it work following a system crash (in which the bomb alert box appears), but it can't hurt to try.

TECHNICALLY SPEAKING ▶ Force Quit From the Finder

If you press Command-Option-Escape when you are at the Finder level, the alert box asks whether you want to quit the Finder itself. You can elect to do this. Because under most circumstances, the Finder must be running at all times, the result of this action is to quit and then immediately relaunch the Finder. Normally, there is little reason to do this. Simply restarting your Macintosh accomplishes the same thing and is more reliable. If you are having problems with the Finder, however, short of a system freeze or crash, quitting the Finder sometimes eliminates the problem without requiring you to restart.

Several shareware/freeware utilities (such as one called Terminator) allow you to quit the Finder directly. It is generally believed that using one of these utilities is a safer way to quit the Finder than using the Force Quit keyboard combination. I have never seen that belief officially confirmed, however. These utilities work only if you want to quit the Finder before you get a freeze, however.

If the Force Quit Succeeds...

If a Force Quit succeeds in giving you back control of your Mac, here's what to do next:

- **Try (again) to save your work** Assuming that the force quit succeeds in bringing your Macintosh back to life, immediately save any unsaved work that is still open in other applications. Otherwise, the danger is that another error may occur again soon, because you have not fixed whatever problem caused the first error to occur. You may even be able to recover unsaved data from the application that led to the freeze, either by searching for temporary files or by using other special recovery utilities.

  SEE: • **"Recover Unsaved Data After a Restart" in the section on System Crashes earlier in this chapter.**

- **Choose Restart from the Finder's Special menu** To be honest, I have recovered from a freeze with a force quit and then continued using my Macintosh for several more hours without any problem. Doing so is a risk, however. You can try it, but don't blame me if it soon leads to another freeze or crash. Problems are especially likely to recur if you were online at the time of the freeze and attempt to reconnect immediately after a force quit.

  Figure 4-7 The Restart and Shut Down commands in the Finder's Special menu

  Instead, restart the Macintosh. This usually corrects the problem that led to the system freeze. The best way to restart is to simply choose the Restart command from the Finder's Special menu. This ensures that all files are properly updated, saved, and closed before the actual restart occurs. This prevents any accidental loss of data and minimizes the (admittedly unlikely) chance of damaging files.

  Some other utility programs contain a similar Restart command. If this command is more convenient, you can use it instead of the Finder's command.

TECHNICALLY SPEAKING ▶ To Sleep...Perchance to Power Down

If you have a PowerBook, and you choose Sleep from the Special menu, the computer appears to shut down. But it doesn't. Power to the hard drive is essentially cut off (to preserve battery power), but enough current is maintained that the information in memory is preserved. On most PowerBooks, pressing any key (except Caps Lock) awakens the PowerBook. On some models, you must press the Power On key. The hard drive then spins up, the screen brightens, and everything returns to normal.

On most recent PowerBooks, just closing the lid puts the PowerBook to sleep. A small blinking light lets you know that the PowerBook is sleeping. Pressing the Reset button on the back of the machine turns it off completely.

All recent desktop Macs have a similar sleep capability. But the Mac continues to make enough noise that you know that it is still on.

SEE: • **Chapters 11 and 14 for more information on sleep and PowerBooks.**

If the Force Quit Fails to Work...Restart

Unfortunately, sometimes the force-quit trick fails to work. Instead, when you click the Force Quit button, your system freeze worsens, from the type in which you can still use the cursor to the type in which now even the cursor is frozen, or the freeze develops into a system crash. In some cases, the force-quit dialog box never even appears. In any of these cases, your main recourse is to restart the Macintosh as you would for a system crash—that is, press the Reset button or the Power button.

SEE: • **"Restart the Macintosh" and "Recover Unsaved Data After a Restart," in the section on System Crashes, earlier in this chapter.**

If the Freeze Recurs

After restarting, you can usually continue your work without another freeze occurring. If the freeze recurs after restarting, you need to try to figure out the cause. As you will see, knowing exactly when the freeze occurs (such as during startup or when you try to launch an application) is useful in diagnosing the cause.

- **Check for disconnected cables** If the freeze reappears immediately upon startup, your best bet is to check the keyboard cable, especially if your mouse is connected to the keyboard rather than to the back of the Macintosh. In this case, a loose or defective keyboard cable prevents both keyboard and mouse input from having any effect. I call this situation a *false freeze.*

    A disconnected cable does not halt any operation in progress (such as a print-ing process), but otherwise mimics a true system freeze. It is not a true freeze because the processing of information has not been disrupted.

    If other cables, such as a printer cable or the SCSI cable (most commonly used for connecting an external hard drive), become disconnected, this can precipitate a true freeze.

    It is strongly recommended that you turn off the Macintosh before disconnect-ing and reconnecting ADB and SCSI cables. Although the threat is generally con-ceded to be minimal at best, why take the risk at all? And even if you do reconnect a cable while the computer is running and nothing adverse happens, the reconnec-tion by itself may not restore the Macintosh to normal. You still probably have to restart the Macintosh.

    On the other hand, it is perfectly OK to disconnect and reconnect USB and FireWire cables.

    SEE: • **Fit-It #14 for more on USB and FireWire cables.**

- **Check whether a cable, the keyboard, and/or the mouse needs repair** It is always possible that a cable, the mouse, and/or the keyboard has suddenly gone belly-up. This situation, too, may mimic a freeze immediately upon startup. If this is the case, try to swap your keyboard and cables for other ones, if other ones are available. (Remember to turn off your Macintosh before removing or connecting any cables.) If replacing components eliminates the freeze, you need to replace the defective components.

- **Check for problems with peripheral devices** If a freeze occurs before extensions start to load, the problem may be SCSI-related. To check for this situation, disconnect external SCSI devices from the Mac and try to restart. See whether the problem goes away. Similarly, check for USB or FireWire devices, if your Mac supports these types of connections.

  If a system freeze occurs whenever you try to mount an external hard drive, try to repair the disk with software repair utilities. If that attempt fails, reformat the disk.

  SEE: • **Chapter 5 on startup problems.**
          • **Fix-It #10 on disk repairs.**
          • **Fix-It #13 on reformatting a disk.**
          • **Fix-It #14 for more information on problems with peripheral devices.**

- **Give the application more memory** Freezes that occur when you launch or quit an application are sometimes due to insufficient memory for the application. To solve this problem, go to the program's Get Info window, increase its Preferred Memory size by at least several hundred K, and try again. Repeat several more times, if necessary, assuming that you have sufficient free RAM. Use virtual memory or RAM Doubler to make more memory available (although watch out for the next item in this list!).

  SEE: • **Fix-It #5 on memory problems.**

- **Turn off virtual memory or other memory-enhancing utility** Freezes are often due to problems with memory-enhancement software. If you are using virtual memory or a utility such as RAM Doubler, turn it off. RAM Doubler is often suggested as a possible cause of freezes while you are running communications and/or networking software.

- **Replace damaged font files** If a freeze occurs whenever you try to launch a particular application, a damaged font file may be the cause. This situation is particularly common with AppleWorks. Damaged font files may also cause a freeze to occur during printing. The solution is to identify the damaged font and replace it from your backups.

  SEE: • **Chapter 9 for more information on identifying and replacing damaged font files.**

- **For freezes that occur during printing, turn off background printing** Freezes that occur during printing are often memory-related. Turning off background printing is a useful first step. Try printing again. You also may have an incompatible printer driver.

  SEE: • **Chapter 7 for more information on printing problems.**

- **Replace the Finder Preferences file (and possibly do a clean install of the Mac OS software)** This technique is particularly likely to work if the freeze occurs only when you are in the Finder or performing system-related activities. A freeze could occur whenever a floppy disk is inserted into a disk drive, for example. Similar situations include freezes that occur when you are copying files or emptying the Trash.

Replace the Finder Preferences file to attempt to correct these problems. If that does not work, you may need to try a complete clean install of the Mac OS software.

SEE: • **Fix-It #2 on replacing Preferences files.**
• **Fix-It #4 for more information on replacing Mac OS software.**

• **Extensions conflicts and other causes**

If none of these suggestions solves the problem, it's time to look elsewhere. Extensions conflicts are the most likely cause at this point.

SEE: • **Fix-It #3 on extensions conflicts.**
• **"Solve It! Recurring System Errors" later in this chapter, for a longer laundry list of things to try.**

Endless Loops

 ## Symptoms:

The symptoms of an endless loop appear, at first, not to be symptoms at all. Everything appears to be perfectly normal. Usually, whenever a process promises to take more than a few seconds to complete (such as a complex transformation in a graphics program), the cursor (most often, an arrow) changes. Typically, it shifts to a watch cursor with rotating hands or a spinning beach ball. This display is perfectly normal; it is the Macintosh's way of telling you to wait a minute.

During this time, the cursor continues to move across the screen in response to mouse movement. All other activity, however, is disabled until the task is completed, at which time the regular cursor (usually, the arrow) reappears.

The signal that you have a problem is that the task never seems to reach completion. The watch cursor appears destined to remain on the screen until at least the turn of the century. Welcome to endless loops! Be especially suspicious of an endless loop any time a task is taking much longer to complete than expected. (Saving a document, for example, should almost never take more than a few seconds.)

A similar situation occurs when the computer's activity is monitored by a progress bar on the screen (as occurs when you are copying disks from the Finder). The dark part of the bar continues to grow as the activity moves to completion. If the progress bar seems to stop, no longer showing any sign of progress, you may be caught in an endless loop.

At a practical level, the endless loop is a first cousin of the system freeze. Your course of action is similar in both cases.

 ## Causes:

Before taking any action, consider that you may not be in an endless loop. The Macintosh may be doing something that takes a very long time to complete. Depending on your printer, for example, it can take more than 10 minutes to print one page of a complex PostScript graphics document.

The other alternative is that you *are* in an endless loop. This problem is typically due to a software bug that causes the program to attempt the same action repeatedly—and indefinitely.

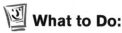 ## What to Do:

Break out of the Loop with Command-Period

Often, a long delay does not mean that you have a freeze; it may just be that the operation really takes an unusually long time to finish. To check for this situation, press Command-period (holding both keys down together). This is an almost universal command for canceling an operation in progress. Hold the keys down for several seconds before letting go. Wait a few more seconds to see whether the operation halts. Typically, the progress bar (if any) disappears and/or the animated cursor is replaced by the arrow cursor. If nothing seems to happen, try again. Continue retrying for at least a minute before giving up.

If canceling does work, you either halted a normal but slow process, or (less likely) you have a forgiving program that was able to break out of an endless loop with this technique.

> **BY THE WAY ▶ Cancelling a Command**
>
> This Command-period technique is useful any time you want to halt an operation that you no longer want to perform, even if there is no suspected endless loop. It does not always work, but it is worth a try whenever you need it. Depending on the operation in progress, it may take as long as a minute or so before the operation is cancelled.

Retry the Procedure

If you were able to break out of the loop, retry the procedure. Wait even longer before resorting to Command-period.

If the process is just a slow one, it may reach completion this time. If the problem was an endless loop, it may have been a one-time-only problem, and it may not repeat.

Otherwise...

If you cannot break out of the endless loop, treat it exactly as though it were a system freeze. In particular, try a forced quit (press Command-Option-Escape). If this doesn't work, restart the Macintosh.

SEE: • "System Freeze," earlier in this chapter, for more details.

Whether or not you can break out of the endless loop, if it continues to recur, you have to figure out the cause.

SEE: • "Solve It! Recurring System Errors" later in this chapter.

Unexpected Quits

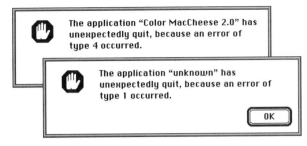

Figure 4-8 Two examples of the unexpected quit alert box

 Symptoms:

An application abruptly and inexplicably quits, returning you to the Finder. Often, you see an alert message informing you that the application *unexpectedly quit.* (I guess that unless the Mac detects that you choose the Quit command, it treats the quit as "unexpected.") This is the most benign of system errors described in this chapter, because the system almost always continues to function after the unexpected quit.

 Causes:

Unexpected quits are usually due to software bugs that affect memory management. Typically, less memory is available than the program needs. Ideally, the program should detect this situation and warn you of the problem. If the program was not written carefully enough, an unexpected quit happens instead.

If this happens, you can consider yourself to be lucky, in a way. The alternative is usually a system crash that would require a restart of the computer.

 What to Do:

Interpreting System Error Codes...Again

An unexpected-quit alert box often indicates the type of error that led to the unexpected quit (such as an error of Type 4). These numbers refer to the same codes that are used for system crashes. Although trying to figure out exactly what these codes mean is not likely to be helpful, you can refer to Table 4-1 earlier in this chapter for guidance. Sometimes, the alert box says that the cause of the quit is of "unknown," making it irrelevant to look up the meaning of the error code.

Save Data in Open Applications

As with almost all system errors, any unsaved data in the application that unexpectedly quit is almost certainly lost. You should still be able to save any data in other applications that remain open, however. You may even be able to recover unsaved data from the application that led to the unexpected quit, either by searching for temporary files or using other special recovery utilities.

SEE: • **"Recover Unsaved Data After a Restart," in the section on System Crashes, earlier in this chapter.**

Restart the Macintosh

To restart, choose Restart from the Finder's Special menu. You probably can continue using your Macintosh without restarting. To be safe, however, you should restart first, because once this problem occurs, the probability that it will recur increases until you restart.

Actually, if you want to return to the problem program, it may be necessary to restart. I have occasionally had a program that would no longer relaunch immediately after an unexpected quit; it simply quit again whenever I tried to launch it. Restarting the Macintosh cleared up this problem.

Increase Preferred Size of Memory

The immediate cause of some unexpected quits is insufficient memory assigned to the application. This can be the case even if you are using the default assignments given to the application. So if the unexpected quit persists after a restart, try increasing the Preferred Size of the application's memory in the file's Get Info window.

If increasing the application's preferred memory size does not work, you may have to increase overall memory availability, as described in Fix-It #5.

Finally, make sure that there is adequate memory in the Font Cache of Adobe Type Manager. You can adjust this setting in the Adobe Type Manager control panel. Adobe recommends using 50K to 80K for every font that needs to be rendered on screen at the same time (including italics, bold, and so on).

SEE: • **Chapter 2 on Get Info window and Fix-It #5 on memory problems, for more details.**

If the Unexpected Quit Occurs During Launch

Unexpected quits often occur in the middle of using an application. Sometimes, they occur as a program is first launched, preventing you from opening the program. If this happens, and the previous solutions did not solve the problem, try removing the application's preferences file from the Preferences folder or, if that technique fails, replacing the application itself. Although a damaged application file may be the cause of any unexpected quit, it is more likely a cause if the quit occurs during launch.

SEE: • **Fix-It #2 on replacing applications and their related files.**

Otherwise...

Sometimes, an unexpected quit develops into a system freeze or a system crash before you can successfully restart. If so, refer to the sections on those topics earlier in this chapter for details on what to do.

Finally, if the unexpected quit continues to recur despite all your attempts at a solution, you need to track down what else may be the cause.

SEE: • **"Solve It! Recurring System Errors" later in this chapter.**

The Finder Disappears

 ## Symptoms:

- The desktop seems to vanish. All disk icons and folder windows disappear. Sometimes, the menu bars at the top of the screen disappear. At the same time, the Macintosh appears to freeze.

- A similar problem has been dubbed the "oscillating Finder crash." In this case, the Finder disappears and is followed by periodic screen flashing.

 ## Causes:

Basically, this is yet another variation on the freeze or endless loop, and it has similar underlying causes. In this case, however, it is more likely that something is amiss with the Finder and/or System files.

 ## What to Do:

Wait a Minute

Occasionally, the Finder reappears by itself if you wait a minute or two, or the oscillating stops (unlikely). If this happens, I would still be suspicious that a more serious error will occur soon. Restart to be safe.

Try a Force Quit (Command-Option-Escape) and Restart

If the Finder does not return on its own, try a force quit. Occasionally, as in a generic system freeze, a force quit may return you to a fully functional desktop.

   If the force quit does succeed, rather than immediately resume your work, you should save any unsaved work and restart the Macintosh by choosing the Restart command from the Finder's Special menu. If the force quit does not succeed, press the Reset button to restart. In either case, the Macintosh should return to normal following the restart.

SEE: • **"System Freezes," earlier in this chapter, for more details.**

Replace the Finder and Its Preferences File

If the problem keeps recurring, replace the Finder and its preferences file. With Mac OS 8.5. or later, also consider replacing Mac OS Preferences, Display Preferences, and Sound Preferences.

   Also, if you are using Mac OS 8.1 or later, and there is a file in your Extensions folder called ObjectSupportLib, delete it.

SEE: • **Fix-It #2 on problems with the Finder preferences file**

Otherwise...

If the oscillating Finder crash happens only when you are online, go to Remote Access's Options Connections tab and disable the option labeled Flash Icon in Menu Bar While Connected. That may help.

More generally, if the Finder continues to vanish, replace or upgrade the entire system software. If even that doesn't work, it's time to look for more esoteric causes.

SEE: • **Fix-It #4 on replacing system software.**
• **"Solve It! Recurring System Errors" later in this chapter.**

Solve It! Recurring System Errors

If you have been directed to this section, you presumably have a recurring system error. If the error recurs, you probably want to eliminate it. Doing so requires using diagnostic guidelines, as follows:

Seek the Cause of a Recurring System Error

Suspect recent changes in the contents of your disk (such as a new system extension or an upgrade of the system software) as being the most likely culprits for a recurring system error. In general, the most common causes of system errors are software conflicts or incompatibilities, software bugs, and damaged software.

What Circumstances, If Any, Reliably Cause the System Error?

To see whether a system error recurs, first try to *exactly* duplicate the precipitating situation (for example, reopen all applications and documents that were open at the time of the error).

System errors can be quite finicky about when they recur. Perhaps the error occurs only when you choose Check Spelling immediately after you select Save, for example. It may happen only when you choose the command while a specific graphics application is also open. Or it may occur only when a specific startup extension is in use. Or it may occur only when many applications are open and memory is running low. You don't really know for sure whether a system error will recur until you repeat the exact circumstances.

More generally, note what process is typically taking place when the error occurs. Does it occur only at startup, when you are launching an application, or when you are printing? This, too, is an important diagnostic cue. Errors that occur while extensions are loading at startup, for example, are almost certainly due to an extensions conflict.

What Variations in Circumstances, If Any, Will Eliminate the System Error?

If you get the system error to reliably recur under a specific set of circumstances, your next step is determining how altering those circumstances affects the error. Suppose that a crash occurs after you choose Check Spelling in your word processor. Does it happen regardless of what documents, other applications, and other extensions are open and/or in use at the same time? Do other commands result in the same type of system error? Does the error recur when you are working with other documents and/or trying similar procedures with other applications?

If the error recurs only whenever a specific document is open, it suggests a problem with the document. If the error happens across all documents within an application, the problem is most likely with the application. If the error keeps recurring during the launch of the program, it usually means there is damage to the application (or one of its accessory files). If it happens across several applications, it is most likely an extensions conflict, a bug, or incompatibility in the system software.

Whatever happens, ideally you can narrow down or isolate the cause of the system error via this approach.

What If the System Error Recurs at Unpredictable Intervals and in Different Situations?

System errors that occur at unpredictable intervals or in apparently unrelated situations are the worst-case scenario, because it is hard to know whether and when the problem has gone away.

The single most likely cause of these types of system errors is a startup extensions conflict. The second most likely cause is corrupted system software, particularly the System file or the Finder. A corrupted font file can also cause system errors. Damage to the directory, the desktop, or the disk driver is also a possible cause. SCSI-connection or other hardware-related problems may similarly lead to system errors. Computer viruses are yet another cause of widespread system errors. Check out the next section of this chapter ("Fix It So That the System Error Does Not Recur") for a complete list of possible causes and where to find out what to do about them.

SEE: • Chapter 3 for more on information general problem-solving strategies.

BY THE WAY ▶ Slow Down

Some system crashes occur because you are trying to do too much too fast. If this seems to be a possibility, slow down. Simply trying everything again, but at a slower pace, may solve the problem. In particular, don't choose several commands in rapid succession, especially from different applications (such as printing in one application and then quickly opening a large graphic document in another). Also, don't have too many background activities going on at one time (such as background printing and copying files).

Fix It So That the System Error Does Not Recur

After you narrow down the cause as much as possible, it's time to do something to fix the problem. This section provides a list of suggestions. Don't worry if you do not entirely understand all the terms (such as *device driver* or *SCSI*). These terms are explained in more detail in the indicated Fix-Its.

TAKE NOTE ▶ Before You Take Another Step

It would take time and effort to try all the Fix-Its listed on the following pages. And most of them (perhaps all but one of them) have little benefit for your particular problem.

If you have followed all the steps in this chapter up to now, however, you may have narrowed down the likely cause. So if a damaged document seems likely, go right to that step. You don't have to try the next strategies in any specific order.

Otherwise, bear in mind that system-error problems are mentioned in different contexts throughout this book. You may want to look in these other, more specific chapters, before checking here.

Still, this section serves as a last resort for the most general case, when you have little or no insight about the cause of the system error and, therefore, have no basis for limiting the scope of your search. The first few causes account for almost all system-error problems. You are unlikely to have to go too far down the list.

SEE: • **Chapter 5 for system errors at startup.**
  • **Chapter 6 for system errors when launching an application or when copying or deleting files.**
  • **Chapter 7 for more information on system errors specific to printing.**
  • **Chapter 11 for more information on system errors specific to PowerBooks.**
  • **Chapters 12 and 13 for more information on system errors specific to online connections.**
  • **Chapter 14 for more information on system errors specific to the iMac, iBook and newer Mac models.**
  • **Chapter 15 for more information on system errors specific to the latest versions of the Mac OS.**

Check for Hardware and/or System Software That Is Incompatible with the Application in Use

If the system error is specific to a particular application, check its manual for any troubleshooting advice. In particular, check for any mention of incompatibilities between the application and either the particular hardware or any version of the system software you are using. An application may crash when launched on a G3 Mac but not other Macs, for example. A game may crash if you try to run it with virtual memory turned on. In general, new versions of an application sometimes do not work with older versions of the system software. Similarly, older versions of the application sometimes do not work with newer versions of the system software.

SEE: • **Fix-It #1 on incompatibilities between software and hardware.**
  • **Fix-It #4 on system software problems.**

Install the Latest System Update (Fixes System Software Bugs)

Apple now releases system software updates on a regular basis. (It claims that it expects to release one at least every three months.) Updates of specific components of its software, such as QuickTime, may get released separately. Apple literally comes out with some sort of update almost every week. Try to stay up to date, as difficult as this may sound. Checking online is the best way to stay current.

SEE: • **Fix-It #16 for more information on getting online help and technical support.**

Check for Software Bugs in the Application

If you suspect a bug in the application, your only recourses are to find a workaround, avoid using the offending software, or get a bug-fixed upgrade to the software (if one is available). Call the software vendor (or check its Web site) to find out about known workarounds and upgrades. Often, publishers release minor maintenance updates designed to fix bugs. Sometimes, they send you these updates only if you call to complain. So call and complain. Remember, you cannot fix buggy software yourself.

SEE: • **Fix-It #16 for more information on getting online help and technical support.**

Turn Off Selected Options in Memory and Turn Off Sharing Setup Control Panels

Turn off File Sharing in the Sharing Setup control panel. In the Memory control panel, turn virtual memory off or reduce its size. Apple reports that setting virtual memory to more than 20MB, for example, can result in a error of type -250. In some cases, *reducing* the size of the disk cache may prevent certain system errors.

SEE: • **Fix-It #5 on the Memory control panel**

Check for Startup Extensions Conflicts

Turn off all your startup extensions (files that load into memory at startup). To do so, restart the Macintosh while holding down the Shift key. Continue to hold down the key until the desktop appears. If this procedure eliminates your system error, you have a startup extensions problem.

Be especially wary of extensions that actively process information in the background, such as antivirus utilities. These utilities are a particularly common source of extensions conflicts. In some cases, you can turn off the offending feature without disabling the entire extension. You can turn off the antivirus option that scans an application on launch, for example, while retaining the rest of its virus-protection features. This can prevent certain crashes that would otherwise occur when you launch an application.

Be especially careful never to use two extensions that do essentially the same thing, such as two screen savers. This is an almost sure way to cause problems.

SEE: • **Fix-It #3 on resolving startup extensions problems.**

Check for Memory-Allocation Problems

Whether or not a software bug is the ultimate cause, the immediate cause of many system errors is a memory problem. Usually, this means that an application or extension is trying to grab some memory that, for one reason or another, it can't have. Memory problems are the most common cause of an unexpected quit.

Some recurring system errors can be solved simply by allocating more memory to the application via its Get Info window. (To access this window, select the application icon and press Command-I). For starters, try increasing the preferred memory size by several hundred K (assuming that you have the memory to do so). Related solutions are covered in the relevant Fix-Its.

If the problem occurs while you're trying to print, try turning off background printing.

SEE • **Chapter 7 for more information on printing-related problems.**
• **Fix It #3 on problems with startup extensions.**
• **Fix It #5 on memory-management problems.**

Zap the PRAM

Zapping the PRAM may eliminate certain system-crash problems or at least make them go away for a while. This technique been especially recommended for Type 11 errors with Power Macs.

See: • **Fix-It #9 for details on how to zap your PRAM.**

Check for Damaged Document Files

If a crash occurred while a document file was open, you may find that you lost what was not saved before the error and also that your entire document is corrupted. It either does not open at all or displays random gibberish.

If such a problem occurs, the crash may have been the cause of the damage to the file. Alternatively, the damage may be the cause of the crash, in which case trying to open the document will surely cause the crash to recur.

In either case, the preferred solution is to delete the damaged file and replace it with a copy from your backups. This technique by itself may solve the system error problem. If you do not have a backup copy of the file, you can try to repair the file or at least recover data from it before you discard it. For starters, if you can open the file (most often, you cannot), try copying the document to a new file by choosing the Save As command. Otherwise, you will probably want help from a recovery utility.

SEE: • **Fix-It #11 for more information on recovering data from damaged files.**

Check for Other Damage

A mixed bag of related causes fall into this area:

- **System software (System, Finder, Updates Finder preferences, and so on)** If you have TechTool Pro, it checks to see whether your System file, Finder, Update, and/or Enabler files are damaged. (Make sure that you have the latest version of the software if you have a new-model Mac.) The freeware version of TechTool does a similar check, but only for the System file.

   If you have an extensions manager, such as Conflict Catcher, it can check for possibly damaged startup extensions (from Apple system software as well as from third-party software).

   Otherwise, replace the System, Finder, and Enabler/Update files if you have backups. Delete the Finder Preferences file (drag the file to the Trash, restart, and then empty the Trash). Make sure that you are using matching and most recent versions of all system software files and that they are designed for your model of Macintosh. If there is any doubt, do a clean reinstall of the entire system software. Make sure that you are using the most recent version of the Mac OS ROM file (and if you are, consider dropping down to an older version to see whether that helps).

   By the way, if a freeze occurs while you are using the Scrapbook desk accessory, the problem is more likely due to damage in the Scrapbook file (located in the root level of the System Folder) than to the Scrapbook desk accessory itself (located in the Apple Menu Items folder). Delete the file after recovering items from it, if necessary, by using a utility such as Can Opener (as described in Fix-It #11). Similarly, for problems with the Clipboard, delete the Clipboard file, if you find one in the System Folder. In either case, the Mac creates a new replacement file when needed.

   SEE: • **Fix-It #4 on selective system software damage.**
      • **Fix-Its #10, #11 and #15 on using TechTool and TechTool Pro.**

- **Program preferences** A program's preferences file may be damaged. To fix the problem, locate and delete the file. Go to the Preferences folder, located in the System Folder, and locate the preferences file that appears to match the problem application (such as Word Settings for Microsoft Word). Delete this file. Do this while the application is closed. Do this after starting up with extensions off, if you are doing it for a control panel.

   The program automatically makes a new preferences file when you next use it. You may have to reselect any customized preference settings.

- **Font files** A font file may be damaged. Also suspect font-related problems, among other possible causes, if you have system errors that occur only when trying to print.

- **Directory** Check for damage to the directory files on your disk. If you find directory damage, and it cannot be repaired, you have to reformat the disk.

   Check for a damaged desktop file by rebuilding the desktop.

- **Media damage** With any type of damaged file, there is the possibility of associated media damage. If so, the disk will probably have to be reformatted.

  SEE: • **Chapter 7 on printing problems.**
  - **Chapter 9, "Damaged Font Files," for how to detect and replace a damaged/corrupted font.**
  - **Fix-It #2 for problems with preferences and accessory files.**
  - **Fix-It #4 for replacing system software.**
  - **Fix-It #8 to rebuild the desktop.**
  - **Fix-It #10 and #11 to check for disk and file damage.**
  - **Fix-It #13 for reformatting the disk.**

Check for More than One System Folder on the Startup Disk

Although opinions on this issue remain divided, the presence of two or more System Folders on the same startup disk could cause system crashes. With recent versions of the Mac OS (8.0 or later), this is *extremely* unlikely. Still, to be safe, if you find more than one System Folder on your startup volume, make all but one unusable. You can do this by dragging the Finder out of the folder and storing it somewhere else or deleting it. Even compressing the Finder and leaving it in the System Folder should work. You can always reverse this procedure if you want to use the System Folder as the active folder at some later point. If you have no use for these additional System Folders, just trash them and regain the disk space they are wasting.

By the way, the folder that is currently considered to be the active System Folder is the one that has a mini Mac OS icon on its folder icon. Removing the Finder from that folder will force a second System Folder on your drive to become the active folder the next time you restart. You cannot delete the active System Folder. If that's what you want to do, restart using the newly active System Folder and then delete the formerly active folder.

SEE: • **Chapter 5 and Fix-It #4 for more on multiple System Folder problems.**

Check for Multiple Copies of Applications and Related Files

Although it is only rarely a source of system-error problems, make sure that you do not have two different versions of the same application on your disk. If possible, check for files related to the application that may have two versions in the System Folder (such as two slightly differently named preferences files). If you find any out-of-date files, delete them. Use only your newest version.

Check for Viruses

Suspect a virus if you are having frequently recurring system errors that show no predictable pattern. It is especially likely if the problem begins immediately after you've added a potentially infected file to your disk.

SEE: • **Fix-It #6 to check for viruses.**

Check for Problems with the Hard Disk's Device Driver

The *device driver* is software contained on a hard disk that the Macintosh needs to recognize and interact with the disk. This software is contained in an area of the drive that is normally inaccessible to the user. It may become damaged. Also, an older version of the driver may be incompatible with newer versions of the system software and newer models of Macintoshes. In such cases, the driver needs to be replaced or updated.

SEE: • **Fix-It #12 to update the disk device driver.**

Check for Hardware Problems:
Cable Connections, Peripheral Devices, SIMMs, and Logic Board

This is an especially likely cause if you are having frequent system crashes and/or ones that occur at apparently random and unpredictable intervals. A system error does not create a hardware problem, but it may be the symptom of an existing hardware problem.

Defective, incorrect, or improperly installed memory is a primary cause of frequent system crashes (assuming that you can start your Macintosh at all!). Persistent Type 1 and Bad F line errors are sometimes caused by nondefective but dirty memory chips. To test for this situation, remove the memory chips and clean them. If you are not sure how to do this, seek outside assistance.

If you are having frequently recurring system errors that seem to occur only when a specific external hard disk (or other peripheral device) is in use, this signals a problem with the way that these devices are connected. Start by disconnecting the cable that connects to the Mac port (SCSI, USB, or FireWire) to see whether the problem goes away.

Crashes that occur in a variety of contexts (such as whenever you launch an application or try to empty the Trash) may indicate a defective logic board.

Hardware problems tend to cause system freezes more often than they cause system crashes. Especially consider (as mentioned earlier in this chapter, in the section on system freezes) whether you might have a false freeze —that is, an apparent freeze due to a defective keyboard, mouse, or keyboard cable. Also note that some hardware-related causes of persistent freezes have been identified by Apple. You may qualify for a free repair or replacement of your Mac's logic board.

Although some hardware-related problems can be fixed easily by even an unskilled user, others require a trip to the repair shop.

SEE: • **Fix-It #14 to check for problems with peripheral devices and connections.**
   • **Fix-It #15 to check whether hardware repairs or replacements are needed.**

Seek Outside Help

If none of the preceding suggestions has helped, and you haven't already done so, it's time to seek outside help.

SEE: • **Fix-It #16 for more information on getting outside help.**

5

Startup and Disk Problems: Stuck at the Starting Gate

Unpleasant Topics

Sad Macs. Dead Macs. Crashed disks. Unreadable disks. Damaged disks. These are the unpleasant topics of discussion in this chapter. Although the emphasis is on those times when you can't even start your Macintosh, this chapter is also about disk-related problems that can happen at any time.

These problems tend to fall into one of three categories. Some problems are specific to the startup process. Disks with these problems cannot act as startup disks but may otherwise function normally. More generic problems, such as an inability to mount a disk, cause problems whether the disk is used as a startup disk or not. Finally, some fairly serious problems have little or nothing to do with startup. Files and folders may begin to vanish from your disk, for example.

Inevitably, some of these problems are caused by damaged hardware, but many are entirely due to software-related causes. And even some hardware problems can be remedied without any repairs. You can do many simple things to solve these problems on your own. So let's get going.

Understanding the Startup Sequence

What Is a Normal Startup Sequence?

For most users, the startup disk is usually an internal hard drive. Assuming that this is the case for you, here's how a normal startup sequence proceeds:

1. Turn on your Macintosh. I am assuming that you already know how to do this. If you have any questions, check the section in Chapter 4 on turning your Mac on and off.

2. The Macintosh immediately begins a series of diagnostic tests that check the condition of the hardware. Because I am describing a normal startup, I will assume that no problems are found.

   In this case, the Macintosh plays its normal startup tone. The tone may be a single note or a chord, depending on what type of Macintosh you are using (yet another example of how Apple continues to make life difficult for those of us who would like to be able to describe these matters without needing to cite numerous exceptions and variations!). The Power Macs have a startup sound not used on any previous models.

3. You may or may not briefly see a folder or disk icon with a ? inside it.

4. The Macintosh checks all available disks (in a prescribed order, to be described later in this chapter) to see whether any of them are startup disks (typically, this means a disk with a valid System Folder on it). If it finds one, you briefly see the (smiling) happy Mac icon. The Macintosh has now passed all of its initial diagnostic tests.

Figure 5-1 The smiling Happy Mac icon, a sign of a successful startup.

5. Eventually, the Mac OS splash screen appears. The words "Welcome to Mac OS" briefly appear below the Mac OS logo, followed by the words "Starting up…"

6. Startup extensions (and related files) load. You can usually identify this activity by the sequential appearance of small icons along the bottom of the screen. These are the icons of the loading startup extensions (see Chapter 1 and Fix-It #3). Not all extensions display an icon here, but you will almost assuredly have at least a few that do.

7. Finally, the Finder's desktop appears. The startup disk icon appears in the top-right corner of the screen. This icon means that the disk has *mounted.*

The term *mounted* is used to describe all volumes, not just the startup disk, that appear on the right border of the desktop. You can have both a CD-ROM disk and an internal hard disk mounted at the same time. The icons for both disks then appear on the desktop.

The icons for other disks, if any, appear below the startup disk's icon. That is, the startup disk is *always* the disk that initially is at the top of the stack of disk icons. You can change the icon's location with the mouse, though this does not affect which disk is the startup disk.

Figure 5-2 When you reach the desktop, the topmost disk icon displayed (Solo in this case) is the startup disk.

8. If you placed any files in the Startup Items folder, these files are launched next, and the startup sequence concludes.

TAKE NOTE ▶ Starting Up NewWorld Macs

The iMac and all Macs newer than the iMac can be collectively referred to as NewWorld Macs. This term refers to a collection of software with names such as Open Firmware, Boot ROM, and Mac OS ROM image file. There are some significant differences between the startup process of these Macs and that of older Macs. I describe all the details in Chapter 14.

What Is a Startup Disk?

Without a startup disk, your Macintosh will not start. That's why it's called a startup disk. To qualify as a startup disk, the disk typically needs a valid System Folder. Although there are ways to create startup disks without a "politically correct" System Folder (a few such methods are mentioned in chapters 2 and 8), I will be ignoring these unusual startup disks in this chapter.

A valid System Folder is one that contains at least a System and a Finder. (Some Macs require a few additional files, especially System Resources and Mac OS ROM.) Usually, a valid System Folder can be identified on the desktop by the miniature Mac OS symbol on its folder icon. A folder with this icon is called a *blessed System Folder.*

System Folder

Figure 5-3 A blessed System Folder has a miniature Macintosh icon on it.

The contents of the blessed System Folder on the current startup disk determine what fonts, sounds, system extensions, control panels, and Apple Menu items are in menus and available for use. The Macintosh ignores information from any other System Folders that may be present.

A working startup disk also needs a valid set of *boot blocks*. This term refers to a special invisible (to you!) area of the disk containing information that the Macintosh checks at startup to initially determine the status of a disk. The boot blocks get their name from the fact that the startup process is sometimes referred to as "booting your computer" (which in turn comes from the expression "pulling yourself up by your own bootstraps").

Most of the time, you can be blissfully unaware of the boot blocks. Creating and writing to the boot blocks is normally handled automatically behind the scenes. Boot blocks are created when you first initialize a disk. Whenever you change the startup status of a disk—by adding a System and Finder, for example—the Macintosh modifies the disks' boot blocks accordingly. It's only when things go wrong that you may need to be aware of boot blocks.

What Determines Which Disk Is the Startup Disk?

Suppose that you have two hard drives connected to your Macintosh, each with a valid System Folder on it. Now suppose that you start your Macintosh with both hard drives running. How does the Macintosh decide which disk to use as the startup disk?

Default Rules for Selecting a Startup Disk

The Macintosh checks the following locations, in the order listed, until it finds an appropriate startup disk:

Floppy drive(s) If your Mac has an internal floppy drive, the Macintosh first tries to start up from an internal floppy drive (if it finds a startup disk there) and then from an external floppy drive (if any).

Internal hard drive This drive is the normal default startup device. It is where you start up from if no floppy disks or CD-ROMs are present at startup and no changes have been made in the Startup Disk control panel.

In some Macs, it is possible to have more than one internal hard drive. One drive is considered to be the default drive, however. If your Mac came with only one hard drive (as almost all Macs do), that's the one that will always be the default drive. Fix-It #14 goes into some more detail regarding multiple internal drives, especially on ATA vs. SCSI issues.

External hard drive(s) This drive is the default choice only if there is no default internal hard drive (with a System Folder on it). If there is more than one SCSI external hard drive, all with System Folders on them, the Macintosh selects one to be the startup disk, based on the SCSI ID numbers of the drives. The drive with the highest ID number (starting from 6 and working down to 0) becomes the default startup disk.

If the Macintosh has failed to find a startup disk it returns to the beginning and tries again. All recent Mac models will check for possible startup drives among any internal SCSI or IDE connected drives. They will also check external SCSI-connected drives. Starting with the Power Mac G4, USB-conneceted drives can also be startup devices. Starting with the Boot ROM version 3.22fl (included with the Power Mac G4's that began shipping in February 2000), it is possible to boot from a FireWire drive. However, this requires upgraded disk drivers. The current version of Drive Setup does not do so.

Starting with Mac OS 9.0.4, you can also startup from a DVD-RAM disc. To do so, use Drive Setup 1.9.2 or later to format the disc.

SEE: • Fix-It #14 for information about SCSI, USB, and FireWire.

Startup Disk control panel selection The current selection in this control panel (described later in this chapter) overrides the default choice. The Startup Disk control panel cannot be used to assign a floppy disk as the default startup disk. Actually, if a floppy startup disk is present, it is selected as the startup disk in preference to any hard disk, regardless of the setting in the Startup Disk control panel. The Startup Disk setting is retained and is used the next time you start up without a floppy disk present, however.

TAKE NOTE ▶ CD-ROM Startup Disks

The Mac OS CD-ROM that ships with all Power Macs can be used as a startup disk. Certain utilities that may need to be run from an emergency startup disk (such as disk-repair utilities) typically ship on a CD-ROM that can be used as a startup disk (see Chapter 2 and Fix-It #10 and #11).

Just having a bootable CD in the CD-ROM drive at startup is *not* sufficient for the Mac to start up from the CD. You must hold down the C key at startup to instruct the Mac to start up from a CD-ROM.

On certain Mac models, if the C key does not work, pressing Command-Option-Shift-Delete at startup may work instead (as discussed later in this chapter). Theoretically, Conflict Catcher can also be used. If you access Conflict Catcher at startup (see Fix-It #3), you should be able to choose the CD-ROM (if it is currently in the drive) from the Startup menu.

As a last resort, select the CD as the startup disk in the Startup Disk control panel and then restart. This method works only if you can successfully start up from your hard drive at the time (which precludes using this technique to deal with a crashed hard drive).

Several other points to note:

- For a CD-ROM to be bootable, it needs the expected blessed System Folder on it. But to act as a startup disk, a CD-ROM needs more. You normally cannot access a CD-ROM drive until after the Apple CD-ROM extension has loaded. CD-ROM startup discs include special instructions that allow them to get around this problem.

- When you are booting normally from a hard drive, the Apple CD/DVD Driver extension must be installed for CD-ROMs to mount when inserted. This means that if you start up with extensions off, no CD-ROM should mount. Bootable CD-ROMs are the exception; they *will* mount. This is because they contain an invisible extension (called .AppleCD) that is part of what allows the CD-ROM to serve as a startup disk. It also allows the CD-ROM to mount even with the Apple CD/DVD Driver disabled.

- CD-ROM startup discs may not always work in CD-ROM drives that are not made by Apple. Some work; others do not. The CDs should still mount as nonstartup disks.

- If you have problems restarting a Mac that used a CD-ROM as a startup disk, do a soft restart (by pressing Command-Control-Power) or press the Reset button. This should cure the problem.

The Startup Disk Control Panel: Changing the Default Startup Selection

You can change the Macintosh's default startup disk by using the Startup Disk control panel. To use it, simply click the icon for the disk you want to make the startup disk. You could use this technique, for example, to switch from your internal to your external drive as a startup disk. The selected disk is used as the startup disk the next time you restart (assuming that there is a valid System Folder on the selected disk).

This control panel lists all mounted hard disks and CD-ROMs. Thus, with this control panel, you can select a CD-ROM to be the startup disk.

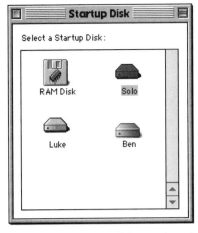

Figure 5-4 The Startup Disk control panel.

A few more points to note:

- **No selection** It is possible to have no drive selected in the Startup Disk control panel. In this case (especially in newer Macs), the Mac may spend a considerable amount of time—30 seconds to a minute or so—looking for a default startup device before starting up. During this time, you simply see the blinking folder icon. At first, you may mistakenly assume that the drive has crashed and will not start at all. Be patient, and you will be rewarded. When you do start up, go to the Startup Control panel and check to see whether any drive is selected (highlighted). If not, make a selection. The delay should vanish next time you start up.

  Zapping the PRAM (see Fix-It #9) or updating the computer's firmware (see Chapter 14) may cause the Startup Disk control panel to revert to a situation where no device is selected as the startup device (nonselection). In this case, you need to reselect the desired device.

  This same delay may occur if the selected disk is not present at startup (such as an external drive that is no longer connected or a CD-ROM that is not reinserted at startup). The Macintosh will eventually start up from the device selected via the default rules listed earlier in this chapter.

- **SCSI cards** A SCSI drive connected to a SCSI card in a blue-and-white G3 Mac may not work as a startup disk even if you select it in the Startup Disk control panel. The problem has to do with using Open Firmware for determining the startup device (as done with the blue-and-white G3 Macs and newer Macs). For such a drive to work, the SCSI card and the drive itself must be Open Firmware-aware. When these new Macs first came out, this problem was common. Updates to the SCSI card (and in some cases, to the disk driver software) have remedied most of these problems, however.

SEE: • Fix-It #14 for more details.

- **Startup Items** Don't confuse the Startup Disk control panel with the Startup Items folder. The Startup Items folder contains files that you want to be automatically opened at startup. The Startup Disk control panel is used to select a particular disk to be the startup disk.

- **Partitions** If you have divided a hard disk into separate partitions (and both partitions contain System Folders), on most recent Mac models, you can select which partition you want to use as your "startup disk" by making the selection in the Startup Disk control panel.

    This technique may not work on all Mac models, however. What happens instead is that the Mac automatically selects one partition as the startup partition—usually, the one listed first in alphabetical order—regardless of what you do in the Startup Disk control panel. You would think that to switch the default startup partition, all you would need to do is rename your hard drives appropriately. I have found this method to be unreliable, however. In general, you can assume that the preferred partition is the one that appears at the top of the stack of icons on your desktop, regardless of their names.

    If you want to start up from a nondefault partition, and the Startup Disk control panel doesn't let you do it, you can try several things. First, your disk formatting utility may have an option that lets you assign a partition to be the startup partition (Drive Setup does not have such an option!). If your utility can do it, this is the most reliable method. A quicker method, which almost always works, is selecting the desired startup partition via a freeware utility from Apple called System Picker. Just launch it and select the partition you want to use. (By the way, System Picker modifies your boot blocks. This means that if you have used any other utility to change your boot-block data, as discussed occasionally in other parts of this book, System Picker erases those changes. Just so you know.)

    If you are still unsuccessful, go to the partition that you do not want to act as the startup disk, and place the Finder in another folder (such as in the Control Panels folder). This procedure "unblesses" the System Folder. Now, when you select the disk in the Startup Disk control panel, the remaining "blessed" partition should act as the startup disk. If you really don't care to save the System Folder, you can even delete it. (If you have more than two partitions, you may have more work of this sort to do!)

    None of these methods is guaranteed. But I have had success with all of them. Much of the variation in success seems to depend on differences among disk drivers (see Fix-It #12). You'll have to experiment a bit to see what works for you.

TAKE NOTE ▶ Where Is My External Hard Drive?

A common use of the Startup Disk control panel is to switch the startup disk from an internal to an external hard disk. I suppose it is obvious that the external drive must be turned on before you can make this switch. It is worth noting, however, that unlike internal drives, external drives usually have a separate power supply from the Macintosh. Thus, they typically need to be turned on separately.

Ideally, an external drive should be turned on at least a few seconds before you start up the Macintosh itself. Otherwise, the drive may not have warmed up enough for the Macintosh to recognize its presence when the Macintosh checks for startup disks. If the drive is not warmed up, the Macintosh recycles its search for a startup disk, stopping at the first one it finds and using it as the startup disk. If your only possible startup drive is the external drive, the Macintosh eventually locates it and starts up from it. If you have an internal drive, however, and it still has a valid System Folder on it, the Mac starts up from the internal drive instead, despite your selection in the Startup Disk control panel. In such a case, the external drive probably will not even appear on the desktop when the startup sequence is over. If this happens, just restart the Macintosh. Everything should now proceed as expected.

This problem is less likely to occur in newer Mac models. Also note that there is a converse situation in which the internal drive does not mount when the external drive is the startup disk (see the following section, "Starting with an Alternative Startup Disk").

Starting with an Alternative Startup Disk

If you are having any problems starting up your Macintosh, an often-recommended (sometimes essential) step is to try restarting the Macintosh with an alternative startup disk. The logic is that if the problem is specific to the normal startup disk, you should be able to start up successfully with the alternative disk.

Start Up with an Alternative Hard Drive or Removable Cartridge

Use the Startup Disk control panel If you have two or more potential startup drives (including any removable cartridge drive, such as a Zip drive) connected to your Macintosh, and you can still start up from the default startup drive somehow (such as by starting up with Extensions Off), the simplest way to switch startup drives is to start up normally, select the alternate desired startup drive in the Startup Disk control panel, and restart.

If you are unable to access the Startup Disk control panel because you are unable to start up from your normal startup drive, you may still be able to switch to another drive, as described next.

Bypass the drive If your current startup disk is your internal hard drive, and you have at least one alternative drive, you can bypass the internal drive at startup and attempt to start up from an alternative drive. To do this:

1. Restart your Macintosh, typically by pressing the Reset button (as I am assuming here that a system error is preventing a normal restart).

   SEE: • **Chapter 4, "System Errors: Living with the Bomb," for more details on restarting.**

2. Press Command-Option-Shift-Delete (COSD) immediately after restarting. Hold these keys down until the Mac OS screen appears. Release the keys. The Macintosh should now start up from the alternative drive (assuming that it has a System Folder on it).

   If you have partitions on the disk, all of which have separate System Folders, see the Partitions item in the preceding section of this chapter for more information.

   If you hold down a number key in addition to the COSD keys (such as COSD1 or COSD2), the Mac starts up from the SCSI device that has that ID number (see Fix-It #14) rather than the device it would otherwise have used. This is a concern only if you have more than one alternative drive that could serve as a startup drive.

3. When you use the Command-Option-Shift-Delete (COSD) technique to bypass an internal drive at startup, the internal drive may not mount (although see: "By The Way: The Internal Drive May Still Mount When You Press Command-Option-Shift-Delete"). Often, this is exactly what you want to happen. Here's why:

   If a startup drive is crashing at startup, there are two possible causes. In the first situation, the crash occurs only when the drive is the startup drive, most likely due to some problem file in the drive's System Folder. In the second situation, the drive causes a crash when it is mounted even if it is not the startup drive, most likely due to some problem with the drive's driver or other corruption of the disk. In the latter situation, even if you bypass the drive as the startup device, it still causes a crash when the Mac attempts to mount the drive at the end of the startup sequence. When you press COSD, the drive does not mount at all, bypassing the crash.

   You can still access the problem drive via disk-repair (see Fix-It #10) and disk-formatting (see Fix-It #13) utilities, ideally fixing the drive so that it can mount the next time without crashing. If the disk can mount without causing a crash, you can mount the disk manually after startup is over, using a utility such as SCSIProbe (see Fix-It #14).

BY THE WAY ▶ Bypassing External Startup Drives

If you selected a drive other than your main internal drive to be your startup device, holding down the D key at startup should force the internal hard drive to be the startup device, at least on NewWorld Macs. Otherwise…

SCSI If your normal startup drive is an external SCSI drive, the COSD technique may not work. Instead, if the external drive has its own power supply, turn off the drive before restarting. This method forces the Mac to use the internal drive instead. You can then turn the drive back on and mount the drive manually, using a utility such as SCSIProbe.

USB or FireWire If your normal startup drive is an external USB drive (possible in some Power Mac G4s and newer Macs) or a FireWire drive, the COSD technique will not work. Instead, simply disconnect the drive from the USB or FireWire chain and restart. Reconnect the drive after the Mac restarts from the internal drive. Assuming that the internal drive has the USB and/or FireWire drivers enabled, the drive should mount automatically.

BY THE WAY ▶ If Removable-Cartridge Drives Eject at Startup

When you use a removable-cartridge drive as a startup disk, you may have problems with the cartridge automatically ejecting when you restart (more likely to occur if you restart via a Restart than via a Reset). If the cartridge does eject, you may be able to reinsert it in time for the Mac to recognize it as a potential startup disk.

Otherwise, consult your drive's documentation for specific advice on what to do. In most cases, the driver software has an option to enable or disable ejecting at shutdown and/or restart. If so, I advise disabling eject at restart and enabling eject at shutdown. This procedure prevents the automatic eject when you are trying to use the cartridge as a startup disk. Ideally, you need to set these options before a startup problem occurs.

BY THE WAY ▶ The Internal Drive May Still Mount When You Press Command-Option-Shift-Delete

When you use the Command-Option-Shift-Delete (COSD) technique to bypass an internal drive at startup, the internal drive may still mount at the end of the startup sequence. There are at least two reasons for this situation:

- In recent versions of the system software, a second check for connected SCSI devices occurs later in the startup sequence. This patch was intended to prevent large-capacity, slow-starting drives from being bypassed during a normal startup. The COSD technique forces the drive to be bypassed at the first check, but the drive still mounts as a result of the second check. Whether this happens depends on which Macintosh model you are using and the size of your hard disk.

  If this happens, a variant of the COSD technique may still allow you to bypass the internal drive altogether (it may not work on all Mac models). The way to do this is to both reset (zap) the Parameter RAM and use the COSD shortcut. This technique works because the second check uses information about connected SCSI devices that is stored in PRAM. With the PRAM zapped, this stored information is erased from the PRAM and thus ignored. In particular: press the Command-Option-P-R keys at startup until you hear the startup tone for a second time (this resets the PRAM); then immediately press Command-Option-Shift-Delete.

- In newer Macs that do not have a SCSI bus on the logic board (such as the iMac and and all new Macs, as described in Chapter 14 and Fix-It #14), the COSD technique may not work at all. This is likely due to the fact that the command is designed to work with SCSI devices only, because these Macs do not have SCSI as a standard feature. In any case, Apple states that at best, the technique bypasses the device selected in the Startup Disk control panel and seeks another startup device. The normal startup drive still mounts at the end of the startup sequence.

  With even newer Macs (such as the iBook and the Power Mac G4), there is an additional option: holding down the Option key at startup (see "Take Note: Using the Option Key to Select a Startup Device").

  If you need to bypass the internal drive at startup, and none of these suggestions work, you may have to take the Mac to an Apple service provider to get the job done.

SEE: • Fix-It #9 for more on zapping Parameter RAM.

Start Up with an Emergency Floppy Disk or CD-ROM

For many users, their startup hard drive is their only hard disk. If that drive fails to start up properly, the alternative is to use an emergency startup floppy disk or bootable CD-ROM (as described in Chapter 2). Ideally, you have already obtained or created such a disk. You cannot create one on a Macintosh that won't start up! Assuming you do have a bootable floppy disk or CD-ROM, here's how to start up from it:

1. If you are using a bootable CD-ROM, insert it in its tray before restarting (assuming that whatever problem you are having does not prevent you from doing so). If you cannot do this, or if you are using a startup floppy disk, skip to Step 2.

2. Restart your Macintosh, typically by pressing the Reset button.

   SEE: • **Chapter 4 for more details on restarting, if necessary.**

3a. Floppy disk For a floppy disk, insert the disk immediately after starting. Recall that the Macintosh uses a floppy disk as a startup disk, if one is present, regardless of what hard disks are also present and what default rules are in effect. If you wait too long to insert the disk, however, the Macintosh again attempts to start up from the problem hard disk—and you may have to begin all over again.

   If you also want to prevent the normal startup drive from mounting at startup, you may be able to do so by using the Command-Option-Shift-Delete combination (described earlier in this chapter).

3b. CD-ROM For a bootable CD-ROM, if you were able to insert the CD before restarting, hold down the C key at startup. This should select the CD as the startup disk (see also: "Take Note: CD-ROM Startup Disks").

   If you were unable to insert the CD before startup, get the CD tray to eject, either by holding down the mouse button or pressing the tray's eject button at startup. Insert the CD-ROM again. Try holding down the C key to start up from the CD. Most likely, it will already be too late for the Mac to select the CD as the startup disk. If so, restart (such as by pressing Command-Control-Power, as described in Chapter 4) and hold down the C key to get the Mac to start up from the CD.

   If you also want to prevent the normal startup drive from mounting at startup, or if holding down the C key does not work, try pressing Command-Option-Shift-Delete instead of the C key.

   If you try the COSD technique, and it results in an external drive selected as the startup disk, rather than the CD-ROM, start up with the power to the external drive turned off. Use COSD to start up from the CD-ROM. Then turn the external drive on and mount it (if necessary) after startup.

TAKE NOTE ▶ Using the Option Key to Select a Startup Device

Starting with the G4 Macs, the iBook and the second-generation iMacs (such as the iMac DV), there is a new option for selecting a startup disk: Hold down the Option key at startup.

Doing this results in the appearance of a row of icons for every potential startup volume currently accessible by the Macintosh, including hard drives and CD-ROM drives. Simply click on the icon that represents the startup device you want. Below this row of icons are two additional arrow icons. Clicking the icon on the left (an arrow that bends 180°) forces the Mac to recheck for potential startup volumes (in case one was missed or added since the first check). The second arrow icon (a straight one), continues the startup with whatever device was selected.

Solve It! When Your Macintosh Won't Start Up

Welcome to every Macintosh user's worst nightmare. You turn on your Macintosh, and nothing happens. Or maybe all that happens is that your screen turns dark except for a ominous-looking Sad Mac icon. Or maybe you keep getting system crashes before the startup sequence is over.

If any of these things happens to you, don't panic. All is not lost—at least, not yet. You are about to go on a tour of the startup sequence, stopping at every place where something can go wrong and learning what to do in each case. You will soon see that the vast majority of startup problems can be completely and easily fixed right from your keyboard.

The Macintosh Is Dead

 ### Symptoms:

You turn on the Macintosh and absolutely nothing happens—no bong, no whirring of the hard drive, no status lights turning on, no nothing.

 ### Causes:

This occurrence is so unlikely that it often means that something embarrassingly simple to fix is the cause (your Macintosh is not plugged in, for example). Otherwise, it implies a major hardware failure (such as a dead power supply).

 ### What to do:

Are All Cables Plugged In and All Switches Turned On?

Make sure that all cords are securely plugged into their respective receptacles. I know—this seems almost too elementary to mention, but check just the same. If you are using an outlet that is controlled by a wall switch, make sure that the switch is on. If you are using a separate power strip, press its reset button.

If you are starting the Macintosh from the keyboard Power key, make sure that the keyboard cable is connected (although to be safe, turn off the Macintosh before attempting to reconnect any cables). If your model of Macintosh requires that an on/off switch be on before the keyboard button will work, make sure the switch is on.

Check Batteries

I discuss PowerBooks more specifically in Chapter 11. But obviously, if you are trying to start up from battery power, it won't work if your battery is dead. Plug the PowerBook into an AC outlet to see whether it starts. If so, your problem is specific to the battery. You need to recharge it. If the battery won't hold a charge, replace it. If the battery is relatively new and it won't hold a charge, check Chapter 11 for some other things to try.

All Macs also have an internal battery, which is used for such things as maintaining the Mac's clock. A dead internal battery can prevent the Mac from starting up. See Fix-Its #9 and #15 for more details, including advice on replacing the battery.

Substitute and/or Switch Cables and Components

If the Power key on your keyboard does not work, the problem may simply be that the connection from the keyboard to the Mac is temporarily not working. Try disconnecting the keyboard cable and reconnecting it, even if everything looks fine. Sometimes, this method fixes the glitch. Otherwise, for ADB keyboards, if your Mac has two ADB ports, try switching the cable to the other port. For USB keyboards, try switching USB ports.

If none of these techniques works, and especially if you can start the Macintosh from the Power button on the Mac itself but not from the Power key on the keyboard, it's time to suspect a defective keyboard or keyboard cable. If so, try swapping the keyboard or keyboard cable (if you have a second one available) to see whether things get moving. If the technique works, you have isolated the problem. Be thankful that the problem is not inside the Macintosh itself. The solution is to repair or replace the faulty component.

See: • **Fix-It #14 for more on ADB and USB ports.**

Is It Just the Monitor?

Sometimes, your Mac appears to turn on with no problem, but your monitor stays black. This situation suggests a broken monitor. But some other possibilities exist.

SEE: • **Chapter 10 for more information on monitors.**

Visit the Repair Shop

If nothing has worked, or if you have already determined that you have a hardware problem, take your Macintosh to an authorized service location to have it checked out. End of story.

SEE: • **Fix-It #15 for more information on diagnosing hardware repairs.**

Sad Macs and Unusual Startup Tones

 Symptoms:

The Sad Mac Icon

The (frowning) Sad Mac icon appears at startup. The screen turns black except for the Sad Mac in the center. This icon is the inverse of the happy Mac that normally appears.

Figure 5-5 The Sad Mac icon appears above a sequence of numbers (and the letters A–F; it's hexadecimal code!)–sort of an Unwelcome to Macintosh greeting.

Unusual Startup Tones

A Sad Mac is typically accompanied by unusual startup tones—that is, tones other than the ones you normally hear almost immediately after turning on or restarting your Mac. These tones have various pessimistic-sounding names, such as Chimes of Death or Chords of Doom. It may be a single note (of a different pitch from the usual one), a chord (again, different from that which you normally hear), a progression of as many as four notes, or the sound of a car crash (new to Power Macs).

A Sad Mac may occur without unusual startup tones, and conversely, these tones may appear without a Sad Mac occurring. In any of these cases, all progress comes to a halt. The startup process stops.

 Causes:

These symptoms occur when the Macintosh's initial diagnostic tests, which occur at startup, discover a problem that prevents the startup from continuing further.

You may have heard that this happens only if you have a serious hardware problem. This is a myth. The truth is that the vast majority of Sad Mac problems are either software problems or minor hardware problems (such as replacing a cable) that you can fix yourself.

Still, these symptoms can also signal serious hardware problems with your Macintosh. The damage could be to the Macintosh itself (a component of the main logic board), a card or memory chip plugged into the main logic board, a disk drive (especially if it is your startup hard disk), or any other peripheral SCSI device. A rare cause is a stuck Interrupt switch.

Software damage in the directory area of the disk could also lead to a Sad Mac. Other, less-ominous causes include a non-system disk in the default startup drive or an incompatible System file on the startup disk.

In general, if the Macintosh can start up from a disk other than the one that first caused the Sad Mac, you probably do not have a hardware problem. Conversely, if the Sad Mac appears immediately after you turn on the power even before trying to access a disk, you most likely *do* have a hardware problem.

Good news: The Sad Mac is likely on its way to becoming extinct. In iMacs and newer Macs, for example, defective memory typically does not result in a Sad Mac—especially if the defective memory is an additional memory module that was added to the iMac's standard memory. In this case, you are likely to see a message at startup that accurately states that the memory is defective. The Mac then simply proceeds to start as normal, using only the memory that is working.

 What to do:

Decode the Message

Sad Mac codes decoded If you already read Chapter 4, which discusses system errors, you know that I don't recommend wasting much time trying to interpret the system-error ID messages. The same is true for the string of letters and numbers that you find below the Sad Mac icon, especially now that the codes appear to be next to meaningless for newer Macs. But for those cases in which the code may still matter, here are a few guidelines:

Below the Sad Mac should be two rows of eight digits. The code is in hexadecimal, which means that the digits can range from 0–9 and A–F. Check out the last digit of the first row. If it's an F, it almost certainly means that your problem is software-related. Sad Macs caused by software problems are most often accompanied by an arpeggiolike four-note startup tone. These are good signs because, as you will see soon, it means that you can probably fix the problem yourself. If you have a Mac Plus or older model, there will be only one row of six digits. In this case, if the first two digits are 0F, these, too, indicate a likely software problem.

Otherwise, the problem is probably hardware-related. The most common hardware cause for the appearance of the Sad Mac icon is a problem with memory chips (SIMMs or DIMMs), especially if the Sad Mac first appeared soon after you added memory to your machine. Some error codes specifically indicate a memory-module problem. In some cases, they even suggest the slot in which the problem memory module is located (though I won't be going into this level of detail here). These codes are not relevant to PowerBooks, the iMac, or any newer Mac models—which is another reason to mostly ignore these codes.

Table 5-1 lists a few of the most common or easiest-to-interpret codes. Some of them refer to floppy drives and NuBus cards (things no longer present in new Macs). Apple has not documented newer codes for newer Macs. This is another indication that the Sad Mac may be fading from the scene and will no longer occur in new Macs. Instead, you will get something like that which is described in "Take Note: The New Power On Self-Test (POST)."

Table 5-1 ▶ Some Common Sad Mac Error Codes*

ERROR CODE**	WHAT IT MEANS	WHAT TO DO
xxxx0001 xxxxxxxx	ROM test failed. The Macintosh ROM has a problem.	Take the Macintosh in for repair.
xxxx0002 or xxxx0003 or xxxxxxxx xxxxxxxx xxxx0004 or xxxx0005 xxxxxxxx xxxxxxxx	RAM test failed. At least one memory module is defective or not seated properly.	Check that memory is inserted correctly. Otherwise, if possible, get replacement memory and use it to replace existing memory to determine which one is defective. Replace the defective memory module. Otherwise, take the Macintosh in for repair.
xxxx0008 xxxxxxxx	ADB failed. ADB refers to Apple Desktop Bus, the ports where the mouse and the keyboard connect to the Macintosh. Either an ADB device or the ADB section of the logic board is defective.	Check whether ADB devices are plugged in correctly. Otherwise, take the Macintosh and all ADB devices in for repair.

Codes are different for Mac Plus and older models and for the Macintosh Portable. Other special codes exist for PowerBooks and Power Macintoshes. Apple Tech Info Library files are available that give more details (see Fix-It #16 for how to access these files).
*** An "x" in the codes listed here means any digit from 0–F.*

Table 5-1 ▶ Some Common Sad Mac Error Codes* *continued*

ERROR CODE**	WHAT IT MEANS	WHAT TO DO
xxxx000A xxxxxxxx	NuBus failed. This term refers to the special NuBus cards (such as graphics cards) and the NuBus slots on the logic board that hold these cards. A NuBus card or a NuBus slot is defective. [It's unclear how this might apply to PCI cards]	If you can, remove the NuBus cards to see whether that solves the problem. If so, the faulty NuBus card needs to be replaced. Otherwise, take the Mac in for repair.
xxxx000B xxxxxxxx	SCSI chip failed. The section of the main logic board (which controls the SCSI port and the devices connected to it) is defective.	Take the Mac in for repair.
xxxx000C xxxxxxxx	Floppy drive chip (called IWM chip) failed.	This is more likely a problem with the chip on the logic board that controls the floppy drive than with the floppy drive itself. You can check Fix-It #14 for some suggestions on fixing floppy drives, but most likely, the Mac will need a repair.
xxxx000D xxxxxxxx	Chip controlling the serial and modem ports (called SCC chip) failed.	Guess what? You most likely need a hardware repair.
xxxx000F 00000001	Bus error, most likely a software error.	Try solutions indicated in text.
xxxx000F 00000002	Address error, most likely a software error.	Try solutions indicated in text.
xxxx000F 00000003	Illegal instruction, most likely a software error.	Try solutions indicated in text.
xxxx000F xxxxxxxx	Most likely a software error.	Try solutions indicated in text.

* *Codes are different for Mac Plus and older models and for the Macintosh Portable. Other special codes exist for PowerBooks and Power Macintoshes. Apple Tech Info Library files are available that give more details (see Fix-It #16 for how to access these files).*
** *An "x" in the codes listed here means any digit from 0–F.*

How soon after startup does the Sad Mac appear? In addition to the Sad Mac code itself, you can sometimes glean useful information from closely following the exact moment when the Sad Mac appears. This can indicate what diagnostic test failed, precipitating the Sad Mac. In particular, the Macintosh's logic board and the memory are among the first items tested, so if you get a Sad Mac almost as soon as you turn the Macintosh on, problems with those elements are the likely cause. A hardware repair looms likely. On the other hand, if the Sad Mac appears shortly after the hard drive begins to start working, a problem with the hard drive or with the SCSI connections is more likely (though software causes are possible, too). If the Sad Mac appears even later in the startup sequence (such as after the Mac OS screen appears), software problems are by far the most likely cause. These problems are also the ones most likely to have the error codes that end with an F on the first row.

TAKE NOTE ▶ The New Power On Self-Test (POST)

Starting with the iMac (and on all new Macs), a new self-test is in the ROM of the computer. It runs at every cold start. If it detects an error, you will hear one of the following beeps (as defined by Apple):

- 1 beep = No RAM installed/detected
- 2 beeps = Incompatible RAM type installed
- 3 beeps = No RAM banks passed memory testing
- 4 beeps = No good boot images in the boot ROM
- 5 beeps = BadROM boot block or processor is not usable

Problems indicated by 1, 2 or 3 beeps could mean defective RAM. Replacing RAM (especially added third-party RAM) may fix the problem. Otherwise, if you hear any of these beeps, you are best advised to take your computer to an Apple Authorized Service Provider for repair.

Error tones decoded For abnormal startup tones, the exact notes and their pattern often indicate the cause of the problem. Trying to learn how to use this information, however, is probably more trouble than it is worth, because Apple keeps changing both the normal and abnormal startup tones in different models, making useful generalizations practically impossible. Unless you are the type of person who enjoys memorizing the names of the episodes of "Gilligan's Island," I don't recommend learning about the different tones. You are unlikely to confront this symptom anyway.

One exception: NewWorld Macs (such as the iMac) have something called POST (Power-on Self Test), which can produce an entirely new set of beeps at startup (see: "Take Note: The New Power On Self-Test (POST)."

Restart the Macintosh

Restart with the same disk as a startup disk Maybe the Sad Mac or error tones will vanish when you restart (but don't bet on it!). To find out, press the Reset button. If the Sad Mac goes away, you can probably forget about it for now. If you really have a problem, it will return soon enough.

SEE: • **Chapter 4 for more details about restarting.**

Restart with an alternative startup disk If you get the Sad Mac icon (or error tones) after your initial restart, it's time to try to restart with an alternative startup disk.

SEE: • **"Starting with an Alternative Startup Disk," earlier in this chapter.**

By the way, if you were already trying to use a floppy disk as the startup disk, it may appear to be stuck in the drive—that is, it does not come out when you restart. If this happens, hold down the mouse button before you restart. Continue to hold it down after you restart until the floppy disk ejects. If you also have a connected hard drive, your Mac should now try to start from this drive. If the software on the floppy disk was the problem, this technique may cure your Sad Mac all by itself.

If the Macintosh Successfully Restarts from an Alternative Startup Disk

You probably have a software problem. As stated earlier in this chapter, this is especially likely if the first line of the Sad Mac error code ends in F. You can try several solutions. The first three solutions listed in this section work only if the problem disk appears as a secondary disk on the Finder's desktop after the restart. The remaining solutions are worth trying whether or not the problem disk mounts.

After each attempted solution, restart the Macintosh with the original startup disk to see whether the problem is solved. Continue until one solution succeeds.

Reinstall the system software You may have a corrupted System file. To check for this problem, reinstall a fresh copy of the System file or (even better) do a clean reinstall of the entire system software.

Upgrade the system software If the version of the system software on your emergency startup disk is different from the version on the disk that generated the Sad Mac, the problem may be specific to the system software version on your problem disk. You probably have an incompatibility between an older, out-of-date version of the system software and your current (presumably newer) hardware. In this case, the solution is to upgrade to a more recent version of the system software.

Most newer Macs will not run older versions of system software.

SEE: • **Fix-It #1 on incompatibilities between hardware and software.**

Rebuild the desktop Apple says this technique is worth trying, but I have never seen it work.

Zap the PRAM I have actually seen this method work, especially for problems with external drives.

Update the disk driver A Sad Mac could also be caused by a corrupted or out-of-date disk driver. Try reinstalling the driver by using your disk-formatting utility (such as Drive Setup). Upgrade to the latest version of the disk driver available.

Repair the directory Your directory files or boot blocks on the problem startup disk may have become corrupted. To repair them, use the appropriate utilities on your emergency startup disk(s). Start with Disk First Aid. Then try Norton Utilities or whatever comparable utility you have.

Even if the disk did not mount from the Finder, the more heavy-duty repair utilities, such as Norton Utilities, may be able to mount it. If repairs fail, these utilities may still be able to recover files from the disk.

Check for SCSI problems If the problem disk is an external SCSI-connected disk, you may have a problem with its connection to the Macintosh. The problem may be caused by conflicting SCSI ID numbers, improper termination, or defective cables, or an SCSI device may need to be repaired. SCSI problems loom particularly likely if the problem first appears after you add a new SCSI device to your computer.

SEE: • **"Technically Speaking: The Sad Mac Makes a Visit," later in this chapter.**

Reformat the disk If all else fails, this is your almost-never-fails last resort.

SEE: • **Fix-It #1 hardware and software incompatibilities.**
      • **Fix-It #4 on reinstalling system software.**
      • **Fix-It #8 on rebuilding the desktop.**
      • **Fix-It #9 on zapping the Parameter RAM.**
      • **Fix-Its #10 and #11 on repairing damaged disks.**
      • **Fix-It #12 on updating the disk device driver.**
      • **Fix-It #13 on reformatting.**
      • **Fix-It #14 on SCSI problems.**

If the Macintosh Does Not Restart from an Alternative Startup Disk

This situation is more likely to mean a hardware problem, but don't despair quite yet. Try the following.

Check for system software problems You may have an out-of-date version of system software that is incompatible with your current hardware. This scenario assumes that the software on your emergency startup disk is the same out-of-date version as on your normal startup disk, which is why you could not start up with the emergency disk. This possibility is unlikely, but I mention it just for the sake of completeness. In this case, you need to obtain a set of system software disks for the most recent version and use them to update your system software.

SEE: • **Fix-It #4 on updating system software.**
      • **"Technically Speaking: The Sad Mac Makes a Visit," later in this chapter.**

Check for SCSI problems You may have a problem with your SCSI devices and/or connections. Turn off your Mac, disconnect the SCSI cable from the back of the machine, and restart. If you restart successfully now (presumably from your internal drive or startup floppy disk), you have a SCSI-related problem. You may be able to fix this problem yourself, though it ultimately may require something as extreme as reformatting your external drive.

In one special case, Apple reports that a Sad Mac may occur if a removable media drive is on at startup and a cartridge is present in the drive (which would seem to preclude using such a cartridge as a startup disk!). This situation is especially likely to occur if you are using File Exchange.

I have never heard of a USB drive or a FireWire drive causing a Sad Mac or related error tone problem, but it can't hurt to disconnect these devices as well. Then try to restart.

SEE: • **Fix-It #14 for SCSI, USB, and FireWire problems.**

Check for hardware problems If all else has failed, you probably have a hardware problem. The most likely hardware cause is an improperly mounted or defective memory (including L2 cache).

If the problem is improperly mounted memory (the module may have gotten loose), you may be able to solve this problem yourself by reseating the memory module in its respective slot on the main logic board inside the Macintosh. If the small clip that holds the memory in place on some models of Macintosh is broken, it may need to be replaced. Otherwise, you probably have a defective memory module that itself needs to be replaced.

If you have a modular Macintosh (or other Mac that allows easy access to the memory inside it), you can usually do most of the work yourself, by removing the lid of the Macintosh and examining the memory directly—assuming that you would recognize memory if you saw it. I am aware that some readers of this book will not feel inclined to open their Macintoshes and start fiddling with the memory. If so, the alternative is to take your Macintosh to a qualified service technician to have it checked out.

SEE: • **Fix-It #16 for more information on memory-related and other hardware problems.**

TECHNICALLY SPEAKING ▶ The Sad Mac Makes a Visit

Here is a Sad Mac problem I had. Defective hardware turned out *not* to be the cause:

A Sad Mac appeared the first time I started my Mac after connecting a new external hard drive. The exact code was uninformative, other than suggesting a nonhardware cause (code = 0000000F; 00000001). Obviously suspecting the newly added hard drive as the root cause, I restarted with that drive off. Everything started OK. I then turned the drive on and tried to mount it by using SCSIProbe (as described later in this chapter and in Fix-It #14). This led to a system freeze. Next, I tried to mount it using a disk-repair utility (see Fix-It #10). After fiddling with some of the utility's options, I eventually succeeded in getting the drive to appear in the utility's list of drives. A check of the drive revealed a bad partition map (see Fix-Its #12 and #13). I had to reformat the drive to fix it. After that, the disk was fine, and the Sad Mac never reappeared.

The Flashing/Blinking ? Icon

 Symptoms:

The ? disk icon or folder icon remains on the screen indefinitely.

 Figure 5-6 The blinking ? icon—a sign of trouble if it does not go away quickly

 Causes:

On older Macs, the flashing question-mark icon was of a floppy disk. On newer Macs, which no longer ship with a floppy disk drive, the icon resembles a System Folder icon.

In either case, the most common cause is that the Macintosh cannot locate a valid startup disk. If so, the Macintosh sits and stares at you with the blinking question-mark (?) icon.

Rarely, the reason why the Mac cannot find a valid startup disk is that no such disk is present. This situation could happen if you inadvertently removed essential files from the System Folder of your internal drive, for example .

Otherwise, it may mean that the Mac is somehow unable to locate a valid startup disk, even though one is present. It's as though the Mac has gotten a bit confused. (I'll provide more details in the "What to do" section.) In some cases, the problem is more of a delay in finding the startup disk than a total inability to do so. The Mac will eventually start successfully if you just wait long enough (usually, about 30 to 90 seconds).

Finally, the startup disk itself or the connections between the startup disk and the logic board may be damaged. The damage may be such that reformatting the disk will remedy it. Otherwise, a repair or replacement is likely needed.

What to do:

Try the following items in turn until one is successful in getting your Macintosh to start up. Remember to turn off all the devices before disconnecting or reconnecting any cables.

Restart the Macintosh

This is almost always a good first thing to try. Simply turn off the Mac's power and try to start up again. Ideally, the problem will disappear. If so, your troubles may be over. If the problem returns later, however, you may have an intermittent problem, such as *stiction*.

SEE: • **"A Hard Disk Won't Mount," later in this chapter.**

If Your Startup Disk Is an External Hard Drive: Check Connections

Make sure that the external drive is properly connected to the Macintosh. Make sure that the drive is on and plugged in to a power outlet. Check that all cables are firmly connected. Restart.

SEE: • **Fix-It #14 on SCSI problems.**

If Your Startup Disk Is an Internal Drive: Disconnect Any External Devices (Especially SCSI Devices) and Restart

Disconnect the SCSI cable from the back of your Mac. If this succeeds in getting your Mac to start up, you probably have either an SCSI connection problem or a hardware problem with one or more of your external SCSI devices.

SEE: • **Fix-It #14 on SCSI problems.**

Check Indicator Lights

Most hard drives have one or two indicator lights on the front of the unit. (The light is built into the front panel of the Macintosh if it is an internal drive.) If there are two lights, one usually indicates that the drive is on; the other goes on only when the drive is being accessed (reading or writing). If there is only one light, it is usually an access light. In either case, the light should go on, at least intermittently, at startup. If it does not, the drive is not functioning (assuming that the light bulb itself is working!). A hardware repair looms likely.

Wait

After the blinking icon appears, wait at least two minutes before doing anything else. The Mac may eventually start up.

Check Startup Disk control panel If a delayed startup occurs, the most likely cause is that no disk is selected as a startup disk in the Startup Disk control panel. To check for this situation, go to the Startup Disk control panel after startup. The drive that you expect to be your normal startup drive should be highlighted. (If the drive is divided into partitions, all the partitions may be highlighted.) If another drive is highlighted or no drive is highlighted, select the drive that you want to be the startup disk, close the control panel, and try restarting. The delay at startup should disappear.

Zap PRAM If the delay still occurs, zap the PRAM and restart. Then, once again, select the desired disk in the Startup Disk control panel and restart again.

SEE: • **Fix-It #9 for more on zapping the PRAM.**

Press the Cuda button If the delay still occurs, and there is a Cuda button on your Mac's logic board, press it. Then start your Mac, select a disk from the Startup Disk control panel, and restart. By now, the delay should be gone.

SEE: • **Fix-It #9 for more on pressing the Cuda button.**

Check for a dead battery There have been reports that if the battery installed on the logic board of your Mac (the battery that maintains the PRAM settings) goes dead, you may not only lose your PRAM settings, but also be unable to start your Mac at all. Fortunately, replacing the battery fixes the problem. No major repair is needed.

On some Macs, a dead battery may result in a normal startup except for no video. In this situation, try zapping your PRAM. If the video comes back, you probably need to replace the battery.

SEE: Fix-It #9 for more on replacing batteries.

Restart with an Alternative Startup Disk

If you waited and waited, and a normal startup never began, try restarting with an alternative startup disk, such as a bootable CD. Simply insert the CD-ROM while the blinking icon is on the screen. In a few seconds, the Mac should begin to start up from this disk. If this method works, check to see whether the problem disk has mounted and is present as a secondary disk (its icon is shown below the startup disk icon on the Finder's desktop). Most likely, it will be there. If this method succeeds, and assuming a valid System Folder is located on the problem drive, follow a similar procedure to the one described in the previous section (If Your Startup Disk Is an Internal Drive…). That is, check the Startup Disk control panel settings (reselecting the desired drive as the startup drive), zap the PRAM, and/or press the Cuda button.

SEE: • **"Starting with an Alternative Startup Disk," earlier in this chapter.**

Check for System Folder Problems

If the procedures in the preceding section were not successful, it's time to take a closer look at the System Folder on the problem drive. Again, restart with an alternative startup disk. Then check for the following problems. Restart the Macintosh, using the problem disk as the startup disk, after each attempted solution to see whether the problem is solved.

Make sure that a System Folder is on the problem disk Presumably, you already know that a System Folder is there. But just in case, check anyway. If one isn't already there, install a System Folder and start again.

SEE: • Fix-It #4 on installing system software.

Ideally, have only one System Folder on the disk Multiple System Folders are not likely to cause startup problems. Still, if you are having a startup problem, play it safe. Delete all but the intended startup System Folder from your disk (unless you deliberately want to maintain multiple System Folders for some reason). If you are unsure whether additional System Folders are present, you can use the Finder's Find command and search for the word *Finder*.

SEE: • Fix-It #4 on system software problems.

Bless the System Folder, if necessary In Icon view in the Finder, check to see whether the System Folder has the mini-Macintosh icon on it. This icon indicates that you have a blessed System Folder. The Macintosh typically does not accept a disk as a startup disk, even if it appears to have a valid System Folder on it, unless it is shown as a blessed System Folder (that is, with a mini-Macintosh icon on the folder).

SEE: • "Understanding the Startup Sequence," earlier in this chapter.

Normally, all System Folders are blessed folders (unless there is more than one on the same volume, as described later in this section). Occasionally, however, a problem may develop when an apparently valid System Folder is not blessed. The System Picker utility, for example, unblesses otherwise valid System Folders. Similarly, if you remove the Finder or System file from a blessed System Folder, it becomes unblessed. Replacing these files blesses the folder again.

Also, an unblessed System Folder may be a warning signal that there is more than one System Folder on your disk. *A disk can have only one blessed System Folder on it*, which is the one that the Macintosh actually uses when it starts up from that disk.

If the System Folder isn't blessed, remove the System file from the System Folder. Close the folder and open it again. Then replace the System file and close the System Folder again. This method usually reblesses the System Folder. You should now see the mini-Macintosh icon on the folder. If so, try restarting with the problem disk as the startup disk. You should succeed.

Check for missing essential files If the System Folder is not blessed (or even if it is), make sure that all essential files are in the System Folder, including System, Finder and—if appropriate for your model—Mac OS ROM, System Resources, and other machine-specific Enablers. In some cases, the Mac begins to start up with some of these files missing, eventually stopping and displaying an error message naming the missing file or stating that startup was prevented because some needed software is missing. In other cases, the blinking icon appears instead. If any of these files is missing, it needs to be installed.

It should be hard to remove these files from the System Folder by mistake. If you do, when you next elect to shut down, you get a message that says: "The startup disk no longer has a valid System Folder. <File name> must be in the System Folder. If you continue, you may not be able to restart. Do you want to continue?" At this point, you can return the file, and all will be well.

I discovered a couple of surprises, however, when I experimented with my iMac:

- If I removed the System Finder or Mac OS ROM files, the iMac did not start up. Removing the Mac OS ROM file, however, did not unbless the System Folder (unlike removing the System or Finder file).

- Removing the Text Encoding Converter extension, which Apple also says is essential, caused a warning message to appear at shutdown. But if I ignored it, the Mac started just fine anyway. I suspect, however, that some problems would crop up if I left the Mac this way; the file has some special relevance for HFS Plus-formatted drives, as discussed in Fix-It #13.

- Removing the System Enabler 462 file (supposedly needed for my iMac) similarly seemed to have no effect on startup. I was running Mac OS 8.5 at the time.

- Removing the System Resources file also precipitated a warning message at shutdown. But if I ignored it, the iMac started up just fine anyway, and I found a new copy of the System Resources file re-created in the System Folder when startup was over. Perhaps if I had trashed the System Resources file instead of just removing it, this method would not have worked. I didn't bother to try.

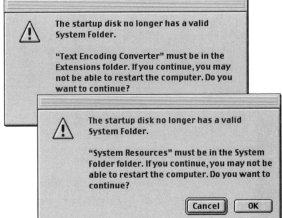

Figure 5-7 Warning message from an iMac if you remove Text Encoding Converter or System Resources files.

Check for damaged or incorrect essential files If all the essential files are present, one or more of them may be damaged. TechTool, TechTool Pro, and Conflict Catcher are useful for checking for damage in these files. Otherwise, to be safe, just replace these files or do a clean install of the system software. You might also try replacing the Finder Preferences file.

You may also be using mismatched versions of some of these files. You could somehow have installed a Mac OS ROM file that is for an older version of the Mac OS than the files in the rest of the System Folder. This situation inevitably leads to problems. Again, if you cannot determine whether this is the case, a general reinstall of the system software is recommended.

SEE: • "A System Error Occurs Just Before or While the Mac OS Screen Is Displayed," later in this chapter.
• Chapter 15 for more on the essential System Folder files in the latest versions of the Mac OS.
• Fix-It #4 for replacing system software.

TAKE NOTE ▶ NewWorld Mac Startup Problems

If you have a NewWorld Mac (an iMac or a newer Mac), here are some special startup problems to watch out for:

- **Boot ROM** It is possible for the boot ROM to get corrupted, preventing a startup. In this case, you probably won't even get as far as the blinking question-mark icon.

- **Mac OS ROM file** This file is in the System Folder. Leave it there! If it gets removed by mistake (or if it gets damaged), the result is similar to losing the System or Finder file. You get the blinking question-mark icon at startup. Nevertheless, removing this file does not cause the System Folder to lose its blessed status.

In any case, check Chapters 14 and 15 for more details.

TECHNICALLY SPEAKING ▶ Boot-Block Problems

Some startup problems can be attributed to corrupted or incorrect data in the boot blocks. This situation is why an apparently valid System Folder may appear to be unblessed. Such a disk does not start up properly.

In some cases, the procedure for blessing the System Folder fixes a boot-block problem. Otherwise, you may have to resort to special utilities (such as Norton Utilities) that repair boot blocks. If a boot block problem exists, these utilities find it, report the problem to you, and fix it. If they cannot fix the problem, your last resort is to reformat the disk.

SEE: • Chapter 8 on boot blocks and Fix-It #11 on disk damage.

Make Disk Repairs

If none of the preceding solutions worked, and especially if the problem disk did not mount when you started up with the alternative startup disk, try repairing the disk, using utilities such as Disk First Aid and Norton Utilities. It may also be worthwhile to defragment/optimize the disk.

One possible complication occurs if the problem disk not only refuses to mount when you start up from an alternative startup disk, but actually precipitates a crash at startup. Possible solutions here are described in "Starting with an Alternative Startup Disk" earlier in this chapter.

SEE: • "A Hard Disk Won't Mount," later in this chapter.
• Fix-It #7 on defragmenting disks.
• Fix-It #10 on repairing disks.

The X Disk Icon Appears

 ## Symptoms:

You should see the X disk icon only if you are trying to start up from a floppy disk (assuming that you have a Mac that still has a floppy drive!). At the beginning of the startup process, the floppy disk is ejected, and a disk icon with an X in the center appears. Assuming that this is the only problem, the Mac then proceeds to start up from your normal startup drive.

Figure 5-8 The X disk icon usually means that there is no System Folder on a floppy disk.

 ## Causes:

This situation is usually no cause for concern. It simply means that the Macintosh did not find a valid System Folder on the floppy disk and so could not start up. The disk is otherwise likely to be a normal, perfectly OK Macintosh disk.

These days, this problem is relatively rare. Normally, if you do get this icon, it is because a floppy disk was unintentionally left in a drive at startup.

 ## What to do:

Do Nothing...At First

If you have a startup internal or external hard disk connected to your Macintosh, do nothing. The Macintosh will start up normally from the hard disk after ejecting the floppy disk.

If you do not have a hard disk connected, you need to do something. Start up with an alternative startup floppy disk.

SEE: • **"Starting with an Alternative Startup Disk," earlier in this chapter.**

Check the problem floppy disk When startup is complete, reinsert the problem floppy disk, ejecting the alternative startup floppy disk, if necessary.

Check for a System Folder There almost certainly isn't one, but check anyway. If there is no System Folder (and you want one on the disk!), install a System Folder on the disk. Then try to start up from the disk again. You should succeed.

SEE: • **Fix-It #5 on installing system software.**

Make sure that the System Folder is blessed If there is a System Folder, you have some problem with the disk. Assuming that the System Folder is recent enough to work on your Mac, the problem may simply be that the System Folder is not blessed. To check, follow the guidelines for blessing System Folders. If the System Folder is valid and has no damaged files, simply opening and closing the System Folder should get it blessed.

SEE: • **"The Flashing/Blinking ? Icon," earlier in this chapter.**

Check for disk damage For more general advice on problems with floppy disks, including dealing with a possibly damaged disk, see: "A Floppy Disk Won't Mount," later in this chapter.

A System Error Occurs Just Before or While the Mac OS Screen Is Displayed

 Symptoms:

A system error occurs while the Mac OS screen is visible. The system error may be a freeze (in which everything just stops), a crash (perhaps with the bomb alert box appearing), or a spontaneous restart (in which the whole process begins again and crashes again at the same spot). A variety of other error messages are also possible.

If you get the system bomb error message at this point, the message may offer advice on how to proceed next (*To temporarily turn off extensions, restart and hold down the Shift key*).

If you are using a startup management utilities, such as Conflict Catcher (as described in Fix-It #3), when you restart after a startup crash caused by a startup extension conflict, you may get a special message alerting you to the problem.

 Causes:

The problem is almost always with a system extension or control panel that loads at startup (previously referred to as startup extensions). The loading of these files corresponds to the appearance of their icons along the bottom of the screen. Some problems may be due to insufficient RAM to complete startup. These problems may also lead to symptoms when the Finder is loading, as discussed in the next section, "Problems While Launching the Finder and the Desktop."

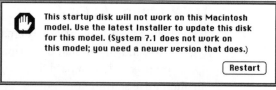

Figure 5-9 One of several messages that you might get at startup, indicating a problem with your system software.

Otherwise, the problem is probably with the system software—typically, a damaged, missing, or incorrect version of a file. In some cases, the PRAM may be corrupted. Occasionally, improper SCSI connections may be the cause.

A spontaneous restart at startup is most likely due to a startup extension problem. Otherwise, it may be due to more general causes, as described later in this chapter.

SEE: • **"Problems with Restart, Shutdown, or Sleep," later in this chapter.**

 What to do:

Try each of the following solutions until you find one that works.

Do You Have the Correct and Latest Version of the System Software?

Suppose you get a message that seems to imply that you need to upgrade your system software. Examples include *This startup disk will not work on this Macintosh model. Use the latest Installer to update this disk for this model* and *The System file on this startup device does not contain the resources necessary to boot this Macintosh. Please use the Installer to update the System file.*

If you are using out-of-date system software, the obvious solution is to update it, as the message suggests.

A message like this may also mean that you are using a version of the system software customized for a Macintosh model that is different from the one you are now using. A System Folder designed to be used with an iMac, for example, may not work if it is used to start up an older model of Mac. The solution is to reinstall the system software, using a version that is compatible with your current model, by creating either a version just for the current Mac or a universal "any Macintosh" option.

SEE: • **Fix-It #4 on installing system software.**

Test for a Startup Extension Problem

If missing or out-of-date system software does not seem to be the cause of your problem, restart with your startup extensions off (by holding down the Shift key at startup). When the Mac OS screen appears, the words *Extensions Off* should appear directly below the Mac OS graphic. This means that you have bypassed the startup extensions. You can now release the Shift key. If a startup extension was the source of the problem, you should now start up successfully.

BY THE WAY ▶ **An Extension Refuses To Load If You Have a Network Connection. Why?**

Though this situation is not actually a system error, an extension may refuse to load at startup because your Mac is connected to a network and it detects another copy of the program with the same serial number installed on another machine. In some cases, disabling AppleTalk can bypass the problem. In other cases, it can occur even if AppleTalk is not active, if the LocalTalk cable is plugged into your Mac. Although I am not recommending that you illegally try to defeat this form of copy protection, you can prevent these problems (assuming that you have a legitimate reason for doing so) by restarting with the LocalTalk cable pulled out. For extensions, you can safely reconnect the cable after the Mac has loaded the extension.

Determine the Problem Startup Extension

If the preceding step indicated a startup extension problem, you want to determine which startup extension is the source of the problem. If you have several startup extensions, the culprit may not be obvious.

SEE: • **Fix-It #3 for more details on how to solve startup extension problems.**

When you isolate the problem startup extension, the most common solution is to stop using it by removing it from your System Folder. You should then be able to restart successfully by using the original startup disk.

Not Enough Memory

Not enough memory to load all extensions Another startup extension problem occurs when you don't have enough memory to load all your startup extensions. With the amount of memory that the latest versions of the basic system software require (and the growing number of extensions that are commonly used), this problem can happen even if you have 32MB or more of RAM installed in your Mac.

You may get a message such as *There is not enough memory to load all of your extensions...To make more memory available, remove one or more extensions from the Extensions folder or reduce the size of the RAM disk and/or Disk Cache in the Memory Control panel then restart your Macintosh.* The advice here is sound. Most likely, you should remove startup extensions from the System Folder until you have reduced the number enough to avoid getting this message.

There is no specific startup extension that must be removed in this case. The amount of memory needed by startup extensions varies from one to the next. Thus, one startup extension may require as much memory as three or four other startup extensions combined. Some startup-management utilities (see Fix-It #3 again) list the RAM use of each startup extension.

Alternatively, of course, adding more physical memory, or using virtual memory or a program such as RAM Doubler, may also solve this problem (see Fix-It #5).

Not enough memory...period Finally, in the most extreme case, you may not have enough memory to successfully start up even with all extensions off. You may see a message at startup such as *Mac OS 8.6 needs more memory to start up.*

In this case, you almost certainly have to add more memory to your Mac to get things working. Using RAM Doubler or virtual memory might help in a pinch. Otherwise, your only choice is to go back to an older version of the system software that requires less memory. Occasionally, reducing the number of sounds in your System file or fonts in your Fonts folder may help (you need to start up from another disk to do so at this point), but don't bet on it.

Here's a little glitch to watch out for: If your physical RAM is below the minimum needed to start up the Mac, the Mac will not let you start up with virtual memory off. Instead, it turns on virtual memory and uses it to supply the needed extra memory. Nice touch. But what if you want to use RAM Doubler instead? You can't. You need to disable virtual memory before you can turn on RAM Doubler, and the Mac won't let you do it. Unless Apple or Connectix finds a way around this problem, the only way to use RAM Doubler at this point is to add more memory!

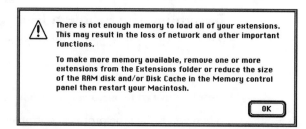

Figure 5-10 A message that may appear if you don't have enough memory to load all your enabled startup extensions—or perhaps not even enough to load essential system software. In this case, only those extensions that could load before you ran out of room will be active when startup is over—or you may not be able to start up at all!

Zap the PRAM

Some of the data stored in PRAM relates especially to drive connections. If the data stored in PRAM becomes corrupted, it can cause problems with a hard disk mounting. Zapping the PRAM restores the data to its default value and should solve this problem.

SEE: • **Fix-It #9 on zapping Parameter RAM.**

Replace or Reduce System Software

If there is no startup extension or PRAM problem, and you seem to have enough memory, the system software may be damaged. Be especially wary of a System file that has suddenly substantially increased in size for no apparent reason. In this case, reinstall your system software. You can also use TechTool or TechTool Pro to check for System file damage.

Finally, if for some reason, you have a System Folder with a System file but no Finder, the Mac may start up successfully but will crash at the point at which the Finder would normally load. The solution is to restart with another disk and install a copy of the Finder in the System Folder.

SEE: • **Fix-It #1 on incompatibilities between hardware and software.**
• **Fix-It #2 on preferences files.**
• **Fix-It #4 for how to replace system software.**
• **Fix-It #5 on increasing memory availability.**

BY THE WAY ▶ CD-ROMs that Cause Startup Problems

The first few tracks of some CD-ROMs contain information that make them appear to the Macintosh to be startup disks, even though they are not. If you start up with these disks inserted in the CD-ROM drive, a crash may occur. Manually eject the disk by inserting a paper clip into the pinhole on the front of the drive, and restart.

Check for Other Problems

Otherwise, check for other file or disk damage, drive connection problems, or a hardware problem.

SEE: • **"A Hard Disk Won't Mount," later in this chapter.**
• **"By the Way: The Iomega Driver Extension Could Not Load," later in this chapter.**

Problems While Launching the Finder and the Desktop

 ## Symptoms:

The loading of startup extensions is complete, the Welcome to Macintosh screen has disappeared, and the Macintosh is ready to launch the Finder and create the desktop. But just when you thought it was safe to start using your Macintosh, something goes wrong.

Typically, problems at this point are signaled by the appearance of an error message. The message may appear at any time from just before the appearance of the desktop to just before the end of the entire startup sequence, as the disk icons appear on the right side of the screen.

If the error occurs before the appearance of the icon for the startup disk, the startup disk is the likely source of the problem. If the error occurs after the appearance of the startup disk's icon but before the appearance of the icon of any other disk that may be mounting as part of the startup sequence (such as a second hard drive), the problem is probably with the secondary disk.

Possible error messages include *Can't load the Finder, The desktop file could not be created, The disk is damaged* and *The disk <name of disk> needs minor repairs.* More rarely, you may get a message that says that the disk is unreadable or even that it is not a Macintosh disk.

Occasionally, rather than an error message, a system freeze or system crash may occur, typically just before the startup disk icon would appear on the screen.

 ## Causes:

Usually, the *Can't load the Finder* error message is a one-time glitch. The exact reason why it happened may never be clear. Otherwise, it is most likely due to defective Finder and/or System files.

The other messages may simply mean a problem with an extension that you may be able to solve by reinstalling software or (conversely) deleting an extension. Otherwise, they typically signal damage to system software (including preferences files) or to the desktop and/or directory files (the critical invisible files that allow the Macintosh to interact with the disk). Sometimes, the problem is SCSI-related.

SEE: • **Chapters 2 and 8 for more details on these invisible files.**

 ## What to do:

Can't Load the Finder

A message that says *Can't load the Finder* may appear near the end of a startup sequence (sometimes with an -41 system error ID code). Following are four potential solutions to this problem.

Figure 5-11 If you get this error message, simply restarting the Mac usually solves the problem.

Restart Restart the Macintosh (typically by pressing the Reset button). Wait to see whether the Finder loads correctly on the next startup sequence. If the startup is successful, the problem may not recur. Otherwise, try restarting again with extensions off. This technique may succeed because it reduces the amount of memory needed by the system software, leaving more memory for the Finder. In this case, it may mean that you cannot use so many extensions without adding more RAM. If the problem recurs even with extensions off, you need to start up by using an alternative startup disk and proceed to the next potential solution.

Replace the Finder and the System and Update/Enabler files Replace the Finder and the System file. Also, to be safe, replace or reinstall any Enabler or Update file (if one is needed).

SEE: • **Fix-It #4 on replacing the Finder and the System file.**

Check for disk damage Use utilities such as Norton Utilities or TechTool Pro. In particular, there may be a problem with the boot blocks, which contain information that tells the Macintosh which file on the disk is considered to be the Finder.

SEE: • **Fix-It #10 on checking for disk directory damage.**

Wrong boot block? If the problem disk is a copy of a floppy disk, and you made the copy using the Finder, make another copy, using a utility such as Disk Copy. If the original floppy disk has customized boot blocks, the Finder does not copy them to the new disk. This situation could cause a startup problem when you use the copy. Disk Copy will copy customized boot blocks.

SEE: • **Chapter 2 for more information on making an emergency startup disk.**

The Desktop File Could Not Be Created

Rebuild the desktop If you get this message, it may mean that the desktop file is damaged. Rebuilding it should fix it.

Be aware, however, that the desktop cannot be rebuilt on a locked floppy disk. Occasionally, this situation may prevent a locked disk from even mounting. The solution is to unlock the disk.

Check for other damage There may be damage to the directory files or SCSI problems.

SEE: • **Fix-It #10 on repairing damaged disks.**
        • **"A Hard Disk Won't Mount" and "A Floppy Disk Won't Mount," later in this chapter.**

Other Unusual Messages at Startup

Sometimes immediately after startup, when you try to open any window in the Finder, you get a message that says the window could not be opened because you are out of memory, even if you seem to have plenty of free RAM available. Although the long-term cause of this problem is not always clear (it may ultimately involve damaged system software), a short-term cure is to use a utility, such as Conflict Catcher, to increase the size of the system heap (as discussed in Fix-It #5).

Following are some other error messages that may appear at startup. What to do about them follows each message in the list (although the solution is often self-evident from the message itself):

This disk must be unlocked in order to perform one-time housekeeping. Unlock the disk!

The System file on the startup disk may be damaged. The Installer can be used to repair this disk. Replace the System file from your backups or do a clean reinstall of the system software (as described in Fix-It #4).

The System file on this startup device does not contain the resources necessary to boot this Macintosh. Please use the Installer to update the System file. Somehow, the System file in use was not created for use on your current hardware. You should do a clean reinstall; an ordinary install may not fix this problem.

Unreadable or Damaged Disk

If you get a message that the disk is unreadable, is not a Macintosh disk, or is damaged, the problem is usually with secondary disks mounted during startup, not the startup disk itself. If the problem had been with the startup disk, it would probably have caused a symptom earlier in the startup process.

For unformatted disks If one of these messages does appear, and you are using a disk for the first time, it may mean that the disk was never formatted. If so, format it. If it is a floppy disk, accept the alert box's offer to initialize it.

SEE: • Fix-It #15 on formatting disks.

For formatted disks If the disk has been formatted previously, don't reinitialize the disk! For floppy disks, you may simply be using the wrong type of disk drive for the disk. If so, the disk is still fine. For other removable media, such as Zip disks, the problem may be due to a wrong disk driver loading at startup (an incorrect version or an incompatible third-party driver). Or the disk directory may need repair. Finally, it is possible that the disk is hopelessly damaged or that the drive itself needs repair.

SEE: • "A Hard Disk Won't Mount" and "A Floppy Disk Won't Mount," later in this chapter.
• Fix-It #13 on formatting disks and Fix-It #14 on problems with disk drives of various sorts.

For RAM disks This unusual situation is described in Chapter 11.

SEE: • "Technically Speaking: An 'Unreadable' RAM Disk" in Chapter 11.

Cursor Alternates Between a Watch and an Arrow (or All Icons in a Window Are Missing)

The alternating cursor is usually caused by the Finder having a problem trying to display the contents of windows that are automatically opened at startup. You probably also have a system freeze.

To solve this problem, restart and hold down the Option key until the Finder mounts. (If you want, you can wait to press the key until just after the Welcome to

Macintosh message disappears.) This method forces the Finder to close all open windows and should resolve the problem. When startup is over, you should be able to reopen the windows without further symptoms.

A related symptom, basically due to the same cause, is the disappearance of all the icons in an open window at startup. Sometimes, just closing and reopening the window solves the problem. Otherwise, leave the window closed and restart.

For Any Other Symptom, Including System Errors

Start by restarting a few times See whether the problem fixes itself. If so, and if things now seem normal, run Disk First Aid, just to be safe. The utility may spot damage that was causing the problem.

SEE: • **Chapter 4 for more on system errors.**
• **Fix-It #10 on Disk First Aid.**

Rebuild the desktop Restart the Macintosh, and press Command-Option until a message appears, asking whether you want to rebuild the desktop. You get a separate message for each disk to be mounted. Click OK for the suspected problem disk(s).

SEE: • **Fix-It #8 for more information on rebuilding the desktop.**

A problem with a corrupted System and/or Finder file One symptom that may result from a corrupted System and/or Finder file is an empty alert box that appears and shimmers, freezing your Mac. You are probably looking at a clean reinstall of system software to fix this problem (or at least a replacement of the System and Finder files).

SEE: • **Fix-It #4 on reinstalling system software.**

Delete the Finder Preferences file This file (located in the Preferences folder) may get corrupted and cause a variety of serious problems, including system freezes and crashes. Deleting the file causes a new one to be created. You have to redo customized changes that you may have made (such as in the Views control panel).

SEE: • **Fix-It #2 for more on how and why to delete the Finder Preferences file.**

Delete other, possibly corrupted preferences files If you check for extension conflicts (using the procedures described in Fix-It #3) and isolate the conflicting extension, you may find that deleting the file's preferences file (rather than replacing or disabling the file itself) solves the problem.

The ObjectSupportLib bug If you are running Mac OS 8.0 or later, you do not need a file called ObjectSupportLib installed in your Extensions folder. The installers for certain applications still insist on installing it, however. Unfortunately, the presence of this file can trigger system crashes, including Finder crashes at startup. If this problem happens, restart with extensions off, and delete this file. To protect against future invasions, create a folder named ObjectSupportLib and place it in your Extensions folder. A file cannot replace a folder with the same name, so a new copy of the extension can never be installed behind your back.

A problem with a Control Strip module I had one case in which a third-party Control Strip module, called Control PPP, caused a system freeze at startup. The cause was somewhat hard to identify. My startup manager initially identified the problem as a triple conflict involving ATM, MacTCP, and Control Strip. Listing Control Strip as a conflict, however, suggested to me that a Control Strip module, rather than the Control Strip itself, might actually be the cause. As I had recently added the Control PPP module, it seemed to be a likely candidate. Deleting it did eliminate the problem.

Did you deinstall At Ease improperly? If you use Apple's At Ease program, it is important that you use its Installer utility to deinstall it. To do so, select the Installer's Remove option and click to remove the software. If you remove the At Ease extension any other way, such as by simply dragging it out of the System Folder, your disk will crash at startup. The other main solution at this point is to do a clean reinstall of your system software.

SEE: • Fix-It #4 on removing software and reinstalling system software.

BY THE WAY ▶ At Ease Is Not Always That Easy

The reason why removing At Ease without using the Installer causes a system crash at startup is that At Ease modifies the boot blocks so that the Mac looks for At Ease rather than the Finder at startup. With At Ease gone, the Mac doesn't know what to start up with. Using the Installer to deinstall At Ease prevents this problem by altering the boot blocks appropriately.

On a related front, if you have password-protected your disk with At Ease, and you forget your password, you can still start up with a floppy disk. Then delete the At Ease Preferences file in the Preferences Folder of the System Folder. This method eliminates the password protection, allowing you to start up from the hard disk again. With the enhanced security options used by At Ease for Workgroups (a special version of At Ease for large multiuser environments), however, you can be prevented from accessing the At Ease startup drive even if you start up from a floppy disk. At Ease accomplishes this feat by modifying the disk driver. This situation is similar to the way that most dedicated security utilities work.

In the past, updating the disk driver eliminated this password protection. With current versions of At Ease for Workgroups, if you forget your password after having used the Lock Startup Volume option, you need a special program called Unlock (which is included with the At Ease package) to unlock the disk again. You will probably also have to call Apple to get a special password to unlock Unlock. If all these techniques fail to work, you will need to reformat the disk to use it again.

Numerous other problems are associated with At Ease. Especially common are problems making copies of floppy disks from the Finder while At Ease is on. At Ease can also cause improper rebuilding of the desktop. If you are having such problems, disabling At Ease is a good way to begin looking for a solution.

More recently, Apple has reported several problems with At Ease for Workgroups on Macs that use IDE drives. Problems include possible Sad Macs at startup and an inability to get At Ease's security features to work on Macs that have unpartitioned IDE drives.

Another issue of concern is that with all versions of At Ease up to 3.0.2, you cannot prevent access to removable media (such as CD-ROM discs) from the Restricted Finder. If this is important, you need to upgrade to at least At Ease 4.0.

More generally, many problems with At Ease can be solved by throwing away the At Ease Preferences, At Ease Setups, and/or At Ease Users files. Deleting all these files, however, requires you to re-create your custom settings. Otherwise, check the read-me file that comes with At Ease (or its updater) for the latest information.

A final note: At Ease is probably on its last legs. Apple is recommending either the Multiple Users feature of Mac OS 9, AppleShare IP, or the NetBoot feature of Mac OS X Server as alternatives (NetBoot is covered again in Chapter 15).

Check for damage If these techniques do not work, you have to start up with an alternative startup disk. Then check for other disk damage (including media damage), corrupted data, or a hardware problem.

SEE: • "A Hard Disk Won't Mount" and "A Floppy Disk Won't Mount," later in this chapter.

Solve It! Generic Problems with Disks

A Hard Disk Won't Mount

 Symptoms:

- A hard disk won't mount, even when it is not the startup disk. This is typically referred to as a *crashed disk.* Most often, no error message or any other indication of a problem occurs. The disk's icon simply does not appear on the desktop. The operation of the Macintosh otherwise proceeds normally.

- In some cases, an error message appears, indicating why the disk cannot mount. Most commonly, the error message says that the disk is damaged, unreadable, or not a Macintosh disk.

- In the worst cases, you may get a system crash.

Note: If the problem disk you are trying to mount is your current startup disk, thereby preventing you from starting up, begin in the preceding section.

SEE: • "Solve It! When Your Macintosh Won't Start Up," earlier in this chapter.

 Causes:

Much of what is stated in this section applies equally well to SCSI, USB, and FireWire drives. Where differences do emerge, this section refers mainly to SCSI and ATA/IDE drives. Occasionally, I will make reference to the newer but less common USB and FireWire drives. Given Apple's push toward USB and FireWire, these drives will likely soon dominate the external drive market. The most common cause is damage to critical invisible files needed for the Macintosh to interact with the disk: the directory and the device driver. (See Chapter 8 for background on the directory and related invisible files.) Otherwise, if the drive is new, the disk may not yet be formatted or the drive may be connected incorrectly.

Hardware problems are also possible, especially if the hard drive appears to make less noise than usual or if its indicator lights do not go on or flash as expected. Also suspect hardware damage if symptoms appear shortly after you've jostled a hard drive while it was in use.

What to do:

If an error message appears, skip ahead to the section that discusses that message. Otherwise, try the following.

Check Power and Connections

For external drives, make sure that the drive is actually on and plugged in. Also make sure that all cables are firmly connected. (Remember to turn the Macintosh off before reconnecting loose cables.)

Restart or Try to Mount the Drive Manually

If you are starting up from an internal drive and a secondary external drive did not mount automatically as expected, the problem may simply be that you did not turn the hard drive on in time for the Macintosh to recognize its presence. Similarly, external hard drives that are turned on when startup is over do not mount automatically. These problems are usually easy to solve. Just choose the Restart command. Everything should now mount as expected.

SEE: • "Where Is My External Hard Drive?," earlier in this chapter, for more information on this problem.

Otherwise, try to mount the drive manually. The easiest way to do this is to use a special control panel, such as SCSIProbe. Select the drive and then click the Mount button.

If SCSIProbe does not even indicate that your drive is present, you can try clicking SCSIProbe's Update button to see whether that gets SCSIProbe to recognize the presence of your drive. If it does, now click Mount to see whether you can get the disk to mount. If this method works, your problems are over.

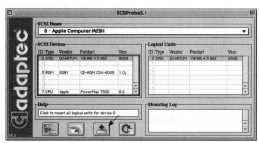

Figure 5-12 SCSIProbe. Click the icon indicated by the arrow to mount a hard disk without restarting the Macintosh.

SEE: • Fix-It #14 for more details on using SCSIProbe.

Note: SCSIProbe sees only SCSI drives. If you have an IDE drive, you can view it with Peripheral View, but you will not be able to use this utility to mount the drive. If Drive Setup supports your IDE drive, you can use it to mount the drive.

Check for SCSI-Related Problems

If you have external SCSI devices, and particularly if you have more than one, check for SCSI-related problems, such as SCSI device ID conflicts and improper termination. The best way to start this search is to try to start up with all SCSI devices detached. Do this by shutting down, detaching the SCSI cable from the back of the Macintosh, and restarting. If things now go well, suspect an SCSI problem.

Be especially suspicious of SCSI-related causes if you have made recent changes in your SCSI connections. In many cases, these problems cause a system crash at startup, typically immediately after the Welcome to Macintosh message appears.

Also, if you have more than one hard drive, Apple's official recommendation is that they all use the same device driver. This may require shifting to a new driver on one or more of your drives or even reformatting disks. I have never seen a problem result from ignoring this advice, however.

Finally, if you are using one of Apple's new Macs (such as G4 Macs) that do not come with SCSI support built into the logic board, you need to add a SCSI PCI card to add SCSI devices. For various reasons, a device that worked fine when connected directly to the Mac may not work when connected to a Mac via a SCSI card. The reasons are covered in Fix-It #14 (see especially "Take Note: Add a SCSI Card").

SEE: • **Fix-It #12 for more details on disk device drivers.**
        • **Fix-It #14 for details on other SCSI-related problems.**

Check for USB-Related Problems

If you have an external USB drive, a problem mounting the drive may be due to any of several USB-specific issues. Basic troubleshooting advice includes:

- If the device has a separate power supply, make sure that it is connected. If the device is connected via a USB hub, make sure that the hub is connected to a power supply.

- Unplug and replug the device.

- Make sure that any needed USB driver software is installed. (For external devices, any needed software should have come with the device itself.) Also use System Profile to make sure that the device is being "seen" by the Mac.

  For USB hard drives, as with SCSI drives, it is possible that a driver installed on the drive itself will allow the drive to mount (if inserted at startup) even if the driver software is not installed on your startup drive.

- Try swapping the USB plugs that go directly into the iMac (or other USB device), such that the plug in Port 1 is shifted to Port 2, and vice versa.

- Apple typically has beta versions of the next generation of USB software available online as part of what it calls the USB DDK, at <http://developer.apple.com/hardware/usb/>. The link to the latest version is at MacFixIt <www.macfixit.com>. Instructions for installing these beta versions are included with the software package. Occasionally, problems with the current release version can be remedied by using these beta versions. For example, a problem in which the Mac crashed when waking from sleep was fixed by installing beta drivers. Eventually, these beta versions become final versions and the fix is official.

  The DDK also comes with a utility called USB Prober. In certain cases, running this utility (which can reset the USB Manager) can get the Mac to recognize a USB device. Otherwise, try restarting the Mac.

- Problems mounting devices connected to a USB adapter (used to provide USB support for older Macs that did not come with a USB port) have been reported. Most of these problems are remedied either by updating the software for the adapter itself or updating Apple's USB software.

USBHIDUniversalModule

FireWire Enabler   FireWire Support

  SEE: • **Fix-It #14 for more advice and details on other USB-related problems.**

Figure 5-13 A USB driver extension (top) and the two key FireWire driver extensions (bottom).

Check for FireWire-Related Problems

As with USB, use of an FireWire-connected device requires that the relevant software be installed. Most especially, you need an extension called FireWire Support.

SEE: • **Fix-It #14 for more advice and details on other FireWire-related problems.**

Special Case: Problems Mounting Removable Media Cartridges

A removable cartridge, such as the kind used with a Zip or Jaz drive, should mount automatically when you insert it. If not, and if it is a SCSI device, you can use a utility such as SCSIProbe to try to mount it. For Iomega drives (Zip or Jaz), if it is an IDE or even a USB drive, you should be able to mount it via the latest version of the Iomega Tools application (part of the software that comes with each Iomega drive).

Problems mounting a removable cartridge are especially likely to occur when you eject a cartridge and insert a different one. Problems are most likely to happen if the new cartridge uses a different disk driver from the previous cartridge, if they were formatted by different utilities. You can remedy this problem by making sure that all cartridges are updated with the same driver.

Finally, if you insert a cartridge and get a message that says the disk is not a Macintosh disk, the disk may simply be a new unformatted disk. If so, do not click the Initialize button. Although that method may work in some cases, in other cases it may not do what is needed to format the disk. Preferably, use your disk-formatting utility to format the disk. If the disk is already formatted and you receive the error message, you may have a damaged disk (see the following section).

BY THE WAY ▶ The Iomega Driver Extension Could Not Load

If you restart your computer with a Zip or Jaz cartridge already in the drive (such as after a system crash), you may get a message such as *The Iomega Driver Extension (version 6.0.4) could not load because an older version (6.0.1) is already installed.* Yet your System Folder reveals that only version 6.0.4 is present. What's going on?

The answer is that there is a hidden copy of the driver on the Zip/Jaz cartridge. When (and only when) you start up with the cartridge inserted, the driver from the cartridge is loaded before the one in your internal drive's System Folder is checked. When the Mac reaches the one in your System Folder, you get the error message. As long as you don't require the new driver, no problems result from this situation. Otherwise, restart with the cartridge removed.

A long-term solution is to update the driver on your cartridge to the newer version. The Iomega software makes updating easy. Simply open the Iomega Drive Options control panel and choose Advanced Options from the Special menu. You will be able to have the driver on the cartridge updated automatically to match the version in your System Folder.

SEE: • **Fix-It #12 for more details on disk device drivers.**
• **Fix-It #13 on formatting disks.**
• **Fix-It #14 for more information on mounting drives and removable media (especially see: "Take Note: Mounting Removable Cartridges").**

Check for Damaged Files and Disks (Disk Is Unreadable or Not a Macintosh Disk)

If none of the previous solutions works, you probably have damaged files on the disk, most likely the directory files. This situation is especially likely when you get the message that says that the disk is unreadable or not a Macintosh disk. Check for this problem with repair utilities such as Disk First Aid, DiskWarrior, or Norton Utilities.

SEE: • **Fix-It # #10 and #11 on repair utilities.**

If these utilities fail to work, round up the usual suspects. Especially try zapping the PRAM.

SEE: • **Fix-It #6 on viruses.**
• **Fix-It #8 on rebuilding the desktop.**
• **Fix-It #9 on zapping Parameter RAM.**
• **Fix-It #12 on updating the hard disk device driver.**

After you try each Fix-It, restart your Macintosh to check whether the problem has been solved. If you succeed, your problem is over. Unfortunately, if the Finder cannot mount your disk, it probably means that most of these techniques do not recognize the drive, either. But they're worth a shot.

Reformat

If all else has failed, reformat the entire drive and start over. (But if you are desperate to try to recover unbacked-up files from your disk, check the following section before you reformat.) After reformatting, assuming that you have backups, restore them to your disk.

With these sort of problems, it often pays to reformat even if previous attempted solutions seem to have fixed the problem. Otherwise, problems may soon return. Reformatting is often necessary for a permanent solution.

SEE: • **Fix-It #13 on formatting disks.**

Hardware Problems: Stiction and Beyond

If reformatting fails, you probably have a hardware problem. If you couldn't even begin to reformat because the disk showed no signs of life, you almost certainly have a hardware problem. In particular, suspect hardware trouble if the drive is either making no noise or not making its usual noises when you first turn it on. Similarly, suspect a hardware problem if the hard drive's indicator light(s) are not going on as expected or are not flashing on and off as they typically do.

Usually, a damaged hard disk cannot be repaired and must be replaced. This can, and often does, mean the loss of all data on your disk. There are, however, a few glimmers of hope even in this case.

Stiction *Stiction* refers to a hardware problem in which the drive gets physically stuck at startup and is unable to reach its normal spinning speed. The result is that the Mac never starts up at all. A sharp slap to the side of the drive case can sometimes get it going again (but the problem will return the next time you try to start up). If this problem happens, immediately back up all your data.

A stiction problem is most severe when the drive is first turned on. So as a temporary fix, do not ever turn the drive off. The Mac will probably continue to run fine as long as you leave it on.

Like other hardware damage to a disk, stiction cannot be repaired. Replacing the disk is the only permanent solution. The temporary fixes should at least allow you to recover any needed data from the disk before you replace it.

Power supply For external hard drives, the problem may be in the power supply, a separate component from the disk itself. When it is replaced, your hard drive will function normally again, and all data on your disk will still be there unharmed.

Otherwise... Otherwise, for internal drives, there is a slim chance that the problem is with the connection cable from the drive to the logic board. This problem should be fixable.

If an external hard drive (or other device) still refuses to mount or otherwise does not work, attach it to another Macintosh. If it exhibits the same symptoms on the second Macintosh, the device is probably at fault.

For suspected hardware problems with an internal hard drive, swapping drives between two machines requires opening the Macintosh case. When the case is open, removing the drive requires unplugging the drive's connecting cables and then prying the drive free of its securing brackets. This operation is fairly simple; in many Mac models, it requires no tools. Still, if you have never done this before, you should probably get some outside help before attempting it.

Finally, if all else fails and you have important unbacked-up data on a damaged disk, try a repair shop that specializes in recovering data from problem drives. Some of these places, such as DriveSavers (800-440-1904), advertise nationally. You can mail your drive to one of these companies, which may succeed where you could not. Do this *before* you try to reformat the disk.

TAKE NOTE ▶ USB and FireWire Devices that Won't Mount

If you have a USB floppy disk drive or a SuperDisk drive, you may occasionally find the inserted disks do not mount. A short-term solution is to unplug the drive from the USB port and reattach it again.

In the long run, the problem is typically due to the USB drivers stored in the Extensions folder. If you are using drivers specific to your drive (e.g., SuperDisk drivers), try disabling them in favor of the generic drivers already built-in to the MacOS. Otherwise, try the reverse: if the product-specific drivers are not installed, install them. If all this fails, you may have a conflict with another USB driver. Use a utility such as Conflict Catcher to determine what it may be. Other possible causes include insufficient power to a USB hub (assuming you use one) or the need for a Mac OS System Software Update.

FireWire devices similarly require software drivers. Solutions to problems mounting such devices follow the same pattern as for USB devices.

A Floppy Disk Won't Mount

 Symptoms:

Upon inserting a floppy disk into a disk drive, one of the following things happens:

- The disk drive makes no sound, as if it does not recognize that the disk has been inserted. Obviously, the disk does not mount.

- The Macintosh appears to recognize the disk and attempts to mount it, but ultimately, a system freeze occurs.

- An error message appears, informing you that the disk cannot be mounted. The most common messages say that the disk is damaged, unreadable, or not a Macintosh disk. Usually, you are given the option to initialize the disk.

 Causes:

The causes vary. In general, as with hard disks, the problem is usually due to damage in the files that the Macintosh uses to recognize and interact with the disk, particularly the directory. If the disk cannot be easily repaired, you have a *trashed disk*.

The problem can also be caused by physical damage to the disk or the disk drive.

TAKE NOTE ▶ If You Can't Get a Disk to Insert

A disk that won't insert is probably due to a stuck or bent shutter—the metal piece at the bottom of the floppy disk. If the shutter doesn't slide freely, it is stuck. If you can't free it, remove it. (To do so, bend it open as though you are trying to straighten a paper clip.) Then insert the disk. If it mounts, immediately copy all data on it to another disk. Discard the problem disk.

If you know that your disk has a stuck or bent shutter, do not even try to insert it into a drive without first straightening the shutter or (if that fails) removing the shutter altogether. Otherwise, even if you succeed in inserting it, you may have even greater problems getting it to eject again. A disk with a bent shutter can even damage the drive.

 **What to do:**

For "Disk Is Unreadable" or "Not a Macintosh Disk" Messages

You may get error messages that say the disk is unreadable or not a Macintosh disk. Typically, the alert box asks whether you want to initialize the disk.

For unformatted disks The messages that the disk is unreadable or not a Macintosh disk appear when you insert an unformatted floppy disk. This situation is perfectly normal. Simply click Initialize (or Two-Sided) to format the disk.

Figure 5-14 *Disk is unreadable* message. Don't give up—your disk may be perfectly OK.

SEE: • Fix-It #13 on formatting and Fix-It #4 on installing system software.

For formatted disks If the disk has been formatted previously, don't reinitialize the disk! The disk may be perfectly fine. Reinitializing it loses any chance you have of saving the disk or recovering any data from it.

Click Eject instead. Then make sure that you are using the right type of disk for the type of drive you have. If you have a very old Mac with an 800K disk drive, for example, it will not recognize the newer HD disks.

SEE: • Fix-It #13 for more on floppy disks and formatting.

Otherwise, proceed to "After You Eject the Disk" later in this section.

For PC (DOS)-formatted disks PC (DOS) computers can now use the same disks that Macintoshes use—but they are formatted differently. If you insert a disk formatted for a PC machine, you may get the unreadable-disk message. Again, don't initialize the disk, and don't ever try to repair it with any Macintosh disk-repair utilities. Most likely, the disk is just fine, and anything you do to it will risk destroying data on the disk. The solution is to use the File Exchange control panel that comes with the Mac OS. With this extension, a DOS disk will mount on the Finder's desktop just as though it were a Macintosh-formatted disk.

In fact, this mounting is done with almost no indication that it is not a Mac disk, except that the disk's icon is different; the letters *PC* should be on the icon. Many users work with PC disks as though they were Mac disks, not even realizing the difference. You can copy files to these disks just as though they were Mac-formatted disks. Also note that File Exchange will help you open PC-format files that may be on the PC disk.

SEE: • Chapter 6 and Fix-It #13 for details.

Finally, if you suddenly have trouble mounting PC-formatted disks and File Exchange is installed properly, the File Exchange Preferences file may be corrupted. Try deleting it.

For "Disk Is Damaged" or "disk error" messages If you get an error message saying
that the disk is damaged, it probably is. You may have a choice of ejecting the disk or
initializing it. Alternatively, your only option may be an OK button that ejects the disk,
giving you no opportunity to initialize it.

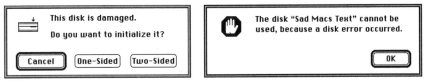

Figure 5-15 The Disk-damage message (left) offers to initialize the disk—decline. You have no
choice but to eject with the disk-error message (right).

Click Eject. Don't reinitialize the disk, if that option is offered! Reinitializing the
disk eliminates any chance you have of saving the disk or recovering any data from it.
Proceed to "After You Eject the Disk" later in this section.

If No Error Message Appears

In some cases, you don't get an error message. The disk simply does not mount. The
Macintosh acts as though you never inserted the disk.

Eject the disk Try to eject the disk by pressing Command-Shift-1. If you cannot get the
disk to eject with this method, see "A Floppy Disk Won't Eject," later in this chapter
Otherwise, proceed to "After You Eject the Disk."

After You Eject the Disk

Hope for the one-time glitch Lock the disk (to protect against any further damage).
Reinsert the disk. See whether it mounts now.

Repeat this procedure a few more times, if necessary. Sometimes, a minor misalign-
ment in the disk drive causes problems that disappear on the next insertion. This problem may occur with some disks but not others.

Floppy disk drives can get pretty finicky about what disks they accept. It might help
to briefly shake the disk or rotate the metal circle on the back side of the disk before
reinserting it. PowerBook floppy drives seem to be particularly subject to these types of
problems. You may have success by inserting the problem disk into another Macintosh,
mounting it, ejecting it, and then reinserting it into the PowerBook.

If reinserting succeeds in mounting the disk, your disk may be OK, but it often means
that you have media damage on the disk. As a precaution, especially if the problem occurs
repeatedly with the same disk and not with others, copy files on the disk to another
disk and then repair or replace the problem disk as described later in this chapter.

Restart with extensions off Sometimes, restarting alone solves this problem. More
rarely, an extension may prevent the reading of a floppy disk. To be extra-safe, when
you restart, hold the Shift key down to keep extensions off. Now try to mount the disk.

SEE: • **Fix-It #3 for more information on dealing with extensions.**

Replace or repair If reinserting or restarting fails to get the disk to mount, you probably have damaged disks and/or damaged hardware.

For damaged disks:

- If you have a backup copy of the disk, throw the damaged disk out. Even if you succeed in repairing the disk, your best bet is to discard the disk. Otherwise, it will probably cause problems again sometime soon. Better safe than sorry. Use your backup copy to make a new copy.

- If you do not have a backup of the disk, and the data on the disk is *not* important, throw the damaged disk out. You could try to reformat the disk, but I prefer to simply throw the disk out. Disks are cheap enough that I would not risk using a defective disk twice. Certainly, if you try to reformat the disk and get the *Initialization failed* message, it's time to discard the disk.

  SEE: • Fix-It #13 for more information on formatting disks.

- If it is important to save the data on the disk that is not backed up, try to repair the disk by using repair utilities. When your attempted repairs are complete, try to mount the disk again and see whether it mounts successfully. If it doesn't mount, use utilities to try to recover files from it to another disk.

  SEE: • Fix-It #10 and #11 on disk repairs and file recovery.

- Otherwise, with a bit of luck, you may be able to recover data from a damaged floppy disk that the Mac says is unreadable without having to resort to repair utilities. Don't eject the disk. Instead, open an application for a document on the disk, and see whether you can open the document from the application. If you can, save it to another disk and then discard the problem disk.

For damaged drives:

- You may have a problem with the disk drive itself, even if you do get the disk to mount. At best, the drive is just a little dirty; at worst, it is beyond repair. To check for this problem, insert other disks into the disk drive. Insert the problem disk into other disk drives. If a specific drive fails to recognize virtually every disk that you insert, but the same disks work fine when inserted into other drives, this is the classic pattern implying a hardware problem with the drive. A hardware diagnostic utility, especially one specifically designed to check floppy disks (such as TechTool Pro), can help determine the problem.

- Because the slot used to insert a disk is uncovered, dirt and dust tend to collect inside a floppy drive. A dirty drive can cause all sorts of unusual symptoms, some of which seem to have little or nothing to do with the drive.

  To clean the drive, place a portable vacuum cleaner near the disk drive opening and turn it on briefly, to try to draw out the dirt. With luck, this method may get things humming again. Disk-drive cleaning kits, such as one that works with MicroMat's TechTool, may also help.

- If the Mac indicates that virtually every floppy disk you insert into a floppy drive is locked (even though you know the disks are not locked), you probably have a problem with the floppy drive itself. In particular, the pin that goes through the hole of a locked disk is stuck in a way that makes all disks seem to be locked. You may be able to fix this problem by opening the drive and cleaning out the gunk that is making the pin stick, but I'd guess most of you would rather take the drive in for professional servicing.

    If the same disk causes problems in other drives, it may mean a physical problem with the disk itself (such as a stuck or bent slide shutter, as described in "Take Note: If You Can't Get a Disk to Insert" earlier in this chapter), rather than the drive.

A Floppy Disk Won't Eject or Unmount

 Symptoms:

You attempt to eject a floppy disk from its drive, using the standard methods, but it does not eject. Sometimes, you can get the disk to eject, but you can't unmount it—that is, the disk image does not disappear when you drag its icon to the Trash.

 Causes:

Many times, the problem is software-based. The problem may be due to insufficient memory to permit the disk to be ejected, although this is not likely in System 7 or later. If so, you should get an error message that describes this situation as the problem. Various bugs in the system software can also cause this problem.

In other cases, the problem has a physical cause. Possible causes include a damaged disk or a defective disk drive. But the cause may be as simple as a disk label that has come partially unglued and is jamming the eject mechanism.

In any case, unless the problem is a recurring one, understanding the cause is not necessarily critical. More important is figuring out how to remove the disk. Regardless of the cause, the methods of removal are the same.

 What to do:

For the sake of thoroughness, I review both the standard and nonstandard ways of ejecting a disk. It may surprise you to discover how many ways there are.

Standard Methods for Ejecting a Disk

From the Finder First, select the disk by clicking its icon on the Finder's desktop. Then try either of the following:

- Choose Eject Disk from the Special menu of the Finder or type Command-E (the Command-key equivalent of Eject Disk, listed to the right of the command). Both techniques do the same thing.

- Drag the icon of the disk to the Trash (no, this act does not erase any data on the disk!), choose Put Away from the File menu, or type Command-Y (the Command-key equivalent of Put Away). All these techniques do the same thing.

Before Mac OS 8, these two commands (Command-E and Command-Y) did different things. Command-E left a dimmed image (called a *shadow*) of the disk icon on the screen, to facilitate mounting a second disk and doing a disk-to-disk copy. Command-Y fully unmounted the disk; the icon vanished, and the Finder acted as though the disk no longer existed. Now both commands do the same thing: they fully unmount the disk. There is no longer an option to leave a dimmed icon on the desktop. Holding down the Option key before choosing Erase Disk used to leave a shadow icon in Mac OS 8.0 and 8.1 (I believe), but this technique no longer works in Mac OS 8.5 or later.

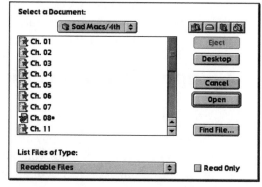

Figure 5-16 Click the Eject button in this Open dialog box to eject a selected disk. (The command is dimmed in this figure because no disk has been selected).

From within an application If you are in an application, such as a word processor, access the Open or Save dialog box, select the disk's name, and then click the Eject button. Surprisingly, this method *does* leave a shadow icon of the disk when you go to the Finder.

From any location Press Command-Shift-1. This method also ejects the disk.

Nonstandard Methods for Ejecting a Disk

All the preceding methods assume that the disk has no problem that would prevent it from being ejected normally. If none of the standard techniques work, it is time to get more serious. Try the following.

Restart your Macintosh This method by itself may eject the disk. It should work for any disk that does not have a System Folder on it.

Restart while holding down the mouse button Restart the Macintosh, holding down the mouse button until the disk ejects. This method should eject a disk even if it has a System Folder on it.

Actually, this technique is a general technique that gets the Macintosh to bypass and eject a floppy disk that is present in a disk drive at startup, whether or not the disk is causing a problem. It does not seem to work on all Macs, however; I was unable to get it to work on my PowerBook.

The Low-Tech Approach

If the disk is physically damaged or somehow stuck in the drive, none of these techniques may work. It is time to try to eject it by inserting a straightened paper clip into the little hole to the right of the drive slot. Ideally, the Macintosh should be off before you try this method.

Gently push straight in until the disk ejects. If you have to push too hard, stop. The disk or metal disk slide shutter may be damaged or caught in such a way that further force would damage the drive rather than eject the disk. It is time for a trip to the repair shop.

Reinserting the Disk

Before you reinsert the disk Check to see whether the disk has a torn label that may be getting stuck in the drive. If so, remove the label. Check to see whether the slide shutter is bent. If so, you may be able to straighten or remove the shutter.

SEE: • "Take Note: If You Can't Get a Disk to Insert," earlier in this chapter.

Reinsert the disk If you can reinsert the disk successfully, congratulations. If the problem recurs, get the disk to eject again. Insert other disks to determine whether the problem occurs with all disks or just that one. If the problem is with only that disk, you probably have to discard it. Before discarding, copy files from it to another disk.

SEE: • Fix-Its #10 and #11 on disk repairs and file recovery.

If the problem occurs with all disks, you may have a problem with the system software. Make sure that you have installed the latest machine-specific update (if there is one), because these updates may have fixes that solve the problem. Otherwise, reinstall the system software.

SEE: • Fix-It #4 on system software.

As a last alternative, you may have a problem with the disk drive itself. Take the drive in for repairs.

SEE: • Fix-It #15 on hardware problems.

Special Cases

Files on the disk are "in use" You cannot use the Finder's Eject Disk or Put Away command if any file on the disk is currently open or in use. If you try, you get an alert message informing you that the disk *could not be put away, because it contains items that are in use.*" The simplest solution is to close all open files from the disk and try again. Close both application and document files, even if a document's creating application is not on the floppy disk.

Even if you have closed all files, and nothing other than the Finder is listed in the Application menu, you still cannot unmount a disk that contains a mounted .img file.

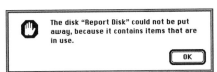

Figure 5-17 A disk cannot be unmounted when applications or documents on the disk are currently open (also see Figure 5-23).

Otherwise, if nothing else appears to be in use, and you run Disk First Aid to see whether a directory problem is the root cause, Disk First Aid may fail, stopping with a message that says *test was interrupted because another program was using the disk*. If this situation occurs, try a force quit from the Finder or a Restart (in some cases, with extensions off). This method should eliminate the problem. The disk will eject, and if you then recheck the floppy disk with Disk First Aid, it should report the disk as being OK.

SEE • **Fix-It #10 for more on Disk First Aid.**

Insufficient memory to eject a disk When you try to put away a disk, the disk may not eject because, according to the error message that appears, there isn't enough memory to move the disk to the Trash. The easiest thing to do is to quit an open application, to free enough memory to allow the disk to eject. Sometimes, increasing the memory size of the Finder or increasing the size of the system heap may help. If the problem still occurs frequently, consider increasing the memory capacity of your machine by adding more memory.

SEE: • **Fix-It #5 on memory problems.**
      • **Fix-It #15 on hardware problems.**

BY THE WAY ▶ More Memory Problems with the Finder

You may receive any of several error messages, each indicating that you cannot mount a disk, eject a disk, or use a disk because of insufficient memory. Normally, these problems are resolved by reducing the number of open applications and desk accessories. If these problems occur frequently, you should increase the size of the Finder's memory, increase the size of the system heap, or add more memory.

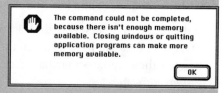

Figure 5-18 The Finder is having a problem because "there isn't enough memory available."

Occasionally, using a disk that is nearly full (besides limiting you to what you can copy to it) results in error messages that appear to be memory-related, such as an inability to update the disk's window. These problems can generally be solved by deleting some items from the disk. Also, rebuilding the desktop generally frees some extra space.

These problems are not limited to floppy disks but can occur with any type of disk.

SEE: • **Fix-It #5 for details on memory management.**

Repeated Requests to Reinsert a Floppy Disk

 Symptoms:

- When you are running certain applications (especially installers) that access multiple floppy disks, the Macintosh may eject a disk and ask that another disk be inserted. You insert what you believe to be the requested disk, but the computer immediately ejects the inserted disk and asks that it be reinserted. There seems to be no end to this repetitive cycle. This problem is especially likely to occur if the installer itself is launched from a floppy disk.

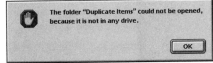

Figure 5-19 The Mac requests that you insert a disk.

- Alternatively, messages may cycle between one asking you to insert first one disk and then a second disk.

 Causes:

Typically, the problem occurs because the application in use needs to update information on the requested disk or otherwise access data from the disk. At other times, it may seem to be asking you to reinsert the disk for no apparent reason.

Reinserting the requested disk may end the problem. If two floppy disks are involved, several swaps back and forth may be required before the system comes to rest. The real problem occurs when the swapping back and forth never seems to end, or when the Macintosh repeatedly spits out the disk that you insert and then asks you to reinsert the same disk. The exact cause is often vague, but the problem is usually attributable to bugs in the system software.

 What to do:

Make Sure You Are Inserting the Requested Disk

You may be inserting the wrong disk, and that is why it is being rejected. The Macintosh may want Disk 1, and you are inadvertently inserting Disk 2. The obvious solution is to find Disk 1 and insert it.

To Break Out of the Cycle, Try Pressing Command-Period

Press Command-period several times. If necessary, hold down the keys until the request to insert a disk goes away (or until you give up in despair). It may take a minute or more for this to happen.

Alternatively, pressing Command-period may lead to another message saying that your command could not be completed, such as saying that your folder could not be opened. If you click OK, the insert-disk message may reappear. If so, press

The folder "Duplicate Items" could not be opened, because it is not in any drive.

OK

Figure 5-20 The message appears after repeated pressing of Command-period to get rid of alert boxes that ask you to insert a disk that you do not want to insert.

Command-period again. Repeat several times, if necessary. Regardless of what messages you see, at some point, you should break out of this cycle. The last message will probably say that the disk *cannot be used, because it is not in any drive.*

If none of these methods works (and sometimes, even if one does), you may have to do a force quit to get out of the installer.

SEE: • **Chapter 4 for more on forced quits.**

Restart with Extensions Off
(or Only Mac OS Base Extensions Enabled)

Restart the Macintosh with extensions off (or only Mac OS Base extensions enabled). Now do again whatever triggered the problem previously. You should be OK.

Bypass the Need for Floppy Disks Altogether

Another workaround is to use Apple's Disk Copy utility (see Chapter 2) to make disk image files of the floppy disks. Alternatively, you could try just making a disk image of Disk 1. In either case, this usually prevents the disk-swapping error from recurring.

A CD/DVD Disk Won't Mount or Play

 Symptoms:

- You insert a CD or DVD disk into a drive, but the disk icon never appears on the desktop. Often, no error message appears. The disk tray may even eject the disk.

- When you insert a CD or DVD disk, the Macintosh displays the message *This is not a Macintosh disk. Do you want to initialize it?*

- You get an error message that says *The DVD hardware cannot be found* when trying to mount or play a DVD disk.

- You get an error message that says *Apple DVD Player has stopped because it is having problems with the disc. The disk may be dirty or scratched or the manufacturer may have encoded the disc incorrectly.*

- An audio CD or movie DVD mounts but refuses to play or plays but with no sound.

 Causes:

Several causes are possible. The driver software or related extensions may not have been installed. You may not have the correct hardware for the type of disk you are trying to use. There may be a problem with SCSI or IDE connections. There may be incompatibilities among the different formats of CD and DVD. Finally, the drive itself may be damaged.

By the way, if you are trying to use the CD-ROM as a startup disk, remember that you may have problems doing this on some models of Macintosh.

SEE: • **"Default Rules for Selecting a Startup Disk," earlier in this chapter.**

 **What to do:**

Problems Mounting a CD or DVD

Make sure that the disk is inserted correctly Insert the disk label side up. While you are at it, make sure that the disk is seated correctly so that the tray can close completely. And make sure that the disk is clean. Otherwise, the tray may automatically eject the disk instead of mounting it.

Make sure that the drive is turned on before you start up If you are using the Apple CD/DVD driver, and you have an external SCSI CD/DVD drive, the drive must be turned on at startup for the driver extension to load (it doesn't matter whether a disk is in the drive or not). If you turn the drive on after startup and then insert a disk, the disk will not mount. No icon appears. The solution is to turn the drive on and restart.

This is not a problem for internal drives, which are turned on whenever you turn on your Mac. Similarly, some third-party CD-ROM drivers prevent this problem. Also, a freeware utility called LoadADrive mounts Apple's CD driver after startup, although I have had problems getting it to work in the latest versions of the Mac OS.

Make sure that the driver is installed in the System Folder and enabled at startup
Similarly, if the CD/DVD driver extension is not installed, you will typically not be able to use the drive. For Apple drives, the name of the extension is Apple CD/DVD Driver.

This driver extension must be loaded at startup for you to use your CD or DVD drive, which means that you can't mount most CD or DVD disks if you started up with extensions off. The utilities mentioned in the preceding item should help you overcome this obstacle.

Figure 5-21 The main extensions needed for CD/DVD software to be recognized and mounted.

Finally, the issue of extensions (on or off) is not directly relevant if you are using your CD-ROM as a startup disk. In fact, as discussed earlier in this chapter, a bootable CD-ROM mounts even when you start up with extensions off, even if you are not using it as the startup disk.

SEE: • "Take Note: CD-ROM Startup Disks," earlier in this chapter.

Make sure that you have Foreign File Access and related extensions, as needed To mount a non-Macintosh-formatted CD-ROM, such as an audio CD or a photo CD, special extensions such as Foreign File Access and Apple Photo Access (and possibly other relevant access files) must be present and loaded at startup. Photo CD disks also need QuickTime 1.5 or later. Otherwise, when you insert a foreign disk, you get the message that *This is not a Macintosh disk.*

Other special extensions are needed for DVD disks, as described later in this section.

You may have damaged files or an extension conflict If you get a *disk is unreadable* message when trying to mount a CD or DVD, and the needed extensions are properly installed, the files may be damaged. Reinstall them. Typically, the files are included as part of the Mac OS that came with your Mac, although it pays to check Apple's Web site for a more recent update.

If this method does not help, you may have an extension conflict (see Fix-It #3).

Special case: problems getting a DVD disk to mount DVD disks of any kind do not work when inserted into a CD-ROM drive. For starters, determine whether the disk that you are trying to mount is DVD, and if so, make sure that you have a DVD drive. Apple System Profiler Version 2.1 or alter will identify the type of drive. Also see the discussion of problems playing a DVD movie later in this section.

Make sure that you have enough memory A CD or DVD disk may refuse to mount if you do not have enough free memory. There will be no error message; the Mac will simply kick the disk back out. The solution is to quit one or more open applications and try again.

Similarly, turn off background processes such as virtual memory and (in some cases, especially with older versions of the OS) file sharing. These operations may prevent a CD or especially a DVD from playing properly.

Clean the disk If the disk has still not mounted by this time, check to see whether other, similar disks will mount. If so, the problem disk may be dirty. Try cleaning the disk with an approved cleaner such as KlearScreen or a soft cloth. Wipe the shiny side of the disk. Look especially for sticky goop on the disk. Wipe from the center to the edge of the disk; do not wipe in circles.

Restart If all else has failed, restart the Mac and try again. If this method still fails, zap the PRAM and try again.

Hardware If you have a SCSI-connected drive, make sure that you do not have a SCSI ID number conflict or termination problem. If the problem persists, it's time to suspect a hardware problem with the drive itself. Call Apple for help or take the drive in for repair.

SEE: • **Take Note: CD-ROM Startup Disks," earlier in this chapter.**
 • **Fix-It #14 for more on CD-ROM drivers, including non-Apple drivers and other SCSI-related problems.**
 • **Fix-It #15 on other hardware problems.**

Problems Playing an Audio CD

No auto-mount? If you expect your CD to start playing as soon as it mounts, but it does not, check QuickTime Settings to make sure that AutoPlay is enabled (but beware of the AutoStart virus, as described in Fix-It #6).

Extended/Enhanced CDs Enhanced (or Extended) CDs are ones that combine a computer data CD-ROM portion with a music-only audio CD portion. Starting in Mac OS 9, when mounting an enhanced CD, the two different portions (data and music) mount as seperate partitions on your desktop. Prior to that, only a single disk icon mounted. So don't worry if you see your CD mount twice; it is not a bug, it's a deliberate feature.

Audio CD halts while playing?

Accessing Save and Open dialog boxes, or even opening Finder windows, can halt the playing of a CD, especially if it is an enhanced/extended CD and you are running Mac OS 8.x or older.

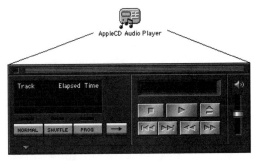

Figure 5-22 Apple's Audio CD Player, used to play audio CDs.

CD-RW disk? Audio CD-RW disks will not necessarily work in ordinary CD-ROM drives. They may work only in the type of drive that was used to create them. CD-R disks (the type that you can write to only once) have greater compatibility and should work with most, if not all, CD drives.

To read CD-RW discs you'll need a CD-ROM drive that is a least 20X speed (in some cases, 24X speed will be required). If you really need to burn discs for use on your older and slower CD-ROM drive, you'll have to use CD-R discs instead of CD-RW discs.

Other possible problems Various bugs may interfere with playing a CD. If you are using a PowerBook G3 with GlobalFax 2.6.5, for example, and your CD-ROM player has a problem playing a CD while GlobalFax is set to receive faxes, the workaround is to go to Global Village Fax Center, click the Setup menu, choose Receiving, and uncheck the Receive Fax checkbox. This bug may be fixed by the time you read this chapter.

Problems Playing a Movie DVD with DVD Player

DVD is a much newer technology than CD. As result, it has growing pains that CDs no longer have. There still is not a single universally agreed-upon DVD format, which can cause problems when you're trying to play a movie in a format that your DVD hardware or software does not support. More recent versions of DVD Player support more formats, so this problem is lessening.

Here are some other issues that may affect your ability to play a DVD disk, especially when you're using Apple's DVD Player to play a movie.

Same problems as for a CD Some of the same problems described in "Problems Playing an Audio CD" earlier in this chapter may apply. Check that section.

Press Command-Option-I If your DVD disk does not mount (especially if you get the error that reads *Apple DVD Player has stopped because it is having problems with the disk. The disk may be dirty or scratched or the manufacturer may have encoded the disk incorrectly*): Press Command-Option-I immediately after inserting the disk and closing the drawer. Continue to hold these keys down until the disk (ideally) mounts, which might take around 30 seconds.

Note: This keyboard trick forces the disk to be mounted as an ISO-formatted volume. This method can work in some cases because the DVD disk may support more than one format. The Mac may not recognize the disk's preferred format and so will not mount. If you force the Mac to try the ISO format (which the disk may also support), the disk may mount.

Starting with DVD Player 1.3, this ISO-related problem has been fixed and you should rarely see this error message anymore—unless of course you really do have a dirty or scratched disk.

You may avoid this error if you hold down Command-Option-I when trying to mount the DVD disk.

DVD Decoder installed? In some Macs you need not only a DVD drive (of course!), but also a DVD decoder card to play DVD movies. Even without the decoder, the drive can work with DVD-ROMs (that is, disks that have ordinary computer data on them) as long as the relevant software is installed. This software includes the basic CD/DVD software (Apple CD/DVD Driver, Foreign File Access, and UDF Volume Access extensions) and certain additional software (especially the ATI and QuickTime extensions). In general, if your Mac came with a DVD drive, the needed software should already be installed. Otherwise, a custom installation of selected software from the Mac OS Installer (choose the Multimedia option) is necessary.

Some original G3 Macs (beige) lack support for Apple's DVD-Decoder Personality card and cannot play DVD movies. To add the capability to play DVD movies to such a configuration, you have to use a third-party solution, such as a PCI MPEG2 decoder card.

With Mac OS 8.6 or later, you can use Apple System Profiler 2.2 (or later) to check for the presence of a decoder. Depending on your Mac model, the Hardware Overview section will have an item that says either Apple Audio/Video DVD Card or DVD Decoder Present if a decoder is installed.

Software-only DVD decoder Starting with Apple's G4 (and all newer Macs, such as the iMac DV), the DVD decoder card is no longer needed. All the relevant DVD information is now in software. In particular, it is built into the DVD Player application (and its associated extensions, such as "DVD Decoder Library" and "DVDRuntimeLib." The version of the player with this support is DVD Player 2.0 or later. This version will not run on older Macs that require a DVD card. They still use the 1.x version of the DVD player.

If you are using DVD Player 2.x, make sure the associated extensions come from the same version. In particular, I found that using the extensions from a 2.0 version of the Player with the later 2.1 version prevented the Player from even launching. A "DVDRuntimeLib could not be found" error occurred.

DVD Player 2.1 or later also fixes an audio/video sync problem where the sound and the video would fall out of synchronization several minutes into watching a movie. Also make sure that you have the latest version of other related OS software, including QuickTime and Apple Audio Extension.

No sounds with a DVD disc? Make sure the sound source, as accessed from the Sound control panel of the Sound Source Control Strip Module, is set for Zoomed Video for PowerBook users. Desktop users should select DVD.

"Driver not installed" error If trying to use the DVD Player results in an error message that says *Apple DVD Player cannot open because the Apple CD/DVD Driver is not installed*, and you recently connected to an AppleShare server, delete the AppleShare Prep file in the Preferences folder and restart.

Stutter When you use the DVD Player, an occasional stutter may be caused by the DVD drive's changing layers on the DVD disk itself. According to Apple, this situation is considered normal. A more persistent stutter may be solved by doing one or more of the following: disabling virtual memory, setting the Energy Saver control panel to maximum performance, turning off Speech Recognition, quitting all other open applications (including background processes, as described in Fix-It #3), or cleaning the disk.

Appearance themes Some third-party Appearance themes cause a conflict with the DVD Player that prevents the DVD movie from playing full-screen. To fix the problem, change the settings in the Appearance Manager back to the default.

ATI extension problems ATI extensions (including those that get installed by the Mac OS for those Macs, such as the blue-and-white G3 Macs, that come with an ATI card preinstalled) have been implicated in problems getting the DVD and/or CD Player applications to recognize disks in a DVD drive. Downgrading to an older or upgrading to a newer version of the ATI software may fix this problem. You'll have to experiment a bit here.

SEE: • **Chapter 10 for more information on multimedia issues, including QuickTime and DVD.**

TAKE NOTE ▶ USING DVD-RAM Disks

Mounting DVD-RAM disks DVD-RAM disks are DVD disks that are writable as well as readable. (DVD-ROM disks and DVD movie disks are read-only.) You can use DVD-RAM disks to store information, as you can with any other writable storage medium, but you cannot use one as a startup disk.

To use DVD-RAM disks, you must have either a DVD-RAM drive or one of the newer (Generation 3) DVD-ROM drives—which means that you cannot use these disks in the drives that came with the first generation of the PowerBook G3 series. You also need the relevant software: the Apple CD/DVD Driver, Foreign File Access, and UDF Volume Access extensions.

Inserting a DVD-RAM disk may cause the computer to temporarily not respond. Just press the manual eject button on the drive. The disk should eject, allowing the computer to function again.

DVD-RAM disks may also require an updated version of Apple's CD/DVD software.

Formatting DVD-RAM disks DVD-RAM disks can be formatted in the Universal Disk Format (UDF), Mac OS Standard, Mac OS Extended, or DOS formats. The UDF format allows you to share information with other computers that support this format (including PCs). You can format a DVD-RAM disk using the DOS format only the first time the disk is formatted, however. After the disk has been formatted, you can reformat it only in UDF, Mac OS Standard, or Mac OS Extended HFS Plus format.

SEE: • **"CD-ROM and DVD-ROM Disks" in Chapter 1, for a basic description of the different disk formats.**

A CD/DVD Disc or Removable Cartridge Won't Eject

 Symptoms:

When you choose Put Away, Eject, or an equivalent command to eject a CD/DVD disk or removable cartridge, it does not eject. Typically, an error message appears that gives you some clue about why it will not eject.

 Causes:

The most common reason that these disks cannot be put away is that the file is "in use." In the same way that you cannot delete a file that is currently open, you cannot eject these disks if they contain a file that is currently open. You get a message that says *The disk <name of disk> could not be put away, because it contains items that are in use.*

Having virtual memory on can also cause this problem. It is also possible that the disk is somehow physically stuck in the drive.

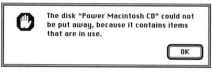

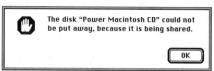

Figure 5-23 Messages that may appear when you are trying to eject a disk. The top one can occur with any type of removable disk (floppy, CD-ROM, or cartridge). The bottom message will not occur with floppy disks.

 What to do:

Use the Put Away Command

Choosing the Put Away command (Command-Y) or simply dragging the icon of the disk to the Trash are the main ways to eject a CD/DVD or removable disk (the same as for a floppy disk). This method unmounts it as well as ejects it. If this method does not work, proceed to the following steps.

If a File on the Disk Is "In Use," Quit the Relevant Application(s)

If you cannot eject a disk because you get the "in use" error message, quit all applications that are currently open on the problem disk or that use documents that are on the problem disk. The disk should now eject.

Turn Off Virtual Memory

Having virtual memory on *may* prevent a CD/DVD disk or removable cartridge from being ejected. If so, you can eject the disk by restarting with virtual memory off (hold down the Command key at startup to do this).

Other Ways to Eject a CD/DVD Disc

- Press the eject (open/close) button, which should be near the drive tray. Normally, this button is used only to open the tray when there is no disk in the tray. It should *not* work when there is a disk present. Still, when you are having problems, this method is worth a try.

- Turn the drive off and then on again (or, for an internal drive, restart the Mac); then immediately press the eject button, repeatedly if necessary. For Macs (such as the Power Mac 6100) that do not automatically turn off when you choose Shut Down, try pressing the eject button when the screen blackens and the "power off" message appears.

- Try holding down the mouse button at startup. The disk may eject.

- Start up with extensions off. Now try the drive's eject button.

- Turn off the drive, take a large straightened paper clip, and insert it into the small hole to the right of the eject button. This method should cause the disk to pop out. On Macs, such as the Power Mac G4, where the CD/DVD drive is behind a door, you must open the door with your fingers to access this hole. On slot-loading iMacs, the eject hole is practically invisible, but it's there: look for it on the far right edge of the slot.

- Follow any other instructions that came with your drive. If nothing works, you may have a damaged drive. Take it in for repair.

SEE: • **"Take Note: CD-ROM Startup Disks," earlier in this chapter, for related information.**

Other Ways to Eject a Removable Cartridge

For most drives, when standard methods fail, the remaining choices are basically similar to the methods for CD/DVD disks described earlier in this chapter. In particular, shut down the Mac and press the drive's stop/eject button. If that fails, insert a unbent paper clip into the small hole near the drive opening (usually provided as a fail-safe for when nothing else works). Check your drive's manual for details.

Note: On some Mac models, the Zip drive's Eject button is blocked by the drive cover. Although Apple officially recommends against doing this, if you feel up to the task you can temporarily remove the covering bezels to gain access to the button. Otherwise, you may have to take a Mac with a stuck disk in for repair.

BY THE WAY ▶ Choosing Restart or Eject When a Removable Cartridge Is the Startup Disk

If you are using a removable cartridge as a startup disk:

- If you choose the Eject command for the removable cartridge, you are likely to get into an endless loop in which the computer asks you to reinsert the cartridge and then spits it out again. Restarting is the only way out of this cycle.

- Choosing the Restart command from the Finder's Special menu causes the removable cartridge to eject, typically resulting in your Mac's shifting to the internal drive as your startup disk. To prevent this shift, choose Shut Down rather than Restart. Then reinsert the cartridge and wait for it to spin up. Finally, turn your Mac back on. The cartridge remains as your startup disk.

A Hard Disk Gets Unmounted

 Symptoms:

- A disk icon of a hard disk can become unmounted. Typically, this means that the desktop icon of the hard disk is gone or is a dimmed shadow icon.

- In some cases, an undimmed hard disk icon may remain on the desktop, but you are unable to access anything on the disk. Attempts to do so may lead to a variety of problems, including system errors.

    SEE: • Chapter 4, "System Errors: Living with the Bomb," for more on system errors.

 Causes:

Removing a Disk Icon

If you drag the icon of a hard disk to the Trash, the disk is unmounted, and its icon disappears from the desktop. The Mac will not let you do this with the startup disk, of course.

As with the similar unmounting of a floppy disk, the Macintosh no longer has any memory of an unmounted hard disk. This situation is not a problem by itself, but it does mean that you no longer have access to anything on that disk until it is remounted.

Dimmed Hard Disk Icons

Normally, if you unmount a drive, its icon should vanish from the desktop. There should never be a remaining shadow icon. If a shadow icon does remain, its cause is usually unclear. Usually, some sort of software bug caused the Macintosh to become confused. It is aware of the presence of the hard disk but does not think that it is currently accessible. A corrupted System file might be the ultimate cause. Whatever the cause, this situation could spell trouble if you try to access anything on the disk.

Turning the Power Off

Turning the power off on an external hard drive *after* you drag its icon to the Trash is not necessarily a problem. To be safe, however, I usually recommend against doing this. If you have several devices attached to a SCSI chain (as discussed in Fix-It #16), for example, turning off one of the devices can prevent the others from working.

If you turn the power off *before* dragging the disk's icon to the Trash, however, you have essentially unmounted the drive without informing the Finder of this fact— a definite no-no. Problems are likely to ensue.

 What to do:

Drag the Disk Icon to the Trash

If you have turned the power off on an external hard drive without first dragging its icon to the Trash, immediately drag the disk icon to the Trash. Do not try to work with any folders, windows, or files from the disk. Doing so will probably lead to a system crash. It may also cause corruption of the hard disk's directory so that it no longer mounts at all.

If you have files that are currently open and in use from that disk, you may have problems no matter what you do. Dragging the disk icon to the Trash may not be enough to save you.

Your best bet is to save what open files you can (on another disk, obviously) before a system crash occurs and then restart. If you don't need to save any files, simply restart.

Drag a Shadow Icon to the Trash

Similarly, if the disk icon appears dimmed, your best bet is to drag the shadow disk icon to the Trash, unmounting the disk before any other problems develop.

Otherwise, some particularly perplexing symptoms may appear. You may get an alert message telling you to reinsert the hard drive, which of course you cannot do. You can try to get this message to go away by pressing Command-period, as you would do for a floppy disk. If this method does not work, you have to restart the Macintosh, as you would after a system error, by pressing the Reset button or by turning the Macintosh off and on again.

SEE: • **Chapter 4, "System Errors: Living with the Bomb," for more on system errors.**

Even if you do not get the reinsert message, if you ignore this situation, a system crash is likely to occur soon. Restart to be safe.

Remount Any Unmounted Disk

Whatever the cause of the unmounting, if you want to use the disk again, you have to remount it. With SCSI drives, to do so without restarting, you have to do so manually, using a utility like SCSIProbe. Otherwise, simply restart the computer, using the Finder's Restart command. This method should remount the disk.

SEE: • **"A Hard Disk Won't Mount," earlier in this chapter.**
• **Fix-It #14 for more on using SCSIProbe.**

TAKE NOTE ▶ Mounting and Unmounting USB and FireWire Drives

USB and FireWire devices are said to be "hot-swappable." This means you can connect or disconnect them from their respective ports while the Mac is running. No need to bother with restarts. In fact, since these devices can potentially run off the power supplied by the port, there may also be no additional power supply to worry about. This is much more convenient than the hassles of dealing with SCSI devices.

Still, be a bit cautious here. Do not disconnect any hard drive while the Mac is currently reading from or (especially!) writing to the drive. This could result in data loss. Also do not connect a device to a chain while other devices on the chain are actively being accessed. For example, if you have a USB chain with a CD-R drive and a Zip drive, do not try to connect the Zip drive while the Mac is reading from the CD-R drive. A system crash or similar error could result. Finally, if you have unmounted a drive and its icon remains on the desktop, drag the icon to the Trash (unless you expect to immediately remount the drive).

I discuss SCSI, USB and FireWire more in Fix-It #14.

Problems with Restart, Shut Down, or Sleep

 Symptoms:

- You choose Restart or Shut Down from the Finder's Special menu. The shutdown process begins normally but is halted by a system error. You may get an error message, or you may simply get a freeze.

- A similar problem may occur when you choose Sleep on PowerBooks (but see Chapter 11 for more general problems with the Sleep command).

- When you choose Shut Down, the Macintosh spontaneously restarts rather than shutting down.

- A spontaneous restart occurs for no apparent reason at any time during an otherwise normal work session.

- A crash or freeze occurs when the Mac is waking from sleep.

 Causes:

When you choose Restart or Shut Down, the Macintosh attempts to save and close all currently open documents and quit all currently open applications before actually shutting down. It also does a final update of the directories of any mounted disks. If for any reason (usually, a bug somewhere in the software) the Finder cannot close a given file, the shutdown process halts. Something as simple as having an unsaved document can cause this problem. Other causes are a problem with an application, extension, or control panel. The problem could also be due to corrupted system software or directory damage.

Corrupted PRAM may also cause an inability to shut down. Finally, you may have a hardware problem, such as a stuck Power key on your keyboard or a bad power supply.

 What to do:

Save Documents, Quit Any Open Applications, and Related Issues

Save any unsaved documents, as requested.

You may also get messages such as one warning that the contents of your RAM disk will be lost when you shut down (assuming that you have a RAM disk). Again, this message halts the shutdown process until you dismiss it. Click OK (assuming that you don't care to save the files).

Sometimes, the Mac cannot close an open application automatically during a shutdown or restart. If you go to the application and manually choose its Quit button, the operation may proceed. If not, try the following techniques.

Check for Background Application Problems

If you try to shut down, and all applications have quit, but the Mac sends you a message that says *can't shutdown because the 'unknown' application can't quit,"* it is probably due to a background application—the sort whose names do not appear in the Application menu, giving you the impression that nothing is left open; sometimes, such applications are stored in the Extensions folder as extensions. The problem may also be caused by some similar process, such as documents left in the PrintMonitor Documents folder).

You can check for open background applications (or processes, as they are sometimes called) via a program such as Peek-a-Boo (described in Fix-It #3). Otherwise, you'll likely have to do a reset (as described in Chapter 4).

This message may also be due to a bug in an ordinary extension (in which case, see the following item).

Check for Startup Extension Problems

If the problem recurs, check for startup extension-related problems. I had an antivirus utility that prevented me from shutting down normally until I rearranged its loading order, for example.

As mentioned earlier in this chapter, startup extensions are an especially likely cause of a spontaneous restart if the restart occurs during startup, while startup extensions are loading. In the worst-case scenario, if continued spontaneous restarts prevent you from completing a startup, try starting up with extensions off. This method is almost guaranteed to work. Then determine the offending startup extension.

SEE: • **Fix-It #3 on solving startup extension problems.**

Restart (by Using the Reset Button, If Necessary)

If you had a spontaneous restart, and your Mac successfully restarted afterward, your problem may be over already. Check it out by trying Restart. If things go smoothly, congratulations. It was probably the old one-time glitch.

Otherwise, especially for a machine that refuses to shut down or restart, treat this problem as a system error. You have to restart your computer by using the Reset button or by turning the computer off and on again. The problem is unlikely to recur after you restart.

SEE: • **Chapter 4, "System Errors: Living with the Bomb," for more on system errors.**

Replace the Finder Preferences File

If the Macintosh fails to restart after you choose the Restart command from the Finder's Special menu, you may have a damaged Finder Preferences file. To fix this problem, restart (using the Reset button, if necessary) with extensions off by holding down the Shift key during startup. Go to the Preferences folder in the System Folder, and drag the Finder Preferences file to the Trash. Restart again (using Reset, if necessary), and empty the Trash.

SEE: • **Fix-It #2 for more information on preferences files.**

Zap the Parameter RAM

SEE: • **Fix-It #9 for how to zap Parameter RAM.**

Replace the Open Application and/or the System Software

If the problem does recur, and if it always seems to involve the same application, you may have a defective copy of the application. Replace it. If this method does not work, contact the company to see whether a bug in the software has been fixed by an upgraded version. Otherwise, do a clean reinstall of the system software.

SEE: • **Fix-It #2 on replacing application software.**
• **Fix-It #4 on updating and installing system software.**

Check for Updates

Some of these problems are caused by bugs in the software (most often, the Mac OS). The solution typically is to get an updated version of some component of the OS that fixes the bug. Problems with a freeze or crash when waking from sleep may occur, especially with PowerBooks. There have been various causes and fixes over the years. Updates of Apple's Open Transport software have fixed several cases. More recently, updating USB software solved a wake-from-sleep problem with newer Macs that come with USB ports.

Check for Disk Directory or Hardware Problems

Run the usual repair software (Disk First Aid, Norton Utilities, or DiskWarrior) to check for directory problems. The most likely hardware cause is a stuck Power key. To check, restart with the keyboard detached. For this problem or other suspected hardware problems, take the Mac in for repairs.

SEE: • **Chapter 11 for more information on PowerBooks and sleep problems.**
• **Fix-Its #10 and #11 on disk repairs.**
• **Fix-It #15 for more information on possible hardware problems.**

BY THE WAY ▶ **Stopping a Shutdown**

If you ever choose Shut Down or Restart and then suddenly realize that you do not want to shut down or restart after all, you may be able to halt the process by quickly launching an application before the shutdown/restart occurs. Also, if an application that was open when you chose Shut Down or Restart asks whether you want to save a document before quitting, clicking Cancel halts the shutdown.

   If you have a RAM disk, and you are using a Mac that can save the contents of a RAM disk after a restart, you may get a message at shutdown warning that the contents of thr RAM disk will be lost. If you click Cancel here, rather than OK, a shutdown is averted (see Chapter 11 for more on RAM disks).

Files Missing from the Desktop

 ## Symptoms:

The most common situation is when many or most files on a particular disk (floppy or hard) seem to have vanished from the desktop. These files are not listed in any Open or Save dialog boxes. Continued use of the disk may lead to system crashes. You can usually tell that something is wrong right away, because the amount of disk space in use (shown in the window header of any window from that disk when you use an icon view) indicates that much more disk space is in use than is accounted for by the files that are still visible.

 ## Causes:

The problem is almost always due to damage in the invisible directory or desktop files that keep track of what is on the disk.

SEE: • **Chapters 2 and 8 for more details on these invisible files.**

 ## What to do:

Close and Reopen the Window

Sometimes, especially if the problem is limited to one or to a few newly copied files, the files are really there and perfectly OK. The Finder may not have been updated properly and thus does not yet display the files. Usually, simply closing and reopening the window that contains the files will get the files to display.

Use Find

Use the Finder's Find command to search for the name of the missing file, if you can recall it. If the command locates the file, the file often becomes visible again, at least temporarily.

SEE: • **"Cursor Alternates Between a Watch and an Arrow (or All Icons in a Window Are Missing)," earlier in this chapter.**
• **Chapter 6, "When You Can't Find, Open, or Otherwise Use a File," for more information on locating a single missing file.**

Rebuild the Desktop

Rebuilding the desktop sometimes solves this problem, at least temporarily. Ideally, use TechTool to rebuild the desktop.

SEE: • **Fix-It #8 for more information on TechTool and rebuilding the desktop.**

Use DiskRepair Utilities

Disk First Aid is especially good at solving these problems. Other utilities, such as DiskWarrior and Norton Utilities, are also likely to be effective. They can fix damage that might otherwise cause these problems to occur in the future.

If you have an immediate problem, and if damage is discovered, repair it or recover data from the disk, as appropriate. If the damage cannot be repaired, you need to reformat the disk. Reformatting is probably a good idea even if you think that you fixed the problem. If the disk is a floppy disk, you should probably discard it instead.

> **SEE:** • Fix-It #10 on using Disk First Aid and other disk-repair utilities.
> • Fix-It #13 on reformatting.

The Macintosh's Speed Is Unexpectedly Slow

 ## Symptoms:

- The primary symptom is that many operations across most or all of your applications are running slower than is typical for your particular Macintosh model. Problems commonly include delays in opening files, saving documents, dropping down menus, and/or responding to mouse clicks. Other symptoms include increased time to copy or delete files and slow redrawing of the screen.

- Sometimes, delays are restricted to particular applications or situations, usually ones that are processor-intensive, such as running QuickTime movies.

 ## Causes:

Having operations run in the background generally slows your machine. Using almost all your available RAM also tends to cause slowdowns. Operations that require frequent disk access, such as compressing and decompressing files, slow the Macintosh as well. More unusual causes revolve around problems with system software or even with the drive itself.

Although some of the causes listed here may not fit perfectly into the scope of this chapter, I include them anyway. The list of solutions is by no means exhaustive, but it covers the most common problems. Some solutions require giving up certain features to gain a speed benefit. You'll have to decide whether the tradeoff is worth it.

BY THE WAY ▶ What Is the Expected Speed of Your Macintosh?

If your Macintosh suddenly starts performing at a snail's pace, you will undoubtedly notice. But what if you have a new Macintosh, and you have no idea how fast your machine should perform? Is there some way of finding out whether it runs as fast as is typical for its model? Yes. A variety of commercial and shareware utilities do this. MacBench (a freeware program) is one example. Norton Utilities has a similar feature.

 ## What to do:

Try any or all of the following, in the general order listed, until you get the speed you expect:

- Quit any applications that you do not need to keep open.

- Stop any background applications or processes, such as communications software that is downloading a file in the background.

- Turn off file sharing. Open the File Sharing control panel, and click the Stop button in the File Sharing section of the Start/Stop panel.

    SEE: • Chapter 11, "Trouble To Go: Portable Macs and Shared Macs," for more on file sharing.

- Turn off any unneeded extensions and restart. Several extensions, particularly those that modify general system functions (such as Apple Menu Options), noticeably slow the Macintosh. The cumulative effect of several of these extensions can be substantial.

    Apple Menu Options can cause an especially long slowdown in system operations when an alias to a hard drive is placed in the Apple Menu Items folder.

    Of special note, one function of most antivirus extensions is to check a file for viruses when it is launched. This check can significantly extend the time required to complete the launch.

    Finally, disable Speakable Items in the Speech control panel, if you have it installed and are not using it at the moment.

- Add certain extensions. If this advice seems to contradict the preceding item, you are right. The resolution of this paradox is that I am talking here about just a certain few extensions that are designed to speed specific operations, particularly those of the Finder. A prime example is Connectix Speed Doubler.

- Turn off virtual memory (as set in the Memory control panel) if you are using it, unless you are using a Power Macintosh). Similarly, if you are using a memory-enhancing utility such as RAM Doubler, turn it off. Typically, this step requires you to restart the Macintosh.

    SEE: • Fix-It #5 for more information on virtual memory.

- The size of the disk cache (as set in the Memory control panel) affects speed. In that regard, note that if you start up with extensions off (by holding down the Shift key at startup), the cache reverts to its default size for that session, not a potentially larger size that you may have previously set. The custom size returns the next time you restart with extensions on. Up to a point, a larger size generally leads to improved performance.

    SEE: • Fix-It #5 for recommended cache size settings.

- Increasing the Preferred Memory size of an application may increase its speed by allowing more of the program to load into RAM, reducing need for frequent swaps to disk (which slow the program).

- Lower your display depth, using the Monitors control panel. All other things being equal, your Macintosh will perform faster when displaying in black and white, for example, than when displaying in 256 colors.

    SEE: • Chapter 10 for more information on setting the display depth.

- Defragment your disk and rebuild the desktop.

    SEE: • Fix-It #7 on defragmenting.
    • Fix-It #8 on rebuilding the desktop.

- Reduce the number of files on your disk, especially if you have folders that contain hundreds of files. This arrangement tends to overwhelm the Mac's operating system and slows things down.

- Turn off Calculate Folder Size in the Views control panel.

- Keeping Key Caps open in the background slows text processing in the foreground.

- If you are using a PowerBook, open the PowerBook control panel. Uncheck the Reduce Processor Speed and Allow Processor Recycling checkboxes. Note: These options may not exist in all PowerBook software versions.

   SEE: • **Chapter 11 for more information on finding and using these options.**

- Otherwise, it's time to check whether you have a hardware problem with your hard drive.

   SEE: • **Fix-It #15 on hardware problems.**

- As a long-term issue, hardware additions (such as adding RAM or a processor upgrade) can increase the overall speed of your machine. Moving up to a faster Mac will also help.

- **Special case: delays at startup.**

   1. If you are having unusual delays at startup, especially before the appearance of the smiling Mac, check your Startup Disk control panel. If no volume is selected, select your desired startup volume. Your startup time should now improve.

      This situation is especially likely to happen if you temporarily set a CD-ROM or removable cartridge to be the startup disk and that volume is no longer available. It can also happen after zapping your PRAM.

   2. The initial startup period (before the appearance of the Welcome to Macintosh message) takes longer with additional physical RAM added. It also takes longer when restarting after a system crash. This situation is normal.

   3. If your Mac suddenly starts taking an unusually long time to start up (with lots of disk activity taking place), it may be that the AppleShare PDS file has become corrupted. To fix this problem, delete the file and re-create your access privileges as needed. Because AppleShare PDS is an invisible file, you need to use a utility, such as DiskTop, that lets you view invisible files (as described in Chapter 8).

   4. Utilities such as Startup Doubler and Speed Startup may significantly decrease your startup time.

      SEE: • **Chapter 4 on starting up after a system crash.**
      • **Chapter 11, "Trouble To Go: Portable Macs and Shared Macs," for more information on file sharing and the PDS file.**
      • **Fix-It #5 for more on RAM checking at startup, including how to disable this check, if desired.**

Frequent System Crashes and Other Disk-Related Quirks

 Symptoms:

In this scenario, the disk apparently mounts successfully, but as soon as you attempt to work with it, you notice serious problems, such as the following:

- Multiple copies of the icon for a mounted hard disk appear scattered across your desktop. Continued use of the Mac is likely to result in a system crash. This unusual symptom is a SCSI-related problem, as described later in this section.

- Frequent system crashes occur at erratic and unpredictable intervals (but only when the problem disk is the startup disk).

- System crashes occur shortly after you attempt any sort of access to a specific disk, such as trying to open an application or document on the disk.

Other strange symptoms may appear. The critical diagnostic clue in almost all these cases is that the problem is specific to one particular disk but involves almost all general activity related to that disk. These problems are all one step short of a total disk crash. If the problem is left unattended, you may soon find that the disk does not mount at all.

 Causes:

The problem is usually due to software damage in the directory or related invisible disk files or to media damage on the disk itself. Other possibilities include a virus, corrupted system files, SCSI problems, or hardware that needs to be repaired. Again, depending on the nature of the damage, it can often be repaired entirely by software techniques.

 What to do:

Check for Damage

Check for damage to the disk, and repair it, if possible. Start by using Disk First Aid. Then try the more industrial-strength repair utilities.

SEE: • **Fix-It #10 and #11 on Disk First Aid and other repair utilities.**

Check for Viruses

A computer virus, although a relatively unlikely occurrence for most people (despite the scare headlines in the media), can be the cause for otherwise unexplained system errors.

SEE: • **Fix-It #6 on viruses.**

System Software and Application Problems

Problems such as frequent system errors (especially Type 2, Type 3, Type 10, and Type 11) are known to be due either to bugs in some versions of the system software or in specific applications.

SEE: • Chapter 4, "System Errors: Living with the Bomb," for more information on system errors.

Startup-Disk Problems

If the problem occurs only when the disk is the startup disk, you should try replacing the system software files. Also consider possible problems with startup extensions that loaded at startup. You can even try rebuilding the desktop.

SEE: • Chapter 4, "System Errors: Living with the Bomb," for more details on system errors.
       • Fix-It #3 on startup extension problems.
       • Fix-It #4 on replacing system software.
       • Fix-It #8 on rebuilding the desktop.

Hard Disk Problems

If the problem is with a hard drive, update the hard disk's device driver. If you have multiple disk drives connected, try to have all disks use the same driver.

For SCSI drives, check for general SCSI-related problems, especially if your symptoms include multiple copies of the hard disk icon appearing across your desktop. This symptom typically indicates a SCSI ID number conflict.

SEE: • Fix-It #12 on disk device drivers and Fix-It #14 on problems with drives in general.

If All Else Fails

If none of the previous steps worked, recover essential files from the disk, if possible.

SEE: • Fix-It #11 on recovering files from damaged disks.

After recovery, if the disk is a floppy disk, discard it. If the disk is a hard drive, reformat it. Make sure that your reformatting utility is a current version.

SEE: • Fix-It #13 on reformatting.

If the problem persists after you've reformatted a hard disk (or, for a floppy disk drive, when you use other floppy disks), you may have a hardware problem with the drive itself. If you have not already done so, now would be a good time to seek outside help.

SEE: • Fix-It #15 on hardware problems and Fix-It #16 on seeking outside help.

6

When You Can't Find, Open, or Otherwise Use a File

It's the Little Things

Maybe you want to open a file but you can no longer remember where on your disk it is located. Or maybe when you do finally find it, the Macintosh refuses to open it. Or maybe when you later try to delete the file, the Macintosh says "no dice." These are the sorts of problems that are the subject of this chapter. If the previous chapter focused on problems that affected your use of an entire disk, this chapter narrows the focus to those problems that are limited to your use of a specific file. You will most likely confront these problems in one of two situations:

- When you are using an Open or Save dialog box from within an application to locate, open, or save a file;

- When you are using the Finder to locate, open, copy, or delete files.

As familiar as these procedures are to most Macintosh users, I should clear up some potential misunderstandings about their use before going any further. Then we'll go on and describe the problems you are likely to confront.

Understanding Opening and Saving

Open and Save Dialog Boxes

There are now two entirely different styles of Open and Save dialog boxes that you might confront: the original style and the new style. The new style is sometimes referred to as the Navigation Services dialog box. When will you see the new style box? First, you have to be running Mac OS 8.5 or later. Second, the application you are using has to be written to be Navigation Services-aware. As I write this, very few applications are Navigation Services-aware. Even some of Apple's own software, such as SimpleText, still uses the old style dialog box. But as updates are released, this is likely to change.

The Open or Save dialog box appears after you select the Open, Save, or Save As commands from the File menu of most applications. These same dialog boxes may occasionally be used for situations where you select or choose a file/folder, rather than open or save it—such as selecting a destination folder for files downloaded from the Web.

"Old" Style Open and Save dialog boxes

You are probably already familiar with this common element of the Mac OS. To briefly review, using these commands is a two-step process:

1. **Navigate to the desired location.** The folder name (which may also be a volume name or simply the Desktop) listed above the scroll box is the name of the folder whose contents are currently displayed in the scrolling list. Double-click any folder listed in the scroll box, and you shift to display the contents of that folder. That

folder's name then becomes the one listed above the scroll box. Conversely, select a folder's name from the pop-up menu that appears when you click the name of the current open folder, and you retreat back to the location you selected. Use these techniques to move to the desired location.

2. **Open or save.** You've arrived at your desired destination. If you are in an Open dialog box, click Open to select the desired file. If you are in a Save dialog box, enter a name for the file (after first clicking in the rectangle where a name is entered, if necessary) and click Save.

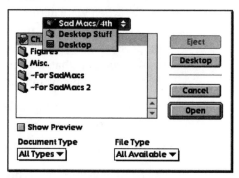

Remember, Open dialog boxes will generally only show those files that can be opened by the application in use. To see a complete list of files on your drive, you need to go to the Finder.

Figure 6-1 Navigating in an Open dialog box: Choose an item from the pop-up menu to go to the selected location.

Navigation Services

If you don't have an application that uses Navigation Services dialog boxes, you can still see what one looks like by accessing certain features in the Mac OS itself. For example, create a dummy file of any sort and make an alias of it (type Command-M). Now delete the dummy file. Finally, double-click the alias. From the message box that appears, click the Fix Alias button. This will lead to a Navigation Services dialog box.

What's "new" in the new Navigation Services -style Open and Save dialog boxes?
The first thing you are likely to notice about the new style of dialog box is that it has the platinum gray background instead of the pure white background. Second, the window is resizable. You can make it wider or longer, as you wish (via the "tab" in the lower right corner). Third, you can sort the listings by columns (Name or Date Modified) just by clicking on the column heading. Also, the list of files now uses disclosing triangles to list the contents of subfolders (as seen in Figure 6-2), rather than limiting you to seeing just one folder's contents at a time. Less obvious, but also useful, you can navigate to any folder via drag-and-drop: just drag the folder to the Navigation Services window and its contents are listed.

Finally, there are three new buttons in the dialog box, each used to access a pop-up menu. From left to right, in Figure 6-2, they represent:

Shortcuts, which let you instantly shift the listing to a different local volume or even another volume on a network. If you aren't yet connected to a network Server, you can select to connect via the pop-up menu's Connect to Server command.

Favorites, which lists all the alias items in the Favorites folder in your System Folder. This button also allows you to add or delete new items from the Favorites list.

Recent Items, which is a list of recently accessed items. This list is determined by the alias items in the Recent Items folder of the Navigation Services folder stored in the

Preferences folder of the System Folder. Every time you open a new file from an Open dialog box or from the Finder (although this does not seem to work as reliably), the contents of this folder should be updated. Older items get automatically deleted after a certain maximum is reached.

In order for the items in Recent Items to be updated as expected, Apple Menu Options must be enabled. The list should then duplicate the contents in the Apple Menu Options Recent Documents and Recent Applications folders.

How do you get to, and select, the Desktop? Navigation Services is missing the Desktop button found in the old style Open and Save dialog boxes. But you can still quickly navigate to the Desktop. One way is to select

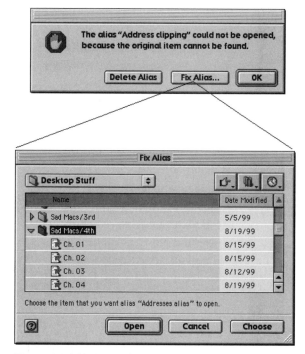

Figure 6-2 A Navigation Services dialog box, as seen after clicking Fix Alias.

Desktop from the pop-up window above the file listing. Another is to type Command-D or select Desktop from the Shortcuts pop-up menu.

But there is now an additional problem: how do you actually *select* the Desktop Folder? In the old-style dialog boxes, the Desktop Folder was included in the file/folder listing. This folder is not listed in Navigation Services. To see how this might be a problem, open the Internet control panel, click the Web tab and then the Select button. From here, navigate to the Desktop. Now try to select the Desktop as your destination. There is no immediately obvious way to do this! But it can be done: simply hold down the Option key and then select Desktop from the Shortcuts menu. Another way is to Shift-Click on the selected item, so that no item is selected; then click the Select button. However, these key combinations only let you select the Desktop Folder of the default drive. There is no direct way to select the Desktop Folder of other mounted volumes. There was no direct way in the old-style dialog boxes either.

Your mileage may vary Your Navigation Services dialog box may look or work a bit differently than those described above. Also, a third-party utility that you expect to modify the Open or Save dialog box may not work as expected. Here are some examples:

Hyphen at start of folder name If the name of a folder begins with a hyphen, you will be unable to select it from a Navigation Services dialog box. This "bug" may get fixed in an update to the OS. Otherwise, the only solution is not to use a hyphen as the first character of a folder's name (not a problem for most users).

Dialog box modified Certain programs, such as Default Folder and ACTION Files directly modify different types of Open/Save dialog boxes, including Navigation Services boxes. For example, Default Folder modifies the listings in each of the pop-up menus, as well as adding its own fourth Default Folder button.

Utility fails to work If you are using a version of a utility that works with Open/Save dialog boxes but has not yet been updated to work with Navigation Services, the utility will typically not

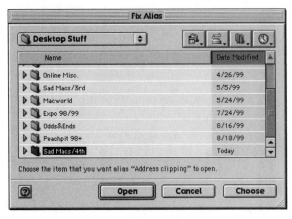

Figure 6-3 A Navigation Services dialog box with Default Folder enabled. The first icon in the row of four icons is for Default Folder.

work when a Navigation Services box is accessed. That is, it will be as if the utility has been disabled.

Utility conflicts Occasionally, a utility, even if updated for Navigation Services, will still conflict in some way with it, at least when accessed within specific applications. In these problem situations, you may be able to selectively turn off Navigation Services. For example, Default Folder has a Preferences option called "Turn off Navigation Services when possible."

Conversely, if you get an error message that says, "Navigation Services cannot be found" when selecting Open or Save, it may be that a utility, such as certain versions of ACTION Files, has turned off Navigation Services. Some applications will balk if this is done. One solution is to disable ACTION Files for that application via the ACTION Files Compatibility list.

Overlapping features Other utilities may have identically or similarly named features as those included in Navigations Services. For example, BeHierarchic maintains its own Recent Items and Recent Folders separately from Navigation Services. Default Folder has its own Default Folder Recent folder. This can admittedly get confusing, especially when some of these folders are being updated as you open new files and others are not. But such is life when you start adding these types of extensions.

Conflicts with other programs Some applications may not work well with Navigation Services (this should become less of an issue as applications get updated). Here are two examples:

Virex 5.9 (and its earlier versions) was known to cause a crash when selecting Open in a Navigation Services dialog box. A workaround was to deselect "Scan files when opened" and "Scan at download" from the Virex control panel. Other similar conflicts may still be lurking.

In the initial 4.0 version of **Adobe GoLive,** you could not name a new site from the Navigation Services window. A workaround is to turn off Navigation Services from GoLive's Preferences options.

For any other problem involving Navigation Services Delete Navigation Services Preferences files (in the Navigation Services folder of the Preferences folder). It may not help, but it's always worth a shot.

SEE: • **Fix-It #2 for more information on preferences files.**

Opening Files from the Finder

You can also open most files (applications or documents) directly from the Finder, either by double-clicking the file's icon or by single-clicking the icon and then selecting Open from the Finder's File menu.

With applications that support *drag-and-drop* (and most now do), you can drag the icon of a document over to an application icon. If the application can read that type of document file, the application icon will highlight. Release the mouse button, and the application needed to open the document launches followed by the document itself. This is an especially great way to open a document with an application other than the application that created the document (which is what would launch if you just double-clicked the document).

Finally, you can open a file by accessing its contextual menu (see Chapter 15 for more information on this feature). The contextual menu includes an Open command, among several other useful commands.

Using Save Versus Save As

When you are saving a document for the first time, the Save and Save As commands do the same thing. The difference emerges when you want to save changes to a previously saved document. In this case, the Save command simply overwrites the previous version and replaces it with the newly modified version. You get no dialog box or alert message when this happens. This also means that (unless you have a backup copy) the previous version is gone forever! It can't even be undeleted (as described in Chapter 2).

The Save As command prompts you to save the document as a separate file with a different name. As a result, you wind up with two documents: the original file and the modified file. After you create the modified document, if you have not closed it immediately, you are now working with the modified document—not the original one.

Be careful not to unintentionally overwrite a file with Save As. When you are using Save As, if you give the document the exact same name as the file you are currently using, you get an alert message asking whether you want to replace the original document. If you click Replace, you essentially wind up with what you would have gotten if you'd simply selected Save instead. If you expected to wind up with two separate documents, you will be sadly surprised.

If you get the Replace alert, even though you have changed the name of the file, it means that some other file with the same name is already at that location. Clicking Replace overwrites that file and replaces it with the current one. Before replacing *any* file, make sure you are not deleting a file you still want.

Finally, remember that until you save it, it ain't saved! Don't be nervous about making sweeping changes to your document and then not being able to return to the original version. Until you select Save, you can always get back

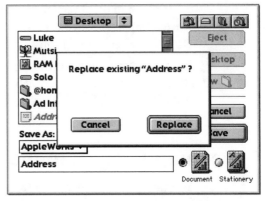

Figure 6-4 Clicking Replace deletes any existing file that has the same name as the file you are about to save.

to the original version simply by closing the document (click No when asked if you want to save it) and then reopening it. A Revert to Saved command, if your program has one, does the same thing. And, of course, if you save your sweeping changes to a new file using Save As (rather than Save), the original version remains available. About the only way to unintentionally save changes is if your program autosaves documents without warning at some regular interval. I would advise against having a program set up to do this.

Solve It! Problems with Files

When You Can't Locate a File

 ### Symptoms:

You are looking for a file that you are fairly certain should be on your disk, but it does not seem to exist. More specifically, one of the two following situations may sound familiar to you.

You Can't Find It in the Finder

You look for a file from the Finder, navigating through all the folders on the desktop, but you are unable to locate the file. Usually, these missing files are document files. You are less likely to lose track of an application, but it can happen.

You Can't Find It in an Open Dialog Box

You are using an Open dialog box from within an application and cannot get the document to appear in the list.

Causes:

Admittedly, a file may really be missing from your hard drive. But before you jump to this conclusion, calm down. Almost always, the file can be found somewhere on your hard drive—and is perfectly okay.

The most common cause of "lost" files is—to put it bluntly—you. Here are typical examples of how users misplace files (more details are given in the What To Do section that follows):

- You misremember what you named the file.

- The file was inadvertently saved to an unintended location.

- The file was moved rather than copied.

- You are looking for the file in the Open dialog box of the wrong application.

- The file was inadvertently deleted.

 What to Do:

Avoid Saving Files to Unintended Locations

When you first use Save or Save As to save a new file, the application you are using may select a default folder to place the file. This location may not be where you intended to save the file. If you do not notice this, and simply click the Save button, the file may wind up buried in a location where you might never think to look. In some cases, you may even save it to a floppy disk when you intended to save it to your hard drive (or vice versa).

When you are using Save for the first time (or whenever you are using Save As), check the pop-up menu above the list of files in the dialog box to see if the selected folder (and disk) location is the one that you want to use. Change it if it is incorrect. Then save the file.

Don't Inadvertently Move a File Instead of Copying It

Moving a file is when you drag a file to a different folder on the same disk. The file is transferred to a new location. There is still only one copy of the file on your disk.

Copying a file is when you save a file to a different disk. In this case, you wind up with two copies of the file: one on the original disk and another on the destination disk.

If you forget this distinction, you may expect to find a moved file still in its original location. Hint: You won't.

BY THE WAY ▶ Copying on the Same Disk

If you want to make a second copy of the same file in a different folder of the same disk, you can do it. Just hold down the Option key as you drag the file. To make a second copy of a file at exactly the same location as the original, use the Duplicate command (Command-D) from the Finder's File menu.

Look for a File from the Finder

Use the Finder's Find File Command If you cannot easily find a particular file, save yourself the headache of searching manually through every folder on your hard drive. Use Sherlock instead (see Chapter 2). Here's how to use the Mac OS 8.5/8.6 version:

1. Select Find from the Finder's File menu or Sherlock from the Apple Menu; they both take you to the same place. If not already selected, select the Find File tab.

2. Restrict the search range, if desired, by selecting a choice from the pop-up menu to the right of "Find items."

3. Type in the name of the file you are looking for (such as MacFixIt Notes) and click the Find button. If you are not sure of the exact name of the file, type in a portion of the name only. Maybe, for example, you can't recall whether you named the file MacFixIt Notes or MacFixIt Stuff. No problem—just type MacFixIt, or even MacF, and Find File locates every file that contains that segment of text.

4. A new window will appear called Items Found. It displays a complete list of all found files. Clicking on any of the files in the top of the window reveals the hierarchical location of the file in the lower pane of the window. Double-clicking any location or file takes you to the location or opens the file.

If none of these steps work, you may have, in fact, given the file a totally different name from what you recall. Perhaps you called it Web Site Info. The Find command can still assist you, however. All you need to do is remember some critical aspect of the file, such as what day you saved it. Let's assume that you know that you saved the file yesterday.

1. To find the file, return to the Sherlock window.

2. Select Date Modified from the first pop-up menu (the one that probably says Name when you first open the dialog box).

4. The current date should appear. Click on the day. Use the arrow buttons that now appear to change the date back to yesterday (or whatever date you want).

5. To find all files created on a single day (or created from that day forward), select *is* (or *is after*) from the middle pop-up menu.

6. Click Find.

7. Once again, the Items Found window will appear, this time with your file listed.

If you wish to reduce the number of entries in the Items Found window, you can combine criteria by selecting More Choices. For example, you can search for all files that contain the word MacFixIt and were created before January 1, 2000.

The overall design of Sherlock is a bit different in Sherlock 2 (introduced in Mac OS 9). The most significant difference (as briefly described in Chapter 2) is that you modify the criteria for the search in a separate More Search Options window, rather than in the Find File window itself.

In either version of Sherlock, you can also search the actual text content of many different types of documents by using Sherlock's Find by Content feature (also briefly covered in Chapter 2).

SEE: • **Chapter 15 for tips on troubleshooting Sherlock's Search Internet feature.**

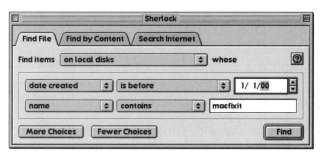

Figure 6-5 Sherlock can find all items created before January 1, 2000 that contain the word "MacFixIt."

Modify the Finder's Window Displays

Close and Reopen the Folder Window In some system software versions, the Finder does not properly update information about files listed in open windows until after the window is closed. A file can be temporarily listed with an older, incorrect modification date. In the most extreme cases, a file can appear to be missing altogether. Simply closing and reopening the window usually corrects this problem (an apparent bug).

BY THE WAY ▶ Wrong Modification Dates

If all of your recently saved documents have incorrect modification dates (usually much older dates than the correct ones), you may have a weak or dead battery in your Mac. The correct date is maintained in PRAM via the battery. Check the date in the Date and Time control panel. If it is incorrect, reset it. If the corrected setting is lost again after you reset it, try zapping the PRAM. If that doesn't work, you probably need to replace the battery. If the PRAM fix fails, replace the System file, which may be corrupted.

There is another date problem that affects, for the most part, Mac OS 8.1 and HFS Plus formatted drives, although there are reports of related problems in later versions of the OS. If you select "Set Daylight-Saving Time Automatically" from the Date and Time control panel, when the time comes to "spring ahead" or "fall back" one hour, the modification date for *every* file on your drive may be changed to the current day. This glitch can cause confusion for applications such as backup utilities that only back up files that have been modified since the last back up. Every file winds up getting backed up even if nothing has changed. The work-around is to turn off the Set Daylight-Saving Time feature and make the time adjustment manually.

SEE: • **Fix-It #4 for information on reinstalling system software.**
SEE: • **Fix-It #9 for information on zapping the Parameter RAM.**

Select Arrange by Name Sometimes, if you are using an icon view, a file is located in the extreme corners of a window, far from the other files, almost inaccessible by normal scrolling. To solve this quickly, Select Arrange by Name (or any other Arrange option of your preference), which will reorder all the icons, and eliminate the big gaps between them.

This command also helps uncover icons that may be hidden from view because they are underneath another icon.

Use View as List Selecting a list view can help locate a file lost in a crowded folder. For example, if you know that a file you want was just saved earlier in the day, select View as List. Then click the Date Modified button. All the newest files are brought to the top of the list. If, instead, you see the oldest files, simply click the pyramid icon in the upper right corner of the window, which reverses the sort order.

Look for a File from an Application's Open Dialog Box

In general, if you are having difficulty locating a file from an Open dialog box, go to the desktop (Finder) to look for it. Use Sherlock if necessary. Otherwise, if you are using the Open dialog box, consider the following reminders:

The Application Is Not Supposed to List the File An application's Open dialog box usually lists only those data files that can be opened by that application. So, for example, don't look for a database document from your word processor's Open dialog box. Make sure you correctly recall the application you used to create your document.

You Are Not Using the Application You Think You Are Using When you select Open from a File menu, ask yourself if you have the correct application. That is, make sure your intended application is the active application. There are several ways to do this:

- **Check the Application menu** The application menu is positioned at the far right of the menu bar. The active application is the one with its icon displayed in the menu bar itself. Additionally, the menu lists all open applications, with a check mark in front of the active one. If the checked application is not the one you want, select the one you want instead.

- **Check the Apple menu** Alternatively, the first line in the Apple menu almost always reads *About <the name of the active application>*. If the active application is not the one you want, you can use the Application menu to shift to the correct one.

Figure 6-6 The Application menu, with AppleWorks as the active application—indicated both by the check mark next to its name in the menu, and its icon and name in the menu bar.

- **Examine the menu bar menus** The menu bar at the top of your screen contains the menus of the active application. If you are familiar with an application's unique menus, you may recognize the active application just by scanning the names of these menus.

- **Click a window** If the application you want to use has any open windows, clicking any one of them makes it the active application.

TAKE NOTE ▶ Clutter Control

Many novice users get frustrated by what happens when they accidentally click in the desktop background while working within an application. Typically, this causes the active application to shift from whatever they were using to the Finder. Windows may disappear or move to a back layer. The user may have no idea what has happened, may not realize they are no longer in their word processing application, for example, and may have some difficulty figuring out how to return.

You can avoid this annoying scenario by selecting "Show Desktop when in background" from the General Controls panel. This feature complements the Hide Others and Hide <application name> commands in the Application menu. With this feature enabled, the Finder essentially vanishes whenever an application is active.

A related convenience feature is the window shade effect you can get by clicking the little square (with two horizontal lines through the middle) in the upper far right corner of a window. This causes everything but the window's title bar to disappear (as if the window had been rolled up like a window shade!). This can reduce screen clutter when you have several applications, each with their own windows, open at once. Click the box again and the window re-opens. If you want, you can access this same feature by simply double-clicking anywhere in the title bar. First select the option to collapse windows by double-clicking from the Options tab of the Appearance control panel.

Even when the window is collapsed, you can still add things to the folder by dragging items to the folder icon in the title bar.

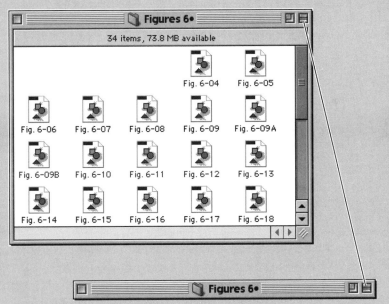

Figure 6-7 Before (top) and after (bottom) collapsing a window via the window shade feature.

Check the Open Dialog Box's Settings Many applications have options to selectively filter which files get displayed in its Open dialog box. If you select a translation filter that does not match your missing file, the file will not be listed. To maximize your chances of a successful file search, make sure the most general option for reading files (such as *All Available*) is selected. If the file is at all readable by the current application, it is now listed.

Check for Unusual File Names Files with unconventional names may get sorted in unpredictable ways. For example, if a blank space precedes the name of the file, an application's sort key may cause it to sort alphabetically to the top of the list in an Open dialog box. If you look for the file based on where it should be, given the first real letter of its name (a file named Zoo Animals should appear at the bottom of the list), you will not find the file.

The solution is to check the entire file list when a file does not appear in its expected location.

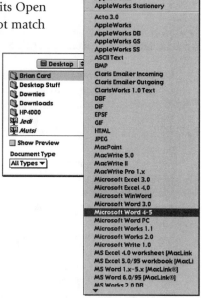

Figure 6-8 A listing of some of the format translators available with AppleWorks—only the files that match the selected format are displayed in the Open dialog box.

BY THE WAY ▶ Finding an Original File of an Alias or a Document's Creating Application

Suppose you want to locate the original file for an alias file. It's easy enough to do. Use contextual menus (a feature described more in Chapter 15): hold down the Control key and click on the alias file. A pop-up menu will appear. One of the items on the menu will be "Show Original." Select it and the Mac opens the folder that contains the original file.

If the link between your alias and original files appears to be "broken," check out "Cannot Open a File from Its Alias" later in this chapter.

In a similar vein, a third-party utility called Reveal Creator adds a contextual menu item that, when selected, will locate the creating application of any document.

Figure 6-9 An example of a contextual menu for an alias. Use the Show Original command (highlighted) to locate the original file of the alias. The Reveal Creator command (second from bottom) is also useful; for documents, select this command to locate the creating application of the original file.

Check the Desktop "Folder" Normally, all files on a disk are listed as being "inside" that disk. Thus, if you click the Desktop button in an Open dialog box, you see the names of all currently mounted disks(or volumes). Double-clicking a disk name results in a list of all the folders and files at the top level of the disk. These are the same items you would see from the Finder, in the window that would open if you double-clicked the disk icon.

However, a file that is located directly on the desktop—that is, not in any window but directly on the background area where the Trash and disk icons are found—is not listed as being inside the disk. This file is listed at the desktop level alongside the names of the mounted disks. All the items on the desktop appear in this one list, regardless of where they reside originally. The point is, you may search in vain for a file by restricting your search to those files and folders inside the disk window. Instead, the file may be relaxing quietly at the desktop level.

TECHNICALLY SPEAKING ▶ The Desktop Folder

Files on the desktop are actually stored in a special invisible folder called the Desktop Folder. Each disk has its own Desktop Folder. The Open dialog box of most applications does not indicate the presence of these folders. Instead, Desktop Folder files are just listed as if they are not in any folder. However, if the Open dialog box does show a Desktop Folder, you probably have to look there for files that would normally be listed directly at the desktop level. Otherwise, simply selecting the Desktop level from the pop-up menu will take you to the desktop. However, if you have multiple volumes mounted on the desktop, this menu will show you the items in *all* the Desktop Folders consolidated in one list.

SEE: • Chapter 8 for more information on invisible files, including the Desktop file and Desktop Folder.

If the File Was Inadvertently Deleted

If, after trying all of the preceding suggestions, you still cannot find your file, it is time to consider that it is really missing. One way this might happen is if you inadvertently deleted the file. Maybe you discarded a folder that contained the file you want, not realizing that the file was inside it. Whatever the reason, the file is now gone. Here's what you can do about it.

Wait! First Make Sure You Really Deleted the File Remember, the Trash is never emptied until you specifically select the Empty Trash command from the Finder's Special menu. Even if you restart the Macintosh, the items in the Trash remain and the Trash can icon continues to bulge. If you haven't yet emptied the Trash, just double-click the Trash icon. A window opens up showing your discarded items. Drag them out of the Trash, and you are back in business.

Unplug your Mac If you have just accidentally deleted a file, you can probably get it back by *immediately* turning off the power on your Mac. Don't select Restart or Shut Down; don't even trust a reset. Pull the plug on the Mac from the wall outlet. Then plug it back in and restart. Chances are your file will be back. I don't recommend this as a regular procedure, but it can be useful in an emergency.

Undelete the File If you really have deleted the file, don't despair yet. All is not lost. You may yet be able to recover the file. This is because when you delete a file, the Macintosh does not erase the data immediately. It simply frees up the space so that it can be over-written with new data as needed. If you have only recently deleted the file, and you have not added too many new files since, the file may still be intact on your disk.

Utilities such as Norton Utilities and MacMedic can recover recently deleted files. As described in Chapter 2, some of these utilities work best if you have previously installed special extensions that the utility uses to keep track of what you have deleted (such as FileSaver for Norton Utilities).

SEE: • **Chapter 2 for more information on installing and using these control panels.**

If you are using Norton Utilities:

1. Run Norton Utilities and select the UnErase option (turn File Sharing off if request-ed to do so).

2. From the next dialog box that appears, select the disk(s) that you believe may con-tain the deleted file(s). Then click the Quick Search button. A list of files appears. If desired, click the View Contents button to view the contents of a selected file. For text files, this feature can help you figure out whether a file is truly the one you want to recover.

3. Assuming that the FileSaver control panel was installed prior to when you deleted the file(s) you want to recover, the desired file(s) should be listed. Select the file(s) (using shift-click to select more than one file) and then click the Recover button. Files are saved to the location you specify.

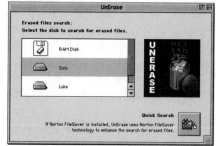

4. If FileSaver was not installed in time, click the Customized Search button in the UnErase window. From the dialog box that appears, select the desired option. Catalog Search gives you the best chance of recovering the file you want. Check the Norton Utilities documentation for details on when and how to use the remaining options. Then click Search. This will create a new list of recoverable files.

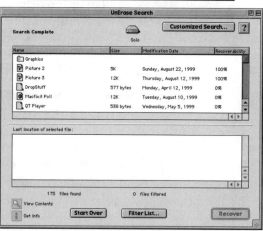

   SEE: • **Fix-It #11 for more information on using UnErase.**

Figure 6-10 Norton Utilities' initial UnErase window (top) and the window that appears after selecting QuickSearch (bottom).

Two important caveats to bear in mind when you are trying to undelete files are that some files may be only *partially recoverable* and that recovered files may appear in a *generic* file format.

- **Some files may be only partially recoverable** Eventually, an erased file is written over by a newly created file. The erased file is then gone forever. In some cases, only part of an erased file may have been overwritten. These files may still be partially recoverable, something that is mainly useful only for text files. Your undelete utility typically lists the recoverability (in percentage terms) of each deleted file. If you have problems opening a partially recovered file, refer to "When You Can't Open a Document" later in this chapter.

- **Recovered files may not open properly** When you double-click a recovered document file, even if it appears to be 100% recovered, launching the file may result in an error message that says the creating application could not be found. Usually, you can still open the document if you select it from within the application using its Open dialog box. If you then save the document to a new name using Save As, the new document should then behave normally.

SEE: • **"When You Can't Open a Document" later in this chapter for more on problems opening files.**
      • **Chapter 8, which covers file types and creators for more technical information.**

If None of the Preceding Steps Succeeds in Locating the File

The File May Be Missing Because of Problems with the Disk Itself This is the last, and most unhappy, possibility. It often means that you have problems that go beyond the immediate loss of one file. Sometimes these problems are repairable, usually requiring a utility such as Norton Utilities or DiskWarrior.

SEE: • **"Files Missing from the Desktop" in Chapter 5.**
      • **Fix-Its #10 and #11 for information on fixing damaged disks.**

Otherwise, the File Is Probably Lost for Good It's time to give up. I hope the file wasn't critical. If it was critical, I hope you have a backup copy.

When You Can't Launch an Application or Control Panel

 Symptoms:

You try to open an application or control panel (or desk accessory) from the Finder, usually by double-clicking its icon, but the application does not open. Usually, an error message appears that indicates why the file did not launch. Often, it also offers advice on how to solve the problem. However, in may cases, an operation may simply fail to work, and no error message will appear (especially if you have several applications open).

In the worst cases, a system error may occur. In this case, refer to Chapter 4, which covers system errors and what to do about them.

Causes:

Insufficient Memory to Launch an Application

The most common reason an application does not open is because there is less available RAM (memory) than the application requires. Whether you have as little as 32MB of memory or as much as 256MB, you can still exceed the limits of your machine. Each time you open an application, you occupy some of that RAM memory. As you leave more and more applications open at the same time, you will eventually have too little memory left to open yet another application.

Actually, some applications require so much RAM that they may not open on your machine even if no other applications are open (other than the Finder, which stays open at all times).

In any of these cases, you will probably get an error message informing you that the problem is due to insufficient memory.

Sometimes, an application starts to open but then quits in midstream, accompanied by a message that says that the program *unexpectedly quit* (a problem described in more detail in Chapter 4). This is also usually a memory-related problem.

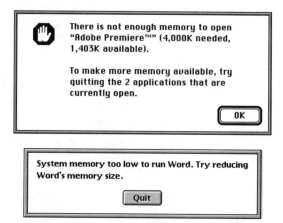

Figure 6-11 Memory-related error messages that appear when trying to launch Adobe Premiere (top) or Word (bottom) with less than the necessary amount of memory available.

Miscellaneous Other Causes

Explanations for each of the following causes is given in the What to Do section below.

- A control panel setting is incompatible with the application.

- You cannot open a file from a broken alias.

- You cannot open a file because it is in a compressed or disk image format.

- You cannot open a file because you have the "wrong" Macintosh.

- Too many files are currently open.

- Damaged fonts can prevent certain files from opening.

- You cannot open damaged files.

⟨image⟩ What to Do:

Insufficient Memory or Unexpected Quit

If an error message offers advice on what to do to remedy this problem, generally follow its advice. Otherwise, try each of the following troubleshooting steps, as needed:

- Quit currently open applications, to free up more memory. Then try to launch the application again.

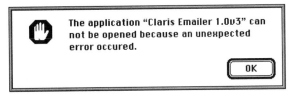

- Restart the Macintosh and try again to re-launch the application.

Figure 6-12 Claris Emailer refused to re-launch after an unexpected quit, showing this error message, until the Mac was restarted.

  Sometimes, due to a memory leak (as described in Fix-It #5), restarting will be required to free up enough memory to get the program to launch. Also, sometimes after an unexpected quit or a forced quit (as described in Chapter 4), the application will refuse to re-launch until after you restart. If you try to re-launch before restarting, you will get another unexpected quit or similar error message.

- Restart the Macintosh with all unneeded extensions/control panels (startup extensions) disabled. This reduces the amount of memory allocated to the system software, freeing up more memory for your application. This is a work around solution (since it means that you no longer have the benefit of the disabled extensions/control panels), but it at least may allow you to launch the problem application. The simplest approach here is to disable all startup extensions by holding the Shift key down at startup. If you need a particular startup extension to remain enabled while using the application in question, you will instead need to selectively disable startup extensions.

  On the other hand, several Mac OS extensions are nearly essential these days. You might instead use Extensions Manager or Conflict Catcher to restart with Mac OS Base or Mac OS All Extension sets enabled.

  SEE: • **Fix-It #3 for information on disabling extensions.**

- You may have to decrease the problem application's Preferred memory size. This is done from the application's Get Info window. If none of the previous suggestions work, there are several other similar memory-related solutions you can try.

  SEE: • **Chapter 2 for information on the Get Info window.**
  • **Fix-It #5 for information on memory management problems.**

Incompatible Control Panel Settings

One common example of an incompatible control panel setting is a program that requires a color depth setting different from your current setting (for example, the application needs 256 colors and you are using 16 grays). Usually, you get an error message that explains this problem when you try to launch the application.

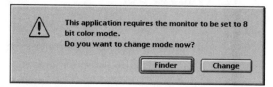

Figure 6-13 the game Crystal Caliburn gives you this message when running in more than 256 colors.

Another common problem, especially with games, is a program that will not run properly with virtual memory (or RAM Doubler) enabled.

For color depth problems, assuming that you have the appropriate hardware to adjust the color depth as needed, the obvious solution is to change the setting by using the Monitors control panel. Most game programs these days make the adjustment for you (if you say OK) when you launch the game.

For Memory control panel problems (or similar sorts of problems with any other control panel), you probably have to turn the relevant control panel options off.

SEE: • Chapter 10 for information on displaying color.
  • Fix-It #1 for descriptions of hardware incompatibilities.
  • Fix-It #4 for information on system software problems.
  • Fix-It #5 for information on memory problems.

You Cannot Open a File from Its Alias

Occasionally, if you double-click an alias file, the original file does not launch. Instead, you get a message that says the "Alias could not be opened because the original could not be found." Usually, this is because the original file has been deleted. Normally, just renaming an original file should not break the link to an alias, but this may happen sometimes. You also cannot open a file from its alias if the original file is on a disk that is currently not mounted, such as a CD-ROM disk or a shared disk (accessed via file sharing). To access these files, you have to remount the needed disk. Then try the alias again.

If the original file is on a currently mounted volume but the alias still does not work, you have a *broken link*. There are various "bugs" that may cause a broken link. The solution is to re-establish the link. Do this by selecting "Fix Alias" from the message box (see Figure 6-14) and then navigating to the original file's location. Finally, highlight the name of the original file and click Choose.

Otherwise, if the alias belongs to a file you no longer have, you can choose to "Delete Alias."

Figure 6-14 This message box appears if you try to open a file from its alias, but the original file is missing or cannot be located.

You Cannot Open File Because It Is in a Compressed, Encoded, or Disk Image Format

This problem is most likely to occur as a result of downloading files from the Internet. These files are often stored in a compressed format. They need to be decompressed before they can be opened. Unless they are stored as self-extracting files, you need special utilities to decompress them. One popular freeware utility of this sort is called *StuffIt Expander*.

To compress a file, use a companion program to Expander called DropStuff, or get the commercial StuffIt Deluxe application. In either case, the current 5.x versions of these applications compress files in a format that cannot be expanded by the older 4.x versions of Expander. If you still use Expander 4.x and you get a message that a file cannot be expanded, get a copy of Expander 5.x and try again.

There are many different types of compression and encoding formats. Each type typically appends its own suffix to the name of the file. Thus you may see files with names such as file.sit or file.bin or file.hqx. StuffIt Expander is able to expand/decode the most common formats. For the remaining types, you will need to install DropStuff as well. Go to Expander's Preferences window and select the Internet Config icon for a list of the types of files Expander can process by itself and with DropStuff.

When StuffIt 5.x first came out, it had numerous problems. I hope that these problems have all been fixed by the time you read this, so I will not give you the gory details here. However, if you are having problems with Expander, check in at MacFixIt (http://www.macfixit.com) for the latest advice.

Finally, Apple uses a disk image format for most of its downloaded software (these files have a suffix of .img; a self-expanding version as a suffix of .smi). Apple's Disk Copy utility is most often used to mount these img files. Expander should also be able to do this, but I have found it to be less reliable. When you open these disk image files, a disk icon appears on your desktop much as if you had mounted a floppy disk or Zip disk.

SEE: • Chapter 13 for more information on problems using downloaded files.
      • Fix-It #4 for more information on disk images and system software.

You Cannot Open a File Because You Have the "Wrong" Macintosh or System Software

This is becoming an increasingly common problem, particularly for control panels and other files from Apple system software. Many of these control panels are designed to work only with certain models of Macintosh (such as just on PowerBooks or just on Power Macs) or with other optional hardware. Some only work with certain versions of the system software (such as Mac OS 8.5 or later) or with certain other extensions installed (such as the Monitors & Sound control panel requiring the SystemAV extension). Also, Apple's Installer may mistakenly

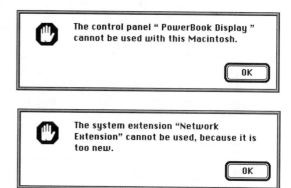

Figure 6-15 Examples of messages that may appear when you try to open a control panel that does not work with your Macintosh model and/or your version of the system software.

install files on a Mac even though they do not work with that model. In any of these cases, when you try to open the file, instead of it opening, you will get a message saying that the file cannot be used (sometimes including an explanation as to why).

However, before giving up, make sure that the control panel is in the Control Panels folder in the System Folder, restart and try again. Sometimes, this type of message appears when you try to open a control panel that was not loaded at startup (such as one that you added since the last time you started up). After restarting, the problems go away.

You can have similar problems with applications. That is, versions of an application that are written specifically for a Power Mac will not run on older Macintoshes (see Fix-It #15) or on older versions of the Mac OS.

TECHNICALLY SPEAKING ▶ You Cannot Open a Control Panel Because NO INITS Bit is Checked

On one occasion, upon trying to open a control panel, I got a message that said the control panel would not open because it had not been loaded at startup. This typically means that the control panel had been disabled via an extension management utility (as described in Fix-It #3). However, in this odd case, I knew it had not been disabled. Even odder, when I checked my extension manager's listing, the control panel was not there anymore! Yet, when I looked in the Finder, the control panel file itself was clearly in the Control Panel folder within the System Folder. What was going on?

What had happened was that a conflict between two other extensions had caused an unusual result: the NO INITS bit on several of my control panels was incorrectly checked. This meant that the Macintosh and my extension manager no longer considered these files as files to be loaded at startup (remember "INIT" is the older, more technical name for startup extensions).

After determining and eliminating the conflicting extensions, I used a utility called Snitch to uncheck the bit. After that, everything worked fine.

SEE: • Chapter 8 for more information on the NO INITS bit and Get More Info.

Too Many Files Are Currently Open

The current limit for Mac OS 8.x is 348 open files. In Mac OS 9, HFS Plus formatted drives have a much greater upper limit (8,169 open files); this should be enough to eliminate any concern about too many open files.

For those still using Mac OS 8.x, being able to open 348 files may seem like more than enough, but in actuality this number is often not sufficient. For one thing, as you add more RAM to your Mac, you can keep open more files at once, pushing you toward the 348-file limit. Second, with virtual memory activated, many files get counted twice. Third, each font file and many of the invisible files working in the background count as open files. Thus, the files (open applications and documents) that you knowingly opened usually represent just a small fraction of the actual total number of open files.

How can you tell how many files are open at any point? Alsoft makes a freeware Control Strip Module called "Open Files Count" that will tell you. Similarly, an Alsoft utility called "List Open Files" tells you the name of each open file, so you can see what's behind the usually surprisingly large number.

If you do reach the Open Files limit when working with your Mac, you will typically get an error message that reads: "The command cannot be completed, because too many files are open." However, just as often you may get any variety of odd messages, including a message informing you that the file you are trying to open cannot be found.

If you find yourself bumping against this limit often, eliminating

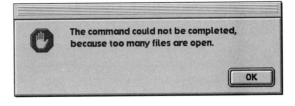

Figure 6-16 Open Files Count shows the number of files currently open.

unneeded fonts can be a good first step toward extending the limit. Temporarily disabling virtual memory may help if this file limit problem occurs only occasionally (or keep virtual memory off altogether if you don't need it).

In an invisible area of your disk called the *boot blocks* (which is described more in Chapters 5 and 8), a number called MaxFiles is typically listed as 10. This is supposedly 1/4 of the maximum number of open files allowed (thus, the maximum would be 40). This number is also technically referred to as the maximum number of File Control Blocks (or FCBs). It is technically possible to increase this number (for example, a utility called "Up Your FCBs" could do it). However, I would not bother with this number anymore. The FCB number is apparently only relevant to System 7 or earlier; it does not play a role in Mac OS 8.0 or later.

SEE ALSO: • **"By the Way: Word Work Files Hassles," in Chapter 4, for another example of a problem linked to too many files open.**

You Cannot Open an Application Because of Duplicate Copies on a Network

Some programs check over a network to see if other copies of the program with the same serial number are running. If there are, the program will not launch. I am not suggesting that you become a software pirate and try to defeat this copy protection. However, if you have a legitimate reason to do so, you can usually launch these programs simply by pulling the network plug out of the back of your Mac before you try to launch the program.

On a related note, in some cases if you use a Force Quit to quit one of these programs, the program may not launch again (even if you are not connected to the network) because it mistakenly detects itself as still running. Usually, turning off AppleTalk will serve as a workaround here. Otherwise, you will have to restart. In some cases, even turning AppleTalk off may not work. In this case, your only option is to actually detach the network cable from your Mac.

You Cannot Open Damaged Files

If a file is damaged, there may be no error message when you try to open it. It may just fail to open. Or you may see an (often cryptic) error message. Or a system error may occur. If you suspect a damaged file:

- Try to open it again, as always, just in case it opens fine the second time.

- Replace the application, its preferences file, and (if necessary) any of its accessory files. There is probably software damage, in which case this is the best and easiest solution.

  SEE: • **Fix-It #2 for information on preferences files.**

- An application may not open because of a damaged font file, rather than a problem with the application itself.

  SEE: • **Chapter 9 for more information on locating and replacing damaged font files.**

- For control panels, if you get a message that the file cannot be opened or used, it may simply mean that the control panel did not properly load at startup (even if the message offers a different explanation). To check, make sure the control panel is in its correct folder (that is, it is not disabled) and that you did not start with extensions off. Then restart normally. The control panel will probably open now. Otherwise, the message's explanation for why you cannot open the file is probably correct.

  If you use an extensions manager (see Fix-It #3), make sure it is not set to disable the control panel at startup.

- If you are having trouble opening the Scrapbook, you probably have a corrupted Scrapbook File (stored in your System Folder) or a problem with the Scrapbook desk accessory itself. If the File is corrupted, you may or may not be able to recover data from it (using a program such as CanOpener). However, if you just remove the Scrapbook File from the System Folder, you will at least be able to use the Scrapbook again (albeit with an empty Scrapbook File). If you don't need anything inside the damaged Scrapbook File, just delete it.

However, if you get a message such as, "Sorry, this disk is full or the system is out of memory," you may really have a memory problem. In this case, you can actually increase the Scrapbook's Memory allocation via its Get Info window.

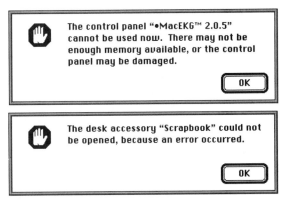

- If you get an error message that says something like, "Unable to read from disk," this suggests possible media damage, typically in the area of the file you are trying to open. Before replacing the

Figure 6-17 Top: this message indicates trouble while opening a control panel that may or may not be damaged. Bottom: this message often implies damage to the Scrapbook file (or sometimes the Scrapbook program itself).

damaged file from your backups, you should first check for and repair any media damage, which usually requires reformatting the disk.

- Otherwise, check for more general damage (such as to system software) that may be causing problems beyond the file in question.

SEE: • **Fix-Its #10 and #11 for tips on fixing damaged files and media damage.**
• **Fix-It #13 for information on reformatting disks.**

TECHNICALLY SPEAKING ▶ A Few Words About Sound And Sound Files

- **Sound file formats** Sounds can exist as independent files on the desktop, much like font files. If you double-click a sound file, the Macintosh will play the sound. If you have sound files that do not work this way, it is probably because these files are not in the standard format. Unfortunately, because Apple failed to provide any standard format prior to System 7, there are a variety of different formats that your sound file could be. Fortunately, there are several shareware utilities that can easily convert most sound formats to the Mac OS standard format. The one that I use most often is called Sound Extractor. SoundApp is another excellent choice.

    These utilities can also be used to change a standard Apple sound file back to other formats (such as AIFF, WAV, or AU) that are commonly needed to use sounds on the World Wide Web. Apple's SimpleSound utility, described shortly, may help out here as well.

    SEE: • **Chapter 13 for more information on the World Wide Web.**

- **Damaged sound files** If you still cannot get a sound file to play when you double-click it, the file may be damaged. In this case, a utility such as CanOpener may be able to recover the sound. Also, for those of you familiar with the basics of using Apple's ResEdit, try to open the sound resource using ResEdit. If the file is damaged, ResEdit will identify the damage and offer to try to fix it for you. If it succeeds, you should then extract the sound resource to a new file.

    SEE: • **Fix-It #11 for general information on fixing damaged files.**

(continues on next page)

TECHNICALLY SPEAKING ▶ A Few Words About Sound And Sound Files
(continued)

- **Sound control panel and sound volume** To adjust Sound parameters, typically you use the Monitors & Sound control panel in Mac OS 8.x. In Mac OS 9.x, Apple has reverted to having separate Sound and Monitor controls panels.

  Giving specific advice here can be tricky, as the rules for adjusting sound volume vary with each update to these control panels. There are also differences that depend on what Mac you are using and what speaker set-up you have. However, in brief, using the Mac OS 9 Sound control panel, you can set the volume of the Mac's Alert Sounds (from the slider in the Alert Sounds section) as well as the overall volume of the Mac's sound (by using the Volume slider in the Output panel, with Built-in selected). You can also separately adjust the sound going to external devices (such as external speakers and headphones) via the multiple sliders in the Speaker Setup panel. If you have external speakers, they may also include their own volume adjustment separate from the Mac altogether. Finally, applications such as Apple's DVD Player and CD Player have separate volume settings that affect sound from DVD/CDs.

  As soon becomes obvious when you begin to fiddle with these controls, the effects of the settings interact. For example, turning up the volume of Alert Sounds may still produce a very low sound if the other sound settings are turned way down. To keep things simple, you may find that you can comfortably keep the volume setting all the way up on all but one of the controls and then regulate volume for everything from the remaining control (such as the Sound control panel's Output slider). Conveniently, the Sound Control Strip module adjusts this Output sound level, so you do not need to go to the control panel to make on-the-fly adjustments.

  If you get no sound at all, make sure you have not inadvertently selected the Mute button in the Sound control panel.

  For more details specific to your Mac and OS version, check the Mac Help information on your drive.

- **Alert sounds** The alert sound is what you hear when the Mac wants your attention for some reason (typically because some error has occurred). You can select from among several different alert sounds. These sounds are stored within the System file but are selected from the Alert panel of the Sound control panel. If you wish to add a new alert sound to the list, you can do so by dragging any compatible sound file to the System Folder icon (or by double-clicking the System file icon and dragging the sound file into the open window). Alternatively, if you wish to record a sound for a new Alert sound, click the Add button in Alerts. If you have a microphone attached and have selected the microphone as the Input Source, you will be able to record your own sound.

  There are several third-party utilities (such as SoundMaster) that can allow you to access sounds from anywhere on your disk and use them as alert sounds. In addition, these utilities allow you to attach these sounds to almost any sort of event (such as Empty Trash or Eject Disk). There is also a way to access sound files that are not in the System file without requiring any specialized software: Change the file's type and creator to match that of a font suitcase. Next, simply place the sound file in the Fonts folder and the System will correctly access it as a sound, listing it as a potential alert sound.

  SEE: • Chapter 8, "Add Alert Sounds Without Installing Them in the System File."

- **Problems retaining sound volume setting** Does your Sound volume setting revert to some default value after a shut down instead of being saved? There are a number of possible causes and cures for this annoying problem (zapping the PRAM, for example, reinstalling the system software, or even repairing hardware may be needed). However, the very first remedy to try is wonderfully simple: delete the Sound Preferences file in your Preferences folder (ideally, you do this after restarting with extensions off). Most of the time, this step will solve your problem. If not, you can try a shareware extension called Unmute-It.

If you use Energy Saver, some muting problems can be solved by making sure that the Notification Preferences option, "Mute sounds while the computer is asleep" is unchecked.

Also, be aware that if you have a cable plugged into the sound-out port (the one with the speaker icon over it), sound will be directed through that port rather than to the built-in speakers. If there are no speakers connected to the cable, you will get no sound at all.

There is a sound bug in the Mac OS 8.6 (and possibly later versions of the OS) that occurs if you halt the startup process (by opening Conflict Catcher, for example) and then let the startup complete. To your dismay, I'm sure, you will have no sound for that session. Any attempted sound will simply result in the menu bar flashing, which is normally how the Mac indicates that the sound level is set to Mute. Restarting again will restore the sound.

- **Recording sounds with SimpleSound** SimpleSound is a utility included with the Mac OS. It can create two types of sound files:

    1. SimpleSound documents, which are standard AIFF files that can be used by most applications that can edit sounds (such as SoundEdit) and are also usable on the Web. To create a SimpleSound document, select New from SimpleSound's File menu.

    2. "System" sounds, which are files that play directly when you double-click them from the Finder. To create these files, click the Add button from SimpleSound's Alert Sounds window. The newly recorded sound file will be stored in the System file initially (where it can be used as an alert sound), but you can drag it out from there, for other uses, if you wish. Just double-click the System file suitcase to see the sound files within. These are the same types of sounds created by the Sound control panel.

- **PlainTalk Speech** Your Mac has the ability to speak Alert messages or speak any selected text in applications, such as SimpleText, that include a Sound menu. The Mac also has the limited ability to recognize commands spoken into a microphone (such as the word "Open") and respond as if you had input the command via the mouse or keyboard. What the Mac can understand is determined by a collection of Speakable Items scripts found in the Speakable Items folder of the Apple menu. You turn these features on or off via the Speech control panel. The generic name for the software is PlainTalk. This software may be installed as part of the Mac OS installation, or you may need to install it separately. PlainTalk also works best with a microphone that is "PlainTalk compatible."

    However, because of the various problems and limitations of this software, Apple appears to be abandoning it. Instead, Apple is moving towards informally adopting the speech technology of third parties, such as IBM's ViaVoice.

Figure 6-18 (Left) The Alert Sounds window from the SimpleSound utility.
(Right) Sound files used for Alert sounds, as located in the System file suitcase.

When You Can't Open a Document

 Symptoms:

You attempt to open a data document, either directly from the Finder (usually by double-clicking the file's icon) or from within an application (using the Open dialog box). In either case, the result is the same: the file refuses to open. Typically, you get an error message indicating the cause of the problem. In the worst case, a system error may occur.

Alternatively, the file may open, but only part of the file's contents remain or the file displays random gibberish rather than the correct data. (More minor display problems, such as incorrect use of fonts or colors, are not covered here. For solutions to these problems, refer to Chapters 9 and 10.)

 Causes:

- The Macintosh cannot find the application needed to open the document (there are several possible reasons for this, as detailed in the following What to Do section).

- The file is in PC/DOS format and/or on a PC/DOS formatted disk.

- The available memory is insufficient.

- The file is not intended to be directly opened (extensions are an example of this type of file).

- The document (or its application) is damaged.

- Many of the same reasons that prevent you from launching an application may prevent you from opening a document file (see the previous section).

 What to Do:

If a Document's Application Can't Be Found by the Finder

You double-click a document file from the Finder, but instead of the file opening, you get an error message that says that the file could not be opened because the application program that created it could not be found.

What exactly is going on here? What's happening is this: the Finder "knows" to which application a document belongs (see Chapter 8 for an explanation). For example, it knows that Excel documents belong to the Excel application. When you try to open an Excel document, the Finder searches the disk until it locates the Excel application. It then launches the application followed by the document. However, if the Finder cannot locate the creating

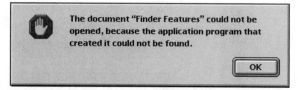

Figure 6-19 The "application could not be found" error message.

application, nothing opens. Instead, you get the error message just described. What you do about the error message depends on exactly why the Macintosh could not find the needed application. There are several possibilities, as outlined below.

The Creating Application Has Been Deleted or Is Not Currently Accessible You create a document file using a particular application. For whatever reason, you later delete that application from your startup disk. Or perhaps you have received a document from a colleague that was created by an application that is not on your hard drive. When you try to launch this document, you probably get the *application could not be found* error message.

The most obvious solution to this problem is to install the needed application on to your hard drive. If you are uncertain about which application is needed, try opening the file from within any application you have that is likely to be of the same category (use a word processor for text files of unknown origin,

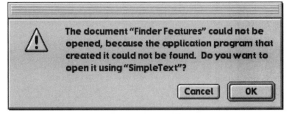

Figure 6-20 Similar to the message in Figure 6-19, this message appears if the file cannot be opened by its creating application (usually because it is not on your disk). However, it can be opened with SimpleText.

for example). You may get lucky and hit the right application (or at least find one that can successfully import the file). Also, the Kind line in the file's Get Info window (see Chapter 2) may indicate the name of the document's creating application.

Finally, you should be aware of several utilities that can assist you in your efforts to open a document:

- **Use SimpleText** When you try to open certain text or graphics files (plain TEXT or PICT documents) that would normally lead to the *application could not be found* error message, you may instead be given the option to open the file in SimpleText (which comes with Apple's system software). At least you will be allowed to view the contents of the file.

    SEE: • Chapter 8 for more information on the types of files (TEXT and PICT) that can be opened this way.

- **Use File Exchange** Open the File Exchange control panel and click the "File Translation" tab. Here you will see two columns: the left one lists the "File Type" while the right one lists the "Application (translator)." Basically, this means that any time you double-click a document that matches one of the file types in the list, it will try to open using the application listed next to it. Thus, if you do not have Application A, but you know that Application B can open documents created by Application A, you can use File Exchange so that Application A documents automatically launch Application B. To set up a new pair, simply click the Add button. You will also typically be given a chance to add a new document-application link directly from the Finder any time you try to open a document where its creating application cannot be found.

File Exchange settings will be used in preference to other default choices. If you no longer wish to continue a particular link, simply select that line from the File Exchange list and click the Remove button. To turn off all translations, uncheck "Translate documents automatically."

If you want even greater flexibility in translations (including the ability to convert documents of one application into a form that can be opened by another application, even though the application itself does not directly support this), you want DataViz's MacLinkPlus.

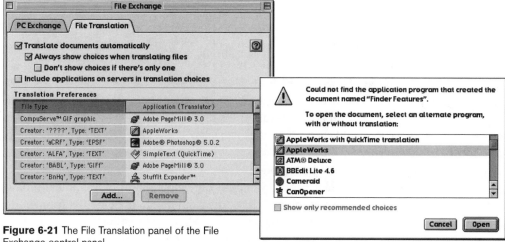

Figure 6-21 The File Translation panel of the File Exchange control panel.

Figure 6-22 This window will appear when you try to open the same file as in Figure 6-20, but now with File Exchange enabled.

- **Other utilities to the rescue** Utilities such as GraphicConverter, and similar shareware alternatives, can open graphics files of almost any format. These can also be used to convert files from one graphic format to another. You can also try to open "unopenable" graphics files with Can Opener.

  SEE: • **Chapter 10 for more information on different graphics formats.**

BY THE WAY ▶ Create Documents That Anyone Can Open

If you plan to give a document to other users who may not have your creating application, you can help them out by saving the document in a way that lets them open the document, no matter what application you used to create it. You need to have special software that can create this document and users of your document need to have the free Reader application to open it. The most popular example of this type of software is Adobe Acrobat and Acrobat Reader. There are also certain programs that can create self-opening documents (such as DOCMaker) that do not even require a reader.

The Creating Application Has Been Replaced with an Upgraded Version When a new version of an application is released, the format of its document files may be changed. Even so, the new version should retain its ability to read files created by its earlier versions by opening the files and converting them to the new format.

However, sometimes this does not work. For example, suppose you are using BusyWorks version 3.0, but you have a file created by BusyWorks 2.0. The file should open in BusyWorks 3.0 without a problem. But in this case, when you try to open the 2.0 document file from the Finder, you get the *application could not be found* error message.

- **Use the Open command** The key here is to try *not* to open the file from the Finder. Open the creating application first, then try to open the document using the application's Open command. If the program is at all capable of reading its older version's files, this solution should work.

- **Check for special commands** Alternatively, you may find that the application itself has a special command for opening files of earlier versions. There may even be a separate special converter utility needed to convert old versions of files to the new version's format. Check the manual for any mention of special commands.

- **Import to another application** You can also try the importing alternative described earlier in this chapter. That is, try to open the file from the Open dialog box of another application that has a translator capability for BusyWorks 2.0.

- **Use the older version** Finally, if all else fails, you can reinstall the deleted older version of the application (assuming you have retained a copy of it—which is usually a good preventive measure). Delete the newer version. Open the document with the now reinstalled older version.

The Document Was Created by a Newer Version of the Application than the One You Are Using This is sort of the reverse of the previous situation. This case is a bit less likely to occur than the previous scenario. It usually happens if you get a file from someone else. For example, perhaps a friend gives you a document created by BusyWorks 3.0, but you are still using version 2.0.

The result is that when you try to open the document from the Finder, you get the *application could not be found* error message.

If this happens, be careful about shifting to the standard alternate approach of trying to open the document from within the application itself (BusyWorks 2.0 in this case). You may succeed on occasion. However, more likely you won't. Usually, the name of the document will not appear in the Open dialog box's file list. Even if it is listed, don't rejoice just yet. When you open it, you may find that the document has lost its formatting or contains garbage data (in addition to the actual data). In the worst case, just trying to open the document may result in a system crash!

A system crash occurs because the application, in the midst of successfully opening a document, may suddenly discover that it isn't in the expected format. Not knowing what else to do at this point, the application decides to crash the system.

- **Upgrade** The easiest (though not necessarily the fastest or cheapest) solution is to upgrade to the new version of the application.

- **Save in a different format** Alternatively, you can see if the person that gave you the file can save the file in a format readable by your version. That is, BusyWorks 3.0 may have an option to save the file in version 2.0 format.

- **Import to another application** If you have new versions of other applications, you may find that one of them has a translator file for BusyWorks 3.0. You can use this application to open the file.

BY THE WAY ▶ Avoid Multiple Versions of the Same Application

When you upgrade to a new version of an application, be sure to delete the previous version from your hard drive. Otherwise, when you try to launch a document created by the application, it may incorrectly launch the old version rather than the new one.

In any event, I would be cautious about opening two different versions of the same application at the same time. While doing this can often work just fine, it can just as easily cause problems, including a system crash.

The Correct Version of the Creating Application Is Present, Yet the Document File Still Does Not Open from the Finder The scenario just described is not supposed to happen. It usually indicates something has gone wrong. Sometimes this happens to a file you have undeleted, in which case, you may also find that the customized icon for the document is lost and that only the generic blank document icon is present. It also sometimes happens with files of a generic type that can be opened by any one of several applications. To try to solve this problem:

- **Drag and Drop** Sometimes, dragging a document to the application icon will force the Finder to successfully open the document with that application even if double-clicking the document fails.

- **Use the Open dialog box** Launch the creating application and try to open the file from within its Open dialog box. If this works, create a copy of the document as a new file with a different name. Quit the application and delete the now unneeded original file. Most of the time, this remedies the situation.

    If the custom icon does not yet appear, select Get Info for the file. This should get the Macintosh's attention and update the icon display. Otherwise, it will probably display correctly after your next restart.

- **Rebuild the desktop** If the preceding steps are unsuccessful, try rebuilding the desktop. The Desktop file stores information about the links between documents and applications. Errors in the Desktop file data can prevent the document from opening. Rebuilding the desktop usually fixes this problem.

    SEE: • Fix-It #8 for tips on rebuilding the desktop.

TAKE NOTE ▶ What to Do About Lost Icons

One day you start up your Macintosh and notice that some or all of the colorful icons that you are accustomed to seeing on your desktop are missing, especially your document icons. This can happen even when there is no problem correctly launching the document. What can you do?

The problem described above is solved simply by selecting Get Info for the file in question, and then closing the window again. Other times, restarting the Mac does the trick. Sometimes changing to a different view, as listed in the Finder's View menu, will make the icon appear. Otherwise, this problem is most often solved by rebuilding the desktop (assuming that the creating application for the document is still available).

Less likely but still possible, you may have an incorrect Creator code (as explained in Chapter 8, "Type and Creator Code Problems"). Finally, the problem may be related to Directory damage, usually a relatively minor problem with the "bundle bit," though sometimes it is due to more serious damage. Norton Utilities and TechTool Pro can typically fix the bundle bit as well as other Directory problems (as mentioned in Chapter 8 and Fix-It #11).

Much more detailed coverage of this entire issue can be found in Fix-It #8.

An Application Does Not Import a Document File, Even Though the Application Has a Translator Available for the File's Format

Suppose you try to open a Microsoft Word file from within the Open dialog box of BusyWorks. You select the *All Available* or *Microsoft Word* option from the pop-up menu that lists the types of readable files. Yet either the file you wish to open does not get displayed in the dialog box or, if it does appear, it does not open when selected.

The most likely cause for this is that the importing translation filter (which is usually stored in the System Folder somewhere) needed to open the file is missing. If you believe the correct filter is present, it may be that it is not an exact match for the file you are trying to import. In particular, the filter may be specific to a different version of the file's creating application from the one used to create the file (if you try to open a Microsoft Word 98 file with a Microsoft Word 3.0 translator, for example, it won't work).

In a related example, Microsoft Word has a Fast Save format option. You can check this option from the Save As dialog box. Doing this is supposed to speed up the process of saving documents. However, files saved with Fast Save may not be recognized by another application, even if the other application recognizes Word files saved in the normal format. Similarly, different types of TIFF document formats exist. A particular translator may be able to open some formats but not others.

The steps that follow are general solutions to the problems described above: re-save the document file in a format that matches the filter; get a filter that matches the file (check availability with the company that makes your application); use another application that can successfully import the file. If none of this works, it's time to abandon trying to import the file.

BY THE WAY ▶ If the Stationery Pad Option Does Not Work...

You check the Stationery Pad option in a document's Get Info window. Yet when you double-click the document, it still opens as an ordinary document, not as an "Untitled" stationery document. The problem may be simply that the application in question does not support this Mac OS option. If so, there is nothing you can do about it. However, many word processors have their own stationery feature, separate from this OS feature, which you can use instead.

The File Is in PC/DOS Format and/or on a PC/DOS-Formatted Disk

The scenario described above is a special case, but really belongs to the previous section on problems with importing files. Many Macintosh applications (such as Microsoft Word and AppleWorks) can read files saved in a PC format (as used on IBM PCs and compatibles), especially those files created using a PC version of their software (such as Word for Windows). However, to successfully access these PC files may require some special preparation.

Make Sure the Macintosh Can Read the PC-Formatted Floppy Disk When you first acquire PC files, they will probably be on a PC-formatted disk. Fortunately, the Macintosh can mount and read files from these disks just as if they were Macintosh-formatted disks. All you typically need to do is make sure that the File Exchange control panel is enabled. If so, when you insert, for example, a PC-formatted floppy disk, it will mount just as if it were a Mac disk. You can copy files back and forth between the PC disk and your Mac volumes.

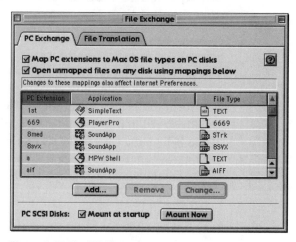

Figure 6-23 The PC Exchange tab of the File Exchange control panel.

One caveat: this control panel has a less -than -stellar history. Among other things, newer versions sometimes have problems reading PC files where older versions did not. If nothing seems to be working as it should, get a copy of an older version of this utility (which used to be called PC Exchange) and try it out.

SEE: • Fix-It #13 for more information on formatting disks.

Make Sure the Application Can Read Files Formatted by the Application That Created It on the PC Some applications have "built-in" translators for reading PC-formatted files. To access these documents, the most reliable method is to open them from within the application, not by double-clicking the document from the Finder. However, with File Exchange installed, you may be able to open the document directly from the Finder. Specifically, PC Exchange will match a DOS suffix (file type) in a document's name to a particular Macintosh application, as set in the PC Exchange window of the File Exchange control panel. Of course, this only works well if the application in question can read the PC-formatted file.

Check for the Correct Suffix If you are trying to import DOS-formatted files (such as a PC Works 2.0 file to Microsoft Works 3.0), make sure the document file has the correct suffix (such as file.*wrk*)—that is, the suffix that would be assigned to that file on a DOS machine. Without the suffix, some Macintosh programs cannot recognize the file when you try to open it later—even though they list a file translator for that format.

CD-ROM Disc Problem If you are having problems opening PC files from a CD-ROM disc, check that you have the Foreign File Access extension installed. If not, install it (either from your System Software disks, or from the CD-ROM Setup disks). Also, the Mac will not recognize long (Windows 95) names of files on a CD.

Use a PC Emulator Another avenue to consider is to purchase a PC emulation program, such as Virtual PC. This software can be used to mimic a computer running, for example, Windows 98. In fact, with Virtual PC, you should be able to simply drag -and -drop the document from the Mac's desktop to the Windows desktop. Once it is on the Window's desktop, you can try to open it. If you have the necessary software installed to open the document, you should be able to open it just as if you were using a PC.

Insufficient Memory to Open the File

Sometimes, even if you can open the application itself, you cannot get it to open a document. This is common if the document is especially large (as with large graphics files, for example) or if you are trying to open several documents at once.

This is usually a memory-related problem. Each application is allocated a specific amount of memory (as determined by the memory size setting in the application's Get Info window). The amount of memory must contain

Figure 6-24 A message that may appear when trying to open a document (in this case, a large graphics file) that is larger than the available memory.

the application itself plus any documents that you open within that application. If opening a document requires more than the allotted amount of memory, you cannot open it (even though the memory setting was sufficient to open the application itself). If this is the case, you usually get an error message accurately describing the problem.

The same sort of error may appear if you try to cut or copy a large selection to the Clipboard. These errors can occur no matter how much memory you have installed in your system. It is a function of the amount of memory assigned to an application, not of the total amount of available memory!

Close Other Documents The easiest solution, if it works, is to close the other open documents within the application, if any. See if the document now opens.

Increase Application's Memory Allocation You can increase the problem application's Preferred memory size from the settings in the application's Get Info window.

SEE: • **Fix-It #5 for details on memory management problems.**

Other Solutions Reduce the size of your system software memory allocation (by turning off extensions at startup) or add more memory hardware.

The File Is Not Intended to Be Opened

Some files are not meant to be opened from the Finder. After Dark, for example, is a screen-saver utility that replaces your display with an amusing image after several minutes of inactivity. It uses numerous plug-in modules to let the user choose what will appear on the screen. Each module is a separate file. Still, if you double-click any of these files, After Dark does not open. Instead, you get the *application could not be found* message. You can only access these modules by first opening the After Dark control panel directly.

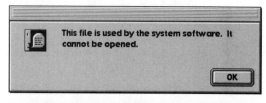

Similarly, many System Folder files are not intended to be opened (such as the Finder itself and most extension files). If you try to open these files, you will get a message telling you that it ain't gonna happen. There is nothing you can do in such cases. The files are not supposed to be opened. So don't try.

On a related note, you cannot use an application to open a file that is already opened in another application. If you try, you will get an error message telling you that it cannot be done.

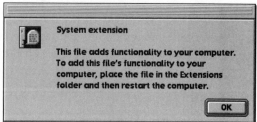

Figure 6-25 (Top) If you try to open the Finder (by double-clicking its icon), it won't open—this message appears instead; (bottom) this message appears if you try to open a system extension.

Opening a Document from the Finder When the Application Is Already Open

You try to open a document file from the Finder for an application that is already open. Instead of opening the file, you get a message saying either that you can't open the document because the application is in use or simply that the document could not be opened.

For example, you double-click a BusyWorks document file from the Finder when BusyWorks is already open. Instead of shifting to BusyWorks and opening the document, you get an error message instead. Technically, this should not happen. You should be able to open the file in this way. However, some programs may give you problems. The solution here is simple. Open the document from within the application, using the application's Open dialog box.

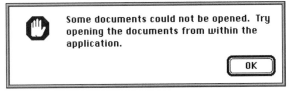

Figure 6-26 This message may appear when you are trying to open a document from the Finder for an application that is already open.

Opening a Document File from the Finder Succeeds, But It Launches the Wrong Application

You create a text file in BusyWorks. The next day, you double-click that file to open it. But rather than the file opening in BusyWorks, it opens in TeachText or perhaps in Microsoft Word.

What happened? Some programs save their documents as plain text files (see Chapter 8). This is common for some programs that are not really word processors although they do produce text reports of some sort. In such cases, if the document is launched from the Finder, it often opens in a generic text application (such as TeachText). This is only a problem if you don't want to work with your document in this format.

Actually, I have the reverse problem just as often. I save a file in a plain text format, expecting it to launch into SimpleText the next time I open it. But instead it opens into the creating application (which may take a lot longer to open).

A related situation can happen if you save the file (inadvertently, perhaps) in a format other than the application's default format (such as saving a BusyWorks file in Microsoft Word format). In this case, trying to open the file from the Finder causes it to launch Word rather than BusyWorks. (Actually, if Word is not on your disk, the file may not open at all—and you will get the *application could not be found* message described earlier in this chapter.)

If a text document does open in the "wrong" application, it is also possible that text formatting (such as the font, the size of the text, the line breaks, and margins) is different from when you saved it.

SEE: • **Chapter 9 for more information on text-formatting problems.**

To get a file to open with the desired application, the solution is usually simple. Open the document from within the application, using the application's Open dialog box, rather than from the Finder. If this does not work, you can fiddle with the document's creator code (see Chapter 8 again). Otherwise, there is not much else you can do.

Internet Problems

If you cannot open a file that you have downloaded from the Internet, the file may be corrupted, only partially downloaded, or encoded/compressed in a format that requires a utility that you do not have. I discuss all of these Internet problems in more detail in Chapters 12 and 13.

The Problem May Be with the Application, Not the Document

If a particular application refuses to open most or all appropriate documents, the application itself may be damaged or there may be a software bug involved. To check, replace the application software. If this fails to open your documents, you may still be able to open them in another application that can read files created by the problem application.

Damaged Preferences

Deleting the Preferences file(s) associated with an application can sometimes help get an application to open a document. For programs originally from Claris (such as AppleWorks), be sure to to delete the XTND Translator List.

SEE: • **Fix-It #2 for more information on Preferences file problems.**

Damaged Documents That Can't Be Opened

When none of the preceding solutions successfully opens a document (or it opens but much of the data appears garbled or lost), the document itself may be damaged. In most cases, the simplest solution is to revert to a backup copy of the file, assuming you have one. If this works, delete the problem copy. Make a new backup copy. You are back in business. If you do not have a backup copy, you can try several options that may repair or recover data from the damaged file.

If you get an error message such as *unable to read from disk*, this usually means media damage to the area of the disk where the file resides. This damage has to be fixed even if you can recover or replace the file.

SEE: • **Fix-Its #10 and #11 for information on fixing damaged files, including media damage.**
• **Fix-It #13 for information on reformatting the hard drive.**

If, after trying this and all of the previous suggestions, you still cannot open the file, there is little or no hope of saving it. Just delete the problem file and go on with your life.

When You Can't Delete a File or Folder

 Symptoms:

You place a file or a folder in the Finder's Trash. You select Empty Trash from the Finder's Special menu, but the item does not get deleted.

Usually, you also get an alert message explaining why the Trash was not deleted. It may say, for example, that *The Trash cannot be emptied ... because... items in it are locked* or *The item <name> could not be deleted because it contains items that are in use.*

 Causes:

Exact causes vary depending on the error message you get.

• Locked files or files on locked floppy disks cannot be directly deleted. They need to be unlocked first.

- Files that are currently open (or in use) cannot be deleted until they are closed, which makes sense. Deleting an open file would be like erasing a videotape while you are in the middle of watching it. Similarly, the System and the Finder on the startup disk cannot be deleted because they are always in use.

- In rarer cases, system software problems, damaged files, or damaged disk media may prevent a file or folder from being deleted. Check the Directory or Finder flags for potential problems.

SEE: • **Chapter 8 for information on the invisible Trash folder and Finder flags.**

BY THE WAY ▶ Exceptional Trash Behavior

Normally, you cannot have two files or folders of the same name in the same location. If you try to do this, the Macintosh asks if you want to replace the existing file (or folder) with the new one. However, the Trash is a partial exception to this rule. If you place an item in the Trash when the Trash already contains an item of the same name, the Macintosh renames one of the items (by appending the word "copy" to the end of the name). Both can then coexist in the Trash—while they await your decision to delete them. You get no message alerting you to this name modification.

 What to Do:

Make Sure the File or Folder Is Really in the Trash

If you can still see the file/folder on the desktop, near the Trash, it is not *in* the Trash. To get it in the Trash, drag it until the cursor arrow covers the Trash and the Trash icon turns black. Then release the mouse. Now select Empty Trash.

If the File or Folder Is on a Floppy Disk, Check if the Floppy Disk Is Locked

A disk is locked if the sliding tab, located in the upper corner on the rear side of the disk, is positioned so that you can see through the hole. Ordinarily you cannot even move an item from a locked floppy disk to the Trash. Certainly, nothing can be written to or deleted from a locked floppy disk.

For a floppy disk that is already inserted, you can check if it is locked without having to eject it. If it is locked, any window from the disk displays a small icon of a padlock in the upper left corner of the window.

To unlock the disk, eject the disk and slide the tab down. Reinsert the disk. You can then delete the file.

If the Mac indicates that virtually every floppy disk you insert to a floppy drive is locked (even though you know they are not locked), there may be a problem with the floppy drive itself. For example, the pin that goes through the hole of a locked disk may be stuck in a way that makes every inserted disk seem locked. You may be able to fix the pin by opening up the drive and cleaning the gunk out that is making the pin stick, but you may prefer to take the drive in for professional servicing.

Check If the File Is Locked

A file is locked if the Locked box in the file's Get Info window is checked (as described more in Chapter 2). If you are viewing files by any view other than an icon view, locked files will have a padlock symbol at the end of its listing line.

If a file is locked, you can still place it in the Trash. However, when you try to delete it, you get a message informing you of the situation. The message tells you that the solution to this problem is to hold down the Option key while you select Empty Trash. This allows locked files to be deleted. If a file refuses to delete, it may pay to hold down the Option key even if the file is not locked (or to deliberately lock the file and then try to delete it with the Option key held down).

Alternatively, you can go to a file's Get Info window and uncheck the Locked box. The file is now unlocked and may be deleted.

SEE: • **Chapter 2 for more information on using the Get Info command.**

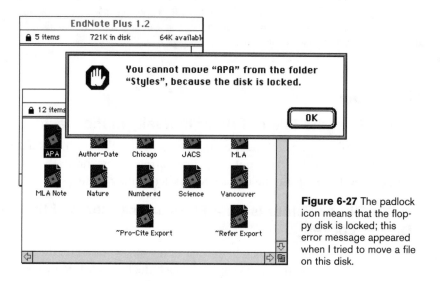

Figure 6-27 The padlock icon means that the floppy disk is locked; this error message appeared when I tried to move a file on this disk.

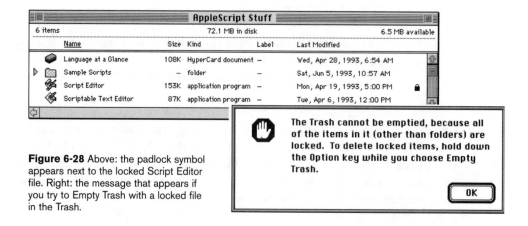

Figure 6-28 Above: the padlock symbol appears next to the locked Script Editor file. Right: the message that appears if you try to Empty Trash with a locked file in the Trash.

TAKE NOTE ▶ Files Locked by the General Controls Control Panel

The Mac OS General Controls control panel has two options called Protect System Folder and Protect Applications Folder. If these options are checked, no files in these folders can be removed, even if the relevant Get Info Locked box is unchecked (by the way, an Applications folder is automatically created when you first check this protect option). To remove files in these protected folders, you must first uncheck the control panel protection options. Otherwise, if you try to move a file, you will get a message that says you cannot do it because you "do not have enough access privileges."

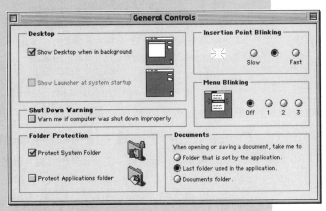

Figure 6-29 The General Controls control panel, with its Protect Applications Folder option unchecked.

Overall, my advice is to avoid using these Folder Protection features at all. They can cause more problems than they solve. In any case, they only prevent removal of files from the main folder; you can still remove files from subfolders of protected folders.

In any case, these features no longer work in Mac OS 9. Apple wants you to use Multiple Users instead (as discussed in Chapter 15).

SEE: • The "Take Note: Clutter Control," section earlier in this chapter, for more information on the General Controls control panel.

Folders Locked via the Sharing Command

If you use file sharing, you probably know that you can use it to restrict the access of other users (on a network) to your files. You do this by selecting Get Info for a folder or volume and then selecting Sharing from the Show pop-up menu in the Get Info window (or by selecting the file and then selecting Sharing from the hierarchical menu off of the Get Info item in the Finder's File menu). From here, you use the check boxes to assign what you wish to share. I discuss file sharing in more detail in Chapter 11. For now, I want to emphasize a lesser known option that can limit your own ability to modify a folder. The option is, *"Can't move, rename or delete this item."* If this option is checked, the folder cannot be moved, renamed, or deleted by anyone, including yourself, whether accessing

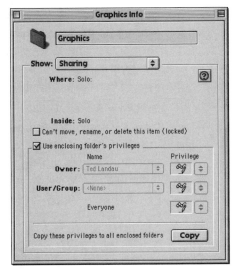

Figure 6-30 Locking a folder via the Sharing command, which only works when File Sharing is on.

it directly or via file sharing—but only as long as file sharing is activated. If you try, you will get a message informing you that the folder can't be moved to the Trash because it is locked. The only solution is to select the folder, go to the Sharing dialog box, and uncheck this option.

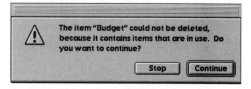

Figure 6-31 This message appears if you try to delete a file that is currently open.

However, assuming that you have access otherwise, you can still remove individual files from the folder and delete them separately.

Check If the File Is Currently Open or in Use

Any application or document file that is currently open cannot be deleted. If you try to do this, you get an error message instead. If you get this message, click Continue to delete any other files that may be in the Trash. Then:

For Applications If the file to be deleted is an application, quit the application. Then select Empty Trash again. The file should now be deleted.

For Documents If the file is a document, it is usually sufficient to just close the document file. Then return to the Finder and select Empty Trash again. If this doesn't work, try quitting the application that created the document. Then try to trash the document.

Occasionally, the document may be in use by some "invisible" applications, making it difficult to quit the relevant application. If this appears to be the case, you can use a utility, such as Peek-a-Boo, that lists open background applications and other invisible "processes"—and allows you to quit them.

SEE   • **Fix-It #3 for more information about using Peek-a-Boo and similar utilities.**

For Essential System Folder Files If the file is an essential system software file on your current startup disk (such as the System, the Finder, or an Update file), you cannot delete it. To do so, you have to restart the Macintosh using an alternate startup disk. Then drag the file to the Trash and delete it. Normally, you only want to do this if you are about to replace these files.

SEE: • **Fix-It #4 for information on replacing system software files.**

For Other System Folder Files (Extensions, Control Panels, Fonts, and so on) If the file is a startup extension or control panel on your current startup disk (or for any other unknown type of file in your System Folder), you may get an error message saying that it cannot be deleted. This often happens if the file gets loaded into memory at startup (a startup extension). In this case, drag the file out of the System Folder. Then restart the Macintosh. You should be able to delete it. You don't need to use an alternate startup disk.

SEE: • **Fix-It #2 for information on deleting Preferences files.**
        • **Fix-It #3 for more information on deleting startup extensions.**

Folders That Remain "In Use" Unexpectedly

Suppose you are working on a file called Daily Report #6. After printing the file, you decide to delete it. In fact, you have a whole folder of daily reports that you now are ready to delete. The folder is called Articles 2. Knowing that you cannot trash an open file, you remember to close the Daily Report #6 file (but you do not quit the application you are using). You then drag the entire folder to the Trash.

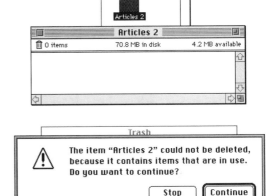

When you select Empty Trash, you get an alert message saying that the Articles 2 folder could not be deleted because it contains items that are still in use. When you check the folder, it is empty. Every file in the folder was in fact deleted. But the folder itself was not. How can anything in it be still in use? What's going on?

The problem is that the Macintosh considers a folder to be in use until you quit every currently open application that has opened any of the files that were within that folder (even if the files have since been closed). In this case, if the word processor (Word, for example) that

Figure 6-32 Top: The folder Articles 2, now in the Trash, is empty. Bottom: Although the folder is empty, it does not get deleted when Empty Trash is selected; instead, an error message appears.

was used to create the Daily Report file is still open, the folder is not deleted, even though you have closed the Daily Report #6 file. The odd thing is that the file itself can be successfully deleted. To delete the folder:

1. Click Stop or Continue.

2. Quit the relevant applications (Word in the previous example).

3. Then select Empty Trash again. It should work now.

An Invisible File in the Folder? A relatively rare problem is if a folder contains an invisible file that is "in use." In this case, the Macintosh will not delete the folder until you either remove the invisible file or quit whatever application is causing the file to be "in use." The best way to check this is with a utility, such as Norton Utilities or DiskTop, which lists invisible files.

The Folder-from-Hell Problem

Occasionally, you may have a folder that is empty but refuses to be deleted no matter what you try. Everything in the folder can be deleted, but the folder itself does not go away. Even after you quit all open applications, even after you restart the Macintosh, even if you hold down the Option key while emptying the Trash, the folder refuses to be deleted. Trying to move or delete the folder may produce various strange symptoms and error messages (such as a -127 error). Often, this problem begins as an aftereffect of a system crash.

This type of folder is referred to as the *folder from hell*. The most likely cause of this problem has to do with the special Directory files that the Macintosh uses to keep track of what is on the disk.

SEE: • **Chapter 8 for more information on the Directory files.**

Without getting too technical here, the problem is typically the result of a discrepancy in information between different areas of the Directory files as to how many files and folders are contained within the problem folder. Because of this confusion, the Macintosh acts as if there is still an "in use" file or folder inside the problem folder, even though there is not. Thus, it does not allow the folder from hell to be deleted. This can be an especially difficult problem to solve. Here's how to try:

Rename the Folder Then try to trash it. It's unlikely to work, but easy to try.

Create a New Folder with the Same Name The easiest solution, if it works, is to create a new folder with exactly the same name as the problem folder. Make sure you create it in a different location (such as within a separate folder) from the problem folder, or you will not be able to give the new folder the same name (since two folders at the same location cannot have iden-

tical names). Then drag the new folder to the same location as the problem folder. The Macintosh asks you whether you want to replace the problem folder with the new one. Click OK. Now try to delete this replacement folder. If it works, the folder from hell is gone!

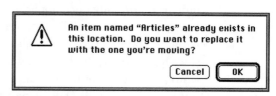

Figure 6-33 Click OK to try to delete the already existing folder from hell.

Utilities to the Rescue Disk First Aid or the other repair utilities (such as Norton Utilities) can usually fix the folder-from-hell problem. A special shareware utility, called *HellFolderFix*, is specifically designed to combat this problem. Utilities such as Apple's *Rename Rescue* or a shareware utility called *UnlockFolder* may also fix the problem. However, none of these utilities have been updated for years and they may no longer work in Mac OS 8.x.

SEE: • **Fix-It #10 for information on disk repair utilities.**

Deleting Damaged Files

Sometimes you will have trouble deleting a damaged file. Often, when you try to do so, you will get an ID = -39 error message. Damaged font files and font suitcases seem particularly prone to this sort of problem. If this happens, try any or all of the following:

Create a New File with the Same Name Create a new file, of any type, with the same name as the problem file. Drag the dummy file to the location of the problem file. The Macintosh should ask whether you want to replace the problem file. Click OK. If it successfully replaces the problem file, now try to delete the dummy file. It should work.

Drag the file out of the System Folder If the file is in your System Folder, such as a font file, try dragging it out of the System Folder and then restarting. Then try to delete the file. For a problem font file, you may have to first drag out the entire Fonts folder.

Restart with Extensions Off Hold down the shift key at startup. Now try to delete the file. This, again, is useful for problem font files, especially if you are using an extension such as Suitcase.

SEE: • Chapter 9 for more specific advice on damaged font files.

When the Preceding Steps Fail to Delete the File or Folder

You may have problems that go beyond your inability to delete a file or folder. It's time, once again , for a more scattergun approach.

Restart the Macintosh If you haven't already done so, restart your Macintosh. This alone may solve the problem.

Rebuild the Desktop Then try to delete the file or folder again.

SEE: • Fix-It #8 for tips on rebuilding the desktop.

Start Up from Another Disk If this does not work, try restarting from an alternate startup disk. Try to delete the file or folder now.

Try a Finder Alternative You may be able to delete the file or folder using a utility such as DiskTop rather than the Finder.

Attempt to Repair the Disk If you haven't already done so, run Disk First Aid and, if necessary, any other disk repair utility you have (such as Norton Utilities or DiskWarrior). Repair any problems that are discovered.

SEE: • Chapter 5 for more details on disk-related problems.
       • Fix-It #10 for tips on disk repair utilities.

Reformat the Disk If the problem persists, reformat the entire disk. First back up the disk, reformat it, and then restore the contents of the disk from your backups. This should almost always solve the problem.

SEE: • Fix-It #13 for tips on reformatting disks.

If None of the Preceding Steps Work If none of this works, there is probably a file, most likely in the System Folder, that you are reintroducing to the disk when you restore the disk from your backup and that is causing the problem. You can continue to search for this problem file by yourself—by testing for startup extension conflicts, for example. But if your patience begins to wear thin at this point, seek some outside help.

SEE: • Fix-It #3 for information about problems with system extensions and control panels.
       • Fix-It #16 for tips on seeking outside help.

When You Can't Rename a File, Folder, or Volume

 ## Symptoms:

You try to rename a file in the Finder, but you are unable to get the I-beam cursor to appear and the text remains inaccessible for editing.

 ## Causes:

Most often, there is nothing wrong. You just need to follow the correct procedures to get the I-beam to appear. Otherwise, for volume names, the problem may be that file sharing is activated or you are experiencing an unusual system software bug.

 ## What to Do:

To get the I-beam to appear, from an icon view, click once in the area where the name of the file is (not the icon). Then wait for the name to highlight and the I-beam to appear. Otherwise, you can click in any part of the icon and press the Return key. You should now be able to edit the name. Remember, a name cannot be more than 31 characters long or contain a colon (:).

For files If the previous step fails to work, the file may be locked. Select Get Info and uncheck the Locked box if it is checked.

Some files have locked names even if their Get Info box is not locked. This is because a special file attribute called *Name Locked* has been checked. This typically would only occur for certain system software files, such as the System and Finder. If for some reason you need to rename these files, you will have to uncheck this attribute and then restart.

SEE: • **"What Are Finder Flags (Attributes)?" in Chapter 8 for more details.**

For volume names (such as hard disks) and/or folders that cannot be renamed
Turn file sharing off. (Alternatively, for folders only, select the folder, then select the Sharing command from the Finder's File menu and make sure that the *Can't move, rename, or delete* option is unchecked.) This will usually solve the problem. Otherwise, you may have a rare bug that may be fixed only with special utilities such as Apple's *Rename Rescue* or a shareware utility called *UnlockFolder*.

Lastly, your computer may be experiencing a more general damaged file or disk problem.

SEE: • **Fix-Its #10 and #11 for more information on fixing damaged files and disks.**

When You Can't Save or Copy a File

 Symptoms:

- **Saving a File** You try to save a file from a Save dialog box, but you are unable to do so. Usually, you get an error message such as *Disk is locked; there is not enough room on the disk* or *Disk is full.*

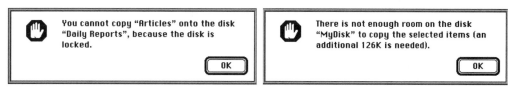

Figure 6-34 Messages that appear when you try to copy files to a locked disk or to a disk with less unused space available than is needed for the file(s) to be copied.

- **Copying or Replacing a File** You try to copy a file (to another disk or to another folder on the same disk), but the copy does not complete successfully. Instead, you get an error message. In some cases, it may say that you cannot copy or replace the file because it is *in use* or because you do not have *access permission.* In more serious cases, it may say *The file couldn't be read and was skipped (unknown error)* or some other similar message.

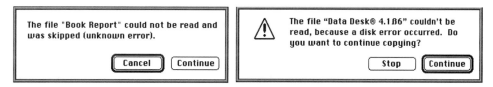

Figure 6-35 Ominous messages such as these may appear when you try to copy files from the Finder.

 Causes:

In most cases, the cause is evident from the error message and easy to solve. If you try to save a 100K file to a floppy disk that only has 20K of empty space left, you get an error message saying that you cannot do this. Similarly, you cannot copy or save anything to a locked floppy disk. Files that are open cannot be replaced and sometimes cannot be copied.

More rarely, you may be unable to save a file from within an application, even though the disk is unlocked and there seems to be sufficient space available. This probably means there is a bug in the application software.

The most troublesome problem is when you get a message that the file you are trying to copy could not be read or could not be written, usually referred to as *disk errors.* This sometimes happens when you are trying to copy too many items at one time. Otherwise, it almost always means a problem with defective disk media, commonly referred to as *bad blocks.* If the file cannot be read (*a read error*), it means that the damage is to the area of the disk where the file now exists. If the file cannot be written (*a write error*), it means the damage is to the area where the Macintosh is trying to create the copy. If you are trying to make a copy from one disk to another, *read errors* refer to the source disk and *write errors* refer to the destination disk.

Sometimes you get a message that says a file could not be *verified.* Functionally, this is similar to a write error. It means that the error went undetected when the file was first written, but was caught when the disk was rechecked (as is normally done by the Finder prior to completing a copy operation to a floppy disk).

Write (and verification) errors are definitely the lesser of two evils. It means that your file is still intact and that the damage is in a presently unused area of the destination disk. Read errors mean that the damage is to the area presently containing the file. In this case, the file is almost assuredly damaged, perhaps beyond repair.

 ## What to Do:

For Problems with Locked or Full Disks

Follow the Advice in the Alert Message These problems are usually remedied simply by paying attention to the alert message that appears. Thus, if the message indicates that the disk is locked, unlock the disk. If the message indicates that the disk is full or that there is not enough room, you either have to go to the Finder and delete some other files from the disk (to free up more space for the file to be saved) or save the file to another disk.

> **SEE:** • "When You Can't Delete a File or Folder," earlier in this chapter, for more information on locked disks.

For "Disk Is Full" Message When Disk Is Not Full If you know that the disk is not full or think that it should not be full, despite the message, try restarting and/or rebuilding the desktop. This alone may cure the problem. Also check for temporary files that may have unexpectedly stayed on your disk (if you use PrintMonitor, be sure to check in the PrintMonitor Documents folder in your System Folder). Otherwise, you probably have a damaged disk. Try to repair it.

> **SEE:** • Fix-It #8 for information on rebuilding the desktop.
> • Fix-Its #10 and #11 for tips on repairing disks.

Full Disk Problem with Virtual Memory

Virtual memory, when turned on, creates an invisible file on your disk needed for virtual memory to work. This file can be quite large. As explained in more detail in Fix-It #5, it is equal in size to the amount of RAM that you have plus the amount of virtual memory that you add (so if you have 164MB of RAM and create 64MB of virtual memory, it will take up 128MB of disk space). If you start up with virtual memory turned off, this file is not created. Thus, in the example given, the user would have 128MB more of disk space when starting up with Extensions Off (or with just virtual memory turned off or when starting up from a floppy disk).

The result is that you may seem to have a mysteriously full disk (preventing you from copying a needed file to it) that just as mysteriously becomes less full when you start up with an Emergency Toolkit disk in order to try to fix the problem. If this happens, it is almost certain that this virtual memory effect is the cause. By the way, RAM Doubler does not share this problem, which is probably the main reason it is often a preferred alternative to Apple's virtual memory.

BY THE WAY ▶ Don't Try to Save a File That is Currently in the Trash

Don't open and select the Save command for a file that is in the Trash. Why anyone would want to do this is unclear to me, but apparently people occasionally try it. Doing this can lead to system crashes and other assorted problems. Using Save As (and saving it to a new location) is okay, but using Save is not.

BY THE WAY ▶ Moving Files on a Locked Disk to the Desktop

If you try to move (or copy) a file on a locked disk (floppy or CD-ROM, for example) to another folder on the same disk, you will correctly get a message that says you cannot do it because the disk is locked. However, if you instead try to move a file from the locked disk to the desktop, you will get a somewhat strange message that says, "Items from locked disks cannot be moved to the desktop." Here, the Mac is telling you that, while you cannot move the file to the locked disk's desktop (because the disk is locked), it will copy the file to your startup disk (if you wish) and place it on the startup disk's desktop. Often, this is what you are trying to accomplish anyway. If so, click OK. Otherwise, for floppy disks, an alternative is to unlock the disk (CD-ROM disks, of course, can never be unlocked).

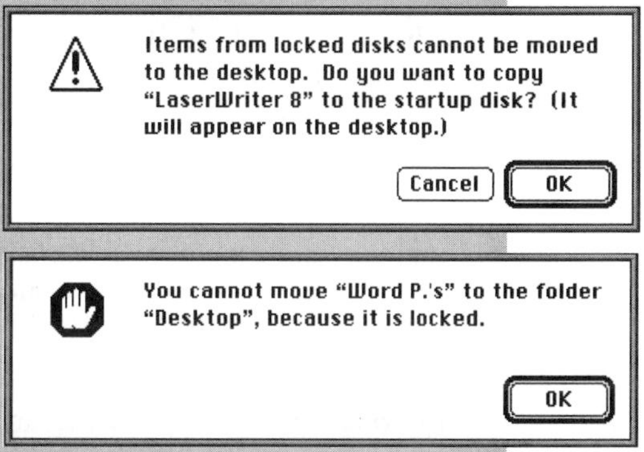

In one strange case, when I tried to move a folder on my hard drive to the desktop, I got a message that said that I could not do it because the Desktop folder itself was locked. Since there was no reason to expect this to be the case, I suspected that some software on the disk was damaged. Rebuilding the desktop did not help. Ultimately, the problem turned out to be due to Directory damage. I was able to fix it using a disk repair utility.

> ⚠ Items from locked disks cannot be moved to the desktop. Do you want to copy "LaserWriter 8" to the startup disk? (It will appear on the desktop.)
>
> [Cancel] [**OK**]

> ✋ You cannot move "Word P.'s" to the folder "Desktop", because it is locked.
>
> [**OK**]

Figure 6-36 Top: this message appears when moving a file to the desktop of a locked floppy disk. Bottom: this message turned out to be prompted by Directory damage.

For Files That Are "In Use" or Have "Illegal Access Permission"

You will find that if you try to replace a file that is currently open or in use (by copying a new file with the same name to the same location as the open file, for example), it won't work Instead, you will get the same "in use" alert message that appears when you try to delete such a file. This is because replacing the file requires deleting the original version. For application and document files, the obvious solution is to close the open file. For control panels and extensions that are in use, drag the "in use" file out of the System Folder to the Trash. Then move the new copy to the intended location. You may have to restart before you can delete the file now in the Trash.

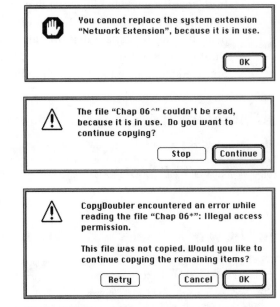

Figure 6-37 One of these messages may appear if you try to replace or copy a currently open file.

SEE: • **"Check If the File Is Currently Open or in Use" in "When You Can't Delete a File or Folder," earlier in this chapter, for more details.**
• **Chapter 9 for special problems related to replacing a font file.**

In some cases, if you try to copy a file that is currently open, you will get another "in use" message. However, if you are trying to transfer an open file across a network, via file sharing, you may instead get a message that says you have "illegal access permission," even if you do have proper access permission. In either of these situations, the simple solution is to first close the document (or quit the application) and then make the copy.

However, when using file sharing, a message that says you do not have the proper "access privileges" may really mean what it says. I discuss this issue more in Chapter 11.

SEE: • **"Take Note: Files Locked by The General Controls Control Panel," earlier in this chapter, for another example of an access permission problem.**
• **Chapter 11 for more information on file sharing and illegal access permission.**

TAKE NOTE ▶ When Copied Files Vanish...Or Cause Your Mac to Freeze

When copying files over a network or to a removable disk (such as a Zip or Jaz disk), you may see errors that don't typically appear when copying more locally. In particular, the copy process may appear to proceed normally; yet when it is finished, you find that some or all of the files you thought you copied are not actually in the destination location. Alternatively, the attempt to copy files may cause the Mac to freeze, requiring a restart to get things working normally again.

The causes of these problems often remain obscure. For Jaz and Zip disks, the problem often originates with the version of the Iomega software you are using. Updating to a newer version of the Iomega driver may eliminate the problem. Otherwise, some other extension is likely to be at fault. In one well-documented case, antivirus software (Virex and Norton AntiVirus) caused a freeze when copying over a network in Mac OS 8.5. Again, an updated version of these utilities fixed the problem. If you are copying to a drive connected to the Mac via an SCSI card, updating the firmware for the card may be the solution. Check MacFixIt (www.macfixit.com) for more specific examples of these symptoms.

Problems Due to a Disk Error

Disk errors refer to those situations when, while trying to save or copy a file, you get an error message that says that the file could not be read or could not be written. If you were trying to copy more than one file, click the Continue button in the error message. This copies any of the remaining files (assuming they are not experiencing problems themselves). Otherwise, you can click Cancel and do the following.

Try to Copy Files Again, in Smaller Groups If Appropriate Check which file(s) did not copy. Try again to copy the file or files that were not copied successfully the first time. Then try one or two more times. Sometimes the problem was a short-lived glitch, and one of your next tries will be successful.

This is especially worth doing if you were trying to copy several files at one time. This can overwhelm the Finder's processing and/or memory capacity, causing the disk error to occur. You may even get a separate error message indicating that there is insufficient memory to copy the files. In these cases, copying one file (or at least a fewer number of files) at a time should solve the problem.

For Floppy Disks, Use a Special Copy Utility If you get an error message that the disk could not be read while trying to copy files from a floppy disk using the Finder, try instead to make a copy of the entire disk using a special copy utility. Disk Copy is a utility from Apple that can be used for this purpose. It sometimes works when the Finder fails.

Also note that if you are using a utility such as Connectix Speed Doubler and you get a "disk error" message when trying to copy files from a floppy disk, the disk may not really be damaged. The problem may instead be with the utility. To find out, disable the utility extension and try the copy again.

If All Copy Attempts Fail

- **Read errors** A read error often means that the file is hopelessly damaged. Your best bet is to replace the file with a backup copy. If you do not have a backup copy, you may still be able to repair or recover data from the disk.

  SEE: • **Fix-It #11 for tips on rescuing damaged files.**

- **Write (or verify) errors** If a write error (or a verification error) occurs, try copying the file(s) to a different disk. This should work fine, since a write error indicates that the problem is with the destination disk, not the source disk that has the original file you want to copy.

  You should then back up all unbacked-up files that already exist on the disk that generated the write error. You may get read errors as you try to do this, indicating that some files on the disk are themselves damaged. Try to recover data from these files, as needed.

  SEE: • **Fix-It #11 on rescuing damaged files**

For both read and write errors, in addition to any attempt to repair files, check for bad blocks: disk errors of either kind almost always mean that there are bad blocks on the disk, usually due to media damage (a term first described in Chapter 2). The damage is on the source disk for read errors and on the destination disk for write errors. If you detect any bad blocks, you probably have to reformat the disk.

If the disk is a floppy disk, you are probably better off discarding it instead of reformatting it. For the price of a floppy disk, why take chances? Even if you had a read or write error that appeared to vanish after repeated attempts to copy a file, do not trust the disk. If the media is bad, the error will return again! Be happy you were able to copy the file first. Get rid of the disk.

By the way, even if you are eventually able to copy a file that triggered a read error, open the file to make sure it is okay. Sometimes, the file is damaged even though the Finder does not report an error.

If the damaged disk is your only copy of an application disk, contact the manufacturer for a replacement. If you are a registered user of the software, you can usually do this for a nominal fee.

SEE: • **Fix-It #11 for information on damaged files.**
          • **Fix-It #13 for information on reformatting.**

When the Going Gets Weird...

 Symptoms:

While you are using an application (or a control panel or a desk accessory), something unexpected happens—something not covered nor explained by any of the previous sections of this chapter.

The problem could be anything: a command that ceases to function (especially one that previously functioned just fine) or a dialog box that doesn't come up when requested. Or the problem could be anything else that seems to run counter to what the software's documentation (or your common sense) tells you should happen.

These glitches fall into a catch-all category that also summarizes many of the suggestions made earlier in this chapter. Though it is hard to generalize here, the list tends to run from the easiest and most common problems to solve to the more complex brain twisters and their causes.

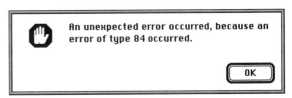

Figure 6-38 One example of an error message that may appear when trying to carry out a command and the "going gets weird." Trying to determine the meaning of the error numbers is not likely to help solve the problem.

 Causes:

Common causes include hardware incompatibilities, software bugs, missing accessory files, corrupted files, startup extension conflicts, and memory problems.

 What to Do:

Scroll, Close, Quit, Restart

An impressive variety of application problems can be resolved by simply scrolling the current display off the screen and then scrolling it back again (to find that everything wrong with the display has been corrected); by closing a window or document and then reopening it; by quitting the application and then relaunching it; or, finally, by simply restarting your Mac. Give these steps a try before proceeding further.

TAKE NOTE ▶ Flashing Icons in the Menu Bar and Unexpected Alert Noises

If you suddenly see a flashing icon in the menu bar, or if an unexpected alert sound occurs, interpret these signals as requests to get your attention.

Most commonly these days, you will see a flashing icon in the Application menu (found on the right side of the menu bar). The icon will always be an application other than the currently active one. If you select the menu, you will notice a diamond symbol in front of the name of the relevant application. This is the Mac's way of telling you that this is the application that wants your attention. Select it. Sometimes what it wants is relatively harmless (for example, an email application that tells you that you have just received some mail). Otherwise, the icon is likely to be an alert or error message of some sort (such as the Finder's message that tells you that your printer is out of paper).

The only other likely cause of flashing icons or alarm sounds is some extension function. For example, Apple's old Alarm Clock desk accessory will flash the Apple menu when its alarm goes off. Similarly, Retrospect's extension will do the same when it is time to run a scheduled backup. In these cases, the program is not listed in the Application menu. You simply have to know what the program is by the identity of the icon.

In any case, once you select the relevant application, the flashing (or sound) should stop.

If the Problem Results in a System Error of Any Kind

Refer to Chapter 4 for information on your particular type of system error. Return to this section only if Chapter 4 fails to provide a solution.

Check for Hardware Incompatibilities Between Your Hardware and the Application in Use

SEE: • **Fix-It #1 for information on incompatibilities between hardware and software.**

Check for Damage to, or Other Problems with, the Application's Preferences File

SEE: • **Fix-It #2 for information on problems with Preferences files.**

Check Whether One of the Application's Accessory Files Is Missing or Misplaced

SEE: • **Fix-It #2 for information on missing or misplaced accessory files.**

Check Whether the Application or Any of Its Accessory Files Are Damaged

Start by replacing just the application file from a copy on the original disk. To do this, first delete the suspected defective file before making the new copy. If this does not solve the problem, reinstall the application together with all of its accessory files. If the program has an Installer utility, use it (if the program requires the use of an Installer utility, you may not have the prior option to replace only the application).

As always, when dealing with potentially damaged files, check for possible media damage to the disk itself. If the original application disk is damaged, you may still have an undamaged version of the files on your regular backups.

SEE: • **"When You Can't Save or Copy a File" earlier in this chapter.**
　　　　 • **Fix-It #11 for information on damaged files.**

Consider Whether the Problem Is Due to a Bug in the Application

There is no way you can repair a bug yourself. Repair must be performed by the software manufacturer by installing a bug-fixed upgrade of the application. If you suspect a bug, you should call the company's technical support personnel to check it out. They may already know about it and be able to tell you what to do.

SEE: • **Fix-It #16 for tips on calling technical support and getting upgrades.**

In general, make sure you are using the latest version of the application, especially if you are using a version of the system software that was released after the version of the application you are using. Newer versions tend to fix bugs and conflicts from earlier versions.

Symptoms due to bugs can be as "simple" as a system scrash or something so weird and convoluted that you might never expect that a bug is the underlying cause. There are no useful guidelines here, unfortunately.

BY THE WAY ▶ Problems with Programs Running in the Background

A program that continues to work even when it is not the active application is said to run in the background. System extensions and many control panels do this, as first described in Chapter 1. Some applications do this as well. For example, the Finder can complete a copy operation in the background. PrintMonitor (see Chapter 7) runs in the background. Background-acting programs make it seem like two things are happening at once, but it is really an illusion. What actually happens is that background activities time-share, grabbing time whenever the foreground application is sufficiently idle.

Depending on the nature of the background activity, you may or may not notice an overall slowing down of the foreground activity as the background action proceeds. For example, cursor movements can become jerky or dialog boxes may take longer to appear. In the most extreme cases, a conflict may occur between a foreground and a background activity, with the result that one or both of the programs cease to function. A system crash may even result.

If you suspect that a problem is due to a background processing conflict:

- **Pause your foreground activity briefly.** Some background activities halt while you type and resume again when you pause. Thus, if you take a brief rest, the background activity is given priority and completes its task faster. When you resume working, you will no longer be hampered by the program's slower response time and jerky cursor movements. Transient problems with PrintMonitor can be avoided in this way. Pausing makes practical sense only if the background activity does not take too long to complete.

- **Turn off the background activity temporarily, if such an option is available.** For example, for control panels, there is usually an on/off button in the control panel window. Turn it back on when you are no longer using a foreground activity that conflicts with the background processing.

  Otherwise, you have to forgo the background processing altogether, either by keeping the potential background activity in the foreground until it is completed, or (when all else fails), by not using the background-processing program.

Note: Beginning with Mac OS X, the Mac OS should handle background activities with greater sophistication, due to a feature called "preemptive multi-tasking." This improvement allows the Mac to assign priorities to different applications, so that the one with the greatest priority gets most of the processor's attention, regardless of whether or not it is a background or foreground application at the moment.

SEE: • **Chapter 15 for more on Mac OS X.**

Check for Startup Extension Conflicts

Startup extension conflicts are a common cause of almost any problem you may have with an application or control panel.

SEE: • **Fix-It #3 for detailed procedures on how to identify and resolve startup extension conflicts.**

Startup extension problems can cause difficulties either with using an application or with using the startup extension itself. Startup extensions that modify either the normal functioning of the Finder or basic system functions (such as Open and Save dialog boxes) are especially likely culprits. RAM Doubler, ATM, and virtually any fax software are among many other common startup extensions that are prone to causing these types of problems.

Similarly, be wary of any extensions that actively process information in the background, such as Disk Express or the prevention checking features of Tech Tool Pro and Norton Utilities. Finally, be careful never to use two extensions that do essentially the same thing, such as two screen savers. This is almost a sure way to cause problems.

In most cases, these startup extensions are regularly updated to resolve identified problems, so make sure you have the latest version.

In general, check the ReadMe files that come with these programs to find out about any already known conflicts. If you have access, check online services for problems reported by other users (often accompanied by answers from the publisher of the software). If you are still stumped, call the program's technical support line.

Here are three more specific recommendations:

- **For RAM Doubler** You can easily start up with just RAM Doubler turned on, and all other extensions off, by holding down the Shift-Option keys at startup. You can similarly start up with all extensions on, except RAM Doubler, by holding down the escape or tilde (~) keys at startup. Lastly, you can compare the effect of using virtual memory vs. RAM Doubler, by turning virtual memory on, which automatically disables RAM Doubler. After doing all of this, you should be able to determine if the problem goes away with RAM Doubler turned off, comes back with RAM Doubler alone turned on and is not a general problem with virtual memory. If all of this is confirmed, then you have almost certainly identified a RAM Doubler conflict. It's time to contact Connectix.

- **For ATM** With ATM, try turning off (or on) the options in the ATM control panel, such as the "Enable Font Substitution" and "Precision Character Positioning" check boxes to see if that fixes the problem. Increasing ATM's cache and/or memory allocation may also help. Check MacFixIt (www.macfixit.com) for more specific advice relevant to a particular symptom.

- **Extensions and Installer utilities** Installer utilities (used to first install a given software product on your hard disk) generally don't get along well with startup extensions. This is particularly true of antivirus software. To be safe, restart with only Mac OS (Base or All) extensions enabled before running any installer. If need be, start up with all extensions off (holding down the Shift key at startup) and try again. You will likely be successful now.

SEE: • Chapter 9 for more information on ATM.
        • Fix-It #2 for information on preferences files.
        • Fix-It #16 for tips on calling technical support and getting upgrades.

Check for Memory-Related Problems

Insufficient available memory is yet another leading cause of problems. In these cases, you will most likely get an error message that tells you the general nature of the difficulty.

SEE: • Chapter 4 for resolving memory problems that lead to a system error, such as a freeze or unexpected quit.
        • Fix-It #5 for more general advice on solving memory-related problems.

BY THE WAY ▶ Apple Events Errors

Apple events are an Apple technology that allows an application to send instructions to other programs. It forms the foundation of AppleScript. Support of Apple events and AppleScript requires that the application be rewritten to understand this feature.

If a program attempts to call another program via an Apple event and does not succeed for any reason, you will likely get an Apple events error message. The cause is usually either not enough memory to open the receiving application or that the receiving application was not able to understand the incoming instruction. For memory problems, you can try to increase your memory availability (as described in Fix-It #5). For the other more specific problems, there is no immediate solution. Contact the application's publisher for possible assistance.

Check for System Software Problems

Some application problems can be resolved by reinstalling the system software. This step is particularly advisable if you get an error message that says needed system resources are missing.

If your version of the software is too old to work with the latest update, strongly consider upgrading (unless your Mac model is too RAM-deficient to use the newer software).

SEE: • **Fix-It #4 for information on system software problems.**

If All Else Fails, It's Time to Round Up the Usual Suspects

The cause may extend beyond the problem application itself. For example, check for a possible virus infection. Check for damage to the invisible Directory files. Let your particular symptoms guide you to the Fix-Its which seem most relevant. Try these Fix-Its first. For example:

SEE: • **Fix-It #6 for tips on how to check for viruses.**
• **Fix-Its #10 and #11 for tips on how to check for damage to the Directory files.**
• **Fix-It #8 for information on how to rebuild the desktop.**

Printing Problems?

This chapter does not cover printing problems, a major topic, and the subject of the next chapter.

TAKE NOTE ▶ A Quick Check for Problems with System Folder Files

Here's a quick way to determine if anything in your System Folder other than the minimally required files, is the source of your problem:

1. Remove the System file and the Finder file (and System Resources and Mac OS ROM files, if present) from the System Folder. (I would also recommend removing the Shared Library Manager, Shared Library Manager PPC, and Text Encoding Converter extensions from the Extensions folder.)

2. Rename the System Folder with a name like "System Stuff."

3. Using the Finder's New Folder command, create a new folder and name it "System Folder." Place the removed files in it. (If it was not automatically created, create a subfolder in the new System Folder called "Extensions" and put the removed extensions in it.)

4. Restart. The Macintosh should use the new, bare-bones System Folder.

   Note: If you get an error message when you try to start up informing you of some missing file, you will need to restart from the Mac OS CD that came with your Mac (or other bootable CD) and move that file into your bare-bones System Folder; then restart again.

5. Check whether your problem remains or is now gone.

If the symptoms remain, the problem is either with one of the files in your bare-bones System Folder, or it has nothing to do with System Folder files. If the problem goes away, one or more System Folder files currently stored in the System Stuff folder is the cause. This technique is similar to starting up with extensions off, but it checks for problems that go beyond extension problems.

In any case, other techniques will now be required in order to determine the precise culprit (whether it be an extension, control panel, preferences file, or whatever) and thereby solve the problem. Such techniques are described throughout this chapter and in relevant Fix-Its (especially Fix-Its #1–#4). The check just described is only a diagnostic technique designed to help narrow your focus.

By the way, to reverse the above steps, return the removed files to their former folder (now called System Stuff), delete the newly created System Folder, and rename the System Stuff folder as System Folder. Restart.

7

When You Can't Print

The Paperless Office?

In the prophesied paperless office of the future, there will be no need for printed output. However, quite the contrary is true today. Printing is one of the most common and critical of all computer activities. For most tasks, the job isn't done until you print it out—which means that if you have a problem printing, you have serious trouble.

This chapter focuses on just one of the many possible printing-related problems you could have. But it is a big one: the failure of a document to print—either because the printing never gets started or because it stops before it is finished.

Many other types of printing problems are either mentioned only in passing or not mentioned at all in this chapter. So, if you are looking for the answer to one of these problems, let me be clear about what is *not* covered in this chapter:

Formatting Problems If the printer spits out your document but the document's appearance is not what you expected, don't look here for help. These sort of problems are the domain of Chapters 9 and 10.

Problems with the Printer Itself This chapter covers some general problems related to printing hardware, such as proper connection of the printing cables. Aside from that, this chapter largely avoids a discussion of hardware-related problems (such as paper jams or replacing the toner). Instead, the focus, as is true throughout this book, is on software-related problems. Check your printer's manual for troubleshooting advice concerning your particular printer's hardware.

Problems specific to certain printers This chapter focuses on laser printers that use Apple's LaserWriter driver. It also has a section on color inkjet printers. In years past, most printers connected to Macs were made by Apple. But Apple no longer manufactures printers. These days, companies such as Hewlett-Packard and Epson dominate the Mac printing market.

TAKE NOTE ▶ Different Types of Printers

Two major categories of printers are commonly connected to Macintoshes: laser printers and inkjet.

- **Laser printers.** Laser printers use a printing method similar to that of a photocopier. Although some color laser printers are now cheap enough that more affluent, mere mortals can afford them, they are still uncommon. The vast majority of laser printers are black ink only. Still, for crisp text, finely detailed grayscale graphics and superior output speed, laser printers are the printer type of choice. These days, the most popular laser printers for the Mac are made by Hewlett-Packard.

- **Inkjet printers.** Inkjet printers work by shooting ministreams of ink from a cartridge onto the paper. Historically, the main advantage of inkjet printers over laser printers was price. Inkjet printers were much slower, the ink had a tendency to run or smudge, and the quality (especially text quality) was noticeably inferior. However, the current generation of inkjet printers has overcome most of these obstacles. They are much faster (although still slower than laser printers) with greatly improved quality. But their biggest selling point is color. For less than $300, you can get a printer that can reproduce a digital photograph with a quality that approaches what you would get by developing and printing traditional film. The leader in color inkjet printers for the Mac is Epson. Epson's Stylus Color printers use black plus three color inks whereas Epson Stylus Photo printers use black plus five color inks (for even more accurate and continuous tone color output of photographs).

  Almost all laser printers support PostScript printing—at least Level 2, often Level 3. Level 3 supports additional features not available in Level 2, but may have some compatibility problems with certain applications not found with Level 2. For most users, Level 2 is all that is needed. Some laser printers, such as those from Hewlett-Packard, do not directly license the PostScript driver from Adobe and instead use their own PostScript (Level 2 usually) emulation. Again, this should be of little consequence for most users. In general, inkjet printers do not directly support PostScript printing (although you can add it in some cases via special software called RIP).

  SEE: • **Chapter 9 on PostScript printers and text printing.**
  • **Chapter 10 on PostScript printers and graphics printing.**

Your Dialog Boxes May Vary

Printer drivers are the files in your Extensions folder that appear in the Chooser window. They have names that generally correspond to the printer you are using (such as LaserWriter 8 or SC 900). In some cases, especially LaserWriter 8, the driver works with a variety of printers and you need to select the specific file that matches your model. I'll explain the details of how this all works in a moment. For now, the point I wish to make is that the information in Page Setup and Print dialog boxes, accessed from most File menus, is determined by what printer driver you use.

Unfortunately, making sweeping generalizations about these dialog boxes and other printer-related commands is nearly impossible. One reason for this is that with the proliferation of different printers differences in the appearance of the dialog boxes are similarly proliferating. However, even if you stick with the same printer and printer driver, these dialog boxes and commands may vary, sometimes dramatically, because of differences in the different versions of the printer driver.

Laser printer drivers For laser printers, we will be assuming that you are using an 8.x version of the LaserWriter driver (probably with a Hewlett-Packard printer). The figures in this chapter will be based on the LaserWriter 8.6.5 or later.

You may alternatively use the AdobePS driver. This is a variation of the LaserWriter driver, made available directly from Adobe, rather than Apple (see: "By the Way: Using AdobePS," later in this chapter).

Inkjet drivers Inkjet printers have their own separate drivers. Different vendors will use entirely different drivers (we will be looking at the Epson driver in this chapter).

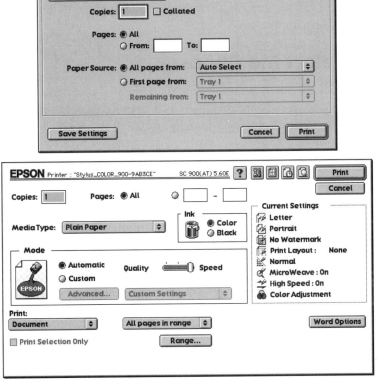

Figure 7-1 The Print dialog box of the LaserWriter 8.6.5 driver (top) and the Epson driver for the Stylus Color 900N (bottom).

When Things Go Right

Before looking at how things can go wrong when printing a document, let's start by looking at what normally happens when things go as expected with printing to a laser printer via the LaserWriter driver (ignoring the use of desktop printers for the moment). The three steps to no-hassle printing are as follows:

1. Select the Chooser.

2. Select Page Setup.

3. Use the Print command.

Remember, for the Page Setup and Print dialog boxes, what you actually see may be different if you are using a different version of the LaserWriter driver. Still, the basic principles remain the same.

Step 1: Select the Chooser

The Chooser is a desk accessory that is an essential part of the Macintosh system software. It's almost certainly already on your startup disk. It should have been installed when your System Folder was initially created. If it was not, you should get it on to your startup disk now.

 When to Use It:

You use the Chooser, as its name implies, to tell the Macintosh which printer to use when printing. Even if you have only one printer connected to your Macintosh, you still need to use the Chooser, at least once, to initially identify that printer for the Macintosh. After that, the Macintosh remembers your choice. You do not have to use the Chooser again unless you want to change your selection.

   Note: If you have Desktop Printing software installed, you can change your printer selection without going to the Chooser, as described in the section on Desktop Printers later in this chapter.

 What to Do:

Select Chooser from the Apple Menu This opens up the Chooser window, from which you make the other selections in this section.

TAKE NOTE ▶ The Fate of The Apple Printer Utility

Apple Printer Utility is the name of a utility that was previously called LaserWriter Utility and called LaserWriter Font Utility before that. It allowed you to do such things as (1) change the name of a LaserWriter printer as it appears in the Chooser, (2) check on the fonts installed in the printer (and download new ones), and (3) stop the startup page that spits out when you turn on certain LaserWriters.

Although it still works with the most recent OS versions, Apple no longer supports or updates this utility. It last appeared with LaserWriter 8.5.1. The latest versions of the Mac OS include it in the CD Extras folder. However, the Read Me file makes it clear that it is designed primarily to work with Apple printers (and Apple no longer makes printers).

If you have a Hewlett-Packard LaserJet printer, you will be able to access comparable features via the HP LaserJet Utility, included with the software that comes with the printer.

A similarly named utility, called Desktop Printer Utility, is an entirely different animal and is described in the section Desktop Printers later in this chapter.

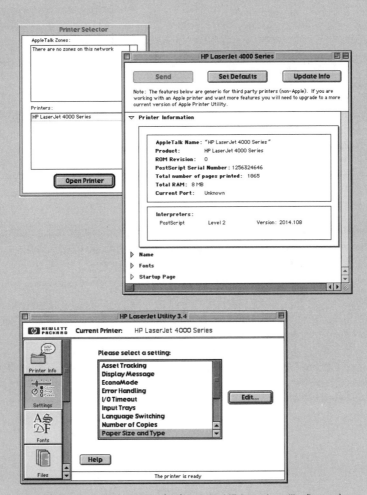

Figure 7-2 Apple Printer Utility (top) and the HP LaserJet utility (bottom).

TAKE NOTE ▶ What Is AppleTalk?

AppleTalk refers to a method of networking computers and peripherals together so that, for example, several users could all share the same printer. It is the equivalent of the language that is used to send information over the network. It is a language that all Macintoshes understand. To make an AppleTalk network connection:

1. Make sure the hardware you want to connect to the network is all AppleTalk-compatible. Every Macintosh computer comes with built-in AppleTalk support. However, not all printers do. Similarly, your printer may support some, but not all, types of connections. For example, it might support LocalTalk but not Ethernet. The manual that came with your printer should provide this information. Otherwise, check with your dealer.

2. Connect the hardware. Usually, this is done via special networking cables. The type of cables you use (and where you connect the cables) will vary depending upon the type of connection you are making.

   If you are using Apple's original networking system, called LocalTalk, you will need a LocalTalk cable (or a compatible cable such as PhoneNet). These are connected via Apple's serial ports. If your Mac has two serial ports you would typically, appropriately enough, use the Printer port, although you can use the Modem port. On the printer end, connect the cable to its serial port. Just remember (especially for PhoneNet-like systems), the cable connected to the device at each end of the chain may need a special terminating resistor, plugged into the empty slot in the phone plug.

   More common today (especially so

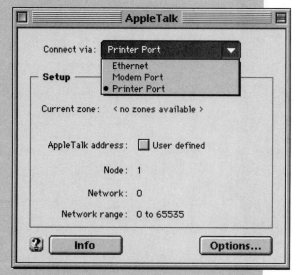

Figure 7-3 Selecting the Printer port from the AppleTalk control panel.

with Apple's newer Macs that no longer include a serial port) is to connect via Ethernet. Here you will use an Ethernet cable connected to the Ethernet port. More details of how to set up an Ethernet connection are described in Chapter 11.

3. Turn on the AppleTalk option (select Active) from the Chooser (or from the AppleTalk control panel or from the Control Strip, as appropriate). Select the appropriate port from the Configure pop-up menu (e.g., printer port vs. Ethernet). You are now ready to follow the remaining steps in this section, starting with using the Chooser.

TECHNICALLY SPEAKING ▶ AppleTalk On and Off?

If you are not using an AppleTalk-connected printer, and are not on any other network, you should keep AppleTalk turned off. Your printer will connect directly to the Mac via a (non-AppleTalk) serial cable to a serial port or via a USB port connection.

If you have a non-AppleTalk printer, you may still want your Macintosh connected to an AppleTalk network for other reasons (such as file sharing). In this case, if you have two serial ports, you could connect the printer through the modem port and connect to the network through the printer port. AppleTalk is now turned on for the network even though AppleTalk is not used by the printer. If you are using some other combination, such as a USB printer and a separate Ethernet network, you have a similar scenario.

If you wish to share such a printer with more than one Mac, there are ways to do so, such as using the Printer Share extension included with at least some versions of the Mac OS. This allows you to access a printer via File Sharing (as discussed more in Chapter 11). However, you can only access the printer if the Mac connected to it is on and file sharing is enabled for that Mac. There no such limitation for true networked printers.

SEE: • **Chapter 11 for more on networking issues.**
      • **Fix-It #14 for more details on connecting peripheral devices.**

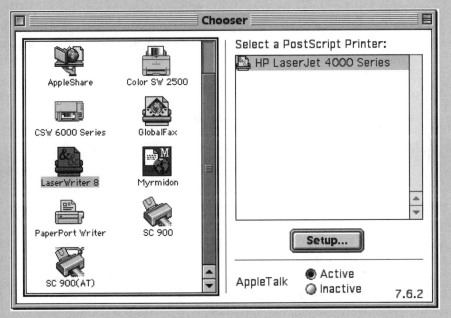

Figure 7-4 The Chooser display with LaserWriter 8 selected. AppleTalk can be made active or inactive from the Chooser (as well as from the AppleTalk control panel or from the AppleTalk Control Strip module).

Make AppleTalk Active or Inactive

Virtually all laser printers require the use of an AppleTalk network in order to work—even if it is just one Macintosh connected to one printer. Historically, this is because when laser printers were first released, they were so expensive that no one expected them to be used by just one person. Today, however, individually owned laser printers are common. Also, other types of printers including inkjets, often come with an option to connect via an AppleTalk connection.

- **For AppleTalk printers, AppleTalk should be active**

  For AppleTalk printers, you need to turn on AppleTalk before you can print anything. Do this by clicking AppleTalk's Active button, located in the lower right-hand side of the Chooser window.

  Occasionally, the AppleTalk Active button may read "Active after restart" indicating that AppleTalk will not be active until you restart. This is especially common after system crashes. Just restart, as it requests, and all will be fine.

  Where best to turn on/off AppleTalk In addition to the Chooser, you can also turn AppleTalk on or off from the AppleTalk control panel or the AppleTalk Switch Control Strip module. However, if any problems develop, turning AppleTalk on or off from the AppleTalk control panel is the preferred choice. Depending upon exactly what version of the software you are using, Apple has confirmed a bug whereby the AppleTalk selection is not retained after restarting the Mac, even if it looks like the setting is correct, unless you make the change directly from the control panel!

- **For non-AppleTalk printers, AppleTalk should be inactive.**

Select a Printer by Clicking a Printer Driver Icon

You tell the Macintosh which printer you intend to use by selecting one from the display of printer icons on the left side of the Chooser dialog box. Normally, you select the icon that corresponds to the particular printer currently connected to your Macintosh.

These icons represent the different printers you can use (as well as possibly some networking options, such as AppleShare, which I will ignore for now). What printers appear in the Chooser window is determined by which printer Chooser extensions (also called *printer drivers*) are located in the Extensions folder of your System Folder. If the icon you are looking for is not present, you need to add that printer driver to the Extensions folder before you can proceed. Printer drivers for all Apple printers are included as part of the system software. The LaserWriter driver is used for most laser printers, whether made by Apple or not. In other cases, the needed printer driver should have come with the printer itself.

SEE: • **"The Macintosh Can't Find the Printer," later in this chapter, for more details.**

At the risk of stating the obvious, selecting a particular icon only lets you use that printer if it is physically connected to your Macintosh. The icon has no magical qualities.

BY THE WAY ▶ Selecting a Printer Driver When the Printer Is Off

If your AppleTalk printer is off when you select the Chooser, you can still select its printer driver. You will not see the name of the printer appear in the scroll box. But this is not a problem as long as you don't intend to print something yet. For non-AppleTalk printers, you can similarly select their printer driver even when they are off.

In either case, doing this forces the document to be formatted as though it will be printed to the selected printer, even though the printer is not currently available. This can be used (as discussed more in Chapter 9) to format documents for printers that may not be currently attached to your Macintosh but that you intend to use for printing later. When you do print later, you may have to reselect the printer driver even though you are not really changing drivers.

Some versions of the AdobePS driver include an option called VirtualPrinter. It allows you to create a desktop printer for a printer that you do not have and save PostScript files of documents you wish to print to that printer. Later, when you have access to the desired printer, you can print the saved file and it will be formatted correctly for the printer.

Select Printer-Specific Options

- **Non-AppleTalk (serial) printers**

  Printer or modem port If you selected a non-AppleTalk printer, you usually have an option to select an icon representing one of the *serial ports:* either the *printer port* or the *modem port.* Select the icon that matches the port where the cable from your printer is connected. You can check the rear of your Macintosh to find out which port this is. Each port has an icon over it that matches the icon in the Chooser display. Despite their different names, the ports are almost identical. A non-AppleTalk printer can be successfully connected to either port.

  Special case: only one serial port? Some Macs (especially many models of PowerBooks) come with only one serial port; it acts as a combined printer and modem port. To connect a non-AppleTalk (serial) printer to these PowerBooks can get a bit complicated. In general, the principle is to make sure that the Modem control panel is set to Internal Modem (or some modem connection, such as a PC Card modem, other than the Modem Port). Then, from the Chooser, select the Modem/Printer port for your printer. Also, if problems persist, make sure AppleTalk is off.

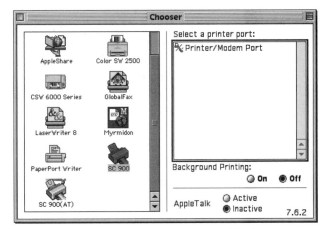

Figure 7-5 A Chooser window showing the combined Printer/Modem port option.

- **Non-AppleTalk (USB) printers**

  For printers connected to the USB port (such as an iMac), the procedure is similar. USB printers typically require special USB driver extensions that are separate from the ones that would be used for a serial connection. Especially if your printer can be connected via both a serial and a USB connection, make sure you have the right software installed for the type of connection you are making.

  Beyond that, you select the printer from the Chooser in much the same way as selecting a serial printer. However, USB printers avoid the complication of the Modem vs. Printer port issue. **Note:** Most USB printers (such as those from Epson) do not support Apple's desktop printing features. Thus you will be unable to make a desktop printer icon for these printers.

  SEE: • **"Troubleshooting Inkjet and/or USB Printers," at the end of this chapter.**
  • **Chapter 14 and Fix-It #14 for more on USB troubleshooting.**

- **AppleTalk Laser Printers**

  Select a printer name If you selected an AppleTalk laser printer, the name of the printer should appear now in the scrollable box on the right-hand side of the dialog box—but again only if the printer is currently turned on and properly connected! Click the name of the printer you are using, if it is not already selected. Unless you are on a network with several printers, there should be only one name listed. For example, after you select a LaserWriter printer driver, the name of your printer appears already selected.

  LaserWriter 8 driver: Click the Setup button After you click the LaserWriter driver icon, a Setup button will appear in the Chooser window. If this is the first time you are using LaserWriter 8 with this printer, you should select the Setup button before you try any printing. To do this, click the name of the printer (as listed in the right-hand side of the Chooser) and then click the Setup button.

  Note: If you have Desktop Printing software installed, the button should say Create, rather than Setup, prior to your first time selecting it. This is meant to imply that selecting the button will create a desktop printer for you.

  (If no printer name is listed in the Chooser or if you have not yet selected a name, the Setup button will be dimmed and therefore unusable. Since a printer's name only appears here if the printer is connected and turned on, you must connect and turn on a printer before you can select Setup for it. If it is important for you to get around this restriction, try a freeware utility, called LaserWriter Patch, that alters the driver so that the Setup button is never dimmed; just make sure the Patch has been updated to match the version of the driver you are using).

  After you select Setup (or Create) the first time, the driver will automatically determine the correct setup for your selected printer. A series of messages will briefly appear on the screen. When they are gone, you're done with Setup/Create. You only need to do this once for a given printer, not every time you reselect that printer. If a Setup has already been completed for a given printer, an icon for that printer will appear to the left of its name. If you see this icon, there is no need to bother with Setup unless you wish to make changes to the current settings.

TECHNICALLY SPEAKING ▶ PPD Files And What Really Happens When You Select Setup or Auto Setup for LaserWriter 8

Want to know a bit more about what happens when you select Setup or Auto Setup? Here's the scoop: If you properly installed LaserWriter 8, there will be a folder within your Extensions folder called *Printer Descriptions.* Within this folder are a collection of files, called *PostScript Printer Description (PPD)* files that cover every different model of LaserWriter that uses the LaserWriter 8 driver (or at least all those models available at the time your version of LaserWriter 8 was released). Non-Apple laser printers may come with their own PPD file that you can install. When you set-up a printer, the Chooser automatically ferrets out the PPD file for your printer and loads it. Additionally, your printer itself is checked for what options it may have available, such as whether an optional paper tray is installed. All of this information is then used to configure your Page Setup and Print dialog boxes to specifically match your printer and its options.

If you never select Setup at all (or if there is no PPD file that matches your printer), the LaserWriter 8 driver will probably default to a PPD named Generic (you can also select Generic from the Select PPD option in the Setup dialog box). If you have a choice, avoid the Generic setup. You will almost certainly be better off by selecting your printer-specific Setup.

By the way, when you create a desktop printer, a second copy of the associated PPD file is placed in a folder called Parsed PPD Folder, located in the Printing Prefs folder of the Preferences folder.

LaserWriter 8

HP LaserJet 4000 Series

LaserWriter 8500

Figure 7-6 The Laser-Writer driver (found in the Extensions folder) and 2 PPD files (found in the Printer Descriptions folder of the Extensions folder).

If you reselect Setup after having already previously set up the printer, you will get a dialog box that lets you select your own Setup options (you can also get this dialog box the first time you select Setup by holding down the Command-Option keys). Most of the time, Auto Setup's choices work fine. However, if needed, you can manually override its selections.

One of the buttons in the Setup dialog box is Auto Setup. Clicking this does exactly the same thing as what probably automatically happened the first time you selected Setup. Unless you are having some problem, there would thus be no reason to select this button.

Another button is the Select PPD button. This will bring up a scroll box listing all the PPD files in your Printer Descriptions folder. Just choose the particular PPD for your printer. It is possible to select a PPD file other than the one that matches your particular printer. If you do so, you may find options in the Print dialog box that your printer doesn't support (or supported options may be missing). However, when you simply select Print, the document should print out OK. Still, I wouldn't recommend doing this.

Next, if desired, click the Configure button to access selection settings for certain printer-specific options. From here, you can select what printer tray options are installed, for example.

The remaining button in the Setup dialog box is "Printer Info." It doesn't allow you to change anything, but gives you a description of your printer's characteristics (such as its resolution, its installed memory, whether it supports PostScript Level 2 or not, and so on) that you may find informative.

Whatever you do, after you are done, close the Setup dialog box.

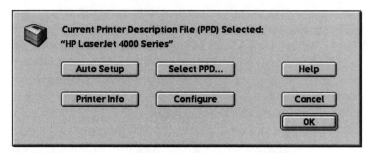

Figure 7-7 The Setup dialog box in LaserWriter 8.

- **Background printing: on or off** Background printing will appear as an option only if your printer supports this feature. With some printers (such as Epson printers), you turn background printing on or off via buttons in the Chooser dialog box. However, with printers that use the LaserWriter driver, this option is absent from recent versions of the Chooser. Instead, you select background printing directly from the Print dialog box.

  Background printing is a useful feature that allows you to regain control of the Macintosh very soon after you select Print, even before the first page is actually printed. The printing process continues in the background while you return to your other work. Thus, you can continue editing your document or work on a different application without halting the printing process. You can even select additional documents to be printed. They will just be added to the waiting queue.

  Without background printing, you have to wait until your print job is completely finished before you can use your computer for something else. Since this can take many minutes, background printing can often be a big time-saver. However, turning background printing off usually speeds up the total time until completion of a given print job—which may be relevant if you are in a big hurry to get the job done. It may also occasionally be necessary to turn it off to prevent certain problems (as described later in this chapter). Still, for most users, background printing is definitely the way to go.

  Using background printing requires the presence of the PrintMonitor and/or Desktop PrintMonitor extensions in the Extensions folder. PrintMonitor is the application that actually carries out the background printing. Normally, you do not need to interact with PrintMonitor in any way. The program handles everything itself automatically as soon as you select Print.

  SEE: • **"Special Case: Background Printing and PrintMonitor," "Special Case: Desktop Printers," and "Problems with Background Printing," all later in this chapter.**

Step 2: Select Page Setup

The Page Setup command brings up a dialog box that is important for formatting a document so that it matches the requirements and limitations of the selected printer. Thus, the options listed in this dialog box differ depending on which printer you are using. Different applications may also add their own custom options to this box.

 When to Use It:

As with the Chooser, you need not select Page Setup prior to every print request. You need only select it after you change printers (from the Chooser) or whenever you wish to change any of its options from their current settings.

 What to Do:

Working with the Page Setup Dialog Box (LaserWriter 8.6.x or Later)

1. Select Page Setup from an application's File menu.

2. There should be a pop-up menu with at least three and possibly more choices: Page Attributes, PostScript Options, and Custom Page Sizes will

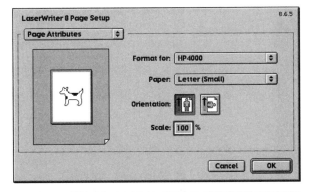

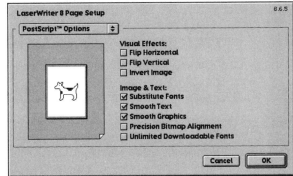

Figure 7-8 The Page Attributes and PostScript Options displays of the LaserWriter 8 Page Setup dialog box.

always be there. In addition, if your application has custom options, there will be an item with the name of the application (such as Microsoft Word).

Page Attributes From Page Attributes you can select Paper (for selecting among different sizes of paper), Orientation (portrait or landscape, as indicated by the icons), or Scale (to change the size of the entire printed output). For most common printing tasks, you should not need to change any of the default settings.

If you have more than one laser printer desktop printer created, there is even an option to select which printer you want the document to be formatted for (eliminating the need to go to the Chooser to do this).

Click the picture of the "dogcow" and you will see the detailed specifications for the paper size you selected.

PostScript Options From here, you choose from among a variety of options, such as Precision Bitmap Alignment and Substitute Fonts, that are covered in more detail in Chapters 9 and 10.

Custom Pages Sizes From here you can create your own page sizes, which can then be selected from the Pop-up menu in Page Attributes.

Application name From here, you get to select special Page Setup options that are specific to the application you are using. Fractional Widths (as described in Chapter 9) might be an option listed here.

You can turn on Balloon Help for some addition guidelines.

3. **Click OK.** This is sufficient to reformat the document to match the require-ments of the selected printer.

Note: Any changes that you make will not be saved. The next time you select Page Setup for a different document, the settings will revert to what they were initially. To save any changes, hold down Option key when you click OK. This will bring up an alert box asking if you want to "Save the current settings as the default settings." Click Save.

SEE: • **Chapter 9 on Page Setup commands and text printing.**
      • **Chapter 10 on Page Setup commands and graphics printing.**

When Changing Printer Drivers

If you change printer drivers from the Chooser, then whenever you quit the Chooser, you automatically receive a message telling you to select Page Setup. If you get this message while an application is open, simply select Page Setup from within the appli-cation and click OK. That's it.

If no application (other than the Finder) is open at the time the Chooser message appears, you can usually ignore the message. Applications should adjust to the newly selected printer automatically when the applications are launched (though see Chapter 9 for some problems that may occur).

Oddly, if you change default desktop printers (as described in the section on Desktop Printers, later in this chapter), you do not get any alert mes-sage like this.

Finally, if you get a message that says that you cannot use Page Setup because you have never selected a printer, go to the Chooser and select a printer, as the message suggests.

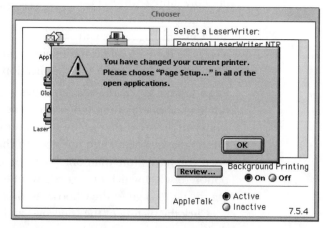

Figure 7-9 If you change printer drivers, the Chooser (when you go to close it) automatically alerts you to select Page Setup.

Step 3: Use the Print Command

The Print command brings up a dialog box that is used to select such options as how many copies you want to print and what range of pages you wish to print. As with Page Setup, its options differ somewhat depending on the printer you are using. Different applications may also add their own custom options to this box.

 When to Use It:

This is the only step that is essential every time you wish to print something.

 What to Do:

Working with the Print Dialog Box (LaserWriter 8.6.x or later)

1. Select Print from the application's File menu.

2. If you have more than one LaserWriter connected, the "Printer" pop-up menu let's you select which one you want to use (again eliminating the need to go to the Chooser to make this change). If you want your print job to be saved as a PostScript file (as described in "Technically Speaking: LaserWriter's "Destination" Option"), you make that choice from the Destination pop-up menu.

3. There should be a pop-up menu with several choices (typically at least eight, possibly more, depending upon your printer and application in use). Several of them involve issues that are beyond what we need to cover here (some, such as Color Matching and Imaging Options, are covered in more detail in Chapter 10). For now, here are the most common options you are likely to need:

   General Here is where you select how many copies you want to print, the page range and the source of the paper.

   Background Printing From here, you can select to print in: "Background" or "Foreground (no spool file)." Unless problems develop, you should leave this selected as Background. This means that control of your Mac is quickly returned to you, while the print job is processed in the "background."

   Layout Here is where you determine how many pages per sheet you want printed.

   Job Logging Here is where you select if and how you want PostScript errors reported (though these error reports will not be all that informative to most users, I would probably still select either the Summarize on Screen or Print Detailed Report options if you are retrying a print job that failed the previous time).

   Font Settings Most users will rarely, if ever, need to fuss with these options. The main one of interest is for selecting to download Type 1 (PostScript) or TrueType fonts. If you have both Type 1 and TrueType versions of the same font installed, this option determines which font type gets downloaded to the printer (if that font is included in a document you are printing). The difference can affect the appearance of the printed output (as discussed more in Chapter 9; especially see "Technically Speaking: Automatic Versus Manual Downloading"). If you have a PostScript printer and/or are using Type 1 fonts via Adobe Type Manager, you will likely prefer to select Type 1. Otherwise, select TrueType.

For most common printing tasks, you will probably only need to worry about the settings in the General window.

Different options may be available depending upon what PPD you have selected. The dialog boxes in the figures here are based on an HP 4000; the Imaging Options and Resolution Options choices (as seen in Figure 7-9) are unique to that printer. If an option you expect to find is missing, you may not have installed the appropriate PPD file (see "Step 1: Select the Chooser"). In some cases, special options may appear if you hold down the Option key when selecting this menu. For example, with my Hewlett-Packard 4000N, I get a special Preferences option by doing this (it gives me access to a long list of rarely needed modifications).

3. Save Settings if desired. Unlike Page Setup, most selections here are not automatically saved when you close the dialog box. They revert to their default option each time you select Print. Thus, even if you change the number of copies from 1 to 3, it will return to 1 the next time you select Print. However, if you want to save the settings, simply click the Save Settings button. Of course, if you select some rarely used settings and save them, you may get surprised the next time you print! Also note that settings appear to be saved globally, rather than separately saved settings for each document.

4. Click Print. The document now prints.

> **SEE ALSO:** • **Technically Speaking: LaserWriter's "Destination" Option.**
> • **Chapter 9 on Print commands and text printing.**
> • **Chapter 10 on Print commands and graphics printing.**

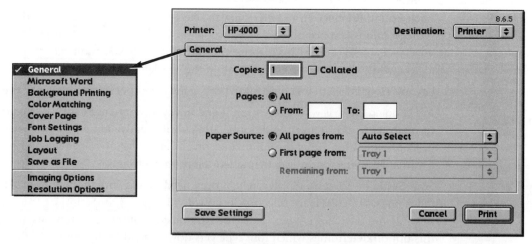

Figure 7-10 The LaserWriter 8 Print dialog box with General selected; other pop-up menu options are shown on the left.

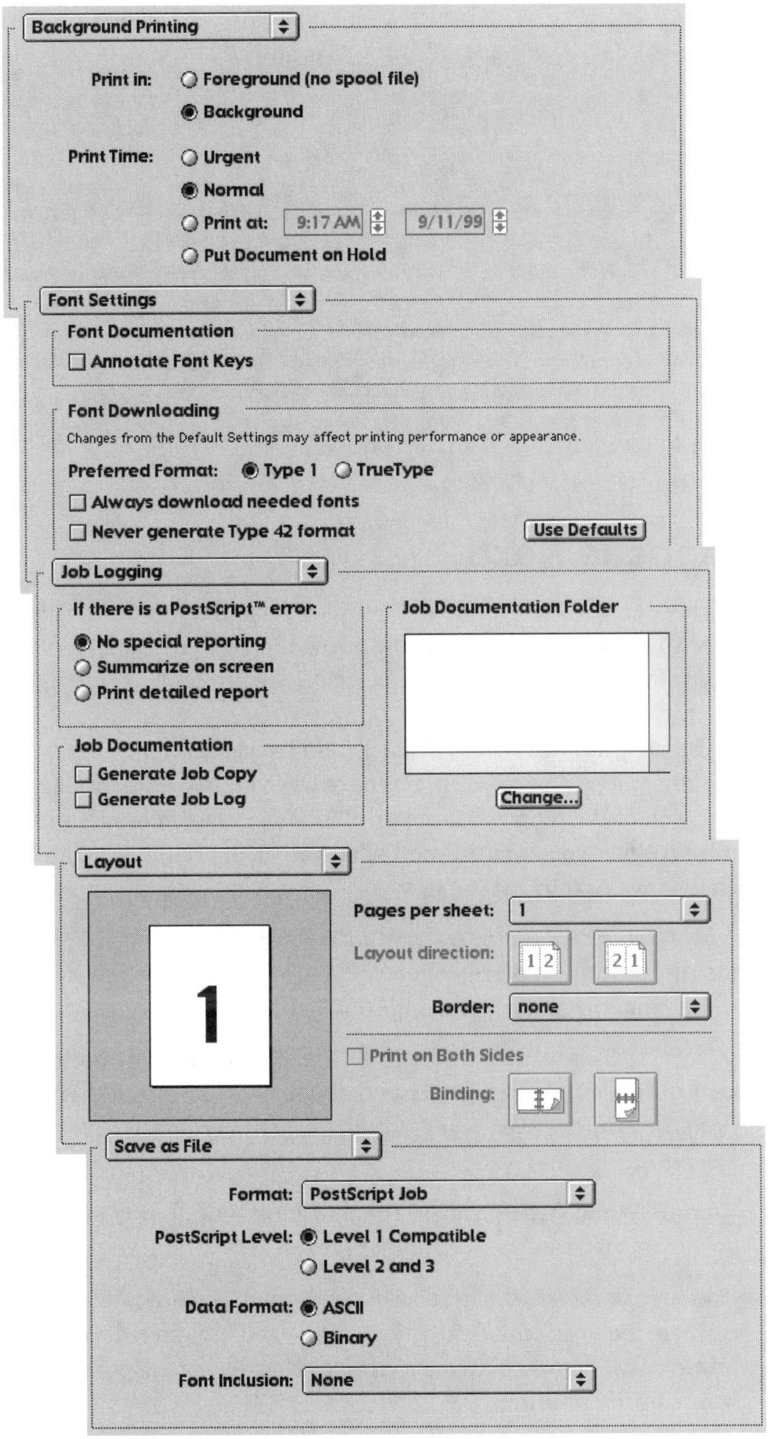

Background Printing ⬍

Print in: ○ Foreground (no spool file)
● Background

Print Time: ○ Urgent
● Normal
○ Print at: 9:17 AM ⬍ 9/11/99 ⬍
○ Put Document on Hold

Font Settings ⬍

Font Documentation
☐ Annotate Font Keys

Font Downloading
Changes from the Default Settings may affect printing performance or appearance.

Preferred Format: ● Type 1 ○ TrueType
☐ Always download needed fonts
☐ Never generate Type 42 format   [Use Defaults]

Job Logging ⬍

If there is a PostScript™ error: Job Documentation Folder
● No special reporting
○ Summarize on screen
○ Print detailed report

Job Documentation
☐ Generate Job Copy
☐ Generate Job Log   [Change...]

Layout ⬍

Pages per sheet: 1 ⬍

Layout direction: [1 2] [2 1]

Border: none ⬍

☐ Print on Both Sides

Binding: [◱] [◲]

1

Save as File ⬍

Format: PostScript Job ⬍

PostScript Level: ● Level 1 Compatible
○ Level 2 and 3

Data Format: ● ASCII
○ Binary

Font Inclusion: None ⬍

Figure 7-11 The Print dialog box display for a selection of the different options from the pop-up menu.

TECNICALLY SPEAKING ▶ LaserWriter's "Destination" Option

In the upper right corner of the Print dialog box is the option to select Printer or File as the destination of your document. Most likely, you will be selecting Printer. If you select File, your document is saved as a PostScript file on your drive, rather than being printed. The exact characteristics of the file are further determined by options you select from the Save as File pop-up menu selection. These options include whether to save the file as a PostScript file or an EPS file (see Chapter 10 for more on EPS), whether to include the font information for your document as part of the file (selecting None for a text document may mean that the document will print in an incorrect font), and whether you want the file to be Level-1 compatible or not.

Why would you ever want to save a document as a file? One use would be to save the print job as a PostScript file so that you can later print it to any PostScript printer, without needing either the original document or its creating application. Another use would be to import a selection from a program that cannot save in EPS format to a program that does support the EPS format.

By the way, as of this writing, you cannot use the Save Settings button to save File as your destination. The Print dialog box always opens up to Printer as the destination.

What Happens Next

After you select the Print command, printing is handled automatically by the Macintosh. Initially, you will see a message on the screen that tells you that the document is printing, usually with instructions that you can cancel the print job at any time by holding down the Command-period keys.

If you are printing to a LaserWriter (and background printing is off), this message is typically followed by the appearance of a second separate message window that informs you of the progress of the print job. The exact messages vary depending on what LaserWriter you are using and what you are attempting to print. But there are generally three or four basic stages:

1. *Looking for <name of printer>* or *Waiting for <name of printer>*. This message means that the Macintosh is searching for the printer currently selected from the Chooser. If the printer is on and properly connected, it will be found.

2. *Initializing.* This message, if it appears at all, appears only during the first print job after turning on the printer. Essentially, information from the Macintosh, mainly from the printer driver, is sent to the printer to establish how the printer and the Macintosh communicate.

3. *Starting job* and *Preparing data*. The Macintosh and printer are working to get the document (referred to as a *print job*) ready to be printed.

4. *Processing job.* This is the final stage before your printed output begins to appear. Here is where the PostScript instructions are finally interpreted. For long documents, the printer may alternate between *preparing data* and *processing job* messages several times before finally printing.

If your document prints without a problem, you can happily ignore all these messages. However, if a problem interrupts the printing process, it can be diagnostically useful to know exactly where in the printing process the interruption occurred.

Special Case: Background Printing and PrintMonitor

Unless you are using desktop printers (described next), using background printing requires an extension called PrintMonitor (however, this software is likely on its way out and may not be supported in future versions of the Mac OS). After you select the Print command, and assuming that background printing is on, PrintMonitor is automatically launched and begins to oversee background printing operations (the situation is a bit different if you are using desktop printers, which is described next). The first step is typically the creation of a special PrintMonitor spool file (see "PrintMonitor Documents Folder," later in this section, for more on this). On screen, an alert box will appear indicating the page-by-page progression of this spooling, which should average about a few seconds per page for text documents (even with laser printers, this process can be surprisingly time consuming with large files, although LaserWriter 8.4 appears to be significantly faster than previous LaserWriter 8 versions).

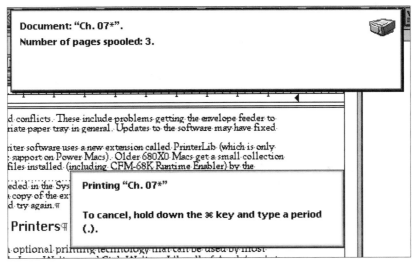

Figure 7-12 The two message windows that typically appear on your screen shortly after selecting to print, when background printing is on.

After this, control of the Macintosh is returned to you and printing begins. Then, after the print job is through, PrintMonitor automatically quits. Normally, that is all there is to it.

However, while PrintMonitor is active, its name will appear in the Application menu (that's the one in the upper right corner of the menu bar). If spooling has just completed, you may have to wait several more seconds before the PrintMonitor name first appears. In fact, it may briefly seem as if your Mac has frozen as it waits for PrintMonitor to gear up. Don't worry. Just wait a bit longer and all will be fine again.

Once its name does appear, you can select PrintMonitor as you would any other application. If you do, it opens the PrintMonitor window.

Note that PrintMonitor usually quits (its name is removed from the Application menu, unless you have its window open) before all your output has been printed. This happens when all the information needed to finish the printing job has been sent to the printer's memory. After that, the Mac itself is no longer involved.

PrintMonitor works fine whether or not you select it from the Application menu. So why would you ever select it? Here's why.

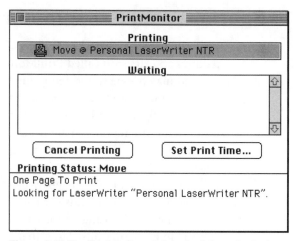

Figure 7-13 The PrintMonitor window: the information in the box under the word Printing indicates that the LaserWriter is about to print the document named Move; no print jobs are waiting in the queue.

Monitor Your Printing

Selecting PrintMonitor allows you to follow the progress of the print job. The messages that would normally have appeared on the screen (if you were *not* using background printing) are instead shifted to the PrintMonitor window. If you have several jobs queued to be printed, you can determine what they are and the order in which they will print. So, if you want to see any of this, select PrintMonitor.

Cancel Printing

If you have queued up several print jobs at once, you can also cancel any waiting print jobs from the PrintMonitor window. Just highlight the document name you want to cancel from the list in the Waiting box. Then click Cancel Printing. This is the only way to cancel a print job at this point. Using Command-period to cancel a print job is *not* an option once PrintMonitor takes over.

Do *not* go to PrintMonitor's File menu and select Stop Printing. If you do, this will stop the current and all subsequent print jobs. To undo this, you will have to return to the File menu and select Resume Printing.

BY THE WAY ▶ Not Quite Cancelling Printing

If you cancel a print job on the LaserWriter, either by holding down Command-Period or by selecting Cancel Printing from the PrintMonitor window, do not necessarily expect printing to stop immediately. As many as a dozen or so more pages may print out before the printer acknowledges your cancel request. The only sure way to prevent these pages from printing is to turn off the printer itself.

Error Messages

PrintMonitor alerts you when any sort of printing error occurs, even if you haven't selected the PrintMonitor window. Exactly how PrintMonitor alerts you (such as whether a general message appears on the screen or whether you see only a flashing icon in the menu bar) is determined by preferences settings that you select, via the Preferences command in PrintMonitor's File menu.

If you get one of these alerts, you need to select PrintMonitor to see the specific error message. Most of the likely messages are described in the next sections of this chapter. With background printing off, the error message would have appeared directly on the screen, without any need to use PrintMonitor. (**Note:** With LaserWriter 8, you may also want to select to report errors via the Error Handling settings in the Print dialog box).

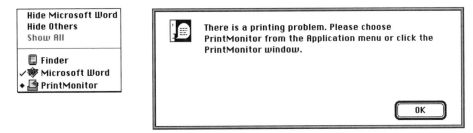

Figure 7-14 Two ways that PrintMonitor may alert you of a problem: a diamond next to its name in the Application menu (left) or an alert message that appears on your screen (right).

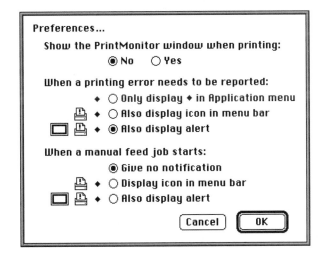

Figure 7-15 PrintMonitor's Preferences window.

Quitting PrintMonitor

When you are done working with PrintMonitor, don't close its window (and certainly don't select Stop Printing from its File menu—which brings all printing to a halt). These choices do not make you quit PrintMonitor. To exit, simply go to another application, either by using the Application menu or by clicking in any window from another application. PrintMonitor looks after itself and quits when it is done.

PrintMonitor Documents Folder

PrintMonitor creates a folder in your System Folder, called PrintMonitor Documents, where it holds temporary "spool" files that it uses to carry out the printing. These files are essentially copies of the documents to be printed, created at the time you selected Print. Thus, the printed output always reflects the state of the document at the time Print was selected. Any changes you make to the document after selecting Print are not included in the pending printout, even if you make the changes before the document is actually printed. A file in the PrintMonitor Documents folder is automatically deleted when the print job is completed.

If you are using desktop printers, these spooled files are instead held as invisible files inside the desktop printer "folder" itself. Actually, if you are using desktop printers, the PrintMonitor file is not even used. Desktop PrintMonitor is used instead (see the next section on desktop printers, for more details).

PrintingLib

PrintMonitor

Figure 7-16 The PrintMonitor and PrintingLib files (found in the Extensions folder) needed for background printing.

Special Case: Desktop Printers

Desktop printers refer to an optional printing technology that can be used by most printers, including virtually all laser printers. This software is frequently updated. The exact version you have will typically depend on which version of the Mac OS you are using or what you installed when you first set up your printer.

The essential idea of desktop printers is that you create icons for each printer that reside on your desktop. Among other things, if you drag a document to a desktop printer icon, the document will print automatically. Similarly, if background printing is on (which it ideally should be to take full advantage of this technology), double clicking the desktop printer icon opens up a window that performs similarly to the PrintMonitor window described in the previous section. Let's look at all of this in a bit more detail.

Desktop Printer Software

The desktop printer software includes Desktop Printer Spooler (an extension in the Extensions folder), Desktop Printer Manager (and extension in the Scripting Additions folder) and Desktop PrintMonitor (an application stored in the Extensions folder). There is also an optional Desktop Printer Utility application.

In older versions of the Mac OS, there was also a Desktop Printer extension, but this was eliminated starting in Mac OS 8.6, as its code was incorporated into the OS itself. When you install Mac OS 8.6 or later, this extension should be removed by the Installer, if it is present. If for some reason the extension still remains, delete it yourself. Otherwise, it may cause a system freeze.

 Desktop Printer Spooler   Desktop PrintMonitor

Figure 7-17 The Desktop Printer Spooler and Desktop PrintMonitor files (found in the Extensions folder), needed for desktop printing.

Creating Desktop Printers

Creating desktop printers could not be easier. One such icon may have even been created automatically the first time you started up after installing the software. Otherwise, go to the Chooser and select the printer

HP4000   Color StyleWriter 2500

Figure 7-18 Two desktop printer icons, as they would appear on your desktop; the bold outline around HP 4000 icon indicates that it is the default printer.

driver icon (and printer name, for AppleTalk printers) for which you wish to create a desktop printer. There should be a button on the right side of the Chooser window that says "Create" (or possibly "Setup"). Click this button.

If nothing happens, just close the Chooser and go to the desktop. Your new desktop printer icon should be there. Alternatively, when you click Create or Setup, a dialog box with several options may appear. One of these will be Auto Setup. Select this and wait for it to finish. Once again, close the Chooser. You should now have the appropriate desktop printer for your printer. You can repeat this for as many printers as you have connected to your Mac (or your network).

Figure 7-19 Left: the Printing menu that appears when you click a desktop printer; among other things, you can go here to select the given printer as the default printer. Right: you can also select a default printer from the Printer Selector Control Strip module.

Selecting a Default Printer

If you have more than one desktop printer, you have to select one to be the default printer. This is the one that the Macintosh will print to the next time you select to print a document. You can identify the default printer because its icon is outlined in a heavier bold line than the other printer icons.

There are several ways you can change the default printer:

- Go to the Chooser and select a different printer driver. Close the Chooser.

- Click a desktop printer icon, and select the Set Default Printer item from the Printing menu that appears.

- If you had the Control Strip installed when the desktop printer software was installed, it should have installed a Printer Selector module. With this, you can select the default printer from the Control Strip. Wait a few seconds for the change to take place before selecting the Print or Page Setup commands from an application.

- With laser printers, you can switch among different desktop printers from the Print dialog box's Printer pop-up menu.

Using Desktop Printers

Once installed, the desktop printer software is in use whether you select a file to be printed from the File menu (ignoring the desktop printer icons) or whether you directly use the icons by dragging a document to a desktop printer icon.

You'll prefer the desktop printer drag-and-drop method if you are printing a number of documents from several different applications, especially if you are sending them to different printers (although remember that doing this opens all of the separate applications, so be sure you have enough memory to do this). Simply drag your documents to your selection of printers, and the desktop printing software sorts everything out. No more need to go to the Chooser to switch printers (though Apple says you may occasionally have problems doing this if documents come from different applications).

And if you use file sharing, you can drag a document to a desktop printer on another mounted Mac. This works even if the printer is not otherwise directly connected to the network in any way.

No matter how you select to print (and again assuming that background printing is on), the major role of desktop printers becomes evident after control of the Mac has been returned to you and the background printing process has begun.

- First, you'll note that the icon for your desktop printer changes. If things are going well, an icon of a piece of paper will appear that will gradually fill up as printing proceeds to completion. If you halt printing a red stop symbol appears. If an error occurs, an yellow alert symbol appears.

Figure 7-20 The changing face of a desktop printer icon: the paper sheet that appears when printing is in progress; the alert symbol that appears if a problem occurs; the halt symbol that appears if you pause printing yourself; and the standard icon that appears when all is done.

- Second, if you click the desktop printer icon, a Printing menu will appear. What is in the menu depends upon what type of printer you selected, but at the very least you can select the default printer from here as well as turn on or off the Print Queue (turning off the Queue brings all printing to a halt). With laser printers, you can also select whether or not you want to Show Manual Feed Alerts. This is a new option in version 2.0 of the software.

- Third (and most significant), if you double click the desktop printer icon, it opens to a window from where you can monitor the progress of your printing in more detail.

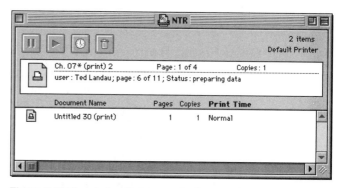

Figure 7-21 The window that opens up when you double-click a desktop printer icon. Here it shows that the document "Ch. 07*" is currently being printed while a document called "Untitled 30" is waiting in the queue.

To hold a document for printing To temporarily Hold printing for a particular item (as opposed to the entire queue), select the item and then click the relevant VCR-like button (in this case the double vertical line button). To Resume printing again, click the button with the triangle on it.

Note: If you hold down the Option-Shift keys these two buttons become Stop Print Queue and Start Print Queue buttons.

To delete a document for printing To completely remove an item from the desktop printer, click the item and select the Trash button.

The remaining button is for setting printing times, an option I will ignore here.

You can also affect the printing process by dragging document items around the window. For example, you can select an item waiting in the queue and drag it so as to rearrange its rank in the queue, making it print sooner or later than its original order. You can even drag an item from the top window (indicating the item currently printing) to the bottom window (the queue) or vice versa.

Note that while you can display documents in the queue in different sort orders by clicking the column headers (for example, clicking the word "Name" displays documents in alphabetical order), the actual printing order does not change in this case.

- This window is also the area where you can follow numerous messages (error and otherwise) that appear during background printing. Thus, if the error alert symbol appears on a desktop printer, and no error message appears immediately in the Finder, open this window to find out what the error is all about.

Finally, there are some more mysterious aspects of how desktop printers work. In some ways they behave like applications. For example, if you select Get Info, you will see that you can adjust the memory size of the printer, as you can for applications (the relevance of which is discussed next in "QuickFixes! Troubleshooting Desktop Printers"). On the other hand, these icons sometimes act as a folder, and may even appear as a folder in some Open dialog boxes of applications. In fact, it is within this "folder" that documents in the print queue are invisibly stored (again, some troubleshooting relevance of this is discussed next).

QuickFixes! Troubleshooting Desktop Printers

Before we get to the main Solve It! section, coming up next, here is a collection of troubleshooting issues specifically relevant to using these desktop printers.

- **How do I disable desktop printing?** You can temporarily turn off desktop printing by disabling the desktop printing extensions at startup (typically done by using a startup management utility). You can permanently remove the desktop printing software by dragging the files to the Trash and restarting.

  Note that using most desktop printing features requires that background printing be active. Thus, you can disable most aspects of desktop printing simply by turning off background printing (although the desktop printing software itself remains active).

  If you disable the desktop printing extensions, you can still use the older PrintMonitor-based method of background printing, as long as the PrintMonitor extension still resides in your System Folder.

- **Why do my desktop printer icons have X's over them?** If your desktop printer icons have X's over them, it usually means that the desktop printing extensions were disabled at startup (either because you selectively disabled them, as just described, or because you started up with all extensions off). You can still print (unless you are using Open Transport and started up with all extensions off), but you don't have access to any of the special features of the desktop printers. Restart with the extensions back on and all will return to normal.

  The printer icons will also have an X over them if the matching printer driver is missing from the Extensions folder for any reason. In this case, you will not be able to print.

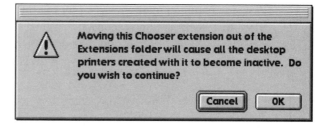

NTR   2400

Figure 7-22 Left: the X for the icons means that the desktop printer software is currently disabled or the needed Chooser extension is missing. Right: an error message that will appear if you attempt to remove (from the System Folder) a Chooser extension linked to a desktop printer.

- **Why can't I trash a desktop printer icon?** To get rid of a specific desktop printer, simply drag its icon to the Trash. However, as long as the software is active, you must always have at least one desktop printer. If you throw away the last one, it will be immediately recreated.

- **Why do I get a message that says the desktop printer cannot be found?** You may get a problem where, when you try to print, you get an alert message that says that your "spool files" have been moved to the Trash because the needed desktop printer could not be found or does not exist. There are two likely causes and solutions to this problem.

    First, it is possible that your desktop printer has somehow become damaged. To fix this, drag the desktop printer icon to the Trash and reselect the printer in the Chooser. I once had to solve this problem by reinstalling my entire LaserWriter and desktop printing software.

    Otherwise, if you have third party printer software, it may be incompatible with desktop printing, particularly Desktop PrintMonitor. In this case, go to the Chooser and turn off Background Printing and try to print again.

    Finally, if you try to print to desktop printer that has been disabled because its printer driver is missing, you may get this sort of message. In this case, you need to return the driver to the Extensions folder.

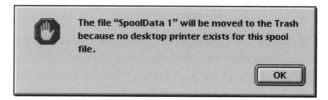

Figure 7-23 If you get this message even though the needed desktop printer is present, it usually means that you have damaged printing software or are using an incompatible application.

- **Why does nothing happen when I try to print certain documents by dragging them to a desktop printer icon?** If you drag a document to a desktop printer and nothing happens, it is likely that the document's creating application is incompatible with this drag-and-drop feature or with desktop printing entirely. There is nothing you can do about this.

Also, unlike most ordinary documents, you cannot print "clippings" files by drag-and-dropping them to a desktop printer icon.

- **Why did I lose my document when I saved it to the desktop printer "folder"?** The Save dialog boxes of applications may list desktop printers as ordinary folders. But don't save a document to these folders. This will not get the document to print. In fact, you will lose access to

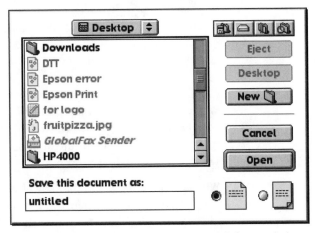

Figure 7-24 A Save dialog box that "erroneously" shows a desktop printer, HP4000, as an ordinary folder.

the document altogether. To get it back, you'll have to start up with extensions off and drag the file out of the desktop printer folder.

- **What do I do to fix a "Desktop printer unknown error -192 at 18" error?** The message is caused by a corrupted print job. To fix it, disable Desktop Printer Spooler and the Desktop PrintMonitor (via the Extensions manager or Conflict Catcher) and restart. You should now get a different error message from Print Monitor telling you about a damaged print job. Select to delete the damaged print job. Restart.

PS Spool File 1

Figure 7-25 A Spool File as you might find inside a desktop printer icon "folder." To see it, start up with Extensions Off (while a print job had been left uncompleted) and then double click the desktop printer icon.

- **What do I do if my Mac continues to crash when restarting after a printing-related system crash?** Occasionally a printing problem may cause the Mac to crash, forcing you to restart. If so, the Mac may crash again near the end of the startup as it automatically retries to print the problem file. The solution? Start up with extensions off. The desktop printer will have an X over it, but double-click it anyway. It will open up like a folder, with the waiting *Spool Files* inside visible as ordinary-looking documents. Drag the document icons to the Trash and restart as normal. Now try printing again. Hopefully the printing problem will not recur; if it does, check out the sections in the remainder of this chapter for more general advice.

- **What do I do about an insufficient memory message when trying to print?**
  Especially if you have several desktop printers, you may get an insufficient memory message whenever you try to print. To solve this, give Desktop PrintMonitor (located in the Extensions folder) more memory by increasing its Preferred memory size as listed in its Get Info window. For starters, increase it by at least 50-100K.

  A related matter: as long as there are any print requests waiting to be printed, Desktop PrintMonitor remains active in memory, even if background printing is off. If you are not printing in the background, remove all print requests from your desktop printer queue. This will "turn off" PrintMonitor, saving you the 160K or more.

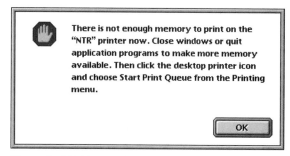

There is not enough memory to print on the "NTR" printer now. Close windows or quit application programs to make more memory available. Then click the desktop printer icon and choose Start Print Queue from the Printing menu.

OK

Figure 7-26 If this message keeps recurring across different print jobs, it often means that it's time to increase the Preferred Size of the Desktop PrinterMonitor file.

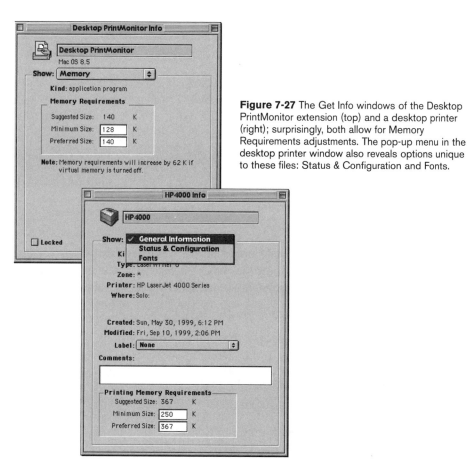

Figure 7-27 The Get Info windows of the Desktop PrintMonitor extension (top) and a desktop printer (right); surprisingly, both allow for Memory Requirements adjustments. The pop-up menu in the desktop printer window also reveals options unique to these files: Status & Configuration and Fonts.

- **What do I do if I get a message that asks if I want to adjust the memory size of my desktop printer?** If you print large complex documents, a message may appear asking if you want to temporarily adjust the memory size of the desktop printer in use. Say OK and all should go well. However, if this adjustment is not sufficient or if this problem happens often, you can permanently increase the printer's memory by selecting the Get Info window for the printer icon itself and increasing its Preferred memory size by about an additional 100-200K.

  SEE: • **Chapter 2 and Fix-It #5 for more on memory adjustments from the Get Info window.**

- **What do I do if I get a message that says I cannot use a desktop printer or otherwise have printing problems, such as freezes and crashes?** If you get a message that says a particular desktop printer cannot be used or if you otherwise cannot get printing to proceed, go to the Preferences folder and delete its Preferences file (for a printer using LaserWriter 8, look for LaserWriter 8 Prefs). Then go back to the Chooser and redo the Setup for the printer. Restart the Mac and try again.

  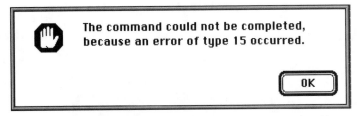

  Figure 7-28 An error message that may appear when trying to print with desktop printers.

  If you are using older versions of the system software and desktop printing software, upgrade to the latest versions.

- **What is Apple's basic advice?** For any other problems with desktop printers, here are Apple's recommended steps to take:

  1. Start with desktop printing disabled.

  2. Trash all desktop printers.

  3. Trash printing prefs folder (located inside the Preferences folder, which is inside the System folder). **Note:** If necessary, save your watermark files before trashing the printing prefs folder, or re-install the watermark files after troubleshooting is complete.

  4. Trash PrintMonitor documents folder (in System folder).

  5. Select Get Info on Desktop PrintMonitor (in Extensions Disabled folder) and add 100K to minimum and preferred memory sizes.

  6. Re-enable desktop printing extensions.

  7. Restart and rebuild the Desktop.

  8. For AppleTalk printers (for example, most LaserWriter printers) try renaming the printer using Apple Printer Utility.

TECHNICALLY SPEAKING ▶ The Desktop Printer Utility

The Desktop Printer Utility can be used to create a variety of different desktop printer icons (also called desktop translators). For example, you can create a desktop translator for a printer that is not connected to the Mac or one that is connected via the Internet, as explained next. You can also create a desktop translator that will automatically convert print requests to PostScript files. The VirtualPrinter feature of the AdobePS printer driver can do the same.

SEE: • **"By the Way: Selecting a Printer Driver When the Printer Is Off, earlier in this chapter.**
• **"By the Way: Using the AdobePS printer driver," later in this chapter.**

TECHNICALLY SPEAKING ▶ Using LPR to Print via TCP/IP

Starting with LaserWriter driver 8.5.1 (which shipped with Mac OS 8.1), you can print to a printer accessed via a TCP/IP connection. You do this via a technology called LPR (Line Printer Remote). Essentially, when you select to Print, you create a Postscript file of your printed output which is sent to the specified IP address. That address must be either for a printer or print server that accepts LPR requests (not all do). The job then prints. To set up your Mac for LPR printing, launch the Desktop Printer Utility. Then do the following (as explained by Apple):

1. Select "Printer (LPR)" and click OK.

2. In the "PostScript Printer Description (PPD) File" section, click on "Change..." and select the PPD for your printer.

3. In the "Internet Printer" section, click on "Change..."

4. Enter the printer's IP address or domain name for "Printer Address."

5. Enter the queue name, if used. Otherwise, leave it blank.

6. Click on "Verify" to verify that the printer was found.

7. Click OK.

8. Go to the File menu and select "Save."

9. Enter a name and location for the desktop printer icon and click OK. The default name is the printer's IP address, and the default location is on the desktop.

10. Quit.

Figure 7-29 The Desktop Printer Utility main window.

Select this newly created desktop printer as your default printer when you wish to use it. Of course, for all of this to work, the printer should be on an Ethernet network, with the TCP/IP control panel set to connect via Ethernet.

LPR to your own printer Of interest, you can use this setup to print to your personal printer connected to your Mac, if it is a networked printer connected via an Ethernet connection. You could then print to the printer via TCP/IP rather than via AppleTalk (the more common method, as described throughout this chapter).

Why do this? There is no reason if the AppleTalk method is working fine. But Apple is expected to eventually phase out AppleTalk in future hardware and software and this LPR method may thus become a necessity. Also, if you use a cable modem or are on any network that supports AppleTalk printing, a problem may sometimes occur where your print jobs are mistakenly routed to AppleTalk server rather than to your printer directly. The result is that you may be unable to print. Using TCP/IP printing can work around this.

One downside is that TCP/IP printing is often slower than printing over AppleTalk.

Solve It! When Things Go Wrong

Most of the time, if you have followed the preceding three steps—select the Chooser, Page Setup, and Print—your printing proceeds without any further problem. Then there are those remaining times, when the printer simply refuses to cough up your request. The following sections detail the myriad of reasons that a printing request may fail and what you can do about it.

TAKE NOTE ▶ **General Advice for All Printing Problems: Try Again**

Before bothering to wade through all of the specific advice in the rest of this chapter, simply try printing again. Maybe you had a one-time glitch and the problem will not repeat itself.

For starters, if you get an error message that includes a *Try Again* button, give it a try (unless you already suspect that you know what the problem is and know that simply trying again immediately will not work). If the error message offers any explanation or advice, make use of it (such as by adding paper or turning on AppleTalk, as indicated) and then try again. You may have to select *Cancel Job* or *Stop Queue* (or whatever) before you can do this.

Otherwise, simply quit the application from which you are trying to print. Launch it again and try to print again. If that fails, turn the printer off; wait about ten seconds or so; then turn the printer back on and try again (this *reinitializes* the printer). If even that fails, shut down the Mac and the printer. Then turn everything back on and try to print the document yet again. Always make sure the printer is correctly selected in the Chooser.

Obviously, if you had a system crash, you may have little choice but to restart and try again.

If it is practical to do so, before trying to print again, close all open applications and documents not needed for the printing to proceed. This frees up additional RAM, which may solve the problem.

Note: If an error message does not appear on your screen (either while in the application or in the Finder), you may have to select PrintMonitor or open the default desktop printer (if you are using this software) before you can see it. In any case, the Mac may seem to freeze briefly before an error message appears. If so, don't worry; the error message will usually show up in a few moments. If not, you probably did not get any error message.

SEE ESPECIALLY: • **"QuickFixes! Troubleshooting Desktop Printers" and "Printing Halts Due to a System Crash, PostScript Error, or Other Printing-Related Error."**

The Macintosh Can't Find the Printer

 Symptoms:

You select Print from the application's File menu and one of the following events happens:

- The Print dialog box does not appear. You immediately get an error message that says the Macintosh *can't open printer*.

- The Print dialog box appears. You click OK. However, then you get the message that the Macintosh *can't open printer*.

- You may get a message that says the printer *could not be found* or *is not responding.*

- An error message of any other sort appears instead of the Print dialog box.

Note: You have to leave your application and go to the Finder to see some of these alert messages. In all these cases, the result is that no printed document ever appears. The good news is that probably nothing is wrong with the printer. Even better, the solutions here tend to be quick and easy.

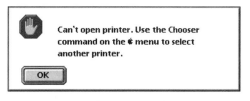

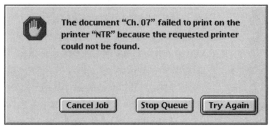

Figure 7-30 Examples of error messages that may occur after you select Print, if the Macintosh cannot locate or access the selected printer.

 Causes:

Typical causes are that the Macintosh cannot locate the printer driver, that the wrong printer driver is selected, or that the printer is not properly connected. If your printer requires an AppleTalk connection, it may be that AppleTalk (or PrinterShare, for those printers that can use this option) is not turned on or that the wrong printer name is selected. The wrong port (printer as opposed to modem) may be selected. Corrupted Parameter RAM (PRAM) can also cause this problem. Or it may be as simple as that your printer is turned off.

Often, you may get an error message that describes the likely cause. For example, it may say *Use the Chooser to make AppleTalk active.* If you get this sort of helpful advice, follow it.

 What to Do:

Try Printing Again

SEE: • "Take Note: General Advice for All Printing Problems: Try Again," earlier in this chapter.

Make Sure the Printer Is Ready to Print

Make Sure the Printer Is Turned On It never pays to overlook the obvious. If the printer is not on, turn it on. If it doesn't turn on, check that it's plugged in. Similarly, make sure the power cord is firmly connected to the printer. You'll know the printer is on when either its status lights are on or the printer at least makes some noise.

Several printers these days have an energy-saving feature that turns the printer off (in a sort of "sleep" mode) when not in use, automatically awakening them when needed. This saves you the hassle of worrying about whether or not the printer is on.

For Laser Printers: Make Sure You Did Not Select the Print Command Too Soon After Turning the Printer On If you select Print too soon, the Macintosh does not recognize the presence of the printer. Wait for the printer to complete its startup cycle. It takes about a minute. You can usually tell this has happened when the printer status lights stop flashing. At this point, reselect the Print command.

Try Plugging the Printer Cable into the Other Serial Port Assuming you are a single user with a Macintosh and a printer, a cable connects the Macintosh to the printer. On Macs with serial ports, this cable usually runs from one of the serial ports on the Macintosh (usually the printer port) to the appropriate port on the printer (there is usually only one port that fits the cable you are using).

For non-AppleTalk printers, if your printer is currently plugged into the printer port, switch it to the modem port—or vice versa. This may help if one of the ports is damaged (which ultimately requires a hardware repair to fix). You will also have to change the port selection from the Chooser. For AppleTalk printers on a LocalTalk network, you can also switch your cable to the other serial port. In this case, you also need to make the switch in software via the AppleTalk control panel.

For printers on an Ethernet network, there is nothing to switch (just make sure the Ethernet cable is connected).

Make Sure You Are Using a Correct Cable If you have never used this printer and/or connecting cable before, there is a chance that you are trying to use an incorrect cable. For example, the cable for connecting a modem to the Macintosh may look identical to the one used to connect a non-AppleTalk printer. But they are not necessarily the same. You may not be able to use a modem cable for printing—or vice versa. Similarly, the cable used to make an AppleTalk connection is different from the standard serial cable used for non-AppleTalk printers (see "Take Note: What Is AppleTalk?" earlier in this chapter). If you are uncertain whether your cable is correct, take your cable to an Apple dealer (or other knowledgeable source) to check it.

For a printer connected to an Ethernet port, you need the correct Ethernet cable (as described in Chapter 11).

Make Sure the Cable Is Firmly Plugged In and Not Damaged Check if the printer cable is loose. Reconnect it if needed. Make sure no pins on the plug are bent or missing. To be certain that a cable is not defective, switch it with a different one that is successfully working with another printer, if possible. If this solves the problem, then the original cable was damaged.

After Completing the Previous Checks, Try Printing Again Even if you didn't find anything amiss, try again anyway. Printing may proceed successfully. If the document still fails to print, proceed to the next step.

TAKE NOTE ▶ Missing or Damaged Preferences (Especially with LaserWriter 8)

If you get an error message, either when selecting to print or when opening the Chooser, that says *The LaserWriter 8 Preferences file may be missing or damaged,* you most likely have not selected the Setup command for your printer. Go to the Chooser, select the printer driver icon, select the printer name, and then click the Setup button. As a last resort for this or related problems, go to the Preferences folder and locate the Printing Prefs folder. A file called LaserWriter 8 Prefs should be inside. Delete the file, then go to the Chooser and select Setup for your printer.

LaserWriter 8 Prefs

Figure 7-31 Trash this file if you keep getting messages that it is missing or damaged.

Check the Chooser

Incorrect settings from the Chooser are a common source of problems at this point in the printing process. However, note that if you are using desktop printer software, you may be able to bypass the Chooser here and, for example, select or switch default printers by a number of other methods.

SEE: • **"Special Case: Desktop Printers," earlier in this chapter.**

If You Cannot Locate the Chooser in the Apple Menu This means that the Chooser is not in the Apple Menu Items folder. If necessary, locate it (either elsewhere on your disk or on a backup disk) and place it in the Apple Menu Items folder in your System Folder. Once you have installed, located, and selected the Chooser, do the following.

Make Sure the Correct Printer Driver Icon Is Selected If you are using a LaserWriter printer, select the LaserWriter icon. If the correct icon is not present, it means that the printer driver for your printer is not present in the Extensions folder. To correct this, locate the correct driver from your Macintosh system software disks (or, if you are using a non-Apple printer that has its own driver, locate this driver), and place it in the Extensions folder.

If You Are Using AppleTalk, Make Sure It Is Active If it isn't, you get a message to this effect when you try to print a document.

If You Are Using AppleTalk, Check That the Name of Your Printer Is Listed and Selected The name should appear after you select the printer driver icon, assuming the printer is already on.

SEE: • **"When Things Go Right" earlier in this chapter.**

If no name appears, it means that the Macintosh does not recognize the presence of the printer. For laser printers, assuming that you have already checked that the printer is on and connected properly (as described previously), it usually means you haven't waited long enough for the printer to warm up after turning it on (some printers now have an "instant on" feature and will not require this warm-up period).

To solve this problem, quit the Chooser (even though this step probably isn't necessary). Wait a minute. Then select the Chooser again. The name should now appear. Select it if it is not already highlighted.

If this fails to work, go to the AppleTalk control panel and reselect the correct port for your printer, even if it is already correctly selected. In one case of a printer connected to an Ethernet port that was not showing up in the Chooser, selecting the Printer port and then reselecting the Ethernet port, finally got the printer's name to appear in the Chooser. For Ethernet-connected printers, the Ethernet hardware and addresses must also have been correctly set up when you first installed the printer (see Chapter 11 if you need more advice about this).

TAKE NOTE ▶ **Problems Printing With Extensions Off: AppleTalk Can't Be Made Active and -23 Errors**

If you start-up with Extensions Off (by holding down the Shift key) and then select Print, you may get an error message that says that AppleTalk is off and that you need to turn it on in the Chooser to get printing to proceed. In some cases, you may instead get a -23 error, which refers to the same problem. In any case, when you go to the Chooser and try to select AppleTalk, you get a message such as one that says "*The printer port is in use. AppleTalk cannot be made active now*" or simply "*AppleTalk cannot be opened.*" What's going on? What do you do?

The answer here is that printing requires Open Transport software. This was disabled when you started with extensions off. The solution is to use Extensions Manager or Conflict Catcher and select the Mac OS Base set of extensions. This should allow you to print.

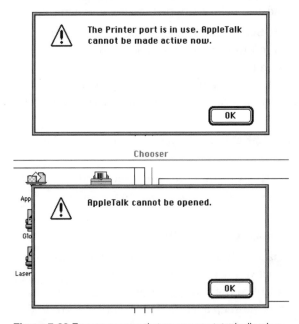

Figure 7-32 Error messages that you may get, typically when in the Chooser, when you use Open Transport and try to print with Extensions Off or with Open Transport software otherwise disabled; doing this prevents you from using AppleTalk which then prevents you from printing to an AppleTalk-connected printer (such as a LaserWriter).

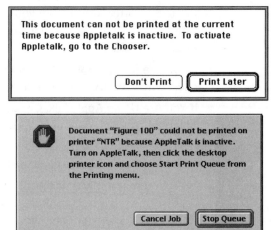

Figure 7-33 If you have AppleTalk turned off when trying to use a printer that requires AppleTalk, you may get a message like one of these.

If you are on a LocalTalk network that has several Macs and/or printers daisy-chained together, be aware that if someone disconnects from the chain (by pulling their cable out) and they are between you and the printer, you will not be able to access the printer. So make sure your fellow office workers keep their cables properly connected.

Finally, note that the top line of the Print dialog box gives the name of the currently selected printer. This may be different from the name of any printer that is now available on your network. For example, if you have a PowerBook and print to one printer at work but another at home, you may be at home but your PowerBook may still list your workplace printer as the selected one. In this case, the Macintosh will claim that it cannot find the selected printer. To solve this problem, again simply select the Chooser and select the name of any currently listed printer.

TAKE NOTE ▶ Finding your Printer Name: When a Shut Down is better than a Restart

If the Chooser refuses to list your AppleTalk printer's name no matter what you do, sometimes the magic of a restart will do the trick. Try it. However, I have occasionally found (particularly with PowerBooks) that even if a restart fails to work, a Shut Down and subsequent Restart will succeed.

For Non-AppleTalk Serial Printers: Check the Port to which the Printer Cable Is Connected Make sure the selected serial port icon is the one that has the printer cable connected to it. That is, if the icon is for the printer port, make sure the cable is in the printer port and not the modem port. Also, it may help simply to turn the printer off and then on again. In some cases, it may be necessary to turn AppleTalk *off* (if you have file sharing enabled, you will have to turn it off in order to turn AppleTalk off).

SEE: • **"When Things Go Right," especially the list item "Non-AppleTalk printers," earlier in this chapter, for more advice, including advice concerning PowerBooks with only one serial port.**

If you are trying to use PrinterShare (or GrayShare or ColorShare) to print to a computer connected to another Macintosh, remember that the computer that the printer is connected to must be turned on as well as the printer itself. Unlike with AppleTalk, it is not sufficient that just the printer be on. Also, in order for the printer to be shared, the Share This Printer option must be turned on for that printer. This is done through the Chooser: Select the printer's icon and then click the Setup button to see this option. Using this feature may also require that the printer be connected to the modem port, not the printer port.

Try Printing Again If you have successfully navigated your way through the Chooser dialog box, close the Chooser, reselect Page Setup if needed, and reselect the Print command. The document should now print.

Investigate Other Possibilities

If none of the preceding suggestions worked, consider any or all of the following, as appropriate.

The Wrong Version of the Printer Driver Generally, you should use either the version of the printer driver that matches the version of your System and Finder or a more recently updated version (see later in this chapter "Take Note: Mixing Versions of Printers, Printer Drivers, and Other System Software," for more on this).

A Corrupted Printer Driver The printer driver may be damaged. To check for this possibility, replace it with a copy from your backups. For example, if you are trying to print using a LaserWriter, replace the LaserWriter driver extension in the Extensions folder with a backup copy. For LaserWriter 8, also replace the PPD files. Reinstall all printing software if in doubt.

Corrupted Parameter RAM (PRAM) The PRAM, a special area of memory, contains information necessary for the serial ports to work. If the PRAM becomes corrupted, information cannot get sent through the serial ports (printer and modem) to the printer. The PRAM then needs to be reset (or *zapped*, as it is often called) before printing can proceed.

SEE: • Fix-It #9 for more about the Parameter RAM and how to zap it.

Hardware Problems If none of the previous suggestions work, a hardware problem looms likely. It's time to take your printer (or perhaps your Macintosh itself) in for repairs.

SEE: • Fix-It #15 on hardware problems.

Printing Halts with No Error Message

 ## Symptoms:

The printing process does not even begin, or it begins but then stops in midstream. In either case, no error message occurs. Everything else seems to be operating as normal. It is simply that a long time has passed and the printer is producing no output.

 ## Causes:

It may be that everything is fine and that the document just needs a long time to print. Otherwise, an *endless loop* type of system error has probably occurred.

SEE: • Chapter 4 for more on endless loops and related system errors.

In the latter case, the document never prints out, no matter how long you wait. If this happens with a LaserWriter, you are likely to notice that the print job seems to be stuck forever in the *preparing data* or *processing job* phase.

The ultimate causes of such system errors are the typical ones: software bugs or damaged files (see also the next section for more on these causes). Occasionally, the problem may be due to insufficient RAM, either in the Macintosh or (in the case of laser printers) the printer itself.

🖳 What to Do:

Is the Queue Stopped?

If all printing seems to have stopped, make sure you have not inadvertently stopped the entire print queue, either by selecting PrintMonitor's Stop Printing command or by selecting desktop printer's Stop Print Queue (in which case a stop symbol will be on the desktop printer icon). If so, select to start/resume printing again.

If You Are Using Background Printing

If you are using background printing, you usually regain control of the computer before the first page prints out. If so, and no error message appears in the Finder, you can check the PrintMonitor window (or desktop printer icon window, if you have this software installed) to make sure no message is waiting there. With desktop printers, you can usually tell that there is a message waiting, because the desktop printer's icon will include a yellow alert symbol. In either case, the Application menu will probably be flashing.

   If no message (or no message with helpful advice) appears, delete the document from the queue (by selecting Cancel Printing in PrintMonitor or by trashing the document with desktop printers) and try printing again.

If You Are Not Using Background Printing

If you are not using background printing, you are probably stuck with some sort of *Now printing* message on the screen. Press Command-period to try to cancel the printing. Press it a few times. Wait a minute or so to give it a chance to cancel the process.

Do a Forced Quit or Restart the Macintosh

If none of the previous procedures has any effect, you can treat this as a system freeze and try a forced quit (press Command-Option-Escape) of the application. Otherwise, you have to restart the computer.

SEE: • **Chapter 4 on forced quits and restarting.**

Reinitialize the Printer

In any case, once you regain control of the Macintosh, reinitialize the printer: turn off the printer, wait a few seconds, and turn it back on again.

Try Printing Again

Return to your application and select the Print command a second time. See if it works now.

SEE: • **"Take Note: General Advice for All Printing Problems: Try Again," earlier in this chapter.**

TECHNICALLY SPEAKING ▶ **What Accounts for Printing Speed?**

Speed of printing is hard to predict because it depends on so many different factors. Similar to automobile mpg, your printing "mileage" may vary.

The first factor is the printer itself. Usually, a printer is rated in terms of pages per minute (ppm). This represents the approximate maximum rate that the printer can produce its output. Most current laser printers are in the range of 10 ppm or even more. The ppm rating is primarily a function of the physical limits of the actual printing machinery. However, printers rarely meet this theoretical maximum.

For example, for laser printers (especially PostScript laser printers), real printing times are also influenced by any computer processing hardware built into the printer. Thus, the faster the processor in the printer can get the information to the printing machinery, the more likely the printer can live up to its ppm maximum. Similarly, the greater the amount of RAM in the printer, the faster that printing generally proceeds.

Speed is also influenced by events that take place before the information ever reaches the printer. The specific version of the printer driver can have an effect. Newer versions often include improvements designed to enhance printing speed.

Sometimes the printing application itself has an effect. Thus, two different word processors may print similar documents at different rates.

The nature of the document itself has a major effect on speed. Simple formatted text usually prints the fastest. Heavily formatted text and (especially) complex graphics slow the operation down considerably. Large multi-colored graphics printed to an inkjet printer can take a very long time indeed.

You can speed up printing somewhat by turning background printing off—but then you lose the advantage of more quickly regaining control of the Macintosh. As always, free lunches are hard to find!

For Laser Printers: Is It a Complex Document?

If the document still fails to print, don't automatically assume that you have a system error. Consider whether you simply have a document that takes a long time to print. For laser printers, where an entire page is printed at once, it is not unusual to have to wait a considerable amount of time before the printing of the page begins. Particularly if the page contains large or complex graphics, it could take ten to fifteen minutes, or even more, for the laser printer to spit it out.

So if you are printing something new and different, where you don't have experience with how long it should take, give it a chance before assuming the worst. If everything else seems to be working normally (for example, the green status light on the printer is blinking as expected), go away for a while. By the time you return, it may print.

Check the Status Lights

There is typically one status light that turns on when you are out of paper. Another light indicates a paper jam. Attend to these problems as necessary. Check the manual that came with your printer for how to remove jammed paper. If both lights are on at the same time (or are flashing in any way), it almost certainly means a hardware repair is needed.

SEE: • Fix-It #15 for more general information on hardware problems.

If None of the Preceding Steps Work

If none of this works, treat the problem as a more general system error. Continue to the next section.

BY THE WAY ▶ **Output Too Light, Too Dark, Or Streaked?**

When LaserWriter output becomes too light or prints with streaks, it probably means that you need to replace the toner cartridge. Too light or too dark output can also be adjusted by changing the print density control, a knob located on the printer (location varies with different models). Sometimes, these symptoms mean that you have to replace a hardware part called the fuser assembly.

Printing Halts Due to a System Crash, PostScript Error, or Other Printing-Related Error

 Symptoms:

Printing halts as a result of any of the following:

- A system crash occurs, usually generating the system bomb error message.

    SEE: • Chapter 4 for more general information on system errors.

- An error occurs that says *the serial port is in use.*

    SEE: • "Serial: Printers, Modems, and Networks," in Fix-It #14, for more on serial port problems.

- A specific printing-related error occurs, usually indicated by a printing-related error message. For example, with PostScript LaserWriters, it is common for the message to read *PostScript error.* These have more specific names such as: *"Set limitcheck," "VM Storage," "Offending command...,"* or *"Range Check."* Usually, additional text follows. Sometimes, this text indicates the precise source of the problem (such as too many fonts in use). More commonly, you cannot make any sense out of the often cryptic content of the message—and it is probably not really worth trying.

    SEE: • Chapters 9 and 10 for more on PostScript.

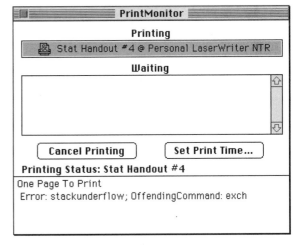

Figure 7-34 A PostScript error, as reported in PrintMonitor.

- An error message appears suggesting a problem with incompatible printer software or system software.

- If you are using PrintMonitor or desktop printers, you may get a message that suggests that they are the cause of the problem (such as a lack of sufficient memory for PrintMonitor to work).

These events may happen even before the first page is printed, or may occur at some point in the middle of a print job. Particularly for LaserWriters, a print job may successfully begin and then halt at a particular page because of a problem specific to the contents of that page.

Remember that the Mac may seem to freeze temporarily prior to the appearance of a printing error message. This is normal. Just wait and the Mac will probably "unfreeze" shortly and the error message will appear.

Many error messages will cite insufficient memory as a cause. However, this message cannot be entirely trusted. Often, something else is the true cause.

 ## Causes:

There are two likely candidates as the source of all of these problems: software bugs or corrupted software.

Bugs in the Relevant Software

Technically, any software that is active at the time of printing could be the offending party. This could include any startup extension or the System file itself. However, the most likely candidates are the printer driver, the PrintMonitor file or desktop printing software, any other non-Apple background printing software you are using, or the application that issued the Print command.

Sometimes the problem may represent an interaction between one of these files and some particular characteristic of the document to be printed, such as the type of font used or a specific graphic element. The bug may be such that the problem occurs only with a specific model of printer, or it may affect all printers.

As is always the case with software bug problems, there is no way to eliminate the bug yourself. That must await a future upgrade to the product. However, some common workarounds may allow you to print a document, despite the presence of the bug.

Corrupted Software

In this case, the problem is that one of the files involved in the printing process has become corrupted. The most likely guilty parties are the same ones as for software bugs, especially the printer driver, PrintMonitor or desktop printers. Additionally, the document itself or font files that the document uses may be corrupted.

The exact events that caused the damage may never be known. However, it doesn't really matter. The important thing is to recognize the problem and to replace the damaged file with an intact copy from your backup disks.

PostScript errors are typically due to corruption in the PostScript output generated when you try to print a file to a PostScript printer. However, these errors also may have nothing directly to do with PostScript output. A corrupted font or graphic image may be the actual cause.

SEE: • **Chapter 2 on damage control, for more general information.**

Other Causes

Other possible causes include the wrong printer driver selected, insufficient memory available, insufficient unused space on the startup disk, and corrupted PRAM. Damaged cables may also cause a PostScript error.

 What to Do:

Try Printing Again

SEE: • **"Take Note: General Advice for All Printing Problems: Try Again," earlier in this chapter.**

If trying again fails to work, try to determine the exact cause of the problem, as described in the following sections. Unless the specific error message you receive offers guidance as to what to do first, there is no particular recommended order for trying these solutions. All other things being equal, try the ones you find easier to do and less disruptive first. I begin with two suggestions that are the most often successful. After that, try the subsequent suggestions until one works.

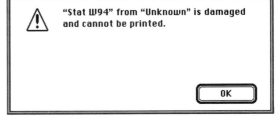

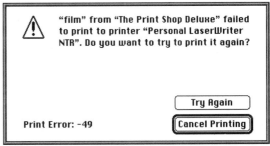

Figure 7-35 Two examples of messages that could mean that a printing problem is due to a damaged document.

Replace Potentially Corrupted Files

If a printing problem is caused by a damaged file, replacing the file should solve the problem. To check for this, do the following.

Replace Printing-Related Files Use your backup disks as a source of uncorrupted copies of these files. In particular, replace the printer driver, the PrintMonitor file (if you are using background printing), and the application file and its accessory files.

Replace the Document File If a document file is corrupted, you will probably notice this as soon as you open the document. The content of the file will probably be partially missing or garbled in some way. In fact, the document may not even open at all. Sometimes you may be "lucky" (in terms of finding a cause) and get an error message indicating a damaged document. However, even if everything seems normal, you may still have damage that somehow prohibits printing of the document. It's worth a try to replace the document with a (hopefully uncorrupted) backup.

Otherwise, you may find that you only have trouble printing a specific page or paragraph. While this could indicate a corrupted font, it may also mean problems with the document itself. You may be able to fix this by simply deleting the problem text and retyping it.

Delete the "Spool" File If, when trying to print a file with background printing on, you get a message that the file could not print because it was damaged, the damage may not be to the original document. Instead, it may be with the "spooled" version of the document that is created when background printing is on. If you cannot delete the document from the PrintMonitor window, the solution is to go to the PrintMonitor Documents folder in the System Folder and delete the document. If you use desktop printers, you instead delete the document directly from the desktop printer icon's window (see "QuickFixes! Troubleshooting Desktop Printers," for exactly how to do this). Then try to print again.

Replace a Potentially Corrupted Font File If a font file becomes damaged, documents that contain that font may display correctly on the screen but not print (this is a particularly likely possibility for TrueType fonts, but it occurs for other font types as well). If a printing problem seems specific to the presence of a particular font, suspect this as the cause. In such a case, you need to replace the corrupted font file (for PostScript fonts replace both the printer font and the screen font).

Shift to a Different Font While replacing a corrupted (or otherwise problematic font) is the recommended course of action, sometimes you may be too rushed to want to bother or maybe replacing the font didn't solve the problem. In these situations, an obvious work-around is simply to shift to a different font. For example, I once had a case where printing in Palatino Bold Italic led to a PostScript error but printing the same text in plain Palatino worked just fine. Shifting fonts does not eliminate the ultimate source of the problem, but it at least gets your document to print.

Even better, in some cases, these errors can be resolved just by changing the portion of text that uses a suspected problem font to another font and then changing it back again to the original "problem" font. Try this before you try more extreme measures.

Retry Printing Retry printing after each replacement. See if the printing problem goes away.

SEE: • **Fix-Its #2, #4 and #11 for more on replacing damaged files.**
     • **Chapter 9, "Damaged Font Files," for specifically how to detect and replace a damaged or corrupted font.**

Serial Port Is Currently in Use?

If you have a serial printer (non-AppleTalk) connected to the Printer port and you mistakenly select the Modem port as its assigned port in the Chooser, and a modem is connected to the modem port, and especially if the modem is in use (whew, that's a lot of "ifs"), you will get a message that says the "serial port is currently in use" when you try to print. The solution is to go to the Chooser and select the correct port. Then try printing again.

In fact, any time the serial port your printer uses is also used by AppleTalk, you will get this message. Actually, this "serial port is currently in use" message may mistakenly occur when the serial port settings have become corrupted. Fixing this requires "resetting" the serial port. The simplest way to do this is by restarting your Mac. If this fails to work, you may have to zap the PRAM (see next item).

It is also possible that AppleTalk is enabled even though the Chooser setting is listed as "off." In this case, select to turn AppleTalk off from the AppleTalk

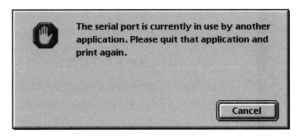

Figure 7-36 This message is often a bit misleading; selecting the correct port from the Chooser, or otherwise simply restarting the Mac, usually fixes this problem.

control panel. This is discussed in the "Make AppleTalk Active or Inactive" section earlier in this chapter (also see the Serial Port section of Fix-It #14).

Zap the PRAM

Consider this especially if you got the message that said printing was unsuccessful because "the serial port is in use." If you get system errors while in the Chooser, zapping the PRAM often solves that problem as well.

SEE: • Fix-It #9 on zapping the Parameter RAM.

Check the Printer Driver

Make sure the printer driver you selected from the Chooser is the one that matches your printer. The wrong selection can result in a variety of unusual error messages.

Shift to a Different Version of the Printer Software

As a rule, you are safe using the printing software that was included as part of the system software you are using. However, you may also want to use a more recently updated version, as long as that version works with your software.

When upgrading, make sure you use the Installer utility on the system software or printer driver installer disk. Don't just drag a driver to your Extensions folder. For one thing, you need to upgrade PPD files as well as the driver. Also, the Installer utility may perform operations that would not be duplicated by simply copying files.

As a rule, don't use printing software from system software that is older than that which you are currently using. However, in certain cases, this may be advised. For example, a new version of the LaserWriter driver may be incompatible with an older version of an application. Shifting to an older version of the driver may eliminate the problem.

If problems persist, try any or all of the following procedures:

Check the Printer Cable

Check if the printer cable is loose. Reconnect it if needed. Make sure no pins on the plug are bent or missing. To be certain that a cable is not defective, switch it with a different one that is successfully working with another printer, if possible. If this solves the problem, then the original cable was damaged. Make sure you are using the right cable.

Turn Off Certain Printing-Specific Options

Some of the following suggestions apply only to certain types of printers.

Turn Off Fractional Character Widths A Fractional Character Widths checkbox option, if your active application includes this feature, may be found in the Page Setup dialog box, though in some applications it may be in a separate Preferences dialog box or even directly in a menu (check the manual of your application to determine where it is located). With the LaserWriter driver, it will typically be in the application-specific pop-up menu. For example, with Word 98, select Microsoft Word from the pop-up menu in the Print dialog box, then select Word Options; Fractional Widths will be one of the options listed. Making changes to this option affects only the current application. Fractional Widths settings in other applications have to be adjusted separately, as needed.

For high-resolution printers, such as virtually all laser printers, checking this option should improve the appearance of printed text by adjusting the spacing between letters. But this option may also cause problems that prevent the document from being print-ed. For example, I once got a PostScript error while trying to print a particular page of a document with Microsoft Word. Turning off Fractional Widths solved the problem. Thus, if you are having printing problems and Fractional Character Widths is checked, uncheck it. Try to print the document again.

SEE: • **Chapter 9 for details on what the Fractional Character Widths option does.**

Don't Use Flip Options and/or Landscape Orientation in Combination With a few applications, you cannot print if you use the Page Setup options for Flip Horizontal, Flip Vertical, and/or the landscape page orientation in combination. Uncheck these if you have problems using them.

Turn Off Unlimited Downloadable Fonts This option, also found in the Page Setup box of LaserWriter drivers (it's in the PostScript Options section), can sometimes be the cause of a PostScript error. If it is on, try turning it off and see if it solves the prob-lem. However, as described shortly, sometimes turning it *on*, rather than *off*, will solve a problem.

SEE: • **Chapter 9 for more on this option.**

Make Sure Enough Free Space Exists on Your Disk

Because of the spool files that get created during background printing, this process may take up a significant amount of disk space (as explained in "PrintMonitor Documents Folder," earlier in this chapter).

The computer always looks for this free space on the startup disk, so it doesn't matter if there is a lot of extra room on any other mounted disk. Unless you are doing a lot of background printing or unless your drive is filled almost to capacity, this is unlikely to pose a problem on a hard drive, as enough free space is almost always available. It is more likely to happen if a floppy disk is your startup disk (itself a rare event these days).

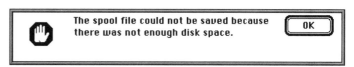

Figure 7-37 This message may appear when printing a large document with background on and too little free space on your disk.

If such problems occur, you usually get a specific error message informing you of the problem. However, if you are using PrintMonitor, the error message may say that you are out of memory, even though the real cause is insufficient disk space.

In any case, the solution here is either to delete files from the disk until you have freed up sufficient space or to use a different startup disk that has additional space already. Then try printing again.

By the way, if you are saving a PostScript print job to a disk file, rather than sending it to the printer, again make sure there is enough disk space available to hold the file.

Check for Insufficient Memory and Related Problems

Does Your PostScript Printer Have Enough Memory? PostScript printers have their own RAM memory. The amount installed varies with different printers. If your document requires more memory than is available in your printer, you will get a PostScript error (insufficient memory in the Mac itself usually generates other types of error messages). Be especially wary of this problem if the error is listed as a "limitcheck error", VMStorage" or "VMerror." PostScript error -8993 is another one that typically means you had insufficient memory to print your document. In some cases, additional RAM can be added to your printer. If so, doing this is the best long-term solution for frequent memory-related PostScript errors. Also, printers that use PostScript Level 2 do a better job of handling memory than was done with the previous PostScript versions. Otherwise, try any of the following suggestions, as may be relevant.

BY THE WAY ▶ How Much RAM Is In Your Printer?

There are two quick ways to check how much memory (RAM) is in your laser printer. Either:

- Open the Chooser and select the LaserWriter driver. With your printer's name highlighted, select Setup and then click the Printer Info button.

- Highlight the desktop printer icon for your printer. Select Get Info (Command-I) and then select Select Status & Configuration from the pop-up menu.

Try Printing One Page At a Time A page of text with complex formatting (such as many fonts of different sizes and styles) can cause printing problems, especially if the page is part of a long document. Similarly, graphics imported into a word processor from draw programs, such as Canvas, may not print—especially if the graphic includes many grouped objects.

Too many fonts is an especially likely problem with laser printers if you are using fonts that are not built into the printer's hardware. Such fonts must be downloaded to the printer's memory before you can print the document. If you have many of these fonts, you can run out of memory to hold them, which then causes problems with printing.

If only those pages with complex formatted text or graphics do not print, try printing that page by itself. Thus, if the problem page is page 5, enter 5 to 5 in the *Pages From: ... To:* area of the Print dialog box.

Similarly, if you were printing multiple copies of a document, try printing single copies instead.

Turn On Unlimited Downloadable Fonts Turning on this option (accessed from the Page Setup dialog box for LaserWriters) may similarly help solve problems with too many fonts in a document.

SEE: • **Chapter 9 for more on this option.**

Simplify the Document If the previous solutions do not work, simplify your page layout, if possible. In particular, if you are using many fonts on the same page, modify the text to reduce the total number of fonts. For problems with graphics combined in a word processing document, cut the graphic from the word processing document and try to print it separately from the text. Sometimes just reimporting the graphic may solve the problem.

Actually, bugs in the printer driver may cause PostScript errors when certain special effects are in use, no matter how much memory you have in your printer. For example, rotated objects with rounded corners or selecting both Invert Image and Smooth Graphics (selected from the Page Setup dialog box) for the same document, have been reported to lead to PostScript errors.

If the object has a lot of separate elements (e.g., a complex object-oriented graphic), see if you can simplify it by reducing the number of elements. Try to print again.

There is nothing you can do about these errors except avoid using the problem effects or upgrade to a newer (hopefully less buggy) printer driver.

Change the Format of a Graphic If the problem appears to be with printing a specific graphic object, sometimes saving it in a different format (such as shifting from PICT to TIFF) may eliminate the problem. For example, PageMaker had trouble printing embedded EPS documents in Mac OS 8.6; shifting to TIFF format instead of EPS worked around the problem.

SEE: • **Chapter 10 for more on graphics formats.**

Use Split Long Paths in PostScript Graphics Programs Check the Split Long Paths option in Illustrator or Freehand. Long paths can cause a system crash if the Postscript interpreter runs out of storage space. Try to print again.

Make Sure Sufficient Memory Is Allocated to the Application Though insufficient application memory is not a common cause of a printing problem, if nothing else seems to be working, try increasing the Preferred (or Current) Memory allocation from the Get Info window of the application you are using. This is likely to help only if you are having a problem printing very long or complex documents.

SEE: • **Chapter 2 on the Get Info command and Fix-It #5 on memory problems for more details.**

Make Sure Sufficient Memory Is Allocated to PrintMonitor or to Desktop PrintMonitor This is discussed in more detail in the next section and in the earlier section on desktop printers. As an alternative, turn Background Printing off.

Problems with Background Printing

This section is relevant only if you are using background printing, particularly as used with LaserWriter drivers. Printing problems related to background printing may or may not be accompanied by an error message. To check if background printing is the cause of your problem, try each of the following suggestions until one works.

Don't Do Anything Else While You Are Trying to Print Don't continue working with your application (actually, it may help to quit the application altogether as soon as the job is sent to the printer). Don't try to copy files and don't do anything else that may use additional memory, until the printing is completed. For example, stop any other nonprinting-related background processing that may be going on at this time (such as a telecommunications program that is working in the background).

All of this minimizes the chance that the problem is caused by overloading the processing capacity of the Macintosh. Of course, this also negates the advantage of using background printing. But hopefully, you won't be required to do this very often. In general, you should be able to carry out other tasks while background printing is in progress. If this does not solve the problem, read on.

Remove Documents from the PrintMonitor Documents Folder If you get a error message with a Try Again option, but selecting it simply leads to the return of the same message, Cancel printing. Then go to the PrintMonitor Documents folder in your System Folder. Delete any documents you find there. You will now have to reselect Print for whatever documents you were trying to print. However, they may successfully print now.

With desktop printer software, it is usually sufficient simply to select to Trash the documents (as selected from the desktop printer's window) and then try again.

Don't Put Your PowerBook to Sleep While Printing Putting a Mac to Sleep while background printing is in progress may halt the printing, especially with PowerBooks. When you wake up the PowerBook, printing may not resume. In this case, you may need to cancel the print job and reselect it.

Turn Background Printing Off Altogether Turn off background printing. Try to print the document again. If you can now print the document, background printing is likely at least a partial cause of the problem. To further isolate the cause, turn background printing on again, as needed, and try the following.

Check for a Conflict Between Background Printing and the Application (or Document) If the problem appears only when you are using background printing in a particular application, a conflict is a likely possibility. You may not be able to do anything about this immediately, other than keep background printing off when using this application.

However, the problem may occur with some documents but not others, so it may pay to turn background printing back on and print a different document, just to check. If you can successfully print most documents, you can turn background printing off only for those rare documents when it is a problem.

Reinstall or Upgrade Background Printing Software I have already mentioned, in previous sections of this chapter, the possibility of a damaged or incorrect version of the PrintMonitor file. If you haven't already done so, replace the file with a copy from Macintosh system software disks that match the system software version on your startup disk. Similarly, reinstall the desktop printing software if you use it. Make sure you are using the latest versions of these files.

TECHNICALLY SPEAKING ▶ Problems with Embedded Fonts

A special problem can occur with background printing of a document that uses fonts that are embedded directly in the document or the printing application, rather than somewhere in the System Folder (a subject I discuss in more detail in Chapter 9). All you need to know now is this: the System is aware of an embedded font only while the document or application that contains the font is open. This means that if you close these files before the software (PrintMonitor or Desktop PrintMonitor) is finished processing the file being printed (normally an OK thing to do), the software will not be able to find the embedded fonts when it needs them. This has been known to cause serious problems, including system crashes.

Thus, you should avoid using background printing with files that have embedded fonts. But how do you know whether a file has such fonts? Well, you can use Apple's ResEdit to check (see Chapter 8). If you find a Font resource for the application, then it has an embedded font. If you find embedded fonts, you can use ResEdit to remove them and transfer them to the Fonts folder, where they can be accessed correctly for background printing to proceed as normal.

However, turning background printing off temporarily also solves this problem. If you are unfamiliar with embedded fonts, you may prefer this simpler, more general solution.

Check for Insufficient Memory for Background Printing You may get an error message that says the document did not print because PrintMonitor or your desktop printer did not have enough memory. With PrintMonitor, the message may say that it will try to print again when more memory is

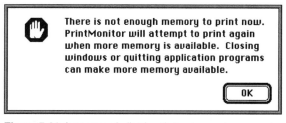

There is not enough memory to print now. PrintMonitor will attempt to print again when more memory is available. Closing windows or quitting application programs can make more memory available.

OK

Figure 7-38 A message indicating that not enough memory is available for PrintMonitor to work.

available. If so, click OK and close any unneeded documents, applications and/or desk accessories. Close any open Finder windows. Printing should now proceed.

Alternatively, the message may offer to allocate more memory to PrintMonitor or your desktop printer. If so, let it. Click OK and try printing again by selecting Print.

Check for Free Space on Your Startup Disk As already mentioned (see "Make Sure Enough Free Space Exists on Your Disk" earlier in this chapter), a document may not print in the background if there is too little free disk space to create the needed spool files. Making matters worse, if this problem occurs, you may get an error message that erroneously says the problems is due to insufficient memory. In either case, if there is very little free space left on your disk, delete some files from your disk. Then try printing again. Alternatively, for multi-page documents, try printing the document in smaller segments, waiting until each one is finished before you try the next one. Or simply turn off background printing.

Otherwise (for PrintMonitor) With any other error message that suggests a problem with background printing when using PrintMonitor, manually increase PrintMonitor's memory as follows:

1. Locate PrintMonitor in the Extensions folder, select it, and then select Get Info from the Finder's File menu.

2. Its Preferred Size should be 167K or higher. Whatever the amount is, increase it by another 100K, assuming you have enough memory available to accommodate this increase.

3. Try printing again. It should work.

Otherwise (for Desktop Printers) If you are using desktop printers, there are similar memory adjustments you can make. These and related troubleshooting tips for desktop printers are described earlier in this chapter.

SEE: • "QuickFixes! Troubleshooting Desktop Printers," earlier in this chapter.

Widen the Search to More General Causes

If all of the preceding fails to work, you are probably dealing with an inherent software bug or conflict in one or more of the programs involved in printing your document. It's time to begin a more general diagnostic hunt to isolate the cause. To do this, try printing using different documents and applications, to determine exactly how specific the problem is. For example, does the problem occur with some documents but not others?

SEE: • **Chapter 3 for general strategy guidelines.**
• **Chapter 4 on general guidelines for system error problems.**
• **Chapter 6 for a more general discussion of file-related problems.**

More specifically, do the following.

Resolve Conflict with the Application The application may turn out to be incompatible with the particular printer you have. Usually, the only immediate work-around here is to stop using the problem application, at least until an upgrade comes along.

It also may be that the application has certain incompatibilities with the printing software. In this case, shifting to an older or newer version of the system (printing) software may help. Check the Read Me files that come with Apple's system software or contact the relevant application vendors for more specific advice.

SEE: • **Fix-It #1 on incompatible software and hardware.**
• **Fix-It #2 on other application-specific problems.**
• **Fix-It #16 on calling technical support.**

Resolve Conflict with an Startup Extension or System Software Similarly, there may be an startup extension conflict or a more general problem related to the system software. Solutions here may require disabling certain extensions or reinstalling your system software. Again, check with the vendor of third-party software for possible workarounds and/or upgrades.

Adobe Type Manager and Adobe Type Reunion have been frequently cited as a cause of printing-related problems (although Adobe has tried to fix this in its latest updates to this software).

SEE: • **Fix-It #3 on problems with system extensions and control panels.**
• **Fix-It #4 on system software problems.**
• **Fix-It #16 on calling technical support.**

Round Up the Usual Suspects If no special problem file can be identified, start rounding up the usual gang of suspects in search of still more general causes. These include rebuilding the desktop and running Disk First Aid. Problems with PRAM, as mentioned earlier in this chapter, are another common source of printer-related problems. See the appropriate Fix-Its for details.

SEE: • **Fix-Its #6 to #10 to check out the usual suspects.**

Hardware Problems Finally, if all else has failed, it's time to assume a hardware problem as the cause, most likely with the printer. Take the printer (and, if need be, the Macintosh itself) in for repairs.

SEE: • **Fix-It #15 on hardware problems.**

BY THE WAY ▶ Using the AdobePS Printer Driver

Adobe makes its own version of Apple's LaserWriter driver called AdobePS. In most cases, if you are using a laser printer that supports Apple's LaserWriter driver, I would recommend sticking with the Apple driver. At one time, Adobe's driver was the default driver included with Hewlett-Packard laser printers. However, HP now supports using Apple's LaserWriter driver. Although there are minor differences, the two drivers are based on the same basic software, so there is no compelling reason to switch if things are working well. In fact, using the Adobe software can sometimes initiate problems that you did not have with Apple's LaserWriter. However, occasionally an application may have problems printing with the Apple's driver but not the Adobe one. In these cases, a switch is in order. For example, PageMaker had several problems printing with Mac OS 8.6; switching to the AdobePS driver was one potential solution. [Selecting Option-Print from the PageMaker File menu also worked in some cases, although this work-around causes you to lose most PostScript printing features.]

Switching to the AdobePS driver is simple enough: get the software from Adobe's Web site; run the installer and restart. Then select AdobePS from the Chooser and create a desktop printer for your printer. You are now ready to print.

One additional caution: AdobePS installs a copy of the PrintingLib file in the Extensions folder, potentially replacing the copy of that file installed by Apple's LaserWriter software. In some versions of AdobePS (such as 8.5.1), the Adobe version of PrintingLib is only a subset of what is contained in the Apple version. The result is that you can no longer use the LaserWriter driver after installing the Adobe driver. The solution is to reinstall Apple's printing software (you can do this via a custom install of the Mac OS, if you do not have a separate installer for the printing software).

The latest versions of AdobePS (8.6 or later) no longer appear to have this problem. These newer driver versions use the identical version of the PrintingLib file. They also install their own supplementary file called Adobe PrintingLib (an older Adobe file called OEMClib is no longer needed and the Installer should delete it if present).

Note: PrintingLib is a collection of libraries which provide many of the driver's functions, including converting QuickDraw to PostScript and parsing PPD files.

If you try to select the AdobePS printer and you get an error message that says, "Sorry, AdobePS cannot be used," try deleting the AdobePS Prefs file. If that fails, reinstall the AdobePS software altogether.

SEE ALSO:
- **"By the Way: Selecting a Printer Driver When the Printer Is Off."**
- **"Technically Speaking: The Desktop Printer Utility."**

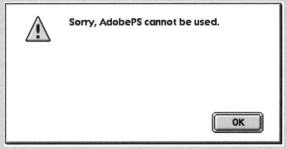

Figure 7- 39 A message that might appear when selecting AdobePS from the Chooser. It probably means the Adobe software is damaged.

QuickFixes!
Troubleshooting Inkjet and/or USB Printers

As described earlier in this chapter (see: "Take Note: Different Types of Printers"), inkjet printers now dominate the low-cost printer market, especially for those who want color printing. Many of these printers also come in USB versions, making them ideal to connect to an iMac or other Mac with USB support. Epson and Hewlett-Packard make the most well-known examples of these printers. In fact, many iMacs are sold bundled with an Epson USB inkjet printer. With all of this in mind, here are some troubleshooting tips specific to working with these printers (Epson Stylus Color printers are used as the prime examples):

• **The basics** Most of the information in the earlier part of this chapter applies to inkjet printers as well as laser printers. For example, you select an inkjet printer from the Chooser, just as with the laser printers covered previously in this chapter. However, unlike most laser printers, each brand of inkjet printer (such as Epson vs. Hewlett-Packard) uses their own printing software. In many cases, there is separate software for different models from the same vendor. Vendor web sites typically have web pages that contain the latest versions of the drivers and associated software. Check and make sure you are using the latest version. An update often fixes problems with older versions.

For Epson printers, the main software will reside in the Epson Folder within the Extensions folder. Additional extensions (located at the root level of the Extensions folder) will include Epson Launcher and EPSON Monitor 3.

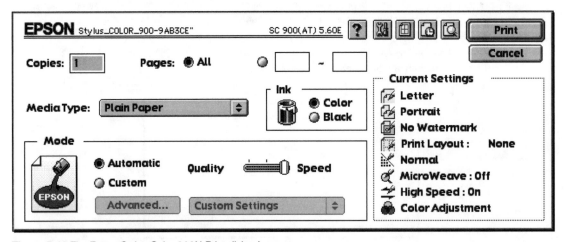

Figure 7-40 The Epson Stylus Color 900N Print dialog box.

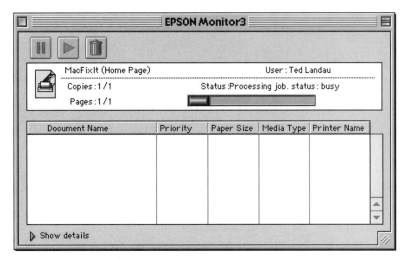

Figure 7-41 The EPSON Monitor3 window.

- **Background printing** Epson inkjet printers do not work with Apple's desktop printer software. However, you can turn Background Printing on (either via the radio buttons in the Chooser or from the Background Printing button in the Print dialog box). If you have background printing enabled, EPSON Monitor 3 (an extension file) launches automatically when you select to print. Its window is similar to the one that appears when you open an Apple desktop printer.

  Background printing typically works a bit differently than with laser printers. Inkjet printers have no built-in memory, so printer data cannot be downloaded. As a result, whenever you print to an inkjet printer in the background, the Mac's processor will be quite busy. If you try to do something else at the same time (such as continue to write in your word processor), the printing speed will be significantly slowed.

  If you are having a problem printing with background printing on, try turning it off (and vice versa). This work-around is known to fix an assortment of problems.

- **The Print dialog box** The Epson Print dialog box is substantially different from the LaserWriter's Print dialog box. Selecting the correct choices here is critical to getting optimal printed output. Several of these choices are described in more detail in Chapter 10. For now, note that you have three main options:

  Media type This refers to the type of paper. Especially for color photographs, the "higher quality" papers will typically yield better results. For example, "photo quality inkjet paper" will give much better results than plain paper; glossy paper will be better still. The downside is that these better papers are much more expensive.

  Inkjet-printed output can smear more easily than laser-printed output, although newer inks are less susceptible to this problem. Still, be especially careful not to get inkjet output wet. Also, using the special coated papers will minimize any smearing or bleeding that might occur directly while the page is printed.

Ink You choose between Color vs. Black, depending upon whether your document has color or not.

Mode Here is where you get to choose whether you want the printer to emphasize speed or quality, via a slider control. If you want to be more selective, you can use the Custom/Advanced options to make individual choices (such as the dithering methods). This can be especially important for getting optimal results when printing color photographs.

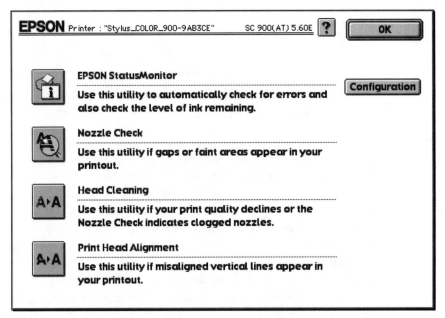

Figure 7-42 The EPSON Printer Utility window, as accessed from the Print dialog box.

- **Problems with the appearance of printed output** Even if you are confident that the settings in the Print dialog box are correct, you may still have problems with the appearance of your printed output—such as wrong colors, missing colors, and horizontal or vertical banding. The most likely cause of these problems are: (1) an ink cartridge that is low or out of ink or (2) a clogged or misaligned print head.

    To help avoid clogged print heads and/or wasted ink, never turn off your printer other than by the on/off switch on the printer itself. When you shut it off via the printer's Power button, it initiates a shut down routine that makes sure the print head is in the correct locked position and checks whether cleaning the head is needed (automatically performing any needed maintenance).

    Another tip for avoiding a clogged printhead is to print at least one page a week, just to keep the ink flowing.

    If the printhead gets clogged anyway, and the printer routines (described next) cannot fix it, you may have to replace the printhead. On some printers, this can be done simply by replacing the ink cartridge (which contains a new printhead). For other printers (including Epson printers) a service call may be required.

Also, for color inkjet printers, one color may run out before the others. So, if only certain colors are printing incorrectly, this probably means that you should replace a tank (if the printer allows individual tanks to be replaced) or the entire cartridge.

Otherwise, here's what to do to check for and fix these problems:

- **Epson Printer Utility** Epson's Print dialog box includes a row of buttons across the top right of the window. Of particular importance is the second one (with the wrench and screwdriver icon). It accesses a utility from which you can check: (1) how much ink is left in the ink cartridges and (2) whether you have clogged nozzles. You can also initiate a head cleaning and print head alignment from here, as well as configure how you want the software to notify you of printing errors.

  If none of this works, you might try putting a few drops of isopropyl alcohol on the clogged ink holes, hoping to dissolve the clogged ink (I have read numerous reports of success with this, although the Epson manual recommends against it).

  (By the way, the remaining buttons in the row are for Help, Layout, Background Printing and Print Preview. The Printer Utility button is also in the Page Setup dialog box.)

- **Printer Check** Another way to check for clogged nozzles is to run a printer check. This essentially duplicates what the Printer Utility's Nozzle Check does, but does it directly from the printer. On most Epson printers, do this by holding down the load/eject button and then pressing and releasing the power button. Wait until a page starts to print. It will print out a pattern that, if any part of it is missing, indicates clogged nozzles or any empty ink cartridge.

- **Status lights** If lights on the printer are flashing when the printer is at rest, this too is a sign of trouble. Depending on what light(s) are flashing, it could mean a paper jam, low ink, or a hardware problem. Check your printer's manual for details.

- **Connecting inkjet printers to a network** Most inexpensive inkjet printers cannot be connected to an AppleTalk network (LocalTalk or Ethernet). However, you may be able to share the printer by using a shareware utility called EpsonShare. It works similarly to Apple's PrinterShare (that is, the Mac connected to the printer must be on in order for the sharing to take place; the sharing is mediated through the Mac).

  Some inkjet printers do have a network capability as an option (such as the Epson 900 vs. 900N). For Epson printers, the network capability is achieved by adding an Epson Ethernet Interface card to the printer. To attach the printer to an Ethernet network, you also have to install the Epson Net!2 software and configure the printer correctly. The manual that comes with the printer and/or Ethernet card provides detailed instructions.

- **PostScript on inkjet printers** Most inkjet printers do not directly support PostScript printing. However, you can get PostScript support via RIP software. Adobe's PressReady and Birmy's PowerRip are two examples.

- **Print speed** Don't be surprised if printing takes longer than you expected. Even under the best conditions, the difference in printing speed between a page of text and a full page color photograph is very, very large. A page of text can take a few seconds. A color photograph will take many minutes.

- **Unable to select printer from the Chooser** If you are unable to select the printer in the Chooser (or the selection does not get retained after a restart), and an error message indicates that this is because AppleTalk is enabled, turn AppleTalk off. If you appear to have AppleTalk turned off already and/or the problem persists: open the AppleTalk control panel and enable AppleTalk; close the control panel; then re-open it and disable AppleTalk. This should resolve the problem.

  If you use an Epson USB printer, make sure you have ink in all tanks of the ink cartridge. An empty tank can prevent the printer from appearing in the Chooser.

- **Printing from Netscape browsers** If you get very tiny output when you try to print from a Netscape web browser to an Epson printer: disable the "Fit to page if possible" option, found in the Page Setup dialog box. Then try to print again. Print should now be normal size.

- **Problems printing with USB printers** Printing to a USB-connected printer is just as simple as printing to a serial printer, maybe even easier (you have no modem vs. printer port issues to worry about). Still, there a few potholes to watch out for:

  Get the right software Serial port printer drivers will not work with USB printers. You need special USB drivers instead. If you don't have this software installed, expect various error messages to appear. For example, an alert may occur during startup stating that the software needed to use the device could not be found. Also, an alert that AppleTalk is active and the serial port is in use may occur after selecting the printer icon in the Chooser. Another possibility is a -192 error (resource not found) when trying to print. While some of these errors could be caused by other problems (such as damaged printing software, indicating that a re-install of the printer software is needed), your first move should be to check if the needed USB software is installed.

  The necessary USB software may not have come with your printer. If the software is missing and if you have an iMac, you may find a folder called "iMac Device Drivers" inside the CD Extras folder on the System Install CD. Inside this folder will be folders that contain the driver software for selected Epson and Hewlett-Packard USB printers. Otherwise, you can get the drivers from the web sites of the vendor for your printer. Get and install the software.

  Conversely, if you are having problems printing to Epson printers via a serial port or Ethernet connection, check if there are *any* Epson USB driver extensions installed in your System Folder (they will typically have the letters "USB" in their name). If so, delete them all. This often fixes the problem.

  USB hubs If you are still having trouble getting your USB printer to work and the printer is connected via a USB hub, try connecting it directly to one of the USB ports on the Mac itself. If this works, there may be a problem with the hub. In particular, if it is not a self-powered hub and you have several devices attached to it, there may be insufficient power for the USB devices to work. The solution is to bypass the hub or get a powered hub.

Using USB adapters If you want to use a USB printer on a Mac that does not have a USB port, or if you want to use a serial printer on a Mac that does not have a serial port, there are numerous adapters that make these conversions possible. The printer vendors themselves make some of these adapters. For example, Epson makes a USB/Parallel Printer Adapter Kit. Farallon, Griffin, and Keyspan are among several other vendors that make USB adapters, allowing for almost any possible arrangement.

Special case: certain Epson files need to be deleted If you are running Mac OS 8.6 (and possibly later OS updates), and you have trouble printing to an Epson printer, delete the following four extensions: Epson USBPrintClass1; Epson USBPrintClass2; Epson USBPrintClass3 ; Epson USBPrintClassA. If even this fails to work, reinstall the Epson printer software altogether.

TECHNICALLY SPEAKING ▶ Using USB DDK software

USB devices, such as USB printers, typically ship with the needed USB drivers and related software on disc. Otherwise, it is available from their web site. Some of this software is derived from files provided to developers by Apple in the form of a USB Driver Development Kit (DDK). These files include USB Support, USB Device Extension, USBHIDUniversalModule, and more (devices typically use only a subset of these USB files). In some cases, there are newer (often beta) versions of these files that reportedly fix problems with the current versions. If you are comfortable with working with beta software intended primarily for developers, you can install these yourself to see if they help solve a USB problem you are having. To obtain the software, go to this web page: *http://developer.apple.com./hardware/usb/index.html.*

SEE : • **Chapter 10, "Problems Printing Color/Grayscale to a Color Printer," for more on inkjet printer problems.**
  • **Fix-It #14 for more on USB troubleshooting.**

8

Getting Under the Hood: The Invisible Macintosh

Peeking Under the Hood

This chapter takes you inside the workings of the Macintosh more than any other chapter in this book. Still, you can understand and use the material in this chapter without any special software or any particular skills other than those already described. So, stick around. Don't rush or skip to the next chapter.

If you make an effort to master this material, you will be amply rewarded. For example, it can aid in solving problems locating or opening files, as described in Chapter 6. It will be immensely helpful in understanding problems with graphics formats, as described in Chapter 10. It bears on how applications import and export files of different formats (as discussed in several chapters). Finally, it allows you to do some neat tricks that you will meet for the first time in this chapter.

File Type and File Creator

How Kind

Every file on your disk is assigned a particular kind. The *kind* is a brief description of the general category to which the file belongs. Thus, all application files have a kind called *application*. Similarly, the kind for a document created by Excel is *Microsoft Excel document*. Note that for document files, the kind description not only lists the general category *(document)*, but also identifies the application that created the document (in this case, *Microsoft Excel*).

As first presented in Chapter 2, you can easily determine the kind for any file by selecting Get Info for that file and reading its kind description. You can also see the kind for all files in a folder at one time by switching to a non-icon view, such as By Name or (even better!) By Kind.

This kind information can help you to identify an unfamiliar file. The Finder similarly uses this information to identify files. For example, if a file's kind is *application*, the Finder knows it can be opened directly and does so when you double-click it. On the other hand, if it is a *system extension*, the Finder knows that it cannot be opened at all and that it belongs in the Extensions folder. If it is a *document*, the Finder uses the kind to determine what application is launched along

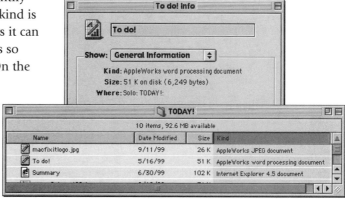

Figure 8-1 Where to find a file's kind: in the Kind line of a Get Info window (top) or the Kind column of a List view (bottom).

with the document when you double-click it. Thus, a problem with a file's kind is one reason you can have difficulty opening a document. This problem, briefly alluded to in Chapter 6, is described more fully here.

Kind and the Desktop File

How does the Finder identify a file's kind? The initial answer is that the needed information is stored in the invisible Desktop files. Every time you add a new file to your disk, the Desktop files are updated to include the kind information for that file. In fact, the Desktop files are the Finder's storage site for virtually all of the information listed in Get Info windows, including what icon a file should have.

SEE: • Fix-It #8 for more on the Desktop files.

So where do the Desktop files get this kind (and other related information) in the first place? Each file on your disk contains this information about itself in a special area of the file reserved for this purpose. When a file is first copied to a disk, this information is copied to the Desktop files where it is then accessed by the Finder as needed. Applications are the primary source of this information (for files other than system software), providing the needed icons and document-linking data for all the application's accessory files and documents.

Specifically, what key information is used to determine a file's kind? A file's kind is determined by two four-letter codes assigned to and initially stored with each file. These are referred to as the file's type and creator codes.

File Type

A file's type determines whether a file is listed as an application, a document, a system file, or whatever. For example, all applications have a type code of *APPL* (for *APPL*ication). System files have several possible codes. For example, the type for desk accessories is *dfil*. For control panels, it is *cdev* (an abbreviation for *c*ontrol panel *dev*ice). For common system extensions, it is *INIT*.

TECHNICALLY SPEAKING ▶ **INIT vs. Extension vs. Control Panel**

As I alluded to in Chapter 1, the type code INIT describes programs that must load into memory at startup in order to work. In particular, this lumps together most system extensions and many control panels. This is the basis for using the term INIT to group these control panels and system extensions together at points in this and other chapters.

SEE: • "Finder Flags (Attributes)" later in this chapter and Fix-It #3 for more details.

For documents, a virtually infinite number of possible type codes is available. Each application uses a unique type code that it assigns to documents that are saved in its unique format. These type codes are determined by the developers of the software. For example, the type code for AppleWorks word processing documents is CWWP, while an AppleWorks spreadsheet document is CWSS.

The type information determines what files get displayed in an application's Open dialog box. Thus, if you select to show only word processing documents in AppleWorks, a spreadsheet file will not be listed. Documents created by applications other than AppleWorks will only be displayed if the application has a "translator" to recognize that type of file (or if you use a third party translator, such as MacLinkPlus). AppleWorks, for example, can recognize a wide variety of formats, including Microsoft Word and WordPerfect.

File Creator

The creator code is used to *bundle* (or link) an application and all the documents that it creates. Thus, an application and its documents generally have the same creator code. For example, the creator code for both the AppleWorks application and an AppleWorks document is BOBO. Creator codes, like the type codes, are selected by the software developer.

The creator code is used primarily at the Finder level. For example, it is what tells the Finder that an AppleWorks document was *created* by the AppleWorks application. This, in turn, tells the Finder to launch AppleWorks when you double-click an AppleWorks document. It also partly determines what icon the Finder assigns to a newly created AppleWorks document.

For documents, the kind description in the Get Info window is determined primarily by the file's creator, not the file's type.

Programs can often save files in several different formats. When AppleWorks saves a file in Microsoft Word format, for example, it assigns Word's document type and creator codes to the file. Thus, when it is finished, there is no way to tell that the file was originally created in AppleWorks and not in Word. When you next double-click this file from the Finder, it launches Word, not AppleWorks (assuming Word is on your disk somewhere). Had it changed only the file's type but not the creator, double-clicking the Word file from the Finder would launch AppleWorks (per the Creator code), which would then correctly interpret the file as a Word file (because of its Word type) and translate it.

To solve problems involving type and creator codes, you need to know what a file's codes are and, if necessary, be able to change them. The next section describes how to do this.

Type and Creator Code Problems

 Symptoms:

One or more of the following symptoms occurs.

Application Could Not Be Found

You are unable to open a document from the Finder because you get an error message that says the application program that created it could not be found. This could happen for many reasons that do not directly relate to type or creator problems (as covered in Chapter 6). The best tip-off that you have a type/creator problem is if you get this error message even though the creating application is presently on a mounted disk.

Wrong Kind

The kind for a data document, as listed in the Get Info window, is listed as *document* (when it should be something more specific, such as *AppleWorks word processing document*). Although a kind of just *document* is the correct listing for some files, this is usually not the case for data documents such as word processing files.

Wrong Icon

A file, most often a data document, does not display its correct icon in the Finder. Typically, it displays a generic (blank-page) icon instead. You will often find this to be the case with documents that have *document* as their kind, as just described. If this is the only symptom you have, you can often ignore it (unless the aesthetic loss bothers you). But if it is linked to a problem opening the file, you probably want to fix it.

TAKE NOTE ▶ Assigning Icons

Most file icons in the Finder are custom icons (sometimes called *bundled icons*, to distinguish them from the truly custom icons that you make yourself). Generally, an application and all its accessory and data document icons share a similar appearance that helps identify them as belonging together.

If no custom icon is present, the Finder instead assigns it one from its standard set of generic icons. The generic document icon, for example, is simply a blank rectangle with a corner turned down. Thus, these generic icons can be perfectly normal, even if they are rarely seen these days.

However, occasionally a file that has previously displayed a custom icon may unexpectedly appear with a generic icon. This is usually a sign of at least minor trouble.

 **Causes:**

As is true for software in general, the area of a file that contains the type and creator codes can become corrupted. These codes can also be mistakenly altered by other programs. Finally, for various reasons, the Finder may have difficulty correctly interpreting a file's type and creator information. More specifically, the following situations can occur.

A File's Type Code or Both Its Type and Creator Codes Are Missing or Corrupted

This situation is relatively rare, but it can happen. Files without type or creator codes can often be quite difficult to open, especially from the Finder. They may not even open from within the creating application. Happily, restoring the proper codes is a quick way to restore the document to working condition

A Document File's Creator Code Is Missing or Corrupted

Be especially suspicious that a document is missing its creator code if you get the message that "the application program that created it could not be found," even though you know the application is on a currently mounted disk. Restoring a document's proper creator code reestablishes the link between the document and its creating application, allowing the Finder to identify the file and open it.

The Creating Application Is Missing

Even if a document has its correct type and creator codes, it cannot be opened from the Finder if the creating application is not currently on a mounted disk. In fact, if the creating application has *never* previously been on the same disk as the document, the document may display a generic icon rather than its correct custom icon.

Bundle Bit Problems

Occasionally, even though a document has its correct type and creator codes and the creating application is on a mounted disk, the Finder still fails to recognize the link between the application and the document. Technically, this is not a type or creator problem. Most often the application's Bundle bit is set incorrectly (as described more in the section on "File Attributes," later in this chapter), or more serious file damage has occurred.

Multiple Versions of the Same Application on Your Disk

If you have two different versions of the same application on your disk, you may find that one of them displays the wrong icon (typically using the icon associated with the other version). Similarly, its documents may display the other application's document icons, or they may display only the generic blank-page icon.

What to Do:

For the fastest and easiest route to success, try the following suggestions in the order given.

Try the Simpler Solutions

Copy the Creating Application to a Mounted Disk If the creating application is not on any mounted disk, you can solve most of these problems easily enough by copying it to a mounted disk. (This suggestion assumes, of course, that you know what the creating application is and that you have access to it.) Not only should this solution allow you to open problem documents directly, it usually fixes any icon display and related problems (after you restart).

Open the File from Within the Creating Application If the creating application is on the disk already, you can usually solve the problem by trying to open the file from within the application's Open dialog box rather than from the Finder. If you can open it this way, save a copy of the file with a new name, quit the application, and delete the original file. This usually solves the problem.

Open the File with Another Application If the creating application won't work, try to open the file from within another application (already on your disk) that can import the problem document file.

SEE: • Chapter 6 for more details on these solutions.

Rebuild the Desktop This fixes a variety of wrong-icon and related problems. If you have two different versions of the same application on your disk, get rid of one of them before you rebuild.

SEE: • Fix-It #8 for details on rebuilding the desktop and much more on generic icon problems.

Use a Repair Utility Run a utility such as Disk First Aid or Norton Utilities' Disk Doctor to check for incorrect Bundle bit settings and/or minor problems with other file attributes. This is all done automatically as part of the utility's routine disk-checking procedures (as described in Fix-It #10). If a problem is detected, the utility alerts you and asks if you wish to fix it. Say yes.

Viewing and Editing Type/Creator Codes

To view and edit the type and creator codes, you can use a repair utility such as Norton Utilities. However, many other utilities let you do this faster or more easily. Two of my personal favorites are DiskTop and Snitch, both mentioned again later in this chapter. The former is a "desk accessory" that is an especially versatile tool for doing virtually any of the functions described in this chapter. Snitch is a shareware control panel that is especially convenient when you want to quickly access the codes for a single file. FileBuddy is another good multipurpose tool.

BY THE WAY ▶ Changing a File's Type Has Its Limits

Other than correcting a lost or damaged type code, there is rarely any reason to consider modifying a file's type (though I'll provide a couple of exceptions later in this chapter). Changing a type code does not change the underlying format of a document. For example, changing a document's type code from WDBN to MWPD does *not* magically change a Word document into a MacWrite Pro document; it only leads to confusion. On the other hand, as described here, changing a file's creator can be useful even when the code is not lost or damaged.

Editing type and creator codes is how, for example, you can restore missing or corrupted code. You can also use these utilities to change a document's creator from a missing application to one that is available. Assuming that the substitute application can import files of the document's type, you would now be able to double-click the document from the Finder and have it launch with its newly assigned application rather than its originally intended one. Other utilities (such as Apple's own File Exchange) accomplish this same goal in a simpler manner (as mentioned in Chapter 6). There are also shareware utilities, such as OpenUsing, that allow you to assign a particular document type to an application other than its creating application. Still, sometimes altering the creator code directly is the only thing that works.

Several specific examples of the potential usefulness of editing a file's creator and type codes will be described shortly. But first, let's see how to use utilities to actually make these changes. (A general warning: before attempting to make any of these changes, make sure the file is closed and that you have a backup of the file.)

BY THE WAY ▶ A Word About Norton Disk Editor

Starting with Norton Utilities 5.0, Symantec removed Norton Disk Editor from the Norton Utilities suite. That is, you can no longer access it from the Norton Utilities menu and it does not get installed when you run the Installer application. However, the program is still on the Norton Utilities CD, in a folder called "Tech Support Tools."

But don't expect much help from Symantec when using it. Symantec now states "Norton Disk Editor is provided only to allow Symantec Technical Support to diagnose problems on a customer's disk. It is not documented and is unsupported except when used in conjunction with a call to Norton Utilities Technical Support."

Actually, there are two versions of Disk Editor included: Norton Disk Editor and Norton Disk Editor +. The Plus (+) version was needed because the regular version is not 100% compatible with HFS Plus formatted drives (although I personally never had a problem in this regard). The Plus version also has a fancier redesigned interface. However, it is missing a few crucial features described here (especially the ability to easily edit type and creator codes). So this chapter still focuses on the older Disk Editor.

Overall, a better idea may be to skip Disk Editor altogether and use the alternative utilities discussed here, whenever possible.

With Norton Utilities

1. Open Norton Disk Editor (either from its Finder icon or by selecting it from Norton Utilities' Utilities menu). This should lead to a dialog box with a pop-up menu of all mounted disks.

2. Select the disk you want and click Open. This opens a window with a directory listing of all files and folders on the disk, including invisible ones. Double-click a folder to reveal the contents of the folder.

3. The Type and Creator codes for each file are already listed in columns to the right of the file name. To edit any of these codes, select the desired file and then click the

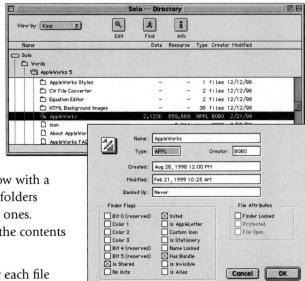

Figure 8-2 Norton Disk Editor shows the type and creator codes of AppleWorks.

Info button at the top of the window. This opens up a new window that lists the Type and Creator (among other things) of the file. From here, you can modify the code by typing in a different one.

With Snitch

1. Before using Snitch, install it in the Extensions folder and restart the Macintosh.

2. Now whenever you select the Get Info window for a file or folder (either by pressing the Command-I keys or by choosing Get Info from the Finder's File menu), Snitch will automatically modify the window to include its added options.

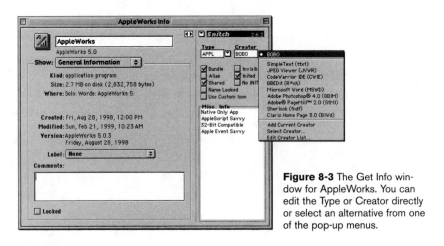

Figure 8-3 The Get Info window for AppleWorks. You can edit the Type or Creator directly or select an alternative from one of the pop-up menus.

3. From here you can view and modify the file's type and creator, as well as several other attributes of the file. Type whatever changes you want. Click OK when you are done.

    The pop-up menus (indicated by downward facing triangles) next to the type and creator fields have a selection of commonly used codes that you can select. For added convenience, you can also add your own codes to these menus.

    Clicking the pop-up menu next to the word "Snitch" reveals selections that lead to other options, including the ability to change the creation and modification dates of the file as well as check the file for possible damage.

Most other competing utilities work in a similar manner. For example, DiskTop works very much like Norton Utilities. You simply open DiskTop, navigate to the file you want, and then choose Get Info from the DiskTop menu (or type Command-I). This brings up a window where you can edit the type and creator codes.

    No matter which utility you use, when you return to the Finder, you may find that the Finder does not yet seem to recognize the changes you've made; for example, the file may still show its old, incorrect icon. If so, choose Get Info for the file. Doing this gets the Finder's attention and forces it to update its information. If your changes still don't show up, restart. As a last resort, rebuild the desktop.

Identifying the Correct Creator Code

The ability to alter a file's creator or type, of course, is not of much value if you do not know what creator or type code you need to enter. For example, perhaps you want to restore a missing creator code to a Microsoft Excel document file, but you have no idea what the proper code is. The simplest answer is to find an existing Microsoft Excel document on your disk, use any of the utilities just described to check what its codes are, and then apply them to the problem document. (**Note:** the use of uppercase and lowercase makes a difference in these codes, so copy codes exactly!)

    If you have no document to use as a guide, there is other software that may help. For example, *Type/Creator Database* is a shareware program that lists over 3000 type and creator codes. Just make sure the version of the application on your disk matches the version listed in the Database. Sometimes an application's creator and type codes are changed when an upgrade is released.

    The commonly used codes in Snitch's pop-up menus will also be of some use here.

TAKE NOTE ▶ A Real-Life Example of Changing a File's Creator In Order to Open the File

I acquired a graphics file from a colleague that was in a format commonly referred to as GIF (the actual file type is GIFF). Because I had an application that opened GIF files, I did not expect any trouble. When I double-clicked the document from the Finder, however, I got the all-too-familiar message that the creating application could not be found. I launched my GIF utility and tried to open the problem document from within the application, but this did not work either.

At this point, I used DiskTop to look at the type and creator of the file. The type was indeed GIF, but the creator was different from the one used by my application. Because at least a dozen or more programs can save in the GIF format, this was not surprising. Even so, the document should have opened, because my GIF utility is designed to open any GIF file, no matter what its creator. Because the document clearly was not opening, however, I decided to see if modifying the creator code might help.

I used Snitch to change the document's creator to match the creator code of the application on my disk. This worked! The file now opened, both from within the application and even from the Finder.

TEXT and PICT Formats: Type and Creator Issues

Some file formats (file types) are *generic*—that is, they are not associated with a particular application. These formats are recognized by most applications of a given category.

For example, the *Plain Text* (or just Text) format is recognized by virtually every word processor.

In fact, even spreadsheets and databases can save their data as Text files as well as read Text files created in other applications. Even if these programs have no special translator files, they typically can still read Text format files. There is a cost, however, to this universal acceptance: Text files do not retain any of the special formatting options (such as font styles or pasted-in graphics) available, for example, when you save these files in an application-specific format.

Graphics formats have a whole collection of generic file formats, each with different qualities. Indeed, many graphics applications do not have a unique format for saving documents, instead, depending entirely on the generic formats. These shared formats make it much easier to transfer graphics information from one graphics application to another.

Probably the most common generic graphic file format is called PICT. Almost every graphics application can read and save PICT files; it is the graphic equivalent of the plain Text format.

SEE: • Chapter 10 for more on PICT and other generic graphics formats.

The file type for plain text documents is TEXT, and the file type for PICT documents is PICT. No single creator code is associated with these file types; each file is assigned the creator code of the application used to save it. Thus, if you create four different PICT files, each with a different application, double-clicking each document from the Finder will launch a different application—even though they are all PICT documents. The same idea applies to TEXT documents.

As a result of all this, you can't trust icons to identify PICT or TEXT files, as each type of file may have any of several different icons, depending on the application that created them.

SimpleText   AppleWorks   JPEGView   Photoshop

Figure 8-4 These icons all represent PICT files, each one created by the application named under the icon.

If the creating application is not on your disk, however, the Finder will not launch a TEXT or PICT file when you double-click it. Instead, as discussed for documents in general, an error message typically informs you that the file did not open because the application program that created it "could not be found." (If you have SimpleText on your disk, the Finder additionally asks whether you want to open the document using SimpleText.)

TAKE NOTE ▶ SimpleText Plus

SimpleText, while useful, is quite sparse in features. For example, you can't open files greater than 32K or paste graphics via the Paste command. To fill this void, there are a variety of shareware programs that function as "enhanced" versions of SimpleText. These include Tex-Edit Plus, QuickTexter and SimpleEdit, as well as a utility that adds features directly to SimpleText itself: SimpleText Enhancer.

This problem, though, only affects opening the file from the Finder by double-clicking. Any application that can read TEXT or PICT files can recognize and open these files from within the application itself. In fact, once the document is open, you can usually use Save to save the document, and it should acquire the creator (and type) code of the application you are using. Otherwise, if you wish, you can directly change the creator code of the TEXT or PICT document using the methods described in the previous section.

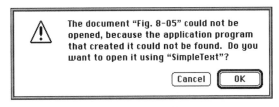

The document "Fig. 8-05" could not be opened, because the application program that created it could not be found. Do you want to open it using "SimpleText"?

Cancel   OK

SEE: • Chapter 6 for more on problems with opening files.

Figure 8-5 This message appears when you try to open a TEXT or PICT document for which the creating application cannot be found.

Four More Good Reasons to View or Change a File's Type/Creator

If you are still not convinced that a working knowledge of how to edit type and creator codes is of value to you, here are a few more practical examples that may change your mind.

Get Documents to Open in SimpleText by Default

Suppose you have saved a text document in a communications program like America Online. The next time you double-click the text document, you would prefer it to open directly in SimpleText (which launches rather quickly) instead of the more cumbersome communications software. Unfortunately, it doesn't. What to do?

Simple. Use Snitch (or a similar utility) to access the file's creator and type codes. The type code should be TEXT; if so, leave it alone. Change the Creator codes, however, from whatever it currently is to "ttxt." The file will now open directly in SimpleText; its icon should also change to the familiar SimpleText icon.

Similarly, for any PICT file, if you change its creator to "ttxt," it should open in SimpleText. You can't edit it from there, but you can view it or copy it to the clipboard. By the way, these are the type of PICT files that are created by your Macintosh when you take a picture of your screen by typing Command-Shift-3 (try it!).

Of course, changing a document's creator is not the only way to get a text document to open in SimpleText by default. You could also open the text document from within SimpleText and then use the Save As command to create a new document containing the same text. This new document will now open in SimpleText by default. Changing the creator is simpler and faster, however. Especially with a utility like Snitch.

Yes Edit   No Edit   Picture

Figure 8-6 SimpleText icons for editable text files (left), uneditable text files (center) and PICT files (right).

Make Uneditable SimpleText Documents Editable

Have you ever come across those uneditable SimpleText documents, the ones with the newspaper icon? If you try just to copy any text from one of these documents (never mind actually altering any of the text!), SimpleText won't let you. The commands are all disabled. What to do?

Easy. Change the file's type code (not its creator). While the file is closed, change its Type from "ttro" to "TEXT." Presto—you now have an editable SimpleText document. Its icon will change accordingly.

By the way, with editable SimpleText documents, you can copy and paste text and copy graphics, but you cannot paste graphics. To place graphics into a SimpleText document, use a utility like ResEdit.

BY THE WAY ▶ Graphics in SimpleText Documents

Did you ever wonder how the SimpleText "Read Me" files that come with some software include graphics in them? It seems impossible, because the SimpleText program itself doesn't let you paste graphics. The way it happens is amazingly complicated (especially for a program named SimpleText) and requires ResEdit, but Apple has a Technote file that spells it all out. If you are on the Web, you can find it at http://dev.info.apple.com/technotes/tn1005.html. Alternatively, you can use a shareware program called Text-Edit Plus.

By the way, if you convert a read-only SimpleText file to an editable one, any editing changes you make may result in the document's graphics being lost or not displayed properly.

Finally, note that while you can't edit graphics files (such as screen snapshots) in SimpleText, the application is still great for quickly copying a selected portion of the file's image to the clipboard. In most "draw" programs, you either cannot do this at all or must first paste the graphic into a special "paint" window to do it.

Add Alert Sounds Without Installing Them in the System File

Open up the SimpleSound utility and you'll see a list of all the alert sounds you can select. This same list is also used by a variety of programs for various purposes, such as for selecting the alarm sound in appointment/reminder programs.

The sounds in this list come from the sounds installed directly in the System file; to install a new sound, you simply drag the sound file to the System file icon. But suppose you would like to add new sounds in the same way that you can add new fonts— simply by placing the sound in a folder, like the Fonts folder, rather than having to install it directly in the System file? This way you could modify your sound list without the damage risk of having to modify the System file each time.

The trick solution here is to change the file type and creator of the sound file to match that of a font suitcase file. In particular, change its type code from "sfil" to "FFIL," and the creator code from "movr" to "DMOV."

Actually, if you have multiple sounds stored in a sound suitcase file, you can change the entire sound suitcase into a font suitcase. Dragging this lone file to the Fonts folder will add all the sounds in one step.

Search for a File Based on Its Type or Creator

Use Sherlock to search for files that have the same "file type" or "creator." These are two choices listed in the "name" pop-up menu. This can be a convenient way, for example, to find all the AppleWorks documents on your drive, wherever they may be.

Finder Flags (Attributes)

What Are Finder Flags (Attributes)?

Finder flags are a set of "on-off" characteristics that have been separately assigned to each file (and folder) on your disks; these flags are also often referred to as a file's *attributes* or *bits*. They determine important aspects of how the Macintosh (especially the Finder) interacts with a given file—for example, whether it is invisible, and whether it loads at startup. Normally, these flag settings are handled without any user involvement, and so you may not even be aware that these flags exist. As you will soon see, however, you can examine and modify these flags by using the special utilities already described in this chapter. Here are six examples of Finder flags that you might have reason to check on or modify.

The Invisible Bit

If the Invisible bit box is checked for a file or folder, it will not be visible on the Finder's desktop; normal access to these files is thus prohibited. The Desktop file is a common example of a normally invisible file. Unchecking this bit for an invisible file will make the file visible on the Finder's desktop, and you can similarly turn any ordinary visible file into an invisible one by checking this bit.

Of course, if a file is already invisible, you may wonder how to find it so that you can change its flags. I'll explain that shortly.

SEE: • "Invisible Files and Folders" later in this chapter.

The Bundle Bit

The Bundle bit is usually turned on for applications. This bit informs the Finder to check the application for information about linked document files, including what icons to assign to documents that the application creates. Programs like Norton Utilities or TechTool Pro, when used to check for disk problems (as described in Fix-It #10), can detect and correct Bundle bit errors (that is, a Bundle bit set to "off" that should be on, or vice versa). This can sometimes help restore the correct icon to a document file. Unless you are sure you know what you are doing, you should depend on these utilities to fix Bundle bit problems rather than altering the Bundle bit yourself.

A utility called Save A BNDL doesn't actually alter the Bundle bit, but it updates the Desktop database for that file, an especially useful function in certain cases where the file would otherwise be ignored by the Desktop database. This can fix a generic icon problem for a specific file without you having to rebuild the entire desktop.

If you really get serious about understanding file icons and what determines when they do and do not appear correctly, you will need to get into using ResEdit and learning about things such as FREF resources. For most people, what is provided here (and in Fix-It #8) will be more than enough.

The Inited Bit

This bit indicates whether or not the Finder has seen the file. If you disable it, you can force the Finder to look at the file again, which can be useful or even necessary to get Finder to recognize changes you have made to other attributes for the file. It may also help to solve a generic icon problem for a particular file. After you uncheck this bit, restart to see if it has any effect. This bit works in conjunction with the Bundle bit to determine the file icons displayed in the Finder.

The Use Custom Icon Bit

This bit indicates that a file's icon has been added by pasting the icon into the icon box of the file's Get Info window. If this icon is not being displayed (and other suggested solutions have failed to work), look to see if this attribute is checked. If not, check it and restart.

The No INITs Bit

The No INITs bit is relevant mainly for certain control panels. If a control panel is designed to act as a startup extension (that is, if it loads into memory at startup along with system extensions), this bit is unchecked. Otherwise, it is checked. You can use this bit to determine which control panels (or extensions) are INITs and which are not.

Normally, you should not alter this bit yourself. In Chapter 6 (see "Technically Speaking: Cannot Open a Control Panel Because No INITs Bit Is Checked"), however, I described one case where certain control panels could not be opened because their No INITs bit had been inadvertently checked. This caused the Mac not to load these control panels at startup, and so they would not work. The solution (after discovering how this had happened in the first place) was to recheck the No INITs bit and restart.

SEE: • **Chapter 1 and Fix-It #3 for more details on startup extensions (INITs).**

The Name Locked Bit

This bit, when checked, prevents the name of the file from being changed from the Finder, regardless of whether the Get Info Locked box is checked or not. This is the reason you cannot change the name of the System, Finder, or Enabler files, for example. If you turn this bit off and then restart, you will be able to change the name of these files.

You might instead, however, simply make a copy of the file, because the copy does not have its locked bit set. You can then change the name of the copy (deleting the original if desired).

Viewing and Editing Finder Flags

One of the conveniences of the Macintosh's design is that you can easily turn these flag settings on or off without any special programming skills—just one click of a mouse can turn an invisible file into a visible one. Still, you don't want to make these changes recklessly. Normally, these flags are set on or off by the developer of the software (or, in some cases, by the Finder), and there is no reason to change them. Nevertheless, a few of these attributes, such as the ones just described, can be relevant to certain problem-solving issues. Even if you don't change them, it pays to know how to check on them.

To access the list of flags/attributes for a file, use the same familiar utilities that you used to check a file's type and creator: Norton Utilities or Snitch (as well as DiskTop or other competing utilities). Here are the exact procedures (the figures showing these utilities, earlier in this chapter, may be useful to look at again here).

With Norton Utilities

1. Open Norton Disk Editor (either from its Finder icon or by selecting it from the Utilities menu of Norton Utilities). This should lead to a dialog box with a pop-up menu of all mounted disks.

2. Select the disk you want and click Open. Doing this opens a window with a directory listing of all files and folders on the disk, including invisible ones. Double-click a folder to reveal the contents of the folder.

3. Select the desired file and then click the Info button. This opens up a new window that lists the file's attributes (as well as its type and creator codes, as described earlier).

4. Check or uncheck a particular attribute as desired.

By the way, you can get a similar list of information from Norton Disk Doctor. Select "Get Info" (for volumes) or "Get Info for..." (for files and folders) from Disk Doctor's File menu.

With Snitch The basic procedure is the same as for getting a file's type and creator codes. One disadvantage of Snitch is that, because it works from the Finder, you cannot use it to select invisible files.

1. Select the desired file from the Finder's desktop and type Command-I; the list of file attributes will appear. This list is somewhat different from the list in Norton Utilities, but they both list the key attributes described in this chapter.

2. Check or uncheck a particular attribute as desired.

Invisible Files and Folders

Lurking on your disk are invisible files and folders. Among the common invisible items you will find on a typical disk are Desktop DB and Desktop DF (the two Desktop files); AppleShare PDS and Move&Rename (used with file sharing); LoadRAMDblr (an invisible file needed by the RAM Doubler extension/control panel in order to work), the Temporary Items folder, the Trash Folder, and more.

Normally, you access invisible files and folders indirectly. Thus, you can rebuild the invisible Desktop file without ever opening it or viewing it in any way. There are occasions, however, when you may want to view or modify these invisible files and folders directly. The next section describes how to do this.

SEE: • **Chapter 2 for more on FileSaver.**
• **Chapter 4 for more on the Temporary Items Folder.**
• **Chapter 11 for more on AppleShare.**
• **Fix-It #8 for more details on Desktop files.**

BY THE WAY ▶ **Two Types of Desktops**

A distinction is usually made between the Finder's desktop (which refers to the display of windows and icons that the Finder creates) and the invisible Desktop file(s). By convention, the word desktop, when used for the Finder desktop, is not capitalized. For the invisible Desktop files, it is capitalized.

Viewing and Editing Invisible Files and Folders

A word of caution before I explain how to work with invisible files: some invisible files only function when they are invisible. Changing their visibility can be equivalent to deleting the file. The Desktop files are an example of this. In general, unless you intend to delete an invisible file, it's best to leave it as invisible when you are done working with it.

With Norton Utilities You can view invisible files and folders with Norton Utilities using the same basic procedures described previously for accessing type/creator codes and attributes. Open a disk with the Norton Disk Editor; from the window that appears, locate the file/folder you want from any currently mounted disk. A complete list of files and folders—both visible and invisible—is displayed. To see the contents of a given folder, open the folder as indicated for each application.

Norton Disk Editor lists *all* files, but they do not make it immediately obvious which ones are normally invisible. If you are familiar with the file you are looking for, such as the Desktop file, this may not be a problem. Otherwise, the only sure way to determine if a file is normally invisible is to select the file and check if its Invisible bit is turned on, as previously described in the section on "Finder Flags (Attributes)."

Norton Disk Editor typically lists only the name and location of these files, so you cannot use them to open a file and examine its contents. Similarly, you cannot directly delete any of these invisible files from these utilities. To do any of these things, you must first make the file visible by unchecking its Invisible file attribute; you can then access the file from the Finder.

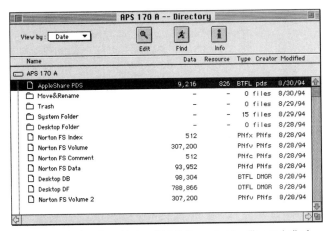

Figure 8-7 A view form Norton Disk Editor; all of the files and all of the folders (except the System Folder) are invisible on the desktop.

For all these reasons, you might prefer another utility for working with invisible files. Fortunately, there are several choices. Here are several examples:

With DiskTop DiskTop deserves special mention here because you *can* use it directly to launch any files or delete invisible files from its listing window. This useful utility, as mentioned, also allows you to modify type/creator codes and file attributes, as well as search by type or creator codes.

1. Open DiskTop; a list of the contents of all mounted disks will be displayed. Double-click a volume or folder name to reveal its contents.

2. The listing should include both visible and invisible files. If invisible files are not listed, select Preferences from the DiskTop menu. Check Technical from the Level options, and return to the file listing. Invisible files and folders will now be listed there.

3. To delete an invisible file or folder, simply select it and click the Delete button, located near the top of the window.

4. To launch any file, just double-click it..

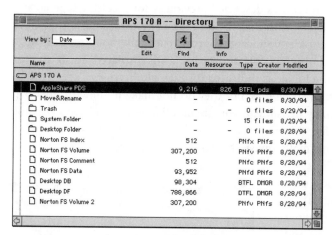

Figure 8-8 DiskTop, still another utility that lists invisible files and folders. This one lets you copy, move, delete or rename them.

With Sherlock From Sherlock's Find File, hold down the Option key, and select the Name pop-up menu. This will bring up four additional options at the bottom of the menu. Select "visibility" as "invisible," then click the Find button. This will give you a list of all invisible files and folders on your disk. You will not be able to open or edit any of these files (and perhaps not even move them). If you try, you will get a message saying that you are unable to open the file "because it is invisible (or is inside an invisible folder)" or that "An unexpected error occurred, because the original item could not be found." Despite these limits, there is not a quicker way to get a list of these files.

By the way, conveniently, another of these special options (name/icon lock) identifies which files have their Name Locked bit turned on.

With Sherlock 2, introduced in Mac OS 9, you access this feature by first selecting to do a Custom search and then clicking the Edit button. This opens up the More Search Items window. From here, you can select "is invisible" from the Advanced Options section. By the way, search criteria can be saved; the next time you want to use the saved criteria, select it from the Custom pop-up menu.

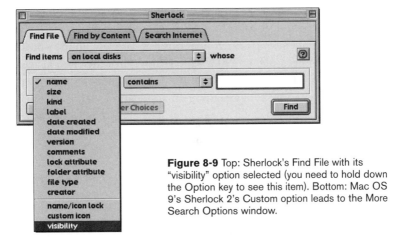

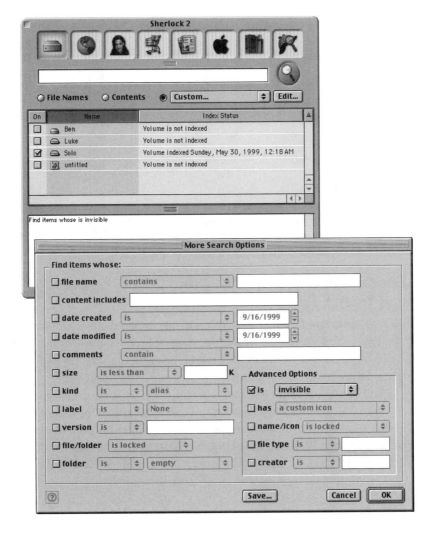

Figure 8-9 Top: Sherlock's Find File with its "visibility" option selected (you need to hold down the Option key to see this item). Bottom: Mac OS 9's Sherlock 2's Custom option leads to the More Search Options window.

With File Buddy File Buddy is a shareware utility that is ideal for locating and modifying invisible files on your disk. Start by selecting "Find Invisible Items" from File Buddy's Cleaning menu and clicking Search. You can now use File Buddy's button bar to manipulate the files. For example, to make a file visible, click the "Reveal selected items in the Finder" button. If you want to examine the contents of the file, open it via File Buddy's "Open With" button, assigning an application such as BBEdit to open the file.

With other utilities Shareware utilities, such as Invisible File Copier and InvisiFile, let you quickly toggle the visibility of a file.

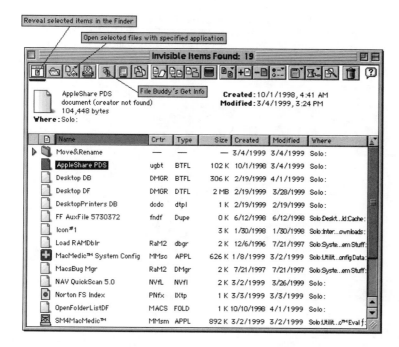

Figure 8-10 File Buddy's window listing all the invisible files on a drive. With File Buddy, you can reveal, open, copy, move, delete or access the Get Info window of any invisible file.

Special Case: Viewing the Contents of the Desktop Folder and Trash Folder

By definition, an invisible folder is not displayed on the Finder's desktop (though it may appear in Open and Save dialog boxes). Similarly, none of the contents of an invisible folder are visible on the desktop (even though the invisible bits for each item in the folder are not turned on).

The special Desktop Folder and Trash folder, however, are exceptions to this generalization. The contents of the Desktop Folder *are* visible; they are seen as the files and folders on the desktop (those items not in any folder nor in the root-level window of a volume). Similarly, just double-click the Trash icon to open a window that displays all items currently in the Trash folder—you can think of the Trash can as a special folder icon.

Each disk maintains its own set of these invisible Desktop and Trash folders. For example, if you use Norton Disk Editor to open the Trash folder on a given disk, it only lists those files that are currently in the Trash from that particular disk. In contrast, if you double-click the Trash icon on the desktop, it lists all files placed there from all mounted disks. If you eject a floppy disk, any unemptied items from that disk disappear from the Trash folder window but return to it the next time you insert the disk.

TAKE NOTE ▶ Invisible Files to the Rescue

Here are a few examples of how a knowledge of invisible files, and how to work with them, can help you solve an assortment of Mac problems:

Cure Finder crashes Finder freezes and crashes can happen for any number of reasons. One reason is a potentially misplaced copy of the invisible OpenFolderListDF file. This file first appeared in Mac OS 8.0. It keeps track of which Finder windows were left open at shut down and whether they are pop-up windows. One copy of this file is in the Preferences folder of the startup disk. Other copies are at the root level of every other disk. An extra copy may sometimes appear at the root level of the startup disk. Apple has stated that this extra copy presents no problem and can be ignored. However, many Mac users found that deleting the extra copy eliminated Finder-related freezes they were having.

SEE: • **Chapter 4.**

Stop persisting shutdown warnings After a system crash, you may get a message during the next startup informing you of the crash (as if you didn't know!). Enabling "Shut Down Warning" in the General Controls control panel is what turns on this feature. However, the message is actually triggered by an invisible file called "Shutdown Check." The Mac creates this file at each startup and then deletes it at each "proper" shutdown (one that uses the Mac's Shut Down command).

If the Mac finds this file still around at startup, it assumes an "improper" shut down and displays the warning message. Occasionally, this message may start to appear at *every* startup. The likely explanation is that corruption of the Shutdown Check file prevents it from being deleted. The simple solution is to delete the file yourself.

SEE: • **"By the Way: The Shut Down Warning Message," in Chapter 4.**

Get file sharing to work If you get a message that says "File Sharing Cannot Be Enabled," the invisible AppleShare PDS file may be damaged. The file maintains information about what folders and disks are being shared, and with whom. The solution is to delete the file (it's found at the root level of the drive). AppleShare will create a fresh undamaged copy the next time it's needed.

SEE: • **Chapter 11.**

Get extensions to load Occasionally, a particular extension may not load at startup. Often, invisible files are the ultimate cause. For example, if Adobe Type Manager refuses to load, claiming that "ATM requires more memory…,"a common cause is a corrupted ATM Temp.ATM file. You'll find it in the Preferences folder. Delete it and ATM will create a new one.

If you move the RAM Doubler control panel to a new System Folder and find that it no longer loads at startup, you did not also move the invisible Load RAMDblr file (located at the root level of the System Folder). Either reinstall RAM Doubler (from its master disk), or locate the invisible Load RAMDblr file and drag it to the new System Folder.

SEE: • **Fix-It #3.**

Eradicate a virus Excessive disk activity, corrupted files and unexpected restarts are just some of the possible symptoms of the AutoStart virus (so named because it can infect your Mac only if QuickTime 3.0's AutoPlay feature is enabled). The virus typically arrives on your drive in the guise of two invisible files: DB (at the root level of your startup disk) and Desktop Print Spooler (in the Extensions folder). The names of these files make them sound as if they are harmless. Indeed, there is a valid visible file in your Extensions folder called Desktop Printer Spooler. But don't be fooled. If you find these files, trash them instantly. Or simply use any up-to-date antivirus utility to get rid of them for you.

SEE: • **Fix-It #6.**

Viewing and Editing *Really* Invisible Files and Folders

Some files are so invisible that they do not even appear in the main listings of utilities like File Buddy or DiskTop. In part, this is because these special files are not files in the same sense as typical documents and applications. A disk's *Directory* file and *boot blocks* are two examples of this. Sometimes, however, you can use other special features of these utilities to view—and even alter—the contents of these files.

SEE: • **Chapter 5 for more information on startup disks and boot blocks.**
      • **Fix-It #10 for more information on the Directory.**

Viewing the Directory and the Boot Blocks

With Norton Utilities

1. Open Norton Disk Editor (either from its Finder icon or by selecting it from the Utilities menu of Norton Utilities). This should lead to a dialog box with a pop-up menu of all mounted disks.

2. Select the disk you want and click Open. This opens a window with a directory listing of all files and folders on the disk, including invisible ones.

3. Pull down the Objects menu. You will see a list of objects that include the boot blocks and the different components of the Directory (such as Extents B-Tree). Note that near the top of the window is an explanation of the function of the selected component; this explanation shifts accordingly each time you select a different component.

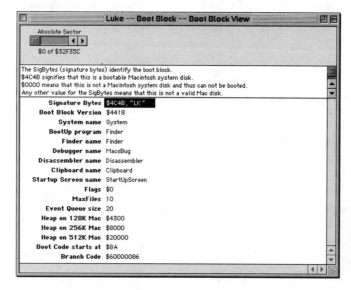

Figure 8-11 Norton Disk Editor's view of a disk's boot blocks; since the Signature Bytes line is selected, the text near the top of the window gives an explanation of what Signature Bytes means.

By the way, the Directory object (the last one in the Objects menu list) is something of a misnomer. It refers to the default listing of the contents of the disk, not to the actual Directory files.

It's technically possible to use Norton Utilities to modify any of this boot block and Directory information. To do so, select the View in Hex or View in ASCII commands from the Display menu. You can now directly modify the data.

TECHNICALLY SPEAKING ▶ Hex/ASCII Data Editing

With Norton Disk Editor, you can get a hex or ASCII listing for any file on your disk just by selecting the file name (when in the Directory view) and clicking the Edit button. There is even a way to access areas of a disk that have not been assigned to any file. Unless you are following detailed instructions or are generally skilled in how to work with hex code, though, I would not mess with any of this. This is the "raw" data level of the computer's contents. Thankfully, you will rarely (if ever) need to edit this information, or even understand more about it than the minimum I have presented here. Refer to the Norton Utilities documentation for more help if you really want or need to try this editing.

When might a person largely unfamiliar with what all of this means have any reason to work at this level? For one example, a vendor helping you to "patch" a program (to fix a minor bug) may provide instructions that require altering the hex code. In this case, you don't need to have any idea what you are actually doing; just follow the vendor's instructions carefully.

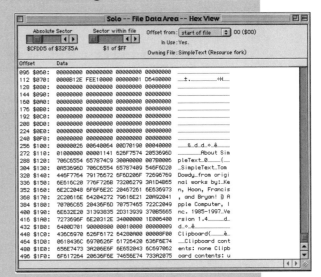

Figure 8-12 A view of the hex code for the SimpleText application, as seen from Norton Disk Editor; Norton lets you edit this code if you want.

Special Case: The Disk Driver and Related Low-Level Data

A hard disk's *driver descriptor map* (which relates to the disk driver first installed when you initialize a disk) and *partition map* (similarly determined when you format a disk) are often referred to as residing in the *low-level* areas of the disk. These areas allow the Macintosh to first interact with a hard disk, identify critical components of its operation, and maintain information about disk partitions.

These areas are physically separate from the rest of the disk and, as such, are inaccessible from every function in Norton Utilities that I have so far described. In fact, the Norton Utilities documentation draws the distinction between the "logical disk" (what we have been working with so far) and the "physical disk" (which includes these additional areas). In essence, this difference is what is implied by saying these areas are at a low level. Normally, you interact with them only indirectly, such as via a disk formatting utility.

If you are really determined, however, you *can* see the driver descriptor map and partition map with Norton Disk Editor. They are listed at the top of the Objects menu. Normally these menu items are grayed out, but you can make them active (leaving the other items grayed out) through a special procedure that requires first selecting "Scan SCSI Bus" from Norton Disk Editor's Open pop-up menu. When Disk Editor finishes this task, select the Open pop-up menu a second time, but now with the Command-Shift keys held down. This brings up a list of the additional names of the physical disks (such as "Quantum drive") that you can open; now you will have access to the grayed out menu items. Check the Norton Utilities manual for more details as needed.

I only mention all of this for the sake of completeness. Typically, you would have no reason to ever work with these areas.

SEE: • **Fix-It #12 for more details on disk device drivers.**
  • **Fix-It #13 for more details on partitioning and disk formatting.**

Figure 8-13 Friends in low places: Norton Disk Editor's hidden options in the Open pop-up menu (right) give you access to the normally grayed-out commands (below).

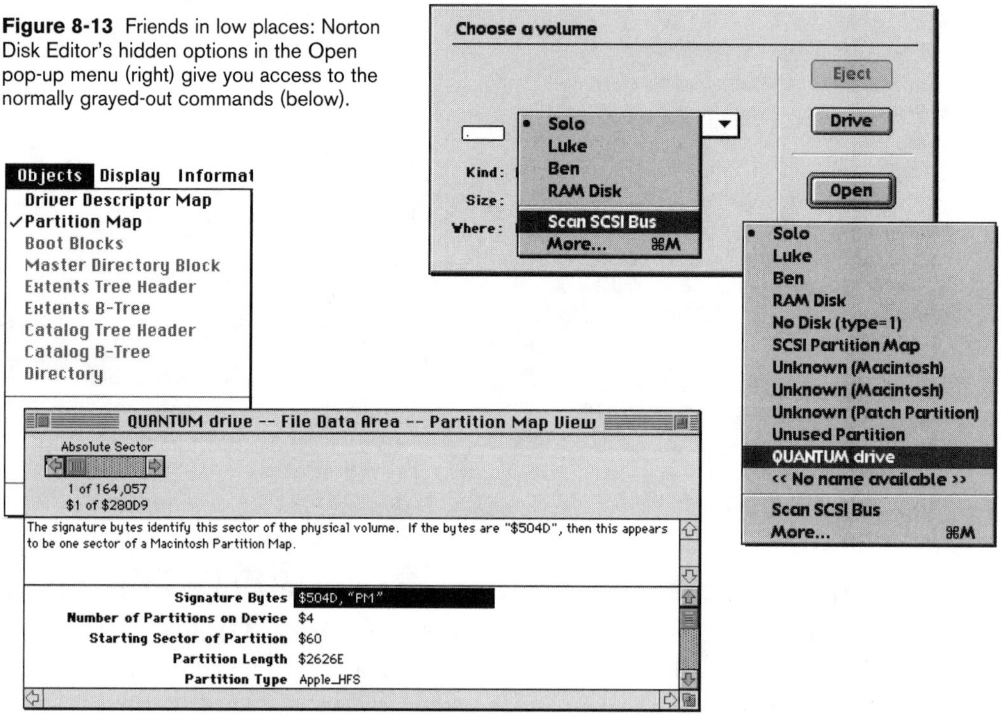

TECHNICALLY SPEAKING ▶ Using ResEdit

Before concluding this chapter, I feel obligated to at least mention the ultimate "under the hood" utility, Apple's ResEdit. It is mainly used to view and edit the variety of *resources* that are stored within a file—such things as fonts, sounds, icons, and more.

Personally, I rarely use ResEdit for troubleshooting. Instead, I use it most often simply to "explore" these resources. By doing so, you can often learn things about the contents of a file that may later prove to be helpful for troubleshooting. For example, you can get a listing of all of the possible error and alert messages that an application might generate or all of the menus generated by an application.

You can also modify all of this stuff with surprising ease: adding custom menus, editing icons, changing the text and default settings of dialog boxes, replacing graphics (including the Mac OS splash screen that you see at startup), and much more.

Finally, you can use ResEdit to do hex editing, as well as modifying the type, creator and Finder flags of any file. It can be a great "Swiss Army knife" utility. If you want to take the time to master it (as easy as it is, it is still more designed for programmers than end users), it can do just about everything that all of the other utilities mentioned in this chapter can do—and then some.

If all of this sounds like it is up your alley, get a copy of ResEdit and try it out. Some sparse documentation may be included with the file; more complete documentation is available from a variety of books and web sites.

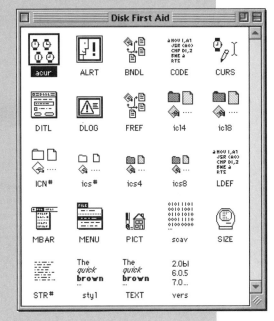

Figure 8-14 Using ResEdit to get inside of Apple's Disk First Aid utility; double-clicking any of the icons opens the door to further exploration of the resources within.

9

Fonts and Text: Write and Wrong

The Write Stuff

No matter what else you do with your Macintosh, sooner or later you use it to write something. It may just be a note to a colleague or a caption added to an illustration, or it may be a full-length manuscript. Whatever it is, you are using the text capability of the Macintosh to write it—and what a capability it is! The power you have to alter the appearance of text on the Macintosh is one of the computer's most impressive features.

These text features and the applications that use them — most notably word processors — are the focus of this chapter. In most of these applications, changes to text are made by selecting items from the Font, Style, and Size menus. For example, you might start by selecting a basic font appearance from the choices in the Font menu (such as Times or Helvetica), then decide on the style (such as *italics* or **bold**) and size (such as smaller or larger) of the font. A quick trip to the menu bar can change "this" to "this." Equally impressive is that when you finally print your text, the output looks virtually identical to what appeared on the screen, sometimes even better! This is the basic "what you see is what you get" (WYSIWYG) appeal of the Macintosh.

What's even better is how easy it is to do all of this. Most people can create and print their text documents without the slightest understanding of how any of these font miracles happen. This is good, because the Macintosh's methods for displaying and printing fonts constitute about the most convoluted topic I'll cover in this book.

Most of the time, the Macintosh succeeds in hiding this complexity from you. Eventually, however, something unexpected happens. Perhaps the line breaks on the printed copy do not match what appeared on your screen, or maybe your document inexplicably displays a different font from the one you expected—or worse. To resolve these problems, you will need to learn at least a little about how all of this works. So take a deep breath, and let's go.

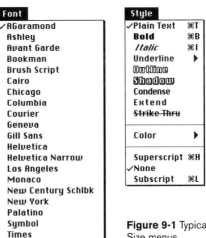

Figure 9-1 Typical Font, Style and Size menus.

Font Basics

Font Files Versus Font Suitcases

Font Files

Font file is the term used to describe a particular individual font as it appears on the Finder's desktop. It can be moved or copied just like any other type of file.

All characters in a font look related, and this basic design is called the *typeface* of the font. All fonts of the same typeface have the same general name and are said to belong to the same family. Thus, Times 10, Times 12, Times (bold), and so on are all part of the Times family of fonts, even though they are a different size and/or style.

The Macintosh can tell which fonts belong to the same family because of special information contained within the font files. Sometimes, because it is common practice, the word font is also used to refer to the entire family rather than just a single file (as in "Select the Times font from the Font menu").

Font Suitcases

It is possible for several font files to be combined into one superfile called a *font suitcase*. To see the contents of a suitcase file, simply double-click the file icon; a new window will open that lists all of the individual font files stored in the suitcase. In most cases (some exceptions are listed in the following sections), you can modify the contents of a font suitcase simply by dragging a font file out of or into the suitcase.

Figure 9-2 Font file (left) versus font suitcase (right) icons.

A font suitcase can contain just one font file, or several (such as all sizes of New York). The fonts in a suitcase do not have to be of the same family; for example, New York and Geneva fonts can be combined into one suitcase.

Where the Fonts Are

Just because a font file is on your disk somewhere doesn't mean it will show up on your Font menus. To be in an application's Font menu, the font file typically has to be in a special location in your System Folder.

Many new Macintosh users, especially if they work with only one application, are surprised to discover that the available fonts are not part of the application itself. Instead, applications get their font listing from the System Folder. Because all applications' font listings are generated in the same way, the same set of fonts is available to all applications running under that startup disk. Thus, if you were to shift from a word processor to a spreadsheet, you would almost always find the same font listing.

The Macintosh system software includes a basic set of fonts that are automatically installed when you first create a System Folder on your hard disk. These are only a tiny sample, however, of what is available (even though they are probably all that most people ever use). Other fonts are available from Apple as well as from many other companies. All told, you can choose from thousands of possible fonts.

How Can You Tell What Fonts Are Installed in Your System?

One way, of course, is to open your System Folder and check directly (assuming you know where to look, as I will describe shortly). A much simpler solution, however, is to open the Key Caps desk accessory that comes with Macintosh system software disks; its Key Caps menu lists all currently installed fonts. The Font menu of most word processors and related applications would have the same menu.

Locating, Adding, and Removing Fonts from Your System Folder

To add a new font to or remove an unwanted font from your Font menu, you have to install or remove the font at its relevant System Folder location. Here's what you need to do (except for special issues that pertain only to PostScript fonts, which will be described later in this chapter).

Fonts in the Fonts Folder

Font files are located in a special folder within the System Folder called Fonts. The Fonts folder can contain both single font files and font suitcases; the Macintosh will deal with both of them appropriately. The Fonts folder must remain in the System Folder, though, in order for applications to access its contents.

Figure 9-3 A Fonts folder containing both suitcase files and individual font files.

Font and suitcase files can be dragged to or from the Fonts folder, similar to how any other set of files and folders on the desktop would work. You can also add a font or suitcase file to the Fonts folder by dragging the file onto the active System Folder icon. This moves the font directly to the Fonts folder, after first giving you an alert message to confirm that this is what you want to do.

You can add font files or suitcases to the Fonts folder even if other applications are open. If applications other than the Finder are open, however, you will typical-

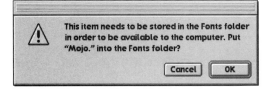

Figure 9-4 A message that appears when you drag a font suitcase or font file to the System Folder icon.

ly get an alert message warning you that the added fonts will not be available to any open applications until after you quit and relaunch them. And you cannot replace a font file with another file of the same name while applications are open, just as you cannot simply remove a file from the Fonts folder while any applications are open. (Sometimes you can remove a font file from a font suitcase within the Fonts folder even though applications are open, but I have found that this doesn't always work.)

The solution in each of these cases, of course, is to quit all open applications before you try to make changes that affect existing fonts.

SEE: • **"Damaged Font Files," later in this chapter, for more details.**

Helpful hint: The system software doesn't always behave by the rules. Sometimes you get these alert messages when you shouldn't, and sometimes you don't get them when you should. For example, to replace a font, even with all applications closed, you may have to remove the existing font file separately and then add the new one—otherwise, you may get the "font is in use" message. Beyond that, if you are still having these font problems, restarting will usually solve them. If that doesn't work, you may have damaged font files (as described later in this chapter).

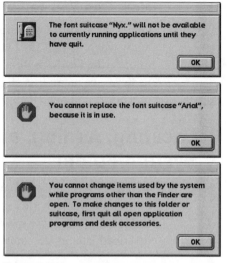

Figure 9-5 Messages that appear when you try to add (top), replace (middle), or remove (bottom) a font file to/from a Fonts folder while applications are open.

Fonts in the System File

A few critical fonts needed for the Macintosh's menus, windows, and message boxes are located in the System file itself, although you will not find them there when you open the System suitcase. The Finder keeps their listing "invisible."

Back in System 7, you could store fonts in the System file by simply dragging a font file to the System suitcase icon. You can no longer do

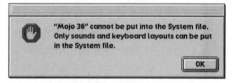

Figure 9-6 This message appears if you try to add a font to the System file by dragging the font file directly to the System suitcase icon.

this. If you try, you will get an error message. While technically you could work around this (such as via some ResEdit hacking), there is no reason to want to do so anymore.

SEE: • **"Technically Speaking: Reserved Fonts And System Fonts" in the "Font Menu Problems" section later in this chapter for more on invisible System file fonts.**

Font Management Utilities and Fonts Anywhere on Your Drive

Although most users will be content storing all their fonts in their System Folder, you can bypass this restriction. To do this, use any one of a collection of font management utilities (such as Adobe Type Manager Deluxe, Suitcase, Font Agent, or Font Reserve). These utilities can be configured to recognize fonts no matter where on your drive they may be. These fonts are then "loaded" and appear in your Font menus, just as if the font was in the System Folder's Fonts folder.

With these utilities, you can also create Font sets. This allows you to turn on and off specific subsets of your complete selection of fonts. This could be useful if, for example, you have some unusual fonts that you only use with one application (perhaps Adobe's InDesign). You can create a set that you only turn on when you use that application.

Why not just leave all your fonts active all the time? There are several reasons. One is simply convenience; you may not like have such a long list of fonts in your Font menu, especially if you hardly ever use most of them. More important, there is a limit of 348 files that can be open at one time (see Chapter 6 for more on this). Each open font file counts as one (or even two, in some cases) files. So eliminating fonts from the "active" list reduces your open files total. However, note that the Mac counts font *files*, not fonts. This means that several dozen fonts in a single font suitcase only counts as one open file. Thus, another way to reduce your open font file total is to combine fonts in separate font files into a single font suitcase (a suitcase can be as large as 16MB). You can similarly merge suitcase files by dragging one suitcase file on top of another.

In Mac OS 8.x and earlier, there is also a limit of 128 font files that can be stored in the Fonts folder (PostScript printer fonts, described more later in this chapter, are not included in this limit). As a suitcase still counts as only one file, combining fonts into font suitcases will allow you to exceed this limit. In Mac OS 9, the limit was increased to 512.

Figure 9-7 Adobe Type Manager Deluxe's list of fonts; the sets on the left are stored outside of the System Folder. Bottom: ATM Deluxe's "Manage Duplicates" window.

You can create a new empty suitcase, if needed, simply by duplicating an existing suitcase and dragging all existing fonts out of the duplicate suitcase. Now you are ready to add new files to it. If there are no suitcases anywhere on your disk, check your system software disks; the fonts included with your system software are typically stored in suitcase format. Otherwise, you can create a new suitcase with a freeware utility called SuitcaseMaker.

It is possible to have two copies of the exact same font file in the Fonts folder at the same time. One way this could happen is if

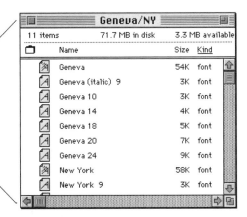

Figure 9-8 Opening a font suitcase to view the font files within.

duplicate font files are contained in two different suitcases. Surprisingly, this usually doesn't cause any problems, but you still want to be careful here. For instance, you wouldn't want to add a duplicate file when you are trying to replace an existing file that you suspect is corrupted. Also you may run into problems with the duplicate fonts having different ID numbers. Utilities such as Adobe Type Manager Deluxe can check for (and delete) duplicate fonts.

SEE: • **"A Document Displays the Wrong Font ;" later in this chapter.**

The Different Types of Fonts

The different categories of fonts described in this section do not refer to the appearance of the font (such as whether it is plain or decorative), but rather to the *technology* the Macintosh uses to create a font, both for screen display and for printing.

The Macintosh's multiplicity of font technologies is evidence of a sorry state of confusion—the result of historical compromises, competing interests, and changing technology. Sadly, it is certainly not the result of a deliberate strategy to make the Macintosh easier to use. As end users, we simply have to make the best of this less-than-great situation.

Bitmapped Fonts

Bitmapped fonts (sometimes referred to as *fixed-size fonts*) are so named because each character is made up of a collection of dots (or *bits*) that create the appearance of the font. Because it is an exact representation of the font, including its size, a separate set of instructions is needed for each different size of a font. Thus a bitmapped font *family* (such as New York) typically would include a collection of separate font files, each representing different font sizes (such as New York 9, New York 10, New York 12, and so on), where each number refers to the *point size* of the font as listed in the Size menu.

Most bitmapped fonts come in a small set of standard sizes, the most common being 9, 10, 12, 14, 18, and 24 points. This is why the Size menus of many applications list only these sizes and do not include odd sizes such as 13 or 17 points. Larger sizes of fonts (greater than 24 points) are similarly rare. This is mainly because, as the font sizes get larger, the amount of disk space needed to store the larger bitmap files increases dramatically.

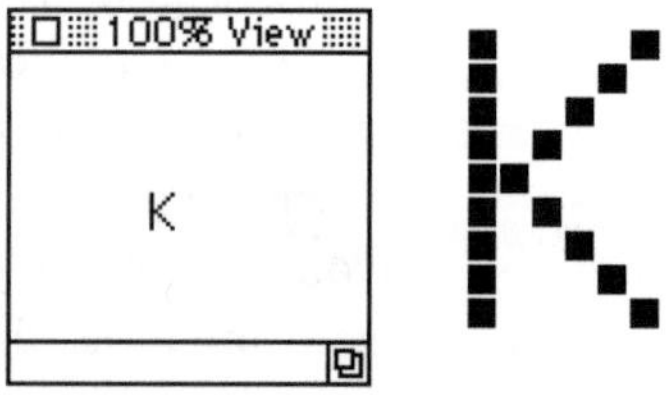

Figure 9-9 A bitmapped letter K, enlarged to show its underlying bit (dot) structure.

Estimating Font Sizes and Styles: The Jaggies

For bitmapped fonts, if you select a font size (such as 13 or 17 points), for which you do not have a corresponding font file installed, you get the *jaggies.* What happens is that the Macintosh tries to approximate the appearance of the font by estimating shape information from sizes that are installed. Unfortunately, the Macintosh cannot do a very good job of this estimation, and so the font appears with an unpleasing jagged look.

New York 14 point with jaggies.

Bitmapped New York at 14 point.

TrueType New York at 14 point.

Figure 9-10 Screen displays of different font types; jaggies occur (top line) when bitmapped New York 14 point is displayed without the 14-point size installed.

Technically, the Macintosh uses the same sort of estimation when you select different font styles (such as **bold** versus *italics*). The changes necessary to alter a style, however, are generally simpler than those needed to change a size. This is why you generally don't need separate bitmapped font files for each different style (although separate files do exist and can improve the appearance of the font over using the estimated style).

At one time in the Mac's history, bitmapped fonts were the only kind there were. Even today, they produce the sharpest screen displays of any type of font, especially at smaller point sizes (12 points or less). Still, because of the jaggies problem as well as their low resolution for printing—bitmapped fonts are designed at 72 dots per inch (dpi), while current printers commonly print at 600 dpi or higher—they have largely been replaced by newer font technologies, as explained in the next sections.

SEE: • Chapter 10 for details on the meaning of resolution and dpi.

How Do You Know What Sizes of Bitmapped Fonts Are Installed?

A quick way to find out what sizes of bitmapped fonts are installed is to select the Size menu of a text application. Here you may see some numbers in plain type (9) and others in outline style (10). The outlined numbers mean that the current System file contains the bitmapped font file for that particular size of the selected font and can therefore produce a smooth display. Attempts to use the sizes shown in plain type will generally result in jagged fonts on the screen.

Of course, which sizes are and are not installed may change each time you select a different font. It depends on which sizes for that particular font are installed in the appropriate System Folder location.

The other sure way to check this information, of course, is to inspect the contents of the System Folder itself to see what font files are located there.

By the way, if all the sizes listed in a Size menu are outlined—even odd sizes that are definitely not installed as bitmapped fonts—it is because you are using a TrueType font (described in the next section).

Outline Fonts: TrueType and PostScript

Outline fonts (sometimes referred to as variable-size or scalable fonts) are an alternative to bitmapped fonts. Essentially, with these fonts, the shape of each character is initially derived from a mathematical formula that describes the curves and lines that represent the character rather than by dot-by-dot mapping. For example, an outline font would derive the letter *O* from the basic formula for a circle (the exact formula differs to account for variations in the letter O for each font). This information is then converted to the pattern of dots necessary to display or print the character, a process called *rasterizing*.

As their name implies, scalable font files are not restricted to a specific size. In fact, with only a single outline font file, you can select any font size you want and never have a problem with the jaggies.

While bitmapped fonts may look better on a typical monitor, outline fonts usually look far superior in printed output. This is because the resolution of outline fonts is *device independent*, taking advantage of whatever resolution is available in the output device. The appearance quality of outline-font text thus improves as the resolution of the printer increases. Laser-printed output, even though it is still a collection of dots constructed similarly to how fonts are displayed on a screen, has a resolution of at least 300 dpi. Because most monitors are limited to about 72 dpi, the appearance of fonts on the monitor display can never match what you can achieve in the printed output from laser printers or any other comparable higher-resolution printer.

SEE: • **Chapter 10 for more on resolution.**

BY THE WAY ▶ Outline Fonts Versus Outline Style

The term *outline*, as applied to outline fonts, has nothing to do with the outline display style of a font. The former refers to a method of generating font characters. The latter refers to the appearance of a particular style of font as selected from a Style menu.

There are two basic types of outline fonts on the Macintosh: TrueType fonts and PostScript fonts.

TrueType Fonts

TrueType fonts are an outline font technology developed by Apple. Virtually all of the fonts that ship with the Mac OS and/or that came with your computer are TrueType fonts. They are now the predominant font type on the Mac.

Only one TrueType font file is needed to display and print all possible sizes. Similarly, you only need the same solitary font file to create the different styles of the font (such as bold or italics), although you may occasionally see TrueType fonts with separate files for different styles (such as Futura Bold and Futura Italic). If you install these additional files, they will be used when you select the Bold or Italic styles from the Style menu.

Otherwise, the Macintosh will estimate the style from the plain-text font file information, as it typically does with bitmapped fonts. This is similar to the situation with PostScript fonts, as described in "Technically Speaking: All in the Family."

How to Identify a TrueType Font Versus a Bitmapped Font

Apple no longer ships bitmapped fonts with the Mac OS, so you will likely not see them around much anymore. But just in case, here's how to quickly identify the type of font you have:

Identifying Fonts from the Finder
If you go into the System folder and look at the icon of the font file, you can see that a bitmapped font icon has one *A*, while a TrueType font icon has three overlapping *A*'s. Similarly, if you double-click a font file, it opens up to display a sample of what the font text looks like. Bitmapped fonts show only a sample in their single fixed size. TrueType fonts show samples in three different sizes.

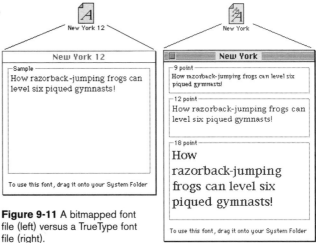

Figure 9-11 A bitmapped font file (left) versus a TrueType font file (right).

Even their names give them away. Bitmapped fonts are always named with a number representing their size (New York 12). TrueType fonts are named without any number (New York).

Identifying a TrueType Font from Within Applications You can usually distinguish the presence of a TrueType font from directly within a text application. First select the font in question from the Font menu, and then check the Size menu. For TrueType fonts, all sizes in the menu should be in outline style—and if there is an Other size option, the word *Other* is also in outline style. If only bitmapped font files are present, only installed sizes are outlined, and the word *Other* is never outlined.

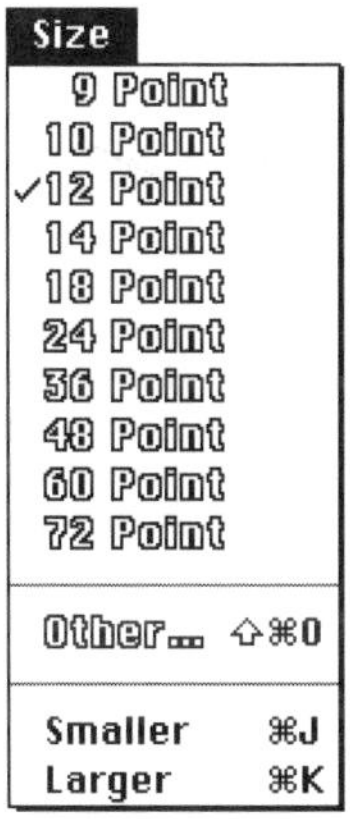

Figure 9-12 The Size menu for a TrueType font.

PostScript Fonts

PostScript outline fonts, which predated the arrival of TrueType fonts by several years, were originally developed by a company called Adobe. They instantly became an essential ingredient of high-quality output on a Macintosh. In fact, one of the reasons that Apple developed TrueType fonts was that it did not want Adobe, or any other company, controlling such an important part of the Macintosh technology. TrueType was Apple's answer to PostScript fonts.

TAKE NOTE ▶ What Is PostScript?

PostScript is a page description language that describes the location and appearance of text and graphics output, usually to a PostScript printer. When you use a PostScript printer, text and graphics (as displayed on your monitor) are translated into PostScript instructions. These instructions, in turn, are used to create the image of each page. The information needed to interpret these instructions and create the final printed output is built into the hardware of a PostScript printer.

PostScript printers can print text created with any type of font. To take maximum advantage of PostScript's capabilities, however, you need special PostScript fonts. Most PostScript printers have a set of PostScript fonts built into the hardware; other PostScript fonts can be downloaded from the Macintosh. Details are described in the main text.

Similarly, although a PostScript printer can print any graphic you see on the screen, it is at its best when printing graphics that directly utilize PostScript instructions (you need special software to create these graphics, as described more in Chapter 10).

The vast majority of Macintosh PostScript printers are laser printers, but not all laser printers include PostScript. Inkjet printers are generally non-PostScript devices (though some inkjet printers include a PostScript interpreter or can optionally add one).

SEE: • **Chapter 7, "Take Note: Different Types of Printers," for more on printer types.**
 • **Chapter 10 for more on PostScript graphics.**

PostScript Printer Fonts Versus Screen Fonts

A PostScript font is often referred to as a *printer font.* This is because a PostScript font file contains the PostScript instructions needed by a PostScript printer to create text output. Printer fonts, however, are completely unable to create an image of the text on the screen (because only the printer has the PostScript interpreter needed to make use of the PostScript instructions). This makes them fundamentally different from bitmapped and TrueType fonts, which can generate both printed text and screen images.

Of course, in order to use PostScript fonts, you must be able to see the text on the screen. This problem was initially solved by the use of *screen fonts,* which are typically ordinary bitmapped font versions of the PostScript fonts' appearance. When you select a PostScript font from a Font menu, you actually select and see the screen font on the screen, but selecting that font also tells the Macintosh to use the corresponding PostScript printer font when you print to a PostScript printer. Both types of font files are necessary to use PostScript fonts on a Macintosh.

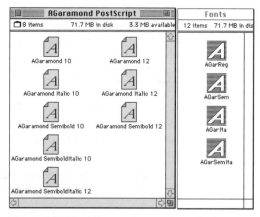

Figure 9-13 The bitmapped screen fonts for the Adobe Garamond (AGaramond) font (left), and the matching printer font files for AGaramond (right).

In general, printer font files are stored in your System Folder (see "Locating, Adding, and Removing PostScript Printer Font Files from your System Folder," later in this chapter, for more details). They are also included directly in the (ROM) hardware of PostScript laser printers; for example, most Apple LaserWriters include Avant Garde, Bookman, Courier, Helvetica, Helvetica Narrow, New Century Schoolbook, Palatino, Symbol, Times, Zapf Chancery, and Zapf Dingbats. Hewlett-Packard laser printers have a different set of fonts in their ROM. Thus, you do not need to place separate printer font files in your System Folder to use these fonts, only the corresponding screen fonts. (If your use of PostScript fonts is restricted to these built-in fonts, you may have never even seen PostScript printer font files.)

Apple Printer Utility and HP LaserJet Utility both show the built-in font lists for their respective printers.

No printer font files are included with Macintosh system software. You acquire them on your own. Adobe has a slew of excellent PostScript fonts, although at rather high prices. Other companies make less expensive PostScript fonts.

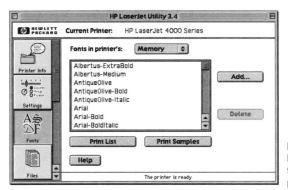

Figure 9-14 The HP LaserJet Utility shows the list of fonts in the printer's ROM.

TECHNICALLY SPEAKING ▶ Type 1 Versus Type 3 PostScript Fonts

You may occasionally hear reference to Type 1 versus Type 3 PostScript fonts (for some reason, there is no Type 2). Type 3 fonts are a relic from a time when Adobe tried to keep secret some of its ways of improving the appearance of fonts: Type 1 fonts contained special appearance-enhancing instructions, called hinting, that could not be used in Type 3 fonts. Only Adobe made Type 1 fonts, while Type 3 fonts were for everyone else. Since Adobe gave up on this restriction several years ago, though, you can pretty much assume that all your PostScript fonts are Type 1.

PostScript Fonts and Adobe Type Manager (ATM) and ATM Deluxe

Because PostScript was not created by Apple (in fact, it was not even developed primarily for the Macintosh), PostScript fonts have not had TrueType's almost seamless integration into the Macintosh system software. Using PostScript for text has traditionally involved several hassles and limitations not found with TrueType. The need for separate printer and screen fonts is one obvious example. (PostScript graphics have their own separate set of problems, as detailed in Chapter 10.)

Fortunately, most of these text-related hassles can be overcome by using a control panel utility called Adobe Type Manager (ATM), which is designed to work exclusively with PostScript fonts. Although Apple's policy can change with each version of the Mac OS, Apple currently includes a version of Adobe Type Manager with the Mac OS. So you probably already own ATM. However, there may be a newer version than the one you have. Updates to ATM are on the Adobe Web site. Make sure you have the latest version. ATM has so many benefits that if you use PostScript fonts at all ATM is nearly essential.

Although ATM may come free with the Mac OS, Adobe markets an enhanced version of ATM, called ATM Deluxe. In addition to having all of the features of ATM, it allows you to create font sets (as described in "Font Management Utilities and Fonts Anywhere on Your Drive," earlier in this chapter). It can also track TrueType fonts as well as PostScript fonts, analyze your fonts to check for possible damaged fonts, and create anti-aliased "smooth font edges" on screen (see relevant sections later in this chapter, such as "Take Note: The Jaggies, Anti-Aliasing, and Related Font Tips," for more details).

Because of the importance of ATM, it is difficult to describe PostScript fonts and how they work without also describing how ATM modifies this process.

BY THE WAY ▶ Accessing ATM Versus ATM Deluxe

With Adobe Type Manager Deluxe installed, you still have access to the ordinary ATM, if you want to view it for any reason. ATM Deluxe is an application, located wherever you want on your drive. ATM is a control panel. ATM is placed in the Control Panels folder (it is actually named "~ATM™"). With ATM Deluxe installed, an alias to the Deluxe application is placed in the Adobe Type Manager folder in the Preferences folder. When you launch the ATM control panel, Adobe uses some trickery to access the alias and actually launch the ATM Deluxe application. If you remove this alias from the folder, when you launch the ATM control panel, you will get the basic ATM program instead of the Deluxe version.

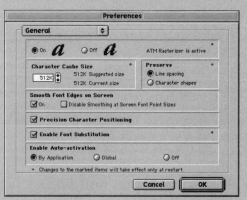

Figure 9-15 The ATM "Lite" control panel (left) and the ATM Deluxe Preferences window (right). Options such as "Line spacing" vs. "Character shapes" choice are described in more detail later in this chapter.

SEE: • **"Take Note: Substitute Fonts," "Technically Speaking: A Primer on Multiple-Master Fonts," "Fractional Widths and ATM," and "Problems with Adobe Type Manager".**

- **What about WYSIWYG?** Although screen fonts are designed to match what the PostScript printed output looks like, the match is almost never perfect. As a result, the Macintosh's normally close WYSIWYG relationship between the display and the printed output is broken. For example, line breaks might not always appear in the printed copy exactly as they appear on the screen.

   A related problem is the return of the jaggies on the screen. For example, suppose you pick a 17-point font size. Because you probably do not have a 17-point screen font, it will *display* with the jagged look described previously in the section on bitmapped fonts. It will still *print* out smooth as silk to a PostScript printer, however, because the printer font file is used to create the printed copy and the printer font uses PostScript (which, as with TrueType, is an outline font technology that prints smoothly at any point size).

- **ATM to the rescue (part 1)** ATM solves most of the WYSIWYG problems just described. In particular, it uses printer font instructions to generate an image of the font on the screen that can be smoothly scaled to any selected size! The jaggies vanish, much like what happens with TrueType fonts. The WYSIWYG matching of lines breaks and character spacing, while not necessarily perfect (especially because of likely differences in the resolution of the monitor versus the printer), will also be improved.

   A minor problem remains with the look of the Size menus. Unlike TrueType, ATM does not affect what sizes are outlined in Size menus. Thus, if the Palatino 18 screen font is not installed, the 18 in the Size menu will not be outlined. Don't be fooled, though—with ATM installed, the font will still print *and* display without the jaggies.

Bitmapped Palatino 14 point

Bitmapped Palatino 18 point

ATM Palatino 14 point

ATM Palatino 18 point

Figure 9-16 Samples of screen displays of bitmapped vs. ATM-generated vs. TrueType Palatino text; there are no jaggies, but each type looks somewhat different.

   Given all of this, you may now be asking: If I use ATM, does this mean that I no longer need screen fonts at all? Unfortunately, you still do need screen fonts. More precisely, you need at least 1 point size of a screen font for every PostScript font you use, because the screen font is necessary just to get the font name to appear in Font menus. Also, since screen fonts at smaller point sizes (12 points or less) generally look better than ATM-generated screen displays, it is common to have 9-point, 10-point, and/or 12-point screen fonts in use, even if you have ATM installed.

   Finally, note that if you are using the PostScript fonts that are built into your PostScript printer (such as the previously mentioned Times, Helvetica, and so forth), you still need to install the corresponding printer font files in your System Folder in order for ATM to create smooth screen displays. ATM cannot access the printer font files in your printer.

- **What if the printer font file is missing?** As I have already implied, if you select a presumed PostScript font from a Font menu but its PostScript font file is missing, it will not print in PostScript, even if you are using a PostScript printer (unless, of course, it is one of the fonts built into the printer). Instead, the screen font prints directly. A PostScript printer, however, will still probably do a better job of printing the screen font than a non-PostScript printer would. This is because a PostScript printer generates a temporary outline-like font file for the font when it goes to print it. It won't look nearly as good as if a true printer font was present, but you may find it acceptable if you have no other alternative. (Life can get more complicated. If the "screen font" is actually a TrueType font, it will print as a TrueType font, as described more a bit later in this chapter.)

  Even if you are using ATM, you still need PostScript printer fonts. If you just have the screen font, ATM is irrelevant; the printed output and the screen display will be the same as if you were not using PostScript fonts at all!

  SEE: • **"Take Note: Substitute Fonts," later in this chapter for related information.**

- **What if you don't have a PostScript printer?** Another traditional problem with using PostScript fonts, again as already implied, is that they require a PostScript printer. If you try to print PostScript text to a non-PostScript printer, the bitmapped screen font once again prints directly (as if it were an ordinary bitmapped font) whether or not the PostScript printer font is present.

- **ATM to the rescue (part 2)** Here is the second major benefit of using ATM: you can use it to print PostScript text even to a non-PostScript printer. In essence, the ATM software substitutes for the printer's PostScript interpreter, which would otherwise be needed.

  With ATM, as long as you have the relevant printer font files installed, text output to a non-PostScript printer looks about the same as the output from a PostScript printer *of the same resolution.* ImageWriter output will never look as good as LaserWriter output, even with ATM, because the ImageWriter is a lower-resolution printer. Output from inkjet printers and non-PostScript laser printers, however, can look almost identical to output from PostScript printers.

  By the way, remember that ATM only affects text. If you plan on printing PostScript graphics (see Chapter 10), ATM is of no help; you still need a PostScript printer.

  SEE: • **"Problems with Adobe Type Manager," later in this chapter, for more help with using this important utility.**

TECHNICALLY SPEAKING ▶ All in the Family

If you have ever purchased a PostScript font and tried to install it, you may notice that things are often a bit more complicated than implied here (as if they weren't already complicated enough!). In particular, you may find that several printer font files exist for the same font family. For example, the Adobe Garamond font includes four printer font files: AGarReg (for plain text), AGarSem (bold), AGarIta (italics), and AGarSemIta (bold and italics combined). All four printer font files are needed for these common styles to appear correctly in printed copy. For example, if you only installed AGarReg, but not the other AGar printer files, Adobe Garamond text will appear correctly in bold or italics on the screen, but will appear as plain text when printed.

This is also why, for example, you can display the Bold style for the Zapf Chancery font (which is a font built into a LaserWriter), but the LaserWriter will not print it as bold. This is because Apple chose to include only the plain text printer font for Zapf Chancery in the printer.

You may also find that a separate set of bitmapped screen fonts is included to match each of the different style variants of the printer font files. For example, there may be screen fonts, at various sizes, for AGaramond (plain text), AGaramond Semibold, AGaramond Italic, and AGaramond SemiboldItalic. If installed, these appear as separate fonts in the Font menu (which can considerably clutter up your Font menu). However, if the font files were created correctly, the Macintosh should still recognize all these variations as belonging to the same font family.

Unlike for the printer fonts, it is usually not necessary to use these screen font style variants. You could still select different styles from the Style menu even without the screen font variants installed, because printed appearance is determined primarily by the presence of the printer files, not of the screen fonts. For example, for printing with most applications, selecting Italic from the Style menu for the AGaramond font usually duplicates the effect of directly selecting the AGaramond Italic font from the Font menu (assuming all the printer font files are installed). Experiment. If your printed output is satisfactory with only the plain text screen font installed, you can skip the others.

Actually, there are advantages to using the Style menu method. For example, if you select Italic from the Style menu for AGaramond text and later change to a different font, the text remains in italics. This would not happen if, instead, you had selected AGaramond Italic from the Font menu.

The main advantage of using the separate style variants of screen fonts is that they typically enhance the WYSIWYG matching of the screen to the printed output, because the Macintosh uses the variant file, when available, to create the screen display rather than trying to approximate it from the plain text file (sometimes called a "false style"). The approximation method usually results in a less accurate matching than using the style variant. For a few applications, character spacing of printed output may also be improved with the use of the style variants.

By the way, don't be surprised if you do not have these variant screen fonts for your PostScript fonts. Not all PostScript fonts come with separate files for different styles. For example, for the PostScript fonts that came with Apple's LaserWriters, Apple included only the plain text screen fonts, without the other screen font variants. You would have the style variants only if you obtained the font directly from Adobe.

Also note that screen font variants may come in forms that are not a direct match for the Italics and Bold styles in the Style menu (e.g., Demi, Light etc. refer to different degrees of "boldness"). This is another reason why selecting the screen font variant may lead to different output than selecting the comparable style from the Style menu. This applies to TrueType fonts as well as PostScript fonts. In general, for TrueType fonts, keeping and using style variants will lead to better display and printing quality.

Similarly, you may have more than one version of a screen font (for example you may have a Times bitmap font from Apple and another from Adobe). One version may more closely match the appearance of the PostScript printed output than the other. Obviously, that is the screen font you should use.

Finally, if you use multiple mater fonts, there are other special factors to consider.

SEE: • **"Technically Speaking: A Primer on Multiple-Master Fonts," near the end of this chapter.**
• **"Font Menu Clutter," later in this chapter, for possible problems with using separate screen fonts for different styles of the same font.**

Locating, Adding, and Removing PostScript Printer Font Files from Your System Folder

In the section on Font Basics, I described where font files are located. All of that applied both to bitmapped fonts (including the screen fonts of PostScript fonts) and TrueType fonts. However, the PostScript printer font files work a bit differently.

First, printer font files cannot be included in suitcases, nor can they be installed in a System file (no matter what version of the system software you are using). Ideally, they should be stored in the Fonts folder of the System Folder together with the screen font version of the font. More generally, wherever the screen fonts are stored, the printer fonts should be in the same folder. Unlike other font types, you can add or remove printer font files to or from the Fonts folder, or any other location, without getting any alert messages, even if other applications are open.

TECHNICALLY SPEAKING ▶ Automatic Versus Manual Downloading

When you print a document that uses PostScript fonts that are not built into the printer, the needed information from the relevant printer font files is downloaded to the printer at the time the document is printed. It is then cleared from the printer's memory when the document is finished printing. This means that the next time you print a document that uses the same font, it has to be downloaded again. This repeated automatic downloading takes time and consequently slows down the printing process.

As an alternative, you can manually download a font to the printer, by using utilities such as the Apple Printer Utility or the HP LaserJet utility. For example, with the LaserJet Utility, select the Fonts tile and then click Add. Manually downloaded fonts stay in the printer's memory until you shut down (but you can download only as many fonts as can fit into the printer's memory at one time). If you plan to use the same few fonts repeatedly, this can be worthwhile. Still, in most cases, manual downloading does not save much time. Most users prefer the simpler and more transparent automatic downloading.

For fonts that are built into a PostScript printer, no downloading of any sort is needed. They are already there.

Finally, a new option in LaserWriter driver 8.6.5 or later, called Font Settings, gives you additional control. For example, you can select to whether to download Type 1 (PostScript) or TrueType versions of a selected font (if both types are available for the same font). You can also select to "Always download needed fonts," which overrides any version of the same font in the printer's memory. The option to "Never generate Type 42 format" is an esoteric way of saying never use TrueType fonts. This would only be needed in the rare case that your printer couldn't correctly print TrueType fonts.

Similarly, with most HP LaserJet printers, if you hold down the Option button when selecting the popup menu in the Print dialog box, you will get a new option called Preferences. From here, you will find a variety of mostly obscure options,

Figure 9-17 The Font Settings dialog of the Print dialog box.

including two called "Ignore fonts in printer when printing" and "Always generate Type 1 versions of TrueType fonts." The former forces the font on your drive to be used in lieu of any identically named font in the printer itself (just in case there are minor differences due to different versions of the same font). The latter is another way of ensuring that a TrueType version of a font is not used in preference to a PostScript version. Obviously, you want not want the settings in these two locations to contradict each other.

SEE: • **Chapter 7, "By the Way: The Fate of The Apple Printer Utility," for more on these utilities.**

How to Identify a PostScript Font

There is no clear way to know if you are using a PostScript font just by checking an application's Font menu or Size menu. To find out if a given font is a PostScript font, check the System Folder for the presence of PostScript printer font files. There are several different possible icons for PostScript fonts, but they will all have "PostScript font" as their Kind in their Get Info window.

For fonts that are built directly into your PostScript printer, there may not be a printer font file present for you to check. For a list of these built-in fonts, use utilities such as Apple Printer Utility or HP's LaserJet Utility to generate a list of these fonts, as described earlier in this chapter.

Also, certain utilities, such as ACTION WYSIWYG, can indicate the font type.

TECHNICALLY SPEAKING ▶ What is FontSync?

FontSync is a new control panel (plus an extension) included in Mac OS 9. You'll find the control panel in the Apple Extras folder. Drag it to the Control Panels folder of the System Folder if you intend to use it. Exactly what it does is still a bit obscure, as Apple has not offered much documentation on it. Apple states: "It provides a common method for identifying fonts based upon the content of the font, rather than just its name, as a document is moved from machine to machine." To use FontSync, applications must be updated to work with it (very few, if any, currently are).

FontSync is intended primarily for publishing professionals, to insure that the how a font looks on the screen used to create a document matches how it looks when printed—especially when the printing is done from a different machine. Apple cites three main reasons that problems occur here, even when you think both machines have the same fonts:

1. TrueType fonts. These cannot be rendered properly on Postscript output devices. Problems are especially likely if you have TrueType and Postscript fonts with the same name (e.g., Times).

2. Different versions of fonts. An older version of the same font may look different than a newer version.

3. Silent failures to access a font. If, for example, there is not enough memory for a printer to open a font (or if the limit on open files is exceeded), the printer may silently substitute a bitmap version of the font.

FontSync is intended to solve these problems. It creates a FontSync Profile based on criteria you set in the control panel. This Profile, when moved to a different machine, will make sure that the screen image and printed output match. If one machine does not have the exact font needed, FontSync may perform some sort of font substitution.

Finally, there has been some speculation that this (or a subsequent) version of FontSync will do Type 1 font rendering on the screen, eliminating the need for ATM. This is not the case as yet.

SEE ALSO: • "Take Note: Substitute Fonts," later in this chapter, for more on font substitution.

Combining TrueType, PostScript, and/or Bitmapped Versions of the Same Font

It is entirely permissible to mix font formats for the same font family within the System Folder. For example, you may have installed the 10-point and 12-point bitmapped versions of Times to use as screen fonts, plus a TrueType version of the Times font. If you are using a PostScript LaserWriter, you also have the PostScript printer font of Times built into the printer.

Are there problems with doing this? Advantages, perhaps? The answer is yes to both questions. To understand why, you first need to understand the rules that determine which font is used for the screen display and for printed output when multiple competing types are present.

Which Font Format Displays?

The font format displayed on the screen when more than one format of the same font is installed is determined according to the following priority list. The Macintosh uses the first format on the list, if it is available, skipping to items lower on the list as necessary:

- Bitmapped font, if the selected size is available.

- TrueType font.

- ATM-generated PostScript font.

- Bitmapped font scaled from a different size (which usually results in the jaggies), if selected size is not available.

Which Font Format Prints?

Which font format is used for printing when more than one format of the same font is installed is governed by a different set of rules from those used for the screen display. Furthermore, the rules vary depending on whether or not you are using a PostScript printer. Also note that some of these preferences, such as PostScript preferred over TrueType for PostScript printers, can be overridden by changing settings in the Print dialog box, as described in "Technically Speaking: Automatic Versus Manual Downloading".

PostScript Printers Use, in Order of Preference:

- PostScript fonts built into the printer's ROM.
- PostScript fonts contained in the active System Folder (with or without ATM).
- TrueType fonts.
- Bitmapped fonts.

Non-PostScript Printers Use, in Order of Preference:

- TrueType fonts.
- ATM-generated PostScript fonts.
- Bitmapped fonts.

What It All Means

Bitmapped fonts get the highest priority for screen display, but they get the lowest priority for printing! Although this may seem illogical at first, it does make sense.

To understand why, return to the previous example. If you have Times 10 and Times 12 installed, these bitmapped fonts are used for the screen display at those sizes. Such fonts generally offer the best possible screen appearance for these small sizes because, as described in previous sections, even if you use an outline font, the screen display itself remains a bitmap (that is, a collection of dots). The outline font instructions must be converted to a bitmapped approximation in order for it to be displayed. Bitmapped fonts at installed sizes, because they do not depend on any approximation, can best utilize the screen display.

The Times TrueType font kicks in at other sizes. This has the advantage of eliminating the jaggies at these sizes without requiring a separate bitmapped file for each size. (You could have used ATM to obtain this same benefit, but this would have also required installing printer font files. In essence you are using TrueType here, instead of ATM, to avoid the jaggies—the matching TrueType font serves as the screen font for the PostScript font. Many times, however, you will not have a matching TrueType font available, so this option will not apply.)

When you print to a PostScript printer, the printer's built-in PostScript Times font takes over, overriding both the bitmapped and the TrueType instructions in order to provide the highest-quality output possible with your PostScript printer.

Still, many experts recommend not combining TrueType and PostScript versions of the same font. This is primarily because TrueType-based screen display may have a different appearance, in terms of line breaks and character spacing, from PostScript-based printed output. Results can be especially hard to predict if you have different screen fonts and different TrueType fonts for different styles of the same font (such as Times Bold and Times Italic). I have made these sorts of combinations in several cases without any problem, however, so experiment for yourself. In any case, placing TrueType fonts and PostScript fonts from different families in the System Folder is not a problem at all.

Which Font Format Should You Use?

Suppose you have bitmapped, TrueType, and PostScript versions of the same font (such as Times). Assuming you would like to use only one of these formats for creating your text, which should you prefer? Or suppose you are considering purchasing a collection of fonts and you need to decide whether you want them to be TrueType or PostScript. Which should you get? Here are some guidelines for solving these and other similar dilemmas.

Limit Your Use of Bitmapped Fonts

Use bitmapped fonts mainly for display of text at small sizes. They make a clearer display and will redraw faster than TrueType fonts. If possible, use bitmapped fonts only in conjunction with TrueType or PostScript (with ATM) versions of the same font, so that the bitmapped version is not used for printing. Otherwise, try to avoid bitmapped fonts altogether, especially with a high-resolution printer.

Occasionally, large point sizes of bitmapped fonts may be useful if you're printing to a low-resolution printer, such as an ImageWriter. They may print better than the ATM or TrueType versions.

If you do print bitmapped text to a PostScript laser printer, it probably will look better than you might expect. This is because (as mentioned earlier in this chapter), a PostScript laser printer creates a temporary outline-like font file for the font, so that the font prints relatively smoothly at any size. ATM may even create a "substitute font."

SEE: • **"Take Note: Substitute Fonts," later in this chapter).**

Checking the "Smooth Text" option from the PostScript Options section of the Page Setup box may also help improve appearance of printed bitmapped fonts (the option is irrelevant for other types of fonts). Still, the converted and smoothed bitmapped output remains inferior to the quality you would get from a true PostScript font.

BY THE WAY ▶ **Printing Screen Fonts as Bitmapped Fonts**

Screen fonts are not usually printed; they serve only to create the screen display for a matching PostScript printer font. If you do not have the matching printer font installed (or if you are using a non-PostScript printer without ATM), however, the screen font prints directly, just like any other bitmapped font. If you try this, you may find that screen fonts do not print as attractively as bitmapped fonts that are specifically designed to be printed.

This is because screen fonts are usually designed with an emphasis more on how well their screen display matches the related PostScript printed output than on how they actually print out. (Of course, if you are using TrueType or PostScript fonts for printing, as recommended, all of this is irrelevant.)

Deciding Between PostScript and TrueType

PostScript (especially with ATM) and TrueType are both excellent font technologies. To a large extent, which looks better depends on the design of the particular font, not the technology. If your primary use of text is for minimally formatted documents, such as reports and manuscripts, either type of font is likely to be adequate.

PostScript, however, does have some advantages. As a group, PostScript fonts tend to be superior in appearance to the corresponding TrueType fonts. A wider selection of PostScript fonts than TrueType fonts is available, though this gap is rapidly disappearing. Most notable, PostScript is the standard font format used by typesetters and is likely to cause them fewer problems than TrueType fonts—an important consideration if you plan to have documents printed professionally by a service bureau. Also, if you plan on using PostScript graphics, you will probably prefer to use PostScript fonts as well.

With PostScript you can create special effects, such as rotated text and shading of text, that are either not possible or difficult to achieve with standard TrueType. There are also special PostScript fonts (called multiple-master fonts) that let you vary the characteristics of a font, including its weight and width.

On the other hand, each Macintosh comes with a selection of TrueType fonts at no extra cost. For some people, that alone is reason enough to prefer them. TrueType also has an advantage in its simplicity and better integration with other system software.

So, should you use PostScript or TrueType? There is no easy answer; I use them both.

Consider Your Printer

- **For PostScript printers** Print with PostScript fonts if you can, using ATM to improve screen displays of these fonts. You can also use TrueType fonts. If you have installed TrueType and PostScript versions of the same font, TrueType is not used for printing.

- **For non-PostScript printers** Prefer to use either TrueType fonts or ATM-generated PostScript fonts.

Keep It Simple

Don't overload your System Folder with fonts you rarely or never use. When you must use bitmapped versions of fonts, keep only those sizes that you use frequently.

Summing Up

Table 9-1 presents a summary of much of the information covered so far in this chapter.

Table 9-1 ▶ Font Basics Summary

	BITMAPPED FONT	TRUE TYPE FONT	POSTSCRIPT FONT*
Icons	or	or	Several possible icons, including: or
Location in System Folder**	Fonts folder	Fonts folder	Fonts folder
Can font be stored in suitcase and/or exist as a separate file?	Font suitcases or separate files	Font suitcases or separate files	Separate files only
Is screen display smooth?	Smooth only if selected size is installed	Smooth at any size	Smooth only if bitmapped font for selected size is installed or if using ATM
Is PostScript printer output smooth?	Generally smooth, but looks best if selected size is installed	Smooth at any size	Smooth at any size
Is non-PostScript printer output smooth?	Smooth only if selected size is installed	Smooth at any size	Smooth only if bitmap font for selected size is installed or if using ATM

* Matching screen font needed to create screen display

** If you use ATM Deluxe or similar utility, fonts may be stored anywhere on your disk. In some cases, fonts may also be stored in the System file directly. In rarer cases, they may be embedded in applications.

Solve It! Text and Font Problems

This section gives specific advice about various problems with the display and printing of text and with using fonts in general. The emphasis is on problems that can occur with almost all Macintoshes and most printers. However, some advice specific to certain printers, such as LaserWriters and ImageWriters, is also included.

SEE: • **Chapter 7 for a more general discussion of printing-related problems.**
   • **Chapter 10 for display and printing problems specific to graphics documents.**

A Document Displays the Wrong Font

 Symptoms:

A previously saved text document is opened. The file opens normally, except that the fonts displayed are different from the ones selected when the document was last saved. For example, the document may have been saved using Garamond, but it now opens using Geneva instead.

 Causes:

The Necessary Font Is Not in Your System Folder

This could occur, for example, if you open a document that uses a font you have since deleted from your startup disk. Or perhaps you are using a document obtained from a colleague, and the font has never been on your disk.

   When this happens, the document typically opens using either a default system font (most likely Geneva or Chicago) or the application's default font (usually Geneva, New York, or Helvetica). You may also get an alert message warning you of what has happened.

   By the way, if you click in an area of text and go to the Font menu, the assigned font name for the text where the I-beam is located

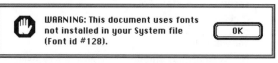

Figure 9-18 The message that appears if you open a document that uses a font not currently installed in your System Folder.

should have a checkmark in front of it. If no font name is checked, this probably means that the assigned font is not available and a substitute font has been used instead. For example, the text might display in Geneva, but the Geneva name will not be checked. If you do not see a checked font in the Font menu when you highlight— rather than just click in—an area of text, however, this could also be because the high-lighted area includes text of two or more different fonts.

A Font ID Number Conflict Has Occurred

Though you do not normally need to be aware of this, every bitmap font file has its own ID number that is initially assigned by the developer who created the file. The

Macintosh uses these numbers to identify the font internally. Within certain limits, what ID number is assigned to a font is arbitrary; as a result, it is possible for two different fonts to wind up with the same ID number.

Two fonts in the same location (the same suitcase file or the same System file) cannot share the same ID number. If you try to install two identically numbered fonts to the same location, the Macintosh automatically assigns a new ID number to one of the fonts to resolve the conflict.

This numbering system is not likely to cause any immediate problems—as long as you stick to your own computer and use only documents you've created. Problems can occur if you send or receive documents to or from other users. For example, suppose you have two fonts, Futura and Frontier, that initially have the same ID number. When you install them both to your System file, Futura is assigned a new ID number to resolve the conflict. Now you create a document using the Futura font. So far, so good—but later, you take this document to be printed elsewhere. Even though the other computer has the Futura font, it probably uses the font's original ID number. As a result, the other Macintosh does not correctly identify the Futura font in your document and probably displays and prints the document in some other font.

The good news is that this problem is becoming increasingly rare, because new ID numbering formats have reduced the probability of two fonts having the same ID number. Similarly, newer software typically identifies fonts by the font's name rather than its ID number; since names should be unique, conflicts are largely eliminated. For people who regularly take their documents to outside sources to be printed, however, this remains a potential source of trouble.

By the way, a font's ID name is separate from the font's file name in the Finder. This means you could potentially change a font's file name without affecting how the font is listed in a Font menu.

A Font File Is Damaged

If a font file is damaged, text using that font may not display in that font.

 What to Do:

Check the Font Menu

If a document opens in the wrong font (and you know what the correct font should be), check whether the intended font is listed in the Font menu.

If the Correct Font Is Not Listed in the Font Menu

Check Key Caps Some applications don't list all installed fonts in their Font menu. You can always use the Key Caps desk accessory to see a complete Font menu list. If the font shows up in Key Caps, check the problem application's manual for how to access the "missing" font.

If you don't see the font in any Font menu, this probably means that the font is not currently installed. To check and fix this:

Quit without saving Quit the application you are using, but *without* saving the document! This prevents you saving any incorrect font information.

Check your System Folder Go to the location in your System Folder where your installed fonts are stored (the System file, Extensions folder, and/or Fonts folder). Check if the font is listed there.

While you're at it, make sure you are using the System Folder. If you are using a startup disk different from the one you normally use, this alone could account for the "missing" fonts.

Get the font If the font isn't in your System Folder, the solution is simple. Assuming you have access to the needed font, get it and install it.

SEE: • **"Font Basics," earlier in this chapter, for more on where fonts are stored and how to install fonts, if needed.**

Check for Font Menu Problems If the font is correctly installed in your System Folder, but still does not appear in the Font menu, check for special problems with Font menu listings.

SEE: • **"Fonts Unexpectedly Appear or Disappear from Font Menus," later in this chapter, for more on locating missing font files and related problems.**

TAKE NOTE ▶ Substitute Fonts

Substitute Fonts From the Page Setup dialog box, select PostScript Options from the pop-up menu. From there you can select the Substitute Fonts option. If the option is checked, any text displayed in Geneva, New York, or Monaco fonts will be printed (to a PostScript printer) in Helvetica, Times, and Courier, respectively (assuming those fonts are available). It will do this whether your screen fonts are bitmapped or TrueType. It will not do this for any other fonts. This option will not only cause your display and printout to have different fonts, but it will result in differing line and page breaks as well.

To avoid this, uncheck the Substitute Fonts option. This forces the document to print using the actual font displayed on the screen. It uses TrueType if it's available for that font. If not, the bitmapped font prints directly.

Alternatively, if you want to print using a PostScript font, then simply select it for display as well. Thus, for example, select all the Geneva font in your document and change it to Helvetica (or any other PostScript font of your choosing).

By the way, the purpose of Substitute Fonts, which originated before TrueType fonts existed, was to use the higher-quality PostScript fonts for printing instead of the bitmapped fonts that were displayed.

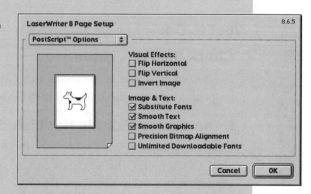

Figure 9-19 The LaserWriter Page Setup dialog box with "PostScript Options" selected from the pop-up menu.

(continues on next page)

Substitute Fonts with ATM With ATM, if a text document includes fonts not currently installed in your System Folder, you can still create a nearly identical substitute version of the font, so that the general appearance and line breaks of the document remain the same.

To do this, open ATM (if you are using ATM Deluxe, open it and select the Preferences command from the File menu and General from the pop-up menu in the window that appears). Then check "Enable Font Substitution."

You will also need a file called ATM Font Database, that is installed at the root level of your System Folder. This file does not come with the Mac OS. However, a version of this file is included with the free Adobe Acrobat Reader. You apparently also need the Adobe SansMM and Adobe SerifMM fonts. Without these files, the "Enable Font Substitution" checkbox will be dimmed.

This feature only works with PostScript fonts and even then may be incompatible with some applications.

More generally, using this feature, Acrobat can create documents that can be viewed and printed in their originally assigned fonts, even if the viewer does not have the needed fonts installed (or even if you are missing the creating application!).

SEE ALSO: • **"Technically Speaking: A Primer on Multiple-Master Fonts," near the end of this chapter, for related information.**

BY THE WAY ▶ Font Not Found

If you select a font from a Font menu and get a message that says "font not found," this may indicate that ATM did not have enough memory to create a substitute font. To solve this, increase the size of the ATM Font Cache from the ATM Control Panel.

If the Font Is Listed in the Font Menu

Check for font ID conflict If the trouble persists, you probably have a font ID conflict. The easiest solution for this problem is to select the text with the incorrect font and then select the correct font from the Font menu. The text should now display properly; if it does, you will probably have no further problems. Save the changed document, and it should open properly next time.

Otherwise, go to the System Folder location of your fonts. Delete both the font currently used to display the text and the font that should have been used, then reinstall both of them from your backups. Try opening the document again, and see if the font now displays as expected.

For documents sent to outside sources If you are regularly plagued by ID conflicts because you send documents to outside sources (such as professional typesetters) and the documents you send print in the wrong font, you may need some special solutions. For example, you could include a copy of your System file and related Fonts and Extensions folders to be used when printing your document.

Check for duplicate ID numbers If you have a utility such as ATM Deluxe, use it to check for duplicate fonts and or font numbers. Select "Manage Duplicates" from ATM

Deluxe's Tools menu. However, in some cases (such as with ATM Deluxe 4.0, but fixed in 4.5 or later), the Mac OS does not recognize that the font ID has been changed by ATM. As a result, duplicate font ID numbers are possible. This should typically only happen if one of the "duplicate" fonts is not stored in the Fonts folder and the other one is. A work-around is to temporarily drag the problem font that is not in the Fonts folder to the Fonts folder. This forces the OS to give it a new ID (so it does not conflict with the same ID number of the font already in the Fonts folder). You should now be able to return the font to its original location with problem fixed.

Replace a damaged font You may have a damaged font file. If so, replace the font from your backups. This should fix the problem unless your backup copy is also damaged.

If You Still Can't Use the Font

If none of this works, or you have no idea what the missing font should be or you do not have access to it, you are out of luck. You have to reformat the text using a font that is available.

SEE: • **"Font Basics," earlier in this chapter, for more on deleting and replacing fonts.**
• **"Solve It! Font File and Font Menu Problems," later in this chapter.**
• **"Problems with Adobe Type Manager," next.**

Problems with Adobe Type Manager

 Symptoms:

- Adobe Type Manager fails to work at all.

- Selected features of Adobe Type Manager appear not to be working.

- A symptom (such as an inability for the Font menu to drop down or a problem printing) occurs in an application. Disabling Adobe Type Manager or Adobe Type Reunion eliminates the symptom.

 Causes:

If Adobe Type Manager (ATM) is not working at all, it may be disabled for some reason, intentional or otherwise. For example, it may be disabled because you started with extensions off, or because it does not have enough memory to load.

Selected features of ATM may not work due to incorrect settings in the ATM control panel or a conflict with another extension. ATM itself is a known source of conflicts that cause symptoms in other programs.

Although the focus of this discussion will be on the basic ATM, it will also include ATM Deluxe and a program included with ATM Deluxe: Adobe Type Reunion. Adobe Type Reunion is a utility that allows fonts in Font menus to be viewed in their own typeface.

SEE: • **"Solve It! Font Menu Problems," later in this chapter for more on ATR.**

What to Do:

- Make sure that ATM loaded into memory at startup. (You didn't hold down the Shift key at startup, did you? If you did, this prevents the loading of all startup extensions and control panels, including ~ATM.)

- The ATM control panel is named deliberately (with a tilde in front of its name) to load near the end of the list of startup extensions. This is to avoid certain potential startup extension conflicts that may prevent ATM from working. Do not rename the control panel.

   SEE: • **Fix-It #3 for more on startup extension conflicts.**

- Check the ATM control panel to make sure ATM is actually turned on. In particular, make sure the option "ATM Rasterizer is active" is enabled. If it isn't, turn it on. Then restart.

- Make sure that all the needed printer font files are present and in their correct location (typically the Fonts folder). ATM will not work for a particular font without the printer font files in your System Folder (even if the fonts are built into your PostScript printer). More specifically, ATM and ATM Deluxe will only work correctly if both a font family's bitmap suitcase and its printer files be stored in the same folder.

- ATM Deluxe also requires that you store bitmap font files and TrueType font files in font suitcases. When a font's files are not stored in a suitcase, ATM will not list the font, so you can't activate it. A statement from Adobe adds: "Fonts are usually distributed so that each Type 1 font family's bitmap font files are contained in one suitcase, and each TrueType font family's font files are contained in one suitcase. You should keep Type 1 bitmap files and TrueType font files in their separate, original suitcases. This will enable you to more easily determine which type of font you have installed."

- If ATM seems to work slowly or improperly when displaying fonts (or if you get a message that says ATM cannot render text because of a low cache size), increase the Font Cache setting in the control panel to as much as 512K or beyond, if you can afford the extra memory. The font cache is used to determine how much memory is assigned to ATM at startup. Especially if you are working with a relatively large number of fonts or are using Adobe's multiple master fonts, proper functioning of ATM may require that the cache size be increased from its default setting.

   Increasing ATM's cache size and/or deleting its Preferences file may also help resolve some apparent conflicts with other applications.

- If the Mac freezes at startup as ATM starts to load: restart with extensions off and delete the invisible file 'ATM Temp.ATM' and the invisible folder 'ATM Temp Fonts.' Both items are in the Preferences folder of the System Folder.

   SEE: • **Chapter 8 for details on how to work with invisible files.**

- From the ATM control panel (or ATM Deluxe Preferences), switch from "Preserve Character Shapes" to "Preserve Line Spacing" (although sometimes making the reverse switch may help). Also turn on the 'Smooth Font Edges on Screen' option, but do *not* check the 'Disable smoothing at screen font point sizes' checkbox. This has been reported to prevent incorrect font displays, overlapping characters, and assorted other symptoms in various versions of ATM.

- Disable ATM and/or ATR as needed.

  For example, with Word 98, you cannot have Word's "WYSIWYG font and style menus" Preference enabled at the same time that ATR is enabled. Otherwise, a typical symptom is an inability of Word's Font menu to drop down. The solution is to disable ATR or disable Word's WYSIWIG option (via its Preferences/General dialog box).

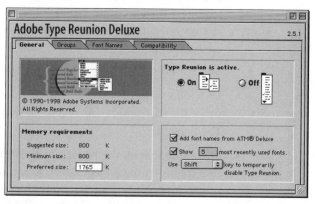

Figure 9-20 Adobe Type Reunion Deluxe; see Figures 9-7 and 9-15 for views of Adobe Type Manager Deluxe.

  ATR has had a conflict with QuarkXPress that has persisted through several revisions of both programs.

  In some cases, Word 98 is reported to crash on launch at just the point that it is "optimizing fonts." Disabling ATM works-around this.

- Replace the ATM file(s), just in case they have gotten corrupted. Restart and try again.

- Check for an upgrade to Adobe Type Manager and/or Adobe Type Reunion that may have fixed the problem.

TAKE NOTE ▶ The Jaggies, Anti-Aliasing, and Related Font Tips

Getting rid of unexpected "jaggies" Happily, with the popularity of TrueType fonts and ATM, jaggies are largely a thing of the past. But problems still crop up from time to time. If text characters display and/or print with ragged, irregular shapes, this is commonly referred to as the *jaggies*. The "expected" reasons for this have been described in "Bitmapped Fonts" and "PostScript Fonts and Adobe Type Manager," earlier in this chapter.

However, the jaggies may also appear unexpectedly in a text document that previously displayed and/or printed without the jaggies. The typical cause is that ATM has been disabled (intentionally or not) and/or no TrueType version of the problem font is available. The solutions, therefore, are to make sure ATM is enabled and/or check in the Fonts folder of the System Folder to confirm that the needed TrueType versions of bitmap fonts are installed.

(continues on next page)

In addition to the reasons cited in the main text (such as a needed printer/outline font file is missing or damaged or ATM's cache size is too small), ATM 4.x may not display a Postscript font smoothly if an older version of a font file is in use (that is, one that does not adhere to the most recent Adobe Type 1 font specifications). If you have used the same Postscript font files for many years, this is a particularly likely problem, especially when you first update to ATM 4.x. The solution is to get a newer version of the problem font. Occasionally, if you have both the TrueType version and the Postscript version of the same font installed, ATM may again not display text smoothly.

Anti-aliasing and text display Even with ATM's rasterizer working correctly and/or TrueType fonts correctly installed, the screen display of your text may still not look as smooth as you might like. The problem is especially apparent with displayed text (as opposed to printed output) because monitors have less resolution than the typical printer. That is, while a printer is printing at 1200 dpi, the screen display may still be 72 dpi.

To further improve the smoothness of the screen display, there is a technique with the strange name of *anti-aliasing* that can come to your rescue. Basically, anti-aliasing (also referred to as "smoothing") is a method of blurring the edges of images so as to make their edges appear more smooth. The effect can be quite dramatic.

To do anti-aliasing, you need software that has an anti-aliasing function. Fortunately, you have the needed software built right into the Mac OS. Here's what to do:

1. Select the Appearance control panel.
2. Select the Font tab.
3. Enable "Smooth all fonts on screen." You also have the option to select the minimum size that will be "smoothed." Generally, very small type (less than 12 point) looks better if it is *not* smoothed.

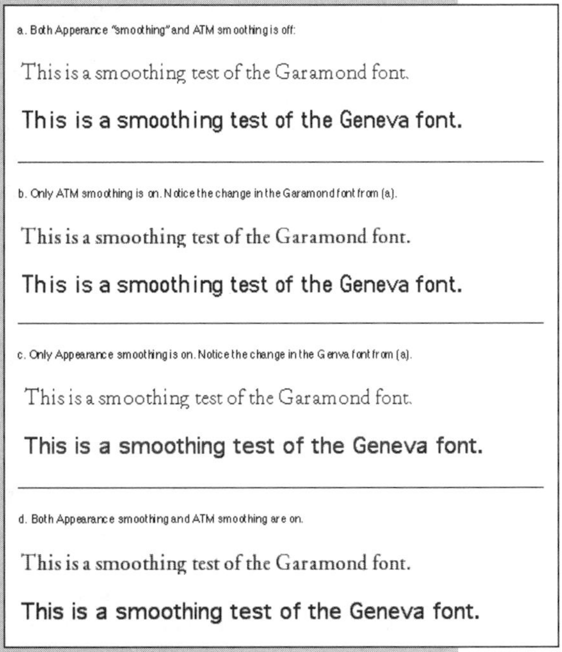

The ATM control panel has a very similar option, except that it only works with PostScript fonts. To enable this option:

1. Select the ATM control panel (or select Preferences/General from the ATM Deluxe application).
2. In the "Smooth font edges on screen" section, enable the On button.

(continues on next page)

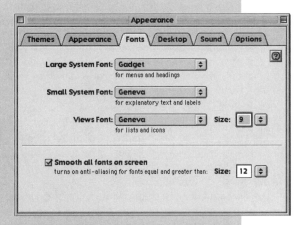

Figure 9-21 The Font tab of the Appearance control panel.

a. Both Apperance "smoothing" and ATM smoothing is off:

This is a smoothing test of the Garamond font.

This is a smoothing test of the Geneva font.

b. Only ATM smoothing is on. Notice the change in the Garamond font from (a).

This is a smoothing test of the Garamond font.

This is a smoothing test of the Geneva font.

c. Only Appearance smoothing is on. Notice the change in the Geneva font from (a).

This is a smoothing test of the Garamond font.

This is a smoothing test of the Geneva font.

d. Both Appearance smoothing and ATM smoothing are on.

This is a smoothing test of the Garamond font.

This is a smoothing test of the Geneva font.

Figure 9-22 Text samples showing the effect of Appearance smoothing vs. ATM smoothing on a display. Garamond is a PostScript font. Geneva is a TrueType font. ATM rasterizing was on in all cases.

TAKE NOTE ▶ The Jaggies, Anti-Aliasing, and Related Font Tips (continued)

3. You can optionally also select whether to "Disable smoothing at screen font point sizes." If you do this, smoothing will not occur for font sizes that have a screen (bitmapped) font available. Again, this is likely only to be for smaller font sizes where smoothing might make the appearance worse rather than better.

You can leave both of these options on at the same time. In fact, it is probably a good idea–as ATM only affects PostScript fonts that do not have a TrueType version also available, and Appearance does not affect these same fonts. Appearance also works for the screen font, thereby affecting the appearance of text in menus. However, if neither option seems ideal, you can try a third-party anti-aliasing utility, such as SmoothType. It uses a different set of "rules" (or "algorithms") for smoothing the text which you may prefer.

We have focused here on anti-aliasing of text. However, anti-aliasing can also improve the appearance of graphic images. It is especially effective with color images. To anti-alias graphics, you will need other specialized software, as the programs described here only work for text. For example, Photoshop and Fireworks can smooth graphics, as can a shareware program called Smoothie (see Chapter 10 for more on dealing with graphics).

Extra help from Postscript printers
Some Apple LaserWriters include an option called FinePrint, accessed from the Print dialog box, that helps smooth out jagged edges, especially of text, even beyond what PostScript normally does. This can be useful

Figure 9-23 Smoothie uses anti-aliasing to eliminate the jaggies, both for text and graphics, in bitmapped images.

even if nothing is really wrong with the text. Hewlett-Packard printers have a similar option called Resolution Enhancement, also selected from the Print dialog box Increasing the resolution of the printer (if your printer has this option) will also reduce the jaggies on the printed page. Obviously, none of this will affect the appearance of text on the display.

BY THE WAY ▶ The Future of Adobe Type Manager

ATM "Lite" (the version that is included free with some versions of the Mac OS as well as with several Adobe applications) may eventually fade from the scene. Most Adobe applications already can render fonts directly, without needing ATM. As a result, Adobe no longer includes ATM with these programs. This will inevitably be true for all Adobe software.

Meanwhile, Apple is increasingly depending on TrueType fonts for use with the Mac OS.

Eventually, only those graphics professionals that need PostScript fonts may need ATM's features and they will be able to get it directly from most of the applications they use. If not, they could still purchase ATM Deluxe, which Adobe will likely continue to support because of its additional font management features.

SEE ALSO: • **"Technically Speaking: What is FontSync?," earlier in this chapter, for an Apple technology that may eventually duplicate ATM's features.**

Problems Copying and Pasting Text Across Applications

 Symptoms:

You select a passage of text and cut or copy it to the Clipboard. However, when you attempt to paste the selection into a document of another application, one of the following occurs:

- The Paste command is dimmed and cannot be used.

- Nothing at all appears when you select Paste.

- Something other than what you most recently copied is pasted.

- The text is pasted successfully, but its formatting is incorrect (such as incorrect font and/or style).

 Causes:

Unless you are working with an application that simply does not accept pasted text, the most likely cause has to do with the operation of the clipboard. Although this may not be immediately apparent to most users, the Macintosh maintains one clipboard for use within an application (called the *application clipboard*) and another for use between applications (called the *system clipboard*). If you copy and paste within the same application, only the application clipboard is used. This generally preserves all formatting, and the copy-and-paste transfer works just fine.

When you transfer to another application, however, the copied information is sent to the system clipboard, which does *not* typically retain application-specific text-formatting instructions—although using drag-and-drop rather than the clipboard can work around this.

More to the point, simply switching among two or more open applications is usually sufficient for information in the application clipboard to pass to the system clipboard and then to the application clipboard for the receiving application. That is why you likely never notice the presence of these separate clipboards. The system clipboard, however, may not always be properly updated. If that happens, whatever is currently present in the system clipboard (which may be totally different from what you just copied) appears when you select Paste in a second application. If nothing is currently in the system clipboard, nothing pastes.

Even if the text is pasted successfully, it may be incorrectly formatted. This may occur (even if the needed invisible characters are included) either because the pasting application cannot interpret the formatting instructions of the original application or because differences between the application and system clipboards cause the instructions to be removed during the transfer. In either case, expect pasted text to conform to the format in effect in whatever document is receiving the text.

This section is limited to problems with the transfer of text. Transfer problems with graphics are covered in Chapter 10 (see: "Unable to Paste a Graphic Across Applications").

☑ What to Do:

If Unable to Paste Text At All

You copy text in one application and select Paste in another, but nothing happens. No text appears. Here's what to try:

- **Select Show Clipboard** Select the Show Clipboard command in the Finder's Edit menu, and look in the Clipboard window to see its contents. If the desired selection is not there, you need to update the system clipboard. To try to do this, go to the next step.

- **Quit the application or go to the Finder** Quit the application you were using when you copied the text (if you get a message such as one that says "Save large clipboard?" select Yes), then return to the receiving application and try pasting again. Alternatively, go to the Finder and then back to the receiving application, then try pasting again. Both of these operations are likely to force an updating of the system clipboard. If neither of them works, copy the selection a second time and try again; it may work now.

- **Transfer the selection in segments** If you are trying to paste a large selection, you may get a message saying that there is not enough memory to copy the selection to the clipboard. If so, the easiest thing to do is to transfer the selection in separate segments rather than all at once. Alternatively, you might try *importing* the selection instead (see the next section), assuming your application supports this option.

- **Make sure the pasting application accepts text** If the previous methods all fail, make sure that the pasting application currently accepts text in your selected location. For example, a database does not accept text into numeric or graphic fields.

If Format Shifts When Pasting Text Across Applications

You copy text in one application and select Paste in another. The text appears, but in the incorrect font or style. Here's what to try:

- **Make sure the needed invisible formatting characters were copied** It may simply be a case of the pasted text adopting the style of the surrounding text.

  SEE: • **"A Paragraph Unexpectedly Shifts Its Formatting" later in this chapter.**

- **Import the text rather than paste it** In many applications you can directly import text from another document, bypassing the clipboard altogether, either via the Open command or via special Import or Insert commands. Doing this successfully depends on the receiving application having a translator capability for the format you want to import (usually listed in a pop-up menu found in the needed dialog box).

  This method is not guaranteed to work, but is worth a try if the clipboard fails. Try importing even if this means having to transfer more text than you need—you can always delete the unwanted text later.

  SEE: • **Chapter 6, "When You Can't Open a Document," for more on importing files.**
  • **Chapter 10, "Take Note: Foreign Imports."**

Use Drag and Drop and Clippings Files

Drag and Drop is a feature that allows you to drag a highlighted selection directly from one document to another, even across applications, without needing the intervening copy-and-paste steps traditionally used by the clipboard.

You can even drag a selection to the Finder's desktop and create a special *clippings* file that can later be dragged to another document, largely bypassing the need for the Scrapbook. You can have multiple clippings files on your desk; double-clicking one of these files opens up a window showing its contents.

Among standard Apple programs, you can drag clippings or selected text directly to or from the Scrapbook, SimpleText, or the Note Pad. Third-party software will work only if it has been designed to use these features.

If these feature does not work at all, and you are using an older version of the Mac OS, make sure you have Clipping extension installed. It should be installed automatically when you select an Easy Install of the system software. With Mac OS 8.0 or later, the Clipping extension is no longer used; this code has been added directly to the System file.

These methods may have no more chance of success than using the clipboard, but they're worth a try.

Among standard App... clipping

Picture 1 clipping

til.info.apple.com/techinfo.ns...

Falcon

Figure 9-24 The four types of clippings files: text, picture, Web page location, and network location. Each has its own custom icon.

TAKE NOTE ▶ Clippings Files: A Closer look

Clippings files are great for those applications that support this feature. Any time I want to save a text selection in a word processing document, I can simply highlight it and drag it to the Finder's desktop. Later on, I can move the file to whatever folder I want or drag it to another open document to paste the text there.

Different types of clippings There are actually several different types of clipping files.

- The most familiar type is a *text clipping*. This is created by dragging a selection of text from its document window to the desktop (but only in those programs that support this feature!). The file is typically named after the first several words of the text you are "clipping." Depending upon the application from which you are dragging the text, the clipping may or may not retain the format (e.g., bold, point size, etc.) of the text.

- If you drag a graphic element (such as by opening a file in SimpleText, selecting an area with the mouse and then dragging that area to the desktop), you will get a *picture clipping* (named "Picture 1 clipping").

- If you drag the text of an Internet URL address (see Chapters 12 and 13 for what these are), you get a *Web page location* clipping file. If you double-click it, it opens a Web browser and launches that URL.

- If you drag a network address (such as an item listed in the Apple menu's Network Browser window), you will get a *network location* clipping. It acts similarly to an alias created of a previously mounted network volume; that is, double-click it and it will attempt to locate and mount the volume(s).

(continues on next page)

TAKE NOTE ▶ **Clippings Files: A Closer look** *(continued)*

Improving on clippings As handy as these clippings files are, there is room for improvement. For example, you cannot edit the text of a clipping file. If you open a clipping, it shows the text. You can copy the text to the Clipboard at this point, but that's it. You cannot directly modify it in any way. You can't even print it. Also, you might like to have the default name of a text clipping be something different than the first few words of the text followed by the word "clipping." You might even want to be able to name the file at the time that you create it (rather than have to separately go to the Finder to change its name).

Happily, a collection of freeware and shareware utilities are available to provide all of these benefits and more. For example, clipEdit allows you to directly edit the text of a clipping file and resave the modified file. It even allows minimal copy and paste editing of picture clippings. You can also use it to print clippings. ClipDragon can convert text, picture, sound files and icon folders into clippings and vice versa. A variety of programs can save text as a clipping file. Of particular interest, a utility such as Net-Print, can directly save selected text from a Web browser as a text clipping. This is convenient because some versions of Web browsers do not support drag-and-drop creating of a clipping. Finally, utilities such as 9Tuner allow you to change the default name assigned to a clipping when you create it.

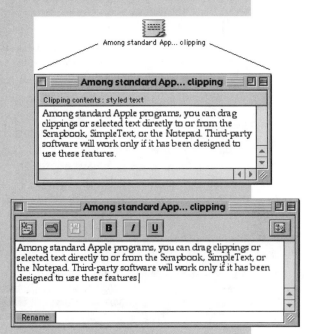

Cosmetic bug with clippings With some versions of the Mac OS, if you open a clippings file, place another window over its open window, and then move the window away, the text in the clippings file may have vanished. In some cases, the text may even mysteriously reappear in other windows and locations on your desktop. It is only a cosmetic bug that will not lead to any system freezes or crashes. If you simply reclose the clippings window and re-open it again, the missing data will return. The bug should be fixed in at least Mac OS 8.5 or later.

Figure 9-25 Top: A text clippings file with its window open; to paste the contents into a document, select Copy when the window is active and then select Paste from within the desired application; or simply drag the file icon to an open document window (if the application supports this feature). Bottom: The same clippings file opened with clipEdit; you can directly editthe text from here.

Otherwise ... Reformat the Text

The only remaining solution is essentially to give up. Paste or drag the text in whatever fashion it transfers and then reformat it as needed.

QuickFixes! An Assortment of Text and Font Problems

What follows is a collection of common font-related problems and their solutions.

Problems with Downloaded Text and Email

Email and text downloaded or copied from the Internet (such as from Web pages) typically will look unattractive when pasted into a standard word processing document.

For example, line breaks will not be correct, with many lines ending after just a few words. This is because the text includes "hard returns" that force a return at that point no matter whether it is at the end of the line or not. In contrast, text you create directly in a word processor has hard returns only at the end of a paragraph, or when you specifically press the Return key; otherwise, the words "wrap" around appropriately at the end of each line, adjusting as you edit the text.

Text copied from Internet applications may also include extra spaces where you do not want them.

To eliminate such problems can be very tedious. Fortunately, there are many utilities that can facilitate this for you. Spell Catcher includes an option to do this. A utility called MagicBullet works especially well, using the Mac's own Copy and Paste commands to effect these changes. Spell Catcher also includes this feature. For bigger jobs, you could consider specialized text cleaning utilities such as TextSpresso.

Incorrect Text Characters and International Keyboard Layouts

If pressing a keyboard key results in an incorrect character appearing on the display (such as "y" appearing when you press the "z" key) or if foreign language characters appear instead of the expected English characters, it probably means that you have inadvertently shifted to an international keyboard layout. Normally you would do this by selecting a layout from the Keyboard control panel, which would be difficult to do by accident. However, a keyboard shortcut, Command-Spacebar (or Command-Option-Spacebar if selected from the Options window of the Keyboard control panel), may also cycle you through the different available layouts. Thus, by pressing this key combination, you may have changed layouts without realizing it.

Actually, this cycling shortcut only works if you have enabled more than one layout from the list in the Keyboard control panel and if you have WorldScript extensions installed. WorldScript software is typically only installed with foreign "Language Kits"; most U.S. users will not have it installed.

Still, if this cycling happens by mistake, go to the Keyboard control panel and reselect the "U.S." layout

Figure 9-26 The Keyboard control panel.

(unless you actually need an international layout). Also, with more than one layout enabled, there will be a flag icon in the menubar, on the right side. Select it to access a list of available layouts.

Afterwards, to prevent this from happening again, you can double-click the System file icon to open its window (this is where the keyboard layouts are stored) and delete all layout files (the ones with names like British, Danish, and French). The default U.S. layout is built in to the system software and does not require a special layout file. Otherwise, you can simply disable the Keyboard extension.

Unlimited Downloadable Fonts and Documents that Print with the Wrong Font

PostScript laser printers: check Unlimited Downloadable Fonts Sometimes, especially if your document uses many different PostScript fonts, the document will print out entirely in the Courier font rather than the fonts you selected.

The cause here is usually that there isn't enough memory in the printer to hold all the different PostScript information needed to print your document. You should get an alert message informing you of this problem, but sometimes things get mixed up and your document simply is printed in the Courier font instead.

One way to try to solve this problem is to select the Unlimited Downloadable Fonts in a Document option (available from the PostScript Options panel of the Page Setup dialog box; see Figure 9-19). This doesn't always work, but it is worth a try. It allows the needed font information to be swapped in and out of the printer's memory as needed, rather than be loaded in all at once (as would otherwise be required). Although this option permits an unlimited number of fonts to be used, it tends to slow down the printing process.

An alternative solution is to simplify the document by using fewer fonts or by dividing up the document into separately printed segments.

PostScript laser printers: Uncheck Unlimited Downloadable Fonts I know, I know, this is the opposite of what I just told you. The resolution of this contradiction is that the advice to *un*check this option only applies when you are printing fonts as part of a graphic (such as an EPS or PICT file) and the fonts print incorrectly. In this case, unchecking this option may help. By the way, printing fonts, especially PostScript fonts, are often a source of trouble with PICT documents. Try to avoid this combination if you can.

Right Font, Wrong Character

Sometimes, particularly with a PostScript font, your text may correctly print out in the same font as displayed on the screen, except that an occasional character is different, usually some special character accessed via an Option key combination. What is probably going on here is that there is a difference between the character set in the screen font file (used to display the text on the screen) and the printer font file (used to create the printed text). While technically this should not happen, it can occur if, for example, the screen font file is from an older version of the font while the printer font is a newer version (or vice versa). Different versions may have minor differences in their character set. If this happens, there is usually not much you can do about it other than switch to a different font (or font version) that does include the desired character, assuming you can find such a font.

Avoid Problems Due to Monospaced Versus Proportional Fonts

Monospaced fonts allocate the same amount of space per letter, regardless of the width of that letter. Thus, an i and a w take up the same space on a line. This simulates how a typical typewriter works and guarantees that each line has the same number of characters on it. However, it tends to have an unattractive, nonprofessional look. Monaco and Courier are examples of monospaced fonts. The alternative is a proportional font, where the space allocated per letter varies appropriately with the width of each letter. Proportional fonts are found in most books, including this one. Most Macintosh fonts are proportional.

> Here is a sample of text in Monaco 12 (a monospaced font).
>
> Here is a sample of text in Geneva 12 (a proportional font).

Figure 9-27 A line of text in Monaco (monospaced font) versus Geneva (proportional font).

By the way, especially with proportional fonts, don't expect to create a table with columns using the space bar to create the space between columns. The text will not line up vertically from row to row, because of the variable length of the proportional text. Instead, use a tab or the application's Table function (if it has one). You can also use the "Tab fill" function of most word processors to create a dotted line or solid line to fill a specific length.

Changes in Appearance Due to Fractional Character Widths

A Fractional Character Widths option, first mentioned in Chapter 7, is found in most text-oriented applications, usually in the Preferences or Page Setup dialog box (it would likely be in the application-specific pop-up menu in LaserWriter 8). Changing its setting from off to on (or vice versa) may change the line breaks and/or character spacing of any text you are currently editing.

This option is designed to be used primarily when printing to higher-resolution printers, such as LaserWriters. The reason is, because of their higher resolution (300 dpi or more), these printers can print thinner (fractional) lines than can be displayed on the screen (which is usually around 72-85 dpi resolution). This means that text can be effectively squeezed closer together in the printed copy than is possible on the display.

With Fractional Character Widths off, the result may be that line breaks are different in the printed output from the way they are in the display.

With Fractional Character Widths on, line breaks on the screen and the printed output should now match correctly, but individual characters in the display may be squeezed together too closely for the monitor to display them properly. This is because the option adjusts the spacing on the screen to match the higher-resolution capability of the printer. This is what causes the irregular, less legible, sometimes even overlapping, character display.

Also, if you are using a solid underline and it prints out as a dashed line, turning on fractional character widths should solve the problem.

Turning on Fractional Widths is generally preferred when printing to LaserWriters. If the screen appearance is less than desirable, don't worry. It should all still print OK.

Fractional Widths and ATM If you are using ATM The ATM control panel has two check boxes that also influence character and line spacing: Preserve Line Spacing and Preserve Character Shapes. These address the same sort of problems as does Fractional Character Widths. ATM has been known to conflict with Fractional Character Widths, leading to improper spacing of text when both are active. You may need to experiment to see which options produce the most attractive output.

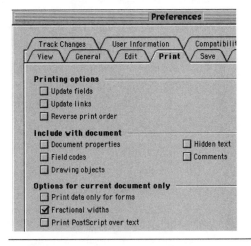

With Fractional Character Widths off, the result may be that line breaks are different in the printed output than they are in the display. Here is how the screen display looks with Fractional Character Widths turned OFF.

With Fractional Character Widths off, the result may be that line breaks are different in the printed output than they are in the display. Here is how the screen display looks with Fractional Character Widths turned ON.

Figure 9-28 Top: the Fractional Widths option in Microsoft Word's Preferences window. Bottom: a sample of text with Fractional Widths turned off (top) and on (bottom).

A Paragraph Unexpectedly Shifts Its Formatting

In a typical word processor, every time you press Return, a special character is created, typically called the *return character* or the *paragraph marker*. This character indicates where a paragraph has ended. It also acts as a marker for all the formatting instructions unique to that paragraph. Other invisible characters are used to identify tabs, page breaks, and paragraph indents.

As implied by their name, these characters are not normally visible on the display or in printouts. However, they can still be deleted, copied, and replaced. Unintended modifications of invisible characters is usually the cause of these unexpected problems. Thus, if you delete a paragraph marker, any customized formatting for that paragraph is lost. Also, the paragraph merges with the adjacent paragraph to form one larger new paragraph.

When copying and pasting text, the key to avoiding problems here is to select the return character when desired and not to select it when not desired. For example, to copy a paragraph and retain the settings of the copied text, you would copy the return character. To copy text to merge with the settings of the paragraph where it is to be pasted, copy the text without the return character.

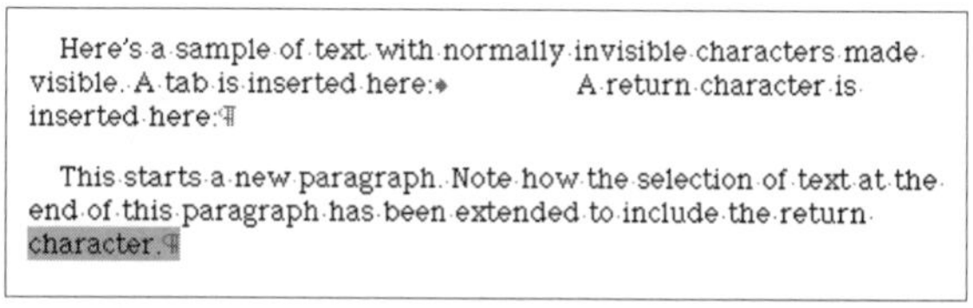

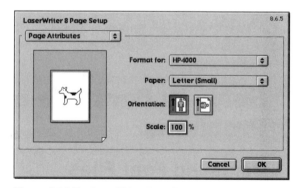

> Here's a sample of text with normally invisible characters made visible. A tab is inserted here:◆   A return character is inserted here:¶
>
> This starts a new paragraph. Note how the selection of text at the end of this paragraph has been extended to include the return character.¶

Figure 9-29 A sample of text from Microsoft Word, with its invisible characters made visible.

To assist in doing this, it often helps to see the return character. To do this, you need to make the invisible character visible. Word processors typically include a command, with a name like Show Invisibles or Show ¶, that makes these characters visible. For Word 98, the options are in the View panel of the Preferences window, under "Nonprinting characters." Select the appropriate command. When you are done with your editing, reselect this command to make the characters invisible again.

If pasting or deleting text results in a format change that you did not want, select Undo immediately(!) and try again.

The Text Is Clipped At the Margins When Printed

If text appears fine when displayed on the screen but is clipped (that is, cut off at the margins) when printed, this is usually because the top, bottom, left, and/or right margin settings for your document (or for a particular paragraph within a document) are set to smaller than the maximum limit that can be accommodated by your printer. Often, you will get an alert message warning that this may occur, such as one that says "Some margins are smaller than the minimum allowed by the printer. Your document may be clipped."

The typical solution is to reduce the margins of your document. Changes to the settings are usually made via Document or Paragraph menu commands within your application. Sometimes, margin settings will be in the Page Setup dialog box.

Figure 9-30 The LaserWtiter Page Setup dialog box with "Attributes" selected from the pop-up menu; see Figure 9-19 for a view of the PostScript Options pop-up menu display.

Alternatively, you may be able to select a "larger" paper size, such as "Letter" rather than "Letter (Small)," although Letter (Small) is generally recommended if you are not having any problems. You may also be able to shift from Portrait to Landscape mode (again via the Page Setup dialog box).

SEE: • **"Problems with Adobe Type Manager," earlier in this chapter, for related information.**
  • **Chapter 7 for a more general discussion of memory-related printing problems.**
  • **Chapter 7 for more on the LaserWriter driver and printer drivers in general.**
  • **Chapter 10 for more on graphic file formats.**

TAKE NOTE ▶ Fonts, FONDS, and a Mac OS 8.6 Font Bug

If you opened up an older font (pre-1991) with a resource editor such as ResEdit (see Chapter 8), you would find a resource called "FONT." With newer fonts, this resource has been replaced with one called "FOND." Mac OS 8.6 had a problem with dealing with these older "FONT" resource fonts. In particular, the Mac OS corrupts these fonts when an application tries to use them. Subsequent use of these fonts can lead to a system crash.

Apple released a utility called Font Manager Update to fix this. It is a combination extension (called Font Manager Update) and a utility (called Font First Aid). The extension prevents further corruption; the utility fixes existing corruption. However, many users have reported problems with this extension; especially delays (or "stalls") in various applications (such as the closing of windows in Internet Explorer). ATM may also be involved in causing these slow downs. In any case, an alternative is to use Alsoft's Corrupt FOND Fixer or DiamonSoft's FONTFixer.
They are both free.

Note: If Font First Aid's check of a drive is terminated with an odd error message, it is likely due to a bug in the program. The work-around is to turn off Platinum sounds in the Appearance control panel and then try again.

The font problem has been fixed in Mac OS 9.0. More precisely, the Font Manager Update code has been built-in to the system software, eliminating the need for the extension. However, the problem with "stalls" due to the Update persisted in Mac OS 9 (especially with QuarkXPress, in operations such as editing text). To fix this, the problem application needs to be updated (as was done with Quark).

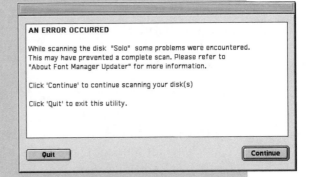

Figure 9-31 Font First error window. If this appears, turn off Platinum sounds and run First Aid again.

Solve It! Font File and Font Menu Problems

Damaged Font Files

 Symptoms:

A damaged font file should be suspected whenever you have any of the following symptoms (especially if other solutions, as described in previous sections of this chapter, have failed to work):

- Text displays in the wrong font or with otherwise unexpected formatting.

- Any document containing a specific font will not print correctly or will not print at all (see also Chapter 7 on printing errors).

- Whenever you try to open a certain application, a system freeze occurs. This can happen even if you are not using a document that contains the damaged font (see also Chapter 4 on system freezes).

- Every time you open or modify any document that contains a certain font, a system error occurs. Sometimes simply selecting the font from a Font menu will result in a crash.

- Trying to open a font file from the Finder results either in a messages that says the file is damaged or in a system crash.

- You are unable to remove a font file from a font suitcase, a Fonts folder, or the System Folder (even if no applications are open). If you try to do so, an error message appears.

- Trying to delete a font file in the Trash results in an error message that says the file could not be deleted.

- The icon for your hard disk looks like a generic text document icon.

Causes:

A font file can get damaged just like any other file. Damaged font files are a potential cause of incorrect font displays and other symptoms as just listed. These problems can occur not only in text-oriented programs, such as word processors, but in virtually any application.

What to Do:

Locate Any Damaged Font Files

Your first job is to determine if you do indeed have a damaged font file and, if so, which one it is. This can be difficult because the symptoms of a damaged font file are so varied and often have other possible causes.

Thus, your first step should be to rule out other likely causes, such as a damaged document or a damaged application. To do this, use the general guidelines detailed in Chapter 3. For example, try different documents and different applications to see how narrow or widespread the problem is. Replace possibly damaged documents and applications with backup copies. Try changing the font of a problem document to see if that eliminates the problem. If the printing problem is specific to a certain page of your document, replace fonts that appear only on that page.

If you decide that a font problem appears likely, you may find that symptoms are indeed linked to the use of a certain font. While this suggests (but does not prove) that you have a font problem, the damaged font may not be the one that you think it is. For example, I once had a problem with a calculator desk accessory that displayed its numbers in an incorrect font, making it difficult to read the numbers. The cause did turn out to be a damaged font file, but neither the correct font nor the one that was being displayed incorrectly was damaged. Replacing a totally unrelated font remedied the problem.

If you ultimately decide that a font problem is likely, a basic (although ultimately tedious) method to identify the font is to systematically remove and return fonts to the System Folder (or enable and disable the fonts via a utility such as Conflict Catcher). However, there are easier alternatives:

Use a Spare System File To Check For Damaged Fonts A neat trick to check for damaged bitmapped fonts is to build a small streamlined System file and drag all your fonts to it. The system checks the integrity of the font before "accepting" it and gives it a unique ID number. If a corrupted font is present, it will flag it. This ID renumbering can also help resolve ID conflicts among these fonts (as described in "A Document Displays the Wrong Font," earlier in this chapter).

Use Utilities To Check For Damaged Fonts There are several utilities that can check for damaged fonts and, in some cases, fix any damage that is found. One that you may already own is Conflict Catcher. To use it, select "Scan Folder for Damage" from its Special menu and select the Fonts folder to be scanned. In the rare case that a font is not damaged but is still somehow causing a conflict with a program on your drive, you can add Fonts to Conflict Catcher's list of files that it manages, and then begin a conflict test (although it may take many restarts before you are done!).

Apple's ResEdit can also check for and possibly repair font damage: select the Verify command from the File menu and pick the file to be checked.

ATM Deluxe will similarly check for font problems: select Verify from its Tools menu. Font Reserve and Font Agent are two other utilities that can check for and repair damaged fonts. Even the control panel Snitch (described in Chapter 8) has a "Verify File" feature that allows you check a particular font file or suitcase.

However, when utilities check to see if a font is damaged, they typically look at something called the file's checksum. Some TrueType fonts have bad checksums even though there is nothing wrong with them. Thus, utilities may erroneously indicate that the font is damaged. There is not much you can do about this. However, if a font that is reported as damaged is displaying and printing fine, and removing the font does not affect any other problems you may be having, I would feel safe in continuing to use the font.

Replace the Damaged Font File(s)

If you don't have a utility that can repair a damaged font, your only alternative is to replace the suspected damaged font file with an undamaged copy from your backups (you *do* have backups, don't you?). Hopefully, the problem is now gone.

Usually, you have to replace only the exact font file that was causing the problem. You shouldn't need to replace all of the files for other sizes and/or styles that are part of the same font family.

In most cases, replacing a damaged font file should be no different from replacing an undamaged font; use the procedures as described earlier in this chapter (see "Font

Basics"). For the sake of clarity, however, here is a specific example of how to replace a suspected damaged font file. Let's assume that the suspected font in this case is a TrueType font called Ashley.

1. First, quit all open applications. You cannot remove *any* font files, damaged or undamaged, from your active System Folder (or Fonts folder within your active System Folder) if any applications besides the Finder, are in use.

2. Open the Fonts folder inside your System Folder and locate the Ashley font. In this case, it is a separate font file (that is, not in any suitcase). If it had been in a suitcase file, you would need to open the suitcase (by double-clicking on its icon) to locate the Ashley font file.

Figure 9-32 The inside of a Fonts folder, with the Ashley font file highlighted.

3. Drag the Ashley font from its location in the Fonts folder to the Trash. Select Empty Trash. (If the Finder says the font file is "in use" and refuses to delete it, restart and try again. It should delete now.)

4. Locate your undamaged backup copy of Ashley. Drag the backup copy of the Ashley font to the Fonts folder. You are done.

Note that I removed the Ashley font from the Fonts folder before adding the new font; I recommend replacing font files this way. The alternative is to drag the replacement font to the Fonts folder before you remove the damaged font, letting the Macintosh do the replacement in one step (after confirming that you want to replace the font). While the one-step method should work—and may sometimes be necessary if the two-step procedure fails—I don't trust it to be as reliable.

This advice is especially important if your suspected damaged font is stored in a suitcase. In this case, if you drag the replacement font to the System Folder icon or to the Fonts folder before removing the damaged font, the damaged font will *not* be replaced. Instead, you will wind up with two versions of the same font stored in your Fonts folder: the problem one in the suitcase, and its replacement loose in the Fonts folder. Alternatively, if your replacement font has the same name as its suitcase, dragging the font to the Fonts folder could cause the entire suitcase to be deleted, not just the single font. To replace a font stored in a suitcase, you should remove the font first and directly drag the replacement font to the suitcase. If it makes things simpler, you could remove and replace the entire suitcase, rather than just one font in it.

Problems Removing a Font File from a Fonts Folder

Occasionally, even when all applications are closed, you may be unable to remove or replace a particular font file (or font suitcase) from your Fonts folder. No matter what you try, you probably get an error message, perhaps saying that you cannot use the font because it is "in use." Assuming it is not being used as a System font (see:

"Technically Speaking: Reserved Fonts and System Fonts," later in this chapter), the problem is usually because the font is damaged. If this happens, try the following:

1. Drag the entire Fonts folder from the System Folder to the desktop.

2. Restart the Macintosh, ideally with extensions off.

3. Drag the problem font file(s) to the Trash. It should now delete successfully.

4. Return the Fonts folder to the System Folder.

SEE: • **Chapter 6, "When You Can't Delete a File or Folder," for more on this problem.**

Check for Problems with Other Files

If all else fails to solve your problem, it's time to suspect more generalized problems, such as damaged system files, startup extension conflicts, or a bug in the application itself. In the worst-case scenarios, you may have to repair the Directory or reformat the entire drive.

SEE: • **Chapter 6 for more general advice on problems with files.**
 • **Fix-It #2 on application problems.**
 • **Fix-It #3 on startup extension conflicts.**
 • **Fix-It #4 on System software problems.**
 • **Fix-It #10 on Directory problems.**
 • **Fix-It #11 for more information on damaged files.**
 • **Fix-It #13 on reformatting the drive.**

BY THE WAY ▶ Damaged Font Suitcase Files

Occasionally, you may be unable to open a font suitcase. When you try, you get an error message that says the font suitcase cannot be opened because it is damaged. This error is unlikely these days and the causes are equally rare. However, if this happens, the best thing to do is delete the entire font suitcase and reinstall a fresh copy from an undamaged backup. Otherwise, replace the individual fonts that were inside the suitcase (assuming you can recall what they were).

If the Macintosh refuses to let you delete the suitcase file, refer to the section on "Damaged Font Files" in the main text.

TECHNICALLY SPEAKING ▶ The 31-Character Font Name Limit

Mac OS file names cannot exceed 31 characters (although technically HFS Plus formatted drives permit longer names, the OS itself still needs to be revised to accommodate this). This limit holds true for font names. If, by some oddity, a font name somehow winds up with more than 31 characters, you may have trouble deleting the font.

The font name refers to an internally stored ID, used by applications to identify the font. This is not necessarily the same as its file name in the Finder, which means that changing its file name in the Finder may not help. Actually, most fonts have their file "name locked" attribute turned on, so that you could not readily change the name anyway (see Chapter 8, "Finder Flags," for how to get around this if you are curious). If you have this rare problem, you may need to use a utility such as ResEdit to change its name.

Fonts Unexpectedly Appear or Disappear from Font Menus

 Symptoms:

You check the Font menu of your word processor (or other text application) and find that either of the following occurs:

- One or more new fonts are listed that were never there before and that you do not recall installing.

- One or more fonts that have always been listed are unexpectedly absent, and you do not recall removing them from their System Folder location.

- One or more font names are listed in the fonts menu but are dimmed.

 Causes:

There are a variety of probable causes for these Font menu disappearing and reappearing acts, none of them very serious, and all usually easy to correct. These include font differences across startup disks, fonts embedded in an application, fonts installed automatically by Installer utilities, and font management utilities inadvertently turned off. In general, remember that a font will not appear in a Font menu unless it is installed in its proper location (usually the System Folder), as detailed in the beginning of this chapter.

Also consider a possible conflict, especially with utilities such as Adobe Type Reunion.

 What to Do:

Check for Font Differences Among Different Startup Disks

You may be using a startup disk that is not the one you normally use. If this new startup disk has different fonts in its System Folder than your normal startup disk, these differences are reflected in the Font menu. The same thing is true, of course, when you are working with someone else's computer; their fonts are probably different from yours.

Fonts are usually installed in the System file or Fonts folder. As stated earlier in this chapter (in "Font Basics"), fonts are usually not part of the application itself. The fonts listed in an application's Font menu vary depending on what fonts are installed in the startup disk's System Folder.

If a change in startup disks is the apparent cause of unexpected changes in your Font menu, simply return to your original startup disk, and all will return to normal. If this is not possible for any reason, you have to either give up on using the missing fonts or install them into the current startup disk's System Folder.

Check for Embedded Fonts in Applications

You *can* install any font directly into an application (similarly to how you install fonts into the System file; such fonts are called *embedded fonts.* It is rare to use embedded fonts these days. If they are used, however, they are listed only in the Font menu of the application that contains them. Thus, when you shift to another application, the embedded font will seem to have disappeared.

SEE: • **Chapter 7, "Technically Speaking: Problems with Embedded Fonts," for a problem with printing documents that use embedded fonts.**

TECHNICALLY SPEAKING ▶ Locating and Unembedding Embedded Fonts

Want to check if a particular application has any embedded fonts? You can use ResEdit of course. If you find any FONT or FOND resources, that's a sure sign you have an embedded font.

Otherwise, try this: make a copy of the application and change the copy into a suitcase file, using a utility that can change a file's Type and Creator (such as Snitch). Change the Type to "FFIL" and the Creator to "DMOV." Then double click the suitcase to open it and embedded fonts, if any, will be revealed. You should even be able to drag the font out of the suitcase at this point.

SEE: • **Chapter 8 for more on ResEdit and Snitch**

Check for Fonts Installed by an Installer Utility

If you recently upgraded your system software or installed a new application that uses an Installer utility, you may have automatically installed new fonts without realizing it. Usually the manual tells you about this, though not all do. Apple's system software Installer, in particular, reinstalls any of Apple's standard fonts that you may have deleted since the previous installation. Most Microsoft and Adobe applications install fonts.

If you wish to delete new fonts that have been added by the Installer, it is usually safe to do so.

Some applications, however, use these fonts for special purposes that may not be immediately apparent, so be careful. Save a copy of the font before you delete it, and be prepared to reinstall it if problems appear when you use the relevant application.

SEE: • **"Locating, Adding, and Removing Fonts from Your System Folder" earlier in this chapter.**

Check If Font/DA Management Utilities Are Turned Off

Font/DA management utilities, such as Adobe Type Manager Deluxe, are system extensions. This means that if you use one of these utilities and you start up with extensions off (for example, by holding down the Shift key at startup), any fonts that are accessed through these utilities now do not appear in Font menus. Anything else that you might do to turn off these utilities has the same result.

SEE: • **"Font Management Utilities and Fonts Anywhere on Your Drive," earlier in this chapter, for more on these utilities.**

Quit Currently Open Applications

If you just made a change to the fonts in your System Folder, don't expect to see it reflected in any currently open applications. To see the change, you have first to quit the application and relaunch it—ideally, you should close all open applications prior to making any changes. In some cases, you may need to restart the Macintosh.

Special Case: Font Names Are Listed In The Fonts Menu But Are Dimmed

If font names are dimmed, it usually means that a program is keeping track of the fonts that were used when a particular document was created and saved (this habit is often characteristic of PostScript drawing programs). If you later open that document on any system where one or more of those fonts is not installed, the fonts will appear in the menu as dimmed. The solution, of course, is either to obtain the missing fonts and install them or to go back to your original system.

In General: If You Are Having Trouble Finding a Specific Font File

To check if a font file has been inadvertently moved from its proper location, or to locate a font file on your startup disk for any reason, you can search your disk for the font (using a search utility such as Sherlock). However, this will not find a font that is inside a font suitcase that is not named after the font itself. In such cases, using Adobe Type Manager Deluxe, Suitcase, or a similar font utility is your surest path to success.

TECHNICALLY SPEAKING ▶ Reserved Fonts And System Fonts

The Macintosh needs certain fonts for displaying system information such as menus and dialog boxes. These fonts (Chicago 12, Geneva 9, Geneva 12, and Monaco 9) are called *reserved fonts*. Because of their importance, you should never delete these fonts from your System Folder. Usually this is not an option anyway, as the Macintosh does not easily let you delete them. In fact, you likely won't find these font files listed anywhere. They are "invisibly" installed in your System file. However, they still appear normally in Font menus.

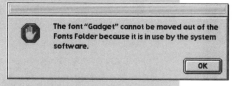

Figure 9-33 The error message you will receive if you try to remove a system font from the Fonts folder.

Traditionally, Chicago 12 is even more reserved than the other reserved fonts; it is included directly in the Macintosh's ROM hardware. It can therefore never be truly deleted, even if you manage to remove all traces of it from your disk. However, with the advent of the Mac OS ROM file on disk (see Chapter 14), even this file is on disk.

Starting with Mac OS 8.5, you can now replace the "Large System Font." This is the one that is used for menus and headings, and has always been Chicago (unless you hacked the System to have it use another font). From the Font tab of the Appearance control panel, you can choose from a limited selection of fonts, including Charcoal, Gadget, Sand, and Techno.

You can also select other fonts for the Small System Font and the Views font, as indicated in the Appearance dialog box. This means you can replace the traditional Geneva with a font of your choosing.

(continues on next page)

TECHNICALLY SPEAKING ▶ Reserved Fonts And System Fonts *(continued)*

Once you have selected one of these fonts via the Appearance control, it is even more difficult than usual to remove the font from its location in the Fonts folder. As described earlier in the main text, you typically cannot remove a font from the Fonts folder when other applications are open. If you try, you get an error message informing you about this. If you try to remove a current System font, you get a different message that simply says the font cannot be removed because it is part of the system software.

Font Menu Clutter

 ## Symptoms:

The only symptom here is a Font menu that seems to contain several separate listings for the same basic font—for the Palatino font, you might see B Palatino Bold, BI Palatino BoldItalic, and I Palatino Italic, as well as Palatino itself.

If you are lucky, all of these fonts may appear together in the Font menu. In the worst cases, the variants of a font are listed in different locations because they do not all start with the same letter. Multiply this by a half dozen or more similarly structured fonts, and you can quickly see the potential scale of this problem.

 ## Causes:

There is nothing actually wrong here. This chaotic listing is what is "supposed" to happen, given the nature of these fonts. The names shown are all style variants of screen fonts, designed to match separate PostScript printer font files for each style. Recall that four (or even more) separate printer font files may exist for the same font (either in your System Folder or built into the PostScript printer); in these cases, you may also have a matching set of four screen fonts.

SEE: • "Technically Speaking: All in the Family," earlier in this chapter, for details on these style variant font files.

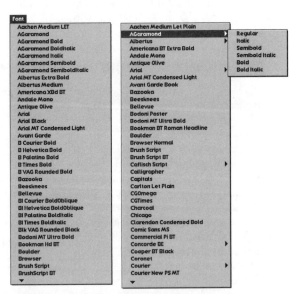

Figure 9-34 Font menu clutter (left) cleaned up with Adobe Type Reunion Deluxe (right). Note how the various AGaramond variations on the left have now been grouped into one Style menu on the right. Also note how the assorted font names that begin with B or BI are no longer separately listed; they are now grouped with their font family (e.g., Courier, Helvitica, etc.). ATR's feature to show fonts in their "actual typeface" is turned off here.

If this part of the Macintosh interface were perfectly designed, all the different screen fonts would be considered part of the same family and would not result in separate listings in the Font menu. For example, your Font menu does not list Times 10 and Times 12 separately as different fonts, even though a separate bitmapped font file may be present for each size. Similarly, this problem does not occur when you install different TrueType fonts of the same family, such as Palatino and Palatino (bold).

As it turns out, however, these style variant screen fonts are often considered to be separate families and thus get listed separately. This is the cause of the menu clutter problem.

What to Do:

Get Rid of the Style Variant Screen Fonts

If you are not using ATM or a PostScript printer, these style variants are irrelevant, so get rid of them. (How did they get there in the first place?)

If you are using ATM and/or a PostScript printer, but the menu clutter still bothers you, just remove all the screen fonts for the style variants. Keep only the plain-text screen font (such as Palatino and AGaramond). You can even use a TrueType font as a screen font if you have one from the same family. In most cases, this should eliminate the menu clutter without unduly affecting the monitor display or printed output.

SEE: • **"Technically Speaking: All in the Family," earlier in this chapter, for more details on pros and cons of eliminating these screen fonts.**

TrueType fonts can also have style variants—such as Georgia; Georgia (bold); and Georgia (italic). But you will only see the font name (Georgia) in the Font menu. You select the variants of the font via the Style menu. It is only PostScript fonts, with their bitmap screen fonts, that contribute to menu "clutter."

Use a Utility to Eliminate the Clutter

If you really want to keep the style variant screen fonts, you can use special utilities such as ACTION WYSIWYG or Adobe Type Reunion Deluxe. These are designed to clean up menu clutter, typically by creating a hierarchical menu off each main font that lists all the variants. Occasional anomalies occur; for example, two common LaserWriter fonts, Helvetica and N Helvetica Narrow, are considered to be from separate families even when you use these utilities.

Adobe Type Reunion has a reputation for compatibility problems, so be cautious with this one. If problems do occur, but only in a specific application, ATR allows you turn it off for just those applications you enter in its control panel.

Do Nothing

If you don't like either of these choices, you can just live with the menu clutter. It will do you no harm.

BY THE WAY ▶ Font Menus: Going in Style

If you pull down a Font menu and each font name is displayed in the "look" of the font itself, you either have installed an extension that provides this feature (such as ACTION WYSIWYG or Adobe Type Reunion Deluxe) or you are using an application that can do this on its own (such as Microsoft Word or AppleWorks).

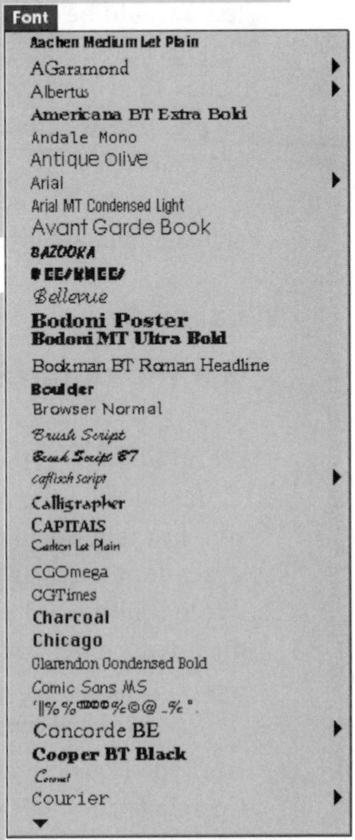

TECHNICALLY SPEAKING ▶ A Primer on Multiple-Master Fonts

Adobe's multiple-master fonts are fonts in which you can vary the style characteristics of the font itself, such as weight (how thick the characters are) and width (how spread apart they are). The details of how all this works are too involved to get into here. If you have at all ventured into the world of multiple-master fonts, however, you are probably a bit mystified by the meaning of all those strange-looking names that appear in your Font menus (yet another contributor to Font menu clutter, these can again be fixed by using a utility such as ACTION WYSIWYG). In any case, here are a few tips that may help you sort things out:

- Adobe Type Manager 4.x includes a button called "Create MM Instances." With this feature, you can easily create a new multiple-master screen font of any weight and width you select. ATM Deluxe has a similar capability, accessed via the "Create Multiple Master…" command in the Tools menu. These functions only apply to multiple master fonts.

- Most of the naming information that follows refers to screen fonts that are stored in a multiple master font suitcase (such as in the Tekton MM suitcase for the TektoMM printer font). Typically, you should not discard these screen fonts or you will lose the multiple master variations of the font.

- "MM" after a name means it is a multiple master font (surprise!).

- Optional designations immediately after "MM" describe the style of the font (such as "Obl" for oblique or "Ita" for italics). Other letters may indicate the company that made the font.

- Letters and numbers that follow the underscore in the name describe the particular attributes of the font (typically its weight and width). For example, MyriaMM_347wt423wd, indicates a weight of 347 and a width of 423. Other fonts with the same numbers should appear comparable in these attributes.

- Alternatively, after the underscore, you may see something like "540 BD" and/or "200 CN." The letters are abbreviations reserved by Adobe to describe the font. In this case, BD means Bold and CN means condensed. The numbers again describe how bold or condensed the font is. If the abbreviations are in caps, this means the specific font was supplied by the company that created the font. If the abbreviations are in lower case, it means that you created the specific font yourself (perhaps by previously using ATM to do this).

Figure 9-35 A Font Menu as it looks with Adobe Type Reunion Deluxe (or other similarly acting feature) displaying the font in its actual typeface.

(continues on next page)

- If the font name begins with "%M," this means it is the master font that all other variations are based on. These typically do not appear in Font menus, but they are critical. If you remove this font from the System Folder, none of the other related fonts will work.

- Adobe SansMM and Adobe SerifMM are two key multiple-master fonts, also not shown in your Fonts menu, that are needed for the "substitute fonts" feature of some versions of ATM. It works in conjunction with a file called ATM Font Database that gets installed at the root level of your System Folder (a mini-version of this file is included with Adobe Acrobat Reader).

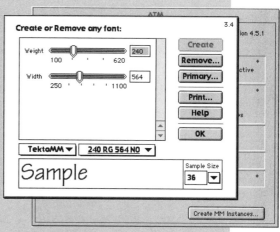

Figure 9-36 The Create MM Instances window of ATM.

TAKE NOTE ▶ On the Horizon: OpenType Fonts

A new type of font is on the horizon. Actually, it is several years old, but still not really in use. As of this writing, it's only available with certain Adobe applications (such as InDesign). But a wider use is expected and it promises to significantly change the font landscape. It is called OpenType. Developed by Adobe and Microsoft, it is an extension of Apple's TrueType format. Essentially, it is a combination of TrueType and PostScript (Type 1) font technologies. The fonts are sometimes referred to as TrueType Open v.2.0 fonts, because they use TrueType's "sfnt" format. As Adobe explains it: "PostScript data included in OpenType fonts may be directly rasterized or converted to the TrueType outline format for rendering, depending on which rasterizers have been installed in the host operating system. But the user model is the same: OpenType fonts just work. Users will not need to be aware of the type outline data in OpenType fonts. And font creators can use whichever outline format they feel provides the best set of features for their work, without worrying about limiting a font's usability."

Adobe Type Manager 4.6 and later supports OpenType, as does Adobe's PostScript Printer Driver 8.7 or later.

10

Graphics: What's Wrong with This Picture?

Picture This

If you think the graphics features on the Macintosh are just for artists and designers, you are wrong. From the Finder's icons to a spreadsheet's charts to a word processor's paragraph borders, the Macintosh lives and breathes graphics that you use and create. Even if you can't draw a straight line, your computer can draw one for you. If you have a scanner, you can use it to convert almost any printed copy into a digitized computer image. You can buy prepackaged images, called clip art, or even have your photographs developed onto a compact disc that can be read by CD-ROM drives.

This chapter deals with graphics-related issues and problems that are likely to confront even the most casual of users; for better or for worse, it is not designed to meet the specialized needs of graphics professionals. As in the previous chapter on text problems, I begin this chapter with some basics about how graphics are created, stored, displayed, and printed. I then shift to specific solutions for a selection of common problems.

Resolution and Display Depth

To solve graphics problems, you first need to understand two issues that are fundamental to the operation of the Macintosh: resolution and display depth. While these issues affect all aspects of Macintosh display and printing, they are particularly relevant to graphics.

Understanding Resolution

How does the quality of the image you see, either on the screen or in a printed copy, relate to the resolution of the display or printing device? In answering this important question, I'll try to avoid technical jargon as much as possible.

Monitor Basics

All monitor screens are made up of a series of square dots (usually called *pixels*). The combination of dots that are on or off at a particular moment makes up what you see as the screen display. The number of dots that fit across an inch of space is referred to as the *dots per inch (dpi)* or *pixels per inch (ppi)* measurement of the monitor. The higher the dpi, the more dots you can fit in an inch of space. "Pixels per inch" is technically more accurate when talking about monitors. "Dots per inch" is a printing term. However, most people use these terms interchangeably.

The *resolution* of the screen refers to how clearly you can see images on the screen and how finely detailed those images can be. The dpi measurement is the most important (but not the only) factor that determines a screen's resolution.

To see how this works, assume you are comparing two different monitors of exactly the same size; the only difference is in the size of the individual dots or pixels. Let's assume Monitor A has 72 dpi, while Monitor B has 144 dpi. Because the screen sizes are the same, this must mean that each dot in Monitor A is twice the size of each dot in Monitor B.

Now, assume further that, despite this difference in dpi, a displayed image takes up the same amount of screen space on both monitors. Thus, if you displayed the same document on both machines, they would both fit the same amount of the document onto the screen. This means that an object in the document that is 2 inches long on either monitor will be 144 dots long on Monitor A, but 288 dots long on Monitor B.

As a result, the object will be seen in higher resolution on Monitor B than Monitor A. For example, if the object displayed is an irregularly curved line, the subtle nuances of the curves can be better captured when you have 288 dots to do so than when you only have 144 dots. To understand this more clearly, imagine how hard it would be to display an intricately curved 2-inch line with a resolution of only 4 dpi. Simply put, you could not do it.

Higher resolution is generally considered desirable, because it offers the potential for smoother, finer, more detailed, and more realistic-looking displays. Similarly, because you cannot create a line thinner than the width of a single dot, the higher the resolution of your monitor, the thinner the lines you can display.

But dpi is not everything when it comes to screen image quality; you must also consider the size of the screen. For example, suppose that the 72-dpi Monitor A we have been considering is a 14-inch monitor, with a typical screen dimension of 640 pixels across by 480 pixels down. Monitor C, with a screen size half as large as Monitor A, also has dimensions of 640 x 480 pixels. Therefore, each pixel in Monitor C must be half the size of those in Monitor A, which means that Monitor C is meas-ured at 144 dpi. Monitor C will thus appear to have higher resolution, but everything on Monitor C will also be shrunk 50 percent compared to Monitor A. For example, a 2-inch curved line in Monitor A will now only be 1 inch long in Monitor C, using 144 dots in both cases. This, of course, makes everything in Monitor C harder to see, even if the images are sharper.

If Monitor C's resolution is 72 dpi, any image will appear just as large as it would on Monitor A (for example, a 2-inch line would display at 2 inches in both cases). Because the Monitor C screen is half the size, however, it could only show half of what Monitor A could show at any one time.

This sort of dilemma has been faced by some users of PowerBooks, whose screens are smaller than the 14-inch or larger monitors common on desktop Macs. Some older PowerBook models maintained 72 dpi resolutions, and by doing so they were unable to show as much on the screen. In particular, these PowerBooks cut off the bottom 80 rows of what would be seen on a desktop screen, using a dimension of 640 x 400, rather than 640 x 480. All recent models of PowerBooks duplicate the 640 x 480 dimensions of desktop monitors by making the pixel size smaller. The actual dpi may be as high as 92, which gives images a crisper look. These PowerBooks display identical images to those on the desktop Macs, but everything on the PowerBook is significantly smaller.

Here's one more complication: the original Macintosh monitor had 72 dpi and all applications were written based on this assumption. Thus, a graphics program wanting to draw a 1-inch line would draw a line that was 72 pixels long. This would be almost exactly one inch long on the screen. The Mac OS and many applications continue to assume a 72 dpi standard, even though a monitor's actual dpi may be different. For example, your monitor may display at 80 dpi. Still, most applications will draw a 72-pixel line for a 1-inch line. With a 80 dpi monitor, this means that a 1-inch line will actually appear as noticeably smaller than 1 inch.

As monitors get larger, their pixel size is usually the same as (or even smaller than) that of smaller monitors. This means they have many more pixels on the screen and can thus show much more of an image at one time than can a smaller monitor at the same resolution. As a result, you will not need to scroll through a document as often with a larger screen.

To summarize: as pixel size gets smaller, the number of pixels per inch (ppi) increases. All other things being equal, this means a higher resolution. By increasing its ppi, a smaller screen may show exactly the same image (though reduced in size) as a larger screen with a lower dpi. Thus the size of the screen and its pixel dimensions both play a role in resolution. Finally, the depth of the display (described in the next section) has an effect on your perceived resolution.

Multiscan Monitors

Multiple Resolutions Multiscan monitors, the most common monitors today, allow you to choose from among different pixel sizes (or resolution) of the display. These are the settings with names such as 640 x 480, 832 x 624 and 1152 x 870, where the numbers refer to the number of pixels on the screen in a row and in a column. As the total size of the screen is always the same, increasing the number of pixels in a row means increasing the ppi. Changing resolution in this way will change how much of an image you can see on the screen at one time. You might choose to use a higher resolution (such as 1152 x 870) when you want to see a lot on the screen at one time (albeit with everything, especially text, smaller and harder to view), but shift to a lower resolution (such as 640 x 480) when you are more interested in a larger image. When a monitor is set to a higher resolution, its ppi may increase to over 80 or, in some cases, even over 90. For example, at the 1024x768 resolution that I use on my 17 inch Studio Display, the ppi is about 85.

LCD vs CRT A flat-panel LCD (liquid crystal display) has more trouble with multiple resolutions than a traditional CRT (cathode ray tube) monitor. Because an LCD screen is actually made up of a series of pixels, it displays best at its natural resolution (that is, the one that matches the number of pixels on the display). To shift to a higher or lower resolution, the display must use emulation (such as making multiple pixels act as if they are one pixel). Depending on the display and the resolution selected, this can work fairly well or lead to an overall much less crisp image than on a traditional CRT display.

Still, LCDs are the wave of the future. Of course, they are already in use in portable Macs. But desktop versions are becoming more and more common (including Apple's stunning 22 inch Cinema Display). LCDs are much lighter and smaller than a CRT monitor of the same size, and display less image distortion.

SEE: • **"Technically Speaking: Web Page Font Size and Resolution," in Chapter 13, for how resolution may affect the display of Web pages in a Web browser.**

Printers

Printed images, like their screen display counterparts, are made up of a series of dots. Printer resolution is thus also measured in dots per inch (dpi). Actually, the situation is a lot less complicated with printers than with monitors, because you don't have to deal with an interaction comparable to that of pixel size versus monitor size. With printers, dpi *is* the total indication of resolution.

These days, almost all printers offer resolutions that are significantly greater than what you will see on the screen. A resolution of 300 dpi is a bare minimum. Resolutions of 600 dpi, 1200 dpi, or even higher are common. With many printers, you can select among different resolution levels (trading off between increased quality vs. decreased printing time). These high levels of resolution are why printed output typically looks better than what you see on the screen. But the discrepancy in resolution between screen and printer also opens the door to potential problems, as you will soon see.

Understanding Display Depth: Color and Grayscale

What Is the Display Depth?

Each pixel of a typical color monitor can be any one of up to millions of different colors. Because of other hardware restrictions in the Macintosh, however, a pixel may be able to show only a subset of these millions of colors in a given situation. More precisely, there is usually a limit to the total number of different colors that can appear on the screen at any one time; this is referred to as the *depth* of the display. Noncolor monitors, by definition, have even greater restrictions on their display depth.

In the simplest case, each pixel—or each bit of the bitmap, to phrase it differently—can be in either one of two states: on (white) or off (black). This simplest case produces a black-and-white display and is called a *1-bit depth*. A basic black-and-white monitor (as used to be available years ago) is only capable of a 1-bit depth display.

With today's displays, each pixel can assume more than just two values. This allows the monitor to display various shades of gray and/or various colors. In fact, almost all monitors sold today are color monitors with a capability to display at least *thousands of colors* (called 16-bit color), and more likely, *millions of colors* (referred to as 24-bit color). Most monitors today will not let you select below 256 colors or grays (8-bit). Whether or not the monitor will actually display all the colors it is capable of showing will also depend upon other factors, such as the amount of video memory installed in your computer and the size of the monitor. Generally, the greater the size of the monitor, the more video memory you need to display a given number of colors.

SEE: • **"Take Note: Problems Displaying Thousands and Millions of Colors," later in this chapter, for more on hardware/software requirements for different color depths.**

Display Depth and Dithering

If you have ever looked at a grayscale graphic on a black-and-white monitor, it may appear that you are actually seeing different shades of gray. But you are not. This illusion is achieved by a careful mixing of dots, called *dithering*. For example, alternating black and white pixels, when viewed at a slight distance, simulates the appearance of a medium gray. By altering the proportion of black to white dots in a given area of the screen, as well as by varying the pattern in which the dots are mixed, a range of shades of gray can be simulated.

The Macintosh uses dithering, with reasonable success, when changing display depths. This is needed because the depth level of a document (determined when the file is created) may be greater than the current display depth. Thus, if you display a 24-bit color graphic at an 8-bit color depth, you get a dithered approximation of the colors that are outside the 256 color range.

This dithering also becomes important when viewing graphics on the Web. For example, the common Web graphic format called GIF allows a maximum of 256 colors. If you convert a graphic image to the GIF format and display it on a Web page, it may look much inferior (because of limitations of the dithering process) to how it originally appeared on your desktop. Fortunately, various graphics software can help you avoid this by "optimizing" your graphic for display as a GIF image.

SEE: • **"Graphics on the World Wide Web," later in this chapter, for more details.**

Figure 10-1 At left, a 256-bit grayscale display of a cat; below, a dithered display (resulting from shifting to a 1-bit display depth) of the same image.

Display Depth and Printing

With resolutions typically of 600 dpi or higher, most current laser printers are great for printing text. They can produce finely detailed fonts in almost any variety. They do equally well with certain types of graphics, as they are capable of printing thinner lines, smoother curves, and sharper, more finely detailed graphics than can be seen on the screen. Most of them, however, are black-and-white printing devices; that is, they have a 1-bit depth. This makes them distinctly limited as devices for reproducing grayscale and color graphics. Any shades of gray that seem to be in an image are accomplished by dithering or by a conceptually similar technique called *halftoning*.

Color laser printers do exist. But they are still too expensive for most users to purchase one. Much more popular are the very affordable color inkjet printers. While they are still not as good (or as fast) as laser printers for producing sharp text, inkjet printers can surpass laser printers in their ability to output near photo-quality color images. If you have any color print, you can transfer it to your computer via a scanner—where you can then edit it and print it. Alternatively, you can start with a digital camera. With one of these, you can download your photograph directly from the camera to the computer with virtually no loss of quality.

SEE: • **"Troubleshooting Digital Cameras," later in this chapter.**
  • **"Problems Printing Color Images," later in this chapter.**
  • **Chapter 7 for more on printing with color inkjet printers.**

Setting the Depth and Resolution of the Display

You have some control over what color depth and (if you have a multiscan monitor) what resolution is actually displayed on your monitor. In Mac OS 8, you make this selection via the Monitors & Sound control panel. In Mac OS 9, Apple divided these into separate Monitors and Sound control panels.

Monitors Control Panels and Display Depth

Exactly what options you have in the Monitors (or Monitors & Sound) control panel will vary depending upon what monitor you are using. (**Note:** In order to use the Monitors & Sound control panel in Mac OS 8.x, the SystemAV extension must also be installed.)

With my Studio Display 17 inch monitor, to select the color depth, I go to the Monitors panel and select either 256, Thousands or Millions. At the 256 level, I can also choose between Grays and Colors. Beyond 256, you must select Colors. If you do not have enough video RAM to display a certain depth (such as Millions), that option will not appear

These numbers refer to the maximum number of different colors the screen can display at any one time. Thus, with an 8-bit (256) display, you display only 256 colors, although you may be able to use other software to vary what 256 colors are actually displayed. This is in essence what you do when you shift from 256 grays to 256 colors, for example.

A setting of 256 grays is sufficient to display a black and white photograph with smooth gradient transitions and subtle shadings. Overall, the image quality is almost equal to that of a photograph. To achieve the same level of image quality for a color photograph, you need 24-bit color.

SEE: • **"Take Note: Problems Displaying Thousands and Millions of Colors," later in this chapter**

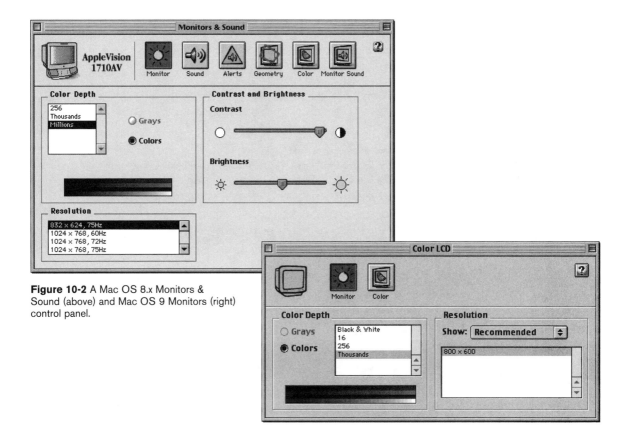

Figure 10-2 A Mac OS 8.x Monitors & Sound (above) and Mac OS 9 Monitors (right) control panel.

Monitors Control Panels and Resolution

The Monitors (or Monitors & Sound) control panel lets you select the resolution (e.g., 640 x 480, 1152 x 870) for multiscan monitors.

Monitors Control Panels, Brightness, Contrast and Calibration

You may be able to set the brightness and contrast of the display from the Monitors control panel. Otherwise, brightness and contrast are set from buttons/dials directly on the monitor.

If you select the Color panel of the Monitors control panel, you may find additional options, including the ability to select a different gamma setting and white point. You can also select a ColorSync Profile, to match your particular monitor; this helps match the colors of the screen display to printed output. At the other extreme, such as with the iMac, there is only one choice: Calibrate. Selecting this opens up the Monitors Calibration Assistant, which walks you through the options to select, explaining the recommended choice in each case. Otherwise, simply using the Mac's default choices will work best in most cases. In general, calibration requires that Apple's ColorSync software be installed. When done correctly, the colors of your display will be the most accurate possible, adjusted for the lighting in your room.

SEE • **"Problems Printing Color Image," later in this chapter, for more details.**

BY THE WAY ▶ The Refresh Rate

On many CRT monitors, you may find that there is more than one option for a given resolution. For example, you may be able to choose between an 800 x 600 resolution at 85 Hz or an 800 x 600 at 60 Hz. This Hz number refers to the refresh rate of the monitor. In brief, the refresh rate (Hz) refers to how many times a second the screen image is redrawn. Generally, the higher the refresh rate, the better. If the refresh rate is too low, you begin to notice this as screen flicker.

If resolution/refresh options are listed in italics, avoid them. These options are generally for when the monitor is hooked up to a PC rather than a Macintosh, and selecting them may lead to distorted displays. The Monitors control panel may give you a choice of Recommended vs. All resolutions. Again, stick with the recommended ones.

In the worst case, after going with a non-recommended resolution, your monitor may actually go black after selecting a "wrong" refresh rate—and you may therefore be unable to reselect the former rate. Solving this may require hooking up your monitor to a computer that works with your selected resolution/refresh rate.

TECHNICALLY SPEAKING ▶ Bit Numbers and Colors

The relationship between the bit number (such as 8 bits) and the number of colors (such as 256) is determined as follows: Each bit of information can have 2 possible values. The total number of different values is thus 2 raised to an exponent equal to the number of bits. For example, an 8-bit display can have 2^8 (or 256) different values.

Setting Display Depth and Resolution from the Control Strip

An alternative way of selecting different display depths or resolutions is via Apple's Control Strip Modules: Monitor BitDepth and Monitor Resolution. These changes are temporary in that the former setting will return the next time you restart your Mac. You typically have to make the change from the Monitors control panel to make it permanent.

Figure 10-3 Selecting resolutions from the Control Strip.

TAKE NOTE ▶ Why 24-bit Color?

The Millions setting on the Monitors control panel is also referred to as 24-bit color. Assuming you have the necessary hardware to select this setting, why would you want to use it? After all, if you were going to draw a picture with crayons, would you feel a need for 17 million different crayons? Probably not. But the Macintosh is a bit different.

- **The pros of 24-bit color.** Higher depths are especially useful for viewing photographic images, such as those digitized from a scanner or used in QuickTime movies. Twenty-four-bit color gives a subtlety and naturalness that far exceeds what is possible with a 256-color limit. Similarly, the color gradient fill commands, found in many graphics applications, produce a much smoother transition of colors with 24-bit color than with 8-bit color. To see this difference, look at the color bar at the bottom of the Monitors control panel when you shift from 256 to Millions of colors. The difference is dramatic. At 256 colors, distinct bands are visible. With Millions selected, the color transitions are so smooth as to be imperceptible. Twenty-four-bit color also eliminates color shift problems (as described in the Solve It section of this chapter).

- **The cons of 24-bit color.** The speed with which the screen image is updated slows down as the depth level increases. Working at the 24-bit color depth can mean, for example, that scrolling through the contents of a window takes significantly longer than at a lower depth (although with today's "super-fast" Macs, this is less of a consideration). Also, because 24-bit documents contain a lot more information than 8-bit (or other lower-depth) documents, they require much more disk space and need more memory to open than comparable 8-bit documents. By the way, creating 24-bit documents requires more than just a 24-bit display; you also need 24-bit capable software (as explained more in "Take Note: Problems Displaying Thousands and Millions of Colors," later in this chapter).

Types of Graphics, Programs, and Files

Bitmapped Versus Object-Oriented Graphics

The Macintosh uses two basic methods to create graphic images: bitmapped graphics and object-oriented graphics. The differences between these two categories are analogous to the distinction between bitmapped and outline fonts (as described in Chapter 9).

Bitmapped Graphics

A bitmapped graphic is created as a series of individual dots (also called *bits*). A bitmapped graphics file contains the instructions that detail the status of every single bit that makes up the image (which bits are off, which ones are on, and with what color). These instructions are called the *bitmap*.

Technically, the bits in a bitmapped image can be of any size (or *resolution*), but the most common size is 72 dpi. This is approximately the same as the minimum dot (or pixel) size of most Macintosh monitors.

This similarity is not a coincidence; it ensures that a bitmapped graphic file stores the exact information needed to re-create a screen image. When you consider that the Macintosh's first printer, the ImageWriter, also had a 72-dpi resolution, you can clearly see the origins of the WYSIWYG aspect of the Macintosh.

Some applications create bitmapped graphics at higher resolutions, such as 300 dpi. These images have a greatly improved printed appearance. If the monitor's resolution is limited to 72 dpi, however, this higher-resolution detail cannot be translated to the monitor display image; at best, it can be approximated. In such cases, the WYSIWYG relationship between the display and the printed output is partially broken.

On the other hand, a bitmapped graphic created at 72 dpi looks no better in the printed output than it does on the screen. Even if the printer has a higher resolution, bitmapped graphics print only at the resolution with which they were created—for instance, 72-dpi bitmapped graphics print out at 72 dpi even on a 300 or 600-dpi laser printer. In some cases, smoothing options are available from the Page Setup dialog box to reduce the jagged look of these images, but this does not alter the basic resolution.

Object-Oriented Graphics

Object-oriented graphics are defined and stored as individual objects (lines, circles, squares, and so on). A document of this type is typically made up of a collection of these separate objects. Analogous to outline fonts (as described in Chapter 9), this method frees the graphic from dependence on a specific level of resolution. Object-oriented graphics display or print at whatever resolution is used by the output device. So an object-oriented graphic will print at whatever the resolution of the printer may be (typically 600-dpi or higher), even though the screen display is still translated into a 72-dpi image. This means that the appearance of printed output is likely to be superior to what you see on the screen.

To further clarify the distinction between bitmapped and object-oriented graphics, consider the differences between a bitmapped versus an object-oriented circle. You create both circles in exactly the same way: select the relevant application's Circle tool from its tool palette, hold down the mouse button, and drag the mouse. Similarly, if both monitors use a 72-dpi resolution, the display images of both types of circles usually are indistinguishable from each other. The increased resolution capability of the object-oriented circle becomes apparent mainly when you print the circles with a higher-resolution printer.

Bear in mind that all Macintosh displays and printed output are necessarily bitmapped. The difference between object-oriented versus bitmapped graphics is that bitmapped graphics begin with bitmapped

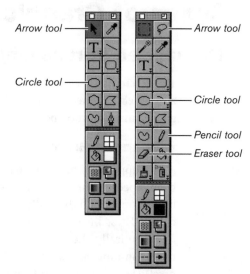

Figure 10-4 At left, a tool palette designed primarily to work with object-oriented graphics (taken from a program's Draw module); at right, a tool palette designed to work with bitmapped graphics (taken from a program's Paint module).

instructions, while object-oriented graphics are converted to a bitmap from the object-oriented instructions.

Object-oriented graphics are often referred to as *vector graphics*, reflecting the fact that objects are generated by mathematical calculations rather than pixel editing.

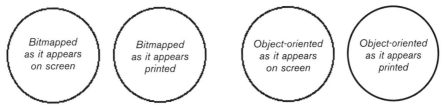

Figure 10-5 The first pair of circles compares a 72dpi bitmapped circle (left) versus an object-oriented circle (right) as they appear on the screen (note the similarity); the second pair compares the same bitmapped circle (left) versus an object-oriented circle (right) as printed by a laser printer (note the difference).

TECHNICALLY SPEAKING ▶ QuickDraw versus PostScript Graphics

In most cases, the basic set of instructions used to create both bitmapped and object-oriented graphics is obtained from the Macintosh's ROM; these built-in instructions are referred to as QuickDraw routines. QuickDraw is used for both screen display and printing.

The alternative to QuickDraw is PostScript, a page-description language used to create and print high-resolution text and graphics. The PostScript language interpreter, which is needed to convert PostScript instructions into printed copy, is built into the ROM of PostScript printers. PostScript can affect only printed output; the screen display is still based on QuickDraw.

PostScript graphics fall into the category of object-oriented graphics. Creating PostScript graphics, however, requires special applications that generate the necessary PostScript instructions (such as Adobe Illustrator and FreeHand). The advantage of these applications, when combined with a PostScript printer, is that you can create and print graphics with finely detailed smooth lines and other special effects that surpass what you can do with the more limited QuickDraw routines.

By the way, all of this is relevant to text as well as graphics. Both bitmapped and TrueType fonts ultimately depend on QuickDraw for printing; you can probably guess what PostScript fonts depend on.

SEE: • **Chapter 9, for related background on PostScript and PostScript fonts**

Editing Bitmapped Versus Object-Oriented Graphics

A major difference between bitmapped and object-oriented graphics, as explained in the previous section, is that the resolution of objected-oriented graphics is device independent. Other notable differences become apparent when you edit these graphics.

Selecting and moving bits versus objects If you draw a circle directly on top of an object-oriented square, the shape and location of the square (now hidden from view) is still remembered. The circle can be later selected, typically by clicking the mouse while the Arrow tool cursor is over the object, and dragging to a new location; the square, now no longer hidden from view, will reappear. It is as if the circle had been stacked on top of the square, which is, metaphorically speaking, exactly the case.

In contrast, when you edit bitmapped graphics, placing a circle on top of a square changes the map of the pixels in that area. There is no separate recognition of a square and a circle; only one layer of dots exists, and nothing can be hidden underneath it. You can still select and move the circle, for instance with a Lasso tool, but you would no longer find a square underneath. There would be only white space.

Pixel-by-pixel versus object-by-object editing Bitmapped graphics can be edited on a pixel-by-pixel basis, while object-oriented graphics can be edited only on an object-by-object basis. For example, with bitmapped graphics, you can use a Pencil tool to add or delete a single pixel from the circumference of a circle; you can similarly use an Eraser tool to remove part of a bitmapped graphic. This precise editing ability is the main reason that bitmapped graphics are the preferred type for creative artwork and image retouching.

With object-oriented graphics, on the other hand, you can make modifications only to an entire object. Thus you cannot remove one pixel from an object-oriented circle; you must instead erase the entire circle (typically by selecting it and pressing the Delete key). Still, this approach has its advantages. For example, you can change fill patterns and line thicknesses of object-oriented graphics at any time with a single command, while comparable changes are far less convenient with bitmapped graphics.

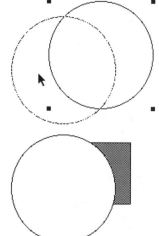

Figure 10-6 At top, an object-oriented circle is selected (indicated by the four "handles" at the corners) and moved (indicated by the dotted-line circle); at bottom, when the move is completed, the square previously hidden underneath the circle is now partially visible.

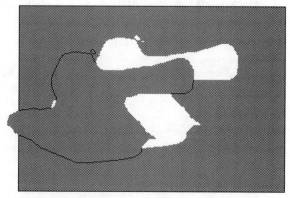

Figure 10-7 Moving this irregularly shaped bitmapped object (selected with a Lasso tool) leaves behind a blank white space; whatever may have been underneath the selection is no longer there.

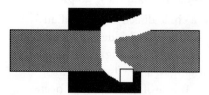

Figure 10-8 Using an Eraser tool to partially erase objects, as shown here, can be done only with bitmapped graphics.

Reducing, enlarging, and rotating bits versus objects For object-oriented graphics, reducing, enlarging, or rotating an object does not alter the quality of the image. For bitmapped graphics, such operations usually reduce the quality of the selected image.

To change the size of an object-oriented circle, for example, the Macintosh uses an appropriate numeric substitution in the formula used to define the circle. The quality and accuracy of the image are maintained as before. In some cases, the screen display may suffer because of the limits of its dpi resolution, but higher-resolution printed output still looks fine.

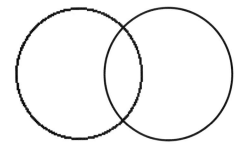

Figure 10-9 At left, the bitmapped circle from Figure 10-5, after enlarging it on the Macintosh; at right, the object-oriented circle from Figure 10-5, similarly enlarged.

For bitmapped graphics, however, these same operations are likely to produce distortions that affect both the screen display and the printed output. Enlarged images tend to have increased jaggies, reduced images lose fine detail, and rotated images look messier. Reductions are a particular problem for bitmapped graphics, since shrinking the image results in a smaller number of bits in the bitmap. For example, if you reduce an irregularly curved line that was 200 dots long to a length of 100 dots, you have only half as many dots to create the same appearance. Some of the details of the original line's twists and turns almost certainly will have to be omitted in this smaller image, since the size of the dots remains the same.

Paint Versus Draw Versus PostScript Programs

How do you know whether you are working with bitmapped or object-oriented graphics? Generally, it depends on the application you are using. Programs (or modules of programs) that work with bitmapped images are called *paint* programs, while those that work with object-oriented images are called *draw* programs. Many applications can work with both types of images. Detailed information should be somewhere in the application's manual.

If you use AppleWorks, you can easily see the difference. When you go to open a new document, two of the choices are Painting and Drawing.

The Painting module works exclusively with bitmapped graphics. The term *paint* is meant to suggest their preferred use for artistic purposes, where the ability to edit pixel by pixel. Any object-oriented graphics that are pasted into a paint program/module become part of the bitmap and lose their object identity. They can now be edited on a pixel-by-pixel basis.

The Drawing module works primarily with object-oriented graphics. This is preferred for architectural and engineering drawings, or any other use where precision and layout are more important than creative touches. However, a Drawing document can include bit-mapped graphic components as separate objects.

Newer programs, such as Macromedia's Fireworks, attempt to combine the best of both worlds, allowing you to edit images as if they were bitmapped, yet retaining the vector paths that make up the image. Fireworks is also especially adept at creating graphics to be used on the the World Wide Web.

PostScript programs such as Adobe Illustrator and FreeHand form a special class that doesn't quite fit into either category. In most ways they are similar to draw programs, because PostScript is basically an object-oriented language. With PostScript, however, what you see on the screen is often only a rough approximation of the printed output, because the PostScript graphic instructions only go to the printer and do not determine the screen display. More details about this distinction are covered in the next section on graphics file formats.

TAKE NOTE ▶ Different Tools in Paint versus Draw Programs

Just as the previous chapter made frequent reference to word-processing programs, this chapter makes reference to graphics applications. In particular, it assumes at least a passing familiarity with the basic array of "tools" used by these programs, such as lasso, eraser, and polygon.

If you don't know whether a program is a paint or a draw program (or whether you are in the paint or draw mode of a program that can do both), you can often figure this out simply by examining the collection of tools currently in its tool bar. For example, paint programs/modules will show an Eraser tool, but draw programs/modules will not. This is because erasing requires editing of individual pixels—something that is possible only with bitmapped graphics in paint programs/modules.

BY THE WAY ▶ PostScript Graphics Without a PostScript Printer

Only PostScript printers can directly print PostScript-based graphics. If you try to print a graphics document that contains PostScript code to a non-PostScript printer, the document will print incorrectly, in lower quality, or not at all. However, there are various software solutions to using PostScript output with a non-PostScript printer. For example, most inkjet printers do not have built-in PostScript capability, but with so-called RIP software you can use these printers to print PostScript files. Adobe's ImageReady is one example of this type of software.

Also remember that printing PostScript graphics requires an applications that supports PostScript graphics. Check with your application's documentation for information on this.

Graphics File Formats

When you save a graphics document, you save it in a particular *file format*. This is really no different from what I have previously described for documents in general, such as with text documents (as described in Chapters 6 and 8). For example, Microsoft Word saves documents in its own Word file format, and generic text is also available in almost all text-oriented applications. To open a text file in a format other than the one specific to the application in use generally requires that the application have a translator file for that format. These same general rules apply in the world of graphics.

Generic Graphics File Formats

There is only one generic text format (called TEXT), but there are several different generic graphics formats. Graphics applications do not depend on application-specific formats to nearly the extent that most other categories of applications do. In fact, many graphics applications do not even have an application-specific format, instead relying entirely on generic formats. When things are working well, this considerably simplifies the process of transferring information across applications by reducing the number of translator files needed.

Each of the different generic formats has different limitations and advantages. For example, some are better for bitmapped graphics, while others are better for object-oriented graphics.

The most common generic graphics formats are PNTG, PICT, TIFF, and EPSF.

TECHNICALLY SPEAKING ▶ Where Do These Names Come From?

Typically, generic file formats are referred to by the four-letter code used to name the file type (not file creator) of the document. Each different format, generic or application-specific, has a unique file type.

SEE: • Chapter 8 for more on file types and file creators.

PNTG or Paint The PNTG format (often referred to as Paint) is a limited format and is rarely used anymore. It can store only black-and-white bitmapped information at 72-dpi resolution. This worked well for accurately transferring the screen image from the original 72-dpi black-and-white Macintoshes to the original 72-dpi black-and-white ImageWriters. But it hardly keeps pace with today's color monitors and high-resolution printers.

A common misconception is that all paint programs use the Paint file format. This is not true. What makes a program a paint program is how it works with bitmapped images, not what file format it uses. Paint programs can use any of several formats, especially the PICT format described next.

PICT The PICT format could be considered the default graphic format for the Mac. For example, when you save a screen image (using the Mac OS's Command-Shift-3 or Command-Shift-4 commands), the screen is captured as a PICT document. It is also the graphic format used when opening graphics with SimpleText.

PICT images can be used by both draw and paint programs and can contain either bitmapped or object-oriented graphics. However, PICT images are notorious for causing problems for PostScript printers, especially those used by professional printers. If you plan to send your documents to a printing service, you will be better off using the TIFF or EPS formats described next.

TIFF TIFF stands for Tagged Image File Format. Like PNTG, it is a bitmapped-only file format. Actually, several different versions of the TIFF format are available. The resolution and color limitations of the format depend on the exact version of TIFF in use (as well as the specific application in use).

TIFF is the preferred format for working with digitized images, particularly scanned photographs. This format is similarly ideal for use in imaging programs, such as Photoshop, that permit brightness and contrast adjustments to a document.

TIFF can save files at very high resolutions, permitting high-quality printouts, but at the cost of requiring enormously large files. As a result, it is common to see special compressed TIFF formats.

EPSF or EPS EPSF (often called EPS) stands for Encapsulated PostScript File. This file format can be used with either bitmapped or object-oriented graphics. The primary reason for using EPS, however, is that it stores the graphic information as PostScript instructions, which are then used to create the graphic on a PostScript printer.

Using EPS files requires an application that supports the use of PostScript instructions; Adobe Illustrator and FreeHand are the two best-known examples of graphics applications that have this capability.

EPS files generally include a separate PICT image of the file in addition to the PostScript information. The PICT image—an approximate visual representation of the PostScript commands—is displayed on the monitor, while the PostScript information is used only when printing. Thus, as is generally true when using PostScript, the screen display of an EPS file is not identical to the printed output.

You may be able to open an EPSF file with an application that does not support PostScript. If so, the display and printing are both generated from the PICT information; the PostScript information is ignored entirely.

By the way, if you are using LaserWriter 8, you can save any file as an EPS file via the print-to-disk option in the Print dialog box (as described in Chapter 7, "Technically Speaking: LaserWriter's 'Destination' Option").

SEE: • **"Unable to Paste a Graphic Across Applications" later in this chapter.**

Application-Specific File Formats

In addition to the generic file formats, some graphics applications have a unique application-specific format, comparable to the specific formats created by most word processors. These unique file formats may allow the creating application to save certain special formatting effects that are not possible with the generic formats.

Graphics programs with application-specific file formats also have options to save files in generic formats. You typically select the type of format you want to use from a pop-up menu in the Save dialog box. In fact, you may have to save in a generic format if you wish to transfer the image to another program, such as a word processor or a page-layout program. Word processors and the like rarely have file-translation filters for application-specific graphics formats. They support only generic formats.

How to Determine the File Type of a Graphics Document

Knowing a graphic document's file type can be the key to solving a problem you are having displaying or printing the file. So how can you tell the file type of a specific document?

AppleWorks PICT GIF

Figure 10-10 Different icons for an AppleWorks document saved in its application-specific format (left) versus a PICT format (center) versus an GIF format (right).

The Kind description in the file's Get Info window, though useful in identifying file types of most nongraphic documents, is generally not helpful here. It tells you only the name of the application that *created* the document, not necessarily the format (or *file type*) of the document. Thus, for example, an AppleWorks document saved as a PICT file will be identified with a Kind of *AppleWorks Picture*.

You may have better luck by checking the icons for each document. Many programs use different Finder icons to indicate the different file formats. For example, the same AppleWorks PICT file will have the word PICT on its icon. If checking icons doesn't help, the best alternative is to use a utility that allows you to view the file type of an application. My preferred choice is Snitch. In the case of the AppleWorks PICT file, you simply select Get Info (Command-I) for the file in question and Snitch will show you that its file type is PICT.

Finally, you can choose to change a graphic file from one format to another using the Save As or Export command of any application that supports saving files in multiple formats. AppleWorks offers a limited set of such options. Programs such as Photoshop or GraphicConverter offer a wider selection.

SEE: • Chapter 8 for more details on file type codes and related utilities.

Graphics on the World Wide Web

Graphics Encoding

For graphics included on Web pages, a primary concern is the speed at which they load. Especially for those connecting to the Web via 56K (or slower) modems, a page with many complex graphics can seem to take forever to load.

As a result, Web graphics are typically encoded using special formats that compress the size of the file, thereby facilitating the speed at which they load. The two most common such encoded formats are *GIF* (Graphic Interchange Format) and *JPEG* (Joint Photographic Experts Group).

GIF files are usually smaller than comparable JPEG files but they cannot display the full range of colors that JPEG files can do. Thus, if you want to include a photograph, or similar full-colored image on a Web page, you will typically use the JPEG format. For most other graphics, including icons, advertisements, and the like, the GIF format is your best bet. Another format that is gaining popularity is *PNG* (Portable Networks Graphics). It combines the smaller size of GIF with the color range of JPEG; so expect to see it more often in the months ahead.

GIF File Variations: Interlacing, Animation, Custom Palettes

Interlacing If you've loaded many Web pages, you've probably noticed that GIF images may load in one of two different ways. An image may load more or less all-at-once (or loading progressively from the top down on slower connections) or it may load with a venetian-blind sort of effect (where the entire image appears in a coarse form at first, progressively getting filled in with more detail). The latter effect is called an *interlaced* image and is again designed to assist those with slower connections. It enables you to see an overview of the image without having to wait for the entire image to load, leaving you to decide if you want to wait for the image to finish or skip on to the next Web page.

Animation GIF images also provide a simple method of having animated images on the Web. They do this by combining a series of images into one GIF file—called an animated GIF. Web browsers correctly interpret this file format and play the animation. In contrast, if you opened an animated GIF in an ordinary graphics program (such as the Draw module of AppleWorks), you would only see a static image.

Custom palettes As already mentioned, GIF images are limited to only 256 colors. This makes it difficult to include graphic elements such as graded transitions (from one color to another) in a GIF file. If you tried, you would typically see unattractive distinct bands of color rather than a smooth transition. A possible solution (other than shifting to JPEG) is to select a custom set of 256 colors to go with the GIF file, rather than the standard palette of colors. This works as long as the total number of colors needed to display the image appropriately does not exceed 256.

Miscellaneous Other Tips for Web Graphics

Use Web-safe colors Historically, Web browsers were limited to display only a set of 216 colors, called the *Web-safe* colors. These are the colors that you are restricted to select from the HTML Picker of Apple's Color Picker (see: "By the Way: Apple's Color Picker," later in this chapter). Newer versions of Web browsers no longer have this restriction. With displays showing Thousand or Millions of colors, the issue is no longer critical. Colors beyond the safe colors may display correctly. Still, if you want to make sure that your graphic image displays correctly, no matter what browser and platform are being used, stick with the safe colors.

In any case, images may display differently in different browsers. It always pays to test out your image in both Explorer and Communicator before assuming that all is well.

Combine graphics Another tip to speed up loading of graphics is to combine several smaller adjacent images into one larger image. As long as the single image is not over-whelmingly large, it should load faster than the collection of separate smaller images. This is because each image on a Web page is transmitted independently. If you have many small images to transmit, this slows down the overall loading time of the page—as compared to having one moderately sized image.

Define the size of the graphic in HTML For those of you familiar with HTML coding, yet another tip is to define the size of the graphic in the HTML code; this typically allows other element of the Web page (such as text) to appear before the graphic even loads. Otherwise, you may have to wait for the graphic to load completely before you see any part of the page at all.

Finally, you may be asking at this point: "How do you achieve all of this control?" That is: "How do I select a custom palette, or create an animated GIF, or select an interlace option?" The answer is that you typically do it with specialized HTML-coding or Web-graphics software. For Web page creation, programs such as PageMill, GoLive, or even BBEdit remain popular. These programs can often manipulate graphic images as well. Otherwise, graphics software such as Fireworks, TypeStyler or ImageReady will do the job. The documentation that comes with these applications will provide the details. With these programs, and the latest versions of Web browsers, you can create and display graphics on the Web using a range of colors and high resolutions that would have only been a dream a few years ago.

SEE: • **Chapter 13 for more on graphics and the World Wide Web.**

QuickTime: Movies, Video, and More

These days, graphics on the Mac means more than just the two-dimensional pictures so far emphasized in this chapter. It means 3-D graphics, animated graphics, QuickTime movies and more. No longer content with having popularized "desktop publishing," Apple now is pushing for "desktop video" as the hot new graphics technology of the start of the new century. What follows is a general overview of these emerging technologies together with specific troubleshooting issues.

Apple's QuickTime is the technology that started it all. It is the major way for viewing "movies" on your Mac. Viewing QuickTime movies requires that the QuickTime software be installed in your System Folder. Make sure you have the latest version, as Apple is constantly improving this file. As of this writing, the current version of QuickTime is 4.x.

Problems Installing QuickTime

QuickTime 4 uses an Internet-based method of obtaining and updating the software. When you "download" QuickTime 4.x, you are actually only downloading a special Installer that requires grabbing files from Apple's server in order to complete the installation. This has inevitably caused problems for some users who, for various reasons (including having firewalls installed) were unable to get this method of installing to work. It also made it difficult to install QuickTime on computers not hooked up to the

Figure 10-11 The Internet-based QuickTime Updater screen, with the Use Web Proxy option unchecked.

Internet. Thus, Apple eventually made a complete version of the Installer available from the Web site. With this version, you can install QuickTime completely offline.

Alternatively, once you have downloaded and installed one copy of QuickTime via the Internet, you can use the QuickTime Installer (or Updater) application together with the QuickTime Install Cache file to install other copies, without requiring access to the Internet. Just drag the Cache icon to the Installer application.

If you are installing QuickTime via the Internet, you may get an error that says "an error occurred trying to download the file VISEData" or "The file 'viseicat.idx'" couldn't be downloaded." This error can usually be bypassed by making sure that that the "Use Web proxy" option (available in the opening screen of the Updater) is disabled. Otherwise, try running the Installer or Updater when Internet traffic is light (such as late at night in the U.S.). Also, to avoid a potential freeze during installation, quit all open applications before launching the QuickTime Installer/Updater.

If you install a new version of QuickTime, the older version should get removed or deleted. However, sometimes the Installer utility does not do this, especially if its name, *as listed in the Finder*, is slightly different than the new version's name (such as QuickTime vs. QuickTime™). In this case, both versions may remain in the Extensions folder after an upgrade. If so, when you try to startup, you will get a message that says that QuickTime cannot be installed because another version is already installed. If this happens, simply delete the older version and restart the Mac. In the meantime, despite what the message says, one of the versions of QuickTime did load. (This exception aside, as a general rule, it is wise not to rename system software files. Otherwise, more problems such as this one are likely to occur.)

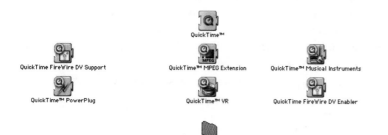

Figure 10-12a Inside the Extensions Folder: QuickTime extensions and the QuickTime Extensions folder.

Figure 10-12b Finder icons for basic QuickTime files, including Player, Plugin, and Installer.

Basic QuickTime Files

The Extensions Folder files The essential file for using QuickTime is the QuickTime extension. Some additional QuickTime extensions include QuickTime FireWire DV Support, QuickTime FireWire DV Enabler, QuickTime™ MPEG Extension, QuickTime™ Musical Instruments, QuickTime™ PowerPlug, and QuickTime™ VR. The remainder of QuickTime's functionality comes from an assortment of files in the QuickTime Extensions folder, located in the Extensions folder of the System Folder. To get some idea what each of these files does, turn on Balloon Help and move the cursor over the file (although some of the descriptions are more humorous than informative).

If you use Conflict Catcher, you will find that it does not list the contents of the QuickTime Extensions folder. If you want, you can change this. To do so, simply add the folder's name to the list accessed via Conflict Catcher's Preferences>Folder>Add command.

SEE: • **Fix-It #3.**

QuickTime PowerPlug and "Can't find QuickTimeLib" If you are using a Power Mac, and you get system crashes when trying to use QuickTime, you probably don't have the QuickTime PowerPlug extension installed. Failure to have this extension installed may also result in a message that says *"Can't find QuickTimeLib."* If you do have PowerPlug installed but you still get this message, it most likely means that there is a bug in the application you are trying to use. Contact the vendor about possible upgrades.

The QuickTime Plugin To enable QuickTime use on the Web, you will need to install the QuickTime Plugin in your browser's plug-ins folder. This may not happen automatically when you install QuickTime. In this case, you will have to manually drag it to the folder.

QuickTime Settings control panel QuickTime includes a control panel called QuickTime Settings. From here, you can select the connection speed of your Internet connection, for optimal access of QuickTime files over the Web. This control panel also includes AutoPlay settings. From here, you can select whether or not you want audio CDs and/or certain CD-ROMs to AutoPlay when inserted. This is also the option that was implicated in the AutoStart virus.

SEE: • **Fix-It #6.**

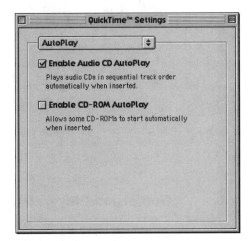

Figure 10-13 QuickTime Settings control panel, with AutoPlay selected from the pop-up menu.

Live Streaming

QuickTime 4 is a major overhaul of Apple's popular QuickTime software. It features a completely redesigned QuickTime Player (formerly Movie Player). Some like the redesigned interface of the new QuickTime Player. Others despise it. Regardless of your reaction, one of the major new features of QuickTime 4 is support for live streaming.

This allows you to view live TV-like broadcasts on the Web in real time (especially so if you have a fast Internet connection such as a cable mode).

What is the difference between QuickTime HTTP streaming (available in QuickTime 3) and live streaming? Apple answers: "The live streaming capabilities of QuickTime 4 are complimentary to the QuickTime HTTP streaming. QuickTime HTTP, otherwise known as Fast Start, downloads the entire QuickTime file to your computer. As soon as enough of the content has been downloaded, it will begin to playback the movie while downloading the rest of the file. QuickTime Streaming does not download the movie to the computer, but loads and plays the movie in real time as the data is received."

You may have to increase the memory allocation of your browser to get good results with live streaming.

Figure 10-14 QuickTime Player window, with a few of the streaming video selections visible along the bottom.

Figure 10-15 QuickTime movie on the Web.

QuickTime Player: Playing and Editing Movies

QuickTime Player, included as part of Apple's QuickTime package, is sort of the SimpleText of movie software. With it, you can view movies and do some simple editing (especially so with the Pro version). To learn more about how QuickTime Player works, especially for editing movies, select the "Online QuickTime Player Help" from the Help menu of the Player.

To get QuickTime Player to play movies smoothly, with good image resolution and proper speed, consider the following:

Lower display depth Playing a movie back at 16-bit or even 8-bit depth, rather than at 24-bit depth can improve the performance of the movie. However, the image will appear grainier (although, for 8-bit depth, there is a way for the creator of the movie to add a "custom color table" that will improve the quality; details of how to do this are beyond the scope of this book).

Reduce screen size Reducing the screen size of a QuickTime movie will improve the smoothness of the display.

Turn virtual memory off (etc.) Turning virtual memory off, quitting other open applications and starting up with only essential extensions can all lead to improved performance when recording or playing back movies.

Get more VRAM and a faster Mac Faster, more powerful Macs, particularly those with the extra video RAM (usually around 8MB or more these days), can play and record video with the best performance capability. If you really need this, you'll need to spend the bucks on better hardware.

A wide variety of other shareware, freeware and commercial programs exist that go beyond the capabilities of Movie Player (including such products as Avid Cinema and Adobe Premiere). At the lowest end, even SimpleText itself can play movies! QuickTime is also not the only way to view live streaming audio and video over the Web. RealPlayer is another popular alternative.

Recording Movies/Video

Prior to FireWire, the typical method for inputting video to your Mac required connecting an input device, such as a camcorder, to the video-in port of a Mac (if your Mac model had such ports) or the video-in ports of a PCI graphics card (such as an ATI XclaVR card) that was installed in your Mac. These methods imported "analog" signals and converted them to a digital image on your computer.

However, currently, the preferred method for video input (and output!) is to use a digital camcorder connected to the Mac via a FireWire port. This uses a digital signal throughout the entire process. The iMac DV even ships with special software, called iMovie, to facilitate this process and to allow you to further edit the movie once you have it on your drive. Of course, higher end Macs would typically use software such as Adobe's Premiere or Apple's Final Cut Pro.

You can use it to record video input (and save it as a movie file), view a TV signal (if you have a TV tuner connected to your Mac) or view MPEG movies.

Once a video has been recorded, another basic option is to open it in QuickTime Player. Here you can do some simple editing and optimizing of the movie. See the QuickTime Help Web site for more details: *http://www.apple.com/quicktime/resources/qt4/ us/help/QuickTime%20Help.htm* .

Note that the speed and smoothness of the movie (as well as the size of the file) are affected by options that you can set from QuickTime Player, especially the compression method and frames per second setting. While details here are beyond the scope of this book, here are a few key points:

Compression In some applications, when recording movies, you can record them at different frame rates (such as 15/sec or 30/sec). Thirty/sec or higher is considered good for producing smooth realistic video. However, older Macs don't have the muscle to record or even playback at that rate and still have the movie appear smooth. In most cases, unless you have a high-speed Mac (such as a newer G3 or G4) with lots of video-RAM, you'll get better results by recording at a slower rate.

There are different methods for compressing videos, each with their own pros and cons. To see a list of the compression options in QuickTime Player, select the Export command, then click the Options button. From the window that appears, click the Video Settings button and finally access the Video pop-up menu.

Three common compression choices (also called codecs, for COmpressor/DECompressor) are: Cinepak ("Commonly used for video movies that require CD-ROM playback. Very slow compressing, but decompresses fast on low-end processors. Good choice for Internet streaming."); Sorenson Video (especially good "…if you plan to stream movies from a QuickTime Streaming Server"), and DV – NTSC ("Used with digital video cameras manufactured in the U.S. and Japan").

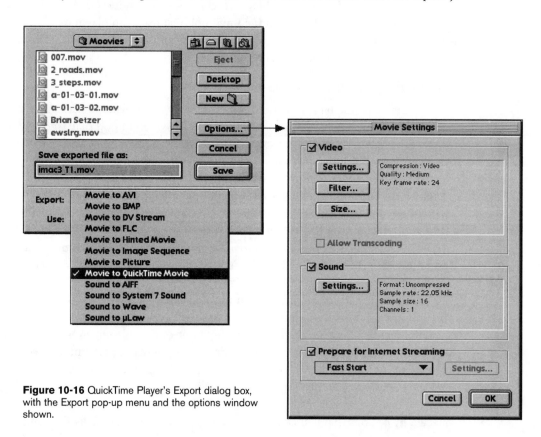

Figure 10-16 QuickTime Player's Export dialog box, with the Export pop-up menu and the options window shown.

With Apple Video Player, recording with Normal or No compression (rather than Most), as found in Apple Video Player's Preferences dialog box, while leading to bigger movie file sizes, will typically improve playback performance.

Record to a RAM Disk or at least a Fast AV Hard Disk Recording movies to a RAM Disk (if you have the RAM to spare), rather than a hard disk, can improve the smoothness of movie playback. Using the fastest hard disk available is advisable if you are recording to a hard disk. Special so-called AV hard disks will also lead to improved performance.

BY THE WAY ▶ Using Apple Video Player

Who can use it? Apple Video Player only works with Macs that have a video input or TV Tuner capability. On other Macs, if you try to run it, you will get a message that incorrectly says the Video Startup extension was not installed properly. Ignore the message. It won't run no matter what you do.

Video Startup On the other hand, for those Macs that *can* use Apple Video Player, it is true that it won't work unless the Video Startup extension is installed.

Insufficient memory If you get a message that says "*An error occurred while trying to copy (via Command–C) the video display to the Clipboard*" when you try to capture a large (640x480) image in the Apple Video Player, or if you get a message that says "*An error occurred while trying to freeze the video display*" when you click the Freeze button, it means that the Apple Video Player is running out of memory. Quit the program, increase its memory allocation (via its Get Info window) and try again.

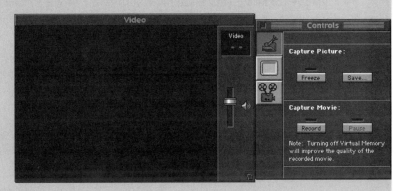

Figure 10-17 Apple Video Player.

QuickTime Movies on the Web

If you pull down QuickTime Player's drawer (along the bottom of its window), you will see it comes pre-stocked with a selection of Web sites that contain QuickTime content. Just click one and, if you are connected to the Internet, you will be taken there.

Saving movies When using QuickTime to play movies on the Web, you can save the movie to your drive after the movie has played. To do this, you access the pop-up menu in the lower right hand corner of the QuickTime window and select "Save as Source" or "Save Movie." However, you will only be able to do this if you register to upgrade to the "Pro" version of QuickTime (as opposed to the "free" version that comes with the Mac OS). Still, if you don't want to register, you should be able to save the movie anyway. To do this, select "Save Movies in Disk Cache" from the Plug-in

Settings window and then locate the saved cache file in the folder where your browser's cache files are stored (it may have a cryptic name, so just look for one of the most recently created and probably larger cache files).

Putting QuickTime Movies on the Web If you design your own Web pages, you should know this: to place QuickTime movies on a Web page, you used to need to "flatten" the movie (that is, remove the resource fork from the file, leaving just the data fork). There are freeware utilities that can do that for you (such as one called FlattenMoov). However, with current versions of QuickTime, you can choose to Export the movie in a format suitable for Internet streaming. To do this, select Export from the File menu. Click Options, and make sure "Prepare for Internet Streaming" is checked. From the pop-up menu, leave the choice at "Fast-Start Movie" unless you know for certain that you want another option (the QuickTime Help Web site provides guidelines).

SEE: • **Chapter 13 for more on the World Wide Web in general.**

Video Formats

Movies can come in different formats (just as graphics files could come in different formats, such as PICT or TIFF). Here are three examples:

MooV (or Mov) This is the basic QuickTime Movie format. You'll need the QuickTime extension to view these files, plus some movie player application (such as QuickTime Player).

MPEG This compressed format was developed for professional video transmissions. However, you commonly see this type of file on the Internet. There are several different versions of the MPEG format, with newer versions having improved quality. QuickTime 4 can work directly with MPEG files.

AVI This is a format from Microsoft and you are likely to see it on the Web from time to time. It is not widely used on the Mac platform. QuickTime Player 4.x can work with some, although not all, varieties of this format.

In particular, when attempting to play an AVI movie, you may get white video frames and the following error message: "You may experience problems playing a video track in 'filename.avi' because the required compressor could not be found." The solution is to get one of the Intel Indeo Video codecs available from Apple's Software Updates web site.

To see a list of formats that QuickTime Player supports for export (both video and sound), select the Export command and check the Export pop-up menu.

BY THE WAY ▶ QuickTime and Sounds

QuickTime 4.0 is not just for movies. It also has the ability to play audio. For example, it can play MP3 files, the popular method of encoding music, with near CD quality, for transfer over the Internet. However, if you really get into using and creating MP3 files, you will want a more full-featured MP3 application, such as Casady & Greene's SoundJam.

QuickTime VR and QuickDraw 3D

Two technologies from Apple are QuickTime VR and QuickDraw 3D. Sometimes it is a bit hard to keep the differences between them straight. Accessing these technologies requires that the relevant extensions be installed in your System Folder and/or that you use applications that were written to take advantage of these features (such as QTVR Player for QuickTime VR).

QuickTime VR QuickTime VR lets you create graphics that a user can navigate around in a 360° space. For example, it could allow you to view a picture of a room and rotate around to see all four walls, look up to the ceiling or down to the floor, even move through a door. The VR software includes a simple VR player application that can be used to view VR documents. If it did not come with your Mac, it is available online.

QuickDraw 3D QuickDraw 3D is a technology that makes 3D rendering easier to do than was previously possible on a Mac. While this is more of a graphic technology than a video one, I placed it here because it is likely to be used in conjunction with movies. For example, QuickTime includes QuickDraw 3D support. If it did not come already pre-installed on your Mac, the QuickDraw 3D software is included on Apple's system software CD-ROM disc. Otherwise, as always, the latest version is available online.

OpenGL Actually QuickDraw 3D is expected to fade out over the next several years. One problem with it was that it only worked on Macs. This meant that authors of 3D games had to completely rewrite the PC version of their software to get it to work on a Mac. Given the Macs smaller market share, many were reluctant to do so—and the Mac game market suffered. Apple's solution was to adopt a cross-platform standard called OpenGL. As Apple states: "OpenGL for Macintosh enables your computer to display three-dimensional graphics using applications designed to take advantage of OpenGL." This software is automatically installed when you do a standard install of the current versions of the Mac OS.

Game Sprockets Speaking of games, another game-related set of software you may spot in your System Folder are files that have the word "sprocket" in their name. Again, as stated by Apple: "Apple Game Sprockets is a set of technologies designed to make writing Macintosh games easier for developers. They are designed specifically to provide the functionality that games need on the Macintosh: drawing to the screen, handling input devices, setting up multiplayer games, and simulating 3D sound sources." There are four kinds of game sprockets: InputSprocket, DrawSprocket, NetSprocket, and SoundSprocket.

SEE: • **"Games on the Mac," in Chapter 15 for more on Sprockets.**

TAKE NOTE ▶ Playing DVD Movies

Recent Macs, such as the second-generation iMac DV, come with DVD drives (see Chapter 1 for more on the basics of these drives). These can be used for playing DVD movies, the same type that you can buy at your local video store for use with DVD players connected to your TV. Here are several tips to help make your movie-watching experience an enjoyable one:

If you get pixelation in dark areas of the screen, try one or more of the following:

- Set the Bit Depth to Millions in the Monitors and Sound control panel.
- Switch resolution to 800x600 or 720x480 if available (only when connected to an external display).
- Choose normal size as opposed to full screen for the best quality image.
- Select Best for video when watching on S-video device such as a television.

If you get low or no sound at all, try one or more of the following:

- Check preferences and make sure Line In audio is not selected.
- Make sure the Sound In source in the Control Strip is set to DVD.
- Try changing the sound setting when playing the movie by selecting the audio button on the DVD Controller.

For more problems with DVD discs, check Chapter 5, "A CD/DVD Won't Mount or Play."

TAKE NOTE ▶ Using Digital Cameras

Basics Digital cameras for "still" photography work similarly to 35mm cameras. You focus, you zoom, you take a picture. However, the resulting picture is not stored on film and does not have to be developed. Instead it is typically stored on a slim little card (about the dimensions of a small Post-It note) which (depending upon exactly what card you have) can hold as much as 32MB of data. Depending on the resolution of the pictures you take, a 32MB card can hold anywhere from about 32 pictures to several hundred pictures. When you no longer want to save the pictures, you can just erase/reformat the card and start all over again. No more film costs ever!

So what's the down side? For starters, the maximum possible quality of the pictures is still not as good as with film (although the differences are rapidly diminishing). However, you may not even be able to get the best possible quality. To create "prints" of your pictures, you need to download the pictures from the data card to your computer (in some cases, you can download directly from a camera to a printer, but this is less common). From your computer, you can now send the image to a color printer. The quality of the resulting output varies dramatically—depending upon what printer you use, what paper you use, and what settings for the printer that you select.

Most likely, you will use an inkjet printer. For example, Epson makes a series of printers with "Photo" in their name. These printers use 6 different colors of ink (including black) rather than the traditional 4 colors. This, in turn, allows for more accurate flesh tones, improving the overall quality of the image. However, 4 color printers, such as the Epson Stylus Color 900, have improved so much in recent years that they come close to matching what the Photo printers can do.

The quality of the print out will also very much depend on the type of paper you use. Glossy photo-quality paper will result in much better output than ordinary typing paper. However, this can get very expensive. Together with the cost of the ink, a single 8x10 photo on glossy paper can cost well over $1.00 to print. In general, use at least the coated paper recommended for inkjet printers to get acceptable photo-quality output.

TAKE NOTE ▶ Using Digital Cameras *(continued)*

Finally, the Print and/or Page Setup dialog boxes for these inkjet printers will include printer-specific options for adjusting the look of the output (such as selecting a particular dithering pattern). I discuss this in more detail in Chapter 7.

SEE: • **QuickFixes! Troubleshooting Inkjet and/or USB Printers).**

You may now be thinking "Why bother? I'll just stick with my Kodak film." Perhaps. But consider this: if you are not satisfied with the results of a particular picture, you can improve it in various ways (increasing its brightness, removing red-eye, sharpening or softening the image and more), using any number of photo-editing programs. These are fix-its that would otherwise be impossible to do without the skills and darkroom equipment of a professional photographer (and maybe not even then). Of course, you can transfer a printed snapshot to your Mac via a scanner. But especially if you intend to use photos directly on your Mac, the quality of the photo will usually be better when taken with a good digital camera.

Getting the pictures on to your computer Once you have taken digital pictures, the next goal is to download them to the computer. Downloaded images are typically saved as JPEG documents. There are two basic ways to transfer pictures from the card in your computer to your computer:

- **Adapter** Get an adapter that allows you to mount the data card directly on the Mac. Then you can use the Finder's copy function to copy the photos to your hard drive. For example, with a PowerBook that has a PCMIA slot, you can get a PCMIA card that allows you to insert the SmartMedia cards used in many digital cameras. For desktop Macs, you can get a PCMIA card reader that accomplishes the same thing. This is much faster than using the cable connection (described next). It is also more reliable, avoiding many of the transfer failures that might otherwise occur.

- **Cable** Attach a cable between the two. Most cameras will have a port where you can connect a cable which then connects to the Mac on the other end (typically via the serial or USB port). You then launch a program that can access the camera and initiate a download. Most likely, one such program came with your camera. If not, there are shareware applications that can do this (such as Cameraid or Camedia).

  Olympus offered the following advice regarding transferring images: "For maximum quality, download your photos without changing any of the default options in the Camedia dialog box. Selecting even 'maximum' quality results in 'recompression' of the JPEG image—which can result in a loss of quality of the image. Every time a JPEG is re-enocded, a quality loss is possible. If you need several iterations of a photo, consider starting with a lossless format such as PICT, making your edits and re-saves, then saving the final image as JPEG."

Battery life and assorted other problems If you use the cable method to transfer files, be sure to attach an AC Adapter to your camera before starting a transfer. Downloading uses a lot of juice and can quickly drain the camera's batteries. In fact, just taking pictures uses a good deal of battery power. This is why it is absolutely essential that you do not use alkaline batteries in your camera (even if the manual says they work). They will get drained too fast to be useful. What you should use instead will vary depending on the camera. I use rechargeable NiMH batteries in my Olympus and find that they work quite well. If your camera's manual says they are okay to use, lithium batteries are another good choice.

Other problems transferring pictures via a cable connection can usually be solved by turning the camera on only after the transferring application has been launched and (in some cases) after the download command has been selected. If that still fails, increase the memory allocation of the application, make sure AppleTalk is disabled and turn off Palm's HotSync Monitor (if you use this). If your Mac can use the SerialDMA Update, install it.

Data cards come in various sizes. For example, SmartMedia cards come in 4MB, 8MB, 16MB, and 32MB sizes. Not all cameras that use SmartMedia can use all sizes (older cameras especially may only be able to use the smaller sizes). And, of course, not all cameras use SmartMedia; they may use another type of data card. You can also use the type of data card your camera supports.

Solve It! Common Graphics Problems

Unable to Paste a Graphic Across Applications

 Symptoms:

You copy a selected graphic to the Clipboard and shift to another application (word processor, page-layout program, graphics application, or whatever) to paste the graphic into a document. Unfortunately, one of the following events happens:

- The Paste command is dimmed and cannot be used.

- Nothing at all appears when you select Paste.

- Something other than what you most recently copied is pasted.

These symptoms are not limited to graphics and may occur whenever you use the Clipboard.

> **SEE:** • Chapter 9, "Problems Copying and Pasting Text Across Applications."

 Causes:

- **The graphic never copied to the system Clipboard**
  Obviously, a graphic image will not paste successfully if it was never copied successfully. This can happen for the same general reason first discussed for text transfers in Chapter 9, which involves the distinction between the application versus system clipboards.

  To review briefly, there are really two clipboards, an application clipboard (used in the creating application) and a system clipboard (used when going between applications). Information is supposed to be converted from the application clipboard to the system clipboard when you switch programs, but it does not always work properly if you have multiple applications open.

- **The application does not support graphics placement**
  If either of these problems occurs, the Paste command will either be dimmed, will paste nothing, or will paste whatever was previously in the system Clipboard.

 **What to Do:**

Check Show Clipboard

To check if the graphic was transferred to the system Clipboard, select the Show Clipboard command in the Finder's Edit menu. Look in the Clipboard window to see its contents.

Update the System Clipboard If Necessary

If the image is not in the clipboard, you will need to update the system Clipboard. To do this, try any or all of the following steps.

Figure 10-18 The Finder's Show Clipboard command, and the Clipboard window that opens when you select this command.

1. Quit the application you were using when you copied the graphic. (If you get a message such as one that says "Save large clipboard?", select Yes.) Then return to the receiving application and try pasting again.

2. Go to the Finder and then back to the receiving application. Try pasting again.

3. Recopy the graphic and paste it to the Scrapbook. Then shift to the application where you wish to paste the graphic. Go to the Scrapbook and copy the desired graphic. Now return to the application and select Paste.

4. Go to the System Folder and locate the file called Clipboard. Drag it to the Trash. A new file will be created automatically, as needed. Now try to recopy and paste your graphic. This may work especially if the Clipboard file was damaged.

5. If none of the above succeeds, try Copy and Paste a few more times. Sometimes, for reasons unknown, it may eventually work.

Check If the Application Supports Graphics Placement

If the image is in the Clipboard but you cannot get it to paste, it is probably because the application doesn't accept graphics. For example, some applications may accept only pasted text, not graphics (such as a spreadsheet that does not accept graphics in its cells). In such cases, when a graphic is on the Clipboard, the Paste command is usually dimmed so that you cannot select it. Even if it is not dimmed, nothing will appear when you select Paste. Check the application's manual for more details as to what can be pasted into it.

Use Drag and Drop, Clippings Files, and Scrapbook

Drag and Drop allows you to directly drag a high-lighted selection from one document to another, even across applications, without needing the intervening copy-and-paste steps traditionally used by the Clipboard.

You can even drag a selection to the Finder's desktop and create a special *clippings* file, which can be later dragged to another document, largely bypassing the need for the Scrapbook. This will work only if the application from which you want to copy the graphic supports this clippings feature. Even if it does work, it may have no more chance of success than using Copy and Paste, but it's worth a try.

SEE: • **"Use Drag and Drop and Clippings Files," in Chapter 9, for related information.**

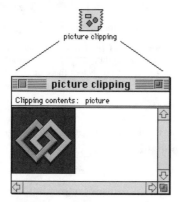

Figure 10-19 A picture clippings file with its window open.

Figure 10-20 The Scrapbook.

Import the Graphic

If none of the preceding suggestions solves the problem, try importing the graphic. This often succeeds even when the clipboard fails.

Successful importing depends on the receiving application having the relevant file-translation filter for the format of data to be imported. Even if you have the correct filter, however, the import may still fail. (If so, you typically get an error message.) This is a particularly common problem with the TIFF format, because there are several variations of the format. You can't do much about a failure at this point, other than return to the original application and see if you can save the file in a different format that will be accepted by the importing application. In general, avoid application-specific formats, as these are the least likely to be importable; use generic formats instead.

SEE: • **Chapter 6 for more on importing problems.**

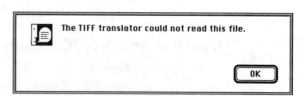

Figure 10-21 This message appeared when a program was unable to import a TIFF file, even though the application had a TIFF format translator.

TAKE NOTE ▶ Foreign Imports

I use the term *importing* to refer to the process where an entire file created by one application is opened in another application. This process bypasses the clipboard. When you import a file, you usually open the entire file via the Open dialog box as a separate document in its own window, exactly as if it were being opened by the application that created it.

In other cases, you may be able to import a file to a specified location of an already open document, rather than opening it as a separate document. Applications that can do this usually have special commands for this feature (with names such as Import, Place, or Insert).

In either case, the import procedure still requires the relevant file translation filter.

Otherwise ...

If none of the previous suggestions succeed, you are probably stuck and will not be able to transfer the graphic to the application in question.

Even If You Do Succeed, Your Problems May Not Be Over

Even if you do finally get the graphic to transfer, you may find that your problems are not over. In particular, you may find that the graphic is no longer in its original file format. The primary cause is that when graphics are transferred across applications, they are typically converted to a PICT format, regardless of the format of the document from which they originated. This is especially a problem with TIFF and EPS files, since these formats contain special printing-related information (such as an EPS file's PostScript instructions) that are lost in the conversion to a PICT format.

If this occurs, here are a couple of suggestions that may help:

- Try importing rather than pasting. It is often more successful.

- Hold down the Option key when selecting to copy PostScript images. In applications that support this feature, this gets the embedded PostScript code of an EPS file to copy along with its PICT image.

- If you want to save the image in EPS format (from an application that does not support this), and you have the LaserWriter driver installed, select "Destination: File" from the Print dialog box. Then select "Save as File" from the pop-up menu and finally select one of the EPS options from the Format pop-up menu. Now Print. This saves the image in EPS format.

- Try to convert the image by opening it in any application that supports a large number of conversion options. Photoshop is a good choice here.

BY THE WAY ▶ Special Problems with the Placement of a Graphic in a Text Document

When you are trying to paste a graphic image into a word processor or similar type of application, you may find that the graphic itself pastes just fine—it's just that you can't get it in the desired location within the document. For example, you may want the graphic to appear to the left of a paragraph of text, or you may want the adjoining text to wrap around the shape of the graphic. Instead, what you may get is the graphic appearing by itself on a separate line below the paragraph, or directly overlaying the paragraph and obscuring your view of the text.

Neither the graphic itself nor a problem related to the clipboard or importing method is responsible for this sort of incorrect placement. Rather, it is inherent in how the application treats pasted or imported graphics. Because different word processors use different methods, you should consult your application's manual for the details of its approach; look especially for features related to "text wrapping."

Many word processors and integrated packages (such as AppleWorks) are now quite flexible in how they handle graphics placement. Still, if you are not satisfied with the limitations of your application, the only solution is to use a different one. If this is a frequent problem, you might consider investing in a page-layout program (such as PageMaker or QuarkXPress). These programs provide the greatest flexibility in how graphics and text can be combined.

Problems Printing Color Images

 Symptoms:

- When you print a color (or grayscale) image to a black-and-white printer (such as most laser printers), the image quality appears distinctly different from the way it appears on the screen (usually worse).

- When you print a color image to a color printer (such as a color inkjet printer), the document prints in wrong colors or the entire image quality is poor. The screen display of the image appears fine.

 Causes:

The printer is the final arbiter of what the printed output looks like. No matter what other hardware and software you have, the quality of the printed copy can never exceed the capabilities of the printer.

Printing to black-and-white laser printers Printing a color or grayscale image to a black-and-white printer requires that the printer try to approximate the look of the image with its limited one-color (black) capability.

Sadly, this approximation is often less than wonderful. The resolution may be great (because it is at 1200 dpi instead of the screen's 72 dpi), but the overall image, in worst cases, may still be reduced to a disconcerting set of large black-and-white blotches that render the image almost indiscernible. The quality of the approximation depends on a number of factors, including the particular application in use, the features of the printer, and the printer driver.

Printing to color printers Color printers have difficulty getting their printed output to match what appears on the screen. This is either due to:

- Problems resulting from the fact that screen colors (which are from a light source) are produced differently from printed color (which is from a pigment source).

- Limitations of the printer technology.

- One or more colored inks may be empty, the print head may need to be cleaned, or there may be other printer hardware-related problems (especially likely with inkjet printers).

SEE: • **Chapter 7, "Take Note: Different Types of Printers," for an introduction to different types of printers.**
• **Chapter 7, for an introduction to the Page Setup and Print dialog boxes, printer drivers, and problems getting any printout to appear.**
• **Chapter 9, for printing problems specific to formatting of text documents.**
• **"Types of Graphics, Programs, and Files," and "File Format Shifts When Transferring Graphics Across Applications," earlier in this chapter, for printing problems related to different graphic formats.**

 ## What to Do:

Switch Applications

Some applications print color graphics better than others. If you have several applications that can print the same graphic document, and the results in the first application you try are not satisfactory, try another.

Similarly, if feasible, converting a graphic document from one format to another (such as from a PICT to a TIFF file) may improve its output. This may also allow you to use special dithering and/or halftoning options built-in to the application that override and improve on the options accessed via the Print dialog box.

Use PostScript Laser Printer Options

Color matching For PostScript laser printers, select the Color Matching option from the pop-up menu in the LaserWriter Print dialog box. From here, make sure that something other than "Black and White" is selected from the "Print Color" pop-up menu. "Black and White" will almost inevitably lead to poor output.

- **Color/Grayscale** The simplest alternative is to select "Color/Grayscale." Doing this causes the printer drivers to generate an improved *dithered* (or *halftone*) output. It does not alter the file or the screen display in any way. In fact, with current versions of the LaserWriter driver and today's faster Macs, there is virtually no need to ever select "Black and White." Leave the setting at "Color/Grayscale" even when printing plain text.

- **ColorSync color matching** This alternative is only relevant if you have a color printer, laser printer or otherwise. I discuss it more in the next section.

- **PostScript color matching** This alternative is only relevant if you have a color PostScript laser printer. Details here go beyond the scope of this book.

- **Printer-specific options** Take advantage of printer-specific options if you have them. For example, my HP 4000 adds an "Imaging Options" item to the Print pop-up menu. From here, you can select either "Enhanced" or "Standard" shades of gray. Enhanced will yield better results.

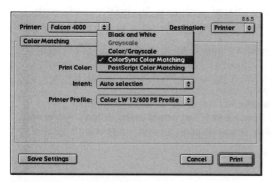

Figure 10-22 The Color Matching window of the LaserWriter's Print dialog box, with a ColorSync option selected.

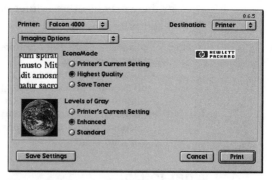

Figure 10-23 The Imaging Options of an HP laser printer.

Use Apple's ColorSync... and Beyond

ColorSync's sole function is to give the user easy automated control over color matching by having one simple set of options that will work with all your different hardware. It is typically installed automatically when you do a full install of any recent version of the Mac OS (if you select to do a Custom Install from the Installer, you will see a separate ColorSync software option listed and checked by default).

To use ColorSync, the first and most important thing you need to do is to select a ColorSync System Profile that matches your monitor. To do this, open the ColorSync control panel and select the item from the System Profile option that matches the name of your monitor. If your monitor name is not listed, this means that a Profile document for it is not included in the ColorSync Profiles folder inside the System Folder. In this case, the manufacturer of the monitor may be able to supply a profile. Otherwise, your best option may be to select "Generic RGB Profile."

For the RGB Default setting, again try to match your monitor's name. For CYMK Default, typically select "Generic CYMK Profile" and for Preferred CMM, leave it at "Automatic." Variations here are primarily for graphics professionals who know more about these settings than I do!

Note: You may also be able to select a ColorSync Profile from the Color panel of the Monitors (or Monitors & Sound) control panel. This accesses the same software as the ColorSync control panel.

Once you have set up your ColorSync profile, you can select to use ColorSync from your printer's Print dialog box. With this all in place and correctly set, the ColorSync software should assure (as much as it is capable of doing) that the color of the printed output matches the color you see on the screen. (**Note:** ColorSync can similarly work with scanners or other imaging devices to help match onscreen color to the color input or output of the device.)

For color laser printers, as I already mentioned, the option to actually use ColorSync when printing is selected from the Color Matching pop-up menu of the Print dialog box.

For a color inkjet printer, if it includes a ColorSync option at all, the location will vary depending on the printer. For example, with my Epson Stylus 900, you access this option by selecting the Custom Mode radio button and then selecting ColorSync from the Custom Settings pop-up menu.

Actually, ColorSync is only one of several options available with an Epson printer. Others include PhotoEnhance3 and Digital Camera. These are alternative methods of creating optimal color output that, depending upon the type of image you are printing, may prove superior to ColorSync. They are especially recommended when working with photographs.

Or you can click the Advanced button and access

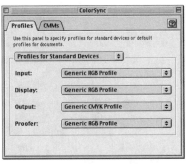

Figure 10-24 Top: The ColorSync 2.5.1 control panel (from Mac OS 8.6) with the Profile for the AppleVision 1710 selected. Bottom: The ColorSync 3.0 control panel (from Mac OS 9).

an entirely new dialog box to make your own customized settings, adjusting items such as Print Quality and Halftoning. With so many choices, it can be difficult to decide what is best to do. Indeed, some experimenting with different settings may be needed to achieve the best results. The manual that comes with the printer will offer some general guidelines.

Figure 10-25 The ColorSync options as accessed from the Monitors control panel. You can also select to calibrate the display from here.

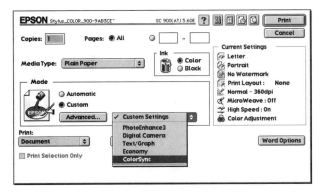

Figure 10-26 The ColorSync (and other color matching options) available from the Epson 900 Print dialog box.

Other printers (such as those from Hewlett-Packard) will likely have other comparable options.

TECHNICALLY SPEAKING ▶ Halftones

Halftoning is the name for a printing process used to simulate the appearance of grays by printing black-and-white dots. It has the same function as dithering. Technically, halftoning is based on a special photographic process where the image is broken up into a series of differently sized dots (small black dots for lighter areas, larger black dots for darker areas). However, on the printers commonly used with a Macintosh, halftoning is not handled the same way, since these printers can only print dots in a single size—such as 600 dpi. Instead, they use digital halftoning, which involves setting up equal-size cells of a given number of dots. The more dots in a cell that are filled in (that is, black instead of white), the darker the shade of gray represented by that cell.

There is a trade-off here. Larger cells allow for more shades of gray (because there are more dots per cell) but result in lower resolution of the image (because the number of cells per inch decreases as cell size gets larger). The result of this trade-off is that, at typical laser printer resolutions, halftoning cannot simulate anything close to the full 256 shades of gray seen on an 8-bit display. Under the best circumstances, you may get only about 90 shades of gray. For many printers, the maximum shades of gray is much less. Still, this may result in satisfactory printouts, at least for nonprofessional uses.

If you need more shades of gray than you can currently get, the best solution is to shift to a printer that has a higher overall resolution. For example, a 1200-dpi laser printer can simulate more shades of gray than an equally featured 300-dpi or 600-dpi laser printer.

This topic is a lot more complex than I have presented here. For example, you soon get into such terms as lines per inch, screen patterns, and screen frequency and angle. For our purposes, it is enough to know that halftoning is a first cousin to dithering—a printing method used to simulate the appearance of shades of gray using only black ink.

TECHNICALLY SPEAKING ▶ Professional Color Matching

If you are really serious about color printing, you need to get into color matching techniques that go well beyond the solutions covered in this section. For example:

- The colors on a monitor are produced by a combination of Red, Green, and Blue lights (RGB), whereas most printers use a combination of Cyan, Yellow, Magenta, and blacK inks (CYMK). Translating an RGB display into a CYMK printed output is not an exact science. The two images are rarely an exact match. Many high-end graphics and page-layout programs have (often complex) features that attempt to compensate for this difference. Apple's ColorSync extension is basically an attempt to make this process more accessible to nonexperts.

- Many specialized graphics and page-layout programs can perform a process called color separation. This is where the document is separated into four (or more) separately colored layers that are each separately saved and then combined by a professional printing process to produce the final multicolor output. This process is essential to professional-level full-color printing, as seen in glossy magazines.

As usual in this area, things are even more complicated than this summary may suggest. You soon find yourself talking about matters such as process versus spot colors, Pantone color selection and more. But take heart! Non-professionals often find that the less-than-perfect output they get, without any knowledge of this stuff or any special effort, is still satisfactory for their needs.

TECHNICALLY SPEAKING ▶ A Word About Scanners

This book doesn't delve much into the use of scanners. However, here is one useful tidbit worth knowing: When scanning something to be printed, you are typically better off selecting a dpi resolution that is *less* than that of your black & white printer (at least half the resolution is often good). This is because, due to how halftoning works, it will typically require at least two dots on a printer to print a dot of scanned image. Actually, a preferred alternative is to scan at a high resolution and then use a program, such as Photoshop, to *downsample* it to the lower resolution.

In general, it doesn't pay to have your finished image at a higher resolution than that of the device (printer or display) you intend to use as the output for your image.

TAKE NOTE ▶ Problems Displaying Thousands and Millions of Colors

In previous editions of *Sad Macs*, I spent several pages describing how to get your monitor to display colors correctly. Much of this revolved around problems that occur only when the monitor is set to display only 256 colors. (**Note:** You can modify this depth as described earlier in this chapter, via the Monitors control panel and/or Monitor BitDepth Control Strip Module.)

As all current Macs default to at least Thousands of colors, this is almost a dead issue. However, here are two general points still worth noting:

- The ability to display colors at the Thousands or Millions level requires that you have enough video memory to support that color depth. The amount of memory that you need, in turn, depends upon the size of the monitor and the resolution you select. Bigger monitors at higher resolutions require more memory to display at a given color depth. Thus, if a particular color depth option is not available at a specific resolution, it likely means that you do not have enough video memory to display that depth.

  On all current Macs, video memory (VRAM) is separate from the rest of the memory your Mac uses. That is, if your Mac is said to have 128MB of memory, this does not include video memory. In some cases, a Mac will ship with less than the maximum amount of video memory it can accommodate. In this case, you can solve a problem of insufficient VRAM by adding more. If you are already at the maximum, your only other option is to get a separate video card (which usually goes in a PCI slot) to bypass your Mac's video memory and instead use the video memory built-in to the graphics card (which is hopefully a larger amount). Actually, Apple's most recent Macs (such as the G3 and G4 desktop Macs) already take this approach, using a separate PCI or AGP based graphics card rather having video memory included directly on the logic board, as had been done on older Macs. For example, as of this writing, the Power Mac G4 comes with an "ATI RAGE 128 graphics card with 16MB of SDRAM graphics memory installed in a dedicated graphics slot (either a 66-MHz PCI slot or a 133-MHz AGP 2X slot)."

- To get the color of your display to be as accurate as possible, you need to calibrate the display (see "Setting Display Depth and Calibration," earlier in this chapter, for more details).

  SEE: • Fix-It #15 for more on terms such as PCI and AGP.

BY THE WAY ▶ Apple's Color Picker

Many applications and control panels that allow a selection of colors for some item (such as colored text) provide both a preset selection of choices (either via a menu of color names or a palette of colors) plus the ability to select your own color (often via an "Other..." menu choice). If you select this "Other" option, you are sent to Apple's Color Picker. For example, open the Appearance control panel, select the Appearance tab and then access the pop-up menu for "Highlight Color." From here, select "Other..."

Note especially that the Color Picker offers several alternative methods of picking a color. For example, non-technically oriented folks may want to use "Crayon Picker." It's like picking colors from a Crayola crayon box. Those working with Web pages may prefer HTML Picker. It can restrict color choices to those considered "Web safe" (see: "Graphics on the World Wide Web," earlier in this chapter). Two other popular options are RGB Picker and CYMK Picker (see: "Technically Speaking: Professional Color Matching," for more on the meaning of these terms).

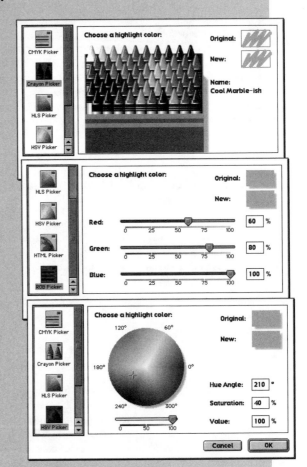

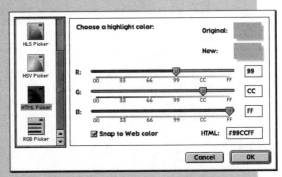

Figure 10-27 Three different ways of picking a color via Apple's Color Picker: crayons (top); RGB sliders (middle) and a HSV wheel (bottom). The second slider option at the very bottom shows the HTML Picker, useful for Web pages.

BY THE WAY ▶ Smoothing Bitmapped Graphics

Bitmapped graphics can be created at a variety of resolutions. Limitations here are mainly dependent upon what your graphics application permits.

However, in many cases, applications (and the Mac OS itself) limit bitmapped graphics to 72 dpi, the resolution traditionally used by monitor displays. This 72 dpi resolution is maintained when the image is printed, even if the printer is capable of a higher resolution. This means that, for example, if a 72 dpi bitmapped image is sent to a 1200 dpi printer, the image will look distinctly inferior (e.g., jagged edges) compared to other text and (non-bitmapped) images on the same page. There is not too much you can do about this. But here's a couple of things to try:

- **Select Smooth Graphics from the PostScript Options of Page Setup**
  If you are using the LaserWriter driver, checking the *Smooth Graphics* option alters the appearance of bitmapped graphics by smoothing out curved lines and reducing jagged edges. This is supposed to improve the appearance of the graphic. However, finely textured artwork may not look any better with this option on. It may even look worse. Similarly, if you selected Color/Grayscale, also selecting Smooth Graphics will probably make things worse. Try it both ways, if in doubt. (**Note:** A *Smooth Text* option offers similar potential improvement for bitmapped fonts).

  The *Precision Bitmap Alignment* (or the related "*Exact Bit Images (Shrink 4%)*" option available in some printers) may also improve the printed appearance of a bitmapped image, especially if you are using a 300 dpi printer. However, in most cases, this option is no longer of significant value.

- **Use Anti-Aliasing**
  Anti-aliasing is a technique that can reduce the jagged edges of objects in bit-mapped graphics, both text and graphics. It can help both for on-screen displays as well as in printed output. Anti-aliasing requires special software (such as Photoshop or a shareware program called Smoothie).

  SEE: • **"Take Note: The Jaggies, Anti-Aliasing, and Related Font Tips," in Chapter 9, for more on anti-aliasing.**

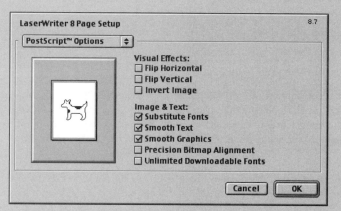

Figure 10-28 The PostScript Options of the LaserWriter Page Setup dialog box (seen after selecting PostScript Options from the pop-up menu near the top of the box).

TAKE NOTE ▶ Solving Monitor problems

Some problems with viewing graphics may not be due to your graphics software or the Mac OS, but are instead directly due to problems with the monitor or display screen. Here is a primer of common problems and solutions:

No display or dimmed display If a monitor shows no sign of life (or is unusually dim), try the following in order:

1. Check that the monitor is on and that the brightness and contrast are turned up. Also make sure that the Mac has not automatically gone to sleep after a period of idle activity, as determined by an Energy Saver setting (see Chapter 11).

2. If the monitor still refuses to show and sign of life, and it is an AppleVision, ColorSync or Studio Display monitor, restart and hold down the Command-Option-A-V keys until the monitor display appears or startup is completed.

3. If this fails, unplug the monitor from the wall outlet for about 30 minutes. Then plug it back in and try again.

4. Zapping the PRAM or resetting the Cuda button (if you Mac has one) may help (as described in Fix-It #9).

5. Otherwise, you probably have a hardware problem with the monitor itself. The monitor will need to be repaired or replaced.

Quality of Display Problems This refers to problems with the quality of the display, rather than the absence of a display.

- **Size and form problems** A display may shrink in size (horizontally or vertically), or the image may start to flicker. This often indicates a power supply problem. For external monitors, the problem is probably with the monitor's power supply. Otherwise, the problem is with the power supply inside the Macintosh. With compact Macintoshes, the built-in monitor and the computer share the same power supply. In any case, if you have a malfunctioning power supply, it needs to be replaced.

- **Color problems and jittery displays** If a color display suddenly shows colored blotches on the screen, it is probably *magnetized*. If your monitor has a *degauss switch,* pressing it should fix this problem. You can often resolve other minor display-size and color problems by adjusting convergence controls, if your monitor has them accessible.

- **Electromagnetic interference** Many display anomalies, such as a jittering display, scrolling horizontal lines or discolorations in the display, can be due to electromagnetic interference (magnets, motors, fluorescent lights and more). If you have such problems, try moving your monitor to a different location. Larger monitors are affected more by these factors than smaller ones.

Screen savers: do you need them? No! Screen savers, such as After Dark, provide some entertainment benefit, but you don't really need them to protect against damage to the monitor. With some older monitors, there was a chance that if the same image was left on the screen for too long, it would cause a permanent "burn in" of the screen image that you could faintly see at all times thereafter. This will not happen with any monitors made in the last several years, and is unlikely even in older monitors.

There is some chance of burn-in on a flat panel display, if you left it on and unattended for weeks!

BY THE WAY ▶ Resolution Shifts at Startup

Depending on the Mac and the display you are using, if you start up with Extensions Off or if you switch the resolutions of the display, the icons on your desktop (that is, those not in any folder) may get all jumbled and re-arranged. When you later revert to your default startup or resolution, the icons may not revert back to their original locations. If you are like me, and keep a lot of icons on your desktop, this can be very irritating.

Fortunately, there are several utilities that help you avoid this problem. Two of my favorites are SwitchRes and Desktop Resetter. For example, with Desktop Resetter, you simply "remember" a particular arrangement. Any time things get messed up, Desktop Resetter can put things back again.

Finally, users occasionally note that, on a given Mac, the resolution may change one or more times during every startup, eventually stopping at the desired resolution. There are various causes of this and there is no guaranteed fix; Apple's official position has been to ignore this as a cosmetic issue that has no impact on the functioning of your Mac.

11

Trouble To Go: Portable Macs and Shared Macs

You *Can* Take It With You

Over the course of four editions, this chapter has undergone more evolution than any other chapter in the book. It began (in the second edition) as a chapter focused on issues unique to Apple's PowerBooks (such as problems with running on battery power). It was then extended to include basic file sharing and networking information (again with the idea that, for most users, connecting a PowerBook to a desktop Mac would be the most common form of file sharing). However, the forces that have guided this chapter have once again shifted considerably.

First, Apple's portables are no longer limited to PowerBooks. The iBook has arrived on the scene.

Second, the gap separating portable Macs from desktop Macs has just about closed. Aside from limited expansion options (you can't put a PCI card into a portable), the capabilities of portable Macs have been bumped up to almost match the feature set of their desktop siblings. And recent desktop Macs (which now include most of the Mac OS software, such as the Control Strip, as well as the hardware, such as optional LCD flat-panel displays, once limited to portables) have narrowed the gap still further. Aside from battery power, there is not much left that is unique to portables.

Similarly, home and small business use of file sharing and networking is no longer primarily limited to portable-to-desktop Mac connections. These days, it is not uncommon for a home to have two or more desktop Macs networked together.

This chapter has been revised to reflect these changes. It still places an emphasis on portable Macs, but any user interested in topics such as Energy Saver, RAM Disks, LCD displays and file sharing will find it worth a look.

Coverage of older PowerBook models (especially ones prior to the PowerPC PowerBooks) has been largely omitted from this edition. On the other hand, coverage of Apple's latest technologies, including the iBook and AirPort wireless connections, has been added.

Portable Mac Basics

This section covers software that is either unique to portables (such as Energy Saver settings for running on battery power) or have special advantages for use with portables (such as RAM Disks).

Control Panels for Portable Macs

Energy Saver

Energy Saver is found in both desktop and portable Macs. However, exactly what you will find when you open it will vary across models. Where differences exist, what we discuss here will be specific to portables.

From the Idle Sleep (also called Sleep Setup) window of Energy Saver, you can select the length of time before the Mac goes to sleep (called "system sleep") or optionally separately select times before the screen dims (called "display sleep") or the hard drive spins down (called "hard disk sleep"). Each of these options save power, which is the main reason to use them.

From the Schedule window, you can select a specific time when you want the computer to automatically wake up or go to sleep. Finally, from Advanced Settings, you may have such options as "Allow processor cycling" (it saves energy at the cost of some speed) or "Turn off the PowerBook display instead of dimming it" (again saving a bit more energy).

In all cases, you can select one set of options for Power Adapter and another for Battery. This allows you to choose settings that will maximize battery life when running on batteries (such as 5 minutes of idle activity until sleep) but have different settings when running from AC power (perhaps selecting for the Mac to never automatically go to sleep).

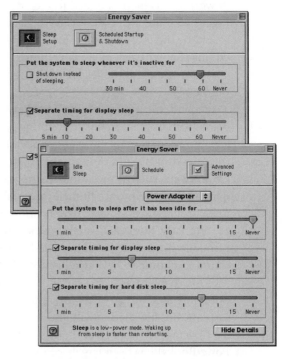

Figure 11-1 Energy saver from an iMac in Mac OS 8.x (top) and from a PowerBook in Mac OS 9 (bottom).

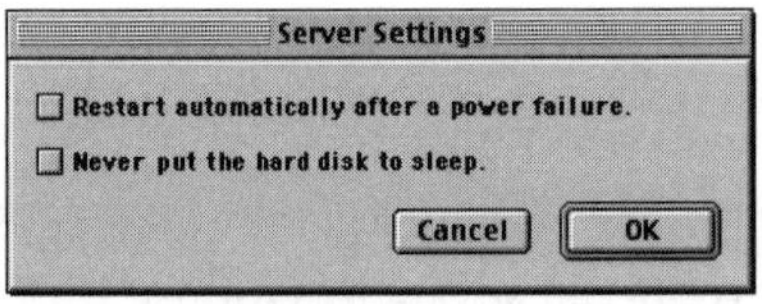

Figure 11-2 Energy Saver's Notification and Server Settings windows from the iMac running Mac OS 8.6.

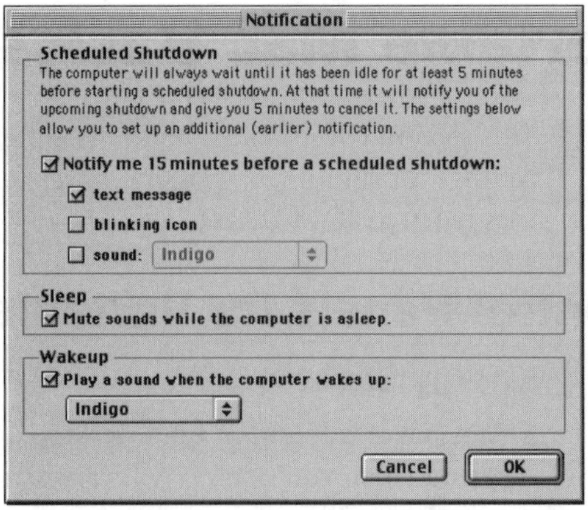

Note: In Mac OS 8.x, Energy Saver included a Preferences menu with two items: Notification and Server Settings. These included several interesting options, including "Restart automatically after a power failure" and "Mute sounds while computer is asleep." In Mac OS 9, this menu has been eliminated in favor of the new "Advanced Settings" Energy Saver panel. While this panel does not contain the options from the old Preferences menu, it has some similar ones, such as "Reconnect to servers on wakeup."

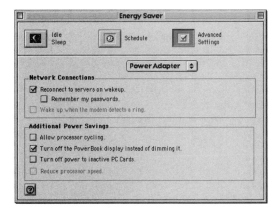

Figure 11-3 Energy Saver's Advanced Settings panel from the PowerBook running Mac OS 9.

BY THE WAY ▶ Bypassing Energy Saver

Despite the obvious utility value of Energy Saver, it has one potentially serious drawback. It has been periodically linked to a host of problems (especially wake-from-sleep crashes). If you want to check whether Energy Saver is a contributing factor to a problem you are having, disable it. However, it is not sufficient to simply disable it via Extensions Manager or a third-party utility such as Conflict Catcher. You must first set the timing of its sleep settings to "Never." Then restart your Mac. You can then disable it. If Energy Saver was causing a problem, the problem should now vanish. If not, leave the settings set to never but do not disable Energy Saver.

If you decide to keep Energy Saver disabled, your next question is likely: "But what about all the great features of the control panel? I don't want to give them up." You don't have to. Use the shareware control panel Sleeper instead. Many users believe Sleeper is superior to Energy Saver even if Energy Saver is working perfectly.

Also note the following statement from Apple: "The Energy Saver sleep settings are not stored in PRAM, they are stored in the Energy Saver Preferences file, located in the Preferences folder within the System Folder. Moving or throwing the Energy Saver Preferences file away and restarting your Macintosh resets the Energy Saver control panel back to the default sleep time of 30 minutes." It will also cause the splash screen that appears the first time you start up with Energy Saver installed to reappear.

TAKE NOTE ▶ Sleep Basics

Putting the Mac to Sleep To put a Mac to sleep, select Sleep from the Finder's Special menu. Alternatively, you can use the Sleep selection in the Control Strip. On some portables, pressing Command-Shift-0 will put the Mac to sleep. So will simply closing its lid.

Waking It Up To wake up a sleeping PowerBook, press any key except Caps Lock (on some models, you must press the Power key). The PowerBook will reawaken almost instantly, returning you to where you left off without requiring you to go through the startup sequence. This is because the RAM content of a PowerBook is maintained while it is asleep. This is a very convenient way to save battery power without having the hassle of a shut down and restart.

 Actually, although the Mac may come to life in an instant when waking up, it may be quite a bit longer before you can actually use it. I find it now takes a minute or longer before the Mac is fully re-awakened, partially diminishing the advantage of the Sleep option.

Why Shut Down When You Can Sleep Instead? When you don't plan on using your PowerBook for a while, an obvious alternative to Sleep is to Shut Down (via the Shut Down command in the Finder's Special menu). But why bother with it? Shut Down means that all open applications are quit, all contents of RAM (including RAM disk contents) may be lost, and that you will have to wait to go through a potentially long startup sequence the next time you restart.

 You can travel with your PowerBook just as well while it is in Sleep mode as when it is Shut Down. You can even safely connect and disconnect cables (such as modem and printer cables) while in Sleep mode (although you need to shut down to connect a Duo to a Duo Dock).

 In fact, the only clear advantage of shutting down a PowerBook, rather than using Sleep, is that a shut down PowerBook drains less battery power than one that is asleep. Shutting down thus makes some sense if you don't expect to use your PowerBook for at least several days and do not have your PowerBook plugged into a wall outlet.

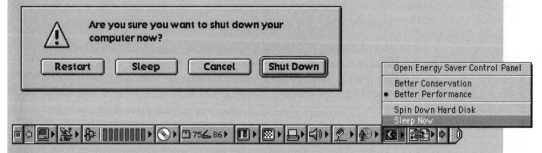

Figure 11-4 Selecting Sleep from the window that appears when you press the Power button (top) and from the Energy Saver Control Strip Module (bottom). You can also select Sleep from the Finder's Special menu.

BY THE WAY ▶ Energy Saver Miscellany

Here are some tips for solving a collection of unusual symptoms related to Energy Saver. They refer primarily to the version of Energy Saver included in Mac OS 8.x. Your mileage may vary.

Can't Get the Hard Drive to Spin Down If your hard disk refuses to spin down at the time interval selected in the Energy Saver's main window, go to Server Settings Preferences and make sure that "Never put the hard disk to sleep" is unchecked. If it is checked, spin down is prevented, despite any other settings to the contrary.

Mac Restarts Instead of Shutting Down If your Mac keeps restarting every time you select to Shut Down, go again to Server Settings Preferences and make sure that "Restart automatically after a power failure" is unchecked. If it is checked, it will likely cause the Mac to restart after any sort of shut down.

Sleep from Energy Saver vs. Sleep from Finder's Special Menu If you do set your Mac to go to sleep automatically via Energy Saver, it may be a different sleep than you get via selecting the Sleep command from the Finder. If you use the Finder's Sleep command, the monitor shuts off completely (the indicator light on the monitor goes off). However, if you wait for the Energy Saver to automatically put the Mac to sleep, it only darkens the screen (the indicator light stays on and pressing a keyboard key brings the screen instantly back).

Persistent Mute If your Mac's sound suddenly goes mute (such as when waking up from Sleep or after a restart), the Energy Saver control panel may be at fault. To possibly solve the problem, select its Notification Preferences and uncheck "Mute sounds while the computer is asleep."

Control Strip

All Macs, not just portables, now include a Control Strip (see "Take Note: Control Strip Basics"). However, a few Control Strip Modules only appear on portables. Most notable is Battery Monitor. It tells you whether or not you are running on battery power and how much battery time you have left. Different models of PowerBook have different variations on this battery display.

If you get Jeremy's CSMs (a popular shareware package), you will find Jeremy's Temperature CSM. It tells you the internal and battery temperature of your portable.

TAKE NOTE ▶ Control Strip Basics

What Is the Control Strip? The Control Strip control panel creates a strip of buttons (called Control Strip Modules or CSMs) that stay on the screen at all times. To use a module, click it and hold down the mouse button; a pop-up menu of choices will appear.

What buttons appear on your Control Strip depends upon what modules are stored in the Control Strip Modules folder inside your System Folder. When you first install the Control Strip, it comes with Apple's basic set of modules. These modules include ones for displaying color depth and resolution (as mentioned in Chapter 10) and changing your default printer (a topic covered in Chapter 7). There are also modules for toggling AppleTalk, connecting online via Remote Access, enabling File Sharing, adjusting the Mac's volume, accessing the Apple CD Player and more. Several control panels, such as Energy Saver, have a Control Strip Module counterpart that you can use to open the control panel or (even more convenient) instantly access a subset of the control panel's features. For example, from the Energy Saver CSM, you can spin down the hard disk or select sleep.

(continues on next page)

TAKE NOTE ▶ Control Strip Basics *(continued)*

There are also various third-party CSMs that add new features to the Control Strip. For example, I particularly like Alsoft's Open Files; it tells you how many files are open on your Mac. Similarly, many applications now include a CSM as part of their package. As with the Energy Saver CSM, these application CSMs allow you to access a subset of the application's features directly from the Control Strip.

Finally, there are a few modules specific to portable Macs, as covered here in the main text.

Moving and Resizing the Control Strip If the Control Strip is in your way but you still want to have it readily available, you can collapse it to just a little tab by clicking its close box (on the strip's left side) or its tab (on the right side). Clicking the tab reopens the strip again. You can resize the strip by click-dragging the tab to the left or right, or move the entire strip to another screen location by click-dragging the tab while holding down the Option key. If the strip has more buttons than it can display at once, click the scroll arrows to see the other buttons.

The Control Strip Control Panel The Control Strip control panel (which is separate from the strip itself) offers only a few options, mainly whether or not to display the Control Strip at all.

What About the "Mirroring" Control Strip Modules? Some modules appear only in certain circumstances. For example, PowerBook G3 Series Macs include an S-Video output port for using a TV as an external display. In this case, the TV Mirroring CSM will appear. Alternatively, if you have a traditional external monitor connected via the video output port, the Video Mirroring CSM will appear. In both cases, these CSMs can toggle "mirroring" on and off. When mirroring is on, what you see on the PowerBook display is also what you see on the external display. With mirroring off, the external display can be used as an extension of the PowerBook display, effectively increasing your display real estate.

Location Manager

Do you use your portable in more than one location? Most likely yes. That's one of the reasons to get a portable, after all. If you do, you will likely find that various settings on your Mac need to be changed from one location to another. For example, perhaps you connect to the Internet via a cable modem at home but need to connect via a 56K modem when you travel. Or perhaps you change your default printer when you go from home to work.

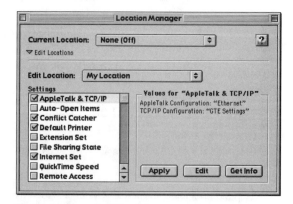

Figure 11-5 Location Manager.

Whatever. The Location Manager control panel allows you to select settings for these options and more and save them as a Location Manager set. You can then switch sets, automatically changing a dozen or so settings all at once. Quite convenient.

Password Security

You won't find the Password Security control panel on all portables. If you do have it, it is a simple utility that, when turned on, requires a password before you can access the Mac when starting up or waking from sleep.

Don't forget your password! If you forget your password, there is no way to bypass it and startup your PowerBook, because the password is written to your drive at the driver level. Even starting from a floppy disk or CD won't work. The only option, according to Apple, is to "take your PowerBook with your proof of purchase (receipt) to an authorized Apple service center where a technician has the means to bypass the security on the system."

One warning: this control panel no longer works in Apple's FireWire PowerBook G3 models. If you try to use it, you will no longer be able to restart your Mac and the drive itself may ultimately need to be replaced.

PowerBook Target Disk Mode

PowerBooks with SCSI ports built in have an option for SCSI Target Disk Mode. With Apple's newest PowerBooks, which have FireWire ports instead of SCSI ports, there is a FireWire-based Target Disk Mode. In either case, this feature allows a PowerBook to be connected to another Mac (SCSI-to-

Figure 11-6 Power Book SCS Disk Mode control panel.

SCSI or FireWire-to-FireWire), as if the PowerBook were an external hard drive. For SCSI connections, a SCSI Disk Mode control panel lets you assign a SCSI ID number to the PowerBook, for when you use this type of setup.

SEE: • **"Transfer Files via an External Drive"**

Portable Mac Battery Conservation

Other than their small size, the single most distinguishing feature about PowerBooks and iBooks is that they can run on batteries. Batteries, though, have a big problem: they can run out of power. If you expect to be away from a convenient power source for any length of time (on an airplane, for instance), conserving battery power becomes a primary concern. Fortunately, there are a wide assortment of battery conservation options. The more of these features you use, the better your battery savings will be.

Use Features That Conserve Battery Power

- **Energy Saver features** Put the Mac to sleep when not using it. Select to spin down the hard drive or dim the screen if you don't want the Mac to go fully to sleep but still want to save some energy during an idle period. If you have a lot of memory and set the Memory control panel's disk cache setting relatively high, you may even be able to work for quite awhile while the hard drive is spun down. However, every time you select to save anything, the hard drive will spin up again.

- **AC power** Use an AC outlet instead of battery power whenever possible.

- **RAM disks** Using a RAM disk helps minimize battery-draining access to the hard drive.

    SEE: • **"Using RAM Disks," later in this chapter, for details.**

- **External battery** Several companies market batteries that attach to the PowerBook (via the AC jack) and thereby extend the time (usually at least doubling it) before you run out of battery power.

Don't Use Features That Especially Drain Battery Power

- **Turn AppleTalk off** This assumes that you don't need it on for any reason. For example, if you were using file sharing, you would want it on.

- **Turn off File Sharing** Turning off File Sharing also saves battery power. Do this from the Sharing Setup control panel by clicking the Stop button in the File Sharing middle section. If the button says Start, file sharing is already off.

- **Don't use virtual memory** If you have enough memory to spare, turn off virtual memory (via the Memory control panel) if you plan to run on battery power. Using virtual memory increases access to the hard disk, one of the bigger eaters of battery power.

- **Turn modem off: Quit communications software** Quit all telecommunications software that you are not using. The modem is on and draining power as long as a telecommunications program is open, even if you are not connected online.

- **Turn down sound volume** Playing sound uses battery power. Keep volume as low as is feasible. Turn it off altogether if you don't need it. You can do all this from the Sound control panel or the Control Strip.

- **Use a "white" desktop pattern** On flat-panel displays, a screen pixel is "on" if it is dark. "On" pixels require more energy than "off" ones. Because your Finder's desktop pattern is frequently on the screen, you can probably save a little power by using a pattern of mostly "off" pixels. You choose the pattern via the Appearance control panel.

Running Out of Battery Power

As you start running low on battery power, a series of messages will appear on the screen (such as "You are now running on reserve power and your screen has dimmed, Very little of the battery's reserve power remains"). Each succeeding message means you have less time until the PowerBook will automatically go to sleep. At the same time, a battery icon should begin flashing over the Apple icon in the menubar. If you can, plug in the power adapter immediately after the first message. This puts a stop to the messages and (once you put the Mac to sleep) starts recharging the battery. Otherwise, if you continue to work on battery power, save your work frequently.

If you ignore all these warnings and wait until the Macintosh finally is forced to sleep, you have about one to two days to get AC power to the PowerBook and recharge the battery before the battery is totally out of juice. If you wait until this happens, the Mac will need to be restarted from scratch after you recharge the battery; any unsaved data will be lost. If you recharge sooner, the PowerBook will wake up where it left off, as after any other Sleep.

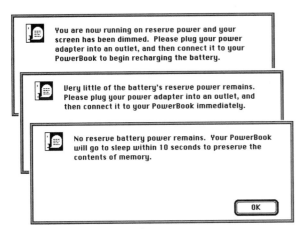

Figure 11-7 Messages that progressively appear as you run low on battery power (the exact messages on your portable Mac may vary from these; but you get the idea).

Figure 11-8 The battery icon that appears in the menubar, over the Apple icon, when battery power is low.

Using RAM Disks

Create and Use a RAM Disk

With the right software, your PowerBook can be "fooled" into thinking that a portion of its RAM is actually a physical disk. This RAM disk appears on the desktop with its own icon, just like any other disk. You can then, for example, copy applications to the RAM disk and launch them just as if they were launched from your hard drive.

RAM Disk

Figure 11-9 A RAM disk icon on the desktop.

You already own the software you need to create a RAM disk: it's the Memory control panel. To use it, just click the On button in the RAM disk section of the control panel and use the slider to adjust how large you want the RAM disk to be. Then restart and presto: your RAM disk will appear.

You will not be able to make changes to the Memory control panel settings for an existing RAM disk while files are on the disk or if file sharing is enabled.

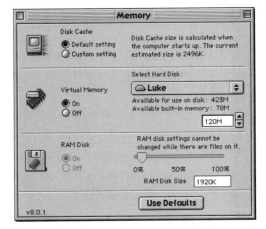

SEE: • Fix-It #5 for more details on creating and removing RAM disks.

Figure 11-10 The RAM disk settings at the bottom of the Memory control panel.

Why RAM Disks?

An important advantage of a RAM disk for PowerBook users is to save battery power. The more the PowerBook can access information from the RAM disk, rather than the hard drive, the longer the hard drive can remain "spinned down" and the less the hard drive will consume battery power. Because RAM disk access is many times faster than hard disk access, you also get a significant speed boost by doing anything from the RAM disk that would have otherwise been done from your hard drive.

The main disadvantage of using a RAM disk, of course, is that it takes up RAM. Unless you have a lot of RAM installed, you may find that you cannot create a reasonably sized RAM disk and still have enough RAM left over to open the applications you want to run. This is because, even though an application copied to a RAM disk is in RAM, it still additionally requires the same amount of RAM to run as it would ordinarily need.

However, when running an application from a RAM disk, you *can* often lower its memory allocation from its Preferred size to closer to its Minimum size and still not see any speed decrement, because, while lower memory allocations typically mean more frequent access to the disk, the disk in this case is RAM, not the slower hard disk! You change an application's memory allocation from its Get Info window.

SEE: • **Chapter 2 and Fix-It #5 for more on the Get Info window.**

Making a RAM Startup Disk; Not Anymore

There are several situations where it would be advantageous to make a RAM Disk serve as a startup disk. For starters, doing this would further reduce access to the hard drive, eliminating all the hard drive access due to calls to System Folder files. It would also be convenient for certain situations when you want to use a repair utility to repair your startup disk, but the utility claims it is unable to repair the current startup disk. The typical solution here is to startup from the bootable CD that usually comes with these utilities. But this may no longer have the latest version of the repair utility (which you downloaded from the Web). A solution would be to place the updated version on a bootable RAM disk and use that instead of the bootable CD.

However, there are two obstacles to doing this. First, with recent versions of the OS, the minimal size of a System Folder needed to place on the RAM Disk is so large that you likely would not have enough RAM to do it.

Second, and more serious, because of changes in the type of RAM used in Apple's recent Macs (including all Macs that shipped with a G3 or G4 processor, except for certain G3 PowerBook models), the option to create a startup RAM disk no longer exists.

More specifically, the startup disk option depended on another now missing feature of RAM Disks. In older Macs, if you did a warm restart (that is, if you selected Restart from the Finder's Special menu), a presently mounted RAM Disk and its contents would be retained in memory. This is what allowed it to be selected as a startup disk from the Startup Disk control panel. However, this ability is no longer present in G3 Macs and newer Macs. The contents of a RAM Disk are now lost with a Restart. As Apple states: "With the SDRAM used in these Macs, the length of time between restart can exceed the period which SDRAM can retain its contents without refresh. Hence the SDRAM can be corrupted and thus result in a corrupted RAM disk after reset. The design choice was to not preserve the RAM disk across restarts."

Given the emphasis on newer hardware and software in this edition of Sad Macs, I have thus decided to largely omit further discussion of this dying capability.

Saving the Contents of Your RAM Disk After a Restart

If you have a pre-G3 Mac, it is likely that it can preserve the contents of a RAM disk when you restart—even if you restart using the reset button after a system crash. However, note that when you select Shut Down, you *will* lose the contents of your RAM disk. In fact, you will normally get a message warning you about this, and asking if you are sure you want to Shut Down.

SEE: • "Technically Speaking: An 'Unreadable' RAM Disk"

But what if you have a newer Mac that does not support the feature to save a RAM disk's contents at Restart? Don't despair. You may still be able to save the contents of

your RAM disk at Restart or Shut Down via the "Save on Shut Down" option in the RAM disk section of the Memory control panel of most newer Macs. This saves the contents of the disk to your hard drive, where it is read and reloaded the next time you start up (you'll even see the cursor change to a RAM disk icon briefly after selecting to Shut

Figure 11-11 Your RAM disk's contents may be lost if you click OK here.

Down; this indicates the contents of the RAM disk are being saved). However, the current contents of the disk will not be saved by this method if you are forced to restart as the result of a system crash, as the normal shut down sequence where the contents of the disk are written to the hard drive would not occur. In this case, when you startup again, you will load the contents that were saved at the last normal shut down.

The RAM disk contents are saved in a file in your Preferences folder called Persistent RAM Disk. The more information stored on your RAM Disk, the larger this file will become.

Despite all of these savings options, it remains solid advice that you should never keep documents on your RAM disk that are not backed up elsewhere. There is too high a risk that the files could be lost if something unexpected occurs (such as a system crash).

Also note that zapping the PRAM at startup will erase any contents of a RAM disk that would have otherwise been preserved in RAM.

SEE: • **"Restarting a PowerBook After a System Error," later in this chapter, for more details.**
  • **Chapter 4 for more general information on restarting after a system error.**

TAKE NOTE ▶ Mounting A RAM Disk When Starting Up From a CD

Here's a great solution to a common troubleshooting problem. Suppose you want to run Utility X (a disk repair or a disk optimizing utility, for example). However, you can not use it on the startup drive or the drive that contains the utility. Unfortunately, your current startup drive contains the utility: a double whammy. Even if you could start up from a bootable CD, your problems are not over unless the CD also contains the needed utility. If you have a Zip drive or some other external storage (or even a partitioned hard drive), you could work around this by placing the needed utility on the alternative location (as explained more in Chapter 2 and Chapter 5). But suppose you don't. Are you just out of luck?

Nope. Here's what to do:

1. Startup normally from your internal drive. Create a RAM Disk

2. Restart, starting up from any bootable CD, such as the Mac OS CD that came with your Mac.

3. The RAM Disk will *not* appear yet. However, launch Disk First Aid. You will see the RAM Disk listed as a volume that cam be verified and/or repaired.

4. Click the RAM Disk icon. From the Options menu, select "Erase Disk...".

5. Select to Initialize or Erase the disk by clicking the button.

6. The RAM Disk will now mount. You can now copy the needed utility to the RAM Disk and run it from there.

TECHNICALLY SPEAKING ▶ An "unreadable" RAM disk

For those of you that still have a Mac that preserves the contents of a RAM Disk after a Restart, here are a few tips:

- With some Macs, every time you shut down, if there are any files on the RAM disk, you will get an alert message warning that the contents of the RAM disk volume will be lost if you shut down. The Mac OS provides no way to prevent this message from appearing, which can be annoying if you want to select Shut Down and then walk away without waiting to respond to the message. There are a few solutions here. The best is to get a utility called RAMShush. Install it and the message is bypassed.

Figure 11-12 An "unreadable" RAM disk. This message usually does not mean that anything is wrong; it may happen when you start up with extensions off.

- If you select Restart (from the Finder's Special menu) and then start up with extensions off (by holding down the Shift key at startup), don't worry about your RAM disk. The RAM disk may or may not appear when startup is over. However, when you then Restart again normally, the RAM disk will be back with its prior contents still intact.

- However, here's a strange situation: you shut down (not restart!). The next time you start up, you do so with extensions off. As startup is completed, you will get a message saying that the RAM disk is "unreadable" and asking if you want to initialize it. If you click Initialize, a new RAM disk is created. If you click Cancel, the RAM disk will not appear at all for that session. In either case, the prior contents are of course lost–unless your Mac supports the "Save on Shutdown" option and you had it enabled.

- Otherwise, if after first setting up a RAM disk you get the message that says *"This (RAM) disk is unreadable by this Macintosh. Do you want to initialize the disk?"*, it probably means that you need to decrease the size of the RAM disk. Experiment until you find a size that works.

Solve It! Basic Portable Mac Problems

Restarting a Portable Mac After a System Error

 Symptoms:

A system crash, system freeze, or other system error has occurred that requires that you restart your PowerBook. You are having trouble figuring out how to do this.

 Causes:

Most causes are the same for PowerBooks as for any other Macintosh. This section focuses specifically on those techniques and problems that are unique to PowerBooks, especially solving the basic problem of just restarting the PowerBook. Some of these techniques were briefly mentioned in Chapter 4, but they are covered in more detail here.

 What to Do:

Restart the PowerBook. Simply said, but not always so simply done. After each step described here, see if the PowerBook successfully restarts. If not, go on to the next step. The last step considers what to do if the system error recurs after a successful restart.

Try the Finder's Restart or Shut Down Menu Commands

Doing this is called a *soft restart* or *soft shut down*. On most recent PowerBook, you can also press the Power button to bring up the alert box that asks if you want to Restart or Shut Down. After most types of system errors, these probably will not work, but give them a try.

Press the Reset Button or Reset Keyboard Combination

- On most recent PowerBooks, you do this by pressing the Command-Control-Power keyboard buttons at the same time (though this may not work after some particularly nasty system crashes).

- On other portable Macs, including the iBook, there is a physical Reset button that can be pressed. In some portable Macs, you will need an unbent paper clip to access it (just like on some desktop Macs, as described in Chapter 4).

- For further information specific to your particular portable Mac, check the documentation that came with it.

Do a Hard Shut Down

Some older PowerBooks had an additional way to shut down if the previous techniques fail. It was called a hard shut down, as opposed to the normal Finder-level soft shut down. With a hard shut down, the normal cleaning up of files and saving to disk that would otherwise have occurred is skipped. In this sense, it is similar to doing a

Reset, except it would work in some cases where a reset would not. The method to get a hard shut down varied with different PowerBook models. In many cases (such as the PowerBook 160 and 180), the method was to hold down the Power button (the same button used to turn on the Mac ordinarily) for several seconds. Pressing this button when the Mac was working normally was the equivalent of a soft shutdown. It is only after a system crash that it worked as a hard shutdown.

In other cases (such as the PowerBook 5300), the method was to press the Power and Reset button at the same time. Because the 500 series PowerBooks have no on/off button, if you can't get a 500 series PowerBook to reset after a system crash, try pressing Command-Option-Control-Power On. If this fails, your only alternative is to remove the batteries and disconnect AC power temporarily. Again, for further specifics, check with the documentation that came with your PowerBook. Apple's newest PowerBooks and iBooks no longer appear to support any separate hard shutdown.

Reset the Power Manager

This is a last resort that should only rarely be necessary to solve a system crash problem (it is more commonly used for battery-related problems, as described in the next section). Still, here are the basic instructions (which unfortunately can and do vary for nearly every portable Mac).

1. Shut down the PowerBook or iBook (not just put it to sleep).

2. Disconnect the power adapter and remove the battery. Let the PowerBook sit for at least 5 minutes. On some portable Macs, removing the battery is not required to reset the Power Manager. But if in doubt, play it safe and remove it. (Actually this step alone should reset the Power Manager on some PowerBooks.) In more recent PowerBooks, such as the G3 Series, you should be able to reset the Power Manager even with the battery in place.

3. Reset the Power Manager. Exactly how to do this step varies with different models of portable Macs. Here are some selected examples (for complete details, check the Apple Tech Info Library article at this URL: *http://til.info.apple.com/techinfo.nsf/art-num/n14449*).

   On a PowerBook 100, 140, 145, or 170 Press and hold the Reset and Interrupt buttons for at least 30 seconds (on all but the 100, you'll need two unbent paper clips to do this rather awkward procedure).

   On any other 100 series PowerBook (except the 190) and 200 and 2300 series Duos Press the Power button on the rear of the machine and hold it for at least 30 seconds. On Duos, some people have claimed that you should simultaneously press both the Power button on the rear of the machine and the Power key on the keyboard. Try it.

On the original PowerBook G3 series Simultaneously press the Shift, Fn (function), Ctrl (control), and Power keys. Wait at least 5 seconds before trying to turn the PowerBook back on (this is important or the reset procedure may not work).

On the PowerBook G3 Series (Bronze Keyboard) Press the reset button on the rear of the computer (it's located between the external video and modem (RJ-11) ports). Wait at least 5 seconds before trying to turn the PowerBook back on (this is important or the reset procedure may not work).

On the iBook Press the reset button located above the power button at the base of the display. You will need an unbent paper clip to press the button. Wait at least 5 seconds before trying to turn the iBook back on. This procedure will cause the date and time to be lost, so you'll need to reset them.

On the FireWire PowerBooks If the computer is on, turn it off. Press the reset button located on the rear panel of the computer between the external video and modem ports. Wait five seconds. Press the power button to restart the computer. This procedure will cause the date and time to be lost, so you'll need to reset them.

4. If you removed them, reinsert the battery, plug in the power adapter (if desired), and turn the Mac on. Hope that your problem is gone.

5. If you still cannot get the Mac to start up successfully, remove the battery again and wait at least 15 minutes before you try the above procedures. Some people claim that you should leave the battery out overnight to be certain that the procedure has succeeded.

    For some PowerBooks, in addition, you may need to remove the internal back-up battery (see "Take Note: What Is the Power Manager?") and let it sit for at least one minute. This is guaranteed to reset the Power Manager. However, although doing this is not that difficult, accessing the backup battery may require opening up the PowerBook case. You may not want to do this yourself. For specifics, consult your PowerBook's manual or simply take your PowerBook to an authorized service provider.

6. Check your Energy Saver control panel. You will have to redo any customized changes you may have made there (because resetting the Power Manager reverts those settings to their default values).

    SEE: • **"Problems Running on Battery Power," later in this chapter, for another situation where you need to reset the Power Manager.**
    • **Chapter 4 for more on reset buttons, power buttons, and what to do to solve system error problems**

BY THE WAY ▶ A Possible Shortcut For Resetting The Power Manager

There is a freeware utility called ResetPwrMgr that, when launched, resets the Power Manager. It saves you the trouble of having to figure out and remember how to do it for your particular model of PowerBook (and with all of the different methods, no one finds it easy to keep it all straight!). The only downside is that it restarts the Mac without the proper checking that is done when you select the Finder's Restart or Shut Down commands. But this is no worse than what happens when you restart after a system crash.

I am not certain if this program works for the latest PowerBook and iBook models. And, of course, it is only useful if your problem is not so serious that it prevents you from starting up your portable.

TAKE NOTE ▶ What is the Power Manager? (And One Reason It May Get Corrupted)

The Power Manager is hardware, sort of like a little microprocessor, located on a portable's logic board (actually all Macs now have some form of Power Manager). It is used to control most battery- and power-related operations. The Power Manager also maintains some information in memory (such as the time settings used by the PowerBook control panel for automatic sleep and screen dimming). This information is preserved, even when there is no AC or main battery power, via the PowerBook's internal backup battery. This small battery is also used to maintain the contents of the PRAM, as a similar battery is used in all Macintosh models.

SEE: • Fix-It #9.

Similarly to what can happen with the PRAM, the Power Manager data can get corrupted. The most common result of this corruption is an inability to start up a PowerBook. Oddly, this may happen even if you are running on AC power. Corrupted Power Manager data may also cause a variety of other symptoms, such as a battery that takes an unusually long time to recharge.

Apple notes the following: "While there are several reasons a PowerBook may need its power manager circuitry reset, most of which involve some kind of power interruption to the unit, there is one very common cause - improper use of the AC Adapter. The PowerBook Power Manager circuitry is most often "corrupted" by the AC Adapter not being plugged into the PowerBook in the proper order. The AC Adapter should *always* be plugged into the AC (wall) outlet before it is plugged into the PowerBook itself. If you are using a power surge protector bar, make sure the power bar is powered on (usually has some kind of indicator light) before you plug the PowerBook AC Adapter into it. Also never turn off the power to the PowerBook by turning off the power bar's switch."

The solution to all of these problems is to reset the Power Manager data (as described in the main text here). For portables, resetting the Power Manager is one of those generic fix-it procedures, much like zapping the PRAM. It may fix many problems beyond the ones specifically mentioned here.

In the worst case, hardware damage to the Power Manager may cause these same symptoms. Fixing this will require a trip to the repair shop.

If the System Error Recurs After a Successful Restart

Try zapping the PRAM. If this fails, consider more general causes and solutions (especially extensions conflicts).

SEE: • Chapter 4 for more general information on system errors.
   • Fix-It #3 on extension conflicts.
   • Fix-It #9 on zapping the PRAM.

Problems Running on Battery Power

 Symptoms:

- After following procedures to recharge a battery, the battery remains uncharged.

- The battery indicator in the Control Strip (or other similar utility) indicates that the battery is nearly out of power even though you just recharged it.

- The battery successfully charges but then drains its charge much more rapidly than expected.

- The portable Mac will not start up at all with battery power but works normally when using AC power.

 Causes:

- The power adapter may be defective or not plugged in correctly. Or it may be the wrong power adapter for your portable Mac.

- The battery may have had a "deep discharge."

- The battery may be dead, or nearly so, and need to be replaced. This is especially likely if the battery either never successfully recharges or loses its charge very rapidly.

- The Power Manager's data may have become corrupted.

- A corrupted PRAM may also cause these symptoms.

- Finally, you may be using your portable Mac in a way that excessively drains battery power.

 What to Do:

Use Battery Conservation Features

If your battery is simply losing power faster than it typically has in the past and if all battery and charger operations otherwise seem normal, you may be using your portable Mac in a way that drains battery power excessively fast, such as using virtual memory or a modem.

SEE: • **"PowerBook Battery Conservation," earlier in this chapter, for details.**

Check for Power Adapter Problems

The typical way to recharge a battery is to use the power adapter. Just connect it to your PowerBook and you are automatically recharging, even as you continue to use the PowerBook (though using it will lengthen the time needed to recharge). If the portable is asleep or shut down, recharging should only take about 2 to 3 hours. If the power adapter doesn't seem to be doing its job, check for the following possibilities:

- Check that the power adapter plugs are correctly and fully inserted at both the portable Mac end and the wall outlet end.

- Check that the power outlet is working. For example, a wall outlet connected to a wall switch will not work if the wall switch is in the off position.

  Don't trust the on-screen icons as a reliable indicator of a charging battery. For example, the lightning bolt icon (indicating a charging battery) in the Control Strip appears as soon as you plug the adapter into the portable, even if the power outlet end is not plugged into anything! (Eventually, if this condition persists, the portable will figure out it has almost no power left and will inform you of this!)

- Remove the power adapter from its power source, wait briefly, then plug it back in. This may correct a problem with the charger stuck in trickle mode.

- Be sure you are using the power adapter that came with your portable Mac or another compatible one obtained from Apple. Using any other adapter may not work and may potentially damage your Mac.

- If possible, check whether the power adapter itself may be broken. Do this by trying to charge the battery with another adapter. If you succeed, this means that the original adapter is broken.

Check for a Dead, Incorrect, or Incorrectly Installed Battery

If your battery will not hold a charge, it may be dead or nearly so. How long a battery lasts depends upon what type of battery you have, how often you use it, and how much demand you place on it when you use it. However, expect it to last for at least 500 charges. Under normal use, this may be expected to take about two years. The solution for a dead battery is to replace it.

While you are at it, check that the battery is installed correctly, following the instructions in your Mac's documentation. Sometimes, an improperly installed battery may be the total cause of your problem.

Also make sure you have the right type of battery for your Mac. Different models of PowerBooks use different types of batteries. Older PowerBooks used NicCad batteries. Later, Apple switched to NiMH batteries. Apple's newest portables use Lithium-Ion batteries.

Even with the same type of battery, different Mac models may use different styles. With different PowerBook, and different battery types, also come different AC adapters. Make sure you are using the right types for your Mac.

Reset the Power Manager

See the previous section, "Restarting a PowerBook After a System Error," for details on how to do this.

Portable Mac Appears Dead

 Symptoms:

- Whether operating on battery power or with the power adapter, the portable Mac shows no sign of life. You cannot even get it to turn on and begin a startup sequence.

 Causes:

- The battery and/or power adapter may be damaged and need to be replaced.

- The Power Manager data may be corrupted.

- If neither of the above, the cause is probably a general one not specific to PowerBooks.

 What to Do:

Check the Battery and Power Adapter

Try another battery, if available. Try a different power adapter, if available. If either of these fix the problem, your old battery may be dead or damaged or your power adapter may be damaged. Replace them.

Reset the Power Manager

Though primarily associated with problems specific to running on battery power, problems here may prevent you from running on AC power as well.

SEE: • **"Restarting a PowerBook After a System Error," for details on this topic.**

Try More General Solutions

Check Chapter 5 ("The Macintosh Is Dead") for other more general possibilities. As a last resort, take the PowerBook in for repair. You may have a damaged Power Manager or other serious problem.

Figure 11-13 The "Preserve Memory contents on sleep" option in the Energy Saver control panel on an iBook.

TAKE NOTE ▶ The iBook and Preserving Memory Contents on Sleep and Restart

Preserve Memory Contents on Sleep In the Advanced Settings panel of the Energy Saver control panel is an option called "Preserve memory contents on sleep." Normally, this is not needed, as the RAM contents are preserved during sleep anyway. The option functions as an additional safety measure, in case all power to the iBook is lost during sleep (which *would* result in the RAM contents being lost). If this option is enabled, the iBook creates an invisible file called Memory Contents on your hard drive and uses it to store the information currently in RAM. If the iBook is awakened normally, this information is restored to RAM. This will require a few more seconds before waking from sleep is completed. If power is completely lost, and you need to restart, the stored information is used to bring you back to where you were when you put the iBook to sleep. Virtual memory must be enabled to use this feature. The FireWire PowerBooks also have this same "Preserve Memory" feature. One potential pitfall here: if the stored contents get corrupted somehow, it can prevent the iBook from waking up or starting up at all. In this case, you will need to restart the iBook and hold down the Escape key until you see the Happy Mac icon. The stored RAM contents are lost when you do this, but the startup should then proceed normally.

Working Around the Lack of a Backup Battery Suppose you are on an airplane and you run out of battery power for your iBook. Fortunately, you have a fully charged spare battery ready to swap with the now discharged one. Great! Or is it?

Unlike all previous Macs, the iBook does not have an internal backup battery (the one that is used to store your PRAM settings). However, there is a small capacitor which will maintain the system clock for approximately 10 minutes. For starters, this means that, when swapping batteries, you should have the iBook connected to AC power; otherwise, all RAM contents will be lost. Even worse, if you go without battery or AC power for more than 10 minutes, all PRAM data may be lost—especially the date and time information (there is still some ambiguity about exactly what gets lost at what time).

A solution here is to make sure that "Preserve memory contents on sleep" is selected. Then put the iBook to sleep and swap the battery. When you next press the power button to wake the iBook from sleep, you will be returned to where you were prior to putting it to sleep.

Otherwise, if you do not have access to AC power, it is best to shut down the iBook before swapping the battery.

Note: On most other PowerBooks, you can safely swap batteries after putting the Mac to sleep. On Apple's oldest PowerBooks, you had to shut down the Mac before you could swap batteries.

Avoid the Reset Button if Possible As it turns out, this is not the only way in which you can unexpectedly lose your PRAM data. Using the Reset button (as may sometimes be needed to restart the iBook after a system crash) also results in most or all of your PRAM data vanishing. Because of this, always first try to use the Command-Control-Power combination to restart the iBook, as this preserves the PRAM contents.

This same situation exists for the PowerBook G3 series (Bronze keyboard).

TAKE NOTE ▶ Deep Discharge and Related Battery Problems

Deep Discharge Apple described a problem specific to the PowerBook G3 Series (Bronze keyboard), but it may apply to other portables as well. The problem is that the battery may go into a deep discharge state if the battery has been left in the computer for an extended period of time without AC power. This means that the battery has discharged to the point where it is no longer recognized by the PowerBook. You will know this has happened if a red X appears through the battery icon in the menu bar.

You can avoid a deep discharge by doing one of the following:

- Recharging the battery when only one of the four green LEDs (Light Emitting Diodes) on the battery is on, or shows one green LED blinking.
- Fully charging the battery and then removing it from the PowerBook for storage.

If you fall victim to a deep discharge problem:

1. Insert the battery in either bay and leave it there for approximately 30 seconds.
2. After 30 seconds, release the battery and pull it out so that it protrudes from the bay approximately one inch; you do not need to fully remove the battery from the bay.
3. Leave the battery extended for several seconds then reinsert the battery for another 30-second interval.
4. Repeat this as many times as needed (10 or 12 times is possible) until the red X no longer appears. The battery should then be able to recharge as normal.
   In general, you will see a lightning bolt symbol on the battery icon in the menu bar and in the Control Strip, when it is charging. When the bolt disappears, the battery is fully charged.
   A Lithium-Ion battery (as used in Apple's newest portables) should take about 2 hours to fully recharge when in sleep mode or when shut down. If the computer is running, the charge time doubles to approximately 4 hours.

Battery Reset Alternatively, for this or any other reason that the battery does not appear to be recognized, use Apple's Battery Reset utility (available from the Apple web site). Running the utility should eliminate the problem.

External Battery Chargers At present, there is a problem where some Lithium-Ion batteries will not charge in an external charger. They will charge when placed in the PowerBook. Hopefully, this problem has been fixed by the time you are reading this.

Can You Hot-Swap a PowerBook G3 Series battery? If the system is connected to AC power or operating with two batteries, then the batteries can be hot swapped. When using a single battery, the battery should be swapped only when the system is in sleep mode or shut down. Otherwise, the system will crash because you have removed the primary power source. You have about 2 minutes to swap a battery in sleep or you may lose data.

Sleep Problems

 Symptoms:

- The Macintosh automatically goes to sleep sooner (or later) than expected or does not go to sleep at all.

- A Macintosh freezes or has a system error immediately before sleep or immediately after waking up from Sleep.

 Causes:

Normally, you put a Mac to sleep by selecting the Sleep command from the Finder's Special menu, pressing the Power button (and then clicking the Sleep button in the alert box), using other keyboard shortcuts (such as Command-Shift-0), or simply closing the lid of a portable.

Normally, you wake up a Mac simply by pressing a key. For the iBook, just opening the lid is enough.

Problems where the Mac does not automatically go to sleep when expected are usually due to incorrect settings in the Energy Saver control panel.

Problems with system crashes and freezes associated with sleep have a variety of causes. Most of them involve extensions. Typically, loading with extensions off will avoid the problem.

While the focus of this coverage remains with portable Macs (PowerBooks and the iBook), some of what follows will also apply to using Sleep with desktop Macs.

 What to Do:

Automatic Sleep Disabled

Automatic sleep refers to when the Macintosh goes to sleep without your specifically requesting Sleep. What determines when this happens is the idle sleep interval, and any schedule, set in the Energy Saver control panel.

For example, if your Mac never goes to sleep, check to see if the system sleep setting has been set to "Never".

If your Energy Saver settings suggest that you should be getting automatic sleep, but it doesn't happen, check for any of the following possible causes. They all prevent automatic sleep from kicking in on at least some Macs (in some cases, they may even prevent manual sleep):

- You are connected to another volume on a network.

- The modem is in use (or if auto-answer is on for an internal modem) or a document is printing, or a serial port is in use for any other reason. In fact, trying to put a PowerBook to sleep while a PPP connection is active can cause a crash.

- Any background activity is occurring. Similarly, some extensions or some applications may cause the Mac to think that the system is busy, thereby preventing sleep.

- An external monitor is in use.

- The Palm Desktop HotSync software may prevent your computer from going to sleep.

- If the Configure pop-up menu in the TCP/IP control panel is set to Using DHCP Server, your computer may not sleep when your Web browser or e-mail application is open or a file server is mounted on your desktop. Quit these applications and dismount file servers when they are not being used.

- An extension called *Insomnia* is included on most Mac OS CDs. If this extension is mistakenly put into the Extensions folder in the active System folder, the Mac will not sleep. Insomnia keeps the Mac from going to sleep during the installation process.

- Newer Macs, such as the iBook, iMac DV and the Power Mac G4, offer a **deep sleep** mode that reduces power consumption to the bare minimum. During deep sleep, the power light on the Mac pulsates in an amber color, rather than the normal green. Certain activities, such as having file-sharing turned on, can prevent deep sleep. These include having file sharing turned on or having a Web page that auto-refreshed every few minutes.

    Note: If the amber light appears other than when the Mac is in deep sleep, it typically indicates a problem with the video hardware.

    SEE: • **"Wake-from-Sleep Crashes/Power Down Sleep Error," in Chapter 14.**

Automatic Sleep Works–But Not At the Expected Interval

In some cases, automatic sleep works, but it kicks in sooner (or later) than you expected. A similar problem can occur with automatic screen dimming. The most likely cause is that the Energy Saver control panel settings are not what you think they are. Check the control panel.

Wake-from-Sleep Crashes

In the last year or so, wake-from-sleep crashes have become an increasingly common problem. Essentially, what happens is that when you wake the computer, the screen comes on but a freeze (or more rarely an actual crash) occurs before access to your Mac is restored. Typically, you are left with a blank gray screen that never goes away.

Unfortunately, there are now a dozen or so known different causes of this symptom, so it is hard to offer generalized advice as to what to do to fix it. The problem is not restricted to sleep on portable Macs; it extends to desktop Macs as well. For example:

- Enabling Energy Saver's "Preserve memory contents on sleep" option may occasionally lead to a wake-from sleep crash.

- Enabling Energy Saver's "Reconnect to servers on wakeup" option may occasionally lead to a wake-from sleep crash, especially if no server is currently connected.

- A corrupted System Preferences file (located in the Preferences folder of the System Folder) may cause this symptom. Try deleting it.

    SEE: • **Chapter 14 for more on wake-from-sleep crashes specific to Apple's new Mac models.**

Symptoms, Causes, and What to do:

Defective Pixels on Active-Matrix Screens

Check for Void or Stuck Pixels PowerBooks with active-matrix screens may have defective pixels (this problem is not relevant to passive-matrix screens). To see if you have this problem, turn your PowerBook on and check for either of the following:

- **"Void" pixels** This means that the pixel is always off (that is, white). For example, if you look at a screen that should have all dark pixels and one or more pixels are white—staring at you like stars in the night sky—you have void pixels.

- **"Stuck" pixels** This means that the pixel is always on (that is, dark). For example, if you look at a screen that should have all white pixels and one or more pixels are dark—looking like periods on a sheet of white paper—you have stuck pixels.

   If you have any doubt as to whether you have defective pixels, a simple test is to use a graphics program to create a large black (or white) rectangle. Now move the window around the rectangle until you have tested all of the screen with it, looking for defective pixels as you go (though you may not be able to test the area of the menu bar this way). Programs that can create slide show presentations can do the same thing. This advice applies best to non-color Macintoshes, though the basic logic is the same in all cases.

Rebuild the Desktop Rebuilding the desktop may sometimes fix defective pixels, but don't count on this.

SEE: • Fix-It #8.

Replace the Screen Apple no longer has an official public policy on how many void or stuck pixels is enough to justify a replacement of the screen. If your screen has enough defective pixels that they bother you, contact Apple for advice.

TECHNICALLY SPEAKING ▶ Passive-matrix versus Active-matrix Screens

All currently shipping PowerBooks include some form of an active-matrix display. Some older PowerBooks came with a passive-matrix display. With active-matrix screens, each pixel is turned on or off individually. In contrast, passive-matrix screens work by activating rows and columns of pixels all at once (a pixel is turned on when an activated row and column intersect).

Active-matrix screens offer much more rapid and precise control over each pixel than do passive-matrix ones. As a result, active-matrix screens have much clearer and sharper images than passive-matrix screens and respond to movement more quickly. An active-matrix screen also does not appear to dim or distort as your angle of view moves to one side (as do passive-matrix screens) and are overall brighter. In addition, active-matrix screens do not have the ghosting/submarining problem described in the main text. The only advantage of passive-matrix screens is that they are cheaper. As the cost of active-matrix screens has decreased, passive-matrix screens have disappeared from the Mac line-up.

Ghosting and Submarining on Passive-Matrix Screens

A disadvantage of passive-matrix screens is that when you move the cursor rapidly, the cursor may temporarily disappear. This is a symptom of a more general display problem with passive-matrix screens, particularly grayscale ones, called *ghosting* or *submarining*.

Of course, moving the cursor more slowly helps resolve this problem. However, a better solution is at hand if you have a recent version of

Figure 11-14 Left: The Mouse control panel, with the Mouse Tracks option on the bottom; Right: The TrackPad control panel.

Apple's Mouse control panel and Assistant Toolbox installed. At the bottom of the control panel should be an option called Mouse Tracks (not Mouse Tracking, which is at the top of the control panel). Selecting longer mouse tracks helps keep the arrow cursor in view by leaving a trail behind it. Checking the Thick I-beam option similarly helps make the I-beam more visible.

Trouble Ejecting PC Cards

PCMCIA stands for Personal Computer Memory Card International Association. PCMCIA-cards (often just called PC Cards) are cards that conform to that Association's standard. All recent PowerBook models include some form of PC Card slot. Common uses of PC Cards include adding a modem, an Ethernet adapter or an adapter that can read the media used in digital cameras. (See Chapter 10.)

Note: PCMCIA PC Cards refer to an older (16 bit; Card & Socket Services v 2.x) PC Card technology. CardBus is the term used to describe the newer (32 bit; Card & Socket Services v 3) implementation of the PC card. Support for the newer CardBus cards began with the PowerBook G3 Sereies portables.

When a PC card is installed, one of the more frequent problems users report is difficulty in ejecting it again. Normally, you do this either by dragging the icon of the card to the Trash or selecting Put Away from the Finder's Special menu (just as you do for disks). If this doesn't work, however, here are some other suggestions:

- If you get a message that says that the card cannot be ejected because it is "in use" and you have quit all open applications, the PCMCIA modem may be in auto-answer mode. To eject the card, you'll have to launch your communications software and turn this option off.

    Otherwise, make sure file sharing is turned off. In either case, try again to eject the card.

- For other eject problems, a paper clip can be inserted into the small hole next to the PCMCIA slot to eject the card manually. Try to avoid pulling the card out of the computer.

- If even this fails, Apple offers the following advice: "You can pull the card out yourself with a pair of needle nose pliers or sometimes with your fingers, if you have strong fingernails. Once the card is pulled out, try inserting the paper clip again to release the spring mechanism. If you hear the springs release, you can try inserting the card (or a different card) again. Of course, the problem may recur." If so, the card may be damaged. If the problem occurs with several cards, the Expansion Module (or bay) may be damaged and need to be repaired.

TrackBall and TrackPad Problems

A few quick fixes for these hardware devices are covered in Fix-It #15.

Transfer Files Mac-to-Mac

If you are fortunate enough to own two Macs, such as a portable and a desktop Mac, you will inevitably find yourself wanting to transfer data from one computer to the other. In the old days, you might have done this by copying the file to a floppy disk and then inserting the disk in the other computer. This is no longer very effective because (1) many of the files you would want to transfer today are too large to fit on a floppy disk and (2) Apple's newest Macs no longer come with a floppy disk.

SEE: • Chapter 14.

Transfer Files via an External Drive

USB and FireWire Drives

If your Macs both have a USB or a FireWire port, all you need is an external USB or FireWire drive. Unlike older, SCSI-based drives, these newer drives can be "hot-swapped." This means that you can simply disconnect the drive from the USB (or FireWire) port on one Mac and connect it to the comparable port on the other Mac—without having to turn off and restart either machine. In addition, these drives may receive power directly from the USB or FireWire port, making an external AC connection unnecessary. Overall, this makes using these drives to transfer data almost as simple as using a floppy disk—except its faster and has a much higher capacity.

Of course, if you have a removable media drive, such as a Zip drive or a SuperDisk drive, you can alternatively use the media supported by these drives to transfer data.SCSI Connections

I cover SCSI connections more generally in Fix-It #14. For now, I just want to emphasize that, if you have an older PowerBook with a SCSI port (Apple's latest models no longer include this port; the Bronze Keyboard PowerBook G3 Series was the last to do so), you can connect an SCSI drive to the port—if you have the special cable needed for PowerBook SCSI connections.

Target Disk Mode

Alternatively, if you also have a desktop Mac with an SCSI port, you can actually connect the PowerBook to the desktop Mac in such a way that the PowerBook acts as an external drive to the desktop Mac. This is called connecting the PowerBook in SCSI Disk Mode (or, as it is more recently called, HD Target Disk Mode). Doing this requires a different cable than the one needed to connect a drive to the PowerBook (it's called a HDI-30 Disk Adapter). The procedure for getting this to work also requires setting the PowerBook's SCSI ID number via the PowerBook Disk Mode control panel. It is also recommended that you shut down the PowerBook and the desktop Mac before making this connection.

Given Apple's abandonment of SCSI, using SCSI's Target Disk Mode will become less and less common in the year's ahead. However, take heart! You can also do this with the latest FireWire-capable PowerBooks via a FireWire connection. Here are the official directions from Apple: To use a PowerBook computer in FireWire Target Disk Mode requires another Macintosh computer with FireWire. To utilize FireWire Target Disk Mode, follow these steps:

1. Make sure that your PowerBook (FireWire) is shut down. Apple also recommends that you connect your computer to AC power.

2. Use a FireWire (6 to 6) cable to connect your PowerBook to a FireWire-equipped host. The host need not be powered down.

3. Start up the PowerBook and immediately hold down the T key. Your computer display will show the FireWire icon, and your internal hard disk icon will appear on the Finder desktop of the host computer.

4. When you are finished transferring files, drag the PowerBook computer's hard disk icon to the Trash.

5. Shut down the PowerBook using the power button and disconnect the FireWire cable.

Transfer Files via File Sharing

File sharing allows your Macintosh to share information with other Macs on the same network. With Remote Access, you can even access a Mac via a modem. Using Web Sharing software, you can share files over a TCP/IP connection, on an Intranet or even the Internet. And in Mac OS 9, you share files via TCP/IP directly; no web server software is needed. With options such as Infrared connections and AirPort, you may even be able to do it without wires. In this section, we will briefly explore all of these options.

Once you set the software up, file sharing is the fastest and most convenient way to get a file from one Mac to another. You can do it all almost instantly without ever leaving your desk.

File Sharing and AppleTalk

As covered in Chapter 7 (see: "Take Note: What Is AppleTalk?"), AppleTalk refers to a method of networking computers and peripherals together. All Macintosh computers have AppleTalk support built-in. This makes it easy to connect them together for file sharing.

Making a connection for file sharing typically requires special networking cables connecting the computers (otherwise you would connect a computer to a server or the Internet). Connections are typically made via the serial port or via the Ethernet port. AppleTalk is also used for connecting via Remote Access (over a modem) and can be used for the Infrared and AirPort wireless connections. Your selection of connection port (Ethernet vs. Printer Port etc.) is made via the AppleTalk control panel.

SEE: • "Take Note: File Sharing via TCP/IP," for an option to share files without using AppleTalk.

File Sharing via the Serial Port

Newer Macs (starting with the iMac) no longer include a serial port. However, for those that still use Macs that have this port: Setting up the wiring for a serial connection between two Macs could hardy be easier to do. Most commonly you would use the "PhoneNet" type connector that plugs in your serial port (these connectors can be purchased from any Mac-friendly computer supplier) and works with ordinary phone wire as the cabling. Apple's original LocalTalk cabling is not used much anymore. If you are connecting more than two devices, you do so in a daisy-chain fashion (device one is connected to device two which is connected to device three and so on). You can do this because the PhoneNet connector contains two outlets. Thus, for device two, one outlet would have phone wire going back to device one while the other would connect to device three. The two devices at each end of such a chain will have a terminator inserted in the outlet that is otherwise unused. If you have two serial ports on your Mac, you need to make sure you use the one that is assigned as the AppleTalk port in the AppleTalk control panel. That's it.

One note: if you ever disconnect a device on an Apple Talk chain, you break the entire chain. This means that all devices "downwind" of you will no longer be able to communicate with any devices on your "upwind" side.

Once the cables are connected, it's time to set up the file sharing software.

SEE: • "File Sharing: Initial Setup".

Serial adapters If you must connect a Mac without a serial port to a serial port network, there are adapters that may let you do so. My favorite is the Stealth Serial Port from GeeThree (*http://www.geethree.com/*). But be careful. Some adapters may let you connect a serial device (such as a printer) but may not work for a serial network (as needed to connect two Macs together). For example, any serial adapter that works via the USB port cannot be used for networking.

File Sharing via the Ethernet Port

All recent Macs have an Ethernet port built in. If you have a Mac not equipped with an Ethernet port, you may be able to add one via an Ethernet (PCI) card.

Setting up the wiring for an Ethernet network, with today's Macs, is almost as simple as for a serial port connection. To connect two Macs, simply get an Ethernet cable and plug each end into their respective Ethernet ports. As described more below (see: "File Sharing: Initial Setup"), you also have to select to "Connect via" Ethernet from the AppleTalk control panel. That's it. You're done.

Crossover vs. standard cables (and Ethernet hubs) Okay, maybe it's not quite that simple. The main trick here is to make sure you are using the correct cable. There are two types of Ethernet cable and you cannot tell them apart visually. One type is called a cross-over cable. It is the type to use when connecting two Macs together. It is also the type that a cable company will use to connect a cable modem to your Mac. The problem arises if you want to connect more than two devices on your Ethernet network (such as two Macs, a cable modem and a printer). Devices on an Ethernet network cannot be daisy-chained together. To have more than two devices, you need to get an Ethernet hub. These come in various sizes. The smallest ones allow for up to five devices to be connected. Larger ones can accommodate 16 or more devices. The advantage of a hub (unlike the daisy chain method used with serial port connections) is that you can disconnect any device from the hub without affecting the working of any other device still connected.

I haven't forgotten the cable problem. Here it is: when connecting an Ethernet device to a hub, you cannot use a crossover cable. You must use the standard (straight through) Ethernet RJ45 cable. A regular cable will not work without a hub and a crossover cable will not work with a hub. So if you find that a connection does not seem to be working at all, checking the cable would be your first step. If you have a hub, you can check the cable by connecting it to a hub and then by connecting it directly between two devices (without a hub). If the connection works one way but not the other, you know that the cable is the issue and you know what type of cable you have. If you need the type of cable you do not have, simply get one.

Two other issues related to using Ethernet hubs:

- **Ethernet hubs and the uplink port** Ethernet hubs typically include an additional port (often called the Uplink port) that is not used for connecting devices to the hub. Most often, it is used for connecting two hubs together, so as to increase the number of devices you can have on the network. Actually, you can use this Uplink port to connect almost any additional device. You use a cross-over cable to connect two devices via the Uplink port. For example, I have a setup where I have 5 devices connected to a 5-port hub. I then connected my cable modem to the Uplink port. The Macs on the hub were all able to access the cable modem.

SEE: • **Chapter 12 for more on cable modems.**

- **Ethernet hubs and 10/100 Mbps speeds** The Ethernet ports on the devices you wish to connect (such as your Mac, your printer, etc.) will typically be one of two speeds: 10 Mbps (called Ethernet or 10Base-T Ethernet) or 100 Mbps (called Fast Ethernet). Faster speeds also exist, but they are less common (and currently you will only get them on the Mac via an Ethernet PCI card). If you have a 10 Mbps hub, 100 Mbps devices may not work with it – and vice versa. Or, if they do work, you will not get the expected speed (that is, the transfer speed of a 100 Mbps device will be slowed down if it is connected to a 10 Mbps port). The best solution is to get a 10/100 Mbps dual speed hub. This will correctly accommodate either speed. Actually, the Ethernet port in newer Macs (such as the iMacs) are also 10/100 ports, so they too will accommodate both speeds. However, the AirPort Base Station is only a 10Mbps device and will not work with a 100Mbps hub.

    One glitch here is that the Power Mac G4 has had problems working with 10/100 devices. However, I expect this to be fixed by the time you are reading this.

    Note: The maximum number of hubs allowed between two devices is four (for 10 Mbps) and two (for 100 Mbps).

Other devices on an Ethernet network Some of the devices on an Ethernet network may need some additional setup. This is especially likely with printers. For example, with my Epson 900N printer, I needed to run the EPSON Net!2 utility before I could use it on my Ethernet network. For my HP laser printer, I needed to run the HP LaserJet Utility. Exact instructions are included with the printer. Of course, all of this assumes that your printer has the needed Ethernet card installed.

Once all this is set up, it's time to set up the file sharing software.

SEE: • "File Sharing: Initial Setup".

Other set-up problems On some newer Macs, you may be unable to see local AppleTalk devices on the network, after initially setting up on an Ethernet network. The solution is to close the Chooser and AppleTalk control panel. Then delete AppleTalk Preferences from the Preferences folder. Finally, restart and zap the PRAM, holding down the keys until the chimes occur twice. This should fix things.

If you have a cable modem, you may find that the cable connection interferes with your local network. This is usually because the cable modem is permitting your AppleTalk packets to go out on to the cable modem's local node, with the result that your Mac mistakenly thinks its connected to some server out on the Internet. Switching to a different cable modem can fix this. Sometimes, the cable ISP can make a change that will fix this. Otherwise, your best bet is to purchase a router. Such a device can be set up (using something called NAT, Network Address Translation) to prevent any direct communication between your local network and the Internet. I recommend the routers from MacSense.

SEE: • Fix-It #9 on zapping the PRAM.

BY THE WAY ▶ Ethernet Extensions

Getting Ethernet to work requires that the essential Ethernet software extensions be installed in your System Folder. Normally, this is done automatically when you install the Mac OS, so it's probably already there and waiting. However, here are a few tips:

- Apparently, the only Ethernet extension needed in Mac OS 8.6 or later 9 is *Apple Enet*.

- In older versions of the Mac OS, you may also find various other Ethernet extensions. In particular, you are likely to find *Ethernet (Built-In)* and/or *Apple Built-In Ethernet*. You probably don't need both. Ethernet (Built-In) is the newer one (used for PCI-based Macs). As their name implies, these were used for the Ethernet capability that is "built in" to all recent Macs. If you are instead using an Ethernet PCI card, you may need other Ethernet software. In general, use the latest versions of these extensions that are available.

    If you have both of these extensions installed, and you are having problems making an Ethernet connection, experiment with disabling one or both of them to see if that helps. If you have only one installed, try installing the other.

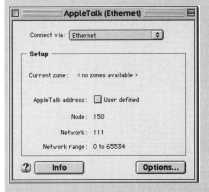

Figure 11-15 The AppleTalk control panel. To turn on AppleTalk, select the Options button.

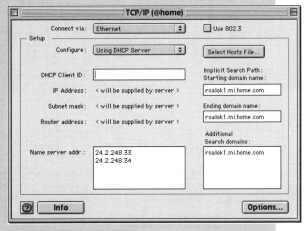

Figure 11-16 The TCP/IP control panel, set for an Ethernet connection.

TAKE NOTE ▶ File Sharing viaTCP/IP

TCP/IP is the protocol initially developed for transfer of information over the Internet. Your TCP/IP connection setup is done via the TCP/IP control panel. For a local (Intranet) connection to a server you would typically select to Connect via: "AppleTalk (MacIP)" (if using LocalTalk or equivalent cabling) or "Ethernet." If your local server is connected to the Internet, this would also indirectly give you Internet access. For a direct Internet connection to the Internet via a cable modem (or similar device), you would typically select to Connect via: "Ethernet." Otherwise, for a dial-up modem, you would select "PPP."

SEE: • **Chapter 12 for further details on how to set up these options.**

With each new revision to the OS, Apple moves more towards using TCP/IP instead of AppleTalk as a general all-purpose transfer protocol. For example, with Mac OS 9, you can now directly transfer files with File Sharing via a TCP/IP connection. In the not too distant future, I expect that AppleTalk will be phased out entirely.

(continues on next page)

TAKE NOTE ▶ File Sharing viaTCP/IP *(continued)*

This edition of *Sad Macs* still focuses on AppleTalk as the basis for file sharing. However, for those wanting to venture into TCP/IP file sharing, here are two examples of how it works (using Mac OS 9 on at least one of the two Macs involved):

1. Assuming you already have the two Macs connected via Ethernet cables, open the TCP/IP control panel and select to Connect via Ethernet. Then select to Configure "Using DHCP Server." Do this on both machines.

2. From one machine (the one running Mac OS 9, if only one Mac is doing so), copy down the numeric IP address that eventually gets listed in the IP Address box of the TCP/IP control panel. It will also be listed in the File Sharing control panel under the Computer Name text box. (With TCP/IP File Sharing enabled, a separate URL address may also appear in the File Sharing section of File Sharing's Start/Stop panel; this works similarly to the IP address.)

3. From this same Mac, make sure that "Enable File Sharing clients to connect over TCP/IP" is enabled in the File Sharing control panel and that File Sharing is turned on (as described in the main text).

Using the Chooser

4. From the other Mac, select the Chooser and click the AppleShare icon. From the window area on the right, click the "Server IP Address…" button (see Figure 11-25). Enter the address you copied down from the other machine and click to Connect.

5. You should now be able to mount the other Mac's hard drive volume(s) as a Guest and/or Registered user (depending upon how you had set up File Sharing).

Using the Network Browser

6. Open the Network Browser. At least in Mac OS 9 or later, the server may be already directly listed under one of the headings (neighborhoods) in the list that appears as soon as the Browser is opened. Depending on the setup, it may be under Local Services or a separate domain name. To check, open the disclosing triangle of the server to see what's there. If the computer is listed, simply double-click it to mount it. Similarly, if you have recently mounted the shared computer, click the Recent Items button (the one with the Clock icon) and it will be listed there. Or, if you added the volume to your list of Favorites, click the Browser's Favorites button (the one with the Folder icon) to access it. These all eliminate the need to know the IP address of the shared volume.

   Otherwise, you can click the Browser's Shortcuts button (the one with the hand icon) and select "Connect to Server" and enter the IP address this way.

The Network Browser in Mac OS 9 is accommodating; it will mount file servers, ftp servers, and Web site servers with equal ease.

Caution: With TCP/IP File Sharing enabled, anyone else on your local network may be able to see your computer. To safeguard your computer in such cases, make sure that you have *not* enabled Guest access. Even better, if you don't need to provide File Sharing access to your computer, turn off the TCP/IP access option or stop File Sharing entirely.

Note: File sharing via TCP/IP requires that the ShareWay IP Personal Bgnd extension be installed. It should get installed as part of Mac OS 9. If this extension is not loaded, the checkbox in File Sharing will remain dimmed. The Mac OS Installer may not install this extension unless you do an Easy or a Clean Install (that is, no Custom Install will install this). If you cannot enable this feature, check for the presence of this extension.

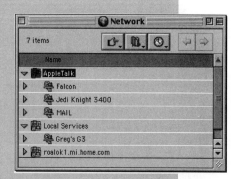

Figure 11-17 The Network Browser. The trio of buttons along the top are the Shortcut, Favorites, and Recent Items buttons.

BY THE WAY ▶ Wireless Connections: Infrared

Infrared connections use a similar technology to that used by remote control devices for your television. Apple has actually used two different Infrared technologies over the years: IRTalk and IrDA. IRTalk is the older of the two (and is an Apple-only technology) and was used in PowerBooks such as the 5300 and the 1400. IrDA is newer and was used in newer PowerBooks (although not in Apple's latest portables) and the original version of the iMac (the PowerBooks with Infrared support allow a choice between IRTalk and IrDA). In order to use Infrared, both computers must have Infrared support and use the same technology. If your computer is not equipped with any Infrared option, and you wish to add it, a few companies have marketed Infrared peripheral devices that attach to your Mac. One example is Farallon's Air Dock.

Make sure that the Infrared control panel and extension(s), as appropriate for your Mac model, are installed and that file sharing is enabled. On most Macs and OS versions, the needed extensions are IrDALib and IrLanScannerPPC. Also make sure that the devices you wish to share are within a few feet of each other and that the infrared beams are facing each other.

IRTalk To se up an IRTalk connection via AppleTalk, select "Infrared Port (IRTalk)" from the "Connect via" pop-up menu in the AppleTalk control panel (this step is only needed if your PowerBook supports both protocols).

IrDA To set up an IrDA connection via AppleTalk, select "Infrared Port (IrDA)" from the "Connect via" pop-up menu in the AppleTalk control panel (if you will be connecting via TCP/IP, select the same option from this control panel). If this choice is not available, make sure that Infrared (IrDA) was selected from the Options section of the Infrared control panel.

If two devices (such as two Macs or a Mac and a printer) are within Infrared range of each other, the Infrared control panel will indicate this. You can select it via the AppleShare selection in the Chooser (as described in the main text). If the device you wish to connect to is a printer, the printer should now appear in the Chooser. Setup a desktop printer for the printer from the Chooser. You should now be able to print.

Tip: You can use Apple's Apple IR File Exchange utility to transfer files via IRTalk, even without selecting Infrared Port from AppleTalk.

TAKE NOTE ▶ Wireless Connections: AirPort

The AirPort was introduced with the iBook. It is now supported in all currently shipping Macs. Essentially, it works like this: An AirPort Base Station is connected to a network, such as an Ethernet network or a PPP connection to the Internet (or even both at the same time). The individual Macs are then equipped with an AirPort card, inserted in the special slot for the card provided on these newer Macs. Now, with file sharing enabled, two AirPort equipped devices should be able to share data via file-sharing just as if there were a wired connection between them. Airport equipped devices should be able to interact with each other within a range of about 150 feet, even if walls are between the devices.

You can even maintain a wireless connection to the Internet via the AirPort (if the Base Station is connected to the Internet). AirPort also includes Network Address Translation (NAT) support which allows multiple computers on a network to share a single IP address connection to the Internet.

You don't absolutely need an AirPort Base Station to use AirPort. You have two alternatives: (1) Apple's G4 and iMac (and newer) computers can run AirPort Software Base Station. This allows the computer itself to serve as a Base Station. (2) Two Macs with AirPort cards can "talk" to each other directly with no Base Station of any kind needed. Simply use the AirPort Control Strip module on both computers to switch from using the AirPort Base Station to using direct computer-to-computer communications.

(continues on next page)

TAKE NOTE ▶ Wireless Connections: AirPort *(continued)*

However, one advantage of the real AirPort Base Station is that it does not require turning on a separate "base station" computer in order for other computers to get a wireless link up the Internet. An AirPort Base Station can also be connected to an Ethernet hub so that wireless and wired devices can be on the same network.

Macs that have a PC card slot, but no AirPort slot may still be able to hook up to an AirPort network via a third party wireless communication PC card that is compatible with AirPort (they must conform to the IEEE 802.11 standard). Farallon makes one such card.

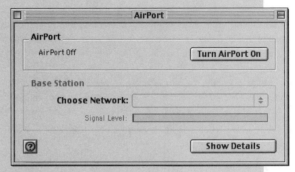

Setting Up an AirPort Connection To set up an AirPort connection, you first need an AirPort card installed in your Mac.

Next, you need to connect a modem and/or Ethernet cable to the AirPort. Exactly what cable you connect depends on your setup. For

Figure 11-18 The AirPort application.

example, if you just want to use the AirPort for a wireless Internet connection, and you have a cable modem, connect an Ethernet cable from your cable modem to the Base Station. However, to be able to file share with other Macs on a local network (that includes Macs not equipped with AirPort), you would likely connect an Ethernet cable from an Ethernet hub to the Base Station. If the hub also has a connection to the cable modem, you will now have access both to the Internet and other Macs on the network.

Finally, you need to install the software (if it was not pre-installed on your Mac). You can then use the AirPort Setup Assistant application to walk you through the remaining installation steps. Alternatively, you can do these steps manually. In brief, you will need to:

1. Set up an AirPort Base Station (or Software Base Station). **Note:** if you do not set up a Base Station from the Setup Assistant, you will need to do so from the AirPort Admin Utility (which is different from the AirPort application); full details of doing this are beyond the scope of this book.

2. Set the AppleTalk and TCP/IP control panels to Connect via AirPort. Choose "Using DHCP Server" from the TCP/IP Configure pop-up menu.

3. From the AirPort application (the one found in the Apple menu or accessed from the Control Strip), select a Base Station or computer to which you want to connect and turn on the connection. You are now done.

Note: The AirPort application lists an AirPort ID and AirPort Base Station ID. These odd looking 12 digit hexadecimal numbers are also referred to as MAC (Media Access Control) addresses. Every device potentially able to connect to an Ethernet network has a MAC address (it has nothing to do with Mac as in Macintosh). The MAC address is built-in to the hardware and cannot be changed. Don't worry about these numbers for now. However, if you run into trouble and seek help, the support person may ask you for one or both of these numbers.

Troubleshooting an AirPort Connection Here are some troubleshooting tips for working with AirPort connections:

• Make sure you have AirPort software 1.1 or later. It is much improved from the original 1.0 version.

- Increase the memory allocation of the AirPort application and utility to avoid system crashes when using the software.

- Apple states: "The AirPort base station supports dial-up connectivity to the Internet using the industry standard PPP connection method. AOL does not currently support this connection method; therefore, AOL is not compatible with the AirPort Base Station. Other Internet Service Providers that do not use the standard PPP connection method are also incompatible." However, if you connect to AOL via a separate ISP (as briefly explained in Chapter 12), you should be able to use AOL.

- If you leave the AirPort card on (as selected from the AirPort Control Strip Module or the AirPort application), AppleTalk will likely be reset to AirPort on restart, regardless of what settings changes you make during a session.

- If you get an error message that states: "The required AirPort software was not found on this computer," it most likely means that the needed AirPort software has been deleted or disabled. However, it can also mean that the AirPort card itself was not correctly seated in the slot when it was installed. To check, try to reseat the card again, carefully following the directions that came with the card.

- Pressing the Reset button on the bottom of the base station for one second temporarily resets the base station password, network password, and IP address, allowing you to change these settings using the AirPort Admin Utility. After entering new passwords and a new IP address (if necessary), make sure to click Re-scan in the Select Base Station window. If you do not click Re-scan, you may be prompted to enter the password and IP address again.

- If you cannot see an AirPort Base Station while using the AirPort Admin Utility, make sure AppleTalk and TCP/IP control panels are set to AirPort, as described above. If these settings are correct, unplug the AirPort Base Station and turn off the computer. Then plug the Base Station back in and restart the computer. Check again to see if the Base Station is listed. Also make sure that there is no interference preventing communication with the Base Station. The AirPort Admin Utility has an option to test signal strength.

- If all else fails, and you still cannot get the computer to locate the Base Station, you can do a "forced reload" of the AirPort Base Station firmware. This reloads the factory default settings of the AirPort Base Station, as stored in the AirPort Base Station Settings file on your computer. You can then use the AirPort Setup Assistant to reconfigure the Base Station, as you did during your initial setup. Here are the instructions for a forced reload, as detailed in Apple TIL article #58613:

  1. Connect your computer to the AirPort Base Station using Ethernet. You can connect directly to the base station using an Ethernet crossover cable, or you can connect through an Ethernet hub using standard Ethernet cables.

  2. Set the TCP/IP control panel to connect using Ethernet and close the control panel. You may notice a brief system delay after closing the control panel.

  3. Disconnect the power adapter from the base station and then reconnect it.

  4. When all three status lights glow orange, insert the end of a paper clip into the reset button hole on the bottom of the base station.

  5. Press and hold the reset button for 30 seconds. The middle AirPort Base Station status light glows orange. If the light glows green, you pressed the reset button too late. Go back to step 3 and try again.

  6. Double-click the AirPort Admin Utility (located in the AirPort folder inside the Apple Extras folder). After a brief delay, a list of base stations appears. If the AirPort Admin Utility is already open, click the Re-scan button.

(continues on next page)

TAKE NOTE ▶ Wireless Connections: AirPort *(continued)*

7. Select your base station from the list and click Configure. (The base station name will be set to the Ethernet ID of the base station, for example "00-50-E4-5B-8F-EA".)

8. Follow the onscreen instructions to reinstall your AirPort Base Station software. **Note:** The AirPort Base Station password is set to "public".

9. Use the AirPort Setup Assistant to reconfigure the base station.

Note: If you use the AirPort Setup Assistant to reconfigure the AirPort Base Station after reinstalling base station software, make sure that you select the correct set of TCP/IP settings to use to configure the base station. Because you changed your current TCP/IP configuration to Ethernet, you may have a TCP/IP configuration titled "AirPort" but that connects via Ethernet. When prompted to select a configuration in the AirPort Setup Assistant, do not use this configuration.

If you want to use the AirPort Admin Utility to reconfigure your base station instead of using the AirPort Setup Assistant, set the TCP/IP control panel back to connect using AirPort, if necessary select the AirPort network from the AirPort application or Control Strip, click Re-scan in the AirPort Admin Utility, select your base station and click Configure, and when prompted for a password enter "public."

Finally, check the About AirPort document that comes with the AirPort software; it has many more useful troubleshooting tips.

File Sharing: Initial Setup

Using file sharing requires special File Sharing extensions and control panels that are a standard part of the Mac OS. The key thing to realize here is that 90 percent of the features in these control panels are designed solely for security: to prevent unauthorized users on a network from gaining access to information on your computer. If all you are going to do is connect your own portable Mac (PowerBook or iBook) to your own desktop Macintosh, security is not an issue. So, what follows is a bare-bones foolproof method of getting file sharing going when security is not a concern. This method eliminates almost all of the hassles you would otherwise have.

However, if you ever use this file-sharing software to connect your Mac to a multi-user network, don't use the method described here! Be especially careful if you enabled TCP/IP file sharing (an option in Mac OS 9 as described more in "Take Note: File Sharing via TCP/IP"). This may allow anyone on the Internet to access your computer when you are online. For details on how to do more secure setups, consult the online Mac OS Help files.

For the sake of simplicity here, I will be assuming that you will be setting up a desktop Mac to allow sharing of its files from a PowerBook (or iBook). However, the same principles apply to any two networked Macs—and can be generalized for setting up more than two Macs on a network. The coverage will assume you are making a serial port or Ethernet connection via AppleTalk. It also assumes you have already set up the network cabling, as described in the previous section. For related information, check out "Take Note: File Sharing via TCP/IP" and "Take Note: Alternatives to Remote Access: Web Sharing and Timbuktu."

Depending upon which Mac model you have, you may also be able to connect one Mac to another via a wireless connection. The first method is via Infrared (IR). Apple has dropped this type of connection from its newest Macs, so don't expect to see any further development of it. The second method is via Apple's new AirPort system. We briefly cover each of these methods in "By the Way: Wireless Connections: Infrared" and "Take Note: Wireless Connections: AirPort."

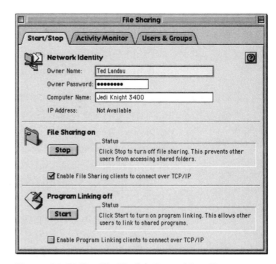

Figure 11-19 The File Sharing Control Panel's Start/Stop panel. File Sharing is currently on, as indicated in the middle section of the panel.

1. **Make sure you have the needed file-sharing software installed** In particular, you'll want the File Sharing Extension and File Sharing control panel and (in Mac OS 8.x) the Users & Groups control panel. For some types of file sharing, you'll also need Open Transport software installed. You may also want (although it is not essential) the Network Browser application. All of this should be installed as part of the recommended set of software installed with the Mac OS.

2. **For AppleTalk networks, turn on AppleTalk for both computers** You can enable AppleTalk from the Chooser or from the AppleTalk Control Strip module. However, the most reliable way to do so is via the AppleTalk control panel (especially if you want to ensure that AppleTalk will remain active after a Restart). To access this option, select User Mode from the Edit menu and select Advanced from the window that appears. Then close the window and click the Options button in the AppleTalk window. From here, select the button to Make AppleTalk Active.

From the AppleTalk control panel, also select the "Connect via" option, typically serial (via the Printer or the Modem port) or Ethernet.

Set up the AppleTalk control panel for both the Macs that will be sharing data.

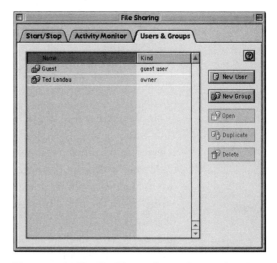

Figure 11-20 The File Sharing Control Panel's User & Groups panel from Mac OS 9 (this is a separate control panel in Mac OS 8.6).

For serial port connections: if your Mac has two serial ports, make sure that the cable is connected to the same port that you select in the AppleTalk control panel.

For an Ethernet connection: you may be unable to select the Ethernet "Connect via" option unless an Ethernet cable is currently in the port.

3. **From your desktop Mac, select File Sharing** In the Network Identity section, you must type in your name (however you want it to appear) and a name for your computer. Once set, you can change these names, but the Mac will not let you leave these spaces blank. You don't have to type a password, but the Mac may send you a warning message, advising against leaving this blank, if you do not.

From the File Sharing section, click Start. Wait a minute or so until this process finishes.

Leave Program Linking off. Program Linking is a rarely used feature that does not affect what we are trying to do here.

Close the control panel.

Note: You can also select to open the File Sharing control panel from the File Sharing Control Strip module. In fact, you can turn file sharing on and off from this module, bypassing the need to go to the control panel at all. However, changes made this way are temporary. That is, the next time you restart, file sharing will revert to what it was (on or off) the last time you selected it from the control panel, not the Control Strip module.

Open the File Sharing control panel and select the Start/Stop tab.

4. **Select to share a volume via Get Info** From your desktop Mac, click once on the icon of a volume (such as a hard disk) that you wish to share and select Get Info (Command I).

From the window that appears, go to the Show pop-up menu and select Sharing.

From the options that appear, click the check box that says "Share this item and its contents."

In the Owner line, make sure that your Name (that is the name you selected in File Sharing) is listed as the owner. From the Privilege icon to the right of your name, select "Read & Write," from the pop-up menu. If security is not an issue, and you want to avoid having to enter a password each time you use File Sharing, also give Read & Write privileges in the Everyone line.

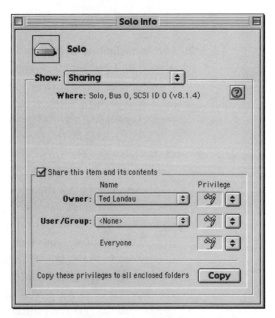

Figure 11-21 The Get Info window's Sharing display for a hard drive volume; in this setup, everyone (including guests) has read/write access.

File sharing is now enabled for every file and folder on your selected volume.

You can make a similar selection for any folder within the volume, thereby overriding the selection for the volume as a whole. In this way, you could make only one folder on your drive sharable. Or you could make your entire drive sharable, except for one folder. In particular, when you open a folder that is within a shared volume or folder, there will be an option to "Use enclosing folder's privileges." In our example, checking this would mean that the folder is using the overall privileges set for the volume (it is likely already checked by default). You could uncheck this option and separately set the privileges for this volume.

Also, you can select "Can't move, rename, or delete this item (locked)" to "lock" a shared folder (although it does not lock the separate contents of the folder). This option is also briefly mentioned in Chapter 6, as it relates to an inability to delete a file or folder.

Finally, you can repeat this step for any additional volumes you want to share.

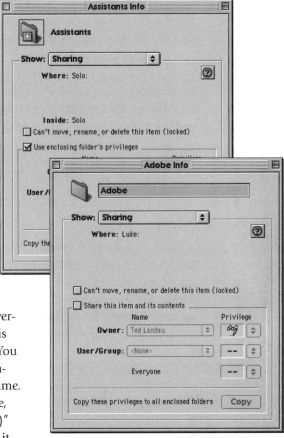

Figure 11-22 Top: the Get Info Sharing panel of a folder within a shared volume, with the "Use enclosing folder's privileges" option selected. If you uncheck this, you can separately set the privileges for this folder. Bottom: the Get Info Sharing panel of a folder not within a shared volume.

SEE ALSO: • **"Technically Speaking: The Sharing Option For Folders," later in this chapter.**

Figure 11-23 A folder's icon when "Share this item and its contents" is selected for the folder. Right: A folder's icon when "Can't move, rename or delete this item" is selected.

5. **From your desktop Mac, select Users & Groups** In Mac OS 8.x, there is a separate Users & Groups control panel. In Mac OS 9, Users & Groups has been combined into the File Sharing control panel as a separate tab.

In either case, you should see two "face" icons here, one with your name on it (with a Kind of owner) and the other called Guest. Double-click the Guest icon. From the window that appears, select Sharing from the Show pop-up menu. Then enable the "Allow guests to connect to this computer" option. Close the icon's window and the control panel. You are now done with the desktop Mac side of the setup.

Again, be warned that doing this means that any user on a network to which you connect will have access to your entire hard drive. As a safer alternative, you can bypass this step and plan to connect using your own name, as listed on the other icon. However, using your name, rather than Guest, will require additional steps to make a file sharing connection, due to the need to enter a password (as set in the Owner profile).

If you are set up for Remote Access, there will be an additional option in the Show pop-up menu called Remote Access. Select it and enable "Allow user to dial into this computer" to allow Remote Access via a modem. However, I would only do this for Owner. I would not enable this for guests; that would be too much of a security risk even for the low-level security described here.

You can also create additional profiles here, but I am skipping over this.

Figure 11-24 The Guest window that appears when you open the Guest item in the Users and Groups panel. Check "Allow guests to connect..." to set up a convenient but zero security connection.

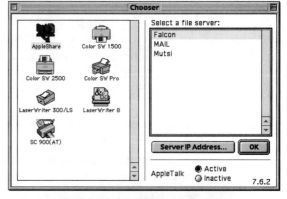

Figure 11-25 Top: the AppleShare option selected from the Chooser, with a list of available file servers on the right hand side. Bottom: accessing the same list of file servers from the Network Browser.

6. **From your portable Mac, access the shared volume on your desktop Mac**

   There are two ways to access the shared volume:

   Chooser From the Chooser of
   the PowerBook or iBook, select the
   AppleShare icon. The name of any
   computers on the network should
   now appear in the window on the
   right. Double-click the name of
   the computer that contains your
   shared volume (or single-click the
   name and click OK).

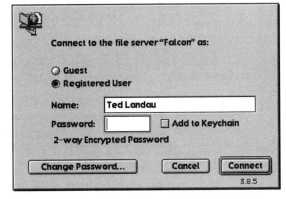

   From the Connect window that
   appears, click the Guest button.
   Then click Connect.

Figure 11-26 The window that appears when you try to
mount a server from the Chooser or the Network Browser.

   Alternatively, if you left Guest
   access turned off in Users and
   Groups, you will need to connect as a Registered User, using the name and password
   you entered in File Sharing on your desktop Mac. If you never entered a password in
   File Sharing (which I would recommend against), you would only need to include
   your name. Guest works more simply… but is less secure.

   After clicking Connect, yet another window will appear. The name of the vol-
   ume(s) you set up for sharing will be in this window (in the simplest case, there
   will be only one—the hard disk volume). If a volume name appears but is grayed
   out, this means that you do not have privileges to use it. Otherwise, to mount a
   shared volume, simply click its name to highlight it (shift-click to simultaneously
   select more than one volume). Then click OK. (Ignore the checkbox to have items
   automatically opened at system startup time.)

   Close the Chooser. Your desktop Mac's hard disk icon (or whatever other volume you shared) should now appear on your portable Mac's desktop. You are
   ready to share files.

   Network Browser Open the Network Browser (as with the Chooser, you should
   find it listed in your Apple menu). You should see an item called AppleTalk. Click
   the disclosing triangle to the left. It should reveal the name of all computers on your
   network. Double-click one of the computer names. This should lead to the same
   Connect dialog box as described above for the Chooser. After connecting successfully, the Network Browser will list all volumes on the computer that you enabled
   for file sharing. Double-click a volume to mount it on your desktop. You are ready
   to share files.

   By the way, you can use the arrow keys (on the top of the Browser window) to
   navigate back and forth in the sequence of Browser screens.

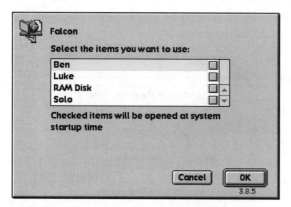

Figure 11-27 The window that appears in the Chooser (left) and the Network Browser (right) after successfully getting past the Connect window in Figure 11-26.

7. **From your portable Mac, make an alias of the shared volume** Before doing anything else, make an alias of your shared volume. Actually, with Network Browser, you can do this by simply dragging the icon of the volume from the Browser to the desktop. Otherwise, highlight the mounted volume and select Make Alias from the Finder's file menu. Place the alias in any convenient location on your desktop. The advantage of this alias will become clear the next time you want to use file sharing, as is described shortly.

    With Network Browser, you may also find the volume listed in the Shortcut (clock icon) menu. You can select it from there as well.

8. **The initial setup is now complete; you can share files** Double-click the volume icon to open its window and reveal its contents. You can now work with this window as if the volume was part of the portable Mac itself. Any time you access the desktop Mac from the portable Mac, you will see a pair of opposite facing arrows flash on and off in the upper left corner of the menubar, to the left of the Apple icon. This is normal.

    Helpful hint: Remember, the previous instructions assume that you intend to share files between a portable Mac and a desktop Mac, that you are the only user doing the sharing, that you intend to share your entire disk, and that you care nothing about security. If you are on a network with other users or if access has been separately set for individual folders for any reason, things can get considerably more complicated. If this is the case, refer to the relevant documentation or other outside help, as needed.

File Sharing: Disconnecting

1. **From your portable Mac, drag the desktop Mac's icon(s) to the Trash** The icon now vanishes from your desktop. The Macs are no longer connected.

2. **If you want, you can now turn file sharing and AppleTalk off and disconnect cables** To do this, select the File Sharing control panel on your desktop Mac and click the Stop button. This has the benefit of reducing the amount of RAM used by the system

software. You can also turn AppleTalk off if you no longer need it for any other operation. Doing this on your portable Mac helps conserve battery power. But don't forget that you need AppleTalk active to use most PostScript printers. In any case, you will need to make sure these features are on again the next time you want to file share.

Finally, if you connected cables between the portable Mac and the desktop Mac only for the purpose of this sharing, you can now disconnect them.

SEE: • **"Problems with Turning File Sharing or AppleTalk Off,"** later in this chapter, for more information.

Accessing File Sharing After the Initial Setup

Once you have completed the initial setup, as just described, accessing file sharing on future occasions is much easier. Here's all you have to do:

1. **Connect your portable Mac to your desktop Mac** If you have to connect any cabling, enable AppleTalk or File Sharing, do so.

2. **From your portable Mac, double-click the alias of the desktop Mac's icon** This is the alias you made in Step 8 of the Initial Setup section.

That's it! The desktop Mac's disk should mount on your portable Mac. You are ready to file-share without any other steps needed. (If you are mounting as a registered user, rather than a guest, you may still get a dialog box where you need to enter your name and password.)

You may have some problems with using the alias if you have changed sharing privileges since creating the alias. In this case, you will need to create a new alias. Also, if AppleTalk, TCP/IP and/or File Sharing are off, the volume will not mount.

TAKE NOTE ▶ File synchronization

Once you have file sharing set up, one of the best uses you can make of it is to update files that you keep on both disks, so that both computers always have the same version of these files. For example, suppose you are working on a report on your desktop Mac. When you leave for a trip, you copy the report to your PowerBook so you can work on it while you are on the road; when you get back home, you replace the now-outdated version on your desktop Mac with the newer copy from your PowerBook.

If you only do this occasionally, it is easy enough to do by simply dragging the file from one computer to another via file sharing. If you do this frequently and with a variety of files, however, you will benefit from a method that automates this procedure and makes sure that everything is updated correctly. Doing this is called *file synchronization*.

There are several utilities for this purpose. Apple includes a decent one, called File Assistant. You'll find it in the Control Panels folder of your PowerBook.

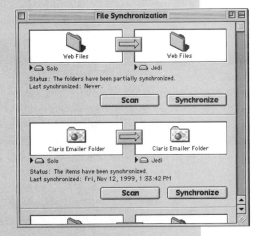

Figure 11-28 Apple's File Assistant.

Transfer Files via a Modem (Remote Access)

If your desktop Macintosh is at home and you are on the road somewhere with your PowerBook, you can still connect the two machines and directly transfer files between them (without requiring e-mail, or similar online feature, as an intermediary). However, you'll need a modem connection and some special software to do this.

The Apple software that does this is called Remote Access. It allows you to connect directly to another Mac via a modem, and then access files through Apple's file sharing.

SEE: • Chapter 12 for more on Open Transport and PPP.

For the details on how to setup and use Remote Access, consult the documentation that comes with the software. However, to give you a basic idea of how all of this works, here is a brief overview of the setup procedures:

1. **Install software and set up file-sharing** You need to have file-sharing software installed and set up as described in the previous section of this chapter: "Transfer Files via File Sharing." You also need to install the Remote Access server software on one of the Macs (the desktop Mac in our example) and the client software on the other (the PowerBook in our case). The client software is included free with all recent versions of the Mac OS. The Server is a separate purchase.

   From the Modem control panel, make sure you have selected to use the modem connected to your machines. Most Macs these days come with an internal modem. In this case, you would want to select to "Connect via Internal Modem" and then select the Internal Modem name from the Modem pop-up menu (such as "iMac Internal 56K").

2. **Select to Answer Calls from Remote Access** From the desktop machine, which will presumably be receiving the incoming calls, open the Remote Access control panel. Select "Answering..." from the Server's Remote Access menu. From the window that appears, check the box to "Answer calls."

   Starting with Remote Access 3.x, you can connect the two Macs via Remote Access's proprietary method (called ARAP or Apple Remote Access Protocol) or via PPP. If you want to allow PPP, also select "Allow TCP/IP clients to connect via PPP."

3. **Select to "Allow to dial in" from Users & Groups** From the desktop machine, go to Users & Groups (you can get there from Remote Access by selecting the Users & Groups command from

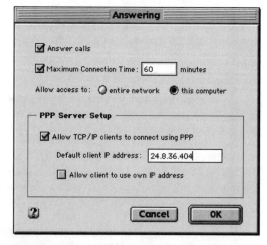

Figure 11-29 Remote Access's Answering Window. Check "Answer Calls" to allow incoming calls to connect to the Mac.

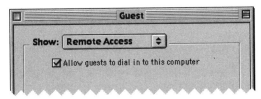

Figure 11-30 The window that appears if you open the Guest item as listed in Users & Groups in Figure 11-20 and select Remote Access from the Show pop-up menu.

the Remote Access menu). Double-click the Guest icon. From the Show pop-up menu, select "Remote Access." Check the "Allow guests to dial in" option. Again, this allows *anyone* to access your system. For greater security (which is especially relevant here, since anyone could dial in over a modem), use the icon with your own name, rather than the Guest icon. From this window, check the "Allow user to dial in" option. This gives you "registered user" access to the Remote Access server on your desktop Mac.

4. **Connect from Remote Access**

   From the PowerBook (the sending machine), open the Remote Access control panel. Select whether you are a Registered User of a Guest. For a Registered User, enter your name and password. In either case, enter the phone number needed to connect to your desktop Mac. Click Connect. That's it. If all goes well, your desktop Mac should mount on your PowerBook desktop just as it would had you been connected via a local network using file sharing.

   To select a protocol, click the Options button (you'll need to select Advanced User Mode from the Edit menu before this button appears). From the Protocol tab, access the Protocol pop-up menu. If you have an Automatic option, it's probably best to leave it there; Remote Access will pick the correct protocol for the attempted connection. Otherwise, select ARAP (to make a direct Remote Access connection) or select PPP (if you want to connect using the same protocol you use when making a dial up connection to the Internet). If one method does not work, try the other.

   If you are still having problems connecting, try ARA's DialAssist

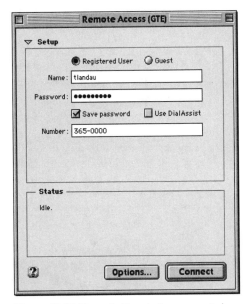

Figure 11-31 The main Remote Access control panel.

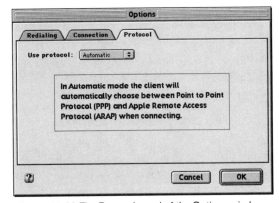

Figure 11-32 The Protocol panel of the Options window of Remote Access.

option (again selected from the Remote Access window). It accesses a control panel that can help you figure out the correct phone number settings. Also see "Problems Using Apple Remote Access," later in this chapter. It covers such matters as when and how to select the Remote Only option.

> **SEE:** • Chapter 12 for more general information on setting up and using a modem and PPP connections.

5. **Disconnect** When you later want to disconnect, select to disconnect via Remote Access's Disconnect button or any equivalent Control Strip Module or Apple Menu item.

TAKE NOTE ▶ Alternatives to Remote Access: Web Sharing, Timbuktu, and iDisk

If you want to share files with someone at a remote location (or even access your own home computer from your PowerBook when you are on the road), you can use Remote Access, as described in the main text. However, there are other alternatives:

Web Sharing The Mac OS now includes a control panel called Web Sharing. From here, you can designate a folder to be a shared folder. When you are connected to the Internet, if you select to start Web Sharing, the software will locate your current IP address (see Chapter 12 for more details on this) and use this as the Internet address for your shared folder. If your folder contains HTML files (see chapter 13), you will have set up your Mac to act as a small-scale web server for your web site (although don't expect it to be very fast or handle much traffic; for big sites you will want a professional strength web server such as WebSTAR). Otherwise, it contain whatever files you want the remote Mac to be able to access. If you do not want everyone on the Internet to be able to access this information, you can select "Use File Sharing to control user access." Now, only those users that would otherwise be able to access your Mac via File Sharing will be able to access your Mac via Web Sharing.

Microsoft Internet Explorer comes with separate web sharing software called Personal Web Manager. You can use this instead of Apple's Web Sharing. They have similar features.

Timbuktu Pro Farallon's Timbuktu Pro can send files over an AppleTalk or TCP/IP connection, much like Apple's File Sharing. In my view, once it is setup, it is even easier to use. But its biggest advantage is that you can use it to remotely view or control another Mac. That is, you can access the other Mac as if you were using the other Mac yourself. You will see the menus and dialog boxes that appear on the other Mac. In fact, you will see exactly what is on the screen of the other Mac as if watching it on TV. This can be great when trying to help someone troubleshoot their Mac over a phone. It will be as if you were in the room with them watching and working with their Mac.

iDisk If you are using Mac OS 9.0 or later, you can use Apple's iDisk feature. Available from the iTools section of Apple's web site, it allows you to set up a 20MB virtual hard disk on Apple's server. The disk is password-protected so that only you can access it. However, there is a folder on the disk, labeled "Public." Items put in this folder can be accessed by anyone who knows the name of your iDisk. They simply enter the name in the "Open Public Folder" text box at the iDisk web site. Thus, you can share files by placing them in this Public folder.

Note: To use iDisk, AppleShare and File Sharing must be enabled.

Apple File Sharing via TCP/IP This was discussed in "Take Note: File Sharing viaTCP/IP," earlier in this chapter.

TAKE NOTE ▶ Troubleshooting Remote Access

If you followed the direction in the main text, and still cannot get Remote Access to work as expected, here are some troubleshooting tips:

Select Remote Only The "Connect via" pop-up menu of the AppleTalk control panel includes an option called "Remote Only." Normally, you do not have to select this to use Remote Access. In fact, it is preferred not to do so, as this prevents use of any other AppleTalk connected devices besides the modem. However, if you believe that all your settings are correct (as described in the main text) and Remote Access still does not work, try selecting this. It may be the solution. Just remember to reselect your original "Connect via" option again when you are done with your remote connection.

    Note: According to Apple, Remote Only "is an extension that allows you to turn on AppleTalk networking when the printer port and/or the modem port on your computer are already in use (for example, for a serial printer and a modem)."

Turn Off "Answer Calls" when not needed With "Answer Calls" selected from Remote Access, the Mac waits for the phone to ring before engaging the modem. In the meantime, any other devices connected to the serial port should still be available for use. However, in some cases, especially with older versions of the Mac OS, the Answer Calls option may prevent access to your other devices on the network and/or software that accesses these devices. If you try to access them, you will get a "Serial Port is in Use" error message. The simplest solution here is to turn off the Answer Calls option until you are done with using whatever device or software was generating the error. Of course, if you rarely or never receive Remote Access calls, you can just leave Answer Calls off by default, turning it on only if and when you need it.

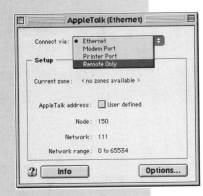

Figure 11-33 The Remote Access option in the AppleTalk control panel (as seen from an older Mac with serial ports).

Getting Your Mac to Answer when It's Off To use Remote Access to call your desktop Mac from your PowerBook, your desktop Macintosh must be turned on. But what if you forgot to leave it on when you left your office (or just don't want to leave it on all the time, so as to save energy and money)? Fortunately, there is a solution. There is a device, called PowerKey Remote (from Sophisticated Circuits), that will automatically turn on a Macintosh when a phone call comes in and turn it off again when the caller hangs up.

Don't Have Both Client and Server Software Installed Problems may occur if you have the Remote Access client and Server software installed on the same machine. In particular, you may not be able to access the Call Answering features. To avoid this, when installing a Mac OS update (which includes Remote Access client), do a Custom Install and only install the Remote Access Modem scripts from the Remote Access package. Then separately install the Remote Access Server. If you believe the "damage" has already been done, run the Installer and click to uninstall/remove all Remote Access software but the Modem scripts from your System Folder. Then run the Server installer. (See Apple Tech Info Library article #30830 for more details.)

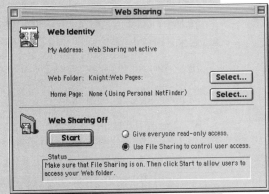

Figure 11-34 Apple's Web Sharing control panel.

Solve It! File Transfer Problems

This section offers solutions to the more common problems you may encounter when trying to transfer files from one Mac to another. Most of the advice here applies to all connections of this sort, not just those involving PowerBooks.

Can't Get File Sharing to Work

 Symptoms:

- When trying to turn on file sharing, you get a message that says "File sharing could not be enabled" or the file sharing startup simply never finishes.

- The file sharing option does not appear in the File Sharing control panel window.

- When trying to connect to another Macintosh, you get a message that says the shared disk could not be opened because it "could not be found on the network."

- When trying to connect to another Macintosh, you get a message that says it can't be opened because you do not have enough "access privileges."

- You cannot enable file sharing or connect to a shared disk for any other reason.

- While sharing information across disks, problems occur, such as system freezes or crashes.

 Causes:

Most causes are due to incompatible software, incorrect software settings, bugs in certain software or corrupted data.

 What to Do:

If You Get a Message That Says "File Sharing Could Not Be Enabled"

In almost all of these cases, the problem is due to a corrupted file that needs to be deleted. By the way, if you succeed in enabling file sharing but still want to delete any of these files, turn off file sharing first.

- **Corrupted Users and Groups data file** The Users and Groups data file is located in the Preferences folder. Locate it and move it to the desktop. Then restart. A new default version of the file will be created. After doing so, see if you can now turn file sharing on. If so, delete the removed file. Otherwise, you can return the file to its original location. If you do delete the original file, you will have to recreate and reset the privileges for the names formerly listed in Users & Groups.

- **Corrupted files in File Sharing folder** The File Sharing folder is located in the Preferences folder. It may contain corrupted files. To check for this, drag the File Sharing folder from the Preferences folder to the desktop. Restart and try again. If file sharing now succeeds, delete the removed folder; a new one is created automatically and its contents restored as needed. Otherwise, you can return the folder to its original location.

- **Corrupted AppleShare PDS file** AppleShare PDS is an invisible file located at the root level of the hard disk. It is used by AppleShare. To check whether the file is corrupted, you need to delete the file. However, since it is an invisible file, you will first need to use a utility, such as DiskTop or File Buddy, that lists and allows you to delete invisible files. Otherwise, you can use ResEdit to make the file visible; then go to the Finder and drag it to the Trash to delete it. After deleting the file, restart. The Mac will automatically create a new PDS file. Check if you can now enable file sharing.

  Deleting the PDS file removes all access privileges assigned to folders. You'll have to reset them.

  By the way, a corrupted PDS file has also been known to be a cause of unusually long startup times. Deleting the file corrects this problem.

BY THE WAY ▶ AppleShare PDS and CD-ROM PDF Files (Enough Acronyms For You?)

If you have a CD-ROM drive and you use file sharing, go to the Preferences folder and look for a folder called File Sharing. Inside, you will see a collection of files with PDF (not PDS!) at the end of their names. The reason these files are created is that, since CD-ROM discs are read-only, the Macintosh cannot create the more typical invisible AppleShare PDS file it would otherwise place on the CD-ROM disc. So instead, it creates these PDF files and stores them in your startup disk's System Folder. You can delete them if you wish. The Mac will recreate them if it needs them again.

By the way, speaking of invisible stuff related to file sharing, you may find an invisible folder on your hard disk, called Move & Rename. It too is created and used by AppleShare. Should you delete it by mistake, don't worry. The Mac will yet again create a new one when it needs one.

For Other Problems with Enabling File Sharing

You may have problems enabling file sharing that do not result in the "file sharing could not be enabled" message and/or do not involve corrupted files. Here are some common situations and their solutions:

- **Needed file-sharing software not installed or not active** In general, make sure that all file-sharing–related software is in place (as described in "File Sharing: Initial Setup" earlier in this chapter). Especially look for AppleShare and File Sharing. Make sure AppleTalk is turned on for both machines (unless you are using TCP/IP). Similarly, make sure that File Sharing is turned on for the host machine.

  Also make sure that Open Transport software is active (as described more in Chapter 12).

- **Corrupted PRAM** Zap the PRAM (see Fix-It #9). You will probably have to turn on AppleTalk again after this.

- **Disk limitations** You should ideally have at least 1MB of free disk space to use file sharing (the minimum may be as low as 360K on some older Macs). Also, some removable cartridge drives do not work with file sharing. Some non-Apple formatting utilities are not compatible with file sharing. Finally, you can't share a PC-formatted volume.

- **Memory limitations** You need at least 340K of memory to use file sharing. If you are having problems, restart with some or all non-file-sharing–related extensions off.

- **Sharing removable media** When trying to access the Sharing panel of the Get Info window, you get a message that says "One or more items could not be shared, because not all items are available for file sharing." This probably means you are trying to share a removable cartridge (such as in a Zip drive) that was mounted after file sharing was turned on. Try turning file sharing off and then back on again. Otherwise restart, making sure the cartridge is present at startup. Then try the Sharing command again. It should now work.

TECHNICALLY SPEAKING ▶ The Sharing Option For Folders

In the main text, I mainly describe selecting Sharing for an entire disk/volume. However, you can select any folder on a disk and similarly select Sharing. If you do so (and assuming you have also turned on "Share this item and its contents" for the whole disk), a variation in the Sharing window will appear. The option to set privileges will read "Use enclosing folder's privileges." If you unselect this, you can separately determine the file sharing options for this folder, overriding whatever options were selected for the disk as a whole.

On the other hand, if "Share this item and its contents" is off for the disk, when you go to set privileges for a folder, the option will now default to the typical "Share this item and its contents" for the folder.

If you make this separate setting, watch the folder's icon change! If you do this and then try to enable sharing for the enclosing volume, you should get a message that says the volume "could not be shared, because there is a shared folder inside it." If this happens, and you no longer want the separate setting for the folder:

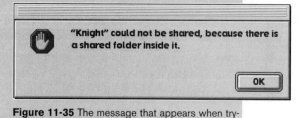

"Knight" could not be shared, because there is a shared folder inside it.

OK

Figure 11-35 The message that appears when trying to enable sharing for a volume where sharing has already been enabled for a folder within the volume.

1. Select the Activity Monitor tab from the File Sharing control panel to get a list of currently Shared Items.

2. Select any and all folders that are within the volume you want to share and click the Privileges button. This will take you to the Get Info window for each folder. From here, unselect "Share this item and its contents" for each folder.

3. Return to the Sharing window for the enclosing volume and select "Share this item and its contents."

4. Click the Copy button to "Copy these privileges to all enclosed folders." The entire volume is now shared with a single set of privileges.

In most cases (again assuming you are sharing among computers that are all your own and you are not part of a larger network), you will have little reason to alter privileges for individual folders. Bottom line: Don't bother them and they won't bother you.

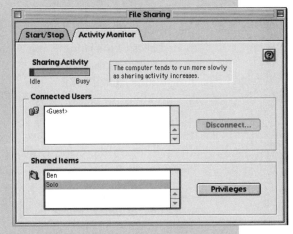

Figure 11-36 The Activity Monitor panel of the File Sharing control panel.

If You Get a Message That Says That the Shared Volume Could Not Be Opened Because It "Could Not Be Found on the Network" (or Similar Error Messages)

Moving from the host computer to the computer trying to access it, there are several possible reasons you may get a message that says that a shared disk "could not be found." The most obvious is that file sharing has not been turned on for the host volume. Other possible reasons include:

Figure 11-37 Message that indicates a problem accessing a shared volume.

- **Cables not connected** Make sure that the cable connecting the two computers is present and plugged into the AppleTalk active ports (probably the printer ports) or Ethernet ports of each Mac.

- **AppleTalk mismatch** If AppleTalk on one computer is set to the Printer port while on the other it is set to Ethernet (or any other similar mismatch), a connection will not be made.

  SEE ALSO: • "Transfer Files via File Sharing," earlier in this chapter.

- **Shared disk not finished with its startup sequence** Even after the startup sequence appears to be over and the desktop icons appear, it may take a minute or so longer before file sharing is actually enabled. So before trying to mount a shared disk, wait until it completely finishes its startup. You can usually tell this has happened when the noise associated with hard disk access at startup stops and the double thick handles appear on folder icons.

- **Alias no longer works** If you are trying to open a shared volume by opening a previously created alias of the volume, the problem may be that something on the shared volume has been modified so that the alias no longer works. The solution is to start over and create a new alias (as described previously in "File Sharing: Initial Setup").

- **Connection Failed, No Response, or other similar errors** When trying to mount a shared volume, you may get an error message that says that the connection failed or that there was no response from the server.

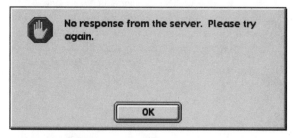

Figure 11-38 Error messages that will usually disappear after restarting the Macs involved.

There are a variety of obscure causes for these errors. However, the simplest solution in almost all cases is to just restart both of the Macs involved.

- **Otherwise...** Check in the next sections for other possible solutions.

TAKE NOTE ▶ File Sharing Freezes and False Freezes

No matter what the cause of "Could Not Be Found on the Network" message, it will likely take 30 seconds or so for this message to appear. During this time, you will be unable to do anything else with your Mac. It may thus seem as if your Mac has frozen. However, this is not the case. Just be patient and the message will appear.

On the other hand, after mounting a shared volume, a true freeze may occur for any variety of reasons. When this happens, the cursor will likely shift to a watch icon and stay that way indefinitely. If you are in the middle of transferring a file, you will also note that the double arrows in the upper left corner of the screen (to the left of the Apple menu icon) will stop flashing. These arrows appear when a shared volume is mounted and the flashing indicates active communication with the volume.

When a freeze occurs, you will likely have no choice but to restart one (or both) Macs to get things working again. A forced quit (as described in Chapter 4) will usually have no effect. The most likely culprit of these freezes is an extension conflict.

However, if you have MacsBug installed, you may just get lucky. Press Command-Power (or the Interrupt button) to drop into MacsBug. Then type (without the quotes): "stopxpp". Next, press Return, "g" and Return again. This should bring you back to the Finder with the Mac unfrozen. All previously mounted networked volumes will be unmounted.

SEE: • **Chapter 4 for more on system freezes and crashes.**
      • **Fix-It #3 on solving extension conflicts.**

If You Get a Message That Says You Can Not Perform a Function with a Shared Volume "Because You Do Not Have Enough Access Privileges"

While trying to connect to a shared disk, you may get a message that says "you do not have enough access privileges" to do so. Sometimes, this is simply because file sharing is not turned on or not yet active on the host machine. The obvious solution here is to make sure file sharing is on, using the procedures outlined earlier in this section.

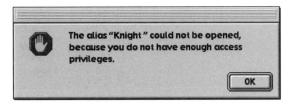

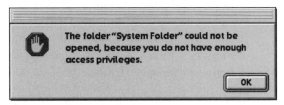

System Folder

Figure 11-39 Top: message indicating insufficient access privileges to open a shared volume. Bottom: similar message indicating an inability to open a folder within a shared volume and the special locked icon associated with this folder.

SEE: • **"Transfer Files via File Sharing,"** earlier in this chapter.

Otherwise, you may have inadvertently limited access privileges via the Sharing option. To fix this, go to the host machine, not the machine where the error message appeared. Select the icon of the problem disk and then select Get Info and access the Sharing item from the Show pop-up menu. Then check for the following:

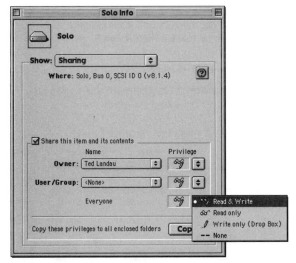

Figure 11-40 The different privileges settings as indicated in the pop-up menu of the Get Info window.

- If the "Share this item and its contents" option is unchecked, it is usually functionally equivalent to having turned off file sharing for the entire disk. When you try to access this volume via file sharing, you may not see it listed at all (from the Chooser or the Network Browser). However, if you double-click a previously created alias for the volume, you will likely get the "do not have enough access privileges" message.

- Even if the "Share this item and its contents" option is checked, you can still separately limit access to Owner, User/Group, or Everyone categories. You do this by selecting the appropriate privilege setting for each category. The options are: Read & Write, Read Only, Write Only, and None.

Normally, for the low-security setups described in this chapter, you would select Read & Write for Everyone. If something else has been selected, you may get a message such as "do not have enough access privileges."

Figure 11-41 Message that appears when trying to move a folder to the Trash when you have Read Only access to the folder.

For example, if None is selected for Everyone, you will not gain access to the volume as a guest—even if access to Guests has been granted in Users & Groups and Share This Item has been checked. As another example, if a Guest is limited to Read access, the Guest will be able to mount and view the disk, but will be unable to make any modifications to it. Should they attempt any modifications, such as discarding a file, an alert message will appear warning that you do not have the privilege to make changes.

- This "not enough access privileges" message will also appear for a folder within a shared volume, if sharing for the volume has been enabled but separate overriding settings have been made for the folder (see "Technically Speaking: The Sharing Option For Folders"). In this case, the folder will also have a special locked icon when viewed from the Mac accessing it.

One exception: the owner of the Mac can access a volume or folder even if "Share this item…" or individual has been disabled for it.

Otherwise, the solution in all cases is to enable file sharing privileges for the volume or folder (by enabling the "Use enclosing folder's privileges" option and/or by separately setting the appropriate privileges for the folder or volume).

SEE: • "Technically Speaking: The Sharing Option for Folders," for related information.
   • Chapter 6, "When You Can't Save or Copy a File," for related information, especially regarding a message that says "Illegal Access Permission."

Problems with Turning File Sharing or AppleTalk Off

If you want to turn file sharing or AppleTalk off, take note of the following:

- When you try to turn AppleTalk off, or change the type of connection (from Ethernet to Printer port, for example) you may get a message warning you that doing so will interrupt any AppleTalk services that are active at the time. Of course, if no shared volumes are mounted, you can just ignore this message. Otherwise, you may want to disconnect first (such as by dragging the icon for a shared volume to the Trash).

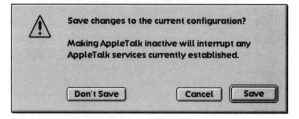

Figure 11-42 Message that appears when you try to turn AppleTalk off.

If you turn AppleTalk off when File Sharing is enabled, File Sharing is also disabled. Don't turn off AppleTalk while a shared disk is actually mounted. This may cause a system freeze or crash.

- You *can* safely turn off file sharing from the host Mac, even while its disk is mounted on another Mac. If you try to do so, you will first get a message asking you to enter how many minutes until file sharing is disabled. This is just provided as a way of giving other users on the network some advance warning, should they be connected to your computer. If it is just your own Macs involved, there are no other users to worry about. In this case, you can safely select zero minutes for immediate disabling.

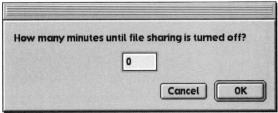

Figure 11-43 This dialog box appears when you try to turn off file sharing from a host Macintosh.

Figure 11-44 The "server has closed down" error may appear for any of several reasons, such as if file sharing is stopped for an already mounted volume.

If file sharing is disabled in this way, while a shared volume is still mounted on another Mac, the other Mac will display an error message stating that the connection has "closed down." The icon for the mounted volume will vanish.

- Similarly, if you uncheck "Share this item and its contents" for an already mounted volume, even though file sharing remains enabled, you will get a message asking if you are sure you want to do it.

If you proceed, the icon for the shared volume will remain on the other Mac's desktop until you try to access it. At this point, you will get a message indicating that you do not have enough access privileges and the volume will then dismount itself (the icon will vanish).

Figure 11-45 A message that appears when unchecking "Share this item and its contents" for an already mounted volume.

- The message that says a connection has "closed down" may occur at other times, such as after a system crash on the host machine. If this happens, and you still see the shared volume's icon on your desktop, drag the icon to the Trash before trying to reconnect to the volume.

Other Problems with Using File Sharing...

The following is a miscellaneous collection of problems and solutions related to file sharing. Several of these problems involve system freezes and crashes. Read it over to see if your problem is contained here:

- When files are being transferred over the network, other operations are likely to slow down. For example, you will notice that moving icons on the desktop, opening and closing windows, launching applications, and copying files will all take longer. This is normal.

- Try not to have other background activities going while a disk is currently being shared, especially while transferring files over the network, and most especially when first trying to access and mount the shared volume. In particular, don't have other file copying or printing in progress, particularly on the host machine. Otherwise, it may lead to a system freeze.

- Be careful about putting a Mac to sleep while a shared disk is mounted. If you do, the connection will be lost. You will get the same "closed down" error described in the previous section. If files are currently being transferred, the transfer will halt. A system crash is possible.

- If you have checked everything, and it all checks out, but you still don't get the shared volumes listed in the Network Browser (or AppleShare option from the Chooser), try this: if you are connecting via Ethernet, for example, shift to connect via another method, such as Remote Only. Save the changes and close the control panel. Then re-open it, reselect the original method (e.g., Ethernet) and save and close again. This can bring a connection back to life.

  If this too fails, it's time to start troubleshooting the network itself, including the cable connections.

    See: • **"File Sharing via the Ethernet Port," earlier in this chapter.**
             • **"Take Note: File Sharing Freezes and False Freezes," earlier in this section.**

12

Road Service for the Infobahn: Getting and Staying Connected

No Mac Is an Island... Anymore

There was a time, not too long ago, when the fact that the personal computer could function free of a network or online connection was perceived as its main advantage. What you could do with your personal computer was not constrained by what the mainframe gods would permit. You were in complete control of your own environment.

These days are over. In fact, connecting the computer to the outside world, particularly the Internet, is probably the single biggest reason that most people buy a computer today. But we have not returned to a world where your computer is little more than a "dumb terminal" with all the "power" concentrated in a mainframe computer over which you have little or no control. You remain in control. The Internet is viewed as empowering users, rather than subjugating them. Via the Internet, you have easy access to more information than people could have possibly imagined even as recently as ten years ago. These days, from cruising the World Wide Web to sending/receiving email, the Internet is *everything*.

These next two chapters cover the world of the Internet: from setting up an Internet connection, to using email and finally to the World Wide Web. Thorough coverage of even a fraction of the topics described here could fill up a book by itself. So, I am forced to be selective. My focus stays on those topics that I believe face the greatest number of users. I am sorry if this means that I omitted a particular topic that you wanted covered.

But cheer up. There are plenty of problems that *are* covered. Chances are good that you'll find what you are looking for.

BY THE WAY ▶ What is the Internet?

The Internet is the name of a loosely organized world-wide network of computers. A network is simply the name given to any setup where at least two computers are connected in such a way that they can communicate with each other. A small network - often called a Local Area Network (or LAN) - can consist of two or three computers in your home or several hundred computers in a place of business. The Internet is actually a large super-network, connecting these smaller networks together. You can view it as a branching tree. Metaphorically, there is a huge trunk that represents the highest level of interconnectivity. Lesser networks are out on the branches. Wherever in the tree you are, it is possible to return to the trunk (more often it's referred to as the "backbone," but we're mixing metaphors here) and get to any other place in the tree. Your computer is probably out there on a distant branch, but it can send a signal to any other place on the Internet.

Amazingly, there is very little central authority on the Internet. It relies on the voluntary cooperation of major institutions that comprise the "trunk" level of the Internet.

TCP/IP and PPP Several key developments fueled the expansion of the Internet. The first was the development of the TCP/IP (Transmission Control Protocol/Internet Protocol) networking protocol in the mid-1980s. TCP/IP breaks the data you send into small packets of information, each of which is separately sent along the Internet. These data packets jump from network to network on their way to their final destination; the exact route is tracked by special computers that act as routers.

(continues on next page)

BY THE WAY ▶ What is the Internet? *(continued)*

This system allowed for faster and more reliable data transfer. It also had the advantage of allowing networks that could otherwise not "talk" to each other (because they each used their own unique networking "language") to communicate. For example, prior to this, CompuServe users could not send email to America Online users because they were on separate non-connected networks. Now, with TCP/IP, the Internet could tie all existing networks together into one super worldwide Internet. Any user could now send email to anyone else in the world who had an email account.

Even if your computer was not directly hooked up to a TCP/IP network, you could dial into one, using a modem and special connection protocols such as PPP (Point-to-Point Protocol). PPP essentially fools the network that you dial up into thinking that you are physically connected to the network, rather than dialing in over a phone line.

Shell access It is only via a TCP/IP connection that you can use the full range of independent Internet software, such as Web browsers, news readers, email clients and so forth. The alternative is to dial up your ISP directly via a terminal emulation program. This makes your computer behave similarly to the old text-only "dumb" terminals that connected to mainframe computers in large institutions. This is rarely done anymore, and we will not discuss it further. However, after making a TCP/IP connection, you might still find it useful to make a terminal or "shell access" connection. You can do this with Telnet software, such as Nifty Telnet on the Mac.

Initially, all Internet services were accessed via text-only connections (such as "shell" or Telnet connections). Shell access is still used today for such tasks as maintaining a Web site on a Unix computer. To run Unix commands needed to manipulate the files on the drive, you would create a shell connection. If you are at a large institution, such as a university, shell access is more common. Many people still use it for email and for accessing specialized software, such as statistics programs.

Non-TCP/IP connections are also still used for logging on to commercial services, such as America Online (although, as we will describe more later on, AOL also now supports TCP/IP access).

Graphics and the Web Another major event in the development of the Internet was the creation of the World Wide Web. Started in 1992, the Web was initially just one minor player among the many services/technologies available on the Internet. Email, newsgroups, and various ways of searching the Internet (such as Gopher and WAIS) were much more popular. However, the Web soon eclipsed them all (with the possible exception of email) and now clearly dominates the Internet. When you see television commercials for .com companies, they are talking about Web sites!

At first, the Web was an all text environment, much like the rest of the Internet. However, with a TCP/IP connection and the right software, it became possible to directly view graphic images over the Internet. This had its greatest effect on the Web, leading to the development of graphical Web browsers, such as Netscape Navigator and Internet Explorer.

By this time, home, office and commercial users had hopped on to the Internet in droves - and soon vastly outnumbered the original government and education institution users. And so we arrive at where we are today.

Getting on the Internet For you to get on the Internet from your computer, you typically need three main components: (1) A means of connecting your computer to the Internet. This is most often a traditional modem hooked up to your telephone line. However, over the next couple of years, there will be an increased use of faster "broadband" connections such as cable modems. Otherwise, if you are in an office environment, you may be able to use a shared Internet connection via your office's local network. (2) A service that provides the means for you to gain an onramp to the Internet. These are most often called Internet Service Providers (or ISPs). (3) Internet software, such as a Web browser. I will look at the details of all of these components in the pages ahead.

As the use of the Internet has exploded, tools to help you get connected have made the task much easier to do. But it still has a way to go before it is as easy as turning on your TV.

TAKE NOTE ▶ Selecting an Internet Service Provider (ISP)

In addition to the hardware and software needed to connect to the Internet (as covered in the main text), you'll also need an Internet Service Provider (ISP). An ISP is a company that has direct, often referred to as "trunk" access to the Internet. From its trunk, it provides users like yourself with a branch from which you can get on the Net. If you use dialup (modem) access to get on the Internet, it is the ISP who you dial up. AOL is probably the biggest single ISP, but it is different from most of the rest because it offers its own AOL-only content as well as Internet access. For cable modem users, the cable company is the ISP. (Your ISP in turn connects to even bigger players–the primary network providers such as UUNET. These then connect directly to the Internet backbone. End users are thus fairly low on the food chain.)

There are thousands of ISPs to choose from. So how do you choose the best one for you? If you want AOL's unique features, your decision is easy. The only way to get them is by signing up with AOL. However, if you are trying to pick from the remainder of the pack, here are several points to consider:

Does it provide support for Macs? All ISPs support Windows. Not all support Macs. There is actually not much difference between what is needed to support Macs vs. Windows platforms. Chances are good that you could use an ISP with a Mac even if the provider does not specifically support the Mac. However, if the ISP provides Internet software and technical support, as most do, you won't get any Mac software or Mac questions answered unless the ISP specifically supports the Mac platform. Currently, Apple and EarthLink <www.earthlink.net> are working together to make EarthLink the biggest (and best?) Mac-friendly ISP.

Is it a local call? With the standard phone service that most people still have, a local phone call is toll-free. If your ISP has a dial-up access phone number that is a local call for you, this can amount to a substantial savings of money over having to pay a per-minute fee for a phone call. If at all possible, choose an ISP that provides local access. If you plan to travel, look for an ISP that has local access numbers around the country or (if you are an international traveler) around the world.

How many lines does your ISP have? When you want to get on the Internet via a modem, you don't want to get a busy signal. Make sure your ISP has enough lines so you can get on when you want. There is no minimum number that is desirable. It depends upon how many users they have. Ask the ISP about how often you might expect a busy signal.

Do they support your modem? This is currently most relevant if you have a 56K V.90 modem. To take advantage of this, your ISP must have implemented V.90 protocol support (we talk about this later in this chapter). Most should have this support by now, but make sure.

Is there a flat-rate payment option? If you plan to be on the Internet for more than about four or five hours a month, you'll want a flat per-month charge, not an hourly charge. With the flat rate, you can log on as much and as often as you want, without worrying that each hour of access is adding to your bill. Flat rates bottom out at about $20-$25 a month, but can go up depending upon the services offered. A common extra is free disk space for setting up your own Web site. With a flat rate fee and a local access phone number, your access to the Internet can be a great bargain (let's just hope that the powers that be don't mess this up and pass laws that force you to pay a lot more).

Understanding Dial-Up Modems

A modem is still the most common way that users hook-up to the Internet—especially individual users not on a network. But modems are not likely to reign supreme much longer. Several alternatives promise much faster speed and 24 hour/day access without having to "dial up." But let's start with a focus on the tried and true modem.

SEE: • Take Note: Beyond Dial-up Modems.

A modem is a hardware device that connects your Macintosh on one end to your telephone line on the other end. A modem may be a separate external unit, a PC Card (slipping in to the PC Card slot of PowerBooks) or an internal card. Some Macs, such as the iMac, come with an internal modem already installed. On older Macs, external modems were connected via the Mac's serial ports. On current Macs, which no longer have serial ports, you can get an external modem that connects via the USB port. With any of these modems and the relevant software, you can connect to other computers or to the Internet or other online information services anywhere in the world.

It is the theme of this book to focus on what to do when things go wrong. In this section, I explain three common modem settings that are important to know about when troubleshooting modem problems: Modem Speed, Flow Control, and Init Strings.

TAKE NOTE ▶ Beyond Dial-Up Modems

V.90 56K modems likely represent the end of the road for traditional modems. The faster the information travels, the cleaner the transmission has to be to avoid errors. Inevitable line noise on ordinary phone lines prohibits speeds faster than 56K.

But alternatives are already here. One such alternative is ISDN (Integrated Services Digital Network). This provides speeds of 56K (and possibly 112K if you have a "dual ISDN line"). You need a special hook-up from your phone company to use ISDN, and you will have to pay extra for it. However, given that it may be not much faster than a 56K modem, and that it is certainly much slower than the remaining alternatives, we predict that ISDN is also a dying technology and we have little more to say about it.

The two most promising technologies today are cable modems and DSL.

Cable modems (which are technically not really modems at all; they should more properly be called converters) connect through the same outlet that you use for cable TV. Cable modems have two distinct advantages over ordinary telephone line modems: they are much, much faster (by a factor of 10 or more) and you are always connected (you don't have to dial up a telephone number to establish a link; you are online as soon as your Mac finishes starting up!). This is definitely the way to go. Check out http://www.home.net for more information.

A couple of other caveats of cable modems: (1) The speed you see is limited by the speed in which the information is sent. For example, trying to load a Web page from a very slow server may not seem much faster with a cable modem than with an ordinary modem. (2) The upload speed on modems is often significantly slower than the download speed. One reason this is done is to prevent "home" users from using their cable connection to run a Web server. However, this is not an inherent limitation of these modems and speeds may be closer by the time you are reading this. (3) Speeds may vary depending upon how many other users in your area are also using the same cable modem "node."

(continues on next page)

When things get busy, speeds can decrease dramatically. You can also expect occasional outages where the modem stops working altogether, although these should not last more than a few minutes. Sometimes simply turning the modem's power off and back on will fix this. Otherwise, if problems persist, you'll need to contact the cable company's tech support. (4) I have seen several reports where cable modem users are able to access the computers of other users on the cable node. This threat should be minimal, especially if you do not have file sharing on. However, be aware that Mac OS 9 allows for file-sharing via TCP/IP, which increases the risks here (see Chapter 11). You can always check MacFixIt (http://www.macfixit.com/) for more information on these matters.

DSL (Digital Subscriber Line protocol; developed by Bell Labs) similarly requires a special type of modem. Like ISDN, this is set up via your phone company. It too often transfers data faster when downloading than when uploading. However, overall its speed is very fast, often surpassing cable modems. And, unlike cable modems, each user is on a separate line; so there is not the problem of slow-downs at busy times. The problem with DSL, for now, is that it is only available in a select few geographical locations. You may also see reference to ADSL (Asymmetric DSL). This is currently the most common type of DSL. The "asymmetric" means that download speeds are faster than upload speeds. Check sites such as http://www.adsl.com for more details on DSL.

Other choices include satellite dish connections (which can achieve super-fast 400K bps speeds) or running your own T1 line (which is almost like becoming your own ISP and can be prohibitively expensive for individual users).

Modem Speed

Dial-up modems can run at different speeds. Faster speeds have the obvious benefit that everything you do, from downloading files to loading Web pages, goes faster. Thus, as is true in every other part of the computer world, *faster is better*.

You would think a modem's speed would be relatively easy to determine and comprehend. I mean if someone says that a car is going 60 mph, it doesn't take a manual to figure out what that means. Sadly, modem speeds are not at all like automobile speeds. So here is what you need to know to get up to speed on modem speed:

Bits Per Second (bps)

Most modems are described as having a basic speed listed in *bits per second* (bps). The bps speed is the maximum speed that the modem is capable of sending and receiving data.

These days, the most common bps for modems is 56bps (also referred to as 56K). The slowest modem still in common use today is 28.8K (anything slower is useless for the World Wide Web and can be interminably slow for downloading software).

By the way, while bps is sometimes interpreted as the same thing as *baud rate*, they are different. The term baud rate is no longer technically correct and is not used much anymore.

56K Modems: A Closer Look

Truth in advertising: the speed of 56K modems is not really 56K. First of all, their upload speed (that is the speed in which you can send things from your computer to another location) is stuck at 33.6K. It is the download speed (the speed by which you receive information) that is at least potentially 56K. Of course, since most users spend most of their time online downloading (browsing a Web is almost entirely a download process), even this one-way speed boost is significant. However, as I will explain shortly, you are not likely to achieve 56K when downloading data.

A related issue is that two of the major modem manufacturers came up with two separate and incompatible methods for achieving this 56K goal. US Robotics devised the **x2** protocol while Rockwell used something called *K56Flex*. In order for you to get 56K performance, you not only need a 56K modem, you also need to connect at the other end to a site that is set up for 56K (it requires special digital equipment as opposed to just another 56K modem). The site also needs to use the same type of 56K protocol as your modem. That is, an x2 modem trying to connect to a K56Flex site would not produce 56K speed. What would it produce? In principle, the two sites should be able to negotiate back down to 33.6K. You would lose the extra speed boost of your 56K modem, but at least you could connect. In reality, the result can be frequent disconnects or even a complete failure to connect.

Happily, this dilemma is now over. USR and Rockwell (and the International Telecommunications Union) got together and produced a multi-vendor common standard called *V.90* (when it comes to acronyms that are totally useless in helping you understand what they mean, nothing surpasses modem technology!). By the time you read this, all 56K sites should have converted to the V.90 standard. If you have an X2 or KFlex modem, chances are good that there is a firmware upgrade that will give it V.90 capability. If not, you may need to get a new modem.

During the transition period, problems abound. For example, if you upgrade your x2 modem to V.90 and, by some chance, you connect to a site that still uses x2, your modem should fall back to x2 or even to the 33.6K protocol. However, often it does not. Instead, once again, it may fail to connect at all. The ultimate solution here will be to wait for your ISP to upgrade its equipment or shift to a different ISP.

To summarize, there are three primary requirements for V.90 compatibility and for 56K speeds to be achieved: (1) you must have a V.90 modem; (2) your ISP must have the necessary 56K digital hardware; and (3) your ISP must support the V.90 protocol.

Why Doesn't My Modem Connect At Its Fastest Speed?

The bps rating, such as 56K, is the maximum speed you can hope to get. However, you will rarely ever achieve this maximum. And the faster the modem, the less likely you will get to its top speed. Here's why.

Line quality The actual transmission speed is determined when you first make a connection and is affected by such factors as telephone line noise. The quality of your phone line can affect the amount of noise on the line. With an especially noisy line, even a 56K modem may do no better than 26.4K. Even with a clean signal, you will be lucky to get over 50K.

In general, the faster your modem, the more likely that line noise will interfere with getting connected at the modem's maximum speed. That is, line noise that might not prevent a 28.8K modem from connecting at 28.8K may very well prevent a 56K modem from connecting at anything even close to 56K.

To some extent, it's like driving a Ferrari in rush hour traffic. It doesn't matter that your speedometer goes up to 200 mph; the needle won't be going anywhere near that range for the moment.

In some cases, your phone line may be so degraded that it does not pay to spend the money to go from a 33.6K to a 56K modem (as you have no hope of achieving the faster speeds). To check for this, you can do a line test. The 3Com Web site has a page (http://www.3com.com/56k/need4_56k/linetest.html) that provides instructions on how to do this.

Of course, if your Mac shipped with a 56K modem already installed (such as is the case with almost all Macs now shipping), you don't have to give up on it and get a slower one. Just be aware that you may not achieve the speed that the modem is capable of delivering.

Connection location As already implied, for a modem to even hope to achieve its maximum speed, both connected sites must operate at that speed (or faster). So if you are trying to connect to a service that sends information at 28.8K, your 56K modem needs to slow down to match the 28.8K of the service. Fortunately, all modems can down shift to lower speeds if necessary, so you don't need a separate modem for each speed.

In years past, an online service such as America Online would have separate phone numbers for different transmission speeds. If you called on a "slow" line, you had no chance of getting a fast connection. Much more common today is a single high-speed line that can accommodate the full range of speeds. Similarly, years ago, services charged extra for connecting at higher speeds. This is usually no longer the case. Now there is a one-price policy regardless of the connect speed.

Modem Data Compression

While your modem may have a limit of 56K, it can increase its apparent transmission speed through compression of the data. This hardware-based data compression is similar to how a software utility like StuffIt works. By analogy, suppose you wanted to send a telegram as fast as you could, but the fastest it could go was 10 letters per second. Your 500-letter telegram would take 50 seconds to send. Now suppose you found a way to eliminate 20 percent of the letters and still retain all the meaning of the telegram. Your message would now only take 400 letters and thus 40 seconds. When the recipient reads the telegram, he essentially "decompresses" it when he reads it. So in some sense he received all 500 letters in less time.

Data compression cannot speed up the transfer of already compressed files (compressed via utilities such as StuffIt Deluxe). However, most other data will go faster if compressed. A typical compression ratio is 4-to-1. This means that data may actually appear to be transmitted at four times the modem's rated bps. Thus a 28K modem may appear to transmit at 115K.

Today's modems also include error-correction protocols to ensure that the data gets transmitted correctly. Both compression and error-correction options may not work well with certain connections, paradoxically slowing down the connection or generating errors. If this happens, you can turn these options off and see if that helps. Often, there is a way to do this from the software that is supplied with the modem or with your operating system. For example, Apple's Remote Access control panel has an option called "Allow error correction and compression in modems." Disable it to turn off these features. Without such an option, your other choice is to directly modify the modem's init string (as discussed later in this chapter).

Carrier (DCE) Versus Connect (DTE) Speeds

The speeds referred to thus far are only half the story of what is commonly thought of as your modem's "speed." What we have described represents the speed with which information travels from its external remote source to your modem (and vice versa). This is technically referred to as the *carrier* (or DCE) speed.

Once the data hits your modem (and gets decompressed), it has to travel to your computer (for external modems, it goes through a serial, USB or Ethernet port). This is called the *connect* (or DTE) speed. It is also referred to as the *port* speed. The fastest connect speed is referred to as the *maximum throughput*. If your software allows you control over the speed setting, the port speed can be (and usually should be) set to higher level than the carrier speed (for reasons explained below).

Selecting the Right Port Speed: Getting Maximum Throughput

The connect (DTE) speed represents a potential bottleneck for a high speed modem. Older Macs (prior to Power Macs) could not always handle the speed that the modem could send the data. You had to carefully select the right combination of speeds to get your modem to work at its best. Happily, this is no longer of much concern. In fact, the most common software in use today no longer even gives you an option to set these speeds. At best, you can select to either have "maximum throughput" option enabled or, if that gives you any trouble, disabled.

How Can I Tell How Fast My Modem Is Connected?

Sometimes you'll want to know what your DCE speed is. Are you really getting the 56K as promised, or are you getting only 28.8K? How can you tell? Usually, the connection software will list a number. Just be sure it is listing the DCE speed and not the DTE speed. The DTE speed will be listed as the same high number (such as 115,200) regardless of variations in the actual connection speed. The DCE speed may vary each time you connect.

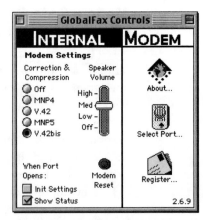

Figure 12-1 Global Village's GlobalFax Controls (sometimes called TelePort) control panel. Connection and Compression are set for V.42bis, the most common and preferred setting.

With Apple's Remote Access control panel, the DCE speed is typically listed in the control panel window after a connection is made. It also displays a bar graph that shows when data is being sent and received. These can be a useful diagnostic to check if your modem connection is truly working (see later in this chapter for more on these diagnostics).

However, be wary of misinterpreting the modem speed as reported by Remote Access (or similar software). First of all, this software only reports that speed at the time you initially connected. If your speed subsequently slows down, the number listed will no longer be accurate. Also, if you shift to a third-party modem script, it can cause Remote Access to shift to listing the DTE speed, making it seem as if your connection just got faster. The true Data Transfer Rate (DTR) can be estimated by using this formula: file size (bytes)/download time (seconds) x 9 = average DTR (bits/second). An Apple Tech Info Library article <http://til.info.apple.com/techinfo.nsf/artnum/n24482> provides more details.

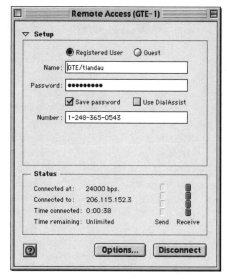

Figure 12-2 Remote Access control panel showing a 24000bps connection (a 33.6K modem was used to make the connection); also note the bar graph indicating that data is being downloaded (a Web page was loading at the time).

Bottom Line?

Your modem data transfer speed at any moment is a combination of the bps and compression technology of the modem, the throughput of the Mac's port, the settings of your software, the type of information being transmitted, the noise in the phone line, and the location to which you are connected. Clearly, your mileage may vary.

BY THE WAY ▶ Checking the Firmware Version with Global Village Software

If you use Global Village's modem software (either for a Global Village modem or the special version that works with the internal modem of iMacs and G3/G4 Power Macs), here is how to check what firmware version you are using: open the Global Village Fax Center software, hold down the Option button and click anywhere on the word "GlobalFax" at the top of the window. The window that appears will include the firmware number. And, if it says you are using an older version than you think you have installed, go to the TelePort/GlobalFax Controls control panel and click the Modem Reset button, then try again. Other modems use other procedures. Check with your modem vendor for specifics.

TAKE NOTE ▶ Updating Modem Firmware and Software

Most modems contain something called firmware or flash ROM. It is a cross between software and hardware. Like software, firmware can be updated. But like hardware, it is a "permanent" part of the circuitry of the modem itself; you cannot directly see it or access it, except through special software that can modify the firmware.

These firmware updates can work such minor miracles as updating a 28.8K modem to a 33.6K one, or converting an x2 56K modem to a V.90 one. Some firmware updates simply provide bug fixes to the ROM. You will find these firmware updates on the Web site of your modem vendor. Once you are on the Web, check to make sure you have the latest version.

However, beware if you have an internal modem that came pre-installed with your computer. While it is most likely manufactured by a major modem maker (such as US Robotics or Global Village), it may be modified in some way so that a firmware update that works with the commercial version of the modem will not work with the version that came with your computer. Check with your computer vendor before attempting to use an firmware update. They may have their own custom version of the firmware update.

Making a mistake here can be very serious. Hopefully, all that will happen is that the updater refuses to run; but don't count on it. Attempting to update the firmware of a modem with the "wrong" updater can incorrectly update the firmware and render your modem useless. The only recourse will be to send the modem back to the manufacturer for replacement or repair.

Even if the firmware update is the correct one for your modem, and installs correctly, you should realize that if problems occur for any reason (such as due to some undiscovered bug in the firmware), you typically cannot "downgrade" back to the older version. You are stuck with a firmware upgrade once you do it, unless the vendor specifically offers a downgrader.

Power users sometimes claim to have found workarounds (or ways to "patch" the updater) that get an updater to work on a modem for which it was not intended to work. Be careful. These power users will not pay to have your modem repaired if the work-around fails.

Your modem may also come with ordinary software (such as fax software) that gets installed on your hard drive. This too can get updated. The same issues apply here, except that an incorrect update will not damage the modem. As long as you have backups of your original software, you should be O.K.

SEE ALSO: • **Chapter 14 for more on firmware upgrades.**

TECHNICALLY SPEAKING ▶ Flow Control

Here are a couple of technical topics that you probably won't need to be concerned with. I just mention them so that in case you hear this jargon thrown around you'll be able to understand it:

Xon/Xoff versus hardware handshake The speed with which your modem sends data to your Mac must be matched with the capability of your Mac to receive that speed. If the modem sends data too fast, data will get lost. This matching is handled by something called flow control or handshake. On old, very low-speed modems, flow control was accomplished by a software method (usually set via options in your communications software) called Xon/Xoff. Higher-speed modems (9,600 bps and above) use a hardware-dependent method, called hardware handshaking. Because it is hardware-dependent (that is, the protocols are built into the modem and handled by dedicated wires), rather than dependent on your communications software, it is faster and more reliable.

This means two things: (1) with today's fast modems, make sure that Xon/Xoff option is disabled (you needn't worry about this in most cases, the modem should have this off by default) and (2) for external modems, make sure the cable that goes from the modem to the computer is hardware-handshaking capable. Again, your modem should have come with one. But if you ever need to buy a replacement, make sure you get the right cable or your modem will not work.

(continues on next page)

CTS and RTS (DTR) versus CTS Only versus RTS (DTR) Only some communications software will give you a choice of the exact type of hardware handshaking you want. There are three options (the fourth option, None, means you don't want hardware handshaking at all): CTS and RTS (DTR), CTS Only, and RTS (DTR) Only. CTS means Clear-to-Send and RTS means Request-to-Send (and no one cares what DTR means). Actually, all you need to know is that most times, you will be best off selecting the "CTS and RTS (DTR)" option. If that appears to cause trouble, try CTS Only.

Modem Scripts and Init Strings

AT Commands and Init Strings

Back in the online Dark Ages, when everyone communicated via a text-only command-line interface, your modem needed a way to know whether the text you were typing was a command to the modem or data to be transmitted. The primary method to do this was to type AT (for ATtention) at the start of a line intended as a modem command. This was followed by a series of numbers and characters that all had special meaning for your modem. Today, you can still do this via a terminal session window, accessible in most communications software. However, this is needed much less often today because current communications software has (happily) assumed the job of doing most of the necessary work for you.

The one place you may still want to enter this sort of information is called the modem's init string. This tells the modem how to initially set up any and all of its parameters, including whether data compression should be on or off, whether hardware handshaking should be used, whether or not the modem's speaker should be on or off, and so forth. When you first try to make a connection, your software initializes the modem based on the init string that you have given it.

Some settings are clearly optional and you can do whatever you prefer (such as turning the speakers off if they annoy you and turning them back on when you want to hear it to do some troubleshooting). However, when trying to make an online connection, especially a PPP connection, some of these options must be set a certain way or you will not get a successful connection.

Selecting Your Init String

The exact init string you should use varies as a function of the brand of modem you are using, the communications software you are using and sometimes even the remote location to which you are trying to connect. It is impossible for me to give general advice here, other than to say that AT&F1 (which signals to use a modem's default settings) is a good starting point if you have no other guidance. AT&F%C0\NO is another possible default choice. Otherwise, your modem's manual, your communications software's manual, or your online service may all have suggestions as to what init string is best for minimizing trouble. Follow their advice.

In most cases, init string decisions are made for you automatically. For example, with Apple's Open Transport, you are essentially selecting a *modem script* when you select a modem name from the Modem pop-up menu of the Modem control panel. These scripts include an init string plus lots of other goodies that will hopefully smooth the road ahead of you. If not, you may have to edit the string (typically based on the advice from other sources) or use a substitute script.

Certain problems, especially failures to connect or frequent disconnects, can sometimes be solved by modifying the init string. ModemHelp.net <http://www.modemhelp.net/> is a good place to go to get suggested init strings and much more modem-related advice.

TECHNICALLY SPEAKING ▶ Editing Init Strings and Modem Scripts

We have made occasional reference in the text to editing a modem script (such as for modifying the modem's init string). What the text does not say is exactly how to do this. Assuming you are using Apple's Remote Access, here's what to do (remember: always work with a copy of the original script file, or save a copy of the original init string, so you can return to it if the changes only makes things worse!):

1. If you can locate a modified script that already includes the changes you want to make, this is preferred. If so, you can ignore the following steps and just place the modified script in the Modem Scripts folder of the Extensions folder; then select it from the Modem control panel. Otherwise, you will first have to determine what exactly needs to be modified in a script. Assuming you cannot do this yourself, you will have to depend upon advice received from Web sites or other sources. For example, a problem with the internal modem of the PowerBook 3400 not reliably making a connection was solved by adding the term "%E1" to the init string in the script for the modem. Once you know what needs to be changed, proceed to the next step.

2. Locate the modem script file that needs to be changed. It should be in the Modem Scripts folder of the Extensions folder. In the case of the PowerBook 3400 example, it is called "PowerBook 3400 Internal 33.6." Always save a backup copy of the file to some other location on your drive, before you modify the original. Just in case.

3. Open a word processor that will attempt to open any type of file. For example, use Microsoft Word and select its "All Files" option. The text editor BBEdit is even better for this purpose. Then navigate to the Modem Scripts folder in the Extensions folder of the System Folder and open the script you wish to modify (such as PowerBook 3400 Internal 33.6).

4. To modify the init string, typically select Find and search for "AT&F"; there may be more than one instance of this. You probably only need to change the first one, although make changes to all instances, if the source of your information said to do so. The string will typically include a long list of terms after it. Change the terms as needed. For the PowerBook 3400 example, immediately after the F, add the term %E1. It should now read "AT&F%E1..."

5. Save the document as a plain text file, using the Text option in the Save As... dialog box.

6. You have now saved the modem script as a text file. However, it needs a different Type and Creator code before it can work as a modem script. These are the special codes that the Mac OS checks to determine whether a file is an application or an extension or a document or whatever and (if it is a document) what application created it. To make the necessary change, any number of disk-editing utilities will do. I use one called Snitch, which allows you to make the change directly from the file's Get Info window. You simply select Get Info for the modem script ad change the Type to "mlts" and the Creator to "slnk."

(continues on next page)

7. Just to be safe, even if you were already using this script, go to the Modem control panel and reselect it. Close the control panel and save the changes when prompted. You are now ready to connect using the modified script.

You can use the same basic method to make other changes.

If you wanted to create a completely new modem script from scratch, you can do it using Apple's *Modem Script Generator* software. It's free and is available from the Software Updates section of their Web site. However, you cannot use Modem Generator to edit an existing script. Check out Generator's Help files for guidance in using it. I can only hope that Apple eventually releases software that makes doing this easier!

If you don't use Apple's modem scripts Two common alternatives to Apple's control panels are FreePPP or connecting directly using America Online's software. In these cases, changing init strings is even easier, because you don't use modem scripts.

With FreePPP, launch FreePP Setup, select the Modem tab and select to edit and existing modem file or create a new one. Now, where it says "Modem init string settings" enter a string in the "Use:" text box or select "AutoDetect init string" and let FreePPP select the one it thinks is best, based on its built-in database of strings.

With AOL, if you are having a problem, you can get advice from AOL tech support on what changes to make to the default settings (normally no changes are needed). The first step to making a change is to select Setup from the AOL Welcome window. After this, what to do varies with which version of AOL you are using. In general, you want to access the Edit Location window for the modem and then click the Modem Options button. From the next window, click the Advanced Settings button. At last, you have arrived at the Advanced Modem Setup window. From here you can edit the modem init string.

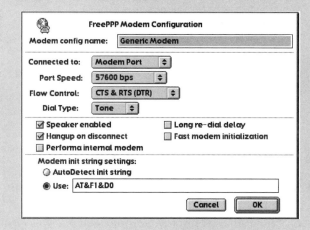

Figure 12-3 The FreePPP Setup control panel, with the option to edit the init string visible at the bottom of this Modem Configuration window; options to set port speed and flow control (described in the text) are also here.

Understanding Open Transport

Open Transport is the general name for the set of files included in the Mac OS that are used for making network connections, especially to the Internet.

TAKE NOTE ▶ What Is Open Transport Software?

Most of the software under the *Open Transport* umbrella is contained in the System Folder.

For starters, on Power Macs, the following shared library files will be in the Extensions folder: Open Transport Library, Open Tpt AppleTalk Library, Open Tpt Internet Library, OpenTransportLib, OpenTptAppleTalkLib, OpenTptInternetLib. The first three files are for running 68K applications in emulation, the latter three are for Power Mac-native applications.

On 680X0 Macintoshes, instead of installing the six library files just listed, it installs just three shared library files: Open Transport 68K Library, Open Tpt ATalk 68K Library, and Open Tpt Inet 68K Library. If these three files appear on Power Macs, they may be deleted. Online performance may actually improve if you do delete them for Power Macs.

Note: In Mac OS 9, the Open Transport Library and Lib files have been eliminated, replaced by two new files: Open Transport and Open Transport ASLM Modules.

As with most extensions, you do not directly interact with any of these files. However, there are several control panels included as part of the Open Transport software that you may work with. These include TCP/IP, Remote Access, and Modem, as described more in this section.

In general, don't remove any of these files from the System Folder unless you are sure you know what you are doing. Otherwise, you are asking for problems.

Note: Prior to the introduction of Open Transport, the Mac OS included a different set of files for connecting to the Internet. They were referred to as *Classic AppleTalk* and featured a control panel called MacTCP. In this edition of *Sad Macs*, I no longer cover this now-obsolete software.

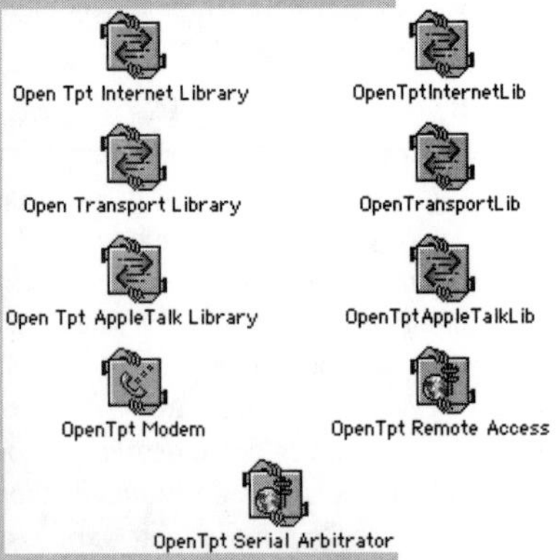

Figure 12-4 The major Open Transport extensions as found in Mac OS 8.x. In Mac OS 9, the top six files have been replaced by Open Transport and Open Transport ASLM modules.

Using Internet Setup Utility Versus Do-It-Yourself

If you have never connected to the Internet before with your Mac, you can start by running the *Internet Setup Assistant* utility that comes with Mac OS 8.x and later. Not only will it walk you through the basics of how all the software needs to be setup, it will even select an ISP for you, if you do not already have one. However, this is mainly a utility you only use once. If you have trouble later on, chances are good that you will need to go directly to the relevant software that the Assistant was modifying behind the scenes. Of course, you can also bypass the Assistant utility and go directly to the "real" software right from the start. Personally, I recommend visiting this software at some point, whether you use the Assistant or not, because you get a better idea of what is actually happening, which will serve you well if and when troubleshooting becomes needed later on.

Apple also includes a few other components with Internet Setup, such as Internet Dialer. This assists in dialing up and Internet connection. Again, there are more flexible ways of handling dialing, once you get comfortable with using your Mac.

Setting Up AppleTalk, TCP, Modem, and Remote Access Control Panels

There are two basic ways to get online via a TCP/IP connection. One is a direct connection (such as via a local network that is hooked up to the Internet or via a cable modem). The other is over a dial-up modem. But with a dial-up modem, there is an additional obstacle to overcome. Besides TCP/IP's translating work, you need a further translator—to send/receive data via the modem transmission. The main way this is done is via a *PPP* (Point-to-Point Protocol) connection. Establishing this PPP connection is a main function of Apple's Remote Access control panel.

Making an Internet connection for the first time requires that a variety of Mac OS control panels be configured properly. Here's what you should know:

Set Up AppleTalk Control Panel

Connect via Open the AppleTalk control panel. It includes a pop-up menu called "Connect via."

If you are connecting to the Internet via an external serial port dial-up modem, and if your Mac has more than one external serial port, you want to make sure that you have not selected AppleTalk to go through the same port as the modem. That is, do not select Modem port as the AppleTalk port if your modem is connected to the Modem port. Typically, you select Printer Port for AppleTalk (although if you use an Ethernet network, you would likely select Ethernet).

If you are connecting to the Internet via a network, then you will want to set AppleTalk to match the port where your connection occurs, typically either Printer Port (for LocalTalk connections) or Ethernet (for an Ethernet hook-up).

Making AppleTalk active and inactive There are at least three ways in which you can turn on and off AppleTalk. Only one uses the AppleTalk control panel:

AppleTalk control panel Open the AppleTalk control panel. If you have not already done so, go to the Edit menu and select User Mode. From the window that appears, click Advanced and then click OK. Next, click the Options button. From the window that appears, select the desired AppleTalk Active and Inactive button.

Chooser Open the Chooser. Select the desired AppleTalk Active and Inactive button in the Chooser.

Figure 12-5 The AppleTalk control panel (top) and its Info (middle) and Options (bottom) windows.

Control Strip Use a Control Strip module, such as AppleTalk Switch. Select "AppleTalk Active" or "AppleTalk Inactive," as desired.

If you are connecting to the Internet via a network, AppleTalk must be active. For a modem connection, it should not matter whether AppleTalk is active or not (although it may matter for using a networked printer!).

In some cases, turning off AppleTalk, regardless of what port it is assigned, may prevent some Internet connection problems. For example, Apple stated in Mac OS 8.0 CD file: "If your PowerBook computer is connected to an AppleTalk network by a LocalTalk connection and you are using your modem for data connections with serial speed setting (between your communications program and the modem) higher than 19200 bps, you should turn off AppleTalk to avoid possible data loss during connections."

TAKE NOTE ▶ **How to *Really* Make AppleTalk Inactive**

If you have modem problems that stem from AppleTalk being active, you may find that the different ways of turning it off are not all equal. The best way to turn AppleTalk off (and make sure it stays off after restarting) is to turn it off from the Options window of the AppleTalk control panel.

However, sometimes even this is not sufficient. Since the main resources are loaded at startup, they may remain loaded even after you turn AppleTalk off–until you restart. Thus, the best way to make sure AppleTalk resources are unloaded and not reloaded is to make AppleTalk inactive from the AppleTalk control panel and then immediately restart. After doing this, check the Chooser to make sure it says that AppleTalk is inactive. If it does, you should now be OK. Any problem due to AppleTalk being active should now be gone.

Having file sharing enabled or connecting to another computer via Apple Remote Access may result in AppleTalk being made active again, despite your efforts to shut it down. To prevent this (assuming that the Apple Remote Access Client software is installed), select "Remote Only" from the AppleTalk control panel's "Connect via:" pop-up menu. This also has the effect of routing AppleTalk off your printer port (assuming that had been your previous Connect selection), freeing the port for use with any non-networked serial port device (such as certain printers). You may not need to bother with this, but it's worth trying if you are having trouble making a connection and cannot determine another cause.

BY THE WAY ▶ **The Info Button**

The AppleTalk control panel includes an Info button. Click it and you get a list of the versions of Open Transport, AppleTalk and AppleTalk driver you are using. While this is not all that useful by itself, it comes in handy if you ever hear about a problem with a particular version. For example, suppose you read, "Your Mac may crash when launching Netscape Navigator if you are running Open Transport 1.2. The solution is to upgrade to version 1.3 or later." The Info button of AppleTalk would be a quick way to check what version you have and therefore learn whether you need upgrading.

Info also lists the unique hardware address of your machine, also called the MAC address (having nothing to do with the name Mac for your computer). You will not likely need to know this number for your own troubleshooting, but you may be asked for this number by a network administrator or tech support person if you are having problems with a network connection.

The TCP/IP control panel has a similar Info window.

Set up TCP/IP Control Panel

1. **Select a User Mode** Select "User Mode" from the control panel's Edit menu. You are probably in Basic mode if you have never done this before. This is fine for most users. However, additional options become available if you select Advanced or Administrator mode. The most relevant of these additional options is the Options button that appears in the main window, which in turn gives you access to the "Load only when needed" checkbox.

2. **Select the desired "Connect via:" setting** If you are connecting via a dial-up modem, and using Apple's Remote Access, you should select PPP from the pop-up menu. (However, if you are using FreePPP, a product that competes with Apple's Remote Access, you should select the FreePPP protocol.)

   For most other types of Internet connections (such as a cable modem), you would select to connect via Ethernet.

3. **Select the desired Configure setting (and related settings)** What options appear in the pop-up menu vary depending upon what you selected in the previous step.

   For example, if you are using a modem connected via PPP and using Apple's Remote Access software, you should select Using PPP Server.

   If you are using another type of connection, such as a cable modem, you would most likely select either Manually or Using DHCP Server. You will be instructed as to which of these to choose from your Network Administrator or Internet Service Provider. BootP and RARP are only rarely used.

   Options to configure manually are only appropriate if you have a static IP address, that is one that is always the same each time you connect (see: "Understanding Internet Addresses," later in this chapter, for more on IP addresses). This would be the case if you were using your computer as a Web server for example,

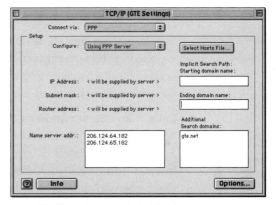

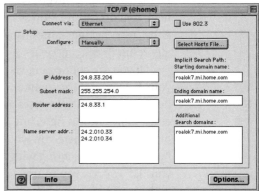

Figure 12-6 The TCP/IP control panel settings for a dial-up modem PPP connection (top) and a cable modem Ethernet connection with a static IP address (bottom).

where you want an IP address that does not change from day to day—so that others know what IP address to use to reach your site. However, if you just use the Internet as a client, to check email and surf the Web for example, you can use a dynamically assigned address. This means that the address is assigned from a pool of addresses that your ISP uses. Which address you get can vary each time you connect. This is why many of the settings in the TCP/IP control panel will say "be supplied by server" and you will not be able to enter them. DHCP is one method of dynamically assigning addresses.

Some cable modem services, such as ATT@home, may use a static IP address. Others use a dynamically assigned address assigned typically via a DHCP Server. DHCP, which stands for Dynamic Host Configuration Protocol, is simply a method that a central server uses to assign IP addresses. Skipping over technical details, protocols such as DHCP also help administrators deal with large networks that include a variety of different computer platforms.

Want to know your current dynamically assigned IP address while you are online via a PPP connection? It's in the "Connected to:" line of Apple's Remote Access control panel (described below). With FreePPP, click the "i" (information) button in the FreePPP Setup window.

Related settings (IP address, Subnet mask, and Router address) will likely be supplied by the server if you use DHCP. If you are connecting Manually, you will need to enter them yourself. In this case, your Internet Service Provider (ISP) or Network Administrator should supply the needed information.

4. **Enter Name Server Address and Additional Search Domains** The Name Server Addresses are not the IP addresses assigned to your computer, but the ones assigned to the machines at some other location that serve as your bridge to the Internet. You typically get these addresses from your ISP. Enter IP addresses into the "Name Server Addr" field and (optionally) enter domain names in the "Search Domains" field. Conversely, if you enter a name in the Additional Search Domains field, entering an IP address in the Name Server Addr field may be optional. In either case, having names listed in the Additional Search Domains field will generally result in faster access.

If you are connecting via a modem, you need to dial up the phone number of your ISP and use the login and password they assigned. But you do not necessarily need to use the IP addresses and domain names they gave you. True, you need to enter some address here, but it can be one belonging to different ISP, such as that of a university where you work. So if you have access to different IP addresses, you might try experimenting with them. They may provide better speed than the one your ISP expects you to use. For example, I work at a university that has its own IP address and I have my own ISP that I pay for separately. I can use whichever IP addresses I wish (or enter all of them). If more than one is entered, the control panel will typically pick the one at the top of the list first. If it senses a problem, it will move to the next one.

BY THE WAY ▶ Using "Load only when needed"

In most cases, with a PPP connection, you should leave "Load only when needed" checked. This is the default setting. This means that the TCP/IP software only loads (and therefore only takes up memory), when you are trying to make an Internet connection. This helps conserve your use of memory and prevents automatic attempts to connect to the Internet that you do not want. Still there are times when unchecking this option is advised.

If you uncheck this option (and restart your Mac), the software loads at startup and remains loaded whether you connect to the Internet or not. As explained more in Fix-It #4, unchecking this option can sometimes prevent memory fragmentation and/or a memory leak, thereby reducing rather than increasing memory use. It also ensures that the control panel has room to load, no matter what applications you may open after startup. If memory-related errors or other unusual problems occur when trying to make an Internet connection, experiment with this option.

Also, some older software may not load Open Transport "as needed." In this case, you must uncheck this option to use this software. Unchecking this option also allows AppleShare servers to mount at startup.

Finally, this option is mostly irrelevant if you are connecting via Ethernet (such as with a cable modem or DSL connection). Apple states that only PPP connections fully respect this setting. In particular, starting in Mac OS 8.6., when using an Ethernet connection, TCP/IP will no longer unload itself from memory after a few minutes of inactivity, even when "Load only when needed" is checked. However, with the option checked, it will still not load into memory until it is needed the first time.

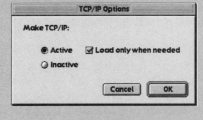

Figure 12-7 The TCP/IP control panel Info (left) and Options (right) windows.

BY THE WAY ▶ DHCP Leases and the Mac OS 8.6 Stall

Many users running Mac OS 8.6 together with a cable modem that used a DHCP Server found that their Mac would "stall" from time to time. By this, I mean that it would stop working for about 30 seconds or so, as if frozen. It would then resume its normal functioning.

It turns out that the cause was that with the DHCP Server setting the Mac checks periodically for a possible new IP address assignment (called a DHCP lease). This should not cause a problem if you are actually connected to the network. But if you are "offline" at the moment, it will fail to report back with this lease information. The Mac may then continue to search for awhile before giving up. This search period accounts for the stall.

One solution is obviously to make sure you are connected to the cable modem or other DHCP Server when your TCP/IP control panel is set to use DHCP Server. However, a better solution will be to upgrade to Mac OS 9.0 or later. This problem was fixed in newer versions of Open Transport.

**TECHNICALLY SPEAKING ▶ The TCP/IP Control Panel:
What Does It Do Exactly?**

The short answer to the title question is that the Internet communicates via a special "Internet protocol" (or IP for short). Your Mac does not "speak" this language. Thus, the TCP/IP control panel functions as a sort of translator that serves as an intermediary between your Mac and the Internet, doing the conversions necessary to so that your Mac can "talk" to the Internet. You may not need this control panel if you are accessing the Internet via some commercial online services (such as America Online) or via certain text-only "shell account" connections. However, TCP/IP is required for most forms of direct access to the Internet. This is typically the case if you use programs such as Netscape Communicator or Outlook Express to access the Internet via an Internet Service Provider (ISP).

Another important aspect of using TCP/IP involves the concept of the domain name. Internet addresses are numeric. Domain names are assigned to these numeric addresses to make it easier for humans to remember them. These domains names and/or their corresponding numeric equivalents should be entered in the Domain Name Server Information area of the MacTCP control panel or the Name Server Addr and Search Domains fields of the TCP/IP control panel. When you try to make a connection (and especially if there is any problem locating a numeric address or if you didn't provide a numeric address), an attempt is made to "resolve" the non-numeric name (that is, it will figure out the actual numeric address that most closely matches the non-numeric domain name you gave). It then uses that address to connect you to the Internet. If it fails altogether, you will get an error message saying something to the effect that it was unable to resolve the domain name. In most cases, your ISP uses special software called a *domain name server*, to try to resolve your domain names when it receives your request.

More rarely, you may instead have a *host file*, provided by your ISP, which you should store at the root level of your System Folder. It contains a table of domain names and IP addresses. This is then used (via the TCP control panel) for domain name resolution. TCP/IP has a button to select a specific host file.

To get the needed domain names and numeric addresses (and indeed for any further location-specific advice on how to get set up), contact your ISP. Never mind if you understand it all, just follow their instructions *exactly*. Some more general guidelines are given in the main text.

By the way, TCP/IP stands for "Transmission Control Protocol/Internet Protocol."

SEE: • **"Troubleshooting Internet Addresses," later in this chapter for more on domain names.**

BY THE WAY ▶ TCP/IP Control Panel: AppleTalk Network Connection

For a AppleTalk network connection, typically select Connect via: "AppleTalk (MacIP)" and Configure: "Using MacIP Server." This can also be used for a AppleTalk network that is connected via a router to a larger network. You may also have to select an AppleTalk zone from the Select Zone window. Again, get specifics from your Network Administrator.

Note: MacIP no longer works with LocalTalk in Mac OS 9 or later. You can only use MacIP when connected to the MacIP gateway through Ethernet.

Set up Modem Control Panel

Obviously, this step is needed only if you are using a dial-up modem. If so, select the port that your modem uses from the "Connect via" pop-up menu. For external modems, it will typically be "Modem port": for internal modems, select "Internal modem". After this, locate the name of your modem in the Setup/Modem pop-up menu and select it.

Generally, the "Ignore Dial Tone" option should be checked only if your phone allows you to dial out without the phone making a dial tone.

That's pretty much it. You are now done.

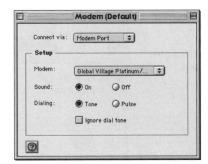 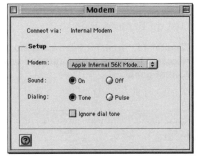

Figure 12-8 The Modem control panel for an external modem connected to a serial port (left) and an internal iMac modem (right).

The only real troubleshooting issue with this control panel concerns what to do if your particular modem is not found in the list. The list is determined by what files are included in the Modem Scripts folder in your Extensions folder. When you install the Mac OS, a default set of scripts are placed there. There are typically additional scripts in a folder called Additional Modem Scripts stored in the CD Extras folder on the Mac OS CD. To use any of them, just drag them to the Modem Scripts folder. Alternatively, you can use the Installer utility in the folder to install all of the additional scripts. In either case, if your modem was not listed by default, check the Additional Modem Scripts folder to see it's there.

If the needed modem script is still not found, check to see if a script came with the software included with your modem. Otherwise, check the vendor's Web site. They typically have the latest versions of the modem scripts for their modems available for downloading. Checking the Web is a good idea even if you have a working script. Vendors may post updated scripts that fix problems with an older script that you may be using. This was especially important when the V.90 56K protocol was released. Most vendors (such as US Robotics, Supra and Global Village) released updated scripts around that time. There are even independent Web sites that have libraries of modems scripts that are supposedly improved over the ones supplied by the modem vendor.

SEE: • **"Modem Scripts and Init Strings," earlier in this chapter.**

Set Up Remote Access Control Panel

Once again, if you are not using an dial-up modem to connect to the Internet (for example, if you use a cable modem), you can skip this step.

For those of you that are using a dial-up modem, this section explains the basics of setting up Apple's Remote Access control panel. If you are using Mac OS 8.1 or older, you may instead be working with a very similar control panel called PPP. Finally, some users may have selected to use a third-party alternative to these utilities, called FreePPP. For simplicity, I will be focusing just on Remote Access.

SEE: • **Chapter 11, "Transfer Files via a Modem (Remote Access)," for more information on using this control panel.**

Figure 12-9 The Remote Access control panel before a connection is made.

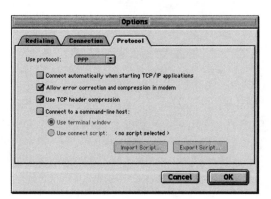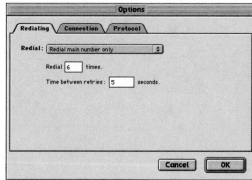

Figure 12-10 The Remote Access Options for Protocol (left) and Dialing (right).

1. **Open the Remote Access control panel and enter basic settings** The important settings here are your user name, password and phone number. These are all supplied by your ISP. If these are not entered exactly as instructed by your ISP, you will never be able to get online. If you want your password to be retained for future use (a possible security risk), check the Save Password checkbox. If you want to have more than one PPP configuration, you can set up and select from different configurations via the Configuration command in PPP's File menu.

    SEE: • **"Take Note: Multiple Configurations for Control Panels".**

2. **Make the connection** At this point, the Connect button should be enabled. Simply click it and, if all goes well, you should get connected. That's it. You are now online.

3. **Using Remote Access's Options (hopefully, you will not need them)** Remote Access includes an Options button. What it contains may vary depending upon

whether or not you selected Basic or Advanced from the Edit menu's User Mode command. Mostly, you will not need to modify these options to get connected. But you may choose to do so for convenience. For example, from the Redialing and Connection tabs, you can set whether or not the software will automatically redial a number if it gets a busy signal, whether the computer will automatically disconnect after 10 minutes of idle activity and a couple of other choices.

The only tab with choices that may be problematic is the Protocol tab. In most cases, you want: (1) "PPP" selected from the Use Protocol pop-up menu; (2) "Allow error correction and compression in modem" and "Use TCP header compression" should be enabled. However, if you are unable to make or maintain a connection, experiment with disabling one or both of these latter options. It may help.

"Connect Automatically when starting TCP/IP applications" allows automatic connection when you open an Internet application. Uncheck it if you are experiencing problems when launching an application. Instead, connect first via Remote Access and then launch the application.

The last option is the most difficult one to use: "Connect to command-line host." You use this only with certain ISPs that require a series of steps to log on that are not handled by PPP's default procedures. Ideally, if a script is needed, your ISP will supply it (it is just a text file). You then select "Use connect Script," import the script using the Import Script command, and you are done. Otherwise, you will have to create your own script. Doing this is beyond the scope of this book. Fortunately, very few ISPs need scripts anymore. (**Note:** If you ever modify an existing Connect Script (which can be done in any word processor), you will need to select to re-import it to get PPP to recognize the changes.)

6. **Disconnect (and Connect Again)** Once connected, the Connect button becomes Disconnect. Click it to break the connection. Macs take an unusually long time to terminate a PPP connection (we are not sure why). But wait about 20-30 seconds and the disconnect will be complete. For subsequent connections, all you need to do is open the Remote Access control panel and click the Connect button again. Or connect from the Remote Access Control Strip Module if you choose.

   DialAssist If you are still having problems, you may want to check for a control panel called DialAssist. This allows you to set parameters for your phone number, such as whether you need to dial "1" or dial "9" or whatever as a prefix. You can enter these prefixes directly in the PPP/Remote Access control panel instead. But be careful: if these additions have been entered in both places, the phone number may not dial correctly.

If you still did not succeed in making a connection, read on. That's what most of the rest of this chapter is about.

TAKE NOTE ▶ Multiple Configurations for Control Panels

You may want to have multiple configuration settings for one or more of the control panels mentioned in this section. In all cases, you do this by selecting Configurations (Command-K) from the control panels' File menu. Then, from the window that appears, select "Duplicate" and give the duplicate settings a new name. Now select the new settings and click "Make Active." This will take you back to the main window. You can now change the settings as you wish. When you close the control panel, you are prompted to save the change. That's it. After this, any time you want to switch back or forth, go to the Configurations window and select which settings to Make Active. Here are some suggested applications of this feature:

- **TCP/IP** Switch between a cable modem and a dial-up modem.

- **AppleTalk** Switch back and forth between Ethernet and Printer ports.

- **Modem** Use this to select among different modems—such as if you use an external modem on some occasions and an internal modem at another.

- **Remote Access** Use this to select different local phone numbers when you are in different locations.

SEE ALSO: • **"Take Note: Solving Problems Getting Connected On The Road," later in this chapter).**

Export and save The Configurations window has an Export button. Use it! In particular, use it to export your settings to a separate file. This comes in handy in two situations: (1) if your settings ever become lost or corrupted, you have a sure backup copy; (2) if you ever need to transfer settings to another computer, you don't have to copy everything down on a piece of paper; just transfer the file and use it to Import the settings on the new machine.

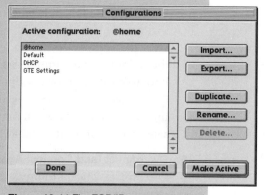

Figure 12-11 The TCP/IP control panel's Configurations window.

You may also be able to transfer settings simply by copying the relevant Preferences file (e.g., TCP/IP Preferences for the TCP/IP control panel).

Still, as an added precaution, make a printout of all of the Internet-related control panel windows (using Command-Shift-3). Keep them handy in case all settings info should somehow get lost.

Other alternatives Having to go to the Configurations window repeatedly can be annoying, especially if you have to do it for several control panels. Fortunately, there are more convenient alternatives. Mainly, they are Control Strip modules. I use a shareware one called FruitSpeak that lets me select among different AppleTalk settings. Perhaps the most useful modules are ones that let you select among different Remote Access settings. Remote Access includes its own Control Strip for doing this. FreePPP also comes with a similarly functioning Control Strip module. With any of these, you can switch configurations "instantly."

All for one; one for all If you need to make changes to multiple control panels on a regular basis, use Apple's Location Manager or Rockstar's GearBox. A shareware utility called NetControl also works well here.

BY THE WAY ▶ America Online Via TCP/IP

For dial-up modems, I have focused here on connecting online via a PPP connection to an ISP using Remote Access. However, you do not need to use a PPP connection to access America Online. In fact, with AOL's built-in Web browser, you can even access the Web without a PPP connection. You simply dial in to one of AOL's own access numbers and you are off and running. No need to bother with the Remote Access control panel at all.

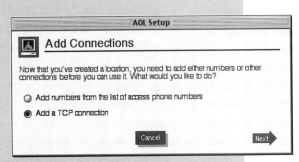

Figure 12-12 AOL's Setup window for creating a TCP connection.

However, if you choose to have a separate ISP in addition to AOL, you connect to your ISP via Remote Access and then log on to AOL directly over the TCP/IP connection. That is, you do not have to disconnect and dial-up AOL every time you want to shift between using your ISP's dial-up connection (and use of any non-AOL Internet software, such as email programs) and AOL.

On the latest versions of AOL, the setup for doing this is quite simple. Start by selecting Setup from the AOL Welcome screen. Then select the "Setup AOL to sign on from a new location..." Next, follow the prompts to select a TCP connection. Now go back to the Welcome screen and make sure that the new location is the one selected in the Location pop-up menu. Finally, get online via Remote Access (for a dial-up modem) or via your Ethernet connection (for a cable modem or other network access). At this point, log on to AOL via your TCP Location. You should log on almost instantly (there is no phone number to dial).

This may well be faster than your normal dial-up connection to AOL (and perhaps cheaper, if your ISP connection is not a toll call and your standard AOL connection is). If you have broadband Internet access, such as a cable modem, you can similarly connect to AOL through it. This is undeniably faster. And, if your AOL number is a toll call, you'll be saving the cost of that as well. In fact, AOL offers a special reduced rate for those who connect this way, saving you yet more money.

BY THE WAY ▶ AirPort and Wireless Connections to the Internet

In the past year, a new way has emerged for connecting your Mac to the Internet: wireless. It is not entirely wireless. That is, there is still a device attached to a wired connection to the Internet. It's just that your Mac connects to this device without the need of wires. With this setup, you can, for example, be online with your iBook from anywhere in your house – with no wires. Cool.

The most popular wireless method for the Mac is Apple's AirPort. The AirPort Base Station device connects directly to the Internet. Wireless connections to the Base Station are made via AirPort cards installed in AirPort slots of recent Mac models. Third-party cards (such as Lucent WaveLAN PC cards) also work with the AirPort Base Station. It is even possible, with the AirPort software and an AirPort card, to set up a Mac as a Base Station, allowing other Macs to wirelessly connect to the Internet through it.

Complete wireless connections (that is with no wiring anywhere at all) to the Internet are not yet available on the Mac. But you can do this with devices such as the handheld Palm VII personal digital assistant (PDA). I am sure that such options will be developed for the Mac before too long.

SEE: • "By the Way: Wireless Connections: AirPort," in Chapter 11, for more AirPort troubleshooting tips.

Internet Diagnostics Utilities

When trying to solve Internet-related problems it's worth keeping in mind that not all problems originate with your computer. You're connected to the Internet, after all. Sometimes the cause of your hassle is out there on the Net, not in your home or office. A failed connection, a Web page that does not load—instead of a problem with your software or your modem, it could instead be a problem with the server you are trying to reach or a problem with the Internet backbone itself. How can you tell?

Giving your ISP a call (or checking a Web page on their site where they list such problems, assuming you can get to the Web) would be a good start. They would know if there is a problem with their hardware or with the Internet at large. Knowing this may not help you solve the problem, but it will at least stop you from wasting time trying to fix a problem that you are unable to do much about. Beyond this, there are some diagnostics tests you can perform yourself.

What Is Ping?

Suppose you cannot get an page in a Web site to load (and error messages that may appear, as described in Chapter 13, do not provide a satisfactory explanation). Or suppose, when you try to send or receive email, the email program claims it cannot connect with your account. A basic technique to try here is to *ping* the host site.

When you ping a host, you send a signal, called a "ping packet," from your IP address to that of the host site. This signal, technically called an "echo request packet," merely requests that a response be sent back to you. If the connection between you and the destination host is working well, the response should come back in less than a second. If things are slow, it could take much longer. If something is down altogether, the echo packet response may never come back.

Figure 12-13 IPNetMonitor's Ping window showing a successful test of the MacFixIt IP address.

Thus, if a ping test fails for a specific site but works well or other sites, it suggests that there is a problem with the specific site, rather than a problem at your end. Probably their server is down. There is little you can do about this except wait for the people responsible for maintaining the site to fix it (although there are some rare cases where your ISP is the only one unable to connect with a particular site, making it your ISP's problem to fix).

If ping tests fail for every host you try, this suggests a problem with your Internet connection (time to contact your ISP for help). Or maybe your modem is not making a proper connection. More rarely, it could mean a problem with the Internet backbone, such as a major router or DNS Server down, crippling an entire geographic region of the network. To determine which it is, you could check with a friend who lives nearby (or works down the hall) to see if he or she has the same problem. The more people that have the problem, the more likely the cause is out there on the Internet.

Ping Testing with IPNetMonitor

There are numerous utilities that can do ping testing. These include MacPing, MacTCP Watcher and IPNetMonitor. My favorite is IPNetMonitor, a great utility that also performs numerous other diagnostic tests. Using IPNetMonitor as an example, here's how to ping:

1. Launch IPNetMonitor.

2. Select Ping from the Window menu.

3. In the name field, type the name of the location you wish to check. For example, to test your ability to connect with Apple, type apple.com. You are not limited to pinging other computers. You can also ping any router or server on the Internet. If it has an IP address, you can ping it.

4. Click the magnifying glass icon next to the name. This will get IPNetMonitor to look up the domain name's IP address, which should then appear in the field above. **Note:** If you know the IP address, but not the name, you can enter the IP address directly.

5. Click the Test button. The button changes to Abort. You can press this to terminate the test at any point.

6. IPNetMonitor will now attempt to send a packet to and receive a packet from the Apple Web site. It will do this 10 times in the default setting. A check mark will appear for each successful send and receive. If the packet is received back, it will also record the time it took.

    A green check mark indicates the corresponding echo datagram was sent or received. A red "X" indicates there was no response within the timeout interval. An orange "X" indicates a "Destination unreachable" response was received.

If IPNetMonitor shows that packets are sent but not received, this indicates that you failed to connect to the site. If the IP address is for a Web site, and you could not get the site to load, this would certainly explain why. As already stated, if you can successfully ping other sites, it strongly suggests that the problem does not originate at your end.

   If the ping is echoed back, but in an unusually long time (more than a second or so), this suggests that the Web page will load but take an unusually long time to do so. To learn more about why this is happening, your might do a Trace Route (described next).

   After you have the results of a ping test, what you do next varies depending whether you are on a local network or connecting via a modem.

Local Network If you are on a local network, a ping failure could indicate a problem with the routers or DNS Servers at your location. You can possibly check for this by pinging another computer on the local network. If the problem is with the router or DNS server, this should succeed even if connections beyond the LAN fail. Check with your network administrator for help here.

If even this fails, it suggests that there is a problem with your computer or with the local network itself. For starters, make sure your TCP/IP control panel settings are correct and your cables are connected properly. You can also try such basic troubleshooting techniques as resetting the PRAM and reinstalling Open Transport software.

If pinging was successful, but you still have connection problems, you might check the DNS Server for problems. You can copy the IP addresses for router(s) and name servers (as listed in the TCP/IP control panel) and paste them in to the IP Address box of the Ping window—and then test them. You can even test your own IP address (which should lead to extremely fast ping response times!). As Apple explains in a support document: "Whenever a host attempts to make a connection using a domain name, that name must first be resolved to an IP address. The name will be sent to the first DNS server listed in the TCP/IP control, and if that server doesn't respond, it will be sent to the second, the third, and so on. Try pinging the DNS servers listed."

If at least some of the name servers in your list fail, contact your network administrator. It may be that the sever is down or that the address you entered is incorrect. While you are waiting for resolution of this, if at least some name servers succeeded, delete the ones that failed and retain the others.

Modem If you are connecting via a dial-up modem and the ping testing suggests a problem, you can similarly check whether your TCP/IP settings are correct and cables are properly connected. Beyond that, it's time to check with your ISP.

Using IP address versus domain name If you type in the name of a Web site (such as www.apple.com), IPNetMonitor will find its IP address and put that in the box above the name. Once you have the numeric IP address, you can use the IP address instead of the Web address when in a Web browser. In fact, if there is a problem with a Domain Name Server, the IP address may succeed even when the name fails. For example, entering http://209.68.14.27 will load MacFixIt just as well as http://www.macfixit.com/. Still, if things are going well, using the name is preferred. One reason for this is that IP addresses for a Web site may change even though the domain name does not.

SEE: • "IP Addresses and Domain Names," in Chapter 13, for related information.

Trace Route testing with IPNetMonitor

Another useful diagnostic test is called Trace Route. To do a Trace Route with IPNetMonitor:

1. Select Trace Route from IPNetMonitor's Window menu.

2. Enter the IP address (in the text box) of the location you wish to test. You can copy the address from the Ping window if you have just completed a ping test.

3. Click the Trace button.

IPNetMonitor will now display every jumping point along the Internet that a packet takes between when it leaves your computer and it arrives at the destination you selected.

If the connection between you and the other site is not working, this may reveal exactly where the breakdown occurs. For example, it may show the name of the jump point where the packet dies.

The Trace Route tries three times at each jump point. If packets (especially in the Received column) are only occasionally dropped (some check marks and only some X's appear), it can be useful to see where the dropped packets occur. In particular, the closer the problem is to the destination location, the more likely that the source of the problem is with the destination location.

If no packets are dropped, but it takes an unusually large number of hops before reaching the destination, this indicates a slow response time from your Web browser. If you do discover a problem here, there is not much you can do about it yourself, but it can be useful information to have when contacting your ISP about the problem. For example, your ISP may have a way to route around the problem location.

Sometimes, dialing up using a different ISP (if you are using a dial-up connection and have more than one ISP) or changing the server addresses listed in the TCP/IP control panel (if you know others that you can use) may resolve these problems.

Some ISPs have better connections to the Internet than others; that is, you may find that one ISP always has shorter trace route paths than another. This might be a reason to prefer one ISP over another.

Also note that if you do Trace Route repeatedly, it may take a slightly different route each time. This is normal.

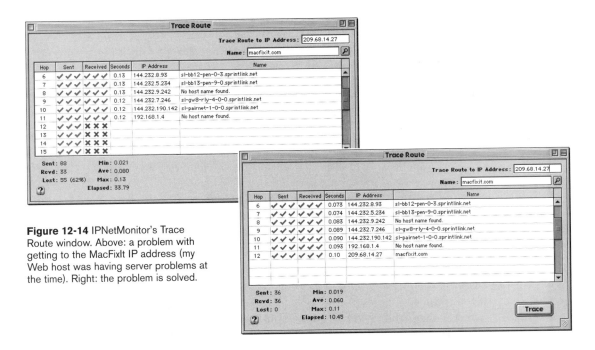

Figure 12-14 IPNetMonitor's Trace Route window. Above: a problem with getting to the MacFixIt IP address (my Web host was having server problems at the time). Right: the problem is solved.

Monitor Activity with IPNetMonitor

One more thing you can do with IPNetMonitor: use its Monitor window to graphically see all the send and receive activity taking place with a connection. If no activity is seen when you make a request, such as to go to a Web page in your browser, it indicates that your modem connection is essentially dead. This is similar to what the graph in the Remote Access control panel indicates, but IPNetMonitor provides much more detail.

Ethernet Checking with EtherPeek

If you are on the Internet via an Ethernet network, a connection problem may be due to a more general Ethernet network problem. There are utilities that can help you determine whether information is traveling over an Ethernet network correctly. The best one is called EtherPeek. But expect to take some time getting to learn how to use it. It is not designed for the technically unskilled user. However, it can be invaluable in diagnosing why a connection does not work. People who use AirPort have found it especially useful in diagnosing AirPort connection failures.

Solve-It! Open Transport Problems

Can't Get Connected or Unusually Slow Connections

 Symptoms:

- When trying to make a connection with your modem, especially a PPP connection, the connection consistently fails.

- After making a successful connection, you still cannot get any response from your relevant applications (for example, pages do not load in your Web browser).

- Online response time is unexpectedly and unusually slow (such as with data transfers).

 Causes:

These problems are typically caused by a bad connection, problems with your modem, problems with your online service (or Internet Service Provider), incorrect settings in your Open Transport and/or PPP software, or software incompatibilities.

Generally, if you cannot even get as far as getting the phone number you are dialing to answer and attempt to establish a connection, the problem is with your modem, modem cables, the serial port, or a problem at the receiving end (a busy signal, the server is down, etc.).

On the other hand, if you get stuck at the point of trying to establish a connection or if a connection appears to be established successfully but you get no response when you try to access the host via your communications software, the problem is more likely due to incorrect settings in your communications software or other software-related issues.

What to Do:

This section assumes that you have already setup and successfully been online at least once, but you are now having problems. If you have never been successful in getting online, start with the previous sections on setting up Open Transport software. Also, make sure all cables (such as phone cables and cables from the modem to the Mac, for external modems) are connected correctly. Check the documentation that came with your Mac or your modem for more details here.

Except where otherwise noted, what follows emphasizes problems with a dial-up modem connection. Dial-up modem troubleshooting is best accomplished if you can listen to the sounds emitted by your modem's speakers. Typically, you can turn sound on or off via the Sound buttons in the Modem control panel. An external modem may also have a separate volume control. Third-party modem software, such as Global Village's GlobalFax Controls, may also include a volume setting. Make sure that these settings are enabled so that you can hear the modem sound while troubleshooting.

Figure 12-15 Remote Access gives you feedback as to the state of your connection attempt; here, the "Starting Network Protocols" phrase in the Status window indicates that a successful connection is about to be established.

It is also advised to keep the Remote Access control panel open when trying to connect. This is where the error messages and other feedback as to the state of the connection will appear.

No Dial Tone or No Answer

If you are having a problem getting online, first make sure that you are getting a dial tone, that the modem is really attempting to dial and that the receiving end is answering correctly. If this is not the case, try one or more of the following (and then try to connect again):

- **Reset the modem.** For an internal modem, you will need software to do this. For example, if you have Global Village's software, use the Reset Modem button in the GlobalFax Controls control panel. If it is an external modem, just turn the modem off and back on again.

- **Disconnect the phone cable from the modem and reconnect it.** This is a good alternative for internal modems that cannot be reset.

- **Restart your Macintosh.**

- **If the problem is that the phone number keeps ringing and never answers, you may be dialing the wrong number.** Check again. Otherwise, your ISP service may be temporarily down due to some repair problem. Call their tech support to find out.

- **Consider whether you have a dead modem.** See if another modem works. Especially if you updated the firmware of your modem and especially if you had any problems or interruptions when doing so, your modem's firmware may now be "history." Contact the vendor for help.

  SEE: • **"Take Note: Updating Modem Firmware And Software," earlier in this chapter.**

Busy Signal

If you get a busy signal, the reason you cannot connect is obvious. The number you are trying to reach is busy. The way ISP connections work, one phone number is "connected" to a bank of modems, called a modem pool. When you dial the number, you are automatically routed to the first available free modem. If all modems are in use, you get a busy signal. This is likely to occur with a popular ISP service that does not have enough modems to meet its peak demand. America Online was notorious for this awhile back, although it is now much better.

The solution is to try again. Sometimes, if you try repeatedly, you may get lucky and get connected on your next try. Your software may have an option to automatically redial if it detects a busy signal, making this sort of repeat checking easier to do. For example, the Remote Access control panel has a Redialing tab in the Options window for doing this. Otherwise, try again later a time known to be less busy (such as late at night).

If it is critical that you connect at a time when you often get a busy signal, contact your ISP for advice. They may have another phone number for you to try that is less crowded. Or they may have a premium service that guarantees access. Or they may be planning to upgrade their modem pool soon. If they can't offer any help, it's probably time to get a different ISP.

Logon Errors

Some times, everything appears to go well with your modem establishing a connection. You get a dial tone, your hear the number dialed and the phone ring. You hear the other end "pick up." A *"Connection established"* or similar message may even appear. But then something goes wrong.

For example, you may ultimately get a message that says *"Waiting for port…"* The message may remain on the screen indefinitely. On you may eventually get a message that says something like *"PPP time out"* followed by a disconnect. In other cases, you may get a message that says *"Authorization failed"* followed by a disconnect.

If you are listening to the sounds the modem makes as it attempts to establish a connection, you may hear sounds that are very different from what you normally hear.

In all of these cases, if Remote Access has not automatically disconnected you, click its Disconnect button. After this, for starters, try the same advice listed in the previous "No dial tone or no answer" section. Then try to connect again. If none of this works, consider the following:

- A common cause of these problems is that the ISP failed to recognize your user name and/or password. So start by checking to make sure these were entered correctly. For example, GTE is one of my ISPs. My GTE user name is "tedlandau." However, it turned out that when I put this in the Name box of the Remote Access control panel, I could not connect. It turned out that I needed to put "GTE/tedlandau." This was mentioned in the documentation I had received, but I had overlooked it. It took a call to GTE Tech Support for me to find this out.

- An *"Authorization failed"* message may occur only intermittently. You may try an hour later and find that everything works. This almost certainly means a problem at the ISP end. There is usually little you can do about it other than try again later. However, sometimes, making a change to your modem's init string can minimize these problems.

  SEE: • **"Modem Scripts and Init Strings," earlier in this chapter.**

- If you get a message that says *"Communicating at an unknown rate,"* this is most often a sign of an incorrect Modem Script file. Open the Modem control panel and check that the Modem file selected is the appropriate one for your modem. To take an obvious example, if you have a USR Robotics modem, you should not have a modem script that says Global Village. If you are using an internal modem that came with your computer, there is probably some default "Internal modem" script for you to select.

When You Can't Get Connected: Miscellaneous Other Advice

What follows is a hodge-podge collection of other suggestions to try if you cannot get online. There is no particular order to try them. Hopefully at least one of them will help solve your problem.

Check your control panel settings   Make sure all the settings in the TCP/IP control panel are correct. If needed, check with your ISP to confirm that you have the right settings. Similarly, make sure the correct modem script is selected from the Modem control panel. Make sure the phone number listed in Remote Access is the correct one for the type and speed of connection that matches your modem. And so on.

If you are using an external modem, go to the AppleTalk control panel and select another Connect Via method (such as shifting from Serial to Remote Only), saving it as a new configuration. Then return to the original configuration. This has been known to fix certain connection failures.

Note: If you zap your PRAM (see Fix-It #9), this will cause some Internet-related control panels (such as AppleTalk) to revert to default settings. After a zap, be sure to check that these control panels are set the way you intend them to be.

"Reset" the TCP/IP control panel   Use Command-K to access TCP/IP's Configurations list (see: "Take Note: Multiple Configurations for Control Panels") and select a different item from the list (create a second item if none exists) that uses a different "Connect via" method. Save and close the control panel. Then open it again, reselect the original configuration and save that. For added convenience, you can use a utility such as NetControl to switch back and forth, saving you the trouble of having to go to the control panel and using Command-K.

By the way, I have found that this trick may also help resolve certain local network access problems with the AppleTalk control panel.

Check the protocol of your ISP Be especially aware of problems using 56K modems (see: "56K modems: a closer look," earlier in this chapter). If your ISP 's phone line cannot accommodate the V.90 protocol that your modem most likely uses, possible solutions are:

- Dial into a different modem pool of your ISP (one that matches the protocol of your modem).

- Downgrade your modem's firmware (so as to match the protocol of the phone number you are using). The modem vendor would have to supply a firmware downgrader to this. For example, you might be able to downgrade from V.90 back to x2.

- Change the modem init string (to disable the V.90 feature). If need be, you can probably disable all 56K protocols and revert back to V.34 (the protocol for 28.8K and 33.6K modems). Contact the modem vendor for specific instructions.

If you are using a cable modem, similar rules apply. Be especially careful that you are using the correct Ethernet settings (DHCP vs. manual)

Shuffle the settings of the TCP/IP control panel If you are connecting via Ethernet, for example, shift to connect via another method, such as PPP. Save the changes and close the control panel. The re-open it, reselect the original method (e.g., Ethernet) and save and close again. This can sometimes bring the connection back to life.

Check for serial port modem problems If you are using a modem connected through the Mac's serial port, and you get a message that says *"serial port in use,"* and it includes an option to reset the port, say "OK." Otherwise, use a freeware utility called SerialKiller to close the serial port. Failing that, you'll have to restart your Mac.

Otherwise, if AppleTalk is on, turn it off. This can resolve some serial port problems. Turning off AppleTalk is also known to improve speed and reduce transmission errors. Try it if you have persistent problems.

SEE: • **"Take Note: How to *Really* Make AppleTalk Inactive," earlier in this chapter.**
        • **"Serial: Printers, Modems, and Networks," in Fix-It #14 for more on serial port problems.**

Check for USB modem problems If an external USB modem does not work, try unplugging it from the USB port and plugging it in again.

SEE: • **Fix-It #14 for more on USB problems.**

Turn off fax software If you have fax software installed, turn it off (or at least disable any "fax receive" options)—when trying to get online. With some modems, this is known to resolve connection problems.

Don't delete the MacTCP DNR file MacTCP DNR file was a file needed by the older (pre Open Transport software). However, if you see a MacTCP DNR file at the root level of your System Folder, you should probably leave it there—even though you are using Open Transport. While technically not required for Open Transport, it is left there for older TCP applications that expect it to be there and won't run without it.

However, if you are having problems getting online or if you get persistent *"can't find DNS entry"* errors, you might try deleting the DNR file. The system software should create a new (hopefully less problem-prone) one if and when it is needed.

Make sure you have the latest updates to your software; reinstall if needed
New versions of communications-related software frequently fix problems with the previous version. If you have some persistent problem, it may have been addressed by a software update (of course, you will likely have to get online somehow to check for these!). Especially check for updates to the Open Transport software from Apple that may be newer than that which comes with the version of the OS you are using. Also check for update files designed to fix machine-specific or modem-specific problems for your machine (such as Apple Modem Updater, released in 1999 for iMacs and PowerBook G3s). One caveat here is that the newest versions of Open Transport do not work with older versions of the Mac OS. To take advantage of the latest versions may mean upgrading your OS (and if you have a really old Mac, it may also mean having to buy a new Mac).

Otherwise, try reinstalling the version of Open Transport you are now using. Just make sure you have a back-up of your settings before you do this, in case they are lost.

SEE: • **"Take Note: Multiple Configurations for Control Panels," earlier in this chapter.**

When You Get an Unusually Slow Connection

You may succeed in getting connected, but every thing you try to do (from loading a Web page to grabbing your email) grinds to a near halt—to the point where you effectively cannot make use of the connection. At a practical level, it amounts to the same thing as a failure to connect.

In some cases, this slowdown may affect all Internet applications you use. In other cases, it may be specific to just one type of application. For example, you may find that you can send and receive email, but you cannot load any Web pages.

While problems specific to the application in use (e.g., Web browser or email program) may be the cause here, it is also possible that it is a more general problem. Especially on the Web, your data transfer rate may vary depending upon a host of factors that are largely beyond your control, such as the speed of the server you are addressing, how many other users are trying to access the page at the same time, and the nature of what you are trying to view (graphics go especially slow).

To check for a more general Internet connection problem, start with the advice in the "No dial tone or no answer" section. If that fails:

Wait If you give up for the moment and wait until a later time, you may find that speed has improved (particularly if the slowdown was occurring at a particularly busy time of day for Internet traffic).

Disconnect and reconnect; restart If your modem connection seems unusually slow, the simplest thing to do is disconnect. Then try to reconnect again. If this fails, restart your Mac and try again. Ninety percent of the time this will fix the problem.

Check Remote Access For dial-up modems, check the Remote Access settings. Here is where you might experiment with turning on or off options previously described (see "Set Up Remote Access control panel," earlier in this chapter).

Check the phone line A particularly weak or noisy phone line may be the cause of a slow connection. To test for this:

- If possible, try another phone line or try disconnecting any phones that may be sharing the same line with your computer.

- Purchase a line noise suppresser, such as one available from Radio Shack.

- Otherwise, your phone company can test the phone line for you. If it finds an above threshold level of noise, it will attempt to fix it for you at no charge. But don't expect any miracles here. Sometimes, the only cure is to run new cables, something that the phone company is unlikely to do just to help with your modem connections

SEE ALSO: • **"Why doesn't my modem connect at its fastest speed?," earlier in this chapter, for related information.**

Check for a revised modem script There may be a bug or non-optimal setting in the default modem script for your modem. With luck, someone has created a revised script that works better. If so, it should be available on the Web. MacFixIt <www.macfixit.com> has links to such scripts and sites.

SEE: • **"Modem Scripts and Init Strings," earlier in this chapter, for background information.**

Don't do too many things at once Any time you try to do several different TCP processes at once, such as loading a Web page while downloading a file while checking your email, the speed of each individual activity will inevitably slow down. Keep your simultaneous activities to a minimum and you will get better response. In particular, when downloading a large file, it often pays to do nothing else at all (unless you have a very fast connection).

If all else fails... Contact your ISP for help or do your own diagnostic testing (see "Internet Diagnostics Utilities," earlier in this chapter).

SEE ALSO: • **"Web Pages Load Slowly or Incompletely," in Chapter 13, for related information.**

Dropped Connections and Freezes

 ## Symptoms:

- A successful connection unexpectedly gets lost (dropped). In some cases, your software may indicate that you are still connected.

- A system freeze occurs while online and/or when trying to disconnect.

 ## Causes:

A dropped connection occurs when, after you are successfully online at a normal speed, your connection is suddenly lost. A related problem is when your connection is not only dropped, but your Mac freezes as well.

A common cause of dropped connections are noisy phone lines. Another cause is a deliberate disconnect by your ISP or your own software, due to a period of inactivity (such as if you leave your Mac online while you take a break). Problems at your ISP end can also lead to dropped connections. If you get a system freeze when your connection is dropped, it suggests a problem/bug with your Mac OS software.

 ## What to Do:

There are two main varieties of dropped connections. In the first type, you get disconnected within a few minutes of connecting; and this happens virtually every time you reconnect. You simply cannot stay connected for long. In the second type, the dropped connection is intermittent, maybe occurring once a day at most, and may occur at any time after you connect. In either case, here is what to consider:

Dropped Connections Due to Idle Activity

Remote Access settings In the Options section of Remote Access, there is an option to "Disconnect if idle for ## minutes." If this is enabled, it will do what it says. Obviously, if this disconnect is not what you want, the solution is to disable this option. FreePPP has a similar option. FreePPP also has an option to "Reconnect automatically if connection drops."

ISP settings Your ISP may similarly have a setting to disconnect after some predefined period of idle activity. Usually, you have no ability to disable

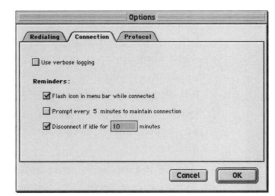

Figure 12-16 Remote Access's Connections options with "Disconnect if idle..." set for 10 minutes.

this setting. It may or may not be preceded by a warning message that it will disconnect you if you do not perform some action in the next few minutes. America Online does this, as do many other ISPs.

For connections that charge by the hour, this is considered a good thing, as it prevents you from being charged for hours of connect time due to you forgetting to disconnect when your left the computer. It is also helps reduce the odds that a user will get a busy signal when they try to get online, due to some other user tying up a phone line that they are not really using (simply because they want to save themselves the hassle of having to reconnect, and possibly getting a busy signal themselves).

However, if you really want to avoid these disconnects, there are utilities that can help. Two such utilities are Keep Me Online and Keep Connection Alive. These work by sending a signal to the ISP at regular intervals, thereby fooling the ISP into thinking that you are using the connection when you really are not. These typically only work when your computer is truly "idle," such as when you are away from your desk. If, instead, you are working at your computer but are just not using your connection (using your word processor, for example), these utilities will not prevent a disconnect. For these instances, there is not much you can do except reconnect again when needed. You could try to contact your ISP about modifying their automatic disconnect for you, but I would not be optimistic of success here.

"Unexpected" Dropped Connections

For dropped connections not initiated by your software or your ISP, there are a number of things you can try to do:

Check the phone line A particularly weak or noisy phone line may be the cause of a dropped connection.

SEE: • **"Check the phone line," in "When You Get an Unusually Slow Connection," previously in this chapter, for advice on what to do.**

Disable call waiting If you have call waiting, a call coming through while you are online can cause a disconnect. To prevent this, make sure call waiting is disabled before getting online. To do so, add "*70," to the start of your phone number string. A checkbox option to do this is included in some non-Apple Internet software.

If you can afford it, a preferred solution is to get a dedicated second phone line just for your computer (or perhaps shared with a fax machine).

Ignore dial tone In certain cases, enabling the "Ignore dial tone" option in the Modem control panel can remedy an unstable connection that is causing frequent disconnects.

Turn off the modem's error correction and/or data compression To do this for Remote Access, go to Options/Protocol and uncheck "Allow error correction and compression in modem" and "Use TCP header compression" options."

Software that came with your modem may also have options to turn error correction and/or compression off. For example, the Global Village software includes this. Otherwise, check the documentation that came with your modem for how to modify the modem's init string to change the default settings of these options.

Making these changes may make the modem operate a little slower, but it should make the connection more stable. Feel free to experiment with what combination of off and on works best for you.

Make changes to the modem init string To do this with Remote Access, you need to edit the Init String in the modem script (see: "Modem Scripts and Init Strings," earlier in this chapter). With AOL, you do it from the Setup window (see again: "Technically Speaking: Editing Init Strings and Modem Scripts"). For FreePPP, there is an Init string option directly in the FreePPP control panel. FreePPP also includes more user-friendly selections that change Inits string setting for you.

- **Change flow control settings** Switching flow control from "CTS & RTS (DTR)" to "CTS Only" may help. With FreePPP, you can change this from the control panel. Otherwise, you need to directly edit the modem init string. Exactly what you need to do to make this change will vary with different modems. Check your modem's manual for details.

- **Add S25=100 to modem init string** If the modem "thinks" that the signal from the ISP has been lost (because it isn't getting a response), it will disconnect. The modem init string can include a setting that modifies the default length of time that the modem will wait before doing this. By increasing the delay, you may prevent a disconnect that would have otherwise erroneously occurred (erroneous because the ISP signal is not really lost). Adding "S25=100" is a typical recommendation. Units are 100ths of a second. 255 is maximum. The default is usually at 25.

- **Other changes** Your ISP may have other recommendations as to how to modify the modem init string.

   SEE: • 'Modem Scripts and Init Strings," earlier in this chapter.

Check with your ISP The cause may (yet again!) be with your ISP end. In this case, you will not be able to reconnect (with any reliability anyway) until they fix the problem.

In one odd case, a particular user name and password combination caused a problem at the ISP end. Nothing could get the user reliably connected until the user changed to a different password.

"Hidden" Dropped Connections

In most cases, after a dropped connection occurs, your Mac will appear to be connected for another minute or so. Then, typically, a message appears on the screen that says you have been disconnected. At this point, the Disconnect button in Remote Access will change to Connect and you will be able to try to connect again.

However, in some cases, your modem and all your software may continue to say you are connected indefinitely, even though you have been disconnected. I refer to this as a "hidden" dropped connection. You can suspect this has happened if all your Internet software suddenly fails to respond.

To solve this: click the Disconnect button in Remote Access; wait for the button to change to Connect and then try again. If that fails, restart the Mac and try again. If that still fails, it's time to assume that the problem is not at your end, but at your ISP's end. It's time to break out your diagnostic utilities and/or contact your ISP.

SEE: • **"Internet Diagnostic Utilities," earlier in this chapter.**

Can't Disconnect or a Freeze/Crash Occurs When Online or When Trying to Disconnect

Finally, there may be times when you click the Disconnect button in Remote Access and nothing happens. That is, the modem never seems to disconnect and the button never changes back to Connect.

In some cases, this develops into a more general freeze of the Mac. More rarely, your Mac may consistently freeze when attempting to *make* a connection, rather than disconnecting from one.

These are almost always caused by a software problem on your drive. In general, restarting the Mac will be at least a short-term solution. That is, the symptom is not likely to return the next time you try to connect. If it does, check for an extension conflict (see Fix-It #3). The cause may also be a bug in the Open Transport software, one that only occurs in certain situations. If so, checking on a Web site such as MacFixIt may tell you what those situations are, how to work-around them and when a bug-fix update to the software is expected.

If the freeze only occurs when trying to load a certain Web page, it may be caused by problems specific to the code on that page, such a Java applet incompatible with the Java engine used by your browser.

SEE: • **Chapter 13 for more about Web browsers.**

TAKE NOTE ▶ Solving Problems Getting Connected on the Road

One of the advantages of having a portable Mac (PowerBook or iBook) is that you can easily take it with you when you travel. However, especially if you stay at hotels, getting online while away from home can present an assortment of problems. Here are the solutions:

Save dollars when you dial If you stretch the definition of troubleshooting to include staying out of debt, here are some useful tips for keeping your costs down when you connect while on the road:

• **Get a local number** With most ISPs charging a flat monthly rate for online access, your biggest potential expense in staying connected is the cost of a long-distance phone call. That's why the first thing you should do before leaving home is check with your ISP to see if they have a local (read "no charge or small flat rate charge for a local call") number at your destination. For example, I use GTE. They maintain a list of local numbers on their Web site at <http://www.gte.net/dialin/>. America Online subscriber? Go to the "Connecting to AOL" screen (exactly how you do this varies with different versions of AOL). Using local numbers will be far cheaper than making a long distance call to the access phone number you use when you are home.

(continues on next page)

- **Get a toll-free number** If there's no local number, your ISP may still have a money saving option: a toll-free (800) number that you can call from anywhere in the country. ISPs charge an hourly rate for using a toll-free number (perhaps around $6.00/hour). But this is still likely to be a bargain compared to dialing your home access number from your travel destination.

- **Avoid the cable modem "solution"** One disadvantage of cable modems is that you can't use them to connect to the Internet when you travel. Therefore, if you travel a lot, you should maintain a separate modem-based ISP. Cable modem companies often provide their own dial-up access for their customers who travel. But the per-minute fees are usually so high that it can wind up costing more than paying for a flat-rate ISP, even if you only travel a few times a year.

- **Don't charge it to your room** If you're unable to get a local or 800 number for your modem access, and you're using a long-distance number, avoid charging the cost of the call to your room. It's almost always far cheaper to charge the call to your home phone, via a calling card number. If you decide to do this, it's important to automate the process so that your Mac does all the dialing. This means adding your calling card number into your phone number sequence, using commas to add the appropriate delays (see "Modifying the phone number string," below, for related details).

Multiple configurations If you do use a different access phone number when traveling, you must enter that phone number in Remote Access. If you connect to the Internet at home via a cable modem, you will also have to change your TCP/IP settings. Of course, you want to be able to change these settings back again when you return home. The best way to handle this is to setup configuration files for the different settings (see: "Take Note: Multiple Configurations for Control Panels," earlier in this chapter). Even better, use Location Manager to handle multiple changes (such as to more than one control panel) in one step.

Modifying the phone number string Beyond changing the phone number itself, there are some additional changes you may need to make to the phone number string in Remote Access.

- Beware if the hotel/motel uses a digital phone system. Not only won't your modem work with it, but it may actually fry your modem if you try. Some better hotels that use a digital system also have a special "data port socket" for use with modems. Ask the front desk about this. Otherwise, you may be able to purchase a digital-to-analog converter to use with your modem. Global Village makes one for its modems called GlobalSwitch; a similar product by Radish Communications Systems is called InsideLine.

- If your hotel uses a special digit (usually an 8 or a 9) to access an "outside" line, this may prevent your modem from working if it doesn't pause long enough to wait for the outside line to "appear." You can probably solve this by adding a couple of commas between the special digit and the rest of the phone number. A comma tells the modem to pause for a second before continuing.

- If commas don't seem to work, you can use the W character to tell the modem to wait for a dial tone. Otherwise, the @ character will cause the modem to wait for 5 seconds of silence. One of these, inserted after the initial special digit (i.e., 8 or 9), should do the trick.

- Finally, some problems may be due to the modem not recognizing the odd dial tone sound that some hotel phone lines use. If none of the previous solutions work, check if your modem supports an AT command for bypassing the need to hear a dial tone. If so, use that command. Otherwise, your software may provide such an option. For example, Apple's Modem control panel has an option to "Ignore dial tone."

(continues on next page)

TAKE NOTE ▶ Solving Problems Getting Connected on the Road *(continued)*

Plugging in When you get to the hotel, you may face still more headaches trying to connect your portable Mac to a wall outlet and phone line. In particular:

- **No modular jacks?** Some older hotels may not have the modular jacks needed for modem cables. If not, my best advice is to stay somewhere else. There are other ways to work around this problem, but the hotel might not appreciate your attempts to modify their wiring.

- **Bring enough cord** Since a wall jack may not be near where you can set up your Mac, bring along an extra long modular phone cord (at least 12 feet). I also bring an adapter that lets you connect two phone cords together. I use this to connect the phone cord that normally goes to the hotel's telephone to the cord that goes to my modem. This way, I never even have to locate the wall jack (which hotel designers are fond of placing behind a headboard in a nearly inaccessible position).

- **Bring an adapter** Pack an adapter for converting a three-pronged (grounded) plug to a two-pronged one; without this, you may be unable to plug in your portable Mac's AC adapter to older-style outlets.

International travel If you are traveling abroad, you'll discover new ways to get overcharged for getting connected. Most important: do not charge the call to your hotel room—unless you wish to use up your retirement savings while online. Also, if possible, avoid using a U.S. long-distance number. Here are some more cost-effective alternatives:

- Check to see if your ISP has international local numbers (CompuServe is an especially good choice here). If so, use these numbers.

- Check if there is a local ISP at your destination that will give you temporary access to their service.

- Use AT&T Direct. With this, you dial an 800 number that gives you a U.S.-based dial tone. From here, you can connect just as if you were calling from within the U.S. Of course, AT&T charges you for the service, but it's almost certainly cheaper than calling your ISP directly. The connection will likely be more reliable as well. Call 1-800-331-1140 for more details.

- Use iPass <http://www.ipass.com/>. For a reasonable charge, this service provides local Internet access from wherever you may roam.

- The telephone jack may be different from the modular plug used in the U.S. TeleAdapt maintains a complete catalog of adapters and accessories, designed to solve these dilemmas. Their Web site <http://www.teleadapt.com/> also has a useful collection of general communications tips for travelers.

TAKE NOTE ▶ Troubleshooting Cable, DSL and Network Connections

Because it is still the most common way to connect to the Internet, this chapter emphasized connecting over a dial-up modem. However, increasingly, users are shifting to faster "broadband" solutions such as cable and DSL connections. If you are connected to the Internet where you work, you may similarly have a direct network connection to a central server that is, in turn, connected to the Internet via a fast connection, such as a T1 line. In all of these cases, you have a much faster connection speed with 24 hour/day instant access, and generally with far less hassle than with an ordinary phone line modem. We covered some troubleshooting basics for these types of connections in "Take Note: Beyond Dial-Up modems," earlier in this chapter. Here are some further troubleshooting tips:

Cable modem down Your cable connection can become temporarily down. This is usually due to some problem not localized to your connection and that you cannot fix yourself. You can usually tell this by looking at the lights on the cable modem itself. Certain lights will stop blinking or change color when the connection is broken. Usually, the cable modem will come back to life on its own in a few minutes. If not, turning the modem off for a few minutes and back on again can sometimes fix this. If the problem persists or if it occurs often, call the cable company to have it come out and check the modem and your cable lines. A repair or replacement may be needed.

Cable modem hijinks and using a router Although my cable connection runs fine most of the time, I periodically experience unusual symptoms that are almost always caused by problems at the cable company's end. In one case, I kept getting an error that another computer was already using my IP address, thereby blocking my access to the Internet. This was fixed after a call to the cable company.

In another case, my Internet access worked fine, but the cable modem connection caused my local AppleTalk network to be shut down. What was happening was that my local network was trying to access a supposed AppleTalk Server on the cable network and failing. There are various solutions to this (as briefly cited in "File Sharing via the Ethernet Port" in Chapter 11), but the guaranteed solution is to add a router to your Ethernet connection, in between the cable modem and the Mac. LinkSys and MacSense make routers that are popular with Mac users. These devices offer firewall protection, in addition to "routing" your network traffic. This means that they can prevent your local devices from being accessed from the Internet (and can similarly prevent local traffic from being routed to the Internet). For more details, check out the MacFixIt web page on this matter: <http://www.macfixit.com/extras/appletalkaccess.shtml>. They also act as an Ethernet hub or switch. **Note:** An Ethernet switch is just a smart hub; it has a small computer inside to direct the flow of internal traffic (inside the hub) in the most efficient manner so there are no traffic jams or packet collisions.

Check connection software settings If the cable modem lights suggest that the connection is fine, but you are still having problems with your Internet connection, make sure your TCP/IP settings are correct. **Note:** how a cable modem connects to the Internet can vary in different regions of the country, even within the same company. For example, as of this writing, ATT@home cable modems may use either Ethernet configured Manually or Ethernet configured via DHCP, depending upon where you live. Make sure you have the correct connections for your region.

Also, if you are using a router with your Ethernet network, you may need to change your cable email and news settings. With my @home account, for example, the mail POP server address was simply "mail." However, after adding a router to my Ethernet network, that address no longer worked. Instead, I now had to use the full address (which in my case was mail@ roalok1.mi.home.com.

@home recommends using a proxy server when connecting to the Web over its cable modem. In particular, they recommend entering "http://proxy:8080/" in the Proxy Server Preferences of your Web browser. However, I have never found this to be helpful. In fact, I have less trouble if I don't use it.

If you are certain the settings are correct, contact the cable company. A problem may have developed with your IP address (such as two people mistakenly assigned the same address) or the company may need to "reset" your modem (something they can do by sending a signal from their offices).

(continues on next page)

TAKE NOTE ▶ Troubleshooting Cable, DSL and Network Connections *(continued)*

More than one Mac on a cable modem A single cable modem can have more than one computer connected to it. How you do this depends upon whether your have a static (Manual) or dynamic (DHCP) IP address. Contact your cable company for details. In either case, there is an additional fee involved. You may be able to set up multiple computers to the same cable modem on your own (at no extra charge), via software such as IPNetRouter or via your own hardware router. However, your cable company is likely to frown on this if they find out you are doing it.

DSL and PPPoE While most high-speed Internet connections use a direct Ethernet connection, some use a special protocol called PPPoE (Point-to-Point Protocol over Ethernet). It is sort of a combination of PPP and Ethernet, where you typically need to run a special application and enter a name and password to access the Internet. PPPoE is often a source of problems. In some cases, the needed PPPoE software (such as one called MacPoET) has conflicted with features of the Mac OS (for example, MacPoET needed to be upgraded to work with Mac OS 9). Also, routers may have problems dealing with PPPoE. MacSense and LinkSys routers have had firmware upgrades to deal with this.

Network connection down If you are connected to the Internet via a local network, the problem may have nothing directly to do with the Internet connection. It may be that your access to the network is down. One way to check for this is to select the Chooser and click AppleShare. If you are on the network, you should see almost certainly see other network devices listed there (such as other servers or computers). If not, and if you are on an AppleTalk network, it may be that one of the devices has been disconnected from the AppleTalk chain. Because of the way that AppleTalk works, this can mean that all computers "downwind" of the disconnnected Mac are now also offline. Check for this. Otherwise, call your Network Administrator to report the problem.

SEE: • **"File Sharing via the Ethernet Port," in Chapter 11 for more on Ethernet hubs.**
• **"Technically Speaking: Ports And Firewalls," in Chapter 13, for more on firewalls and routers.**

13

Road Service for the Infobahn: The World Wide Web, Email and Beyond

Internet Basics

In the 1960s movie "The Graduate," the "one word" was "plastics." If that movie were updated for today, the new word would surely have to be "Internet." And the biggest slice in the Internet pie would be the World Wide Web.

The World Wide Web. It started out in a backwater of the Internet in the early '90s. Initially, it was supposed to be just for academic and government researchers, designed to help them link and locate information on the Internet. The idea that there might be some commercial value to the Web, and that home users would find it of interest, was probably never even considered. Yet in perhaps the most stunning example of explosive growth this century, the World Wide Web is well on its way to becoming an integral part of our society, both culturally and financially. It's a shopping mall, library, meeting place, and news and entertainment center all rolled into one. And it seems as if everyone from General Motors to half the general population now have their own Web page.

The key requirement for surfing the Web is a Web browser application. Today's Web browsers do more than just load Web pages. You can also use them to download files and (sometimes in conjunction with a partner application) get mail or read newsgroups.

Getting Your Web Browser

To surf the Web you need a Web browser. It is the job of the Web browser to interpret the underlying code of a Web page and produce the finished images and text that you see on your screen.

These days, the Web browser market has narrowed down to two main players: Netscape Communicator (with Navigator the name of its Web browser component) and Microsoft Internet Explorer. The Mac OS comes with both Internet Explorer and Netscape Communicator. If a newer version is available, you will find a free update for it on the Web (MacFixIt is one of many places that will post this information). Updates may also be included on CD disks that come from other sources, such as the monthly CD included with each issue of *MacAddict* magazine.

Note: Internet Explorer 5 came out after I finished writing this chapter. I added information about its new features, as relevant, in the sections that follow. In general, the troubleshooting matters covered here are equally accurate for Explorer 4.x and Explorer 5.x. The current version of Netscape is 4.7.x, although a 6.x version is on the horizon. Another browser, called iCab, has a small but loyal following.

TAKE NOTE ▶ Web browsing via America Online

If you have America Online, you can connect directly to AOL and use the Web browser that gets installed as part of the AOL installation. With AOL, you can get to the Web in one of several ways:

1. From the Internet menu on the task bar, choose "Go to the Web."

2. Type a URL directly in the Go text box and then click the Go button (or press Return).

3. Click any underlined link in anything you are doing from within AOL or AOL email and it will take you to the Web site.

4. Click any Web page listed in the Favorites menu on the task bar.

AOL's built-in browser is currently a variation of Internet Explorer (although AOL can always change that in the future). However, once connected to AOL, you are not limited to using this browser. You may use any Internet browser (**Note:** This only applies to the browser itself, not email or other specialized Internet software that makes non-Web connections). Thus, you can use the separate Explorer or Netscape browsers, even while you are logged on to AOL. You can even have multiple browsers running at the same time.

Finally, I recommend getting both an AOL and another ISP account (such as EarthLink). With this, you can bypass AOL altogether, except when you want to use AOL's proprietary features, such as its forums or chat areas. If you do not use AOL much (such as just for email), you can sign up for the cheapest AOL rate possible (currently $4.95 per month for 3 hours or less of use). Or you can sign up for AOL's special reduced "Bring your own access" rate for those who only access AOL via a second ISP. It has no monthly usage limit. So, for just a little more than AOL alone might cost, you can have the best of both worlds (see Chapter 12 for more on setting up an account with an ISP).

BY THE WAY ▶ Web Portals

With the exception of AOL, most of what used to be called "online services" (such as CompuServe and eWorld) have disappeared or been vastly cut back. In their place, we have "*Web portals.*" These serve as a jumping off point to other parts of the Web, and (if the services are successful) the place you keep returning to after you venture elsewhere. They feature news headlines, stock prices, and assorted other information and links. A portal page will typically be your browser's default home page.

Essentially, this means that instead of needing proprietary software to access the special features of the service, you access everything from a Web site. In many cases, these services are free. Or you may need to pay for password-protected access to the site.

In addition to former online services, sites that have always been Web-based are seeking to be your Web portal. These include search engines such as AltaVista and Excite. Apple's default home page, assigned in the browsers that ship with new Macs, is based on Excite (http://apple.excite.com/).

Understanding Internet Addresses

IP Addresses, Domain Names, and URLs

Every Web page (actually every separate Web element, such as a graphic within a Web page) has its own specific address. The root element of all of these addresses is something called an *IP* (Internet Protocol) *address*. Just like the address for where you live, IP addresses identify a specific location. You use the address to tell your browser where you want to go.

IP addresses are simply a string of numbers, separated by periods (such as 206.124.64.253). However, even if you are a long time Web surfer, you may never have seen these numeric IP addresses. This is because each IP address can be assigned a name, called a *domain name*, that is easier to remember. A domain name is a string of words or letters, separated by periods (such as www.apple.com). When you enter a domain name in your Web browser, a *Domain Name Server* (DNS) matches domain names to their "real" numeric IP addresses so that you can navigate the Web using just the names.

You can still use the numeric addresses if you wish, but it's not required. Actually, there is one time when the numeric address is preferred: if there is some problem with the DNS. In this case, you may be unable to get to a site by its domain name but its numeric address may still work. To find out a site's numeric address, you'll likely need a utility such as IPNetMonitor.

SEE: • **"Internet Diagnostics Utilities" in Chapter 12.**

The domain name address for the Apple Web site is www.apple.com. Like most addresses for the main page of a site, it has three components separated by periods (or "dots"). The first component "www" means that the Web page is part of the World Wide Web. Most Web page addresses start this way, but it is not an absolute requirement. The second component "apple" tells you the distinguishing name of the specific site. The third component "com" is the domain category. This identifies the type of domain. Common domain types are com (commercial), org (non-profit), edu (education) and gov (government). Domain names outside the U.S. typically end in a two-letter abbreviation for the country (such as .de for Denmark or .au for Australia).

Technically, the full address of the Apple Web site is http://www.apple.com. The "http" stands for *HyperText Transfer Protocol*. Using "http" is what tells the browser to interpret the address that follows as a Web page or Web page element (such as a graphic image). As I will soon explain, there are other protocols besides http. The "://" is simply the convention used to divide the protocol designation from the rest of the address. The entire address is often referred to as a URL (or *Uniform Resource Locater*).

The initial part of all Web URLs is the domain name/IP address of the Web site. This can be the entire URL. However, as explained more in the following sections, the URL may also contain additional elements. It is by using these longer URLs that a Web site with a single IP address can have a separate URL for each page that makes up the site.

TECHNICALLY SPEAKING ▶ Where Do Domain Names Come From?

How does a Web site obtain a domain name address, particularly a top-level address such as www.apple.com? You have to apply for these addresses. The major agency in charge of the well-known top-level domains (com, net, org, and edu) is InterNIC, a cooperation of the National Science Foundation and a private profit-making operation. When you apply, InterNIC makes sure that the name you request has not already been assigned to someone else. The name is then assigned and linked to the numeric IP address that you have been assigned by your Internet Service Provider (ISP). You have to pay an annual fee to keep the address. Check the InterNIC Web site http://internic.net) for more details. You can also look up important information about whether a domain name is available, who owns the rights to a particular domain, and how to contact the owner or technical provider for domains by checking this InterNIC page: http://internic.net/cgi-bin/whois.

Most common and potentially popular domain names (such as www.loans.com or www.autos.com) are already taken. In some cases, people have been offered millions of dollars from companies seeking to purchase these names!

You do not need to have your own personal domain name to have a Web site. Instead, you can set up your Web site within someone else's domain, assuming you have permission to do so. The downside of this is that you have a less simple, harder to remember address. For example, most universities allow their students and staff to set up their own Web sites on the university computer. For example, if Mark Jones went to Yale University, he might wind up with a Web address such as www.yale.edu/~jones/.

America Online lets its members create their own Web site within AOL's members.aol.com domain. Here you might have an address such as members.aol.com/~jones.

To get your browser to go to a specific address on the Web, you can enter its URL in the appropriate text box (the Location box of Netscape or the Address box of Explorer). Just be careful to enter the address *exactly* how it is written. Even the most seemingly trivial variation may result in the address being rejected (that's why users depend upon ways of saving URLs they intend to use again, such as via bookmarks, as covered later in this chapter). You can also cut and paste a name into an Address box.

HyperText Links

In many cases, you will be navigating the Web, not by typing in URLs, but by clicking hypertext or graphic image links on a Web page. In this case, the URL for the destination is obtained from the Web page itself, rather than by you. Otherwise, the basic mechanism is the same.

These links are typically seen as colored and/or underlined text or as special graphic images. The standard colors are blue (if the linked site has not been visited recently) and purple (after you have recently visited the site). But the specific colors are set and can be changed by your browser preferences (options). The browser's cursor typically changes when you pass over one of these links (such as to a hand), indicating that the text or graphic has an underlying link. Graphic images with attached links often (although not always) are surrounded by a colored border. In any case, the URL of any link that your cursor is over should appear in a box at the bottom of the browser window. If you click the mouse at that point, the browser opens the Web page of the linked URL.

The Structure of a Web Site: Home Pages and Subdirectories

The Apple Web site URL (http://www.apple.com/) takes you to what is referred to as the *home page* of the site. A Web site may consist of just this home page. Or it may consist of any number of additional pages (which is the case for Apple). These additional pages are typically organized into separate subdirectories (or folders) much like the organization of the files on your computer's desktop. Similar to a table of contents, you can navigate to these other locations from links on the home page.

This structure is reflected in the addresses of each Web page within a Web site. In particular, the URLs of the additional pages are usually based on the home page name. For example, to go to the part of Apple's Web site specific to the iMac, you would go to http://www.apple.com/imac/. The additional single slash before the word "imac" indicates that you are going to a subdirectory location of the main www.apple.com site.

For most Web pages, the URL must end in the name of the page you are loading. And most Web pages are named with either *.html*, *.htm*, or *.shtml* as a suffix. Thus to load a page that contains a list of downloadable files from my own MacFixIt Web site, you would type: http://www.macfixit.com/library/a-f.shtml. This loads the Web page named a-f.shtml. Technically, there should be no slash at the end of this URL. However, if you mistakenly add a slash, most browsers will simply ignore it and correctly load the page anyway.

All Web files on a site are contained within one or more directories (or folders). Within each directory, one file can be designated as the default (or home) page of that directory. This is the page that loads if no file is specified in the URL. The name of such a file is either *index.html* or *default.html*. Thus, if you type http://www.macfixit.com/, you will actually be loading http://www.macfixit.com/ index.shtml. This is the "true" URL of the MacFixIt main home page.

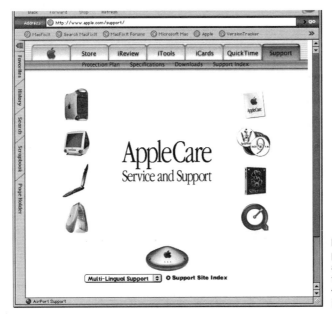

Figure 13-1 Apple's root Web page for all of its support locations as viewed from Internet Explorer; the URL for the page <http://www.apple.com/support/> is in the Address text box.

Note that while URLs that specify a page do *not* end in a slash, URLs that specify a directory *do* end in a slash. However, once again, browsers are forgiving of this and if you omit the slash, the URL should still work. In fact, these days browsers are intelligent enough to guess what page you are looking for from even less information. For example, if you just type "MacFixIt" as a URL, it will take you to http://www.macfixit.com. By the way, this provides a convenient way to guess at the name of a Web site. (Looking for the Web site for a company called MacWidgets? Just enter the name in the browser's text box and see what comes up.)

If there is no default page in a directory, the browser will instead load a catalog list of all the files/pages in the directory. You could click any one of them to load the page. However, if a Webmaster wants to prevent you from seeing this list, he can set it up so that a message such as "Access Forbidden" appears if you try this. Or he could simply create a "dummy" index page that is completely blank. This sort of arrangement is common for directories that are not intended to be directly accessible (perhaps a list of files for downloading, where the file to be downloaded is selected from a page in another directory).

In some cases, when you enter a specific URL, you may find that you get taken to a page that has a different URL than the one you entered. The most likely reason for this is that the Web site is using one URL as a "referrer" to the other URL. This may be done for any of several reasons. For example, the real URL may be a long and complicated one. By using a simple referring URL to indirectly access the page, the Webmaster gives the Web surfer an easy URL to remember.

Finally note: the home pages described here are separate from what is called the home page of your browser. The browser's home page is the one that opens by default when you open the browser (which you can determine via a setting in the browser's preferences).

TECHNICALLY SPEAKING ▶ What's HTML? And How Do You View HTML Source Code?

The main text states that most Web pages end in a suffix of either html, htm, or shtml. These suffixes are derived from the name HTML (HyperText Markup Language), which refers to the language used to create Web pages. You can see the underlying HTML *source code* of a Web page from within your browser. For example, from the View menu select Page Source Netscape) or Source (Explorer). The source code is basically just a text file. None of the graphics that appear on a Web page are contained in the source code. Instead, the source code provides instructions as to where the desired graphic is located and where on the page it should appear. It is the job of the Web browser to interpret this and produce the finished page that you actually see.

From the users' perspective, there is no difference between the htm, html and shtml suffixes. However, if you were a Web page designer, you would know that shtml refers to pages that include a special type of instruction called *server-side includes*. This allows the Web page to have different content each time it loads. For example, this is one way that Web pages can have advertising banners that rotate each time you load the page.

(continues on next page)

While Web browsers understand HTML, the language itself is constantly being improved and expanded. It is possible for a Web page to contain "new" HTML instructions that the browser does not yet understand. This can result in the page not loading properly. This is one reason that a Web page may look different on one browser than it does on another.

One other important HTML principle: traditional HTML instructions are relative rather than absolute. This means, for example, that an HTML instruction may say to make a given line of text smaller than the preceding line (by indicating that it should be an H5 level heading rather than the larger H4 level). But exactly how large is H4 or H5? The HTML language does not decide this. This is decided by the browser itself. This is another reason that the same HTML may look different in different browsers. More recent versions of HTML language (particularly what is known as HTML 4) includes ways of more specifically addressing the size of text and even selecting the specific font and style of text (known as dynamic fonts). In this latter case, the font information is actually built in to the HTML file.

BY THE WAY ▶ A Word About Web Page Authoring and HTML

Just how do you go about creating a Web site? To do so, you create a text document written in HTML. The document is then loaded to a *Web server* and assigned a specific address. Once on a server, your Web pages can be viewed by anyone with access to the Web.

The basics of using HTML are quite simple (much simpler than learning a programming language). It depends on special tags that indicate instructions on how the page should appear. Your Web browser then interprets these instructions to construct the page. For example "<TITLE>Ted Landau's Home Page</TITLE>" tells the browser that "Ted Landau's Home Page" is the title of the page. Note that the actual text needs to be correctly enclosed by an opening tag and a closing tag (which has the slash). This is a general principle of almost all HTML "commands."

Still, designing fancy pages can get complicated quickly enough. That's why there are a host of Web page editors on the market to help you out. The recent trend is for these editors to completely hide the HTML code from you, allowing you to lay out a page almost as easily as you can in a word processor or page layout program. However, the very easiest-to-use of these WYSIWYG editors (such as Adobe's PageMill) have fallen by the wayside. Most popular now are more industrial strength editors, such as Adobe GoLive and Macromedia's Dreamweaver. There are also graphics programs, such as Fireworks and ImageStyler, geared especially towards designing Web page images.

(continues on next page)

Figure 13-2 Left: part of a Web page as viewed in a browser. Right: part of the source code behind the Web page (with Communicator, select Page Source from the View window to see this source code).

BY THE WAY ▶ A Word About Web Page Authoring and HTML *(continued)*

There are, of course, a host of troubleshooting issues that might confront a Web author trying to get a page to look and work exactly as desired. But that's a subject for another book. Well, OK, before I leave this topic, here are a few key troubleshooting reminders for those of you who have started working on your own Web pages and are having problems:

- If you are entering your own HTML code, make sure that opening tags have a matching closing tag.

- When using HTML to control the font, size and formatting of text, you can never tell for sure how it will look until you actually see it in a Web browser. So test the page in both Netscape and Explorer browsers before going public. You can do this by simply opening your finished page in your browser while offline.

- GIF and JPEG are graphic formats directly supported by most Web browsers. Other graphic formats may require special plug-ins to be viewed. Graphics of each type usually have a suffix indicating that name, such as banner.gif. Both GIF and JPEG images are encoded files (designed to be smaller in file size than they otherwise would be, which is especially nice for Web pages where increased size slows down the loading of the page).

  GIF graphics are especially flexible. There is a special GIF-89 format used to create *transparent* GIF graphics (that let the page's background show through). You can also create *interlaced* GIF graphics (that load progressively, thereby speeding up the initial view of the graphic). There are even *animated* GIFs that provide a simple way to have movement on your page, without needing any plug-ins or fancy tricks.

- Creating forms and using counters and some types of imagemaps generally require special software on your server, called CGI scripts, that do most of the work. Simply setting up a form on your Web page will not, by itself, get the form to work.

  SEE ALSO: • **Chapter 10 for more on different graphic formats.**

BY THE WAY ▶ A Word About Using Your Mac as a Web Server

Mac or remote? If you do create a Web site, you will most likely upload it to a remote server (often it's the same ISP you use to access the Web for surfing). If the server is a Unix server, you'll have to learn the basics of Unix to access your files.

However, your Macintosh can be set up as a Web server with very little effort or expertise. You can do it with high-powered software (such as WebSTAR) or more personal-oriented software—such as Personal Web Sharing (that comes with the Mac OS) or Personal Web Server (included with Internet Explorer). Or, if you have more advanced skills, you can use Mac OS X Server.

While using your Mac has numerous advantages over using a remote server (you have much more control over how the site works and can customize it more easily), it has one big disadvantage: it can be a lot more expensive. This is because of the connection costs. A dial-up modem will simply not be fast enough to support any sort of decent-sized Web traffic; neither will an ISDN line. And with a dial-up modem, even if you get a separate dedicated line for your server (another expense!), you still won't have the reliable 24-7 link to the Internet that a Web server should have. A cable connection should be sufficient, but home accounts typically prohibit using your computer as a server. Instead, you'll need a more expensive work account. You may also have to invest in a router (for security purposes), adding still more to the cost.

(continues on next page)

Finally, you will need a *static IP address*. This (as opposed to a *dynamic address*) is one that stays the same every time you connect. Without this, visitors to your site will not be able to use the same URL to return to it next time. Again, static addresses are often more expensive to get.

To be fair, remote servers can also get expensive, especially if your site starts getting a lot of traffic and if you want to use additional server features (such as cgi scripts). Still, a simple and low-traffic site can be set-up for very little cost. Sometimes it will be a free bonus that comes with your ISP account.

While Personal Web Sharing (or Web Server) cannot support a high level of traffic, you can use them as a convenient way to share information with a small group of friends and/or relatives. Another simple alternative is to see up a Web site directly on the Web itself, such as via Apple's iTools.

The risks of using a Web server on your Mac When you set up your Mac as a Web server, you are allowing at least some public access to your drive. If you do this, it is critical that you limit this access to those Web pages that you wish to be public, with the rest of your drive strictly off limits.

In principle, the settings of the software make this easy to do. For example, with Microsoft's Personal Web Server, the default setting limits public access only to those files in the folder designated as My Personal Web Site. However, if you enable the "Let Me Access Mounted Disks From My Home Page" check box, and you have file sharing turned on, any one who knows or can guess your Owner Password could have access to your entire disk. Again, this is not a likely situation, but it is worth knowing.

SEE ALSO: • **"Web Security," later in this chapter, for more on security matters.**

Navigating the Web

So far, we have discussed two of the main ways to move from one Web page to another: typing an address in the Address box and clicking hypertext and graphic links. In this section, I briefly introduce a few other common navigational methods. They are relevant to troubleshooting issues covered later in the chapter.

Bookmarks/Favorites

Having to remember potentially long and complicated URLs can be a real pain. The easiest way to avoid this is to save the URL as a Bookmark (in Netscape) or a Favorite (in Explorer). For example, to save the URL for the current page in Navigator, use the Add Bookmark command. The URL will now be listed in the Bookmarks menu. Simply select it any later time you wish to return to that URL.

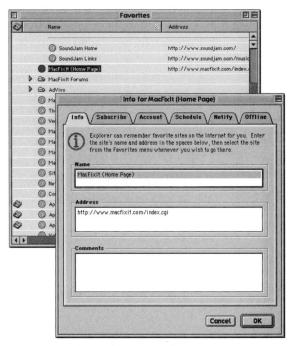

Figure 13-3 In the background is the list of Favorites as seen in Explorer after selecting the Organize Favorites command. In the foreground, the Get Info window for the MacFixIt favorite.

You can also save a bookmark for any hypertext link within a Web page. To do so, click and hold down the mouse button until a pop-up menu appears. Select the "Add Bookmark" (or similarly worded) command.

You can edit the contents of your Favorites, such as to delete ones you no longer want. To do so, select Edit Bookmarks (Netscape) or Organize Favorites (Explorer). Especially with Explorer, select to Organize Favorites, click a Favorite, and then select Get Info (Command-I). Here you will see an almost dizzying array of further options, including the option to have Explorer automatically check for when a particular page has been updated. It is beyond the scope of this book to detail all of these options here.

Go, Back, and Forward

Browsers have a *Go* menu, which tracks recently visited pages. You can select a URL from there to return to any recently visited page. The Go menu in Explorer is especially convenient; it groups your previously visited URLs according to the day that you visited them.

If you have very recently visited a Web page, the *Back* button will also take you back to it. In fact, if you click the Back button and hold down the mouse button, you'll see a list of all the pages you have visited from this window since it was opened.

With Netscape, hold down the Option key when clicking the Back button and you will be taken to the most recently previously visited Web site (rather than the previous Web page).

Bear in mind that the Back button only backs you up along your most recent path. This means that if you back up six pages and then move forward to two new pages, when you start backing up again, you will no longer be able to back up to the six pages you previously retraced. These pages are no longer on your most recent back up path.

The *Forward* button works similarly, except it goes forward of course.

Each browser has various shortcuts for these and other functions. For example, in Internet Explorer 5, pressing the Delete key is the same as using the Back button. Shift-Delete is the equivalent of the Forward button.

Links from the Desktop

The exact rules of the game here seem to change with each update to the browser software but in general:

www.macfixit.com/   MacFixIt (Home Page)

Figure 13-4 The URL file icons that appear when you drag a URL to the desktop from Explorer's address box (left) and Netscape's Location box (right).

- If you drag a link from a Web page to the desktop, you will save a copy of the file. The actual link may be in the Comments box of the Get Info window of the file (especially with Navigator).

- If you drag a link from the browser's Address/Location box to the desktop, you get a file that is essentially just the link itself. (With Netscape, you have to click the bookmark icon directly to the left of the Location box and drag that.) Double-click this file and, if you are online, it will load the page from the Web.

Utilities for URLs

If you want URL management features that go beyond what is included with your Web browser, there is an assortment of third-party utilities available. My personal favorite is URLManager Pro.

Beyond the Web: Using Your Browser for Email, Newsgroups, and More

In a sense, the Internet is not just one service network, but a loosely held collection of several different services. That is, you can use the Internet not only for accessing the World Wide Web, but also for email, for downloading files, and for checking out newsgroups.

There are specific Macintosh applications for accessing each of these types of services. For example, there is Eudora for email, NewsWatcher for newsgroups, and Anarchie or Fetch for downloading and uploading files.

However, one of the beauties of Web browsers, such as Netscape Communicator or Microsoft's Internet Explorer (in combination with Outlook Express), is that you can access all of the services from the browser itself. The browser has evolved into something much more than a tool just for viewing Web pages. It has become a sort of Swiss-Army-knife Internet tool. The other applications are not obsolete by any means. They retain certain advantages, offering more features that the Web browser could include. But for many users, the Web browser will be all they need.

The main reason this can work is that all of these different services can be referenced via the same URL system I have already described for Web addresses. The http:// designation is just one type of URL protocol. Your Web browser can also download files, via an FTP:// protocol. Similarly, it can access newsgroups via a news: protocol or set up to send email via the mailto: protocol. For example, a URL to send email to MacFixIt is: mailto:feedback@macfixit.com. **Note:** By convention, the double slashes that usually follow the http and FTP protocols in URLs are not used for mailto and news URLs. However, in truth, most browsers will now correctly recognize any of these URLs with or without the double slash.

Accessing news and email either (a) takes you to special sections/windows of the browser that are separate from the Web browser, or (b) takes you to a separate application altogether (such as Outlook Express). You are not limited to the browser's default settings. From a browser's preferences, you can select which applications you want to use for email, newsgroups, etc.

SEE ALSO: • **"Downloading and Uploading Files," 'Downloading and Helper Problems," "Solve-It! Email Problems," and "By the Way: Newsgroups," later in this chapter, for information on these "Beyond the Web" topics.**

TAKE NOTE ▶ Saving and Printing Web Pages

Here are some tips for saving and/or printing Web pages:

Save a selection of text from a Web page As of this writing, browsers do not support dragging text to the desktop to save it as a clippings file (you can drag linked text that way, and save the link, but not text). As an alternative, you can copy and paste. But you will find it more convenient to use a utility that allows you to directly save text as a clipping file and/or SimpleText file. For example, ClipFiler allows you to drag-and-drop text from your browser.

Net-Print is another personal favorite. In addition to saving selected text, Net-Print also cleans up the text eliminating unwanted characters and extra spaces, etc.). Another alternative is to copy the text and use a separate utility to clean it up (such as Magic Bullet or TextCleaner).

By the way, you may find pages where you cannot select a portion of the text, although you can select the entire page of text (using Command-A to Select All). Explorer seems particularly vulnerable to this on pages that use many HTML tables in their layout. There is nothing you can do to work around this. Just select the entire text and cut what you do not need when you open the text in your word processor. Hopefully, an upgrade to the browser will fix this.

Other times when you may not (or will not) be able to select text include when you have text that is really part of a graphic or text that is based on a style sheet (an "advanced" HTML feature that Web page designers may use). In these cases, if you don't care to save the text in an editable form, you can always use a screen capture to save a portion of a Web page (use Command-Shift-4 to save exactly the area you want).

Save a graphic from a Web page Most graphic images can be selected and saved by directly dragging them to the desktop.

Save an entire page At the most basic level, saving an entire Web page is easy to do. Simply select Save As from your browser's File menu, save the file, and you are done. From this dialog box, both Netscape and Explorer give you the option to save just the Text of a Web page or the HTML (Source code) of a Web page. By saving it as HTML, you have the advantage of being able to load the page back in a Web browser and seeing it exactly as it looked originally (minus the graphics, if you are offline). Even its links will still be intact. When you save as Text, formatting and links are lost. If you later need a plain text version, you can still create this from the HTML version.

By the way, you can choose to see the source code before printing it. To do so, choose the Source option from the View menu.

With Explorer you have a great third option called *Web Archive*. Web Archive saves a page *exactly* as it looks when you view it from a Web browser, including all graphics. It even has options to save the pages that are linked from the page you are saving, so that if you load the Web Archive file when you are not connected to the Internet, the links actually load the additional pages. To do this, click the Options button in the Save dialog box. In the Download Links option, you get to select how many layers deep you want the links to go.

(continues on next page)

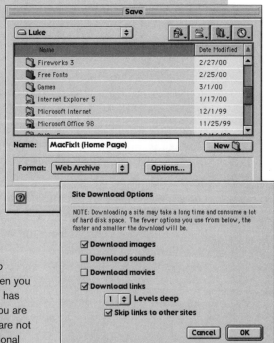

Figure 13-5 Top: Explorer's option to save a page as a Web Archive as listed in the Save dialog box. Bottom: the window that appears after clicking the Options button.

To try this out, save a Web Archive and then select Work Offline from Explorer's File menu; now load the Web Archive file by double-clicking it and click some links.

The main disadvantages of Web Archives are that they can get quite large in size and only Explorer can open them. For Netscape, you would have to turn to any of several third-party utilities (such as Web Whacker) for a similar function.

There are also ways of saving a page by dragging a link to the desktop (as described in "Links from the Desktop," in the main text).

Saving pages with frames If you are saving a page with frames, beware. The Save command may just save the frame shell rather than the contents within the frame. This is probably not what you want. To get around this, you can open the frame contents as a separate window before saving. To do this, click and hold down the mouse button while the cursor is over the frame; you should get an option such as "New window with this frame"; select it. Then select to Save.

Printing a page Printing a page is as simple as selecting Print from the File menu. To reduce the size of a Web page that is wider than the paper you are using, you can use the scaling option in Page Setup. Or you can shift to Landscape orientation and hope it fits that way. Even better, with Explorer, use Print Preview. It has an option to shrink a page to fit the paper—as well as an assortment of other useful choices. Take a look.

New in Explorer 5 With Internet Explorer 5, you can for the first time simply drag any selection of text to the desktop. Explorer saves the selection as a text file, complete with its original formatting (font, style, size and color)! You can even drag a selection directly into a document of another application (such as AppleWorks).

Web Security

One of the more frequent concerns about using the Internet is security. The concerns generally fall into two categories: (1) protection of your data (for example, making sure an intruder can not gain access to your computer and read or erase your files); and (2) protection of privacy (for example, making sure that when you send credit card or other personal information over the Internet, prying eyes cannot view it). While both concerns are legitimate, the extent of the danger is often exaggerated. Let's take a brief look.

Cookies and Security/Privacy

A cookie is defined as a bit of text that a Web site can store on your hard drive and retrieve when you revisit the site. Netscape stores this cookie information in a file called MagicCookie. Explorer stores this information in the Internet Preferences file.

The usual purpose of these files is innocent enough. They are designed to store information about you that would be useful for the Web site to know on a return visit. For example, suppose a site has a special page that greets first-time visitors. It could leave a cookie file that would identify you as a returning visitor, thereby bypassing the first time visitor screen.

However, from a security point of view, users worry about two aspects of these cookies: (1) can unscrupulous Web site designers use cookies to leave "dangerous" stuff on your hard drive, such as a virus that might erase your drive? (2) could sensitive material (such as credit card numbers) be stored in these cookie files and then accessed by people who do not have the authority to have this information?

In general, the answer to these questions is no. It is unlikely, although not impossible, for a cookie to be used in this way. However, for those that feel you cannot be too safe, there are a variety of options for dealing with cookies. The two main options are: (1) clear out existing cookies and (2) prevent new cookies from being created. Not too long ago, doing these things required a utility separate from your browser. However, current versions of browsers now handle cookie management quite well on their own.

Control your cookies You can block your browser from accepting certain or all cookies. You can even delete existing cookies.

Netscape Communicator To do this in Netscape, go to Edit/Preferences/Advanced and click "Do not accept cookies." You should probably also enable "Accept only cookies that get sent back to the originating server." This prevents the Cookie information from being sent back to a site other than the site than sent it. It is a minimal form of security. Finally, you can choose to decide whether or not to accept a cookie on a case-by-case basis. To do this, select "Warn me before accepting cookies." Now you will get a prompt, to which you must answer yes or no, each time a cookie is sent.

If you want to actually see a list of existing cookies and edit it, you need a third-party utility such as Cookie Cutter.

To delete completely all existing cookies, simply delete the MagicCookie file, located in the Netscape f folder in your Preferences folder.

Internet Explorer To do this in Explorer, go to Edit/Preferences/Receiving Files/Cookies. Similar to Netscape, a pop-up menu allows you to choose between "Always accepting," "Never accepting," "Ask for each site," or "Ask for each cookie." Better than Netscape, you see a complete list of all current cookies. From this list, you can select individual cookies to be deleted entirely. Or you can select to delete all of them.

By selecting "Ask for each site," you can avoid the annoyance of having the browser repeatedly ask if you accept cookies for the site before the page even loads. With this option selected, if you say yes once, it assumes you have said yes for all other cookies on that site. Thus, the messages do not appear again.

If you have the "Ask for each site" option selected, you can also select to "Decline cookies" from a specific site from the Preferences display. This stops all cookies from being accepted from that site but does not delete the current cookie. You can later turn the cookie back on.

Cookies and forms You've probably visited a site where there are text boxes for you to fill in. When you complete the text boxes, you hit a button, such as Send or Submit, and the information you filled in gets sent to the receiving Web site. This is often used to register software, purchase items, or fill out online surveys. This is a potential security issue itself, especially if the information you send includes items such as a credit card number (we'll get to this in a moment). However, if you set your browser to never accept cookies, you may have another problem: some sites that use forms require that you accept a cookie before they will accept your form information. If this is the case,

the error message you receive may not tell you what is happening. You may simply get a message that says that sending the form's information was rejected.

It is similarly possible that other Web site features may not work with cookies disabled. If this happens, change your preference to accept cookies, and try again. If you are concerned about the cookie, you can accept the cookie and delete it immediately after leaving the site.

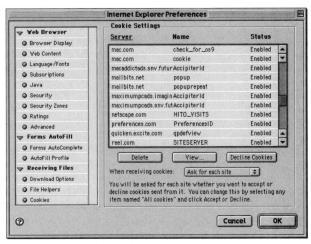

Figure 13-6 The Cookies list from Explorer's Preferences window.

TECHNICALLY SPEAKING ▶ Ports and Firewalls

Ports A port number is a number used to identify a specific type of transaction or service over the Internet. A port number, for example, distinguishes a Web server (HTTP), mail server (SMTP), and file transfer (FTP) server that may all be at the same IP address. The port number uniquely identifies which server application is to be accessed. For example, the default port number for HTTP is 80.

As a typical end user, you almost never need to enter port numbers, as your Internet software (such as your Web browser) assumes the default numbers based on the address you enter. That is, www.company.com is assumed to be a Web address and is sent to the Web server automatically.

However, occasionally an IP address may have more than one port number for a particular service (because it is using two different servers for that service), or a host may simply not use the default number for some reason. In this case, you would need to enter the default port number to access the server. You typically do this by adding a colon, followed by the port number, to the end of the address, such as <http://www.company.com:80>.

Also note: the email protocol SMTP uses port 25 and POP uses port 110. Email programs assume these latter two ports are the ones to use for sending and receiving mail respectively. In the rare case that your ISP has assigned a different port number, you may not be able to send or receive mail. The only solutions here are to use an email program that allows you to specify a port or get your ISP to change their ways.

Firewalls (and proxy servers) A firewall is a name for any form of security protections that stands between your computer (or local network) and the Internet. It offers security by protecting your local network (or even a single computer) from potentially hostile outside intrusion. There are various forms of this sort of protection.

One type of firewall is accomplished by using a *router*. A router is a hardware device (although there are some software programs that can serve as a router). For example Apple's AirPort Base Station, in addition to being a wireless connection device, is also a router (and its Software Base Station acts as a software based router). You connect your local network to a router and the router in turn connects to a larger network, typically the Internet.

(continues on next page)

TECHNICALLY SPEAKING ▶ Ports and Firewalls *(continued)*

Routers are used to monitor incoming traffic from the Internet and properly route the traffic to its intended destination in your local network. If this was all a router did, it would not offer significant firewall protection. However, most routers include additional firewall features that allow you to block/filter certain incoming traffic, based on criteria you set, from ever getting through to your local network.

One such firewall feature is called port inspection. This allows the router to block outside access to selected ports. In this way, if you had an intranet Web server set to port 80, and you did not want anyone other than employees on the local network to be able to access it, you could set a router so that any external requests for port 80 are rejected.

Some routers can be set up as NAT (Network Address Translation) servers. With this setup, your router can give local IP addresses to multiple computers on your Local Area Network (LAN) and have them all use one Wide Area Network (WAN) IP address to connect to the outside world. The result is that the outside world only "sees" the IP address of your router, another form of firewall protection.

A different form of firewall is a proxy server. In this case, a server may be setup to store the Web pages requested by users on the local network. When a user requests a page, it gets it from the server rather than the Web. This protects the user from direct access to the Internet. If there is no proxy service set up for a particular protocol (such as FTP), devices on the local network are blocked from accessing that protocol. You can set up a Mac as a proxy server but typically, this is done on a central server of a local network. Beyond that, there is little reason for you to set up a proxy server on your own although Connectix's Surf Express was essentially a personal proxy server designed to intelligently cache Web pages with the intent of speeding up your browser.

Finally, a software program called NetBarrier offers personal firewall protection for any Mac user.

Problems with firewalls Unfortunately, firewalls can interfere with your ability receive certain types of Web content. This has been a particular concern for QuickTime streaming video. Apple has an entire Web page <http://www.apple.com/quicktime/resources/qt4/us/proxy/> explaining how to set the options of the QuickTime Settings control panel to work around most firewall-related problems.

Another potential problem with firewalls is that they may block attempts to download files via FTP. Usually, this can be avoided by using FTP in passive (PASV) mode. Briefly, FTP usually tries to open a connection from the server first and then to the client. This is prevented with certain firewalls in place. In passive mode, the server is told not to open a connection until the client does so first. This works. Most browsers now default to using passive mode. Otherwise, you can overtly select this option from the Advanced/File Transfer panel of the Internet control panel: enable the "Use Passive Mode" checkbox.

This subject rapidly escalates beyond my area of expertise. When confronted with these problems, I either follow the advice of pages like the Apple page just cited and hope for the best, or seek outside help.

SEE ALSO: • **"Take Note: Troubleshooting Cable, DSL, and Network Connections," in Chapter 12.**

BY THE WAY ▶ Using Go to Spy

We have already noted that a browser's Go menu lists all the sites that have been visited in the recent past (see "Navigating the Web," earlier in this chapter). If someone has access to your computer, they can use this to spy on what sorts of Web sites you've been visiting.

On the plus side for parents, if your child was using the Web browser earlier in the day (unless they are savvy enough to cover their tracks by deleting the file that stores the data), you could use this to check what sites were visited.

SEE ALSO: • **"Web Pages Load Slowly or Incompletely," later in this chapter, for how to delete the data used by the Go menu.**

Secure Web Pages

Is it safe to provide a credit card number to a Web site? The short answer to this question is yes. It is certainly no more risky than telling someone your credit card number over a telephone (especially a cordless phone!). Of course, the more you trust the firm behind the Web site, the safer you are. Sending information to Amazon.com is far less risky than sending your credit card to some unknown Web site that is offering you some qet-rich-quick scheme.

Still, even with a trusted Web site, you might have some concern about a third party intercepting your message and stealing your information. Web browsers help out here by providing additional security. The primary method is via special "secure" Web pages. These Web pages typically use a technology called SSL (Secure Socket Layer) that encrypts the information, so that if it is intercepted en route to its destination, it will be of no value to the person intercepting it.

HTTPS If a page contains a form that you fill out to send information, and the information is sent as encrypted data, the URL for the page will likely begin with the term *https* rather than the more common *http*.

An additional sign that you have entered this type of secure page is that the padlock icon in the lower left of the window will be closed (Netscape) or that the padlock icon will appear (Explorer).

If you click Netscape's padlock icon, you will be taken to a panel that contains a listing of Netscape's security options. Select the Security Info item and you will get information about the security level of the active page.

A Web browser will also display a message whenever you enter or exit a secure Web page—so you know when

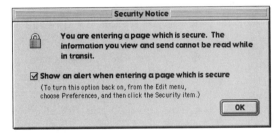

Figure 13-7 Top: The message that appears in Explorer when you enter a secure Web page. A similar message appears in Netscape browsers. Bottom: the closed padlock icon at the bottom of Netscape's window indicates you are on a secure Web page.

you have this protection and when you don't. It may also display a warning any time you send data that is not encrypted. However, you can optionally turn off these warning messages. In Netscape, you do this from the same security window that was just mentioned. Click the Navigator item to see your choices. With Explorer, select Preferences/Web Browser/Security.

Of course, none of this protects against the intended recipient using the information improperly. Also, be aware that if you are a recipient of encrypted information, your Web browser unencrypts it before displaying it. It therefore also stores the information in the disk cache in an unencrypted form. This too could be a security risk.

Certificates If you try to send data from a secure page and you get an odd error message that says that you are unable to send (or receive) the data, it may be that the page works with a certificate. The error typically means that a certificate is required and either you do not have the certificate, the certificate's expiration data has passed or you are using a computer other than the one you used when you obtained the certificate.

Certificates are used to confirm the identity of the organization sending/receiving the data and allow the data to be encrypted. A list of certificates available to your browser can be found in the same locations cited in the previous section on HTTPS. Most users need not worry about the details here, as the Web browser itself generally takes care of making sure you have up-to-date versions of the commonly needed certificates via updates to the browser software. However, if you have problems with a particular Web site, contact the site for further advice on how to obtain the needed certificate or otherwise proceed.

Figure 13-8 An error message that may appear when trying to access a secure Web page with an expired certificate.

128-bit encryption Explorer and Netscape browsers come in two forms: a standard form (that typically uses a 40 bit or 56-bit level of encryption) and a 128-bit encryption version. The 128-bit version provides an extra measure of security, as it will be more difficult to decode should someone intercept the message. Until just recently, this version was only open to U.S. citizens, due to some government restriction about making the encryption technology available to other countries, and you had to "sign" a statement saying you were a U.S. citizen before you were permitted to download it. However, this restriction has now been eased. As a result, Internet Explorer 5 only comes in a 128-bit version.

Security Leaks

If you keep up with computer-related news, you will inevitably hear about the latest "security leak" or "security hole." Typically, the description may sound something like this: "A security leak has been discovered in the latest version of Internet Explorer. Users who know how to exploit it can gain access to your computer while you are online and {fill in the blank}." Depending upon the leak in question, the phrase "fill in the blank" could be "read files on your drive" or "erase files on your hard drive," or any of a variety of other unwelcome activities. These security risks are certainly something to worry about. And the people who write browser software (or any Internet software) take them very seriously. As a result, these security leaks are usually plugged within a few days of being discovered.

What about the as yet undiscovered ones? I would not be too concerned. The vast majority of Web users will never be affected by any security leak. Even if you are vulnerable, it still takes someone to seek you out for attack before you are affected by it. Yes, it can happen—in the same way that you can get mugged on your way to your car in a parking lot. It's worth taking reasonable precautions in both cases (for the Web, these precautions include the advice given in this section on security). But I would not let the risks prevent me from ever going to a mall again or ever using the Web again.

Java (and scripts in general) and security Later in this chapter (see "Problems due to Java and JavaScript"), I provide some background about Java and related scripting technologies. For now, I merely want to point out that they are also a potential security risk. A Java applet is a software program that gets run on your computer when you load a Web page that contains the applet. An unscrupulous Web page designer could write an applet that might seek to gain information from your hard drive or actually damage your hard drive. The security built-in to your browser is designed to prevent this access. But hackers sometimes find "leaks" that allow them to bypass these safeguards. As always, these leaks tend to get plugged as they are discovered.

Downloading and Uploading Files

One of the more popular things to do online is to download software. This is a convenient way, sometimes the only way, to obtain the wealth of freeware, shareware, and updates to commercial software. Combined with an online payment option, it is also becoming a common way of obtaining full versions of commercial software. Finally, it is how you obtain many of the documents (such as those in PDF format) available on the Web.

Downloading a file simply means getting a copy of it from some remote location and transferring it to your Mac via an online connection. Typically, downloading a file is as simple as clicking a hypertext link or button and letting your software (usually your browser) do the rest of the work. However, if problems occur, solving them will be easier if you understand some downloading basics.

HTTP vs. FTP

When you click a link to download a file, the URL is almost always going to begin with either http or FTP. If it begins with http, it means that you are downloading the file via the Web's own HyperText Transfer Protocol. If it says FTP, it means that you are downloading the file via the older File Transfer Protocol.

To the end user, it typically makes little difference which protocol is used. However, if you are running a Web site, the protocols do make a difference. You can place a file anywhere on your Web site's HTML directory and link to it to set up an http download. But to use FTP, a separate FTP server must be set up and the files placed in that server.

So why do Webmasters bother with FTP? Its main advantages are that (1) it is often faster and more reliable than http and (2) programs other than browsers, known as FTP clients, can also download the file; sometimes these clients can succeed in downloading a file where a Web browser would fail. These FTP client applications can also be used for uploading files to an FTP server. You cannot do this from a Web browser.

Downloading Files

For either protocol, to download a file from a Web browser simply click the link to the URL for the file. There is usually a slight pause while the browser prepares to download the file. This is followed by the actual transfer of data, which you can typically monitor, either via a window that opens (in Netscape) or the Download Manager window (in Explorer). These windows list the name of the file you are downloading and indicate the progress it is making (how much of the file has downloaded; and how fast it is downloading). Relevant information may also appear in the text bar along the bottom of the browser's window. When the download is complete, the file is now on your drive.

The speed of the download can vary dramatically, depending on the type of connection you have, the speed of the server where the file resides, how busy the server is, and the overall level of Internet traffic. Speeds are usually measured. On a 56K modem, download speeds of at least around 3.0K/sec are common. They may go as high as 5K/sec. With broadband access, such as a cable modem, speeds can increase to over 100K/sec! [**Note:** the K in a modem's 56K is measuring something different than the K in the download speed; the K in the modem is equal to 8x the K indicated for download speed. Thus, a 56K modem should be able to transfer a file at a download speed of about 7K. In fact, you will virtually never get that fast.]

Once the browser indicates that a transfer has begun, you can close the Web page that contains the link to the downloading file; the download will proceed anyway.

Decoding and decompressing downloaded files

After the file has been downloaded, it is probably not immediately ready to be used. It will likely need to be decoded and/or decompressed. Your browser may or may not do this automatically. If it does not, you'll need to do it yourself, via a utility such as StuffIt Expander (ideally enhanced with DropStuff).

Encoded Files: Binhex (.hqx) and MacBinary (.bin) In this context, encoding a file means converting the data to a format that facilitates its tranfer online. If a downloaded file ends in the suffix *.hqx*, this means it has been encoded as a *binhex* file. If it ends in a *.bin*, this means it has been encoded as a MacBinary file. MacBinary is preferred if it works, as its file size is generally smaller and potential problems opening a decoded file are minimized. However, successfully transferring MacBinary files over the Internet has not been as reliable as for BinHex. So BinHex has been more common. In the last few years, the kinks seem to have been worked out because MacBinary is becoming more and more common (although it still does not work well when used in email attachments, as described
later in this chapter).

A binhex file is essentially a ordinary text file. However, the content of the file is in "code." The code, in turn, can be decoded with the right software to re-create

Gauge PRO.sit.hqx   Gauge PRO.sit   Gauge PRO

Figure 13-9 The icon for a downloaded file in binhex format (left); after decoding the binhex file into a StuffIt (.sit) format (center); after unstuffing the .sit file into a usable file (right).

the original Mac document or program. The first line of a binhex file will typically read *"(This file must be converted with Binhex 4.0)."* The remaining text will be appear to be meaningless nonsense (which, of course, is the coded information). If needed (because of file size restrictions in certain cases), a program can be converted into several smaller binhex file segments, with each

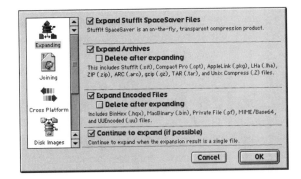

Figure 13-10 What binhex coding looks like if you load an "hqx" file into a word processor.

segment rejoined when it is decoded, so as to re-create the original single file.

A MacBinary file is not a plain text file, which is one reason that it can be more difficult to transfer successfully.

Compressed Files Even after decoding (or if decoding was not even used), the file may still not be usable. This is because it may be in a compressed format (such as a StuffIt archive, which will typically have the suffix: *".sit"*). Sometimes these files are

"self-extracting," (often with a suffix such as *".sea"*). If so, they can be decompressed simply by double-clicking the file (a new uncompressed copy of the file is created). Otherwise, StuffIt Expander is once again the utility of choice for decompressing all of the common formats.

Apple software updates may be in disk image (.img) format. When these are opened they appear as a mounted disk on your computer. You then run the software (typically an Installer) from the mounted image.

SEE ALSO: • **Fix-It #4 for more on image files and updating Apple software.**

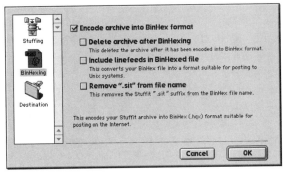

Figure 13-11 Some of Aladdin's Expander (top) and DropStuff (bottom) Preferences settings.

Uploading Files

Unless you run your own Web site on a remote server, your need to upload files will be minimal. If you do upload files, you will typically do so either via an upload feature built-in to your Web authoring software or via an FTP client (such as Fetch or Anarchie). DropStuff can be used to encode files in BinHex format. For other formats (and there are *many* more), you will need a more full-featured utility, such as DropStuff's parent application: StuffIt. You can also use these utilities to compress files.

When uploading files, you will need to specify in your FTP program what type of file is being transmitted. Text files and Binhex (".hqx") files will transmit as *Text*. Other files will most commonly transmit as *Binary* (or *raw data*). However, if you are sending a Mac program to another Mac user, encoded in MacBinary format, you should choose *MacBinary* or *Macintosh* (if you have one of these options). The difference between Binary and MacBinary is that MacBinary files include the data to recreate the "resource fork" used with Macintosh applications. Thus, plain Binary could not be used to upload an application.

Beware of duplicating your effort. That is, make sure you do not try to compress or encode files that have already been compressed or encoded.

Finally, if you use Apple's iDisk, it allows you to upload and download files to its server without any encoding or protocol information needed. Moving files to and from an iDisk works almost as simply as moving files from one folder to another on your Mac. This may well be the future of file transfers.

Solve-It! Web Browser Problems

The focus of this section is clearly on the Web browsing part of Web browser software (as opposed to a browser's newsgroup or email features). Still many of the points covered will have a general applicability to these other components, as well as to any online software.

TAKE NOTE ▶ Web Troubleshooting Basics

It is a maxim of all troubleshooting that a multitude of symptoms have a minimum of causes. Or, to put it another way, most problems, despite how varied the symptoms may appear, can usually be solved by a small number of general fix-its. So, before you begin a hunt for a specific solution to your specific problem, give these general troubleshooting tips a try:

Try again If a Web page won't load for some unspecified reason, select to reload it: click Reload (Navigator) or Refresh (Explorer). If necessary, halt the current attempt to load the page first, by clicking the Stop button or pressing Command-period.

If the page still won't load, try again an hour or so later. The vast majority of these problems clear up by themselves, as they are due to temporary glitches on the Internet or at the Web site you are trying to view.

(continues on next page)

If this does not fix the problem, check to see if the same problem occurs on other pages. If the problem appears to occur on any and all Web pages and/or if you get an error message that indicates that a connection was not established, you have a problem with your connection. This is covered in Chapter 12.

Give the browser more memory Browsers tend to be memory hogs; they will benefit from memory far in excess of the minimum they claim to need. And the more plug-ins you use, the more memory you will need. Whether it's an inability to launch a browser, a crash while using a browser, or an unacceptably slow speed of loading pages, increasing your browser's memory allocation is likely to help.

To increase a browser's memory size, go to the Get Info window of the browser and increase its Preferred Memory size. If you don't have enough memory to spare to do this, get more physical RAM (using virtual memory to get the additional memory may work, but having more physical memory is much preferred).

Reinstall or update the software Many problems are solved by getting a newer version of the browser. Check to see if one exists. If not, it may be that your current copy has gotten corrupted in some way. To fix this, you can simply reinstall the same version again, from the original Installer. It is preferred to actually delete the currently installed software before reinstalling (by dragging the existing files to the Trash or using the Uninstall feature of the Installer utility), but this should not be necessary in most cases.

If you do delete files, be careful not to delete the Bookmark and Favorites files, unless you don't care if your list of Bookmarks is lost. In particular, for Netscape, save a backup copy of the Bookmarks.html file that is in the User Profile folder with your Profile (as located in the Preferences folder of the System Folder). There are likely to be other Bookmarks.html files on your drive. But this should be the critical one. If in doubt, open it in your browser to see if it lists your current Bookmarks. For Explorer, save the Favorites.html file in the Preferences/Explorer folder. If need be, return the back-up copies to their System Folder location after reinstalling the browser software.

With Netscape, you may also want to delete the Netscape Preferences file; this alone can eliminate a variety of problems, saving you the hassle of a reinstall of the complete software. With Explorer, try deleting the file called Internet Preferences (used by the Internet control panel). However, if you do this, you will need to re-create the settings in the Internet control panel.

One problem with reinstalling can occur if you have updated your software with Smart/Active Updates from the Web. In this case, your original version of the software (as contained on a CD-ROM disc most likely) does not contain the version you are currently using. In this case, you would need to reinstall the update files from the Web again - which can be a time-consuming pain (especially via a dial-up modem connection). Alternatively, you can download the complete new version and install that.

SEE ALSO: • **Fix-It #5 for more on memory, including special issues involving temporary memory, memory leaks etc. as they apply to Internet connections and Web browsers.**

TAKE NOTE ▶ The Internet Control Panel

What is it? Apple's Internet control panel is used to set Preferences that can be accessed by any Internet application assuming the application is written to take advantage of this). This saves you the trouble of having to repeatedly enter the same information (such as your email address) for each application.

For example, Internet Explorer uses the Internet control panel settings. This means that changes you make to the Internet control panel settings will affect the Preferences settings from within Explorer itself (and vice versa).

(continues on next page)

TAKE NOTE ▶ The Internet Control Panel *(continued)*

Actually, Microsoft has an additional control panel called Configuration Manager that is a virtual duplicate of Explorer's Preferences options—and similarly interacts with those settings. However, Configuration Manager also affects other Microsoft Office applications, such as Word. For example, if you click a Web link in a Word document, Configuration Manager determines what browser will open.

Netscape browsers do not automatically use the Internet control panel settings. Netscape maintains its own preferences. However, you can force it to override at least some of its preferences and use the ones from the Internet control panel instead. To do this, go to Preferences/Mail & Newsgroups/Identity and enable the "Use Internet Config" check box. Doing this can lead to some surprises if you are not careful. For example, if Netscape and Internet are set to have different default home pages, when you select to "Use Internet Config," you will use Internet's selected home page, not the one in Netscape's Preferences. In fact, if you go to Preferences/Navigator, you will see that the home page option is dimmed and cannot be selected at all! Similarly, when clicking an email link, Internet may access another email program rather than Netscape's built-in email feature.

Why does Netscape call it "Internet Config?" This is because the Internet control panel is based on an older freeware program called Internet Config. If you use the Internet control panel, you no longer need the Internet Config application. However, the Internet control panel still uses the Internet Config Extension. So leave that where it is! And make sure that third-party installers do not replace this with an older version of the extension. Have a backup of this extension available, just in case.

Finally, some applications may offer to modify your Internet control panel settings when you install the program (such as GraphicConverter asking if you want it to be your default application for handling graphic files). Feel free to say yes or no, depending upon your personal preference. A few applications may make these sort of changes without asking or telling you. If this happens, and you don't like the changes, you will have to reset the preferences after the installer is done.

(continues on next page)

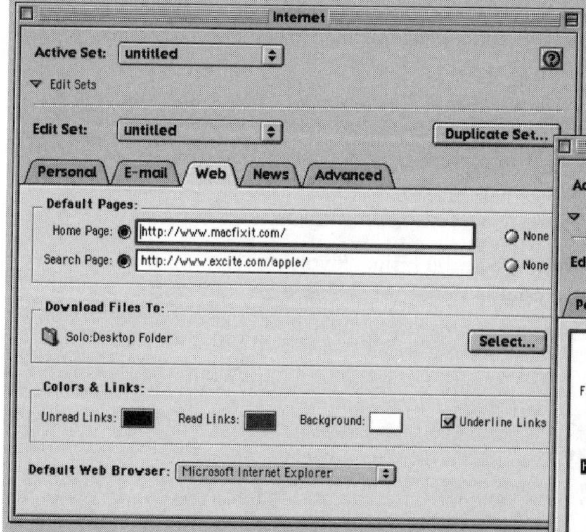

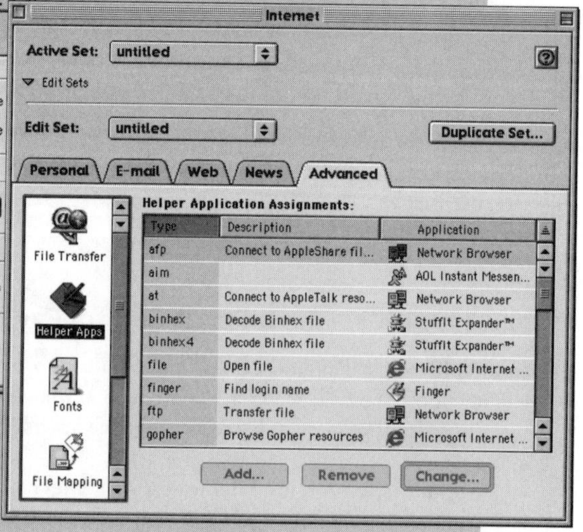

Figure 13-12 Above: the Internet control panel's Web tab; you can pick a default home page from here. Right: the Advanced tab with File Helpers displayed.

How to use it Using the Internet control panel is simple enough. You access the Personal, Email, Web, or News tabs and enter the requested information. For example, to set the home page for your browser, select the Web tab, and fill in the desired home page in the text box labeled Home Page. From the Default Web Browser pop-up menu, you can even select what browser will be opened by default from other applications that support hypertext links (such as Microsoft Word). For options that are unfamiliar to you, other sections of this chapter provide some guidelines (such as the information on setting up an email account in "Solve-It! Email Problems"). Otherwise, you'll need to seek outside help.

If you want to have different preference settings for different uses, you can even create different sets and switch among them.

Finally, go to the Edit menu and select User Mode. From here, select the Advanced option. This will open up a new tab, called Advanced. With this tab selected, there will be a column of icons along the left side, with names such as File Transfer, Helper Apps, File Mapping, and Firewalls. You shouldn't often, if ever, need to mess with these Advanced settings. However, for those times that you do, I go into detail about certain of these options (especially Helper Apps and File Mapping) later in this chapter.

SEE: • **"Downloading and Helper Problems".**

Web Pages Won't Load

Symptoms:

- Pages won't load at all. There is no error message. Or the browser gives an error message immediately upon launch.

- One or more pages won't load. Any of a variety of error messages appears.

Causes and What to Do:

No Pages Load

If your browser steadfastly refuses to load any pages at all, you are probably not really connected or you have a bad connection. Even if your modem seems to have connected successfully, there may still be problems. Specific messages in this category include *Netscape was unable to create a network socket connection* or *Attempt to load <name of page> failed.*

Most likely, these messages appear from the first moment you launch your browser. However, these problems can also appear, due to a dropped connection, at any point in your use of a browser. If you are using a modem, your PPP software may indicate that you are connected even though you are not.

- **Are you really connected?** If you are using a dial-up modem, your first step should be to quit your browser, click the Disconnect button from your PPP software, and start all over, reconnecting and then relaunching your browser. If you have an external modem, turn it off and back on again before reconnecting.

    If you are using a cable/DSL modem, confirm that the modem is actually successfully connected to the Internet. Usually, a change in the pattern of lights on the modem will indicate if the connection has gone down. Check with your provider for details. Cable modems are often finicky and, on a bad day, may go down for brief periods.

If all seems well but you still can't load any Web pages, restart your Mac and try again.

- **Is your ISP really connected?** If problems persist, there may be a problem with your ISP (perhaps their hardware is down). Try to check by giving them a phone call.

- **Check your settings** Otherwise, you probably have a problem with your control panel settings (such as in the TCP/IP control panel) or perhaps a hardware problem (such as with the modem). Check Chapter 12 for more help here.

BY THE WAY ▶ Pages Load Even When You Are Disconnected. How?

Sometimes after you have been dropped from your connection, you may find that some pages still appear to load. Inevitably, these are pages that you have recently visited which are still stored in your browser's cache. The browser is drawing the page from the cache file rather than from over the connection. If you want to see if your browser has really lost its connection, try to go to a new page or *reload* the current page by selecting its Reload button.

SEE ALSO: • "Web Pages Load Slowly or Incompletely," later in this chapter, for more on cache files.

A Specific Page/Site Does Not Load

You may be able to successfully get to almost all locations you try. But one Web page or one entire Web site may not load. The exact error message may vary depending upon which browser you are using and the exact cause of the error. Some common examples include "Unable to connect to host," "Invalid host," "The server does not have a DNS entry," "404 Not Found," "The server could not find ....," "The attempt to load…failed," "Network connection refused by server," and "The name is illegal." There are several possible causes here:

- **The site you are looking for does not exist** Perhaps you are typing a URL from memory and you have the wrong URL. Or you may have misspelled the URL. Leaving out even one letter (such as www.macfixt.com) can cause an error. You'll either find out that the URL does not exist at all, or it will take you to an entirely different site.

- **The site or page no longer exists** If it is an old URL, the site you are trying may no longer exist. Perhaps that Web page listing the changes in the retail price of pepperoni over the past 10 years has simply packed its bags and gone home.

  Or if it is just a page from a site that you cannot access, that page may have been moved to a new URL or deleted altogether. Sometimes a Web site will inform you that a page has been moved, and may even have the page set up to automatically take you to the new location. But in many cases, you will just reach a dead end.

  SEE ALSO: • "Problems with URLs and Bookmarks/Favorites," later in this chapter, for more advice.

- **The server is too busy** If you are trying to access a very popular Web site, especially one not prepared for a sudden surge in traffic, the server you are trying to reach may be getting more traffic that it can handle. If so, you will be unable to reach the site.

  Even if you do finally connect, an overloaded server can also lead to agonizingly slow data transfer times no matter how fast your modem or network connection is. As the source of the problem is not at your end, there is not much you can do about any of this. Trying again later (hopefully at a less busy time) is the time-honored solution.

  In fact, this has been used as a method to bring down a site deliberately; that is, hackers will set up a situation where a site is flooded with traffic (via ping requests, as described in Chapter 12) so that no one can reach the site. This is called a *Denial of Service (DoS)* attack. Again, if this is happening, there is nothing you can do except to wait till it is over or the server personnel find a way to block it.

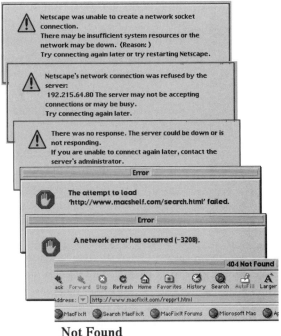

Figure 13-13 Some messages that may appear when your browser can't load a requested page.

  SEE ALSO: • **"Web Pages Load Slowly or Incompletely," later in this chapter, for more advice.**

- **The server is down or page is "gone"** In some cases, the server hosting the Web site might crash, just as your Mac can crash. In this case, you will be unable to reach the site until the server is up and running again.

  In a related situation, the message *File Contains No Data* may mean that the Web page exists but it is a "blank" page, empty even of the needed header information for the browser to load it as a blank page. This happened to my home page once when my Mac crashed just as I was uploading my home page to the server that hosts MacFixIt. The result was that just a fragment of the page existed, and readers trying to get to the page got the "No data" error.

  In a few cases, the page may be there intact. But there may be a problem getting to it, for any number of obscure reasons. If so, try adding a port number of 80 to the URL (such as "http://www.macfixit.com:80/). Or use its numeric IP address.

  SEE ALSO: • **"Understanding Internet Addresses," and "Technically Speaking: Ports & Firewalls," for background information.**

- **The Internet is down** Well, not really. But there are occasions where there is a disruption in a major trunkline of the Internet. This can affect all sites that originate in a certain geographic area where the problem occurs (such as the entire Northeastern United States). If your ISP also originates from that area, your problems could get worse: the disruption will likely affect all your online activity, not just a few particular Web sites you try to visit! The solution here is to do something offline until the problem is fixed. Perhaps take a nice walk.

- **Access is forbidden** A "403 Forbidden," "Access Denied," or similar error message mean that access to the site is blocked. If a dialog box appears asking for a password, you can get to the page if you know the password. Otherwise, the page may simply be entirely blocked from access via the Web.

  Bear in mind that these messages do not always mean you are completely locked out from the content of that page. For example, it is common to get one of these messages if you try to access a directory that does not have a default page (as explained in "The Structure of a Web Site: Home Pages and Subdirectories," earlier in this chapter). Still, it is possible that individual files/pages in the directory are accessible either by entering the file name URL directly (in the browser's Location/Address box) or indirectly (via a link from another page that you can access). Thus, typing http://www.macwidgets.com/files/ might lead to an access error. However, you still might have access to a file in that directory, such as http:/www.macwidgets.com/files/help.html. This helps only if you know what full URL to try.

  For accessing FTP sites (described more in "Downloading and Uploading Files," and "Downloading and Helper Problems," elsewhere in this chapter), you may get a related message that says something like: "Maximum number of anonymous log-ins exceeded. Try again later." This means that the site allows a minimum number of users to access the site without a password and that minimum has been exceeded. The solution again is to try later, when it is less busy.

- **Firewall/security restrictions** If you are on a network that maintains a firewall (see "Technically Speaking: Ports & Firewalls," earlier in this chapter), it may be that the firewall is set up to prohibit access to certain URLs, including the one you are trying to reach. Check with your network administrator about this.

To some extent, the exact wording of the error message may give you a hint as to which of the above possibilities applies to your current situation. For example, a "No DNS entry" error would more likely mean that the Web site no longer existed than that it is simply busy. "Host unavailable" typically means that the host's server is temporarily down, but the site is still there.

  Similarly, if an error message comes up almost instantly after clicking to go to the page, this typically means that the URL is wrong. If there is a long pause before an error message appears, this is more likely to mean that the URL is correct but you cannot reach it now for some reason.

Web Pages Load Slowly or Incompletely

 Symptoms:

- Pages load but at a very slow rate or with a long delay before starting to load.

- Web pages start to load but stall indefinitely before completing.

- Some elements of a page, such as certain graphics, never load at all.

 **Causes and What To Do:**

Start With Some Basics

If your requested page does not appear as soon as you enter its URL, don't despair. For starters, you may have a connection problem and be able to fix it.

SEE: • **"Can't get Connected or Unusually Slow Connections," in Chapter 12.**

Or you may be accessing a site with a slow server or a server that is very busy. In this case, the page may still load successfully. Just be patient and see what happens.

If your requested page actually begins to display on your screen, don't applaud yet. The page may be loading so slowly that you begin to wonder whether someone pressed the pause button. If the cause is not a connection problem, it is most often due to a page that contains large or many graphics. Text transmits a lot faster. The precipitating cause can be at your end (where even a 56K modem is not all that fast for some graphics-rich pages) and/or at the server's end (where they may be using equipment that not fast enough or does not have enough bandwidth to support many simultaneous requests for access).

Other than wait patiently and take a coffee break, curse your computer (which rarely has any effect), or install a faster connection, what can you do to speed up these slowdowns? Not all that much. Still, these suggestions may help:

- **Click any link button as soon as it is visible** There's no need to wait for the entire page to load if all you want is to click a link to go to some other page.

    One caution: some links take you to another location on the same page. Such links, called *anchors*, typically end in a # symbol, followed by some text. If you click an anchor link that goes to a location lower down on the page and that part of the page has not yet loaded, loading of the page will instantly halt and you will not go to the requested link location. To solve this problem, you will need to reload the page and wait for the part of the page with the link destination to appear.

- **Click your browser's Stop button** While this stops the loading of the remainder of the page, it also forces whatever has already loaded (even though it may not yet be displayed) to appear on your screen. If you are lucky, whatever you need will already be there. If not, you can always click the Reload button and try again. Sometimes it loads a lot faster on its second try.

TECHNICALLY SPEAKING ▶ Image Loading Speed: Web Authors Can Help You

In some cases, no text will begin to appear on your page until after all graphic images begin to appear, no matter what Web browser options you choose. There is nothing you can do about this. The problem is in the design of the Web page itself. It is possible for the Web page author to include instructions about the size of graphic images on his page. If this is done, the text should start appearing almost immediately. Otherwise, the text does not appear until after all the graphic size information has been calculated, which can only happen after the images have started to appear. Not all authors include this helpful size information.

You will also notice that some graphics appear first in a very blurry form (or in a partial form that looks a bit like a series of slats in a window blind). Gradually the parts fill in until you have a finished image. Called an interlaced image, this is another technique used to help speed things up. It allows you to see an approximation of the image before it is completely loaded. Again, there is nothing you can do to turn this feature on or off. It is determined by the Web page author.

SEE ALSO: • **"By the Way: A Word About Web Page Authoring and HTML."**

- **Tell your browser not to load any graphic images at all** To do this in Communicator, go to Preferences/Advanced and uncheck "Automatically load images…"In Explorer, go to Preferences/Web Browser/Web Content/ and disable the option to "Show Pictures."

    In some cases, your browser (or a third-party utility) may be able to selectively disable certain types of graphics, such as just animated GIF files (typically used for banner ads). Explorer has an option to do this.

    In any case, you still have the option to manually load any desired graphic, either by clicking the image and then clicking the load images button from the browser's toolbar, or accessing the contextual menu while clicking the image and selecting the Load Missing Image (or similarly worded) item.

    Even if you have graphics enabled, sometimes images may still not load. If this happens, you can try to load an individual image manually. Assuming the image is still at

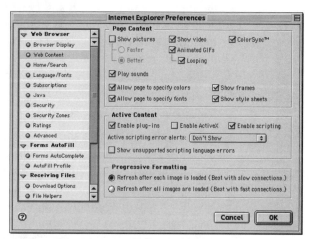

Figure 13-14 Explorer's Page Content Preferences with "Show Pictures" disabled.

the correct location on the Web site, this will usually succeed. If not, the Webmaster may have mistakenly moved or removed the graphic.

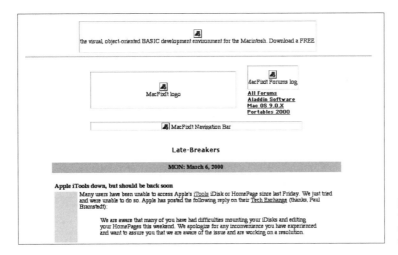

Figure 13-15 The top of the MacFixIt home page seen with "Show Pictures" disabled.

On a related note, trying to run a Java applet (described more later in this chapter) can similarly slow down the loading of a Web page or even bring it to a halt. If necessary, you can turn off Java options from the Preferences settings of your browser. For example, in Explorer, select the Java item and uncheck *Enable Java*.

- **Select to see the low-tech version of the site** Some sites may include an optional "low graphics" or "text only" version of their site for the benefit of those with slow connections. Use these to speed things up if viewing the graphics is not needed for your use of the page.

- **Increase your browser's memory** Insufficient memory can cause slow loading of all your pages. To solve this, increase the amount of RAM allocated to the browser from the Get Info window of the browser (see Fix-It #4 for details). If this does not work, proper use of your browser's cache can help speed page loading.

  SEE ALSO: • **"Take Note: Web Troubleshooting Basics."**

- **Delete your browser's "history"** Explorer and Netscape both keep a list of recently visited Web pages. These appear in the Go menus of the browsers. If the list becomes too long or the file maintaining the list becomes corrupted, it can slow down your browser.

  To solve this with Netscape browsers, delete the Global History and/or Netscape History files in the Netscape Users and/or Netscape ƒ folders. Do this with Navigator closed. You can delete as many of these files as you find. Look especially for the one with the most recent modification date. New, empty files will be created by the browser when you next launch it.

  With Internet Explorer, go to Preferences/Web Browser/Advanced/History and click the Clear History button.

  Of course, clearing these lists means you lose the data that would have otherwise appeared in the Go menu.

Browser Cache Settings, Browser Speed, and Avoiding Disk Damage

A browser can cache information to speed up its operation. A browser's cache is similar in concept to the disk cache of the Memory control panel (see Fix-It #5). When your browser reads a Web page, it typically creates a *cache file* of the page (with separate files for each graphic element on the page), either temporarily in RAM or in a special location on your disk. Their value is that, if you revisit a page, the browser can use the cache data to load the page rather than grabbing the data from the Internet. This results in much faster loading times, especially for a page with many graphic images that would take a long time to transfer.

Note that, when returning to a page either by clicking a browser's Back button, clicking the Home page button or clicking similar links on a Web page itself, the page should load from cache (assuming

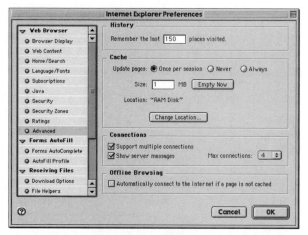

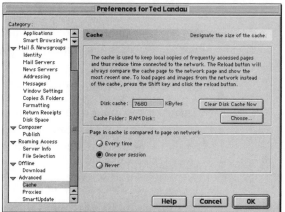

Figure 13-16 Explorer's (top) and Netscape's (bottom) Preferences for setting cache options.

you have enabled the cache features, as described below). Theoretically, this means that the page should almost instantly snap into view. In practice, whether or not this happens depends upon what browser you use (Explorer does a better job here) and what button you press, what your exact preferences settings are and possibly the humidity level in Venezuela. In other words, it is hard to predict exactly what will happen in each case.

A browser may have one (or both) of two types of cache: disk cache and memory cache.

Figure 13-17 Explorer's cache.waf file and various Netscape Communicator cache files.

Disk cache By default, Internet Explorer stores disk cache information in a file called cache.waf, located in the MS Internet Cache folder in the Preferences folder. Netscape browsers store multiple cache files in a folder called Cache ƒ buried in the Netscape folders of the Preferences folder. Even America Online's Web browser has its own cache, located in a folder called Browser Cache in the America Online Preferences folder.

In general, a larger cache (double or triple its default size, assuming you have the disk space for it) should speed up the loading of a greater number of recently accessed pages and may even prevent certain system crashes and low memory errors.

Paradoxically (and similar to the situation with the history files), a very large cache (or potentially corrupted cache files) can slow down your browser. In some cases, a corrupted cache file can prevent you from even loading your browser. Corrupted cache files can also lead to more general Directory-related problems of the sort that Disk First Aid is needed to fix.

SEE: • Fix-It #10.

The value of a cache gets lessened when you have a fast Internet connection, such as cable or DSL. This is because any potential speed boost from a cache is swamped by the overall speed of the connection itself. In these cases, reducing or eliminating the cache may be preferred.

Sometimes, simply moving the storage location of the cache is just what the doctor ordered.

Clearly, you may have to experiment with different cache sizes to see what works best in your particular situation. Here's how to make these changes:

- **Empty the cache** With Internet Explorer, go to Preferences/WebBrowser/Advanced/ Cache. To empty the cache, click the "Empty Now" button.

  With Netscape, go to Preferences/Advanced/Cache display. To empty the cache, click the "Clear Disk Cache Now" button.

  You can also empty the cache by deleting the cache file(s) directly from the Finder's desktop. However, do not do this while the browser is open. In fact, you should only need to do this if a possible cache problem is preventing the browser from launching successfully.

- **Increase/decrease the size of the cache** You can also adjust the maximum size of the cache. When the cache reaches this limit, older files are deleted automatically to make way for more recent ones. To do so in Explorer, enter an amount in the Size/Disk Cache text box. A similar option exists in Netscape.

  If you want to give up on using a disk cache altogether, you can set the cache size to zero.

- **Change the storage location of your cache files** Another option in the Cache Preferences displays is to change the location where the cache is stored on your disk. To do this, use the Change Location button in Explorer or the Choose button in Communicator. Typically, you have to restart your Mac for this change to take effect.

  In most cases, there is little reason to make such a change. But here is one case where it might pay: create a RAM Disk and select to store your cache on the RAM

Disk. This offers two advantages: 1) it makes loading pages from the cache faster (since the data is stored in RAM rather than on a disk); 2) if your cache files get corrupted, they cannot cause more general problems for your hard drive.

SEE: • **Chapter 11 for details on creating a RAM disk.**

Why is potential corruption of disk cache files such a concern? And why exactly does using a RAM disk help? Because of the frequency with which these cache files are added and updated, your browser writes to your disk especially often. Each write access is a chance for something to go wrong (especially so if a system crash occurs while the file is being written). By writing to a RAM disk instead of your hard drive, you don't actually modify the drive's Directory (which is most likely where this data corruption will occur). Thus the chance of a problem developing is greatly reduced. If a problem does occur, simply wiping out your RAM Disk and creating a new one will fix it.

To check to see if you already are a victim of this type of corruption, use a utility such as Disk First Aid. If the utility often reports damage, especially "B-tree" errors, shortly after using a browser, suspect this sort of cache file problem.

SEE: • **Fix-It #10 for more on Disk First Aid.**

One potential inconvenience with storing the cache on a RAM disk is that the cache data is lost when you shut down (or, on some Macs, even when you restart). Personally, I find this an advantage overall, as I like to clear the cache regularly and this does it automatically. However, if you want to save the cache across restarts, you have at least two options:

- Select the Save on Shutdown option from the RAM Disk portion of the Memory control panel (if your Mac supports this feature).

- Use a disk image file (created with Disk Copy) rather than a RAM Disk to hold the cache. To create such a file, select the Create New Image command from Disk Copy's Image menu. Store the .img file in the StartUp Items folder so that it automatically mounts with each startup.

BY THE WAY ▶ Explorer's Download cache

Internet Explorer maintains yet another cache file called Download Cache (stored in the Preferences folder of the System Folder). It may mysteriously start growing in size, reaching over 100MB in some cases. As its name implies, it stores information about files you have downloaded. This file is unrelated to the disk cache, and is not cleared when you empty the disk cache. To recover the disk space it uses, you may choose to delete this file. To do so, simply locate the file and manually drag the it to the Trash.

Memory cache Netscape browsers use an additional cache called memory cache. It holds the same sort of information that the disk cache holds, except it is stored in RAM, rather than on disk. Apparently, Web page data are cached in both locations when you visit a page. The upside here is that information is retrieved even faster from the memory cache than it is from the disk cache, as loading from RAM is faster than loading from disk. The potential downside is that the stored information is permanently lost every time you quit Netscape (as this clears the memory cache).

In principle, to get the best overall benefit, the browser should check the memory cache first and then check the disk cache if necessary. In actuality, it has been hard to pin down exactly what the rules are. In particular, it may be that the memory cache is ignored unless the disk cache is set to zero. In other words, paradoxically, setting the disk cache to zero may improve speed more than a large disk cache setting. This is especially likely to be so with broadband Internet connections. Experiment to see what works best for you.

You cannot directly change the size of Netscape's memory cache from a Netscape Preferences setting. Rather, its size is indirectly linked to the browser's Preferred (memory) Size (as set in the Get Info window). The more memory you give Netscape, the more memory cache you will have.

However, if you are determined, there is a way to directly modify the size of the memory cache. Some users report that doing so significantly speeds up loading of cached pages, especially if you also set the disk cache to zero. Just be careful not to increase the memory cache so large that it exceeds the total allocated to the browser (via Get Info). This could lead to system crashes.

To do this memory cache hack, you need ResEdit. Here's what to do (remember to save a copy of the Netscape application and Preferences files first, in case you do not like the effect of these changes):

1. Using ResEdit, open a copy of your Netscape application.

2. Open the "TEXT" resource.

3. Open the "allprefs" (ID: 3010) item.

4. Scroll until you find the line that reads: pref("browser.cache.memory_cache_size", 1024). The 1024 number is the size of the cache in RAM.

5. Replace 1024 by a larger number (4096 for example), assuming you have enough RAM to support this increase.

6. Save your changes and quit ResEdit.

7. Launch your edited Netscape browser and see if its speed has improved.

SEE: • **Chapter 8 for more on ResEdit.**

Note: If no text is visible when you open allprefs, do not try to further edit the file. Instead, you can add a line (such as: user_pref("browser.cache.memory_cache_size", 4096) to the Netscape Preferences file in the Netscape ƒ of the Preferences folder. To make this change, you'll have to open the file in a text editor such as BBEdit.

Perhaps the next generation of Netscape browsers will incorporate these features, making this hack unnecessary.

TAKE NOTE ▶ Netscape About Tricks

If you enter the expression "about:"—followed by a variety of different terms— into Netscape's Location box, you can get some very useful troubleshooting information. For example:

- **about: cache** Gives you statistics about the items in the disk cache.
- **about:memory-cache** Tells you the number of items in the memory cache.
- **about:global** Gives more detailed information about what is stored in Netscape's History file. This one can be especially interesting. When I tried it once, it gave me a list of the last 4979 URLs I had visited, each listed as a hypertext link (each GIF image on a page was listed as a separate URL)!

BY THE WAY ▶ Explorer and Temporary Memory

In general, a Macintosh application cannot use more memory than the amount assigned to its Preferred Size in its Get Info window. However, there is one major exception: a feature called *temporary memory* which allows an application to use otherwise unused memory on a temporary basis (if the memory is later needed by another application, temporary memory is purged). Because of this feature, you may occasionally find that an application's memory allocation (as listed in the Apple menu's About This Computer window) is larger than the Preferred Memory size.

Internet Explorer is one application that definitely does this. It's not exactly the same as Netscape's memory cache, but it's in the same ballpark.

Also, if a Mac application uses shared library files, and all browsers do, the memory for these files is allocated to the system software memory rather than the application itself. This is another way that a browser technically exceeds its Preferred Size restriction.

SEE ALSO: • **"Take Note: Temporary Memory and Memory Leaks," in Fix-It #5.**

TAKE NOTE ▶ Disk Cache and Getting the Most Recent Copy of a Web Page to Load

Using Preferences settings The whole function of your browser's cache is to use it as a source for loading pages, when requested, rather than going to the Internet itself. But there is an inherent problem in doing this. What happens if the Web page has been modified since it is was placed in the cache? In this case, you will get an old out-of-date version of the page to load, rather than the updated copy. This can be a significant problem with Web pages that you visit every day for the daily news updates they provide.

To prevent this, you can instruct the browser when to load from cache and when to check the Internet. In Explorer, you do this via Preferences/WebBrowser/Advanced/Cache, where you select how often to check for an updated Web page: Once per session, Never, or Always. Netscape has similar options in Preferences/Advanced/Cache.

The default is Once per session. This means that each time you quit your browser and relaunch it, it will check for a possible newer version of the Web page and update it accordingly. Setting it to Always makes sure that the latest version is always loaded, but may unnecessarily slow down your browser (by bypassing the cache) when no update is needed.

(continues on next page)

Conversely, selecting Never means that you will miss all subsequent updates to a Web page after you first load it (unless you manually select to Reload/Refresh the page or clear the cache). However, it may be useful to enable this temporarily when you are using your browser while offline. This way you don't have to worry that your browser will try to access the Web to find a page that is already in your cache, leading to an error if you are not connected to the Internet at the time. Alternatively, you could select the offline browsing options from Netscape's and Explorer's File menus.

Even if your browser is set to update your pages once per session, it may update them more frequently, depending upon what method you use to return to a page. For example, using the browser's toolbar Back button is less likely to update a page than using a Back button found on a Web page itself. Again, you may have to experiment a bit to see what does what.

Using Reload/Refresh and Super Reload Regardless of the Preferences setting, select Reload (Netscape) or Refresh (Explorer), and the browser should reload the current page from the network rather than the cache—especially if the page has been updated from the cached version.

At least with some versions of Netscape, if Reload does not seem to work, hold down the Shift (or Option) key when you select Reload. This is called a Super Reload and should absolutely always force the page to load from the Internet. Except when it doesn't (due to some bug).

On recent versions of Netscape browsers, here is a surer way to force a Super Reload:

1. Select Reload and press and hold down the Option key while the page continues to load.

2. When the page is done loading, still holding down the Option key, go to the View menu.

3. Reload should now say Super Reload. Select it.

Updating a graphic Especially with Netscape browsers, graphic images that get continually updated (such as an image from a video camera or a Web page counter) may not get updated even after an otherwise successful Super Reload. To fix this, click and hold down the mouse button on the image. From the pop-up menu that appears, select Open this Image, Netscape will open up the image in a separate window. This, by itself, typically shows an updated image. Reloading (or even just returning to) this page should now show the updated image on the page.

Proxies If pages still seem to load from a cache, you may be using a proxy server that delivers pages from its cache (see also: "Technically Speaking: Ports & Firewalls," earlier in this chapter). With Netscape, to check for whether you are using a proxy, select Preferences/Advanced/Proxies. If you have "Direct connection to the Internet" selected, you are not using a proxy. Otherwise, you are. To bypass the proxy, shift to the "Direct connection" option. With Explorer, go to Edit/Preferences/Network/Proxies and uncheck the Web proxy checkmark, if enabled.

In some networks, you may be forced to use a proxy. Some cable companies recommend using one, primarily for security reasons (@home does, although it will work well without a proxy). However, using a proxy can also interfere with access to certain Web sites. If so, and you still want the proxy enabled in general, you can temporarily disable the proxy. In any case, check with your network administrator for advice on what your proxy settings should be.

By the way, with a proxy server, a page may load from the proxy cache even if the server is not connected to the Internet at the moment. Thus, it may seem as if you are online when you really are not.

Empty the cache Occasionally, probably due to some bug, a page continues to load from the cache even though, based on your settings and/or the button you click, it should not. Usually, you can solve this by emptying the disk cache (although even here the problem may persist if the page is stored in the memory cache).

Quit and relaunch As a last resort, quit the browser and relaunch it. This should almost always work as long as you have not set your cache option to "Never" update. As a very last resort, quit the browser, trash its cache file(s), restart the Mac and relaunch the browser.

Downloading Files

Downloading a file uses up more "bandwidth" than most other online activities. Thus, you may notice significant slowdowns when trying to do anything else, such as loading a Web page, while a file is being downloaded in the background. The only solution here is to wait for the file to finish downloading.

SEE ALSO: • **"Downloading and Helper Problems,"** later in this chapter.
• **"Web Page Display Problems,"** later in this chapter, especially the section on Java and JavaScript.

BY THE WAY ▶ Speed Tip: Use Multiple Windows

If you are going to a page that you anticipate will take a long time to load, or if you know you will want to go back to a page you are about to leave, save time and open the new page as a separate window. This allows you to retain the previous page on the screen, so you do not have to waste time going back to it. You can also continue to read one page while the other page is loading. As always, exactly how you do this depends on your browser. In general, there should be a contextual menu item to "Open link in new window." With Explorer, Command-clicking a link does the same thing.

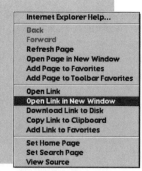

Figure 13-18 The Open Link in New Window command is selected from the contextual menu accessed via a link in Explorer.

Problems with URLs and Bookmarks/Favorites

 Symptoms:

- Your Bookmarks/Favorites menu is unexpectedly empty or returned to the default list that existed when you first used the browser.

- You select to load a Web page from a saved URL, but the page no longer loads. Various error messages may appear.

- You copied or typed a URL from another source, but it does not seem to work.

 Causes and What to Do:

As described previously (see: "Navigating the Web"), Bookmarks and Favorites are where your browser stores those URLs that you select to save.

Bookmarks Menu Is Empty

If your Bookmarks/Favorites menu suddenly shows up empty (or just shows its original default list of links), here is why and what to do:

The file is corrupted Netscape stores Bookmarks in a file called Bookmarks.html. Explorer stores its equivalent Favorites list in a file called Favorites.html. Both of these files are located in the respective browser folders in the Preferences folder of the

System Folder. If the file gets corrupted, the Bookmarks or Favorites menu may no longer list any URLs. To fix this:

- Replace the file with a backup copy, if you have one.

- Otherwise, drag the corrupted file out of its location and to the Desktop. When you next launch the browser, it will make a new default copy of the file. The menu will still be empty. At this point, try to import the contents of the original, possibly corrupted, file. To do this with Explorer, select to Organize Favorites from the Favorites menu and then select Import from the File menu. With Netscape, select Edit Bookmarks from the Edit menu and then select Import from the File menu. Hopefully, this does not re-import the corruption.

Bookmarks.html   Favorites.html

Figure 13-19 Netscape's Bookmarks.html and Explorer's Favorites.html files (also see Figure 13-3).

If this too fails, you can try to open the original file as a page in the Web browser. If this works, you can select each link and use the Add command to re-add it to the Favorites/Bookmarks list.

Netscape Profile has changed Netscape has a feature called Profiles that allows for different users of the same Mac to have a customized list of Bookmarks. If you opened a profile other than the one you usually do, your bookmarks will not appear. To check for this, simply make sure you are opening the desired Profile when you launch Netscape.

TAKE NOTE ▶ Create a New Netscape User Profile to Solve Problems

When you are done installing Netscape the first time, you will be asked to create a Profile. The New Profile Setup dialog boxes will walk you through the process. Profiles allow different users to have different settings (including bookmarks) and still use the same copy of Netscape. You can create a new profile at any time (and delete the old one) by using the User Profile Manager located in your Communicator folder.

Creating a new Netscape user profile for yourself (and then deleting the existing one) is another recommended procedure for solving a variety of ills with Netscape. It is especially likely to be helpful if you have gone through several upgrades of Netscape. To do this:

1. In your Navigator or Communicator folder, locate the file called User Profile Manager. Launch it.

2. Select New Profile.

3. Enter your user information. Give the profile a slightly different name than your current profile name.

4. Quit the utility.

If the errors have now gone, you can delete the old profile. To do this, start User Profile Manager again, click the old file name, and select Delete.

WARNING! There is a bug, at least in some recent 4.x versions of Netscape, such that when you launch Communicator after installing a new version you get a screen that says you have duplicate profiles (two profiles with the same name, presumably your name). You will be asked to delete one of them. Don't! Due to this bug, agreeing to delete the Profile data may delete *all* your profile data (resulting in a loss of your saved bookmarks) and, in some cases, can delete files on your drive having nothing to do with Netscape! Hopefully, this will be fixed in a Communicator update.

The Bookmark/Favorites file is missing or incorrectly located Especially after you update to a new version of a browser, or switch to a new System Folder, you may have either inadvertently deleted an existing Bookmark/Favorites file or the browser may no longer access the file because it is in an incorrect location. If the needed file is still on your drive, you can use Sherlock to locate it and move it to the correct location (in your active System Folder). If the file has been deleted, and you do not have a backup nor can otherwise recover the file (such as via an unerase utility, as explained in Fix-It #11), there is nothing you can do. You'll just have to start over.

However, if you use both Explorer and Netscape, you should be able to import the Bookmarks from one program into the other, using the same basic technique as described previously in this section. If you have a similar list of URLs in both pro- grams, this could re-create a list that is lost in one program but not the other.

A Typed or Copied URL Does Not Work

If a typed or copied URL does not take you to the page you are seeking, you may have mistyped the URL in some way. Web browsers can sometimes successfully guess at what you meant to type, but don't count on it. If you at least get to the desired site, but not the desired page, you may get a special page informing you that the page you are requesting does not exist. Less well-designed Web pages will simply display a basic "page not found" error message. In other cases, you may wind up at an entirely wrong site or no site at all. In all of these cases, here is what to do:

Check for typos Check for spelling or typographical errors. Especially note: using a hyphen instead of an underline, or any other minor variation from the exact URL, can cause the URL to fail. Exactly matching capitalization is not usually required, but if problems occur, check for this as well.

Check for unwanted characters If you copied a URL from a text document, you may have inadvertently copied a return character or a space that does not belong in the URL. In the former case, only part of the URL may get pasted into the Location/Address box. In the latter case, the space will be added to the URL. In either case, the URL will not work.

Actually, punctuation that is not considered "legal" in a URL may get converted to an equivalent "hexadecimal" term that is "legal." Such terms are preceded by a % char- acter. For example, a space is not allowed in a URL. If you include a space in a URL, the browser will convert it to %20. So, if you type *http://www.net advice.com/*, what the browser will likely actually use is *http://www.net%20advice.com*. If the space is an inten- tional part of the URL, the converted URL is correct and will work. If the space is the result of a typing error on your part, you will get an error message. Conversely, if the space is required, but the "%20" is not inserted, the URL will fail.

Otherwise The Web page or even the entire Web site may no longer exist.

If you suspect that page exists but may have a changed URL, try deleting the last part of the URL (that is, everything after the last or next to last slash). For example, if the URL is http://www.netadvice.com/archives/news.html, delete "news.html." You may get taken to a directory that lists all of the files in it. From here, you may see that the file has been renamed news1.html. Click it and you are there.

You can keep experimenting with the remaining levels until you have found what you want or have exhausted them all. In this case, for example, try next deleting "archives/"; this should take you back to the home page. Here, you may find the link to the page you want.

If the site includes a site map page, go there and see if you can locate the URL you are seeking.

If the site has a search engine, try that.

SEE ALSO: • **"The Structure of a Web Site: Home Pages and Subdirectories," earlier in this chapter for more details.**

A Linked or Bookmarked URL No Longer Works

The symptoms are similar to those in the previous section. For example, you may get a "page not found" or related error. However, now you are selecting a URL directly from a link or a bookmark, so there is no chance you mistyped anything. Here is why this happens and what to do:

Page should not be bookmarked In some cases, a Web page will be generated as the result of a script that is run, often in response to a form you filled out. Examples include the results page of a search or the acknowledgment page after submitting a purchase online. In such cases, the resulting URL may be a temporary one. If you try it the next day, it will no longer work. You should especially suspect this if the URL is a very long, complex-looking one. The solution here is to not bother bookmarking these pages. They won't work.

Page content has changed After selecting a bookmark, you may get a Web page that appears normal but is simply not the one you bookmarked the previous day. For example, if you saved a URL to an article on a news service site, when you return to it, it may be a different article entirely. Or you may get an error message indicating that the article cannot be found anywhere on the site. This is particularly common with sites that post a new series of articles every day. The Web site is structured such that the URLs for the current day's articles are temporary. Much like the home page of sites that are frequently updated, a "today's news" URL remains the same even though the articles in them change. Usually, the original article still exists under a new "permanent" URL somewhere else on the site. Using the Web site's search engine (which it hopefully provides) should locate it.

Link is bad If you click a link on a Web page and it takes you to a location other than the one intended, the link may have been entered incorrectly by the Webmaster. I have certainly been guilty of this on my own MacFixIt site. Often, if you are familiar with the structure of URLs, the typo will be obvious and you can make a change to fix it. For example, if a link on MacFixIt reads: "http://www.macfixit.com/http://macwidgets.com/," you probably want to delete everything up to the second http. Then try the link again. It should work. Or if there is no colon after http, just add one. If you can't figure out the fix yourself, contact the Webmaster for help.

Also remember that, for the same reason as described in the previous section, a link on a Web site that was good yesterday may no longer work today.

Otherwise Old bookmarks and/or links on pages that are months old may stop working because the destination page or site no longer exists. Or a page's URL may have changed. To try to find it, follow the advice in the "Otherwise" item of the preceding section.

BY THE WAY ▶ Using Search Engines

Sometimes the problem is not a URL that refuses to work. The problem is that you don't know what URL you want. For example, suppose you want information on the history of computers. Where do you begin?

That's what search engines are for. I'm talking here about the big ones that search the entire Web, not just a particular site. Apple's Sherlock taps into these search engines (such as AltaVista and InfoSeek) or you can go to them directly via the Search features of your browser or by directly using a particular search engine's URL. Here are a few tips for using these search engines more effectively:

- Most of the popular search engines work by scanning the entire Web and maintaining an updated index of the Web sites it finds. They do this 24 hours a day. When you type in a term to request a search, it searches its index, not the Web itself. This means their results will only be as current as the last time a page was checked. This could be weeks or months ago. So don't expect to use these search engines to find something that was just posted yesterday.

  A few search engines only (or primarily) list sites that are submitted to it. They do not actually scan the Web. Yahoo works this way. This obviously limits what you may find.

  With either type of search engine, there may be an option to search by selecting from a list of general categories, rather than by typing in a search term. If one approach fails, try the other.

- Generally, when you enter two or more words, the search engine will find every page that lists at least one of these words (called a Boolean OR search). This means that if you search for "antique cars," you will likely get every page that mentions either the word "car" or antique." Clearly, this will yield a long list of Web sites, almost all of which will have nothing to do with antique cars. How to narrow in on your desired choice varies with different search engines. The best solution is to find a way to get the search engine to only return pages that have *all* the words you listed (a Boolean AND search). Sometimes putting the word "and" between terms will do this. Sometimes, putting the words in quotes works (this may even further limit the results to pages that have the quoted words next to each other on a page, exactly in the order typed). Check with the search engine's Help option for advice here.

  Even with an OR search, the results at the top of the list should be the most "relevant," which usually means they include all the terms you entered. This may be sufficient to find what you want.

- Often, what you are looking for is not a match of words, but a match of topics. For example, someone looking for "Macintosh troubleshooting help," might be happy to have MacFixIt come up, even if the words "Macintosh troubleshooting help" were not on the site's home page. This can be difficult for a search engine to do.

  Web page authors help out here via the use of the META tags at the top of the HTML source code of the page. These words are not visible when you load the Web page in its normal view, but search engines pay special attention to them when deciding the relevance of your page in reply to a search request. For example, if MacFixIt had the words "Macintosh, troubleshooting, help" in its META tags list, it would increase the odds that it would appear in a search for those terms.

- No two search engines work in exactly the same way. As a result, each one has its pros and cons in terms of how likely it is to find what you are seeking without also finding a bunch of pages that you are not seeking. So if the first one comes up a bust, try a second or third one.

System Freezes, Crashes, and Errors

 Symptoms:

- A system freeze or crash occurs while trying to load your Web browser or while using it.

- Utilities such as Disk First Aid report frequent disk repair problems, especially B-tree Directory errors.

 Causes and What to Do:

For most system crash and system freeze problems, your best bet is to turn to Chapter 4. However, there are some special instances of these problems that are unique to using a Web browser. Here's a brief list of what to do:

- **Follow the "basics"** Follow the advice in "Take Note: Web Troubleshooting Basics," earlier in this chapter. Especially try giving the browser more memory and deleting appropriate preferences files.

- **Increase the browser's cache** Increase the size of the browser's disk cache (as covered in "Browser Cache Settings, Browser Speed, and Avoiding Disk Damage," earlier in this chapter) by at least a couple of megabytes.

- **Move the browser's cache** Move the disk cache to a RAM disk or a disk image file, to minimize the risk of disk corruption (again as covered in "Browser Cache Settings, Browser Speed, and Avoiding Disk Damage").

- **Check for missing shared libraries** Latest versions of Web browsers make use of Apple's Shared Library Manager extension (Explorer also uses Microsoft's Shared Code Manager). These extensions are needed, in turn, to use additional "library" files specific to the Web browser. Without these extensions and library files installed and active, the browser either will not launch or will likely crash soon after launching. The needed files should be automatically installed by the browser and/or are part of a standard installation of the Mac OS. Be careful not to delete these files. If you do, unless you can identify and locate a copy of the deleted file, you may have to reinstall the entire browser software and/or the OS itself.

- **Avoid betas** Avoid using beta versions of browsers and any other files (especially those related to getting online) that go in your System Folder.

  It has become especially common for software developers to release "public beta" versions of their software. In essence, it turns all of us into beta testers for software that, in many cases, should not yet be in general release. Beta software is beta for a reason. That reason is usually that there are still known bugs in the software. Often these bugs can lead to system crashes.

  If you are determined to use these beta programs, make sure you are prepared to uninstall them (and go back to the last non-beta version, if one exists) if any problems occur shortly after installing the program. To assist in this, keep the Installer log of the original installation (assuming one is created), so you know exactly what was installed and where it went. You should find such a log at the root level of your startup drive.

SEE ALSO: • **Fix-It #5 for more details on increasing memory size, and related issues of memory leaks and temporary memory.**
• **Fix-It #10 on repairing directory damage.**

Web Page Display Problems

 Symptoms:

- You go to a Web page that claims to include animation (or some other special feature), but you find that all you see are static images that don't move anywhere (or don't otherwise display the special feature). Sometimes, a symbol with a diagonal line or an X through it (indicating that something is wrong) will appear. Other times, an error message may appear.

- Text and/or graphics overlap, are missing, or are in an incorrect location.

- Colors on a page are wrong.

 Causes and What to Do:

Problems Due to Plug-Ins

Get the missing plug-in These days Web pages can do much more than simply display text and a limited number of graphics. They can use streaming video to turn your browser into a TV set. They can play music that rivals the quality of an FM radio station. You can play games, complete with sophisticated animations. And more.

Most of these effects require supplemental files, called plug-ins, that work in conjunction with the main browser application to extend the capabilities of the browser. These files are usually stored in the Plug-ins folder within your browser's folder. In Mac OS 9, there is also an Internet Plug-ins folder in the System Folder where they may be stored. These files are often developed by third parties (not the browser vendor). As such, most plug-ins are not included when you install your browser. You need to obtain them separately.

Some plug-ins are special variations of stand-alone applications. The difference between accessing a separate application vs. a plug-in is that separate applications work independently of the browser whereas plug-ins work within the browser. For example, if you select to view a QuickTime movie, and you have the QuickTime plug-in, it should open right on the Web

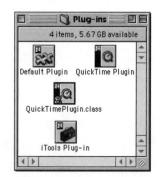

Figure 13-20 The contents of an Explorer Plug-ins folder.

page itself. Otherwise, the browser may try to open QuickTime Player and show the movie from there. Similarly, to open Acrobat files from within your browser, you need the PDF (Portable Document Format) plug-in.

In some cases, there is no matching stand-alone application. In this case, there is no choice but to use the plug-on. Otherwise, a page can not display any content that requires the plug-in. For example, to take advantage of the special graphic animation features provided by Macromedia's Shockwave, you need the Shockwave plug-in. You can obtain and install this from the Macromedia Web site.

Most recent versions of Web browsers will alert you to a missing plug-in, giving you some error message and perhaps even offering to search on the Web for where you can download the plug-in you need. For example, with Explorer, you may get a message that says: "You do not have the plug-in needed to view 'application' type of information on this page." If this happens, click the View Plug-in Directory button in the message to locate and download the missing plug-in.

Once you have the plug-in installed, you will still have to quit your browser and relaunch it before you can use the plug-in.

If you can't locate or choose not to install a particular plug-in, note that some Web sites have alternate views of a page, one that requires the plug-in and one that just uses standard browser features. If so, choose the plain version of the page. That way, even though you do not have the plug-in installed, you still see a page that "works" as intended.

Update or disable a problem plug-in On the downside, be aware that plug-ins can increase the amount of memory needed by your browser. This can be a problem if you don't have memory to spare.

A plug-in may also have bugs that lead to system crashes. Or crashes may occur due to corruption of the plug-in file. In these cases, the problem can be solved by updating to a newer version or reinstalling the existing version. Ideally, you should trash the existing plug-in before updating or reinstalling. Note that some Installers that place a plug-in in your browser's Plug-Ins folder may not do so for all browsers on your drive. For example, it might do so for Explorer but not for Netscape. If you use both browsers, and discover this has happened, you will have to manually drag a copy to the needed location of the browser that is missing the plug-in.

If problems still occur, you will likely have to remove the plug-in or not go to the page that triggers the problem. With Explorer, you can choose to disable *all* plug-ins by going to Preferences/Web Browser/Web Content/Active Content and unchecking "Enable plug-ins."

Plug-in listings You can easily view a list of all installed plug-ins and what type of files use them.

To do so with Internet Explorer, select "About Internet Explorer" from the Apple menu, then click Support. You will get a list of all the plug-ins that are installed and what types of files will trigger use of the plug-in. For example, it might say that "video/quicktime" is handled by QuickTime.

With Netscape, go to the Help menu and select "About Plug-ins." You will get a similar list.

You can also edit what types of files are linked to what plug-ins. For example, suppose you want your browser to use SoundJam as your default MP3 player when accessing MP3 files from the Web (rather than the QuickTime plug-in). To do this in Explorer, you would go to the File Helpers in the Preferences settings and change the setting for the .mp3 extension. Similar editing can be done in Netscape browsers. Details are covered in "Downloading and Helper Problems," later in this chapter.

Problems Due to Java and JavaScript

What is Java? Very briefly, Java is a programming language. Java programs, called applets, can be run from a Web page. They may be automatically run when you load the page. Often, they are used to create a variety of special effects, such as needed to play graphical games on the Web. One advertised advantage of Java is that it is "platform independent." That is, the same Java program can run on a Mac or a Windows machine without modification. This is why they can be incorporated into Web pages without regard for the platform that will be used to load the page.

However, in order for your Web browser to correctly recognize and run a Java applet, it needs special software called a *Java engine*. At least one flavor of Java engine is built into all current browsers. Different Java engines have different capabilities. Thus it is possible that a given Java applet will run correctly with Netscape but not with Internet Explorer (or vice versa).

How would you know if a page was even trying to run an applet? Because, as the page loads, there is typically a message that appears somewhere in the browser window (often in the message area at the bottom of the window) that says something such as "Loading Java applet." In effect, the Java applet is being downloaded to your computer (typically to the same place where cache files are stored) prior to running it. Depending upon the size of the applet, this may take a considerable time (several minutes in some cases, if you have a slow connection), so be prepared to wait. Once it is downloaded, the page will load and run the applet as needed.

Note: Shockwave and Flash plug-ins depend on Java for their implementation. Thus, problems that occur when loading pages that use these plug-ins may have a similar Java-related cause.

The downside of Java There are several obvious costs to using Java: it eats up memory, it can significantly slow down your Web page loading and (due to bugs in its software) it can even lead to system crashes. Especially if your browser crashes when the phrase "loading Java applet" appears on the screen, suspect Java as the cause. Depending on the browser you use, this could occur on launch of the browser or when you first try to load a page that uses Java.

You may also get an error message while the applet is loading. Typically, it appears in a separate window. The message is usually arcane, and will be nearly unintelligible to someone who does not understand Java. Again, much of this can be browser-specific. For example, a given applet may load fine in Explorer but not in Netscape, or vice versa.

The result of all of this is that, unless using Java is critical to your enjoyment or value of the Web pages you view, Java may be more trouble than it is worth. In some cases, emptying the browser's disk cache can solve a Java problem. You might also notify the Webmaster of the problem page. These errors almost always are due to bugs in the Java applet; so perhaps the Webmaster can fix them. Otherwise, you either have to avoid the problem page or turn off Java altogether.

Enable/Disable Java

To enable/disable Java in Internet Explorer, select Preferences/Web Browser/Java and check/uncheck the Enable Java checkbox. In Explorer, you may have a choice

of which Java engine to use: either *Microsoft Virtual Machine* or *Apple MRJ* (Macintosh Runtime for Java). You select your choice from the pop-up menu in the Preferences window. If your version of Explorer did not come with MRJ, you have to separately obtain and install it (the latest version is available from Apple's Web site). If you are having problems with Java, but still want to use it, you may try switching engines before disabling Java altogether (assuming your browser allows this). However, Explorer 5.0 and later only use MRJ. If you are restricted to MRJ, make sure you have the latest version.

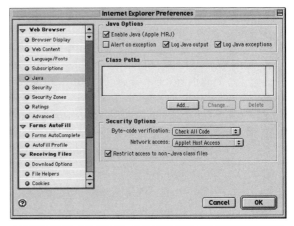

To enable/disable Java in Netscape browsers, go to Preferences/Advanced and enable/disable the Enable Java checkbox.

Note: If no Java applets load on any Web pages that use Java, you may have previously disabled Java via these settings. If so, re-enabling Java should solve the problem.

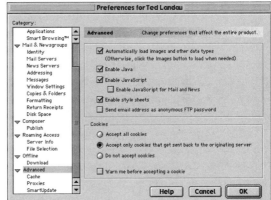

Figure 13-21 Top: Explorer's Java Preferences. Bottom: Netscape's Preferences for Java/JavaScript (and more).

What about JavaScript? JavaScript has little in common with Java except their names. JavaScript routines are directly included within the HTML code that makes up a Web page. Thus it is a scripting language much like HTML itself, rather than a true programming language (such as Java). This makes it far simpler to implement than Java, since no separate applets need to be written and downloaded. No separate engine is needed either. JavaScript can be used for such "cool" effects as graphic images that change when your cursor glides over them, scrolling messages that appear on a page, text that appears in message area at the bottom of the browser window, pop-up windows that appear after a page loads, and more.

How can you tell if a page uses JavaScript? The surest way is to select to view the source code of the page (see "Technically Speaking: What's HTML? And how do you view HTML source code?") and search for a phrase that reads: "SCRIPT LANGUAGE=JavaScript."

If there are mistakes in the JavaScript code, you may have an error message appear when the page loads. This error message typically appears in a special JavaScript error window. If a certain JavaScript routine only runs after you take a certain action, such as clicking a button, an error message may occur only at that time. Alternatively, a symptom may simply occur with no error message. For example, a JavaScript error could prevent a page from loading at all. As with Java errors, there is little you can do about JavaScript errors except contact the Webmaster of the site and request that they fix the script—or disable JavaScript altogether.

However, overall, JavaScript uses less memory and has less problems than Java. That's why I would generally leave JavaScript enabled, even if you decide to disable Java.

Enable/Disable JavaScript With Netscape, you can choose to enable or disable JavaScript via the "Enable JavaScript" checkbox in the same Advanced Preferences window where you select to enable Java.

With Explorer, go to Preferences/Web Browser/Web Content/Active Content and enable/disable the Enable Scripting checkmark. However, I believe this will disable more than JavaScript and may cause problems with accessing the features of some pages that use other types of scripting. Still, you can turn these options on or off, as needed, for particular pages.

Color and/or Text Is Not As Expected

Text If the text on your Web pages is too small, too large, the wrong font or anything else, your first stop should be the Preferences section of your browser. You can modify the default settings from Language/Fonts in Explorer and from Appearance/Fonts in Netscape. This will affect virtually all text in all Web pages you visit.

A given Web page can have instructions to override your default choices, but most pages will let them stand. From Netscape Fonts panel, you can choose to prevent a Web page from overriding your choices.

More recently, Web pages may use a new feature called dynamic fonts. These allow a level of control over the font and size of text that is comparable to what you can do in a word processor. Netscape allows you to select to override dynamic fonts (again, the option is in the Fonts panel). Otherwise, you are simply stuck with what the Web page sets up.

These same areas of the Preferences display also have options to select the default colors for text, background, and text links. Experiment to get what you like best.

If much of the text on a Web page seems too small to read, it may be that the page was designed with PC viewers, rather than Mac viewers, in mind. For an explanation of why this happens and what to do, check out "Technically Speaking: Web Page Font Size and Resolution."

Otherwise, simply reloading the page may fix a temporary glitch.

If none of this works, the problem is probably a "bug" in the HTML code of the Web page itself. Your only hope here is to get the Webmaster to fix it.

TECHNICALLY SPEAKING ▶ Web Page Font Size and Resolution

Font Size Most Web designers assign the size of text on a relative scale, where numbers from 1 to 7 indicate size, with 3 being the default size. On a Mac, the typical default size for Web browsers is equivalent to 12-point text. On a PC, it is 16-point. Thus, text at any given relative size looks bigger on a PC than on a Mac. If a Web page designer expects his site to be viewed primarily by PC users, he will likely select smaller relative text sizes than if he was catering to a Mac audience. The result for Mac users is a page that may have text that is too small to read. With Internet Explorer 5, you can compensate for this by selecting a larger default font size from the Size pop-up menu of the new Fonts and Size Preferences settings. For an even faster on-the-fly change in the displayed text size, without altering the default size or needing to open the Preferences window, type Command-Plus (for larger text) or Command-Minus (for smaller text). Netscape's Fonts Preferences include options to select separate default sizes for variable width and fixed width fonts. For most Web pages, Mac users will remain happiest with a 12-point default.

Font Resolution Why, you may ask, do PCs and Macs have different default text sizes? The answer has to do with the different assumptions about monitor resolutions made by each platform. Macs traditionally assume that the monitor has 72 dots per inch (dpi), also referred to as ppi (pixels per inch). Since there are also 72 points per inch, this works out nicely in translating text point size to pixels. PCs assume a resolution of 96 dpi. In theory, this means that 16-point text on a 96 dpi PC should be the same size as 12-point text in a 72-dpi Mac ($16/96 = 12/72 = 1/6$). However, because the relationship between points and pixels is even more complicated than I have indicated, 16-point text on PCs winds up looking larger than 12-point text on a Mac.

The higher resolution of PCs also allows smaller point text to be more legible on a PC than on a Mac, which is yet another reason that PC-centric Web designers may choose smaller font sizes, sizes that will be totally incomprehensible on a Mac's 72-dpi monitor.

To help out here, Internet Explorer 5 includes a Resolution option in Fonts & Size Preferences. Here you can select the Mac's 72-dpi resolution, the PC's 96-dpi—or any other size via the Other option. Surprisingly, switching the resolution from 72 dpi to 96 dpi has absolutely no effect on text assigned a relative size. You'll only see a difference if an absolute point size is used, such as 12 points. This is not often done, but is possible with the style sheets feature of HTML. In any case, on pages where changing the Resolution setting has a noticeable effect, shifting from 72 to 96 dpi should result in text size displaying somewhat larger, as the Web designer intended. (Netscape 6 will also have a resolution option.)

Of course, with today's multi-resolution monitors, a Mac's display is not really 72 dpi anyway. For example, my 17-inch Studio Display is currently set at 1024x768 resolution. This translates to about 85 dpi (1024 divided by the width of the display in inches). For the overall best text appearance on most Web pages, Microsoft recommends setting Explorer's Resolution to match that of the monitor.

The Resolution setting, like all Fonts and Size settings, only affects text. Web page graphics look the same no matter what changes you make here.

SEE: • **Chapter 10 for more on monitor resolution.**

Color HTML defines colors either by the use of certain names ("blue," "red") or by special hexadecimal values that code for that color. For example, the hexadecimal code for blue is "OO33FF." Essentially, any 6-digit code made up of pairs of 00,33,66,99,CC, or FF can represent a color. Because all Web browsers, on whatever platform, should display these colors correctly, they are referred to as the *Web-safe colors*. There are 216 such colors.

However, today's Web browsers can display additional colors (especially so as part of graphics such as JPEG images). Exactly how they look can vary significantly among different browsers. They may look as intended, or they may be a "dithered" approximation of the true color (giving the graphic an undesirable speckled appearance). Or you may wind up getting an entirely wrong color. If it does not look the way you like, there is not much you can do about it. It is something that the creator of the Web page needs to fix. But at least now you know why it is happening.

One bit of good news: if your monitor's resolution is set for thousands or millions of colors (rather than 256 colors), this issue may be largely moot, as even non-safe colors should display correctly. All new Macs and Mac displays now default to at least thousands of colors.

SEE ALSO: • **"Graphics on the World Wide Web," and "By the Way: Apple's Color Picker," in Chapter 10.**

Try a different browser If a page just looks "wrong" no matter what you do, you can try switching browsers. Sometimes, a bug or missing feature in one browser will cause problems for the display of a page. The same page may display perfectly in another browser. This can mean switching from Explorer to Netscape (or vice versa) or upgrading to a newer version of the same browser. Again, experiment.

BY THE WAY ▶ Dealing With Frames

Some Web pages use frames. These are pages that consist of two or more separate windows, each of which can scroll independently. You may also note that when you go to a new "page" within a frame, the URL for the page (as found the Browser's Location/Address box) does not change.

Saving Frames can cause problems if you use your browser's Save command to save a Web page that contains frames. You may find that when you open the saved file, almost all of the page's contents are missing. This is because you only saved the frame structure and not the contents of the frame windows. Sometimes just clicking within the desired frame before selecting to Save will work well enough, but don't count on it. The surest solution is to open the Frame in a separate window—one that does not contain any frames. To do this, typically hold down your mouse button within the frame you wish to save, until a pop-up menu appears that includes a choice that says something such as "Open Frame in New Window."

Moving Back One old complaint about frames was that they prevented a browser's Back and Forward commands from working as desired. When you select to go back to a previous frame of a page, you are taken back to the page you were viewing prior to the frame-based page loading. Latest versions of browsers fix this.

Not seeing frames at all If pages that use frames do not display correctly, you may have turned off your browser's option to display frames. For example, in Explorer, check in Edit/Preferences/Web Content/Page Content.

SEE ALSO: • **"Take Note: Saving and Printing Web Pages," earlier in this chapter.**

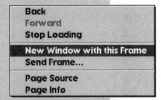

Figure 13-22 The pop-up menu that appears when clicking a frame in a Netscape browser window.

Downloading and Helper Problems

 Symptoms:

- Your browser does not call or cannot find a needed helper application or plug-in. The result is that certain actions (such as attempting to play a QuickTime movie) do not occur as expected.

- You try to download a file but the file either does not successfully download or does not work after it is downloaded.

 Causes and What to Do:

Most pages that you view with your Web browser are HTML documents. These are the typical Web pages that contain the links and graphics for which the Web has become famous. Reading and displaying HTML documents is what your browser was mainly designed to do. It can do the same with a few limited other file types (such as GIF and JPEG graphics). For any other type of file, your browser requires helper applications or plug-ins. Most of the time this works just fine without you even being aware of what's going on behind the scenes. However, when things may go wrong, it pays to understand in more detail how this works.

The previous section ("Web Page Display Problems") covered problems with plug-ins as they affect the appearance of the display and offered some basic advice. This section takes a more technical look at the broader picture—with a special focus on issues involving downloading files.

Checking Your Helpers Lists

Locating and editing Helper lists When called upon to do something that is not in its built-in repertoire, a browser calls for outside help—typically in the form of separate applications or plug-ins stored on your hard disk. For example, a browser may "call" the QuickTime plug-in when you click to view a QuickTime movie. These plug-ins and applications are referred to as "helpers."

But how does a browser know which helper application to open? The secret is a table that your browser checks when needed. It matches various types of files/documents to the helper that the file requires. When your browser tries to load an unfamiliar file type, it checks this

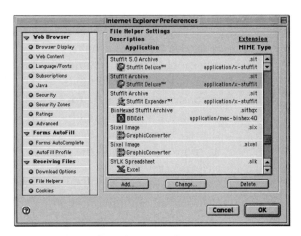

Figure 13-23 Explorer's File Helpers list.

table to determine if any helper is available and if so, how to use it. You can view and edit the items in this table. Each browser comes with a list of items already built in to the table. They cover most common situations. So you may rarely or ever need to look here. But just in case...

With Communicator, go to Preferences/Navigator/Applications.

For Internet Explorer, go to Preferences/Network/Protocol Helpers. Explorer also maintains a separate table, mainly for deciding how to deal with downloaded files. To see it, go to Preferences/Receiving Files/File Helpers.

Actually, Explorer uses the same lists that are accessed via the Internet control panel at Advanced/Helper Apps and Advanced/File Mapping.

Although there is overlap, each of the two Explorer lists functions a bit differently. For example, Protocol Helpers lists http as a protocol and indicates that the Web browser itself (Internet Explorer) is used for this protocol. In contrast, File Helpers lists html as a file type extension and indicates that Explorer should be used to open files with that extension (useful info for when you save an .html file to your drive). Both lists contain similar items about what application is used to decode a BinHex file. Protocol Helpers lists StuffIt Expander as the application to use with the mac-binhex40 protocol. File Helpers lists StuffIt Expander as the application to be used to decode files with a .hqx extension. One more example: the Protocol Helpers list tells the browser what email program to use when you double-click an "mailto" link; there is no comparable item in the File Helpers list.

With Explorer's Protocol Helpers, you can turn on or off a particular protocol by clicking the checkmark on the right

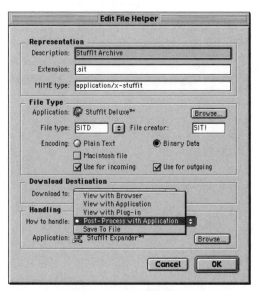

Figure 13-24 The StuffIt Archive listing that was highlighted in Figure 13-23. Note that while StuffIt Deluxe is listed as the File Type, the pop-up menu indicates that post-processing should be done by StuffIt Expander.

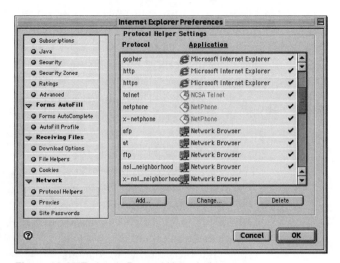

Figure 13-25 Explorer's Protocol Helper's list.

side of the row where the protocol is listed. When it is unchecked, it will act as if you have no protocol selected. If the application listed for a particular protocol is dimmed, this means that the browser could not locate the application on your drive. Most likely, this is because it is not there. To solve this, you can go to the Web and download the file (most of the listed applications are shareware or freeware and are available on the Web). Or if you have another application that serves the same function, you can assign it to be the new application for this protocol. To do so, click the Change button and then click to "Choose Helper." You can similarly Delete a protocol or Add an entirely new one.

Explorer's File Helpers list works similarly. You can Add, Delete, or Change an item. However, there is an important additional function accessed only from this list, called "Handling." From here, you can select what you want the browser

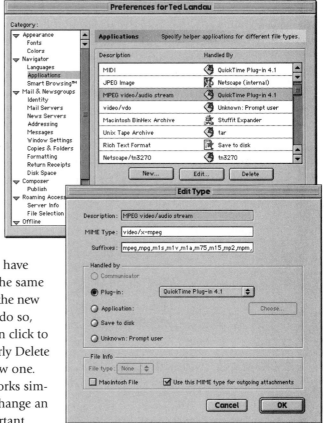

Figure 13-26 Netscape Communicator's Applications Preferences, with the MPEG video item selected and displayed.

to do when it accesses a file with a particular extension/suffix. For example, from the "How to handle" pop-up menu, you can select to save the file to your drive, open it in the browser, or post-process it with another application. This last option requires a bit more explanation, and is covered in the next section.

Communicator similarly has a "handling" capability. From its Applications Preferences, double-click a helper item (or select to Edit it). You can then select whether a particular file type should be handled by a plug-in (as selected from a pop-up menu of all available plug-ins), an application (which you select by clicking the Choose button), or saved to disk.

Occasionally, due to a bug in the software, you may find the exact same item listed more than once. Or you may find the same extension listed more than once, but with a different helper each time. In general, I would advise deleting all duplicates except the one you wish the browser to use.

This hardly exhausts everything that could be said about the options in these admittedly esoteric listings. But it should get you through most situations.

Post-processing Post-processing can be used to assign an application to handle a file that is different than the application listed in the File Type section of an item's Edit/Change window. A common use of the post-processing option is with compressed and/or encoded files. With post-processing selected, you not only save the file to disk, but you have the browser automatically open your choice of an application that can decode/expand it. For example, Explorer may list ZipIt as the application linked to compressed files with a .zip extension. At the same time, it can list StuffIt Expander as the application to process these files. Thus, any time you download a Zip file, Expander will attempt to expand it (not ZipIt, which you probably don't have on your drive anyway). The Handling feature includes a Browse button that lets you select which application you wish to use for post-processing.

You can also access post-processing from the Internet control panel's Advanced/File Mapping option: select to Change an item and then click the "Show Advanced Options" button. Here you see the "Handle by" section.

SEE ALSO: • **"Web Page Display Problems," earlier in this chapter, for more on plug-ins.**
• **"Take Note: The Internet Control Panel," earlier in this chapter, for information on using this control panel.**
• **"Technically Speaking: Understanding MIME and Downloading" and "Technically Speaking: Understanding MIME and Email," for related information.**

TECHNICALLY SPEAKING ▶ Yours or MIME: Understanding MIME and Downloading

The main text describes the use of Helpers lists to match a file type with the application or plug-in that needs it. The critical information that the browser attempts to use in making this determination is the file's MIME type.

MIME (which stands for Multipurpose Internet Mail Extensions) was developed to permit sending email attachments that extended beyond plain text files. Each different category of file has its own MIME name (usually divided into a main type and a subtype). For example, the MIME for a binhex file is "application/mac-binhex40" (where "application" is the main type and "mac-binhex40" is the subtype). Similarly, for QuickTime movies, the MIME is "video/quicktime." For most HTML Web pages, which are essentially text files, the MIME is *text/html*. When one of these files is placed on a Web site's server, it is assigned its appropriate MIME type (usually also identified by the suffix of the file's name; such as .hqx for binhex files). When your browser receives the file, it also receives its MIME name. Your browser than compares this MIME with those listed in its Helpers table. Both the Explorer and Netscape lists include a line called MIME Type, where this information is found.

When it locates the item with the correct MIME, it determines what Helper is linked to it (such as StuffIt Expander for binhex files or QuickTime Player for QuickTime movies) and takes the appropriate action. It also assigns the correct file type and creator to download files (see Chapter 8 for background on type and creator codes).

Occasionally, the server may fail to send the MIME type or it may send a MIME type that your browser does not recognize. Or a particular extension in the Helper's list may not have a MIME type included. In these cases, your browser checks the extension/suffix of the filename and again compares it to the list of suffixes in the Helpers table (such as "hqx" for binhex files or "mov" for QuickTime movies) to determine the appropriate action.

(continues on next page)

If, after all of this, your browser is still unable to sort things out, it will treat the file according to the browser's default MIME, which is typically "text/html". When this happens, the file, whatever its contents, will appear as text characters on a Web page (which is usually not what you want). To fix this, you may need to add a new or edit an existing Helper listing. However, in some cases, even this won't help. When this happens, it usually means that the problem is at the server end. For example, the server may incorrectly list a file's MIME. To solve this, you'll have to contact the Webmaster of the server for assistance.

Finally, you may be wondering how a particular MIME name is decided. It is handled by a central registry called the Internet Assigned Numbers Authority (IANA). Developers of new file types submit requests here to register new MIME names. Getting permission to add a new subtype is fairly easy. To add a new main type, you'll have to convince the registry that it is really necessary.

Check That You Have the Needed Software

Missing and wrong helpers If you don't have a particular helper application or plug-in that the browser includes in its list, the browser will not know what to do when it comes across a file with that type of extension. If this happens, you will likely get some error message informing you of this.

To solve this, you can either get the missing helper and install it on your drive, or (if you have another helper that serves just as well), edit the item to assign the helper you do have. Do this via the Browse/Choose buttons in the window that opens when you select to Edit/Change a Helper item in the Preferences window of your browser.

Sometimes, your browser may claim it cannot find a specific Helper even though you know it is there. For example, it may claim that it cannot find Expander even though it is clearly on your drive. There are several possible reasons for this. For example, this could happen if you change the name of the application or upgrade to a new version. The solution is the same: select or reselect the desired application by using the same Browse/Choose button.

Occasionally, rebuilding the desktop may also help.

In other cases, your browser may find the listed Helper but it will not be the one you want. For example, perhaps you want to use Eudora as your email program, rather than Outlook Express. You can go to Protocol Helpers and edit the item for mailto so that it sends mailto links to Eudora. In this particular case, you could alternatively select your desired email program from the Internet control panel's Default Email Application setting (under the Email tab).

SEE ALSO: • **"Problems due to plug-ins" in the "Web Page Display Problems" section, earlier in this chapter.**

Helpers specific to downloading files The vast majority of files that you download will need to be decoded and/or expanded before you can use them (see "Downloading and Uploading Files," earlier in this chapter). The most common software used for this task is Aladdin's StuffIt software (either the commercial StuffIt Deluxe or the freeware/shareware Expander and DropStuff). Expander comes with the Mac OS and may also come with your browser. You probably have it already on your drive. Still, before doing any other troubleshooting for download problems, make sure this software is installed. If you have more than one version on your drive, delete all but the latest version. Also note that Expander 4.x cannot open files compressed with StuffIt Deluxe 5.x or DropStuff 5.x versions, so also check to make sure you have the latest version of this software.

For some files, especially from Apple, you may also want Disk Copy, in order to mount disk image files (described more in Fix-It #4). However, Expander can also mount disk image files, so Disk Copy is not a necessity.

Finally, if you are downloading a document, such as a graphic image, you need an application that can open the document. For example, if you download a GIF or JPEG graphics file, and want to open the file and edit it, you need an application that can do this. Happily, there are programs, such as GraphicConverter, that are good at working with a wide variety of graphic formats. You won't need a different application for each format. Make sure you have at least one of these programs on your drive. QuickTime Player should be able to open most movie and even sound files (although again, there are shareware programs that go beyond the limits of what QuickTime can do). In certain cases, such as for a PowerPoint presentation, you will need the precise creating application (e.g., PowerPoint or PowerPoint Viewer); no substitutes will be accepted.

Finally, you may inadvertently download a file that is actually an application intended to run in Microsoft Windows. Such files cannot be used on the Mac, unless you have Windows emulation software, such as Virtual PC.

If you are sure you have the software you need, try opening the file from within the application (using the Open dialog box), rather than double-clicking the document from the Finder.

SEE ALSO: • **Fix-It #4, "Take Note: Why Can't I Open The System Software I Just Downloaded?"**
• **"Movies, Video and More," in Chapter 10, for more on graphic/video file formats.**

File Download Data Transfer Does Not Begin

Occasionally, when you click to initiate a download a file, your browser will show signs that it is trying to begin the download, but no data will ever begin to transfer. An error message may ultimately appear. Or you may have to click a Stop button to get the transfer to halt. The most common reason for this is that the site is overloaded with requests for the file. For example, if a vendor that makes a very popular program has just announced a major free update to their product, their Web site may get jammed with requests to download the file.

If the file is on an FTP server, there may be a limit to how many users can log on to the Web site at any one time. If that limit has been reached, you will get a message to that effect and you will not even be able to reach the location page.

By the way, even though most FTP sites require a special login (including a user name and password) in order to access the site, they usually support a limited number of anonymous logins. These are open to anyone, even if they do not have specific password to access the account. Your Web browser will usually get you on via anonymous

FTP without you having to enter anything. However, if the FTP site does require a "real" password, you will not be able to access it at all (unless you have the required password of course). Web pages can also be password protected, although this is not commonly used for downloading of files from an http protocol.

For any of these situations, the standard solution is to try at a later time (such as late at night; or at least the time that is late at night for when most people will be accessing the site) or simply wait a few days and try again. Otherwise, popular updates are also soon posted at additional sites that may better handle the load. Check there. For example, if a small vendor posts a free update on its Web site and soon becomes swamped with requests, check for the same update at the Web sites of major magazines, such as *Macworld* and *MacAddict*, or at places such as Download.com.

SEE ALSO:
- **"Downloading and Uploading Files," earlier in this chapter.**
- **"Web Pages Won't Load," especially the section on "A Specific Page/Site Does Not Load," earlier in this chapter, for more general advice.**

File Download Data Transfer Is Unusually Slow

Sometimes a file download may begin but proceed at such a slow pace that even a small download will take hours to complete. The cause for this is usually similar to what is described in the previous section: a site's server is near its overload point. It is not so overloaded as to prevent you from logging on and accessing the file, but its bandwidth is not enough to support so many simultaneous requests. The result is that everything slows to a crawl.

The main solution is thus the same as before: try again later. Sometimes, if you had a bad connection to the server, simply trying again a minute or so later may be enough. But more likely, you will have to wait until a less busy time.

Also, if you are downloading more than one file at a time, you can expect the download rate of each file to be a fraction of what it would otherwise be. Thus, if you download two files at once, each will download at half its expected rate.

File Download Fails to Complete

Sometimes, when downloading a large file, a download will partially complete and then stop. Most often, this happens if you have a dial-up connection. And it usually means that you have lost your Internet connection in the middle of the download. As discussed in Chapter 12, ISPs will automatically disconnect you after a period of inactivity. The downloading from a remote site may not be sensed as activity coming from your computer, and may thus not prevent an automatic disconnect. Sometimes, you just get disconnected, seemingly at random. Line noise or a problem at your ISP's end could be the cause. In any case, you will have to reconnect and try again. You may also want to contact your ISP about whether they can do anything to minimize frequent unwanted disconnects.

If a file transfer stops even though you remain connected to the Internet, the cause may be with the particular application you are using to download the file. In this case, if the file you are downloading is on an FTP site, you might try using an FTP client (such as NetFinder or Fetch) rather than a browser to download the file. These are known to succeed where the browser fails and they tend to have better "resume download" features. To access a site from an FTP client, copy the "FTP://" URL from the browser and paste it into the window used to identify the host for a new connection.

Occasionally, one browser may work where another does not. Just switching browsers may be enough to solve the problem.

The best solution for problems with disconnects while downloading is to get broadband access, such as a cable modem. These download at much greater speeds and do not have the disconnect problems of dial-up modems.

Resuming downloads Getting disconnected in the middle of a download can be *very* frustrating, especially if you were several hours into downloading a large file and find you now have to start all over again. Fortunately, some programs allow you to pick up a download from where you left off. Internet Explorer lets you do this, via its excellent Download Manager.

Download Manager maintains a list of all your recent requests to download files. To use it to resume a partially downloaded file, reconnect to the Internet and then select Download Manager from Explorer's File menu.

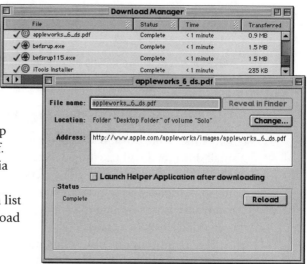

Figure 13-27 Internet Explorer's Download Manager.

Locate the file that you were downloading and double-click it. From the window that appears, click the Reload button. You should even be able to quit Explorer and relaunch it at a later time, and still resume the download. However, I find that this does not always succeed.

Netscape Communicator may also resume a download if you reconnect before exiting the page that contains the link, and click the link again to restart the download. But again, I find success here to be very variable.

Post-processing Does Not Work As Expected

When a download is complete, your browser should automatically decode and decompress (if necessary) the file. If you are using Explorer and this does not happen for a BinHex or MacBinary file, your first stop should be to Preferences/Receiving Files/Download Options/Download Manager Options. Make sure that the options here to "Automatically decode..." are enabled. If they are enabled, then the problem is most likely with the settings in the File Helpers list. To check for this, select File Helpers and locate the .hqx and/or .bin extensions. Make sure the correct post-processing application has been selected. This applies to Netscape browsers as well.

SEE ALSO: • "Checking your Helpers lists," earlier in this section, for details.

With Explorer, another thing to try is to enable the "Launch Helper Application after downloading" option while the file is downloading. It's in the window for the downloaded item, as accessed from the Download Manager.

Unfortunately, there is a history of bugs both in Web browsers and in StuffIt software (e.g., StuffIt Deluxe and Expander) that have led to a variety of post-processing oddities. For example, some versions of Explorer have a bug where the post-processing selection may be ignored. The result is that the Helper's File Type is used as the processing application, even when the post-processing setting lists a different application. This can cause StuffIt Deluxe to open after downloading a file, even though Expander had been selected for post-processing. If you do not have StuffIt Deluxe on your drive, there may be no post-processing attempt at all. The best solution to these problems is to update to a version of the browser that fixes the bug, assuming one exists. Otherwise, there may be a work-around you can use.

SEE: • **"By the Way: Getting Netscape to Call Expander" for a work-around to a Netscape processing bug.**

If a file apparently downloads successfully, but does not automatically expand as expected, simply drag the icon of the file to the Expander icon on your drive. If Expander can recognize the file type, it should expand it successfully. If not, check Expander's Preferences. For starters, click the Expanding icon and make sure "Expand Archives" and "Expand Encoded Files" are checked. Also check the Internet Config settings, as explained in "By the Way: Getting Netscape to Call Expander."

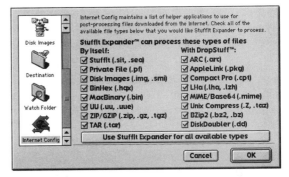

Figure 13-28 StuffIt Expander's Internet Config Preferences window.

One word of caution. Expander's Preferences can be set to "Delete after expanding." This means it will automatically delete an encoded/compressed file after it decodes and/or expands it. I recommend disabling this option. Just in case something goes wrong, it's nice to have the original file to start over with. After you have succeeded in getting the expanded file to work, you can manually delete the original file.

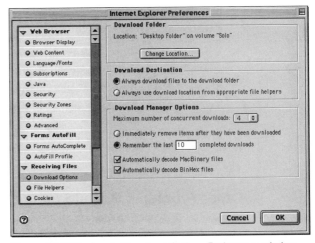

Figure 13-29 Explorer's Download Options Preferences window.

BY THE WAY ▶ Getting Netscape to Call Expander

Sometimes Netscape calls, or tries to call, StuffIt Deluxe instead of Expander. This happens only if you previously edited the settings for Expander in Preferences/Navigator/Applications. Even if you retain Expander as the selected application, Netscape puts the incorrect information into its Preferences. If this happens, first make sure you have set Expander to be the helper application for those files types you wish it to expand. To do this:

1. Launch Expander and selecting Preferences from the File menu.

2. Select the Internet Config icon and click the "Use StuffIt Expander for all available types" button (or be more selective, if you wish, and check just those types you want Expander to handle).

3. Click "OK" and quit Expander.

Then find your most recent copy of Netscape Preferences (using Sherlock) and discard it. The next time you launch Netscape, a new default set of Preferences will be created. Post-processing should now work correctly. However, do not later attempt to change any of Netscape's settings related to Expander or you'll end up back in the same boat again. Hopefully, this will be fixed in an update to Netscape Communicator.

File Will Not Expand or Expanded File Will Not Launch

Sometimes after successfully downloading a file, when an attempt is made to expand the file, an error will occur. For example, a message may appear that says the file is corrupt. Or, the file may expand successfully but, when you double-click the expanded file to finally launch it, a system crash or similar error occurs. There are three main causes and solutions for this:

- The file may have gotten corrupted during downloading. The solution here is to download it again.

- The file was corrupted before it was uploaded. The solution here is to contact the Webmaster and alert them to this possibility. If you downloaded a file twice and had the same problem both times, I would do this. Hopefully, they will re-upload a corrected version of the file.

- A bug in the StuffIt software may be at fault. This is likely to be limited to relatively rare situations (such as only when downloading very large files), or it would have been spotted and fixed already. In any case, your best bet here is to make sure you have the latest version of the Aladdin software. Hopefully, it fixes the bug.

If you simply get an error that says that an application can't be found to open the document, you may not have the required software.

SEE: • **"Check that you have the needed software," earlier in this section.**

Other Problems Downloading Files

BinHex vs. MacBinary downloads As discussed earlier in this chapter (see "Downloading and Uploading Files"), most downloadable Macintosh files will be in one of two formats: BinHex (hqx) or MacBinary (bin). If you have a choice of both formats for a file, you can try MacBinary first (because it is always a smaller file and will thus take less time to download) and shift to BinHex if MacBinary does not work. Or if you want to play it safe, just start with the BinHex version (avoiding possibly having to download the file twice, if the MacBinary transfer fails).

With Netscape, if you see that a file is a MacBinary file, hold down the Option key when clicking the link. This will cause an Open dialog box to appear (in which you name the file you are about to download). This method increases the odds of a successful MacBinary download.

Don't forget that some files may be both encoded and compressed. For example, after decoding a BinHex file, you may have a .sit file that needs to be expanded. Normally Expander will do both steps automatically. However, if it does not, again simply drag the file to the Expander icon.

BinHex download appears as text in the browser window When clicking to download a BinHex file from a Web browser, you may occasionally find the BinHex text loads in the browser window rather than downloading as a file. This is more likely to happen if the URL for the file is a http address than an FTP one. In any case, this is obviously not what you want.

One possibility here, especially if this happens with almost every download, is that the Helper file and/or the MIME has been incorrectly assigned.

SEE: • "Checking your Helpers lists," earlier in this section; see especially "Technically Speaking: Yours or MIME: Understanding MIME and Downloading".

If you can't solve this problem, you may still be able to work-around it, especially if the download is a relatively small file. To do so, allow all the text to load in your browser window. Then save the text as a text file. Finally, drag the text file to your Expander icon. If Expander recognizes it as a BinHex file, it will expand it.

Can't find a file after you download it? Your browser may specify where a downloaded file gets placed on your hard drive. For example, with Explorer, you can view this from Preferences/Receiving Files/Download Options/Download Folder. You can also change the location by clicking the Change Location button. This should make it a sure thing to find your downloaded files. Otherwise, use Sherlock to search for the missing file.

Solve It! Email Problems

Part of the advantage of having a Mac is being able to use Mac programs (such as Eudora, Outlook Express, and even the now-orphaned Claris Emailer) for receiving and sending email. These programs download received email from the (probably Unix) server where it is stored and upload email back to the server to be sent to its intended recipients. In between, you get to work with a familiar Mac interface, rather than the more arcane Unix one you would need to use if you worked directly from the server. You can even read and write email when offline. Very convenient. Still problems can occur. This section should help you solve most of them.

If your email problem appears due to the fact that you do not have an Internet connection at all, check back in Chapter 12 for advice. Otherwise, keep reading.

TAKE NOTE ▶ Setting Up an Email Account

The key to successfully sending and receiving mail is correctly setting up the account information in your email program. Exactly what to do varies from program to program. I will present some general guidelines here.

The essential idea is to take the specific account information, as provided by your ISP, and enter it into the appropriate text fields of your email program's account window. The exact names may vary from program to program. For example, the user name may be referred to as the Account ID.

You will typically need to enter the following:

- **POP server address (where POP stands for Post Office Protocol)** This is the domain name of the incoming mail server, used to receive email (such as mail.pair.com). In some email programs you combine the server domain name with your email name to create an email account name (such as ted@mail.pair.com). This is not the same thing as the email address used to send you mail.

- **User Name and Password** This is used to access the POP server. In some cases, only the password is actually required.

- **SMTP server address (where SMTP stands for Simple Mail Transfer Protocol)** This is the domain name of the outgoing mail server, used to send email.

- **Email address** This is the address that people will use when they want to send you email. This is what you are probably already familiar with; it will be something such as ted@macfixit.com.

Figure 13-30 The Account settings window for Claris Emailer.

POP vs. IMAP vs. Web email An alternative to a POP server for receiving email is an IMAP server (where IMAP stands for Internet Messaging Application Protocol). The main difference between the two types is that with an IMAP account the email stays on the server, whereas with a POP account the email is downloaded to your computer. IMAP can be an advantage if you frequently access your email from more than one computer, as you will always see the same thing no matter where you connect. With a POP account, once you download mail to your computer, it is no longer accessible from the POP server. But using IMAP means that you can only work on your email while you are online.

With a POP account, your email program may have an option to tell the server to leave the messages on the server even after downloading them (so that they *can* be accessed from another computer at a later time). This is useful, for example, if you are viewing your mail while on vacation from a friend's computer and still want to be able to download your email when you get home. However, this is not the same as actually working with files directly on the server, as IMAP does.

IMAP accounts are still a distinct minority. In order to use an IMAP account, your email program must support this protocol. This chapter focuses on POP accounts.

(continues on next page)

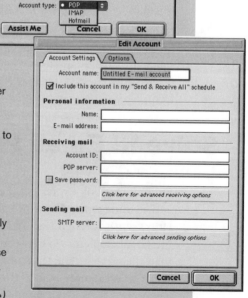

Figure 13-31 Setting up a POP account in Outlook Express.

By the way, popular Web-based email services, such as yahoo.com, are functionally equivalent to IMAP servers. That is, you don't download messages to your hard drive. You view them on a special Web page directly from the mail server. While email programs are generally unable to receive Web-based email, you can usually have the messages automatically forwarded to another account that *can* be accessed from your email software (assuming you have a second such email account). This way, you can read your yahoo (or whatever) email without having to go to the Web.

Problems Sending Email

 ## Symptoms:

- You try to send a message but your email program is unable to do so.

- You try to send a message and your email program appears to succeed, but you later get a message back that says your email was not delivered.

- You send a message but it arrives with an incorrect date and/or time.

 ## Causes and What to Do:

SMTP Server problems

If an email problem is related to your SMTP server, you will get an error message immediately upon trying to send any email from that server. The message will vary depending upon the exact cause. However, in general, here's what to do:

Check your SMTP settings In "Take Note: Setting Up an Email Account," I explained the basics of entering the settings for an email account. If any of this information was entered incorrectly, or has changed since you entered it, you may not be able to send email. Especially check the SMTP Server entry, as this is what is needed to send email.

Check if the server is down If the settings are correct, it may be that the SMTP server is down. Other than notifying your ISP, there is little you can do about this except wait for them to fix it. However, you may be able to work around this problem by using another SMTP server in the mean time. You can usually use an SMTP server without needing any password. In theory, this means that you could use *any* SMTP server for which you know the domain name. It could be the one from an ISP that you no longer use, for example. Or one that a friend uses.

Does your ISP block relays? There is a potential roadblock here. The fact that anyone can use an SMTP Server has been taken advantage of by those people who send junk email (known as "spam"). They may try to use someone else's server as a "relay" to send their piles of junk. Needless to say, the people whose server is being usurped do not appreciate this, so steps have been taken to stop it.

In some cases (more and more often), the ISP may set it up so that you can only send email when logged in directly via their account. For example, I cannot send email via my university's SMTP server unless I access the Internet via the university's dial up access (which of course requires that I use a password). Less stringent is a procedure where you can only send email for a given number of minutes after you receive email (usually around 15 minutes). Because you need a password to receive email, this too protects the ISP from spammers.

Unfortunately, all of this can make it difficult for "legal" users to access these SMTP servers. For example, returning to my university example, I cannot send email from their SMTP server when I am connected via my cable modem. The solution is to enter my cable modem's SMTP domain name into my university account. If the email program has a reply address setting (and most do), email sent from this account will still list my univer-

> Sending mail using "relay.pair.com"
> ** Couldn't complete the last command because a network stream error occurred.

> Sending message "testing"
> ** 550 <landau@macfixit.com>... we do not relay landau@oakland.edu
> ** SMTP server error "503 Need RCPT (recipient)"

> Checking email account "landau@cliff.acs.oakland.edu"
> ** Couldn't complete the last command because the connection timed out.

> Checking email account "tlandau@mail.gte.net"
> ** Pop server error "-ERR invalid user name or password."

Figure 13-32 Examples of email error messages (generated by Claris Emailer in this case). The first two occurred after relay errors (each is from a different ISP); the third message occurred after a temporary problem at the ISP end prevented access to their POP server; the last one occurred after an attempt to receive mail using an invalid password.

sity address as the "sent-from" and "reply-to" address, even though it was not sent from my university's SMTP server. Thus, people receiving the email will see no difference, no matter what SMTP server is used. Usually, this is what you want.

This works fine except when my cable modem goes down and I have to switch back to dial-up access for the time being. Then the cable modem SMTP domain name will no longer work (it only works when connected via the cable modem). It also causes problems when I am on the road and cannot use my cable modem. At these times, I am required to dial up to the university account if I want to send email from that address. I then have to change the account's SMTP setting to accommodate this shift. Of course, none of this affects my ability to receive email from the university account.

SEE ALSO:
- "Take Note: Avoiding Spam," later in this chapter.
- "Technically Speaking: Ports & Firewalls," earlier in this chapter, for information about SMTP ports.

Address Problems

If you are having problems sending only certain email messages from a given account, check for the following:

Incorrect address Make sure you have typed the address correctly.

SEE ALSO:
- "Take Note: Email Address Basics."

Alternate reply-to address Some email programs allow a person to specify one address to send the mail from, but list another as the desired "reply to" address. In some cases, if you do not use the reply-to address, the message will not get sent at all. In general, this is designed to defeat spammers (see "Take Note: Avoiding Spam") or for any situation where the person doesn't want to receive an automatic reply. If you click the Reply button of your email program, to automatically set up a reply message, it often does not use the reply-to address. Thus, the email would not get delivered. In this case, you need to manually type the correct reply address.

TAKE NOTE ▶ Email Address Basics

Internet email addresses are based on the domain name scheme described at the start of this chapter ("Understanding Internet Addresses"). An email address is divided into two parts: the user's name and the user's location. The two parts are separated by the @ symbol. So, for example, one of my email addresses is *landau@oakland.edu*. This essentially identifies me (*landau)* as located at Oakland University (*@oakland.edu*).

Here's one more example. My America Online name is *Ted Landau*. However, if you want to send me email to that account over the Internet, you will have to send it to *TedLandau@aol.com*. Note that the space between my first and last name is eliminated on the Internet-based address (Internet addresses do not permit spaces). The location name tells you that it is an America Online location (*aol*) and that America Online is a commercial institution (*com*).

There should be no need to worry about correctly capitalizing email addresses. Mail will get sent correctly regardless of how you mix lowercase and uppercase in the address.

Email Failure Notices

If an email message is successfully sent by your server but is not successfully received, you will almost always get a message back informing you of the failure. This is sometimes referred to as the message "bouncing" back to you. Usually the "sender" of the failure notice will be a "Mailer-Daemon."

In some cases, it may just be a warning, telling you that the mail server will try to deliver the message again later. This could mean that the person's mail box is "full" or that there is some other local problem preventing the email from being received. Typically, when an attempt is made to deliver it again later, it will succeed.

Otherwise, you will get a failure notice, indicating that the email was not delivered and no further attempts to do so will be made. If this happens, check once again that you are using the correct email address.

If you are sure you are using the correct email address, try sending the message from another SMTP server, or even via another ISP connection. Sometimes, there is a problem with a particular route on the Internet highway that will not occur if you take another route.

If this fails, and you are sending a large file (such as with a graphic attachment), it may be that you are exceeding the size limit for messages imposed by the recipient's ISP. If you can successfully send a smaller message, this is the likely problem. In this case, contact the intended recipient for advice. You may need to break up the file into smaller components or find some other way to give the recipient access to it—such as by uploading it to a mutually accessible FTP server or iDisk (if you use this Apple feature).

Often the exact wording of the failure notice will give you a hint as to what is going on. For example, if the message says "not enough space," then it probably means you are sending too large a file.

```
Hi. This is the qmail-send program at relay1.pair.com.
I'm afraid I wasn't able to deliver your message to the following addresses.
This is a permanent error; I've given up. Sorry it didn't work out.

<mailto@webmail.co.au>:
196.2.147.68 does not like recipient.
Remote host said: 550 <mailto@webmail.co.au>... Mailbox disabled for this recipient
Giving up on 196.2.147.68.

--- Below this line is a copy of the message.

Return-Path: <landau@macfixit.com>
Received: (qmail 3908 invoked from network); 7 Mar 2000 12:33:26 -0000
Received: from c689362-a.roalok1.mi.home.com (HELO ?192.168.1.104?) (24.9.40.101)
   by relay1.pair.com with SMTP; 7 Mar 2000 12:33:26 -0000
X-pair-Authenticated: 24.9.40.101
Subject: Re: billing information
Date: Tue, 7 Mar 2000 07:34:59 -0500
x-sender: macfixit@mail.macfixit.com
x-mailer: Claris Emailer 2.0v3, January 22, 1998
From: Ted Landau <landau@macfixit.com>
To: <mailto@webmail.co.au>
Mime-Version: 1.0
Content-Type: text/plain; charset="US-ASCII"
```

Figure 13-33 An example of an email failure notice; the exact wording will vary depending on why the failure occurred and what server is sending the message. This is just the top part of the message; the remainder was a copy of the text of the message that failed to be sent.

Messages Sent with the Wrong Date

Most email programs on the Mac use the Mac's date and time, as set in the Date & Time control panel, to assign a date and time. If the control panel setting is incorrect, your email will be similarly incorrect.

BY THE WAY ▶ Dealing with Your Email: Reply, Copy, Forward, and Redirect

Replying to email When you receive an email message and you wish to reply to it, simply click the appropriate Reply button in your email program. It will automatically address the reply. All you have to do is type in the text of your message and send it.

Depending upon your program, and the options you have set, it may also include the text of the message you received as part of your reply. It does this with each line preceded by a > symbol. This is called quoted text. Including it helps the recipient recall what they sent you. For example, if a person asks "How about we meet tomorrow at 2:00?" and you reply simply "Okay"—without the quoted text the person might not recall what you are agreeing to do.

Copies and Blind copies Have you ever gotten an email message that did not have your name on it as the recipient? Sure you have. Often it is junk mail being sent to many users at once. These messages probably do not list the names of anyone else who was sent the message. You can similarly send email this way. To do so, look for your email program's option to send a "blind carbon copy" (Bcc, as opposed to CC or To). If you select this, the names of such persons will not appear in the copies sent.

With some programs, you need to include at least one non-blind copy to send a message. If this is the case, and you want everyone on the list to receive a blind copy, make yourself the non-blind recipient.

Forward and Redirect Other common sending options include the ability to forward and redirect a message. These two options are similar.

With forwarding, you send someone else a complete copy of an email message you received. You are listed as the sender and you can add text to the message.

(continues on next page)

A redirected message arrives as if the person who sent it to you also sent it to the redirected recipient. If the recipient replies to the message by clicking their Reply button, the recipient will reply to the person who sent it, not to you. The only way that the recipient knows that you redirected it is because the "from" information will list you as the "redirector." For example, it might say: "From: Larry Smith, larry@atomic.com (by way of Ted Landau, <landau@macfixit.com>)."

Automated replies etc. With most email programs, you can set up rules (or actions) that can automate sending replies. For example, if you want every message that you receive from your accountant to be redirected to your attorney, you can set this up so that it happens automatically without you needing to remember to do it.

More generally, if you have created separate folders to hold different categories of email you receive, these rules/actions can be set to automatically filter your incoming email to these folders according to criteria you enter. Consult the documentation of your email program for details.

Problems Receiving Email

 Symptom:

- You try to check for your email but your email program is unable to do so.

 Causes and What to Do:

If your problem is because you can't even launch your email program or because you are unable to get connected to the Internet, seek help in other chapters of this book, as appropriate (especially Chapter 12 for Internet problems). Otherwise, if you still can't receive incoming email messages from a given email account, here's what to do:

Incoming Mail (POP or IMAP) Server Settings

In "Take Note: Setting Up an Email Account," I explained the basics of entering the settings for an email account. If any of this information was entered incorrectly, or has changed since you entered, you may not be able to receive email. Especially make sure you have the correct password.

Pop Lock Errors

If you receive an error message that says something like "-ERR .username.pop lock busy!," there are two common possibilities. The first is that you (or someone else!) is already logged into your email account from another application (or from another computer). If you are sure you have not done this, and it happens often, someone may have stolen your password and is logging into your account. Change your password!

Otherwise, this error can appear if your email program crashes while accessing your mail. The server does not realize you are "gone" and considers you still connected. In this case, wait about a half hour and try again. The POP server should have automatically closed your connection by then, allowing you to log back in.

For some bizarre reason, in a few occasions where this error persisted with one of my email accounts, I was able to fix it by simply deleting the entire email account and setting up a new one—even though the settings were identical. Go figure.

If none of this works, check with your ISP. There may be an error causing the server to permanently lock you out. They can fix it.

Wait!

The speed of your Internet connection, even with broadband connections such as cable modems, can vary tremendously across time. Some days it may be blazingly fast; on other days it may slow to a snail's pace. If you are having trouble receiving email, or if it is received very slowly, consider waiting and trying again later.

One odd bug: I've noticed that when Microsoft Word is open, there is an occasional bug where I need to keep clicking the mouse to get a download of my email to keep going (about one click for each email message). Actually, this bug affects all online performance (e.g., Web pages load only if I keep clicking the mouse).

TAKE NOTE ▶ Avoiding Spam

Spam is the nickname given to the email equivalent of junk mail. If you have had an email account for any length of time, you know what I mean. They're the messages that are trying to get you to buy some product or service that you have no interest in and never asked to receive. Just like with telemarketers, it is difficult to stop this onslaught. There are ways to "filter" email so that most of the junk never reaches your mailbox. Outlook Express includes such a Junk Mail Filter. America Online also offers options to block junk mail. However, they are never 100 percent effective. Your best defense against spam is to keep off the mailing lists the spammers use. Here are a few tips for doing this:

- Never reply to a spam message even if the message says you should reply to be removed from their mailing list. It's just a trick. Once they find out you actually read and reply to their junk, they will send you even more.

- Minimize how often you post your email address on other Web sites. Scanning publicly posted addresses, such as in online message boards, is a prime way of getting names for a spam lists. Even better, use a separate email address for online postings. Check with your ISP about how to do this. With America Online, you can do this by setting up a separate screen name. With this second address, at least if you get spam there, it won't clutter up your main email account.

- A similar trick is to use a phony reply-to address, setting up an alternate one as the real one. In this way, if a spammer acquires your email address, they will likely get the phony one, so you won't get their spam. However, it may also confuse people whose replies you *do* want to receive. So use this cautiously.

- If you use America Online, don't set up a Member Profile. Spammers look here for email addresses.

TECHNICALLY SPEAKING ▶ Yours or MIME: Understanding MIME and Email

The subject of MIMEs was first covered in the section on downloading files (see: "Technically Speaking: Yours or MIME: Understanding MIME and Downloading"). Here we look at the relevance of MIMEs to email, which is where the concept originated in the first place.

MIME and email Email can only send plain (ASCII) text. To send full-fledged Macintosh files, from formatted word processing files to graphics documents to applications, you must encode the file into an all-text format. The recipient then decodes the text and puts the file back together again. In most cases, this process is handled automatically by your email program, using something called MIME (Multipurpose Internet Mail Extensions). MIME-encoded files typically appear as attachments when decoded.

There are numerous different encoding formats. Each different type assigns a suffix to the name of its encoded files. This helps identify how a file was encoded. The most popular encoding methods for Mac users are BinHex (.hqx) and MacBinary (.bin). BinHex is much preferred for email. With other methods, the recipient may be unable to open the file. BinHex works by converting the resource and data forks of a file (described more later in this chapter) to a single data file and then encoding it.

Before encoding a file, you might also choose to compress it. Compressing makes a file smaller (thus reducing the time needed to send and receive a large file). The most common compression method on the Mac is Aladdin's StuffIt format (.sit).

If your email program is "MIME-compliant," and recognizes the just mentioned formats, it may be set to compress/decompress and encode/un-encode attachments automatically when you send and receive email. Virtually all current Macintosh email programs do this. If not, you may have success by separately converting a file by opening it with Aladdin's StuffIt software.

Viewing the header You can get information about the MIME format of an email message, as well as other technical data, by looking at the message's header information. Many email programs hide this data from you (as it is the equivalent of clutter 99% of the time). At best, you see primarily the Date, Subject, To and From listings. However, if you need to see the full header, there should be a preferences option to allow it. For example, in Emailer (which I still use), go to Preferences/Incoming messages and enable "Long headers." With Outlook Express, go to Preferences/Display and select "Show Internet headers." These long headers will also appear in the text of sent email that gets bounced back to you (see "Email failure notices").

(continues on next page)

```
Date:        2/17/00 4:40 PM
Received:    2/17/00 4:54 PM
From:        Brian Landau, brian.landau@oberlin.edu
To:          Ted Landau, landau@macfixit.com
```

```
Received: from mercury.cc.oberlin.edu (mercury.cc.oberlin.edu [132.162.1.220]) by
macfixit.com (8.9.1/8.6.12) with ESMTP id QAA23868 for <landau@macfixit.com>; Thu, 17
Feb 2000 16:38:41 -0500 (EST)
X-Envelope-To: <landau@macfixit.com>
Received: from [132.162.237.247] (DHCPP6817.resnet.oberlin.edu [132.162.237.247]) by
oberlin.edu (PMDF V5.2-32 #38929) with SMTP id <0FQ300J0TG6XK5@oberlin.edu> for
landau@macfixit.com; Thu, 17 Feb 2000 16:40:09 -0500 (EST)
Date: Thu, 17 Feb 2000 16:40:09 -0500
From: Brian Landau <brian.landau@oberlin.edu>
Subject: Just stuff
X-Sender: sbjl8181@oberlin.edu
To: landau@macfixit.com
Message-id: <0FQ300J0UG6XK5@oberlin.edu>
MIME-version: 1.0
X-Mailer: Claris Emailer 2.0v2, June 6, 1997
Content-type: text/plain; charset=US-ASCII
Content-transfer-encoding: 7BIT
X-UIDL: c5a9cc866a11cc688816d6f216525e57
```

Figure 13-34 Top: an example of the "short" header for a received email message. Bottom: the "long" header for the same message. The MIME type is indicated in the line that reads: "Content-type: text/plain.

TECHNICALLY SPEAKING ▶ **Yours or MIME: Understanding MIME and Email** *(continued)*

Formatted text A partial exception to the above generalizations: you *can* have formatted text (including different fonts and styles) appear directly in the text of an email message, rather than as an attachment—if your email program (and the program of the person you are emailing) has this option. To do so, the program must support at least one of two MIME protocols for embedding format commands in text: *enriched text* or *HTML text.* For example, with HTML formatted text, the message is sent as HTML code rather than plain text (just as if it were designed to load as a Web page); on the receiving end, the email program interprets this and displays it in formatted form (again, similar to what a Web browser would do with the HTML code).

In all of these cases, the email program knows which type of MIME protocol is in use because of the MIME header that is added to the message. For example the header for HTML formatted text would be something such as "Content-Type: text/enriched; charset="us-ascii."

One advantage of HTML over enriched text is that the recipient can usually view it correctly, even if the receiving program does not support HTML. The email program will typically display the actual text (just as if you were viewing the source code of a Web page). The recipient can then save the text as a file and load it in a Web browser. Alternatively, if the email program automatically saved the text as an attachment, just open the attachment file directly in your Web browser.

SEE ALSO: • "Downloading and Uploading Files" and "Downloading and Helper Problems," earlier in this chapter for more on encoded and compressed files.

Problems with Attachments

 ## Symptoms:

- You receive your email, but there are attachments that you cannot open. Or similarly, you send email with an attachment and the recipient claims that it cannot be opened.

- Your receive your email but the message includes (or is entirely) encoded text.

- You are especially having problems exchanging attachments with Windows/PC users.

 ## Causes:

If you send a separate file, such as word processing document or Photoshop file, as an email attachment, you will need to encode (and probably compress) it. Often, your email program does this for you automatically. However, if your encoded message is not one that can be decoded by the recipient or conversely if you receive a message via an encoding method that your software cannot decode, you have a problem. Here are some potential solutions.

SEE ALSO: • "Yours or MIME: Understanding MIME and Email," for more background.

⬛ **What to Do:**

Attachments That Are Not Decoded

If, for whatever reason, your email program does not properly decode an attachment, the "file" may appear as text in the body of the email, rather than as an attachment. If so, save the encoded text as a text file (deleting all extraneous text that does not appear to be part of the encoding) and use a program such as StuffIt Expander to attempt to expand it. This will usually work.

If not, contact the sender about sending the file again, using an alternative encoding and/or compression method that your software can recognize.

If the file appears to decode correctly but still does not open when you double-click it, try opening it from within its intended application. Sometimes the creator information needed to open the file directly from the Finder gets lost in the transmission, yet the file itself is otherwise intact.

The next section gives more specific advice for cross-platform email.

Problems Sending Attachments to PC Users

Selecting the compression and encoding method A common problem exchanging files with a PC user is that their email programs typically cannot handle the common Macintosh compression and encoding formats (such as .sit and .hqx). Instead, they have their own PC-specific formats. The Mac actually has an easier time dealing with PC formats than vice versa, so PC users are more likely to have a problem with files that you send them. You typically want to encode (and possibly compress) the file in one of the recognized PC formats before sending it to a PC user.

Some email programs may have an option that lets you make these choices directly. Otherwise, you will need to use a program such as Aladdin's Expander, DropStuff or StuffIt Deluxe. For example, a common compression format on the PC is Zip (.zip) and common encoding formats are UUencode (.uu) and Base64 (.mime). [**Note:** Because of its suffix, Base64 is sometimes used as a synonym for MIME, but MIME is really a more general term, as described elsewhere in this chapter.] If in doubt about what to use, check with the intended recipient as to how they would prefer the file to be sent.

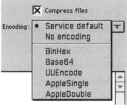

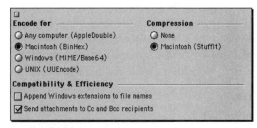

Figure 13-35 The compression and encoding options for sending mail from Emailer (top) and Outlook Express (bottom).

Resource fork problems Another problem specific to sending Mac files to PC users is that Mac files have both a data and resource fork. If you are not familiar with what this means, just think of them as two separate components to a file. Most Mac applications have their information primarily in the resource fork. Conversely, most documents store all their essential information in the data fork. PCs can deal with the data fork but the idea of a resource fork is unknown to them.

This means that trying to run a Mac application on a PC will be useless (although this would still be the case even if PCs *did* understand resource forks). So don't even bother sending applications to PC users (unless you are just doing it to store a file for later transfer back to a Mac).

The outlook is much better for Mac documents. They can be successfully emailed and potentially opened on a PC. However, for a Mac file to be able to open on a PC, it will likely need some help. For starters, if it has a resource fork (and most documents do not), you will want to strip it out before you send it. This is called "flattening" the file. ResEdit can do this (just cut all the resources it displays and save the modified file) as can programs such as Resource Remover. Some email programs will also assist here by only encoding the data fork when you select a file to be encoded in formats commonly used with PCs (such as Base64 and UUencode).

Note: The AppleDouble format is preferred by Outlook Express as general purpose format for all computers. It splits a file into two files, one containing the resource fork, the other containing the data fork. These forks are then encoded, typically using Base64. Mac users (assuming their email program recognizes AppleDouble) will put the file correctly back together again. PC users can just trash the resource fork file and retain the data fork component. The AppleSingle format, similar to what BinHex does, combines both forks into one file; as such, it would not be recommended for sending to PC users.

Application problems Even if your PC colleague successfully receives, decodes, and expands a flattened file, she will still not be able to open the file unless she has an application that can recognize that format. For example, sending a TypeStyler document to a PC user is useless. There is no PC program that opens TypeStyler files, at least not yet (a Windows version of the program is in development). However, TypeStyler can export files to various formats (including JPEG and Photoshop) that can be opened by a PC program. Even so, the exported file will likely not have all of the attributes available in the original file. This can be especially critical with exports of word processing files, where the exported file may lose much of the fancy formatting that the original version had. That's why a preferred alternative is to use a cross-platform program (i.e., one that exists in both PC and Mac versions, such as Microsoft Word); it should be able to save files that can be opened by its cross-platform sibling, with all the file's fancy formatting intact and often without any special exporting required. Again, contact the recipient about what format they can potentially use.

Otherwise...

If you believe you have followed all of the preceding suggestions, and the file still cannot be opened, the MIME information of the attached file may have been corrupted when the file was sent. To check for this, resend the file (or if the problem is with a file someone sent to you, ask that they resend it).

BY THE WAY ▶ Newsgroups

Newsgroups are essentially message boards, where anyone can post a message or read messages others have posted. They are separate from the World Wide Web (and existed years before the Web was born). With the growth of message boards on the Web itself, newsgroups are not as popular as they once were. But they are still quite active. And Mac newsgroups, such as comp.sys.mac.system (accessed from your browser via the URL: <news:comp.sys.mac.system>), are still a useful, if unfiltered, source of information.

You can access newsgroups from the Newsgroup feature of Netscape Communicator, the News feature of Outlook Express, or specialized programs such as NewsWatcher. In order to get started, you'll first need to set up a news server account (similar to setting up an email account) in your software of choice. If your ISP supports access to a news server, they should provide you with the needed information to do this.

These days, you can also access many newsgroups directly from the Web. A popular site for doing this is Deja.com (try: http://www.deja.com/usenet or http://www.deja.com/categories/comp.shtml). The main part of the site has become a place for buying stuff; this is not what you want for locating newsgroups.

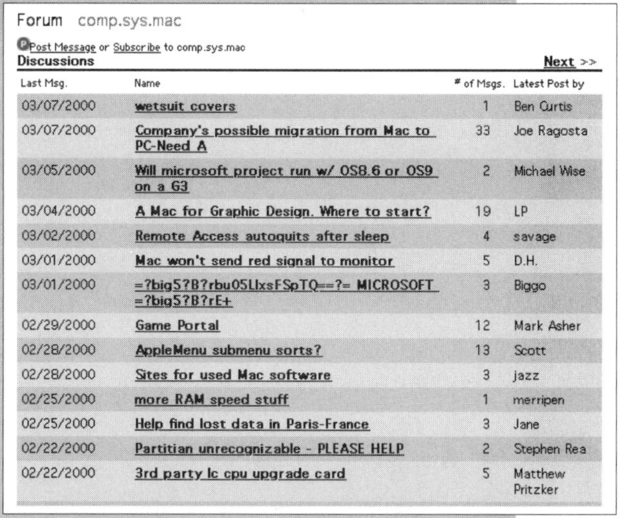

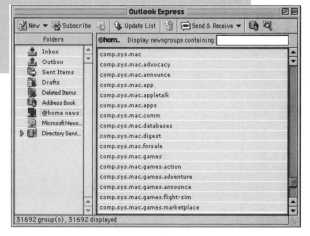

Figure 13-36 An example of the comp.sys.mac newsgroup listing, as viewed from Deja.com.

Figure 13-37 A listing of some of the comp.sys.mac.x newsgroups, as viewed from Outlook Express.

BY THE WAY ▶ Vcards, Security and such

Do you ever get email that has a tiny file attached, with a name that includes an odd suffix such as .vcf? This is a signature card. Netscape Communicator allows you to send email with these attachments. To do so, select the VCard option in the Mail & Newsgroups/Identity Preferences.

These cards act as a sort of business card, with information such as your name and address included. They may also provide a measure of security that the person claiming to send the message is really the person sending it. Personally, I find these attachments annoying and simply trash them as soon as I receive them.

If email security is really a big concern, you'll be better off using something such as PGP Personal Privacy. This can actually encrypt the message so that only the intended recipient can even read it, even if the recipient does not own PGP.

14

Think Different: the iMac, iBook, Power Mac G4 and Beyond

It's a Whole New World

If you are reading this book, it's safe to assume that you already know about the phenomenal success of the iMac. Released in August 1998, it set sales records not only for Apple, but for the computer industry as a whole. It almost single-handedly saved Apple from the brink of financial doom.

The iMac was also the first Mac to introduce a host of new features that have since spread throughout the rest of the Macintosh line—to the iBook, the Power Macintosh G3 (blue-and-white model) and the Power Macintosh G4—and to all newer models that may be out by the time you read this.

To those who were concerned that all of this change, all of this "newness" and all of Apple's "Think Different" philosophy meant that older software wouldn't work with these new Macs, Apple said "Think Again." The good news is that these new Macs are fundamentally still familiar old Macintoshes. Sure, there are some programs and some hardware peripherals that were incompatible with these new Macs. This was inevitable. But most of these problems were handled by relatively minor updates to software or firmware. Most of the rest of existing software and hardware worked just fine with no change at all. In fact, when the iMac was first introduced, based on feedback received at my MacFixIt web site, I commented that the iMac was the most trouble-free new Mac model that Apple had ever introduced. The success of the iMac is not simply based on how cool it looks. It also works very well. New users really can unpack an iMac and be on the Internet in fifteen minutes.

OK, but what about those inevitable problems? That's what the rest of this chapter is about. It focuses on what's new and different about these new Macs, and how it all affects troubleshooting your Mac.

NewWorld Macs

As noted in Chapter 1, all Macs have something called a ROM chip located on their logic board. Traditionally, this ROM not only contained the instructions necessary to initially start up (boot) the Mac, but it contained the code for many of the common Mac OS interface components—such as menus and dialog boxes. This common set of tools has tremendous advantages. It allowed all Mac applications to share these common interface components, giving all applications a similar look and feel, without requiring that the programmer of each application re-invent the wheel to accomplish this.

However, having this information in ROM also had its disadvantages. Primary among them is that it is difficult to modify and update the ROM, as it requires either a hardware replacement (which Apple virtually never does) or a series of software "patches" (in the form of extensions and/or enablers) that can lead to a series of different files needed for each model of Mac. The obvious solution (especially as a Mac's typical RAM and hard drive sizes increased) was to move the ROM to the hard drive and then load the information into memory (RAM) at startup.

This is essentially what is behind what Apple refers to as its NewWorld architecture. It was initiated in the iMac and is found in all newer Macs (iBook, blue-and-white G3 Macs, G4 Macs, bronze keyboard PowerBook G3 Series and whatever else has come along since writing this). Much of the details of what NewWorld is and how it works is something only developers need to know. The typical end user's experience is much the same regardless of whether they startup with a NewWorld Mac or an "old world" one. Still, for troubleshooting purposes, there are some basics you should master. Here they are.

Boot ROM

Instead of the single large hardware ROM, there is now only a much smaller ROM— called the Boot ROM. It provides only the essential functions needed begin to start up the Mac and to load an operating system.

Boot ROM Is Firmware Upgradable

The Boot ROM is firmware upgradable. This allows Apple to make changes to the Boot ROM without having to make a hardware replacement.

Some background: the term firmware refers to a hybrid that is midway between software and hardware. Akin to software, firmware can be upgraded. Akin to hardware, the firmware data is actually stored in special hardware chips, rather than as data on the hard drive. You typically update firmware by running a special firmware update utility.

BY THE WAY ▶ Other Firmware Updates

The Macintosh Boot ROM is not the only Mac component that is firmware upgradable. The internal modem also works this way. For example, the Apple Modem Updater updated the firmware of the original 56K modem in the iMac, to make it compatible with the latest V.90 protocol (see Chapter 12). SCSI cards (as found in Power Macs) can also have firmware updates to fix bugs. CD-ROM and DVD drives similarly have firmware that can be modified by these upgrade utilities. One of the first updates for the iMac was a CD Firmware update that fixed CD drives that were too noisy. More recently, a DVD-ROM update modified the firmware on this drive included with the iMac DV.

How Do You Know What Boot ROM Version You Have?

Given that the Boot ROM is upgradable, how can you check what version you have? There are at least two ways. The simplest is to use Apple System Profiler (version 2.1.2 or later). From the System Profile window, open the disclosing triangle for Product Information. There you will see lines for Boot ROM version (such as 3.0.f3) and Mac OS ROM version (such as 1.1). [There will also be lines for ROM revision, serial number and software bundle.]

The other way to learn the Boot ROM version is via the Open Firmware screen (detailed a bit later in this section).

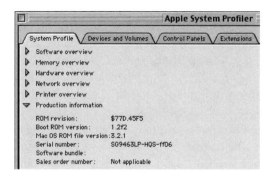

Figure 14-1 Apple System Profiler window listing the Boot ROM (1.2f2) and Mac OS ROM (3.2.1) version numbers from an iMac DV running Mac OS 9.0.

How Do You Install a Firmware Update?

The instructions to install a firmware update are a bit tricky and may vary from Mac model to Mac model. Happily, each firmware update comes with very specific step-by-step instructions as to what to do (read them carefully and follow them *exactly*!).

In some cases, running the Updater application will lead to a message that says the firmware needs to be updated. Clicking the Update button will install the firmware update. At this point, you are done. Couldn't be more simple.

In other cases, the procedure will be more complex. For example, here is a procedure used to install one version of an iMac firmware upgrade (the procedure gets a bit simpler with the latest upgrades):

1. Run the Updater application. Wait for a message to appear.

2. You will eventually get a message that says you need to shut down your computer. Do so (typically just click the Shut Down button in the message box).

3. Press the Programmer's button (see Chapter 4).

4. Press the power button on the keyboard or the iMac itself (while still leaving the Programmer's button depressed), and wait until you hear a long tone (different from the normal startup tone). You can then let go of both buttons.

   (If you hear the normal startup tone, you probably were not pressing hard enough on the programmer's button. Try again.)

5. The update will then proceed. A progress bar will appear at the bottom of the screen as the update takes place.

6. After startup is completed, if the update process was successful, a message appears saying the firmware is now up-to-date. Click OK. If a message appears saying the update was not completed successfully, go back to step 1 and begin the update process again.

Firmware Update Problems

If the Firmware update does not install The updater may fail to install for any variety of reasons. These can include such benign reasons as the update was already previously installed or the update is not intended for the model of Macintosh in use. In these cases, you typically get a message informing you of the failure to install the upgrade and the reason for it.

If you get a message that says the firmware was not installed and you believe that you are running the correct Mac for the upgrade and it has not yet been installed, the cause may be a bug in the installer or a conflict with some extension. For example, with the first G3 Firmware Update, the update did not install on some models that had an early version of the Boot ROM. It mistakenly said that the old version was actually a newer version.

To find out exactly what is going on with a particular update, check a site such as my own MacFixIt.

Firmware install is interrupted More serious is if the firmware update process begins but then halts before it is finished for some reason (such as an untimely power failure). In this case, the firmware may be only partially updated. If this was for an update to the Boot ROM, you may now find that your Mac does not startup at all! Essentially, you now have a corrupted Boot ROM. The Mac tries to protect against this by keeping a second back-up copy of the Boot ROM that it can use if the first copy gets corrupted. But occasionally even this backup may fail. If such problems happen, try running the updater again. If that doesn't work, you may need to take the Mac in for repair (essentially to replace the firmware chip).

Downgrading? In most cases, you cannot downgrade firmware. That is, once you update to a newer version of the firmware, you typically cannot go back to the older version. Normally, you would never want to downgrade. But occasionally it turns out that the new version unexpectedly causes a more serious problem than what it is designed to fix. There is little you can do at this point other than hope for a yet newer update that fixes all of the problems.

Bottom-line advice: Take installing firmware updates very seriously. Be careful to install them correctly and install them only if you know you have the symptoms that they are designed to fix.

Mac OS ROM

After the Boot ROM, the rest of what used to be in the ROM chip was mainly higher-level Mac OS routines that were not stored in the System file. In current Macs, these are now stored in a file in the System Folder called (appropriately enough) Mac OS ROM. This file is loaded into RAM at startup. This file is as essential, if not more so, as the System and the Finder files.

Mac OS ROM requires about 3MB of memory. It is loaded into a special area of memory that the Mac reserves for it. However, this memory use means that NewWorld Macs will require more RAM than a similarly configured older Mac. On the plus side, some of this loss is offset by the need for fewer RAM-occupying patches with NewWorld. Another tradeoff is that these newer Macs should perform faster with these data in RAM, rather than ROM.

Of the many items in the Mac OS ROM, I want to mention one here, because it relates to the previously covered Boot ROM: the *bootinfo* "file." This contains various information about the current startup device (such as where the System Folder is located on the drive). The Boot ROM checks this information after the Mac OS ROM loads, so that the startup process can proceed.

Mac OS ROM Updates

Occasionally, Apple may provide an updated version of the Mac OS ROM without updating the entire OS. For example, Apple released a package called Audio Update which, among other things, included updated files needed for the iMac DV to work with the iSub subwoofer. The package included an updated version of the Mac OS ROM file. If you want to find out what OS ROM file you have, Apple System Profiler (as just described) will tell you. Of course, you can also tell simply by selecting Get Info for the file itself.

Mac OS ROM

Figure 14-2
The Mac OS
ROM file.

Before running any Apple Installer that replaces your Mac OS ROM file, make sure you have a backup of the current file. There have been several instances where a ROM update caused more problems than it fixed. Reverting to the older version was the work-around. For example, the Mac OS ROM file that was part of early versions of the Audio Update was known to cause start-up crashes in certain cases. Reverting to the prior version of the ROM file eliminated the problem.

If you don't save a back-up, as a last resort, you can reinstall the version of the file that came with your Mac by using the system software CD.

Updates to Mac OS ROM files should largely eliminate the need for separate machine-specific enablers.

Open Firmware

Open Firmware is the name of special code that resides in the Boot ROM. It is responsible for loading the initial key components of the operating system software and then transferring control of the Mac (and the loading of the rest of the OS) to the software on your drive.

Open Firmware is something that predates NewWorld Macs. It is a cross-platform firmware standard for controlling hardware. It was originally conceived as part of an ill-fated project that would allow Macintosh models to boot from any variety of different operating systems. The user would choose the desired OS at startup (Mac OS, Linux, etc.). At one point, it was even hoped that Windows would be included as a potential OS. However, the project died with the death of the Macintosh clones (see: "By the Way: Where are the Clones," later in this chapter). Still, all Power Macs from the original PCI-based Power Macs (see Fix-It #15) to the present models use Open Firmware booting. In fact, NewWorld Macs require Open Firmware to startup. While the original vision for this feature may have vanished, Apple has still partially implemented it in its current use of Open Firmware (as described shortly). Further, the version of Open Firmware in these NewWorld Macs (version 3.0 or later) is much more full-featured than the original version.

Open Firmware Loads RTAS

Open Firmware loads into RAM certain features stored in the Boot ROM that will likely be needed, no matter what OS is running. These features, officially called Run-Time Abstraction Services (RTAS), include the clock data and NV-RAM (which contains the PRAM, as described in Fix-It #9).

Use Open Firmware to Startup an Alternate OS

The Macintosh boots into the Mac OS by default, just as if Open Firmware were not involved. As such, the typical end user will not even be aware that something called Open Firmware is present. However, one of the advantages of Open Firmware is that it is OS-independent. That is, it loads before any OS loads. This means that you can use it to choose a different OS than you would normally load. Here's how:

1. Turn on the Mac

2. Hold down the Command-Option-O-F keys at startup until the Open Firmware screen appears.

3. The screen will display some initial information, such as the version of Open Firmware and Boot ROM installed. Here's what it may look like on an iMac (with the X's filled in of course).

   > Apple iMac Open Firmware X.XX built on XX/XX/98 at XX:XX:XX
   > Copyright 1994-1999 Apple Computer, Inc.
   > All Rights Reserved.
   > ok

   This will be followed by a > symbol, after which you can type your command.

4. To access the Mac OS, type "mac-boot" or "bye" and press return. The Mac should now startup as normal. Actually, you will briefly see an odd Mac icon with strange code beneath it (almost like a Sad Mac); then the normal startup sequence will resume.

For any other OS, follow the instructions provided as part of the OS installation. To boot from another OS, you will also have to have OS software already installed on your drive. You may even have to create a separate drive or partition just for the OS. There may also be a way to get the alternate OS to load by default, eliminating the need to boot into the Open Firmware window at each startup. For example, starting with Mac OS X Server, a new utility called System Disk can be used to select the OS that will boot at the next startup.

SEE: • **Chapter 15 for more on Mac OS Server.**

If you are at the Open Firmware screen and want to boot back into Mac OS, simply type "mac-boot" without the quotes at the command prompt and type the 'return' key to exit Open Firmware. The iMac should exit Open Firmware and continue booting into Mac OS.

Note: When you type mac-boot you must not type the hyphen; it comes up automatically. If you type the hyphen, a message comes back stating "unknown word."

Startup with a NewWorld Mac

In Chapter 5, we described the basics of the startup sequence. While the overview remains largely accurate even for NewWorld Macs, there are some significant differences in the details. Here are the essentials of the startup sequence of a NewWorld Mac booting the Mac OS:

Power On Self Test (POST) This is the first thing that runs when the Mac is turned on after a shut down (it does not run after a restart). This software, located in the Boot ROM, performs the initial diagnostic test of the hardware when the Mac is first tuned on. Older Macs perform similar tests. However, the "beep" codes that may occur if a problem is detected are new.

1, 2 or 3 beeps: mean problems with installed memory modules. It could mean defective RAM or the incorrect type of RAM (see Fix-It #15). Replacing RAM (especially added third-party RAM) may fix the problem.

4 or 5 beeps: means that the Boot ROM appears corrupt (technically referred to as bad checksums). If this occurs, you are best advised to take your computer to an Apple Authorized Service Provider for repair.

SEE ALSO: • **Chapter 5, "Take Note: The New Power On Self Test (POST)."**

Open Firmware This is the second code to execute. It loads in to RAM.

Mac OS ROM The Mac OS ROM file is loaded into RAM via Open Firmware. A file called bootinfo is run, followed by the nanokernal (the core of the operating system), the 68K emulator (which allows non-PowerPC programs to run on a Power Mac) and finally the Mac OS itself.

BY THE WAY ▶ Booting into Open Firmware by mistake

If things are working well, you should never see the Open Firmware screen unless you type Command-Option-O-F at startup. However, for some reason (almost certainly some obscure bug), your Mac may boot into the Open Firmware screen even if you think you started up normally. If this happens, don't worry. Once again, typing "mac-boot" should get your normal boot working. Almost certainly, this screen will not return the next time you start up.

TECHNICALLY SPEAKING ▶ The Startup Disk Control Panel and Open Firmware

When you run the Startup Disk control panel in a NewWorld Mac, it looks and acts no differently than it did in older Macs. But under the hood, there are many differences. The main change is that the Startup Disk now interacts with Open Firmware to locate a startup device. Here is a slightly edited quote from an Apple technical document that explains the details:

- Open Firmware now bears responsibility for locating a startup device. This is very different from previous Mac OS systems where the Mac OS ROM had responsibility for locating the startup device. In NewWorld Macs, since the Mac OS ROM file is on the startup disk, it cannot be used to determine the startup disk. The startup device decision must be made earlier in the startup process. Previous systems stored the user's selected startup device in PRAM. The startup device was set in PRAM (or more technically, NVRAM) when the user selected a device in the Startup Disk control panel. This device was honored by the Mac OS ROM unless the selected device was unavailable or was overridden by the user. The startup disk routine for NewWorld Macs, rather than setting Mac OS PRAM, sets an Open Firmware config variable called boot-device. This setting is honored by Open Firmware unless the selected device was unavailable or was overridden by the user."

- **Selecting the Startup Disk at startup** As detailed in Chapter 5 (see: "Take Note: "Using the Option Key to Select a Startup Device"), with Apple's most recent Mac models, holding down the Option key at startup brings up a screen from which you can select the startup drive.

TAKE NOTE ▶ Open Firmware and Devices Connected to SCSI Cards

NewWorld Macs do not come with a SCSI port built into the logic board. If you want to connect external SCSI devices to a Mac such as the blue-and-white G3 Macs or G4 Macs, you must add a SCSI card in one of the Macs PCI slots. You then connect SCSI devices to the port on this card.

Startup devices You may find that a SCSI drive connected this way cannot serve as a startup drive, even though the same device worked as a startup drive when connected to older Macs. The reason for this is that for a drive connected to a SCSI card to be a startup drive, the firmware on the SCSI card must be "Open Firmware aware." By the time you read this, I suspect this will largely be a moot point, as all SCSI cards will have met this requirement. However, when the blue-and-white G3 Macs first came out, many existing cards did not allow startup device connections. A drive connected to these cards would mount as a secondary drive, but would not work as a startup drive. Firmware updates largely resolved the issue. In some cases, updates to the driver software on the drive itself are also needed.

The technical reason behind this problem: if Open Firmware code is not included in a card's firmware, the card cannot be recognized by the computer until after the OS starts to load. Of course, since the OS now resides on disk (initially in the Mac OS ROM file), this means that the card cannot be recognized until after a startup device has been located. Therefore, no drive connected to the card can serve as a startup drive.

Scanners and such A somewhat different problem is an external SCSI device, such as a scanner, that is not recognized as connected by the scanner software, even though SCSI utilities (such as SCSIProbe) recognize the device as present. The problem here appears to be that devices connected to the SCSI port of older Macs were considered to be on Bus 0. However, the SCSI card on NewWorld Macs lists devices as connected on Bus 1. Some software is written such that it only checks for the relevant device on Bus 0. As a result, it never finds the device (such as a scanner) connected to the SCSI card. The typical solution here is an update to the device software (such as the scanner driver software).

There are other reasons that a particular device may not work with a particular SCSI card. For example, the card may transfer data too fast for the device. In this case, a slower SCSI card may work.

SEE: • Fix-It #14 for more on SCSI connections.

Mac Models: A Closer Look

Following the introduction of the iMac in 1998, Apple completely overhauled its hardware line-up, introducing models that were radically different from all previous Macs. This section provides a brief overview of what is new and different about each of these Mac models. It also offers a collection of troubleshooting tips specific to each model.

Hardware: iMac, iBook, and Power Mac G3/G4

iMac

There are now many versions of the iMac. There is the original Bondi blue iMac (these are the only ones that included an infrared port). Then there are the original 5-colored iMacs. These were followed by the second-generation iMacs, as exemplified by the iMac DV. Because the second-generation iMacs all include a slot-loading CD/DVD drive (as opposed to the older drives that used a tray), Apple refers to them as the slot-loading iMacs.

The iMac laid the ground rules for the major changes in the Mac line-up. After you got past the stunning design of the iMac, the first thing that old-time Mac users noticed was the hardware that was missing:

- No floppy drive.

- No SCSI port.

- No serial port.

- No ADB port.

- No fan (in the slot-loading iMacs).

The major new additions were:

- USB ports. Actually, you get two of them. One of them is used to connect the keyboard and mouse. The other is left for you to use as you wish. In the second generation of iMacs (the ones with the slot-loading CD/DVD drives), the two USB ports are independent. This means they are not on the same bus, which theoretically means that you can attach more devices (especially self-powered devices) to the two ports before reaching a limit where they do not work.

- FireWire ports (only in the iMac DV).

- AirPort card support (in all slot-loading iMacs).

    SEE: • **Fix-It #14 for more on the various Mac ports.**

The absence of the floppy drive and the Mac's traditional ports (together with virtually no internal expansion options, such as PCI cards) required some significant "adjustments," especially if you were upgrading to an iMac from an older model. If you had an ADB writing tablet and a serial port modem and a LocalTalk networked printer and an external SCSI Jaz drive, suddenly you had no way to connect them to your iMac. If you had floppy disks, suddenly you had no way to use them.

Fortunately, a variety of mostly inexpensive adapters and drives came along to solve (or at least reduce the impact of) these problems. Here's a sampler of the solutions available:

- Need a floppy drive? You can get one that attaches to the iMac's USB port. Or you can get a SuperDisk drive. As explained in Chapter 2, a SuperDisk drive reads both ordinary HD floppy disks as well as its own 120MB SuperDisk formatted disks.

- Need a Zip drive? There is a USB model available.

- There are even USB-connected external hard drives on the market, such as one by LaCie.

- Need to connect your old serial inkjet printer? It can be done via a serial-to-USB adapter (such as one made by Keyspan). Still, in my view, you will be happier investing in a USB inkjet printer, such as the ones by Epson or Hewlett-Packard.

- Need to connect other serial port devices to your iMac? These same serial-to-USB adapters work. Keyspan even makes one specific for connecting a Palm cradle.

- Need to connect a LocalTalk network to your iMac? You could shift to Ethernet instead (the iMac does have an Ethernet port). Or you can get Farallon's iPrint LT. It allows LocalTalk connections to the iMac's Ethernet port.

  Note that while USB is a serial communications channel, it is not a replacement for LocalTalk. This is because you cannot connect two Macintosh computers together via USB. For networking iMacs, your best bet is to use Ethernet.

- Need to connect an ADB device? Try Griffin's iMate ADB-to-USB adapter.

- Have an external modem? Don't worry about how to connect it. The iMac comes with its own internal modem. And, if you really want an external modem, there are now USB versions available.

The list goes on, but you get the idea. Another thing that becomes clear here is that almost all of these "solutions" depend upon the iMacs now all-important USB ports. What's so good about USB anyway?

As covered more in Fix-It #14, USB stands for Universal Serial Bus. It has numerous advantages. First, it is widely used in the PC world. This means that hardware vendors no longer have to make one version of their hardware for the Mac and another for the PC. The same USB version can work on both platforms. All the vendor needs to do is create special software drivers unique to the Mac.

USB is also hot-swappable. This means that you can plug and unplug USB devices while the Mac is running. This was not recommended for ADB and SCSI devices. You can also have as many as 127 USB devices connect to one iMac. They can even draw power from the Mac's USB ports (eliminating the need for a separate power supply in many cases). However, if you have several USB devices connected to the iMac, you are advised to get a USB hub. This is a device, with its own power supply, that allows five (or more, depending upon what model you get) USB devices to connect to it.

And USB is fast. It's faster than either serial or ADB connected devices. Unfortunately, it is significantly slower than SCSI. This means, for example, that a USB Zip drive will be slower than an SCSI Zip drive on an older Mac. Even worse, most USB drives cannot even match the theoretical maximum speed of the USB connection. So they are even slower than they might appear to be. That's why those Mac users who crave speed will never be satisfied with USB hard drives. Fortunately, on the newer iMacs, you can use FireWire hard drives, which can be even faster than SCSI.

The iMacs also come with a zippy G3 processor and (currently) an ATI Rage 128 graphics accelerator. These may be consumer Macs, but they are fast machines!

When combined with Mac OS 9 (or in some cases a special version of Mac OS 8.6 that shipped with the computers), the iMacs (as well as all of the other Macs covered in this chapter) have another new feature: the F1 through F12 function keys are programmable. Apple states: "To set up a programmable function key, open the Keyboard control panel under the Apple menu. Or, if the keys have not been programmed yet, simply pressing one of them brings up a dialog box that leads you to the Keyboard control panel. Apple has preprogrammed F1 through F6 with such common control functions as screen brightness, speaker volume, and so on. F7 through F12 can be programmed for your personal choices."

Finally, a note about the lack of a floppy drive: this was the biggest complaint about the iMacs when they were first released. But Apple was betting on the future, a future where floppy disks were clearly fading as a too slow, too low-capacity storage medium. For years, its only advantage has been its ubiquity; they were everywhere. Now that the iMac has been out for a few years, I believe Apple's decision has been largely vindicated. The only time I would want a floppy drive anymore is (1) to load some old software that I still only have on a floppy disk or (2) when I want to transfer a small document to a Mac at another location. The first situation has become so rare as to be just about non-existent; as for the second situation, there are usually other ways to transfer the file that are just as convenient (or more so). And as a last resort, you can always buy a USB floppy drive.

iBook (and PowerBook)

A list of what's new and different about the iBook would look nearly identical to what I just described for the iMac. For example, it too has abandoned ADB and serial ports for USB. And it too has no floppy drive. One difference, compared to the new iMacs, is that there are no FireWire ports in the iBook. Also, there is no built-in microphone or video out capability.

The "bronze keyboard" PowerBook G3 Series (so named to distinguish it from an older PowerBook G3 Series Mac that had a different-colored keyboard) is a "NewWorld" Mac. It includes a USB port and has no floppy drive. Apple's most recent version of this PowerBook added FireWire ports and an AirPort slot.

Power Mac G3 (Blue-and-White) and G4

The Power Mac G3 that came in a blue-and-white case is the G3 Mac covered here. To distinguish it from the older beige-colored G3, Apple referred to the newer one as the blue-and-white Power Mac G3.

The Power Mac G4s are the first Macs to use the G4 processor as well as an AGP slot (as opposed to a PCI slot) for the graphic accelerator card. AGP is faster than PCI, allowing for improved graphics performance. At first, the low-end model of the G4 did not have the logic board that came with an AGP slot. Instead, it had a slightly modified version of the blue-and-white G3 logic board that came only with PCI slots. However, it was upgraded to the AGP logic board about 3 months after the G4s were released. To distinguish the two types of logic boards originally used in the G4, Apple referred to them as Power Mac G4 (PCI) vs. Power Mac G4 (AGP).

The Power Mac G4s also are the only Macs that work with Apple's current line of Studio Displays and the gorgeous Cinema Display.

The G4 processor itself features something that Apple calls the Velocity Engine (also known as AltiVec). When combined with software that is Velocity Engine-aware (such as the latest versions of Photoshop), this allows for processing speed gains that are phenomenally higher than with any previous Mac (or any previous desktop computer of any kind). Put more technically, what AltiVec does is introduce a separate vector processing unit (32 specialized 128-bit "vector" registers and 162 new instructions for working with them) that is in addition to the more traditional integer units and single (double-precision) floating-point unit of other PowerPC processors.

Beyond all this, these Power Macs are very similar to the iMac in terms of what's new and different. That is, for example, they come with USB and FireWire ports and no floppy drive. One key difference is that because these Power Macs retain the PCI slots of the older Power Macs, you can add a SCSI card to them. This allows you to easily attach your legacy SCSI peripheral devices to these Macs. The Power Mac G3 retained an ADB port, but this has been dropped from the G4.

Quick Fixes: iMac, iBook and Power Mac G3/G4

Despite all that's new in these new Macs, much of the basic troubleshooting advice, from starting up with extensions off to zapping your PRAM, remains largely the same. However, there are some issues that are either unique to these new Macs or occur more often in these machines.

Restarting After a Crash

On the iMac, unlike older Macs, the Control-Command-Power key combination (pressing all three keys together) will not cause a restart after a system crash (or at any other time for that matter). This is a general issue with USB keyboards. Pressing the Power button on the keyboard is thus also not going to work. However, pressing the Power button on the iMac itself may work (to give it a fair try, hold down the button for at least seven seconds). Otherwise, your main option is to restart using the Reset button on the side of the iMac. The situation is similar on the Power Mac G3/G4s.

On the iBook, Command-Control-Power *does* act as a reset after a system crash. Should that fail, there is also a Reset button (located near the Power button). However, only use the Reset button as a last resort. Unlike with other Macs, resetting the iBook also wipes out the PRAM data, which means that you will lose your date and time settings and all other customized settings stored in the PRAM.

Note: When not dealing with a system crash, exactly what the Power button does varies with the exact circumstances. If the Mac is off, pressing it turns it on. If it is on, pressing it either puts the Mac to sleep or presents the Shutdown dialog box (depending on exactly which Mac you are using). If it is already asleep, pressing it should wake up the Mac and present the Shutdown dialog box.

SEE: • Chapter 4 for more on starting up after a system crash.
  • Fix-It #8 on zapping the PRAM.

Restarting from a RAM Disk

Due to a different type of memory module (RAM) in all of these new Macs, starting up from a RAM Disk is no longer possible.

SEE: • Chapter 11 for more on RAM disks.
  • Fix-It #15 on memory modules.

Blinking Folder Icon At Startup

If you get a blinking folder icon (with a question mark in it) at startup that lasts for an unusually long time but is eventually followed by a normal startup, the problem is most likely that a startup device is not selected in the Startup Disk control panel. To fix this, open the control panel and select your normal startup drive.

SEE: • Chapter 5 for more on using the Startup Disk control panel.

No Emulated SCSI Bus

Newer iMacs, iBooks, and G4s are different from older iMacs and blue-and-white G3s in that they don't have an emulated SCSI bus 0. Of course, none of these Macs come with a SCSI port on the logic board. However, having an emulated SCSI bus in the Mac OS apparently solved a problem for software that checked for this bus when loading. Without this emulation, an extension that did this check at startup would likely precipitate a system crash when it failed to find the bus. Certain third-party CD-ROM drivers are an example of software that were guilty of this. Happily, by the time you read this, all of this software should have been updated to fix this problem.

SEE: • Fix-It #14 for more on the SCSI bus.

iBook: "Preserve Memory Contents on Sleep" and the Lack of a Back-Up Battery

The iBook does not have an internal back-up battery. As a result, if you remove the main battery for more than 10 minutes (when not connected to AC power), date and time information will be lost (remaining PRAM data is preserved). On the other hand, the Energy Saver control panel for an iBook contains an option called Preserve Memory Contents on Sleep. As explained more in Chapter 11, this can be used to save the contents of memory when the iBook's main battery is removed, such as when swapping batteries.

However in Mac OS 9, a situation was discovered where, when waking from sleep with this option enabled, you could corrupt data on your hard drive such that you might be unable to successfully restart. FireWire PowerBooks (which have this same option) were also affected. This was later corrected via an update/patch to the Mac OS.

SEE: • **Chapter 11, "Take Note: The iBook and Preserving Memory Contents on Sleep and Restart," for more on this option.**

Figure 14-3
The iBook's "Preserve Memory Contents on Sleep" option.

Wake-from-Sleep Crashes

Wake-from-sleep crashes have been an irritatingly common problem in these new Macs. As the name implies, the primary symptom is that when you try to wake up your Mac from sleep, it simply freezes. Typically, you have to restart to get the Mac working again. There is more than one known cause for this symptom.

USB devices attached Many iMac and iBook users have found that their Mac crashes when waking from sleep if certain USB devices are attached. Apple's USB mouse and keyboard do not seem to be a problem here. This is likely a software problem that will be fixed with updates to the relevant USB driver software (hopefully, it has already been addressed by the time you read this). One work-around is to keep USB devices detached when they are not in use. Another work-around, in some cases, is to delete the USB drivers specific to the USB device attached and hope that Apple's default USB software works as well. This has been known to prevent crashes associated with Iomega USB Zip drives.

iBook: Corrupted Memory Contents file In some cases, most likely due to corruption of the Memory Contents file (created by the "Preserve memory contents on sleep" feature described above), the iBook may be unable to wake-up from sleep when "Preserve memory…" is enabled. If this happens, restart the iBook and press and hold down the Escape key until the Happy Mac icon appears. This forces the iBook to bypass loading of the Memory Contents file (which of course means that all of the data preserved there are lost). Writing new contents to the file (which happens automatically) should fix whatever corruption caused the problem. If problems persist, you may have to disable the "Preserve Memory..." option and manually delete the file.

SEE: • Chapter 8 on working with invisible files.

iBook: Startup CD error Apple states: "If you start up from a CD and then put the iBook to sleep (or let it go to sleep by itself), it will not come out of sleep properly. Instead, the hard drive spins up but the screen remains black. At this point you can press Command-Control-Power or press the reset button to recover."

Power down sleep error The iBook and the Power Mac G4 introduced Power Manager 2.0, a hardware and software combination that, among other things, allows these Macs to achieve a power level when sleeping that is exceptionally low, almost as low-power as when the computer is off. This is typically referred to as "deep sleep."

However, many SCSI cards (at least initially) did not support this power down mode. Thus, a Power Mac G4 with one of these (single-channel) SCSI cards installed would not go into this power down mode when put to sleep. They would instead go into an "old-fashioned" higher power level sleep. This was already disappointing for those hoping to take advantage of this new energy-saving feature. However, it got worse. When these Macs did go to sleep, the computer would sometimes incorrectly assume the SCSI card supported this power down mode and as a result, freeze when waking from sleep. The only work-around was to disable sleep altogether in the Energy Saver control panel. This was fixed in Mac OS 9.0.1.

"Reconnect to servers" enabled Enabling Energy Saver's "Reconnect to servers" option may cause wake-from-sleep crashes, especially if there are no servers available to reconnect.

Multiprocessing folder removed There is a folder called Multiprocessing in the Extensions folder. Leave it there. Removing this folder may cause wake-from-sleep crashes.

SEE ALSO: • Chapter 11 on wake-from-sleep crashes and other sleep problems with portable Macs.

Apple's G3 Firmware Update 1.1 and G4 Upgrade Block

If you have an older blue-and-white G3 Mac and you install Apple's G3 Firmware Update 1.1 (or if you have one of the later G3s that came with this update already pre-installed), you supposedly have the benefit of the update's "improved PCI performance." Unfortunately, it also prevents a G4 processor upgrade from working in these Macs. Manufacturers of G4 upgrades have found ways around this "G4 block" (typically via a software utility that comes with the upgrade card). But be sure to check with the vendor about this matter before purchasing a G4 upgrade for your G3.

DVD Audio/Video Synch Problem

Starting with the Power Mac G4 and the slot-loading iMac, Apple changed the way it supported the playing of DVD movies. It shifted from a method that required a hardware-based decoding card to an all software method. One glitch that developed after this change (especially with the iMac DV) is that, when playing certain DVD movies, the audio and video got "out of sync" after several minutes of playing. Keeping virtual memory off sometimes prevented this from happening. Otherwise, the only choice was to stop the movie and restart it.

A combination of updates to the Mac OS (including updates to the DVD-ROM firmware, the DVD software and QuickTime software) provided the permanent solution, at least in most cases. Check on MacFixIt <http://www.macfixit.com> for the latest status of this problem.

SEE ALSO: • "A CD/DVD Won't Mount or Play," in Chapter 5.

Troubleshooting USB and FireWire

The introduction of USB and FireWire ports in these new Macs inevitably led to new troubleshooting problems. These are covered in Fix-It #14.

Dangers of Mixing System Software Versions

Power Mac G3 (Blue-and-White) and first-generation iMacs can run Mac OS 8.5. However, do not move any Mac OS 8.5 system software components into a Mac OS 8.6 or later System Folder on these Macs. Also, do not move the Mac OS ROM file from a Mac OS 8.6 or later System Folder into a Mac OS 8.5 System Folder. Doing so may prevent these Macs from starting up.

Similarly, early versions of the iBook, iMacDV and Power Mac G4 came with a special version of Mac OS 8.6. If you do a clean install of a generic version of Mac OS 8.6 on these Macs, you will not be able to startup. Use only the version that came with your machine or use any version of Mac OS 9 or later.

Finally, if you have an iMac DV and you upgrade via a clean install from the Mac OS 8.6 that came with the machine to Mac OS 9, you will need to drag three DVD extensions from the Extensions folder of the old System Folder to the new one. Otherwise DVD Player will not work, giving an error that says "DVDRuntimeLib could not be found." These files are DVD Navigation Manager, DVD Region Manager, and DVDRunTimeLib.

Get the Updates

Apple continues to release updates to the Mac OS that fix problems (such as the DVD problem just mentioned) specific to Apple's new hardware. The most recent general OS release is Mac OS 9.0.4, which includes a PowerPC Enabler file (needed for Apple's latest hardware to run the OS).

With all that's new in these new Macs, it's not surprising that certain third-party software programs do not work with them. Unless the software is no longer being supported by the vendor, these problems are inevitably fixed by updates to the software. Thus, the standard advice here is to check that you are using the latest versions of your software.

SEE: • Fix-It #16, for more on obtaining updates and getting other troubleshooting help from the Web.

BY THE WAY ▶ **What Happened to the Mac Clones? Where are the Performas?**

In the third edition of *Sad Macs*, I talked about the arrival of the Macintosh clones, such as those from Power Computing. At the time, they seemed to hold the promise of greatly expanding the installed base of Mac users, much the way sales of PCs expanded when clones of the original IBM models were introduced.

However the analogy to PCs is not a perfect one. For starters, Apple (unlike IBM) makes its own operating system. This can be a tremendous advantage in terms of being able to design the hardware and software to perfectly match each other. But it can present difficulties if you start allowing other companies to also make hardware (which may have differences that mean they do not work as well with the software).

In any case, when Steve Jobs returned to Apple, he decided that Mac clones were more likely to hurt Apple's success than enhance it. As a result, he killed the clone licenses and the clones all vanished. At the time, it seemed to me to be a terrible decision. However without it, we may never have seen the iMac and iBook and the resurgence of the Mac market that followed.

Jobs also decided, soon after returning to Apple's helm, that its hardware lineup was too diverse and confusing, with too many too similar models. Most especially, Apple's attempt at a consumer line of Macs, dubbed the Performas, was deemed to be a failure. So they too were killed (a move that was already underway before Steve's return). Apple's hardware choices were then reduced and simplified to the iMac, iBook, Power Mac and PowerBook. This was a change I heartily welcomed.

15

Troubleshooting Mac OS 8.x, Mac OS 9.x, and Mac OS X

Why This Chapter?

When the last edition of Sad Macs was published, Mac OS 8.0 had not yet been released. Since then, we have seen the release of Mac OS 8.0, 8.1, 8.5, 8.5.1, 8.6, 9.0 and 9.0.4. Mac OS X Server is also out. Within the next few months, Mac OS X will be released. We have seen new software technologies emerge, such as Game Sprockets, OpenGL and QuickTime Streaming. And we have seen the death of once-touted technologies such as OpenDoc and QuickDraw GX. There can be no doubt that the Mac landscape is radically different than it was three years ago.

Information about much of what is new in these latest OS updates—from Sherlock to Navigation Services to the Network Browser to the new Mac OS Installer—are integrated throughout *Sad Macs*. But that still leaves more than a few new topics that did not find a comfortable spot elsewhere in this book. That's the purpose of this chapter. It's a collection of troubleshooting tips specific to these latest OS releases. If you don't find what you are looking for here, check out the appropriate section of the rest of this book (for example, check Chapter 7 for printing problems, even if they are specific to Mac OS 9).

BY THE WAY ▶ Apple's Read-Me Files

Read-me (or About) files have always been included with system software disks. But they are especially relevant now. They contain important late-breaking information sometimes not available elsewhere. Read these files!

To get more help from Apple, check their disk-based Mac Help or their Web site.

SEE: • Chapter 1 for background on Mac Help
and Balloon Help.
• "Take Note: Getting Help from Apple,"
in Fix-It #16 for more details.

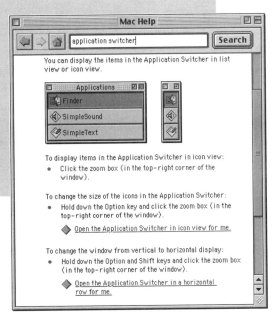

Figure 15-1 Using Mac Help; the window shown here provides help in using Application Switcher.

QuickFixes! Mac OS 8.x-9.x Problems

Contextual Menus

If you have never used contextual menus, you are missing out on one of the most useful features of the Mac OS. Try this: Click the Finder's desktop background; now, holding down the Control key (note the little menu icon that appears next to the cursor arrow when you do this), click and hold down the mouse button. In a short time, a menu

will pop up near the mouse cursor. It will include almost all the options found in the Finder's View menu plus a Change Desktop Background option. As implied by the name of this feature, the commands that appear in these menus vary according to the appropriate context. For example, Change Desktop Background only shows up when the desktop background is the current location. To see how things can change, access the contextual menu for a folder or file icon. You will now see a selection of items (such as Open and Get Info) from the Finder's File menu. If the selected file is an alias, the menu will even have a Show Original command (which is why the Find Original button no longer appears in an alias' Get Info window!).

Figure 15-2 A contextual menu that appears when clicking the Finder's Desktop background (FinderPop is installed, as are plug-ins for Snitch and BeHierarchic).

Contextual menus only work in applications that have been programmed to be "contextual menus aware." This means that older applications especially may not take advantage of this feature. A few programs (Microsoft Office applications are an example) use contextual menus exclusively for their own application-specific options. Generic choices that would otherwise appear are suppressed.

Shortly after contextual menus were introduced, Apple released an extension called Contextual Menu Enabler. Its purpose was to allow contextual menus to work with applications that had not been updated to work with contextual menus. However, Apple no longer supports this extension. It is not included on Mac OS 9 and may even conflict with it. I guess Apple assumes that, by now, most software has been updated for contextual menu compatability and this initial work-around is no longer needed.

Some applications may have conflicts with contextual menus, leading to freezes, crashes or other odd symptoms. In this case, you either need to avoid using contextual menus in these programs or disable the Contextual Menu Extension at startup.

Many applications, especially utilities, offer contextual menu plug-ins that provide access to the features of the application from within a contextual menu. These work by placing a special plug-in file in the Contextual Menu Items folder in the System Folder. For example, you can access BeHierarchic's menu of all the files on your drives via a BeHierarchic Contextual Menu Item listing. With the StuffIt Magic Menu plug-in, you can click a file and select a contextual menu command to stuff or expand the file, as appropriate.

The extension *SOMobjects for Mac OS* must be in your System Folder for some contextual menus to work. Normally it is installed by the Mac OS. But if you disable or remove it, you may have problems. Check that it is there.

A personal recommendation: get FinderPop. It is a control panel rather than a true Contextual Menu Items plug-in. But it offers a wide range of enhancements to contextual menus. For starters, it can add menu items that provide a list of all open background processes (see Fix-It #3) or all open windows (allowing you to select a window to make active). It also has a feature that allows you to access the contextual menu by simply holding down the mouse button (without need of the Control key). Alternatively, if you have a two-button mouse, you can typically program the second button to bring up contextual menus.

SEE ALSO: • **Chapter 1 for more background on contextual menus.**

Sherlock (Internet Searching)

In Chapter 2 and 6, we covered mainly the Find File and Find by Content features of Sherlock that were used for finding files on your drives. However, these features were mainly an enhanced version of what was already available in the Find File function of older versions of the Mac OS. Here we focus on the one entirely new feature of Sherlock: its ability to search the World Wide Web.

Searching the Internet

In the original Mac OS 8.x version of Sherlock, you accessed Sherlock's Internet searching feature by selecting its Search Internet tab. With Sherlock 2 (first shipped with Mac OS 9 and which I emphasize here), you instead click any icon in the Channels row along the top of the Sherlock 2 window (except the first icon, which is for the traditional Find File and Search by Index searches of your drives). A list of search engines for various Web sites will appear in the lower part of the window. You can enable or disable any site's search engine by clicking the "On" checkbox to the left of its name. Disabling a specific site means that it will not be included in any search results.

Next, type in a search term in the text box and press Return (or click the Search magnifying glass icon). This initiates a simultaneous search of all of the active search engines listed in the lower part of the Sherlock window.

The results will appear in the window below, replacing the list of search sites.

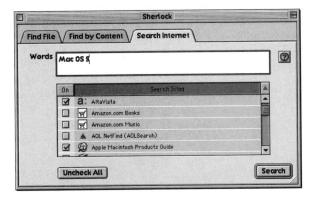

Figure 15-3 The original Sherlock's Search Internet display.

Sherlock Plug-ins and Channels

What sites are available for Sherlock to search are determined by what Sherlock plug-ins (files that have a .src suffix) are in the Internet Search Sites folder of the System Folder. In addition to the "built-in" plug-ins that ship with the Mac OS, you can get many other plug-ins from the Web (for example, I have one for my own MacFixIt site).

For Sherlock 2, there is a separate subfolder for the contents of each of the Sherlock channels (such as Internet, Shopping, Apple, Reference, etc.). Each of these channels contains a subset of all the available channels. Actually, all of these different channels fall into one of four channel types: Searching (or Internet), Shopping, People, and News. Each type conducts a search in a different way and gives different results (for example, a shopping search gives the price listed on each site for the item you are seeking). So you would not, for example, want to put to put a shopping plug-in in a non-shopping channel. Unfortunately, it is not easy to tell one type of plug-in from another. Fortunately, Apple helps you to avoid making a mistake. In particular, to add a plug-in to a channel: drag the icon of the plug-in file from the desktop to the icon of the desired destination channel in the Sherlock window. Sherlock should only allow the plug-in be moved if it is a match with the destination channel.

You can use My Channel (the last built-in icon in the row) to create your own custom list of Internet search sites. Just add your selected plug-ins to it. You can even add the built-in plug-ins to My Channel by going to the Internet Search Sites folder and Option-dragging the desired plug-ins from the folder to the My Channel icon in Sherlock 2. Although it will probably work, I would generally avoid dragging a plug-in directly into a Sherlock subfolder (such as the My Channel subfolder); let the Mac OS do it for you (via the Sherlock 2 window) and you will likely sidestep problems down the road.

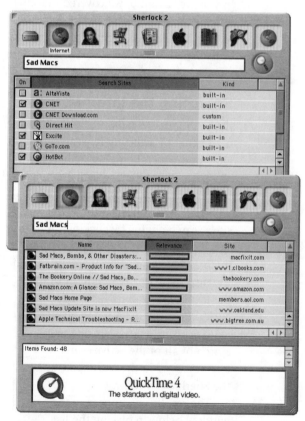

Figure 15-4 Searching the Internet with Sherlock 2. Top: the row of icons along the top of the window are for the different channels. Currently, the second icon (Internet channel) is selected. Bottom: The results of a search on the term "Sad Macs".

You can also create additional custom channels, if desired, by selecting New Channel from the Channel menu. By the way, the ability to have multiple channels is the major new feature of Sherlock 2. The only way to do this with the original Sherlock was with third party add-ons, such as Casady & Greene's Baker St. Assistant.

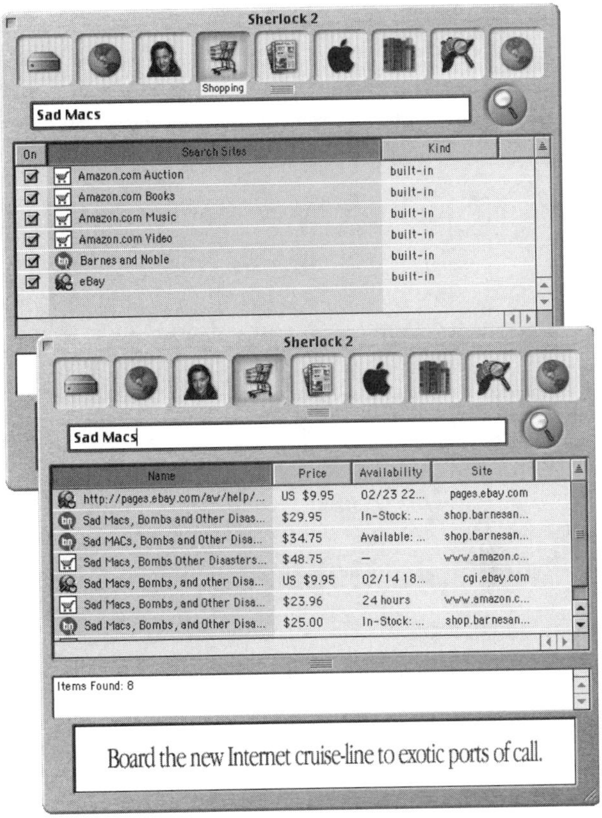

Select Search Criteria via Contextual Menus

The contextual menus feature works well with Sherlock. In any application that supports contextual menus, simply highlight the text you wish to search for, Control-click the text to bring up contextual menus and select "Search Internet." This will automatically launch Sherlock and initiate an Internet search for the highlighted text.

Figure 15-5 Top: the Sherlock 2 window with the Shopping channel selected. Bottom: the results of a search on the term "Sad Macs".

If Sherlock's Internet Searches Won't Work

Most problems with getting Sherlock's Internet searches to work can be easily fixed. Your first step should be to increase the memory of the Sherlock application (located in the Apple Menu Items folder). Increase it by as much as 2MB if you can spare the RAM.

Otherwise, make sure you have the latest versions available of your Sherlock plug-ins (as newer versions may fix bugs in older versions). With the original version of Sherlock, do this by selecting Update Search Sites from the Find menu. With Sherlock 2, just wait for Sherlock to do it for you. In most cases, if a new plug-in exists, you will get a message asking whether it is okay to download it at the time that you try to use the plug-in.

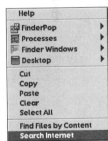

Figure 15-6 A contextual menu that pops up after selecting text. The Search Internet item is selected.

If problems persist, disable all but one plug-in and try the search. Do this until you find one plug-in that works. Then keep re-enabling plug-ins and repeating the search until the problem reappears. The most recently added plug-in is the most likely source of the problem. Go to the Web location where the plug-in is available (typically the

Web site in question or the Sherlock section of Apple's Web site) and make sure a newer version is not available. If not, try reinstalling a clean copy of the plug-in. If that fails, you'll simply have to stop using that plug-in for now.

For any remaining problems, try deleting the files in the Sherlock Prefs folder, especially Sherlock Preferences.

Multiple Word Searches: A Limitation

If you enter more than one word in Sherlock when doing an Internet search, be aware that different search engines may treat them differently. In one case, they may be treated as joined via a Boolean OR while another engine may treat them as joined by a Boolean AND. Similarly, enclosing words in quotes may force one search engine to treat the enclosed words as a single unit (only pages where the words are found next to each other in that order will be reported) while for another search engine you need to connect the words with hyphens to accomplish this. This is an inevitable limitation of doing multiple term and multiple search engine searches with Sherlock.

Multiple Users

Multiple Users is a new feature in Mac OS 9. Its main function is to allow customized settings for different people using the same computer. It combines this with security features, including use of passwords, that prevent other users from logging on to the computer via your settings. Thus, you can set up your Mac so that you log on as normal, with full access to your Mac, your normal desktop background, and so forth. At the same time, your kids can have a separate log on where they choose their own desktop background and have restrictions as to what they can or cannot access (preventing them from opening the System Folder and your checking program, for example).

There are three types of Multiple User accounts: Normal (full access except for those administrative powers granted only to the Owner), Limited (looks just like Normal except that there are places you are restricted from going), Panels (prevents access to the Finder altogether, restricting you to a Panel display where the accessible items are listed). The Owner is typically the one to set up new accounts and determine what restrictions they have (such as what applications they can open). This is all done via the Multiple Users control panel. In particular, to set the exact restrictions for Limited or Panels user accounts, open the account from Multiple Users, click to "Show Setup Details," and go to the Applications

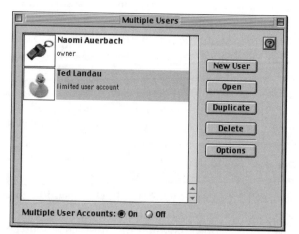

Figure 15-7 The Multiple Users control panel.

and Privileges tabs. For more information on how all of this works, click the Help (question mark) icon in the Multiple Users control panel.

To start using Multiple Users, simply click the On button for "Multiple Users Accounts" at the bottom of the Multiple Users control panel main window. The next time you start up, you will be presented with a Logon window. From here, you select the desired account, enter the password, and you will be logged in. (**Note:** Starting up with extensions off does not bypass this feature; you'll still need to enter a password.)

To shift to another account, you do not have to restart. Instead, select the Logout command that is added to the Finder's Special menu when Multiple Users is on.

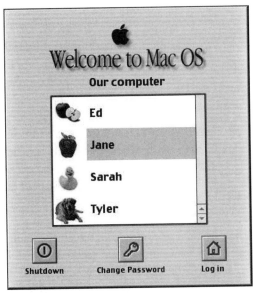

Figure 15-8 The Multiple Users logon window that appears when starting up or when changing users via the Logout command.

How It Works

The "secret" to how Multiple Users works is the Users folder at the root level of your startup drive. Inside this folder you will find a subfolder for every Limited and Panels account. There is also a Shared Documents folder, used for documents accessible to all accounts.

Inside each account subfolder will be a set of further subfolder (many of them with the same names as subfolders in your System Folder, such as Favorites, Preferences, Launcher Items). When you log on via a given account, the Mac uses the information in these folders, rather than the System Folder (or elsewhere on your drive, as appropriate), to determine exactly what the account owner can access. Some of the files in these account folders will be aliases pointing to the actual file; others will be copies of the original file.

It is best not to make modifications to these folders directly from the Finder. Make changes to the Multiple Users control panel settings, which in turn will modify the contents of these folders.

Problems with Limited and Panels Accounts

Multiple Users can present difficulties for some third-party software, especially programs that need to access Preferences files stored in the Users folder for Limited or Panel accounts.

For example, applications such as Office 98 open an installer or self-repair application the first time they are run. At this point, certain files (such as Shared Library files) are placed in the System Folder. The problem is that a user with a Limited or Panel account, even if they are given access to Office 98, will not be able to open the applications because they likely don't have specific access to modify the contents of the System Folder. They probably also do not have access to the needed Microsoft First Run application. The solution is to have the Owner launch the Office 98 applications at least once. The other accounts should then be able to access them—at least until the next time Office 98 tries to update itself for some reason.

Reader Rabbit programs present a slightly different problem. When trying to launch current versions of Reader Rabbit, you get a message saying that the program cannot launch because additional hard disk space is required—despite the fact that you have plenty of unused disk space. The real problem is that the Reader Rabbit software keeps track of a user's responses via a file created and saved to the disk. This requires writing to the disk at launch. If the Multiple User account is set up to prevent writing to disk (at least in this location), the error will occur.

Most other problems of this sort are caused by the fact that Multiple Users stores Preferences files for Limited and Panels accounts in the Users folder. Many applications, not updated to recognize this new feature, will not work properly with Limited, and/or Panel access because they will not be able to locate and/or store the Preferences in this location. You may get messages about being unable to access or modify needed Preferences, for example. Making an alias to the needed Preferences file, or making a copy of the file, and placing it directly in the Users folder, will solve the problem in most cases.

Accessing printers can also present a problem with Multiple Users. For example, in order for users to print to Epson printers with Multiple Users enabled, the owner must give the user access to "All Printers" via the Allowed Printer popup menu in the Privileges section of the user's account. Additionally, as Apple states: "A user in the Limited or Panels environment should configure the Epson printer driver to use a spool folder located in the user's folder, or another location where the user can create files. To do this, go to the Epson print dialog box, click the Tools button, then click Configuration. Then change the Temporary Spool and Temporary High Speed Copies folder locations."

Rebuilding the Desktop

With Multiple Users enabled, if you want to rebuild the desktop (see Fix-It #8), don't waste your time holding down the Command-Option keys until after you have logged in. As soon as you enter your password, hold down the Command-Option keys and the rebuild should work.

General Controls Options Gone

The "Protect System Folder" and "Protect Applications Folder" items in the General Controls control panel are dimmed and cannot be selected in Mac OS 9. This is Apple's not-so-subtle way of saying that you should now use Multiple Users to obtain this protection.

At Ease Trashed

Apple's At Ease software duplicated many of the features of Multiple Users. As a result, Apple has now discontinued At Ease. In fact, if Multiple Users is simply installed in your System Folder, even if it is not turned on, the Mac OS cheerfully trashes any At Ease software that it finds.

Password Non-Protection

With Multiple Users, you must supply a password to log on to an account. Although this may make it *seem* that your hard drive is protected from intruders, it really isn't.

Startup from a CD All someone needs to do is stick a bootable CD in your drive and restart with the CD as the startup drive. This bypasses all password blockades. It's now open season on your hard drive's contents.

There is a benefit to this. If you ever forget your password, you can use a CD to access your drive. Then delete the Multiple Users Preferences file and restart without the CD. Your Mac will now start with Multiple Users off, thus allowing you to startup without needing your Password. You can now change the password to something you will hopefully not forget.

Other security leaks Even without a CD handy, an unscrupulous user can potentially break through Multiple Users' barrier. Here's one way to do it: The Multiple Users control panel has an option to "Lock the Screen" if user is idle for *x* minutes. After the selected interval of idle activity, a "lock screen" appears. You need to enter your password to resume. This helps keep your computer secure should you walk away from your desk for a few minutes. Or so you would think.

The trouble is that there is an option besides Resume in the lock screen: Logout. If you click Logout and you have any unsaved documents open, you will be asked to save the document(s) before the logout actually occurs. From this dialog box, you can select Cancel rather than Save. If you do this, there will be a period of at least a few seconds before the same dialog box reappears. Selecting Cancel essentially does nothing. However, during the interval between Cancel requests, you (or anyone else trying out this sequence in your absence), has full access to the contents of your machine. An intruder who knows this trick could delete files or even change your Multiple Users' password.

If you find that Multiple Users is not adequate for your security needs, turn instead to AppleShare IP or Mac OS X Server.

BY THE WAY ▶ Setting Up Voiceprint

A really cool feature of Multiple Users is to have a Voiceprint password rather than a typed password. With this setup, you speak a password into a microphone in order to log on. Here's what to do to get your Mac to recognize your voiceprint password:

1. Assuming you are the owner of the Mac, open the File Sharing control panel and enter a name and password for yourself.

2. Open the Multiple Users control panel. Your name will appear there as the Owner. The password you entered in File Sharing will be the password for your account.

3. Enable Multiple User Accounts by clicking the On button at the bottom of the window.

(continues on next page)

BY THE WAY ▶ **Setting Up Voiceprint** *(continued)*

4. Click the Options button. From the Login tab, enable the checkbox for "Allow Alternate Password" (the pop-up menu to the right should say Voice Verification). This is important. Otherwise, the Alternate Password tab (in Step 6) will be dimmed and inaccessible. Close the Options window.

5. Select your name from the Multiple Users window and click the Open button.

6. Click the Alternate Password tab. Here you will see a button that says "Create Voiceprint." Continue as directed, recording your voice when prompted.

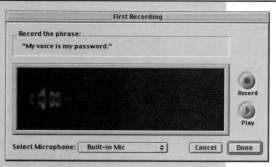

"Lost" microphones If you get a "No microphone found" error at login, and you know your microphone is there, it may be that you don't have a compatible version of Apple's Speech Recognition software installed. You need the version that came with Mac OS 9 or a newer version) for voiceprint passwords to work. To check for this, open the Get Info window of the Speech Recognition extension. It should say version 2.0.1 or later.

The "No microphone found" error may also occur if you are using a microphone other than the one you use to first record your phrase. As Apple explains, voiceprint recognition "takes into account the inherent properties of the microphone." To solve this, simply re-record your voiceprint phrase using the current microphone.

Figure 15-9 Two windows that appear while setting up a Voiceprint password from the Multiple Users control panel.

Know when to stop While trying to record a voiceprint phrase, you may get an error that says: "You may have clicked the Stop button too soon. Try recording the phrase again." This happens if you are still talking (or if there is too much extraneous noise) when you click the Stop button. The software interprets this as meaning that you weren't done entering your phrase.

If you are using one of the new "fanless" iMacs, Apple says that this "stopped too soon" message can be triggered by the noise of the iMac's hard drive. I guess the masking noise of a fan would otherwise prevent this error. There is not much you can do about this except try again—and keep other extraneous noise to a minimum.

Memory Problems

Starting in Mac OS 8.6, some applications will require about 300K more memory than needed in Mac OS 8.5 in order to work. To apply this boost to programs too old to have been "boosted" by the vendor, select Get Info for the file, select Memory from the Show pop-up menu and increase the Preferred Size by 300K.

Scrapbook Memory (and Related) Problems: A Special Case

The Scrapbook is an application, not a desk accessory or a control panel (actually this was true even in System 7). This means that you can change its memory allocation from its Get Info window. This is important because "out of memory" messages may appear when you try to cut from or paste to the Scrapbook (especially if you have a large number of items in the Scrapbook file). Sometimes, these commands simply refuse to work, with no error message appearing. If any of this happens, try each of the following, as needed:

Scrapbook   Scrapbook File

Figure 15-10 The Scrapbook application (left) vs. the Scrapbook file (right).

- Restart the Mac and try again. Sometimes, this is all you need to do.

- Quit the Scrapbook, go to its Get Info window, and increase its Preferred memory size by 100 to 200K (or more if you can afford it).

- Cut unneeded items out of your Scrapbook.

- Drag the file called *Scrapbook file* from the root level of your System Folder (not the Scrapbook program in the Apple Menu Items folder) to the desktop. Now when you open the Scrapbook, a new empty Scrapbook file will be created and used. You can still access the original Scrapbook file by double-clicking its icon.

- In a few cases, the problem may be a damaged Scrapbook file. In this case, you can try to recover images from the file, using a utility such as CanOpener. After that, delete the Scrapbook file.

- Use a third-party utility that substitutes for the Scrapbook. There are several, such as MultiClip and ScrapIt Pro.

Assorted Mac OS 9 Fixes and Tips

Here's an assortment of Mac OS 9 tips and problems (and their solutions).

Type 119 Error

In general, we are not going to talk about programs that don't work with a particular version of the Mac OS. This is because these compatibility conflicts are almost always fixed by updates to the relevant software and these updates would likely be released before this book ever reached the shelves. So what would be the point of citing it here? It's enough simply to say that such conflicts exist whenever a new version of the Mac OS is released and that you should check with your software vendor (or a site such as MacFixIt) for information about such problems whenever you update your Mac OS.

That said, there is one particular type of conflict worth mentioning here: The Mac OS 9 Type 119 error. When you try to launch certain applications, you may get a Type 119 error message and the program will fail to launch. The origin of this is a change that Apple made to something buried deep in the system software, called the Mac OS File Manager. The reason for the change is a good one. In Mac OS 9, you can now open larger files (greater than 2GB) and have many more files open at once (8169 to be exact) than you ever could before. But to accomplish this, Apple changed the way the OS tracks files. The problem occurs with software that tries to use the old tracking method and finds it no longer exists. The result is a Type 119 error, a number invented especially for this Mac OS 9 situation!

Even Apple's own software is not immune: AppleWorks 5.0.4 Updater (included on the Mac OS 9 CD) is needed to bring AppleWorks into compliance. Adobe Type Manger (both the Free and Deluxe versions) and Adobe Type Reunion were identified as having this problem even before Mac OS 9 was released. To fix these programs, updated versions came out within two weeks after OS 9 shipped. This same bug also bit Netscape Communicator. However, in this case, you could fix things without an update: just remove the Talkback folder from the Communicator folder.

Alsoft has released a utility called Mac OS 9 File Mgr Compatibility Checker that checks the programs on your drive to see if they are susceptible to this error. The Checker will also determine a related issue: whether or not a given application can create and open files larger than 2GB in size.

Software Update Control Panel

Mac OS 9 introduced a new control panel called Software Update. If you are online, this control panel can check if there are any updates to Mac OS 9 software that you need, and, if so, download and install the software.

The control panel does not always work as expected. It may sometimes stall or freeze. At other times, it may report that you need software that you already have or it will fail to report software that you do need. In some cases, the problem is that Apple's server is down or too busy. The solution here is to try again later. Otherwise, make sure you are using the latest version of the control panel (check Apple's Software Downloads for this). Finally, try deleting the control panels preferences files: *Software Updates Pref* and *Updatable Items.*

Note: The control panel may insist on closing all open applications before down-loading software. This is normal, although it can present a catch-22 for certain types of Internet connections (particularly common with PPPoE connections) that require a special application remain open for the connection to the Internet to be maintained.

Control Panels Don't Work

A few control panels don't get along well with Mac OS 9. These are mostly older ones that insist on loading into the same memory space as used by the Finder. This used to be OK but Mac OS 9 now insists that control panels open in their own memory space. The result is that these control panels don't work. One notable example of this is Microsoft Office 98 Manager. In particular, when you select the Customize command, the Customize window doesn't appear.

Fortunately, Apple built a solution into Mac OS 9: you can force the control panel into the Finder's memory space by holding down the Command and Control keys.

This is just a stopgap solution. The technique only works for control panel files containing a 'cdev' resource (see Chapter 8). Further, Apple warns that this work-around will not be included in the next update to the Mac OS. The ultimate solution is for vendors to update their software.

Package Errors

At some point after installing Mac OS 9, a folder's icon may mysteriously change to a blank document icon. When you try to open this folder, you get a cryptic message that says: "The package could not be opened...Try reinstalling the package." The cause of all this is a problem with a new feature of Mac OS 9, called packages.

Happily, Apple has provided a simple fix: drag the problem folder's icon to the Package First Aid utility (which you'll find hidden at the bottom of the Utilities folder on the OS 9 CD). That's it.

Just what is a package? It's a way of grouping an application and related files (such as its Help files) into a single folder called a "package." More technically, a Package is a folder with the "package bit" set that contains exactly one alias file at its root level. Normally, a package will consist of an application and a number of support files organized into subfolders.

The Finder views the package almost like an application. That is, the package acquires the icon of the application whose alias is at the root level. When you double-click the package, that same application is launched. All the additional files in the package are hidden from view, so that you cannot modify or delete them.

The problem occurs when an ordinary folder is mistakenly set to be a package (which Apple claims could happen after a system crash). In this case, the Finder will treat such a folder as a "damaged package" and its icon will appear as a blank document with the kind string set to "package." By the way, if you want to experiment with deliberately creating packages, there are utilities (such as Tape, Instant Package, and even Snitch) that allow you to do so.

The old style Open and Save dialog boxes do not recognize packages. As a result, they may allow you to navigate inside a package to open files there or save documents there. Don't do it. Stay out of these packages. The newer Navigation Services dialog boxes do recognize packages and correctly block access to them.

Mac OS 9 Install Glitches

Hard disk not recognized Apple has identified an issue with a limited number of hard drives that will result in a message, when trying to install Mac OS 9, that says your hard disk is unrecognizable and asks if you want to initialize it - if you startup from the Mac OS 9 CD by holding down the C key at startup. Apple states: "The files and directory structure on these drives are not modified or damaged in any way. Simply select cancel in the dialog box and restart the machine without pressing the 'c' key. After having started up from the computer's hard disk, launch the Startup Disk Control Panel and select the Mac OS 9 disc. Restart the computer and proceed with the Mac OS 9 installation."

Need to start up from OS 9 CD If you have a Power Mac 6100, 7100, or 8100 Mac, Apple has stated that "the computer must be booted from the Mac OS 9 installation CD" in order to install Mac OS 9.

Installer omissions Installers often won't install newer versions of certain files unless it finds the older version already on your drive (this applies to Mac OS 8.x as well). In a few cases, it won't install the new version even if the old version *is* on your drive. For example, if you have moved Sherlock from its default location in the Apple Menu Items folder, the Mac OS Installer will not place the new version on your drive. Similarly, if you have renamed any Mac OS extensions or control panels (perhaps to modify their loading order), these may not get updated—because the Installer does not recognized the altered name.

If you are still having problems getting the Installer to install what you want and just what you want, consider using TomeViewer.

SEE: • Fix-It #4.

Mac OS 9 Alert Boxes

One pleasant new feature of Mac OS 9 is its less obtrusive alert box messages. They are smaller and non-modal. This means that you can ignore them and continue to work without having to dismiss them until you want to take the time to look at them. Not all alert boxes have been converted to this new format.

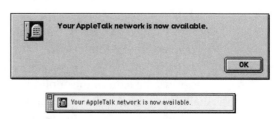

Figure 15-11 An example of the old style (top) and Mac OS 9 style (new) alert boxes.

Mac OS 9's Smarter System Folder Icon

When you drag files to the System Folder icon, the Mac is smarter than ever about knowing the subfolder to which the file belongs. For example, I tried dragging a Desktop Picture file and it was automatically placed correctly.

Assorted Mac OS 8.x/9.x Fixes and Tips

Games on the Mac

Until recently, Apple's reputation as a game machine was not the best. Not only was the selection of games much greater on the PC, but the software and hardware needed for the most demanding games (especially those that pushed speed and 3D effects to the limit, such as top-of-the-line graphics accelerator cards) were lacking on the Mac. Now Apple has aggressively begun to reverse this trend. On the hardware side, Macs come with much faster graphics acceleration cards (via continually updated versions of ATI's Rage cards). On the software side, here's what's happening:

USB The Mac's support of USB has allowed many game hardware devices (such as gamepads and joysticks) developed for the PC to be easily adapted to the Mac. Typically, the only thing needed to get the device to work on a Mac is to write a piece of software called a USB driver. In some cases, the hardware vendor does not even have to write a separate driver for their device. The generic USB software that ships with the Mac OS may be sufficient or, in some cases, preferable.

As with all USB devices, if a gamepad doesn't work (or especially if it appears to precipitate a system crash at startup), restart with the device disconnected. Connect it again after startup is over. This workaround fixes most such problems.

SEE: • Fix-It #14 for more on using USB drivers.

Sprockets Apple has integrated its Sprockets software in the latest version of the Mac OS. These files, stored in the Extensions folder, work with Mac OS 8.1 or later. Apple states: "Apple Game Sprockets is a set of technologies designed to make writing Macintosh games easier for developers. They are designed specifically to provide the functionality that games need on the Macintosh: drawing to the screen, handling input devices, setting up multiplayer games, and simulating 3D sound sources."

There are four kinds of game sprockets: InputSprocket, DrawSprocket, NetSprocket, and SoundSprocket. You will find these files in your Extensions folder. Each of these files provides a different type of game support. For example, InputSprocket is needed to use many of the USB joysticks, gamepads, mice, and keyboards with games that support this Sprocket software.

If you are having problems with playing a certain game, it can often be traced to a problem with one of these Sprocket files. Updating to a newer version, if available, may fix it. As is often the case, occasionally a problem is solved by downgrading to an older version of one of these files. If you are unsure whether or not a version change is required, Web sites (such as my own MacFixIt) will let you know.

BY THE WAY ▶ Generic vs. Device-Specific USB and Sprockets Drivers

Apple's USB and Sprockets software includes "generic" versions of support files. For example, the *USB HID Driver* is a generic driver from Apple that will be used for most unknown USB gaming devices, such as gamepads. If a company makes its own device-specific driver, such as Gravis' *InputSprocket Gravis USB,* this should be used instead. This would mean that when configuring a Gravis GamePad within a game, you should see specific reference to the Gravis device, not a generic device.

However this may not happen. There is a bug in Mac OS 9 that can result in the generic driver being used in error, even if a vendor-specific driver is present. This specific bug will likely be fixed by the time you read this. You should still be aware of this general generic vs. specific driver issue, however, in case similar problems occur down the road.

Open GL OpenGL is a technology that "enables a computer to display three-dimensional graphics using applications designed to take advantage of OpenGL." More specifically, it is used by many 3D games, such as Quake. Since OpenGL is also used on platforms other than the Mac, this makes it much easier for a game developer to port a game from the PC platform to Mac.

OpenGL files are stored in the Extensions folder of your Mac. They include OpenGLEngine, OpenGLUtility, and more. Once again, Apple keeps updating this software. The latest version is available from their Web site. If you are having problems with a game that uses OpenGL, check if a newer version is available. It may be the cure you need.

OpenGL software comes with the Mac OS 9. Newer versions may ship with games that use them.

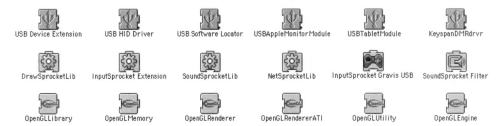

Figure 15-12 Examples of USB (top row), Sprocket (middle row) and OpenGL (bottom row) extensions in the Extensions folder.

TECHNICALLY SPEAKING ▶ Generic vs. Machine-Specific Versions of the System Software CD

A version of the OpenGL software is included on the generic Mac OS 9 CD. However on the machine specific versions that ship with a Mac, you may also find a special folder called Macintosh Computer Software (buried in the Software Installers folder on the CD). This contains a disk image file that includes the OpenGL software as well as some other machine-specific software. The Installer on these CDs will only work on the machines they are designed for (and on these machines an Easy Install should automatically install this software). The Get Info window for these files indicates that they are part of "Mac OS CPU Software" rather than "Mac OS 9.x." On my iMac DV, it installed a newer version of the OpenGL files rather than the ones that came with the generic Mac OS 9 CD.

SEE ALSO: • Fix-It #4 for more on installing system software.

Simple Finder Surprise

Is the Get Info command missing from your File menu? Do other Finder oddities abound? Make sure you have not inadvertently enabled Simple Finder from the Finder's Edit/Preferences/General menu.

List View in Reverse

Are all the files in a Finder window seen in List view in reverse alphabetical order? If so, just click the "pyramid" icon above the scroll bars on the right hand side of the window.

Name	Date Modified	
Fig. 15-15	Today, 12:09 PM	
Fig. 15-14	Today, 12:16 PM	
Fig. 15-10	Today, 12:17 PM	
Fig. 15-09	Today, 12:03 PM	
Fig. 15-08	Today, 12:02 PM	
Fig. 15-07	Today, 12:02 PM	

Figures 15 — 12 items, 76.3 MB available

Figure 15-13 The "sort order" pyramid icon in Finder windows (just above the cursor); it's upside down now, indicating a reverse order sort.

Mac OS 9 Servers Startup Stall

An occasional problem in Mac OS 9 is an extremely long startup time. This can occur in any recent OS version if the correct startup disk is not selected in the Startup Disk control panel. But in Mac OS 9 additionally check the Servers folder in the System Folder. Delete all files located there. The stall should vanish.

SEE ALSO: • **"By the Way: DHCP Leases and the Mac OS 8.6 Stall," in Chapter 12.**

Hardware Data Corruption Risk

Some Mac OS 8.5 users were bit by a bug that caused corruption of data on their hard drive possibly leading to a failure of the drive to mount. Although this only rarely occurred, it is obviously a serious problem if it happens to you. Happily, this was fixed by updating the disk driver using the Drive Setup 1.6.2 version that came with Mac OS 8.5.1. All later versions of Drive Setup also prevent this.

SEE ALSO: • **Chapter 5 on disk problems.**
                   • **Fix-It #12 on updating the disk driver.**

Apple Menu Options Trouble

In Mac OS 8.5/8.6 you may notice an unusual slow down when switching themes or changing the system font in the Appearance control panel. Similar slowdowns can occur when selecting any menu after just switching from one open application to another.

The slowdown is due to a bug in the OS that relates specifically to the Apple Menu Options control panel. It happens only if you have Apple Menu Options enabled and also have an alias to a large folder or volume in your Apple menu (either at the root level or in the Favorites folder).

To solve the problem, delete the alias or if that doesn't do the trick, disable the Apple Menu Options control panel. If you decide to abandon Apple Menu Options but don't want to give up on its features, try one of several shareware alternatives (such as BeHierarchic and MenuChoice).

This bug appears to be fixed in Mac OS 9.

Resolution Shifts

Does your monitor start up in 640X480 resolution and then switch to your preferred resolution later in the startup sequence? If so, this is probably not a bug, but a feature. Most likely, there is a newer video driver in the Mac OS software than the one in the ROM hardware of your Mac. If so, the correct resolution does not appear until this newer driver loads. In fact, if you startup with extensions off, the resolution may never shift and you will wind up with a 640x480 display even after startup is over. Exactly if and when this happens depends upon what Mac you are using, what monitor you have and what version of the OS you are running.

ObjectSupportLib

ObjectSupportLib is an extension from System 7.x that is no longer needed in Mac OS 8.0 or later. The problem is that some third-party software installers still mistakenly install it. Even worse, if it gets installed by mistake, it can lead to a system crash. So if you have otherwise unexplained crashes, especially in the Finder shortly after starting up, check for this file.

A "trick" to prevent this OSL file from getting installed in error is to create a blank document (say from SimpleText and name it "ObjectSupportLib." Next lock this document by checking the "lock" checkbox in the file's Get Info window. Finally, move this file to the Extensions folder. This will block an Installer from installing the real file with the same name.

Note: The OSL file is still found on installer CDs, such as the Mac OS CD that ships with your Mac. This is OK. Don't worry about it.

And Elsewhere in *Sad Macs*

Mac OS 8.6 Font bug

SEE ALSO: • "Take Note: "Fonts, FONDS and a Mac OS 8.6 Font bug," in Chapter 9.

Navigation Services

SEE ALSO: • "Open and Save Dialog Boxes," in Chapter 6.

Network Browser, File Sharing via TCP/IP

SEE ALSO: • "Transfer Files via File Sharing," in Chapter 11.

HFS Plus

SEE ALSO: • "Take Note: Mac OS Standard (HFS) vs. Mac OS Extended (HFS Plus) Formats," in Fix-It #13.

BY THE WAY ▶ **"Hidden" Mac OS Features**

Here are some lesser-known "hidden" features of the Mac OS.

Mac OS 9 About This Computer hidden features The About This Computer window has been enhanced with some new capabilities in Mac OS 9. For example, if you double-click any name in the list of open applications, you are now directly taken to that application. You can similarly drag a document icon to the application's name and (assuming the application can read the document) the document will open in that application. If you Command-click the Mac OS 9 logo and you are online, you will be taken to the Mac OS 9 home page.

Application Switcher hidden features There are a number of "hidden" options when using Application Switcher, also known as Application Menu (it's the menu on the far right side that lists applications' names):

• **Tear it off** You can create an Application Switcher window on your desktop by dragging the cursor from the dropped-down Application menu to the desktop. Try clicking and Option-clicking or Option-Shift-clicking the zoom box in the upper right of this window for some more surprises. (**Note:** There are some special options only available by clicking links in the ""Switching between open programs" page of Mac Help. If you use them, you may have to use them a second time to "undo" their effect.)

(continues on next page)

- **Drag and drop** If you drag a document icon to an application listing in the floating Application Switcher, it will open the document in that application, just as if you had dragged to the document's icon to the application icon directly. This can be especially convenient if you want to open a document (an HTML file for example) in an application other than the one that created it and the desired application's icon is not readily accessible.

- **Changing Command-Tab** Application Switcher's use of Command-Tab to select among currently open applications overrides whatever function Command-Tab may have had within a given application. If this is a problem for you, you can assign something other than Command-Tab to the Application Switcher. To do this, go to Mac Help, and locate the item called "Switching between open programs." Then locate the link that says "Help me modify the keyboard shortcuts." Click it and follow the instructions.

- **Auto-hide** If you Option-Click an application in Application Switcher, the application becomes active *and* the previously active application becomes "hidden."

Screen capture hidden features Most people know that Command-Shift-3 takes a "screen-dump" of your Macintosh screen, placing a PICT file of the screen on your desktop. But did you know that Command-Shift-4 lets you select an area to capture with your cursor? And that Command-Shift-Caps Lock-4 takes a picture of just the window that you click with the mouse? Finally, Command-Shift-Control-3 sends the screen dump directly to the Clipboard rather than creating a file on the desktop. This was all first introduced in Mac OS 7.6.

Still more Press Command-Delete after selecting an item and the item is automatically moved to the Trash. Select an alias and hit Command-R and you will "reveal" the original file. In older versions of the Mac OS, you needed shareware utilities such as 8Tuner (which does not work with Mac OS 9) and Jerry's Finder Patch to "unlock" these features. Starting with Mac OS 8.5, at least some of these features (including the two just mentioned) are built directly into the Finder.

    With these same shareware utilities, you will be able to add even more new features to the Finder. These include adding Command-key shortcuts for virtually any Finder command as well as changing the default suffixes/names assigned to aliases, copied files and untitled folders.

SEE ALSO: • **Chapter 6 for more on the Application Menu.**

Figure 15-14
Two variations of the Application Switcher menu display after it has been "torn off" of the menu bar.

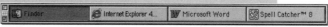

TAKE NOTE ▶ Mac OS 9 Upgrades

Mac OS 9.0.4 was released in April 2000. It is a bug fix upgrade, especially fixing some USB and FireWire problems. It also improves networking performance and audio/video functionality. It introduced no new features. Mac OS 9.0.2 and 9.0.3 shipped with some Macs prior to the release of Mac OS 9.0.4. They were essentially "beta" versions of 9.0.4. All of these Mac OS 9.0.x updates include a PowerPC Enabler file, not present in the original Mac OS 9. This file is needed for compatibility with Apple's newest hardware.

    Released at the same time as Mac OS 9.0.4 was DVD Player 2.2. You will need it after updating to Mac OS 9.0.4. DVD Player 2.0 or earlier will not work with Mac OS 9.0.4.

Mac OS X

Mac OS X Server and NetBoot

From their names, you might think that Mac OS X Server and Mac OS X are very similar. You would be wrong. At least at present, Mac OS X Server has none of the spectacular user interface features that are drawing attention to Mac OS X (described below). Instead, with Mac OS X Server, you are likely to be typing Unix commands in a command-line interface. Very much not "Mac-like." The main thing that Mac OS X and Mac OS X Server have in common, besides their similar names, is the underlying Darwin core.

SEE: • **"Technically Speaking: What's under the hood of Mac OS X?.**

As its name implies, Mac OS X Server is designed to run on a machine that serves software to a variety of other client machines connected to it on a local network. In this regard, it is similar to AppleShare IP, which Mac OS X Server will eventually replace.

Apple is quite clear. The Mac OS X Server machine itself is not intended for end users. It is for "experienced system and network administrators, who typically have had previous experience with configuring and managing AppleShare IP, At Ease for Workgroups, complicated networks, (including routing between subnets) and/or other Unix servers (such as Solaris and Linux)."

It is the client machines connected to the Server that are used by end users. For example, a classroom computer lab would be a great place for a Mac OS X Server connected to a dozen or more client iMacs. Client Macs can only be NewWorld Macs (iMacs or newer, as defined in Chapter 14).

Because the OS is not for end users, coverage of Mac OS X Server is beyond the scope of this book. However, in case you ever use a Mac OS X Server client machine, there is one thing that you should definitely know about: NetBooting.

NetBoot

The most spectacular feature of Mac OS X Server is NetBooting. This allows client Macs on the network to start up from a NetBoot "startup disk" on the Server, rather than from the client's own internal hard drive. I saw a demo of this with 50 NetBooted iMacs running off of one server—all playing the same QuickTime movie. It was very impressive!

For NetBooting to work, you must have an Ethernet network; 100Base-T is almost required if you want decent speed.

The user of a client Mac chooses at startup whether to boot from the machine's own drive or to NetBoot. To NetBoot, just hold down the N key at startup. Or select Network Disk as the startup disk from the Startup Disk control panel

All NetBooted Macs share the same startup disk System Folder, as stored on the Server. This greatly simplifies the task of maintaining the client Macs with the same (and the latest) version of shared software. Still, a NetBooted Mac *can* appear to make changes (such as adding a font) to the NetBoot startup disk's System Folder. However, the change is only temporary. What actually happens is that the changes are made to a shadow image version of the startup disk image. The Server maintains a separate shadow image for each client Mac. But the shadow image is discarded when the client shuts down their Mac, which means that none of the shadow image changes are saved across sessions.

If you are running from a NetBooted Mac, expect a few oddities. For example, information in the Memory control panel may be incorrect. To view the actual memory settings, choose About This Computer from the Apple menu. Also, applications that store Preferences in the application's folder rather than in the System Folder may have problems because the Applications HD image (used to store applications accessed via NetBoot) is read only. Check Apple TIL articles (http://til.info.apple.com/) for the latest details and workarounds.

Mac OS X and Aqua

Mac OS X is a complete overhaul of the Mac OS. It is not an update to the Mac OS. It is really a new OS altogether. Its roots are in the NeXTStep OS that was acquired by Apple when it purchased NeXT. NeXTStep, in turn, is based on Unix, a not very user-friendly OS that was originally designed for mainframe computers rather than desktop ones. During the long development of Mac OS X, many people began to fear that this new OS was going to abandon the user-friendly interface that has been the core of Apple's success in favor of a possibly more powerful but certainly more arcane Unix-based OS.

This anxiety has now been vastly reduced. Partly this is because Unix, in the form of the Linux variation now available for many platforms including the Mac, has become quite fashionable. Some analysts even see Linux as an eventual threat to the dominance of Microsoft's Windows OS. So basing a Mac OS on Unix is not nearly so frightening a prospect as it once might have seemed.

The other mitigating factor is that (at least based on previews) not only will Mac OS X be retaining the Mac OS's inherent interface advantages, but it will be greatly expanding them. The Unix base, while still there, will be largely hidden from the user experience. Instead, users will see a dramatic new interface that Apple has named Aqua.

If things go well, Mac OS X could prove to have almost as much impact on the computer industry as the original Mac OS did more than 15 years ago. For now, here's what we do know.

Will There Be Multiple OS Versions Supported Simultaneously?

No! Apple will be pushing for all Mac users to eventually upgrade to Mac OS X. Mac OS 9 will be the last version of the old Mac OS to be developed. By January of 2001 Apple expects to be shipping all of their Mac hardware with Mac OS X pre-installed. So Mac OS X is in your future.

Will My Old Mac OS 9 Applications Still Run in Mac OS X?

Yes. All applications that currently run in Mac OS 9 will run in Mac OS X. However exactly how they will run requires a bit more explaining. There will be three Mac OS X modes:

Classic In Classic mode, Mac OS 9 applications will run just as they do in Mac OS 9. They will take absolutely no advantage of any of the new features of Mac OS X.

Carbon A Mac OS 9 application can be "carbonized" by the developer. This requires making some changes that Apple claims are rather minimal and easy-to-do (although I have seen some conflicting reports that suggest things may not work quite as smoothly as Apple suggests). After making these changes, a Mac OS 9 application will run in Mac OS X and also take advantage of most of the major new features of the OS. I expect that most popular applications will be Carbonized. Those that are not will be doomed to eventually fade away.

Cocoa This is the environment for those applications that are written more-or-less from scratch for Mac OS X. They will be able to take advantage of the new OS's object-oriented features. An email program, to ship with Mac OS X, will probably be the first available Cocoa application.

What Macs Will Be Needed to Run Mac OS X?

As of this writing, Apple has still not made an official pronouncement about this. But the general opinion is that Mac OS X will run at least on any Mac that originally shipped with a G3 or G4 processor: from the original beige G3s through the iMacs, iBooks, and G4s. Whether older Macs upgraded with G3 processors will be able to run Mac OS X is still an open question. My guess is that the official answer will be no, although inventive third parties may find away around this.

TECHNICALLY SPEAKING ▶ What's Under the Hood of Mac OS X?

The core OS of Mac OS X is called Darwin. This is where features such as protected memory and preemptive multi-tasking originate. This is also where its Unix-based kernel and networking support can be found.

Layered on top of Darwin are three graphics technologies that form the foundation for how things will look and work. These are Apple's familiar QuickTime (for video), the more recently added OpenGL (for 3D graphics; see "Games on the Mac," earlier in this chapter), and the brand new Quartz (for 2D graphics). Quartz is based on Adobe's PDF (Portable Document Format) technology (the same format used in Acrobat). This means that Quartz delivers "on-the-fly rendering, anti-aliasing and compositing of PostScript graphics with pristine quality." Most of the "look" of the Aqua interface depends on the use of Quartz.

The next layer includes the Classic, Carbon, and Cocoa modes referred to in the main text. And sitting on top of all of that is the Aqua interface itself.

What's New in Mac OS X and Aqua of Special Interest to Troubleshooting?

For troubleshooting, Mac OS X provides several welcome and long-promised additions:

Protected Memory Although not one of the glitzy new features of Aqua, this may well be the one that I most welcome. With protected memory, each open application runs in its own "separate" memory space isolated from each other. The result of this is that, if an application crashes, it only brings down the application itself. Everything else continues to run as normal. This means that you should never (almost never?) have to restart your Mac after an application crash (avoiding all the lost data and time wasted that this typically entails).

Improved Virtual Memory Mac OS X has improved on the virtual memory feature found in previous OS versions. It works with protected memory so that "you no longer have to worry about how much memory an application like Photoshop needs to open large files. When an application needs memory, the virtual memory manager automatically allocates precisely the amount of memory needed—no more and no less." The result? Out-of-memory messages may practically vanish altogether.

Preemptive Multitasking These days, most Mac users are doing multiple tasks on their Mac at the same time. For example, they may be working on a memo in a word processor while waiting for a Web page to load. With preemptive multitasking, the Mac prioritizes these tasks, giving most of the Mac's resources to the tasks deemed most important, and in general trying to maximize the overall performance of everything currently running. No more will the activity of some minor background process be able to hog all the processor's attention while a much more critical foreground task grinds practically to a halt.

The Finder and the Desktop are separate
In Mac OS 9 (and all earlier versions of the OS), the words "Finder" and "Desktop" were almost synonymous. When the Desktop was active, with all of its icons and windows in the foreground, you were also said to be in the Finder. In Mac OS X, this is no longer the case. The Finder is now a separate application, much like any other application, with its own Finder window. The Desktop is a separate entity that forms the background environment.

Figure 15-15 Two views of the Finder in Mac OS X's Aqua interface: the single window view (top) and the column view (bottom).

Further, you can navigate the Mac OS X Finder in three different ways. In the first way, opening a folder opens a new window, essentially as it works in Mac OS 9. In the second method, when you open a folder, the contents of the just opened folder replace the contents previously displayed in the same window. Back and Forward buttons allow you to navigate among the folders you have opened. Both of these methods can use the Icon and List views of Mac OS 9.

The third variation is a navigational column view. It uses columns to list the contents of each folder. Clicking a folder creates a new column view (of the contents of the new folder) to the right of the previous folder view. The column view can also display previews of files, and let you watch portions of movie files.

What Else Is New in the Mac OS X/Aqua Interface?

Windows and the Dock Desktop windows in Aqua have three jewel-like buttons on their title bars for closing, maximize, and minimizing the window. If "minimizing" sounds reminiscent of the MS Windows Task Bar, you've only got the basic idea.

The Mac OS X "task bar" is called the Dock. It rolls up from the bottom of the display when you move your cursor there, or you can have it displayed full time. It includes the Trash, and thumbnails of minimized windows. When you click the minimize button, the window morphs into the Dock, looking like it's pouring into a thumbnail. These thumbnails are live, too, so if you minimize a QuickTime movie, it continues to play.

When the Dock gets full, it shrinks to accommodate more thumbnails. You can also set the Dock's size. When Dock is tiny, a feature called Magnification enlarges the thumbnails when you move the cursor over them. You can also change the size of icons on the Desktop.

A really useful feature promises to eliminate desktop clutter. A button in the upper right of each window puts the desktop into "single Window mode," which puts all other windows in the Dock. When you pick another window in the Dock, it switches places with the open window, so that you only have one open window at a time.

New Save dialog boxes When you save a document in Aqua, it no longer brings up a modal Save dialog box. Instead, the Save features are attached to the window of the document you are trying to save, scrolling down from the title bar, so you always know exactly what file you will be saving.

Extensions gone Extensions that currently load at startup will not work in Mac OS X.

What else is new? The interface makes liberal use of translucent 3-D, drop-shadow enhanced buttons, sliders, windows and icons, giving everything an almost-liquid appearance—hence the name Aqua. For more information, visit Apple's Mac OS X Web site: http://www.apple.com/macosx/. Or if it is out by the time you read this, try out Mac OS X yourself.

Using MacFixIt

I am sure by this point in the book, my final advice will be far from a shock: to get the latest troubleshooting information about Mac OS X and as well as whatever other OS version you may be using, check out MacFixIt (http://www.macfixit.com). Think of MacFixIt as a free update to this book.

PART III

Disaster Relief: The Fix-Its

Meet the Fix-Its. The Fix-Its are a collection of sixteen topics that cover the entire range of problem-solving techniques. Think of them as a set of descriptive troubleshooting tools, the metaphorical equivalent of hardware tools such as a screwdriver or a hammer. Where previous chapters are organized according to symptoms, the Fix-Its are organized according to the tools themselves. There are two ways to use this Fix-It section.

First, and most common, you are sent here via a cross-reference from an earlier chapter of this book. In this case, these Fix-Its are an extension of the step-by-step procedures listed in the previous chapters. Assuming you are still hunting for a solution to your problem, here is where you continue the hunt. These Fix-Its detail frequently cited techniques, avoiding the need to repeat this information every time it is relevant.

Second, I have tried to make each Fix-It stand as a self-contained tutorial on its subject. Thus, if you want to learn about viruses (what they are, how they originate, and how to protect yourself against them), turn to Fix-It #6. This can be useful regardless of whether you are referred there from a previous chapter. To make these Fix-Its independent, some material presented earlier in the book is repeated here, but I have tried to keep this to a minimum.

Each Fix-It is divided into five parts:

1. **Quick Summary.** This briefly describes the key procedure(s) of the Fix-It.

2. **When to Do It.** This section summarizes the common situations and symptoms that suggest the use of the Fix-It. When to Do It is especially useful if you are browsing through the Fix-Its, without having been directed here from a previous chapter.

   Be aware that many of the symptoms described in this section appear in more than one Fix-It. For example, a system crash may point to many different causes, including an extension conflict, a damaged preferences file, a virus, or more. Therefore when you see your symptom listed for a particular Fix-It, do not immediately assume you have found the cause of your problem. To diagnose a particular problem, you are better off starting your search in Part II, which also gives suggested sequences for trying the Fix-Its, the precise order varying according to the particular problem at hand.

3. **Why to Do It.** This section briefly summarizes the rationale behind each procedure and what you can expect it to accomplish. Here, more than in the other sections, you can gain insight as to why a given solution works.

4. **What to Do.** This is the main section of each Fix-It. Here is where you'll find the actual procedures and step-by-step instructions. Some of these sections are relatively brief; others are lengthy. In general, they follow the What to Do format of the previous chapters.

5. **For Related Information.** This last section is a list of cross-references that tell you where to go to further investigate selected topics mentioned in the Fix-It.

Disaster Relief: The Fix-Its

Fix-It #1: Resolve Hardware and Software Incompatibilities

▶ **QUICK SUMMARY**

Read the manuals (as well as any on-disk Read Me files) that come with your software and hardware in order to determine what known incompatibility problems may exist. Check to see if upgrading, downgrading or modifying settings of software may be able to work around the problem. Check for adapters or cards that may enable a hardware device to work.

 When to Do It:

- Before installing or using any new hardware or software. Even better, if you can find out incompatibility information before you purchase a product, you may save yourself from buying a product you cannot use.

- If an application fails to launch successfully (possibly even causing a system error) the first time you use it.

- Similarly, if an application fails to launch successfully the first time you try it after having made a change in your hardware configuration.

- If a hardware device fails to work properly, or does not work at all, the very first time you try to use it.

 Why to Do It:

Few things are as frustrating as opening up a new software package or unpacking a new piece of hardware only to find that it will not work on your Mac because of a hardware incompatibility. In recent years, there is both good news and bad news in this regard.

The good news is that Apple has dramatically simplified its product line. This means you no longer have to worry about whether some new program will work with any or all of 30 or more different Mac models. There are only 4 basic Mac models: the iMac, the G3 desktops, the iBook, the desktop PowerMacs and the PowerBooks.

The bad news is that the newest Macs represent a major departure from previous Mac models. None of the current Macs come with a floppy disk drive. This means that unless you buy a peripheral floppy drive, any software you have that comes on a floppy disk is instantly unusable. I describe more issues with peripheral devices and new Macs later in this Fix-It.

Beyond this, there are still a myriad of ways that Macs can be modified, each of which can introduce potential compatibility problems with existing or future software.

For example, you may get a CPU upgrade, a RAM upgrade, a new third party monitor, or a new printer.

The software itself can introduce other incompatibilities. In particular, a given piece of software or hardware may require that the OS be at least Mac OS 9.0. Or it may require at least a G3 processor with at least 64MB of RAM. Unless you meet such requirements, you will not be able to use the software.

What to Do:

General Strategies

1. **Check manuals, Read Me files, and Apple Guide Help.** The first thing to do to check if a problem is attributable to an incompatibility between a particular product and your current hardware and software is to check the documentation that came with the product. The basic requirements are usually clearly stated (although in fine print) right on the box. Check this out before you even open the box. This will tell you if you have the right Mac OS, processor, amount of RAM, and so on. Otherwise, check the Read Me file or printed documentation that came with the product. Manuals typically inform you of potential incompatibilities as well as minimal hardware requirements. For example, if an application requires a PowerPC processor or Mac OS 9.0, the manual should tell you that.

   Of course, conflicts with products that were not released until after the manual was published will not be mentioned. Thus problems may occur that are not cited in the manuals.

   If this information cannot be found in the product you just bought, check the manual(s) that came with your existing hardware and software for possible help. For example, if you added a PCI card to a Mac, it may list compatibility issues relevant to other hardware that you may later add.

   Increasingly, vendors are depending on the use of Apple's Help for their critical documentation, rather than printed material. So check there as well. Another trend: shipping the documentation on the same CD-ROM disc (often in Acrobat format or as HTML files) that contains the application. Finally, you may have to go to the vendor's Web site to get the needed help.

   If you cannot find the relevant manuals, or they don't contain the information you are seeking, call the manufacturer of the program directly.

TECHNICALLY SPEAKING ▶ **Learning the Lowdown on Your Hardware**

The more you understand the characteristics of your Macintosh model, the easier it will be to discover hardware incompatibilities. Throughout this book, I have referred to the different characteristics of the different models of Macintosh but often only in a general way. These days, to get a good summary of the details of the hardware for every Mac ever made, check out Apple Spec, a FileMaker document that Apple updates periodically after new models come out. It's available at many online locations including Apple's software updates sites (such as <http://asu.info.apple.com/swupdates.nsf/artnum/n11135>). For details on your particular Mac, select Apple System Profiler from the Apple menu.

2. **Adjust settings.** Some hardware-related incompatibilities can be partially solved by a work-around with your current software. In particular, certain control panels and Get Info settings have options that inactivate or modify problem-causing hardware features, enabling you to use otherwise incompatible applications. There is an possible trade-off here: you may lose the advantage of whatever feature you turn off or reduce in order to obtain the needed compatibility.

   Many of these options are described elsewhere. Here are three common examples:

   Memory control panel settings. Increasing (or in some cases, decreasing) the size of the disk cache may help. Increasing the disk cache to at least the default level (if it is not there already) will usually boost overall performance of your Mac. In order to make adjustments to the disk cache size, first select the "Custom setting" radio button.

   Monitor depth and resolution. Some problems only occur with certain resolution sizes or color depths. Try changing these from the Monitors & Sounds control panel(s) or from the matching Control Strip modules. This issue is particularly likely to come up when playing games.

   Increase an application's memory. Do this by adjusting the Preferred Size in the Memory control panel (see Fix-It #5).

   More generally, games often place particularly hard demands on the processor and memory. As such, their Preferences settings may offer various options to help reduce that demand for Macs that don't have enough hardware power. For example, they may turn off music or eliminate certain details in the graphics.

3. **Upgrade software or hardware, as needed.** With luck, a new version of the relevant software either already exists or will be released shortly that eliminates the incompatibilities. In any case, as a preventative measure, you should keep your software current.

   If you have a current version of the application, it may be your system software that is not current. Assuming your hardware supports the upgrade, you may need to upgrade from Mac OS 8 to Mac OS 9, for example.

   For hardware devices, such as printers or scanners, upgrading the software driver used with the device may solve the problem.

   Otherwise, you may need to purchase new hardware that eliminates the incompatibilities. This can include anything from adding more memory to getting a logic board upgrade that essentially transforms your machine into a newer model. In the most extreme case, you may have to purchase a new Macintosh.

4. **Don't be a pioneer.** In general, you can keep compatibility problems to a minimum by not rushing to be the first on your block to purchase a newly released model of Macintosh or upgrading to a major revision in the operating system. I try to wait at least 4 to 6 months after a machine comes out before I consider buying it. By then, most of the software companies have had a chance to upgrade their software to meet the demands of the new machine, and Apple has had a chance to correct any

minor glitches in the product. For system software upgrades, I confess to upgrading immediately (but I often pay for this with frequent problems for the next several months until the kinks get worked out).

A Few Common Hardware Incompatibilities

Graphics Accelerators, Video RAM

If you want to play today's 3-D super-realistic games, and you want them to have smooth motion, textured graphics, great 3-D effects and more, you need a video accelerator. Fortunately, such a capability is built into all current Mac models. The G4 Macs, for example, currently ship with a Rage Pro 128 accelerator. If you have an older Mac, that does not have such a card, you will need one for game playing. The Voodoo 2 card is another popular choice.

A graphics accelerator card typically includes its own video RAM. This VRAM (as described more in Chapter 10) is the basis for the limits on how many colors you can see on the screen at one time and what the resolution of the monitor can be. If you find that there is a resolution or color depth that you want or need, but your Mac will not let you select it, you may need to add more video RAM. In some cases, you can add this extra RAM to the graphics accelerator card. In other cases, your only alternative may be to get a new card. If your Mac does not have a separate accelerator card, it will typically use separate VRAM that is included directly on the logic board. In most cases, you are able to add additional VRAM up to some limit associated with the machine. However, your Mac may already ship with the limit reached.

G3/G4 Processor Upgrades

Perhaps the best feature of Apple's PCI Macintoshes (which began with the 7500, 8500, and 9500 back in 1995) is that they have an upgradable processor slot. This means that you can simply remove the processor that came with the Mac and replace it with another, presumably faster one. It is as easy as adding RAM. Users who purchased a Power Mac 7500 with its original 100MHz 601 PPC processor were soon using a much faster 200MHz 604 PPC processor. Even greater benefits came to those who waited to upgrade to a G3 processor. These cards have been among the hottest selling products for the Mac. For the first time in the history of the Mac, upgrading your Mac's processor was often more cost effective than simply selling your old Mac and buying a new one.

In newer Macs, processor upgrades are no longer done via a processor card but via a Zero-Insertion-Force (ZIF) module. However the principle remains the same.

But occasional problems cropped up. In a bizarre symptom, some software installers (including Apple's own Mac OS updates) failed to work with certain processor upgrade cards. The only solution here was to temporarily return the original processor (assuming you still had it) to perform the installation. In another case, there were reports of hard drives corrupted when certain G3 upgrade cards were in use, especially if the Mac also had a separate PCI SCSI card installed (although the drive that would get corrupted need not be connected to the SCSI card). This problem has now been largely resolved by fixes to the cards themselves. But if you have an older card (circa 1998), you should check with the vendor about this potential problem.

Of more widespread significance, older non-G3 Macs that are upgraded with G3 or G4 processors may not be able to run software that Macs that were "born" with a G3 processor can run. Perhaps the first example of this was Connectix's Virtual Game Station. This Sony PlayStation emulator was recommended only for true G3 Macs. The reason for this did not really have anything to do with the processor itself. It was because the system bus speed (see Fix-It #15 for more on bus speeds) was faster on the newer Macs, and this increase in speed was needed to run the game. As we go to press, the word is the Mac OS X will similarly only run on Macs that have G3 or G4 processors from birth.

There is a more general truth here: upgrading an older Mac with a newer processor, while providing a significant speed boost, will not give you a Mac that is as fast as a new machine with the same processor. New machines benefit from more than just a faster processor.

Finally, if you have a Mac that is not even a PowerPC, there is much software that you will be unable to use. Although developers originally wrote software in both 68K and PPC versions, the trend is towards just having a PPC version now.

SEE: • "Processor Upgrades," in Fix-It #15, for more information on this topic, especially "Take Note: G3 and G4 Upgrades: Speculative Addressing and Altivec Support."

Epson Printers

For some reason that I do not entirely understand, problems seem to crop up that are associated with Epson inkjet printers more often than for any other type of printer. Maybe it's just that they are so popular that there are more people to report these problems. Don't get me wrong, these are great printers, producing photo-realistic print-outs that rival taking your film to be developed by Kodak, but they have their quirks.

Here are two recent examples: (1) When trying to print anything from AppleWorks 5.0.4 (as well as several other applications) to an Epson Color Stylus 900, some letters and/or numbers only print halfway. An updated version of the driver fixed this. Otherwise, selecting a different font or font size may work around the problem. (2) You cannot select the Epson driver from the Chooser if any of the ink cartridges are empty. However you will not get a message informing you of the cause; instead, it will simply seem as if there is something wrong with the Chooser.

Connecting Peripheral Devices to Newer Macs

The iMac (and all other current Mac models) do not have serial ports, ADB ports, or SCSI ports. This means, for example, that an external modem, a graphics tablet, or any other device that used the serial port cannot be directly attached to the iMac. Similarly, any SCSI devices (such as the popular Zip and Jaz drives) cannot be attached. Fortunately, there are many alternative solutions.

For starters, the iMac does have USB ports. USB ports are much faster than serial or ADB ports (although significantly slower than SCSI). Companies like Iomega now

Fix-It
#1

make USB versions of their drives. Depending upon the product, you may be able to get a special adapter cable that lets your serial device plug-in to the USB port (HP printer example) or you may get a separate "hub" that lets you plug any of an assortment of devices into it. This can be especially useful if you wish to connect an iMac on a LocalTalk network (as the iMac has no built-in LocalTalk connection; it communicates over networks only via Ethernet). Conversely, if you have an older Mac that does not have a USB port, you can get a device that allows you to use USB devices.

Apple's newest Macs also have FireWire ports. FireWire is Apple's replacement for SCSI. You can now get FireWire hard drives, CD/DVD drives and scanners. However if you have legacy SCSI devices, you can still connect them to desktop Power Macs via a SCSI port, if you purchase a SCSI card for one of the PCI slots in the Mac. Even here, there is some reason for caution. Some SCSI cards may allow you to startup from drives connected to the card, while others will not. If you expect to want to use a SCSI hard drive as a startup drive, make sure you get a card that supports this. For the iMac, you cannot add a SCSI card. Your only option here is to get a SCSI-to-USB adapter. While this will allow you to use your SCSI device, it will be slowed down to the USB speed. Also, due to various potential incompatibilities (such as with the USB software), not all SCSI devices will work when connected via these adapters.

 ## For Related Information

SEE: • Fix-It #4 on system software problems.
• Fix-It #5 on memory-related problems.
• Fix-It #12 on disk drivers.
• Fix-It #14 on USB, SCSI, FireWire and other peripheral device connection issues.
• Fix-It #15 on diagnosing hardware problems.
• Fix-It #16 on calling technical support and seeking outside help.
• Chapter 10 on monitor-related problems.
• Chapter 11 on PowerBooks.
• Chapter 14 on Power Macs.
• Chapter 15 on new system software.

Fix-It #2:
Delete or Replace Preferences, Plug-ins, and Related Files

▶ QUICK SUMMARY

Delete a program's preferences file and/or system software preferences file (such as Finder Preferences), usually found in the Preferences Folder of the startup disk's System Folder. Similarly, make sure plug-in (and other accessory) files are correctly installed and updated. If the latest version is already installed, consider replacing it.

 ## When to Do It:

- When any changes you have made to preference settings are unexpectedly lost. For example, customized settings in a word processor, such as fonts and margin settings, may be different from the defaults.

- Whenever you have a problem using a specific feature of an application or control panel, such as a command that does not work or a dialog box that does not appear as expected. Be especially suspicious if that feature worked properly on previous occasions.

- Whenever an extension does not load or work; especially suspect system software preferences files such as Finder Preferences. Examples of system software known to have preferences file-related problems include the Finder, the Network extension, and PC Exchange.

- If an application specifically requests that you locate a missing accessory file either via an Open dialog box or via an alert message.

- If selected features (such as menu commands or dialog box options) of an application are dimmed, missing, or do not work. Rarely, the program may not even launch.

 ## Why to Do It:

Preferences Files

Basics Preferences files are used mainly to store customized settings. For example, a word processor may include a checkbox to turn smart quotes on or off. Whichever selection you make, the program remembers it even after you have quit the application. It usually does this by storing your choice in the application's preferences file. This way, you do not have to reselect the desired settings each time you relaunch the application or open a new document.

Preferences files typically have names like Word Settings or Excel Preferences and they are usually located in the System Folder. They are usually in a special folder called

Preferences. In some cases, preferences files can be stored in the same folder as the application. Or they may be found in the Application Support folder of the System Folder. Usually the program finds its preferences file whether it is with the application or in the System Folder. Not all programs have preference files, but most do.

Many control panels (including those that come with the System Software) also have their own Preferences files. These include, for example, Apple Menu Options Prefs, Sound Preferences, and Display Preferences.

Deleting Preferences files Preferences files are among the most often modified files on your drive. Certainly every time you change a preference setting, the file gets modified. For some programs, the preferences files is updated every time the program is launched. As such, they are especially at risk for becoming "damaged." This damage in turn can lead to a variety of symptoms, including system freezes and crashes. If this happens, the solution is to delete the preferences file. The application then recreates a new default preferences file the next time the program is launched. This probably means that all of your customized settings are lost, but at least you no longer have the symptom that led to your decision to delete the file.

A related issue can occur when you upgrade to a new version of a program. Often, even if you exactly follow the program's upgrade instructions, the previous version's preferences file is not replaced during the upgrade procedure. This can leave you with two preferences files for the same application (often with slightly different names, such as "Excel Settings (4)" and "Excel Settings (8)"). Normally, no harm will come from this. But, to be safe, it is best to delete the old, now unused Preferences file, as soon as you confirm that the updated application is working as expected.

More than just Preferences in the Preferences folder In recent years, the contents of the Preferences folder have expanded to include items that go way beyond ordinary Preferences files. Many applications now even install one or more folders in the Preferences files, each of which contain an assortment of files. Web browsers, such as Netscape Navigator and Communicator, are well-known for doing this. For example, the Netscape ƒ contains Netscape Preferences, Bookmarks.html, Global History, MagicCookie, and several more items, including yet another folder-within-a-folder called Java. Some of these items are automatically recreated the next time you launch the application. Others are not; if you delete these, the only way to get them back is to reinstall them. Also, many applications store a file that contains registration data, needed to even launch an application, in a Preferences folder. This means that you can no longer be so cavalier about trashing preferences files. Certainly, you should never simply trash the entire Preferences folder. Some files are recommended to delete when trouble strikes. Others are not. For example, deleting the Java folder would be a bad idea. It will result in Netscape browsers no longer being able to run Java applets. On the other hand, deleting the Global History file is known to solve cases where Netscape is loading pages particularly slowly.

Instead of simply deleting your entire Preferences folder, your best bet is to try to determine what, if any, Preferences file is causing a problem and then delete that specific file. If you are uncertain of what can or cannot be deleted, check your software's manuals or ask for outside help.

Shifting System Folders One other preference file related oddity may occur: if you start up your Mac with a different System Folder and/or startup drive (such as a second hard drive) than the one you typically use, you will shift to the Preferences files in that System Folder. This means that you are likely to lose any custom settings you may have made. If this becomes a common problem, you will likely want to copy over your custom preference files to each System Folder you use. Of course, if you are starting up from a CD-ROM drive, you won't be able to do this, as you cannot write to a CD-ROM disc.

There is one unusual exception here: Netscape browsers use the Preferences file in the System Folder that was assigned when the application was installed, even if you shift System Folders.

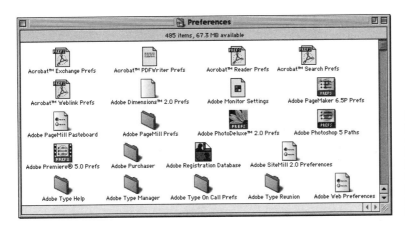

Figure F2-1 A peek inside a Preferences folder. There are 485 Preferences files and folders within (and some of the folders have dozens of additional files within). In this peek, just about all you see are Preferences files related to Adobe software.

Plug-Ins and Other Accessory Files

Another type of file that can cause problems in a way similar to Preferences files are plug-in files. Most applications do not use plug-ins, but several important applications do. These include Photoshop (and several other Adobe applications) and Web browsers (both Netscape browsers and Internet Explorer). These files typically reside in a folder (often called Plug-ins) that is stored in the same folder as the application itself. In other cases, they may be stored in the Preferences folder. Or they may be stored, possibly together with other application-related files, in the Application Support folder of the System Folder.

Problems related to these plug-ins fall into one of three categories:

Plug-in is missing or mislocated. If the plug-in is not in its expected location, the application will typically not recognize its presence and whatever feature the plug-in is supposed to provide will be missing. Normally an application's Installer should place such files in their correct location, but it may make a mistake. Or you may inadvertently move (or even delete) these files.

Plug-in is the wrong version. It is possible that an application will install an out-of-date version of a plug-in. In doing so, it may even overwrite (and therefore delete) a newer version that was already on your drive. This is especially of concern with plug-ins for Web browsers, as applications other than the Web browser itself may install browser plug-ins. For example, Apple's QuickTime installs a QuickTime Plug-in in the plug-ins folder of your browser. In this regard, if you use both Navigator and Explorer, remember that you will have to install browser plug-ins for both browsers, in order for the plug-in to be available to both.

Plug-in has a bug or is corrupted. If a plug-in file has a bug or if the file itself is corrupted in some way, it can cause problems directly related to the plug-in feature of course, but it may also cause more general problems with the application itself. For example, a bug in a plug-in that kicks in to play sounds on Web pages could cause your browser to crash every time a Web page with sound is loaded. An application may have many other accessory files beyond plug-ins. For example, a word processor will use dictionary and thesaurus files. A Web browser has a host of files related to using Java. Microsoft Office has dozens of accessory files both in its own folder and in the System Folder. In the latest versions of the Mac OS, there will be a subfolder in the System Folder called Application Support. Apple is encouraging software developers to move all of their System Folder accessory files into that folder. Exactly what some of the more obscure accessory files do can be hard to determine. If you suspect a problem here, you may need to seek outside help in learning more about the function of these files.

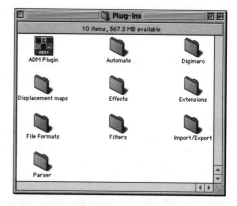

Figure F2-2 Two examples of accessory file folders: at top, Photoshop's Plug-Ins folder, normally located with the Photoshop application; at bottom, the inside of the Application Support folder located in the System Folder.

 What to Do:

1. **Quit the problem application (or close the problem control panel).** If a problem is specific to a particular application that is currently open, quit the application before taking any further steps. Relaunch the application only after you have completed these changes.

2. **Before replacing/deleting preferences files for control panels, restart with extensions off.** When deleting preferences files of control panels, first restart with extensions off. Otherwise, even though you delete the preferences file, the new preferences file may be created from the corrupted information still present and in use in RAM.

3. **Find and delete (or replace) suspected corrupted or incompatible preferences files.**
   If you suspect a corrupted or incompatible preferences file, delete it. Remember, many control panels now use preferences files. So check for both application and control panel preference files, as relevant.

   If you are having trouble locating a specific preferences file, remember to check for it in both the System Folder (especially in the Preferences folder) and in the folder that contains the application. Also note that in some cases, preferences files may be contained in a special folder (created by the application) located within the System Folder. A well-known example of this is the preferences files in the Claris folder (a folder created and used by virtually all Claris applications).

   If you are still having trouble locating a preferences file for a particular program, use Sherlock to search for all files that include the name of the program.

   If even this fails to locate a specific preferences file (perhaps because it has an unusual name that you do not recognize as belonging to the application), do the following:

   a. **Get a utility, such as Snitch, that can list a file's Creator code.** Use it to learn the code for your problem application ("BOBO" is the creator for AppleWorks, for example). See Chapter 8 for more details on doing this.

   b. **Next, use Sherlock (or Find File in older OS versions) to search for all files that have the desired Creator.** To do this, from the Find File tab, select Creator from the "Name" pop-up menu. Type in the name of the Creator code exactly (including capitalization). Click to Find. In the Search Results that appear, check for the relevant Preferences file.

   With Sherlock 2, in Mac OS 9, you would do this by first clicking the Edit button to access the More Search Options window. Then select the Creator from Advanced Options.

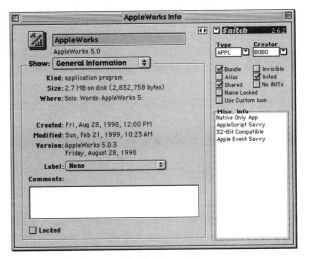

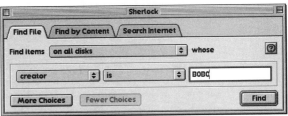

Figure F2-3 After determining the creator for AppleWorks is BOBO (top), do a search for all files with that creator (bottom); this should locate any AppleWorks-specific preferences files (although, in this case, you may miss some more general preferences that apply to all applications originally developed by Claris, such as XTND Translator List).

c. Assuming you find the desired Preferences file, delete it. If you find two similar preferences files (such as Excel 4 Preferences and Excel 5 Preferences), delete just the older one (check the files "Created" date, in the Get Info window, to determine this). If this fails to fix the problem, delete both.

4. **Restart, launch the problem application and see if the problem has been fixed.** Typically, a new preferences file will be created when you launch the application. This should have happened automatically at startup for some control panels. You may have to reset some custom preferences at this point. However, if a Preferences file was the source of the problem, it should now be fixed.

TECHNICALLY SPEAKING ▶ Problems Deciding What Preferences File to Delete

Deciding what preferences files to delete can get more complicated than just a difficulty in locating a specific file. For example:

- Some preferences files are used by several applications. For example, XTND Translator List is a quasi-preferences file shared by most Claris applications (including AppleWorks, which was originally called ClarisWorks) and is located in the Preferences folder. Deleting such files, in addition to or instead of any application-specific Preferences files, may solve certain Preferences file-related problems.

  Note: Claris Corporation no longer exists. AppleWorks is now marketed directly by Apple, and uses an AppleWorks folder in the Application Support folder of the System Folder. However AppleWorks still may use files stored in the older Claris folder, so do not delete the Claris folder.

- Sometimes a symptom may give no suggestion that a Preferences file for a particular program is the cause. This is particularly true for control panel preferences: in these cases, figuring out what to do may require getting advice from others who have been down the same road before and figured out the solution. Here are two examples:

  Apple Menu Options Prefs The most notorious example is the Preferences file for Apple Menu Options (Apple Menu Options Prefs). Problems with this file can lead to a loss of the hierarchical menus in the Apple menu (in which case, the link to the Prefs file would be obvious), but it can also cause a variety of apparently unrelated symptoms, including memory errors at startup and an overall slowdown in the speed of your Mac.

  Finder Preferences (and related files) The Finder has its own preferences file located in the Preferences folder. It stores settings that affect the Finder's display, especially the options set by selecting Preferences from the Finder's Edit menu (in older OS versions, you would select the Views control panel). If the Finder's desktop display seems askew in some way, deleting Finder Preferences is obviously worth trying. However, symptoms may not immediately suggest a link to this file. For example, Finder crashes at startup may be due to a corrupted Finder Preferences file.

  To delete the Finder Preferences file, drag the file out of the System Folder, and then restart the Macintosh. A new Finder preferences file is created. You can then delete the old file. This procedure is necessary because the Macintosh may not allow you to delete the Finder preferences file of the current startup disk. Actually, to make absolutely sure that the old (possibly corrupted) preferences data is not simply recreated, your best bet is to restart from an alternate startup disk and then delete the Finder Preferences file.

  If deleting the Finder Preferences has no effect, there are a few other related Mac OS software Preferences you can try deleting as well. These include: Mac OS Preferences, Display Preferences, and Sound Preferences.

TAKE NOTE ▶ Cleaning Up Unneeded Preferences Files

One of the more common complaints among Mac users is that "uninstalling" an application is often not as easy as installing it (particularly when the application's Installer forgot to include a "Custom Remove" or "Uninstall" option). You delete the application but often leave behind a bunch of related files, such as Preferences files, that should also be deleted. Coming to the rescue here are several utilities that help you identify files linked to an application, and then help you decide whether or not to delete them. The two most well known of these utilities are Yank (and its commercial sibling, Yank Pro) and Aladdin's Spring Cleaning. PrefsCleaner and Clean Sweep are two other shareware alternatives. Spring Cleaning has many additional features beyond handling Preferences files; these include fixing orphaned alias files and checking your fonts.

None of these utilities are perfect in their cleanup detection. For example, they will not typically spot third party extensions or fonts that may have been installed by a given application's Installer. For cases such as this, the Installer may include its own Uninstall option which may be more thorough. Of particular note, Microsoft Office 98 has several uninstall options of differing degrees of thoroughness. One reason for this flexibility is that some files may be used by more than one application. In such a case, you may want to retain a file installed by Office, because it is also needed for Internet Explorer (which you are not uninstalling).

As a last resort, you will simply have to do an uninstall manually (search your drive for relevant files to delete). The only other alternative is to ignore this issue and let these files collect on your drive like junk in your attic. As long as you have the drive space, there is usually no harm in doing this.

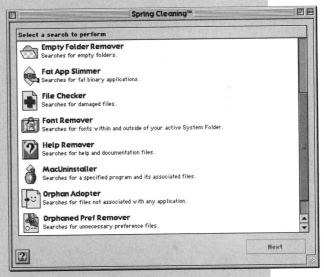

Figure F2-4 Spring Cleaning can help you clean up your unwanted (orphaned) Preferences files.

5. **Determine if you have missing or mislocated accessory files.** If the symptom remains, regardless of whether or not you discover a problem with a Preferences file, you may have a missing, out-of-date, or wrongly located plug-in or other accessory file. To check for this, consider the following:

   When an Open dialog box appears. If an application cannot locate a needed accessory file needed for a feature you are trying to use, it may present you with an Open dialog box requesting that you locate the file. This could happen, for example, if you select an application's Help command and it cannot locate the needed Help file.

   When an alert message appears. If you get an alert message that says an accessory file is missing but you do not get an Open dialog box, this also means the application could not locate the needed file. This may happen, for example, when opening a Web page that requires a certain plug-in or when downloading a file that requires a certain helper application.

When no dialog box or message appears. Missing or mislocated accessory files can cause problems even though no dialog box or alert message appears. For example, a given menu command or a dialog box option may be dimmed or missing. Similarly, if an application does not list as many file-translation formats as the manual says it should, it probably means that the needed translator files are not properly located or were never installed.

6. **Locate missing or mislocated accessory files.** Try the following suggestions, in the order given, to locate the needed file(s):

   a. **Use the Open dialog box.** If you get an Open dialog box and the mislocated file is on your disk, use the dialog box to find the file, select it, and then click Open or Select. This usually solves the problem. If so, the Open dialog box should not reappear the next time you use the feature. If the Open dialog box does reappear, you may have to move the accessory file to a particular location where the program expects to find it (see Step 3). Simply showing the file's location to the program was apparently not good enough.

   b. **Go to the expected location.** Otherwise, to find a missing or mislocated accessory file, go to the file's expected location (typically the System Folder or the application folder) as described in the Why to Do It section of this Fix-It.

   c. **Check other mounted disks with System Folders, if any.** If you have two or more mounted hard disks, both with System Folders, be careful when installing an application onto your nonstartup disk. This is because some Installers automatically place accessory files in the System Folder of the same disk that contains the application, while others place accessory files in the startup disk's System Folder, regardless of where the application is placed. If accessory files wind up in the System Folder of the nonstartup disk, they are not accessed by the application when you launch it (since it looks only in the startup disk's System Folder). If you think this has happened, you have to either reinstall the application to your startup disk or locate the needed accessory files in the secondary disk's System Folder and move them to your startup disk's System Folder.

   d. **Use Sherlock (Find File).** Follow the same basic procedures as outlined for Preferences files in Step 3b.

7. **Relocate, replace or upgrade the plug-in or other accessory file, as needed.**

   If you cannot locate the desired plug-in file: Reinstall the plug-in file from your back-ups or from the Installer of the software. If you use the Installer, check for a Custom Install option that lets you install just the plug-in and nothing else. Otherwise, consider using TomeViewer to access the needed file. If in doubt, reinstall the entire application software, as if you were installing it for the first time.

   SEE: • **"Take Note: Use Tome Viewer, in Fix-It #4.**

If you can locate the desired plug-in file: If you suspect the file may be damaged, replace it from your back-ups or via the Installer of the software, as just described.

If the file is in the wrong location, move it to the correct location. The documentation that came with the software should help you establish what the correct location should be.

If neither of these procedures have any effect, make sure you are using the latest version of the software. If you don't have the latest version, get it and install it. (Of course, it is always possible that a newly introduced bug results in the latest version being the cause of the problem; in this case you may need to downgrade to an older version or wait for the next bug-fix upgrade).

> **SEE:** • "Take Note: Staying Up to Date, in Fix-It #16, for more on checking for the latest versions.

8. **Try related solutions.** If the previous steps do not solve the problem, the problem is not with the preferences file. The application itself or its accessory files may be damaged and need to be replaced. Damaged control panels or system software damage are also possible.

BY THE WAY ▶ LOCATION, LOCATION, LOCATION

Here's one unusual variation on an accessory file location problem — one that also involved a preferences file. An application would not list its plug-in modules in the appropriate menu, even though the modules were properly located according to the manual. It turned out that the application's preferences file needed to be placed in the same folder as the modules in order for the application to use the modules. When I moved the preferences file to the plug-in modules folder, the problem was solved.

Here's another unusual case. Both Photoshop 5.0 and Microsoft Office 98 use a file called OLE Automation. However, as I write this in Spring 2000, each application required a different version of the file. In particular, installing Photoshop after installing Office 98 could cause problems for Office 98. Here was Microsoft's official advice on how to prevent such problems:

If neither application is installed:

1. Install Photoshop 5.0.
2. Move the OLE Automation 2.06 library from the System Folder to the Photoshop program folder.
3. Install Office 98 and run an app to execute the First Run Install.

If Office 98 is already installed:

1. Remove OLE Automation and OLE Library files from System Folder:Extensions.
2. Install Photoshop.
3. Move the OLE Automation 2.06 library from the System Folder to the Photoshop program folder.
4. Run Word 98 to restore the proper OLE versions using First Run Install.

**FIX-IT
#2**

> **TAKE NOTE ▶ Mac OS 9 Multiple Users and Preferences problems**
>
> Mac OS 9 includes a new feature called Multiple Users. It allows for different customized preferences for each person that uses a given Mac. Each user logs in to their own account at startup and then "sees" their selected preferences. This is achieved in part by the use of a new Users folder (at the root level of the startup drive). Inside this folder are subfolders for each user account (except for the "owner" account which uses the System Folder itself). And inside these subfolders, in turn, are Preferences and associated files for that user.
>
> The problem occurs with some older third party software that does not know to look in the Users folder and thus cannot correctly use these files. This, and related problems, are especially likely to occur with Limited or Panel access. You can work around this by creating an alias to the relevant file or folder in the System Folder and placing the alias in the User's account folder. This won't allow for a custom preference for each user, but it may get a feature to work that was failing altogether. For example, with some Hewlett-Packard printers, placing an alias of the PrintMonitor Documents folder in each user's folder is needed to enable background printing for those users.
>
> **SEE:** • **Chapter 15 for more on Mac OS 9.**

 For Related Information

> **SEE:** • **Fix-It #4 on Installer utilities and replacing system software.**
> • **Fix-It #11 on damaged files.**
> • **Chapter 2 and Chapter 6 for more on using Find File and Sherlock.**
> • **Chapter 13 on Web browser plug-ins and helper applications.**
> • **Chapter 15 for more on Multiple Users.**

Fix-It #3:
Check for Problems with Extensions and Control Panels (Startup Extensions)

▶ **QUICK SUMMARY**

Temporarily disable all startup extensions (system extensions and certain control panels that load into memory at startup). Typically, do this by holding down the Shift key at startup. If the symptoms disappear as a result, you have a startup extension problem. To solve it, first identify the offending startup extension(s). Then you will typically need to either rearrange the loading order of the problem startup extension(s), remove the startup extension(s) or replace the startup extension(s).

 When to Do It:

- When a system crash occurs at startup, particularly while the Welcome to Macintosh (Mac OS) screen (or alternate custom startup screen) is visible. Typically, the crash occurs at exactly the same point (such as just after a certain icon appears along the bottom of the screen) each time you start up.

- When a startup extension does not load at startup, even if the startup sequence otherwise proceeds normally.

- When a system error or other disruption occurs while you are using a specific system extension or control panel.

- When a specific command or function in a given application does not work, possibly resulting in a system error. This problem can have numerous causes, a startup extension conflict being one of them. A startup extension conflict can be the cause even if the problem appears unrelated to the functioning of the startup extension.

- When a problem occurs in similar situations across several or all applications, such as when you are trying to save a document. Again, this type of symptom has many possible causes besides problems with startup extensions.

- Whenever a message appears at startup (from system software or other startup utilities) that indicates that a likely startup extension conflict occurred during your previous startup.

- Just about any other time something isn't working as expected. Startup extension conflicts are one of the most common sources of Macintosh problems.

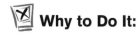

Why to Do It:

Some (but not all) of the extensions and control panels in your System Folder load into memory during the startup sequence. These files perform any number of (largely background) functions, such as placing a clock in your menubar or monitoring for virus infections or enabling file sharing. Apple includes many such extensions and control panels as part of its system software. Some are almost essential. Others, including many from third parties, are desirable because they greatly enhance the capabilities of a bare-bones system. Whatever the case, we call them startup extensions.

On the helpful side, icons for startup extensions typically appear along the bottom of the Mac OS screen as each startup extension loads into memory. By identifying the icons, you can get a sense of which extensions and control panels load at startup and which do not (though unfortunately not all startup extensions display these icons).

Startup extensions, like any software, are subject to the general problems associated with software bugs or corrupted files. However, the two most specific problems associated with startup extensions are startup extension conflicts and startup extensions that do not load or run.

TECHNICALLY SPEAKING ▶ Terminology: Startup Extensions vs. INITs

Even though some startup extensions are control panels and even though not all extensions load into memory at startup, Apple generally refers to these programs simply as *extensions*. Is this confusing? You bet it is. To try to disentangle this, as described in Chapter 1 (see "Take Note: What's a Startup Extension?"), I typically refer to all of these special programs as *startup extensions*. In previous editions of *Sad Macs*, I referred to these files by their more technical, but correct, name: INITs (where INIT is the file type of typical system extensions). However, except in a few cases (such as in the discussion of the "No INITs" bit in Chapter 8), I have dropped the term INIT for this edition.

TECHNICALLY SPEAKING ▶ Where in Memory are the Startup Extensions?

Applications and documents occupy an area of memory (RAM) referred to as the application heap. Startup extensions, on the other hand, load into the special area of RAM reserved for the system file and related software called the system heap. You can check how the size of the system heap is affected by the presence of startup extensions. Select About This Computer from the Apple menu when you are in the Finder to see a bar representing the amount of memory occupied by the Mac OS (as explained more in Chapter 2). As you add to or subtract from the number of startup extensions that load at startup, the bar becomes larger or smaller accordingly on subsequent restarts.

This has some practical implications. For example, if you do not have enough memory available to launch a particular application, you can free more memory by disabling a few rarely needed startup extensions and restarting. There may now be enough free memory to permit the application to launch. Similarly, the less RAM in your machine, the fewer startup extensions you can load at startup before you run out of memory. Startup management utilities (as described in this Fix-It) are especially useful for temporarily disabling selected startup extensions.

SEE: • **Fix-It #5 for more on application and system heaps.**
• **Chapter 5 for more on memory and startup problems.**

Startup Extension Conflicts

Most startup extensions remain in memory, working in the background, from the moment you start up until you shut down. This presents a unique challenge for these programs: they must function smoothly no matter what other startup extensions or applications you are using at the same time, and they must not prevent the normal functioning of these other startup extensions or applications. Failure to meet these goals is referred to as a *startup extension conflict*.

Sometimes these conflicts are easy to diagnose. Other times, they can be *very* subtle. For example, an application may have some quirk that appears only when you are using a new AutoSaver startup extension while running with virtual memory turned on and the QuicKeys startup extension also installed.

Regardless of the symptoms, the cause of these conflicts is typically a software bug (though developers may argue among themselves whether the source of the bug is in the startup extension or in the software with which it conflicts). Three basic types of startup extension conflicts occur, as follows:

Conflict with another startup extension Conflicts with another startup extension are often the hardest to diagnose because even when you think you have found the problem startup extension, another one may be at least partially responsible. This type of conflict is the one most likely to lead to system crashes during the startup sequence.

Conflict with another application The symptoms of a conflict with another application may show up as a malfunction of the startup extension or as a problem with the application (often seemingly unrelated to the startup extension functioning, such as a menu command that does not work).

Conflicts with system software The worst-case scenario is when the startup extension is incompatible with the version of the system software you are using. In this case, problems are likely to occur in a variety of contexts across applications. The startup extension may not work at all. Startup problems are also possible.

Although a startup extension conflict is not the only possible cause of many of these symptoms, it is usually an easy one to either confirm or eliminate. That's why it should be one of the first things you check.

Startup Extensions That Do Not Load or Run

A startup extension may simply not work at all—even without any sign of conflict with other software. Typically, this is because the startup extension never loaded into memory at startup (which it must do in order to work!). A startup extension conflict may still be the underlying cause here, but other causes are possible. For example, remember that you cannot use a newly installed startup extension without first placing it in the System Folder (typically in the Control Panels or Extensions folders) and then restarting.

What to Do:

Described here are the three main steps to solving startup extension conflicts: (1) Disable startup extensions to determine if you have a startup extension conflict, (2) identify the problem startup extension, (3) resolve the conflict. The final section of this Fix-It deals with what to do for a startup extension that appears not to load or run at all.

Disable Startup Extensions to Determine if You Have a Startup Extension Conflict

The logic is simple. Temporarily disable *all* of your startup extensions. If the problem goes away, then you know you have a startup extension conflict. There are three different ways to disable your startup extensions: hold down the Shift key during startup, use a startup management utility, or remove all startup extensions from your System Folder.

To quickly disable all of your startup extensions, nothing is better than the Shift key method. It is simple, easy to do, and guaranteed to disable almost all system extensions and startup extension-type control panels in your System Folder.

Using a startup management utility is more likely to leave some startup extensions enabled (including itself of course!). But it is still fine to use if those remaining startup extensions are not the source of your problem.

Dragging startup extensions out of the System Folder is recommended only for extreme cases where you have some reason to believe that the Shift key technique (or a startup manager) did not disable what you wanted to disable (as described in "Technically Speaking: Startup Extension Oddities," later in this Fix-It).

Here are the details of each method:

TAKE NOTE ▶ Startup Extension is Disabled But Its Settings Remain

The settings of some control panels (especially those that come with Apple's system software) remain in effect even if you start up with extensions off. For example, this is true for the battery conservation settings of the PowerBook control panel. The reason for this is that, although you need the control panel to change the settings, the current settings are stored in the Mac's Parameter RAM (PRAM) (see Fix-It #9) or Power Manager (see Chapter 11), which remain active even when startup extensions are off.

Similarly, the settings for the Energy Saver "control panel" used with PCI-based Macs are retained even if you later disable the extension. If you want to turn these settings off, you should set the settings to "Never," in the control panel, restart, and then disable the separate *Energy Saver Extension* (or simply leave it enabled with the settings at "Never").

Method #1: Disable Startup Extensions by Holding Down the Shift Key at Startup

To disable all of your startup extensions at startup:

1. **Restart the Macintosh.**

2. *Immediately* **press and hold down the Shift key.** If you do not press it soon enough, it will not work. If it fails to work, restart and try again. The first sign that

it worked is that, when the Welcome to Macintosh screen is displayed, the words *Extensions off* appear directly below the words *Welcome to Macintosh.* You can now release the Shift key; your startup extensions have been disabled for this startup. No startup extension icons will appear along the bottom of the startup screen. This is all only a temporary change. Everything returns to its previous condition the next time you start up.

By the way, if you are using a customized startup screen that replaces the Welcome to Macintosh screen, the *Extensions off* message does not appear. To be safe here, hold down the Shift key until the startup screen disappears.

This Shift key technique also bypasses any programs found in your Startup Items folder (which is totally separate from your startup extensions!). Actually, if you wait to hold down the Shift key until just after extensions have loaded, you can bypass Startup Items files without similarly disabling extensions.

Method #2: Disable Startup Extensions by Using a Startup Management Utility

Startup management utilities are themselves startup extension-type control panels. Casady & Greene's Conflict Catcher, and Apple's Extensions Manager are the two major examples.

BY THE WAY ▶ Startup Management Utilities: Control Panels and Extensions

Today's startup management utilities work as a combination of an extension and control panel. The main file that you deal with is the control panel. However, Conflict Catcher also uses an extension called Conflict Extension. Extensions Manager uses EM Extension. When you enable or disable these startup management utilities, make sure you enable or disable both parts or unexpected effects are likely to happen (such as control panel options that do not work even though the control panel is installed).

Apple's Extension Manager has one major advantage over Conflict Catcher: It is free. That's it. In every other way, Conflict Catcher is superior. For example, Conflict Catcher lets you reorder the load order of extensions; Extensions Manager does not. Conflict Catcher lets you manage fonts and virtually every other type of file in System Folder, beyond what are typically thought of as extensions. Extensions Manager does not. Conflict Catcher lets you do automated conflict testing (hence its name). Extensions Manager does not. And so on. Conflict Catcher also allows you to list an extension's name during startup, rather than just the icon, and can scan the System Folder for damaged files. Extensions Manager does allow you to set up different extension sets and individually turn extensions on and off, but little else of note. As a result, the discussion in this Fix-It will focus primarily on Conflict Catcher. Where Extensions Manager can match Conflict Catcher, the method to use will be similar. [**Note:** Do not try to install both extensions at the same time. This will lead to problems.]

Sets: Mac OS Base and All

Both Extensions Manager and Conflict Catcher include one feature immediately relevant to the topic at hand. The Mac software has now gotten so complex that disabling *all* startup extensions, by holding down the Shift key, may disable more than you wish. For example, suppose you suspect that an extension conflict may be the root cause of why you cannot connect to the Internet. Holding down the Shift key at startup will not be useful, because doing so

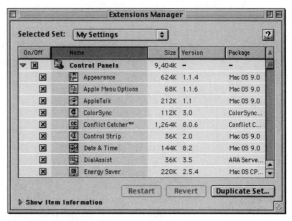

Figure F3-1 Apple's Extensions Manager.

FIX-IT #3

will disable a variety of extensions (most especially Apple's Open Transport files) that are needed to connect to the Internet. Thus there will be no way to test whether disabling other extensions has any beneficial effect. To get around this, these two utilities have two options called Mac OS 9.x Base and Mac OS 9.x All. If you are still using Mac OS 8, they will similarly say 8.x. (Actually, they will not say 8.x; they will say whatever version of the Mac OS was current when the latest update to the program was made. For example, it might say Mac OS 8.6 Base.) Selecting one of these options (either from Extensions Manager's Selected Set pop-up menu or Conflict Catcher's Active Set pop-up menu) either enables just a core group of extensions that came with the Mac OS (Base) or all startup extensions that came with the Mac OS (All). Use these options to test for problems with third-party extensions when disabling all extensions would prohibit the necessary test.

You can use these same Sets options to selectively create your own Custom sets (such as a limited set for when you are planning to run memory and processor intensive applications).

To use Conflict Catcher to disable startup extensions at startup, do one of the following:

- **Hold down the space bar at startup.** This interrupts the startup process at the point that Conflict Catcher's extension loads. The Conflict Catcher window will appear. At this point, you can make any changes you wish. To disable all extensions, simply select *Disable All Startup Files* from the Active Sets pop-up menu (or alternatively select one of the Mac OS sets, if desired). Then click the Continue Startup button. Later in this section, we will explain how to be more selective about what you turn on and off.

- **Use another Conflict Catcher shortcut.** Conflict Catcher offers numerous startup shortcuts. Engaging the Caps Lock key does the same thing as holding down the Space Bar. If you forget to do either of these two things in time, press Command-R at any point that the remaining extensions are loading. This forces an immediate restart, giving you a second chance to access Conflict Catcher. Command-P pauses the startup process until you press Command-P again; just in case you need some time to think about what you want to do.

One other option: with Conflict Catcher, you can assign a letter to each set. Holding down that letter at startup will select that set. For example, to do this for Mac OS Base, selected "Edit Sets" for the Sets menu. Then select Mac OS Base, and click Modify. This will bring up another window, where there will be an option to define "Set Activates by Startup Key." Type in the desired character ("b" for example). Close the windows. Now the next time you start up, if you hold down the b key at startup, it will automatically select the Mac OS Base extension set. Just remember to revert back to your full set when you are done experimenting. (Conflict Catcher does have an additional option to define a set as a Default set, so that it will automatically load the next time to restart normally, even if it was not the set you selected previously).

Normally any changes that Conflict Catcher makes are "permanent." That is, they remain in effect until the next time you make a change. However, you can tell Conflict Catcher to only make changes "temporary." This means your extensions list will revert to its previous state after your next restart. To do this, select "Continue (Temporary Changes)" from Conflict Catchers File menu (this option only appears when you access Conflict Catcher at startup).

You are not limited to using Conflict Catcher only at startup. You can access it at any time, as you would any control panel. You can make the same sort of changes at these times. Changes will be in effect the next time you start up.

SEE: • **"Take Note: How Startup Management Utilities Do (And Do Not) Disable Startup Extensions" and "Technically Speaking: Startup Extension Oddities," for more on disabling startup extensions.**

FIX-IT #3

Figure F3-2
Casady & Greene's
Conflict Catcher.

**TAKE NOTE ▶ How Startup Management Utilities Do (and Do Not) Disable
Startup Extensions**

What exactly does a startup management utility do to a startup extension that prevents it from loading at
startup? They simply move the disabled startup extension to a special folder.

Here's how this works: the Mac OS or the management utility creates folders with names like
"Extensions (disabled)" and "Control Panels (disabled)" and places these folders in your System Folder.
Any startup extensions that you select to be disabled are then placed in these folders by the management
utility. Removed from their normal location, these startup extensions do not load at the next startup. A
minor disadvantage of this approach is that when you select Control Panels from the Apple menu,
disabled control panels do not appear (since they are now in a different folder). At first, you may think
they have disappeared. Don't panic. They're still on your disk. They return to the Control Panels folder
automatically after you use the management utility to turn them back on. You can also reenable these
startup extensions manually, simply by dragging them back to their previous folder location (except that
some startup management utilities may move them back to the disabled folder the next time you restart—
until you re-enable them in the startup management utility listing).

Also note that there are differences between what may get disabled by selecting to skip all
extensions via your startup management utility vs. via holding down the Shift key at startup. For example,
Apple's Extensions Manager's All Off setting switches off Chooser extensions while holding the Shift
key down at startup does not.

Finally, Conflict Catcher has an option to *link* extensions (as mentioned in "By the Way: Create Links
With Conflict Catcher," later in this Fix-It). This is so that, for example, if one extension is turned on, the
other is automatically turned on (or off). This is designed to prevent known problems that would otherwise
occur. The result is that if you disable a linked extension, but do not disable the link itself, the extension
may get re-enabled automatically the next time you restart. Conflict Catcher comes with a built-in set of
links, so check for these if you are having a problem getting a change to "take."

TECHNICALLY SPEAKING ▶ Startup Extension Oddities

Most extensions have a file type "INIT" and most control panels have a file type "cdev." These are the
ones that consistently function in the typical way described throughout this Fix-It. However, there are
numerous exceptions. Here is a sampling of the more noteworthy "exceptions to the rule."

- **Early startup files** Some extensions are required to load at the beginning of the startup process,
  even before the startup management utility itself loads. While you can use Conflict Catcher to enable
  or disable these extensions, you cannot change their load order. You can also turn these extensions
  off when accessing your management utility at startup. After disabling the extension, the utility will
  force the Mac to restart (this time with the early loading extension disabled). With Extensions Manager,
  you need to hold down the Command key when you close its window in order for this to occur.

- **Extensions that cannot (or usually should not) be disabled** Certain extensions from Apple's
  System Software may be required for your Mac to startup. These cannot be disabled. Conflict
  Catcher is generally aware of this, and will not let you startup with these extensions disabled. Text
  Encoding Converter is one such file. While its exact function is a bit obscure, it is required for current
  versions of the OS to operate properly, especially so if you use HFS Plus formatting (see Fix-It #15).

  A few other extensions, while not essential for startup, are so important to normal use of the
  Mac that you would generally not want to work without them. For example, you cannot use
  AppleScript functions without the AppleScript extension enabled. Only when you are testing for
  extensions conflicts would you typically disable these. Similarly, a CD-ROM drive and a monitor
  typically require certain extensions in order to function normally.

(continues on next page)

Special Enabler files and related System Software files (see Fix-It #4), typically found at the root level of the System Folder, are also essential for certain Mac models. These are usually not even listed in Conflict Catcher's or Extensions Manager's list, and cannot be disabled. Certain driver extensions, such as FireWire drivers, are not disabled by holding down the Shift key at startup.

- **Background-only applications (*appe* files)** There is a category of extensions that have a file type of *appe*. These are sometimes referred to as background-only (or faceless) applications. They are sort of a hybrid of extensions and ordinary applications. Apple includes several of these in the System Software. Application Switcher and Desktop Printer Spooler are two examples. These special extensions do not really launch until the end of the startup sequence, regardless of where their startup icon may appear during the startup process. In some cases, they may only launch when their function is needed. In general, Conflict Catcher lists these appe files and should allow you to disable them. Holding down the Shift key at startup should also disable them.

  SEE: • **Take Note: Process Manager Utilities, for more about these files.**

- **Shared Library files** Apple's Shared Library Manager extension defies logic by having a file type of *INIT*, but still having its "No INITs" flag checked. This extension is needed to make use of additional files called shared library files. These shared library files (such as the Open Transport Library or Game Sprocket files) have a file type of *shlb* or *libr*. While they are stored in the Extensions folder, they are not typical extensions. These files typically do not load into memory at startup. They only load when needed by an application that uses the shared library. Still, the presence of these files can be critical for other files to work. For example, without the Open Transport shared library files present, you will be unable to use the TCP/IP or AppleTalk control panels).

- **Wild things (*thng* files)** Files of the type *thng* (such as System AV and Conflict Catcher itself) are also found in the Extensions and Control Panels files. Technically referred to as "component resources," they are special types of extensions that may be used by one or more other files.

- **Applications in the System Folder** Some files (such as Print Monitor or Energy Saver 2.x) are stored in the Extensions and Control Panels files but are really applications (of the type *APPL*).

- **Chooser extensions** Chooser extensions (as described in Chapter 1) usually do not have a startup extension code and do not load at startup. But some, such as AppleShare (with a file type of *rdev*), break this rule and act as typical startup extensions.

- **RAM Doubler** Then there's RAM Doubler. It actually consists of two extensions. The first one to load, called *Load RAMDblr*, is invisible and located at the root level of the System Folder. The other extension, called RAM Doubler, is visible and located in the Control Panels folder. The Load RAMDblr extension loads prior to virtually all other startup extensions, including the RAM Doubler control panel. Load RAMDblr is the critical file needed to actually install RAM Doubler. If it does not load at startup (which it may not do the first time after RAM Doubler has been previously disabled and turned back on again), the icon for the control panel will appear with an X over it. When startup is complete, you will get a message that says that RAM Doubler did not load but will load correctly the next time you start. To solve this problem, just restart as it suggests.

  If you disable the visible RAM Doubler file at startup, using Extensions Manager or Conflict Catcher, RAM Doubler will still be active for that startup because the Load RAMDblr file has already loaded (thus overriding your disabling attempt). You will have to restart again to really disable RAM Doubler.

  Finally, if you simply drag the RAM Doubler control panel to a new System Folder, RAM Doubler will not load, because you did not also move the invisible Load RAMDblr file.

  SEE: • **"Take Note: The Loading Order of Startup Extensions or What's in a Name?," later in this chapter, for more on dealing with startup extensions that load before a startup manager.**
  • **Chapter 8 for more on file types and Finder flags.**

TAKE NOTE ▶ Process Manager Utilities

There are certain types of files, called background-only or faceless applications, that run in the background without you typically being aware of them. They are not listed in the Application menu or in the About This Computer window. In the latter case, the memory they use is lumped in to the Mac OS allocation. So how do you know which, if any, faceless applications are running?

Fortunately, there are a multitude of utilities that let you see a complete list of all open "processes" (a term which refers to the combination of ordinary and faceless applications). Even better, these utilities typically let you kill any given process. This is important because, if you suspect that a faceless application is causing a problem, you would ordinarily have no way to select and quit it (other than restarting with its extension disabled) because it is not accessible from the Application menu.

My current favorite of these utilities is Peek-a-Boo. It not only lists open processes, it lists the percentage of CPU time each one is using and lets you adjust this as well. This

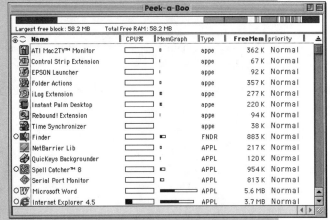

Figure F3-3 Peek-a-Boo displays a list of open processes.

can help speed up your Mac by giving a higher priority to an application that you want to get most of the processor's attention.

Note: Although most background applications are opened at startup (either as an extension or as a file in the Startup Items folder of the System Folder), they can be launched at any time. For example, using the Extensions Strip control panel, you can launch and kill the process that creates this Control Strip substitute.

BY THE WAY ▶ Don't Depend On a Control Panel's On/Off Buttons

Some control panels have on and off buttons. In some cases, selecting the off button instructs a startup extension-type control panel not to load at the next startup. However, this is not always the case. Often, selecting a control panel's off button simply stops the immediate background functioning of the control panel. It still remains in memory, available to be turned back on (without having to restart) if desired. It also may continue to load into memory (although in the off position) at subsequent startups. Even though it is "off," since it loads into memory, it can still be the cause of a startup extension conflict.

Identify the Problem Startup Extension

If your problem disappears as a result of turning off all your startup extensions, you have a startup extension conflict. The next step is to determine which startup extension or combination of startup extensions is the source of the problem. To do this you will have to selectively enable and disable startup extensions. Of the three methods for disabling startup extensions described in the previous section, a startup management utility is clearly the best here. It offers the maximum in convenience and flexibility.

Dragging startup extensions in and out of your System Folder from the Finder also works, but it is much more time-consuming. The Shift key technique is useless here; you cannot selectively disable startup extensions with it.

Bearing this in mind, try the following suggestions, in the order indicated, as appropriate.

Check Recently Added Startup Extensions

If you added a startup extension to your startup disk just prior to the appearance of a problem, this startup extension becomes a prime suspect. To check it out, disable just that startup extension. To do this with a startup management utility: Access the list of startup extensions from the manager's control panel window, enable all the startup extensions that you normally use, then disable the suspect startup extension. Then restart. If the problem disappears, you have identified the likely problem startup extension (though the problem may also involve a conflict with another startup extension already on your disk).

Conflict Catcher can help here by listing files in the order that they were installed. Simply select "By Date Installed" from the pop-up menu above the list of extension names in the main window.

By the way, if you made a list of all extensions and control panels installed by the Mac OS and all the ones you installed yourself, you would probably find that there are still a healthy number of additional files in these folders. These are typically installed when you install other applications, such as Microsoft Office or Web browsers. As a result, even if you consider yourself a "power user," you may have little or no idea of what exactly certain extensions do or even where they came from. There is help on Web for figuring this out (see Fix-It #16), but in the end, you probably have to resign yourself to not knowing the function of every file in your System Folder. The system software has just gotten too complex for all but a few experts to have this information at hand.

Check Suspicious Startup Extensions

If the symptoms suggest a particular startup extension or group of startup extensions as the cause of the conflict, disable these startup extensions and restart. For example, if a problem appears across a variety of applications whenever you try to save documents, and you use an autosave control panel, this control panel is a likely source of the problem. Start by disabling it. See if the problem goes away.

Check for Known Incompatibilities and Bugs

Chances are, you are not the first person to experience your particular startup extension conflict. If so, others may be able to identify and solve the problem for you. Check the documentation of all of your startup extensions for any advice. If you discover a likely culprit, disable it to see if the problem goes away. Check with the software vendor for specific help, if needed.

Similarly, if you are having a problem only with a particular application and you suspect it may be caused by a startup extension conflict, contact technical support for that application. They may be able to identify the problem and offer a solution.

However, when there is a conflict between a startup extension and an application, it can be hard to determine whether the cause is the startup extension or the application. Occasionally, you may get a run-around. For example, if startup extension A conflicts with Application X, the startup extension developer may blame the application developer for the problem, and vice versa. Unfortunately, while each one waits for the other to correct the problem, you are left without a solution.

Do a Conflict Test to Isolate the Problem Extension(s)

If none of the preceding methods succeed, it's time to systematically disable and reenable all your startup extensions. This is a potentially long and tedious process, especially if you have many extensions. Not only does it take a long time, but it requires your active involvement throughout the process. This means you can't just walk away for an hour and come back after the procedure is over. You must constantly be present to watch what happens and respond accordingly.

In previous editions of *Sad Macs*, I described a procedure for "manually" doing this sort of isolation. It basically involves systematically shuttling extensions in and out of your System Folder, restarting each time, until you figure out which extension is causing the problem. However, using Conflict Catcher is a so much better alternative that I am no longer going to waste the space to discuss any other way to do it. If you are serious about tracking down extension conflicts, get Conflict Catcher. Conflict Catcher can also include fonts and Control Strip modules and other related files in a conflict test.

1. **Click Conflict Catcher's Conflict Test button; check for damage.** Open Conflict Catcher and click the Conflict Test button. You will be asked if you wish to scan files for possible damage. Say Yes. If damage is identified, Conflict Catcher will offer to try to repair it. Give it a try. If it fails, immediately disable the damaged extension(s) to see if it is the source of the problem.

   By the way, it is a good idea to check Fonts for possible damage, as this is a surprising common cause of more general problems. If no Fonts are damaged, remove Fonts from the list prior to doing a conflict test (so as to speed up the test). You do this by selecting Preferences from Conflict Catcher's Edit menu and then clicking the Folders icon. Here you will find a check list of folders; check or uncheck the ones you wish.

2. **Do the conflict test.**
   Conflict Catcher will walk you through the rest of the procedure (check the excellent Conflict Catcher manual if you have any questions that the software help does not answer). Essentially what will happen is that after asking a few questions, Conflict Catcher will

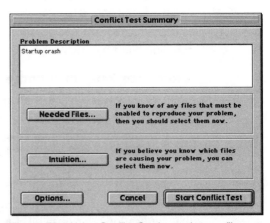

Figure F3-4 Using Conflict Catcher to do a conflict test.

disable a subset of your startup extensions (and other files if so selected) by moving them to the "(Disabled)" folders in your System Folder. It then restarts your Mac. It will do this repeatedly, each time modifying which files are enabled and disabled. After each restart, you will be asked whether the original problem is still present or not. When Conflict Catcher completes all its restarts, it will either identify the problem-causing extension or tell you that no extension appears to be the cause.

Multiple extensions involved Conflict Catcher will also alert you that more than one extension may be involved in causing your problem and will give you an opportunity to test further for this. Generally, to save time, I would pass on this option unless disabling the identified extension does not solve your problem.

Startup management utility is the cause If Conflict Catcher claims that no extension is an identifiable cause, remember that, in rare cases, Conflict Catcher itself can be the cause. Especially suspect this if the problem goes away if you disable all startup extensions with the Shift key technique but not with your startup management utility. You may want to manually disable Conflict Catcher, by dragging its extension and control panel out of the System Folder and restarting, to check for this. Otherwise, Conflict Catcher has a special feature that can help determine if Conflict Catcher itself is the source of a problem at startup. To do this, click its Prefs button; then click Disable Startup Features and restart. If Conflict Catcher was the cause of a problem at startup time, the problem should now go away.

Codependent extensions Conflict Catcher may also have problems properly testing codependent start-up extensions.

SEE ALSO:
• **"Is It a Codependent Startup Extension Problem (or Other Startup Extension Conflict)?,"** later in this Fix-It.

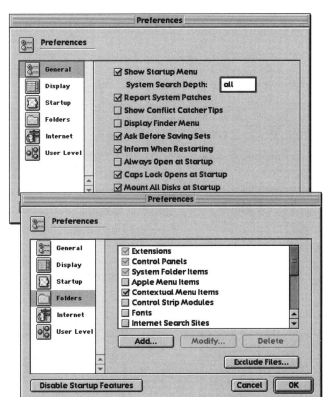

Figure F3-5 Two panels of Conflict's Catcher's Preferences window: General and Folders.

3. **Confirm that you have identified the problem startup extension.** Once you have identified the suspected problem startup extension, reenable all startup extensions except the problem one. Restart. If the problem no longer occurs, the lone disabled startup extension is confirmed as the problem startup extension.

As an extra check, disable all startup extensions except the problem startup extension. If the problem reappears, this is added confirmation that the lone enabled startup extension is the problem.

If these tests do not confirm the identity of the problem startup extension, you probably have one of the special cases described in the following sections.

TAKE NOTE ▶ Conflict Catcher Catches Startup Crashes

If your Mac crashes while extensions are loading during startup, Conflict Catcher can optionally identify the extension that was trying to load at the time of the crash. It will automatically open and list the suspect extension at startup the next time you restart. It will further give you the option to disable the extension. To turn on this option, select Preferences from Conflict Catcher's Edit menu and click the Startup icon; then check "Detect Startup Crashes."

Once you have identified the suspected problem startup extension, reenable all startup extensions except the problem one. Restart. If the crash no longer occurs, the lone disabled startup extension is confirmed as the problem startup extension. However some startup crashes are "one time events" and will not recur on subsequent restarts. Before giving up on the extension, enable it again to see if the crash still occurs. If it doesn't, you may continue using it. You might also try installing a fresh copy of the extension, just in case the current copy has some undetected damage.

TAKE NOTE ▶ Shared Library Manager Conflicts

If Conflict Catcher reports that that the offending extension is Shared Library Manager and/or Shared Library Manager PPC, don't believe it. OK, Conflict Catcher is not exactly wrong; it's just not able to interpret this situation correctly. These two extensions are needed to use any of the various Shared Library files that are also in the Extensions folder. If one of these library files is corrupted, it can precipitate the problem—perhaps a system crash or an odd message about an inability to load some Lib file. The Lib file name may not even be the name of any of the Library files in your Extensions folder; rather it may be some "file" stored within the individual Shared Library file, not the Shared Library file itself.

The critical point here is that the problem is not with the Shared Library Manager but with one of the Shared Library files.

You can use Conflict Catcher to test for this by marking Shared Library Manager and Shared Library Manager PPC as a "needed file." This means that they always remain enabled during the conflict test. With a little luck, Conflict Catcher will then hone in on the real problem file.

This happened to me once recently. It got even a bit weirder. It turned out that the identified Library file was still not the exact cause. Rather it was the Preferences file associated with the file that was the cause. In general, before assuming you have to disable a supposed problem-causing extension, check if there is a Preferences file with a similar name. If so, remove it from the System Folder and see if the symptom vanishes.

SEE ALSO: • **"Technically Speaking: Startup Extension Oddities," earlier in this chapter, for more on Shared Library files.**
• **Fix-It #2 for more on Preferences.**

TAKE NOTE ▶ Conflict Occurs Only When Using a Startup Extension

Sometimes a conflict may be apparent only when you actually access a startup extension's features (such as selecting a pop-up menu created by the extension). If so, you cannot disable the startup extension to check if the problem goes away. For these cases, Conflict Catcher gives you the option to keep certain extensions permanently enabled and then do a conflict test to see what other extension(s) may be interacting with the enabled extension to cause the problem. If no other extension is identified as a cause, the problem may simply be due to a bug in the original extension itself. The only solution here may be to give up on the extension until a bug-fix update comes along.

SEE ALSO: • **"If the Startup Extension Does Not Load or Run," later in this Fix-It.**

Resolve the Conflict

Once you identify the problem startup extension, the simplest solution is to stop using it. Alternatively, if the startup extension causes problems only with one application, you might find it preferable to stop using that application. However the ideal solution is to find a way to continue to use all of your startup extensions and applications, but minus the problems. This may be possible. Here's how to give it your best shot.

Rearrange the Loading Order of Startup Extensions

Sometimes a startup extension causes a problem only if it loads before (or after) a certain other startup extension. Rearranging the order in which the startup extensions load can thus eliminate the problem. Typically, to test this out, move a problem startup extension toward the start of the loading order or (if that fails to work) toward the end of the loading order. Restart to see if the problem goes away.

The manual that comes with a startup extension may offer advice about where the startup extension should load and what other common startup extensions should precede it or come after it (be careful not to reverse the order of codependent startup extensions, as described in "If the Startup Extension Does Not Load or Run," later in this Fix-It). Otherwise, you have to experiment. Of course, there is no guarantee that any amount of reordering will help. If a few reshuffles don't seem to do anything, give up.

TAKE NOTE ▶ The Loading Order of Startup Extensions or What's in a Name?

Startup extensions load in alphabetical order according to the name of the startup extension. Thus, a startup extension named AutoSaver loads before a startup extension named VirusKiller.

There is one important exception to this alphabetical loading order: all startup extensions in the Extensions folder load first, then startup extensions in the Control Panels folder load, and finally any startup extensions in the top level of the System Folder load. Within each location, items load in alphabetical order. Thus a system extension named VirusKiller, located in the Extensions folder, loads before a control panel called AutoSaver, located in the Control Panels folder. Remember, loading order is determined by folder location, not by the type of startup extension. A system extension placed in the Control Panels folder loads alphabetically with the other control panels, not with the other system extensions in the Extensions folder.

(continues on next page)

**TAKE NOTE ▶ The Loading Order of Startup Extensions or
What's in a Name?** *(continued)*

For some startup extensions, it is critical (from a functional point of view) that they load early in the loading process. For example, you want an antivirus startup extension to load first so that it can detect possible viruses in other startup extensions. Similarly, you want a startup management utility to load first (or just after an antivirus startup extension) so that it can manage all the remaining startup extensions. To accomplish this, creators of these startup extensions give them special names designed to move them to the top of the loading order. A typical trick is to place a blank space in front of the name of the startup extension, since the Macintosh considers a blank space to be alphabetically before the letter A.

Adding a blank space to the start of a startup extension's name can be tricky since the Finder does not ordinarily let you type a blank space as a first character. To circumvent this prohibition, select the startup extension's name, type any letter as the first character, follow it with a blank space, and then delete the initial letter.

A few startup extensions (such as startup management and antivirus utilities) always seem to load near the start of the list, even though they may not appear to have a special character in front of their name. Most often, they do have a special character. Typically, they use a control character. For example, at least some versions of SAM use Control-A. This loads even before a blank space.

To place a control character in front of any startup extension's name, go to the Key Caps desk accessory. Type Control-A (or Control-B, or whatever). Copy the character symbol that appears. Now go to the startup extension file in the Finder, select its name, and place the text cursor in front of the first character. Finally, select Paste. To cut a control character from a name, you must also select a character adjacent to the control character.

Other startup extensions (Adobe Type Manager is one well-known example) work best when they are loaded last (or late) in the loading process. To ensure that this happens, Adobe adds a tilde (~) to the name of its extension, which the Macintosh arranges after the letter Z.

In general, unless you use a startup management utility to maintain the loading order, you should not change the name of startup extensions that begin with these special characters because you do not want to alter their intended loading order. Finally, note that some special startup extensions load at the start of the startup sequence, regardless of their name. Typically, you cannot use a startup management utility to rearrange the loading order of these special startup extensions, even if the utility lists their name.

SEE: • **"Technically Speaking: Startup Extension Oddities," earlier in this Fix-It.**

To rearrange the loading order of startup extensions, try one or more of the following suggestions, as appropriate:

- **Use Conflict Catcher.** Using Conflict Catcher is the preferred method of rearranging startup extensions. Simply go to the utility's dialog box that lists all startup extensions. Make sure you have selected to view files "By Load Order." You can now reorder the names of the startup extensions by dragging them to new locations in the list. The listed order is the order in which the startup extensions load, regardless of the names of the startup extensions and regardless of whether they are in the Extensions or Control Panels folder.

- **Rename the startup extension.** If you don't use Conflict Catcher, you must rename a startup extension to change its position in the alphabetical hierarchy. For example, if you want a startup extension to load late, go to the Finder, select the startup extension's icon, and add a tilde in front of its name. To get it to load early, add a blank space or a control character. Of course, simply putting an extra A or Z in front of the name often works just as well, though it is less aesthetically pleasing.

  SEE: • **"Take Note: The Loading Order of Startup Extensions or What's in a Name?,"**
  earlier in this Fix-It, for details on how to add a blank space or control character
  to a name.

  One word of caution: some startup extensions work only with their original name. Often these startup extensions have their name "locked" so that you cannot change it. Ideally, the startup extension's manual should alert you to this. In any case, I would leave these names alone. If you are determined to change one, you can unlock its name (as explained in the section on Finder Flags in Chapter 8).

- **Use an alias.** Using an alias is especially useful if you have a startup extension located in the Control Panels folder that you want to load prior to a startup extension in the Extensions folder. Normally, all items in the Extensions folder load before any items in the Control Panels folder. Simply renaming the startup extension, no matter what name you choose, does not change this rule. Of course, you could get the control panel to load earlier by moving the control panel to the Extensions folder. But then it would no longer appear in the Control Panels window.

  To solve this dilemma, create an alias for the control panel. Place the control panel in the Extensions folder and the alias in the Control Panels folder. Now it loads with the Extensions folder, but the alias shows up in the Control Panels display.

  Of course, if you use a startup management utility that permits reordering of loading order, using the utility is more convenient than this alias technique. Still, the alias technique may be useful for establishing the loading order of the startup management utility itself or for a control panel that you want to load prior to the startup management utility (such as an antivirus utility). In these cases, this alias technique is useful even if you don't have a startup extension conflict that you are trying to resolve.

  In most cases, utilities that need to be concerned with this dilemma are designed to solve the problem automatically, as part of their installation process. For example, the Extensions Manager control panel uses a companion EM Extension.

  SEE: • **"Take Note: The Loading Order of Startup Extensions or What's in a Name?,"**
  earlier in this Fix-It, for more details.

FIX-IT
#3

BY THE WAY ▶ Create Links With Startup Management Utilities

Conflict Catcher has a feature that can create special links among any group of startup extensions. These links can prevent certain startup extension conflicts involving two or more startup extensions. For example, you can create a link that guarantees that one startup extension will always load later than another one, that both startup extensions get turned on (or off) if either one gets turned on (or off), or that certain incompatible pairs of startup extensions cannot both be on at the same time. Once you identify one of these problems as the cause of your symptoms, these links provide a permanent solution.

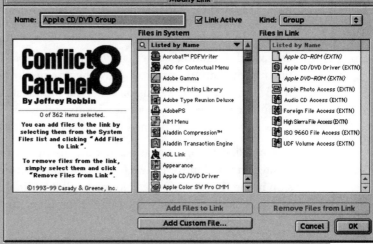

Figure F3-6 Conflict Catcher's Links list for the Apple CD/DVD Group.

Upgrade the Problem Startup Extension or Other Software

Many of these startup extension problems are due to bugs in the extension(s) (or the application with which it conflicts). If nothing so far has succeeded, check if there is a newer nonconflicting version of the startup extension available. If this is the case, get the upgrade and check if it resolves your problem. Upgrading the application, if a newer version is available, may offer another route to a solution.

If the startup extension conflict appears to be with the system software, upgrading to a newer version of the system software (or downgrading back to the previous version, if the problem began as a result of an upgrade) can also eliminate the conflict.

SEE: • Fix-It #5 for checking on system software incompatibilities and upgrading system software.

Replace Potentially Damaged Files

Conflicts due to damaged files can obviously be resolved by replacing the files with undamaged copies. To check this out:

• **Replace a control panel's preferences file.** Some control panels have their own preferences files, located in the Preferences Folder. These files may get corrupted and need replacement. To do so, restart with the suspected control panel temporarily disabled. Then delete the potentially corrupted preferences file. The control panel will make a new one automatically, as needed.

- **Replace the startup extension or application or system software.** Delete the problem startup extension (as described in the next section) and replace it with a fresh copy from your backups. Alternatively, if the problem only occurs when using a specific application, replace the application software to see if that helps. Some startup extension conflicts may be traced to corrupted System and/or Finder files; consider replacing them if all else has failed.

Recall that Conflict Catcher has a feature that scans your startup files to test for damaged resources that may cause these startup problems. To access this, select either the Scan Files for Damage or Scan Folder for Damage… items from Conflict Catcher's Special menu. However, be aware that this will not detect all possible sources of damage. It mainly detects for corrupted resources, similar to what ResEdit can check for. A utility such as Disk First Aid may find a different type of damage.

SEE: • **Chapter 8 for more on ResEdit.**
  • **Fix-It #10 for more on Disk First Aid.**

Check for Memory-Related Problems

Some problems involving startup extensions are not directly caused by the startup extension. For example, if you are using many startup extensions, insufficient memory may be the cause. Memory problems are covered in Fix-It #5. However, for starters, turn off virtual memory (accessed via the Memory control panel) and file sharing (accessed via the File Sharing control panel) if they are on.

There may also be occasions when you need to increase the memory allocation of certain extensions.

SEE: • **Fix-It #5 for more on memory.**

Delete the Problem Startup Extension

If nothing so far has helped, you probably do have to stop using the startup extension altogether. Sometimes, as previously discussed, a problem may be caused by a conflict between two different startup extensions. In this case, removing one of the startup extensions is likely to resolve the problem. If not, remove them both.

Most often, if you decide to permanently stop using a startup extension, you want to place it in the Trash and delete it from your disk. However, if the startup extension is currently in use (that is, if it was loaded into memory at startup), this may be tricky. If you try to empty the Trash when an active startup extension is in it, you may get an alert message that says that the startup extension cannot be deleted because it is in use. Even if you can trash the startup extension, be careful. The startup extension is probably still present in memory and functioning. If it subsequently tries to access its disk file, it will find it missing. This can cause problems, including system crashes.

The safest way to delete an active startup extension is: (1) drag the startup extension from the System Folder to the desktop, (2) restart the Macintosh, (3) now drag the startup extension to the Trash and discard it.

If the Startup Extension Does Not Load or Run

A startup extension may not load at startup, though the startup otherwise proceeds normally. Alternatively, a startup extension may appear to load properly, but still not function. For control panels, you may even be unable to open the dialog box. If any of these or similar problems happen, ask yourself the following questions.

Is It a Codependent Startup Extension Problem (or Other Startup Extension Conflict)?

Codependent startup extensions are two or more startup extensions, typically from the same software package or same company, that must load in a specific sequence in order to run properly. Typically, one startup extension needs to load first in order for the second startup extension to function. For example, in order to use CE Software's QuicKeys startup extension, you must first load the CEToolbox startup extension (QuicKeys ships with both startup extensions). Without these toolbox startup extensions installed, the second startup extension of the pair will not load or will not function properly.

The solutions to this type of problem are either to install the missing codependent startup extension (if only the second startup extension is present) or to rearrange the loading order of the startup extensions (so that the one that needs to load first does).

In the end, this is just a special case of the general problem where any startup extension can cause a conflict if it loads before (or after) a certain other startup extension. Sometimes an incompatibility between two startup extensions is such that if one of the startup extensions is present (especially if it loads first) the other startup extension will not load or function. The quickest way to check this is to disable all startup extensions except for the one that did not load. Now restart the Macintosh. If the startup extension now loads and runs properly, there is a conflict between that startup extension and another startup extension on your startup disk, probably one that loaded prior to the problem startup extension. Often rearranging the loading order will solve the problem. Otherwise, you may have to disable one of the incompatible startup extensions.

SEE: • **"Resolve the Conflict," earlier in this Fix-It, for more general advice.**

Did You Restart After Installing the Startup Extension?

Remember, because startup extensions load into memory at startup, they do not immediately work when they are first installed on your startup disk. To get them to work, restart the Macintosh after installing the startup extension.

Is the Startup Extension in the System Folder?

Startup extensions do not disappear from your System Folder by themselves. However, don't forget that if you switch to a different startup disk, the new startup disk may contain different startup extensions. In this case, some of those you normally expect to see are not present.

Is the Startup Extension in Its Proper Location in the System Folder?

Remember, startup extensions load only if they are in one of the following locations: the Extensions folder, the Control Panels folder, and the root level of the System Folder (that is, not in any subfolder). Some startup extensions work properly only if they are in one, but not either of the other, of these locations.

Normally, to add a new startup extension to the System Folder, either use the startup extension's Installer utility or drag the startup extension file to the System Folder icon (*not* the System file icon and *not* the System Folder window). In the latter case, the Finder determines the startup extension's correct folder (Extensions or Control Panels) and asks you if you want it to be placed there. If you add startup extensions by any other method, you may inadvertently place them in a wrong location. In such cases, they may either not work properly or not load at all. However, I must admit that this automatic method sometimes makes mistakes itself. For example, ordinary applications designed to look like control panels and go in the Controls Panel folder will be placed in the root level of the System Folder instead. Recent versions of the Mac OS make less of these mistakes, especially if developers follow guidelines for how the file types of these control panels should be assigned).

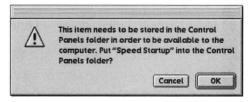

Figure F3-7 Drag a control panel to the System Folder icon and you'll typically get this message.

If problems do occur, the solution is to determine the startup extension's correct location (check its documentation if needed) and move it there. Then restart the Macintosh.

Helpful hint: If a control panel is located outside the System Folder, you may still be able to open it successfully. However, if it is a startup-type control panel, any changes you make to its settings will likely have no effect—until you correctly locate it and then restart.

Was the Startup Extension Disabled by Your Startup Manager?

Conflict Catcher has a user-definable hot key that, when held down at startup, prevents all startup extensions from loading. This is faster than having to access the manager's control panel at startup. Be careful not to inadvertently press this key at startup. Be especially careful if you define Caps Lock as the hot key, because this can be left locked and will thus prevent your startup extensions from loading even if you aren't touching the keyboard!

Also recall that you can set Conflict Catcher to disable a particular startup extension or automatically skip all startup extensions (by selecting its Skip All, or equivalent, command). Make sure you do not do this unintentionally.

Similarly, both Conflict Catcher and Extensions Manager can save different startup sets (listing which startup extensions are on or off), which you can then select (making it convenient to selectively turn some startup extensions on only when you know you will need them). If you do this, make sure you are using the set you think you are.

Finally, be aware that Conflict Catcher has an optional preferences setting that automatically disables any newly added startup extensions. In such cases, you must manually enable the startup extension from the startup manager's control panel window before the startup extension will load. Then, of course, you still need to restart the Macintosh.

Also, any extension links that have been established (see "By The Way: Create Links with Startup Management Utilities") may result in one extension being turned off automatically as a result of the presence or absence of another extension.

In general, simply make sure that the startup extension is not currently disabled by your startup management utility.

Is the Startup Extension Turned On?

Many control panels have on/off buttons in their dialog box. These buttons must be in the on position for the control panel to work, even if the control panel file is in its proper location at startup. If you discover a startup extension in the off position, turn it back on. If this has no immediate effect, restart the Macintosh. This should get it to work again.

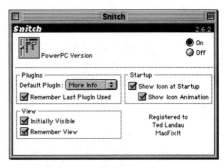

Figure F3-8 The Snitch control panel, with On and Off buttons in the upper right corner.

Special Case: Startup Icons Appear with an X Over Them or Disappear

Many extensions have an assigned key or key combination that can be used to selectively disable it at startup. No other startup extension is affected unless it too uses the same hot key(s). (By the way, although these hot keys can selectively disable startup extensions, I would avoid using them as a means of diagnosing startup extension conflicts. Instead, stick with the other methods described earlier in this Fix-It.)

If you disable a startup extension with this hot key method, the startup icon (in the Welcome to Macintosh screen) for the relevant startup extension may appear with an X through it, indicating that the startup extension did not load. Alternatively, the startup icon may disappear altogether. This is all perfectly normal. Just be careful not to inadvertently hold down these hot keys at startup or you may get a surprise. By the way, sometimes turning off a startup extension from its control panel (as described in the previous section) will also cause an X'd icon to appear.

If these possibilities do not account for the X'd icon, consider the following:

- You may be trying to use a startup extension that does not work on your Macintosh model (such as trying to use the AppleVision extension on a Mac that does not support this feature). This will typically result in an X'd icon.

- The startup extension's preferences file may be damaged. Locate it and delete it.

   SEE: • **"Replace Potentially Damaged Files," earlier in this Fix-It.**

- For startup issues involving RAM Doubler, see "Technically Speaking: Startup Extension Oddities," earlier in this Fix-It.

   SEE ALSO: • **Fix-It #5 for more on RAM Doubler.**

- If the problem persists, the startup extension itself may be damaged or it may have a bug that has been fixed in an upgraded version. Replace the startup extension. If that fails, contact the startup extension's vendor for help.

 For Related Information

   SEE: • **Fix-It #2 on problems with preferences files.**
   • **Fix-It #4 on system software problems.**
   • **Fix-It #5 on memory problems.**
   • **Fix-Its #10 and #11 on damaged files and disks.**
   • **Fix-It #16 on seeking outside help.**
   • **Chapter 1 on System Folder subfolders.**
   • **Chapter 4 on system errors in general.**
   • **Chapter 5 on system crashes at startup.**
   • **Chapter 8 of file type and creator assignments.**
   • **Chapter 11 on file sharing.**

Fix-It #4:
Check for Problems with
System Software

▶ **QUICK SUMMARY**

If a system software problem is suspected, update or replace the system software files as needed. Generally do a "clean reinstall" of the system software, using the Installer utility that came with your Macintosh system software disks.

 When to Do It:

- Whenever you have made a change to your system software version shortly before the onset of the problem.

- Whenever you have a specific problem using system software (such as a problem with the functioning of the Finder).

- Whenever you have a problem with recently added software that does not appear to be due to the causes described in previous Fix-Its or any other identifiable cause—even if you have made no changes to the system software.

- Whenever a symptom, such as a system crash, occurs in a variety of different contexts or across a variety of applications.

- Whenever you need to upgrade to a newer version of the system software.

I would not automatically do a clean install of the system software in all of the above cases. But it remains something to consider. For some of these symptoms, other causes exist, but system software remains a prime candidate.

 Why to Do It:

System software, particularly the System and the Finder, forms the essential background against which all other programs must work. It is in use from startup to shutdown. Thus, because the system software is never dormant, you should suspect it as the potential cause of almost any problem—especially one that is not easy to diagnose.

Besides the System file and the Finder, Macintosh system software includes other files normally found in the System Folder, such as various control panels, extensions, and Apple menu items. The definitions and explanations of all categories of system software files are described in Chapter 1. If these distinctions are unfamiliar, check Chapter 1 before proceeding.

Most system software problems fall into two familiar categories: incompatibility problems and corrupted file problems.

Incompatibility problems For example, a new upgrade of your favorite application may only work with the latest version of the system software. If you are still using an older version, you have trouble.

Because the symptoms can be so nonspecific, it can be difficult to know for sure whether a particular problem is due to incompatible system software. Fortunately, there are several ways to get some help.

SEE: • **"Take Note: Identifying System Software Compatibility Problems and Bugs,"** next.

Corrupted file problems Any system software file may become corrupted. However, the ones of most common concern are: the System file, the Finder, the System Resources file, Mac OS ROM file, PrintMonitor, printer drivers, and font files. The System file is particularly prone to damage, mainly because it is modified more often than other files. It gets modified almost every time you use your Macintosh, even though you are not directly made aware of this. Making matters worse, damage to the System file is likely to cause more serious symptoms than damage to other system software files. The main solution in all cases is to replace the corrupted file. (**Note:** This is not a type of "damage" that is typically fixed by disk repair utilities.)

FIX-IT #4

TAKE NOTE ▶ Identifying System Software Compatibility Problems and Bugs

You have a problem that may be due to a system software incompatibility, but you are not certain that this is the cause. Before you rush to unnecessarily do a complete system software reinstall, check out the following.

Check any printed documentation and Apple Guide files that came with your software for possible advice. Read Me files often have last-minute information about discovered bugs and conflicts. Otherwise outside help, in the form of technical support lines, magazines, users groups, and online services may provide the answer (see Fix-It #16 for details).

On a related note, sometimes a problem may be caused by a bug in the system software itself, rather than with other programs incompatible with the system software. Actually, no version of the system software is free of bugs. Apple tries to eradicate bugs, via updated versions of the Mac OS (as described more elsewhere in this Fix-It), but it never entirely succeeds. In fact, new system software may introduce new bugs as much as fixing old ones. Reinstalling system software, as advised in this Fix-It, will not fix bug-related problems. Fixing these problems will require waiting for the appropriate bug-fixed upgrade. The best you can do in the meantime is to try to stay informed about such bugs, so that you can understand the cause of whatever symptoms they produce.

TAKE NOTE ▶ Reference Releases vs. Updates

Apple's current policy is to periodically release two types of system software upgrades.

The first type is called a *reference release*. This contains all the necessary software to do a clean reinstall. It also contains all (or almost all) of the updated files from previous releases. After a reference release upgrade, you should never need to go back to earlier system software releases.

(continues on next page)

> **TAKE NOTE ▶ Reference Releases vs. Updates** *(continued)*
>
> The other type of upgrade is called an *update*. These are primarily bug-fixes, with perhaps some minor new features added. Typically, these can only be used to update existing system software. You could not do a complete clean reinstall from an update. And it may not contain key software found on the reference release because there are no updated changes to those components. To do a clean reinstall here, you need to start with the previous reference release and then install the update (as explained more in the main text).
>
> Occasionally, a system software version may exist in both forms. For example, there may be an update for people who have the previous reference release, but there may also be a reference release for people purchasing a new Mac, who therefore do not have a previous reference release.
>
> Also note that updates typically do not add updated software unless the older files are already in your System Folder. For example, an update may include a new version of Energy Saver. Still, it will not install it unless it finds the older version of Energy Saver already in your System Folder.

 What to Do:

This section is divided into two parts: "Complete Install/Reinstall of System Software" and "Selective Install/Reinstall/Deletion of System Software." The simplest and most direct approach to most system software problems is to completely reinstall the system software. How best to do this is explained in the first part. Sometimes less drastic solutions are possible, such as just replacing a single file known to be damaged. These solutions are described in the second part.

Clean Reinstall of System Software

When you use the Installer utility on your system software disks to install system software over existing system software, the Installer may update an existing file by modifying it rather than by completely replacing it. Similarly, it may fail to modify or replace a file if the new version is not any different from the version already on your drive. This is actually preferable in many situations. For example, you may have customized a System file with your own set of sound files. A normal reinstall will update the System file, if needed, but will leave the customized sounds intact. The problem with this approach is that if the System file is damaged, the damage may be left intact. To solve this problem, you need to do what is called a clean reinstall. In this case, you completely replace all existing system software files. Essentially, you create an entirely new System Folder, as if there were no current System Folder on your startup disk. This new System Folder then replaces your old one, which is then deleted.

While a clean reinstall is intended primarily to deal with suspected damaged files, doing a clean reinstall will do no harm (other than possibly losing some customized settings) even when no damage is suspected. I typically do a clean install every time I upgrade to a new system software reference release. Actually, if your main hard drive is divided into at least two partitions (as mine is), you can do a clean install on one partition, leaving your previous System Folder intact. You then shift to using the partition with the new System Folder as your startup partition (by selecting it in the Startup

Disk control panel, as explained more in Chapter 5). This way you can always revert back to the old System Folder if, for any reason, the clean install of the new version causes more problems than it solves.

Some experts recommend a clean install every few months simply as a preventative measure—even if there is no new version of the system software to install. Other experts claim that a clean install, at any point, is almost always a waste of time. I don't agree with either extreme.

In this section, I cover both how to do a clean install on a drive that has an existing System Folder as well as how to do an ordinary install (such as when installing system software on a disk for the first time). If instead, you wish to replace just a selected subset of system software files, skip ahead to the next section, "Selective Install/Reinstall/Deletion of System Software."

In previous editions of *Sad Macs*, I went into considerable detail explaining how to "manually" do a clean reinstall of System Software. However, especially with Mac OS 8.5 or later, the Mac OS Installer makes this process nearly automatic. So with this edition, I will focus mostly on using this "automated" method. Conflict Catcher (among several other utilities) also includes a feature that further helps to simplify and automate a clean install, as we will discuss shortly.

Apple keeps changing and improving its Install software with each OS release. So it is possible that some details of the following procedures may have changed by the time you read this. But the general procedure will remain accurate.

FIX-IT #4

TAKE NOTE ▶ The iMac: Software Restore vs. Software Install CD-ROM discs

The iMac (as well as some other recent Mac models) comes with two system software CD's: Software Restore and Software Install.

Software Restore The Restore disc should only rarely be used. It not only affects your System Folder software, but it reinstalls all other software (including applications such as AppleWorks) that came preinstalled on your drive. You have three variations on how to do this.

In the default case, all the software currently on your drive is placed in a folder called "Original Items." At the same time, all the preinstalled software is re-installed on your hard drive. Of course, this assumes there is enough unused space on your hard drive to accommodate this. After this is done, you can select to move or delete the files in the Original Items folder.

A second option is "Restore in Place." This replaces existing copies of all your preinstalled software with fresh copies. An Apple TIL article <http://til.info.apple.com/techinfo.nsf/artnum/n31204> describes how to use this option as an alternative way of doing a clean install of the System Folder (assuming that the current OS on your drive is still the same basic version as on this CD). However, I don't see any clear advantage to this method.

The third option is to "Erase before restoring." This erases your hard disk before reinstalling your preinstalled software. You would thus lose any additions that you made to the drive, unless they were backed up elsewhere. This essentially restores your drive to how it was the day that it shipped from the factory. With a Restore in Place, most of your custom preferences settings are retained. However, Preferences files actually installed by the Restore will overwrite existing files. These include preferences for America Online, and Internet Explorer, as well as the TCP/IP and Internet control panels. So save a copy of any Preferences files that you would not want to risk losing. Otherwise, you will have to recreate them after the restore. Of course, if you Erase before restoring, *all* preferences are lost.

(continues on next page)

**TAKE NOTE ▶ The iMac: Software Restore vs. Software Install
CD-ROM discs** *(continued)*

I would only consider this approach if your hard drive's contents appeared so "messed up" that anything short of a complete restore would not likely solve your problem. Even here, I would generally prefer to restore from my personal back-up files (assuming I had them) rather than start over from ground zero. That's why I consider this method to be one of last resort. Still, I suppose it's an attractive option to have if you decide to sell your iMac and want to return the drive to the way it was the day you bought it.

Software Install This is the disc that most closely mimics a Mac OS reference release CD. However, it also includes separate Installers for whatever other preinstalled software was on your drive (such as AppleWorks). Thus you could use this not only for a clean reinstall of the system software but to replace any selected applications as well.

By the way, if the latest reference version of the Mac OS is still the same as the one that shipped with your computer, use this Install CD for doing any system software reinstalls - in preference to any generic Mac OS CD you may have acquired. A generic Mac OS CD (even if it says it is the same system software version) may predate your Mac and not include special system software files that are specific to your Mac model.

Doing a clean install, rather than an Easy install (as described in the main text) carries a risk of losing preferences settings for your Internet-related and networking software (such as TCP/IP and AppleTalk). So save a copy of these settings before doing a clean install (see Chapter 12 for details on how to do this).

Note: This Software Install CD, even though it is functionally identical to the retail version of the Mac OS CD, will only work on the type of machine (e.g., an iMac) that it came with. For a generic version of the Mac OS installer, that works with all machines that can run the OS, you need to purchase the retail product.

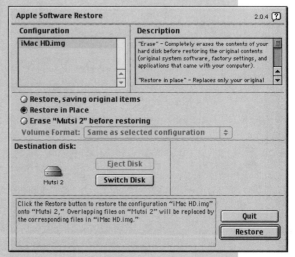

Figure F4-1 The Software Restore application window.

1. **Launch Mac OS Install.** To do a clean install, you need to use a reference release CD, not a system software update. If there is a newer update that you wish to use, you will need to install it after doing the initial clean install.

   You will typically want to start-up from the Mac OS CD prior to doing the install. To do this, have the CD-ROM disc already in the tray at startup and hold down the C key as soon as you turn the Mac on (if this does not work, see Chapter 5 for more advice). If you are doing an install on a volume that is not your active startup disk, you need not startup from the CD. Otherwise, it is recommended that you do so.

   If you are not starting up from a CD, you should probably restart with the "Mac OS All" or "Mac OS Base" set of extensions enabled (see Fix-It #3). This is now preferred to starting up with Extensions Off (which was the previous recommendation).

After startup is over, find the icon on your CD called Mac OS Install and double-click it.

Fix-It #4

Figure F4-2 The initial window of the Mac OS Install utility.

2. **Select a Destination Disk.** From the pop-up menu in the Select Destination panel, select the volume where you want the new System Folder to be installed. It should normally be the same drive where your current startup System Folder is. If there is any problem with the drive you selected, such as not enough room to install the needed files, a message will appear in the text box at the bottom of the window. The solution will typically be suggested by the symptom. Thus, if there is not enough room on a selected volume, select another volume or delete files from the present one.

Figure F4-3 Top: Select a Destination Disk from this Mac OS Install window. Bottom: This window appears if you select the Options button in the window seen at the top of this figure. Here is where you select to do a Clean Install.

3. **Select to do a Clean Install.** Click the Options button in the Select Destination panel. Select the checkbox for the Perform Clean Installation option. Click OK to close the Options window. Click the Select button. This should move you to the Read Me file display. Read it if you have not already read the duplicate file that is on the CD itself. Follow any advice it gives that is relevant to your particular setup. Hit the Continue button; agree to the Mac OS License.

Figure F4-4 The window that appears after selecting the Options button in the Install Software panel of the Mac OS Install utility.

4. **Select the Install Options.** You are now at the Install Software panel. Click the Options button. One of the options should be Update Apple Hard Disk Drivers. This is probably checked by default. If so, you should probably uncheck it. You have already updated the drivers previously, if this is indeed a clean *reinstall* of the same version of the OS you previously installed (or that came installed with your Mac). Also, you may have since updated to a newer version of the drivers than what are on the CD. Leaving this option checked could then downgrade you to an older version. If you are doing a clean install of a newer version of the Mac OS than what is currently on your drive, it is possible that you need to update your drivers. Even here, I would leave this unchecked. Instead, run the Drive Setup utility (included on the CD or a later version if you have it) to update the drivers immediately after the installation is complete and you restart.

SEE: • **Fix-It #12 for more on updating drivers.**

The other option in this window is to Create Installation Report. I would leave this checked. It creates a file on your drive that shows everything that was installed, deleted and/or replaced by the Installer. It is useful if anything appears not to work after the install; for example, you can use it to check whether or not some file you expected to get installed or updated actually did install.

Figure F4-5 The Install Software panel of the Mac OS Install utility, after selecting the Customize button.

5. **Install the software.** You are now ready to install the software. Simply click the Start button at this point and you are off to the races.

However, if you suspect that there are some components that you do not wish to reinstall, click the Customize button. You will now see a list that starts with an item that reads "Mac OS" and continues with other items, such as Internet Access, Personal Web Sharing and Text-to-Speech. If, for example, you know that you will never use Personal Web Sharing, you can uncheck the option so that it is not installed.

Further customization is possible by selecting an option from the pop-up menu to the right of each component's name. The default choice is "Recommended Installation." The other two choices are "Customized Installation" and "Customized Removal" (not all software components include these options; in such cases your only choice is to enable or disable the checkbox to the left of the component's name). For a clean reinstall, it is doubtful that you will need to make selections here. I discuss the use of the Customized Installation option for selected reinstalls later in this Fix-It.

Once you are done with any Customize selections, click Start. The rest should be automatic.

When the installation is completed, you should have a new clean System Folder. The contents of the old System Folder should have been moved to a separate folder called Previous (or Old) System Folder. You can now restart your Mac as normal (the Installer will likely force you to restart after you are done with the installation). Your Mac should now use the new System Folder as the startup System Folder.

One warning: if you cancel a Clean Install in progress, your original System Folder may be left with the name Previous System Folder (with an empty folder named System Folder now on your disk) and it may even be unblessed (that is, the System icon will not be on the folder). This can cause problems for your use of System Folder files and may even prevent you from restarting successfully. The solution is to delete the empty folder, rename your original System Folder correctly, and then open and close the folder (to rebless it if needed).

6. **Merge contents of previous and new System Folder.** With the basic clean reinstall complete, the major hassle of the job is still in front of you: what files from the "Previous System Folder" folder do you copy back to the new System Folder, and what files do you instead delete? In general, you want to copy back the following: most (if not all) of the stuff in your Preferences folder, any special third party folders and files (such as the Claris folder) that may reside in your System Folder, and (most difficult to manage), any third party extensions, control panels, fonts, Apple Menu items, Control Strip modules, etc. that may reside in Apple's System Folder subfolders. If you are knowledgeable about what is in your System Folder, you can probably do this manually.

If, when dragging files from the old to the new folder, a message appears saying that you are about to replace a newer (or older) file with the one you are dragging, I would generally decline the offer (click "Cancel"). Otherwise, you are likely to

Fix-It #4

replace one of the "clean" files installed by the clean install with a "dirty" file that you intended to replace. One exception here are the Preferences files. If you do not replace these, you will lose your custom settings.

Use Conflict Catcher If you get the impression that this procedure can be a pain to do, you are right. That's why several software utilities exist that make this job easier. Happily, if you already have Conflict Catcher (as recommended in Fix-It #3), you already have one such tool. To get Conflict Catcher to help here, go to its Special menu and select *Clean-Install System Merge* (it is best to do this at startup after starting up from the new System Folder). From here, the utility will walk you through the procedure. Essentially, Conflict Catcher compares both the new and old System Folders and creates a list of every file that it believes should be transferred from the old folder to the new folder. It is quite intelligent in its selection. For example, if you are doing a clean install of a newer version of the Mac OS than the one currently on your drive, Conflict Catcher will not list certain Apple system software files in the old folder that are not in the new folder—if these files are no longer required in the new OS (typically because the file has been merged with or replaced by another file). It will also replace the new default Scrapbook file with your old one, based on the assumption that the old one has items that you added and wish to save. A few other similar system software items may also be replaced.

You then have the option to deselect any items that you do not want transferred (the utility's Help feature offers descriptions of each file to assist you with deciding what to do about files you are not familiar with). Conflict Catcher even has an option called "Merge System File Resources" that will copy over settings that you could not as easily do with the "manual method," such as your choice of default desktop printer and any sounds you have added to your System file. You can also choose to apply color labels to transferred files, so you can tell later on what files came from what source. When you are done setting this all up, you simply click Merge Systems, and Conflict Catcher does the rest. When it's done, restart.

Helpful Hint: In some cases, as an added precaution, you may want to reinstall third party files from their original discs, rather than merge them from the old System Folder. You can easily do this after the initial merge is complete. This protects against the possibility that the currently installed version is contributing to or causing the problem that led you to do a clean install.

6. **Delete the Old System Folder.** At this point, there should be no more need for the remaining contents of the Old System Folder. You can safely delete it. You are now done.

Hopefully, your problem has not returned. If it does, it remains possible that non-Apple files in your System Folder that were not replaced were the source of the problem. For such problems, refer to other relevant Fix-Its, as needed.

FIX-IT
#4

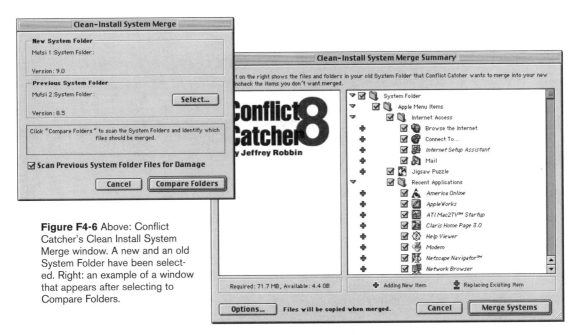

Figure F4-6 Above: Conflict Catcher's Clean Install System Merge window. A new and an old System Folder have been selected. Right: an example of a window that appears after selecting to Compare Folders.

BY THE WAY ▶ A Clean Install Without Selecting "Perform Clean Install"

An alternative method to doing a clean install is to install a new System Folder on a different volume (partition, drive, etc.) than the current startup volume. In this case, you do not have to check the Perform Clean Installation option. Simply do an Easy Install. Then use Conflict Catcher to do a System Merge. You will now have two functional System Folders, one on each volume. This can be especially useful when doing a clean install as part of updating to a newer version of the Mac OS.

A general hint when merging: you may prefer to reinstall some third-party software from your backups rather than from your old System Folder, just in case the copy currently on your drive is corrupted and is the source of the problem. I would not do this for all software, as it is long and tedious to do. But if you can isolate your suspects to any few particular programs, definitely reinstall those.

BY THE WAY ▶ Preserving Custom Changes to Your System File

Removing and saving the resources inside your System file may not save all the customized changes to your System file. In particular, some Installer utilities for other software modify the System file itself, often without telling you they are doing this. No later examination of the System file will directly tell you that this modification has been made. In such cases, when you reinstall the basic system software (even assuming that it is the same version you used previously), you will lose these customized changes. If this happens, you may notice that certain features have disappeared.

The main solution here is to rerun the Installers for the other newer software (assuming you remember which ones you need!) when you are done with the system software reinstall. You may also use Conflict Catcher's "Merge System File Resources" option, as described in the main text.

TAKE NOTE ▶ System Enablers, System Resources, and Mac OS ROM file

Here's the scoop on a trio of critical files, beyond the basic Finder and System files, that may be in your System Folder:

System Enablers When Apple releases new hardware, such as the iMac, current versions of the Mac OS may not work on it. Rather than release a new Mac OS, Apple may release a special file called an Enabler. This file is machine-specific; that is, it is only needed for the Mac that it is designed to "enable."

For example, the original iMacs came with a file called System Enabler 462. Without this file in the System Folder, the iMac would not startup. Older Macs did not need this file. If it was present, it would be ignored.

Similarly, when Mac OS 9.0.4 was released in March 2000, Apple included a file called PowerPC Enabler 9.0.4 that was needed for Apple's latest hardware to work with the new OS.

When an update to the Mac OS comes out, the data from any existing Enabler files are typically rolled into the System Software and these Enabler files are no longer needed. After installing an Update, you may thus find that the Enabler file has vanished. If so, don't worry; it's supposed to happen.

A possible problem involving these Enablers is with startup CD-ROM discs. For example, a startup CD that contains the latest version of the Mac OS may still not work with Apple's latest Macs, if these Macs require an Enabler that is not in the CD's System Folder.

System Resources and Mac OS ROM Starting with Mac OS 8.5, Apple introduced a secondary System file called System Resources. From the users point of view, it contains the same sort of information as found in the System file itself. It is an essential file for startup.

Starting with the iMac, and continuing with the new Macs introduced in 1999, Apple added an important new file to the System Folder: Mac OS ROM. More details about both of these files are provided in Chapter 1 (in the System Software section) and Chapter 14.

BY THE WAY ▶ Mac OS 9.0.4 Installation Oddities

Two oddities that may occur when installing Mac OS 9.0.4 (which may similarly remain true for subsequent updates):

Trashing and updating System Resources After starting up a Power Mac G4 after updating to Mac OS 9.0.4, you may find a copy of the System Resources file in the Trash. This can happen if, for any reason, the System Resources file is an older version than is required to work with the PowerPC Enabler file. If this happens, the older file is moved to the Trash and a new up-to-date System Resources file is automatically created.

File System Map error Updating to Mac OS 9.0.4 from a previous version of Mac OS 9 is not completed until you restart. Final changes to the contents of the System Folder are made during this initial post-installation startup. This can be a problem if you have installed a Mac OS 9.0.4 System Folder on a bootable CD before these final changes have been completed. Because you cannot write to a CD (certainly not at startup, even if it is a read/write CD in a CD-RW drive), starting up from the CD will fail, typically with a "file system map inconsistent" error. The solution is to startup from the System Folder on your hard drive before copying it to a CD.

Normal Install of System Software

If you want to install or reinstall System Software without using the Clean Install option, as just described, the procedure is quite similar:

1. **Follow steps #1-#4 of "Clean Reinstall of System Software," except don't select to "Perform Clean Installation" in Step 3.**

2. **Decide whether to Customize the Installation of not.** You are now ready to install the software. If you want to install everything that Apple recommends, simply click the Start button. If you wish to be selective about what you install, select Customize prior to selecting Start.

   Fix-It #4

   You will now see a list that starts with an item that reads "Mac OS" and continues with other items, such as Internet Access, Personal Web Sharing, and Text-to-Speech. In most cases, you should probably leave these settings alone. But if, for example, you know that you will never use Personal Web Sharing, you can uncheck the option so that it is not installed. Also be aware that some of these options are unchecked by default. If you want any of these options, you will have to specifically select them.

   Further customization is possible by selecting an option from the pop-up menu to the right of each component's name. The default choice is "Recommended Installation." The other two choices are "Customized Installation" and "Customized Removal" (not all software components include these options; in such cases your only choice is to enable or disable the checkbox to the left of the components' name). In general, I cover the use of Customized Installation in the next section of this Fix-It (see "Selective Install/Reinstall/Deletion of System Software"). However, there are two choices that should be covered right now:

   Universal Installation From the Installation Mode popup menu for the Mac OS, select "Customized Installation." At the top the window that appears will be a Selection pop-up menu. Its default choice will be Recommended Installation. The choice beneath it will be Universal Installation. If you select this option, you will wind up installing all the files you need for your Mac plus many files that have no relevance to your particular model. For example, files that are only relevant to a PowerBook will still get installed on a desktop Mac. However, these extras can be useful if you are installing to a removable cartridge (or other "portable" form of storage). In this case, you will have a cartridge that can be used as an emergency startup disk for virtually any Mac model. If you work in an environment where there is a mix of Mac models, this can prove to be invaluable. Otherwise, I would avoid using this. It will simply waste space on your drive with unneeded files.

   Another caution: if you select the "Universal" option when you first install system software, you may have a problem if you later try to update using the option to install software only for a specific Mac model. In particular, it may still install the "Universal" set of software (newer versions of the Installer may not do this). This is because, during the initial installation, the Installer places information in the System file about the type of installation selected. This information is used for updates, rather than the information you select from the Installer. To get around this problem, the solution is to do a clean reinstall or simply remove the System file from the System Folder prior to your update installation.

Core System Software If you make any changes to the individual items listed below the Selection pop-up menu, you instantly shift to a Custom installation. A key item in this list is the first item is Core System Software. If you select this and deselect everything else, you will install a minimum set of software needed to enable you to startup from the volume getting the software. There was a time when "minimum" meant small enough to fit on a floppy disk. No more. In Mac OS 9.0, for example, the Core System Software is about 18.5MB. If you want a System Folder that fits on a floppy disk, it may be possible to do (I discuss this more in Chapter 2), but not via this method. Anyway, Apple has made it clear that the floppy disk is on the way out, so there is less and less need to worry about this. Overall, I can't see any compelling reason for a Core-only install. A full Easy Install (of the Mac OS and other checked items, such as Internet Access) will not fit on a 100MB Zip disk; but even a Zip disk can likely hold the entire Mac OS Recommended Installation.

By the way, if you are ever unsure about what this or any other option does, click the "i" button at the far right of the line. This will open a window describing some (usually skimpy) details about what this item installs.

3. **Install the System Folder.** Once you are done with the Options and Customize selections, click Start. The rest should be automatic. When the installation is completed, you will have a new System Folder installed. You can now restart your Mac as normal (the Installer will likely force you to restart after you are done with the installation).

If you had previously selected the volume that contains the new System Folder to be your startup volume (via the Startup Disk control panel), your Mac should now use the new System Folder as the startup System Folder. Otherwise, if you want it to be the startup drive, select it from the Startup Disk control panel and restart.

4. **Install additional updates and software, if needed.** There may be an update to the reference version of the system software you just installed (such as the Mac OS 9.0.4 update to Mac OS 9.0). If so, you will need to separately install this as well. In most cases, you simply launch the Installer and when you get the window that has a Start button, simply click it. There will probably not be any Customize options.

Also, there is typically other software on the Mac OS CD, especially in a folder called CD Extras, that is not installed by the Mac OS Install utility. Each of these programs are optionally separately installed. They include HyperCard, America Online, and more. In some cases, they will have their own separate Installer utility. In other cases, you may simply need to drag the files to the appropriate location on your hard drive. It is beyond the scope of this Fix-It to provide details about these additional installations.

If you had previously installed newer versions of files that are also contained on the software you are now installing, you may need to reinstall these newer versions. What often happens is that you get messages during the initial system software installation asking whether it is OK to replace a newer version of a file with an older version. You may have to click OK in order to let the installation proceed. If so, do so. For example, the installation system software may contain an older version of QuickTime than the current version you are using. It may replace the newer version with the older one. If so, you need to separately reinstall the newer QuickTime to get it back.

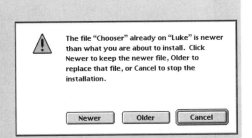

Figure F4-7 The Customized Installation window for the Mac OS 9 item in the Mac OS 9 Installer.

Finally, it is likely that you wound up with files that you do not need. For example, you probably have printer drivers for printers that you will never connect to your Mac. These can be deleted if you choose. Or you can just leave them there. As you get more familiar with what you use and do not use in your System Folder, you can always make decisions to trash files later on. Unless you need the extra disk space that the files occupy, there is no reason to be in a hurry to delete them.

TAKE NOTE ▶ If the Installation Fails

Occasionally, an attempt to install system software will fail, yielding any one of a variety of error messages. There are an equal variety of causes for these messages.

Corrupted fonts are one possible source of these problems. However, a corrupt font will likely only cause problems if the Installer attempts to install a font (as is common in printing software installations) that has the same name as a corrupt font currently in your System Folder. To work around this, remove the Fonts folder from the System Folder before installing. Then discard all the fonts with names identical to the new ones that were installed, returning the others to the new Fonts folder.

If you downloaded the software from an online source and you get a message that says: "An error occurred while trying to complete the installation. Installation was canceled leaving your disk untouched" while trying to install the system software, you probably got a corrupted copy of the software when you downloaded it. Try to download the software again, perhaps from another source.

(continues on next page)

> ⚠ The file "Chooser" already on "Luke" is newer than what you are about to install. Click Newer to keep the newer file, Older to replace that file, or Cancel to stop the installation.
>
> [Newer] [Older] [Cancel]

Figure F4-8 This error message may appear in the Installer window if the Installer is trying to install a version of the file that is older than the version that you already have. What to do here depends on the file. Sometimes an "older" file will be considered newer if you have modified it in some way (which would change its modification date); generally, these files should be discarded in favor of the truly new version you are about to install. Other times, the file in your System Folder already is a truly new version that you separately installed; these you should keep; otherwise you will have to reinstall them again later!

FIX-IT
#4

TAKE NOTE ▶ If the Installation Fails (continued)

When running an Installer, make sure that all system software files in your current System Folder have not been renamed from their original name. Wrong names can confuse the Installer and cause problems.

Be aware that if you try to run an Installer for a version of the system software that is too old for your hardware or not intended for your hardware, the Installer will refuse to let you do it (as it should!). For example, do not run an iMac-specific update on any other Mac. Similarly, do not run a Mac OS 7.*x* Installer on an iMac.

If you get an error that says the installer failed because a "resource has been modified," this usually means that some change was made to the application that causes the updater not to recognize it. The usual solution is to go back to the original version found on the CD you got when you purchased the product. Then apply the updater directly to this re-installed version.

Otherwise, if problems persist, try zapping the PRAM.

If you are using a CD-ROM as a startup disc, dirt on the disc may cause an installation failure. To check for this, wipe the shiny side of the disk gently with a soft cloth or tissue. Look especially for sticky "goop" on the disk. Wipe from the center to the edge of the disk; do not wipe in circles.

In one unusual case, I was unable to install Mac OS 8.*x* as long as I had a 200MHz 604 processor upgrade card in my Power Mac 7500. The Installer just quit in the middle with a message that the installation had failed. When I reverted to the original processor card (temporarily), the installation finished without a hitch.

BY THE WAY ▶ Saving Files that the Installer Replaced

When you update an existing System Folder, it removes any files that have been replaced by updated versions or that are no longer needed at all. However, if you are updating the currently active System Folder, it does not immediately delete these files (because they may still be in use until you restart). This gives you an opportunity to locate and save these files—which could turn out to be useful if some new file introduces more problems than it solves and you wish to revert to the older version. Here's what to do to hold on to these files:

1. With your hard drive as the startup disk, run the Installer.

2. After the installation is complete, restart with extensions off (hold down the Shift key at startup).

3. In your System Folder, find a folder called "Installer Temp" and drag it out. This folder contains all the files that were replaced by newer versions. Save this folder on a backup disk. Note that if you did not start up with extensions off, this folder gets deleted at startup.

4. Restart again with extensions on.

5. You can now replace files in your System Folder with files from the saved Installer Temp folder should you ever want to downgrade.

TAKE NOTE ▶ "Why Can't I Open The System Software I Just Downloaded?"

These days, if you download any Mac OS or other software update from Apple's Web site, it is likely to arrive as a file with a .smi suffix. This stands for self-mounting image. Double-click the image file to open it. This will result in a disk image appearing on your desktop, similar to what would happen if you had mounted a floppy disk or zip cartridge. The Installer application is contained on the mounted image. Simply double-click the Installer application to start the ball rolling.

Update Mac OS 9

Figure F4-9
A self-mounting image (.smi) icon for a Mac OS Update "disk."

If instead of an smi file you wind up with a file that has a .img suffix, this is also an image file but it is not self-mounting. If double-clicking this file results in the "application cannot be found" error message, it means that you do not have Apple's Disk Copy application available. It is typically found on the Mac OS CD that came with your Mac. However more recent versions, which fix inevitable bugs, may be available online.

If the downloaded file ends in a .sit, .bin, or .hqx suffix, this means that the file has been compressed and/or encoded to facilitate downloading. Check out Chapter 14 for more details about this.

Selective Install/Reinstall/Deletion of System Software

Basis for a Selective Install/Reinstall

The main purpose of a clean reinstall of your system software is to solve a problem that may be due to damaged or incompatible system software files. However, in some cases, you may be able to solve such problems by replacing only one or a few selected system software files, saving yourself the time and hassle of a complete reinstall. Examples follow.

Selective Damage/Bug Suspected You may suspect, because of the nature of your symptoms, that damage is to a particular file (such as if your problem is only with the Scrapbook, you obviously suspect the Scrapbook file). If so, you can choose to just replace that file. It typically pays to delete any associated Preferences files as well.

Otherwise, for any system software problem, the main suspects are the System file, Finder, and (if present) the System Resources, Mac OS ROM and Enabler files.

- To check for potential damage to the System file, try to open the System suitcase (by double-clicking its icon). If it refuses to open, it is almost certainly damaged and should be replaced. Unfortunately, if it does open, it does not guarantee that it is not damaged.

- If a Mac cannot maintain the correct date or time, and a battery problem appears ruled out, it may mean a corrupted System file.

- The freeware utility TechTool includes an option, called System Analyze, that checks if your System file is corrupt and needs replacement. However, make sure you have a version of TechTool that is current for the system software you are using. Otherwise, Tech Tool will either refuse to do this check or may even falsely claim that you have a corrupted file. Also, if you have applied any unofficial patches to the System file, TechTool may similarly claim that the System file is damaged. This is because TechTool works by comparing your System file to a database of the resources it expects to find—and it presumably does not know about your patch.

Tip: If you hold down the Option key when selecting Analyze, you will get a report of the number of system resources analyzed by TechTool and exactly which ones, if any, did not "pass." This can sometimes help (if you are familiar with such matters) diagnose why TechTool thinks your file is damaged, and therefore whether or not it really is.

Figure F4-10 TechTool's System Analyze feature can check for a corrupted System file; Conflict Catcher has a similar function.

Conflict Catcher can also check for a wider range of possible damage to System Folder files. (It too typically needs to be updated to accommodate new Mac OS releases). Even Apple's ResEdit can be used in this manner (if a file is damaged, ResEdit will give you an error message when you try to open it). ResEdit and Conflict Catcher may be able to fix damage that they discover. Disk repair utilities, such as Norton Utilities, may also be of use here, although their main function is to check for other types of damage.

SEE: • Fix-Its #10 and 11.

• Also consider checking for media damage (with Norton Utilities or equivalent), especially if you receive any sort of error message that says the Macintosh was unable to successfully replace a suspected damaged file.

• Finally, consider that the problem might be due to an incompatibility with a particular application rather than the system software alone. In this case, you may be able to solve the problem by upgrading to a newer version of the application rather than by dealing with the system software.

Files or resources missing Some system software problems are not due to damaged software but to missing software. This is especially likely if you initially did a Custom Install. For example, you may not have installed the files needed for file sharing or EtherTalk because, at the time, you did not intend to use these features. If you later try to access these features, you will probably get a message that says that needed resources are missing. Similarly, your System file may have been customized for your particular model of Macintosh. If you later copy the same System file for use on another type of Macintosh, it may not work properly. In this same situation, you may not have the Enabler needed for that Macintosh. In yet another case, certain applications expect specific fonts, available from the Macintosh system software disks, to be installed on your startup disk. If these are not installed, you get a message saying that the font is missing. Subsequent screen displays and printed output may not be correct.

BY THE WAY ▶ System Software Version Matching

To see the version of the Mac OS you are using, open the About This Computer window. It's the top item in the Apple menu when you are in the Finder. On the upper right-hand side, it may list the version number, and possibly some related Enabler or Update file name (such as PPC Enabler). Alternatively, there may be a line on the left side that says "Version:" followed by the current version number.

Other utilities (such as Apple System Profiler, also available from the Apple menu) will also provide this information.

Be aware that the version number of your System file and your Finder, as listed in the files' Get Info windows, may not be the same. This is probably okay as long as the difference is only in the digit after the second decimal place (such as System 8.5.1 vs. Finder 8.5.0). Otherwise, you probably have a Finder/System mismatch, in which case one or both of the files need to be replaced. With other system software files, it is impossible to make any reliable generalizations about whether or not version numbers should match each other.

If you do decide to check the Get Info windows for system software version information, check both the line below the name of the file (at the top of the window) and the Version line. The version number below the name (such as Mac OS 8.5.1) indicates what Mac OS version the software came from. The version number in the Version line is specific to the software file itself and is often different from the overall Mac OS version. To confuse things a bit more, Mac OS 9.0.2, 9.0.3, and 9.0.4 all simply said "Update Mac OS 9," rather than any specific version number, in the line below the file name.

With newer Macs, the About This Computer window may also list the Mac OS ROM version (see Chapter 14 for more details on this). This

Figure F4-11 Top: the Finder's Get Info window in Mac OS 9.0, indicating "9.0" in two locations (below the word "Finder" and in the Version line). Bottom: the About This Computer window indicating "Version: Mac OS 9.0" with "Mac OS ROM 3.1.1" installed.

FIX-IT #4

file may get updated separately from the OS, so it is possible to have a newer version of this file than the one placed their by your most recent Mac OS Installer. However, you should not have an older one there (unless you deliberately placed it there as part of some troubleshooting experiment, to see if it fixed a problem with the current version).

Install/Reinstall/Remove Selected System Software Files

To resolve any of the problems just described in the previous section, you can try installing or reinstalling selected files to your System Folder, rather than doing a complete reinstall. There are three basic ways to do this. Choose the one that is most appropriate for your situation.

Reinstall files from your backups. You can do this if you suspect that, or simply want to check if, a particular file is damaged, as long as you believe that your backup copy is still okay. For System, Finder, System Resources, Mac OS ROM and Enabler files, you could maintain a special separate set of backups, separate from your system software disks and your hard disk backups, just for this purpose.

To replace these files, you do not need to first start up from another disk. For example, to replace the Finder, drag the Finder from your System Folder to the desktop. Then copy the replacement Finder to your System Folder. Then restart. You will restart using the new Finder. You can now trash the old Finder.

For most other system software files, simply replace the file from your backups as you would for any file.

Install/reinstall files using the Mac OS Installer. When you run the Mac OS Installer and select a volume that already had that version of the OS installed, a dialog box will appear asking whether you want to do a new installation or want to add/remove files in the current installation. Select the latter. To replace specific system software files, you typically use the Customized Installation option described previously (see "Normal Install of System Software" earlier in this chapter). From here, peruse the list for the exact item you want. If you cannot find it, it may be part of a set of related files. For example, the Open Transport item in Networking & Connectivity actually is a collection of several Open Transport files. Sometimes, if you click the i button to the right of the item, you will find a list of the files that get installed if you select that item. More often, it will only provide a generic description of the function of the files. In any case, if you suspect that even your backup copies may be damaged, the custom installation method is the preferred way to go.

By the way, if you open the folder called Software Installers (on the Mac OS CD), you will find folders containing all the separate installer documents that are listed in the final Mac OS Install window. In some cases, if you open these folders, you will find the actual software files to be installed (such as Web browsers). In other cases, you will find a separate Installer utility. These are similar to the "old" style Installers that Apple used years ago. In most cases, you can launch these utilities separately and bypass the global Mac OS Install. If you get an error message when you try to launch one of these Installers, try holding down the Option key and launching again. This usually succeeds. If you are comfortable with this bypass, you may find it quicker and more convenient than using Mac OS Install. However, in some cases, files here may only be accessible from the Mac OS Install utility. In fact, with Mac OS 9, the Installer applications are gone altogether. Only the Installer documents remain and these can only be accessed by the top level Mac OS Install utility. It appears that Apple no longer wants you to access these Installers separately.

Remove files using the Mac OS Installer. Occasionally, you may want to completely remove certain system software from your drive — either prior to replacing it or without intending to replace it at all. For example, if Apple Menu Options is causing you trouble and you never use it anyway, you might as well trash it. In a case like this, it is sufficient to simply drag the file to the Trash icon and empty the Trash. In other situations, you may be uncertain exactly what file(s) you wish to delete, but you know the general category you wish to delete. For example, you may wish to delete all printing related software and then instead install the printing software that came with your printer. Or maybe you want to permanently delete all software related to Personal Web Sharing. In these cases, you can use the Installer's Customized Removal option. To access it, click the Customize button in the Install window and then select the desired Customized Removal item from the popup menu next to the software category that contains what you wish to delete. From the next window that typically appears, you can choose to delete All or just a Custom subset of the selected software.

**Fix-It
#4**

Whatever method you chose, when you are done, restart the Macintosh using the now modified disk as the startup disk when you are done. If your problem is gone, congratulations. If none of this worked, you may need to do a complete reinstall of the system software after all (as described in "Normal Install of System Software").

BY THE WAY ▶ Fooling the Installer

Sometimes an Installer may balk at opening. Even holding down the Option key when you launch the Installer won't work. This is usually because the Installer believes that it has nothing appropriate to install on your particular Mac. For example, an Installer for iMac software may refuse to open on any machine other than an iMac. However you may still wish to install the software. For example, perhaps you heard that software X, intended only for Mac OS 8.5 or later, actually works just fine in Mac OS 8.1 (which you still use). The only problem is the Installer refuses to run if it does not see Mac OS 8.5 installed. The solution here is to fool the Installer into thinking you are running the version of the Mac OS that it expects. Here's how (proceed at your own risk and always save a backup!):

1. Make a duplicate of your System file and drag it out of the System Folder to the desktop.
2. Open the System file that is still in your System Folder with Apple's ResEdit utility. (You'll get a warning that Apple does not recommend you do this. Ignore it: as long as you follow these instructions, you'll be okay.)
3. Open the vers item and open each of the two resources listed.
4. The top line of each should say Version Number followed by three boxes that together contain the actual version number. Change the number to the version the Installer expects to see. For example, change 8.1.0 to 8.5.0 in this case.
5. Save the change and quit ResEdit.
6. Launch the reluctant Installer. It should now work.
7. After the installation is complete, change the version number back to its original number.
8. Restart and make sure everything is working as expected. If so, you can now delete the backup copy of the System file on your desktop.

TAKE NOTE ▶ Use TomeViewer

The Installer utility is the key to installing almost any software these days – whether from Apple or some third-party software company. Many companies use some version of Apple's Installer, as described here.

You may be wondering, "Must I use an Installer, or could I copy the files directly using the Finder?" These days, you must use the Installer. The files are almost always stored in a special compressed format, typically called "tomes." The Installer extracts the needed files from these tomes and then places them in their correct location, saving you the increasingly complicated hassle of figuring out where everything goes. The files inside these tomes are not directly accessible from the Finder.

To access just one file, you might try using the Installer's Customize option. However, the Installer does not always give you selective access to every file in a tome. In cases such as this, it's time to turn to an Apple utility called TomeViewer. Apple's official policy is that this program is just for developers and it does not support its use for end users. However, it is quite easy to use and extremely effective. It creates a list of every file in any tome you select to open and permits you to extract any file or collection of files in the list. Just select a file and click the Extract button in the upper left corner of the window.

TomeViewer may also be useful to run prior to running an Installer. It will give you a preview peek at what the Installer might install.

One caution: using TomeViewer as a total substitute for running the Installer is not recommended. The Installer may perform operations beyond just installing the tome files (such as modifying the System file).

ID	Name	Type	Creator	Full Size	Compressed	Saved	Version
51	'Apple Video Player'	'APPL'	'mtv2'	745,296	338,007	55%	1.7.3
52	'Apple Video Player Guide'	'poco'	'reno'	298,551	79,779	74%	1.6
53	'apple.cnl'	'TEXT'	'fndf'	3,520	1,099	69%	3.0.1
54	'Apple.src'	'issp'	'fndf'	3,995	1,543	62%	3.0.1
55	'Apple/GV 56K'	'mlts'	'slnk'	15,229	5,637	63%	1.0.7
56	'AppleCD Audio Player'	'APPL'	'aucd'	157,145	61,272	62%	2.3.1
57	'AppleCD Audio Player Guide'	'poco'	'reno'	126,075	42,246	67%	1.0.2
58	'AppleScript'	'thng'	'ascr'	768,839	317,828	59%	1.4
59	'AppleScript Guide'	'poco'	'reno'	3,950	1,805	55%	1.0
60	'AppleScriptLib'	'shlb'	'cfrg'	11,611	3,560	70%	1.4
61	'AppleShare'	'RDEV'	'afpt'	645,228	318,885	51%	3.8.5
62	'AppleTalk'	'cdev'	'atdv'	211,617	99,240	54%	1.1
63	'AppleTalk & TCP/IP'	'almn'	'fall'	33,345	18,831	44%	1.1
64	'AppleTalk Preferences'	'pref'	'atdv'	1,075	679	37%	1.1.2
65	'AppleTalk Switch'	'adev'	'dav5'	17,393	7,121	60%	2.0.2
66	'AppleTIL.src'	'issp'	'fndf'	3,747	2,467	35%	3.0.1
67	'Application Switcher'	'appe'	'apsw'	87,023	42,612	52%	1.0
68	'Applications'	'find'	'fndf'	694	461	34%	3.0.1
69	'Arabic Encodings'	'utbl'	'encv'	36,206	10,650	71%	1.5
70	'ASLM Preferences'	'pref'	'aslm'	475	341	29%	n/a
71	'ATI 3D Accelerator'	'shlb'	'tnsl'	742,252	177,115	77%	4.8.4
72	'ATI Driver Update'	'ndrv'	'ATI©'	592,669	290,722	51%	1.4.8
73	'ATI Graphics Accelerator'	'INIT'	'ATI '	611,663	193,971	69%	4.7
74	'ATI MPP Manager'	'shlb'	'ATII'	59,815	19,417	68%	1.2f1
75	'ATI Rage 128 3D Accelerator'	'shlb'	'tnsl'	703,368	146,972	80%	5.6.6
522 Files		Totals:		90,278,605	42,795,267	100%	

Figure F4-12 Top: from the Mac OS 9 CD, if you open the Software Installers folder, then the System Software folder and finally the Mac OS 9 folder, this is what you will see. The Install System Software file is the "script" file accessed by the Installer utility. The Big System Morsels and System Extras files are ResEdit documents and can be viewed by that application. The Installation Tome file contains the balance of what gets installed when you install the basic Mac OS 9 software. Bottom: the window that opens if you use TomeViewer to peek into the Installation Tome file.

TAKE NOTE ▶ Beyond Mac OS install

The Mac OS Install utility is only one of many Installer utilities you are likely to meet. Even if you stick with just Apple software, you may see a variety of other installers. When you install an upgrade to system software (such as an Apple Displays Software update), you may see a utility similar to Mac OS Install, called Upgrader. It actually works in conjunction with a special version of Apple Software Restore (mentioned previously in this Fix-It in "Take Note: The iMac: Software Restore vs. Software Install CD-ROM Discs") which is found in a companion folder called Upgrader Files. The tomes that contain the actual update files are in a separate folder called Installation Files.

Other software (from Apple or from third parties) may still use Apple's older Installer utility, or it may use popular third party Installers such as one by Aladdin called StuffIt Installer.

One annoyance with almost all Installers is that they force you to quit all open applications before they begin (there is no getting around this). In many cases, they also want you to restart immediately after the installation is over (usually because they installed extensions or other software that requires a restart before they start to work). This can be annoying if you plan to do several installations. You don't want to have to restart after each one. Happily, recent versions of Installers now usually give you a choice of quitting or restarting. Otherwise, a Force Quit (Command-Option-Escape) of the Installer can typically bypass the "Restart now" requirement.

Another annoyance with Installers is that they often don't tell you everything they installed. This can lead to problems if the Installer incorrectly installed something you would rather not have (such as a copy of ObjectSupportLib in Mac OS 8.x – which is known to lead to problems). You would want to know this so that you can remove the file after it is installed. Happily, many Installers now create a log file (usually placed at the root folder of your drive) that lists all files installed. Check there to see what got put where.

Special Case: Delete Multiple System Folders

Multiple System Folders on your startup disk are a potential source of problems (see "Take Note: The Multiple System Folder Controversy [or Why Worry About More than One System Folder on Your Disk?]"). To eliminate them:

1. **Check for any multiple System Folders on your startup disk.** The simplest way to locate multiple System Folders is to use the Finder's Find command to search for all files that contain the word *System*. Alternatively, the Apple System Profiler Utility (used by most recent Mac models) can check for this. Simply select the "System Folders" tab from the Profiler window.

   By the way, there is no problem with having another disk with a System Folder on it mounted at the same time as the startup disk. The potential problem is restricted to multiple System Folders on the same startup volume.

2. **Delete any extra System Folders that you find.** If you find more than one System Folder on your disk (no matter how deep into how many folders they are buried), you may want to delete all except the one that you intend to be the startup System Folder. Restart immediately.

   If the System Folder you want to delete is currently the blessed System Folder, you may need to change this before you can delete it. To do this, drag either the Finder or the System file out of the folder. Open and then close the System Folder that you want to preserve. This folder should now have a Macintosh icon on it.

3. **Restart.** The correct System Folder should act as the startup System Folder. You can now delete the unwanted System Folder. Alternatively, you could restart with an alternate startup disk and then discard any System Folders from the original startup disk.

TAKE NOTE ▶ The Multiple System Folder Controversy (Or Why Worry About More Than One System Folder On Your Disk?)

It is best to have only one valid System Folder on your startup disk. Or, more precisely, only one System file and Finder should be on your startup disk.

With more than one System Folder present, you may develop problems with applications that store accessory files and preferences files in the System Folder. If these files are stored in one System Folder and a second System Folder on the same disk is used for startup, the applications will not access their accessory and preferences files and thus may not function as expected. In general, confusion may develop as to which of the multiple System Folders should be the blessed, or startup, System Folder.

More serious problems, including system crashes, may result when the Macintosh tries to access conflicting information from both System Folders. However opinions are divided on the likelihood of these more serious problems occurring. Some experts claim that you should absolutely never have two or more System Folders on the same startup disk. Others claim that the predicted dire consequences of doing this are highly exaggerated. Everyone seems agreed that problems are especially unlikely in recent versions of the Mac OS. Even Apple now admits that you can (and I quote) "safely store multiple System Folders on your drive."

Nonetheless, my advice is to play it safe: avoid having extra System Folders on your startup disk, unless you have some deliberate need for them (such as if you wish to be able to switch between two different versions of the system software).

If you are determined to have multiple System Folders on the same disk, a freeware utility called System Picker enables you to easily select or switch which System Folder you intend to use as the startup System Folder.

Also, if a drive is divided into multiple partitions, you can safely have a System Folder on each partition, even if one partition is the current startup volume.

 For Related Information

SEE:
- Fix-It #1 on incompatibilities between hardware and software.
- Fix-It #2 for more on replacing preferences files.
- Fix-It #12 on updating the disk device driver.
- Fix-Its #10 and #11 on damaged files, disks, and media.
- Fix-Its #15 on diagnostic software.
- Chapter 1 for details on the locations of system software files.
- Chapter 5 on startup problems and blessed System Folders.
- Chapter 9 for more on replacing damaged font files.
- Chapter 15 for more on problems specific to latest version of the Mac OS.

Fix-It #5:
Check for Problems with
Memory Management

▶ **QUICK SUMMARY**

Increase free memory by closing unneeded documents and applications, adjust an application's memory allocation from its Get Info window, or make more global adjustments to memory allocation (such as by modifying options in the Memory control panel).

 When to Do It:

- When you cannot perform a task because of insufficient free memory. Most often this occurs when you are trying to open an application or a document. Usually, you get an alert message such as *"There is not enough memory to open <name of application>."*

- Whenever you get an alert message stating that memory is running low.

- When software is running unusually slow, often with frequent disk access.

- Whenever an application suddenly and unexpectedly quits. Insufficient memory is not the only reason for an unexpected quit, but it is a common one.

- Whenever you get a system freeze, a system crash, or any less serious malfunction while using an application, particularly if you were doing a memory-intensive operation at the time (such as making a change to a large area of a complex graphics file). No error message need appear. The only system acknowledgment of the error may be a system beep.

- Whenever applications and/or system software have less (or more) memory assigned to them than you expected.

 Why to Do It:

No matter how much RAM you have, it is not enough. It may seem like enough now, but some day soon, it will not be. As memory becomes cheaper, computers include more and more memory in their standard configurations. But as soon as software developers expect users to have more RAM in their machines, they develop software that requires the additional RAM. The original Apple II computers came standard with as little as 4K of RAM. Today, most Macintoshes come standard with anywhere form 32MB to 128MB of RAM standard. Users often upgrade their Macs to even higher limits. Programs are already on the market that make effective use of these mega-amounts of RAM. This Fix-It can help you deal with the inevitable memory-related problems you will face, especially when you are not fortunate enough to have as much memory as you might like.

Almost all of your Macintosh's memory is divided into two components: the *system heap* and the *application heap*. The system heap contains the memory needed for the System file as well as for most extensions and control panels. The application heap contains the memory needed by applications and their documents.

TECHNICALLY SPEAKING ▶ SYSTEM HEAP VERSUS SYSTEM SOFTWARE

In the About This Computer window (as selected from the Apple menu), there is always a bar representing the size of the memory occupied by the Mac OS. This is not exactly the same as the size of the system heap. In particular, the Finder, as it is technically an application, is located in the application heap. However, its memory size is combined with the system heap size to calculate the Mac OS size in the About This Computer window. That's why you don't see the Finder listed as a separate bar.

Many control panels are actually applications and will be loaded into the application heap. Others function more like extensions and will be loaded into the system heap.

The size of the system heap can vary depending on such things as how many extensions are in use. Whatever is left over is assigned to the application heap. For example, suppose you have 64MB of RAM in your machine and that the system heap is occupying 20MB. That leaves 44MB of RAM for all applications. Every application needs a minimum amount of RAM to open and run properly (the amount is listed in the Memory area of the file's Get Info window). If insufficient RAM is available, the application does not open. Thus, in this example, you could never open an application that required more than 44MB of RAM.

All open applications share the available RAM in the application heap. Each application has a maximum amount of RAM that it occupies. It does not exceed this value even if more memory is available (although there is an exception to this that we will explore later in this Fix-It). Again, this limit is determined by the Memory settings in the file's Get Info window. Documents opened within an application use the memory space assigned to the application. So even if an application successfully opens, it may not have sufficient memory for all its documents that you wish to open.

If you work at the limits of your total available RAM, you are likely to get frequent memory-related alert messages. Occasionally, you may even get a system error, such as an unexpected quit, a freeze, or a system crash. These errors generally happen when, as a result of the low memory availability, the program gets "confused" and tries to address an area of memory that does not exist or has already been assigned to another use. Ideally, a program should avoid these errors and simply warn you about low memory via an alert message. However, this ideal is not always attained.

SEE: • Take Note: "About 'About This Computer and 'Get Info'," for more on these features.

What to Do:

This section is divided into four parts: "Memory Problems When Trying to Open an Application," "Memory Problems When Using an Open Application," "Special Case: Finder-Related Memory Problems," and "How to Increase Overall Memory Availability."

TAKE NOTE ▶ About "About This Computer" and "Get Info"

If you have any problems with memory management, it's useful to assess the allocation of your Macintosh's memory. Some details of how and why to do it were first given in Chapter 2. Here's a summary of the essential steps:

FIX-IT
#5

1. Select About This Computer from the Finder's Apple menu. Check the size of the Largest Unused Block. The Largest Unused Block is a measure of how much memory is still free to be assigned to applications or other uses. It can never be larger than the Total Memory size minus whatever is used by the Mac OS. Any application that needs more memory than this cannot be opened without first increasing the size of the Largest Unused Block (as described in the main text).

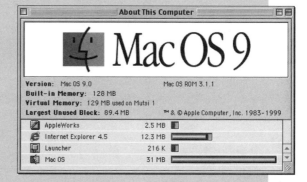

2. Select Get Info (from the Finder's File menu) for the application you wish to open. In the Get Info window, select "Memory" from the Show pop-up menu. The Minimum size is the minimally required amount of RAM needed to open the application. The application will use more than its Minimum, if memory is available, up until it reaches the Preferred size. The Preferred size is the typical maximum that the program will use. The more closely a program opens toward its Minimum rather than its Preferred size, the more likely it is to have memory-related problems (such as an inability to open large documents).

3. Compare the information in the application's Get Info window and in About This Computer. If the program's Minimum size is larger than the Largest Unused Block, you cannot open the program. This is probably the most common reason for the appearance of memory-related alert messages. Solutions to this are described in the main text of this Fix-It ("Memory Problems When Trying to Open an Application"). Also, note that the filled part of the bars in the About This Computer window will get larger as you open documents for the application or make active use of it. When a bar is nearly completely full, you will also be more likely to have memory-related problems with that application.

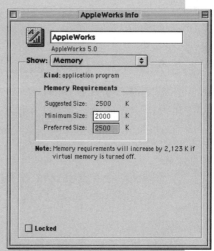

(continues on next page)

Figure F5-1 Check these windows for helpful information about memory allocation: the About This Computer window (top); an application's (AppleWorks) Get Info window (bottom).

TAKE NOTE ▶ **About "About This Computer" and "Get Info"** *(continued)*

Finally, note that some programs use special memory allocation schemes that differ from the standard procedures outlined here. For example, Adobe's Photoshop has its own virtual memory allocation method that may not be reflected in the About This Computer display. Some programs also use Temporary Memory, as described later in this Fix-It.

SEE: • **"Take Note: More About 'About This Computer': Bar Shading," "Take Note: Still More About 'About This Computer': Built-In Versus Total Memory," and "Take Note: Temporary Memory,"** for more on this feature.

TAKE NOTE ▶ **Quick Fixes To "About This Computer" Oddities**

Occasionally, the information displayed in the About This Computer window may suggest that something is wrong. Here are two common examples and their quick solutions. More details are given in the relevant sections of this Fix-It:

- **Problem:** The sum of the memory used by all software together with the Largest Unused Block size is substantially less than the Total Memory size.

  Solution: You have memory fragmentation or a memory leak. Quit all open applications. If this does not work, the surest (although not necessarily the most convenient) solution is to restart your Mac.

- **Problem:** You have more than 8MB of RAM installed, but everything over 8MB is allocated to the System Software line.

  Solution: If there is a 32-bit addressing option in your Memory control panel, make sure it is turned on; then restart. If 32-bit addressing is already on (or you do not have this option), restart anyway (as this may fix a similar but unrelated problem).

Memory Problems When Trying to Open an Application

You try to open an application or desk accessory. Instead of opening you are greeted with an alert message that says *"There is not enough memory available to open."* When this happens, here's what to do.

Check the Advice, If Any, in the Alert Message

The alert message may offer advice on how to solve the memory problem. For example, it may say *"Closing windows or quitting application programs can make more memory available."* If you get such advice, it usually pays to follow it. However, occasionally you may get an alert message that says that less memory is available than a program ideally needs, yet it asks, *"Do you want to open it using available memory?"* Usually, I would *not* click OK here. Even if the application successfully opens (and it may not), it is likely to give you problems. I prefer to seek other solutions instead.

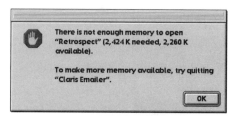
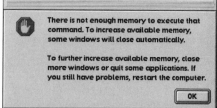

Figure F5-2 Two examples of alert messages indicating insufficient memory to open an application.

In particular, the main solutions to any of these problems are either to make more free memory available or to reduce the amount of free memory needed by the application. To do this, try one or more of the following, as appropriate.

Quit One or More Other Open Applications

Quitting open applications frees the memory occupied by those applications. Assuming you have enough total memory available, quit as many programs as necessary to free enough memory to launch the problem application. Now try to relaunch the problem application. If this works, you may also be able to reload the other applications that you have just closed (see "Check for Fragmented Memory Space," shortly, for how this works).

Reduce the Size of a Large Clipboard

Select Show Clipboard from the Finder's Edit menu. If it indicates that a large segment of data is there (such as all of a 50-page document), get rid of the selection. Storing a large selection in the Clipboard can take up extra system heap memory. Reducing its size may increase the Largest Unused Block enough to allow the application to open.

To try this, go to the Finder, select something small (such as one letter of text in a file's name), and copy that selection to the Clipboard. This replaces the large selection, hopefully reducing the Clipboard's memory allocation.

Check for Fragmented Memory Space

What is Fragmented Memory? You may find that an application does not open, even though enough unused memory is available to meet the requirements of the application. Here's what is probably happening: picture the total memory space as a long loaf of bread that gets divided into smaller slices, where each slice represents an open application. Ideally, the slices should be adjacent to each other, so that the remaining unsliced bread forms one big block. However, if for some reason you removed slices from random locations in the loaf, the unused portion of the bread would be broken into smaller noncontiguous segments.

This can happen with memory, as it can for bread. Normally, applications open into contiguous (that is, adjacent) memory space. However, if you have opened and closed and opened several applications over the course of a session, this adjacency may be gone. Noncontiguous or fragmented memory blocks may exist (note that this is not the same as disk file fragmentation, the subject of Fix-It #7).

The Largest Unused Block size in the About This Computer window indicates the largest contiguous block. If memory is fragmented, this amount is less than the amount of unused memory. This would mean that the sum of all the memory used by open applications plus the Largest Unused Block size would be less than the Total Memory.

If you want to see if your memory is currently fragmented, several utilities let you do so. Two that I frequently use are Memory Mapper and Peek-a-Boo. For example, Figure F5-3a shows the division of memory among the numerous applications open on my drive as I write this. The map is on the left (it's in color on your Mac, making it easier to see what is going on). On the right is a sequential listing of each application shown on the map. Note that every time you see the word "Free," this indicates unused memory. If you see the word "Free" more than once, this means that you have fragmented memory. In this example, the sizes of the fragments are rather small and a huge block

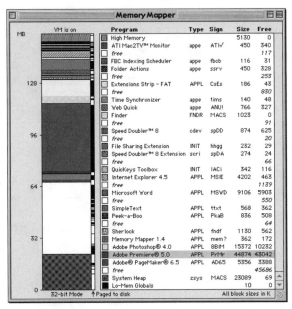

Figure F5-3a Memory mapper shows distribution of memory. Each "free" segment is a memory fragment.

of free space remains open. Thus, fragmented memory is not likely to be a problem.

In Figure F5-3a, the application Adobe Premiere (which I set to be a memory guzzler at almost 45MB of RAM) is highlighted. Figure F5-3b shows what happens after quitting Premiere. Note the new large block of free memory that appears as Premiere gives up its allocation. More importantly, note that this block is still isolated from another large block of free memory by the still-open PageMaker application. Because the blocks are not contiguous, any application that needed both blocks in order to open would not be able to do so. Figure F5-c shows what happens after also quitting PageMaker: the two

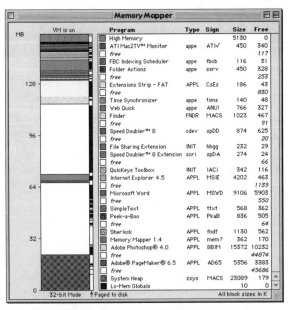

Figure F5-3b The same Mac after quitting Adobe Premiere. Note the additional block of free memory that appears.

isolated blocks of free memory, as well as the space previously occupied by PageMaker, have combined into one larger block. Now, any application that needed that much space could use it. Thus, even though sufficient memory was already free, quitting PageMaker became a necessary step to making use of it.

System vs. application heap growth

While looking at these figures, note that the application heap is represented by all of the files at the top of the map, while the system heap is the large block at the bottom. Generally, each heap grows towards the middle as more memory is needed, minimiz-

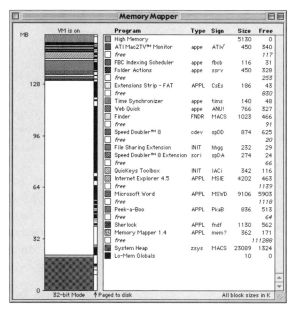

Program	Type	Sign	Size	Free
High Memory			5130	0
ATI Mac2TV™ Monitor	appe	ATIv	450	340
free				117
FBC Indexing Scheduler	appe	fbcb	116	31
Folder Actions	appe	ssrv	450	328
free				253
Extensions Strip - FAT	APPL	CsEs	186	43
free				830
Time Synchronizer	appe	tims	140	48
Web Quick	appe	ANU!	766	327
Finder	FNDR	MACS	1023	466
free				91
Speed Doubler™ 8	cdev	spDD	874	625
free				20
File Sharing Extension	INIT	hhgg	232	29
Speed Doubler™ 8 Extension	scri	spDA	274	24
free				66
QuicKeys Toolbox	INIT	IACi	342	116
Internet Explorer 4.5	APPL	MSIE	4202	463
free				1139
Microsoft Word	APPL	MSWD	9106	5903
free				1118
Peek-a-Boo	APPL	PkaB	836	513
free				64
Sherlock	APPL	fndf	1130	562
Memory Mapper 1.4	APPL	mem?	362	171
free				111288
System Heap	zsys	MACS	23089	1324
Lo-Mem Globals			10	0

32-bit Mode ⬆ Paged to disk All block sizes in K

FIX-IT #5

Figure F5-3c The same Mac after also quitting PageMaker. Not how the two large separate fragments of free memory have combined into one larger one.

ing any chance that they get in each other's way. However, this can occasionally lead to problems. For example, if you fill the application heap to the point where it is almost adjacent to the system heap, this leaves little or no room for the system heap to grow. Should an action then require an increase in the system heap, a system crash could result (see also: "Increase the Size of the System Heap," later in this Fix-It). This problem is more likely to occur if you have very little physical memory to begin with. This is one reason that having a large amount of memory can prevent system crashes.

How Can You Eliminate Fragmented Memory? We already implied one answer to this in the example of quitting PageMaker. To be specific: unlike disk storage, where a file can be stored in fragments, an application must load into RAM as a single contiguous block. Thus, any application you want to open must fit within the Largest Unused Block (as listed in the About This Computer window). So if an application needs 800K of RAM, and only two separate 500K blocks of RAM are currently unused, the application does not open, even though 1000K of memory is available. The solution here is as follows:

1. **Quit one or more applications, saving your work first.** In the example just described, quitting PageMaker would likely be sufficient to solve a fragmented memory problem. Of course, the trick here is knowing which application is the key one to quit. That's where a utility such as Memory Mapper comes in handy. If even this is not sufficient, or you simply want to maximize the size of the largest unused block, quit all your open applications and reload them. Ideally, load them in an

order such that the applications you expect to quit first are launched last. This will minimize future fragmentation.

If you still don't have enough memory for the task at hand, go to the next step.

2. **Kill open background processes or (even better) restart the Macintosh.**
Occasionally, even after quitting all apparent open applications, you will still have fragmented memory. There are two main reasons for this.

The first is that you likely have background (or "faceless") applications open (see: "Technically Speaking: Startup Extension Oddities" and "Take Note: Process Manager Utilities" in Fix-It #3). These may be fragmenting memory. For example, in Figure F5-3a, note the two "free" fragments between Folder Actions, Extensions Strip, and Time Synchronizer (all of which are faceless applications). These fragments are small and can probably be ignored as possible help in opening applications, but occasionally you may see bigger ones. Although you can use a process manager (such as Peek-a-Boo) to kill particular background applications, assuming you know that you do not need the process open, it might be simpler (although more time consuming) to simply restart your Mac.

RAM Doubler is another utility that has a convenient way to see a list of all of these "invisible" files that are using memory. Click RAM Doubler's Application Details tab, scroll down to the System Software item and click the triangle icon to open the list contained within. Here you will see all of the open processes that are taking place behind the scenes. It is the sum of these processes that make up the Mac OS allocation in the About This Computer window.

The second reason for seeing fragmented memory even after quitting all open applications is that you have a memory leak (as described next). In this case, restarting is likely the only remedy.

Check for Memory Leaks and "Unreleased" Memory (A Step Beyond Memory Fragmentation)

What is a memory leak? A problem similar to the fragmented memory problem is when all or part of an application's memory does not get "released" when you quit the application or when the application otherwise no longer needs it. Instead, it may get rolled into the system software's memory allocation, making it much larger than normal. Or it may simply seem to "disappear." When this happens, you do not regain your expected free memory when quitting applications. Especially if this happens repeatedly, you can wind up with a substantially reduced amount of memory available for other applications. This is called a *memory leak*.

In the worst cases of a memory leak, memory continues to get used up by the offending application (or absorbed by the Mac OS allocation) until you run out of memory altogether. In these situations, you may be able to open the About This Computer window and watch the bar representing the application's memory continue to increase and increase, even beyond the supposed limit set in the application's Get Info window. This can lead to a crash or to the program displaying an out of memory message.

I must add here that the difference between memory leaks and memory fragmentation is sufficiently subtle that one problem may be frequently mistaken for the other. Some confusion of this sort may be contained right on these pages. For example, what appears to be a leak (because it occurs even when all applications are closed), may really be fragmentation due to a background application that you are not aware is still running. Basically, anytime you have a suspected memory loss of this type, try solutions relevant for both fragmentation and leaks.

What causes a memory leak? The most common cause for this problem is a bug in Apple's system software. Read Me files for system software updates frequently cite that they have fixed some of these "leaks." But others always seem to remain. Sometimes bugs in the application itself may cause a memory leak.

Also, programs that use shared library files may result in a particular type of memory leak. This is because shared library files load into the system heap memory when needed. The memory they use may remain in system heap even after quitting the application that needed it. Web browsers have been an especially common source of such memory leaks. Microsoft Office does this as well—intentionally. Making matters more confusing, some programs that indicate how much memory is free may mistakenly list the shared library memory as free even though it isn't. On the other hand, programs that correctly identify the shared library memory as allocated may not tell you what's going on, leaving you with the impression that the memory has somehow vanished.

SEE: • **Take Note: "Temporary Memory and Memory Leaks," elsewhere in this Fix-It.**

What can you do about a memory leak? The ultimate solution to memory leak problems is for developers to fix the software that causes the leak.

The most common memory leak problems revolve around software that uses Open Transport and TCP connections to the Internet (see Chapter 12). That's why several of the solutions point to these programs. More generally, the solutions divide into two categories: (1) how do I get rid of a memory leak that I now have? and (2) how do I prevent memory leaks from recurring in the future?

How Do I Get Rid of a Memory Leak That I Now Have?

- First, quit all open applications. See if this reclaims the amount of memory you expect to be available. This makes sure that your "leak" is not merely memory fragmentation.

- Try using certain utilities that may plug a leak. Over the years, utilities such as Mac OS Purge and FixHeap have been able to refill the memory lost to a leak. But I have found these to be relatively ineffective in the most recent versions of the Mac OS. But some new utility coming down the road may turn out to be more successful. In any case, these rarely make matters worse, so they are worth a try.

- Quit the Finder. Use a utility such as Terminator Strip, a Control Strip module that can send a Quit command to the Finder, without requiring that you restart. This is more graceful and less likely to have undesirable side-effects than a traditional Force Quit from the Finder (via Command-Option-Escape), as described in Chapter 4. But any Force Quit may succeed here in a pinch. Try it.

- Memory leaks related to Open Transport can be minimized by, immediately after starting up and getting online, opening up a Open-Transport dependent application that requires only a minimum of RAM and then quitting it. You will have a leak here but it will be a small one. Subsequent applications that you open, that use much more RAM (such as Netscape), should then not "leak." However, for this to work, you will have to redo this each time you restart your Mac.

- Otherwise, the only other short term solution is to restart your Mac. As with memory fragmentation, this is guaranteed to work!

How Do I Prevent Memory Leaks From Recurring in the Future?)

- If you use a dial-up Internet connection, go to the TCP/IP control panel. If you are in Advanced or Administration User Mode, there is a button called Options. Click it. From the window that appears, make sure that the "Load Only When Needed" checkbox is checked (although in the voodoo of how this works, some users report that *unchecking* this can help avoid the memory leak problem, so you may want to experiment here). This should prevent many (though not all!) memory leaks that are specific to using Open Transport and applications (such as Web browsers) that use Open Transport.

    SEE: • **"Using 'Load only when needed,'" in Chapter 12, for related information.**

- Do not enable the "Connect automatically when starting TCP/IP applications" checkbox in Remote Access' Protocol options (or any similar option in whatever other PPP utility you may use). For some reason, it may also contribute to memory leak problems.

- Upgrading to the latest version of the Mac OS may help. Each new version generally fixes memory leaks discovered in the previous version.

- Check for an updated version of the leaking program that may have fixed the leak.

- Turn on virtual memory (even at a 1MB size) or install RAM Doubler. This appears to reduce memory leak problems, at least on Power Macs. This is especially so for "memory leaks" that would otherwise occur due to use of shared library files. Of course, users with sufficient physical RAM are reluctant to do this, as it slows down your Mac. You'll have to decide what is more critical on these occasions.

- Increase the amount of memory that a program uses (to delay the effect of the leak).

- Install more RAM. Even if this doesn't prevent memory leaks, it makes them less noticeable (as you are less likely to run out of RAM when you have a lot more installed).

TAKE NOTE ▶ Temporary Memory and Memory Leaks

In the Mac's days of yore, each application had an absolute maximum amount of memory that it could use. This was generally equal to the Preferred Size setting, as listed in the application's Get Info window. If a program needed more memory after you opened it, you would have to quit the application, increase its Preferred Size, and launch it again.

In recent years, the Mac OS now permits the use of temporary memory. Essentially, if a program needs additional memory beyond what it has been allocated, and there is free memory available, it can request that the Mac OS assign additional memory to the application on a temporary basis. If the Mac OS perceives that the memory is more critically needed somewhere else, such as to open an application that you just launched, it can reclaim this temporary memory (assuming it is not currently actively in use). These increases and decreases in memory for an application take place dynamically, without the need to quit and relaunch the application.

This only happens if a program is specifically written to request temporary memory. The Mac OS does not otherwise do it on its own. Internet Explorer is one well known program that does this.

In Mac OS 8.0 and later, the About This Computer window shows temporary memory as part of the Application heap (e.g., the increases are added to the memory listing of each application that uses temporary memory). In Mac OS versions before 8.0, temporary memory was included as part of the System heap (the amount of memory the window indicates the System Software is using).

A potential problem with temporary memory can occur if, due to some bug, the program fails to give up its temporary memory when requested to do so. In fact, it might continue to request more and more temporary memory and never give it up. In essence, this is a form of memory leak.

FIX-IT #5

Reduce the Minimum/Current Memory Size

What can you do if you want to open an application that has a Minimum size of 2000K, but you cannot afford to free more than 1800K of memory? You could reduce the application's Minimum size to 1800K and see if it now opens. Technically, if 2000K is truly the minimum needed to open the application, this should not work. In fact, when you try to make this change, you will get a message warning you about the potential dire consequences of what you are about to do. However, often the posted Minimum is not really the rock-bottom minimum, so the application may successfully open. I would only consider doing this if you do not intend to go very far below the Minimum size (and if the default Minimum size is not too far below the Suggested size). Otherwise, you truly are asking for trouble in the form of an eventual system error.

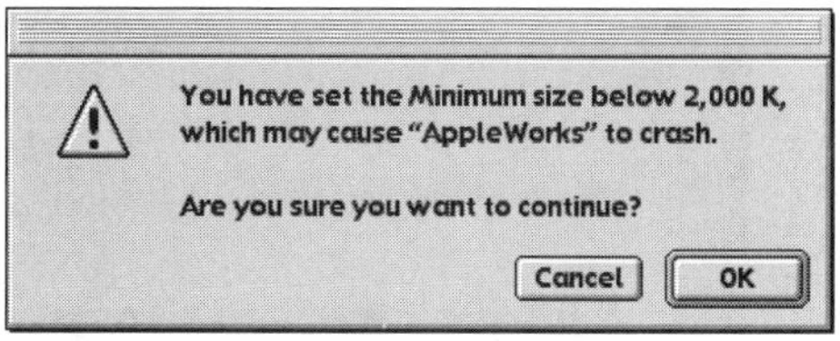

Even if the application opens at reduced memory settings, you may find that not all of its features work. Still, if you only need to do this on rare occasions, it can be preferable to not being able to open the application at all.

By the way, if you do change an application's Minimum (or Preferred) Memory setting, there is no button you can click to get the settings to return to their default values. If you forget the default values, you may need to check with a backup copy to find out what they were (though the message you get when trying to go below the Minimum value at least tells you the default Minimum value).

You have set the Minimum size below 2,000 K, which may cause "AppleWorks" to crash.

Are you sure you want to continue?

Cancel   OK

Figure F5-4 The Macintosh warns you not to set the minimum below its preset default value.

Power Macintosh Alert: If you have a Power Macintosh, turning on virtual memory may reduce the Minimum size needed to open an application.

SEE: • **"Increase the Total Available Memory," later in this Fix-It, for more details.**

Remove Plug-In Modules and Other Accessory Files

If reducing the memory size did not succeed in getting the application to open, and if your application uses plug-in modules or other accessory files (such as a grammar checker included as part of a word processor), delete any modules you do not need. Since each of these modules typically uses a portion of the application's allocated memory, removing them reduces the amount of memory needed to run the program. If so, the application may now open in your reduced memory size setting.

By the way, if an application already successfully opens at a given memory size, you can still decide to remove unneeded modules. Doing this leaves a greater portion of the application's allocated memory available for documents to be opened within the application (a problem discussed more generally later in this Fix-It).

If None of the Preceding Advice Works

If you are using a new, more memory-hungry version of an application, you can return to the previous version, assuming it is compatible with your other software. Alternatively, try methods to increase the amount of unused memory available. For example, eliminate unneeded extensions or turn on virtual memory.

SEE: • **"How to Increase Overall Memory Availability" later in this Fix-It.**

TAKE NOTE ▶ Unexpected Quits and Other System Errors

If you get an unexpected quit message, either while trying to launch an application or anytime after it has opened, this is a form of system error. The cause is usually a memory-related software bug in the application. It is more likely to occur when your demands on memory are high, such as when you have several applications and documents open at once. Sometimes, after an unexpected quit, you can simply relaunch the application without a problem, but just as often doing so will result in a recurrence of the unexpected quit. Memory problems may also lead to other types of system errors (including system freezes, system crashes, or a spontaneous restart of the Macintosh). Most often, simply restarting the Macintosh (if it hasn't already done so itself!) and relaunching the application clear up these problems. Sometimes, increasing the Preferred memory size of the application, as described in this Fix-It, may help. Otherwise, refer to Chapters 4 and 6 for more specific advice.

Memory Problems When Using an Open Application (Such As an Inability to Open a Document)

There is something of a paradox here. When, as just described, you can't open an application, the solution typically requires freeing up more memory. However when you can't open a document within an open application, freeing up even an infinite amount of memory is not likely to help. This is because, if the application has already opened in its Preferred memory size, freeing up more memory will not affect how much memory the application can use (barring the possible use of temporary memory). For example, a program that has a Preferred memory size of 1MB will use no more than 1MB of memory even if 32MB of free memory is available. Thus, these problems require a different set of solutions than those just described.

TAKE NOTE ▶ More About "About This Computer": Bar Shading

Once again, the About This Computer window can help diagnose potential memory problems here. In particular, the light shaded portion of each application's bar indicates how much of its allocated memory is still unused. If this area is very small for a given application, memory problems may be imminent. Remember, turning on balloon help and placing the cursor over a bar will give you the exact amounts represented by the shaded areas.

The sum of a bar's dark and light shaded portions is the application's total memory allocation (and is equal to the number to the right of the application's name).

For the Mac OS bar, don't worry about how little white space there is. The system software is designed so that there will always be very little white showing. If the Mac needs more memory for the system software, it can dynamically increase its allocation (up to some limit, of course).

Common memory problems within an application include an inability to open a document or the application's failure to carry out a selected command (such as copy or paste). Typically, these symptoms are signaled by an alert message. For example, you may get a message that says *"There is not enough memory..."* to open a document. Or you may get an alert message that says *"Out of memory"* or *"memory low."* Finally, you may simply get a system error (such as an unexpected quit or a system crash).

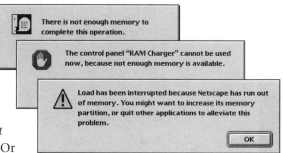

Figure F5-5 Three examples of out of memory alert messages.

For system errors, see "Take Note: Unexpected Quits and Other System Errors." Otherwise, try one or more of the following solutions, as needed. Then retry opening the document (or carrying out whatever other operation was not working).

Close Any Open Documents That Do Not Need to Be Open

This increases the amount of unused memory available to the application and may permit your requested operation to proceed successfully.

Reduce the Size of the Clipboard

In some cases, the Clipboard uses the application's memory allocation. Reducing the size of the Clipboard is thus another way to increase the unused portion of the application's memory. To do this, select something small (such as one word from an open text document) and copy it to the Clipboard.

Do Not Try to Open the Document from the Finder

When an application's unused memory is low, you may be able to open a document from within the application that would not open if you double-clicked it from the Finder.

Quit the Application and Relaunch It, Restarting If Needed

Select Save and then quit the application. Then relaunch it. Often, this alone will solve the problem. If you are trying this in response to an "out of memory" warning message, do this before trying either of the previous two suggestions. This is because such messages are typically a warning that it is time to bail out immediately. If you ignore this warning, unexpected quits, system freezes, or crashes are likely to occur very soon.

After relaunching, if you had several document windows open previously, work with fewer open documents this time. This will help avoid the return of these memory-related problems.

If relaunching alone does not work, restart the Macintosh and then relaunch. If this still fails to work, you probably don't have enough memory allocated to the application. To correct this, continue to the next step.

Increase the Preferred Memory Size

Allocate more memory to the application (assuming you have free memory available). To do this, you need to increase the Preferred memory size of the application, as listed in its Get Info window. This is somewhat the reverse of what you try to do when the application cannot open at all. There you try to reduce the amount of memory the application needs in order to open. Here you will increase it.

1. **Quit the application.** You cannot modify the memory size of an application while it is open.

2. **Check the About This Computer window.** Check the About This Computer window to see the size of the Largest Unused Block. This tells you the maximum size that you can set as the Preferred size of the application.

3. **Increase Preferred/Current Memory size.** Assuming free memory is available, increase the Preferred/Current memory size in the application's Get Info window (and select "Memory" from the Show pop-up menu). For starters, I typically increase the size by about 1-2MB or double its current size (whichever is smaller).

   If you have enough free RAM, increasing this size is a good general preventative measure to forestall memory related problems in almost any application.

   If the application's allocation is less than its Preferred size. The method above assumes that the application is currently open at its Preferred memory size. If it isn't, there may be a simpler solution. You can check for this by selecting About This Computer before you quit the application. It lists the application's actual memory allocation (see "Take Note: More About 'About This Computer': Bar Shading"). Compare this to its Preferred size. If the application's allocation is less than its Preferred size, and other applications are open, it probably means that there was not enough free memory available (when you launched the application) for the program to open at its Preferred size. To remedy this, quit all open applications and launch just the problematic application. It should now open in its Preferred size. You can probably now open the problem document(s). If not, quit the application again and increase the Preferred size, as described above.

4. **Repeat the process, if needed.** Relaunch the application and try opening the document that would not open previously (or try whatever other memory-related problem you were having). If it still does not work, repeat this process, increasing the memory size further, until you succeed or you run out of memory.

   If you do not have enough free memory available to sufficiently increase the application's memory allocation, try to increase free memory availability by using methods described later in this Fix-It.

   SEE: • **"How to Increase Overall Memory Availability," later in this Fix-It.**

Fix-It
#5

5. **Divide the document into smaller files.** If you succeed in getting the application and document to open by increasing the Preferred or Current memory size, consider dividing the document into separate files for future use. For example, if it is a large word-processing document, divide it into two smaller segments and save each one as a separate document. You may now be able to reduce the memory size to its previous level and still avoid a recurrence of this problem. Obviously, this technique does not work as well for graphics files or other documents that do not lend themselves to being subdivided.

6. **Reduce memory demand of graphics files.** Bitmapped graphics, such as TIFF files, can require a large amount of memory to open. Bear in mind that when creating these files, the lower their depth and resolution, the less memory they will require to open (I am talking here about how they are saved, not how they are displayed). That is, using 256 grays rather than millions of colors, using 72 dpi rather than 300 dpi, and so on, will help reduce memory demands. If you need the higher depth and resolution, so be it. But don't use more than you need. If you succeed in getting the document to open, consider resaving it with a reduced depth or resolution to reduce its memory demands in the future.

   SEE: • **Chapter 10 for more on depth and resolution.**

BY THE WAY ▶ The Reaper and Memory Adjustments

The Reaper is a shareware utility that provides several useful functions for managing your memory. First, it allows you to change the memory allocation of any application without having to adjust the settings in the Get Info window. You can select an absolute change (e.g., 2MB) or a relative change (e.g., 100% increase over the Get Info setting). Its "Smart Heap" function is especially cool. Have you ever tried to open a huge JPEG graphic in AppleWorks only to be told that you don't have enough memory? While you can adjust AppleWork's allocation to fix this, you probably will want to undo the change when you are done—because most of what you do with AppleWorks does not need this additional RAM. These changes back and forth can get to be a pain. With "Smart Heap" Reaper will give AppleWorks the added memory only when it needs it. It's like having a "Temporary Memory" feature even for those applications that were not programmed to use it.

(continues on next page)

BY THE WAY ▶ The Reaper and Memory
Adjustments (continued)

Figure F5-6 The Reaper.

Finally, Reaper can increase the memory allocation of applications stored on CD-ROM discs or other "read-only" media; these sizes cannot be modified using the Finder. In fact, you can use the Reaper to increase the memory allocation of the Finder itself, as well as any other files (such as most extensions) that have a memory allocation but do not have memory size settings in their Get Info window.

SEE ALSO: • "Special Case: Finder-Related Memory Problems."

FIX-IT
#5

BY THE WAY ▶ Increasing Memory Size of Extensions

Many extensions request a specific memory allocation when the Mac starts up. You can see how much memory has been assigned to an extension by using Conflict Catcher (see Fix-It #3). Check out the Memory Use column. Many will have no memory usage at all, but others will. Background-only applications (often referred to as appe files also have an assigned memory size. **Note:** The memory use number may be in boldface for some files. This means that the file is using more memory than it requested at startup. While you can often ignore this, it can sometimes be a cause of system crashes. One thing that might help is to enable the "Guarantee System Heap" option in Conflict Catcher's Startup Preferences panel.

A more general solution is to increase the memory allocation of the file. The problem here is that, as with the Finder, these files do not normally have a Memory Requirements box in their Get Info window. So you cannot use this method to increase the memory allocation of these files, should you need to do so.

However, these changes can be made. Using Reaper is one way. For those familiar with ResEdit, you can also do it by opening the file and directly editing its Size resource. Alternatively, you can actually get the file's Get Info window to display a Memory Requirements box. There are several ways to perform this trick. I will describe one that uses a utility called Snitch (described more in Chapter 8). You can do the same thing with utilities such as File Buddy, OtherMenu, or ResEdit (again). Pick the method you like best. You should always be working with a backup copy when making changes to a file.

How to increase memory size of extensions with Snitch:

a. From the Get Info window of the file you want to fix, change its Type to APPL.

b. Close the Get Info window.

c. Make a copy of the file with the Finder's Duplicate (Command-D) command.

d. Open the Get Info for the duplicate file. The Memory Requirements box will now be there.

e. Make the increase in memory as desired. Change the Type back to appe (or whatever it was).

f. Close the Get Info window. You can now delete the original file and rename the copy.

   The Memory Requirements box now remains visible in Get Info even though it is an appe file again. It may go away after a restart. Otherwise, if you want it to disappear, you need to once again make a copy of the file. The copy will not show the Memory Requirements box.

   This method can also be used to adjust the memory size of the Finder as well as desk accessories.

More recently, control panel applications have shifted to using the APPC file type. This file type does provide for memory adjustments in the Get Info window, just as with "ordinary" (APPL) applications.

SEE: • Chapter 8 for more on changing file types.

Special Case: Finder-Related Memory Problems

Like every other application, the Finder has a memory size assigned to it. Normally, this size is adequate and does not need readjustment. At times, however, the Finder may have insufficient memory to carry out a request. Most often, this occurs when you are trying to copy files, eject disks, show the Clipboard, or open folder windows.

Usually, you get an appropriate alert message informing you of this problem. Here's what to do.

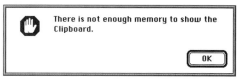

There is not enough memory to show the Clipboard.

OK

Figure F5-7 Message that may appear after the Show Clipboard command is selected from the Finder's Edit menu; if the object on the Clipboard is not unusually large, this message probably means that the Finder is running low on memory.

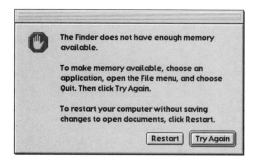

The Finder does not have enough memory available.

To make memory available, choose an application, open the File menu, and choose Quit. Then click Try Again.

To restart your computer without saving changes to open documents, click Restart.

Restart   Try Again

Figure F5-8 A message that directly indicates insufficient memory to run the Finder.

Quit Applications and Close Windows

Quit any applications that do not need to be open. Next, close all open Finder windows that you do not currently need. Try again. If this fails to work, restart the Macintosh and try the desired operation again, still maintaining a minimum of open applications and/or Finder windows.

If you get a memory error only when you are trying to copy several files at once, you should also try copying the files in smaller groups. This reduces the memory demand for each copy request.

Increase the Finder's Memory Size

If Finder-related memory problems occur often, you may be able to permanently resolve the problem by increasing the memory allocation of the Finder. Remember that doing so reduces the amount of memory remaining for other applications to use, so don't be in a hurry to do it.

As a rule, you should not have to bother with this. Apple has assigned what it believes to be an adequate amount of memory to the Finder. And usually it is (especially if you have 12MB or more of memory). Still, if you start getting out of memory messages when trying to open windows or move files (or whatever) in the Finder, it could mean you have a Finder memory (or possibly even a system heap) problem. In this case, increasing the Finder's memory is worth a try.

The simplest way to increase the Finder's memory size is via a utility. Currently, I recommend using Reaper to do this. Using Snitch is another alternative (as described in "By the Way: Increasing Memory Size of Extensions"). You could also try FinderFixer or Finder Heap Fix; just launch the utility, type in your desired memory allocation for the Finder, quit the utility, and restart. However, beware: these latter two utilities may not be updated to work with the latest versions of the Mac OS. For example, Finder Heap Fix was mainly designed to fix a problem in System 7.5.5 and has not been updated since. It still appears to work in Mac OS 9, but I would be cautious.

SEE: • **By the Way: The Reaper and Memory Adjustments.**
• **"Increase the Size of the System Heap," later in this Fix-It, for related information.**

**FIX-IT
#5**

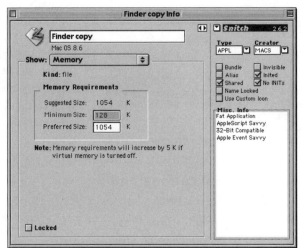

Figure F5-9 Above: Finder Heap Fix can increase the Finder's memory allocation. Right: Using the Snitch trick described in "By the Way: Increasing Memory Size of Extensions" to access the Finder's memory allocation.

How to Increase Overall Memory Availability

The previous sections of this Fix-It focus on techniques that affect a single application (such as adjusting Memory settings in the application's Get Info window). If memory problems persist, despite trying those techniques, or if memory problems occur across numerous applications, you need to try more general solutions.

After you try any of the following techniques, relaunch the problem application and/or documents (as well as the other previously opened programs, if enough memory is available). See if all goes well.

TAKE NOTE ▶ The Memory Control Panel

Many of the solutions described in this section make reference to the Memory control panel. This note serves as a brief and general introduction to how and why to use it.

Always remember, you typically must restart the Macintosh before any changes you make to Memory settings take effect.

The options listed in the Memory control panel window may differ depending on which model of Macintosh you are using and what version of the OS you have. The most common ones include:

• **Disk cache** The disk cache is a specified amount of RAM that has been set aside to hold information that has recently been accessed from your disk. When you access new information from your disk, the new information replaces what is currently in the cache.

(continues on next page)

By itself, this offers no benefit. However, if you request information that is already waiting in the cache, it is accessed directly from the cache rather than from the disk. Theoretically, this speeds up the operation since, as discussed in Chapter 1, RAM access is much faster than disk access. Thus, the disk cache primarily speeds up the performance of operations that would otherwise require repeated reading of the same disk-based data. The larger the size setting, the more RAM it uses, and the more performance benefit you can get – at least up to a point. You'll have to decide how to make this trade-off.

Recent versions of the Mac OS have become quite smart about deciding the optimal size for the disk cache (it estimates about 32K multiplied by your MB of installed RAM). Thus, if you click the "Default setting" button, you will usually be fine. However, if you need to go lower (to conserve memory for some other use) or decide to go higher, simply check "Custom setting" and enter your own size.

Connectix Speed Doubler's Faster Disk Performance is an alternative to Apple's Disk Cache. However, Apple's cache has become so good in recent OS versions, that Speed Doubler is actually slower in this feature. As a result, Speed Doubler omits this option from its control panel when running newer OS versions. Speed Doubler no longer works in Mac OS 9 (and as of this writing, it looks as if Connectix will not be updating it.)

- **RAM disk** A RAM disk is a specified amount of RAM that has been set aside to act as if it were a physical disk mounted on the desktop. A RAM disk's icon, which looks similar to a floppy disk icon, appears on the desktop just like any other disk. For reasons similar to the rationale for a disk cache, the speed of operations involving files copied to the RAM disk should be greatly increased. The effect can be spectacular, since items on a RAM disk are always accessed from RAM–not just if they are repeatedly accessed.

Because the contents of a RAM disk are stored only in RAM, you cannot permanently save files to a RAM disk as you can to a physical disk. Any information on a RAM disk is lost whenever the RAM is cleared. Typically, this will happen every time you shut down or restart. However, many Mac models will preserve the contents of a RAM disk when you do a "warm" restart (select Restart from the Finder's File menu). This can be especially convenient if you want to set up a RAM disk as a temporary startup disk. You can simply copy the necessary files to the RAM disk, select it as the startup disk from the Startup Disk control panel, and restart. The most recent Macs (starting with the iMac) no longer can do this, because they use a different type of memory.

Even if your Mac can save a RAM disk's contents via a restart, it will not do so when you shut down. If there are files on your RAM disk when you shut down, you will typically get a message (after selecting Shut Down) warning you that all files on the disk will be lost if you continue. However, there is one exception to this. Some Macs, primarily PowerBooks and all newer Macs, have an option in the RAM Disk section of the Memory control panel called "Save on Shut Down." With this checked, the Mac saves a copy of the RAM disk's contents in a special file called "Persistent RAM Disk," stored in the Preferences folder of the System Folder. When you next start up, the contents of this file are copied back to the RAM disk.

To create a RAM disk, select the disk's size by adjusting the slider in the RAM disk area of the control panel. Then select the On button and restart. To change the size of an existing RAM disk (or to turn it off altogether), you must first delete all files currently on the RAM disk. At a practical level, the size of a RAM disk is limited by your total available memory. However, many users will need almost all the memory they have to adequately run their software. In such cases, a RAM disk is a dispensable luxury.

The RAM disk option will be dimmed if you do not have enough free RAM to create the minimal sized RAM disk that the OS permits.

(continues on next page)

**FIX-IT
#5**

FIX-IT #5

TAKE NOTE ▶ The Memory Control Panel (continued)

- **Virtual memory** While the disk cache and RAM disk options use up available RAM, virtual memory is a way to increase your apparent available RAM. Virtual memory is like the mirror image of a RAM disk. Rather than allocating a portion of RAM to act like a disk (which is what a RAM disk does), virtual memory allocates a portion of a disk to act as if it were RAM. With virtual memory, you can open applications that require more memory than you physically have in memory chips. Connectix RAM Doubler is an alternative to Apple's virtual memory; you should not try to use both at the same time.

    On Power Macintoshes, using virtual memory also decreases the amount of RAM needed to launch all PowerPC native applications (see later in this Fix-It for more on this feature). For this reason, it is often advised to keep virtual memory set at a minimum of 1MB, even if you don't need the extra RAM directly. However virtual memory inevitably slows down your Mac. That's why certainly applications (such as Adobe Premiere, Windows emulators, and many games) recommend not using it at all when running these applications. Turning off virtual memory requires restarting the computer before the change takes effect.

    Also note that virtual memory requires an amount of hard drive space equal to the virtual memory setting plus the amount of physical RAM installed. It's stored as an invisible file called VM Storage. Thus, if you have 96MB of RAM, adding 1MB of virtual memory will require 97MB of disk space. The Memory control panel at least lets you assign which drive will hold this invisible file. If disk space does become a problem, one solution, other than keeping virtual memory off, is to use RAM Doubler. It doesn't require the disk space that virtual memory does. Finally, Apple recommends that the size of your virtual memory be no greater than 50% of your physical RAM. RAM Doubler obviously does not limit itself to this recommendation.

    In a few rare cases (such as if a disk driver does not support virtual memory), the Virtual Memory box may be missing from the Memory control panel.

- **Startup memory tests** If you hold down the Command-Option keys when launching the Memory control panel, an additional "secret" option appears: Startup Memory Tests. Every time your Mac starts up, it tests the integrity of your physical RAM, giving you an error message if it finds any problem. The more RAM you have, the longer this test takes. For RAM-rich Macs this can add a minute or two to your startup time. If you are confident that your RAM is fine, you can avoid this wait by selecting to turn off Startup Memory Tests.

- **Gone but not forgotten** On some 680X0 Macs (but not on any Power Macs) you will find an option called *32-bit Addressing*. If you find it, turn it on. Without it enabled, you will not be able to use more than 8MB of RAM. Also, System 7.5.5 is the last version of the System Software that will run on a Mac that does not support 32-bit addressing.

    On Power Macs running older versions of the Mac OS, you may find an option called *Modern Memory Manager*. If you find it, turn it on. Turning it off may make your Mac run a bit slower. The only reason to do this is to prevent compatibility problems with the new Manager; but this should be irrelevant unless you are running very old software.

    SEE: • **Chapter 11 for more on RAM disks.**

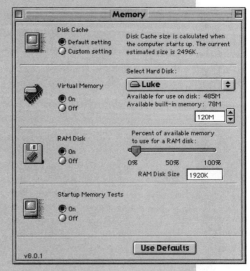

Figure F5-10 The Memory control panel with its "secret" Startup Memory Tests option visible.

Reduce Applications' Preferred/Current Memory Size

Many applications have a Preferred size that is larger than the program typically needs in order to run. If you reduce this setting for these applications, they will be assigned less memory when opened, leaving more free memory remaining for other applications to use. I do not recommend doing this as a general rule, but it can be useful occasionally if you frequently find yourself without enough memory to do what you want.

This technique is similar to what was described previously in this Fix-It as a way to get a specific application to open when free memory is low. Here the emphasis is on changing the Preferred size (rather than the Minimum size) in order to allow more applications to stay open at the same time.

To see if this technique is viable for a particular application, check its Get Info window. If its Preferred memory size is set higher than its Suggested size, reduce it to as low as its Suggested size. If this causes no problems with your use of the application, leave it that way. You can get a hint if this is likely to work by initially selecting "About This Computer" when the application and a typical number of its documents are open. If the unfilled area of the bar representing the application's memory allocation is quite large, it means that you are not using much of the memory assigned to the program. If so, you can try to reduce it.

Fix-It #5

If need be, you can reduce the Preferred size all the way down to the Minimum size (though this is likely to cause other memory-related problems). You shouldn't set the Preferred value below the Minimum (the Macintosh gives you an alert message if you even try).

SEE: • "Take Note: More About 'About This Computer': Bar Shading," earlier in this Fix-It.

Reduce the Memory Size Needed by System Software

The system software on your startup disk occupies a portion of memory at all times. Its size varies, depending on the particular activity you are doing each moment, but it generally stays within a relatively narrow range during any one session. To make substantial reductions in the size of the system software requires that you make changes that affect its initial startup size. Doing this should make more memory available for use by applications, which should hopefully solve your problem. In particular, you can turn off or remove nonessential startup extensions, turn off file sharing, remove unnecessary fonts and sounds, and reduce the size of (or turn off) the disk cache and RAM disks.

Turn off or remove nonessential Startup Extensions (INITs). Startup extensions take up memory. Turn off startup extensions that you do not absolutely need. Remember: simply turning off a control panel by selecting its Off button (assuming it has one) may not free any RAM. To recover any memory, you must disable the startup extension at startup (typically via a startup management utility or by dragging the startup extension out of the System Folder before you restart). In extreme cases, you may need to disable all startup extensions (by holding down the Shift key at startup).

Remember, not all extensions use memory at startup. Conflict Catcher will tell you how much memory each extension is using, if any.

SEE: • Fix-It #3 for more on solving startup extension problems.

Turn off file sharing. File sharing involves several related extensions. When in use, it takes up about 200 to 300K of system software memory. Turning it off recovers this memory for other uses. To turn File Sharing off, you do not have to dis-

Figure F5-11 The File Sharing section of the Start/Stop tab of the File Sharing control panel. File Sharing is currently off.

able the extensions at startup. Instead, open the Sharing Setup control panel. If File Sharing is on, the button in the File Sharing field of the control panel will read "Stop" and the Status description will say that "File sharing is on." To turn File Sharing off, click Stop. Obviously, you should only do this if you do not plan to use this option for the time being. You typically use File Sharing to connect to other Macintoshes over a network.

SEE: • Chapter 11 for more on file sharing.

Remove unnecessary fonts and sounds. Fonts and sounds require memory. Actually, fonts take up very little system software memory (just enough to keep track of their names), no matter how many fonts you have. However, they may increase the amount of memory needed by any application that includes a Font menu. Sounds, on the other hand, are assigned to system software memory (typically sounds are stored in the System file itself) — so the more sounds you have, the more memory you use. In any case, it is best to delete fonts and sounds that you rarely or never use. Detailed instructions for removing fonts are described in Chapter 9. The procedures for removing sounds are similar.

Reduce the size of (or turn off) the disk cache and/or RAM disks. The memory required by these options is included in the system software allocation. Turning them off, while obviously eliminating whatever speed enhancement benefit they had, allows you to recover the memory they would otherwise use. You access these features from the Memory control panel.

- **Disk cache** The disk cache cannot be turned off. However, you can lower its size (to as low as 128K) via the arrow keys to the right of the current cache size listing. The Mac will warn you that doing this can severely slow down your Mac. This is true. You need to restart the Mac for the change to take effect.

- **RAM disks** You can reduce the size of a RAM disk or turn it off altogether. Just remember that you must delete *all* files from the RAM disk before you can change its size or turn it off. To do this, drag all files on the RAM disk to the Trash or simply select Erase Disk from the Finder's Special menu (don't worry if you get a message that says "Initialization failed"). Although any modifications to the RAM disk settings should result in the disappearance of the RAM disk icon, you must still restart the Macintosh to see any change in memory allocation.

BY THE WAY ▶ Driver-Level versus System-Level Disk Caches

Certain third-party disk utilities have options to create a drive-specific disk cache separate from the one created by the Memory control panel. If you own a third party hard drive, cartridge drive, or CD-ROM drive, such a utility may have come with your drive. The disk cache created by these utilities should show better performance benefit than Apple's disk cache. This is because they operate at a machine-specific device driver level rather than a more generic system software level. Additionally, to avoid duplication of effort, these utilities come with an option to "Disable System Cache" (essentially preventing data used by the cache from also being sent to Apple's disk cache).

If you are using one of these utilities, be sure to check it, rather than the Memory control panel, to reduce the size of the disk cache, if needed. Also, if you select the driver's Disable System Cache option, you can lower the size of Apple's disk cache to conserve RAM (though note that Apple's cache will still be used by any devices not using the third party driver).

FIX-IT #5

BY THE WAY ▶ Running Applications From Ram Disks versus Hard Disks

When an application opens, whether from a hard disk or a RAM disk, it loads into RAM. Thus, you might think that running an application from a RAM disk offers no speed advantage over running it from a hard disk. But this is not the case. In fact, running applications from a hard disk is typically slowed down by frequent required hard disk access. This is because only a portion of the application is in RAM at any one time. Different parts get swapped in and out as needed, accessing the drive each time a swap is made. Some applications have an option to load entirely into RAM, but this is not common.

Actually, even if you run an application from a RAM disk, it will still access the hard disk whenever it requires information from the System Folder. Avoiding even this access is the rationale behind creating a startup RAM disk (although this is not a practical option for most people these days, given the increased size of a minimum System Folder and the fact that most newer Macs no longer permit startup RAM disks).

By the way, when running an application from a RAM disk, you can often lower its memory allocation from its Preferred size to closer to its Minimum size and still not see any speed decrement. This is because, while lower memory allocations typically mean more frequent access to the disk, the disk in this case is RAM, not the slower hard disk.

For PowerBooks, a RAM disk has the additional benefit of saving battery power (because RAM access uses less power than disk access).

SEE: • Chapter 11 for much more on RAM disks and PowerBooks.

Increase the Size of the System Heap

If you are experiencing periodic system crashes (or other strange and serious symptoms) across a variety of applications, you may have a system heap size problem. If you cannot load all of your extensions at startup due to insufficient memory, increasing the size of the system heap may help (although simply getting more memory would be even better!).

A system heap problem may also underlie apparent out of memory messages in the Finder, such as when opening a lot of windows (or strangely even with all applications quit and all windows closed). Thus, although they affect different areas of memory (remember that the Finder is really in the application heap!), increasing the size of the system heap may fix some of the same problems fixed by increasing the Finder's memory size (a technique explained in "Increase the Finder's Memory Size," earlier in this Fix-It).

The size of the system heap is dynamically regulated. This means that the Macintosh automatically adjusts the system heap's size as needed to accommodate additional files, theoretically eliminating the need to readjust the heap size yourself. Thus, these adjustments should be only rarely needed. However sometimes this dynamic size readjustment is insufficient because the Mac finds itself needing more system heap space than it can create. This can happen, for example, when several RAM-hungry applications and startup extensions are all active simultaneously. The system heap needs room to grow. Sooner or later, you run into the limitation set by how much physical memory you actually have.

However, some system heap limitations may be due to a blockade by application heap memory. Here's what is going on: the system heap and the application heap ultimately share the same total memory space. You can picture the situation if the system heap starts at the bottom of the memory space and grows upwards, while the application heap starts at the top and grows downward. In the middle, there is a common area where the space could be assigned to either heap as needed. Thus, if the system heap grows large enough, and if space in this middle area is currently empty, the system heap will use an area that might otherwise be assigned to an application. Further, since the system heap must be one contiguous block of memory, any application currently occupying the space near the system heap/application heap border will block the growth of the system heap—even if there is free memory available higher up in the application heap. That is why the Mac tries to assign applications to this "border" area as a last resort. If a block such as this does occur, you may run out of system heap room even though there is free memory still available. When this happens, you will start getting system heap related "out of memory" messages.

Quitting open applications, notably the potential blocking application, will help here. Beyond that, you can minimize the chance of this happening by guaranteeing more initial space for the system heap. This means reserving more area that can never be used by the application heap (realizing that this leaves less memory for applications). Also, you may be able to clear the system heap of unneeded data. Here's how to do all of this:

- Use Conflict Catcher. Go to the Startup Section of its Preferences window. Click the "Guarantee System Heap" option. You can adjust the guaranteed size. Typically, 30% is a good choice. Increase a bit more if it is already set there.

- When you find yourself faced with the symptoms of a probable system heap problem, it may be too late to adjust the system heap size (without restarting). In this case, you might try to clear the system heap of unneeded data, such as memory which is assigned to extensions that load when used but is not cleared when the extensions are no longer needed. The freeware utility, Mac OS Purge, may be able to do this.

    If you use a lot of extensions and don't have a lot of physical RAM, you will eventually reach a limit beyond which the system heap size cannot reasonably increase. If this becomes a problem, your best immediate alternative is to reduce the system software memory size by following the advice in the previous section ("Reduce the Memory Size Needed by System Software"). Otherwise, just get more memory (as described next).

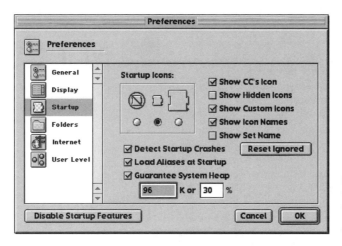

Figure F5-12 Conflict Catcher's Preferences, showing "Guarantee System Heap" option at the bottom of the window.

Increase the Total Available Memory

To increase the total available memory, you can: use virtual memory, use RAM Doubler, or add more physical RAM.

Use virtual memory. Virtual memory, accessed from the Memory control panel, fools the Macintosh into treating part of your hard disk space as equivalent to RAM. After you turn it on, select the desired size of total memory (physical plus virtual) by clicking the arrows on the right side of the control panel. It does not let you select a higher value than your Macintosh and disk can accommodate.

Virtual memory is quick and easy to use and is a lot less expensive than buying more physical RAM. However, there are some limitations to using this feature. First, some software may be incompatible with virtual memory (though this is relatively rare now). Second, if you do not have enough unused disk space to accommodate what virtual memory needs (see: "Take Note: The Memory Control Panel," earlier in this chapter), you cannot use it. Third, your Macintosh will run somewhat slower when it uses virtual memory. Still, as long as no single open application requires more memory than is available with physical (built-in) memory, the slowdown should not be significant. This is because the Macintosh shifts the active application into the faster physical (built-in) memory whenever possible.

Helpful hint: Once virtual memory has been set from the Memory control panel, you can turn it off "temporarily" by holding down the Command key at startup. This will disable virtual memory for that startup, but not any other Apple startup extensions. However, it is possible that some other non-Apple startup extension uses the Command key to similarly disable it at startup so check for this. Virtual memory will return automatically the next time you start up. Thus, this technique allows you to toggle virtual memory on and off without having to go to the Memory control panel each time.

TAKE NOTE ▶ Still More About "About This Computer": Built-In Versus Total Memory

You can of course use the Memory control panel to see if you have virtual memory turned on and, if so, how much virtual memory you have. However, you can also check this from the "About This Computer" window. If virtual memory is in use, a new listing called Built-in Memory appears above the Total Memory listing. The difference between these two numbers is how much virtual memory you have. Using RAM Doubler similarly results in the appearance of the Built-in Memory versus Total Memory distinction.

Also, on Power Macs, the Total Memory may be larger than expected when virtual memory is on. This is not a cause for concern; everything will still work fine (although you really don't have the extra memory). Without going into details here, the mislisting is a consequence of how the Power Mac deals with the presence of its 68040 emulator (needed to run non-native applications on a Power Mac).

Figure F5-13 The "About This Computer" window with Virtual Memory off (top) or with (1 MB of) Virtual Memory on (bottom). Note how the Power Mac native applications (AppleWorks and Explorer) take up more memory when Virtual Memory is off. Using RAM Doubler has similar effects.

Use RAM Doubler. RAM Doubler behaves in many ways just like virtual memory. It even results in the same Built-in Memory versus Total Memory listing appearing in the About This Computer window. In fact, Connectix (the makers of RAM Doubler) refer to both of these techniques as examples of *extended memory*. However RAM Doubler accesses the hard disk much less than does Apple's virtual memory (which is why it is usually faster than virtual memory) and does not require nearly as much disk storage space (because it first tries to expand memory capacity by compressing data in RAM rather than immediately moving the data to disk).

RAM Doubler effectively doubles or even triples your apparent RAM, getting your Macintosh to act almost identically to how it would if you actually added an equivalent amount of physical RAM. Speed decrements may occur at times (especially as you approach the limits of available memory), but they are usually minor. Also note that RAM Doubler works best when you use it to open more programs at once, rather than to assign increasing amounts of memory to a single program.

Because of its pervasive effect on your system, compatibility problems with RAM Doubler are more common than with most other programs. To keep these to a minimum, always check with Connectix to make sure you are using the latest version of RAM Doubler.

Helpful Hint: you can turn off RAM Doubler at startup, leaving all other extensions on, by holding down the tilde [~] or escape keys at startup. Conversely, you can startup with all extensions off, except RAM Doubler, by holding down Shift-Option at startup.

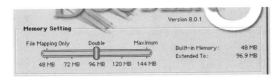

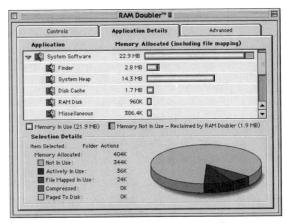

Figure F5-14 Above: The Memory Setting slider from the RAM Doubler control panel. Note especially the "File-Mapping Only" option on the left (the function of this is described in the main text). Right: RAM Doubler's Application Details shows the separate RAM allocations for the different components of the system software; this can help you identify precisely what parts of the system software are the biggest RAM guzzlers.

Virtual memory, RAM Doubler, and PowerPC (native) software. If you have a Power Macintosh, you may notice that the Get Info windows for PowerPC native code applications have a message about virtual memory at the bottom of the window. These messages basically tell you that the amount of memory needed to open the application will change when virtual memory is on. Programs running in native mode require significantly *less* RAM (as much as several megabytes less) with virtual memory turned on than they would with it off.

This is due to do something called *file mapping.* Indeed, if you turn virtual memory on (even using as little as 1MB), the Suggested, Minimum, and Preferred values will all change to lower numbers. When you turn on or off virtual memory (and restart), the numbers in the memory requirements boxes will shift accordingly.

Check it out. For Power Macintoshes, turning on virtual memory has a double benefit: it makes more memory generally available to all applications plus it allows native code applications to open in less memory.

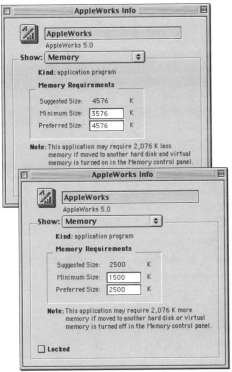

Figure F5-15 The memory savings effect of using virtual memory as seen from the Get Info window. Top: the Get Info window for a native code application (AppleWorks) as seen on an iMac with virtual memory off. Bottom: the Get Info window of AppleWorks when virtual memory is on. Note the reduced RAM requirements.

If you should change any Preferred or Minimum values with virtual memory on, the values that appear when you turn virtual memory off will be altered by the same absolute amount (and vice versa).

RAM Doubler works similarly to virtual memory and leads to similar messages in Get Info windows. If you don't really need RAM Doubler to give you any additional memory, you might still select its *File-Mapping Only* option (at the left end of the Memory Setting slider). This enables this feature that reduces the memory requirements for native PowerPC applications, but does not add any more extended memory. This will minimize any performance slow downs associated with RAM Doubler.

With virtual memory (or RAM Doubler) on, some Power Mac native applications may actually load faster than with virtual memory off. Aside from that, virtual memory still slows down your machine (exactly how much of a slow down you get depends on how much physical RAM you have and how many applications are open, etc.).

TECHNICALLY SPEAKING ▶ Why Do Native Applications Need Less RAM When Virtual Memory Is On? (File Mapping and Code Fragment Manager)

Skipping over some really technical details (which are not relevant to your troubleshooting efforts anyway), here's the basic idea: native code applications are written in a way that allows the Mac to perform a neat trick when virtual memory is on. With 680x0 applications, there is a certain amount of data that must be loaded into memory (physical and/or virtual) before the application can even open. There is a similar requirement for native software when launched with virtual memory off. However, with virtual memory on, a significantly smaller portion of this information is loaded into memory (actually it goes exclusively to physical RAM). Additionally, a "file map" of the remaining data that would normally be loaded is created on the area of the disk used by virtual memory. This map points to the locations within the application file (as stored on the main part of the disk) that the Mac needs to go to to find the data. This map takes up a lot less space than if the actual data had been loaded. This is the source of the memory savings. This *file mapping* is handled by something called the *Code Fragment Manager* (instructions built in to the Macintosh ROM and/or system software). 680x0 Macs relied instead on something called a Segment Loader (although Apple now has Code Fragment Manager software extensions that 680x0 Macs can use.)

A side effect of this is that application developers must now ensure that their applications are not self-modifying in any way. Otherwise, if the file on the disk is altered while the application is open, the map in memory may no longer be accurate. System crashes would likely result.

SEE: • Fix-It #15 for more on PowerPC processor and Code Fragment Manager.

Add more physical RAM. As a last resort, if memory problems persist, you can solve them by adding more physical RAM to your Macintosh. If you frequently find yourself short of needed RAM, adding memory should not be a last resort! There is no better solution to memory problems. It has no disadvantage other than price (and, as of this writing, prices are incredibly low!).

Adding additional memory is a hardware modification that, depending on your particular model of Macintosh and your willingness to try, can be easy to do yourself or may require that you take your Macintosh to a dealer. The documentation that came with your Mac should include details on how to add RAM to your model. Essentially, you insert the memory into special slots located on the computer's main logic board. One important caveat: whenever you add or replace memory, there is a chance that the memory may be of the incorrect type, defective, or incorrectly installed. This can lead to *very* serious problems, including an inability to start up the Macintosh. The details of which types of memory to buy, how to install them, how much you can increase your RAM and in what increments, vary significantly among the different Macintosh models. Additional details on these matters are covered in Fix-It #15. If you need still more information, contact an authorized Apple dealer or seek other outside help.

 For Related Information

SEE:
- Fix-It #3 on extensions and control panels.
- Fix-It #15 on PowerPC issues and memory upgrades.
- Fix-It #16 on seeking outside help.
- Chapter 1 on hardware terminology (SIMMs, processor, and so on).
- Chapter 2 on the Get Info command and the About This Computer window.
- Chapter 4 on unexpected quits and other system errors.
- Chapter 5 on startup problems.
- Chapter 6 on applications and files that will not open.
- Chapter 9 on installing and removing fonts.
- Chapter 11 on RAM disks.
- Chapter 12 and 13 for memory issues related to Open Transport and using Web browsers.

FIX-IT #5

Fix-It #6:
Check for Viruses

**FIX-IT
#6**

▶ QUICK SUMMARY

Use an updated anti-virus utility to scan your disk for viruses. Replace any infected files with clean copies from your backups. If no backup is available, use the anti-virus utility to eradicate the virus and repair the infected file.

 ## When to Do It:

- Whenever you get a warning message from your anti-virus utility that a virus attack has occurred.

- If you have frequent and unpredictable system crashes.

- When you replace an apparently corrupted file and it soon becomes damaged again.

- If the Macintosh system beep, or any other sound, occurs at unusual times and for no discernible reason.

- If files have been inexplicably erased from your disk.

- If a strange or nonsensical alert message unexpectedly appears on your screen.

- If you have just installed an anti-virus utility for the first time or are using a new disk that has not been previously checked for viruses.

- When any of an assortment of system-level problems occur, such as: applications take unusually long to open, documents do not print from all (or almost all) applications, cursor movement is erratic, or windows refuse to open or close. These symptoms have several possible causes, as covered in other Fix-Its. The probability that a virus is the cause increases if you have recently engaged an activity that is a high risk for virus infections (see "Take Note: How to Catch a Virus" later in this Fix-It).

These are just some of the more general symptoms associated with various viruses. For more specifics, see "Technically Speaking: Viruses at the Millennium."

TECHNICALLY SPEAKING ▶ Viruses at the Millennium

Until the last year or so, viruses tended to be a minor issue on the Mac. Though it was always prudent to take precautions against them, the odds of actually getting infected were quite low. Moreover, at least compared to the Windows platform, the actual number of viruses was quite small as well.

Mac users got a wake-up call in 1998 with the arrival of at least two major new viruses. Both spread rapidly and widely. One of them even occasionally found its way on to CD-ROM discs shipped from major vendors (inadvertently, of course). With the arrival of the new millennium, virus protection is again a hot issue. Here's the scoop on these two latest invaders (the text is adapted for information included with the Virex anti-virus utility):

- **666 or SevenDust** The 666 (also known as SevenDust) family of viruses has several variants. The final variants are polymorphic. This means that they can partially self-modify their code, making it more difficult for anti-virus utilities to detect them. One variant of this family is the "**Graphics Accelerator**" virus, so named because it first appeared as a file by that name on certain online shareware archives. An infected machine will erase all non-application files, if started during the 6th hour of the 6th or 12th day of any month. Damage also includes overwriting an application's menu resource with the f character (Hex 66). Infected applications will also generate the "Graphics Accelerator" extension if it is not present. Some variants of this virus leave a file called 666 in your Extensions folder; the System file may also be an initial site of infection.

- **AutoStart 9805** The AutoStart 9805 family of worms can be transmitted via almost any HFS disk volume, including floppy disks, most removable-cartridge drives, hard disks, and even disk images. AutoStart worms spread via disks that contain an invisible application file in the root directory. This file is designated in the boot sector of the disk as the AutoStart file. When the infected disk is inserted in a Macintosh running QuickTime 2.0 or later, the application is launched automatically if the CD-ROM AutoPlay option is enabled in the QuickTime Settings Control Panel. Upon launch, the worm application copies itself to the Extensions folder and changes into an invisible, faceless background application. The background worm application is now automatically launched whenever the computer system starts up. It periodically examines the mounted volumes. If any are not already infected, it attempts to infect them by copying itself to the root directory and setting up the disk's AutoStart information. Most writable HFS disks or volumes are successfully infected. The notable exception is server volumes, which do not have the necessary boot block fields for AutoStart operation.

  The original AutoStart 9805 application is named "DB" and its background application is named "Desktop Print Spooler." Immediately upon infecting, it restarts the computer system. This worm triggers every thirty minutes to infect mounted volumes and to damage files. It conducts a case-insensitive search for files whose names have certain endings. Files ending with "data", "cod", and "csa" are targeted if the data fork is larger than 100 bytes. Files ending with "dat" are targeted if the entire file is larger than about 2 megabytes. When a targeted file is found, it is damaged by overwriting the data fork (up to approximately the first 1 megabyte) with random data. A through F variations of the virus subsequently appeared, each with a minor variation on this theme.

Of course, both major anti-virus utilities (Virex and Norton AntiVirus) can deal with these threats. But each virus has also spanned a collection of freeware and shareware utilities designed to specifically target these viruses. For example, WormFood and WormScanner deal with the AutoStart worm, while Agax wipes out the SevenDust virus.

**FIX-IT
#6**

TAKE NOTE ▶ The Y2K bug

Speaking of the millennium, I could not write this new edition without at least mentioning the infamous Y2K bug. This is not really a virus at all, but I'll mention it in this context anyway. Y2K stands for Year 2000. The bug refers to the fact that, at least on certain computer platforms, software (especially older programs) encoded the year as just two digits rather than four digits (98 instead of 1998). This was designed to save memory and data storage space, which was in very short supply years ago. Unfortunately, it also meant that when the year 2000 arrived, the program might assume that the year 2000 was actually the year 1900. This could potentially wreak all sorts of havoc. For example, if this happened to your credit card billing system, it could suddenly decide that you were 100 years behind in your payments, charging you an enormous finance fee and canceling your card. An enormous amount of time and money was spent in averting these problems, mainly by updating vulnerable software. Happily for Mac users, almost all applications and the Mac OS itself were already immune to the problem, as they already used 4 digit years. It was primarily an issue for other platforms, mostly older mainframe computers.

For example, here is a statement from Apple on how the Mac OS (particularly in combination with ClarisWorks and AppleWorks, although likely to apply to other programs as well) handles two digit years:

Beginning in the year 2000: Two-digit years (mm/dd/yy) can be used as follows:

- Years 91-99 will be recognized as being 1991-1999, respectively

- Years 00-90 will be recognized as being in the 21st century

- For dates in the 20th century prior to 1991, it will be necessary to use four-digit dates throughout a file (as described further below).

- Beginning in the year 2011: All two-digit years will be recognized as being in the 21st century. For dates in the 20th century, it will be necessary to use four-digit dates.

In any case, the year 2000 arrived with virtually no serious Y2K bugs to be found on any platform. Either the problems were averted through all the preparation, or the fears were largely unwarranted. Or a combination of both.

TAKE NOTE ▶ Scriptable Viruses

Scriptable viruses are an odd variation on the basic virus theme. One type is in the form of HyperCard scripts (using the HyperTalk language). They only infect HyperCard stacks. One example is the "Merryxmas" virus, that was inadvertently present in some copies of (a now out-of-date version of) Apple's SIMM Stack. It does no active harm to your Mac (that is, it makes no attempt to deliberately damage or delete files on your drive). "HC 9507" is yet another recently reported HyperCard virus. It types the word "pickle" and makes the system behave strangely.

Another form of scriptable virus is the group of Word Macro viruses. These can infect Microsoft Word 6.0 documents and templates. Examples include viruses named "Word Macro 9508" or "WordMacro.Concept." They are written in the Microsoft Word macro-language Word Basic. They have an effect only when using Word 6. Infected documents appear with the template icon, rather than the usual document icon. The simplest solution here is to delete infected files. Otherwise, a file available online from Microsoft, called "mw1222.hqx," can supposedly eradicate the virus.

Although older anti-virus utilities, including Disinfectant, ignore these HyperCard and Word macro scriptable viruses, latest versions of NAV and Virex do check for them.

☒ Why to Do It:

Viruses A virus is a special type of software program. It has two main purposes in life. Its first (and most critical) is to duplicate itself—in particular, to spread copies of itself to other disks and other computer systems. Its second function is to carry out some activity on each disk where it resides. This activity can be as benign as sending a message that says "Peace" or as vicious as erasing your hard disk.

Viruses duplicate themselves in a variety of ways. The most common method of virus attack is for a newly arriving virus to locate a specific system software file on your disk and infect it (that is, place a copy of itself within some file's code/resources). For example, suppose you install an already infected application on your disk and launch it. This triggers the virus, with the result that it initiates a search for its target file (let's say it's the System file here) and infects it. Then it uses the System file as a base of operations for further infections. (By the way, at this point deleting the original infected application will be of no help). Any other system software files, particularly the Finder, control panels, and extensions, are also potential initial sites of infection (it varies according to the particular virus).

Fix-It #6

Once the virus has successfully infected a file on your disk, the virus code typically acts as a startup extension (see Fix-It #3), loading into memory at startup. From here, it executes its code, with instructions on how and when to duplicate itself as well as whatever else it may have been programmed to do. For example, every time an application on the disk is launched, the virus code is alerted and typically infects that application. Occasionally, a virus might attach itself to a driver (such as a printer driver) and execute its code when you access the driver (such as when you attempt to print something).

Transfer of the virus to a different disk usually involves some inadvertent help from the user. For example, a virus on a hard disk can transfer to a floppy disk either when you copy an infected file to the floppy disk or if you run an application from the floppy disk while the infected hard disk is mounted. When the newly infected floppy disk is mounted on another computer, the process begins anew with the virus transferring to the startup disk of the other machine.

A few viruses work by attaching themselves to a disk's invisible Desktop file (see Fix-It #8 for more on this file). These viruses spread to other disks as soon as an uninfected disk is inserted and mounted. No copying of files across disks or launching of applications is necessary.

Viruses are created by unscrupulous programmers. Other than creating a sense of misplaced pride among their creators, viruses have no purpose other than to cause trouble for unsuspecting users. Fortunately, most viruses are relatively benign. That is, they do not deliberately alter or damage your software other than to do what is necessary to duplicate the virus. Unfortunately, since legitimate software is not designed to accommodate viruses, even a so-called benign virus can cause problems. Frequent system crashes or damaged files can easily result. Viruses occasionally have bugs that result in their causing even more harm than their creator intended.

Trojan Horses A few viruses are deliberately destructive. Most threatening in this regard is a variation on viruses called a Trojan horse. A Trojan horse is a phony program, often disguised as a game. However, the real purpose of the program is to do damage to your disk, often erasing all the files on it. When you launch the program, it begins its insidious task. The only good news is that, unlike a true virus, a Trojan horse cannot replicate itself. To transfer to another disk, the user must deliberately copy it.

Worms Worms are similar to viruses in that they can spread from computer to computer on their own (unlike Trojan Horses). However, they are self-contained applications that simply replicate themselves rather than infecting other programs. The good news here is that this generally makes them easier to eradicate than a virus. Delete the worm files and the worm is gone.

Virus, worm or Trojan horse, benign or malicious—the bottom line is that you do not want them around.

Fix-It #6

TAKE NOTE ▶ How to Catch a Virus

The only way your files can get infected by a computer virus is to come in contact with a file that is already infected. The probability that this will happen depends on the nature of your computer activity. Activities that place you at higher risk include the following:

- Downloading files from the Internet or any online service. You can become infected if you attempt to use a downloaded file that contains a virus. The major services and Web sites check files for viruses before they list them for downloading, so it would be rare for you to get a virus this way. However, it does happen.

- Opening files received as attachments in email, especially if the message comes from a person you do not know or if it seems like some sort of chain letter. The file may contain a virus that is triggered when you open the file.

- Using a disk or cartridge given to you by someone else. It doesn't matter whether the person giving you the disk is a close friend or a total stranger. A friend could give you an infected disk without realizing that it contains a virus.

- Inserting an unlocked floppy disk or other removable media (such as a Zip disk) into a computer other than your own and then later inserting it into your computer.

Conversely, the odds of coming in contact with a virus are relatively low if you stick to using only shrink-wrapped copies of commercial software, downloaded files from those sites that are known to check their files for viruses, disks from reputable user groups that virus-check their files, and disks from friends that you are confident take adequate precautions against viruses. Also, keep your disks locked as much as possible, especially when taking them from one machine to another.

TAKE NOTE ▶ Virus Hoaxes (and Getting Viruses From Email and Downloads)

Hoaxes Dealing with real viruses is enough of a pain. Now you also have to worry that the latest virus threat you read about is really a hoax. The most well-known example of this is the "Good Times" virus. Basically, if you get an email message that warns you to beware of any email message with the subject "Good Times," because even reading such a file could erase your hard drive or destroy your processor, do not believe it. It is a hoax! There are many variations on this theme; the name of the supposed virus file changes but the basic idea remains the same. The F-Secure Web site <http://www.datafellows.com/news/hoax.htm> is one of several excellent sites where you can check if some supposed virus threat is a hoax or not.

More generally, at least on a Mac, there are no known cases where you can get a virus from an email message itself (although you could get one from a file that someone sends you attached to an email, if you launch the file).

Similarly (although I worry about exceptions to this rule!), you cannot get infected from any file that you download until you attempt to open the file.

Protection In any case, if you use Virex or Norton AntiVirus (NAV), you can set them to automatically scan downloaded files for possible virus infection. If anything you download has a virus, the anti-virus utility should stop it before it spreads to the rest of your drive. For example, NAV's SafeZone works this way. You can additionally choose to scan a compressed file at download, catching the threat before you even extract the file.

A related option is Virex's "Scan Files When Opened" (NAV has a similar option: "Scan for known viruses when files are opened and applications are launched"). This checks a file each time it is opened, just in case it was infected since the last time you used it and you had not done a general scan to check for possible infections.

The downside of these options is that they tend to slow the overall performance of your Mac. They also tend to be the feature of these programs that most often cause conflicts with other software. For example, when Mac OS 8.5 was first released, you would get a system freeze when trying to copy files over a network, if these options were enabled. Updated versions of the anti-virus utilities eventually fixed the problem.

The real thing Despite these hoaxes and the protection afforded by anti-virus utilities, it still pays to be wary of any unsolicited email attachments you receive. From the infamous Melissa virus to newer ones such as BubbleBoy, email attachment viruses are a real threat. As usual, Windows PCs are more at risk. And, on the Mac, risks are greater with some email programs than with others (Outlook Express appears to be riskiest because of its unique features, such as Active X, that viruses use to assist in their attacks).

FIX-IT
#6

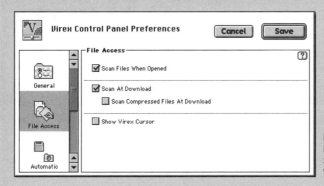

Figure F6-1 Virex control panel's Preferences window, showing the Scan at Download and Scan Files When Opened options.

⟨image⟩ **What to Do:**

Your best defense against viruses is to prevent them from infecting your disks in the first place (see "Take Note: How to Catch a Virus"). Failing that, check for ones that may already be present and get rid of any that you find.

Install and Set Up an Anti-Virus Utility

Install an Anti-Virus Utility

Your main line of defense against viruses is a current version of a good anti-virus utility. Install one on your startup drive. As mentioned in Chapter 2, the two major anti-virus utilities available for the Mac are Norton AntiVirus (NAV) and Virex.

Anti-virus utility packages typically include an application plus a system extension or control panel. The application can scan a disk (or just selected folders/files within a disk) and eradicate all copies of any virus it detects, either by deleting or by repairing infected files.

The extension is designed primarily to detect a virus before it infects your disk and thereby stop an infection from occurring. For example, once installed, the extension continually monitors for potential attempted infections, working in the background while you do other tasks. It can also be set to scan removable media as they are mounted, as well as scan your hard drive at each startup or shut down.

For Virex, there are a Virex application and a Virex control panel. NAV has the NAV application and the Auto-Protect extension.

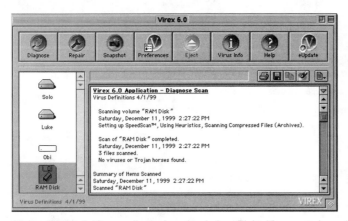 

Figure F6-2 Left: Virex application's main window. Right: Virex control panel.

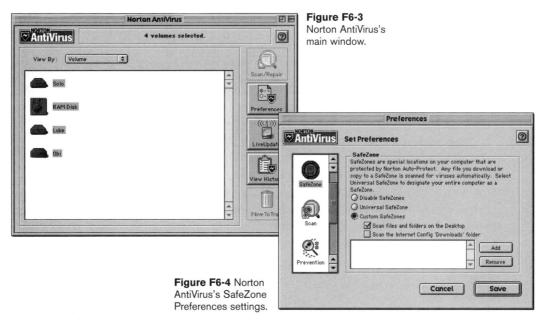

Figure F6-3
Norton AntiVirus's
main window.

Figure F6-4 Norton
AntiVirus's SafeZone
Preferences settings.

Keep Your Anti-Virus Utility Up-to-Date

When you install Virex or NAV, a Virus Definitions file is placed in your System Folder. For Virex, it is in the Virex Preferences folder inside the Preferences folder of the System Folder. This file contains the information needed by Virex to identify and repair specific viruses. New versions of this file are released every time a new virus is discovered. Actually, these days a monthly update is typically released regardless of what new viruses may or may not have arrived. You can get these updates free from the Networks Associates Web site (for Virex) or the Symantec Web site (for NAV). Symantec has said it will charge for updates after a year of owning NAV, but the charge will be nominal at most. NAV also has a LiveUpdate feature that can be set to download NAV's latest virus Definitions file and other updated additions. Virex now has a similar feature. If you want to reliably detect new viruses, you need to periodically replace your Definitions file with updated versions.

Customize Your Anti-Virus Utility

Customization preferences vary between Virex and NAV, but the overall logic is similar. Among other things, NAV allows you to decide whether or not floppy disks should be scanned automatically when mounted, what folders on your computer should be designated as SafeZones (that is, where checking for viruses is automatically done when a file is placed in the folder), whether to check an application for viruses each time it is launched, whether to check for possible unknown viruses, and what level of "Auto-Protect" checking for viruses should be done. NAV also lets you select what types of compressed files to check, if any.

Virex preferences let you control when to scan floppy disks as well as other removable media. You can also check whether or not to scan compressed files. Virex has a special "Snapshot" feature, useful for detecting unknown viruses. It compares your current drive's state to that of the previously saved "snapshot," looking for differences that might indicate a virus infection. For Virex, different preferences are set from the Virex control panel vs. the Virex application. For example, the control panel is where you set whether or not to scan files that have just been downloaded.

In NAV, you set what sort of activities to consider "suspicious" via the Prevention Preferences. You also can select to "Protect against unknown viruses" in the Scan Preferences. This works a bit like Virex's Snapshot feature.

Both NAV and Virex also let you decide whether to automatically try to repair an infected file, or instead give you the option of deciding what to do with the file. NAV gives you more control over selecting individual files and/or folders to scan, rather than having to scan the entire disk.

Fix-It #6

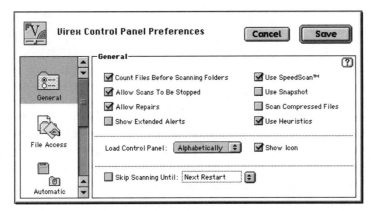

Figure F6-5
One view of the Virex control panel's Preferences options.

Detect, Repair, and/or Delete Infections

If your antivirus utility's "background scanning" feature ever detects an infection or attempted infection by a known virus, an alert message will appear. The message will tell you the name of the virus and which file is infected. Depending on your preferences settings, you typically can choose to repair the file, go to the main application to check the entire disk for other possible infections, or simply ignore the virus and continue.

In almost all cases, you should choose to repair an infected file, if the option is offered. Unless the infected file(s) are not backed up, I would delete them and replace them with clean backup copies—even though they may have been repaired. Better safe than sorry. I would next check all mounted volumes for possible virus infections—again doing so even if the alert message says that the detected virus was successfully repaired. Of course, if your anti-virus utility is unable to repair the file, you have no choice but to delete it.

Trojan horse and worm files are typically automatically deleted when found; there is nothing to repair. For example, you can set Virex to automatically do this (via its Repair Preferences).

If a virus is ever detected on removable media, such as a floppy disk, immediately eject the disk; don't risk even trying to repair it. Instead, restart your Mac from the bootable CD that contains your anti-virus utility and then try to repair the virus. This minimizes the chance that the virus can spread to your hard drive. If you detect a virus on a CD, or other read-only media, trash the CD. Call the vendor for a replacement.

If you are scanning a volume as a precautionary measure, rather than responding to an alert message, viruses are similarly flagged when detected. If you were using Virex's Diagnose option, you would then click the Repair button. With NAV's Scan/Repair option, you are given the opportunity to repair infected files as they are found.

To be extra safe, if any infected files were found and repaired or deleted, check the volume a second time after you are done.

Suspicious activities Bear in mind that if you have your utility set to detect unknown viruses and other suspicious activities, not every alert means that you really have a virus. A "Suspicious Activity" alert could be a false alarm. In fact, if you are confident that what

you are doing is harmless, you can click to Remember this activity, so that you are not similarly alerted again (you may have to turn on "Show Remember" from Alert Preferences, before you see this button). In general, if you keep up to date with your virus definitions, you need not be too concerned about unknown viruses and can choose not to check for them.

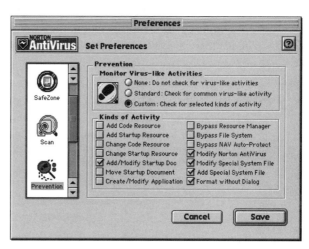

Figure F6-6 Norton AntiVirus's Protection Preferences window.

TAKE NOTE ▶ Infected Desktops

As mentioned in the "Why to Do It" section, some viruses attach to the invisible Desktop file on your disk. Anti-virus utilities typically report when this has happened and may automatically disinfect the file. Still, the surest way to eradicate these viruses is to completely rebuild the Desktop file. This creates a new, uninfected file.

SEE: • **Fix-It #8 on rebuilding the Desktop file.**

If the Anti-Virus Utility Didn't Solve Your Problem

If you use your anti-virus utility and update it as needed, you should be safe from almost any type of virus infection. Therefore, if your problem persists despite these efforts, it's probably not a virus-related problem. It's time to look elsewhere. However, you might first check the vendor's Web site (or other Web sites that cover virus news, including MacFixIt) to see if more is known about your suspected file and/or symptoms.

Otherwise, if you remain concerned that you have an unidentified virus, you could reformat the entire disk and restore it from (what you hope are) your uninfected back-ups. This should eliminate any virus infections, even if they were not detected by your anti-virus utility. Normally, though, this should not be necessary.

By the way, if a virus or Trojan horse did succeed in infecting your disk and appears to have erased files, don't despair yet (even if the files aren't backed up!). It may only be the disk's Directory that has been damaged or erased. If so, you may be able to repair or restore the disk, as described in Fix-Its #10 and #11.

**FIX-IT
#6**

Determine the Source of Your Virus Infection

Whenever you find a virus on any of your disks, try to determine where the original infected file came from. Use this knowledge to prevent future infections. For example, did symptoms start shortly after you used a particular floppy disk borrowed from a friend? If so, alert your friend to the problem, and be more careful the next time you borrow a disk from him or her!

 ## For Related Information

SEE: • Fix-It #3 on extensions and control panel problems.
       • Fix-Its #10 and #11 on repairing damaged files and disks.
       • Chapter 2 on preventative maintenance.
       • Chapter 4 on system crashes.

Fix-It #7:
Defragment/Optimize the Disk

▶ **QUICK SUMMARY**

Use a disk-optimizing utility (such as Speed Disk from Norton Utilities) to defragment/optimize the files on your hard disk.

 When to Do It:

- Whenever the overall speed of operations on your disk slows down significantly.

- Whenever symptoms appear that get worse as less and less free space is available on your disk—especially problems opening or correctly displaying a document.

- Whenever your undelete utility is unable to restore or only able to partially restore even the most recently deleted files.

- Whenever you use a defragmenting utility to analyze a disk and it suggests that defragmenting is desirable.

**Fix-It
#7**

 Why to Do It:

This is one of several Fix-Its that refer to topics first mentioned in Chapter 2, under the heading "Give Your Macintosh a Tune-Up." At that time, I briefly considered them as preventative maintenance procedures. Here, I look at them in more detail, as specific problem-solving techniques. For this Fix-It, the problem is file fragmentation. Suppose that a 50K file is stored on your disk, tucked between two 900K files. If the 50K file is deleted, it leaves a small 50K gap between the two larger files. The larger files cannot automatically slide over to fill in the gap. Files can be moved to different physical locations on a disk only when they are copied or modified. (Remember, *location* refers to the physical area of the disk that the file occupies. This is different from its location on the desktop, which refers to the folder where it resides. It is also different from the area of memory occupied by a file after it is launched.) After you've spent months adding, deleting, and modifying files on your disk, the unused space on your disk may consist mostly of these small gaps.

Now suppose that you want to copy a new 1200K file to your disk but no longer have a single block that large anywhere on the disk. A total of 5000K of unused space may be on the disk, but it is all in blocks smaller than 1200K. By itself, this is not a problem. Fortunately, the Macintosh can divide the physical storage of a file into separate fragments. These fragments, which don't have to be stored near one another on the disk, then fit into the smaller empty blocks. This is called *disk fragmentation* or (more accurately) *file fragmentation*. Similarly, existing files on your disk can become more fragmented each time they are modified (such as when you save changes to a document file).

The information needed to link together the data from all of a file's fragments is stored in the invisible files that make up the Directory area of the disk (as described in Chapter 8). By accessing this information, the Macintosh can combine a file's fragmented data as needed (for example, it would do this when opening a file and loading its data into memory). This does not actually eliminate the fragments; it just allows the Mac to work around them. Thus, most of the time, you could not tell the difference between using a file that is stored as a single block versus using the same file stored in fragments.

If the amount of fragmentation gets too great, however, it can become a problem, albeit usually a minor one. Because of the added time needed to skip around the hard drive to find the fragments of a file, the operational speed of the Macintosh may slow down noticeably. Also, especially if an individual file is severely fragmented, you may have trouble using the file. A fragmented word-processing file, for example, may unexpectedly display incorrect formatting. Also, disk-repair utilities and some undelete utilities work less effectively with highly fragmented disks. Finally, if your free space is fragmented, you may have trouble using certain virtual memory utilities that require contiguous free space in order to work (Apple's virtual memory does not have this restriction). If you are experiencing any of these problems, and you haven't defragmented your disk recently, it's time to check it.

Fix-It #7

There is a minority that says "to hell with optimization." These users have never optimized their drives and claim to never have noticed any deficits as a result. Personally, I tend to lean in that direction myself. I typically don't even think about optimization more than once a year or so. However, Apple has confirmed a rare situation where a heavily fragmented drive may fail to startup, stalling at the "happy Macintosh" icon. The only solution here is to startup from another disk and defragment (or reformat) the drive.

What to Do:

Optimizing/Defragmenting Basics

Defragmenting and optimizing refer to different but similar operations. *Defragmenting* means to restore fragmented files to single undivided files. *Optimizing* means to rearrange the location of files on your disk so as to minimize future fragmenting. Optimizing works on the principle that files can only get fragmented as they get used and especially as they get modified. Thus, you can minimize fragmenting by locating all rarely modified files (such as most applications) in one location and frequently accessed files (such as most documents) in another. A related optimizing technique is to combine all unused space into one block. In general, when you say you optimized a disk, it implies that you also defragmented it. That's how I will use the term here.

You use special utilities to optimize a disk. The most well-known is Speed Disk from Norton Utilities. We will use it for the examples in this Fix-It. The same principles should apply to other optimizing utilities.

Disk Express is noteworthy because it can optimize your disk in the background, working whenever your Macintosh is idle for a few minutes. When you resume work, it halts. At your next break, it returns to where it left off. However, as of this writing, it has not been updated to work with the latest versions of the Mac OS.

Before You Optimize

Check for damage Optimizing an already damaged disk can further damage files, resulting in irretrievable loss of data that could have otherwise been saved. So before you optimize a disk, first check for possible damage. With Speed Disk, this is done automatically when you select Check Disk from the Speed Disk window. Otherwise, run Disk First Aid or a comparable utility (as covered more in Fix-It #10).

Other precautions For reasons explained more in later sections of this Fix-It, you should make sure you have a current backup of the disk to be optimized, that all files on the disk to be optimized are closed, and that you have deleted all unneeded files from the disk. Ideally, start up from a disk other than the disk you want to optimize.

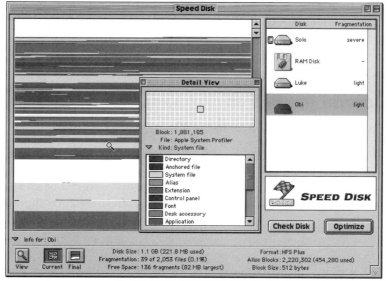

Fix-It #7

Figure F7-1 Norton Utilities' Speed Disk shows the current fragmented state of a hard drive. The area under the magnifying glass icon is displayed in the Detail View window. It is currently over a fragment of Apple System Profiler.

Optimize the Disk

1. **Launch your optimizing utility and select the disk you want to optimize** After launching Norton Utilities, click Speed Disk from its Main Menu. From the window that appears select the disk you want to optimize.
2. **Select the command to display the current status of the disk** For Speed Disk, click the Check Disk button in the Speed Disk window. This creates a graphic map showing the distribution of files across the entire disk. Different types of files are assigned different colors (or shades of gray, if you don't have a color display), based on the key shown in each window.

   The overall level of fragmentation is indicated by words such as "Moderate" or "Severe" listed next to the name of the drive. If anything worse than Moderate is indicated, consider optimizing the drive.

The bottom of the window also lists the number and percentage of total files that are fragmented (open the disclosing triangle to Show Info if needed). As a general guideline, and assuming you are concerned about framentation problems at all, if fragmentation is greater than 5 percent, I would defragment the disk.

3. **Prior to defragmenting/optimizing, select desired options** With Speed Disk, the *Optimize For* command in the Options menu gives you a choice of different optimizing arrangements, depending upon your primary use of the drive. If you select Multimedia, for example, instead of General Use, Speed Disk will arrange your defragmented files in a different way. Defragmentation will be complete in all cases; just the optimization locations will vary. In most cases, selecting the default General Use is your best bet.

    You can see how the Optimization will look for an option you select, prior to actually doing the Optimization, by clicking the Final button at the bottom of the window (open the disclosing triangle to Show Info if needed).

4. **Optimize** Click the Optimize button to begin optimization/defragmentation of the disk. Wait until it is finished. This can take quite awhile.

Beyond the Basics

Check for Fragmentation of Individual Files

Prior to defragmenting a disk, defragmenting utilities can report the number of fragments of any specified file. Even if the overall fragmentation percentage for a disk is at an acceptably low level, a particular file on the disk may still be excessively fragmented. If you are having problems with a file, check its fragmentation. To do this:

1. **Display the current status of the disk** Follow the instructions in Step 2 of "Optimize the Disk."

2. **Select the option to display fragmentation of individual files** With Speed Disk, select Show Fragmented Files from the Explore menu. If a file cannot be defragmented because it is currently open or because there is not enough free space ("disk is too full"), this will be indicated as well. From this list, you can select individual files and defragment only those files.

    Also, if you click the View button at the bottom of the main window, it will open up yet another window. Now, when you move your cursor over any section of the graphic map of your disk's file fragmentation, the additional window will show a close-up view of what is located there. The name of the file will also be indicated.

3. **Decide whether to defragment/optimize** As a general guideline, if a file is divided into more than five or six fragments, and if the file has been causing any problem, strongly consider optimizing it.

Make Sure Files Are Free to Defragment/Optimize (Startup Disk Problems and More)

Open files typically cannot be defragmented. Similarly, the System and the Finder on the startup disk cannot be defragmented, as they are considered to be open files. If you optimize the disk that contains the optimizing utility, the utility itself cannot be defragmented, as it is an open file.

Defragmenting a disk with files that cannot be defragmented reduces the effectiveness of the procedure. Therefore, ideally you should close all files on the disk to be defragmented and not defragment the startup disk or the disk that contains the optimizing utility.

Speed Disk will not even attempt to Optimize a startup disk. It will only defragment (and even that may be incomplete).

To defragment your normal startup disk, it is best to startup from the bootable CD that contains your optimization utility. (Disk Express is an exception. It can effectively defragment the disk that contains it, even if the disk is the startup disk.)

Create Free Space

Successful defragmentation requires a minimum amount of free space on your disk. If your hard drive is almost full, you may not be able to completely defragment your disk. In particular, you may not be able to defragment larger files.

The solution is to remove files from your hard disk to create enough free space for the optimizing utility to work. Ideally, at least 10 percent of your hard drive should remain unused. Delete any and all unneeded files from your disk.

Maximizing the amount of free space available on your disk minimizes future fragmentation. The Macintosh prefers to store files in a single large block. However, as the total amount of free space on your disk declines, large blocks become increasingly rare and file fragmentation becomes increasingly common.

Don't Optimize Floppy Disks

In general, don't bother optimizing floppy disks. They are not large enough for fragmentation to be a significant problem.

A Disk Is Optimized When You Reformat and Restore It

Reformatting a hard drive and restoring its files from backups also completely defragment the disk. I would not usually reformat and restore a disk simply to defragment it. But if you are going to do this for some other reason, it's nice to know that you are also optimizing the disk.

Be Careful if Your Have an HFS Plus-Formatted Drive

If you have an HFS Plus-formatted drive (see Fix-It #13), make sure you don't use an out-of-date utility that is incompatible with this format (also called Mac OS Extended). If your utility does not work with HFS Plus, you could conceivably destroy the data on the drive. For Speed Disk, you need version 4.0 or later.

FIX-IT #7

Fix-It
#7

TECHNICALLY SPEAKING ▶ Speed Disk, DiskWarrior, and Extent Fragments of Deleted Files

When Speed Disk optimizes a disk, it may leave "extent fragments" of deleted files on the disk, rather than zeroing out these fragments. These are file fragments of files that have technically been deleted and therefore contain irrelevant data. Norton believes this is a useful feature that may aid in later attempts to unerase files. However, these same extent files may lead other repair utilities to report that the disk is damaged, when really it is just fine. Early versions of DiskWarrior made this error, but the latest versions have been modified so this no longer occurs.

SEE: • Fix-It #10 for more on extent fragments

The Downside of Optimizing and Defragmenting

If you follow the preceding steps, defragmenting/optimizing should proceed smoothly. However, a few cautions to note are described in the following paragraphs.

Defragmenting Takes Time

Defragmentation can take a lonnnnng time. You could easily have time for a leisurely lunch (and probably dinner too) while a 4GB or larger hard drive is optimized. However, current versions of Speed Disk (4.0 or later) are much faster than earlier versions.

Defragmenting Can Erase Files that Otherwise Could Have Been Undeleted

Defragmenting your disk can eliminate the capability of undelete utilities to undelete previously deleted files, because the optimizing process usually overwrites files that have been deleted but that otherwise would have still been recoverable.

With any optimization utility, of course, defragmentation does not prevent the recoverability of files deleted after the defragmentation process is completed.

Defragmenting Can Cause Disk Damage

The optimizing process rearranges and rewrites so much data that, if there is a bug in the optimizing utility, the process could easily damage files on your disk (although the publisher of the utility will almost certainly release upgrades that fix these bugs as soon as they become aware of them). Even without a bug, there is a small risk that damage may occur if there is an unexpected interruption in an optimization, such as from a system crash or a power failure.

To save yourself from potential disaster here, make sure your backups are current before you optimize your disks.

 For Related Information

> **SEE:** • Fix-Its #10 and #11 for how to check for and repair damaged files and disks.
> **SEE:** • Chapters 2 and 6 on using undelete utilities.

Fix-It #8:
Rebuild the Desktop

▶ **QUICK SUMMARY**

To rebuild the desktop, hold down the Command-Option keys at startup until a dialog box appears asking whether you want to rebuild the desktop. Click OK.

 When to Do It:

- If a file's desktop icon displays as a blank, generic icon rather than its correct custom icon.

- If a file's desktop icon displays an icon for an older version of the software rather than its current version.

- When you drag a document icon to its application, the drag-and-drop highlighting does not occur and the application does not launch, even though it worked previously.

- When you double-click a document to open it, a message appears saying that the creating application is missing, even though the application is not missing (or other unusual error messages appear)

- If the overall response speed of the Macintosh slows down significantly.

- If the size of available space on a disk, especially a floppy disk, is considerably less than what you would expect based on the files visibly located on your disk.

- If files are inexplicably missing from the Finder's desktop.

- When you get a message that says *The disk needs minor repairs,* and clicking OK does not remedy the problem.

 Why to Do It:

There are two desktop files: Desktop DB and Desktop DF. The DB file stores icon information, while the DF file stores the information about where on the desktop files are located. These two invisible files are created on each volume when the volume is first initialized. They are stored at the root level of each volume. They store information about the contents of the disk that is particularly important to the Finder. For example, they keep track of what custom icons are assigned to files, the links between documents and their creating applications, and the links between aliases and their original files. The text in the Comments boxes of Get Info windows is also stored here. Every time a file is added, deleted, or modified, the Desktop files are updated accordingly.

Note: System 6 used only one Desktop file, called Desktop. You may occasionally still see the single Desktop file on disks. If you discover this Desktop file on a current system, you can usually safely ignore it. However, it is also safe to delete it. Floppy disks use the lone Desktop file even in current versions of the Mac OS. This is because a volume needs to be greater than 2MB before it uses the dual Desktop files.

Without the Desktop files, the Finder could not create its desktop display. When you rebuild the desktop, it means that the Desktop files are largely recreated from scratch by scanning the current contents of the disk to get the required information. Here's why you would need to do this:

The Desktop Files Can Become Bloated

Even after a file is deleted, the Desktop files retain the information about that file, such as its icon. Particularly because they retain this now-unneeded information, the Desktop files can become quite large over several months of adding and deleting files. Rebuilding the desktop purges unneeded information from the Desktop files and thus reduces the size of the files. This frees up some disk space (especially relevant for floppy disks) and can help speed up Finder operations. You can see exactly how much disk space you recover (it can be as much as several hundred kilobytes) by comparing available disk space immediately before and after rebuilding the desktop.

The Desktop Files Can Become Corrupted

Like all software, the Desktop files can get corrupted. If this happens, the link between a document and its creating application can get lost. As a result, the *Application could not be found* error message can appear when you double-click a document file to open it from the Finder. Occasionally, a damaged Desktop file may cause system crashes. A likely solution to all of these problems is to rebuild the desktop.

Generic Icon Problems

These days, virtually every program and document on your hard drive has its own unique, customized icon. These icons give the Finder's desktop a wonderfully varied and colorful appearance, an aesthetic experience that you may miss if you select the "By Name" or other non-icon view from the Finder's View menu (although even these views can show custom icons if you select the relevant option from the Views control panel).

Figure F8-1 The generic document icon (left) and the generic application icon (right).

Unfortunately, if the Desktop files are not correctly updated, a file's custom icon may not display. Instead, document(s) may sport the boring generic "blank" document icon or (more rarely) applications may display the generic application icon. This is considered a Desktop file (rather than a Finder) problem because the Desktop files are where all of the icon information used by the Finder is stored.

For example, custom icons often get "lost" when you upgrade to a new version of an application, if the new version uses a different icon from the older version. The Macintosh may get confused about which icon to use. The result is that the new version's files continue to display either the old version's icon or a generic icon.

Happily, rebuilding the desktop updates the Desktop files and usually fixes these icon problems (though some incorrect icon displays can be caused by a problem with a file's bundle bit, as described in Chapter 8).

TAKE NOTE ▶ Two More Invisible Files Related to the Desktop Files

Starting in Mac OS 8.0, two new invisible files made their appearance on your desktop.

OpenFolderListDF The first one is OpenFolderListDF. It contains information about the location of open windows/folders on the desktop, especially the new tabbed folders introduced in Mac OS 8.0. The file on a startup drive also maintains information about folder placements on read-only media, such as CD-ROM discs, that were previously mounted.

On a startup drive, the file should be found in the Preferences folder. On all other volumes, it will be in the root level of the volume.

You may find a copy of the file at both locations on any given volume. According to Apple, this should not cause problems; you need not delete one or the other of these files. However, other reports suggest that deleting the older of these two files and then rebuilding the desktop may fix certain Finder freezes. In particular, if you get a persistent watch cursor at startup, just before items in the Startup Items folder would normally launch, deleting this file may help (you'll probably need to start up with extensions off to get past this freeze). Note that sometimes, simply holding down the Option key just prior to the onset of the freeze may also help (as described in Chapter 5).

In one case, a user kept getting a "*Files are open*" error message when trying to optimize his disk with Norton's Speed Disk. Deleting the duplicate OpenFolderList files eliminated the problem.

DesktopPrinters DB The other new invisible file is DesktopPrinters DB. As its name implies, it is used to keep track of the desktop printer icons on your desktop. It need not concern us here. (Chapter 7 has more on desktop printers.)

 **What to Do:**

Rebuilding Basics

The basic procedure for rebuilding the desktop was described in Chapter 2 (in the section called "Give Your Macintosh a Tune-Up"). I explain it in more detail here.

1. **Hold down the Command and Option keys at startup** To rebuild the Desktop file on the startup disk (or any other disk mounted at startup), hold down the Command and Option keys during the startup sequence until you see an alert box asking *Are you sure you want to rebuild the desktop file on the disk <name of disk>?*.

    To rebuild the Desktop file on any other disk, at any time, hold down the Command and Option keys prior to mounting the disk. For example, for a floppy disk, do it just prior to inserting the disk. If you want to rebuild the Desktop file on a floppy disk (or other removable media) that is already mounted, eject the disk using the Put Away command from the Finder's File menu. Then reinsert the disk while holding down the Command and Option keys. In all cases, wait for the alert box message to appear before releasing the keys.

    Note that, when rebuilding the desktop at startup, the message asking you whether you want to rebuild will not appear until after all startup extensions have loaded. If you have a lot of extensions, this can take a while. Be patient. Actually, you don't even have to hold down the Command-Option keys until the end of the extension loading sequence approaches.

When running Mac OS 9's Multiple Users, the rebuilding the desktop message does not appear until after you have logged in, so don't bother holding down the keys until then. In fact, you can use this feature to rebuild the Desktop without restarting: Log out of your Multiple Users account and log back in; hold down the Command-Option keys while logging in and the option to rebuild the Desktop will appear. However, with limited or panel access, you will not be able to rebuild the Desktop at all.

SEE: • **Chapter 15 for more on this Mac OS 9 feature.**

Figure F8-2 Alert box that appears when you hold down the Command-Option keys to rebuild the desktop.

2. **Click OK to the alert box message** Click the alert box's OK button and wait. A progress bar should appear, monitoring the rebuilding process. In a few minutes the Desktop file is rebuilt, and the progress bar disappears. You are done.

If you have more than one volume (such as two drives or one drive with multiple partitions) that gets mounted at startup, you get a separate message request for each disk. Click OK just for the volumes you want to rebuild. You do not have to rebuild all of them. However I have occasionally fixed an icon display problem on my internal hard drive by rebuilding the desktop of my external hard drive. This might happen, for example, if a document on my internal drive was created by an application on my external drive. It usually pays to rebuild all regularly mounted volumes if you are having problems.

BY THE WAY ▶ Rebuilding the Desktop on Potentially Damaged Disks

Just a reminder: if you plan to rebuild the desktop because of symptoms that suggest file damage on the disk, it is a good idea to first run Disk First Aid or a similar utility to check for and repair possible Directory damage (see Fix-It #10). Otherwise, there is a slim chance that rebuilding the Desktop can make things worse.

In this regard, note that the Desktop is not the primary method by which the Macintosh keeps track of the contents of disks. The Directory is far more critical for this task. Only the Finder needs the desktop.

---

3. **Restart again if needed** Restarting may be required to get correct icons to appear. This is especially likely for Desktop files rebuilt at times other than during startup.

Beyond the Basics
Fixing Generic Icon Problems

As described in the Why to Do It section, rebuilding the desktop can fix problems with incorrect (generic) icon displays. However, there are cases where simpler solutions are preferred or where rebuilding the desktop will not work. Here are a variety of such cases.

Icon problems for individual files If you are having an icon problem with just one or two files, you probably can avoid the time and hassle of rebuilding the desktop and instead selectively update the information just for the problem files. A freeware utility called Fix Icons can do this, as can various other utilities.

Otherwise, open the Get Info window of the file, click on its icon box, and then select Copy, Paste and Cut. (This is not guaranteed to work, but may be worth a try).

Generic icon problems with unmounted disks If you save a document to your startup hard disk from an application stored on a floppy disk or other removable media, the document should still display the appropriate icon. However, the next time you restart without the application disk/media mounted, the document may have a generic icon (especially if the creating application has never been copied to the hard disk). This is because the icon information on the unmounted disk may never have been copied to the Desktop file on your hard drive.

Getting the correct icon to display typically requires that the necessary disk/media be present at startup. If you mount it later, the correct icon will still not display.

You can usually solve these problems by copying the creating application to your startup disk. Then launch the application, open the document, and save it (using Save As). The correct icon should be restored. If not, you need to rebuild the desktop after all—ideally with all relevant disks mounted. This almost always works.

After that, you can delete the application from your startup disk, if desired. However, if you do so, the generic icon may return if you later rebuild your desktop (as explained in "When Rebuilding the Desktop Causes Generic Icon Problems," later in this section).

Generic icon problems with disk partitions, external drives, and removable media This situation is similar to the one just described. However, in this case, the problem can occur even if all relevant files are on your startup disk. It can also occur with external drives and removable media, even if they are mounted at startup.

The problem is typically specific to document icons or aliases that are stored on the startup disk's desktop area (that is, not in any folder). In this case, these files may display generic icons if the creating application is on a different volume (partition or disk), even if the other volume mounts at startup. The reason is that the Finder checks for the icons of files on the desktop before the secondary volumes mount. If the icon data is not present in the startup disk's Desktop files, the generic icon is displayed. A similar situation can arise if the file is in a folder on the startup drive whose window is set to open at startup.

**Fix-It
#8**

The problem can be avoided if the Finder does not have to actually display the icon until after the secondary volume(s) are mounted. So the easiest solution is to keep these icons off your desktop and out of any windows that are automatically opened at startup.

If you must keep these icons on your desktop, you can use a program such as SCSIProbe that allows for mounting of SCSI volumes during the time that extensions load (which is earlier than the volumes would normally load). This will mean that the volume(s) are mounted prior to the Finder loading—with the result that the icons appear correctly.

If the file is an alias, another solution is to create the alias on the non-startup volume and then drag it to the desktop. This keeps the alias file on the non-startup volume. If you create the alias directly on the desktop, it is stored on the startup volume and will likely display a generic icon when you restart.

Lastly, a quick fix is to do a Force Quit or otherwise use a utility that quits the Finder (such as Terminator Strip). When the desktop reappears, the custom icons will be restored. Similarly, rebuilding the desktop will bring the icons back. However, with these fixes, the problem is likely to return next time you restart.

When rebuilding the desktop causes generic icon problems Occasionally, a file may display its correct custom icon and then lose it *as a result* of rebuilding the desktop. Most often, this happens to a document file whose creating application has been deleted from the startup volume prior to rebuilding. Rebuilding the Desktop file purges all information about the deleted application, including what is needed to display the document's custom icon. There is no solution to this other than to return the deleted application to your drive (rebuilding the desktop again if needed).

When the System, Finder and/or Enabler/Update files become generic If your System and Finder (and possibly Enabler/Update) icons become generic (sometimes *after* rebuilding the desktop), this typically means that the System file's Bundle bit information has gotten corrupted in the Desktop files or (more likely) the file's Bundle bit attribute has somehow gotten unchecked.

In the first case, rebuilding the desktop should get the icon back. However, you can again save yourself the hassle of a complete rebuild by simply updating the desktop for the System file alone—via utilities such as Save a BNDL. Otherwise, using a utility such as Snitch (as described in Chapter 8), look to see if the System file's Bundle bit is unchecked. If so, turn it back on. While you are at it, *uncheck* the Inited bit. Then restart. This should get your icons back. If nothing else works, doing a clean reinstall should get the job done.

In any case, this is only a cosmetic problem that does not signal any other problems with your software.

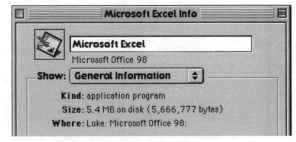

Figure F8-3 A box appears around the icon in the Get Info window when you click on it. This indicates that you can cut or copy the icon or paste a new one over it.

TAKE NOTE ▶ Custom Icons vs. Really Custom Icons

The expression *custom icon* often has two different meanings. One refers to the normal, non-generic, application-specific icons used by almost all applications and their documents. These icons are established by resources stored in application files, placed there by the creator of the application. This is the main meaning of the term *custom icons*, as used in most of the discussions in this Fix-It. Sometimes these may also be called *bundled icons*.

The other meaning of the term is when you create a personal custom icon by pasting an image into the icon box of a file's or folder's Get Info window. With this method, you can change the icon for any file, folder, or volume. More specifically, here's one way to do it:

1. Select a file that has an icon you like. Open its Get Info window and click on its icon picture. A box should now surround the icon. Select Copy. (You can otherwise get icons from any other source, including making one yourself in a graphics program.)

2. Now go to the Get Info window of the file whose icon you want to change. Click on its icon and select Paste. The copied icon now replaces the existing icon. This overrides any bundled icon that an application or document would normally have. However, the bundled icon information is not lost. If you subsequently cut your personal custom icon, the bundled icon will return.

By the way, if you want to create a folder icon that looks like a generic folder icon but with a smaller custom icon "inside" it (as is the case for the System Folder icon), you can do it easily with a shareware utility called Folder Icon Maker.

TAKE NOTE ▶ 32-Bit Icons

Starting in Mac OS 8.5, Apple introduced 32-bit icons. Compared to the previous 8-bit icons, these allow for new levels of icon delight: up to millions of colors and 256 levels of transparency. These icons can have smoothly detailed and intricate effects, with color gradients and various transparency effects. However there's a problem if you want to create or edit icons using this new format: as of this writing, most utilities that can manipulate icons (such as ResEdit) have not been updated to work with 32-bit icons. One exception is a utility called IconBuilder (it works as a plug-in for Adobe Photoshop).

Bear in mind that these 32-bit icons can only be viewed if you are running Mac OS 8.5 or later. Older versions of the OS will ignore them or display them incorrectly. However, a utility called IconDropper can help by ensuring that a custom icon can be seen no matter which OS version you are using.

Finally, note that there was a bug in Norton Utilities 4.0.x such that it reported certain 32-bit icons as needing to be fixed. If you fixed them, the 32-bit icon was lost and all you saw was a generic (or ResEdit) icon.

Problems with custom icons for folders and volumes The information about custom icons for a particular program (and its document files) is stored in the resource area of the program as well as in the volume's Desktop file. This is true for both bundled icons and true custom icons.

Custom icons for folders and volumes work a bit differently. Since there is really no file that corresponds to a folder or volume, their icon information is stored in special invisible files, named *icon*, located within each folder that has a custom icon. Thus, if volumes or folders with custom icons unexpectedly revert to displaying generic icons, rebuilding the desktop is not likely to have any effect. Here are some solutions that should work:

- In general, use a utility such as Snitch to make sure that the folder/volume's "Use Custom Icon" bit is checked.

- If the missing custom icon is for a volume (such as a hard disk), check the disk's formatting utility to see if icons can be selected from there. If so, use it to reselect the one you want.

- For folders and volumes, an unexpected generic icon can mean that the custom icon file is damaged. If so, you may be able to fix or create a new icon via the Get Info window method (as explained in "Take Note: Custom Icons vs. Really Custom Icons").

- For folders, if the file damage is such that the Get Info method does not work, try this alternative: remove all files from the folder, trash the folder (the invisible icon file goes with it), create a new folder, and make a new custom icon. As an alternative, utilities such as File Buddy can locate and delete unwanted icon files.

- For volumes, the invisible icon file may be missing or "lost" but the volume's "Use Custom Icon" bit is still set (which means that it thinks the icon is still around). In this case, if you try to use the Get Info method to paste a new custom icon over the generic icon, you will probably get a message such as *The icon could not be deleted because the file can not be found.* To get around this, try using a freeware utility called Disk Rejuvenator.

- Running Disk First Aid may correct certain "Custom icon missing" problems. If running Disk First Aid seems to make icon appearances worse, restart the Mac; the situation should get better.

- If all of this fails, use any utility that can delete invisible files and use it to delete the invisible icon file. Then add a new custom icon.

- As a last resort, reformat the entire disk.

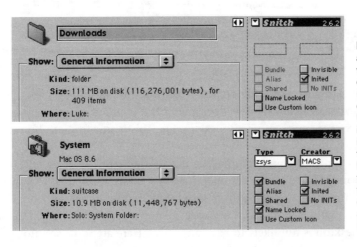

Figure F8-4 Top: A portion of a Get Info window for a folder, with Snitch enabled. For missing custom folder or volume icons (and sometimes even for missing custom file icons), make sure that Use Custom Icon is checked. It isn't checked here because there is no custom icon in use. Bottom: for problems with your System file having a generic icon, make sure that the Bundle bit is set and that the Inited bit is not set. In all cases, restart your Mac when you are done. Hopefully, the missing icon(s) will return.

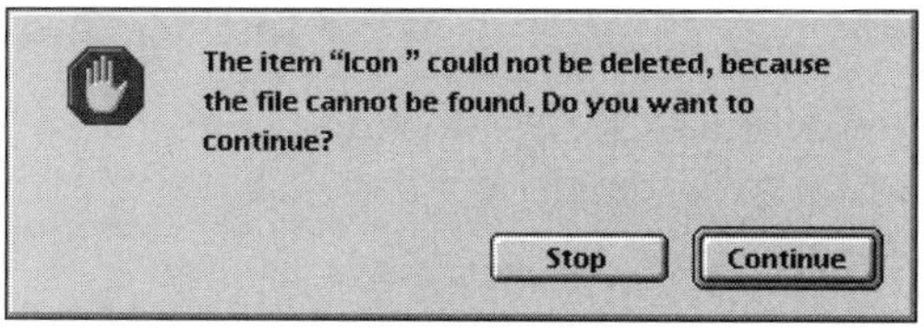

Figure F8-5 If you get this message when trying to paste a custom icon into the Get Info icon box of a folder, try using Disk Rejuvenator.

Bundle bit damage and other more unusual problems If the preceding fixes do not help, use Norton Disk Doctor or similar utility to check for bundle bit problems or possible damaged files. Otherwise, try a "complete" rebuild of the desktop with TechTool (see later in this Fix-It).

You may be able to fix some nasty icon problems by using ResEdit to directly modify a file's icon resources. But this gets beyond the scope of this book.

Finally, be aware that not all generic icon problems need fixing. For example, back in the days when QuickDraw GX was still around, I found that if, after installing QuickDraw GX, I restarted with QuickDraw GX disabled, many of the custom icons associated with GX switched to generic icons. When I returned to GX, everything reverted back to custom icons.

SEE: • Chapter 8 for more on invisible files, bundle bits, other file attributes, and related information.

BY THE WAY ▶ Weird SimpleText Icons

If your SimpleText document icons are missing their left border, don't fret. It is merely a cosmetic problem and is usually remedied by rebuilding the desktop.

The actual cause appears to be out-of-date or damaged copies of TeachText/SimpleText that are on your disk. The long-term solution is to get rid of all copies of the application except the most recent version.

Losing (and Saving) Get Info Comments After Rebuilding the Desktop

If you select Get Info for a file, you will see a Comments area. You can type whatever text you like there. Starting with System 7.5.3, these comments are retained when you do a basic (Command-Option) rebuild of the desktop. In older versions of the system software, they were lost.

However, if you use a third-party utility to rebuild the desktop (such as TechTool), it is likely that the text in these comments fields will be lost. This is because TechTool completely deletes the Desktop files rather than just updating them (as described more later in this Fix-It). However, you can save the Desktop files (including comments) before rebuilding. This could be useful, for example, if a rebuild of the desktop has no effect on whatever problem you were trying to solve and maybe even makes the situation worse. If so, you can replace the original Desktop files and get the comments back.

Don't Bother to Rebuild the Desktop After Initializing a Disk

Any time you reinitialize a disk, it creates a new Desktop file. You do not have to separately rebuild the desktop.

Desktop Files and Reusing Floppy Disks

Many users reuse floppy disks without reinitializing them. That is, they drag all the files on the disk to the Trash and then begin to fill the disk with new files. I don't recommend this. Instead, when you start over with a disk, reinitialize the disk first. Not only does this confirm that the disk is not damaged (otherwise, initialization would fail), but it also forces a rebuild of the desktop. This, in turn, purges unneeded information from the Desktop file and may thus reclaim a significant amount of disk space (over 100K in some cases). If you don't want to reinitialize the disk, at least rebuild its desktop (after deleting all items from the disk).

The Desktop Rebuilds Every Time You Start Up

A file named Desktop on your desktop What is happening is that the Macintosh is confused into thinking that the file is actually a System 6 Desktop file (see the "Why to Do It" section at the start of this Fix-It). This causes the Macintosh to repeatedly try to rebuild the desktop (among other problems it may cause).

Keep Extensions Off When You Rebuild?

Some extensions may cause problems when you rebuild the desktop, even going so far as to prevent the rebuild from successfully completing.

For example, with some versions of anti-virus programs running, rebuilding the desktop may not correct all icon problems. To avoid this, and most other extension-related problems, the general solution is turn off all extensions prior to rebuilding. To do this, hold down the Shift key at startup until the Extensions Off message appears; then let go of the Shift key and immediately hold down the Command-Options keys to get the desktop to rebuild.

Unfortunately, there are a few exceptions even to this generalization. For example, if you rebuild the desktop with StuffIt SpaceSaver disabled, all files that had been compressed may adopt the compression utility's icon instead of the file's own icon. If this happens, rebuild again, with the compression utility on. More generally, if a rebuild problem can be traced to any particular extension, rebuild again with that extension enabled.

Apple recommends keeping File Exchange enabled when rebuilding the desktop, especially with Mac OS 8.x.

If none of this works, and you still have problems (such as a system error) when trying to rebuild the desktop, you probably have a more serious directory-level problem. You will need to try to repair the disk.

SEE: • Fix-Its #10 and #11 on repairing disks.

Really Rebuild the Desktop

The information in this section is sufficiently important that I've separated it out from the rest of "Beyond the Basics." When you rebuild the Desktop file(s) using the Command-Option key method, it does not *completely* rebuild the desktop. It is more like a thorough updating of the existing file(s) as opposed to deleting them and replacing them with new ones. This can be a problem if you are rebuilding the desktop because you suspect a corrupted Desktop file. In this case, rebuilding may not repair the damage, and the symptoms may persist. In such cases, it pays to delete the Desktop file(s) and thereby force completely new one(s) to be created. (The Mac will create the new ones automatically when it finds the old ones missing). This may solve a problem that a normal rebuild would not.

Completely deleting the Desktop files may also enable you to rebuild the desktop on those occasions when the standard Command-Option technique does not work.

Of course, reinitializing a disk accomplishes a complete rebuild, but there are less drastic ways to do this. Here's how.

Use TechTool (or File Buddy) My favorite way of completely rebuilding the desktop is to use a freeware utility called TechTool. To use it, just launch the utility and click the "Rebuild Desktop" button. TechTool will then ask permission to quit any open applications. Let it do so. You will then have the option to select which disks to rebuild, if more than one is mounted. After you have made your selection, TechTool deletes the Desktop file(s) and initiates a rebuild. The rebuild occurs without restarting the Macintosh. When the rebuild is finished you are returned to the Finder.

You can also Save the Desktop database files prior to a rebuild. You can use this to later Restore your original data after a rebuild. This can be desirable in cases where the Desktop files were actually perfectly okay and rebuilding the desktop had no beneficial effect on your problem.

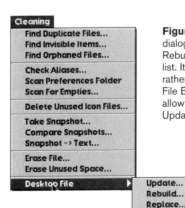

Figure F8-6 Left: the TechTool dialog box with the Desktop Rebuild button at the top of the list. It actually replaces the files rather than rebuilding them. Right: File Buddy's Desktop File options allow you to chose between an Update, Rebuild, or Replace.

A shareware program called File Buddy also lets you rebuild the desktop, giving you three different choices:

- Update: Updating the desktop will add new information but not remove icons and references that are no longer valid.

- Rebuild: Reset the desktop database file and enter all current information from scratch. This is the most common action. This is similar to what Apple's Rebuild command does.

- Replace: Delete the existing desktop database file, create a new one, and enter all current information from scratch. This is similar to what TechTool does.

Use Desktop Reset Another solution is to use a freeware system extension called Desktop Reset. When it is installed, you still request a rebuild the normal way—by holding down the Command-Option keys at startup. When you do this, however, the extension intercepts the normal procedure, gives you a slightly different alert message, and (after you click Reset) deletes the Desktop files, initiating the complete rebuild.

Use Norton Utilities or DiskTop Utilities such as Norton Utilities or DiskTop (as described in Chapter 8) let you view and modify invisible files. Use one of these utilities to move the invisible Desktop DB and DF files from their location at the root level of the disk to inside a folder on the disk (also making them visible when you do this). This should force a complete rebuild, creating new Desktop file(s) when you restart. After restarting, delete the now obsolete Desktop file(s) from the folder where you moved them. However, I see no reason to bother with this method, since the previous methods work just as well and are easier to do.

In fact, Apple generally recommends against anything but a normal rebuild of the desktop, unless it clearly fails to work. For one thing, the more extreme deleting of the Desktop files will cause all Comments to be lost.

 For Related Information

SEE: • Fix-It #3 on turning extensions on and off.
        • Fix-It #11 on damaged disks.
        • Chapter 2 on preventative maintenance.
        • Chapter 6 on files that do not open.
        • Chapter 8 on invisible files and on icon problems.

Fix-It #9:
Zap the Parameter RAM

▶ **QUICK SUMMARY**

Hold down the Command-Option-P-R keys at startup until the Macintosh restarts itself a second time. Then release the keys and let startup proceed normally. This resets the parameter RAM (PRAM).

 ## When to Do It:

- Whenever control panel settings, such as the current date/time and volume level, are inexplicably incorrect (especially if, after you reset these values, the settings are wrong the next time you turn on your Macintosh).

- If your Mac starts up in Black-and-White or Grayscale, even though you have selected Color from the Monitors control panel.

- Whenever you are unable to start up from a hard drive, especially an external hard drive. Symptoms as serious as a Sad Mac may occur.

- If you cannot mount or otherwise access any externally connected SCSI, USB, or FireWire device.

- Whenever you cannot access a modem or other serial port device because its port is claimed to be in use.

- When you cannot get documents to print at all or if garbage characters print instead of the correct output, especially if an error message appears indicating a problem with the serial port.

- If, in certain PowerBook models, you lose sound from your speakers.

- If a monitor's screen does not come on at startup.

- If, after you select Shut Down from the Finder's Special menu, the Macintosh restarts instead of shutting down.

- If you get persistent and frequent system errors at random times.

 ## Why to Do It:

Parameter RAM, usually referred to as PRAM, is a small amount of RAM maintained by special hardware on the main logic board of the Macintosh. It is separate from both the main memory (see Fix-It #5) and the video memory (see Chapter 10) to which I have referred most often elsewhere in this book.

Fix-It
#9

So what exactly does PRAM do? Primarily it stores the settings of several control panels included with the Macintosh system software. Most notably, the PRAM stores the current date and time, the choice of Startup disk (set by the Startup Disk control panel), and whether AppleTalk is active. It also stores settings from various control panels, including General Controls (insertion point and menu blinking rates), Memory (disk cache size), Mouse (mouse tracking and double-click settings), Sound (alert sound selection), Keyboard (key repeat settings), and Appearance (highlight color). The PRAM also stores information regarding the status of ports, such as the serial and SCSI ports. Some data not technically stored in PRAM is also reset to default values when you zap the PRAM. These include the settings for the desktop pattern and the color depth of the monitor.

The rationale for storing this information in PRAM is that, unlike other forms of RAM, PRAM information is retained after the Macintosh is turned off (or even after you unplug it!). That is why, for example, you do not have to reset the time each time you turn on your Macintosh.

At this point, you may be recalling that I said (in Chapter 1) that RAM gets wiped out when you turn the Macintosh off. This is true. But the PRAM is saved because a battery inside the Macintosh keeps the PRAM powered at all times (similar to how some bedside alarm clocks use a backup battery to keep going in the event of a power failure).

The problem is that the information stored in PRAM can get corrupted. A good sign that this has happened is if the time and date are suddenly wrong and, even if you reset them, the corrected settings are not retained. Another similarly common symptom is when control panel settings, such as the Monitors control panel, are not retained when you restart. If this happens, all other PRAM settings are likely to have the same problem.

A corrupted PRAM can also prevent the Macintosh from transmitting information to or receiving information from the Mac's ports (SCSI, serial, USB, FireWire), causing problems with all devices connected to those ports.

These PRAM problems do not occur often. But when they do, the solution is to "zap the PRAM." This is a cute way of describing the method for erasing the presumably corrupted current PRAM data and returning all PRAM settings to their default values. If zapping the PRAM does not eliminate these symptoms, it may mean you have a dead battery or system software damage.

Finally, note that some third-party extensions may use parts of the PRAM for their own purposes, contrary to Apple's guidelines. This usage may conflict with Apple's own changing uses of PRAM, leading to freezes and crashes, etc. The only solution here, short of an upgrade to the extension, is not to use the problem third-party software. Contact the vendor for information if you suspect this is a problem.

Fix-It
#9

BY THE WAY ▶ PRAM vs. the Finder Preferences File

The Finder Preferences file also stores some user-selected settings. In particular, the Finder Preferences file stores: the Finder version; all settings from the Finder Preferences window except Label colors and names (which are kept in the System suitcase file); last window size and position for Clipboard, Copy windows and the About this Computer window; where Sherlock was last located; and location of the Trash. It also stores the on or off status of the "Warn Before Emptying" check box (located in the Trash's Get Info window). These settings are separate from PRAM settings and are not reset when you zap the PRAM. Problems with these preferences settings are usually solved by replacing the Finder preferences file, as described in Fix-It #2.

By the way, there are a variety of other system preferences files that are important, such as AppleScript Preferences, Display Preferences, and Sound Preferences. None of these settings are reset when you zap the PRAM.

 What to Do:

Zapping Basics

If corrupted PRAM is preventing your startup hard disk from mounting, especially if it causes a Sad Mac to appear, you may need to start up with a floppy disk, such as your Emergency Toolkit disk, before you can zap the PRAM.

FIX-IT #9

TAKE NOTE ▶ Warning for Users of RAM Disks

Zapping the PRAM will erase all data on a RAM Disk created via Apple's Memory Control Panel. Be sure to back up any critical data on your RAM disk before you zap!

For all 680x0 Macs and NuBus Power Macs

The title here refers to all Macs that are not Power Macs and all first-generation Power Macs (6100, 7100, and 8100 models).

1. Simultaneously hold down the Command-Option-P-R keys at startup. Wait until the Macintosh startup tone chimes again and the Mac restarts itself a second time.

   Actually, if you continue to hold down these keys, the Mac will continue to chime and restart indefinitely. Some reports suggest holding down these keys until three or more starts have occurred. However, Apple's official position is to say that just the two starts are enough.

2. Release the keys and let startup proceed as normal. That's it.

For All Other Macs

The title here means all Macs newer than the ones in the previous section. These Macs store some display data in yet another special area called non-volatile RAM (NVRAM). You can clear this NVRAM area at the same time as you zap the PRAM. Actually, the PRAM is considered a subset of the NVRAM, so clearing the NVRAM clears the PRAM as well. But you'll have to be a bit more precise about what you do. In particular:

1. Shut down the Mac (do not use Restart).

2. Then restart and *immediately* hold down the Command-Option-P-R keys. Wait for the Mac to chime twice. (If you don't hold down these keys immediately, you will only reset the PRAM.**)**

3. Release the keys and let startup proceed as normal.

4. After the startup has been completed, go to the Preferences folder and trash the Display preferences file (ideally this should be done on a startup where extensions were disabled by holding down the Shift key at startup; you can still do this after zapping the PRAM).

By the way, current versions of TechTool and TechTool Pro (as described later in this Fix-It) do *not* zap the NVRAM. According to MicroMat (makers of TechTool), zapping the NVRAM is still planned for a future version. Also note, as mentioned in Fix-It #1 (see: Technically Speaking: G3/G4 Upgrades and Speculative Addressing), that zapping the NVRAM can eliminate a special fix placed there when you install certain G3 and G4 upgrades on older Macs. Without this fix, the Mac may be unable to start. A special bootable disk is necessary to reinstall this fix. Otherwise, you may have to temporarily downgrade your processor to get things working again.

Fix-It #9

BY THE WAY ▶ iBooks, New PowerBooks and PRAM Settings

The iBook stores PRAM differently from other Macs. In particular, an iBook doesn't have a PRAM battery that stores the date; instead it relies on the AC adapter or its lithium battery. This means that if you remove the battery without first attaching the iBook to an external power source, all non-default PRAM settings may be lost. You probably have about a 10-minute window here, due to a small capacitor that preserves the settings for this duration. Similarly, unlike desktop Macs, if you press the Reset button (see Chapter 4) on an iBook, customized PRAM settings are lost. This includes the current date and time, which will then have to be reset. If this happens, the modification dates of all files on your drive may also change. Apple's recent G3 PowerBooks (such as the FireWire PowerBook) share this "feature." That is why Apple recommends using the Control-Command-Power keyboard command to restart a Mac after a crash, using the Reset button only as a last resort.

This is decidedly less convenient than the way other Macs work. I can only hope that Apple fixes this in future revisions to the portable line.

SEE: • **Chapter 11 and Chapter 14 for more on this and other matters regarding the iBook and newer PowerBooks.**

Optional: Remove the Battery

If you want to be absolutely positively certain that you zapped the PRAM, you can remove the Mac's internal battery (the one that is used to maintain this PRAM information after you turn the Mac off).

The battery is located on the Mac's logic board. This means you will have to open up the Mac's case to remove the battery. It also means that you will have to learn where the battery is located and any specific information about how to remove it on your particular model (details may have come with your Mac). This may be more than you care to learn—especially with Macs such as the iMac that are not designed to have their "insides" easily accessible. Note that in some cases, the battery is soldered to the board. If so, you almost certainly want to take the Macintosh in for servicing to get it replaced. Otherwise, you can try to remove it and replace it yourself.

If you do decide to do it, first shut off your Mac. Then remove the battery. Then wait at least a half hour to let the capacitor that maintains the PRAM information "drain." Finally, insert the new battery, close up your Mac, and turn it back on.

More details on how to replace these batteries can be found at various sites on the Web. Check MacFixIt <www.macfixit.com> for the latest links on this subject.

SEE ALSO: • **"The Logic Board Battery," in Fix-It #15.**

After Zapping the PRAM

- **Reset customized settings** Zapping the PRAM wipes out any customized changes you may have made to your control panel settings and returns all values to their default state. Thus, you will now need to reset any changes you had previously made. For example, you will probably need to reselect "Internal Modem" from the PowerBook Setup control panel if you use an internal modem.

  However, in most cases, if the time and date were correct before you zapped, you should not have to reset them. These two settings are temporarily stored elsewhere while the PRAM is reset and then written back to the PRAM afterward (but see: "By The Way: iBooks, new PowerBooks and PRAM Settings").

- **Replace a dead battery** If your newly reentered settings are lost again after you turn off the Macintosh, you probably have a weak or dead battery. Replace it.

  But don't worry too much about this happening—a battery should last at least five to seven years. Many users will replace their Macintosh before the battery wears out!

  However, be aware that a dead battery can cause some surprising and disturbing symptoms, well beyond lost control panel settings. These symptoms range from a monitor display that will not turn on to a Mac that appears completely dead.

  Want to check if you have a weak or even a dead battery? A shareware program called Battery Checker can do it for you. You just run it immediately after turning on your Mac.

- **Replace a corrupted System file** If you still have a problem with an incorrect date and/or time, you may have a corrupted System file. Replace it. The freeware utility TechTool can both zap your PRAM and check for a corrupted System file.

FIX-IT #9

Also, check the Date & Time control panel to make sure you have actually entered the correct date and time there and have set the formatting for how you want them displayed.

SEE: • **Fix-It #4 on reinstalling system software.**

TECHNICALLY SPEAKING ▶ The Cuda Button and the PMU: Solving Startup Problems

Cuda button Most recent Mac models have a small, circular, usually red, button on the logic board (called the Cuda button) that, when pressed, resets the Mac's "permanent" settings even more thoroughly than a reset of the PRAM. You should only need to use this button as an absolute last resort for PRAM-related problems.

Its location varies from model to model, but a visual scan of the logic board should reveal it. On the iMac it is located near the RAM modules. On the Blue and White G3 Macs, if you open the computer, you will see two buttons behind the PCI slots marked "Power On." The left one (as you face the front of the Mac) is the normal Power button. The right one is the Cuda button.

Pressing the Cuda button is often advised if your Mac does not start up after installing a RAM or processor upgrade. The Cuda button may also help if your hard drive is unwilling to even start spinning at startup. It is similarly advised *any time* the Mac completely fails to startup, especially if the failure is very early in the startup sequence (such as a failure to even produce a startup tone). Also possibly helpful for this problem is to remove and reseat all RAM, because defective RAM can also cause these symptoms.

One other problem where pressing the Cuda button may help out is if your monitor screen goes black and stays black even though its power light is on and everything else seems to be working normally. If restarting and zapping the PRAM has no effect (or only works sporadically), try the Cuda button.

More technically, what the Cuda button does is reset the data stored in the Cuda Microcontroller Chip. According to Apple, the main functions of this chip are to:

• Turn system power on and off.

• Manage system resets from various commands.

• Maintain parameter RAM.

• Manage the Apple Desktop Bus (ADB).

• Manage the real-time clock.

• Let an external signal from either Apple GeoPort serial port control system power.

PMU On the iMac DV and other very recent Macs, there is no Cuda button. Instead, a button (again on the logic board) resets the PMU (Power Management Unit). Resetting the PMU can similarly resolve many system problems, such as failure to power up, no video on power up, or a gray screen on power up.

Apple states that the PMU is a "microcontroller chip that controls all power functions for the computer. The PMU is a computer within a computer. It has memory, software, firmware, I/O, two crystals, and a CPU." Its functions are to:

• Tell the computer to turn on, turn off, sleep, wake, idle, etc.

• Manage system resets from various commands.

• Maintain parameter RAM (PRAM).

• Manage the real-time clock.

Unfortunately, this button is relatively inaccessible on an iMac, so you are not likely to be able to use it. If resetting the PMU is indicated, take the Mac to an Apple Authorized Service Provider.

SEE: • **Fix-It #15, for more on hardware-related problems.**

FIX-IT #9

BY THE WAY ▶ Resetting the Power Manager on PowerBooks

PowerBooks have another special type of RAM called the Power Manager, similar to the PRAM, that is primarily used to maintain information regarding operating a PowerBook on battery power. As with the PRAM, the Power Manager data may get corrupted and may need to be reset. The details of exactly why and how to do this are described in Chapter 11.

Really Zap the PRAM: Use TechTool

Unfortunately, the standard method (Command-Option-P-R) of zapping the PRAM does not reliably zap *all* the PRAM data. If the remaining unzapped portion of the PRAM is corrupted, the previous zapping of the PRAM will not fix the problem. This seems to happen particularly with the PRAM data that affects the SCSI and serial ports. For example, you may find that, even after zapping the PRAM, you cannot access external SCSI devices. Or it may be that when you try to use your modem you get an error message that says the serial port is "in use." In these cases, you need to *completely* zap your PRAM.

Removing the Mac's battery or using the Cuda/PMU button will completely zap (and then some), but there's an easier way: use a software utility. Several utilities completely zap, but TechTool is my first choice. (Yes, this is the same utility used to completely rebuild the desktop, as described in Fix-It #8.) As an added bonus, TechTool will save your PRAM settings before you zap, allowing you to restore them when you are done. TechTool Pro also has these same features. Here's what to do, using TechTool:

FIX-IT #9

- **Click the PRAM Save button** Doing this saves a copy of your current PRAM data for later use by TechTool. Obviously, the ideal time to do this is *before* you suspect that your PRAM is corrupted. Otherwise, you may be saving corrupted data. On the other hand, if you have not previously saved the PRAM before you zap, you might as well do it in any case. If, after you zap, the symptoms still remain, then the PRAM was not the cause. In this case, you can safely restore your just-saved PRAM data.

- **Restoring the mandate** The PRAM maintains data about the date of manufacture of the Mac and its hours of use. This data is lost when zapping the PRAM and is set back to a default value. However, TechTool preserves this data prior to zapping the PRAM, and then restores it the next time you start up. This is called *restoring the mandate*. TechTool will do this even if you did not select to save and restore the remaining PRAM data.

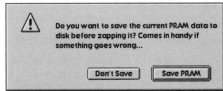

Figure F9-1 Top: TechTool's PRAM Zap and System Analyze button, seen listed below the Desktop Rebuild button. Bottom: the message that appears after you click on the Zap button.

- **Click the PRAM Zap button** Active applications must be closed before you can zap the PRAM. The Macintosh will restart as part of the zap process.

  Note: After selecting the Zap button, a dialog box will also appear that asks: *"Do you want to save the current PRAM data to disk before zapping it?"* If you have already saved a copy of the PRAM that you want to use, say no here. Otherwise, you will be saving PRAM data that you suspect is corrupted (which is not what you want to do).

  There is a small risk that zapping the PRAM will make things worse rather than better. Check TechTool's Help file for more details about this concern.

- **Click the PRAM Restore button if zapping the PRAM had no effect** If you have previously saved your PRAM (and the saved data appears to be uncorrupted), return to TechTool and click the Restore button.

  The PRAM data are now restored to what they were when you last saved them, eliminating the need to manually re-create customized control panel settings.

  One caution: never restore data saved from one machine on to another machine. Doing so could prevent your Mac from starting up; you will have to remove the battery to fix the problem.

- **Optional: click the System Analyze button to check for a corrupted System file** If the results of running Analyze indicate that the System file is corrupted, replace the file. Remember that you must use a version of TechTool that is at least as recent as the version of the system software you are using or Analyze may provide inaccurate results (see: "Selective Install/Reinstall/Deletion of System Software," in Fix-It #4).

- **Optional: Zap the NVRAM** You may also want to zap the PRAM again, via the standard method, in order to zap the NVRAM (as described in "Zapping Basics").

Fix-It #9

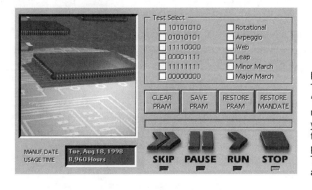

Figure F9-2 The PRAM zapping options from TechTool Pro (Expert Interface mode). Note: "Restore Mandate" will restore the original manufactured date and hours of use (from your saved PRAM data) without restoring the rest of the PRAM data; this allows you to preserve these data when zapping the PRAM. TechTool (the freeware version) does this automatically; there is no option to not do it.

 For Related Information

SEE: • Fix-It #12 on disk device drivers.
- Fix-It #14 on problems with **SCSI** devices and connections.
- Fix-It #15 on hardware problems.
- Chapter 2 on preventative maintenance.
- Chapter 5 on startup and disk-mounting problems.
- Chapter 11 on resetting the power manager and on file sharing and modem problems.
- Chapter 14 on special problems with iMacs and iBooks.

Fix-It #10:
Repair Corrupted Disk Directory

▶ **QUICK SUMMARY**

Use a disk repair utility (such as Disk First Aid, Norton Utilities, or DiskWarrior) to check for and repair corruption of the Directory area of a disk. If you have more than one of these utilities, and the first one you try does not fix the problem, try the others.

 ## When to Do It:

- Whenever you cannot start up your Macintosh with a known startup disk, especially if the symptom is a flashing disk or folder icon at startup.

- Whenever you are unable to get a properly formatted disk to mount to the Finder's desktop. Especially with floppy disks you may get a message that says the disk is *unreadable, not a Macintosh disk,* or *damaged* and that asks if you want to initialize it.

- Whenever you have system-wide problems with a particular disk, especially problems related to keeping track of files. These commonly include an inability to open, copy, or delete files/folders on the disk, as well as files/folders that mysteriously disappear.

- Any time you have a problem that is not easily diagnosed or solved. Using these utilities, especially Disk First Aid, is such a simple and effective procedure that it is almost always worth trying.

 ## Why to Do It:

Directory Damage

Amid all the bad news about things that can go wrong with your Mac, here is one piece of very good news: some of the most serious of Mac problems (such as an inability to start up your Mac) are often quickly and easily solved by a repair utility. This is because many of these problems can be traced to a damaged Directory, and these utilities can often fix the damage quickly. Here are the details:

The Directory The Directory area of a disk, as detailed in Chapter 8, is a collection of invisible data that contains the essential information that the Macintosh needs to access the disk and the files on it. Each area of the Directory has its own (often esoteric) name, such as *extent BTree* or *catalog hierarchy*.

The Directory maintains a continually updated catalog of the names, sizes, and locations of all files and folders on a disk. It is essentially a database. One very important function of the Directory is to keep track of the number of fragments of each file (see Fix-It #7) and where each fragment is located. For example, if a file is stored on a disk in fragments, the Directory contains the information needed to link all the fragments together when you launch the file. Without this information, fragmented files on the disk are unusable. Because almost all files on your disk are likely to be fragmented if you have not optimized recently, this can spell serious trouble.

The Directory (together with related "hidden" areas of the disk) also contains the critical information necessary for the Macintosh to recognize whether the disk is a Macintosh-formatted disk as well as whether it is a startup disk. Even a small amount of damage to the Directory can render an entire disk virtually inaccessible.

If anything is ever incorrectly updated, the Directory is considered damaged. Because the Directory is continually modified as you change the contents of your disk, and because most disk damage occurs when a file is modified, it is common for the Directory to become corrupted. Minor problems may cause symptoms so subtle that you do not notice them—at least not at first. This is why, in Chapter 2, I recommended using Disk First Aid as a preventative measure even if nothing seems wrong. You should eliminate even the most minor Directory problems as soon as you discover them, because minor problems tend to get more serious if left unfixed. Serious Directory problems can render the files on a disk inaccessible—you may not even be able to mount the disk.

Fortunately, if Directory damage occurs, there is still a very good chance that your disk, or at least most of the data on it, can be saved, because the remaining areas of the disk, where the documents and applications actually reside, may still be unharmed. The files contained on the disk are often all usable, if only they can be accessed. Working with a disk with a damaged Directory is a bit like trying to use a library without a catalog. The books are all fine, but there may be little hope of finding the ones you want.

Repairing the Directory Apple builds in sufficient redundancy to the structure of a disk so that even if a disk's Directory gets corrupted, a good repair utility can scan the undamaged portions of a disk, determine where the Directory errors are, and fix them. If this works, it is the ideal solution. It is almost like magic. An apparently dead disk can be restored to full working order in a matter of minutes, with no loss of data.

Disk First Aid Apple makes an excellent disk repair utility. It is called Disk First Aid and it is included free with every copy of the Mac OS. You will find it in the Utilities folder on the Mac OS CD. It will also be installed on your hard drive (in a Utilities folder) when you install the Mac OS. A copy was probably already there when you first booted your Mac. Finally, at least as of this writing, the Mac OS CD includes a Disk Tools image file that can be used to create a bootable floppy disk that contains Disk First Aid. It's called the Disk Tools disk. This is important because it may be necessary to start up from another disk, such as the Disk Tools disk, before you can repair your startup drive. Of course, in most cases, you can startup instead from the Mac OS CD itself, but for those Macs that still have floppy drives, the Disk Tools disk can sometimes be more convenient.

FIX-IT
#10

In general, I would use this first, before trying any other utility. I recommend it because, assuming you have the latest version of the utility, it may contain special fixes known only to Apple that will fix your problem where other utilities might not. However at least as often Disk First Aid will fail where other competitors might succeed. If Disk First Aid fails to solve the problem, simply move on to the next utility.

Beyond Disk First Aid There are currently three other popular disk repair utilities on the market. The first two are Norton Utilities for the Macintosh (especially the Norton Disk Doctor module) and TechTool Pro. Both do many more things beyond disk repair. For example, they may have the ability to check for media damage, recover files, unerase files, and/or optimize disks. We cover such matters in other Fix-Its (especially #11). Here we focus just on disk Directory repairs. The third utility in this category is DiskWarrior. As with Disk First Aid, all DiskWarrior does is Directory repair. However, DiskWarrior does it in a different way, completely replacing the Directory rather than trying to repair the existing one (the latest versions of TechTool Pro offer a similar option).

For the examples used in this Fix-It, I will use mainly Disk First Aid and Norton Disk Doctor. A "Take Note" with more information on the other repair utilities is included near the end of this Fix-It.

What all of these utilities do is check for possible damage to a disk's Directory. They can then repair many, although not all, of the problems that they find. For preventative maintenance, run one or more of these utilities about once a month. If you have suspected Directory problems, immediately run the utility (or directory-checking module of the utility).

There are other causes of some of these symptoms, besides a damaged Directory (see the list at the end of this Fix-It). But if Directory damage does turn out to be the cause, and the damage is so severe that none of these utilities can repair it, usually your only remaining options are to reformat the disk or (for a removable media disk) discard it.

FIX-IT #10

TAKE NOTE ▶ Be Careful If You Have an HFS Plus Formatted Drive

If you have an HFS Plus, also called Mac OS Extended, formatted drive (see Fix-It #13), make sure you don't use an out-of-date utility that is incompatible with this format. If your utility does not work with HFS Plus, you could conceivably further damage the data on the drive. The most recent versions of all utilities mentioned here are HFS Plus-compatible.

HFS Plus caused many headaches for disk repair utilities. Programmers spent a good part of 1998 trying to rewrite the utilities to work with this new format. Initial updated versions of these utilities often caused unexpected problems, including damaging disks that did not have any problems until after they were checked. The latest versions of these utilities appear to be much more reliable.

If you do develop a problem here, Disk First Aid 8.5 or later may be able to undo it. Give it a try.

What to Do:

Using Disk First Aid

Start by making sure you have the latest version of Disk First Aid. Check Apple's Web site for the latest version. At the very least, use a version no older than the one that came with the version of the Mac OS on your startup drive.

Getting Started

1. **Before you launch Disk First Aid...** Although Disk First Aid can always verify a disk (that is, check for problems without making any repairs), repairing a disk requires that certain preconditions be met. In particular, Disk First Aid cannot repair a write-protected disk (including CD-ROMs). It also cannot make repairs when there are any other open files.

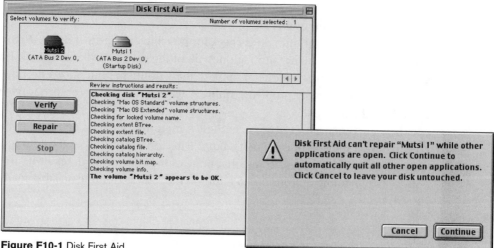

Figure F10-1 Disk First Aid.

Figure F10-2 This message will generally appear when you select to "Repair" a disk with Disk First Aid. Click Continue if you want to proceed with the repair attempt.

Current versions of Disk First Aid can repair the startup disk and/or the disk from which Disk First Aid was launched. Older versions of Disk First Aid could not repair such disks. And it seems to work well. Still, it is recommended to start up from a disk other than the one you want to repair; this allows Disk First Aid to more reliably verify and repair your disk. Thus, to save time, before you even launch Disk First Aid:

a. Restart your Macintosh from a bootable CD-ROM (such as the Mac OS system software disk), floppy disk (such as a Disk Tools disk) or secondary hard drive volume or removable cartridge. This may be a requirement, rather than an option, if a problem with your startup drive prevents you from starting up from it.

    b. Make sure any floppy disks or removable cartridges that you want to repair are not locked.

    c. Do not open any other applications prior to launching Disk First Aid. Ideally, also turn off File Sharing.

You can choose to bypass these steps for now and just verify or attempt to repair a disk. However, if a problem is found, and the repair attempt is unsuccessful, you will probably have to make these adjustments and start over.

2. **Launch Disk First Aid** If you ignored Step 1, you may get warning messages concerning the matters just described. It may offer to close all open applications. Choose OK. Eventually, you will get to Disk First Aid's window, where a brief set of instructions is displayed. If you have not read them yet, do so. You are now ready to begin.

Verify or Repair a Disk

1. **Click the disk icon of the disk you want to check** From the Disk First Aid window, click the icon of each disk you want to check. Shift-click to select more than one volume at once. By the way, if a disk is so damaged that it cannot be mounted from the Finder, Disk First Aid may still list it as openable. Give it a try. (Insert floppy disks that cannot be mounted into a drive only after Disk First Aid is open and currently selected as the active application.) If Disk First Aid cannot access the damaged disk, try other repair utilities, such as Norton Disk Doctor, as discussed later in this Fix-It.

2. **Click the Repair button to begin verification and repairs** If the repair button is dimmed, you cannot select it. You can only verify the disk. (The reasons this might happen were described in "Getting Started.") Or:

   Click the Verify button to just verify the disk Most users will do this only if the Repair button is dimmed. However, even if Repair is enabled, you might consider verifying first. This way, if problems are detected, you can back up critical files on the disk before repairing (just in case the repair makes things worse).

3. **Wait while Disk First Aid goes to work** Whichever you select, Verify or Repair, the instructions in the window to the right of the buttons will be replaced by a growing list of items that indicate what Disk First Aid is checking. You will see things such as "Checking extent BTree" and "Checking catalog file." Don't worry about what any of it means. Just wait for it to finish.

4. **If no problems are found** Whether you selected Verify or Repair, you will see a message that says "*The volume <volume name> appears to be OK.*" for each volume checked. If this happens, you should still run Disk First Aid a second time, just to confirm the diagnosis. If nothing pops up this time, you can quit. Go to Step 6.

FIX-IT #10

5. a. **If a problem is found after having selected Repair** If you clicked Repair and Disk First Aid spots problems, one of two outcomes will generally occur:

   - **Disk First Aid cannot make repairs** You get a message that says *"Test done. Problems were found, but Disk First Aid cannot repair them."* This means either that Disk First Aid detects identifiable damage but does not know how to fix it, that the disk has an unfixable problem, or that the disk is sufficiently damaged that Disk First Aid cannot identify the problem.

     Similarly, if you get a message such as *"Unable to read from disk"* or *"The disk is damaged,"* these imply damage to the disk, probably media damage to the Directory, that prevents Disk First Aid from successfully completing its tests. In these cases, testing is aborted or never begun.

     Most likely, Disk First Aid cannot repair such disks no matter what you do. Still, before giving up, try running Disk First Aid a few more times. Sometimes, layers of problems exist, and repairs are made incrementally. Disk First Aid may fix one problem but still report that the disk could not be repaired because of other remaining problems. It may take Disk First Aid several runs before it detects and repairs all problems. With luck, you may eventually get the *OK* message.

   - **Disk First Aid successfully repairs the disk** If this happens, you will get a message something like *Repair done. The disk is OK*. As a precaution, run Disk First Aid a few more times even if you get this sort of message. It may still detect and repair other problems on subsequent runs.

   b. **If a problem is found after having selected Verify** If you clicked Verify, and Disk First Aid spots problems, one of the same basic two outcomes described in Step 5a will occur. The only difference is that Disk First Aid will not attempt a repair when verifying—even if it can fix what is wrong. If Disk First Aid detects a problem, and if it can repair it, you will get a message such as *"The volume <name of volume> needs to be repaired"* (other messages may appear if Disk First Aid does not know how to make the repair). To make repairs, you will have to click the Repair button. If that button is not enabled, you will have to do whatever is necessary to enable it (as described in the Getting Started section). In either case, make sure critical files on your disk are backed up before proceeding with repairs.

6. **If Disk First Aid could not make repairs or if symptoms persist, try other repair procedures** No matter what the outcome of the test, even if Disk First Aid initially or eventually reported no problems, you may still have problems with the disk, because there are problems that Disk First Aid does not detect. If symptoms persist despite your use of Disk First Aid, or if Disk First Aid found problems that it could not repair, you need to use other procedures to try to fix them. Your next step should be to try a different repair utility, as described next.

TECHNICALLY SPEAKING ▶ What Do Those Symptom Messages Mean?

If it finds a problem, Disk First Aid will often (but not always) include a line describing what it is. For example, it might say *"Invalid sibling link, 4, 5"* or *"Invalid PEOF."* Most of the time, these provide very little insight into how to solve the problem, if Disk First Aid is unable to do so.

In case you are interested: I don't know for sure what an invalid sibling link is (although I suspect it has to do with links between fragments of the same file). However, I do know that an invalid PEOF refers to an "invalid Physical End of File." This typically means there is a file on the disk that is bigger or smaller than the Mac's Directory thinks it is. More precisely, the Mac makes a distinction between the PEOF and the Logical End of File (LEOF). It is okay for the LEOF to be smaller than the PEOF (because this means the end of the file falls within the physical limit set by the PEOF), but not vice versa. If the PEOF is too small, you will get the invalid PEOF error message. If you get this message and Disk First Aid cannot fix the problem (and it usually can't), try Norton Utilities and/or MacTools. Even if repairs are successful, you may still need to replace the affected files. Also, rebuild the desktop. If the problem persists, the System or Finder files are probably corrupted and should be replaced. If all else fails, you will have to reformat the drive.

For those interested in more details about what Disk First Aid checks when it checks a disk's Directory, here's the scoop: Disk First Aid checks the Partition Map (which stores the locations of partitions, if any, on your drive), the device driver, the Boot Blocks (where booting instructions are stored along with directions for locating the system and Finder files), the Master Directory Block (which contains volume information such as the date and time of volume's creation and number of files the volume contains), the Volume Bitmap (a record of which logical blocks in the volume are allocated to files), Catalog File/Tree (which stores the hierarchical location of each file and folder), Extents File/Tree (which stores information about how a file is fragmented into segments), and Finder attributes (such as file type, creator, and bundle bits settings).

Errors in the catalog and Extent trees are commonly referred to as B-tree errors. These errors and Volume Bitmap errors are the most common errors that Disk First Aid is likely to fix.

BY THE WAY ▶ Disk First Aid's Erase Disk Option

Disk First Aid's Option menu includes a command called Erase Disk. You would likely only use this for floppy disks that you want to reformat (typically because they are reported to have problems that cannot be repaired). Even here, you may want to try other repair utilities, such as Norton Utilities, before erasing the disk. You typically would not want to use this to erase a hard drive.

SEE: • Fix-It #13 for more details on erasing/reformatting disks.

FIX-IT #10

BY THE WAY ▶ Disk First Aid at Startup

With Mac OS 8.5 or later, when you restart after a system crash, you may get a message during the next startup informing you of the prior crash (see also Chapter 4). If this happens, the Mac will typically also run Disk First Aid during the startup sequence, as a precaution against the system crash having caused any Directory damage. If you want to bypass all of this, go to the General Controls panel and uncheck the *"Warn me if computer was shut down improperly"* option.

(continues on next page)

BY THE WAY ▶ Disk First Aid at Startup (continued)

Why would you want to do that? Two reasons: first, it takes a lot of extra time and is rarely worth it. Ninety-nine percent of the time, a system crash does not cause any further damage. Second, occasionally running Disk First Aid may cause a new problem. For example, there was a version of Disk First Aid (no longer current) that caused many custom icons to revert to generic icons—until you restarted a second time. If you had this problem, you would want to avoid this inconvenience by running Disk First Aid only when essential to do so.

Similarly, if you get an error at startup that says *"Sorry, a system error occurred. International Utilities not present...,"* restart with extensions off (by holding down the Shift key at startup). This prevents the Disk First Aid check of the drive, which is what was triggering the error. After startup is over, run Disk First Aid manually and let it repair any problems it reports. The error should now go away at your next startup. Otherwise, you can work around it by disabling the "Warn me if computer was shut down improperly" option in the General Controls panel. As a last resort, you can bypass this error by deleting the invisible Shutdown Check file that the Mac uses to determine whether or not you are restarting after a crash. If you still get this error, it probably means a damaged System file. Try replacing the System file with a clean copy.

By the way, the version of Disk First Aid that runs at startup is not the First Aid application on your drive. It is a special version "hidden" in the System Resources file in your System Folder. This means that if you update to a newer version of the Disk First Aid application, the startup run of Disk First Aid will still use the older version built-in to the System Resources file.

SEE: • **"By The Way: The Shut Down Warning Message," in Chapter 4.**
      • **"Take Note: Invisible Files to The Rescue," in Chapter 8.**

Using Norton Disk Doctor

Getting Started

FIX-IT
#10

1. **Before you launch Norton Disk Doctor...** Current versions of Norton Disk Doctor can repair the startup disk and/or the disk from which Norton Disk Doctor was launched. Still, it is recommended to start up from a disk other than the one you want to repair, allowing Norton Disk Doctor to more reliably examine and repair your disk. For some types of damage, Norton cannot repair the current startup disk. If this happens, when the damage is detected, you will get a message advising you to start up from a different disk and try Norton Disk Doctor again. Thus, to save time, before you even launch Norton Disk Doctor:

   a. Restart from the Norton Utilities bootable CD. If you have a Mac that requires a newer version of the system software than is on the CD, you will have to request an updated CD from Symantec. Alternatively, you can create a startup disk that contains Norton Utilities on removable media, such as a Zip cartridge. One of these procedures may be a requirement, rather than an option, if a problem with your startup drive prevents you from starting up from it.

   b. Make sure any floppy disks or removable cartridges that you want to repair are not locked.

2. **Copy critical files** If the damaged disk can be mounted from the Finder, and there are critical files on the disk that are not backed up, back them up now to another disk. This protects against the chance that trying to repair the disk will only make things worse.

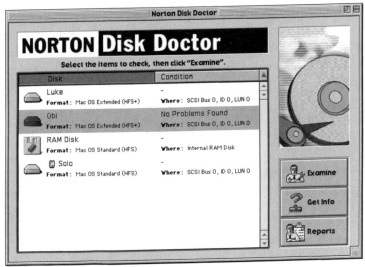

Figure F10-3
Norton Disk Doctor's main window.

3. **Launch Norton Disk Doctor (and get the damaged drive to appear in the list)**
Launch Norton Utilities and then click the Norton Disk Doctor button. A list of all mounted drives should appear. Even if your drive did not mount from the Finder, it will often appear here. If it still does not appear, try using the Show Missing Disks or Add Custom Disks options from the Disks menu (check Norton's documentation for more details).

Fix-It
#10

If mounting any removable media or external drive causes a crash at startup, you might try inserting the media (or powering up the external drive) only after you have launched Norton Disk Doctor. This may allow the drive/media to be recognized by Disk Doctor without crashing the system.

For a damaged internal hard disk, hold down the Command-Option-Shift-Delete keys at startup until the *Welcome to Mac OS* message appears. The Macintosh should bypass the internal drive so that it does not mount at all. Only your active startup disk (most likely a bootable CD) and any other secondary disks will mount (see Chapter 5, "By the Way: The Internal Drive May Still Mount When Using Command-Option-Shift-Delete"). This can avoid a crash that would otherwise occur when the Finder attempts to mount the startup drive. Again, after launching Norton Disk Doctor, the drive may still appear. If this does not work, you may have to zap the PRAM and try again.

Similarly, if as a result of inserting a damaged floppy disk when your repair utility is not active, a dialog box appears asking if you want to initialize the disk, do not do so. Eject the disk instead. Then launch the repair utility and insert the floppy disk.

If none of this gets the disk to mount, it's time to give up on Norton Utilities for this disk. Other solutions are discussed elsewhere (such as Chapter 5 and Fix-It #14). Ultimately, you may have to reformat the disk (losing all the data on it) or discard the disk.

Assuming the damaged volume eventually appears, your first order of business will likely be to try to save any files that are not backed up elsewhere. If you cannot do this via the Finder, for whatever reason, you may choose to use Norton Utilities Volume Recover function (see Fix-It #11) before proceeding. This may allow you to recover these critical files (again, do this just in case a repair attempt makes the situation worse).

Repair a Disk

1. **Set Preferences (via the Preferences command in the Edit menu)** You should not have to do this often (maybe only the first time you use Norton). In most cases, you can leave the Preferences at their default settings.

   Still, you may want to turn off "Check for Defective Media" as this check takes a long time and defective media is rarely the source of a problem. You would most likely want to check for bad blocks only when you are having a problem with a specific file that suggests that bad blocks are the cause, such as a read or write error- when trying to copy a file. What to do in that case is more specifically covered in Fix-It #11 ("Special Case: Recover/Repair Files Damaged Due to Bad Blocks"). In the worst case, if bad blocks are located in the Directory area of a disk, Disk Doctor may not even be able to successfully scan the disk. In this case, you will likely need to reformat the disk.

<table>
<tr><td>**FIX-IT**
#10</td></tr>
</table>

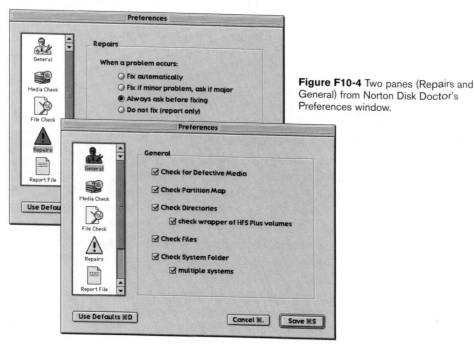

Figure F10-4 Two panes (Repairs and General) from Norton Disk Doctor's Preferences window.

If you don't want to turn off this media check preference, you can always choose to "Skip" the test while the test is running (as described next).

You may also want to uncheck one or more of the file check options, such as Bundle Bits and Custom Icons. In my experience, they often find problems that don't really need to be fixed.

One option I would never check is "Fix Automatically" in the Repairs section. It's always safer to see what the utility intends to do before it actually does it. There are times when you may even want to skip a particular repair (which you cannot do if "auto fix" is on).

SEE: • **Chapter 2 and Fix-Its #11 for more background information on bad blocks.**

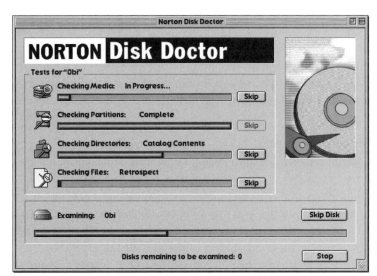

Figure F10-5
Norton Disk Doctor checking a drive.

2. **Attempt to repair the disk** Click on the name of the disk you want to check and click the Examine button. The program now begins to check the disk. If it discovers a problem, it stops to alert you. Under the default options, a window appears that describes the nature of the problem and suggests what to do about it. It usually gives you the choice to repair the problem (if possible) or skip over it (if desired). In general, repair any problem that is detected and can be repaired (though you can ignore minor problems, such as incorrect modification dates, without affecting your ability to use the disk). In some cases, it may recommend deleting a file (typically a Preferences file that will be rebuilt the next time it is needed); usually you should agree to delete the file.

After making your choice, the analysis then proceeds, pausing again as needed until the entire disk is checked. Normally that's all there is to doing repairs.

One word of caution: if a repair utility reports an unusually large number of problems when you are not experiencing any problems using the disk, or if it reports a problem with a specific file that is not giving you any problem, be a little skeptical. Do not automatically select to repair this problem. It is sad but true that even programs designed to detect problems may have bugs of their own!

Some repair utilities have the ability to undo any repairs they make, in case they make matters worse. Norton Disk Doctor does not currently have this ability.

3. **Check the disk again** If the utility has reported no problems with the disk, or if it has claimed to successfully repair any problems it found, check the disk again anyway. As with Disk First Aid, problems may be detected on subsequent runs that were not spotted or not fixed on the first run. Ideally, check the disk at least until no problems are detected on two consecutive runs. Symantec says this should no longer be necessary. But I still prefer to err on the side of caution.

4. **If repairs are successful** If your utility detects no further damage on retesting, your problems should be over. Quit the utility and restart the Mac. Try using the problem disk to see if it now works as expected. If so, you are done.

If the disk seems okay for the moment but the same problem recurs within a few days, you should probably reformat the disk rather than repairing it again. In the meantime, make sure your important files are backed up, just in case disaster strikes.

5. **If repairs aren't successful** Norton may detect a Directory problem but report that it is unable to repair it. In some cases, a disk is so damaged that the utility either cannot start or cannot complete its analysis of the disk. In rare instances it may claim to have repaired a problem, but when you return to using the disk, the problem remains. For example, you may have *cross-linked files*. This occurs when the Directory indicates that two different files are occupying the same sector of a disk. This usually means that one or both of the files are damaged, with lost data almost a certainty. Although a repair utility may offer to repair the incorrect Directory listing, it can't entirely repair the damaged files.

If Norton Utilities cannot fix a certain problem, it may directly launch its Volume Recover function. Using this is discussed more in the next Fix-It. In other cases, it may simply report that it cannot repair the volume.

Whenever you are unable to successfully repair a damaged disk, try to recover any files that you want to save (that have not already been recovered or backed up). You may then try yet another repair utility. If all attempts fail, it's time to reformat the disk. After successfully reformatting, restore the data from your backups. You are done.

**Fix-It
#10**

TAKE NOTE ▶ Using Other Repair Utilities and Using More Than One Repair Utility

TechTool Pro TechTool Pro features three separate user interfaces: Simple, Standard, and Expert. Each give you a completely different view (or lack of view in the case of Simple) of the myriad tests that TechTool Pro can perform. For doing disk repairs, I recommend shifting to the Standard interface. Have just Drives and Other checked from the top row of options. In the scrollable window, leave all the options checked except Surface Scan and Optimization. Then select the drive you want to check and click Run.

The strong suit of TechTool Pro is its ability to check for various hardware problems, something that none of its competitors can do. Like Norton Utilities, it can also perform file recovery and optimization. It also has the desktop rebuilding and PRAM zapping features of its freeware sibling, TechTool.

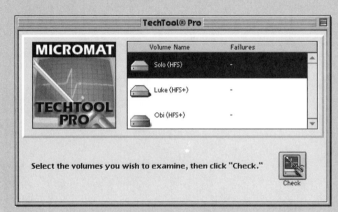

Figure F10-6 TechTool Pro's main window in its Simple interface. You can optionally select a Standard or Expert interface, which include more options.

DiskWarrior All DiskWarrior does is repair the Directory. However, it does it in a way that is different from its competitors (although recent versions of TechTool Pro include a "Rebuild Volume" command in the Control menu that performs a similar function). Rather than trying to fix a damaged Directory by correcting each error as it is found, DiskWarrior builds an entirely new Directory all at once. It does this by using the existing Directory data as well as, if necessary, by "scavenging" the contents of the remainder of the disk. It simultaneously optimizes the Directory when it builds the new one; this means that it re-orders the contents of the Directory to maximize hard drive performance.

DiskWarrior offers a Preview feature that allows you to mount the volume using the rebuilt Directory simultaneously with the volume mounted using the existing Directory. This allows you to compare the effect of the rebuilding before any irreversible changes are written to the disk.

Overall, this Directory rebuild approach can fix certain types of damage that the other methods are incapable of handling.

To use DiskWarrior, simply select the disk you want to check from the popup menu. Then click Rebuild. After the rebuilding is completed, and errors have been fixed, click Preview to compare the results. If all looks well, click Replace and you are done.

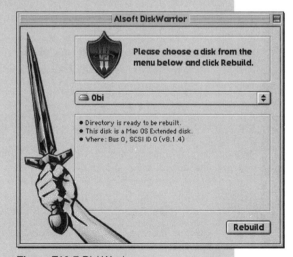

Figure F10-7 DiskWarrior.

FIX-IT #10

(continues on next page)

TAKE NOTE ▶ Using Other Repair Utilities and Using More Than One Repair Utility *(continued)*

DiskWarrior cannot rebuild either the current startup disk or the disk that DiskWarrior is on. In such cases, you may need to start up from a DiskWarrior CD or other startup disk that you have created.

Using more than one repair utility In general, I recommend using as many repair utilities as you have on hand when trying to fix a disk. At least keep trying if the one you already tried did not succeed. However, some caution is warranted here.

Occasionally, one utility may "undo" a repair made by another, potentially leading to an endless cycle of repairs as you switch back and forth between utilities. For minor problems, such as a bundle bit error, you can probably ignore this and just stop at the end of one utility's analysis. For more serious problems (such as a B-Tree Header problem), this endless cycle may result from each utility spotting separate damage to the same area, with neither one able to effect a complete repair. In these cases, once again, reformatting may be your only solution.

On the plus side, one utility's repair may allow the other utility to spot damage that it would have otherwise missed. If I had all the repair utilities mentioned here, I would probably try Disk First Aid first, followed by DiskWarrior. If neither of them worked, I would try Norton Utilities and TechTool Pro in no particular recommended order.

SEE: • **"Recover Selected Files from a Damaged Disk," in Fix-It #11.**
• **Fix-It #13 on reformatting disks.**
• **Chapter 2 on restoring from backups.**

BY THE WAY ▶ Automated Checking and Repairs

Norton Utilities and TechTool Pro both offer options to periodically scan a disk in the background (while the computer is otherwise idle), at startup and/or at shutdown. Norton Utilities does this background scanning via FileSaver. TechTool Pro uses a control panel called TechTool Protection. Having one of these options enabled can also assist in volume recovery, should that become necessary.

DiskWarrior includes an extension option called DiskShield. It attempts to prevent disk damage by checking the validity of any data being written to the directory. It also checks the validity of any directory data read from disk to alert you of any existing directory damage. Finally, it continually updates the directory to prevent a loss of data due to a crash or power failure.

SEE: • **Chapter 2, "Protect Against Disk Damage" in the "Install Protection Utilities" section for more on setting up these autoscanning options.**

BY THE WAY ▶ Disk Damage and Web Browsers

Web browsers, such as Netscape Navigator and Internet Explorer, probably write more often to your disk than any other applications you own, mainly due to frequently updating their cache files. The result of all this activity is an increase in the risk of data corruption occurring while running your browser. If you often use a Web browser, check your disk regularly for directory damage with your disk repair utilities. If your utility frequently reports B-tree or other related errors, your Web browser should be a prime suspect.

SEE: • **"System Freezes, Crashes and Errors," in Chapter 13 for more details on how to minimize this risk.**

Further Damage Checks

Disk repair utilities cannot fix all damage-related problems to your disk. Neither do they address all possible causes of startup problems. If problems persist, here are some other suggestions (details are covered in the other sections of the book listed at the end of this Fix-It):

To Check for Software Damage:

- Check for defective media (bad blocks). Norton Disk Doctor typically does this as part of the same procedure that checks for Directory Damage. Note that disk-formatting utilities can also check for defective media.

- Use utilities such as TechTool, TechTool Pro, Conflict Catcher, Adobe Type Manager, Font Box, ResEdit and a variety of others to check for damage to specific system software files. These files include System, Finder, extensions, and fonts.

- Use TechTool or TechTool Pro to repair possible damage to the Desktop file and the Parameter RAM (or use the standard procedures for rebuilding the desktop and zapping the PRAM).

- Update the disk driver using a disk-formatting utility (such as Drive Setup) to repair possible problems due to a damaged driver.

- Check for viruses. Viruses can sometimes damage files or result in symptoms that mimic those caused by damaged files. Also, there are cases where an anti-virus utility spots damage that repair utilities missed. For example, NAV may give a messages that says *"This is probably not a valid resource."* This may indicate a damaged file, rather than a virus-infected one.

To Check for Hardware Damage:

- Use TechTool Pro (or other competing utilities) to test for problems with an extended selection of hardware components, including memory, drives, modems, monitors, and just about anything else.

Fix-It #10

 For Related Information

SEE:
- Fix-It #1 on hardware/software incompatibilities.
- Fix-It #3 on solving extension conflicts.
- Fix-It #4 on system software problems.
- Fix-It #6 on checking for viruses.
- Fix-It #8 on rebuilding the desktop.
- Fix-It #9 on zapping the Parameter RAM.
- Fix-It #11 on repairing files.
- Fix-It #12 on updating the disk device driver.
- Fix-It #13 on damaged media and reformatting disks.
- Fix-It #15 on hardware troubleshooting.
- Chapter 2 on preventative maintenance.
- Chapter 5 on startup and disk problems.

Fix-It #11:
Check for Damaged Disks and Files:
Replace, Recover, Restore, or Repair

▶ QUICK SUMMARY

If possible, replace damaged or erased files from backups. Otherwise, use a data recovery utility (such as Norton Utilities) to recover specific files on a damaged volume or to unerase files on an undamaged volume. In certain cases, you can use these utilities to restore an entire volume. If appropriate, attempt to fix damaged files, especially document files. Check for and repair bad blocks.

 ## When to Do It:

- If you cannot mount a volume and cannot fix the problem via a disk repair utility—and you have files on the drive that are not backed up and you want to recover.

- If you accidentally erase a hard disk with the Finder's Erase Disk command.

- If you accidentally (or intentionally) erased a file that you now want back.

- Whenever launching an application consistently results in a system crash, freeze, or other serious malfunction.

- Whenever a program's feature that worked correctly on previous occasions now causes problems or simply does not work.

- Whenever opening a document consistently results in a system crash, freeze, or other serious malfunction.

- Whenever a document opens but displays only part of its contents or displays unintelligible gibberish rather than its expected data.

- Whenever specific documents will not print but other similar documents print without a problem.

- Whenever the error message *"Unable to read from disk"* appears when you try to open a file.

- Whenever you cannot successfully copy a file, especially when attempts to do so result in an error message such as *"File could not be read (or written or verified) and was skipped."* These messages indicate bad blocks (media damage) on at least one of the disks involved in the copy operation.

- If you are using a floppy disk (or other removable disk media), a bad block is also indicated by a distinctive and uncharacteristic whining or clicking sound that emanates from the drive as it attempts to read from the defective area of the disk.

Be aware that several of these problems have other causes besides damaged disks or files. See Chapter 6 for a more general discussion of file problems.

Why to Do It:

Restore Volumes

Sometimes a disk's Directory corruption is so extensive that it cannot be repaired, usually resulting in a crashed disk. Similarly, if you accidentally erase a hard disk (via the Finder's Erase Disk command), the original Directory information is hopelessly lost, resulting in the Finder listing the disk as empty. In both cases, however, the rest of the files on your disk may still be perfectly okay (in the case of the "erased" hard disk, this is because the Erase Disk command does not actually erase or reformat a hard disk—it only alters the Directory, as described more in Fix-It #13.

You may still be able to resurrect the hard disk by using a recovery utility to completely replace the current, presumably damaged or erased Directory with an undamaged backup copy.

Recover or Unerase Files

If attempts at disk directory repair have failed, and restoring a disk is not an option or also fails, you are probably facing reformatting your hard drive. However you may have files on your hard drive that you have not yet backed up and that you want to recover before reformatting.

Similarly, you may have deleted a file previously from your drive (intentionally or not), which you now wish you had back.

In both cases, recovery utilities may be able to find and recover, or unerase, the desired files.

If you have a damaged file, you want to replace it or fix it. In Chapter 2, the causes of damaged files were briefly described in the section entitled "Damage Control." Here is a closer look at how these causes apply to solving problems with damaged documents and applications.

Repair Damaged Files

A file may no longer open or launch as expected. One reason for this may be that the data in the file itself is corrupted or damaged. In certain cases, especially if the file is a document, you may be able to repair the damage and regain use of the file. Otherwise, you may still be able to extract critical data (such as the plain text of a word processing document) from the file. To fully understand how this works, you need to know more about how such files may get damaged:

Damaged files due to miscopied information Many damaged files appear to be normal on the desktop. They can be moved or copied without any problem. However, when you try to open the file, problems appear. Applications may crash when launched. Documents, if they can be opened at all, display only part of the expected contents or display garbage data. In these cases, the file damage is usually due to some alteration in the data that makes up the file. The damage usually originates as an error made when the file is copied, saved, or modified in any way. Because many files, such as the System file, are regularly modified as part of their normal use, this damage can happen to a file without your directly modifying it. This software damage is analogous to a book that has some words misprinted. There is no problem reading the book—it's just that the words don't always make sense.

Damaged files due to bad blocks The other common type of damage is usually referred to as *bad blocks*. As explained in Chapter 2, bad blocks are usually the result of *media damage* (that is, physical damage to the disk media) in a given area (*block* or *sector*) of a disk. Technically, this is not a file-related problem; it is a disk problem. In fact, a bad block can occur in an area of the disk where there is no file at all. Similarly, a bad block can occur in the Directory area of a disk, usually resulting in a crashed disk and almost certainly requiring reformatting the disk.

However, when a bad block occurs in an area where a document or application file exists, it is also considered a file problem. In these cases, you have two separate problems to solve.

First, the file is damaged. Even small files are usually several blocks in size, so a single bad block damages only a small part of most files. Still, this damage can render an entire file unusable. The information in the bad block region is most often permanently lost in any case. Usual solutions here are either to replace the file, if you have a backup, or (if it is a document file) to try to recover at least some of the data from the damaged file. If the bad block problem is intermittent, which happens occasionally, you may be able to recover the entire file.

Second, regardless of what you do to recover the file, the bad block problem remains and must also be remedied, typically by marking the block so that it will no longer be used. Otherwise, the bad blocks lie in wait, ready to cause problems the next time the Macintosh accesses that area of the disk.

Overall, floppy disks are much more susceptible to bad blocks than hard disks.

Fix-It
#11

TECHNICALLY SPEAKING ▶ Media Damage Explained

Why are my blocks bad? Media damage can affect virtually any storage medium. For hard drives and floppy disks, it can result from media material flaking off or being scratched or by an assortment of other related possibilities. The probability of media damage increases as a disk ages, even if it is just a floppy disk sitting on a shelf. Other cases of media damage are harder to categorize. They are most often the result of a loss or disruption of the magnetic field needed to store data in the block. For example, exposure to strong magnetic fields can cause such bad blocks to appear.

Whatever the cause of this media damage, the symptoms are the same, and the solutions are similar. You cannot read any data from a bad block. Often, you cannot write (that is, copy to or save) any data to a bad block.

Intermittent bad blocks Occasionally, a bad block problem may be intermittent. That is, the damaged area of the block may "flip" back and forth between its correct and incorrect state, such that sometimes the block behaves normally and other times it responds as a bad block. Left alone, the intermittent response usually worsens until it always responds as a bad block. Data written to an intermittent bad block has a reasonably good chance of recovery. The idea is to read the block over and over again until you catch it on one of the times when it reads correctly.

(continues on next page)

Repairing bad blocks Although some types of bad blocks can be repaired, real repair is usually not possible. When a utility, such as Norton Utilities, claims to find and repair a typical bad block, the best the utility can do is to mark the block to prevent that block from being used in the future. As long as not too many blocks are damaged, this should have a negligible effect on your disk capacity.

Bad blocks are marked in one of two ways. One method is to write a special invisible dummy file over the block. This prevents the block from being used to store other files. Called *sparing* the block, this can be done on any type of disk, floppy or hard. The other method is to map out the block by listing it as a bad block in a special area of the disk's Directory. This instructs the Macintosh not to use any of these blocks. The latter method is the more reliable and the one most commonly used with current software.

In some cases where utilities such as Norton Utilities cannot successfully deal with a bad blocks problem, your only recourse is to reformat the disk. If even this fails, you may be facing discarding the drive altogether.

What to Do:

This Fix-It describes four related topics: restore a damaged or accidentally erased disk, recover/unerase selected files from a disk, repair damaged files, and recover/repair files damaged due to bad blocks.

Restore a Damaged or Accidentally Erased Disk

You may never need to restore a disk. However, for irreparable Directory damage or an accidentally erased hard disk, restoring a disk can sometimes save the day (but see "Take Note: Use Backups Instead of Restore or Recover" for some cautions about restoring).

I will use Norton Utilities for the examples in this section. With Norton Utilities, you try to restore a volume using its FileSaver and Volume Recover features.

Before Attempting to Restore a Disk

1. **Make sure Norton FileSaver is installed and active** Restoring a disk requires that you have installed and activated Norton Utilities' FileSaver prior to the occurrence of the problem. This creates and updates the required invisible files. In particular, make sure the On/Off button in the FileSaver control panel is on and that the option to "Update Disk Directory Info" is enabled for each disk you want to protect. This creates a series of invisible files (that all begin with the phrase "Norton FS") that will be needed when you want to recover files or an entire volume.

   If you have not done this prior to a recovery attempt, the best you can do for an immediate problem is to recover files as described in a subsequent section of this Fix-It, "Recover Selected Files from a Damaged Disk."

   If you had these files on your drive but they were erased when you accidentally erased a volume, you may be able to use Norton Utilities' UnErase to get them back.

2. **Recover recent files that are not already backed up** A restore, even if successful, may not restore your disk to the *exact* state it was prior to the crash. In particular, recent changes and additions may not get restored (see "Take Note: Use Backups

Instead of Restore or Recover" for details). For this reason, before attempting a restore, you should try to recover files that may have been added, modified, or created since FileSaver's most recent update—unless you know that you already have these files backed up elsewhere. To do this, use methods as described in "Recover Selected Files from a Damaged Disk" later in this Fix-It.

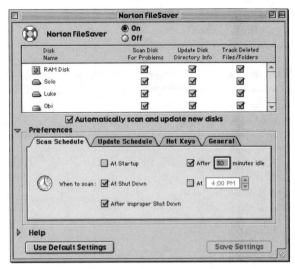

Figure F11-1 Norton FileSaver control panel.

When and how often the FileSaver information is updated are set from the FileSaver control panel. If you are unsure when the last update was performed, you will get this information as you carry out the steps in the next section.

SEE: • Chapter 2 for more on setting up FileSaver.

TAKE NOTE ▶ **Use Backups Instead of Restore or Recover**

There are limitations with using Norton FileSaver's recover ability. That's why having backups of your files is the preferred method for file recovery. For example:

- If you have not installed and activated FileSaver prior to the crash, the restore won't work.

- Even with FileSaver active, the restore doesn't always work. For example, if the disk damage involves the FileSaver files, they are rendered useless. Also, FileSaver cannot restore files damaged because of bad blocks.

- Most notable, these protection files cannot necessarily restore a disk to the state it was at the time of the crash or erasure. The recovery can restore the Directory only to the state it was the last time these protection files were updated. Depending on luck and how you configured FileSaver, the last update may have been made just before the problem occurred—or it may have been made several weeks before. Any changes made since the last time the protection file was updated are not restored. In fact, trying to restore a disk with an out-of-date Directory may cause problems of its own (such as if a file listed in the outdated Directory has since been deleted from the disk).

Unless the last update was made relatively close to the occurrence of the problem (or you have made very few recent changes to the contents of your disk), I would not consider using this restore feature. Neither would I want to depend on a utility's recover feature. Frequent backups remain your best protection against data loss (which you should always maintain, whether you use FileSaver or not)! True, backing up also requires regular updating to be effective, and restoring a disk from backups can be time-consuming. But backups are much more reliable than the alternative methods. If you have an up-to-date set of backups, successful recovery is almost guaranteed.

Restore the Disk

1. **Access Norton Utilities' Volume Recover** Launch Norton Utilities. From the main menu, click the Volume Recover button. A window listing all mounted volumes will appear. **Note:** In general, you should only try Volume Recover if, after running Norton Disk Doctor, Disk Doctor suggests to use it.

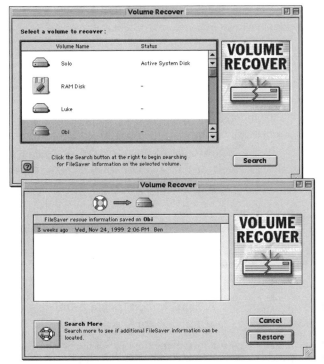

Figure F11-2
Norton Utilities' Volume Recover; first, select a volume (top) and then start the restore (bottom).

Fix-It #11

2. **Select the disk to be restored** Select the volume you want to restore and click the Search button. You cannot restore the startup disk or the disk that contains the active copy of the Norton Utilities. In these cases, starting up from an alternate disk is required.

3. **Attempt to restore the disk** After selecting Search, Volume Recover searches for the needed FileSaver data. The window will next display a list of all available FileSaver files. You can also try the Search More option. When several files are listed as available, pick the most recent date (unless you suspect the damage occurred prior to that date). Then click Restore.

    Note that if the FileSaver file's date is much older than the current date, your restore is unlikely to result in a good match to the current status of your disk (as described in "Take Note: Use Backups Instead of Restore or Recover").

4. **If the restore is successful** If the restore succeeds, your disk should be returned to normal. Congratulations. Return any separately recovered files (as described in

"Before Attempting to Restore a Disk") that were not restored. To be safe, now run Norton Disk Doctor, or other repair utility (as described in Fix-It #10).

If the restore fails If the initial restore attempt fails, you can try to restore again using another FileSaver backup file (if available). Alternatively, you can go to Disk Doctor to see if it can now repair the disk despite the apparently failed restore attempt. Otherwise, recover any unbacked-up files that you have not already tried to recover (using methods described in the next section). Then reformat the disk and restore it from your backups and recovered files.

Recover/UnErase Selected Files from a Disk

This section covers the procedure for recovering specific files from: (1) a damaged disk that cannot be mounted by the Finder and/or (2) an intact disk from which you erased files that you want to unerase.

Once again, we will use Norton Utilities as the example utility. And once again, having installed Norton FileSaver prior to the recovery attempt will greatly increase the probability of a successful recovery. [**Note:** as an alternative, Data Rescue is a great shareware utility that may be able to recover files even if Norton cannot.]

1. **Replace the file from backups, if you have them** Don't even bother using a utility such as Norton Utilities if you have a backup of the file. It is more reliable and often faster. For applications, you hopefully still have the original disks or, if you downloaded the file, the original copy stored on a separate medium (such as a Zip disk). If so, use this. For documents, you hopefully have a backup that you created.

2. **Launch your recovery utility (in this case, Norton Utilities) and select UnErase** If you don't have a backup, it's time to reach for your recovery utility.

   SEE: • Chapter 6, "If the File Was Inadvertently Deleted" in the "When You Can't Locate a File" section, for a related description of undeleting files

Fix-It #11

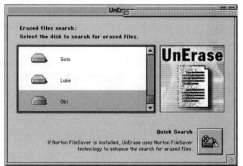

Figure F11-3 Left: Norton Utilities UnErase main window. Below: the results of an UnErase QuickSearch of a volume.

3. **Generate a list of recoverable files** Select the disk from which you want to recover files and click the QuickSearch button. A new window will open. When the search is completed, it will include a list of all files that UnErase can recover. A key item here is the column called Recoverability. Unless it says 100%, you can only expect partial recovery. And unless you are recovering a document (where partial recovery is better than nothing), less than 100% is often the practical equivalent of 0%. Sometimes, even when 100% recovery is promised, the file is still not fully restored. But if there is no other copy of the file, small hope is better than none at all.

4. **Do a Customized Search, if needed** If the initial search results do not include the file(s) you want (especially likely if FileSaver is not installed and tracking files), click the Customize Search to initiate a search that does not require FileSaver. You would also use this option to recover files that have not been erased.

   Three options are listed in the window that appears: catalog search, file type search, and text search. Only catalog search has a reasonable chance of recovering files intact, but you may still try the others if you are desperate.

   You also have the choice here to search for either "erased files" vs. "real files." You would select real files if you are trying to recover files from a damaged disk that cannot be mounted, where the files you want are not erased. Otherwise, select erased files.

   After making your selection, click the Search button. Once again, a list of recoverable files is generated.

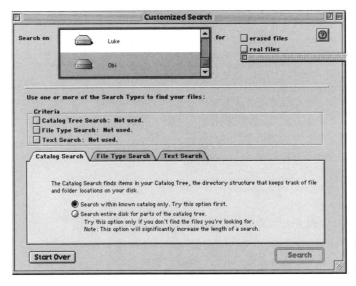

FIX-IT #11

Figure F11-4 The UnErase Customized Search window.

5. **Attempt to recover files** Select the file(s) you want to recover and click the Recover button. Be sure to save the files to another disk (not the damaged disk!), when prompted to select a destination disk.

Note: After recovering a file, such as a word processing document, you may find that the file will still not open in its creating (or any other) application. In this case, you can highlight the file name in the UnErase window and click the View Contents button. With the Data Fork option selected, you should have a view of the text contents of the file. You can now save this to the Clipboard and paste it into a text document.

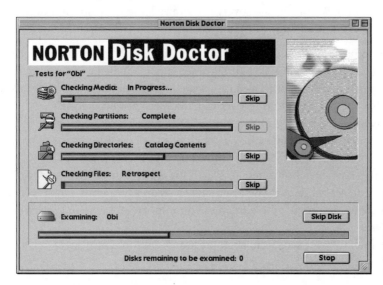

Figure F11-5 Click View Contents for a selected file, and you will get a window such as this one. For example, with this HTML file, you can actually view and copy the source text.

6. **Check on success or failure of recovered files** When the recovery is done, quit the utility. If possible, go to the Finder (restarting the Mac with an appropriate startup disk, if necessary). Recovered files should be on your selected disk, typically in a folder called Recovered Files. Try to open the files. If documents do not directly open from the Finder's desktop, they usually open from within their creating application (see Chapter 6 for more on how to deal with this problem).

With luck, the files are intact or (for text files) only require minor reformatting. However, some documents may have only partial contents or will be otherwise unusable. In any case, what you now have is the best you are likely to get by this method.

FIX-IT
#11

BY THE WAY ▶ TechTool Pro's Trash Cache

Although I have emphasized using Norton Utilities in the examples in this Fix-It, TechTool Pro is worth a special mention. It has an option called Trash Cache (accessed via the TechTool Protection control panel). If you have this feature enabled, it will track deleted files in a manner similar to FileSaver. However, in my experience, if TrashCache can recover the file at all, it is likely to do a better job than Norton's UnErase. Almost all files recovered by Trash Cache are 100% intact. Norton's advantage is that it remains the court of last resort. It offers the best chance of recovering at least some data from the widest possible range of missing files.

7. **Repair and/or reformat** If you were trying to recover files from a damaged disk, and you have not yet done so, proceed to try to repair the damaged disk. If repair attempts fail, any files that are still unrecoverable probably cannot be saved. Some disk repair companies (most notably DriveSavers) specialize in recovering data from disks that you have given up for dead. If you absolutely must get your data back, they are worth a try.

   Otherwise, it is time to reformat the disk (for floppy disks, it's safer to discard the disks rather than reformat them). If the hard disk fails to work after reformatting (or if you can't reformat the disk), you have more serious problems. Hardware damage is a likely possibility.

Repair Damaged Files

If you suspect that a file cannot be opened because it is damaged, and you do not have a backup, you may be able to repair the file. The value of repairing applies mainly to document files. For applications, extensions, etc., you should almost always simply be able to replace the file.

Make a Copy of the Damaged File

Make a copy of the file, ideally to another disk. There are two reasons for this: first, if your recovery attempts make things worse, you have a duplicate copy with which to try again. Second, sometimes copying a file from the Finder succeeds in recovering it, either fully or partially.

1. From the Finder, copy the file to another disk.

2. Try to open the newly copied file.

3. If the copy works normally, make a new backup copy of the now recovered file and delete the damaged copy. You are done.

4. If the copy seems just as damaged as the original (or if you get only partial recovery), proceed to the next section, called "Try to Open the Damaged Document."

5. If, when you try to make a copy, you get a message that says the file could not be read, this indicates that a bad block is the cause of the damaged file. In this case, proceed to "Special Case: Recover/Repair Files Damaged Due to Bad Blocks" later in this Fix-It.

Try to Open the Damaged Document

Sometimes, even though a document appears damaged (as indicated by an inability to copy the document from the Finder), you can still open it. You may find that some data is lost or incorrect when the document is opened, but the document nevertheless opens.

1. Try to open the document. Try first from its creating application. If that doesn't work, try opening it using another application that reads the damaged file's format (for example, try opening a Word file with AppleWorks).

Fix-It
#11

2. If you can get the document to successfully open, even if it displays only partial contents or gibberish, save the contents to a new file, using the Save As command. Now open the newly created file to check if the problem symptoms are gone. As with making a copy of the file from the Finder, this sometimes completely repairs a damaged file.

3. If the Save As technique does not work, copy any usable data from the damaged file to the Clipboard. Open a new document and paste the data into it. Save the new document.

4. For partially recovered or unrecoverable files, if the damage occurred recently and if you have installed a utility such as Spell Catcher's GhostWriter feature, you may be able to find at least some of the missing data in the special recovery files created by these utilities (see Chapters 2 and 4 for details). Even better, if you have a backup copy of the document, but it is insufficient because it is an older version that does not contain recent modifications to the file, you may be able to combine the backup document with the more recent data recovered from GhostWriter to fully reconstruct the current version of the document.

File Repair/Recovery via CanOpener

If all the preceding techniques have failed, you may still be able to use special recovery utilities to extract the text or graphics from the file. However, for text files, even if you succeed in doing this, you will lose all the text's formatting (such as font selections, styles, and margin settings). Still, this is a small price to pay to recover the complete text (or even just part of the text) of a long manuscript.

There are many file-recovery utilities on the market. My favorite one is CanOpener. CanOpener works with almost any file—damaged or undamaged, document or application. It can extract graphics (of several different formats) as well as text that may be contained within a file. It can even extract sounds and QuickTime movies. With Version 3.5 or later of CanOpener, you get some additional Internet-related features, including the ability to strip HTML code from a text file, so you can wind up with a clean text extract.

Although other utilities may have similar features, CanOpener is generally both more effective and easier to use. To use it:

1. Launch CanOpener.

2. Locate the damaged file in CanOpener's scroll box, much as you would use an Open dialog box.

3. Double-click the damaged file's name. This opens a list of what text, pictures, sounds, and movies are recoverable from that file, each one listed as a separate item.

Fix-It
#11

4. Double-click an item to view its contents. You cannot edit the displayed text or graphic in any way. However, you can view it to check if it is what you want to recover.

5. Once you have found the desired text or graphic, go to the Item menu and select Save As to save the item. This command saves text to a separate plain text file and graphics to a separate PICT file (see Chapter 8 for more on these file formats).

6. Quit CanOpener and access these saved files, for further editing if needed, in other applications (such as word processors or graphics applications). For example, text files may contain extraneous gibberish text that you want to delete.

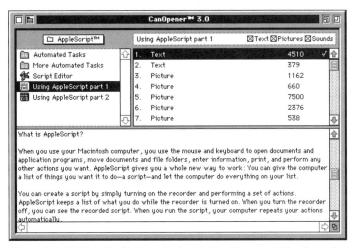

Figure F11-6 Using CanOpener: double-clicking the name of the file on the left produces the list of text and picture items on the right; double-clicking the highlighted text item opens the text display below.

If a file contains bad blocks or the disk is severely damaged, CanOpener may not be able to open the file, or the file's name may not even appear in the initial list. If this happens, you have to address the bad blocks problem before you can use CanOpener (see "Special Case: Recover/Repair Files Damaged Due to Bad Blocks" later in this Fix-It).

Checking/fixing files with Norton Utilities The "View Contents" feature of Norton Utilities UnErase (mentioned earlier in this Fix-It) works similarly to CanOpener. Also, utilities such as Norton Disk Doctor check files for a variety of minor problems, such as bundle bit errors, invalid creation dates, and missing custom icons. Finally, see Chapter 8 for how to deal with files that have problems due to incorrect File Types and Creators.

Fix-It
#11

TECHNICALLY SPEAKING ▶ **Repairing System Folder Files**

This section of this Fix-It refers mainly to repairing documents. As described at several points elsewhere in this book, various System Folder files, from fonts to the System file itself, can become damaged. Various utilities can detect this damage and alert you that the file needs to be replaced. Some may even be able to repair the file.

For example, those of you who use Apple's ResEdit utility should know that ResEdit has some built-in repair capabilities. For example, I had a sound file that I could not use (that is, I could not get the sound to play). When I tried to open the file in ResEdit, it reported the file as damaged and offered to fix it. ResEdit was able to resurrect this file well enough that I could recover the sound intact!

TechTool and especially TechTool Pro check for damage to the main System Folder files (such as System and Finder). Conflict Catcher checks for a variety of System Folder damage, from extensions to fonts. Adobe Type Manager and Font Box are two utilities that can check for corrupted fonts and related font problems.

Special Case: Recover/Repair Files Damaged Due to Bad Blocks

If bad blocks are present in the area of a disk occupied by a file, usually you cannot open or copy the file. If you try, you get an error message that says a file could not be read. On the other hand, if you get a write or verify error when you try to copy a file, this also indicates bad blocks. However, the file itself is not damaged. Rather, the bad block is in the presently unused destination location for the file copy (though there may also be more bad blocks on this disk, in locations that *are* occupied by files).

This section explains how to repair and/or recover files that have been damaged due to bad blocks.

Use repair utilities (such as Norton Disk Doctor) When you run Norton Disk Doctor, in addition to its checks for Directory damage (as covered in Fix-It #10) and file problems (as mentioned just previously), it can also check for defective media (bad blocks). Because this takes a long time, you can choose to skip this test unless you suspect media damage. If you do test for this, and bad blocks are found, Norton Disk Doctor may offer to repair the bad block (as described in "Technically Speaking: Media Damage Explained," earlier in this Fix-It). In addition, if a file exists where the defective media is located, and the Media Check Preferences is set to "Fix the file automatically," Disk Doctor will attempt to copy the file to a different location. Sometimes this alone "repairs" the file. You will be able to open the copied version of the file—or at least extract data from it via CanOpener.

Other disk repair utilities, such as TechTool Pro, also check for media damage. For example, with TechTool Pro, select the Advanced interface and go to Surface Scan. However, it does not directly support file recovery of files with media damage.

Fix-It #11

Reformat to "repair" bad blocks I still find the most reliable method for dealing with bad blocks is to reformat the disk. This means using a utility such as Drive Setup (see Fix-It #13 for more details). Of course, this does nothing to save files on the disk; it simply makes the disk usable again. It also means you need to have all your files backed up first, as reformatting erases the contents of the disk. Occasionally, if you need to back up the disk before you reformat it, you may find that the bad blocks prevent a normal backup. In this case, do try to first mark the bad blocks with a recovery utility. Then back up the disk (except for files possibly damaged by the bad blocks for which you already have a current backup) and reformat.

For floppy disks with bad blocks, I usually don't even bother with reformatting. I just discard the disk. But if you have a file on the floppy disk that you want to save…

Recover files from floppy disks with bad blocks First, try to copy the floppy disk via a utility such as Apple's Disk Copy. To do this with Disk Copy, launch Disk Copy and insert the damaged floppy disk. (**Note:** For USB floppy drives, you may have to reverse these steps. That is, mount the disk *before* launching Disk Copy. However, this can be a Catch-22 if the Finder spits out the disk because it claims it is damaged.)

Once in Disk Copy with the disk mounted, select to Save the disk image. Then select Make a Floppy from the Utilities menu. Select the mounted image of the newly created .img file. Insert a floppy disk as requested and initiate the copy.

If you have a copy utility that has an option to "skip bad blocks" when copying, use that utility (with the option enabled). Older versions of Norton Utilities included a program called Floppier that worked like this; sadly, it is no longer included in current versions. Without such a utility, attempts to copy the disk will likely also copy the bad block data, which leaves you no better off than you started. Or, due to bad blocks, you may not be able to make a copy at all. This is a potential problem with Disk Copy. You could similarly try copying the disk via the Finder, but if a bad block is the problem, it too will typically abort the copy process.

By itself, bypassing the bad blocks does not mean that the damaged file is recovered (the data that were in the bad block area may now be missing), but it's a start. At least you now have a copy of the file that does not contain bad blocks.

Fix-It #11

Whether or not you bypassed bad blocks with your copy, your next step is to try to open the newly created copy of the damaged file from within its creating application. If this does not work (and it usually doesn't), next try to open the damaged file using CanOpener or other comparable utility (this usually works, even if CanOpener could not open the original damaged file). If you succeed in opening the file at all, extract data from it using the method previously described (see: "File Repair/Recovery via CanOpener," earlier in this Fix-It).

⚡ For Related Information

SEE: • Fix-It #2 for information on corrupted preferences files.
• Fix-It #3 on startup extension conflicts.
• Fix-It #4 on replacing damaged system software.
• Fix-It #8 on rebuilding the desktop.
• Fix-It #10 on repairing directory damage.
• Fix-It #13 on reformatting disks and for problems with floppy disks that appear to be damaged but are really not.
• Fix-It #14 on SCSI-related problems that may prevent a disk from mounting.
• Fix-It #15 on hardware repairs.
• Chapter 2 for information on disk damage, backing up your disks, and installing invisible files needed for restore and recovery.
• Chapter 4 on system errors.
• Chapter 5 for more details on startup problems and other problems mounting disks.
• Chapter 6 for more on problems opening, copying, saving and undeleting files.
• Chapter 8 for more on the disk Directory, bundle bits, and other file attributes.
• Chapter 9 for problems with corrupted font files.

Fix-It #12:
Update the Disk Device Driver

▶ **QUICK SUMMARY**

Use a disk formatting utility to update the device driver on hard disks and removable media cartridges. With Apple's Drive Setup, select the Update Driver command from the Functions menu. Although it is not always required, it is best to startup from a separate disk that contains the formatting utility before updating a driver. If your drive or cartridge was formatted by software other than Drive Setup (such as Hard Disk ToolKit, Silverlining, or Iomega Tools), you should generally prefer to use that software to update the driver.

 When to Do It:

- Anytime a new version of the driver is released, especially if you have upgraded your hardware or software and the new driver is needed to use selected new features or bug fixes present in the previous version of the driver.

- If you are experiencing frequent system crashes or other serious problems, especially if the problems do not occur when you are using a floppy disk as a startup disk.

- If you cannot get your Macintosh to start up. Obviously, this is only one of many possible causes of this symptom.

- If you cannot get virtual memory to work properly.

 Why to Do It:

A hard disk's *device driver* is software. It is located in a special section of the disk that is created when the disk is first formatted. Any hard disk you are now using most likely came preformatted came with a driver already on it. The driver is normally completely invisible and inaccessible to the user. Even disk-repair utilities, such as Norton Utilities, do not directly access it when making disk repairs.

The driver contains critical *low-level* instructions that tell the Macintosh how to initially communicate with the drive. A copy of a disk's driver is loaded into memory whenever the disk is mounted. Without the driver in memory, the disk cannot be mounted.

The whole updating process takes only a few seconds, and it leaves the rest of your drive untouched. You do not normally have to reformat the drive in order to update it. This is convenient, because reformatting would erase all the data on the drive (requiring that you restore the files from your backups) and would take much longer to do.

If you "update" your disk driver with the same version of the utility that originally installed it, it will simply replace the existing driver with a duplicate. However, similarly to system software, disk-formatting utilities are periodically upgraded. Updating the driver from a newer version of the formatting utility will replace the older version with the newer one.

Drive Setup vs. third party formatting utilities Updating a disk driver requires using the same formatting utility that you would use to reformat the disk (see Fix-It #13). Apple's formatting utility is Drive Setup. It is included on the Mac OS CD that ships with all Macs. If you purchase a drive from another company, such as LaCie, it may come with its own formatting software. For example, LaCie drives come with Silverlining. These utilities may only work on the brand of drives that they ship with. A few companies make "universal" formatting software that is sold independently of any hardware and may be used with almost any drive. The most well known example here is FWB's Hard Disk ToolKit. A version of this also ships with many third-party hard drives.

Finally, removable-cartridge drives typically use their own drivers. The most well-known examples are the Iomega drivers for Zip and Jaz cartridges. The Iomega software is included when you purchase a Zip or Jaz drive. It is also now included as part of the Mac OS (you'll find it in the CD Extras folder on the Mac OS CD).

In terms of problem solving, there are four basic reasons to update a driver: to accommodate new system software, to accommodate new hardware, to fix bugs in the existing version of the driver, or to repair damage to the driver installed on your drive.

Update to Accommodate New System Software and/or Fix Driver Bugs

When Apple releases a new version of its system software, newly added features may require changes to disk drivers. Similarly, the upgrade may include a new version of Drive Setup that fixes bugs in the previous version. In one example, the version of Drive Setup that came with Mac OS 8.5 was discovered, in rare cases, to damage the data on a drive in such a way that reformatting was often the only way to regain use of the drive. A new version of Drive Setup was released with Mac OS 8.5.1. You needed to update the driver with this new version in order to prevent the possibility of this disk damage.

Fix-It #12

Update to Accommodate New Hardware

Occasionally, you may need to update to a new version of a driver in order to accommodate features added to newer Macintosh models. For example, when Apple came out with its "blue and white" G3 Macs, it included a new version of Drive Setup that was needed for that Mac model. If you purchased an additional drive for the G3, and it used Drive Setup, you would need to make sure it used this latest version.

In a related example, the version of Silverlining Lite that was current at the time that the blue-and-white G3 Macs were released could cause of loss of data on the drive if used with these Macs. LaCie soon released an updated version that fixed this problem.

Update to Repair Damage to the Driver

Despite its relative inaccessibility, the driver (like any software!) can get damaged. For example, sudden power failures, particularly during startup, can cause it to be damaged. A damaged driver usually causes serious problems, including an inability to mount the disk on the desktop. Updating the driver can repair the damage and eliminate the problem.

A special problem with the write cache of some disk drivers (solved by updating to a newer driver that addresses the problem) is covered more in Fix-It #13 (see: "Take Note: The Write Cache Problem and Data Corruption").

TAKE NOTE ▶ Beware: Updating the Drive May *Cause* Problems (Not Fix Them)!

The disk driver lives on your hard drive in an area referred to as the driver partition. When a disk is first formatted, a certain amount of space is set aside for this partition. When you update a driver, it may be that the new driver takes up more space than the space allotted to the driver partition. When this happens, your formatting utility should warn you and prevent the update. The solution is to reformat your drive with the new formatting utility (or not to do the update at all).

However, in some unfortunate cases, the format utility may incorrectly try to fit a too-large driver into a too-small space. The result is that you wind up with a corrupted driver. When you next try to start up your Mac, it won't work. Symptoms include startup system crashes, the disk icon with the blinking question mark, or a Sad Mac. You may be able to reinstall your previous driver at this point. However, more likely, you will have to reformat your disk. So make sure you have things backed up before updating a driver.

Suppose you have a drive that is currently formatted with Drive Setup and you want to switch to using Hard Disk ToolKit. Can you simply update the driver with the Hard Disk ToolKit utility? Or must you reformat the drive first? Here again, simply updating the driver will often succeed. But the chances that it won't succeed are even greater than if you are simply going to a newer version of the same utility. Thus, in general, I would recommend reformatting the drive here.

Occasionally, a bug in an update to a driver introduces problems not seen in the previous version. In such cases, downgrading to the previous version may be the solution. For example, many users reported problems copying files to Zip/Jaz disks, after upgrading to the 6.x version of Iomega's drivers. Downgrading to a 5.*x* version fixed the problem in many cases.

 ## What to Do:

Get the Latest Version of the Formatting Utility

You should almost always use the latest version of your formatting utility, even if you are not experiencing any of the problems described in "Why to Do It." At the very least, the new version probably contains fixes to bugs found in the previous versions. For Apple drives, you will most likely use Drive Setup. I will use it for most of the examples included here.

Drive Setup can be used in all Apple Macs (unless you have a very old Mac that requires Apple's old disk formatting utility, called Apple HD SC Setup). In the past, Drive Setup could only be used with drives that shipped directly from Apple. If you tried it on another type of drive, the utility would claim to be unable to work with it.

However, recent versions of Drive Setup now work with almost all the popular brands of drive. Still, beware: if you switch from Drive Setup to another utility, there remains a chance that Drive Setup will no longer work with the drive if you try to return to using it later.

Still, some users may prefer the added features of a program such as Hard Disk Toolkit or PowerTools. If so, similarly make sure you have the latest version of this utility.

If you have several drives in addition to your startup drive, my general advice is to use the same driver on all of them, if possible. Although the risk is a small one, this minimizes the chance of a conflict between the drivers themselves causing problems.

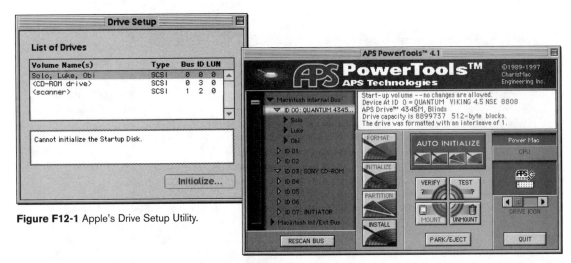

Figure F12-1 Apple's Drive Setup Utility.

Figure F12-2 APS PowerTools; one of several alternatives to Drive Setup.

TAKE NOTE ▶ Removable Cartridge Drives: Drivers And Extensions

With removable cartridge drives, such as those using Iomega Zip disks and Jaz cartridges, there is an extension in your System Folder that serves as a driver, in addition to a more typical "invisible" driver found on each cartridge. The extension allows the driver to load even when there is no cartridge inserted at startup (as long as the drive is turned on at startup). That way, the drive is ready to mount a cartridge as soon as you insert it.

However, if a cartridge is present at startup, the driver from the cartridge typically loads before the one in your Extensions folder is checked. If the two drivers are different versions, you may get an error message such as *The Iomega Driver Extension (version 4.3) could not load because an older version (4.2) is already present.* This is normally nothing to worry about (although you probably should update to get everything using the same driver).

Note: You can force the driver on a disk to be automatically updated to match the version of your startup drive by setting the option to do so in Advanced Driver Options window—accessed via the Advanced Options command in the Special menu of the Iomega Drive Controls control panel.

(continues on next page)

A similar driver conflict situation can occur with any format utility that uses an extension to mount drivers at startup (such as Hard Disk ToolKit). These may try to mount a driver for an Iomega drive (if no cartridge is present at startup). If so, when the Iomega extension later tries to load, it will be unable to do so. Again, you will get some error message saying that the driver could not load because another driver is already present. The solution here is to change the loading order of the extensions so that the Iomega extension loads first. Alternatively, you could give up on one of the drivers altogether (deleting the extension from your disk) and just use the other driver. Since the Iomega driver only works with Iomega drives, this is often the one you would give up. In these cases, make sure you also update your cartridges with the alternate driver.

However, exceptions occur even here. Iomega recommends against using anything other than Iomega drivers on its Zip or Jaz disks. Although many have ignored this advice without incident, others take it very seriously. Personally, I would stick to the Iomega drivers if possible. However, the other side of the coin is that, in some cases, the Iomega drivers have been known to cause problems that are avoided by shifting to another driver. For example, when the blue-and-white G3 Macs first came out, you could no longer startup from Zip or Jaz disks that used the Iomega drivers. It was possible to shift to a different driver that allowed the disk to serve as a startup disk.

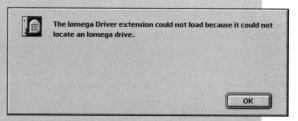

Figure F12-3 Here's a message that may appear if you startup your Mac with the Iomega Driver extension installed, but with the Iomega Zip or Jaz drive off.

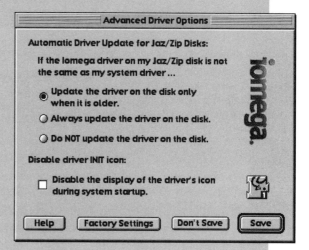

Figure F12-4 The Advanced Driver Options window of the Iomega Drive Options control panel allows you to select if and how the driver on a cartridge/disk is updated as compared to the version in your startup drive's System Folder.

SCSI vs. USB Iomega now makes both SCSI/ATA and USB versions of the Zip drive. For the SCSI and ATA versions, the driver is called Iomega Driver. For USB drives, there is a pair of drivers called USB Iomega Driver and USB Iomega UT Driver. These are included with the Iomega Tools software. You cannot use the USB software on a SCSI/ATA drive or vice versa. If you have problems with the USB Zip drive, users report that trashing the Iomega USB drivers and simply defaulting to the default USB driver software included with the Mac OS (USB Mass Storage Extensions and USB Mass Storage Support) may work better.

SEE: • **"Take Note: Formatting Iomega Disks (and the 'Click of Death'),"** In Fix-It #13.
 • **"Take Note: Mounting Removable Media Cartridges,"** and **"USB"** In Fix-It #14.

FIX-IT #12

BY THE WAY ▶ Who Really Made the Drive?

The name *Apple* on a drive doesn't mean that Apple really made the drive. The actual drive mechanism is made by a company that specializes in drive manufacturing (such as Quantum). These vendors sell their drives to various other companies who package them and sell them to end users. Nevertheless, some versions of Drive Setup may recognize only an Apple drive because of the special coding information that Apple put on the drive before it shipped.

In any case, you can find out the drive vendor by using Apple System Profiler. Select Devices and Volumes, locate the drive, and open its disclosing triangle. You may be more surprised to learn that some Apple drives are manufactured by IBM!

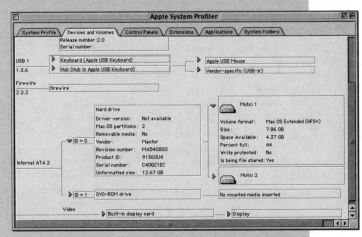

Figure F12-5 The Devices and Volumes tab of Apple System Profiler. Here it shows that the hard drive that shipped with my iMac DV SE was made by Maxtor.

BY THE WAY ▶ Checking the Version Number of The Driver

If you want to know the version number of your formatting utility, it's simple enough. It is usually present somewhere in the window that appears when you launch the utility. Otherwise, just open the Get Info window and check the line labeled "Version." But what if you can't find this utility anymore or want to confirm that your currently installed driver is the one actually installed by this utility? Check the version number of the driver itself. You can usually do this by selecting Get Info for the disk in question. In the line labeled "Where" you should see a version number. In many cases, the version number here matches the version number of the formatting utility itself. However, it is not uncommon for it to be an entirely different number (unfortunately, this is the case with Drive Setup). In this case, you may need to contact technical support of the company that made the utility. This should enable them to tell you if you are using the latest version of the driver. Otherwise, the information may be available on the vendor's Web site. For Apple, check its Tech Info Library.

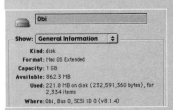
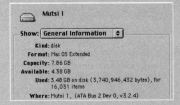

Figure F12-6 A segment of the Get Info window of a SCSI drive (left) and an IDE/ATA drive (middle), both formatted by Apple's Drive Setup. The version numbers listed here (8.1.4 and 3.2.4) will be different for these two types of drives, even if the same version of Drive Setup was used in both cases. The version number (1.8.1) of Drive Setup itself (as seen in the bottom Get Info window segment) will be different again. Yes, this can get confusing.

Update the Driver

1. **Make sure your data are backed up and your disk is not damaged.** As with most of these types of procedures, there is the slim chance that updating will do more harm than good. So, before attempting any updating, make sure all your data are backed up. It is also a good idea to check for possible disk damage (see Fix-Its #10) before updating or switching drivers.

   SEE: • **"Take Note: Beware: Updating the Drive May *Cause* Problems (Not Fix Them)!,"** **earlier in this Fix-It.**

2. **Restart from a startup disk other than the one you want to update, if needed.** With some formatting utilities, you cannot update the current startup disk or the disk from which you launch the formatting utility. The simplest solution for this problem is to start up from a bootable disk that contains the utility (see Chapter 2 for information on creating your own emergency startup disks).

   With Apple's Drive Setup, you *can* update the driver on the current startup disk, but you will still have to restart before the new driver is actually used.

   (If you are unable to start up because the problem disk causes a crash at startup, even when using an alternate startup disk, check with Chapter 5, "Starting with an Alternate Startup Disk," for advice.)

3. **Launch the formatting utility and select to Update.** With Drive Setup, select Update Driver from Drive Setup's Function menu. In either case, wait a few seconds, and you are done.

   For most other formatting utilities, the procedure is essentially the same: locate the Update button and click it.

Figure F12-7 Drive Setup's Functions menu. Here is where you select to Update Driver.

BY THE WAY ▶ Warning for Password Security Users

Some software can "lock" access to a password-protected disk so that you cannot access the hard drive even if you startup from a floppy disk. It does this by modifying the disk's driver. If you lose the password, you may still be able to regain access to the drive by updating the disk driver. But some security programs will even block this. In this case, you will need to reformat the drive.

  Users of the PowerBook password security software face this problem. If you forget your password, contact Apple for what to do.

FIX-IT #12

4. **If the Update selection is dimmed and cannot be selected (or if the update process fails for any reason).** If you are using Drive Setup and you find that the Update Driver command cannot be selected, the reason for this will typically be displayed in the text box of the Drive Setup window. One reason may be that you just launched a version of the utility that is older than the version of the driver that is currently installed; in some cases, the utility will not let you downgrade.

The update may also be prevented if the current version of your driver is so old that the new utility cannot update it. Or it may mean that your driver (or partition map, a related low-level area of the drive) is damaged. In these cases, you will likely need to reformat the disk before you can use the utility with it.

TAKE NOTE ▶ Updating the Driver When Installing System Software

When you select to install or reinstall the Mac OS, and you run the Mac OS Install utility, when you get to the Install Software screen, there will be an Options button. If you click this button, you will find an option to "Update Apple Hard Disk Drivers." This option is typically checked by default. This means that when you install the software, you will also automatically upgrade to the version of the driver included with the OS. This is normally a good idea if you are moving up to a newer version of the OS. However, it is possible that you already have used a newer version of Drive Setup than the one that came with the OS. In this case, it is possible that leaving this option checked would downgrade to the older version. This is not a good idea. In such cases, you would uncheck this option. You can always update the driver later by running Drive Setup.

Also, while this option claims to do nothing (even when checked) if you are using a utility other than Drive Setup, some users have reported that it overwrites their non-Apple driver. In such cases, play it safe and disable this option.

---

5. **Whatever you do, do *not* click the Initialize button!** Clicking Drive Setup's Initialize button sets up to reformat the entire drive (with other utilities, the button or command will more likely be called "Format" (as explained more in Fix-It #13). Reformatting your disk will irretrievably erase all data on the disk, which is probably not what you want to happen when you are just trying to update a driver.

     Actually, the situation with Drive Setup is a bit more complex. While it does not have separate Initialize and Format buttons, it does include separate options to "zero all data" or do a "low level format." Again, this is described more in Fix-It #13.

     True, the driver gets updated when you reformat/initialize a disk. But reformatting a disk just for this reason is like using a machine gun to swat a fly. However, as noted (see "Beware: Updating the Drive May *Cause* Problems (Not Fix Them)!"), I would consider selecting Format/Initialize, rather than Update, if I were switching to a different driver entirely (after first backing up my data, of course).

6. **Quit the utility and restart the Macintosh.** After updating is complete, quit the format utility. If you started up from a startup disk other than the one you are updating, the updated hard drive may be unmounted as a result of the update, its icon vanished from the desktop. Don't worry. Restart the Macintosh. The hard disk should now mount using the new driver.

     If after updating and restarting, you still have problems, such as a failure to start up normally, start up from another volume (such as the System Software CD). The problem disk will likely mount. If so, run the prior version of Drive Setup and "downgrade" the driver. This should get your startup drive working again. To get the new version's driver to work, there are various workarounds you may try, such as zapping the PRAM. If nothing else works, reformatting the drive with the new version of Drive Setup should almost always work.

 ## For Related Information

SEE: • **Fix-It #13 on reformatting disks, partitioning disks, and formatting utilities in general as well as more detailed coverage of Drive Setup.**
• **Fix-It #14 on SCSI and USB problems.**
• **Chapter 5 on problems mounting disks.**

Fix-It #13:
Format, Initialize, and Verify Disks

▶ **QUICK SUMMARY**

For floppy disks and SuperDisks, use the Finder's *Erase Disk* command to reformat the disk. For Iomega Jaz and Zip disks, typically use the Iomega Tools application. For most other media, especially hard drives, use a formatting utility (such as Drive Setup) to reformat the disk; launch the utility and click its *Initialize* or *Format* button, as appropriate.

 ## When to Do It:

- Whenever everything else you have tried has failed to fix your problem, especially when your recovery utilities (such as Disk First Aid or Norton Utilities) report damage to a disk that they are unable to repair or when you cannot otherwise get the disk to mount at all.

- Whenever you have a problem with bad blocks, especially on a hard disk. This usually becomes apparent when you try to copy a file and get a message such as *File could not be read and was skipped.*

- Prior to a complete restoration of your hard disk from your backup files.

- Whenever you want to restore a disk to like-new condition, making sure that virtually all data on it are truly erased.

- Whenever you have an unformatted or incorrectly formatted disk.

- For Zip and Jaz disks, it *may* be recommended in some cases where the disk fails to mount (but see: "Take Note: The Click of Death," later in this Fix-It).

- If you want to move from a HFS to HFS Plus formatted disk and do not want to purchase a special utility to do this.

- If you want to change a disk from a PC format to a Mac format (or vice versa).

 FIX-IT #13

 ## Why to Do It:

All disks need to be formatted before they can be used. Otherwise, you cannot even mount the disk. So why cover formatting of disks here, near the end of this book? It would appear that formatting should be one of the first things to do, not one of the last things to consider.

The answer is that *re*formatting of disks is an important problem-solving tool. It is an all-purpose last resort for dealing with many of the problems covered in previous Fix-Its. In particular, if you have a damaged disk that cannot be repaired by utilities such as Disk First Aid (as described in Fix-It #10), reformatting may be the only way to bring the disk back to life. Reformatting also fixes problems resulting from improper updating of a disk driver (Fix-It #12). Similarly, if you have a problem with bad blocks on a hard disk (as described primarily in Fix-It #11), reformatting is the most reliable way to solve the problem. Reformatting a disk also rebuilds the desktop (Fix-It #8) and reinstalls the disk driver (Fix-It #12). Finally, when you restore files to a reformatted disk, they are defragmented (Fix-It #7). In other words, in one bold stroke, reformatting can cure a variety of ills. Reformatting is also advised whenever you want to recycle an old floppy disk, even if you do not suspect any problems with it.

The only real disadvantages of reformatting are that it can take a relatively long time (especially for hard disks) and that it erases everything on the disk (requiring you to back up and subsequently restore your disk's contents in order to get back to where you were before reformatting, which adds even more time and hassle to the whole procedure).

The focus of this Fix-It is on how and when to reformat problem disks. This Fix-It also tells you when *not* to reformat a disk. In particular, there are several situations where the Macintosh *incorrectly* claims that a perfectly fine disk is unreadable and requests that you reformat it. Don't reformat these disks, or you will unnecessarily erase data. Finally, this Fix-It briefly covers some problems that may occur when you try to format or reformat any disk.

The common use of the term *format* may actually refer to up to six separate processes, only the first of which is what is technically meant by formatting. (1) *Formatting* affects every block on the disk. It lays down the initial background of data that allows a disk to be recognized as a Macintosh disk. (2) For hard disks and some removable media, the next step (which is optional) is to *partition* the disk, which means to divide the disk into separate volumes, each of which then acts as if it were an independent disk. (3) Again just for hard disks and some removable media, the third step is to *install the disk's driver*, a critical piece of software that allows the Macintosh to communicate with the disk. (4) *Initializing* the disk occurs next, which primarily means to create a new set of Directory files. (5) Again a sometimes optional step is to *verify* the disk, which is essentially to check that the preceding steps, especially the formatting step, were successfully carried out. A final check for bad blocks may also occur here. (6) *Mounting* the disk, which means to have the disk appear on the Finder's desktop, comes last.

In some cases, especially when talking about floppy disks, the terms formatting and initializing are used interchangeably to refer to the entire set of steps. Thus, all of these steps are typically performed in response to a single disk-formatting (Format or Initialize) command (although with most hard disk formatting utilities, you can also separately select each step). Verifying a disk can be done separately as a test of an already formatted disk, usually as a way to check for possible media damage.

FIX-IT
#13

What to Do:

This Fix-It is divided into three topics: (1) floppy disks, (2) hard disks, and (3) verifying disks and media damage.

Floppy Disks

Floppy disks are history. None of the currently shipping Macs include a floppy drive, not even as an option. If you still want to use floppy disks, you'll need to buy a third party USB floppy drive. In recognition of this, I have drastically cut back the coverage of floppy disk troubleshooting—here in this Fix-It and elsewhere in *Sad Macs*.

Formatting an Unformatted Disk

When you insert an unformatted floppy disk into a drive, a message appears that says that the *disk is unreadable* and asks whether you want to initialize it. You will typically be given an opportunity to name the disk; if you ignore this, the disk is named "Untitled" by default (you can always rename it later if you want). You may also be given the opportunity to select a type of Format. The Format you should definitely see is "Mac OS Standard 1.4MB," If you have File Exchange enabled, you will also see options to format the disk as a DOS disk. Unless you later intend to mount the disk on a PC (running DOS or Windows), there is no reason to use these DOS formats.

If you click the Erase button, the message *Erasing disk...* will appear on the screen. This may be followed by messages that read: *Verifying format ...* , and *Creating directory.* When it is finished, the newly formatted disk appears on the desktop.

If you decide you don't want to format the disk, click Cancel (or Eject, if that option is available).

Reformatting an Already Formatted Disk

Erase Disk You can reformat a floppy disk at any time by selecting the disk and then selecting the Erase Disk command from the Finder's Special menu. A message similar to the Format alert message appears, asking you to confirm that you really want to completely erase the disk. You can also rename the disk here. Click the Erase button and the format process begins. This formats the disk in exactly the same way as

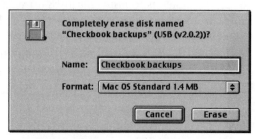

Figure F13-1 The Erase disk window for a floppy disk inserted in a SuperDisk drive.

when the disk was first formatted. All information currently on the disk is completely erased and forever irretrievable! If you got here by mistake, click Cancel.

Command-Option-Tab As a shortcut to initiate reformatting, hold down the Command-Option-Tab keys prior to inserting a disk. Continue to hold down the keys when you insert the disk, until a message appears such as the one that says *Completely erase the disk....* It appears before the disk is mounted.

This shortcut is especially useful if there is a problem with the disk that results in a system crash when the Macintosh tries to mount the disk. By bypassing the mount attempt, you can still reformat the disk.

TAKE NOTE ▶ 800K and 400K Floppy Disks: Ancient History

The only floppy disks you are likely to come across these days, assuming you come across any, are the 1.4MB disks referred to as High Density (or HD) disks. In days gone by, there were also 800K and even 400K disks. Recent Mac models may not even accept such disks (especially the 400K ones). Similarly, the USB SuperDisk drive will only mount 1.4MB floppy disks; it treats 800K floppy disks as unreadable and offers to initialize them as 720K DOS disks (if File Exchange is enabled).

    On the other hand, if you have a really old Mac, the floppy drive may not recognize the HD disks.

    By the way, you can tell if a disk is an HD disk in two ways: (1) there should be an HD icon on the disk; (2) there will be an second small hole on the disk (the first hole is where the tab is that is used to write-protect the disk).

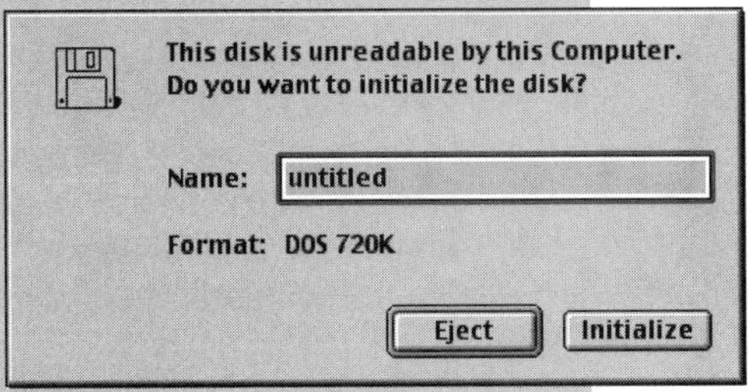

> This disk is unreadable by this Computer. Do you want to initialize the disk?
>
> Name: untitled
>
> Format: DOS 720K
>
> [Eject] [Initialize]

Figure F13-2 The message that appears when inserting an 800K disk in a USB SuperDisk drive.

Reformatting Vs. Deleting

Reformatting a floppy disk is an effective way to erase all files on the disk. As an alternative, you can delete all files from a disk by dragging them to the Trash and selecting Empty Trash from the Finder's Special menu. Although this is usually faster than reformatting the disk, I don't recommend it as a method for recycling a disk. Unlike reformatting, using Empty Trash does not rebuild the desktop, nor does it check for bad blocks. Thus, if there are problems with the disk, deleting the files with Empty Trash does not eliminate them—nor does it really erase the files. It only eliminates the references to the files in the disk's Directory, thus allowing the space occupied by the files to be used for new files as needed. This is why you can use undelete utilities (as described in Chapters 2 and 6) to recover files that have been deleted in the Trash.

    Thus, in general, use the Erase Disk command to completely erase floppy disks. Only use Empty Trash if you want to preserve the chance to undelete files or if you want to delete selected files.

Fix-It #13

File Exchange and PC-Formatted Disks

PC computers can use the same HD disks as do Macintoshes. File Exchange is a control panel that allows PC-formatted disks to be mounted on the Finder's desktop just as if they were Macintosh-formatted disks. File Exchange is also what allows you to format disks as DOS disks when you use the Finder's Erase Disk command. [Although less often done, File Exchange can also be used to mount PC-formatted hard disks. If you need to do this, consult the documentation that came with the software or seek other outside help.]

If you start up with File Exchange disabled, and insert a PC-formatted disk, the Mac will likely claim that it is unreadable and will offer to initialize it. Do not do so or you will erase any data on the disk. The solution is to restart with File Exchange enabled.

TECHNICALLY SPEAKING ▶ Using File Exchange for Opening Files

The PC Exchange tab of File Exchange includes a list of PC file extensions and the Mac applications that will be used to open PC files that have those extensions. For example, under the default settings, text files with an "ascii" extension will be opened in SimpleText. You can modify these settings by clicking the Change button. This was described in more detail in Chapter 6 (in the "When You Can't Open a Document" section).

Note: PC Exchange was a separate control panel in older versions of the Mac OS.

Also note: if you open the Internet control panel, select User Mode from the Edit menu and enable Advanced, a new Advanced tab will appear. If you select this tab and then click the File Mapping icon, you will get to essentially the same settings as accessed by PC Exchange.

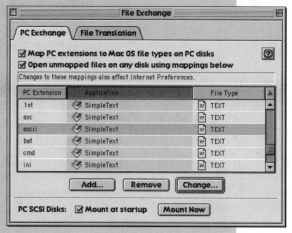

Figure F13-3 The File Exchange control panel.

Damaged Disks

Occasionally, when you insert a disk, you may get a message that says a disk is *unreadable*, is *not a Macintosh disk*, is *damaged*, or *cannot be used*, even though you know you have previously correctly formatted the disk. In this case, you probably do have a damaged disk. If you do not need to recover the data on the disk, you can immediately try to reformat it. If it reformats without a problem, it is probably OK (but see "Verifying Disks and Media Damage," later in this Fix-It). Otherwise, discard the disk. Alternatively, if you do need to recover files from the disk, see Fix-It #11. Also, refer to Chapter 5 for a general discussion of problems with floppy disks that do not mount.

Fix-It #13

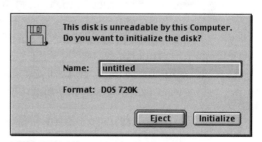

Figure F13-4 One of several messages that may appear when you try to mount a damaged disk.

TAKE NOTE ▶ Reformatting SuperDisks

With the arrival of the iMac in 1998, there was a surge of interest in the SuperDisk format. A SuperDisk looks almost identical to a floppy disk, except that its capacity is 120MB instead of 1.4MB. As a bonus, SuperDisk drives, such as the one made by Imation, can mount ordinary floppy disks as well as SuperDisks. This is what makes them so attractive as an add-on to the otherwise floppyless iMac.

To format or reformat a SuperDisk, you use the Finder's Erase Disk command, just as you would for a floppy disk. If the SuperDisk drivers are installed (which they must be for the disk to even mount), you will typically get a choice of three options for formatting a SuperDisk: Mac OS Standard 120.3 MB, Mac OS Extended 120.3 MB, and DOS 120.3 MB. Choose either Mac OS option (preferably the Extended format if your Mac supports it) and click Erase. That's it.

If you get a SuperDisk, it may come already formatted for DOS. If so, you can use this procedure to reformat it for the Mac. You can check the format by selecting Get Info (Command-I) for the disk and reading the Format line. If it says DOS, that's what you have. It may still mount as a DOS disk (if File Exchange is installed) and seem to work no differently than a Mac disk. Still, unless you intend to share the disk's contents with PC users, the Mac format is preferable.

For some reason, one of my Mac-formatted SuperDisks says "Do not reformat" on it. I don't know why. I reformatted it several times, just as a test, and it continues to work perfectly. Maybe it just means that you don't *need* to reformat it.

SEE: • **"Take Note: Mac OS Standard (HFS) vs. Mac OS Extended (HFS Plus) Formats," later in this Fix-It.**

BY THE WAY ▶ Installers That Must Run from a Floppy Disk: A Solution for iMacs and Other Macs Without a Floppy Drive

With iMacs and other Macs that do not come with a floppy disk drive, users who want a floppy drive will either purchase an external drive or a SuperDisk drive (which reads both ordinary floppy disks and 120MB SuperDisks). In either case, these drives connect via the USB port. They also typically only work with the HD 1.4MB floppy disks.

An added problem is that certain applications require installing from a special floppy disk, as a form of copy protection. These disks often will not work to install the software when run from these USB drives. A solution is to get a freeware extension called USB Floppy Enabler. It allows these copy-protection schemes to work, so that the software can be installed. In the long run, vendors will eliminate these floppy disk installers altogether in favor of CD-ROM discs. But if you still have one, you now have a solution.

Fix-It #13

Hard Disks
Formatting and Reformatting in General

You may be surprised to learn that hard disks need to be formatted just like floppy disks. Because most hard disks come preformatted and, in many cases, never have to be reformatted, many users have no experience with formatting hard disks. However, as described in the "Why to Do It" section, sometimes you want to reformat a hard disk (for example, if a hard disk is damaged in a way that your data recovery utilities cannot remedy).

To format or reformat a hard disk or removable cartridge, you need a special disk-formatting utility. Apple includes such a utility, called Drive Setup, with the Mac OS. **Note:** Old Mac models using old versions of the Mac OS may still use an older Mac formatting utility called HD SC Setup. This utility is no longer covered in *Sad Macs*.

If you buy a drive from another vendor, it typically comes with its own utility. There are also utilities (such as Hard Disk ToolKit) that you can purchase independently of any drive purchase. Third-party utilities tend to offer more options than the rather minimal features of Drive Setup. Using universal utilities can be especially desirable if you own several hard drives from different sources and you want to use the same formatting utility for all of them (which Apple officially recommends that you do), as Drive Setup may not work with all drives.

In general, make sure you are using the latest version of whatever utility you use, as updates fix problems (sometimes serious ones!) with the previous version. This is especially critical when Apple comes out with major new hardware. Existing versions of formatting utilities may be incompatible with the new hardware. In fact, simply using a drive that had been formatted with an older version of a formatting utility could damage the drive. Check Web sites (such as my own MacFixIt) or the utility vendor's Web site for update info and advice.

The major functions of these utilities are the same, no matter which one you use. These include formatting the hard drive, updating the device driver, partitioning the disk, and testing the drive for media damage. Additional functions may include checking the performance of the drive and other special features designed to increase speed (such as disk caches) or assist in troubleshooting. A third party utility may also have more specialized options, such as the ability to set a removable cartridge to automatically eject at restart and/or shutdown.

**Fix-It
#13**

SEE: • **Fix-It #12, on updating disk device drivers, for a general introduction to these different types of formatting utilities and why you might switch from one to another.**

You should have a current backup of the data on your disk (as explained in Chapter 2) before reformatting, unless you no longer care to save the data. However, if your disk is damaged, you may not be able to perform a needed backup (in this case, refer to Fix-Its #10 and #11 for advice).

TAKE NOTE ▶ Mac OS Standard (HFS) vs. Mac OS Extended (HFS Plus) Formats

Starting with Mac OS 8.1, you have the option to format your hard disks (and most other media except for floppy disks) via one of two formats: Mac OS Standard (also known as HFS, for Hierarchical File System) or Mac OS Extended (also known as HFS Plus or HFS+). HFS is the format that existed prior to Mac OS 8.1. HFS Plus is the new one. These days, all Macs ship with drives formatted using HFS Plus. However, if you have an older Mac, your drive may still use HFS. In this case, you might want to convert to HFS Plus. Why convert? How do you convert? What problems might occur if you do or do not convert? Here are the answers:

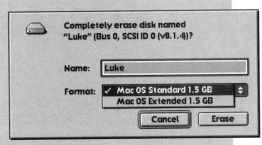

Figure F13-5 Mac OS Standard and Mac OS Extended options in the Erase Disk window popup menu.

What is HFS Plus and why should I use it? The main purpose of HFS Plus is to reduce the amount of space used by files stored on your disk, thereby significantly increasing the total storage capacity of a drive.

A "feature" of HFS is that the minimum amount of disk space that a file requires gets larger as the size of the drive gets larger. For example, the minimum size (or *allocation block size*, as it is technically called) on a 120MB drive is 2K. For a 720MB drive, the minimum is 12K. Thus, a 2K text file would take up only 2K of disk space on a 120MB drive but would require 12K of space on a 720MB drive (wasting 10K). For any file, no matter what its size, disk space requirements increase in increments of the minimal file size. Thus, a 13K file would require 14K of disk space on a 120MB drive (2K x 7 = 14K) but would require 24K on a 720MB drive (12K x 2 = 24K), again wasting 10K. Thus, if you have a large capacity drive with a lot of small files on it, you are wasting a significant amount of disk space. With larger and larger drives becoming the common standard (6GB is now about the minimum size hard drive you can buy), we are talking about a *lot* of wasted space.

With HFS Plus, the minimum file size is reduced so that it is always 4K, no matter how large the drive is. Thus with HFS a 4 GB hard drive a file containing a 4K file requires 64K of space, whereas with HFS Plus, it would only require 4K! With this same drive, a typical user might easily recover 1 GB or more of space by moving from HFS to HFS Plus.

Want to know the minimum file size for your volume(s)? Just create a blank SimpleText document. Check the Size in its Get Info window. That's the minimum allocation block size for the volume on which the file resides.

How do I tell if my drive is using HFS Plus? Easy. Click the drive icon and select Get Info. If it is using HFS Plus, you will see the phrase "Mac OS Extended" on the Format line. Otherwise, it will say "Mac OS Standard."

What do I need to use HFS Plus? Basically, all you need is a Mac OS 8.1 startup disk. However, the Text Encoding Converter extension and the Text Encodings folder must remain in the startup drive's System Folder in order for HFS Plus to function properly. If you are using HFS Plus, do not ever try to remove these files!

A volume must be 32MB or larger to be formatted with HFS Plus. If you attempt to format a smaller disk, using Drive Setup, you will receive an error message that states: "Initialization Failed." Floppy disks can not be initialized with Mac OS Extended format.

One caution: unless you have a bootable CD or other startup disk that uses Mac OS 8.1 or later, do not format your startup drive with HFS Plus. Otherwise, if you need to startup from the "emergency" bootable CD because of a problem with your startup drive, you will not be able to access the drive.

(continues on next page)

Fix-It #13

TAKE NOTE ▶ Mac OS Standard (HFS) vs. Mac OS Extended (HFS Plus) Formats
(continued)

Also, only Power Macs can use an HFS Plus disk as a startup disk, no matter what OS version you are using. Similarly, only Power Macs can use HFS Plus disks as the location for the invisible VM Storage file as used by the Virtual Memory option of the Memory control panel (see Fix-It #5).

How can I convert a drive to HFS Plus? Once again, this is easy enough. Simply select Erase disk from the Finder's Special menu. Here a Format pop-up menu will give you the choice between Mac OS Standard and Mac OS Extended. Choose the Extended option and select to Erase. You cannot do this for the current startup disk of course. Warning! Doing this erases all the files on your drive. Make sure they are backed up first!

Alternatively, launch Drive Setup (version 1.4 or later) and select Initialize. A dialog will be displayed where you can specify Mac OS Extended format, as well as other initialization options. One potential advantage of using Drive Setup over the Finder's Erase Disk command: Drive Setup can partition a disk into multiple volumes and you can even choose to use HFS Plus for some but not all volumes. Other third-party disk formatting utilities provide similar options.

Can't I convert to HFS Plus without having to erase my disk? Yes you can. There are several non-Apple utilities that let you do this. The most well-known is Alsoft's PlusMaker. This utility also lets you preview how much disk space you will recover by the conversion. Mac OS Extended Calculator is a shareware utility that also provides these previews. PlusMaker makes the conversion without erasing anything. Still, to be safe, back up first - just in case something goes wrong.

Note: The maximum block size for an HFS Plus volume is 4K (smaller volumes may use as little as 0.5K per block). You can squeeze some more space from a hard drive by forcing even large volumes to use a maximum that is less than 4K. Apple's system software won't let you do this, but another Alsoft utility, called PlusMaximizer, will (as will a variety of other utilities). You can reduce the maximum to as low as 0.5K with these utilities. But there is a small risk of increased compatibility problems and (according to some experts) a performance decrease. Personally, 4K seems small enough for me; I would recommend against fiddling with this.

What happens if you are running from a Mac OS 8.0 or earlier startup disk and you try to mount an HFS Plus volume? You need Mac OS 8.1 or later to see the contents of an HFS Plus drive. Every HFS Plus volume contains an HFS "wrapper" that can be recognized even by older versions of the system software. The wrapper contains a Read Me file that informs you that you need to run Mac OS 8.1 or later in order to read the remaining contents of the volume. No damage is done to the drive and all its contents remain intact. Just start up from a Mac OS 8.1 or later System Folder and the contents will appear.

One exception: if you are accessing an HFS Plus volume over a network via AppleShare, you can mount and access the contents of the volume even if you are not running Mac OS 8.1 or later.

Are there any problems to watch for after converting to HFS Plus? Assuming the conversion process itself did not cause any problems, there should be no further hassles. However, this assumes you are using the most current versions of your software. For example, when HFS Plus first came out, disk repair and disk optimization utilities, such as Norton Utilities and TechTool Pro, did not work with HFS Plus formatted disks. In some cases, trying to repair an HFS Plus disk with ones of these utilities could actually damage the disk to the point where only reformatting could salvage it. However, these problems have no been remedied. For most users, using HFS Plus will present no problems that are not also present in HFS.

Finally, Apple warns: "When using a Mac OS Extended formatted drive as your start up disk, the Password Security control panel will not function properly. Do not use the Password Security control panel if you plan to password protect and then start up from a Mac OS Extended formatted volume." (This appears to be fixed in Mac OS 9 for some Mac models. Still, I no longer trust this utility. If it doesn't work, it can wind up trashing your entire drive. There are safer options, including Mac OS 9's Multiple Users and several third party utilities.)

Fix-It #13

TAKE NOTE ▶ Mac OS Server (UFS) Format

Mac OS X Server supports three file system formats: Mac OS Standard (HFS), Mac OS Extended (HFS Plus), and UFS (or Unix File System). There are actually two flavors of UFS. Mac OS UFS is for Mac OS X. Mac OS Server UFS is for Mac OS X Server and can only be chosen when running MacOS.app in Mac OS X Server.

Drive Setup 1.8.1 or later can format partitions in any of these formats.

Mac OS 8 or 9 cannot read UFS disks or files, but Mac OS X Server can read all three formats.

SEE: • **Chapter 15 for more on Mac OS X.**

TECHNICALLY SPEAKING ▶ Formatting a Disk and Virtual Memory

Ideally, you should make sure virtual memory is off before trying to reformat a disk. Also have all extensions disabled.

However, if you try to reformat a hard disk after starting up with the Apple Mac OS CD that came with your Mac, you may get messages that say the reformatting cannot be done because virtual memory (VM) is "on" (even though you have not turned it on) or because files are "in use." The apparent problem is that some versions of these CDs set VM to on (and thus place the invisible VM file on your disk which then leads to the symptoms described). A simple work-around is to hold down the Command key when starting up from the CD. This turns virtual memory off for that session.

Reformatting Using Drive Setup

Current versions of Drive Setup work not only with drives that ship from Apple, but many other drives as well. They can also reformat removable cartridges, such as Jaz and Zip cartridges. As a result, Drive Setup is the most commonly used formatting utility. We will use it for the examples here. If you use another utility, check its documentation for exact details.

If a particular drive is not supported by Drive Setup, it should still appear in the Drive Setup window when the drive is mounted. However, if you select to format it, you will get a message such as: *Cannot modify a disk in an unsupported drive.* If the drive is a removable cartridge, such as a Zip or Jaz cartridge, try disabling any driver extension in the System Folder (such as *Iomega Driver*). Then restart. This should now allow Drive Setup to recognize and reformat the cartridge. Otherwise, you may not be able to use Drive Setup for that drive.

Figure F13-6 Apple's Drive Setup.

FIX-IT #13

If you get a message that says *Unrecognized driver*, this usually means you have an Apple drive but you have used a third-party software to reformat it or update its driver and Drive Setup will no longer "work" with the drive. (This is much less common than it used to be). In this case, you cannot use Drive Setup and must use a third party utility instead.

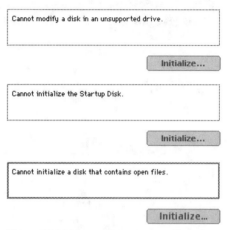

Whatever utility you use, be aware that it may indicate a problem where none really exists. The culprit is the hard drive spin-down feature of the Energy Saver control panel. If the drive spins down during the test, it will indicate a failure. To avoid this, make sure you select "Never" from the Sleep Setup option in the control panel prior to performing any function with a drive formatting utility. Also, turn off any security software before attempting to update or reformat your drive.

Figure F13-7 Some error messages that may appear in the Drive Setup window.

To reformat a disk with Drive Setup:

1. Start up with a disk other than the disk you want to reformat. If you intend to reformat your normal startup hard disk, restart with a Disk Tools disk, Mac OS System Software CD (or other Emergency Disk that you custom created for this purpose).

2. Launch Drive Setup and select the desired drive by clicking its name. If you don't see the name of the disk listed, try selecting the Mount Volumes or Rescan Bus command from the Functions menu.

3. Click Initialize. If another window appears, click the Initialize button in that window as well. That's it. If the first Initialize button is dimmed, it means you cannot initialize the disk. Typically the program will give you a message explaining why (such as that you cannot initialize the startup disk).

Instead of just initializing, consider the following options first:

Zero all data Initialization doesn't actually erase all the data on the disk. It essentially just erases and creates new Directory files. In this sense, it is fundamentally similar to what would happen if you selected the "Erase Disk" command from the Finder for a hard disk (as explained in Fix-It #11). This means that, with utilities such as Norton Utilities, you might be able to recover data from an initialized disk. If you want to prevent this from happening, typically for security reasons, select Initialization Options from the Functions menu and check the "Zero all data" option. Then initialize the disk.

Low-level format The other option available from the Initialization Options window is "Low level format."

Apple recommends against selecting low-level format for a routine initialization, as it takes much longer to do. Apple recommends using low-level format only if the disk has never been formatted before (even from the factory) or if there is a problem with the disk that initialization alone does not fix.

If Drive Setup spots a problem with a disk that requires a low-level format to fix, it may inform you that this is required. If so, Drive Setup will perform this format even if this option is not checked.

SEE: • **"Take Note: Understanding Drive Setup's Initialization Options" and "Take Note: Understanding Drive Setup's Test Disk Option" for related information.**

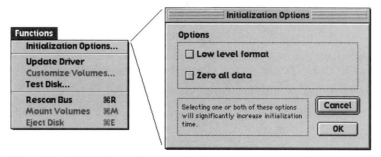

Figure F13-8 Drive Setup's Function menu and Initialization Options window.

4. Most likely, the reformatted disk will not be mounted (that is, it will not yet appear on your desktop). To mount the disk, you can use Drive Setup's Mount Volumes command. Otherwise, simply restart the Macintosh. The disk should now mount and function normally.

SEE: • **Chapter 5 and Fix-It #14 for more on problems mounting drives.**

5. If the reformatted disk was your normal startup disk, it obviously needs to have the system software reinstalled before it can serve as a startup disk again. To do this, either restore the contents of the disk from your backups (using a startup disk that contains your backup utility) or start fresh with a new set of system software (using the system software's Installer disk as the startup disk, as detailed in Fix-It #4). In either case, restart when finished.

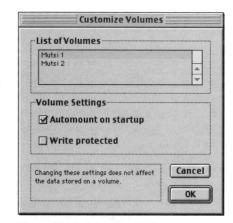

Figure F13-9 Drive Setup's Customize Volumes window (typically leave it with its default selections, as shown).

FIX-IT #13

TAKE NOTE ▶ Understanding Drive Setup's Initialization Options

High-level format If you select Drive Setup's Initialize button, with no options selected, it performs what it called a "high-level format." This means it erases and creates a new Directory, but leaves the rest of the hard drive untouched. For all practical purposes, the drive has been erased, but file recovery software (such as Data Rescue and Norton Utilities' UnErase may still be able to resurrect it). When you are reformatting a disk because Disk First Aid (or other repair utility) could not fix a problem with it, a high-level format is what you should try first.

Low-level format and Zero all data If you select the Initialization Options command from Drive Setup's Functions menu, you will be given two additional options: "low-level format" and "zero all data."

If you select "low-level format" and then click to Initialize, it performs a "true" physical formatting of the hard disk, recording the magnetic markers that divide the total usable space into sectors and tracks. This takes much longer than a high-level format. It also removes information, such as the computer's serial number, that may be recorded in an otherwise protected area of the disk. The serial number of an iMac, for example, can be conveniently viewed in Apple System Profiler 2.x, but only if the hard drive that contains it has never been low-level formatted. Thus, a low-level format is recommended mainly when a high-level format fails or if Test Disk was unable to repair damage to the media.

A low-level format does not completely zero all data on the disk, so some software might still be able to recover information from the drive. To prevent this, also select *Zero all data*.

Low-level format is mainly used for SCSI drives. Starting with Drive Setup 1.7, you cannot select to do a low-level format for ATA disks (as used for the internal drive in all currently shipping Macs). This is because, for these drives, the low-level format option was actually doing the same thing as the "zero all data" option.

SEE: • Fix-It #14 for more on SCSI vs. ATA drives.

Reformatting vs. Erasing vs. Deleting

In general, do not use the Finder's Erase Disk command to format a SCSI or IDE hard disk. If the disk has never been formatted, it will not correctly format the disk. If it has been formatted, it will not truly reformat it. Erase Disk is mainly for floppy disks, USB disks, and limited other situations (such as for converting a drive from HFS to HFS Plus).

For formatted hard disks, Erase Disk erases only the Directory, replacing it with an empty one. The net result is that the Macintosh, after checking the Directory, now considers the disk to be empty. This is similar to what would happen if you selected all the files on the disk, placed them in the Trash, and deleted them using "Empty Trash." That's why recovery utilities (such as Norton Utilities UnErase) can restore a hard disk accidentally erased via the Erase Disk command (as explained in Fix-It #11). Selecting Erase Disk for a formatted SCSI or ATA drive is actually virtually identical to doing a high-level format via Drive Setup. Still, I'm a bit of a stick-in-the-mud here; for any sort of reformatting of a SCSI/ATA drive, I prefer to use Drive Setup.

SEE: • "Take Note: Understanding Drive Setup's Initialization Options" and "Take Note: Understanding the Finder's Erase Disk command" for more details.

Fix-It
#13

TAKE NOTE ▶ Understanding the Finder's Erase Disk Command

Why and when should you use the Finder's Erase Disk command in lieu of Drive Setup's Initialize command?

Floppy Disks: Use Erase Disk. It does both a low-level and high-level format. You cannot use Drive Setup on floppy disks.

SCSI and ATA hard disks: In general, avoid Erase Disk. While it should do a high-level format, I would trust Drive Setup as more reliable - especially if a newer version has been released since the release of the OS version you are running. If you use a formatting utility other than Drive Setup, definitely do not use Erase Disk, as it will force a shift to a different driver.

USB disks (hard drives and SuperDisk drives): Use Erase Disk. It does a high-level and, in most cases, a low-level format. USB devices often do not come with their own formatting utility and Drive Setup does not work with them, so the Finder's Erase Disk is typically your only option.

Iomega Zip and Jaz drives: Avoid using Erase Disk. Use Iomega Tools preferably; although other software may be used instead. Drive Setup may work, but not in all cases.

BY THE WAY ▶ Formatting CD-R, CD-RW, and DVD-RAM Disks

You can write to, as well as read, CD-R, CD-RW and DVD-RAM disks. To format these disks, you would typically use a third party program such as Toast (see Chapter 2). This is especially true if you want to make a bootable CD.

DVD-RAM discs can be formatted using the Universal Disk Format (UDF), Mac OS Standard, Mac OS Extended, or DOS formats. The UDF format allows you to share information with any computer platform that supports UDF 1.5.

Starting with Mac OS 9.0.4, you can format and startup from a DVD-RAM disc. To do so, use Drive Setup 1.9.2 or later to format the disc.

Partition the Disk

A hard drive can be subdivided into separate *partitions*. These partitions then act as if they are totally separate disks (technically, each partition is referred to as a separate *volume*). Each one mounts separately and has its own icon.

Helpful hint: Partitioning a disk (or even modifying the size of existing partitions) requires reformatting the disk and thus erases all data currently on it. Also, reformatting a disk to add new partitions (and then restoring your data to newly named partitions) will typically result in all the links between aliases and original files (and other similar types of links) being broken. So be careful!

Why Partition? Partitioning a disk is not required, and many users choose never to partition their drive. Still, there are two main advantages to partitioning larger-capacity drives.

- **Speed** Partitioning can improve disk access speed. For example, a fragmented file (as described in Fix-It #7) always has all of its fragments contained within a single partition. Thus, when trying to open a fragmented file, the Mac will have less "distance" to go to search for fragments if it only has to search within an 1GB partition

Fix-It #13

of a 6GB drive than if it has to search within the entire 6GB drive. However, this speed advantage is diminished if you use your partitions in such a way as to require the Mac to frequently traverse partitions. For example, if your application is in one partition and your document is in another, the speed advantage will be less than if both files are in the same partition.

- **File Size** If you are using HFS formatting, the minimum file size gets larger the larger the hard drive you have (as detailed in "Take Note: Mac OS Standard (HFS) vs. Mac OS Extended (HFS Plus) Formats"). This can mean a good deal of wasted space on large capacity drives. The best solution these days is to use HFS Plus, if your Mac supports it. Otherwise, partitioning the drive into smaller volumes can help.

- **Alternate startup volume** I prefer to have at least two partitions on my main internal drive. I keep a System Folder on both drives. This allows me to shift from one volume to the other as the startup volume. This can be useful when upgrading to a new version of the Mac OS (you can test it out on one volume while keeping the old System Folder untouched on the other volume). It can also be useful if you need to do a repair on a volume that cannot be done on the startup volume. Usually, if you simply restart from the alternate volume, you can make the repair (as long as the problem is not so severe that the drive cannot mount at all).

- **Alternate OS** Less common but significant: partitions can also be used to set up a volume formatted for a different operating system (such as Linux).

How to Partition (with Drive Setup) Apple's Drive Setup can create standard (Mac OS) partitions of any size you choose. For example, to use Drive Setup to create partitions:

1. Start up with a disk that contains Drive Setup. This disk should not be the one you want to partition.

2. Launch Drive Setup and select the name of the drive you want to format/partition.

3. Click the Initialize button.

4. Click Custom Setup from the window that next appears.

5. Select the desired Partitioning Scheme from the pop-up menu (two or three equal sized partitions would be a common choice). You can create partitions of unequal sizes either by dragging the bar handle of the partition box in the graphic depicting the partitions or by changing the number in the Size box for a selected partition.

6. When you are done, close the window and click the Initialize button.

7. Use the "Customize Volumes" option of the Functions menu to select whether or not to have a volume automatically mount at startup (typically you would want them all to mount).

8. Quit Drive Setup and restart.

Fix-It
#13

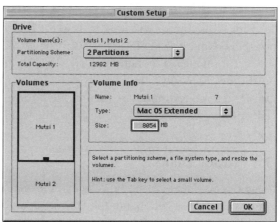

Figure F13-10 Above: click Drive Setup's Custom Setup button to get the Partition window. Right: Drive Setup's Partition window; use the Partitioning Scheme pop-up menu to select the number of partitions you want.

BY THE WAY ▶ The "Extra" Partition

When partitioning a disk, you may notice that there is an "Extra" partition (of about 5MB or so) at the bottom of the partition graphic (with Drive Setup, you may need to use the Tab key to see the listing of such a small partition on a large-capacity drive). Apple says the extra partition is used by some duplicating and copying software utilities. However it is not essential and can be deleted or at least reduced to some minimum size (to do this with Drive Setup, for example, you would enlarge another partition to its maximum size and then reformat the disk). Personally, I would not bother doing this merely to reclaim 5MB. With today's large-capacity drives, it is not worth the effort.

Other small partitions contain essential driver-level information. Do not even try to delete them!

TECHNICALLY SPEAKING ▶ What's an Interleave?

You may have heard that changing something called the *interleave factor* on your hard disk can improve its speed. The basic idea is this: hard disks are constantly spinning from the moment they are turned on. A drive "reads" requested data from this spinning disk as the relevant portion of the disk passes by the disk's drive head. In some cases, especially with older drives, the drive cannot read data from the disk as fast as the disk can spin by the drive head. This means the drive has to wait for the next revolution of the disk to read the next sector of data, which can slow things down. Changing the interleave factor alters the way data is written to a disk so that it partially compensates for this problem (essentially, it spaces out data so that the drive does not have to read from contiguous sectors; related sectors are spaced far enough apart so that the drive can read data from them without having to skip over and return to them on subsequent revolutions). The result is that performance speed improves.

The ideal is for the drive to read fast enough to use an interleave factor of 1 (this means that the drive can keep up with the rate of spinning). All current drives are fast enough to do this and come preformatted with a interleave factor of 1. As such, most users can ignore this as an issue. Drive Setup doe not even include an option to change this. If you really need to adjust this, you would have to use a third-party formatting utility.

Changing the interleave factor requires that you reformat the drive.

**FIX-IT
#13**

Verifying Disks and Media Damage

Verifying a disk means checking each sector (block) on the disk to make sure that no media damage (bad blocks) exists. Usually, this is done automatically whenever a disk is formatted, although there are ways in which you can choose to do this at other times. Typically, if bad blocks are detected, they are *marked (mapped out or spared)* so that they cannot be used in the future. If successful, this allows the disk to verify despite the bad blocks. Otherwise, the verification fails. For more specific details, read on.

For Floppy Disks

Using the Macintosh to verify When you format a floppy disk, such as with the Finder's Erase Disk command, the Macintosh automatically verifies it.

In System 7 or newer, if any media damage is detected during the verification, the disk is verified a second time, during which any bad blocks detected are spared. When this happens, a message saying *Updating disk* should appear during the formatting sequence. Reverification takes much longer than the initial verification. Reverification usually succeeds unless there are too many bad blocks or the damage is in the critical area of the disk needed to store the Directory. In these cases, you get a message that

says *Initialization failed!, Disk Initialization failed!* or *Erasing the disk failed.* If this happens, it's time to discard this disk. Actually, I take a conservative approach and discard any floppy disk that needs to be reverified, even if it ultimately formats successfully. In my experience, once bad blocks appear on a floppy disk, the probability increases that more will appear soon. Why take chances?

Figure F13-11 A message such as this appears if the Macintosh is unable to verify a floppy disk that it is attempting to format.

Occasionally, I have had a disk problem that appeared to be due to bad blocks (such as a write error when copying a file). Yet when I reformatted the disk, it surprisingly formatted successfully without any reverification needed. I am more optimistic about the continued use of such a disk than those that require reverification. However, the cause may well be an intermittent bad block problem that will inevitably soon return. So be cautious.

If you begin to have problems with many or all disks failing to verify, there is probably a problem with the floppy drive mechanism.

SEE: • Fix-It #15 for more on hardware repairs.

Using other utilities to verify Utilities such as Norton Utilities' Disk Doctor can verify a disk without having to format it. To do this, use the commands for checking the disk media (as described in Fix-It #11). These utilities typically can mark any detected bad blocks, similarly to how the Finder's Erase Disk verification works. Still, if bad blocks are detected, I would discard the disk.

TECHNICALLY SPEAKING ▶ **Bad Blocks and Sector Sparing**

Bad blocks Damage to the physical formatting structure means bad sectors - blocks of the disk that can no longer be written to or read from successfully because the magnetic markers that define them have either been removed or altered.

Sector sparing Depending upon the kind of damage and where it is located, and the utility in use, a low-level format typically either repairs the affected sectors by recreating those markers, or works around them by sector sparing, also known as block reallocation: recoverable data is moved to good blocks, and the bad block is rendered unavailable for the disk driver to write to in the future.

SEE: • **Fix-It #11, "Check for Damaged Disks and Files: Replace, Recover, Restore, or Repair, "** **for more extended information about bad blocks.**

For Hard Disks

Testing a hard disk Most disk-formatting utilities can test a hard disk for bad blocks without having to reformat the disk. For Drive Setup, select "Test Disk" from its Functions menu. This feature works most thoroughly if the disk can be unmounted for the test (the startup volume cannot be unmounted, for example).

Recovery utilities, such as Norton Utilities' Disk Doctor, can similarly check a disk for bad blocks (as described in Fix-It #11). Recovery utilities can map out any bad blocks that they detect.

Testing for bad blocks can take several minutes or more. Be prepared to wait.

Mapping out bad blocks If media damage is detected, I would generally recommend to reformat the disk. Although recovery utilities can map out bad blocks, reformatting is the most reliable method for permanently preventing these blocks from being used again. Unless an unusually large number of bad blocks exist (which would almost certainly indicate a more serious problem with the disk), reformatting should remedy any bad block problems. After you reformat, restore the disk's contents from your backups.

If your hard disk formatting utility has an option to format without verifying (to save time), don't take it. Without verification, bad blocks will not get mapped out.

SEE: • **"Understanding Drives Setup's Test Disk option," for more details.**

Although I recommend discarding floppy disks with bad blocks, even if the disk ultimately verifies, I obviously would not recommend this for hard disks! You would not want to discard an expensive drive unit for a single bad block, especially if the block is successfully mapped out.

A few bad blocks on a hard disk are no cause for concern, once they are mapped out. Actually, many new hard drives come with bad blocks already on them (mapped out before they were ever shipped from the factory). Still, if you are careful with the use of your hard drive, you may never have any problems with bad blocks. Bad blocks are much more common with floppy disks. However if new bad blocks frequently appear on a hard disk shortly after you have formatted it, you probably have a hardware problem. In this case, the disk drive needs to be repaired (if possible) or replaced.

FIX-IT #13

TAKE NOTE ▶ Understanding Drives Setup's Test Disk Option

Using Test Disk When you select Test Disk from Drive Setup's Functions menu, it will check the disk for bad blocks and (if the drive is not the startup disk and can be unmounted) attempt to repair them if found. This is preferred to also doing a low-level format to fix bad blocks because you do not have to erase/reformat the disk to fix the errors. However, a low-level format may needed in some cases where Test Disk alone does not work.

Test Disk, Low Level format, and sector sparing In general, Test Disk will report back with messages that indicate whether the test was successfully completed or whether errors occurred that indicate you should try a low-level format instead. If you do a low-level format, you should still follow it by running Test Disk. This is because Drive Setup's low-level format does not verify blocks, and thus does reallocate (spare) bad blocks.

   If problems still persist, you may have a drive that is beyond the help of software "repairs." If you still want to try to save the drive (or the data on it), take it to a drive repair service, such as DriveSavers (see Chapter 5).

SCSI vs. ATA disks Test Disk is mainly used for SCSI disks. For ATA disks, Test Disk is only a read-only test; it will not make repairs. In general, ATA drives are "self-fixing," sparing a bad block whenever there is an attempt to write to it. Zeroing all data makes such an attempt. Thus, to actually reallocate bad blocks with Drive Setup, you must Initialize the disk with the "Zero all data" option enabled. Follow this by running Test Disk (to check for the success of the operation).

TAKE NOTE ▶ Formatting Iomega (Zip/Jaz) Disks and the "Click of Death"

Formatting Iomega disks Although you can use almost any disk formatting utility to format Iomega disks (Zip and Jaz cartridges), Iomega strongly recommends using their own software: Iomega Tools. If you select the Erase/Initialize option from the Tools window, you will have a choice of a Short or a Long Erase. This is more-or-less equivalent to the high-level and low-level formatting with Drive Setup. Iomega Tools also includes a Diagnose option that does a quick test for problems (although it does not appear to do a through test for bad blocks, as does Drive Setup's Test Disk). Using another feature of Tools, you can use Create Rescue Disk to quickly create a startup Zip or Jaz disk.

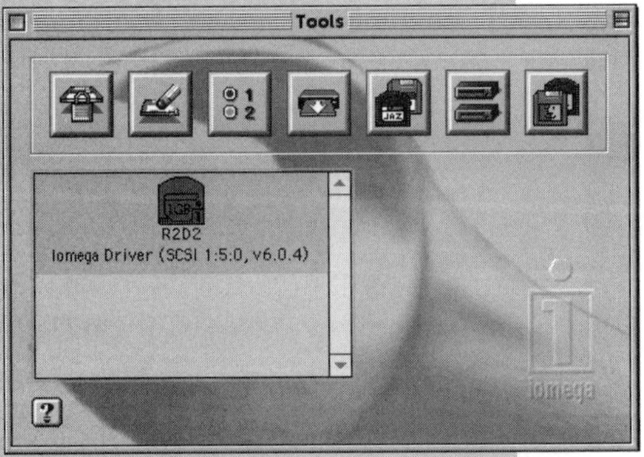

Figure F13-12a The Iomega Tools main window.

   One caution: Iomega's software has a tradition of having numerous shortcomings – such as an inability to copy files, system freezes, and problems using a disk as a startup disk. Despite Iomega's recommendation, many users report better luck using other software (including Drive Setup). Check MacFixIt <http://www.macfixit.com> for the latest details. For more general Iomega troubleshooting advice, check these Apple tech Info Library articles: http://til.info.apple.com/techinfo.nsf/artnum/n20881 and http://til.info.apple.com/techinfo.nsf/artnum/n30380.

   Other removable cartridge systems, such as ORB disks, similarly have their own custom tools software, although other third-party software may also be used.

(continues on next page)

Fix-It #13

Damaged disks and the "Click of Death" If you ever insert a Jaz or (more likely) a Zip cartridge in its drive and hear an unpleasant clicking sound and the cartridge refuses to mount, you have what Iomega users affectionately refer to as the "Click of Death." It almost certainly means your cartridge is now ruined; hence the name. There has been much controversy surrounding this phenomenon: what causes it and what if anything might fix it or prevent it from happening again? Many answers have been given, although no definitive consensus opinion has been reached. Here's what we do know:

*   If you get the Click of Death, do not try to reformat the disk. It is unlikely to work and could make matters worse. **Note:** An Apple support document claims that this noise is due to using a Zip disk with an old version of the Iomega driver on it, and that reformatting the disk will fix it (just let the disk continue to click until the "Initialize" dialog appears and then Initialize). However, I am very skeptical of this advice.

*   Whatever caused the Click of Death for the cartridge, using it in a drive can cause damage to the drive head. This in turn can lead to damage of otherwise intact cartridges when you insert them in the drive. So if you get a Click of Death, remove the cartridge immediately and do not use it again. If the next cartridge you insert is also damaged, it's time to suspect that the drive itself is now damaged.

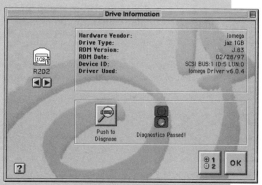

*   In either case, contact Iomega (or the vendor that marketed the drive) for replacement of the damaged cartridges and/or drives.

*   There is debate about whether reformatting a cartridge with a utility other than Iomega Tools can be a cause of the "Click of Death." Iomega asserts this is so, and warns against using other utilities. However, many users have ignored this advice and had no problems. In fact, doing so has sometimes worked around a problem that appeared to be due to the Iomega driver (including problems copying files to cartridges or using a cartridge as a startup disk).

*   If there is data on a "dead" cartridge that you really are desperate to save, and you are willing to risk damage to the drive, you can sometimes save it by launching a utility, such as Norton Utilities, and then inserting the cartridge. From here, you can try to recover files with UnErase (see Fix-It #11).

(continues on next page)

Figure F13-12b The Erase/Initialize window, the Drive Information window (with the Push to Diagnose button), and the Create Rescue Disk window.

FIX-IT #13

TAKE NOTE ▶ Formatting Iomega (Zip/Jaz) Disks and the "Click of Death"
(continued)

If you try to do a "long erase" of a Jaz or Zip cartridge, using Iomega Tools, it will sometimes fail, usually giving various "disk write" error messages. Again, if this happens repeatedly on more than one cartridge, you may have a damaged drive, or at least one that needs a firmware upgrade. Contact Iomega or your drive vendor. Actually, Iomega suprisingly states that any long erase of a Jaz cartridge risks damaging the cartridge and should be avoided.

If a removable cartridge is damaged, due to something other than the Click of Death, you may get an error message when you try to mount it that resembles the message you get when you try to mount a damaged floppy disk. In this case, you may be able to repair the disk with tools such as Disk First Aid or Norton Utilities. However, it is more likely that you will need to reformat the cartridge.

SEE: • **"Take Note: Removable Cartridge Drives: Drivers And Extensions," in Fix-It #12, for related information.**

 For Related Information

  SEE: • **Fix-It #5 on disk caches.**
  • **Fix-It #12 on using formatting utilities to update the disk driver.**
  • **Fix-Its #10 and #11 for more on bad blocks and using recovery utilities.**
  • **Fix-It #14 on SCSI-related problems.**
  • **Chapter 1 on basic terminology regarding disks.**
  • **Chapter 5 on problems starting up and mounting drives.**

Fix-It #14:
Check for Device and Connection Problems: SCSI, ATA (IDE), FireWire, USB, ADB, and Serial

▶ **QUICK SUMMARY**

Use a utility, such as SCSIProbe or Drive Setup, to mount a SCSI device that will not otherwise mount. Check for other possible SCSI-related problems, such as ID conflicts and improper termination. Similarly, troubleshoot ATA, FireWire, and/or USB device problems, such as by updating drivers. For older Macs, check for ADB and serial port problems.

 When to Do It:

- When a device connected to a SCSI, ATA, USB, FireWire, or ADB port does not mount or does not function as expected. This includes fixed-format disk drives, removable media cartridge drives, CD-ROM drives, printers and more.

- When a system crash or freeze occurs as a result of accessing an externally connected device. For example, when trying to open any or almost any file on an external drive or CD-ROM drive results in a system crash. Or if a freeze occurs when trying to access a scanner.

- When you cannot start up your Macintosh because a Sad Mac appears.

- When you cannot start up your Macintosh because a system error occurs, particularly if the error occurs immediately after the Welcome to Macintosh message appears.

- When you lose access to external devices connected to your Macintosh. For example, if SCSI devices are not recognized by a SCSI utility, or if a USB printer is not listed in the Chooser.

- Whenever problems develop immediately after you add, remove, or rearrange the order of these devices, especially SCSI or ATA devices.

- If the Mac does not respond to mouse and/or keyboard input.

- When multiple copies of the disk icon of a SCSI disk device appear scattered over the desktop.

- If you get any of a variety of error messages that indicate a problem with peripheral devices. USB device error messages are especially common.

- Any other time a peripheral device is a likely suspect as the cause of a problem.

FIX-IT
#14

Why to Do It:

Ports and buses If you want to add any device to your Macintosh, there is an assortment of ways to do so. Each method has its own functions and limitations, advantages and disadvantages. Here is a brief overview of the major types of ports used to connect devices:

- **Serial ports** The iMac signaled the end of the serial ports. No Macs released since the release of the iMac have them. Traditionally, there are two separate serial ports, a *modem port* and a *printer port* (although some models, especially PowerBooks, just come with one port). The names give away their function: these ports are mainly used for connecting to modems and printers. They are also used for hooking up a Mac to a LocalTalk network, including "networked" printers, such as most laser printers. Despite their different names, the two ports are virtually identical and can generally be used interchangeably.

  For the iMac (and newer Macs), these functions have been taken over by the USB and/or Ethernet ports, as well as (in some Macs) by an internal modem slot.

- **Apple Desktop Bus (ADB)** Until the iMac and USB came along, this was the bus that was used to connect your keyboard and mouse. Other input devices, such as pen tablets, might also use it. Beyond that, it was not used much. Apple's blue-and-white G3 Macs still have one ADB port, as a legacy input option. With the Power Mac G4, Apple dropped the ADB port altogether.

- **Universal Serial Bus (USB)** This bus is included on the iMac and all Macs shipped since the iMac. It is used to connect the keyboard and the mouse. It is also used to connect all non-networked printers (such as most Epson Stylus Color printers). Finally, it can be used to connect any of a large variety of other peripherals, from digital cameras to scanners to Zip drives and SuperDisk drives. As a replacement for serial ports, they are much faster. As a replacement for SCSI ports, they allow more devices to be connected and are easy to work with (for example, there are no problems with connecting or disconnecting a device while the Mac is on). However, the USB port is much slower than a SCSI port, so you cannot read and write to a USB hard drive nearly as fast as a SCSI one.

  One big advantage of USB over SCSI is that USB is also popular on PCs. This means that USB devices for the PC can be easily adapted to run on a Mac. Generally, all that is needed is to create a new software driver; no hardware modifications are required. This means that cameras, joysticks and even printers designed for the PC can easily run on a Mac as well. Because SCSI was largely restricted to the Mac and required special hardware, manufacturers too often rejected a move to the Mac platform as not cost-efficient if a SCSI implementation was needed.

- **Small Computer Systems Interface (SCSI–pronounced "scuzzy")** Starting with the Macintosh Plus, and ending with the last Macs before the iMac, all models of Macintosh had a port in the rear of the machine called the *SCSI port* or *SCSI bus*. You used this port to connect most external hard drives, CD/DVD-ROM drives,

FIX-IT #14

scanners, and backup devices. You could even use it to connect a PowerBook to a desktop Mac. It was the most high-speed port available on the Mac, and thus the preferred port for all high-end non-networked devices or whenever the maximum in speed was desired.

- **Integrated Drive Electronics (IDE); also known as Advanced Technology Attachment (ATA)** IDE and ATA mean almost the same thing. IDE (ATA) was originally designed for hard disks only, not removable devices such as Zip or CD-ROM drives. To accommodate this, Advanced Technology Attachment Packet Interface (ATAPI or just ATA) was created. ATAPI devices still use the same old IDE connector. IDE was originally developed on the PC. IDE is slower but less expensive than SCSI. As such, the first Macs to employ IDE used it as a less expensive alternative to SCSI for the internal hard drive. These were the low-end (now extinct) Performa Macs. Over the years, the speed capability of IDE has improved to the point where it now rivals SCSI. As such, even high-end Macs now come with internal IDE hard drives and CD-ROM drives.

- **FireWire** If you followed along through all of this, you may have noticed that, with the demise of SCSI on Apple's newest Macs, the Mac lost its fastest external port. To replace SCSI, Apple introduced FireWire. From a troubleshooting perspective, it eliminates almost every problem that plagued SCSI: it is faster (much faster) than SCSI, you can connect as many devices as you could possibly want, there are no issues with cable length, ID numbers, and termination (as described here shortly) and you can even "hot-swap" (connect and disconnect) FireWire devices while the Mac is on. FireWire even supplies its own power source, so low power FireWire devices can work without having to be plugged into an separate wall outlet. This is clearly the wave of the future.

Cables and icons Each type of port is different and has its own cable associated with it, as well as its own icon symbol used to identify the port and cable. Figure F14-1 shows the icons for SCSI, USB and FireWire.

Figure F14-1 The FireWire (left), USB (center), and SCSI (right) icons.

SEE: • **"By the Way: SCSI Cable Connection Confusion," later in this Fix-It, for more details on the various SCSI connectors and ports.**

Problems Each type of port also has its own problems. If you have SCSI, ATA, USB, FireWire and/or ADB devices connected to your Mac, and they all work as expected, you can skip the rest of this Fix-It for now. But if anything isn't working quite right, read on. As you will soon see, problems here can often be traced to problems with how these devices are connected, what cables are used, and settings on the device itself.

Note that some of the more general advice in the SCSI section of this Fix-It also applies to other sections. For example, Iomega makes SCSI, ATA, and USB Zip drives. While some Zip issues are specific to the exact device, others will apply to all the Zip

Fix-It #14

drive variations. So no matter what type of drive you have, look over the SCSI section for possibly relevant information.

Finally, note that many of the symptoms described here (such as system crashes) have other causes besides "port" problems. These other causes are covered throughout this book, as appropriate.

BY THE WAY ▶ Other Ports in a Storm

The ports described in this Fix-It are the ones most commonly used to attach the greatest variety of peripheral devices. But they do not exhaust the list of ports you may find on your Mac. Here are the others:

Infrared "port" Some Macs also have an Infrared "port." You can use this to communicate with a variety of similarly equipped devices, including other Macs, printers and Palm PDA. The original iMacs included infrared support, but it was dropped in the Revision C models. Infrared communication is discussed in Chapter 11.

Ethernet port This port is used for hooking up a Mac to an Ethernet network. Even if you are not part of an office-wide network, you might use it to connect a networkable printer, such as a laser printer. It is much faster than, and therefore much preferred to, LocalTalk. Ethernet is covered in Chapter 11 ("Transfer Files Mac-to-Mac").

Monitor port The monitor port is where your monitor attaches to your Mac (unless you have a PowerBook or an iMac or other Mac with a "built-in" monitor). Display problems are covered in Chapter 10.

Sound ports Microphone (sound in) and headphone (sound out) ports are covered briefly in Chapter 6.

 ## What to Do:

SCSI

In the previous edition of *Sad Macs*, this Fix-It was devoted exclusively to SCSI connections. With SCSI fading from the Mac scene, I've expanded the Fix-It to include other connection technologies. Still, SCSI devices are likely to remain in use for many more years. And they are still a common source of problems. It's a good place to start out.

SCSI Basics

SCSI chain Only one device can be connected directly to a SCSI port, such as the port on the back of many Mac models. However each external SCSI device is typically equipped with two SCSI ports. So, for example, if you connect an external hard drive to a Macintosh, this will still leave one SCSI port empty on your external drive. A second SCSI device can be connected to this port. This arrangement can continue, creating a *daisy chain* of SCSI devices. If all devices are connected correctly, the Macintosh will recognize all of them, even though only one device is actually plugged into the Mac.

SCSI ID numbers Each SCSI device has an ID number. The Macintosh uses these numbers to differentiate one SCSI device from another. ID numbers can range from 0 to 7. ID 7 is reserved for the Macintosh (which, despite its number, is technically not part of the SCSI chain). ID 0 is reserved for internal hard drives (which *are* considered part of the SCSI chain).

Thus, you can attach up to *seven* SCSI devices to one Macintosh (however, see "Technically Speaking: More Than One SCSI Bus; More Than One Type of Bus" for an important exception to this). With an internal hard drive, you can connect six external SCSI devices, with ID numbers from 1 to 6.

Some Macintoshes can have more than one internal SCSI device (such as both an internal hard drive and a CD-ROM drive). Each device will have its own ID number (internal CD-ROM drives, for example, should have their ID number set to 3).

You assign the ID number to each external device. Usually, you do this by pressing a button located somewhere on the device. Each time you press the button, you cycle to another ID number, which should be indicated in a display next to the button. The number currently in the display is the ID number for that device. These ID numbers do not have to be assigned in the order that the devices are connected. For example, the first external device in a chain could have an ID of 4, and the second device could have an ID of 2.

All other things being equal, assign ID numbers based on how often you use a device, giving higher ID numbers (where six is higher than five, for example) to those external devices that you use more often. The device with the higher number is given priority when two devices are simultaneously competing for access to the SCSI bus.

The most important rule to remember is that each device must have a different ID number. To repeat: **No two devices can have the same ID number (on the same SCSI bus).** Otherwise, problems will certainly result.

TECHNICALLY SPEAKING ▶ More Than One SCSI Bus;
More Than One Type of Bus

Multiple buses Depending on the Mac model you have, your Mac may have more than one SCSI bus. In particular, many PCI-based desktop Mac models have two buses. This allows for more than seven SCSI devices to be attached to a Mac. The external port connects to one bus, while most (although not necessarily all) internal SCSI devices use the other bus. Each bus can hold up to six devices beyond the Mac itself (the Mac is listed as ID 7 on all buses). The internal SCSI bus is typically bus 0, with other buses numbered incrementally. The internal bus, although having a 7 device limit, may actually be more limited - due to the constraints of how many devices can fit inside the box.

Having multiple buses means, for example, that you can have two devices with an ID of 3, one on bus 0 and the other on bus 1. Normally this is not a problem. However some hardware has problems unless it has an ID that is not assigned to any other device on any bus. UMAX scanners have been plagued with this problem.

Note: With multiple buses, each device actually has a "long name" ID that identifies it uniquely. For example: ID 1.3.0 means Bus 1, Device 3, logical unit 0. Allowing multiple logical units for one device is rarely implemented on the Mac; don't worry much about it. If only one unit is used, it will be assigned ID 0.

(continues on next page)

FIX-IT
#14

TECHNICALLY SPEAKING ▶ More Than One SCSI Bus;
                              More Than One Type of Bus *(continued)*

For a device to work properly with a multiple bus Mac, the device must be "SCSI Manager 4.3 compliant." This refers to the Mac OS software that controls the SCSI communication. If a device is not compliant, you may (for example) have trouble assigning the same ID number to different devices even if they are on different buses.

Fast, Ultra, Narrow, Wide There are multiple variations on the SCSI standard. Each new variation is associated with increasing speed of data transfer. For example, there is Fast SCSI (which is faster than regular SCSI) and Ultra SCSI (which is faster still). There is also Wide SCSI, which is faster than Narrow SCSI. Wide vs. narrow refers to the transfer bandwidth (it's like measuring the diameter of a water hose). The Fast and Ultra types refer to the speed of the transfer (it's like the water pressure determining how fast water is pushed through the hose). Ultra-Wide is as fast as it gets–except that there are also multiple variations of a given designation (where Ultra-2, for example, is faster than ordinary Ultra).

If your Mac has more than one SCSI bus, they may be of different types. In particular, the internal bus is often faster than the external bus. To take advantage of the faster SCSI drives, you need to hook them up to a SCSI port that can carry the data at the same speed. For example, connecting a Fast/Wide drive (which can transfer data at 20MB/sec) to a port that can only carry data at 5MB/sec will defeat the advantage of the fast drive. This is one reason for getting a PCI card with a SCSI port. The card can be designed to handle faster drives than the port built in to the Mac (see also: "Take Note: Adding a SCSI Card," later in this Fix-It).

Note: A SCSI card, if you add one, is typically assigned its own bus; on Macs that do not have any built-in SCSI port, the card will likely be assigned bus 0.

SCSI Termination SCSI termination may sound like what you want to do to a drive that has just crashed for the third time this week, but it is nothing of the kind. But SCSI termination is a messy topic, so let me disentangle it for you.

I am the first to admit that I don't really know the nuts and bolts of what termination is all about. Fortunately, to fix most termination problems, you don't have to know very much.

Essentially, termination tells the Mac where a SCSI bus begins and ends, preventing signals from getting mixed up by reaching the end of a chain and bouncing back again. It is also important for keeping signal strength at an appropriate level and maintaining transmission speed at all locations across your cables. The longer your chain, the more likely it is that termination problems will appear.

That said, **the main thing you need to know is that a typical SCSI chain needs to be terminated at both ends of the chain.** Most Macintoshes with internal drives are considered terminated at the Macintosh end. In those cases, all you need to do is make sure the opposite (external device) end of the chain is terminated. The most common method to do this is to get a special SCSI plug called a terminator. It looks like an ordinary SCSI plug with no cable attached. Simply plug it in to the second (empty) port on the last SCSI device in a chain, and you are done.

If you have no external SCSI devices attached, you can skip this whole discussion. If you have two or more external SCSI devices attached, you will likely need to be concerned about termination issues.

FIX-IT
#14

Mounting SCSI Devices with SCSIProbe (or Other SCSI Utility)

A nearly essential tool when working with SCSI devices is a SCSI utility. An excellent popular (and free!) SCSI utility is SCSIProbe. I will use it for most of the examples described here. Another useful similar utility is Mt. Everything. Some hard disk formatting utilities (as described in Fix-It #13) can double as a SCSI utility. These may also include a companion control panel that functions similarly to SCSIProbe. Even Apple's Drive Setup can handle SCSIProbe's most critical mounting functions (and as a bonus, it recognizes ATA drives as well as SCSI ones).

The primary use of any SCSI utility is to mount SCSI devices. There are two common occasions when you need to do this: when you need to mount a SCSI device turned on after startup is completed and when a properly connected mountable SCSI device, turned on at startup but not the startup disk, does not mount automatically.

Bear in mind that some SCSI devices will be listed in SCSIProbe but cannot be mounted. Scanners are an example here. The scanner does not appear as a device on the desktop (such as a hard drive would). But if it is listed in SCSIProbe, it should still work when the appropriate scanner software is launched. If it doesn't, this can indicate problems with the scanner software or the SCSI connections (see "Troubleshooting SCSI," later in this Fix-It).

Also bear in mind that some hard drives, CD-ROM drives and other devices may be on an ATA bus, not a SCSI bus. SCSIProbe will not list these.

For devices that can be mounted, here's what to do:

1. Make sure the SCSI device you want to mount is turned on and the cables are securely fastened in their respective ports. SCSIProbe can recognize only devices that are turned on.

    If you are having any trouble securing a plug to a SCSI port, check for bent connecting wires on the end of the plug. If you find any, straighten them and try again. If a wire breaks off, you have to replace the cable. Remember: Only disconnect and connect cables when the Macintosh is off.

2. Open SCSIProbe. A window appears that lists every active device connected to your SCSI chain. Each device is listed next to its assigned ID number. This will help right away to identify a possible ID number conflict!

    All devices, whether mounted or not, should be listed here. SCSIProbe also lists the type of each device, such as whether it is a hard disk *(disk)* or CD-ROM *(ROM)* drive.

3. Select the desired bus. If your Mac supports multiple buses, you will need to select the correct bus before you can see your device. Do this via the pop-up menu in the SCSI Buses section at the top of the window.

    Note: If you select "Show All SCSI Information" from SCSIProbe's Preferences (the first button in the bottom row), you will get an expanded window that contains a list of "logical units" (which you can generally ignore) and a log of what SCSIProbe is doing (which can sometimes be useful to examine if something goes wrong).

Fix-It
#14

4. If the device you want to mount is not listed, click the Scan button. It's the last button in the row of buttons along the bottom of the window. This forces SCSIProbe to rescan the SCSI bus and locate any devices that it may have missed when it initially opened.

   If this still did not work, hold down the Option key and click the Scan button again. This "resets" the bus currently displayed. If there was some problem with the data transfer, this should clear it up. You can now try to scan the bus again, if needed. If even this fails, you might try restarting and zapping the PRAM (see Fix-It #9).

   Unless your device is damaged or improperly connected, it should be listed now. If not, skip ahead to "Troubleshooting SCSI problems," later in this Fix-It.

5. Highlight the name of the device you want to mount by clicking it. Then click the Mount button (it's the third one in the row). This should mount the device.

   If you hold down the Option key when clicking the Mount button, SCSIProbe tries to mount *all* devices on the bus, not just the highlighted one.

6. Close SCSIProbe. You're done.

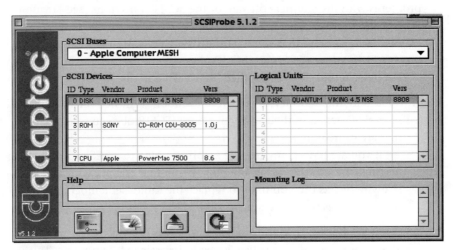

Figure F14-2 SCSIProbe's main window (this is on a Mac with dual SCSI buses; Bus 0 is displayed here).

TAKE NOTE ▶ Mounting Removable-Media Cartridges

Removable-media cartridges (such as those used with Zip and Jaz drives) present a special problem. As with fixed hard disks, each cartridge contains its own device driver, an invisible software file necessary for the Macintosh to interact with the disk (see Fix-It #12 for more on device drivers).

In many cases, there are two sources of this driver: an extension in your startup disk's System Folder and a "hidden" driver on a cartridge itself. The former source is used if there is no cartridge present at startup; the latter is used if there is a cartridge present at startup. The latter case in particular can present some special problems.

When you insert a cartridge into a removable media drive (at startup and sometimes on other occasions), its driver is copied from the disk and loaded into RAM. It is the RAM copy that is actually used. If you switch cartridges after startup, you may be switching to a cartridge that uses a different driver from the one initially present. This could happen if the cartridges were formatted using different format utilities (see Fix-It #13 for more on formatting utilities), as might especially be the case if you are using cartridges obtained from sources other than yourself.

The problem here is that, when you switch cartridges, the Macintosh may not automatically replace the RAM copy of the initial driver with the driver now needed for the newly inserted cartridge. A conflict occurs because the Macintosh attempts to use the wrong driver (the one from the previous cartridge) to interact with the current cartridge. This can cause various problems, including an inability to mount the cartridge or a loss of data from the cartridge. The simplest solution to this problem is to make sure that all of your cartridges use the same driver.

To do this with Iomega drives, open the Iomega Drive Options control panel and select Advanced Options from the Special menu. Select either "Update the driver on the disk only when it is older" or "Always update the driver on the disk," as appropriate. These will force a copy of a driver on a cartridge to be updated to match the version in the startup disk's System Folder (either always or only if the driver on the cartridge is older). This is normally a good idea.

If you formatted a Jaz/Zip cartridge with something other than Iomega's software, the formatting software may include an option to set the driver to mount a cartridge automatically when inserted after startup. If this option is not enabled, the cartridge will not mount when inserted. If this happens, use a utility such as SCSIProbe to mount the cartridge.

Finally, you can mount an Iomega cartridge by attaching a Iomega drive to a computer, even if you have not installed the Iomega driver in the System Folder. This is useful if you just want to attach the drive on a friend's computer to transfer some data. To do this, you use the Iomega Guest application. Alternatively, if you simply restart with the Zip drive attached and the cartridge inserted, it should mount automatically. You can also use Guest to mount a cartridge inserted after starting up with extensions disabled (which of course would include the Iomega driver extension).

SEE : • Chapter 5, "Special Case: Problems Mounting Removable Media Cartridges" in the "A Hard Disk Won't Mount" section, for more discussion of these problems.
        • "By The Way: Removable Cartridge Drives: Drivers And Extensions," in Fix-It #12.
        • "Formatting Iomega (Zip/Jaz) Disks (and the 'Click of Death')," in Fix-It #13.

**FIX-IT
#14**

TAKE NOTE ▶ Mounting CD-ROM Discs

SCSIProbe may not work to mount a device if a separate driver needed to be mounted at startup and was not. For example, it will not work for a CD-ROM drive if the Apple CD-ROM extension did not load at startup. If this happens, you need to restart with the CD-ROM extensions enabled. **Note:** If you have an external drive, the extension will not load at startup, even if it is enabled, unless the drive is turned on prior to startup.

SCSIProbe may also not work to mount a device if the device driver extension is corrupted or needs to be updated to work with new hardware or Mac OS software. Thus, if problems persist, make sure you have the latest version of the driver, reinstall it, and make sure it loads at startup.

Also, some nonstandard format CD-ROM discs, such as PhotoCD discs, will not mount unless additional extensions are also installed (such as Apple's Apple Photo Access and Foreign File Access extensions). Check your CD-ROM drive's manual for more details.

As described in Chapters 1 and 5, some CD-ROM discs (with system software on them) can act as startup discs. This ability may still strike you as involving a paradox: for a CD-ROM disc to boot at startup, it must load before the supposedly required CD-ROM driver extension has loaded. How can this be? The answer is that, in addition to the required System Folder being on the disc, these CD-ROM discs have special instructions, presumably in the boot blocks, that allow the Mac to mount them as startup discs. These same invisible instructions are what let the CD act as a startup disk even when booting with Extensions Off.

One tip: if you are having problems with an application that is unable to use files from a CD-ROM disc that is in a nonstandard format and you have the needed extensions installed, hold down the Option key when you insert the disc and keep it held down until the disc mounts. This should solve the problem.

And one more tip: with today's large hard drives, it is even possible to create a disk image (using Disk Copy) of an entire CD. You can then mount the disk image exactly as if it were the CD itself.

SEE: • **Chapter 5 for more on problems mounting and ejecting CD-ROM discs.**

TAKE NOTE ▶ Disks That Don't Automatically Mount at Startup

If you are using an internal hard drive as your startup disk, any external drive that is turned on at startup should mount automatically as a secondary drive. That is, when startup is completed, its icon should appear on your desktop. However, a hard drive needs time to warm up before the Macintosh can detect its presence. If you turn on the external drive too late (such as after the Macintosh is already on and startup has begun), the Macintosh may check for external SCSI devices before the drive is sufficiently warmed up. In this case, the external drive is passed over and does not mount.

Similarly, if the external drive is your default startup disk (as selected by the Startup Disk control panel), and you turn it on too late, the Macintosh will start from its internal drive instead (assuming there is an internal drive and it has a System Folder on it). Again, in such cases, the external drive may not mount at all. SCSI utilities, such as SCSIProbe, are not essential to solving this type of problem. However, they are usually the most convenient solution.

In some cases, especially with most recent versions of the system software, an external disk may mount even if it warms up too late to be recognized by the Macintosh at its first startup check. This is because the Mac makes a second check later in the startup process. However, the effect of these checks may not be identical. For example, I noted that when mounted via the second check, the custom icon for my disk was absent.

FIX-IT #14

(continues on next page)

To solve the immediate problem of a disk that does not automatically mount at startup, try one of the following:

- **Restart the Macintosh.** Assuming they are all turned on, the hard drive(s) will now mount correctly. This is the only solution for an incorrect startup disk selection.

- **Mount the disk manually with a utility such as SCSIProbe** (as described earlier in this Fix-It). Even if you think the drive had sufficient time to warm up and should have mounted automatically at startup, try using SCSIProbe now. There may have been a one-time glitch. If SCSIProbe mounts the drive, chances are that the next time you restart, the drive will mount automatically as expected. To prevent this problem from recurring, do either of the following.

- **Remember to turn the drive on at least several seconds before turning on the Macintosh.** This gives the drive enough time to warm up. By the way, if a disk fails to mount even when you gave it sufficient time to warm up, it may be that you are using a disk-formatting utility that has an option (typically called "auto-mount") to turn on or off automatic mounting of a drive. With this option set to off, the drive will only mount manually after startup is over. The solution is to make sure this option is on. Launch your disk-formatting utility or its companion control panel to check.

- **Use a special option available with SCSIProbe called** *Mount SCSI Volumes During Startup.* Select this from the SCSIProbe Preferences window (accessed by clicking the first button in the bottom row of SCSIProbe's main window). This causes SCSI devices to mount during the time when extensions load at startup. This is significantly later in the startup sequence than when the Macintosh first checks for the presence of SCSI devices. As a result, SCSIProbe recognizes and mounts SCSI devices that are turned on but were skipped over by the Macintosh's initial check. Usually, this is late enough for a hard drive to be detected even if it was not turned on until *after* the Macintosh was turned on. This option is useful only for mounting drives as secondary drives. It does not switch startup disks.

    Conflict Catcher also has a "Mount all disks at startup" Preference.

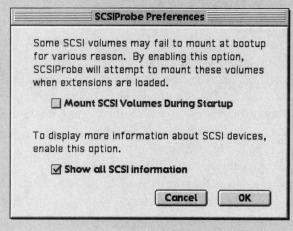

Figure F14-3 SCSIProbe's Preferences window.

BY THE WAY ▶ **Switching Startup Disks at Startup**

As discussed at several points in this book, if you hold down the Command-Option-Shift-Delete keys at startup, the Macintosh bypasses the internal hard drive and instead uses an external hard drive as the startup disk, assuming one is available. It does this regardless of the setting in the Startup Disk control panel. Although it is most often used to bypass an internal drive that is crashing at startup, it is also a useful shortcut technique for switching startup disks even if there is no problem with the internal drive. The only inconvenience of this method is that the internal drive may not be mounted during startup. Its icon is absent from the desktop when startup is completed.

However, with SCSIProbe installed on your external drive and its Mount SCSI Volumes During Startup option selected, the bypassed internal drive does mount automatically as a secondary drive at startup.

As another alternative, Conflict Catcher, if accessed at startup, has an option to switch the assigned startup disk and immediately restart.

With Apple's newest Macs, you can also select a startup disk by holding down the Option key at startup. This will bring up a window from which you can select the desired startup disk.

SEE: • **Chapter 5 for more on selecting a startup disk.**
• **Chapter 14 for more on Open Firmware and startup.**

Troubleshooting SCSI-Related Problems

If you are having any problems with SCSI devices, from a device that will not mount (or be recognized by the software designed to work with it) to system crashes (especially "bus errors") at startup due to SCSI problems, here is a brief "checklist" of what to do:

General advice Always shut off the Macintosh and all SCSI devices before disconnecting or reconnecting any SCSI devices. Otherwise, you could damage your hardware. Restart after each change to test its effect.

In general, turn on all devices on a SCSI chain before turning on your Mac.

If you decide to turn off a mounted SCSI device while the Mac is running (which I would advise against), absolutely make sure you unmount the device before turning it off. That is, drag the device's icon to the Trash or use the Finder's Put Away command to unmount it. Trying to access the icon of an unmounted device is asking for a system crash.

If your problem remains, the next logical diagnostic step is to disconnect the SCSI chain from the Macintosh. To do this, simply shut off all devices and unplug the cord that connects the first device in the chain to the rear of the Macintosh. Restart.

If the problem persists, it is probably not a SCSI problem. You can reconnect your SCSI chain and look elsewhere. System software problems loom likely. Check Chapter 5 for a general overview of possible causes.

If the problem vanishes when the chain is disconnected, a SCSI problem is the likely cause. Although the precise problem may be due to a damaged SCSI device, it is more likely a problem with how the SCSI devices are connected (cables, ID numbers, or termination). At this point, dealing with SCSI problems becomes something of a black art. However, most problems will be solved by the following steps:

FIX-IT
#14

- **Make sure no two SCSI devices have the same ID number** If two or more SCSI devices on the chain have the same ID number, you have an ID conflict. If one of the conflicting devices is a hard drive, a possible symptom is the appearance of multiple copies of the disk icon scattered across the desktop. System freezes and crashes are likely to follow. Loss of data on your disk is a real risk. In other cases, the device simply does not mount. In any case, correct this problem immediately!

    1. Turn off your Macintosh and all SCSI devices.

    2. Check each device's ID number by examining the location on the device where the number is listed. If you cannot locate it, check the device's manual to learn where its ID number is listed.

    3. If you find a conflict, change the ID number to correct it. Remember, all external devices should have numbers between 1 and 6. (However, in certain odd cases, where a SCSI device is connected to the USB port of a Mac via a SCSI-to-USB adapter, changing the ID of the device to zero (0) allowed the device to mount.)

    4. Reconnect SCSI devices to the Macintosh (if necessary) and restart the Macintosh.

    Remember to consider the ID number of any internal SCSI devices, beyond the internal hard drive, that may be present. For example, an external device cannot use the same ID number as used for an internal CD-ROM drive (typically 3) if the two devices are on the same bus.

    While the Macintosh is on, a utility such as SCSIProbe should be able to tell you what these ID numbers are. However don't rely on it to show an ID conflict, as it may get too confused by the conflict to sort things out. You can use SCSIProbe when you are done with your ID changes to confirm that all is now well. SCSIProbe lists the ID location of each mounted device. If each device has a unique ID number, the conflict is probably resolved.

    Another way to see a SCSI device's ID number, if it is a device that mounts on the desktop, is to select the desktop icon for the device and then select Get Info. The Where listing often (though not always!) lists the device's ID number.

- **Make sure all SCSI devices are properly terminated** Improper termination may leave you unable to access any of the SCSI devices in your chain. However it does no permanent harm to your hardware. Correctly adjusting the termination should get things working again.

    As explained earlier in this Fix-It, the last device in an external SCSI chain should be terminated. Sometimes the first external device also needs to be terminated. Generally, no other external SCSI devices should be terminated. If your chain is not set up this way, you should add or remove termination as appropriate.

    In reality, these rules are often broken. In particular, for short chains (one or two devices with short-length cable), the system may work even without a terminator at the end of the chain (even if your Mac's manual says one is needed). For long chains, a third terminator in the middle of the chain may be required.

FIX-IT
#14

(Fortunately, in this regard, most external terminators have an outlet on their rear side where another cable can be plugged in, thereby permitting the chain to continue beyond the termination point.) So experiment. If you are having problems that you think may be solved by adding or removing a terminator, try it. Some people may warn you against this, fearing that turning on an improperly terminated system can permanently harm your hardware, but I have never found that to be the case.

Note: Some SCSI devices include a feature called Digital Active Termination (DAT) which attempts to adjust the termination on a chain, as needed - eliminating the need for you to fiddle with it. It may even allow you to connect or disconnect SCSI devices without having to worry about first shutting the power off. But don't trust this to be 100 percent effective. Following the advice here is still a good idea.

- **Reconnect, rearrange and/or switch** If the previous solutions have failed to solve your SCSI problem, it's time to delve still deeper into the black art of SCSI problem solving. For example, if you have more than one external SCSI device, try reconnecting them one at a time. If necessary, remove and reconnect them in various combinations (such as only Device 1 connected, then only Device 2 connected, then both connected). Also rearrange the order in which devices are connected along the chain (such as Device 1 followed by Device 2, and then reverse the order). For obscure reasons, a device may work if it is earlier in the chain than another device but not later in the chain (or vice versa).

  Try switching cables and/or ID numbers, even if nothing seems wrong with them. This sometimes helps. Using a shorter, high-quality cable may solve a problem caused by a longer low-quality one.

BY THE WAY ▶ SCSI Cable Connection Confusion

If you start rearranging or disconnecting SCSI devices, or whenever you add a new SCSI device, you may find that you do not have the proper cables to accomplish your goal. This is because there are several types of SCSI ports and connectors.

Traditionally, the most common types of ports are a 25-pin port on the back of the Mac (and on some SCSI devices) and a large 50-pin port on many external SCSI devices. Thus, to attach a typical external drive to a Macintosh, you would need a cable with a 25-pin connector on one end and a 50-pin connector on the other end. As you add devices, however, you may find that you need cables with a 50-pin connector on both ends or a 25-pin plug on both ends.

More recently, the SCSI cards that are now often installed in G3 and G4 Macs (i.e., the Macs that do not have an SCSI port built-in) have either a 50-pin "Ultra Narrow SCSI" port or a 68-pin "VHDCI" port (this latter port is used mainly with high speed "SCSI-3" connections). To use these ports with older cables, you will need an adapter plug to convert the cable's connector from one type to the other.

None of these cables will work directly with most PowerBook SCSI ports, which have an altogether different 30-pin squarish SCSI outlet, requiring a special matching cable! In fact, as explained in Chapter 11, there are two variations of this cable, depending upon whether you want to attach a drive or use the PowerBook in "target mode."

**Fix-It
#14**

TAKE NOTE ▶ The Write Cache Problem and Data Corruption

There is a problem that can occur with hard drives whereby the disk data may occasionally get corrupted at the time of shutdown. This should only happen if the drive is an internal drive stored on bus 0 (which is certainly the bus where your drive will be if you only have one internal drive) and is set to be your startup drive.

The problem is due to what is called a *write cache*. With a write cache, the drive instructs the Mac to hold data in an area of RAM (reserved for the cache) with the intention that it be written to the disk later, presumably at a time when the Mac and the drive are less busy. This results in faster access times for the drive. When you select to shut down your Mac, any data currently in the cache and not yet written to the disk is of course written to disk before the Mac actually shuts down. At least, it is supposed to do that.

What can mistakenly happen is that the Mac fails to recognize the action of the write-cache operation. In this case, the write-cache may sometimes still be writing data to the drive from the RAM buffer at the time the Mac shuts off. The result is that some data is only partially written to the drive so that the data winds up being corrupted. This is most likely to affect your Directory files, which may in turn lead to problems starting up or mounting the drive on your next restart.

Most current drivers have been updated to prevent this, although they may not always succeed. If you suspect this problem, your formatting utility may have "Disable write cache" as an option. Try this. It will slow down your drive's performance, but decrease the chance of a write cache problem.

Hardware damage? In the end, you may find that nothing works. At best, you may find that your SCSI chain only works with one or more devices removed from the chain. In these cases, if a device is a hard drive, try repairing its Directory via a utility such as Disk First Aid (see Fix-It #10). If that fails, reformat the drive. Otherwise, you likely need a hardware repair, either for the SCSI device or the Mac itself.

TAKE NOTE ▶ Add a SCSI Card

Apple's latest Macs no longer include a SCSI external port connected to the logic board. So what do you do if you have an external SCSI device (such as a scanner or a hard drive) that you still want to use? The answer is: get a SCSI card. These cards can even be used on Macs that already have a built-in SCSI port. The cards plug into one the Mac's PCI slots (see Fix-It #15) and add a SCSI port to the back of the machine (typically also adding another SCSI bus, if you add one of these cards to a Mac that already has an SCSI port).

Note: The iMac does not have any PCI slots. However, the Revision A and Revision B (Bondi Blue) versions of the iMac included an unsupported slot, called the Mezzanine slot. Apple didn't want people to use it (apparently, Apple intended to use it at some point but then changed its mind). Apple eliminated the port altogether in the 5-colored (and newer) iMacs. But if you have one of the original iMacs, third party developers have created SCSI cards that go in the Mezzanine slot.

(continues on next page)

FIX-IT #14

TAKE NOTE ▶ Add a SCSI Card *(continued)*

Once you get a SCSI card, your problems may not be over. Here's what to watch out for:

- If you want to start up from an external SCSI drive, the SCSI card needs to be Open Firmware aware (see Chapter 14 for more on Open Firmware). This is needed so that the Mac can check devices attached to the card early enough in the startup sequence to use them as a startup disk. Otherwise, the device may mount without a problem, but cannot be used as a startup device. If you need this feature (for example, if you have a SCSI Jaz drive, and want to use it as the startup drive on occasion), make sure your SCSI card is "bootable." If it is not, it is possible that the card vendor has released a "firmware" update that fixes this problem. Check the vendor's Web site for help on this. Firmware updaters change the code in the ROM of the card, sometimes irreversibly.

  In order to be bootable, some devices may also need their drivers updated.

- Some cards may also support internal SCSI connections. This is useful if you want to add an internal SCSI drive to a Power Mac G4, for example.

- Some SCSI devices do not work at all via a SCSI card. Apple's own Apple Color One Scanner falls into this category. Iomega drives had problems initially, although their latest drivers seem to work well. Some devices may only work with certain SCSI cards. For example, at first, UMAX recommended only the Adaptec 2906 and 2930U cards for use with their scanners.

  Software updates can often fix these problems. For example, a software update to UMAX's MagicScan and VistaScan software did address most of the scanner-related problems. Firmware updates to the SCSI card itself fix other problems.

  For the OneScanner problem, Apple released an update to the OneScanner driver. To get it to work, they further advised: "Place the latest version of the SCSI Probe control panel (available from Adaptec's Web site) in your Control Panels folder, open it, select Preferences, and choose to "Mount SCSI volumes during startup." Place version 4.3 of the scanner extension in your System Folder (not in the Extensions folder or any other folder within your System Folder)."

- In some cases, problems are due to the fact that the device expects to connect via SCSI Bus 0, while the SCSI card uses another bus. As a result, the scanner software does not "see" the scanner. There may also be problems related to what SCSI ID may be assigned to the device. This is generally because the SCSI device (not the card) is not SCSI Manager 4.3 compliant, which means that the device cannot recognize that there is more than one SCSI bus in use. In this case, problems will develop if two devices have the same ID number, even if they are on different buses.

- SCSI cards vary in terms of the speed of their bus. For example, some may support only Ultra, while others support Ultra-2. Some may support Wide drives, while others only support Narrow.

  Of course, all of this is true for SCSI devices and/or SCSI cards used with older Macs as well—not just the newer G3 and G4 Macs. In fact, it is precisely because the SCSI port in many older Macs is a slow narrow one that power users have added SCSI cards even to Macs that already have a SCSI port. Thus, if your Mac's bus is narrow, and you want the speed boost of a wide bus, adding a SCSI card will accomplish this.

  However, remember: to take full advantage of this speed boost, make sure the device itself is of the same type. For example, if you have an Ultra-Wide bus, connect only an Ultra-Wide hard drive to it. An Ultra Wide SCSI-3 chain can transfer data at up to 40 MB per second.

- Different types of SCSI devices connected to a SCSI channel operate only as fast as the slowest device on the chain. For example, an SCSI-2 (10MBps) tape drive and an SCSI-1 (5MBps) hard disk on the same SCSI channel will both operate at 5MBps.

FIX-IT #14

TAKE NOTE ▶ Booting from Devices Connected to Ports

As mentioned in the preceding Take Note, you can boot from SCSI devices connected to newer G3 and G4 Macs via a SCSI card - if the card is Open Firmware aware and the device's firmware is similarly compatible with booting from SCSI card connections.

As also covered elsewhere in this book. you can boot via drives connected to the USB ports of newer Macs (such as the G4 and the iMac DV).

With Macs that use the Unified Macintosh Architecture chipset and Boot ROM version 3.22f1 or later, you can now also boot from a FireWire hard drive. These Macs include the latest Power Mac G4 models and the PowerBook (FireWire).

All of this assumes that the USB or FireWire driver used by the hard drive supports booting from the device.

Finally, if you are connected to a Mac running Mac OS X Server, you might be able to "NetBoot." This is a new option that allows you to startup from a System Folder on the server, rather than on your local Mac. This should prove to be a boon for server administrators. No longer will you have to update the System Folder of the fifty Macs connected to your network. Instead all users will share the one on the server. The user simply holds down the N key at startup to access the Net-Boot option. (See also Chapter 15 for more on NetBooting.)

TAKE NOTE ▶ Port "Switching" wIth Adapters and Cards

With the demise of SCSI, ADB and serial ports, owners of newer Macs have looked for ways to connect their legacy devices to these new machines. Conversely, owners of older Macs are sometimes interested in using a device that requires the newer USB and FireWire ports. To meet these needs, third party vendors have produced a wide assortment of adapters and cards. Among the most popular vendors for these adapters and cards are Newer Technology, Farallon, Asanté, Microtech, and Keyspan. Here are some examples:

- To hook up SCSI devices to newer Macs, install a SCSI card in your Mac's PCI slot (as discussed more in "Take Note: Add A SCSI Card," elsewhere in this Fix-It). For iMacs (which do not have PCI cards), you can get a SCSI-to-USB adapter. However, using an adapter means that the speed of your SCSI device will slow to the speed of the USB port. Also, many especially older SCSI devices are incompatible with these adapters and/or the USB driver software.

- To hook up serial devices to new Macs, you can get a serial-to-USB adapter or (if your Mac has PCI slots) get a PCI card with serial ports. However, if you want the serial port for making a LocalTalk serial connection (such as for older networked printers that do not support Ethernet), these devices will not work. In this case, you may be able to use Farallon's iPrint, which allows you to connect a LocalTalk serial device to an Ethernet network. Not all serial devices will work with these adapters. Before making a purchase, make sure you can return the device if it fails to work.

- To use ADB devices on newer Macs, try Griffin's iMate Mini-ADB adapter.

- To hook up USB devices to older Macs, you can get a USB (PCI) adapter card. To use them, you will need Apple's USB Adapter Card Support software. Similar options now exist for FireWire as well.

FIX-IT #14

ATA/IDE

ATA buses generally have many fewer problems than SCSI ones. Still, in case things do go wrong, here's what you should know:

- **ATA channels: slave and master** A Mac typically supports up to two ATA "channels": a primary and a secondary channel. Some Power Macintosh G3 models and all Power Mac G4 computers can have two ATA/IDE devices on the same ATA/IDE channel. One device is called the *master* while the other is called the *slave.* The internal hard drive is almost always the master device on the primary channel. In fact, only the master device can serve as a startup disk. Beyond this, the master device does not have any special status compared to the slave. The slave device does not rely on the master device in any way.

  A second hard drive, an internal CD-ROM drive and/or a Zip drive can be on almost any other combination of the remaining locations (although the Zip drive will usually be on the secondary channel). Thus, these Macs could support up to four ATA devices. These are all internal devices; there is no external ATA connection.

  Normally, you need not worry about any of this, especially if all of these ATA devices came pre-installed on your Mac. But if you start installing ATA devices yourself, it can be a concern. In particular, a device that works well as a slave may not work well as a master, or vice versa. You may also need to get into adjusting the jumpers on the device itself. This gets beyond the scope of *Sad Macs.* However, details should be included with the manual that comes with the device. Iomega, in particular, has a great technical manual that comes with its internal Zip drive.

  Another concern: for an ATA drive to work with a Mac, the manufacturer needs to configure it in a certain way—a way that is not done for all ATA drives (because ATA drives are also used with PC machines where some of these specifications are not needed). So before you buy an ATA drive, check with the vendor to make sure it is Mac-compatible.

  ATA channels can be of different speeds, much like SCSI buses. For example, your Power Mac could have a fast Ultra ATA bus, used for the hard drive, and a slower, standard one used for the CD-ROM drive.

- **Mounting and using ATA Drives** SCSI utilities, such as SCSIProbe, do not list ATA devices. If you have an internal ATA hard drive or CD-ROM drive, don't be surprised when they appear to be missing. They will still show up in Apple System Profiler, although this cannot mount a drive. However, any formatting utility that has been updated to work with ATA drives (and this includes Drive Setup) can be used to mount any ATA drive. For Drive Setup, just highlight the drive and select the "Mount Volumes" command from the Functions menu. Similarly, Iomega Tools can be used to mount ATA (and even USB) Zip and Jaz cartridges.

  If you just want to view a list of all your SCSI and ATA devices, what bus/channel they are on, and whether or not ATA devices are slave or master devices, another useful utility is Intech Software's freeware Peripheral View.

Fix-It #14

In general, make sure you have the latest driver software for each device, as they fix problems with older versions. For example, some first-generation Power Macintosh G3 computers came with an ATAPI internal Zip drive. You could not start up from a Zip cartridge in this drive unless you updated to version 6.0 or later of the Iomega driver. The driver had to be installed on the cartridge itself. You can also use Iomega Tools to mount cartridges in ATA (and even USB) drives.

FireWire

FireWire is the name Apple uses for a technology that is also called IEEE 1394 or i.Link. Whatever it's called, it's incredibly fast (in excess of 50 or even 100 MB per second). As I write this, FireWire is still too new and untested for much troubleshooting advice to be known. Still, here are a couple of points to keep in mind:

- **Check FireWire connectors** There are 4-pin and 6-pin FireWire connectors. Macs only accept the 6-pin connector. Other devices (such as digital cameras) may use the 4-pin. You will need a cable that has the correct connector on both ends.

   Not all digital camcorders work with FireWire (and/or with applications that use FireWire, such as Final Cut Pro). An Apple Web page <http://www.apple.com/finalcutpro/techspecs/qualification.html> provides a list of what works and what does not.

- **Check FireWire drivers** Using FireWire depends upon having Apple's FireWire driver extensions (e.g., FireWire Enabler and FireWire Support) installed in the System Folder. If you are using FireWire to download from a digital video camera, you will also need DV Enabler and DV Support. Devices attached to the FireWire port will likely require additional separate FireWire-specific drivers.

   In some cases, these drivers conflict with other software. At least with the early versions of these drivers, users reported that disabling these extensions solved certain problems starting up the Mac and/or using the ATI Rage 128 extensions on the blue-and-white G3 Macs. Disabling these extensions is fine only if you do not plan to add any FireWire peripherals.

   Similarly, older versions of these drivers may cause a startup crash when installed with a newer version of the OS. For example, Mac OS 9.0.4 installs version 2.3.3 of these files. If (perhaps due to a third party installer), you instead wind up with version 2.1, your Mac will crash at startup. Even worse, these extensions load even if you startup with Extensions Off (by holding down the Shift key at startup). Thus, to access the drive and remove the problem extensions, you will need to startup from a bootable CD or similar emergency startup disk.

- **Unmount before hot-swapping** Although you can hot-swap FireWire devices (that is, disconnect and reconnect them while the Mac is running), be sure you unmount a FireWire hard drive (on the Finder's desktop) before disconnecting the drive from the FireWire chain. Do this by dragging the icon of the drive to the Trash.

Fix-It #14

Certainly do not disconnect a FireWire device while it is in use, such as disconnecting a hard drive while data is being written to it.

- **If a FireWire device does not work as expected, try the following (in order):**

  1. Disconnect and reconnect the device.

  2. Turn the device off and back on.

  3. Restart the Mac.

  4. Make sure all software that came with the device is installed.

  5. Try switching to the other FireWire port on the Mac. If you have multiple devices connected to one port, try moving the device to the other port by itself.

  6. If the device is self-powered, consider getting a powered FireWire hub and connecting the device to the hub.

  7. Some of the advice for USB troubleshooting (described next) may apply for FireWire as well. Read on and see.

USB

USB, although simpler to use than SCSI, is far from problem-free. If you are having trouble getting a device connected to the USB port to work, consider the following:

- **Check for power** If the device has a separate on/off switch, make sure it is on. If the device has a separate power supply, make sure it is plugged in. If a USB device does not work at first, give it several minutes to warm up.

- **"Not enough power" errors: use a powered hub for multiple devices** If you are going to add several USB devices, consider getting a USB hub. This may even be required if you have USB devices that only have a single port (thereby preventing you from chaining additional devices to them). Because the USB port supplies its own power, the hub need not have a separate power supply. However a powered hub is recommended, as it will minimize problems that may occur due to a device not getting sufficient power. This is especially likely to be the cure if you get a message that says: *The device can't operate because it needs more power than is available* or *The device may not provide all of its functions because it requires more power.*

    Sometimes, this error may be due to a bug in the Mac OS ROM file software. Upgrading (or downgrading, if you are already using the latest version) to a different version of the ROM file may eliminate the error.

**Fix-It
#14**

- **Failure to shut down? Check if it's caused by a USB hub or other USB device** If you select the Shut Down command and your Mac restarts instead of shutting down, this could be due to a USB device connected to your Mac. This happens most often with USB hubs. Sometimes zapping the PRAM (see Fix-It #9) or doing a clean install of the system software (see Fix-It #4) will fix this. Otherwise, the solution will likely require fixing or replacing the problem USB device.

- **Reconnect and/or switch cables (especially for startup and shut down problems)**
  Try disconnecting and reconnecting the suspected problem device to its USB port. Also try switching ports on the Mac itself. That is, move the cable from USB Port 1 to USB Port 2 (or vice versa).

  Note: There are two types of USB ports (Type A, as found on the Mac, and Type B, as used on many external devices). To connect a USB device to your Mac, you will need a cable with the matching connectors on each end.

  USB devices have been implicated in some wake-from-sleep crashes (see Chapter 14), as well as various startup and/or shut down freezes. The usual work-around is to disconnect or power down the problem USB device before taking the action that triggers the freeze (e.g., disconnect the USB device before starting up and then reconnect the device when startup is over). The permanent fix typically requires getting updated versions of relevant USB driver software (either from Apple or from the vendor of the problem device). If you get a wake-from-sleep freeze, you can often regain control of the Mac via a Force Quit (Command-Option-Escape); restarting the Mac is not typically required (see Chapter 4 for more on freezes).

  More generally, turning a USB device on before you start up may solve some problems. Other times, turning it on only after the startup sequence is over may be what is needed to succeed. Not totally unlike SCSI, there is a bit of "voodoo" developing here as to what will or will not work.

- **"No driver found" error: check for USB software** USB devices often ship with their own driver software, needed for the device to work. These drivers are installed in the Extensions folder. Make sure they are installed. The Mac OS will generate a *No Driver Found* message if the Mac checked for a driver for the USB device you just connected but could not find one. Install (or re-install) the driver as needed.

  Apple now includes a set of USB drivers with the Mac OS. They have names such as USB Support, USB Device Extension, USBPrintDriver, and USB Mass Storage. In many cases, these files can serve as substitutes for the device-specific USB drivers that ship with a device. So if you are having problems getting the Mac to recognize a USB device, try removing its driver software from the Extensions folder. Surprisingly, this might be the solution!

  Note: Some of these USB files are built-in to the latest versions of the Mac OS ROM file, so you may have them installed even though you do not see their names in the Extensions folder.

- **Use Apple System Profiler: disable drivers as needed** One way to check for a possible problem with a USB device is to use Apple System Profiler. Select its "Devices and Volumes" tab. If a USB device is currently recognized by the Mac as properly connected, it will be listed there. If not, it typically means either that the needed software driver is not installed or there is a hardware-related problem. For example, it may mean that you need to separately connect the device to a powered USB hub rather than to a chain of USB devices connected to the Mac's USB port.

  If the device is shown in the Apple System Profiler, but does not work, it most often means a problem with the device's USB driver. You either need to update to a

Fix-It #14

newer version of the driver, eliminate the driver (in favor of using Apple's default drivers), or resolve a conflict with another USB driver.

For example, I could not get my SuperDisk drive to work after updating to Mac OS 9. The solution was to delete the SuperDisk drivers installed by the SuperDisk Installer and go with the Mac OS 9's "built-in" drivers. Later, I once again could not get the SuperDisk drive to work. This time, I discovered the problem was the Olympus USB SmartMedia card reader drivers that I had just installed. If I deleted them, the SuperDisk worked. With such conflicts, you may be able to fix things by switching the loading order of the drivers (assuming that there are drivers for each device in the Extensions folder; sometimes the driver is instead built in to the Mac OS software). Otherwise, you will simply have to enable and disable the relevant drivers (and likely restart) each time you need to switch to use a given device.

SEE: • **"Take Note: Booting From Devices Connected To Ports," earlier in this chapter, for information about starting up from a USB drive.**

- **Check for Apple updates**

   USB drivers Apple continues to update its USB drivers. There may be a newer version than the one you are using that fixes a problem you are now having. Check on Apple's Web site for updates (or, if you are using Mac OS 9, you can use Apple's Software Update control panel).

   InputSprockets If you are using your Mac to play games, and especially if you are connecting USB peripheral devices (such as a game pad or joystick), also be certain to get Apple's latest InputSprockets files: USBHIDUniversalModule and a collection of extensions that all begin with the word InputSprockets. One version of these files should be included on your Mac OS system software CD and were probably already installed on your hard drive when it first arrived. However, Apple's Web site may have newer versions.

   Other updates For example, in late 1998 Apple released iMac Update 1.1. Apple stated that it "improves the iMac's ability to identify USB devices when starting up, improves the startup time when many USB devices are connected, and enables new USB solutions." The update was simply a replacement for the Mac OS ROM file in the System Folder, presumably with updated USB-related code. Apple will likely have further updates along these lines.

- **Special problems with USB printers** Even if the device is connected correctly and drivers are installed, you may get one or more of the following problems:

   - An alert may occur during startup stating that the software needed to use the device could not be found.

   - An alert that AppleTalk is active and the serial port is in use may occur after selecting the printer icon in the Chooser.

   - A -192 error (resource not found) may occur when trying to print

   - The printer may not appear at all in the Chooser.

   - The printer may refuse to print for various other unspecfied reasons.

In all of these cases, the problem is usually traced to the printer driver software or the Apple firmware. In particular, make sure you are using the latest versions of the driver software and especially make sure it is a USB-specific version of the driver. The same printer may have a serial-port version of the driver. This driver will not work with a USB version of the printer.

- **USB modem** If you have an external USB-connected modem, the Modem control panel should list the USB modem as a new option in its "Connect via" pop-up menu. This is what you should select.

- **Try general troubleshooting** Beyond this, if your problem has not been solved, it's time for more general troubleshooting, such as checking for an extensions conflict.

BY THE WAY ▶ Why Your USB- or Firewire-Connected Drive is Not as Fast as You Think It Should Be

The data transfer speed of a given USB or FireWire hard drive will likely not match the quoted maximum possible speeds for its respective port. Here are some reasons why:

- Using a SCSI-to-USB adapter, it is possible to add a SCSI drive to a USB port. However, its speed will be limited by the speed of the USB port, which is much slower than the drive would be if connected to a SCSI port.

- Some USB drives come formatted for DOS. While you may be able to use these, you will generally get better performance if you reformat them for the Mac OS. Use Erase Disk to do this (as described more in Fix-It #11).

- Both USB and FireWire can operate at different speeds. For example, USB has a low-speed (1.5 Megabits per second maximum) and high-speed (12 Mbps maximum) data transfer rate. The maximum speed is an inherent characteristic of each device; it is not determined by the Mac. Thus a 1.5Mbps USB hard drive is not capable of attaining the speed of a 12Mbps drive, even though both are connected to the same USB port of the same Mac. By the way, the maximum speed of FireWire is 400 Mbps; this means that even the fastest USB drive will never come close to matching a fast FireWire drive.

    However, USB 2.0 is a new USB standard that will eventually replace the current implementation of USB. It promises to be faster than FireWire. Still, USB 2.0 is not likely to spell the end of FireWire. FireWire will remain preferred for certain uses, such as connecting to digital camcorders. No Macs support USB 2.0 as of this writing.

- If you have multiple devices connected to a single port, the speed of devices at the distant end of the chain can be no faster than the fastest device between itself and the Mac. Thus, connect devices to the chain such that the slowest devices are furthest away from the Mac.

- There is a native mode for FireWire hard drives. This mode is needed for FireWire drives to realize FireWire's promised throughput speeds. However, as of this writing, no native FireWire drives exist. All FireWire drives are actually ATA drives with a ATA-to-FireWire adapter card built-in to the unit. Thus, they will not really be much faster than ATA drives. By 2001, native FireWire drives should be on the market.

Fix-It #14

ADB: Keyboard and Mouse/Trackball/TrackPad

This section covers problems with the ADB port and the common devices (mouse and keyboard) connected to this port. This is mainly for the benefit of those users with older Macs that still have these ports. Some of the information, such as for cleaning a mouse, may also apply to USB versions of these devices.

- **Keyboard cable** If you are having problems with your keyboard, check the cable before you assume it is a hardware problem with the keyboard itself. To do this, try using a different cable (assuming you have one). If the problem disappears when you switch cables, simply replace your original cable with a new one.

- **ADB ports** Many models of Macintosh have two ADB ports. One, but not the other, may be defective. Try switching cables to see if only one port is associated with the problem. If so, you have a defective port. You need a repair.

  Occasionally an ADB-related problem may be software-based, typically caused by a specific application that somehow conflicts with ADB port communication. Ideally, such applications come with special fixes (usually in the form of an extension, such as one called ADB Fix) that are used to get around this problem. Unfortunately, sometimes the presence of such extensions can be the cause of the problem. In this case, the simple solution is to discard the extension.

- **Defective keyboard or mouse** If your keyboard seems dead but your mouse functions fine (or vice versa), switch the keyboard (or mouse) with one from another computer. If the second keyboard (or mouse) works fine on your computer, the original keyboard (or mouse) is probably defective. Usually these items are not repairable and need to be replaced.

- **A false freeze** On many Macintosh models, you can choose to attach your mouse to either the ADB port on the rear of the Macintosh or the one on the side of the keyboard.

  If you attach the mouse to the side of the keyboard, and the keyboard or keyboard cable is defective, then *both* the mouse and the keyboard cease to function. This may seem to resemble a system freeze (as described in Chapter 4). However, it is really a hardware problem. You can usually spot a false freeze because, with defective hardware, the cursor does not respond to the mouse even in the earliest stages of the startup sequence. In general, if the problem recurs no matter what software techniques you try, suspect a false freeze. Again, the simple solution is to replace the defective cable (or keyboard).

- **A false alarm (A beeping occurs whenever you press a key on the keyboard)** If you hear a beeping sound whenever you hit a key on your keyboard and no character appears on your screen, you have turned on the Slow Keys feature of the Easy Access control panel. This is not a hardware problem. The character will appear if you hold down the key long enough. If the control panel is installed, this feature is turned on by holding down the Return key for more than 5 seconds. This control panel is designed for people with disabilities. Turning it off will fix the problem. Most other users should simply trash this control panel to avoid this problem in the future.

BY THE WAY ▶ Are Individual Keys Defective?

Sometimes a problem with a keyboard is limited only to specific keys. A quick way to check for this is to use Apple's Key Caps desk accessory. Press the suspected defective key. If the matching screen image of the key darkens, then the key is okay. Conversely, if there is a key in the Key Caps display that is darkened before you press it, this is a stuck key. Depending on what key is stuck, this can cause a variety of different symptoms (imagine, for example, if the Mac thinks the Command key is always depressed!). This should work with both ADB and USB keyboards.

- **Cursor doesn't respond to mouse/trackball movements** The inside of the mouse (or trackball), where the rubber ball lies, collects dust and dirt. Eventually, this may prevent the rollers inside the mouse/trackball from turning properly. The result is that the mouse/trackball responds intermittently, with jerky movements, or not at all. Fortunately, you can easily clean the inside of a mouse or trackball. Here's how:

  Clean the mouse/trackball On most mice, press on the ring that surrounds the rubber ball and rotate it counterclockwise from its locked to open position. Turn over the mouse and let the ring and the ball fall out into your other hand. On some mouse models, the ring does not rotate; it slides out and snaps back in. In either case, once the mouse is open, blow briefly and strongly into the mouse to remove any loose dust. Use a cotton swab dipped in isopropyl alcohol to clean the rollers. Use tweezers, if necessary, to remove stuck-on dirt. Reverse the steps to reassemble the mouse, making sure the ball is dry and free of dirt.

  Older PowerBooks have a trackball (the newer models use a TrackPad). As with the mouse, this ball also may need to be cleaned. To do so, turn the ring around the trackball counter clockwise until it pops out. Now you can lift out the ball.

- **TrackPad unresponsive or erratic** For a TrackPad (as found on newer PowerBook models and on the iBook) that is unresponsive, try the following: 1) Put your PowerBook to sleep (by closing the display) and then wake it up (by pressing any key on the keyboard); 2) Press the PowerBook's reset button; 3) Zap the PRAM.

  If the cursor is jumpy or erratic when you try to move it, make sure you are touching the TrackPad with just your finger (and not also your hand or wrist, for example). Similarly, make sure you are not accidentally touching the TrackPad as you are typing (a shareware utility called TapGuard can help avoid this). Also wipe off any moisture that may have collected on the TrackPad.

- **Numeric keypad doesn't work** Some applications do not respond to numeric keypad input unless *num lock* is on. To turn it on, on most standard keyboards, press the *num lock/clear* button on the numeric keypad. The num lock light, above the keypad, should now come on. You should now be able to use the numeric keypad. Other programs do not respond to numeric keypad input no matter what you do. There is no fix for this.

FIX-IT
#14

- **USB** If your keyboard and/or mouse are USB devices, ADB-specific tips will not apply. Check the previous section. Also note that certain Mac OS keyboard shortcuts (such as Command-Control-Power to restart your Mac) work with ADB keyboards but typically do not work with USB keyboards (as discussed in Chapter 4).

BY THE WAY ▶ A Defective Mouse Prevents a Mac From Starting Up

As described in Chapter 5, sometimes a disk icon with a question mark inside it will appear at startup. The startup sequence halts at this point. This is usually caused by the Mac's failure to find a hard disk with a System Folder on it or by a damaged hard disk. However, I am aware of one unusual case where this was caused by a defective mouse. One clue here was that this older Mac would not even start up with a startup floppy disk. The disk would just be ejected. However, when a replacement mouse was connected, all worked fine. Go figure.

Serial: Printers, Modems, and Networks

Common problems with devices attached through the serial ports are more often software-related than hardware-related. For example, many serial printer problems revolve around making the correct selections from the Chooser desk accessory. These, and other printing problems, are explained in Chapter 7. Some problems with modems and with networks (especially as related to file sharing) are covered in Chapters 11 and 14.

To check for more general hardware problems with devices connected through the serial port, check the serial cables, the serial port, and the serial port peripheral device.

- **Check the serial cables** Except for the oldest models of Macintosh (which required 9 or 25 pin cables), serial connections use a round, 8-pin serial cable. However, while all 8-pin serial cables may look identical on the outside, they can have quite different wiring inside. For example, a serial cable for non-AppleTalk printers is different from one used for modems. Either cable works correctly with either port. However, printer cables may work only with printers, and modem cables may work only with modems.

  The cables used to connect devices on an AppleTalk network (LocalTalk, PhoneNet, etc.) are a third type of serial cable.

  Note: Newer Macintosh models can use a separate Ethernet port, with its own type of cable, for connecting to a network. Apple's newest Macs no longer have a serial port at all, and must use the Ethernet port for networking.

  If you are having a problem from the first time you connect a serial port device, check to make sure you are using the right cable. If in doubt, consult with the place where you purchased your equipment or seek other outside help. As always, if problems persist even though all cable connections appear correct, you may have a damaged cable. Swap cables from another Macintosh, if possible, to check for this

- **Check the serial port** If you are still unable to get a response from a device connected to a serial port, try restarting the Mac. Also, try turning the serial port device

FIX-IT #14

off and back on again. These two techniques should solve most serial port problems (for example, it should reset a modem that is not responding and get it working again). If these fail to solve the problem, you may have a corrupted PRAM. To fix this, zap the PRAM (as described in Fix-It #9).

Otherwise, one of the two serial ports (assuming your Mac model has two ports; some only have one) may be damaged. To test for this, if your device can work from either serial port, try switching the cable to the other port. To get things to work after switching ports, you probably also have to readjust Chooser settings (as discussed for printers in Chapter 7). If the device now works, the original port is probably damaged. Take the Macintosh in for repair.

- **Check the serial port peripheral device** Finally, the peripheral device may be damaged. If so, indicators on the device often provide additional clues. Consult your device's manual for specific details. For example, the different patterns of status lights on Apple LaserWriters indicate different problems. In particular, if both the paper jam and out of paper lights are on at the same time, or are flashing together, a hardware repair is probably needed.

- **Check for serial port modem (and printer) problems** If you are using a modem connected through the Mac's serial port, and you get a message that says *Serial port in use*, and it includes an option to reset the port, say "OK." Otherwise, use a freeware utility called SerialKiller to close the serial port. Failing that, you'll have to restart your Mac.

  Otherwise, if AppleTalk is on, turn it off. This can resolve some serial port modem problems. Turning off AppleTalk is also known to improve speed and reduce transmission errors. Try it if you have persistent problems.

  The best way to turn off AppleTalk is via the AppleTalk control panel (see: "Take Note: How to *Really* Make AppleTalk Inactive," in Chapter 12). As a last resort, also try setting AppleTalk's "Connect via" selection to "Remote only."

  Some of these suggestions apply as well to similar "serial port in use" errors with printers (as covered more in Chapter 7).

 ## For Related Information

SEE: • Fix-It #1 on hardware and software incompatibilities.
- Fix-It #3 on extension conflicts.
- Fix-Its #10 and #11 on fixing damaged disks.
- Fix-It #12 on damaged disk device drivers.
- Fix-It #15 on hardware repairs.
- Chapter 5 on startup and disk problems.
- Chapter 7 on printing problems.
- Chapter 11 on networking problems.
- Chapters 12 and 13 on connecting to the Internet.
- Chapter 15 for more on Input Sprockets.

FIX-IT #14

Fix-It #15:
Check the Hardware: Logic Board, Memory, Processor, and PCI slots

▶ **QUICK SUMMARY**

Check for possibly damaged logic board components, by using software utilities or otherwise diagnosing symptoms. Make sure cards are properly inserted on the Macintosh's main logic board. Try other hardware tests as your skills permit.

 When to Do It:

- If the Macintosh doesn't turn on at all.

- If the Sad Mac icon appears at startup (especially if there are no F's in the code numbers below the sad Mac). This symptom is most often caused by defective memory.

- If a Macintosh does not play a normal startup tone when you turn it on, and it subsequently refuses to start up. This is again most likely a memory problem. Alternatively, you may actually get an error message at startup describing a memory problem.

- If you are having crashes or other similar problems that begin shortly after installing additional RAM, a SCSI card or a processor upgrade.

- If the borders of the monitor's display image has shrunk or the display is showing other unusual symptoms, especially if they disappear if you connect the same monitor to another Mac (this often indicates a power supply problem).

- If you have any problem with the Macintosh and you have exhausted all other possible causes, as described throughout this book.

 Why to Do It:

Virtually all Macs provide a way for you to add or replace memory to the appropriate slots on the Mac's logic board. Most of Apple's desktop machines (such as the Power Mac G3 and G4) similarly include the ability to add PCI cards or upgrade the processor. Unlike certain other "repairs," these components are so easy to access (at least on most Mac models), that users typically do these jobs themselves. This Fix-It focuses on troubleshooting issues involving these components: when you need to add or replace one of them, and what could go wrong when you do. This Fix-It will also cover certain other problems with the logic board itself and its other major components (such as the power supply).

This Fix-It also covers some general hardware troubleshooting advice. For more specific help with other hardware, such as modems, drives, monitors, keyboards and mice: check other parts of this book (especially Chapters 5, 10 and 11 and Fix-It #14).

Fix-It
#15

TECHNICALLY SPEAKING ▶ Working Inside the Macintosh

Some hardware checks and simple repairs require opening the Macintosh's case. These include the main focus of this Fix-It: inserting or removing cards, and adding or removing RAM.

If you have even the slightest ability in this area, it is probably more than enough to get the job done. This is not an area I consider to be my strength. Yet in the last year or so, I have added memory to an iMac (the first-generation models, before Apple redesigned the iMac to make this a snap to do) and replaced the TrackPad button in my PowerBook 3400. I would not have been able to do either operation without a detailed set of instructions. Fortunately, Apple's Help information (available via the Help command in the Finder) provided the instructions for the iMac. For the TrackPad button, I found the instructions on the Web. Armed with the instructions, the procedures were quite easy to accomplish. A screwdriver was the only tool needed (true, for the PowerBook, I needed a special size of Torx screwdriver that is not so easy to find). Over the years, and across many models of Mac, I have similarly swapped hard drives and CD-ROM drives, as well as adding PCI cards and processor upgrades - all without incident.

Overall, Mac models vary in terms of how easy it is to get inside them. Happily, Apple's G3 and G4 Macs are the most accessible Apple has ever made. Just pull a handle and it's open. In contrast, the old Power Mac 8500 was a low point in Apple design. Just opening it once is enough to convince you never to try it again.

In any case, it's always wise to turn off the Mac before opening the case. (I once received an email from someone who had replaced his RAM while the Mac was running. He innocently inquired if this could be why he could no longer start up his Mac.) Also be careful to avoid damage due to static electricity; touch something metal before touching any other internal components.

Beyond that, I don't provide too many specific details in this book on how to do hardware repairs or get inside your Mac. In general, the necessary instructions should come with whatever component you wish to add or replace—or should be readily available from Apple's Help command or the Web.

 ## What to Do:

This Fix-It is divided into four main topics (1) Logic board, (2) PCI slots, (3) Processors and processor upgrades, and (4) Memory.

TAKE NOTE ▶ Make Preliminary Checks

If you suspect a hardware problem that requires opening up your Mac, there are a few things you should check before you potentially waste your time:

1. Make sure all cables are plugged in tightly and in their correct port.
2. Make sure devices are connected to an outlet and that, if the outlet is connected to a wall switch, the wall switch is on.
3. If you have a surge suppresser, make sure the fuse is reset.
4. Make sure a device's on/off switch is on.

FIX·IT #15

TAKE NOTE ▶ Use Diagnostic Utilities

A variety of software tools can help you diagnose hardware problems. Here are some top choices:

- **TechTool Pro** checks for possible hardware problems with almost every part of your Mac, from modems to memory. However, even if it does not spot trouble, you may still have defective hardware.

- **Apple System Profiler** (which comes included with the Mac OS) provides a wealth of diagnostic information. For example, if Profiler does not even "see" an externally connected device, this suggests a hardware or driver-software problem. If you want the details on the name, version number, firmware number or serial number of your internal hardware, this is also a good place to look. Otherwise, try the shareware utility TattleTech.

Figure F15-1 TechTool Pro's memory test options, one of its many hardware checks.

- **Gauge Pro** is a useful freeware tool that gives you information about the amount of RAM you have installed, the speed of your processor, the size of your L2 cache, and more.

- **Norton Utilities** has a System Info feature that allows you to compare speed benchmarks across different Macs. MacBench is another tool that does this.

- **Disk formatting utilities**, such as Hard Disk ToolKit, also provide numerous diagnostic features for assessing hard drive functioning.

The main limitation of all of these utilities is that using them assumes that you can successfully start up your Macintosh. This can be a real Catch-22. For example, how can you run a utility to check for defective memory if the defective memory is preventing you from starting up your Mac? You can't! Second, and not surprisingly, these utilities cannot repair any of the hardware problems they discover.

Still, these utilities can be useful as a preventative measure or when the problem is not so serious as to prevent using the utility.

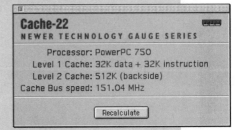

Figure F15-2 NewerTech's Cache-22 utility gives you the specs on your Mac's processor.

Often, defective hardware initially produces only minor symptoms, as the component continues to function albeit in a "weakened" state. Major symptoms appear later, when the component fails altogether. These programs can help you detect impending disaster, when the symptoms are still so minor that you may not even notice them and the Mac is still running apparently OK. Other symptoms are intermittent, which means you can check the Mac on those occasions when the symptom is temporarily on vacation.

Once the problem is diagnosed, you can then determine if it is something you can try to fix yourself, or if you need to take the component (or the entire Mac) in for repairs.

**Fix-It
#15**

Logic Board

The logic board is the heart of the computer. In a sense, it *is* the computer. Every other part of your computer must connect to it in order to function. So let's start with the big enchilada itself.

The Logic Board

A logic board problem can be a minor hassle (such as the wire that runs from the logic board to the computer's speaker being loose, thereby eliminating all sound to the speaker; just plug in the wire and sound is restored) or a major disaster (such as critical integrated circuits on the board shorted out; the board will need to be replaced to get things working again).

Except for the most minor cases, logic board problems almost always require taking the Macintosh in for repair. In fact, Apple's official solution for most logic board problems is to replace the entire board. This can be an expensive repair for what may only be a defective resistor somewhere on the board. Still, it's the safest way to go. If you want to risk it, non-authorized dealers may be willing to replace individual components of the board, at a considerable savings.

There are a couple of clear exceptions to this "replace the entire board" policy:

The Logic Board Battery

The battery on the logic board typically maintains PRAM information that would otherwise be lost when you turn the Macintosh off. However, a dead battery can lead to more serious symptoms than a loss of stored PRAM data. For example, if your Macintosh is one that can be turned on by the keyboard's Power key (not all models use this key), a dead internal battery can actually prevent your Macintosh from starting up. Other symptoms that may mean a dead battery include a Sad Mac on startup and a monitor screen that does not come on. Fortunately, the remedy is simply to replace the battery (rather than the much more expensive logic board replacement). Thus, checking your battery is always a good thing to do before assuming the worst. According to some reports, if your Mac has a physical on/off switch, turning it on and off rapidly a few times can temporarily revive a Mac with a dead battery problem (letting you get some work done while you wait for a battery replacement).

The trick with replacing the battery is (1) finding where it is on your Mac, and (2) finding where to get a replacement battery. The specifics tend to vary with each Mac model, so there is little in the way of easy generalizations. The documentation that came with your Mac usually does not provide much help either. However an Authorized Apple Service Provider should be able to tell you what battery to get and how to get it. They will even install it for you if you want (for a fee of course). Otherwise, check the Web for information. One site in particular worth checking is http://www.academ.com/info/macintosh/.

SEE: • **Fix-It #9 for more on PRAM and battery troubleshooting.**

**Fix-It
#15**

Power Supply

Distortions in the monitor display (such as a reduction in the usable area of the screen) are often an early sign of power supply problems. The ultimate sign of a completely failed power supply is, of course, a dead Macintosh. In either case, get the power supply replaced.

If your Mac is so completely dead that turning it on does not produce even the slightest response, this too usually means it's time to replace the power supply.

TAKE NOTE ▶ Apple's Repair Extension Program

In 1996, Apple announced what is essentially a free seven-year extended warranty, called the *Repair Extension Program*, to fix certain problems with 5200, 5300, 6200, and 6300 series desktop Macs as well as 190 and 5300 series PowerBooks. A variety of symptoms are covered under this program. Among the most notable are:

- System freezes caused by specific, known component issues that have been identified by Apple (this means that not every cause of a system freeze is covered!).
- Sudden or intermittent changes in the monitor's color hue on Power Macintosh and Performa 5200 and 5300 series computers (due to a particular cable).
- AC adapter problems (the adapter does not fit or the Mac takes longer to start up with the AC adapter than with battery power) with PowerBook 190 and 5300 series PowerBooks.

Note: If your PowerBook has an "AA" in the lower right corner of the serial number label, you should be OK. Apple also has freeware utilities, including one called 5XXX/6XXX Tester, that may help determine whether your Mac qualifies under this program. Otherwise, if you own any of these Mac models, and have not yet been contacted by Apple, call 1-800-SOS-APPL or 1-800-801-6024 for more details as to whether or not you qualify and what you should do. Repairs may include a free logic board replacement.

Apple has periodically offered other similar extension programs. Some are "unofficial," meaning that Apple does not publicize them but will replace the component free of charge if you call to complain. So before you pay for an out-of-warranty repair, call Apple Tech Support to see if they will pay for the repair (don't assume your local service provider will know). For example, I got my AppleVision 1710 monitor repaired free by doing this. Apple's old 15" MultiScan monitor was also the beneficiary of an extended warranty.

PCI Slots

PCI (Peripheral Component Interconnect) slots are on the logic board of most of the recent desktop Macs. There will be at least three of them.

PCI slots are used to hold PCI cards. These cards are like mini-logic boards and act to extend the functionality of the computer. Common examples include graphics cards such as ATI's XCLAIM VR card (for increased graphic speed and improved 2D and/or 3D rendering), DOS compatibility cards, and SCSI cards (described more in Fix-It #14).

There isn't much troubleshooting to worry about with PCI cards. You simply open up the Mac and insert the card in its slot. Make sure the card is oriented the correct way to fit in the slot (the plug part is typically off-center so that it can only be inserted in one direction). Then make sure the card is firmly in place. Close up the Mac and you are done.

Fix-It #15

In some cases, there may be compatibility problems associated with a particular card. For example, when the Power Mac G4 first came out, most SCSI cards prevented the Mac from entering its low power sleep mode. There have also been problems with some SCSI devices not working with certain SCSI cards (again, as covered more in Fix-It #14). Generally, firmware updates to the card and/or connecting devices fix these problems.

Each card draws power, as needed, from the Macintosh's power supply. There is a limit on the total combined power that should be used by all cards. If you have several cards, you need to be concerned about exceeding this limit. In rarer cases, even the order in which you fill the slots can be of importance. If so, the vendor who made the card should be aware of this; contact them for help if needed. Otherwise check Mac sites on the Web for possible help (such as my own MacFixIt).

The Power Mac G4 added a new type of slot called AGP. This slot is typically filled by the graphics accelerator card (such as the ATI Rage Pro 128, or newer version of this card, that ships with the G4). This eliminates the need to use a PCI slot for a graphics card.

BY THE WAY ▶ Before PCI There Was...

If you ever see reference to terms such as NuBus or PDS slots, these refer to the type of slots that were present on Mac models before Apple converted to PCI. PCI-based Macs started with the Power Mac 7500, 8500 and 9500. Essentially, everything before that is not PCI.

You absolutely cannot use a NuBus card in a PCI slot (or vice versa). If you have an older Mac, you won't find much in the way of NuBus or PDS cards any more; the current market only supports PCI.

Processors

Every Mac model since the Power Mac 6100 back in 1994 is a Power Mac. For this edition of Sad Macs, I am assuming that you have a Power Mac. This section focuses on Power Mac hardware issues, but also delves into the ways in which the processor hardware and software interact.

What Makes a Power Mac Different from Other Macs?

Power Macs vs. 680x0 Macs The defining characteristic of a Power Mac is that it has a *PowerPC processor* (originally developed by Motorola and IBM). The first PowerPC processors had names like PPC 601 and PPC 604. The newest ones are called G3 and G4 processors. In general, each new generation of the processor is significantly faster than its predecessor. Further, within each basic processor type, there are variations that run at different speeds, as measured in megahertz. Thus, you may have a 350MHz G3 or a 500MHz G4. All Macs with a G3 processor are referred to as *G3 Macs*. Thus, even the iMac is a G3 Mac.

Older Macs use an older Motorola series of processors called the 680x0 series. Specific processors had names such as 68030 and 68040.

SEE: • Chapter 1 for some basics on exactly what a processor is.

FIX-IT #15

PCI-based Macintoshes The second generation of Power Macs (starting with the Power Mac 7200, 7500, 8500 and 9500) were the first to be called PCI-based Macs. Although, technically, this simply means that they come with PCI slots (as described previously in this Fix-It), they also introduced several significant changes to the Mac design, including the first upgradable processor slots. Virtually all Macs since these first ones are PCI-based, including Apple's newest desktop machines.

The iMac and beyond Starting with the iMac and continuing through the G4 Macs, Apple took yet another leap forward. These are the first to use USB and/or FireWire. They are also the first to have the Mac ROM loaded in RAM from a system software file, rather than from hardware. These, and other differences, are discussed more in Chapter 14 (on the iMac and newer Macs).

Multiple-Processor Macs Finally, although we won't be discussing it much here, some Mac models are capable of running more than one processor simultaneously. This can offer greatly increased speed advantages (it's almost like having two Macs working at the same time). But taking advantage of this requires that application software be rewritten to be multi-processor aware. This has hardly happened; as a result, multi-processor Macs remain a rarity.

- **Processor type** One such consideration is the type of processor. For example, a G3 processor is inherently faster than a 604 PPC processor even at the same MHz clock speed. This is because clock speed mainly refers to how fast the data can "move." Another limitation is how fast the data can be processed. For example, a processor that can handle eight instructions for every clock cycle will process data faster than one that can only handle 4 instructions per clock cycle, even if the processors have the same megahertz speed.

- **Bus speed and multipliers** The bus speed of the logic board itself plays a limiting role in the processor's speed. The *bus speed* determines how fast information can shuttle in and out of the processor. The logic board bus speed is not "advertised" as much as processor speed. You may have to dig a little to find out what it is for your model. Still, it can have a significant effect on the performance of your Mac. For starters, the same processor attached to a logic board with a 50MHz bus speed, for example, will generally run faster than one attached to a 40MHz board.

  Things get even more complicated when you consider yet another factor: the *multiplier*. Essentially, your processor must work at a speed that is an integer ratio (or multiplier) of the bus speed (typically in sizes such as 3:1 or 4:1 or 5:1). This ratio is an inherent part of the processor's design. This means, for example, that a 150MHz processor with a 3:1 multiplier will attain its 150MHz maximum speed when hooked up to a bus that goes at 50MHz (50 x 3 = 150). But when hooked to a bus that goes at 40MHz, it will only be able to achieve 120MHz (40 x 3 = 120). A processor may have more than one multiplier built-in, allowing it to choose the optimal one. Also, devices called clock-chip accelerators may help circumvent some factory-set limitations and push the processor beyond its stated specs.

  There are still other complications (aren't there always!), including the fact that the processor can actually set the bus speed itself. But enough for now. The bottom line is that all of these factors combine to determine the "true" speed of your processor.

- **L2 cache and other factors** L2 RAM caches are a special high-speed RAM, whose purpose is to increase the speed of your Mac by allowing for more efficient use of your processor. An L2 RAM cache can give you a speed boost, usually about 10 percent to 20 percent. How does it do this? Here's how:

  The Mac's CPU operates only on data in its "registers." If these registers don't have the needed data, it looks for it first on the CPU's on-chip (L1) cache (usually about 32K in size). If the on-chip cache doesn't have it, it then searches the L2 RAM cache, if one is present (these currently run in size from about 256K to 1MB). If it still can't find it, it will search the (slower) main RAM (including any disk cache, as described in Fix-It #5). Failing that, it reads the needed information from your hard drive (which is the last resort because it has the slowest access of any of these options).

  A Level 1 (L1) RAM cache is always built on to the processor itself. L2 RAM caches used to be separate modules that you added into special slots on your computer, much like ordinary RAM. However, starting with the G3 Macs, L2 cache is included on the processor itself. It is called "backside" L2 cache. [A few 604 processors had a similar arrangement referred to as "inline" L2 cache.] With backside cache, another megahertz speed measurement comes into play: the bus speed between the processor and the cache. The best case scenario is if the speed is equal to the speed of the processor. Thus if you saw a reference to a G3 300/300 with 1MB of backside cache, this would mean that you had a G3 processor running at 300MHz with 1MB of backside L2 cache attached, communicating with the processor along a 300MHz cache bus.

(continues on next page)

FIX-IT
#15

TECHNICALLY SPEAKING ▶ Speed of Your Power Mac:
                          Beyond Processor MegaHertz *(continued)*

If you have an older Mac that supports adding a L2 cache card, and you upgrade the processor to a G3 (which comes with L2 cache included), a separate L2 cache card will no longer be accessed. Whether or not you have a L2 cache card installed is thus irrelevant. Whatever type of L2 cache you have, utilities such as Newer's Gauge Pro or MicroMat's TechTool Pro will check for the presence and size of the cache.

Finally, there are a host of more general items that affect the overall speed of your Mac: the amount of RAM, the speed of the disk drive, etc.

In the end, at least two things are clear: (1) a 500MHz G4 processor is unbelievably fast, (2) a year from now, it will seem slow.

SEE: • "Processor Upgrades" later in this Fix-It, for more on processor (especially G3/G4) issues.
       • Chapter 5, "The Macintosh's Speed Is Unexpectedly Slow, " for more on speed-related issues.

PPC Software

Running in emulation vs. native mode The single most amazing thing about Power Macintoshes, especially so when they were first introduced, is that when you start to use one, they do not seem any different from the older 680x0 Macintoshes. I mean this in the positive sense; that is, the Finder and the desktop are still there and work the same way they always have. Almost all the software that runs on older Macs still runs on Power Macs. At this level, the fact that you are using a completely different processor seems almost irrelevant. In other words, a Power Macintosh is still a Macintosh.

To fully appreciate the significance of this accomplishment, consider this: software is written to match a particular processor. This means that software written for a 680x0 processor should not be able to run on a machine using a PowerPC processor. Thus, a person upgrading to a Power Macintosh would be faced with the prospect of having to throw out all of his or her existing software. Not at all a happy prospect! Apple solved this dilemma by including a *68040 emulator* in the ROM of all Power Macintoshes. This emulator is essentially a set of instructions that allows the Power Mac, when needed, to imitate a 680x0 Macintosh. This is why a Power Mac can still run almost all of your old software.

When you launch an application, the Power Macintosh automatically determines whether the application is written for a 680x0 Macintosh or a Power Macintosh. If it is a 680x0 application, the Power Mac shifts into *emulation mode*. If it is a Power Mac application (also referred to as a *native code* application), the Power Mac shifts into *native mode*. In native mode, the PowerPC processor is used directly, without any intermediary emulation. The Power Mac can even accommodate software in which part of the software's code is native while other parts are not, again switching modes automatically and transparently as needed. (Unfortunately, this compatibility across machines is a one-way street: there is no way to run Power Mac software on a 680x0 Mac.)

**Fix-It
#15**

This isn't to say that there is no cost to using emulation mode. The main problem with emulation mode is that you lose the PowerPC processor's speed advantage—which was the primary rationale for developing the Power Mac in the first place. Emulation mode, almost by definition, can be no faster than the speed of the 680x0 Macs that it is emulating. Actually, running software in emulation mode on a Power Mac can result in *slower* speeds than running the same software on a true 68040 Macintosh. This was particularly true of the first generation of Power Macintoshes, released in 1994. However, things have gotten better with the improved version of the emulator included in PCI-based Power Macs (specifically called the DRE, or *Dynamic Recompilation Emulator*) Also, the Speed Emulator component of Connectix's Speed Doubler offers an alternative emulator that generally outperforms Apple's emulator. Combined with their ever-faster processors, today's Power Macs equal or outperform all 680x0 Macs, even in emulation mode.

Still, emulation mode can never equal the performance you can get when running in native mode, so ideally, you want all your software to be native-code applications. When the Power Mac was first released, there was virtually no native software available. It took until 1995 before the floodgates finally opened. Now, almost all popular software has a native version.

Mac OS is still not entirely native Even if you are running a native application, you will still not necessarily get the maximum speed benefit you might expect. This is because you may be shifted into emulation mode even when using a native application.

The main reason for this is lingering Mac OS software that is still not converted to native code. Happily, by Mac OS 8.5 or later, most of the Mac OS has now been rewritten in native code. (For example, starting in Mac OS 8.5, AppleScript is native.) This is important because system software kicks in regularly while using almost any application. For example, opening and saving documents are typically handled by system software, not by the application itself. Thus, even when running a native application, if the OS is still non-native, you will be temporarily switched to emulation mode when you open or save a document. There is a double penalty here. Not only are things slowed down as a result of being in emulation mode, however briefly, but just the act of switching from one mode to another slows things down a bit. The more often you switch back and forth, the more of a slow-down penalty you pay.

Finally, some system software, including the Finder, is still not PowerPC native. This means that whenever you go to the desktop (which is almost always lurking behind your application windows), you go into emulation mode.

With each new version of the Mac OS, more and more of it gets rewritten in native code.

Extensions/control panels that are not native Control panels and extensions running in emulator mode can cause unexpected slowdowns. For example, versions of ATM (Adobe Type Manager) prior to 3.8 run in emulator mode. ATM is active any time a program, such as a word processor, needs it for the display or printing of text. This means that the Mac will be shifting into emulator mode for ATM even if the application itself is in native code. This can cause a slowdown of as much as 15 percent or more.

Fix-It
#15

The solution is to use native versions of all startup extensions, whenever possible. In the case of ATM, use version 3.8 or later.

Programs that need a math coprocessor (FPU) The Power Mac's 68040 emulator is technically a 68LC040 emulator. The relevance of this is that this flavor of 68040 processor does not include an FPU (floating point unit, also called a math coprocessor). This means that non-native versions of programs that use the FPU, such as statistics and scientific software, will run much slower on a Power Mac than on a 68040 Mac with an FPU. In the worst cases, the program may not run at all, giving you a "No FPU Installed" or "No Coprocessor Present" error message.

You may be able to partially solve this problem by using an FPU emulator called Software FPU, but don't count on it. The best solution is to get the native code upgrade to your problem application (hopefully, there is such an upgrade!).

By the way, your Power Mac does have an FPU. It is built in to all PowerPC processors, but can only be accessed by programs running in native mode.

Installing PPC-Native Software

Some software just exists in Power Mac native form. You can't get a version that runs on 680x0 machines. However, most software today still comes in both Power Mac and 680x0 versions. If the program comes with an Installer, there may be separate versions for Power Mac and 680x0 Macs. Or, more commonly, there is just one Installer; selecting Easy Install installs the correct version for your Mac. If you select Custom Install, you may get a choice between a 680x0 version, a Power Mac version, or a combined *fat binary* version. The fat version combines both the 680x0 and Power Mac code in the same file. This has the advantage of allowing the same copy of the program to run on either type of machine. However, these fat versions, as their name implies, take up more disk space.

In a few cases, a fat binary version is the only option. This means you get stuck with non-native code in your software even if you don't want it. While there are a few programs out there that can strip out the unwanted code (Spring Cleaning is one), I would be cautious about doing this. It may lead to problems down the road (for example, if you do this to Apple system software, you may have trouble updating the software later).

Is It Native or Not?

Native code software may identify itself as "Accelerated for Power Macintosh" right on its package and/or manual. But suppose you have an application already installed on your Macintosh and you are not sure whether or not it is native code. How could you quickly find out? Just open its Get Info window. If you see a message at the bottom of the window saying how turning on (or off) virtual memory (or RAM Doubler) will decrease (or increase) the memory requirements for the application, the application is native.

SEE: Fix-It #5 for more on virtual memory and PowerPC (native) software.

BY THE WAY ▶ Utilities Tell You When You Are Running Native

As described in the main text, your Mac can slip back and forth between emulation mode and native mode, even when running a native application. If you want to find out precisely when your Mac is or is not in native mode, check out a freeware extension called PowerPeek. It puts a little "light" in your menu bar that flashes green when the Mac is in native mode and red when it's in emulation mode. This not only gives you an indication of when mode switching occurs, it can confirm whether a supposed native mode application is really running in native mode.

Another shareware utility, PowerPCheck, can check any selected application and report whether or not it contains native PowerPC code.

Shared Library Files

Power Macintosh native applications increasingly use a technology called *shared libraries.* This is a method designed to minimize the need to have the same code in RAM more than once at the same time. Thus, if two programs use essentially the same code, it can be stored in a special shared library file that both programs can access (called *dynamic linking*).

While this should help to reduce the total amount of RAM needed to keep multiple applications open, the memory requirements listed in an application's Get Info don't include any extra memory that may be needed to access a shared library. Thus, you may need more memory to open an application than the Get Info window would suggest. In some cases, this may mean that you do not have enough available memory to open the application.

SEE: • **Fix-It #5 on how to solve problems due to insufficient available memory.**

If a needed shared library file is missing from your hard drive, this too can prevent an application from opening. If this happens, try reinstalling the application software, making sure to use the application's Installer utility (if it includes one) and carefully following the directions given. This should get the needed library file on to your disk.

Shared Library Manager and documents The key files that you need to use shared libraries are the Shared Library Manager and Shared Library Manager PPC extensions. Power Macs need both Managers (despite their names suggesting that only the latter is needed). Older Macs need only the Shared Library Manager file.

One example of a shared library "document" files that ship with the system software is AppleScriptLib. Used especially with AppleScript, it is also used by several other third party programs, so do not discard it. Open Transport (see Chapter 12) also depends on shared library files. The files that end in the word Lib are used for running native code applications; the ones that end in the word "Library" are needed to run 680x0 applications in emulation mode. Neither file type loads into RAM at startup. They are loaded only when needed.

Note: There is a similarly named (and similarly functioning) extension called Shared Code Manager. This is not part of Apple's system software, but is a Microsoft extension that is used in conjunction with some Microsoft applications.

FIX-IT #15

Code Fragment Manager The Code Fragment Manager (CFM), is essentially a replacement technology for the Shared Library Manager. In this setup, all code (including applications) is considered code fragments; a shared library document is just one type of code fragment. Eventually, as software gets updated to use the CFM, this should technically eliminate the need for the separate Shared Library Manager extensions. But they are still included in Mac OS 9.0

There is no CFM extension. It is built directly into the system software. On 680X0 Macs, you may find a file called CFM-68K Runtime Enabler. This allows Code Fragment Manager-dependent software to run on these Macs.

Shared Library error messages Occasionally, you may get an error message such as *Can't Find SoundLib* or *Can't Find MathLib* when launching or using an application. This means that the application could not locate the shared library files it expects to find. Not surprisingly, if you search for this file on your drive, you will likely not find it. If such a file does exist, the solution is fairly simple: locate the Installer that installs the file and reinstall it (although this can sometimes be tricky since it may not be obvious where the file in question came from). However, more likely a search for the file will be a waste of time—because no file with that name exists (at least not in the version of the OS you are using). What has happened is that the code for this library file has been rolled into some other file (an extension or even the System file itself). The application is thus really looking for this other file. In the SoundLib example above, it is likely looking for the Sound Manager extension. If the Sound Manager extension is missing, you simply need to reinstall it.

But what if you get this message and the supposedly missing file (e.g., Sound Manager extension) is correctly installed? This is surprisingly the most likely scenario. This means one of two things: (1) The application reporting the error has not been correctly updated to search for the file in the correct location, hence it does not find it. The solution here will require an update to the application. (2) The extension is not the correct version or has become corrupted or something similar that prevents the application from accessing it. The solution here is to reinstall the software, checking that you are using the appropriate version. The appropriate version will usually be the one that came with the version of the OS you are using (although occasionally there may be a newer version that is needed) or the application that you are using. In the "MathLib" example, the file is actually built-in to the System file. If this message persists, it may mean that a clean install of your System Software is in order. (By the way, the shareware application, InformInit, provides an excellent list of these library files and where they are located.)

Shared Library version conflicts Occasionally, two different applications may require different versions of the same Shared Library file. This has happened particularly with different Microsoft applications (such as word and Internet Explorer needing different versions of the Microsoft Component Library file). As you cannot keep two versions of the same file in the Extensions folder, this can present a problem. The typical solution is to place one version of the file in the same folder as the application that uses it, leaving the other (typically more recent) version in the Extensions folder. Applications will use a version found in their folder before seeking one in the Extensions folder before seeking one in the Extensions folder. Thus, this arrangement allows each application to use the correct version.

ObjectSupportLib This shared library file deserves special mention. Its function is a bit esoteric, dealing with sending and receiving of Apple Events. Of more importance to you are two facts: (1) This separate extension is no longer needed in Mac OS 8.0 or later. Its code has been rolled into the System file. (2) If you have this extension mistakenly installed in a Mac OS 8.0 (or later) System Folder, it can precipitate system crashes. Especially common are crashes in the Finder just at the end of the startup sequence. Even more irritating is that several third-party applications mistakenly install this file behind your back. So you can wind up with this hassle even if you are sure you never personally installed the file. The solution (if you are getting a crash at startup) is to start up with Extensions Off and trash this file if you find it. A preventative measure is to create a folder called "ObjectSupportLib" and put it in your Extensions folder. An Installer will be unable to replace this folder, thereby preventing the installation of the problematic file.

Note: You'll find ObjectSupportLib on Mac OS Installer CDs in a folder called Upgrader Files. This is OK. It is supposed to be there.

Processor Upgrades

The good news Starting with the first PCI-based Macs (Power Mac 7500, 8500 and 9500), Apple included a slot on the logic board where a processor card is inserted. In the past, the processor was soldered directly to the logic board. This new arrangement allowed the processor to be replaced or upgraded without having to replace the entire logic board. In the past, when your Mac's speed was not fast enough to keep apace with the current software, it was almost always cheaper to buy an entirely new and faster Mac than to upgrade an existing one. With processor cards selling for a low as a few hundred dollars, this was no longer true.

Initially, users upgraded from a slower 60x processor to a faster one (such as from a 601 to a 604, or from a 200MHz 604 to a 300MHz 604). With the arrival of the G3 processor, users left the 60x series behind for the G3 card—and upgrading Mac processors became a booming business. For a 60x user, upgrading to a G3 offered tremendous speed boosts for a fraction of the cost of getting a new Mac. A G3 upgrade also eliminated the need for a separate L2 cache card (because G3 processor come with a "built-in" L2 cache that supersedes any separate cache card).

Over time, processor upgrade vendors even found ways to provide G3 upgrades to Macs that did not have a processor upgrade slot. For example, you can now upgrade the original generation of PowerPC Macs (6100, 7100 and 8100) as well as the PowerBook 1400. Unfortunately, upgrading an iMac remains largely elusive (although there are options for upgrading first-generation Bondi blue iMacs, as described in Chapter 14).

With the arrival of the G3 Macs (that is, Macs that came with G3 processors right from Apple). Apple shifted from a processor slot that resembled a PCI slot to a different squarish slot called a Zero Insertion Force (or ZIF) slot. Having a G3 did not mean you no longer could benefit from an upgrade. Speed-hungry users began replacing slower G3 processors with faster ones and with G4 processors.

Fix-It #15

A reality check Amidst all of this good news about cost-effective speed jumps, let's pause for a reality check:

- The fastest upgrade cards are still very expensive. Unless you really want to hold on to your existing Mac for some reason, getting these top-of-the-line cards is often a poor deal. It can be better to get a new Mac altogether.

- Getting a G3 or G4 upgrade card for a 60x Power Mac does not give you all of the speed benefits of a new G3/G4. For example, Macs that initially came with a 60x processor typically have a system bus speed of about 50Mhz (or less). Apple's current G4 Macs have a bus speed of 100MHz. Adding a G3/G4 card to an older Mac has no effect on the system bus speed. This means that G3 and G4 Macs will always have a speed advantage over an older non-G3/G4 Mac upgraded with the same G3 or G4 processor. It is mainly for this reason that some software is recommended to be used only on Macs that came initially with a G3 or G4 processor. Connectix Virtual Game Station is a prime example here.

- Apple's newest Macs have many other features, unrelated to the processor, that you will miss out on by simply upgrading your older non-G3/G4 Mac (or even older G3 Mac in some cases). For example, if you want to use the NetBoot feature of Mac OS X Server (see Chapter 14), you will need an iMac or newer Mac. Older Macs also do not come with USB and FireWire ports. So there are still many reasons to consider getting an entirely new Mac rather than a processor upgrade (which is good news for Apple, as it is not in the processor upgrade business).

Troubleshooting Overall, a processor upgrade is a simple modification. It is as easy to do as installing RAM—which means most users can do it themselves. And, after the upgrade is in and working, there are very few potential problems to worry about. Still, occasional problems appear. For example, certain SCSI cards (installed in PCI slots) caused system crashes after a Mac was upgraded to a G3 processor. This is a rare problem these days, as vendors have generally fixed the cause of the problem.

See: • **"Take Note: G3 and G4 upgrades: Speculative Addressing and AltiVec Support," for related matters.**
  • **"G3/G4 Processor Upgrades," in Fix-It #1, for more on possible incompatibilities.**

TAKE NOTE ▶ G3 and G4 Upgrades: Speculative Addressing and AltiVec Support

The following two issues affect mainly older Macs that are upgraded to G3 or G4 processors.

Speculative Addressing Speculative Addressing (also called *Speculative Access* or *Speculative Processing*) is a method of achieving greater microprocessor performance. Technically, the processor fetches extra data from locations near where it is currently getting data. The processor is fetching this other nearby data speculating that the processor will eventually need it as the current execution stream proceeds. However, it can cause unintended problems on older Macs that aren't properly set up to handle Speculative Addressing. This has been an issue with G3 upgrades and now G4 upgrades in certain (primarily older) Power Macs (such as Power Mac 7300 to 9600 models).

If this problem is not corrected, data corruption may occur due to the processor writing data to the wrong sector of the hard drive.

(continues on next page)

There are two ways that this problem can be avoided: a firmware fix and a software fix. The firmware approach is for the "fix" to be built directly into the processor hardware. The second solution involves Open Firmware software. In the latter case, the fix is installed in the computer's non-volatile video RAM (NVRAM) where it loads at startup. The problem with this approach is that, if you should ever reset the NVRAM (as described in Fix-It #9), the "fix" gets lost and the Mac may become unable to startup from all but special floppy or CD disks (included with the processor upgrade). Fortunately, these special disks include an Installer application that can reinstall the needed fix. Check with the processor vendor for details as to how they handle this issue. See this MacFixIt page for more details: http://www.macfixit.com/extras/G4speculative.shtml.

None of this is relevant to Macs that ship with a G3 or G4 processor already installed (such as the iMac or Power Mac G3/G4s).

AltiVec support To get the maximum performance speed from a G4 processor, you need to take advantage of its AltiVec Component. Apple also refers to this as the "Velocity Engine." AltiVec is similar to a co-processor built onto the chip in that it can dramatically speed up certain operations. It achieves this speed gain primarily because it can process data in 128-bit chunks, instead of the smaller 32-bit or 64-bit chunks used in most other processors. However, it can only do this with software that is aware of and designed to take advantage of AltiVec. As of this writing, most software is not yet AltiVec-aware. So the full potential of the G4 processor is yet to be realized.

Also, older Macs that are upgraded with a G4 may not be able to fully utilize AltiVec, because they have an older ROM that does not include the needed instructions. Again, the processor vendor can come to the rescue here by providing a software fix that provides the necessary support. For example, Newer Technology does this with its Velocity Enabler software.

Memory

Basics: Why and How to Add Memory

Adding memory to your computer is the single most common (often the only) hardware modification that the average Mac user will make. The terms *memory*, *RAM*, and *DRAM* (Dynamic Random Access Memory) will be used pretty much interchangeably here. But that's hardly the end of it. There are many more acronyms to confront before we are done.

Memory is added to your computer in the form of "memory modules" (also called "memory cards" or "memory chips") that fit into special "RAM slots" on your Mac's logic board. These modules look a bit like miniversions of PCI cards described earlier. These memory cards provide the RAM (random access memory) for your Macintosh (as first described in Chapter 1). Thus, if someone claims to have "128 megs of RAM" in their machine, this means that a total of 128MB of memory modules are installed on the Macintosh's main logic board.

Every Macintosh comes with some memory already installed. Otherwise your Macintosh could not work. In all recent Macs, at least some (if not all) of the installed memory is in slots in which existing memory cards can be removed and/or new cards installed. In some cases, slots may initially be empty, allowing you to add memory without having to remove any existing modules. In most cases, especially with Macs that open up to allow easy access to the inside of the machine, adding memory is a quick and easy procedure.

Fix-It #15

There are two main reasons to add or replace memory in your Macintosh:

- **Add memory in order to increase the RAM capacity of your Macintosh** If you find that your available RAM is insufficient to meet your needs (as covered in Fix-It #5), adding more memory is the best long-term solution. Minimum recommended memory requirements get larger every year. What is the typical amount of RAM you should have? Experience has shown that whatever I say here will be out of date by the time you read this. As of now, 64MB is the bare minimum to expect to have. Suffice it to say that it makes sense to get as much RAM as you can possibly afford. There is no such thing as too much RAM. If you can afford it, get at least 256MB.

- **Replace defective memory** Memory modules may be defective from the moment they are installed or, as with any electronic component, they may go bad over time. Defective memory modules cause the most serious types of symptoms. Your Macintosh typically will refuse to start up at all, show the Sad Mac icon, and/or sound unusual startup tones (as detailed in Chapter 5, on startup problems). If you do succeed in starting up, despite the bad modules, you may be plagued with frequent and apparently unrelated system errors.

  In such cases, if you are at all lucky, the Macintosh may remain stable long enough for you to use diagnostic utilities, such as TechTool Pro (as described earlier in this Fix-It), to determine if a defective module is the cause. Otherwise, determining which of your several modules is the defective one typically requires swapping modules in and out of their slots and testing the Macintosh after each swap to see if the problem goes away.

  Depending on what model of Macintosh you have, you may be able to remove a memory module and start up just with the modules that remain. If the problem goes away, you know that the module(s) you removed were the source of the problem. In other cases, you may need to replace a potentially defective module with a new one before you can even try to start up. If you do have a defective memory, it must be replaced. Defective memory modules cannot be repaired.

  If you get a Sad Mac at startup due to a defective memory module, the Sad Mac error code may help identify which one is the defective module. Various documents are available online that help you interpret these codes (also see Chapter 5 for more on interpreting Sad Mac codes). However, with recent Mac models, these numbers are pretty much meaningless, if they appear at all. More likely with newer Macs, if your Mac has a memory problem, you will hear unusual startup tones. If you know how to interpret them (as again explained more in Chapter 5), these can help you determine if there is a memory problem.

  Note: Newer Macs may function even with defective memory installed. For example, when I received my first iMac, the first thing I did was add an additional 64MB of memory. However, the memory card turned out to be defective. I found this out because the Mac runs diagnostic tests at startup to check if the memory is working properly. When I started up the Mac after installing the memory, an error message appeared during the memory check, warning me that there was a problem with the memory. After dismissing the message, startup proceeded otherwise normally. When startup was over, everything seemed to work just fine—except of course that the additional memory was not there. I now knew I had to replace the card, which I did. This is much preferred to getting an ominous startup-stopping hard-to-diagnose Sad Mac or startup tones.

SEE: • **"Take Note: The Memory Control Panel," in Fix-It #5, for how to disable the memory tests at startup.**

TECHNICALLY SPEAKING ▶ Memory Modules That Only Seem Defective

Sometimes a memory module that is not properly seated in its slot will mimic the symptoms of a defective module. To check for this, make sure that each module is firmly in its slot and that its wires are unbent.

On some models of Macintosh, modules are held in place by tabs that clip into holes on the module. When you install a module, make sure that the tabs on the slot click into holes at either end of the module. Removing this type of module requires that you carefully pry back the tab without breaking it off. A broken tab can prevent proper seating of the module with the result that the module appears to be defective, so be especially careful when removing these modules. An inexpensive tool, sold by many places that sell modules, can assist in this removal task.

On many Macs, the slots have a "tang" on one end that, when pressed down, pops up the chip that is installed there. To get a new chip inserted properly, slide it in from the non-tang end first. When it is lined up properly, push straight down. This often requires that you press down on the chip harder than you might otherwise think is needed (or even advisable!). When it is really "in," you should hear a distinct "click." If your Mac does not show the additional memory when you are done, check again to make sure you have seated it properly before assuming you have damaged RAM. If you can pull out the memory chip without opening the slot's "tang," it was not seated properly.

Sometimes (as mentioned in Chapter 4) modules that are merely dirty will behave like defective modules, causing frequent system crashes or startup problems. Using a handheld vacuum cleaner to clean out the inside of your Macintosh may help. Otherwise, you may need to remove each module and clean it. In most cases, just blowing dust off of it and wiping it gently with a soft cloth should be enough. In really bad cases, you may want to apply a specialized cleaning spray (such as one called DeOxlt). Most users should rarely, if ever, find this necessary. In any case, remember to take precautions against static electricity damage (see "Technically Speaking: Working Inside the Macintosh" earlier in this Fix-It).

Getting the "Right" Memory for Your Mac

Once you decide to add memory to your Mac, your main task is simple enough: purchase the memory in the quantity you need. However, several complicating questions typically arise here:

- "I want to add 128MB of RAM to my machine; how do I know if this exceeds the maximum possible for my Mac?"

- "I want to add 128MB of RAM to my machine; assuming I have the option, is it better to add one 128MB module or 2 64MB modules?"

- "There seems to be a dizzying array of different types of memory. How do I know which one is the right type for my machine?"

FIX-IT #15

The easy answer to these questions is simply to trust the salesperson from where you purchase the memory. Especially if you buy via a reputable mail order vendor that specializes in Mac memory, you are likely to get good advice. Simply tell him what you want and he will make sure that you get the right memory. To find recommended vendors, the best place to start is on the World Wide Web. There are sites that maintain constantly updated lists of reliable vendors, with the latest prices from each vendor (RAMWatch <http://www.macresource.com/mrp/ramwatch.shtml> is one example). In general, it won't matter which vendor you use from among these recommended vendors, so you can go mainly by price. Memory prices tend to fluctuate more than any other component, so always check before buying. But beware of unusually low prices from non-recommended vendors. They may be selling inferior RAM that will likely cause you trouble.

If you are purchasing a new Mac, you may choose to purchase additional memory at the same time, often having the vendor install it before you even take possession of the Mac. This usually works out fine, although (unless the added memory is part of some special promotion), you'll probably pay more for this memory than if you purchase it from a vendor who specializes in selling memory.

If you are not satisfied with trusting a salesperson to know everything (and I am with you here), there are two documents (available on the Web) that I recommend you get. The first is from Apple. It's called *Apple Spec*. It is a database of virtually all technical specifications for every Mac model ever made. Apple periodically updates it when new Mac models come out. Apple also has another document, specific to memory, called *Apple Memory Guide*. To access these documents, search for them at Apple's Software Updates <http://asu.info.apple.com/swupdates.nsf/Search?OpenForm >. Apple Spec is also directly viewable online <http://support.info.apple.com/info.apple.com/applespec/applespec.taf>. The second option is to get NewerRAM's GURU (*Guide to RAM Upgrades*). Again, assuming you follow knowledgeable advice on what memory to buy, you typically do not need to know much more of the technical details about memory. Just decide how much memory you want, buy it, plug it in, and you are done. However, for those interested in what these technical concerns are, here is a sampling of what you should know:

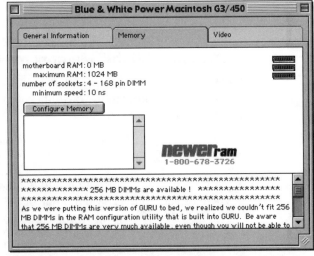

Figure F15-3 GURU lists memory information about a G3 Mac.

The Maximum Allowable RAM

Different Macintosh models have different limits on the maximum amount of RAM that they can use. If you install more than this maximum (assuming this is even possible), at best the Macintosh will not recognize it. At worst, it may lead to system crashes.

For example, Power Mac G4 computers come with at least 64 megabytes (MB) of memory. You can increase this to 1.5 gigabytes (GB) by adding Dual Inline Memory Modules (DIMMs) to the four DIMM slots on the main logic board.

Note that if you use virtual memory (as explained in Fix-It #5), the maximum allowable total combined (physical plus virtual) RAM may exceed (sometimes by a wide margin) the maximum allowable physical RAM.

The Size of the Memory Module

The amount of memory on an individual memory module can vary. This means a Mac can have the same amount of RAM but use different-sized modules and thereby fill a different number of slots. For example, the Power Mac G4 computers come with 4 memory slots. In this case, you could have 128MB of RAM by having one 128MB module in one slot or by having two 64MB modules fill two slots.

Memory module sizes usually double as they increase. Common module sizes today are 32, 64, 128 and 1256MB. Note that the word *size* in this context does not refer to the physical dimensions of the module, but rather to its MB capacity.

In general, although it may cost a bit more initially, using larger memory modules is recommended. This is because it allows for future expansion by filling in the remaining empty slots. Thus, if you had 128MB of RAM via 4 32MB modules, any future expansion would require that you remove one of the modules. In this example, adding a 64MB module would only give you 32MB additional memory. If you had a slot empty, there would be no loss of RAM. However, it is sometimes the case that the largest modules, because they are also usually the newest developed and least tested, have compatibility problems. Thus, if you are adding a large amount of RAM, it may be best (and more economical) to stick with a module one or two sizes below the maximum.

For other possible restrictions and limitations, check with Apple Spec.

The Speed of the Memory Module

Memory module speed is measured in nanoseconds (ns)—the lower the number, the faster the speed. Different Macintosh models require a different minimum speed. Generally, faster machines require faster memory.

For example, in recent years, Mac memory was typically either 70 ns or 60 ns. It is OK to add memory that is faster than the minimum needed, but this will usually just cost you more money without giving you any increase in performance. For example, a Mac that requires 70 ns RAM will not run faster as a result of using 60 ns RAM.

However, some experts claim that the faster RAM, even when not needed, provides a "margin of error" in the manufacturing of the RAM. So even if it is slightly slower than its listed specs, it will still be fast enough to exceed the needed minimum.

Fix-It #15

In any case, to avoid problems, do not add RAM that runs slower than the minimum required speed. Otherwise, at the very least, the speed of your Mac will decline.

Technically, as long as all the RAM exceeds the minimum requirement, you can even mix and match RAMs of different speeds. Again, some experts warn against this, citing increased system crashes as a possibility.

The original G3 Macs required an especially fast 10ns RAM. The current G3 and G4 Macs now use a different measurement of speed. You will see reference to PC-100 SDRAM DIMMs. This is Intel standard for DIMMs compatible with Intel 100 MHz systems. Macs now also use these same DIMMs (see "The Type of Memory" on SDRAM for more details).

The Type of the Memory

Even if two Macintoshes both use the same size and speed memory, there may still be differences in exactly what module each model uses. Apple is notorious for using a different type of memory in virtually every new line of Macs it releases. One implication of this is that you should not count on taking your memory with you. That is, don't buy memory for a Mac that you are about to replace on the theory that you can put the memory in your new Mac when you get it. Chances are, it won't work in the new Mac. If you do need a new type of memory, you may not even be able to insert the old memory in the slot of your new machine (because the module may have a different number of pins). Even if you can, it won't work and may damage your Mac.

Note: PowerBook models often use special memory cards that are specific to that model and cannot be used in any other Mac.

Here's a brief overview of the different types of memory you may confront:

- **SIMMs (Single Inline Memory Modules)** Used in the oldest of Macs. There are 30-pin SIMMs and 72-pin SIMMs.

- **DIMMs (Double Inline Memory Modules)** Used in more recent Macs, including the first PCI-based Macs. DIMMs provide a wider data path than SIMMs, which means they can carry more data and thus allow for faster performance. DIMMs typically have 168 pins. The DIMMs on the iMac have 144 pins. There are multiple flavors of DIMMs.

- **Fast-Page Mode (FPM) memory** Macs that support FPM can generally access a specific memory address faster than without this support. Most Macs prior to the Mac G3s support and use FPM memory. The G3s and G4s use a different type of memory where this is no longer an issue.

- **Extended Data Out (EDO) memory** EDO memory is a superset of FPM memory, allowing for even faster access of memory addresses, thereby reducing "wait states" (that is, the time that a processor has to wait for the memory to complete its task). However, this may not be very relevant if most of the processor and memory interaction is taking place between the processor and the L1 and L2 cache, rather than the memory itself. Most computers that can use FPM memory can also use EDO memory.

However, unless the Mac specifically supports EDO, there will be no performance gain in using EDO. There are two types of EDO memory: 5-volt and 3.3-volt. These cannot be used interchangeably. You need to find out which type your Mac model uses and then use only that type. Installing any type of EDO memory in Macs that cannot use it can damage the Mac's logic board and other memory.

- **SDRAM (Synchronous Dynamic Random Access Memory)** This type of memory is technically also a DIMM. Actually, it is typically an SO-DIMM (or "Small Outline" DIMM, which is smaller than the DIMMs used in older Macs). Apple explains SDRAM as follows: "The processes performed by a computer are coordinated by an internal clock, but memory access has traditionally used its own fixed timers for reading and writing data. Rather than synchronizing its actions with those of the internal clock, memory access had set times for reading and writing data regardless of the actual time the processes required. This would sometimes result in periods of wait cycles where nothing was happening. Because of this, memory was considered to be asynchronous.

  However, SDRAM eliminates this difference between memory speed and processor speed because SDRAM has a clock synchronized with the computer's central processing clock. Thus, SDRAM uses only the time required to read/write data which increases data transfer rates by eliminating non-productive periods of waiting. The clock coordinates with a computer's central processor's clock so that data can be delivered continuously to the microprocessor. The timing coordination between memory, the microprocessor, and other support chips permits more efficient memory access and eliminates wait states. This results in memory access speeds of up to 20% faster than EDO."

  Other issues that may come up here are whether the memory needs to be "buffered" and/or "dampered." Again, this is technical stuff that you need not really understand. All you need to know is Apple's recommendation for what type the memory should be (or trust your memory vendor to know it).

  The iMac and desktop G3 and G4 Macs use SDRAM. They are typically either 144-pin or 168-pin modules.

- **SGRAM Synchronous Graphics Random Access Memory)** Apple explains SGRAM as follows: "SGRAM functions similarly to SDRAM except that it has added graphics support. Graphics support is provided by adding block write and masked write (or write-per-bit) functionality.

  Block write enables the graphics engine to do block transfers of graphical data, such as tiling, and to interpret these larger data packets. Block write is often used in 3-D operations to clear the buffers or to prepare them for new rendering. With the block write function in the graphics memory, the graphics engine is free to do other tasks which increases performance. Masked write simplifies changing selected bits in a block of data. Masked write increases graphics performance with tasks such as color management of the display."

  Some Macs may allow SGRAM only for video memory, not main memory. The main memory will use SDRAM instead.

**FIX-IT
#15**

TECHNICALLY SPEAKING ▶ Memory Placement Restrictions

If your Mac has multiple memory slots, and especially if you only fill some of them, does it matter which ones you fill and which ones you leave empty? Yes, it can.

Older PCI-based Macs The first generation PCI-based Power Macintoshes (such as the 7500, 7600 and 8500) have 8 DIMM slots. They are labeled A1-A4 and B1-B4. You have maximum flexibility here. You can put memory modules in anywhere from one to all eight of these slots, in any location, and the Mac should work fine.

Still, for optimum performance speed, where you put the DIMMs does matter. First off, these Macs support a memory technology called "interleaving." Interleaving lets the computer read and write data to memory at the same time other reads and writes (such as to a hard disk) are occurring, thereby improving performance. Avoiding more details here, this means that you will get better performance if you have memory installed in matching pairs. A matched pair means having DIMMs in both an A and a B slot of the same number (such as A4 and B4). These labels are visible on the motherboard when you open up your Mac. So, for example, having two 8MB DIMMs in slots A4 and B4 will give better performance than one 16MB DIMM in slot A4 or even two 8MB DIMMs in A4 and B1.

A matched pair of DIMMS should be of the same size for interleaving to work. For absolute best performance, these matched DIMMs should also be of the same speed.

With a 604 or faster processor, interleaving can boost speed by as much as 15%. With a 601 or slower processor, the speed boost will be almost negligible. By the way, the Power Mac 7200 does not support this interleaving feature.

Next, assuming that you are only going to partially fill up your DIMM slots, does it matter which ones you fill up first? Officially, Apple says it should not matter. However, many experts have stated that starting with the highest numbered pair (A4/B4) and working your way down to the lowest number pair (A1/B1) is best. One report suggested an exception if you have 4 DIMMs: in this case A4, B4, A1 and B1 is the best selection (supposedly this helps to minimize the effects of "noise" across the DIMMs). Other reports say that if you have pairs of DIMMs of different sizes (such as one pair of 16MB DIMMs and another pair of 8MB DIMMs), the higher capacity DIMMs should preferably go in the highest number slots (that is, A4/B4).

Finally, there have been sporadic reports of 16MB (of higher) DIMMs working properly in some slots but not in others. So if you suspect a DIMM problem, try re-arranging the slot locations of the DIMMs before assuming that you have a defective one.

Worrying about most of this for what may only result in a minimal speed boost may be more than you care to worry about. But speed freaks gobble this stuff up like M&Ms.

Even Older Macs In many older models of Mac, all SIMMs in a given Mac had to be the same size. Thus, you could not put a 1MB SIMM in one slot and a 4 MB SIMM in the next slot. In some cases, the Mac had two separate *banks* of SIMM slots (called A and B). In this case, all SIMMs within a bank must typically be of the same size, though each bank can have a different size. Sometimes, the slots in a bank must either be all full or all empty in order for the Mac to work properly. The Macintosh IIci is a classic example of this type of Macintosh. It has two banks of 4 slots each.

Virtually all Macs that use SIMMs needed the SIMMs to be installed in complementary pairs. Thus, in Power Macintoshes 6100, 7100, and 8100, both memory slots must be filled with SIMMs of the same size and speed in order for the Mac to work properly. Newer Macs (that use DIMMs) typically have none of these restrictions.

For any other Mac model, check its technical specifications (usually buried somewhere in the documentation that came with the Mac or available online, such as with Apple Spec or other Apple support documents) for any restrictions specific to that model.

(continues on next page)

Newest Macs On Apple's newest Macs, there are little or no restrictions regarding memory placement. For example, the Power Mac G4 comes with 4 PC-100 DM slots. It usually ships with just one slot occupied. When adding memory to the additional slots, there is no performance benefit to matching DIMM sizes or installing them in pairs.

For any other Mac model, check its technical specifications (usually buried somewhere in the documentation that came with the Mac or available online, such as with Apple Spec or other Apple support documents) for any restrictions specific to that model.

TECHNICALLY SPEAKING ▶ Video RAM and Printer RAM

Video RAM Except for a few older Mac models, the RAM needed to generate the video display is obtained from RAM separate from the main memory. This additional RAM is called video RAM (VRAM or NVRAM). On some Mac models, there are separate slots on the logic board specific for video RAM. If so, it may be that some of the slots are empty. This means that you can expand the video RAM capacity of your Mac. In other cases, you may have a separate video PCI-card. Apple G4 Macs use an entirely new type of card and slot called AGP. In these cases, the video RAM is located on the card. Some cards allow for memory expansion; others do not. If you have a video/display/graphics card, its VRAM is used instead of whatever VRAM may be included on the logic board.

The amount of VRAM installed determines, among other things, the maximum number of colors that your monitor can display at one time. For example, without enough VRAM, you cannot get 24-bit color at some resolutions (see Chapter 10).

How do you know how much video RAM you have installed? Both Apple System Profiler and TattleTech list this information.

Figure F15-4 TattleTech lists the NVRAM of a Power Mac 7500.

Printer RAM Laser printers typically have their own RAM. On some models, you can add additional printer RAM. Adding RAM will allow the printer to print faster and to better handle complex documents.

For more details and specifications on VRAM and printer RAM, check out Apple Spec or otherwise get outside help.

For Related Information

SEE: • Fix-It #1 on incompatibilities between hardware and software.
• Fix-It #3 on extension conflicts.
• Fix-It #5 on memory problems.
• Fix-It #9 on zapping the PRAM.
• Fix-It #14 on SCSI problems.
• Chapter 4 on system crashes.
• Chapter 5 on startup and disk problems.
• Chapter 7 on printing problems.
• Chapter 11 on portable Macs.

**FIX-IT
#15**

Fix-It #16:
Seek Technical Support or
Other Outside Help

▶ **QUICK SUMMARY**

If you are unable to solve a specific software or hardware problem, contact technical support of the company that makes the product (via a phone call or by checking out its Web page or other online support). Otherwise, seek help from more general online services, users groups, magazines, books, and/or colleagues, as practical.

 ## When to Do It:

- Whenever symptoms suggest a bug or incompatibility problem.

- Whenever you have searched the relevant manuals for the answer to a question but were unable to find it.

- Whenever you have a problem that you were unable to solve using the advice given in this book.

 ## Why to Do It:

Even if you memorize everything in this book, there will still be times when you cannot solve some problem. Perhaps you need some detailed information about your model of Macintosh (such as, "What type of memory does my Mac use?"). Maybe you want some guidance on a particular procedure you have never tried before (such as installing memory). Or maybe you simply can't find the answer to some application- or hardware-specific problem (such as "How do I import Word documents into this program?" or "Why do I get a system freeze whenever I select to save in this program?"). In all these cases, when you have exhausted your own resources, it's time to seek outside help.

 ## What to Do:

This Fix-It divides help into two separate categories: (1) vendor technical support, and (2) Web-based technical support.

Vendor Technical Support

Telephone Technical Support

When to call technical support Telephone support is still probably the most frequently used method of getting technical support. Basically, it is a help line for problems specific to the company's products. The phone number for technical support should be in the manual that came with the product. Arrangements for technical support lines vary. Some phone numbers are toll-free, others are not.

Increasingly, tech support is no longer a free option. Even Apple no longer provides free support beyond 90 days. Depending upon the vendor, you either have to pay a subscription fee (which entitles you to a certain number of incident requests or provides tech support for a specific duration of time) or you pay a per-incident fee each time you call. If it turns out that the problem is due to something that needs to be fixed under warranty, the fee is typically waived.

There are two types of problems that suggest a quick call to technical support.

The first is when, having carefully followed the product's installation instructions, a problem still occurs the first time you try to use a product.

The other is when a familiar program develops an unknown illness and, after using all the diagnostic skills at your disposal, you are still unable to solve the problem. This means you should at least try common checks, such as checking for extension conflicts and directory damage. Otherwise, when you do call, they are almost certainly going to advise you to try them anyway.

In general, for symptoms that do not clearly point to a likely cause, it pays to call technical support fairly early in the search process. If you are lucky, they already have the answer to your problem. If so, the phone call can save you from wasting a substantial amount of time and effort looking for a solution on your own.

Still, even here, it might pay to pause for a moment before you grab the phone. I have had more than my share of embarrassing moments as I hastily made a call only to discover the all-too-obvious solution to the problem while I was talking to the support technician ("Well, what do you know, my surge protector *is* unplugged from the wall outlet.") When this happens, I apologize gracefully and hang up as fast as I can, regretting that they already know my name and are probably adding my conversation to their "Stupid Questions Hall of Fame."

In any case, before you call, don't forget to check manuals, read-me files, Apple Help files or any other online help that may be available. This is especially true if your problem is more of a "how do I do this?" than a "I think something is wrong" issue.

Technical support is especially helpful for problems due to software bugs and incompatibilities with a company's software. The manufacturer is privy to the latest information (and what is being done to resolve the matter). If there is an upgraded version of the program that remedies these problems, you can order it (sometimes you may even get it free!). Occasionally, minor bug-fix upgrades are released that are not generally announced to registered users. Calling and asking for it (or describing a problem that the upgrade version addresses) is the only way to get it. Otherwise, the

FIX-IT
#16

manufacturer may suggest some way to work around the problem. Technical support is also a good source of information about the obscure features of a program that are not adequately explained in the documentation.

On the other hand, if the technical support people do not know the answer to your problem, all they can do is suggest the same techniques described in this book. That is why it pays to try the simpler solutions before calling technical support. If these techniques succeed, you have saved yourself a call. If not, you are in a more informed position to make your call.

Be prepared before you call Assuming you have decided to call technical support, the key to getting help from technical support is to be prepared. If the technical personnel don't have an immediate answer to your problem, expect them to ask questions about the circumstances surrounding your problem. This information is critical for technical support to successfully diagnose the problem. Here is how you can be prepared to deal effectively with technical support:

- Have your product's registration number ready. Some companies will require this before they help you.

- Have a *specific* description of the problem. Under what circumstances does the problem occur? Is it random or predictable? If an error message appears, what does it say? If you have done any of your own detective work, what did you find?

- Know the details of your hardware and software (such as what Mac model you are using, what version of the system software you are using, how much RAM you have installed, what version of the application you are using and more).

- Be at your Mac when you call, so that you can try out any suggestions that the support person may make. Also, be prepared to write down what you do so that you can remember it later.

Any attempts you made to solve the problem can pay dividends now, even though they were ultimately unsuccessful. The information you gathered helps to isolate the cause. For example, consider these two differing descriptions of the same problem:

- "I don't know what's going on. I was in the middle of writing my report, and all of a sudden the whole application crashed."

- "The application crashes as soon as I attempt to cut a selection of text, but only if I do it immediately after saving the document. At other times, the Cut command works fine. I know this is not a startup extension conflict, because it happens even when all of my startup extensions are turned off. It isn't a damaged document, because it happens with any document I use. I tried replacing the application with a backup copy, and that didn't help either. If you want to know the details of my hardware or system software, I have that available. Just ask what you want to know."

Which statement do *you* think is likely to be more helpful to a tech support person?

Fix-It
#16

As an added bonus, the information in the more detailed statement already provides an initial work-around solution: do not use the Cut command immediately after you save a document. Type a few characters first. Then cut.

Using utilities to help get prepared What if you don't know all the system information you should know before calling technical support? And what if you have no idea where to get this information? Not to worry. Any one of several utilities can come to your rescue. They analyze the current state of your System Folder, examine the overall contents of all your mounted disks, and determine the details of your hardware configuration. When they are finished, they create a report of all this information, which you can then print. For most users, Apple System Profiler, which is included with the Mac OS, will be the utility of choice.

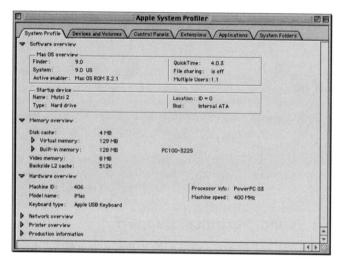

Figure F16-1
The System Profile tab of Apple System Profiler for an iMac DV SE.

Make the call When calling technical support, make sure you are dialing the technical support number, not the customer service number. The two services are entirely different. Customer service deals primarily with sales and generally knows little or nothing about technical problems. Some companies offer only one phone number. In this case, there is usually an automated system for making a choice after the call is answered.

When you get to the technical support location, you will probably be placed on hold. Be patient. Depending on the company's staffing and the popularity of the product, you may be on hold for a minute or for half the day.

When you finally get to speak to someone, be courteous but be persistent. Restate your question if the initial answer was not helpful. While most technical support people are knowledgeable about their company's product, some may seem like they were just hired yesterday. If the person answering the phone seems incapable or unwilling to help, ask to speak to someone else. You should eventually get transferred to someone who knows the product well enough to answer your question.

TAKE NOTE ▶ Registration and Upgrades

Whenever you purchase a computer product, you almost always find a registration card enclosed. Fill it out and mail it back! You will not regret it. Registering computer products, especially software, is more valuable to you than for almost any other type of product you purchase. Here's why:

- Some companies provide technical support only to registered users. (Otherwise, if you haven't registered, they may require that you tell them the serial number of your software before they help you.)

- Registering your product puts you on the company's mailing list. This means you get the company's newsletter, if any, which often contains useful hints and tips about the product.

- Finally, when an upgrade to the software is released, registered users are given an opportunity to purchase it at a substantially reduced cost. Usually, at least for commercial software, you will be automatically mailed (or emailed) a notification about the upgrade offer. This is by far the greatest benefit of registering your product. It's like being able to get a new car at a fraction of its normal selling price, simply because you own an older model of the same car. Sometimes, especially if the upgrade is released primarily to fix bugs in the previous version, the upgrade is free and available to all registered users.

It is true that not all upgrades are worth buying. Some add more style than substance, primarily making the product larger, more RAM-hungry, and slower to use. If you are content with your present version, there may be little to gain by upgrading. More often, however, the upgrade adds significant and valuable new features, fixes bugs, and generally addresses user complaints about the previous version. It also may be the only version compatible with Apple's most recent system software version, which is important if you are staying current with system software.

In most cases, getting an upgrade is worth the cost. However, registering the software is always free and at least gives you the option to decide about the purchase of any upgrades. So register your product!

Other Options for Vendor Technical Support

Instead of calling a company's technical support phone line right away, it pays to first consider a company's other support options. These days, the most common other option is Web-based technical support. Other possibilities include email support and fax-based support. However, even if you just want to send an email message to a company, you may need to go its Web site to find out their email address.

Often you may get a quicker (and sometimes more accurate or more detailed) response by using these services rather than using the phone to talk to tech support. With the phone, you may have to wait on hold or even leave a message and wait for someone to call you back. And the person who finally responds may know less about your problem than the information available on the Web. Plus, companies often charge for telephone support; Web support is always free.

Typically, the documentation that comes with a product should include a listing of all of a company's support options.

SEE: • "Web-based Technical Support," later in this Fix-It, for more general information about using the World Wide Web and other Internet resources for getting technical support.
- "Take Note: Getting Help from Apple," for information about Apple's Internet-based and other technical support options.
- Chapters 12 and 13 for more basic information about using the World Wide Web.

TAKE NOTE ▶ Getting Help from Apple

If you want help with your Mac from Apple, Apple provides three main ways to get it:

- **Mac Help** Years ago, your Mac would come with a manual that was about the size of a dictionary. It provided answers to most of the questions you were likely to have. These days, the manual is no more than a pamphlet and answers almost nothing. (This is an industry-wide trend, not limited to Apple. And in one sense, I guess I should be grateful, as it makes books like this one more in demand.) To compensate for this loss of printed documentation, Apple has beefed up its disk-based help system. Just select Help Center from the Help menu, when in the Finder, and you'll get a list of several Help options (see also "Application Support," in Chapter 1, for related information). The key option to select is Mac Help (which you can also access directly from the Help menu). From here, you can use the table of contents listing or the search feature to find out much more detailed information about your

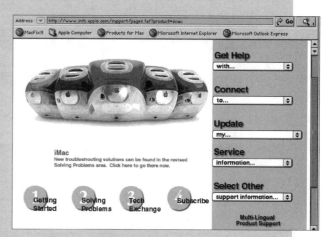

Figure F16-2 Apple's iMac support page.

Mac than is included in the pamphlet manual. For example, if you are stumped trying to figure out how to set up a Voiceprint password in Mac OS 9's Multiple Users, Mac Help will give you step-by-step instructions.

- **Telephone support** For any Apple product, you have 90 days of free technical telephone support from the date of purchase. To access this help (in the U.S.) call 800-500-7078 or 800-767-2775 (SOS-APPL). After the ninety-day period is over, technical support will still be free if the problem turns out to be something that Apple covers on its one-year hardware warranty. To avoid charges beyond these limits, you can pay for AppleCare Extended Services (currently a three-year Protection Plan that you can purchase at the time you buy the hardware or any time while it is still under warranty). In recent months, Apple has improved the wait times for telephone support, although it can still be 15 minutes or more before your call is answered.

- **Web-based support** For starters, product-specific pages in Apple's main Web site can be mined for useful, albeit usually basic, information about virtually all of Apple's products. If you are not sure what URL to enter for the product you have in mind, go to the Apple site map (http://www.apple.com/find/sitemap.html).

   Otherwise, check out AppleCare Service and Support at http://www.apple.com/support/. Here you will get to choose specific support options to match the particular hardware or software you own. For example, for help with your iMac, go to http://www.info.apple.com/support/pages.taf?product=imac.

(continues on next page)

TAKE NOTE ▶ Getting Help from Apple *(continued)*

Whatever Apple products you own, there are three additional support pages that you will want to check from time to time:

- **Tech Info Library** (http://til.info.apple.com/) This is Apple's database of troubleshooting and technical documents. If you have a question about any Apple product that goes beyond the stuff you find in their advertising and spec sheets, this would be the place to check first.

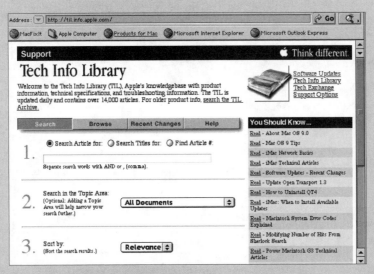

Figure F16-3 Apple's Tech Info Library search page.

- **Tech Exchange** (http://support.info.apple.com/te/te.taf) This is a bulletin board where users post questions and other users (and sometimes Apple Support) provide answers. The signal to noise ratio is low here (that is, you'll have to wade through a lot of "junk" messages to find useful information). But it's a good place to find out if other users are complaining about the same thing that you are having trouble with.

- **Apple Software Updates** (http://asu.info.apple.com/) This is where you'll find almost every free update that Apple has available. You can download any file from this library to your own computer. Click the Recent Changes tab to see Apple's newest updates. If you are using Mac OS 9, the Software Update control panel (see Chapter 15) may be a more convenient alternative (as it does the searching for you). But the Software Updates Web site will show you updates for software not on your computer (and therefore not flagged by the control panel).

If you are more technically inclined, there are two other Web pages you will want to visit:

- **Hardware Developer Documentation** (http://developer.apple.com/techpubs/hardware/) This has a list of Developers Notes. These Notes contain developer-level technical information about Apple's current hardware.

- **Technical Notes** (http://devworld.apple.com/technotes/index.html) Again, these are intended mainly for developers. But when a new version of the Mac OS is released, the Technote on that OS almost always has tidbits that even non-developer troubleshooters will want to know about.

FIX-IT #16

Web-Based Technical Support

Virtually all companies maintain technical support for their products on the World Wide Web. This may include (1) databases of Frequently Asked Questions (FAQs) and other support documents; (2) bulletin boards (also called message boards or forums) where you can post a question and get an answer (ideally from the vendor's technical support staff), and (3) a section where you can download the latest free updates to the vendor's software (see: "Take Note: Staying Up To Date").

However vendor technical support, by definition, is focused on the product the vendor publishes. It is not prepared to answer questions about more general problems you may have. Occasionally, vendor technical support may even be unaware of some problem with their own product (or unwilling to talk about it). At these times, you'll want to look to independent sources of information for help. Again, the most popular place to find these independent sources is on the World Wide Web.

For general Mac information, there are an abundance of independently run Web sites, from slick e-zines to simple tips pages. Many of these sites contain some form of troubleshooting help. For starters, you could visit my own MacFixIt site.

MacFixIt *MacFixIt* (http://www.macfixit.com) focuses exclusively on Macintosh troubleshooting. *Sad Macs* readers will find it especially useful for information that goes beyond that covered in this book or that is too new to have been covered here.

The MacFixIt home page contains the site's most recently posted information. Older information can be accessed via the Archives. There are also special reports on major topics, such as on each new version of the Mac OS. You can go directly to any page or you can use MacFixIt's search feature to locate what you are seeking.

There is also a Download Library of troubleshooting-related software, including links to almost all of the freeware and shareware utilities mentioned in this book.

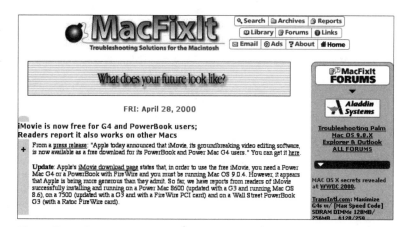

Figure F16-4 The top part of my MacFixIt home page (like everything else in this fast-changing environment, the design may be different by the time you read this!).

Finally, the MacFixIt Forums is a bulletin board where you can post a question about any troubleshooting matter. Within a few hours to days, you should get an answer—often several answers—from some of the most knowledgeable Macintosh users in the world. Actually, just by searching through existing messages, you may find the answer to your question.

Figure F16-5 The MacFixIt Forums main page.

TAKE NOTE ▶ Staying Up to Date

In addition to the major releases of the Mac OS, Apple releases a steady flow of minor updates to the OS. For example, as of this writing, recent updates included DVD Software 2.2, Input Sprockets 1.7.4 and QuickTime 4.1.2. Happily, if you are using Mac OS 9 or later, running the Software Update control panel will make sure (with very few exceptions) that you always have all of the latest software. QuickTime updates are one example of something that this control panel does not handle. For this, you would have go directly to Apple's QuickTime Web page <http://www.apple.com/quicktime/> or use the QuickTime Updater on your drive. As mentioned in "Take Note: Getting Help from Apple," you can also get most Apple updates from Apple's Software Updates Web page.

It similarly pays to make sure that you have the latest version of all of your third-party software. With each update to the Mac OS and with each release of a new model of Mac, some third-party programs that were working just fine will no longer work. In response, the author updates the program to fix the conflict. These updates typically also fix assorted bugs in the previous version and add new features. Many times, these updates are free. To check for the latest version, you can go directly to each vendor's Web site. Or you can depend upon more general Web sites—such as my own MacFixIt or Version Tracker <www.versiontracker.com>. Finally, there are third-party programs, such as Insider's UpdateAgent, that (much like Apple's Software Update control panel does for Apple software) will check all the software on your drive for what needs updating and offer to download the updates for you.

FIX-IT #16

BY THE WAY ▶ America Online: More Than Just an ISP

An Internet Service Provider (ISP) provides a way for you to access the Internet (typically via a modem). It typically includes an email account (and perhaps some personal Web space) and little else. EarthLink is an example of a popular ISP for the Mac.

America Online (AOL) is a bit different. It is both an ISP and a content provider. This means that although you *can* use it to access the Internet, you can also use it for AOL's unique features (such as the news, sports, travel, and other links listed on AOL software's Welcome screen). Only AOL subscribers can access its unique content (although some of it is freely available via www.aol.com). A few other services similar to AOL still exist (such as CompuServe), but AOL is by far the biggest one.

In this book, I focus only on content available to all Internet users, mainly via the World Wide Web, rather than those just available to users of a specific service such as AOL.

BY THE WAY ▶ Newsgroups and Mailing Lists

While the World Wide Web is the major information resource on the Internet today, there are other sources still in use that were available even before the Web was created. The two most popular of these other resources are newsgroups and mailing lists.

Newsgroups Newsgroups cover every imaginable topic (including some of the most notorious pornographic ones). However, for Macintosh users there are a series of newsgroups that all begin with "comp.sys.mac" that are your best bet for technical support. For general questions, the best of the best is "comp.sys.mac.system."

SEE: • "By the Way: Newsgroups," at the end of Chapter 13, for how to access newsgroups.

Mailing lists A mailing list is basically an email service that functions similarly to a newsgroup. You post messages as email. Everyone who is subscribed to the list then gets your message (either immediately or as a combined "digest" of all messages received within the last 24 hours). Subscribers can then respond to the message. You subscribe via email (some lists maintain a Web site where you can access subscription information). Subscribing is usually free. At any time, you can unsubscribe (by following instructions that are sent to you when you first subscribe). The only software you need for a mailing list is your email program.

Note that some mailing lists do not accept postings. They just send information, typically in the form of electronic magazines or press releases or whatever.

To get information about or to sign up for a specific mailing list, check out the Web site created by the group that runs the mailing list. Apple maintains a list of some popular Mac-related mailing lists at http://lists.apple.com/.

Still More Options: Beyond the Web

You can also get troubleshooting help by (1) joining a local Macintosh User Group (MUG), if one exists in your area; (2) reading popular Mac magazines, such as *Macworld* and *MacAddict*; (3) reading books, such as the one you are holding!; (4) taking a training course or workshop, such as those available at *Macworld Expo* (http://www.macworldexpo.com) or through separate companies, such as *Complete Mac Seminars* (http://www.macseminars.com/); or (5) simply asking a friend, colleague or consultant who knows more than you do.

 For Related Information

SEE: • Chapter 3 on general problem-solving strategies.
• Chapter 12 and 13 for information on accessing the Internet and especially the World Wide Web.

Appendix: Stocking Your Troubleshooter's Toolkit

Throughout this book, I have described a variety of troubleshooting software. In previous editions of *Sad Macs*, I spent several pages explaining where and how to get this software. For this edition, due to the growth of the World Wide Web, recommendations are much simpler. On a related topic, the last section of this Appendix includes a list of common troubleshooting keyboard shortcuts.

Commercial Software

If you know the vendor of the software you seek, find their Web site and go to it. They will almost certainly either sell the software directly from their site or have links to other sites where you can get it. For example, if you want Alsoft's DiskWarrior, go to this page: <http://www.alsoft.com/alssales.html>. From here, you can either order it directly or link to any one of several distributors that sell it.

If you don't know the vendor's name, or if you are just in the mood to browse through a large catalog of software (and hardware!), you can go directly to a software retailer's Web site. There you can find almost all the commercial software available for the Mac. Among the best ones are:

- MacMall <http://www.macmall.com>

- MacZone <http://www.maczone.com>

- MacWarehouse <http://www.macwarehouse.com>

- Outpost.com. <http://www.outpost.com>

Most of these retailers also provide phone numbers, should you prefer to speak to a salesperson and/or order via the phone.

For Apple products, you can also order directly from the Apple Store <http://store.apple.com/>.

In general, I recommend against going to a retail store to buy software. You will almost certainly find that the selection of software for the Mac is poor, and prices will tend to be higher than from online sources. However, if you insist on going retail, your best bet in a national chain is CompUSA. Locally, you may find a better choice.

Shareware and Freeware

What is shareware and freeware?

Many of the troubleshooting utilities mentioned in this book fall into the category of shareware or freeware. These include utilities such as Data Rescue and TechTool. You won't find these in any of the commercial outlets just listed. Although this may make them a bit harder to find, the best ones are well worth the effort. They offer professional-quality features often not available from any other product at a fraction of what a comparable commercial software program might cost.

Freeware and shareware are similar in most ways. The difference is only in how much you pay for them.

As the name implies, freeware is completely free. You need pay nothing.

For shareware, you are obligated to pay a fee (usually about $10 to $40). But you need to pay this fee only if you continue to use the program. The idea is that you get to try out the software for a limited time risk-free. It is a sort of honor system: if you use the program, you pay for it; otherwise, you don't. You pay the shareware fee by mailing a check or by paying online, either directly to the developer or via a payment processing agency (most likely Kagi.com). The instructions on how to do this are invariably included with the program or on the Web site where it is listed. In some cases, shareware products are distributed in a restricted form. For example, you may need a password to access all the features of the program. To obtain the password, you must pay the shareware fee.

Where do you get shareware and freeware?

Once again, to obtain shareware and freeware, turn to the World Wide Web. Especially for the utilities mentioned in this book, start at the Download Library at MacFixIt: <http://www.macfixit.com/library>. If that doesn't have the program, a search of MacFixIt will likely turn up a link to a Web site that does have it.

There are also a few sites that maintain a very large catalog of shareware/freeware. These include Download.com <http://download.cnet.com/> and the Info-Mac Archive (<http://hyperarchive.lcs.mit.edu/> is a link to a mirror version of the archive that I prefer to use).

Otherwise, locate the Web site of the programmer who wrote the software. You can download the software from there. VersionTracker <http://www.versiontracker.com> is another good place to search for such sites.

Once you get the software, you'll want to check online from time to time to make sure you still have the latest version. These days, programs sometimes get updated a couple of times a week! So you can't check too often.

SEE: • **"Take Note: Staying Up to Date," in Fix-It #16 for more advice on staying up-to-date.**

Common Troubleshooting Keyboard Shortcuts

Here is a listing of the most notable troubleshooting-related keyboard shortcuts cited in *Sad Macs* together with the page number where each one is primarily described. Some commands may not work with all Mac OS machines nor with all versions of the system software.

Keyboard shortcuts that are listed in menus are not listed here. For more shortcuts, go to the Help menu when you are in the Finder, choose Mac Help and then select "Shortcuts and Tips." Especially check out the "Keyboard shortcuts" item in the list that appears.

TO	PRESS	PAGE
Access Conflict Catcher at startup (assuming you have CC installed)	Space bar at startup	698
Access the Open Firmware screen	Command-Option-O-F at startup (on some Macs only)	630
Bypass the internal drive at startup	Command-Option-Shift-Delete at startup	130
Cancel an operation	Command-Period(.)	106
Empty the Trash with locked files in it	Option while selecting Empty Trash command	232
Erase a disk automatically when you insert it	Command-Option-Tab	846
Force Quit (from a freeze)	Command-Option-Escape	101
Option to restart, sleep or shut down	Power key	91
Rebuild the desktop	Command-Option at startup or when mounting a non-startup volume	785
Restart (will not work after a crash on Macs with USB keyboards)	Command-Control-Power *or* Command-Control-Shift-Power	93-94
Select startup drive at startup	Option key at startup (on certain NewWorld Macs only)	132
Start up from a bootable CD-ROM disc	C key at startup	126
Start up from internal drive (if drive is not already the current selection)	D key at startup (on some Macs only)	130
Start up with extensions disabled	Shift at startup	693
Start up with virtual memory off	Command key at startup	763
Zap the PRAM	Command-Option-P-R at startup	797

Index